Dictionary of Literary Biography

1. *The American Renaissance in New England,* edited by Joel Myerson (1978)
2. *American Novelists Since World War II,* edited by Jeffrey Helterman and Richard Layman (1978)
3. *Antebellum Writers in New York and the South,* edited by Joel Myerson (1979)
4. *American Writers in Paris, 1920-1939,* edited by Karen Lane Rood (1980)
5. *American Poets Since World War II,* 2 parts, edited by Donald J. Greiner (1980)
6. *American Novelists Since World War II, Second Series,* edited by James E. Kibler Jr. (1980)
7. *Twentieth-Century American Dramatists,* 2 parts, edited by John MacNicholas (1981)
8. *Twentieth-Century American Science-Fiction Writers,* 2 parts, edited by David Cowart and Thomas L. Wymer (1981)
9. *American Novelists, 1910-1945,* 3 parts, edited by James J. Martine (1981)
10. *Modern British Dramatists, 1900-1945,* 2 parts, edited by Stanley Weintraub (1982)
11. *American Humorists, 1800-1950,* 2 parts, edited by Stanley Trachtenberg (1982)
12. *American Realists and Naturalists,* edited by Donald Pizer and Earl N. Harbert (1982)
13. *British Dramatists Since World War II,* 2 parts, edited by Stanley Weintraub (1982)
14. *British Novelists Since 1960,* 2 parts, edited by Jay L. Halio (1983)
15. *British Novelists, 1930-1959,* 2 parts, edited by Bernard Oldsey (1983)
16. *The Beats: Literary Bohemians in Postwar America,* 2 parts, edited by Ann Charters (1983)
17. *Twentieth-Century American Historians,* edited by Clyde N. Wilson (1983)
18. *Victorian Novelists After 1885,* edited by Ira B. Nadel and William E. Fredeman (1983)
19. *British Poets, 1880-1914,* edited by Donald E. Stanford (1983)
20. *British Poets, 1914-1945,* edited by Donald E. Stanford (1983)
21. *Victorian Novelists Before 1885,* edited by Ira B. Nadel and William E. Fredeman (1983)
22. *American Writers for Children, 1900-1960,* edited by John Cech (1983)
23. *American Newspaper Journalists, 1873-1900,* edited by Perry J. Ashley (1983)
24. *American Colonial Writers, 1606-1734,* edited by Emory Elliott (1984)
25. *American Newspaper Journalists, 1901-1925,* edited by Perry J. Ashley (1984)
26. *American Screenwriters,* edited by Robert E. Morsberger, Stephen O. Lesser, and Randall Clark (1984)
27. *Poets of Great Britain and Ireland, 1945-1960,* edited by Vincent B. Sherry Jr. (1984)
28. *Twentieth-Century American-Jewish Fiction Writers,* edited by Daniel Walden (1984)
29. *American Newspaper Journalists, 1926-1950,* edited by Perry J. Ashley (1984)
30. *American Historians, 1607-1865,* edited by Clyde N. Wilson (1984)
31. *American Colonial Writers, 1735-1781,* edited by Emory Elliott (1984)
32. *Victorian Poets Before 1850,* edited by William E. Fredeman and Ira B. Nadel (1984)
33. *Afro-American Fiction Writers After 1955,* edited by Thadious M. Davis and Trudier Harris (1984)
34. *British Novelists, 1890-1929: Traditionalists,* edited by Thomas F. Staley (1985)
35. *Victorian Poets After 1850,* edited by William E. Fredeman and Ira B. Nadel (1985)
36. *British Novelists, 1890-1929: Modernists,* edited by Thomas F. Staley (1985)
37. *American Writers of the Early Republic,* edited by Emory Elliott (1985)
38. *Afro-American Writers After 1955: Dramatists and Prose Writers,* edited by Thadious M. Davis and Trudier Harris (1985)
39. *British Novelists, 1660-1800,* 2 parts, edited by Martin C. Battestin (1985)
40. *Poets of Great Britain and Ireland Since 1960,* 2 parts, edited by Vincent B. Sherry Jr. (1985)
41. *Afro-American Poets Since 1955,* edited by Trudier Harris and Thadious M. Davis (1985)
42. *American Writers for Children Before 1900,* edited by Glenn E. Estes (1985)
43. *American Newspaper Journalists, 1690-1872,* edited by Perry J. Ashley (1986)
44. *American Screenwriters, Second Series,* edited by Randall Clark, Robert E. Morsberger, and Stephen O. Lesser (1986)
45. *American Poets, 1880-1945, First Series,* edited by Peter Quartermain (1986)
46. *American Literary Publishing Houses, 1900-1980: Trade and Paperback,* edited by Peter Dzwonkoski (1986)
47. *American Historians, 1866-1912,* edited by Clyde N. Wilson (1986)
48. *American Poets, 1880-1945, Second Series,* edited by Peter Quartermain (1986)
49. *American Literary Publishing Houses, 1638-1899,* 2 parts, edited by Peter Dzwonkoski (1986)
50. *Afro-American Writers Before the Harlem Renaissance,* edited by Trudier Harris (1986)
51. *Afro-American Writers from the Harlem Renaissance to 1940,* edited by Trudier Harris (1987)
52. *American Writers for Children Since 1960: Fiction,* edited by Glenn E. Estes (1986)
53. *Canadian Writers Since 1960, First Series,* edited by W. H. New (1986)
54. *American Poets, 1880-1945, Third Series,* 2 parts, edited by Peter Quartermain (1987)
55. *Victorian Prose Writers Before 1867,* edited by William B. Thesing (1987)
56. *German Fiction Writers, 1914-1945,* edited by James Hardin (1987)
57. *Victorian Prose Writers After 1867,* edited by William B. Thesing (1987)
58. *Jacobean and Caroline Dramatists,* edited by Fredson Bowers (1987)
59. *American Literary Critics and Scholars, 1800-1850,* edited by John W. Rathbun and Monica M. Grecu (1987)
60. *Canadian Writers Since 1960, Second Series,* edited by W. H. New (1987)
61. *American Writers for Children Since 1960: Poets, Illustrators, and Nonfiction Authors,* edited by Glenn E. Estes (1987)
62. *Elizabethan Dramatists,* edited by Fredson Bowers (1987)
63. *Modern American Critics, 1920-1955,* edited by Gregory S. Jay (1988)
64. *American Literary Critics and Scholars, 1850-1880,* edited by John W. Rathbun and Monica M. Grecu (1988)
65. *French Novelists, 1900-1930,* edited by Catharine Savage Brosman (1988)
66. *German Fiction Writers, 1885-1913,* 2 parts, edited by James Hardin (1988)
67. *Modern American Critics Since 1955,* edited by Gregory S. Jay (1988)
68. *Canadian Writers, 1920-1959, First Series,* edited by W. H. New (1988)
69. *Contemporary German Fiction Writers, First Series,* edited by Wolfgang D. Elfe and James Hardin (1988)
70. *British Mystery Writers, 1860-1919,* edited by Bernard Benstock and Thomas F. Staley (1988)

71 *American Literary Critics and Scholars, 1880–1900,* edited by John W. Rathbun and Monica M. Grecu (1988)

72 *French Novelists, 1930–1960,* edited by Catharine Savage Brosman (1988)

73 *American Magazine Journalists, 1741–1850,* edited by Sam G. Riley (1988)

74 *American Short-Story Writers Before 1880,* edited by Bobby Ellen Kimbel, with the assistance of William E. Grant (1988)

75 *Contemporary German Fiction Writers, Second Series,* edited by Wolfgang D. Elfe and James Hardin (1988)

76 *Afro-American Writers, 1940–1955,* edited by Trudier Harris (1988)

77 *British Mystery Writers, 1920–1939,* edited by Bernard Benstock and Thomas F. Staley (1988)

78 *American Short-Story Writers, 1880–1910,* edited by Bobby Ellen Kimbel, with the assistance of William E. Grant (1988)

79 *American Magazine Journalists, 1850–1900,* edited by Sam G. Riley (1988)

80 *Restoration and Eighteenth-Century Dramatists, First Series,* edited by Paula R. Backscheider (1989)

81 *Austrian Fiction Writers, 1875–1913,* edited by James Hardin and Donald G. Daviau (1989)

82 *Chicano Writers, First Series,* edited by Francisco A. Lomelí and Carl R. Shirley (1989)

83 *French Novelists Since 1960,* edited by Catharine Savage Brosman (1989)

84 *Restoration and Eighteenth-Century Dramatists, Second Series,* edited by Paula R. Backscheider (1989)

85 *Austrian Fiction Writers After 1914,* edited by James Hardin and Donald G. Daviau (1989)

86 *American Short-Story Writers, 1910–1945, First Series,* edited by Bobby Ellen Kimbel (1989)

87 *British Mystery and Thriller Writers Since 1940, First Series,* edited by Bernard Benstock and Thomas F. Staley (1989)

88 *Canadian Writers, 1920–1959, Second Series,* edited by W. H. New (1989)

89 *Restoration and Eighteenth-Century Dramatists, Third Series,* edited by Paula R. Backscheider (1989)

90 *German Writers in the Age of Goethe, 1789–1832,* edited by James Hardin and Christoph E. Schweitzer (1989)

91 *American Magazine Journalists, 1900–1960, First Series,* edited by Sam G. Riley (1990)

92 *Canadian Writers, 1890–1920,* edited by W. H. New (1990)

93 *British Romantic Poets, 1789–1832, First Series,* edited by John R. Greenfield (1990)

94 *German Writers in the Age of Goethe: Sturm und Drang to Classicism,* edited by James Hardin and Christoph E. Schweitzer (1990)

95 *Eighteenth-Century British Poets, First Series,* edited by John Sitter (1990)

96 *British Romantic Poets, 1789–1832, Second Series,* edited by John R. Greenfield (1990)

97 *German Writers from the Enlightenment to Sturm und Drang, 1720–1764,* edited by James Hardin and Christoph E. Schweitzer (1990)

98 *Modern British Essayists, First Series,* edited by Robert Beum (1990)

99 *Canadian Writers Before 1890,* edited by W. H. New (1990)

100 *Modern British Essayists, Second Series,* edited by Robert Beum (1990)

101 *British Prose Writers, 1660–1800, First Series,* edited by Donald T. Siebert (1991)

102 *American Short-Story Writers, 1910–1945, Second Series,* edited by Bobby Ellen Kimbel (1991)

103 *American Literary Biographers, First Series,* edited by Steven Serafin (1991)

104 *British Prose Writers, 1660–1800, Second Series,* edited by Donald T. Siebert (1991)

105 *American Poets Since World War II, Second Series,* edited by R. S. Gwynn (1991)

106 *British Literary Publishing Houses, 1820–1880,* edited by Patricia J. Anderson and Jonathan Rose (1991)

107 *British Romantic Prose Writers, 1789–1832, First Series,* edited by John R. Greenfield (1991)

108 *Twentieth-Century Spanish Poets, First Series,* edited by Michael L. Perna (1991)

109 *Eighteenth-Century British Poets, Second Series,* edited by John Sitter (1991)

110 *British Romantic Prose Writers, 1789–1832, Second Series,* edited by John R. Greenfield (1991)

111 *American Literary Biographers, Second Series,* edited by Steven Serafin (1991)

112 *British Literary Publishing Houses, 1881–1965,* edited by Jonathan Rose and Patricia J. Anderson (1991)

113 *Modern Latin-American Fiction Writers, First Series,* edited by William Luis (1992)

114 *Twentieth-Century Italian Poets, First Series,* edited by Giovanna Wedel De Stasio, Glauco Cambon, and Antonio Illiano (1992)

115 *Medieval Philosophers,* edited by Jeremiah Hackett (1992)

116 *British Romantic Novelists, 1789–1832,* edited by Bradford K. Mudge (1992)

117 *Twentieth-Century Caribbean and Black African Writers, First Series,* edited by Bernth Lindfors and Reinhard Sander (1992)

118 *Twentieth-Century German Dramatists, 1889–1918,* edited by Wolfgang D. Elfe and James Hardin (1992)

119 *Nineteenth-Century French Fiction Writers: Romanticism and Realism, 1800–1860,* edited by Catharine Savage Brosman (1992)

120 *American Poets Since World War II, Third Series,* edited by R. S. Gwynn (1992)

121 *Seventeenth-Century British Nondramatic Poets, First Series,* edited by M. Thomas Hester (1992)

122 *Chicano Writers, Second Series,* edited by Francisco A. Lomelí and Carl R. Shirley (1992)

123 *Nineteenth-Century French Fiction Writers: Naturalism and Beyond, 1860–1900,* edited by Catharine Savage Brosman (1992)

124 *Twentieth-Century German Dramatists, 1919–1992,* edited by Wolfgang D. Elfe and James Hardin (1992)

125 *Twentieth-Century Caribbean and Black African Writers, Second Series,* edited by Bernth Lindfors and Reinhard Sander (1993)

126 *Seventeenth-Century British Nondramatic Poets, Second Series,* edited by M. Thomas Hester (1993)

127 *American Newspaper Publishers, 1950–1990,* edited by Perry J. Ashley (1993)

128 *Twentieth-Century Italian Poets, Second Series,* edited by Giovanna Wedel De Stasio, Glauco Cambon, and Antonio Illiano (1993)

129 *Nineteenth-Century German Writers, 1841–1900,* edited by James Hardin and Siegfried Mews (1993)

130 *American Short-Story Writers Since World War II,* edited by Patrick Meanor (1993)

131 *Seventeenth-Century British Nondramatic Poets, Third Series,* edited by M. Thomas Hester (1993)

132 *Sixteenth-Century British Nondramatic Writers, First Series,* edited by David A. Richardson (1993)

133 *Nineteenth-Century German Writers to 1840,* edited by James Hardin and Siegfried Mews (1993)

134 *Twentieth-Century Spanish Poets, Second Series,* edited by Jerry Phillips Winfield (1994)

135 *British Short-Fiction Writers, 1880–1914: The Realist Tradition,* edited by William B. Thesing (1994)

136 *Sixteenth-Century British Nondramatic Writers, Second Series,* edited by David A. Richardson (1994)

137 *American Magazine Journalists, 1900–1960, Second Series,* edited by Sam G. Riley (1994)

138 *German Writers and Works of the High Middle Ages: 1170–1280,* edited by James Hardin and Will Hasty (1994)

139 *British Short-Fiction Writers, 1945–1980,* edited by Dean Baldwin (1994)

140 *American Book-Collectors and Bibliographers, First Series,* edited by Joseph Rosenblum (1994)

141 *British Children's Writers, 1880–1914,* edited by Laura M. Zaidman (1994)

142 *Eighteenth-Century British Literary Biographers,* edited by Steven Serafin (1994)

143 *American Novelists Since World War II, Third Series,* edited by James R. Giles and Wanda H. Giles (1994)

144 *Nineteenth-Century British Literary Biographers,* edited by Steven Serafin (1994)

145 *Modern Latin-American Fiction Writers, Second Series,* edited by William Luis and Ann González (1994)

146 *Old and Middle English Literature,* edited by Jeffrey Helterman and Jerome Mitchell (1994)

147 *South Slavic Writers Before World War II,* edited by Vasa D. Mihailovich (1994)

148 *German Writers and Works of the Early Middle Ages: 800–1170,* edited by Will Hasty and James Hardin (1994)

149 *Late Nineteenth- and Early Twentieth-Century British Literary Biographers,* edited by Steven Serafin (1995)

150 *Early Modern Russian Writers, Late Seventeenth and Eighteenth Centuries,* edited by Marcus C. Levitt (1995)

151 *British Prose Writers of the Early Seventeenth Century,* edited by Clayton D. Lein (1995)

152 *American Novelists Since World War II, Fourth Series,* edited by James R. Giles and Wanda H. Giles (1995)

153 *Late-Victorian and Edwardian British Novelists, First Series,* edited by George M. Johnson (1995)

154 *The British Literary Book Trade, 1700–1820,* edited by James K. Bracken and Joel Silver (1995)

155 *Twentieth-Century British Literary Biographers,* edited by Steven Serafin (1995)

156 *British Short-Fiction Writers, 1880–1914: The Romantic Tradition,* edited by William F. Naufftus (1995)

157 *Twentieth-Century Caribbean and Black African Writers, Third Series,* edited by Bernth Lindfors and Reinhard Sander (1995)

158 *British Reform Writers, 1789–1832,* edited by Gary Kelly and Edd Applegate (1995)

159 *British Short-Fiction Writers, 1800–1880,* edited by John R. Greenfield (1996)

160 *British Children's Writers, 1914–1960,* edited by Donald R. Hettinga and Gary D. Schmidt (1996)

161 *British Children's Writers Since 1960, First Series,* edited by Caroline Hunt (1996)

162 *British Short-Fiction Writers, 1915–1945,* edited by John H. Rogers (1996)

163 *British Children's Writers, 1800–1880,* edited by Meena Khorana (1996)

164 *German Baroque Writers, 1580–1660,* edited by James Hardin (1996)

165 *American Poets Since World War II, Fourth Series,* edited by Joseph Conte (1996)

166 *British Travel Writers, 1837–1875,* edited by Barbara Brothers and Julia Gergits (1996)

167 *Sixteenth-Century British Nondramatic Writers, Third Series,* edited by David A. Richardson (1996)

168 *German Baroque Writers, 1661–1730,* edited by James Hardin (1996)

169 *American Poets Since World War II, Fifth Series,* edited by Joseph Conte (1996)

170 *The British Literary Book Trade, 1475–1700,* edited by James K. Bracken and Joel Silver (1996)

171 *Twentieth-Century American Sportswriters,* edited by Richard Orodenker (1996)

172 *Sixteenth-Century British Nondramatic Writers, Fourth Series,* edited by David A. Richardson (1996)

173 *American Novelists Since World War II, Fifth Series,* edited by James R. Giles and Wanda H. Giles (1996)

174 *British Travel Writers, 1876–1909,* edited by Barbara Brothers and Julia Gergits (1997)

175 *Native American Writers of the United States,* edited by Kenneth M. Roemer (1997)

176 *Ancient Greek Authors,* edited by Ward W. Briggs (1997)

177 *Italian Novelists Since World War II, 1945–1965,* edited by Augustus Pallotta (1997)

178 *British Fantasy and Science-Fiction Writers Before World War I,* edited by Darren Harris-Fain (1997)

179 *German Writers of the Renaissance and Reformation, 1280–1580,* edited by James Hardin and Max Reinhart (1997)

180 *Japanese Fiction Writers, 1868–1945,* edited by Van C. Gessel (1997)

181 *South Slavic Writers Since World War II,* edited by Vasa D. Mihailovich (1997)

182 *Japanese Fiction Writers Since World War II,* edited by Van C. Gessel (1997)

183 *American Travel Writers, 1776–1864,* edited by James J. Schramer and Donald Ross (1997)

184 *Nineteenth-Century British Book-Collectors and Bibliographers,* edited by William Baker and Kenneth Womack (1997)

185 *American Literary Journalists, 1945–1995, First Series,* edited by Arthur J. Kaul (1998)

186 *Nineteenth-Century American Western Writers,* edited by Robert L. Gale (1998)

187 *American Book Collectors and Bibliographers, Second Series,* edited by Joseph Rosenblum (1998)

188 *American Book and Magazine Illustrators to 1920,* edited by Steven E. Smith, Catherine A. Hastedt, and Donald H. Dyal (1998)

189 *American Travel Writers, 1850–1915,* edited by Donald Ross and James J. Schramer (1998)

190 *British Reform Writers, 1832–1914,* edited by Gary Kelly and Edd Applegate (1998)

191 *British Novelists Between the Wars,* edited by George M. Johnson (1998)

192 *French Dramatists, 1789–1914,* edited by Barbara T. Cooper (1998)

193 *American Poets Since World War II, Sixth Series,* edited by Joseph Conte (1998)

194 *British Novelists Since 1960, Second Series,* edited by Merritt Moseley (1998)

195 *British Travel Writers, 1910–1939,* edited by Barbara Brothers and Julia Gergits (1998)

196 *Italian Novelists Since World War II, 1965–1995,* edited by Augustus Pallotta (1999)

197 *Late-Victorian and Edwardian British Novelists, Second Series,* edited by George M. Johnson (1999)

198 *Russian Literature in the Age of Pushkin and Gogol: Prose,* edited by Christine A. Rydel (1999)

199 *Victorian Women Poets,* edited by William B. Thesing (1999)

200 *American Women Prose Writers to 1820,* edited by Carla J. Mulford, with Angela Vietto and Amy E. Winans (1999)

201 *Twentieth-Century British Book Collectors and Bibliographers,* edited by William Baker and Kenneth Womack (1999)

202 *Nineteenth-Century American Fiction Writers,* edited by Kent P. Ljungquist (1999)

203 *Medieval Japanese Writers,* edited by Steven D. Carter (1999)

204 *British Travel Writers, 1940–1997,* edited by Barbara Brothers and Julia M. Gergits (1999)

205 *Russian Literature in the Age of Pushkin and Gogol: Poetry and Drama,* edited by Christine A. Rydel (1999)

206 *Twentieth-Century American Western Writers, First Series,* edited by Richard H. Cracroft (1999)

207 *British Novelists Since 1960, Third Series,* edited by Merritt Moseley (1999)

208 *Literature of the French and Occitan Middle Ages: Eleventh to Fifteenth Centuries,* edited by Deborah Sinnreich-Levi and Ian S. Laurie (1999)

209 *Chicano Writers, Third Series,* edited by Francisco A. Lomelí and Carl R. Shirley (1999)

210 *Ernest Hemingway: A Documentary Volume,* edited by Robert W. Trogdon (1999)

211 *Ancient Roman Writers,* edited by Ward W. Briggs (1999)

212 *Twentieth-Century American Western Writers, Second Series,* edited by Richard H. Cracroft (1999)

213 *Pre-Nineteenth-Century British Book Collectors and Bibliographers,* edited by William Baker and Kenneth Womack (1999)

214 *Twentieth-Century Danish Writers,* edited by Marianne Stecher-Hansen (1999)

215 *Twentieth-Century Eastern European Writers, First Series,* edited by Steven Serafin (1999)

216 *British Poets of the Great War: Brooke, Rosenberg, Thomas. A Documentary Volume,* edited by Patrick Quinn (2000)

217 *Nineteenth-Century French Poets,* edited by Robert Beum (2000)

218 *American Short-Story Writers Since World War II, Second Series,* edited by Patrick Meanor and Gwen Crane (2000)

219 *F. Scott Fitzgerald's* The Great Gatsby: *A Documentary Volume,* edited by Matthew J. Bruccoli (2000)

220 *Twentieth-Century Eastern European Writers, Second Series,* edited by Steven Serafin (2000)

221 *American Women Prose Writers, 1870–1920,* edited by Sharon M. Harris, with the assistance of Heidi L. M. Jacobs and Jennifer Putzi (2000)

222 *H. L. Mencken: A Documentary Volume,* edited by Richard J. Schrader (2000)

223 *The American Renaissance in New England, Second Series,* edited by Wesley T. Mott (2000)

224 *Walt Whitman: A Documentary Volume,* edited by Joel Myerson (2000)

225 *South African Writers,* edited by Paul A. Scanlon (2000)

226 *American Hard-Boiled Crime Writers,* edited by George Parker Anderson and Julie B. Anderson (2000)

227 *American Novelists Since World War II, Sixth Series,* edited by James R. Giles and Wanda H. Giles (2000)

228 *Twentieth-Century American Dramatists, Second Series,* edited by Christopher J. Wheatley (2000)

229 *Thomas Wolfe: A Documentary Volume,* edited by Ted Mitchell (2001)

230 *Australian Literature, 1788–1914,* edited by Selina Samuels (2001)

231 *British Novelists Since 1960, Fourth Series,* edited by Merritt Moseley (2001)

232 *Twentieth-Century Eastern European Writers, Third Series,* edited by Steven Serafin (2001)

233 *British and Irish Dramatists Since World War II, Second Series,* edited by John Bull (2001)

234 *American Short-Story Writers Since World War II, Third Series,* edited by Patrick Meanor and Richard E. Lee (2001)

235 *The American Renaissance in New England, Third Series,* edited by Wesley T. Mott (2001)

236 *British Rhetoricians and Logicians, 1500–1660,* edited by Edward A. Malone (2001)

237 *The Beats: A Documentary Volume,* edited by Matt Theado (2001)

238 *Russian Novelists in the Age of Tolstoy and Dostoevsky,* edited by J. Alexander Ogden and Judith E. Kalb (2001)

239 *American Women Prose Writers: 1820–1870,* edited by Amy E. Hudock and Katharine Rodier (2001)

240 *Late Nineteenth- and Early Twentieth-Century British Women Poets,* edited by William B. Thesing (2001)

241 *American Sportswriters and Writers on Sport,* edited by Richard Orodenker (2001)

242 *Twentieth-Century European Cultural Theorists, First Series,* edited by Paul Hansom (2001)

243 *The American Renaissance in New England, Fourth Series,* edited by Wesley T. Mott (2001)

244 *American Short-Story Writers Since World War II, Fourth Series,* edited by Patrick Meanor and Joseph McNicholas (2001)

245 *British and Irish Dramatists Since World War II, Third Series,* edited by John Bull (2001)

246 *Twentieth-Century American Cultural Theorists,* edited by Paul Hansom (2001)

247 *James Joyce: A Documentary Volume,* edited by A. Nicholas Fargnoli (2001)

248 *Antebellum Writers in the South, Second Series,* edited by Kent Ljungquist (2001)

249 *Twentieth-Century American Dramatists, Third Series,* edited by Christopher Wheatley (2002)

250 *Antebellum Writers in New York, Second Series,* edited by Kent Ljungquist (2002)

251 *Canadian Fantasy and Science-Fiction Writers,* edited by Douglas Ivison (2002)

252 *British Philosophers, 1500–1799,* edited by Philip B. Dematteis and Peter S. Fosl (2002)

253 *Raymond Chandler: A Documentary Volume,* edited by Robert Moss (2002)

254 *The House of Putnam, 1837–1872: A Documentary Volume,* edited by Ezra Greenspan (2002)

255 *British Fantasy and Science-Fiction Writers, 1918–1960,* edited by Darren Harris-Fain (2002)

256 *Twentieth-Century American Western Writers, Third Series,* edited by Richard H. Cracroft (2002)

257 *Twentieth-Century Swedish Writers After World War II,* edited by Ann-Charlotte Gavel Adams (2002)

258 *Modern French Poets,* edited by Jean-François Leroux (2002)

259 *Twentieth-Century Swedish Writers Before World War II,* edited by Ann-Charlotte Gavel Adams (2002)

260 *Australian Writers, 1915–1950,* edited by Selina Samuels (2002)

261 *British Fantasy and Science-Fiction Writers Since 1960,* edited by Darren Harris-Fain (2002)

262 *British Philosophers, 1800–2000,* edited by Peter S. Fosl and Leemon B. McHenry (2002)

263 *William Shakespeare: A Documentary Volume,* edited by Catherine Loomis (2002)

264 *Italian Prose Writers, 1900–1945,* edited by Luca Somigli and Rocco Capozzi (2002)

265 *American Song Lyricists, 1920–1960,* edited by Philip Furia (2002)

266 *Twentieth-Century American Dramatists, Fourth Series,* edited by Christopher J. Wheatley (2002)

267 *Twenty-First-Century British and Irish Novelists,* edited by Michael R. Molino (2002)

268 *Seventeenth-Century French Writers,* edited by Françoise Jaouën (2002)

269 *Nathaniel Hawthorne: A Documentary Volume,* edited by Benjamin Franklin V (2002)

270 *American Philosophers Before 1950,* edited by Philip B. Dematteis and Leemon B. McHenry (2002)

271 *British and Irish Novelists Since 1960,* edited by Merritt Moseley (2002)

272 *Russian Prose Writers Between the World Wars,* edited by Christine Rydel (2003)

273 *F. Scott Fitzgerald's* Tender Is the Night: *A Documentary Volume,* edited by Matthew J. Bruccoli and George Parker Anderson (2003)

274 *John Dos Passos's* U.S.A.: *A Documentary Volume,* edited by Donald Pizer (2003)

275 *Twentieth-Century American Nature Writers: Prose,* edited by Roger Thompson and J. Scott Bryson (2003)

276 *British Mystery and Thriller Writers Since 1960,* edited by Gina Macdonald (2003)

277 *Russian Literature in the Age of Realism,* edited by Alyssa Dinega Gillespie (2003)

278 *American Novelists Since World War II, Seventh Series,* edited by James R. Giles and Wanda H. Giles (2003)

279 *American Philosophers, 1950–2000,* edited by Philip B. Dematteis and Leemon B. McHenry (2003)

280 *Dashiell Hammett's* The Maltese Falcon: *A Documentary Volume,* edited by Richard Layman (2003)

281 *British Rhetoricians and Logicians, 1500–1660, Second Series,* edited by Edward A. Malone (2003)

282 *New Formalist Poets,* edited by Jonathan N. Barron and Bruce Meyer (2003)

283 *Modern Spanish American Poets, First Series,* edited by María A. Salgado (2003)

284 *The House of Holt, 1866–1946: A Documentary Volume,* edited by Ellen D. Gilbert (2003)

285 *Russian Writers Since 1980*, edited by Marina Balina and Mark Lipoyvetsky (2004)

286 *Castilian Writers, 1400–1500*, edited by Frank A. Domínguez and George D. Greenia (2004)

287 *Portuguese Writers*, edited by Monica Rector and Fred M. Clark (2004)

288 *The House of Boni & Liveright, 1917–1933: A Documentary Volume*, edited by Charles Egleston (2004)

289 *Australian Writers, 1950–1975*, edited by Selina Samuels (2004)

290 *Modern Spanish American Poets, Second Series*, edited by María A. Salgado (2004)

291 *The Hoosier House: Bobbs-Merrill and Its Predecessors, 1850–1985: A Documentary Volume*, edited by Richard J. Schrader (2004)

292 *Twenty-First-Century American Novelists*, edited by Lisa Abney and Suzanne Disheroon-Green (2004)

293 *Icelandic Writers*, edited by Patrick J. Stevens (2004)

294 *James Gould Cozzens: A Documentary Volume*, edited by Matthew J. Bruccoli (2004)

295 *Russian Writers of the Silver Age, 1890–1925*, edited by Judith E. Kalb and J. Alexander Ogden with the collaboration of I. G. Vishnevetsky (2004)

296 *Twentieth-Century European Cultural Theorists, Second Series*, edited by Paul Hansom (2004)

297 *Twentieth-Century Norwegian Writers*, edited by Tanya Thresher (2004)

298 *Henry David Thoreau: A Documentary Volume*, edited by Richard J. Schneider (2004)

299 *Holocaust Novelists*, edited by Efraim Sicher (2004)

300 *Danish Writers from the Reformation to Decadence, 1550–1900*, edited by Marianne Stecher-Hansen (2004)

301 *Gustave Flaubert: A Documentary Volume*, edited by Éric Le Calvez (2004)

302 *Russian Prose Writers After World War II*, edited by Christine Rydel (2004)

303 *American Radical and Reform Writers, First Series*, edited by Steven Rosendale (2005)

304 *Bram Stoker's* Dracula: *A Documentary Volume*, edited by Elizabeth Miller (2005)

305 *Latin American Dramatists, First Series*, edited by Adam Versényi (2005)

306 *American Mystery and Detective Writers*, edited by George Parker Anderson (2005)

307 *Brazilian Writers*, edited by Monica Rector and Fred M. Clark (2005)

308 *Ernest Hemingway's* A Farewell to Arms: *A Documentary Volume*, edited by Charles Oliver (2005)

309 *John Steinbeck: A Documentary Volume*, edited by Luchen Li (2005)

310 *British and Irish Dramatists Since World War II, Fourth Series*, edited by John Bull (2005)

311 *Arabic Literary Culture, 500–925*, edited by Michael Cooperson and Shawkat M. Toorawa (2005)

312 *Asian American Writers*, edited by Deborah L. Madsen (2005)

313 *Writers of the French Enlightenment, I*, edited by Samia I. Spencer (2005)

314 *Writers of the French Enlightenment, II*, edited by Samia I. Spencer (2005)

315 *Langston Hughes: A Documentary Volume*, edited by Christopher C. De Santis (2005)

316 *American Prose Writers of World War I: A Documentary Volume*, edited by Steven Trout (2005)

317 *Twentieth-Century Russian Émigré Writers*, edited by María Rubins (2005)

318 *Sixteenth-Century Spanish Writers*, edited by Gregory B. Kaplan (2006)

319 *British and Irish Short-Fiction Writers 1945–2000*, edited by Cheryl Alexander Malcolm and David Malcolm (2006)

320 *Robert Penn Warren: A Documentary Volume*, edited by James A. Grimshaw Jr. (2006)

321 *Twentieth-Century French Dramatists*, edited by Mary Anne O'Neil (2006)

322 *Twentieth-Century Spanish Fiction Writers*, edited by Marta E. Altisent and Cristina Martínez-Carazo (2006)

323 *South Asian Writers in English*, edited by Fakrul Alam (2006)

324 *John O'Hara: A Documentary Volume*, edited by Matthew J. Bruccoli (2006)

325 *Australian Writers, 1975–2000*, edited by Selina Samuels (2006)

326 *Booker Prize Novels, 1969–2005*, edited by Merritt Moseley (2006)

327 *Sixteenth-Century French Writers*, edited by Megan Conway (2006)

328 *Chinese Fiction Writers, 1900–1949*, edited by Thomas Moran (2007)

329 *Nobel Prize Laureates in Literature, Part 1: Agnon–Eucken* (2007)

330 *Nobel Prize Laureates in Literature, Part 2: Faulkner–Kipling* (2007)

331 *Nobel Prize Laureates in Literature, Part 3: Lagerkvist–Pontoppidan* (2007)

332 *Nobel Prize Laureates in Literature, Part 4: Quasimodo–Yeats* (2007)

333 *Writers in Yiddish*, edited by Joseph Sherman (2007)

334 *Twenty-First-Century Canadian Writers*, edited by Christian Riegel (2007)

335 *American Short-Story Writers Since World War II, Fifth Series*, edited by Richard E. Lee and Patrick Meanor (2007)

336 *Eighteenth-Century British Historians*, edited by Ellen J. Jenkins (2007)

337 *Castilian Writers, 1200–1400*, edited by George D. Greenia and Frank A. Domínguez (2008)

338 *Thomas Carlyle: A Documentary Volume*, edited by Frances Frame (2008)

339 *Seventeenth-Century Italian Poets and Dramatists*, edited by Albert N. Mancini and Glenn Palen Pierce (2008)

340 *The Brontës: A Documentary Volume*, edited by Susan B. Taylor (2008)

341 *Twentieth-Century American Dramatists, Fifth Series*, edited by Garrett Eisler (2008)

342 *Twentieth-Century American Nature Poets*, edited by J. Scott Bryson and Roger Thompson (2008)

343 *Mark Twain's* Adventures of Huckleberry Finn: *A Documentary Volume*, edited by Tom Quirk (2009)

344 *Nineteenth-Century British Dramatists*, edited by Angela Courtney (2009)

345 *American Radical and Reform Writers, Second Series*, edited by Hester Lee Furey (2009)

346 *Twentieth-Century Arab Writers*, edited by Majd Yaser Al-Mallah and Coeli Fitzpatrick (2009)

Dictionary of Literary Biography Documentary Series

1 *Sherwood Anderson, Willa Cather, John Dos Passos, Theodore Dreiser, F. Scott Fitzgerald, Ernest Hemingway, Sinclair Lewis*, edited by Margaret A. Van Antwerp (1982)

2 *James Gould Cozzens, James T. Farrell, William Faulkner, John O'Hara, John Steinbeck, Thomas Wolfe, Richard Wright*, edited by Margaret A. Van Antwerp (1982)

3 *Saul Bellow, Jack Kerouac, Norman Mailer, Vladimir Nabokov, John Updike, Kurt Vonnegut*, edited by Mary Bruccoli (1983)

4 *Tennessee Williams*, edited by Margaret A. Van Antwerp and Sally Johns (1984)

5 *American Transcendentalists*, edited by Joel Myerson (1988)

6 *Hardboiled Mystery Writers: Raymond Chandler, Dashiell Hammett, Ross Mac-*

donald, edited by Matthew J. Bruccoli and Richard Layman (1989)

7 *Modern American Poets: James Dickey, Robert Frost, Marianne Moore,* edited by Karen L. Rood (1989)

8 *The Black Aesthetic Movement,* edited by Jeffrey Louis Decker (1991)

9 *American Writers of the Vietnam War: W. D. Ehrhart, Larry Heinemann, Tim O'Brien, Walter McDonald, John M. Del Vecchio,* edited by Ronald Baughman (1991)

10 *The Bloomsbury Group,* edited by Edward L. Bishop (1992)

11 *American Proletarian Culture: The Twenties and The Thirties,* edited by Jon Christian Suggs (1993)

12 *Southern Women Writers: Flannery O'Connor, Katherine Anne Porter, Eudora Welty,* edited by Mary Ann Wimsatt and Karen L. Rood (1994)

13 *The House of Scribner, 1846–1904,* edited by John Delaney (1996)

14 *Four Women Writers for Children, 1868–1918,* edited by Caroline C. Hunt (1996)

15 *American Expatriate Writers: Paris in the Twenties,* edited by Matthew J. Bruccoli and Robert W. Trogdon (1997)

16 *The House of Scribner, 1905–1930,* edited by John Delaney (1997)

17 *The House of Scribner, 1931–1984,* edited by John Delaney (1998)

18 *British Poets of The Great War: Sassoon, Graves, Owen,* edited by Patrick Quinn (1999)

19 *James Dickey,* edited by Judith S. Baughman (1999)

See also DLB 210, 216, 219, 222, 224, 229, 237, 247, 253, 254, 263, 269, 273, 274, 280, 284, 288, 291, 294, 298, 301, 304, 308, 309, 315, 316, 320, 324, 338, 340, 343

Dictionary of Literary Biography Yearbooks

1980 edited by Karen L. Rood, Jean W. Ross, and Richard Ziegfeld (1981)

1981 edited by Karen L. Rood, Jean W. Ross, and Richard Ziegfeld (1982)

1982 edited by Richard Ziegfeld; associate editors: Jean W. Ross and Lynne C. Zeigler (1983)

1983 edited by Mary Bruccoli and Jean W. Ross; associate editor Richard Ziegfeld (1984)

1984 edited by Jean W. Ross (1985)

1985 edited by Jean W. Ross (1986)

1986 edited by J. M. Brook (1987)

1987 edited by J. M. Brook (1988)

1988 edited by J. M. Brook (1989)

1989 edited by J. M. Brook (1990)

1990 edited by James W. Hipp (1991)

1991 edited by James W. Hipp (1992)

1992 edited by James W. Hipp (1993)

1993 edited by James W. Hipp, contributing editor George Garrett (1994)

1994 edited by James W. Hipp, contributing editor George Garrett (1995)

1995 edited by James W. Hipp, contributing editor George Garrett (1996)

1996 edited by Samuel W. Bruce and L. Kay Webster, contributing editor George Garrett (1997)

1997 edited by Matthew J. Bruccoli and George Garrett, with the assistance of L. Kay Webster (1998)

1998 edited by Matthew J. Bruccoli, contributing editor George Garrett, with the assistance of D. W. Thomas (1999)

1999 edited by Matthew J. Bruccoli, contributing editor George Garrett, with the assistance of D. W. Thomas (2000)

2000 edited by Matthew J. Bruccoli, contributing editor George Garrett, with the assistance of George Parker Anderson (2001)

2001 edited by Matthew J. Bruccoli, contributing editor George Garrett, with the assistance of George Parker Anderson (2002)

2002 edited by Matthew J. Bruccoli and George Garrett; George Parker Anderson, Assistant Editor (2003)

Concise Series

Concise Dictionary of American Literary Biography, 7 volumes (1988–1999): *The New Consciousness, 1941–1968; Colonization to the American Renaissance, 1640–1865; Realism, Naturalism, and Local Color, 1865–1917; The Twenties, 1917–1929; The Age of Maturity, 1929–1941; Broadening Views, 1968–1988; Supplement: Modern Writers, 1900–1998.*

Concise Dictionary of British Literary Biography, 8 volumes (1991–1992): *Writers of the Middle Ages and Renaissance Before 1660; Writers of the Restoration and Eighteenth Century, 1660–1789; Writers of the Romantic Period, 1789–1832; Victorian Writers, 1832–1890; Late-Victorian and Edwardian Writers, 1890–1914; Modern Writers, 1914–1945; Writers After World War II, 1945–1960; Contemporary Writers, 1960 to Present.*

Concise Dictionary of World Literary Biography, 4 volumes (1999–2000): *Ancient Greek and Roman Writers; German Writers; African, Caribbean, and Latin American Writers; South Slavic and Eastern European Writers.*

Dictionary of Literary Biography® • Volume Three Hundred Forty-Six

Twentieth-Century Arab Writers

Dictionary of Literary Biography® • Volume Three Hundred Forty-Six

Twentieth-Century Arab Writers

Edited by
Majd Yaser Al-Mallah
Grand Valley State University
and
Coeli Fitzpatrick
Grand Valley State University

A Bruccoli Clark Layman Book

ST. PHILIP'S COLLEGE LIBRARY

Detroit • New York • San Francisco • New Haven, Conn • Waterville, Maine • London

**Dictionary of Literary Biography,
Volume 346: Twentieth-Century
Arab Writers**
Majd Yaser Al-Mallah and Coeli Fitzpatrick

Founding Editor: Matthew J. Bruccoli

Advisory Board: John Baker,
    William Cagle, Patrick O'Connor,
    George Garrett, Trudier Harris,
    Alvin Kernan

Editorial Director: Richard Layman

@ 2009 Gale, Cengage Learning

ALL RIGHTS RESERVED. No part of this work covered by the copyright herein may be reproduced, transmitted, stored, or used in any form or by any means graphic, electronic, or mechanical, including but not limited to photocopying, recording, scanning, digitizing, taping, Web distribution, information networks, or information storage and retrieval systems, except as permitted under Section 107 or 108 of the 1976 United States Copyright Act, without the prior written permission of the publisher.

This publication is a creative work fully protected by all applicable copyright laws, as well as by misappropriation, trade secret, unfair competition, and other applicable laws. The authors and editors of this work have added value to the underlying factual material herein through one or more of the following: unique and original selection, coordination, expression, arrangement, and classification of the information.

For product information and technology assistance, contact us at
Gale Customer Support, 1-800-877-4253.

For permission to use material from this text or product, submit all requests online at **www.cengage.com/permissions**
Further permissions questions can be emailed to
permissionrequest@cengage.com

While every effort has been made to ensure the reliability of the information presented in this publication, Gale, a part of Cengage Learning, does not guarantee the accuracy of the data contained herein. Gale accepts no payment for listing; and inclusion in the publication of any organization, agency, institution, publication, service, or individual does not imply endorsement of the editors or publisher. Errors brought to the attention of the publisher and verified to the satisfaction of the publisher will be corrected in future editions.

EDITORIAL DATA PRIVACY POLICY. Does this publication contain information about you as an individual? If so, for more information about our editorial date privacy policies, please see our Privacy Statement at www.gale.cengage.com

LIBRARY OF CONGRESS CATALOGING-IN-PUBLICATION DATA

Twentieth-century Arab writers / edited by Majd Yaser Al-Mallah and Coeli Fitzpatrick.
    p. cm. — (Dictionary of literary biography ; v. 346)
"A Bruccoli Clark Layman book."
Includes bibliographical references and index.
ISBN 978-0-7876-8164-7 (hardcover)
1. Authors, Arab—20th century—Biography. 2. Arab countries—Bio-bibliography. I. Al-Mallah, Majd Yasser. II. Fitzpatrick, Coeli.

PJ7521.T84 2009
892.7'16—dc22
[B]
                                2008041243

ISBN-13: 978-0-7876-8164-7   ISBN-10: 0-7876-8164-4

Gale
27500 Drake Rd.
Farmington Hills, MI 48331-3535

Printed in the United States of America
1 2 3 4 5 6 7 12 11 10 09 08

To Shorouq, Layth, and Qays Yaser
  —*Majd Al-Mallah*

To Philippe and Eli with love
  —*Coeli Fitzpatrick*

Contents

Plan of the Series xv
Introduction xvii

Muhammad 'Abduh (1849–1905) 3
   Yasir Ibrahim Almallah

Mas'udah Aboubakr (1954–) 10
   Hager Ben Driss

Mohammed Arkoun (1928–) 15
   Ursula Günther

Sadik Jalal al-Azm (1934–) 24
   Sebastian Maisel

Liana Badr (1952–) 30
   Angela Saliba Bajalieh

Halim Barakat (1936–) 35
   Jared Reene

Rachid Boudjedra (1941–) 40
   Boutheina Khaldi

Slaheddine Boujah (1956–) 45
   Hager Ben Driss

Assia Djebar (Fatima-Zohra Imalayène)
(1936–) 52
   Boutheina Khaldi

Gamal al-Ghitani (1945–) 58
   Ayman A. El-Desouky

Kahlil Gibran (1883–1931) 68
   John Walbridge

Emile Habiby (1922–1996) 80
   Kamal Abdel-Malek

Sonallah Ibrahim (1937–) 84
   Mara Naaman

Yusuf Idris (1927–1991) 91
   Wyoma vanDuinkerken

Isma'il Fahd Isma'il (1940–) 101
   Sebastian Maisel

Jabra Ibrahim Jabra (1920–1994) 106
   Kamal Abdel-Malek

Mohammed 'Abed al-Jabri (1935–) 112
   Mohamed Ourya

'Aziz al-Sayyid Jasim (1941–1991?) 119
   Hager Ben Driss

Ghassan Kanafani (1936–1972) 125
   Kamal Abdel-Malek

Sahar Khalifeh (1941–) 131
   Ahmad al-Mallah

Raif Khuri (1913–1967) 137
   Malakeh Khoury and Goetz Nordbruch

Abdallah Laroui (1933–) 141
   Mohamed Ourya

Amin Maalouf (1949–) 147
   Coeli Fitzpatrick

Naguib Mahfouz (1911–2006) 153
   Majd Yaser Al-Mallah

Fatima Mernissi (1940–) 164
   Azza Basarudin

Hanna Mina (1924–) 171
   Toufoul Abou-Hodeib

Abdelrahman Munif (1933–2004) 178
   Sebastian Maisel

Mushin al-Musawi (1945–) 185
   Hager Ben Driss

Emily Nasrallah (1931–) 193
   Pennie Johnson

'Abd al-Hakim Qasim (1935–1990) 198
   Christina Phillips

Sayyid Qutb (1906–1966) 203
   Ovamir Anjum

Nawal El Saadawi (1931–) 208
   Coeli Fitzpatrick

Muhammad Baqir al-Sadr (1935–1980) 215
   John Walbridge

Contents

Edward W. Said (1935–2003) 221
   Matthew Abraham

Tayeb Salih (1929–) 232
   Majd Yaser Al-Mallah

Anton Shammas (1950–) 238
   Mahmoud Kayyal

Hanan al-Shaykh (1945–) 244
   Wyoma vanDuinkerken

Bahaa' Taher (1935–) 252
   Ayman A. El-Desouky

Fuad al-Takarli (1927–2008) 257
   Imed Nsiri

Zakaria Tamer (1931–) 264
   Mahmoud Kayyal

Hasan al-Turabi (1932–) 269
   Carol Bargeron

Latifa al-Zayyat (1923–1996). 274
   Ellen McLarney

Constantine K. Zurayk (1909–2000) 279
   Noomane Raboudi

Books for Further Reading 283
Contributors 287
Cumulative Index 291

Plan of the Series

... Almost the most prodigious asset of a country, and perhaps its most precious possession, is its native literary product—when that product is fine and noble and enduring.

Mark Twain*

The advisory board, the editors, and the publisher of the *Dictionary of Literary Biography* are joined in endorsing Mark Twain's declaration. The literature of a nation provides an inexhaustible resource of permanent worth. Our purpose is to make literature and its creators better understood and more accessible to students and the reading public, while satisfying the needs of teachers and researchers.

To meet these requirements, *literary biography* has been construed in terms of the author's achievement. The most important thing about a writer is his writing. Accordingly, the entries in *DLB* are career biographies, tracing the development of the author's canon and the evolution of his reputation.

The purpose of *DLB* is not only to provide reliable information in a usable format but also to place the figures in the larger perspective of literary history and to offer appraisals of their accomplishments by qualified scholars.

The publication plan for *DLB* resulted from two years of preparation. The project was proposed to Bruccoli Clark by Frederick G. Ruffner, president of the Gale Research Company, in November 1975. After specimen entries were prepared and typeset, an advisory board was formed to refine the entry format and develop the series rationale. In meetings held during 1976, the publisher, series editors, and advisory board approved the scheme for a comprehensive biographical dictionary of persons who contributed to literature. Editorial work on the first volume began in January 1977, and it was published in 1978. In order to make *DLB* more than a dictionary and to compile volumes that individually have claim to status as literary history, it was decided to organize volumes by topic, period, or genre. Each of these freestanding volumes provides a biographical-bibliographical guide and overview for a particular area of literature. We are convinced that this organization—as opposed to a single alphabet method—constitutes a valuable innovation in the presentation of reference material. The volume plan necessarily requires many decisions for the placement and treatment of authors. Certain figures will be included in separate volumes, but with different entries emphasizing the aspect of his career appropriate to each volume. Ernest Hemingway, for example, is represented in *American Writers in Paris, 1920–1939* by an entry focusing on his expatriate apprenticeship; he is also in *American Novelists, 1910–1945* with an entry surveying his entire career, as well as in *American Short-Story Writers, 1910–1945, Second Series* with an entry concentrating on his short fiction. Each volume includes a cumulative index of the subject authors and articles.

Between 1981 and 2002 the series was augmented and updated by the *DLB Yearbooks*. There have also been nineteen *DLB Documentary Series* volumes, which provide illustrations, facsimiles, and biographical and critical source materials for figures, works, or groups judged to have particular interest for students. In 1999 the *Documentary Series* was incorporated into the *DLB* volume numbering system beginning with *DLB 210: Ernest Hemingway*.

We define literature as the *intellectual commerce of a nation:* not merely as belles lettres but as that ample and complex process by which ideas are generated, shaped, and transmitted. *DLB* entries are not limited to "creative writers" but extend to other figures who in their time and in their way influenced the mind of a people. Thus the series encompasses historians, journalists, publishers, book collectors, and screenwriters. By this means readers of *DLB* may be aided to perceive literature not as cult scripture in the keeping of intellectual high priests but firmly positioned at the center of a nation's life.

DLB includes the major writers appropriate to each volume and those standing in the ranks behind them. Scholarly and critical counsel has been sought in deciding which minor figures to include and how full their entries should be. Wherever possible, useful refer-

*From an unpublished section of Mark Twain's autobiography, copyright by the Mark Twain Company

ences are made to figures who do not warrant separate entries.

Each *DLB* volume has an expert volume editor responsible for planning the volume, selecting the figures for inclusion, and assigning the entries. Volume editors are also responsible for preparing, where appropriate, appendices surveying the major periodicals and literary and intellectual movements for their volumes, as well as lists of further readings. Work on the series as a whole is coordinated at the Bruccoli Clark Layman editorial center in Columbia, South Carolina, where the editorial staff is responsible for accuracy and utility of the published volumes.

One feature that distinguishes *DLB* is the illustration policy—its concern with the iconography of literature. Just as an author is influenced by his surroundings, so is the reader's understanding of the author enhanced by a knowledge of his environment. Therefore *DLB* volumes include not only drawings, paintings, and photographs of authors, often depicting them at various stages in their careers, but also illustrations of their families and places where they lived. Title pages are regularly reproduced in facsimile along with dust jackets for modern authors. The dust jackets are a special feature of *DLB* because they often document better than anything else the way in which an author's work was perceived in its own time. Specimens of the writers' manuscripts and letters are included when feasible.

Samuel Johnson rightly decreed that "The chief glory of every people arises from its authors." The purpose of the *Dictionary of Literary Biography* is to compile literary history in the surest way available to us—by accurate and comprehensive treatment of the lives and work of those who contributed to it.

The *DLB* Advisory Board

Introduction

Dictionary of Literary Biography 346: Twentieth-Century Arab Writers provides readers an introduction to some of the prose writers from the Arabic-speaking Middle East, a geographical area marked by a diversity of languages, religion, and cultures. While the Arabic-speaking Middle East immediately conjures up the Arab League, the institution founded in 1945 to foster cooperation between Arab countries, we should also note that other Middle East countries such as Israel, Iran, and Turkey have Arabic-speaking communities. There are twenty-two Arab countries, spread out from the Persian Gulf in the East to the Atlantic Ocean in the West, and from Syria in the North to the Indian Ocean in the South. The Arab countries in the Asian continent include Bahrain, Iraq, Jordan, Kuwait, Lebanon, Oman, Palestine, Qatar, Saudi Arabia, Syria, United Arab Emirates, and Yemen. In the African continent, the Arab countries include Algeria, Djibouti, Egypt, Libya, Mauritania, Morocco, Tunisia, Sudan, and Somalia. The Comoros Islands, off Southeast Africa, is also a member of the Arab League. All of the writers in this volume were born and spent at least part of their lives in the Arabic-speaking Middle East. Titling the volume "Muslim Writers" would not have reflected the religious diversity of writers included here nor of the Arab world itself. Many of the writers in this volume migrated to the West or lived in the West for a good portion of their lives: Edward W. Said, Tayeb Salih, and Muhammed Arkoun, for example. Although most of the authors in the volume wrote in Arabic at some point in their careers, some write in other languages, most commonly English and French.

Because the volume covers a vast cultural landscape, we chose regionally representative authors in compiling our list of subjects. Unfortunately, several limitations compelled us to make difficult decisions on the list of writers to include in the volume. We include authors from the Arabian peninsula, the fertile crescent, Egypt and Sudan, and the North African countries. Although these writers use different forms of expression (novels, short stories, essays, and nonfiction books), they are all influenced, one way or another, by the impact of colonialism and postcolonialism. In other words, the legacy of foreign subjugation of the Arab World and the development of society and political thought before and after independence is evident in their works.

The modern colonial period begins with Napoleon Bonaparte's military campaign and subsequent control of Egypt in 1798. One of the reasons Napoleon's campaign is significant is that it included many scientists and researchers—men who were charged with "recording" Egypt. The volume of their production was enormous, and presented to Europeans, for the first time, a chronicle of the Orient. These studies provided Europe with a one-sided view of what "characterized" the Egyptian people; they notably did not include any recording of Egyptians' understandings of themselves. Napoleon's rule in Egypt came to an end very quickly (in 1801), largely as a result of the competing interests with the British who destroyed the French navy, leaving Napoleon with no option but to return to France. However, the experience as a whole proved to be important and formative in the historical and intellectual developments in the nineteenth and twentieth centuries. On the historical level, when the French left Egypt, a strong leader by the name of Muhammad 'Ali emerged as the ruler of Egypt in 1805, filling the power vacuum that Napoleon created with his withdrawal from Egypt. Muhammad 'Ali had an ambitious agenda in Egypt, including modernizing the country's military, education, and economy. He wanted to imitate Western—particularly French—advancements due to the Industrial Revolution. To further this end, he sent Egyptian students to learn and gain experience in France. Although Muhammad 'Ali's reforms were largely unsuccessful in producing fundamental changes in Egypt, the interaction with France brought about some modernization, exposure to new ideas and styles of writing, but it also brought a sense of bewilderment amongst some Arab intellectuals as to why the Arab people seemed to be so far behind the West and were so easily able to be exploited by Western interests.

This feeling became even more pressing in the wake of direct colonialism and subjugation in the majority of Arabic-speaking provinces. France, for example, occupied Algeria in 1830 (and stayed there until Algeria's independence in 1962); Britain controlled Egypt in 1882 (and stayed, with various forms of direct or indirect influence, until 1952). With the end of World War I, the vast majority of the Arabic-speaking world was under either direct or indirect political, economic, and social influence of a European country (mainly Britain and France, with the exception of Libya which came under Italian control, and portions of Morocco which came under Spanish control). As a result of this control, European hegemony was felt in some form or another in most of the Arabic-speaking provinces.

Writers responded to European colonialism, which left a lasting impression on people in the Arab world, in varied and complex ways. Literary figures and intellectuals alike began their reaction to colonialism by questioning how and why they came to be subjugated to European powers so easily and how they (as writers) could respond to the root causes of being so weak militarily compared to Europe. Such a focus led to feelings of cultural inferiority (reinforced by Europe) that were often embraced by Arabs themselves. In Egypt, a French-educated lawyer by the name of Qasim Amin argued that Arabs were lazy, inherently illogical, and unable to see the value in their natural resources. Although this perception was by no means uniform, it was widespread enough to have created a vibrant discussion and questioning of how the once-rich Arab and Islamic civilization had come to reach such a state of "decay." Amin's writings can be seen as the catalyst for the women's movement in Egypt. The writers and intellectuals of the late nineteenth and early twentieth centuries were more concerned with how they could respond to this "decay."

There were several types of responses, with three major streams of thought that began in the nineteenth century and continued well into the twentieth. Some writers and intellectuals looked to the West as a model of development and an inspiration for their political, literary, and intellectual pursuits. Often these were writers who had spent some time in Europe or in European schools. Other writers looked at the Arabic and Islamic civilization as a source of inspiration and renewal. The most prominent writer of this sort is the Egyptian writer Muhammad 'Abduh (died 1905), whose intellectual legacy serves as a major school of thought that provided a bridge to some of the newer forms of Islamic renewal in the twentieth century. A student of Jamal al-Din al-Afghani, one of the first Muslim intellectuals whose writings specifically addressed the issue of imperialism in the Muslim world, Muhammad 'Abduh wanted to respond to imperialism both by looking inward to see what was weak in Arab society owing to its own negligence and by examining what kind of indigenous response could be rallied to confront Western colonialism. Finally, there were the anti-imperialist Islamists, such as Sayyid Qutb, who viewed the West as depraved, corrupt, and full of ideals detrimental to Islam. All of these kinds of responses to Europe continued to provide "competing" ideologies and ways of dealing with the West and responding to the challenge of modernity and development, both while the Arab world was under European rule and also after independence.

In literature, contemporaries of Muhammad 'Abduh founded a strong movement of revival or renaissance (the transliterated Arabic word is *al-nahdah*) to conquer "decay." Literary figures wanted to revive the cultural richness of the Arab heritage by turning to the classical literary tradition as a source of inspiration. In poetry, it was certainly appropriate, and in many cases easy, to go back to the masters of classical Arabic poetry, who were highly regarded in their art, and who were considered the main foundation of Arabic literature. In the area of fiction, writers turned not only to the classical literary tradition, particularly the *maqamah* (a form of medieval tale) as a model for indigenous writing, but also to the West. Indeed, unlike poetry, which had a very old pedigree in the Arab world, literary forms such as the novel never really existed in the earlier Arabic literary tradition. Literary historians trace the beginnings of the novel and the short story to the translation movement, which came about as a result of the interaction with the West. Some authors felt that the best response to Western domination was an embracing and emulation of Western culture. They reasoned such embracing of Western ideas would strip Western countries of the ability to claim that the Orient was backward. Al-Tahtawi (died 1873), who traveled to Europe during the period of Muhammad 'Ali, translated Fénelon's *Télémaque,* and in doing so set into motion calls for more translations. The public interest in reading novels led to the emergence of the "historical" or "romance" novel, whose most prominent writer is Jurji Zaydan (died 1914). His novels focused on a "romance" between two "fictional" lovers in the context of a major event in Islamic history. According to many literary critics, *Zaynab* by Muhammad Husayn Haykal, published in 1913, is considered to be the first novel in Arabic literature with some literary merit. The Egyptian writer Taha Husayn (died 1973), a prominent literary and intellectual figure in the twentieth century, also contributed to the beginnings of the novel, through the publication of his autobiography in the 1920s. His nonfiction work *Mustaqbal al-Thaqafah fi Misr* (1938; translated as *The Future of Culture in Egypt,* 1954) was also an important part of Egyptian nationalist writings. The artistic Arabic novel, however, does not emerge until Naguib Mahfouz, Egyptian author (and later Nobel laureate), popularizes the novel as a major and serious literary form (see entry). Arab writers in Egypt formed the New

School group to promote and discuss literary works. Members of this group founded a weekly literary journal, *al-Fajr* (Dawn) which disseminated literary works throughout Egypt, as well as the Levant.

It was quite common for Arab writers in the twentieth century to imitate purely European models. Romance novels, such as those written by Egyptian author Ihasan 'Abd al-Quddus, became popular as light entertainment and continue to be read. The writers included in *DLB 346: Twentieth-Century Arab Writers,* however, were not writing merely to entertain. Their works offer nuanced responses to the complex changes through which their countries were rapidly going. Naturally, many of these writers focused on the theme of social justice as their way of responding to European colonialism and the suppression of native ideas and influences that persisted even after colonial powers left the Arab world. For example, Mahfouz's Cairo Trilogy–*Bayn al-qasrayn* (1956; translated as *Palace Walk,* 1991), *Qasr al-shawq* (1957; translated as *Palace of Desire,* 1991), and *al-Sukkariyyah* (1957; translated as *Sugar Street,* 1992)–is rife with tales of Egyptian interaction with Britain, particularly the popular quest for independence in 1919, which dominates a good portion of *Bayn al-qasrayn*. One recurrent scene in the fiction of the Egyptian feminist writer Nawal El Saadawi is of the student demonstrations in Egypt against the British presence in the country.

Across the Arab world, writers addressed their people's experience with colonialism as well as the larger issues of social and political justice, including how society should be constructed after independence from the colonial powers. Tunisian writer Slaheddine Boujah deals with political and social justice in a subtle way. Examining issues of both personal and national independence, Boujah's novel *al-Taj wa al-khinjar wa al-jasad* (1992, The Crown, the Sword and the Body) tells the story of Sidi Farhat, a Sufi mystic who led a rebellion against the oppression of the king in the eighteenth century. In his first novel, *al-Masabih al-zurq* (1954, Blue Lanterns), Syrian writer Hanna Mina describes clashes with the French occupation authorities during World War II. In Iraq, 'Aziz al-Sayyid Jasim, a one-time member of the Communist Party who lived under the repressive regime of Saddam Hussein, followed a generation of writers much influenced by Marxism. In his fiction, however, Jasim depicts his disillusionment with the Communist Party in Iraq and criticizes the political oppression from the time of the monarchy until the establishment of the republic and on to the reign of the Baath Party and the rule of Saddam Hussein. Another important Iraqi writer, Fuad al-Takarli, sets his most important novel, *al-Raj' al-ba'id* (1980; translated as *The Long Way Back,* 2001), against the backdrop of political turmoil that Iraq was experiencing in the late 1960s.

The impact of war is a major theme in the work of Arab authors. The most prominent of these wars, and probably those most ingrained in historical memory of the region, are the wars of 1948 and 1967. The 1948 War resulted in the creation of the State of Israel, and consequently resulted in a major population of Palestinians, estimated in the hundreds of thousands, who suddenly became stateless refugees in other Arab countries. The Six-Day War of June 1967 between Israel on the one side and Syria, Jordan, and Egypt on the other resulted in a crushing defeat for the Arab states (and for the Palestinians in whose name they went to war) and the occupation by Israel of the West Bank and Gaza strip, as well as the Egyptian Sinai Peninsula and the Syrian Golan Heights. Both wars were highly demoralizing, not only for the Palestinians but also for many Arabs throughout the Middle East. The wars live on in the fiction and essays of many of the authors featured in this volume. Novelist and sociologist Halim Barakat depicts the impact of war and the cruelty of the fighting during 1948 and 1967. Ghassan Kanafani, one of the most prominent Palestinian writers, addresses the Palestinian issue by focusing on the refugees who left their homeland after the wars. Emile Habiby, a prominent Arab author who became a citizen of Israel after the 1948 War, depicts how the Palestinians who stayed dealt with the development of the new Israeli state. In addition to these authors, many other Arab writers from across the Middle East address the impact of the Palestinian plight, including Saudi author Abdelrahman Munif and Palestinian author Jabra Ibrahim Jabra. Edward Said, who was living in the United States at the time of the Six-Day War, said that he was completely absorbed by the academic life of an English professor until the 1967 War, when something inside of him was forever changed. From that point on, he felt himself directly involved in Palestinian life, even though he was living thousands of miles away. His writings went from being confined to the study of English and French literature to politics, including the study of how the humanities disciplines affect and are affected by politics.

The civil war in Lebanon, a brutal and destructive fifteen-year-long affair (1975–1990) in which more than twenty thousand people (most of them civilians) were killed, is another historical event that was the focus of the writing of some of these intellectuals. The Lebanese writer Hanan al-Shaykh provides a vivid depiction of the disturbing impact of war on women's lives through her most memorable character, Zahra, in her novel *Hikayat Zahrah* (1980; translated as *The Story of Zahra,* 1986). In her novel *Tilka al-dhikrayat* (1980, Those

Memories), Lebanese writer Emily Nasrallah also examines the subject of war and its profiteers.

In Algeria, the war for independence from the French lasted eight years (1954–1962). It was, as one scholar called it, a "savage war of peace" wherein more than one million Algerians lost their lives. Some of the North African writers use this war as backdrop to their novels. Assia Djebar's *Les Impatients* (1958, The Impatients) and her *Les enfants du nouveau monde* (1962; translated as *Children of the New World,* 2005) are both set during this time period. She also memorialized the brutality of Algeria's civil war in her novel *Ombre Sultane* (1987; translated as *A Sister to Scherazade,* 1988). These and other authors have given voice to the many victims of war who would otherwise be forgotten.

Arab cultures, buffeted by internal as well as external forces, have experienced bewildering and profound changes in the twentieth century. In Egypt, Mahfouz explores the impact of change in the Cairo Trilogy through the life and tribulations of one Cairo family that he follows from World War I until World War II, brilliantly depicting the complexity and surprising developments of Egyptian society. In contrast to the urban setting of Mahfouz, Yusuf Idris explores life in countryside, sometimes using his experiences gleaned from his practice as a doctor in his intimate and close descriptions of those plagued by disease. Other Egyptian writers have focused on the structure of political systems in the Arab world. One of the most vocal of such critics, Sonallah Ibrahim writes fiction that challenges Arab political regimes and governments.

Beyond Egypt, many other Arab writers have turned inward to examine issues affecting their societies. Tayeb Salih, Sudan's most famous writer, describes fascinating characters involved in village life, but he also addresses the impact of change, particularly through his villagers' interaction with the West and the quest for modernization. His masterpiece, *Mawsim al-hijra ila al-shamal* (1969; translated as *Season of Migration to the North,* 1969), looks at the relationship between East and West and the difficulty of reconciling competing and often contradictory impulses in the individual's quest for a fulfilling identity. Abdallah Laroui and Mohammed 'Abed al-Jabri, both Moroccan intellectuals, criticize "Arab thought" for limiting its founts of inspiration to those found within European modernity. They advocate a reexamination of Arab tradition in order for Arab thought to free itself from the confines of both an understanding of tradition that is locked in a particular "glorious past" and an understanding of tradition which acts as if the Arab world and the West have similar historical experiences.

Changes in Arab countries are not, of course, limited to political ones. There are also important social and economic changes that authors address. The beginning of feminism as a movement in the Middle East can be traced to Huda Sha'rawi's shocking decision to defy social convention by publicly removing her veil in Egypt in 1923. But as for feminism as a discipline for intellectual criticism, we can point to the works of Nawal El Saadawi and Fatima Mernissi to find nearly always controversial discussions of the role and status of women in the Arab world. Like other veins of criticism, feminism took varying forms and styles of writing. El Saadawi is critical of the patriarchy of Islam and finds little sympathy for feminism within the religion. On the other hand, the Moroccan sociologist Mernissi takes on the *interpretation* of Islam (specifically how the Qur'an and Hadith sayings of the Prophet Muhammad were interpreted over the centuries after his death) rather than the religion itself. She argues that a compassionate and ethical Islam has been overshadowed by centuries of largely unchecked misogyny. She believes that if one could scratch through the layers of (often deliberate) misinterpretation and misrepresentation of the religion, the "spirit" of Islam encourages the quest for equality and justice for both sexes. In her novels–many of which were banned in the Arab world because they were too controversial–Lebanese author Hanan al-Shaykh employs women characters to examine marriage and divorce in patriarchal societies.

Male authors such as Qutb and Hasan al-Turabi also take up the issue of women in society. Qutb spent time in the United States, where he found himself deeply troubled by what he saw as the exploitation of Western women. He saw his criticisms as aimed at protecting women from Western society. Qutb praised Islam for mandating equality between the sexes while lambasting the West for allowing women to work in what he called an "atmosphere of the smoke of incense and opium." Such an approach is notably different from El Saadawi and Mernissi, each of whom in different ways is critical of what they saw as the exploitation of women by Islam. In his writings on women and Islam, al-Turabi contends that a revolution against the condition of women in traditional Muslim societies is inevitable, arguing for a reading of *shari'ah* (Islamic law) that is more compatible with the ideal Islam (in the contemporary sense). In fiction written by men, women are often represented as positive and hopeful characters–Zohra's character in Mahfouz's *Miramar* (1967; translated, 1978) and Yu'ad in Habiby's *al-Waqa'i' al-gharibah fi ikhtifa' abi al-nahs Sa'id al-Mutasha'il* (1974; translated as *The Secret Life of Saeed, The Ill-Fated Pessoptomist: A Palestinian Who Became a Citizen of Israel,* 1984) are only two of many examples.

The understanding of the colonial legacy in the Middle East was forever changed in 1978 with the publication of Said's monumental study *Orientalism*–the work that many cite as the beginning of postcolonial theory. Said examines what he calls the "material culture" produced in Europe during the centuries of colonialism–a culture of art, history, philosophy, science, geography, and literature–that very often was used to justify and promote the colonial endeavor by normalizing the image of the "Orient" as set apart from and lesser than the "Occident" and therefore "in need of being made civilized." Said argues that the relationship between the Occident and the Orient as one of power, domination, and hegemony is so firmly entrenched within the minds and cultures of people living in the Occident that it will take a serious and concerted effort–a profound reinterpretation of Western history–in order to escape its consequences and promote a new future. It is not simply enough to "tell the truth" about the Orient, he writes, because "any system of ideas that can remain unchanged as teachable wisdom (in academies, books, congresses, universities, foreign-service institutes) from the period of Ernest Renan in the late 1840's to the present in the United States must be something more formidable than a mere collection of lies." He calls upon his readers as a first step to grasp what has happened through the "creation" of the Orient by European culture. Said's work generated (and continues to generate) a considerable amount of scholarship both in support of and against his thesis.

In philosophical and political writings, the response to both imperialism and Islamic revivalism started by 'Abduh in the late nineteenth century has been refined by thinkers in the twentieth century. Lively debates ensued between thinkers in the vein of what has sometimes been called "liberal Islam" and these continue through the present day. At issue are important questions such as who has the right to practice *ijtihad*, or interpretation of the Qur'an; how Islam should address contemporary notions of human rights; and whether or not Islam is compatible with democratic government. In the latter part of the twentieth century, we have seen a proliferation of thinkers who are interested in addressing such questions–and the debates have gained a new urgency since 11 September 2001. After that day, it became even more common for Westerners to view all of Islam as fundamentalist Islam, in the name of which the attacks on New York and Washington, D.C., were carried out. Mohammed Arkoun and Said are only two of many authors who have engaged in this important intellectual debate.

There is no doubt the authors presented in this volume have either shaped or, at the very least, enriched the intellectual discussions that have been taking place in various countries in the Arab world. While some of them were imprisoned in their respective countries because of their works or attacked for their ideas, it is important to say that the very existence of such voices is indicative of the rich and complex intellectual ideas that are produced in the Arab world. Some of these authors migrated to the West, and the volume includes such voices and considers them invaluable in the intellectual development of the Arab world. Exile creates its own particular problems, but also brings about a unique perspective.

DLB 346: Twentieth-Century Arab Writers is being published at a time when stereotypes and misrepresentations of Middle Easterners threaten to undermine the ability of Westerners to understand and effectively interact with the Arab world. Said wrote that we find ourselves confronted with a "limiting discourse" when we allow fear to dictate how we understand the world. What is important to realize is that the same debates taking place across the United States and Europe today–whether Islam is compatible with democracy; what the role of women is in Islam; what a just peace might look like; and what the future holds for the prospects of peace in this ever-shrinking world–are all, without exception, and often at risk to the authors, being addressed by Arab writers. Their fiction and critical writings provide firsthand insights into the challenges that continue to be faced by Middle Eastern societies. These are authors who know that there is much at stake and the risks are high, but are willing to search for answers for the sake of the world, East and West.

–*Majd Yaser Al-Mallah and Coeli Fitzpatrick*

Note on Transliteration

For titles that were originally published in Arabic, the editors decided to use a simplified transliteration system that is suited for a non-specialist audience. Diacritical marks are not used in this volume. In order to accommodate readers who are familiar with Arabic and its transliteration, we decided to use the single opening quotation mark (') for the 'ayn and a single closed quotation mark (') for the hamzah. We have used a consistent transliteration system for authors' names, except when an alternate spelling of an author's name was established in Western publications.

Acknowledgments

This book was produced by Bruccoli Clark Layman, Inc. George Parker Anderson was the in-house editor. He was assisted by Philip B. Dematteis and Richard Layman.

Production manager is Philip B. Dematteis.

Administrative support was provided by Carol A. Cheschi.

Accountant is Ann-Marie Holland.

Copyediting supervisor is Phyllis A. Avant. The copyediting staff includes Frederick C. Ingram and Rebecca Mayo. Freelance copyeditors are Brenda L. Cabra, Jennifer Cooper, David C. King, and Katherine E. Macedon.

Pipeline manager is James F. Tidd Jr.

Permissions editor is Dickson Monk.

Office manager is Kathy Lawler Merlette.

Digital photographic copy work and photo editing was performed by Dickson Monk.

Systems manager is James Sellers.

Typesetting supervisor is Kathleen M. Flanagan. The typesetting staff includes Patricia M. Flanagan.

Library research was facilitated by the following librarians at the Thomas Cooper Library of the University of South Carolina: Elizabeth Sudduth and the rare-book department; circulation department head Tucker Taylor; reference department head Virginia W. Weathers; reference department staff Marilee Birchfield, Karen Brown, Mary Bull, Gerri Corson, Joshua Garris, Beki Gettys, Laura Ladwig, Tom Marcil, Bob Skinder, and Sharon Verba; interlibrary loan department head Marna Hostetler; and interlibrary loan staff Robert Amerson and Timothy Simmons.

Dictionary of Literary Biography® • Volume Three Hundred Forty-Six

Twentieth-Century Arab Writers

Dictionary of Literary Biography

Muhammad 'Abduh
(1849 – 1905)

Yasir Ibrahim Almallah
Al-Quds Open University

BOOKS: *Risalat al-Tawhid* (Cairo: 1897); enlarged, with notes and additions (Cairo: 1908); translated by Ishaq Musa'ad and Kenneth Cragg as *The Theology of Unity* (London: Allen & Unwin, 1966);

Tafsir al-Qur'an al-Karim (Bulaq: Al-Matba'ah al-Amiriyyah, 1904–1905); enlarged as *Tafsir al-Qur'an al-Hakim,* 12 volumes, edited and completed by Muhammad Rashid Rida (Cairo: Dar al-Manar, 1906–1935);

Al-Islam wa al-rad 'ala muntaqidih (Cairo: Al-Maktabah al-Tijariyyah al-Kubra, 1928);

Nash'ati wa Tarbiyati (Cairo, n.d.).

Collection: *Al-A'mal al-Kamilah,* 4 volumes, edited by Muhammad 'Imarah (Beirut: Al-Mu'assah al 'Arabiyyah, 1972).

OTHER: Ali b. Abi Talib, *Nahj al-Balaghah,* introduction and commentary by 'Abduh (Cairo, 1876);

Al-Waqa'i' al-Misriyyah (Cairo), edited by 'Abduh, 1880–1882;

Al-Urwah al-Wuthqa (Paris), edited by 'Abduh, March–October 1884;

Badi' al-Zaman al-Hamadhani, *Maqamat Badi' al-Zaman,* introduction and commentary by 'Abduh (Beirut: Jesuit Press, 1888);

Herbert Spencer, *Education: Intellectual, Moral, and Physical,* translated by 'Abduh (Cairo, n.d.).

SELECTED PERIODICAL PUBLICATIONS–
UNCOLLECTED: "'Id Misr wa matla' 'istiqlaliha,'" *Al-Waqa'i' al-Misriyyah* (Cairo), July 1880;

"Wakhamat al-Rashwah," *al-Waqa'i' al-Misriyyah* (Cairo), December 1880;

"Al-Tamaddun," *al-Waqa'i' al-Misriyyah* (Cairo), January 1881;

Muhammad 'Abduh (Britannica Online Encyclopedia)

"Al-Wataniyyah," *Al-waqa'i' al-Misriyyah* (Cairo), March 1881;

"Hukm al-shari'ah fit ta'adud al-zawjat," *al-Waqa'i' al-Misriyyah* (Cairo), March 1881;

"Al-Kutub al-'ilmiyyah wa ghayruha," *al-Waqa'i' al-Misriyyah* (Cairo), May 1881;

"Nayl al-ma'ali bi al-fadilah," *al-Waqa'i' al-Misriyyah* (Cairo), October 1881;

"Al-Khurafat," *Al-Waqa'i' al-Misriyyah* (Cairo), January 1882;

Al-Islam wa al-Nasraniyyah ma'a al-'ilm wa al-madaniyyah, essays collected in *Al-Manar* (1902).

Muhammad 'Abduh is one of the most important and influential Arab thinkers and scholars, with a career that stretches from the nineteenth century into the twentieth century and an intellectual legacy that remains relevant in the twenty-first century. It is not an exaggeration to say that 'Abduh's lifelong drive for change and reform has had a profound impact on many, if not most, contemporary Arab intellectuals. 'Abduh's experience at a time of great change and interaction between the East and the West serves as a precursor to much of the intellectual discussion about the direction of Arab countries in the context of colonialism and independence. Although 'Abduh's ideas and actions were sometimes controversial, few can deny his significant contribution in the intellectual development of Egypt and the Arab world. His most famous original contribution is his book *Risalat al-Tawhid* (1897; translated as *The Theology of Unity,* 1966), but during his lifetime he was best known as an important editor and commentator whose essays and serialized contributions appeared in leading newspapers and magazines. Although his writings for periodicals began to appear in book form shortly before his death, some were also collected years after his death. As a testament to 'Abduh's enduring influence, his works have gone through multiple editions, with several scholars editing collections of his essays.

'Abduh was born in 1849 to Junaynah bint Uthman and 'Abduh ibn Hasan Khayr Allah al-Turkumani, both peasants from the village of Hasat al-Bashir, part of the larger village of Mahalat Nasr, in al-Buhayrah province in Northern Egypt. Because Hasat al-Bashir was not a remote or isolated village, 'Abduh grew up in an environment that was connected to the larger historical developments in the country and specifically the capital, Cairo. At the time, the Egyptian government (a monarchy in the line of Muhammad 'Ali) had been attempting to "modernize" Egypt, but in the process the government neglected the basic needs of the people and turned to superficial changes that were aimed mainly at the elite in the Egyptian community. King Isma'il, for example, compiled great debt in his effort to build a new and modern section next to the old city of Cairo. Discontent among Egyptians was met with heavy-handed suppression by the government—'Abduh's family was directly affected when his father was imprisoned on charges of sheltering army deserters.

'Abduh began to learn reading and writing in his family's home after he turned ten years old. He joined the Qur'an school—he was the only student at the time—and was motivated enough to memorize the entire Holy Qur'an in only two years. Seeing his son's ability and talent for learning, his father in 1862 sent 'Abduh to further his Qur'an study in the city of Tanta at al-Ahmadi Mosque, where he took classes for a year and a half. Discouraged by the traditional teaching methods and the difficulty of the courses in Arabic grammar and Islamic law, 'Abduh ran away from the mosque to live with his maternal uncles for three months. Although his brother found him and wanted to force him to return to al-Ahmadi Mosque, 'Abduh instead returned to his village, where he decided to get married, settle down, and work as a farmer. After only forty days of marriage, however, 'Abduh was prevailed upon by his disappointed father to go back to al-Ahmadi Mosque. But on the way 'Abduh again ran away to Kanisat 'Urin, the home of his maternal uncles. There, his uncle Shaykh Darwish, a Sufi, transformed 'Abduh into a new person, helping him to learn in a "gentle" and less threatening way. In 1865, upon gaining confidence in his ability, 'Abduh decided to resume his studies at al-Ahmadi Mosque.

From al-Ahmadi Mosque, 'Abduh moved to al-Azhar University, at the time the most important institution of Islamic religious training and learning. The instruction followed a traditional method in which the professor read from a book, explaining each sentence as he read. The students asked questions, sometimes to the dismay of the professor, who wielded full authority in the class. Any deviation from the traditional curriculum or teaching method was frowned upon, sometimes even considered blasphemous. When the renowned nineteenth-century reformer Jamal al-Din al-Afghani (died 1897) came to Egypt in 1869, bringing with him new ideas for change, the establishment in al-Azhar sided against him and ordered students not to attend his classes. 'Abduh, however, ignored the dictate of the university. When Shaykh 'Ilish, a senior professor in al-Azhar, found out about 'Abduh's attending al-Afghani's classes, the professor and the student became engaged in a heated argument.

Because of al-Afghani's teaching, 'Abduh became attuned to the conflicts and tribulations of political, intellectual, and social life in Egypt. He began to write in *Al-Ahram,* the leading daily newspaper in the country, as early as 1876. Also around this time, 'Abduh began one of the most important projects of the *nahdah,* or revival movement: editing, providing commentary, and publishing some of the major classical Arabic works, authored during the height of Islamic civilization (roughly from C.E. 622 to 1258). In 1876 'Abduh published an edited version of *Nahj al-Balaghah* (The Path of Rhetoric), authored by 'Ali b. Abi Talib (cousin to the Prophet Muhammad and fourth successor to the Prophet). In 1877 'Abduh attained his degree, which further established his credentials as a scholar. Although the Egyptian government, fearing al-Afghani's ideas and charismatic personality, exiled him to Hijaz (now Saudi Arabia) in 1879, 'Abduh continued to be inspired by his example and teaching. Like his mentor, he became a vehement proponent of change and reform in Egypt, which in a few years led to his own banishment from the country.

After graduating from al-Azhar, 'Abduh taught at the school for two years, though unlike other professors who began their teaching with grammar and Islamic law, 'Abduh taught logic, philosophy, *tawhid* (unity of God), and other sciences. He incorporated translations of European authors into his teaching. In 1879 he left al-Azhar to teach history at *Dar al-'Ulum* (Institute of Science), where he was an innovative and effective teacher, reportedly authoring a book for his students on sociology and architecture (the book was lost and there is no longer a copy). A few months after his appointment, however, he was fired from *Dar al-'Ulum* because the state perceived his teaching as a threat to its authority—he was seen as a promoter of the dangerous ideas for which al-Afghani had been banished.

In 1880 a new prime minister, Riyad Pasha, came to power and appointed 'Abduh to edit the first official Arabic newspaper, *al-Waqa'i' al-Misriyyah* (Egyptian Events). 'Abduh not only edited the newspaper but also wrote many articles during his tenure, which lasted until 1882. He established an independent section of the newspaper devoted entirely to literary and social essays, and in his own articles he promoted a variety of social and political reforms. One of his first essays, appearing in July 1880, is "'Id Misr wa matla' istiqlaliha" (Egypt: The Beginning of Its Independence), in which he addresses Egypt's desire for independence in the context of the major financial debt that the government had accumulated. Often a strong critic of society, 'Abduh wrote to expose corruption in his December 1880 article "Wakhamat al-Rashwah" (Problems with Bribery). In a January 1881 essay titled "Al-Tamaddun" (Modernity), 'Abduh argued for the value of a "genuine" quest for modernity and progress but opposed simply adopting the superficial appearance of European modernity. 'Abduh addressed issues many considered taboo, including criticizing the practice of polygamy in his March 1881 essay "Hukm al-Shari'ah fi ta'adud al-zawjat" (Polygamy according to Islamic Law). He encouraged his readers to abandon superstitions in such articles as "Al-Kutub al-'ilmiyyah wa ghayruha" (Scientific and Other Books, May 1881), "Nayl al-ma'ali bi al-fadilah" (Achieving Greatness through Nobility, October 1881), and "Al-Khurafat" (Superstitions, January 1882).

With the support of the reform-minded prime minister, 'Abduh instilled important and revolutionary values through his influential position at the newspaper. He pushed to compel governmental agencies to write to the press about initiatives that they intended to implement. This practice allowed the press to criticize governmental agencies and their programs and to question every institution about the criticism directed at it in the newspapers. The prime minister and 'Abduh believed in gradual reforms and changes, rather than immediate and complete transformations. Both believed that the solutions to Egypt's problems would result from spreading good education among people, fighting corruption, a firm commitment by the prime minister to implement needed reforms, and gradual movement toward a parliamentary political system. Riyad also wanted to resolve issues with the British and French through dialogue and understanding. Another camp, led by 'Urabi Pasha, argued for giving personal freedoms to individuals, allowing total political freedom in criticizing the government, and establishing an independent parliament to oversee the workings of the government.

At first 'Abduh argued for Riyad's approach of gradual reforms, and advised 'Urabi to give reforms more time before declaring a revolution. He made the following argument about the need for more education and time:

> Now, we must pay attention to education for a few years, convince the government to be just, ask the government to consult people in special committees from various provinces, and allow these actions to be the precursor to the goal of questioning the government. It is not advantageous or beneficial to surprise the country with something (i.e., parliament) before we are prepared for it–it's almost like giving money to a child before he reaches maturity; he will certainly lose the money! (Quoted from 'Abbas al-'Aqqad in his *Muhammad 'Abduh*)

However, when the 'Urabi revolution came about in 1882, 'Abduh supported it because he believed that the people demanded change and did not want to go against the general sentiment in the country.

The 'Urabi revolution failed after the British invaded the country in 1882 to "fix its finances." The government arrested 'Abduh for his support of the revolution–he spent three months in jail; then he was exiled to Lebanon for three years (but the exile actually continued for six years). From Lebanon, 'Abduh con-

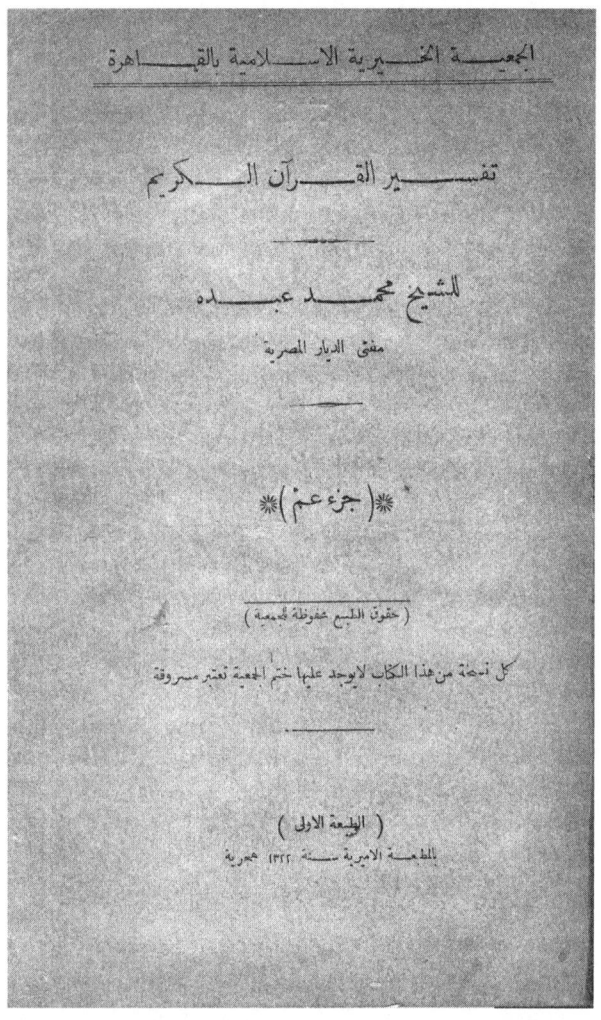

Title page for 'Abduh's study of the Qur'an that was published in 1904–1905 (Van Pelt Library, University of Pennsylvania)

tacted his mentor al-Afghani, who at the time lived in France, through several letters that he wrote shortly following his exile (probably in the year 1882). After one year of living in Beirut, 'Abduh traveled to Paris to work with al-Afghani, and began editing a magazine, titled *al-'Urwah al-Wuthqa* (Strong Brotherhood) after an important reformist group, in 1884. Although the publication of the magazine stopped after publishing only eighteen issues from March until October of 1884, for the duration of its publication it served as an outlet for an organization that had members in Egypt and throughout the Muslim world. 'Abduh's essays, published in this magazine while he resided in Paris, outlined his reformist agenda.

Unlike al-Afghani, who believed in change through political activism and continued dialogue with the Ottoman sultan and other Muslim leaders, 'Abduh thought that the emphasis should be on reforming people's hearts and minds through education. He once proposed to al-Afghani that he should become fully devoted to teaching their reformist agenda to a few youths, who would in turn teach it to others–initiating a process that would eventually lead to a profound change, though one that would take more time. Al-Afghani, on the other hand, wanted to continue his dialogue with Muslim leaders, in the hopes of convincing one of them to adopt his reformist agenda, thus implementing it from the top down.

"Abduh also became more vocal in his criticism of Britain's occupation of Egypt. On a visit to London he declared his position forcefully:

> Why don't you leave our country at once? The British taught us only one thing, which is to unite in asking them to leave. . . . We complained about the Turks because they were foreigners to our country, and we wanted to reform and modernize following the advancement of Europeans toward freedom, but now we know that there is something worse than the oppression of leaders, and worse than the oppression of the Turks, and there is no one in Egypt who wants your help despite any oppression that they [have suffered]. We want from you only one thing, and that is to leave our country immediately and never come back. (Quoted from al-Aqqad)

In 1885, after *al-'Urwah al-Wuthqa* had ceased publication, 'Abduh returned to Beirut, where he continued his own reformist agenda by focusing on education through teaching and publishing. He taught at al-Madrasah al-Sultaniyyah (The Sultanate School) and wrote essays for the Lebanese newspaper *Thamarat al-Bayan* (Fruits of Rhetoric). Following Sultan 'Abd al-Hamid's call for reforming schools and education, 'Abduh wrote an important letter that he sent to the Ottoman capital in 1886, in which he advocates the inclusion of religious education in the curriculum. He argued that Muslims needed to free themselves from superstition and become genuinely knowledgeable in matters of religion. He suggested that Friday sermons needed to be "reinvigorated" with passion and ideas that would educate people and serve as a forum for reform. In 1888 'Abduh published an edited commentary, with an introduction, of *Maqamat Badi' al-Zaman*, a collection of stories from the classical period. The practice of editing and commentating that 'Abduh initiated in this volume is recognized as a first step toward the renaissance of Arabic culture.

Upon returning to Egypt in 1889, 'Abduh realized that his country had changed tremendously in the years that he spent in exile. The most obvious difference was the authority that the British wielded in every venue of Egyptian government or public life. The king, called the *khediwi*, lacked any power and followed British directions. While reluctant at first to work with the British and the monarchy, 'Abduh decided that he needed to if he were to accomplish his goal of reforming education in Egypt. 'Abduh's good relationship with the king and the British was based on mutual interests: he wanted to push his agenda; the king thought that he could take advantage of 'Abduh's strong personality and public influence; and the British believed that the proposed reforms did not contradict their goals. But 'Abduh's relationship with the king deteriorated over the years because he opposed some of the king's decisions, as when he insisted that the king pay the proper price when the king wanted to trade for property designated as religious endowment land *(waqf)*. On another occasion, 'Abduh stood in the way of the king when he tried to appoint one of his closest allies to a high position at al-Azhar. During the last fifteen years of his life, 'Abduh worked in the courts, as a judge for some time and also as a *mufti*.

In 1897 'Abduh published his first original book, the critically acclaimed philosophical treatise titled *Risalat al-Tawhid*. In his introductory remarks to the book, 'Abduh writes that his work was based on lectures on the subject of Divine Unity that he had given while living in Beirut. Because he had not written down his lectures and believed that they "survived only in the notebooks of the students," he had planned to write to some of his students in the hope that they would send him their notes. But he soon discovered that his brother had copied down the lectures, which upon review he found to his liking. Nevertheless, he significantly revised his earlier work, adding or deleting where he saw fit. He explains that while he was teaching in Beirut, he noticed the difficulty that students had in understanding the subject, as what he regarded as the major works authored on the topic of Divine Unity "were beyond their comprehension and the intermediate text-books were in the idiom of another time." One may wonder at 'Abduh's desire to resume his work on the subject of Divine Unity so many years after having given the lectures in Beirut. He begins to answer this question in his introduction when he asserts that he realized the subject "belonged with the very structure of serious existence." But what does that mean, and how does this subject relate to 'Abduh's lifelong project of reform? The answer lies in the thrust of the argument that the author makes in *Risalat al-Tawhid*.

The table of contents for *Risalat al-Tawhid* makes no mention of reform whatsoever. The book has seventeen chapters, beginning with one on the basic definition of the unity of God, followed by several chapters that deal with divine attributes. 'Abduh then turns to a discussion of human beings, with a focus on the Prophet Muhammad as God's helper, followed by a discussion of the Qur'an as God's revelation. The final chapters focus on Islam as a religion, how it has been the culmination of human progress, and the need to accept Muhammad's message. Throughout the book, but especially toward the end, the reader sees 'Abduh's constant emphasis on the centrality of reason in the author's thought and arguments. 'Abduh argues that reason is a characteristic of Islam—that most, if not all, aspects of the religion conform with reason. Apart from some minor exceptions, he argues that reason and the mind have a primary role in his faith. Although philosophical and complex in nature, the *Risalat al-Tawhid* can be said to be the culmination of 'Abduh's thought and a continuation for his reformist agenda, which always aimed at combating *taqlid* (blind imitation). "Religion is guidance and reason," 'Abduh asserts toward the end of the book, claiming that he has unveiled the true nature of Islam—its conformity to reason—while also blaming "those Muslims who by their conduct have become an argument against it." Central to 'Abduh's lifelong project, these quotations reveal one of the lasting legacies of his career: his contention that Muslims' backwardness did not come as a result of the religion but rather as a consequence of people's lack of knowledge and their constant reliance on imitation and superstition, instead of renewal and innovation.

Critics have seized 'Abduh's book as being essential to the larger Arab intellectual transition into the twentieth century. As Kenneth Cragg writes in the introduction to the translation of the book, 'Abduh's *Risalat al-Tawhid* is "a work of central importance in the study of the changes and the continuities of mind that belong with Islam as it approaches the close of its fourteenth century." The book servers as a precursor for his more ambitious project, to provide a modern, progressive reading or exegesis of the Qur'an—an interpretation based on logic and reason, one that looks closely at the original text, not the commentaries that came with it throughout the centuries.

In 1899 'Abduh was appointed Grand Mufti and began his public lectures to provide a new and innovative *tafsir* (exegesis or explanation) of the Holy Qur'an. Undoubtedly, his work on the exegesis of the Qur'an is one of his most ambitious and, in many ways, his most important achievements, one that encompassed the remaining years of his life. He provided commentary on the first four chapters of the Qur'an (though he was unable to finish the fourth chapter completely) as well as commentary on several of the final short chapters of the Qur'an. His student Shaykh Rashid Rida wrote down 'Abduh's exegesis and finished the project after

Title page for the translation of 'Abduh's first book, which was based on lectures he gave in Beirut in the 1880s (Thomas Cooper Library, University of South Carolina)

his teacher's death. 'Abduh's Qur'anic exegesis was initially serialized on a monthly basis in *al-Manar* (Lighthouse) magazine, beginning in May of 1900 and continuing until May of 1912. It began to appear in book form, under the title *Tafsir al-Qur'an al-Karim* (Exegesis of the Holy Qur'an), in 1904 to 1905.

In his reading of the Qur'an, 'Abduh focused on the original text rather than relying on extensive and excessive commentaries and superstitious readings. He insisted that the Qur'an, as the word of God, is intended to help people reach fulfillment in their life and to find practical solutions to everyday problems and practices. He argued that only by reading the Qur'an in a modern and direct way can Muslims achieve their goals of renewal, reform, and change. Most importantly, 'Abduh believed in providing an exegesis that people can understand and to which they could relate their own experience. His approach of going directly to the text, while seemingly intuitive, was revolutionary at the end of the nineteenth century and the beginning of the twentieth century. Critic Yvonne Haddad asserts that 'Abduh "initiated the twentieth-century trend of individual interaction with and interpretation of the Qur'an." Haddad argues that for 'Abduh "The Qur'an is worthy of being called the book of freedom of thought, of respect for reason and for the shaping of the individual through research, knowledge and the use of reason and reflection." But 'Abduh also believed that the Qur'an should be the guide for Muslim society; he saw his work on the Qur'an as a continuation, indeed, a true fulfillment, of his major reform project.

In 1900 'Abduh served as president of the Institute for Reviving Arabic Books, an organization dedicated to preserving Arabic books and publishing classical volumes. The same year he wrote several essays defending Islam for *al-Mu'ayyad* (The Supported One) magazine in which he responded to M. Gabriel Hanoteaux, at the time France's minister of foreign affairs, who had criticized Islam and argued that it was a prime cause for conflict between the West and Muslims. 'Abduh refuted claims that Christianity—and by extension Western culture—is superior and more adaptable to renewal and modernity. These essays were posthumously collected and published as *al-Islam wa al-rad 'ala muntaqidih* (1928, Islam and Responding to its Critics). In 1902 he wrote several essays—serialized and collected by *al-Manar* magazine under the title *al-Islam wa al-Nasraniyyah ma'a al-'ilm wa al-madaniyyah* (Islam and Christianity with Science and Modernity)—in response to Farah Antoon, editor and publisher of *al-Jami'ah* (Association) magazine. In an essay on the Muslim philosopher Ibn Rushd, Antoon had argued that Christianity was more welcoming and more accepting of science and advancement than Islam, ultimately the reason, according to Antoon, for Arabs' "backwardness." 'Abduh refutes Antoon's arguments and points out Islam's encouragement of science. 'Abduh begins by looking at the history of Christianity, arguing that it opposed and suppressed science for many years. On the contrary, he asserts that Islam's primary emphasis on reason is evidence that it has no contradiction with science, that in the cases where reason seems to contradict a "superficial" rule, one should go with reason. 'Abduh also points out that Europe's renaissance and modern scientific venture has its roots in the golden age of Islam, and the transfer of knowledge to Europe through Muslims' scientific achievements. 'Abduh remained in his position as the Grand Mufti until his illness and death in 1905.

'Abduh's approach to seeking change—his decision to work from inside the political and religious system, rather than being a critic from the outside—has led to a divided opinion among researchers and critics. A group of intellectuals and critics regard him as a visionary reformer and an excellent scholar. His most important advocate is his student Shaykh Muhammad Rashid Rida, whose *Tarikh al-Ustadh al-Imam* (The History of the Teacher and Imam, 1906-1931) is probably the most important source on 'Abduh's life and contributions. Rida justified 'Abduh's decision to work with the king and the British authorities on the grounds that he had no other viable option—had he not done so, he would have been exiled and accomplished little. In addition to Arab intellectuals such as Ahmad Amin and 'Abbas Mahmoud al-'Aqqad, who agreed with this assessment of 'Abduh, Westerners such as Evelyn Baring, Lord Cromer, Wilfred Blunt, and Sir Hamilton Alexander Gibb also gave high praise to 'Abduh and his reformist agenda. Lord Cromer praised 'Abduh in his annual report of 1905 because he helped the British resolve some thorny issues by issuing a *fatwa* (religious opinion) that allowed Muslims to invest their money in savings accounts. For 'Abduh's admirers, his legacy is his continuous and unwavering quest for change and reform, seen most obviously in his essays and practical proposals for change in the educational system.

"Abduh also had his critics who, while acknowledging his achievements, were critical of the compromises he made in dealing with the British authorities and the king. Among them is Ghazi al-Tawbah, who points out 'Abduh's "mistakes" in his book *al-Fikr al-Islami al-mu'aasir; dirasah wa taqwim* (1977, Modern Islamic Thought: A Study and Analysis). For example, al-Tawbah criticizes 'Abduh's decision to seek Lord Cromer's assistance to reform education for the benefit of Egyptians while Cromer represented the occupation force. Al-Tawbah also faults 'Abduh's cooperation with the British in issuing religious opinions that "fit their objectives." While some might consider 'Abduh's interpretations of the Qur'an modern and progressive thinking, this group of critics believe that 'Abduh was used by the British to legitimize their objectives.

Not even Muhammad 'Abduh's harshest critic, however, would deny him a place among the most influential thinkers and intellectuals in the nineteenth and early twentieth centuries. His so-called practical approach yielded undeniable results. Indeed, 'Abduh's drive for reform and the devotion of his whole life for this single cause has been inspirational and truly formative in later thinkers calling for change and reform. Perhaps his most important contribution was his willingness to have an open mind and his advocacy of a well-rounded approach to the study of Islam, combining close reading of the Qur'an, Hadith, and Islamic law with deep study in the broader discipline of philosophy—both Islamic and non-Islamic. He believed in an Islam that is open to change and free of superstition, one that, after centuries of a deep slumber, accepts modern advancements. He personally advocated the study of all sciences at a time when al-Azhar and its leaders only favored the study of Islam and Islamic law because they feared that a broader approach would lead to infidelity and lack of faith. 'Abduh, on the other hand, saw that these ideas were not consistent with Islam, and fought all his life to combat them by encouraging education in all areas. He truly believed that Arabs and Muslims needed such an approach at a time when ignorance and the inablity to accept change put them behind and led to their occupation and defeat.

References:

'Abbas al-'Aqqad, *Muhammad 'Abduh* (Egypt: Ministry of Culture, n.d.);

Ahmad Amin, *Zu'amaa' al-islah fi al 'asr al-hadith* (Beirut: Dar al-Kitab al-'Arabi, n.d);

Wilfred Blunt, *My Diaries: Being a Personal Narrative of Events 1888-1914* (New York: Knopf, 1921);

Blunt, *The Secret History of the British Occupation of Egypt* (New York: Knopf, 1922);

Kenneth Cragg, "Introduction," *The Theology of Unity* (London: Allen & Unwin, 1966);

Evelyn Baring, Lord Cromer, *Modern Egypt*, 2 volumes (London: Macmillan, 1908);

Yvonne Haddad, "Muhammad Abduh: Pioneer of Islamic Reform," in *Pioneers of Islamic Revival*, edited by Ali Rahnema (London & New Jersey: Zed Books, 1994);

Muhammad 'Imara, "Introduction," *Al-A'mal al-Kamilah*, 4 volumes, edited by Imara (Beirut: Al-Mu'assah al-'Arabiyyah, 1972);

George Ambrose Lloyd, first Baron of Lloyd, *Egypt Since Cromer*, 2 volumes (London: Macmillan, 1933);

Muhammad Rashid Rida, *Tarikh al-Ustadh al-Imam*, 2 volumes (Egypt: Maktabat Al-Manar, 1906-1931);

W. C. Smith, *Islam in Modern History* (Princeton: Princeton University Press, 1957);

Ghazi al-Tawbah, *Al-fikr al-islami al-mu'asir; dirasah wa taqwim* (Beirut: Dar al-fikr, 1977).

Mas'udah Aboubakr

(19 February 1954 –)

Hager Ben Driss
University of Tunis

BOOKS: *Ta'm al-ananas* (Tunis: Al-Atlasiyyah, 1994);
Laylat al-ghiyab (Tunis: Dar Sahar, 1997);
Turshqana (Tunis: Dar Sahar, 1999);
'Iqdu al-marjan (Gabes: Al-Khadamat al-Sari'a, 2000);
Wada'an Hammurabi (Tunis: Dar Cérès, 2002);
Lu'lu' li jidi al-kalam (Tunis: Dar al-Ithaf, 2002);
Walimah khassa jiddan (Tunis: Dar Sahar, 2004);
Juman wa 'anbar (Tunis: Dar Sahar, 2005).

Mas'udah Aboubakr occupies a special position in the Tunisian literary scene. Versatile and prolific, she stands as the voice of the lower classes, the proletariat and the marginalized. Indeed, her books give voice to the muted, narrate the suffering of the poor, and relocate the marginalized in history. Because she is mainly concerned with social issues, her work can be classified as social realism. Her writing is characterized by her ability to mix the ideological with the poetical. Her texts are not mere social and political oratory; she has managed to keep the artistry of the creative work while raising serious issues.

Mas'udah Aboubakr was born on 19 February 1954 in Sfax, a town in the south of Tunisia. Her mother, Majida al-Shami, was originally from Sfax, and her father, Ahmad Aboubakr, was Moroccan. One year after her birth, her parents moved to Tunis. They settled in Jbal Jloud, some three kilometers away from the capital. Aboubakr spent her childhood and girlhood in that small village where she had her primary education. While studying in the primary school, she also went to the *kuttab,* a type of traditional school where she learned the Qur'an and Arabic grammar. From the age of six to twelve, the *kuttab* had a major role in shaping her creative mind. The *meddeb* (teacher), who told stories to the children, opened the first gate of Aboubakr's imagination.

While the *kuttab* inspired Aboubakr's interest in creativity, the quarter where she lived provided the foundation for the development of her political consciousness. Accompanying her father to the café, the child followed with keen interest men's discussions

Mas'udah Aboubakr (from the back cover for Ta'm al-ananas, *1994; University of Arizona Library)*

about the wars in Algeria and Palestine. She witnessed her father collecting money to help the resistance in Algeria. Men gathering around the radio, eager to hear the latest news about Arab struggles, was a vivid image deeply stored in the child's mind and reproduced later in the adult's fiction. The radio became a recurrent leitmotif in almost all her highly politicized works.

Aboubakr's free wandering in the male's world, however, came to an end when she reached her twelfth year. Considered a grown-up girl, she was not allowed to play anymore outside the house or go with her father to the café. She started writing secretly at that early age—a way to articulate her "frustration" as she confessed much later when speaking about her novel, *Turshqana* (1999), which explores Arab cultural constructions of masculinity and femininity.

In 1960 Aboubakr was awarded her certificate of primary education and moved to the secondary school of Montfleury in Tunis. Her father, who worried about his daughter because she was no longer under his direct watch, obliged her to stay for hours every day in the library of Les Soeurs Blanches (The White Sisters), a missionary institution run by French nuns. Aboubakr had access to books of art and devoured the works of Alphonse de Lamartine and Arthur Rimbaud. She was particularly impressed by Emile Zola's novels, which furthered her interest in social problems and the strife experienced by workers.

Although Aboubakr dreamed of having an academic career, she was obliged to leave school in 1967 because of her father's financial difficulties. At the age of nineteen, she started a secretarial job in the embassy of Morocco. After two years, she took secretarial courses and got a job in a private company where she still works. In 1978 Aboubakr married but soon divorced as she found herself confined to a barren intellectual life. Her husband tried to stifle her creativity. Rebellious and defying, like her fictional heroines, Aboubakr managed to free herself from intellectual inertia.

Aboubakr started publishing short stories in 1981. Her first story, "Al-Wafa" (Fidelity), was published in *al-Bayan,* a popular Tunisian weekly newspaper. She continued publishing short stories in Tunisian newspapers even though her work did not attract any critical attention.

In 1984 Aboubakr got married again. With an understanding husband and a stable family life, her creativity thrived. In 1987 she was awarded the prize of Mahrajan al-Udaba' al-Shubban (Festival of Young Writers) for her short stories. At the beginning of the 1990s, she directed al-Salun al-Adabi li Ittihad al-Udaba' al-Tunisyyin (Literary Salon of the Tunisian Writers' Union). In 1994 she began writing for major Tunisian newspapers. Her literary column, "'Iqdu al-Marjan" (Coral Necklace), in *al-Hurrya* (Liberty) newspaper, attracted much attention. Her columns were collected as *'Iqdu al-marjan* in 2000.

In 1994 Aboubakr published her first collection of short stories, *Ta'm al-ananas* (The Taste of Pineapple), which received an enthusiastic critical assessment and established her reputation on the Tunisian literary scene. Composed of thirteen short stories, *Ta'm al-ananas* depicts social and economic alienation, featuring characters such as a homeless orphan, a poor young girl keeping her family, and a destitute old woman whose house is flooded by rain. Hmida Souli concludes his reading of the collection by stating that "studying these stories helps understanding the social background

Cover for Aboubakr's first book, Ta'm al-Ananas *(1994, The Taste of Pineapple), a collection of thirteen stories depicting the difficult lives of the poor in Tunisia (University of Arizona Library)*

and leads to locate obstacles in order to get rid of them."

Ta'm al-ananas was initially banned from circulation because the title story, placed last in the collection, was found to make insidious allusions to the violence of the police. The story is about a young man, Hadi, who promises to give the children of his poor village a taste of pineapple. This fruit, rather rare and expensive in Tunisia, stands for the symbol of class division—pineapple being inaccessible to lower classes. One day Hadi finds himself at the heart of a popular demonstration caused by the rise in the price of bread, the so-called Revolution of Bread that took place in Tunisia in January 1984. As the demonstration turns violent and people break windows and pillage shops, Hadi sees a pack of canned pineapple. As he takes the pack, he is shot in the leg by the police but still manages to hide his stolen fortune. When he goes back later, however, he finds that the pineapple has disappeared, leaving him with

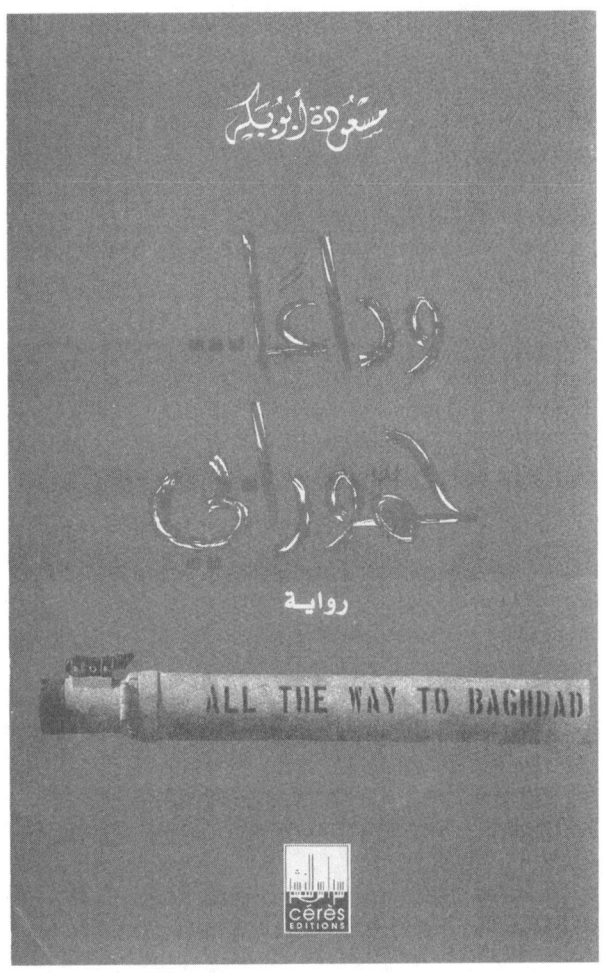

Title page for Aboubakr's third novel, Wada'an Hammurabi (2002, Farewell Hammurabi), which depicts the fallout from the First Gulf War on a northern Tunisian village (Harlan Hatcher Graduate Library, University of Michigan)

the shame of being unable to fulfill his promise to the children of his village.

If Aboubakr tried in her first collection of short stories to give voice to the ostracized, her first novel was an attempt to represent a muted individual. *Laylat al-ghiyab* (1997, The Night of Absence) uses first-person narration to explore the deep recesses of the self. *Laylat al-ghiyab* is the story of Fayqa, who discovers at the age of twelve that her real father left her mother before she was born. Her mother married again, and Fayqa was adopted by her stepfather, whom she grew up believing was her real father. At the age of thirty, Fayqa, divorced and emotionally wounded, comes back from abroad to attend the funeral of her real father, Muhammad al-'Arabi, whom she calls "sahib al-nutfa" (the owner of the sperm). The narrative is a montage of the dead/absent father's life through the reports of several characters.

Critically well received, *Laylat al-ghiyab* won the Prize of the Municipality of Gabes for the novel. In "Laylat al-ghiyab: Bahth 'an al-ubuwwa fi ma'naha al-wijdani" (*Laylat al-ghiyab:* The Search for Fatherhood in Its Emotional Meaning), Rachida Cherni states that "the heroine Fayqa Mahfudh looks for a solution to her crisis of consciousness. She does not look for fatherhood in its biological meaning, but rather in its emotional and human significance." When interviewed about the significance of the father in *Laylat al-ghiyab*, Aboubakr answered that at the superficial level of the novel the distorted image of the father functions to destabilize the inherited ethical hierarchy that is the respected image of the father. At a deeper level, however, the novel translates the state of the Arab nation: a terrifying orphanage in "the absence of Arab consciousness, a sacred ideal and real leadership."

In 1997 Aboubakr also received the Presidential Badge for Cultural Merit (Fourth Category), which encouraged her to write more. Two years later, she became the first Arab writer to deal openly with the topic of transsexuality in *Turshqana* (1999)–the strange title being the nickname of Murad al-Shawwashi, the major character of the author's second novel. The protagonist's name, Aboubakr explained in an unpublished essay on *Turshqana* she presented in 2002 at Bayt al-Hikma Foundation, comes from "the mocking sounds emitted by young people in popular quarters upon seeing an effeminate person. They clap their hands and shout 'tursh . . . qan . . . tursh . . . qan', imitating thus the sound of the qubqab (wooden slippers) often used by the effeminates."

Turshqana tells the story of a man who wants to become a woman. Murad al-Shawwashi defies his family, as well as religious and social taboos, to claim his feminine identity. The main story intersects with a sub-narrative in which Nura, Murad's friend, transforms Murad's story into a fictional work. In her text, Murad goes abroad, gets an operation, and succeeds in becoming a beautiful young woman called Nada. Nura, however, stresses Nada's suffering and despair as she is unable to be transformed into a full woman able to bear children. Nura's novel closes in an ambiguous way that mirrors the ambiguity of Murad's sexual identity. Discovering Nura's manuscript, Murad feels hurt and betrayed. The text ends with his disappearance.

Turshqana "emerges from my memory," declares Aboubakr in her unpublished essay. "He used to frequent our feminine meetings in a natural way. We addressed him as a female. He seemed happy while infiltrating our feminine world. I cherished and admired him. But I knew he was terrified, I knew it from his eyes." Being taken from her memories may have given the novel its great strength and credibility.

Indeed, *Turshqana* has received an excellent academic assessment rarely given to other Tunisian writings. Jean Fontaine presents Aboubakr as the first Tunisian woman writer who "subverts taboos." He claims that the novel "shows the originality of Tunisian literary production." In "Riwayat Turshqana: Tarafa wa Jura" (*Turshqana:* Originality and Audacity) the Tunisian academic Jalloul Azzouna describes it as "a bold novel that raises major issues related to identity, freedom and the right of difference and choice."

The novel, however, raised a heated debate, as Aboubakr reports that her work was attacked as immoral and vindictive. She recalls a Tunisian writer asking her, "what the hell are you looking for in this bottleneck?" Others, she continues in the essay she presented, "thought I was avenging the image of the devalued woman in the Arab novel through the portrait of an effeminate and perverse man."

In 2002 two books by Aboubakr were published: her first volume of poetry, *Lu'lu li jidi al-kalam* (Diamonds for the Neck of Words), and her third novel, *Wada'an Hammurabi* (Farewell Hammurabi). Aboubakr started writing this novel during the First Gulf War (1991), but she could only finish it years later. The original title she gave to her manuscript was "La'nat al-kam" (The Curse of Mushrooms). In his article "Wada'an Hammurabi: Intisar al-fanni 'ala al-idyulugi" (*Farewell Hammurabi:* The Aesthetic Defeating the Ideological), Kamal Riyahi reports that Aboubakr together with the publisher made a questionnaire to test the readers' reaction to the title. The writer quickly realized that the word *kam* (mushroom) was not only unknown to many people but also they found it difficult to pronounce.

Titled after the king who famously codified laws governing Babylonian life, *Wada'an Hammurabi* re-creates the impact on Tunisian society of the 1991 United States–led invasion of Iraq. The novel is set in a small, poor village in North Tunisia, al-Rajin. Feelings of deep sorrow are shared by everybody: poor and rich, educated and illiterate. The intense reaction against the war is compounded by the inability to understand what is regarded as Western aggression and the incapacity of the villagers to take effective action. The reaction of this small village encompasses the general feelings of injustice felt by most Tunisians during the conflict.

The war in Iraq is juxtaposed to a social, political, and psychological turmoil in the village, as the oppressed people cope with the devastating feeling of impotence. Highly polyphonic, the narrative gives voice to different social classes, including the thief, Zaqqouma, who is arrested in a demonstration against the war on Iraq, and the old aunt who keeps repeating, "Where are men, aren't they tired of talking?" The narrative also records the influence of war on five intellectuals: Mnawwar, the primary-school director who tries to launch a free newspaper; Sami, the poet, who remains sarcastic and cynical till the end; Fuad, the painter, who sinks into madness as a way to escape the absurdity of the war; Mundhir, the teacher, who becomes sexually impotent after the war; and Rim, the secondary-school teacher who dies on her way to Baghdad after the end of the war. Rim's death is particularly bleak, as she responded to the beginning of the embargo on Iraq by joining an Arab women's aid association to help the children of Iraq and is killed when their ship carrying food and medicines is bombarded by American troops. The novel ends on an optimistic note, however, as Mnawwar succeeds in gathering his friends to launch his newspaper.

Wada'an Hammurabi was awarded Ja'izat al-Komar al-Dhahabi (Golden Komar Prize), a prestigious Tunisian literary honor. When the novel was published in 2002, the U.S. government was moving toward its second war on Iraq. The novel was seen as especially relevant by Arab readers who were anticipating for the second time a Western assault on an Arab land. With her title *Wada'an Hammurabi* Aboubakr reminds her readers that war overturns all laws—a particular irony in a land that had established its laws as early as the eighteenth century B.C.E.

A similar set of characters to those in *Wada'an Hammurabi*—intellectuals, artists, and socially marginalized people—is found in Aboubakr's second collection of short stories, *Walima khassa jiddan* (2004, A Very Special Feast). The twenty-four stories of the collection show again Aboubakr's adherence to the realist aesthetic as well as her continuing concern with social issues. In his review of *Walima khassa jiddan* in the 12 April 2004 issue of *La Press,* the Tunisian academic Habib Salha emphasizes Aboubakr's narrative power to "astonish, disturb and move."

In 2005 Aboubakr received for the second time the Presidential Badge for Cultural Merit (Third Category). The same year, she published her fourth novel, *Juman wa 'anbar* (Pearls and Amber). The novel is difficult to adequately summarize as it takes a Chinese-box–like structure: a story within a story. The narrative opens with Kamal Miftahi, a drum player in a dance band, confessing to a friend his feelings of failure and sorrow. Thurayya, the girl he loves and a dancer in the band, is in love with another man and has become a famous actress. The story then moves to the film *Marmar al-dhakira* (The Marble of Memory) in which Thurayya takes the role of Huriyya, an artist living in the Medina, the old town of Tunis. The film, which celebrates the old town and discloses the secrets of its houses, concentrates on Shamma al-Bayya,

Huriyya's grandmother, who before she settled in the Medina had worked as a servant in the castle of the Bey (Ruler of Tunisia) before he was dethroned and independence declared in 1956. The narrative juxtaposes the events of the first story (Kamal, Thurayya, and the dance band) and the events of the film (the story of Shamma, the love story between Huriyya and a sculptor). Aboubakr uses the same narrative techniques adopted in *Turshqana* to draw connections between the real world and the dreamworld of the movie. Contrary to the ambiguous end of *Turshqana*, *Juman wa 'anbar* closes in an optimistic way as the band manages to reunite and continue its activities in a locale in the old Medina.

Aboubakr employs multiple voices as a basic narrative component in all of her fictional works and often has her characters move about to different settings. In *Laylat al-ghiyab*, the heroine moves between Tunisia, Morocco, Greece, and Strasbourg. The story in *Turshqana* moves between Tunisia, Morocco, and France, settings that give rise to the character's dreams, disillusions, and hopes.

Even though Aboubakr denies any type of feminist commitment, her female characters stand out as being strong and outspoken. "I don't place myself on the feminist terrain," she declares in her essay on *Turshqana*: "my goal transcends the cleavage man/woman as perceived by either the feminist or anti-feminist discourse." Yet, women in her texts are fully liberated; they have control over their bodies and destinies.

Whether male or female, characters in Aboubakr's fiction strive to change the world around them. They are portrayed in a perpetual search for identity. Throughout all her texts, she uses the figure of the marginalized artist who tries to provide another vision of the world. In *Turshqana*, Murad is a painter who endeavors to break the taboos around sex and gender. *Jumah wa Anbar* gathers sculptors, musicians, and dancers who fight to preserve memory. *Wada'an Hammurabi* also includes a poet and a painter who witness the weakness of the Arab nation. The artist stands for the aesthetic consciousness that aims to fight the ugliness of the collapsing modern world.

With six fictional works, a volume of poetry, and a collection of literary essays, Mas'udah Aboubakr stands as the most prolific and versatile Tunisian woman writer. Her novels and short stories embrace universal values through Tunisian reality. While she uses local language and settings, her concern with poverty, class division, and marginalized people make her works relevant to other cultures in the Arab world and beyond.

References:

Jallul 'Azzunah, "Riwayat Turshqana: Tarafa wa Jura," *Al-Hayat al-Thaqafiyya*, no. 120 (December 2000): 132–136;

Rashidah Sharni, "Laylat al-Ghiyab: Bahth 'an al-Ubuwwa fi ma'naha al-wijdani," *Al-Hayat al-Thaqafiyyah*, no. 94 (April 1998): 126–130;

Jean Fontaine, "La Transsexualité dans Turshqana de Massouda Aboubakr," *Le Magreb Littéraire*, 4, no. 7 (2000): 71–76;

Kamal Riyahi, "An Interview with the Tunisian Writer Mas'uda Aboubakr," *Amman*, no. 95 (May 2000): 28–37:

Riyahi, "*Wada'an Hammurabi*: Intisar al-fanni 'ala al-idyulugi," *Amman*, no. 101 (November 2004): 54–57;

Hmida Souli, "Thaman al-ananas al-ladhi tabakhara," *Al-Hayat al-Thaqafiyyah*, no. 96 (June 1998): 132–133.

Mohammed Arkoun
(February 1928 –)

Ursula Günther
University of Hamburg

BOOKS: *Deux épitres de Miskawayh* (Damascus: Bulletin d'études orientales, 1961);

Aspects de la pensée musulmane classique (Paris: Sevpen, 1963);

L'humanisme arabe au IVe/Xe siècle: Miskawayh, philosophe et historien (Paris: Vrin, 1970);

Les Musulmans. Consultation islamo-chrétienne entre Mohammed Arkoun et Youakim Moubarac (Paris: Beauchesne, 1971);

Essais sur la pensée islamique (Paris: Maisonneuve et Larose, 1973);

La pensée arabe (Paris: PUF, 1975); translated as *Arab Thought* (New Dehli: S. Chand, 1988);

L'islam hier-demain, by Arkoun and Louis Gardet (Paris: Buchet-Castel, 1978);

L'étrange et le merveilleux dans l'islam médiéval: Actes du Colloque tenu au Collège de France à Paris, en mars 1974, by Arkoun, Jacques Le Goff, and others (Paris: Editions du J. A., 1978);

Islam: Religione e Società, by Arkoun, Mario Arosio, and Maurice Borrmans (Turin: ERI, 1980);

Lectures du Coran (Paris: Maisonneuve et Larose, 1982);

Pour une critique de la raison islamique (Paris: Maisonneuve et Larose, 1984);

L'islam: Morale et politique (Paris: UNESCO-Desclée, 1986);

Rethinking Islam Today, Occasional Papers Series (Washington, D.C.: Center for Contemporary Arab Studies, Georgetown University, 1987);

Ouvertures sur l'islam (Paris: J. Grancher, 1989); enlarged as *Penser l'Islam aujourd'hui* (Algiers: Laphomic, 1993); revised and enlarged as *L'Islam: Approche critique* (Paris: J. Grancher, 1997); revised and enlarged as *ABC de l'Islam* (Paris: Grancher, 2007); translated and edited by Robert D. Lee as *Rethinking Islam: Common Questions, Uncommon Answers* (Boulder, San Francisco & Oxford: Westview Press, 1994);

Religion et laïcité: Une approche laïque de l'islam (L'Arbrelle: Centre Thomas More, 1989);

Mohammed Arkoun (courtesy of Ursula Günther)

Littérature et oralité au Maghreb: Hommage à Mouloud Mammeri, by Arkoun and Tassadit Yacine (Paris: Harmattan, 1993);

Islam & de Democratie een outmoeting, by Arkoun and Frits Bolkestein (Amsterdam: Contact, 1994);

Islam, Europe and the West (London: I. B. Tauris, 1996);

Islam et Judaïsme: Dialogues avec le protestantisme, by Arkoun, Jean-Claude Basset, and others (Paris: Cerf, 1999);

The Unthought in Contemporary Islamic Thought (London: Saqi, 2002); revised as *Islam: To Reform or to Subvert?* (London: Saqi, 2006);

De Manhattan à Bagdad: Au-delà du bien et du mal, by Arkoun and Joseph Maïla (Paris: Desclée de Brouwer, 2003);

Humanisme et islam: Combats et propositions (Paris: Vrin, 2005).

OTHER: Ibn Miskawayh, Ahmad ibn Muhammad, *Traité d'ethique,* translated into French, with an introduction and notes, by Arkoun (Damascus: Institut Français de Damas, 1969);

"Actualité d'ibn Rushd musulman," in *Multiple Averroès: actes du Colloque international organisé à l'occasion du 850e anniversaire de la naissance d'Averroès, Paris 20–23 septembre 1976,* edited by Jean Jolivet (Paris: Belles Lettres, 1978), pp. 55–56;

"Dialogue islamo-chrétien et nouvelle pensée religieuse," in *La foi en marche: les problemes de fond du dialogue islamo-chrétien: Premier Congrès International à Distance, organisé par CRISLAM* (Rome: PISAI, 1990), pp. 35–41;

L'islam et les musulmans dans le monde; Études islamiques, Volume I: L'Europe occidentale, edited by Arkoun, Rémy Leveau, and Bassem el-Jisr (Beirut: Centre Culturel Hariri, 1993);

"Contemporary Critical Practices and the Qur'an," in *Encyclopaedia of the Qur'an,* 5 volumes, edited by Jane Dammen McAuliffe (Leiden: Brill, 2001), I: pp. 412–431;

"For a Subversive Genesis of Values," in *The Future of Values, 21st Century Talks,* edited by Jérôme Bindé (New York: Berghahn Books, 2004), pp. 47–54;

Les Cultures du Maghreb, edited by Arkoun, Maria-Àngels Roque, and Paul Balta (Paris: Harmattan, 1996);

Histoire de l'islam et des musulmans en France du Moyen-Age à nos jours, edited by Arkoun (Paris: Albin Michel, 2006).

SELECTED PERIODICAL PUBLICATIONS– UNCOLLECTED: "L'exemple arabo-islamique," *Axes,* 5, no. 1 (October/November 1972): 20–31;

"Les Arabes vus par Jacques Berque," *Esprit,* new series, 43, no. 11 (November 1975): 727–734;

"Scholars whose learnings knew no bounds," *UNESCO Courier,* 30 (30 December 1977): 18–22;

"L'Islam et la laïcité," *Bulletin du Centre Thomas More,* 24 (1978): 5–26;

"Propositions pour une autre pensée religieuse," *Islamochristiana,* 4 (1978): 197–206;

"Comprendre l'Islam," *Die Welt des Islams,* 22 (1982 [i.e. 1984]): 134–137;

"The Adequacy of Contemporary Islam to the Political, Social and Economic Development of Northern Africa," *Africa Studies Quarterly,* 4 (1982): 34–53;

"Jérusalem: au nom de qui? au nom de quoi?" *Islamochristiana,* 9 (1983): 225–230;

"Deux médiateurs de la pensée médiévale: Averroës et Maïmonides," *UNESCO Courier,* 9 (September 1986): 14–20;

"Réflexions sur la notion de "raison islamique," *Archives des Sciences Sociales des Religions,* 63, no. 1 (January–March 1987): 125–132;

"Les tâches de l'intellectuel mu sulman. Intellectuels et militants dans le monde islamique au VIIe-XXe siècle," *Cahiers de la Méditerranée,* 37 (December 1988): 1–34;

"The Notion of Revelation: From Ahl al-Kitab to the Societies of the Book," *Die Welt des Islams,* new series 28, no. 1 (1988): 62–89;

"The Topicality of the Problem of the Person in Islamic Thought," *International Social Science Journal,* 117 (August 1988): 407–421;

"New Perspectives for a Jewish-Christian-Muslim Dialogue," *Journal of Ecumenical Studies,* 26, no. 3 (1989): 523–529;

"Avec Mouloud Mammeri à Taourirt-Mimoun," *Awal, Cahiers d'Etudes berbères* (1990): 9–13;

"Islam, pensée islamique, islamisme," *Peuples Méditerranéens,* 50 (January–March 1990): 107–113;

"Algérie 1993. Réflexions sur un destin historique," *Revue du monde musulman et de la Méditerranée,* 65 (1992/1993): 197–207;

"Réflexions d'un musulman sur le 'nouveau catéchisme,'" *Islamochristiana,* 19 (1993): 43–54;

"Is Islam Threatened by Christianity?" *Concilium,* no. 3 (1994): 48–57;

"Clarifier le passé pour construire le futur," *Confluences Méditerranée,* 16 (1995/1996): 17–30;

"Transgresser, déplacer, dépasser," *Arabica,* 53 (1996): 28–70;

"Du dialogue inter-religieux à la reconnaissance du fait religieux," *Diogène,* 182 (1998): 103–126;

"Peut-on parler d'humanisme en contexte islamique?" *Israel Oriental Studies,* 19 (1999): 11–22;

"The Answers of Applied Islamology," *Theory, Culture and Society,* 24, no. 2 (2007): 21–38.

Mohammed Arkoun is a versatile intellectual and academic, one of the pioneers among contemporary scholars and thinkers in the field of Islamic Studies. His concepts challenge both Muslim and non-Muslim perceptions and approaches to Islam, taking up various intellectual, scientific, religious, and political currents and tensions. His contribution consists in applying findings and insights developed in social sciences to the study of Islam while simultaneously augmenting them with his own ideas. Arkoun's intellectual flowering paralleled the formation of great contemporary philosophical movements such as structuralism, semiotics, structural anthropology, discourse analysis, and poststructuralism–discourses that he has intensely studied and that have affected his evolution as a thinker. He confronts the field of Islamic Studies as well as Islamic thought with the *unthought* and *unthinkable*–two interconnected concepts he developed in the late 1980s–by calling into question putative certainties and by going beyond the orthodoxy established and defended by and within the various Muslim communities and the field of Islamic Studies. Appropriating methods that traditionally are not part of what is considered to be Islamic Studies or the study of Islam, he advocates a paradigm shift through his approach to Islam by asking fundamental questions and outlining new strategies of interpretation. Familiar with two civilizations and intellectual traditions–the North African as well as the European–Arkoun is able to articulate a double critique while simultaneously building cultural bridges and tracing new ways out of the limitations and difficulties of the discourses specific to each tradition.

Although many of his publications date to the mid 1980s, Arkoun's writings did not stir widespread interest until the 1990s. Since then, his star has been rising. Arkoun is now regarded as one of the most exceptional thinkers to come from the Arab-Muslim region, an estimation underscored by the many awards he has received. The University of Exeter awarded him an honorary doctorate in 2001. His life's work was honored with the Georgio Levi Della Vida Award in 2002. In 2003 he received the Ibn Rushd Prize for Free Thought. An examination of Arkoun's life reveals that his personal experience often provided the impulses that guided his thought and criticism–a finding with which Arkoun himself agrees. He has stated that it was existential experience, not academic training, that turned him into an intellectual.

Mohammed Arkoun was born in the village of Taourirt-Mimoun in Great Kabylia, northern Algeria, in February 1928. Of Berber ethnicity, he grew up with nine younger siblings, two of whom died of intestinal inflammation at a young age because of inadequate medical care, the nearest doctor practicing seventy kilometers away. His family was traditional and religious, and they lived in poverty. His mother, born Mohdad Debia, remained illiterate, speaking only Kabyle, one of the various Berber languages of the Maghreb, which never became an official language in Algeria. The position and history of his father's family–the At-Warab–within the community is indicated by the location of their house in the lower part of the village, at the foot of the hill on which the old settlement was built. They did not originate in Taourirt-Mimoun but settled there in the late eighteenth or early nineteenth century, after having been expelled from their home in the region of Constantine. As relatively poor newcomers, their influence in the village Taourirt-Mimoun society was comparatively small.

Arkoun attended school in his home village until the age of nine, when he left the region to live with his father, a shopkeeper in the wealthy French settlement of Aïn-el-Arba, east of the northwestern city of Oran. He learned his father's trade while continuing to attend school. The move, and its attendant culture shock, affected him deeply. He learned painfully that, as a Berber, he belonged to a minority of lesser status than the Arabs, who faced problems communicating and making their voices heard outside of the Berberophone districts. Higher social status (even among the Berber population) was accorded to speakers of French and Arabic, with Arabic as the language of the Qur'an and of instruction in Islamic studies being accorded greater respect than French.

Arkoun recalls these moments of his youth in an interview with Hassan Arfaoui in 1995: "This was my first particularly painful experience; being a little Algerian, alone among his francophone and arabophone peers. I had to learn two languages at once, and very quickly, all the while experiencing what it meant to be part of a minority rejected, even disdained by two socio-cultural groups whose languages dominated public space . . . This daily reasserted marginality was all the harder to bear as a distinction had to be made between the disdain all natives suffered equally under the colonial system and the gaps in sensitivity, collective memory and socio-cultural references that separated arabophone and berberophone Algerians." He continued to encounter similar experiences in the future.

Arkoun was given the opportunity to follow his own path by his mother's brother, a member of a religious brotherhood and supporter of mystic Islam, who arranged for him to receive a good education. This uncle also introduced Arkoun to the basics of Islamic scholarship and the Qur'an at the *madrasa* (Islamic school), and he accompanied Arkoun and his father to meetings of the religious brotherhoods and village council meetings. Religion and religiosity were integral parts of everyday community life.

Arkoun began to explore Christianity at the age of thirteen. His family's financial situation did not allow him to attend a lycée in Algiers, but he had the opportunity to attend the *collège secondaire* (secondary school) in a neighboring village which was run by the Pères Blancs (White Fathers) Jesuit order. Instruction there was free, which allowed him to pursue the *baccalauréat,* a degree in the French school system that is equivalent to a high-school diploma in the United States. He describes this period as one in which he explored Latin culture and literature, especially the African church fathers Tertullian, Cyprian, and Augustine. He investi-

Front cover for the 1994 translation of the book Arkoun first published in 1989 as Ouvertures sur l'islam (Richland County Public Library)

gated the relationship between Christianity and Islam. He was impressed particularly by the concept of Christian charity, as exemplified by the monks who dedicated themselves to educating the youths of the region without questioning their Islamic identity.

With the colonial French school system then dominant in Algeria, Arkoun's intellectual development was influenced by his study of French literature and history as well as of Latin. He remembers reading Virgil, which became part of his love for the whole of Mediterranean culture. The lessons treating the African church fathers, who lived in the Maghreb, had a lasting influence on his perception of the Mediterranean as a common cultural space. In his interview with Arfaoui, Arkoun mentions that his studies gave him "confidence in the possibility of recovering a continuous historical memory encompassing not only the Maghreb, but the entire Mediterranean, including Roman Italy, Muslim and Christian Spain, and Southern France."

A bursary from the French ministry of education allowed him to attend the Lycée Lamoricière in Oran for the final years before graduation. He was one of the few Muslims to attend French schools and was later able to finance his studies of Islamic literature at the University of Algiers (1950–1954) by teaching at a lycée. He describes his university experience as unsatisfying compared to the stimulating instruction he had received from the Pères Blancs and in Oran. He found the purely descriptive lessons both sterile and badly taught. Personal interest and intellectual curiosity led him also to attend courses in law, philosophy, and geography. He also read Arabic philosophy and longed for the opportunity to study in Paris. His rebellious side was strengthened not only by the poor conditions at the university and the restrictive approaches to instruction but also by his personal conflict with Henri Pérès, the director general of Arabic studies in Algeria, who was strictly opposed to Arkoun completing his studies in

Paris and obstructed his progress at every opportunity. In his interview with Arfaoui, Arkoun sees this trying period as crucial to his intellectual development and particularly his characteristic approach to Islam: "there lie the roots of my revolt as a young student and my resolve to transgress the cognitive practices of flamboyant Orientalism, difficult though it was to free myself of them."

Arkoun was finally able to leave Algiers on 1 November 1954, the eve of the War of Independence, to study Arabic language and literature at the Sorbonne under Régis Blachère, Carles Pellat, Évariste Levi-Provençal, Robert Brunschvig, and Henri Laoust. He graduated with an *Agrégation* in 1956. During this time he supported himself by teaching at a lycée. Between 1956 and 1959 he taught at the university and the Lycée Kléber in Strasbourg and studied religious philosophy. Claude Cohen, then also teaching at Strasbourg University, introduced him to the Annales school and its then novel approach to the history of the Islamic Orient that emphasized an orientation to structures and mentalities rather than events. Once again, the intellectual gap between the universities in Strasbourg and Paris and that at Algiers struck Arkoun.

French intellectuals in the mid to late 1950s and 1960s were ready for what may be termed "New Beginnings." More and more criticism of established academic methods and perspectives prevailed, and the desire to leave worn paths brought forth many new movements or schools, including structuralism, structural anthropology, historical discourse criticism, and the Annales school. Political debate centered around the anticolonial struggle of the so-called Third World in general and the Algerian War in particular. A new political awareness was emerging, known as *tiers-mondisme* (third worldism), as nonaligned states and former colonies began to make their voices heard and advocated a "third way," apart from the agenda of the Cold War antagonists.

Arkoun, like many North African students, placed high hopes in a new era that was to follow the independence of Algeria in 1962 and that of the other Maghrebin nations. With the return of the Arabic Muslim world to the stage of history, he and many others believed that neglected problems would be addressed and that a new spirit would reinvigorate endeavors in all fields. Such a hope–at least partly–informed Arkoun's academic motivation, until the crushing disappointments of the mid 1960s. The overthrow of Algeria's first elected president following independence in the coup by Houari Boumédiennes in June 1965 and the disastrous results of the the Six-Day War of June 1967 marked the beginning of the end of Arkoun's enthusiastic belief that Arabs would be able to once again write their own history.

Maghrebin intellectuals of Arkoun's generation were formed by the French culture and yet remain rooted in Arabic Muslim or Berber-Arabic Muslim culture. This rich cultural background holds, and always has held, a particular problem of identity, not just since Algerian independence. With the end of the War of Independence, in the context of a rising tide of nationalism, the belief gained currency that a new, unified Algerian identity had come into existence. Arkoun and others like him found it difficult to integrate into polarized worldviews they did not share, and it left them open to attack from both sides. Arkoun states in the interview with Arfaoui: "The most saddening aspect of this, on the French side, is that Maghrebin intellectuals, formed and influenced by French culture and thought, and thus in turn capable of enriching it, are never adequately recognized in either French culture or society. . . . This is an experience I share. The French invariably regard 'us' as people who have come from somewhere else."

Arkoun faced a dilemma that was not uncommon to North African students of the time. Educated in the French system, he had not engaged in the struggle for independence, which made it difficult for him to begin an academic career in Algeria. In addition, he found the intellectual climate of France with its specific challenges and opportunities vital to his work. But France was not congenial to him, either. He eventually was able to gain a post as *Maître de conférence* (associate professor) at the Sorbonne in 1961, a position which he held until 1969. He then faced many conflicts before completing his dissertation on the Islamic scholar Ibn Miskawayh in 1968. Many of his superiors would have preferred to see him return to Algeria.

Arkoun's initial dissertation project was to be a study of the religious practices of Kabylia. However, the Algerian War made this project impossible as the political situation did not allow for fieldwork. Following the advice of Brunschvig, Arkoun decided instead to write his dissertation on Miskawayh and Arab humanism of the tenth century. He later came to regard his change of topic as crucial to his career, as it both provided him with the conceptual tools needed to develop his critical approach and drew his attention to the importance of an intellectual critique of religious thought.

The study of Miskawayh and his intellectual environment led Arkoun to understand how Islam had been reduced over the centuries to Arabism and Sunnism. He was particularly impressed by Miskawayh's openness to other traditions such as Greek and Persian. He also discovered that in the context of *adab* (the study of cultivation and knowledge) religious reason could adopt elements of philosophical knowledge without provoking the opprobrium of legal and theological scholars, the defenders of orthodoxy. He recognized the importance of Miskawayh and tenth-century contemporaries such as Abu Hayyan at-Tauhidi for the development of Arab and Islamic thought, which motivated him to undertake his long-term project of a criticism of Islamic reason within the context of religious thought.

In the early 1960s orientalists agreed that an Arab humanism, analogous to the European humanist movement that advanced from the fourteenth to the sixteenth centuries, had never existed. Through his research and work, Arkoun began an academic debate to establish the term *Arab humanism,* which became part of the title of his dissertation when it was published in 1970 as *L'humanisme arabe au IVe/Xe siècle: Miskawayh, philosophe et historien* (Arab Humanism of the Fourth/Tenth Centuries: Miskawayh, Philosopher and Historian).

In *L'humanisme arabe au IVe/Xe siècle: Miskawayh, philosophe et historien* Arkoun refutes the assumption that the Arab culture of this period produced purely imitative, unoriginal literary works through his reevaluation of the writings of Miskawayh. Through his analysis of the case of Miskawayh, Arkoun explores the conditions under which an intellectual and his work may appear and then disappear from public consciousness. The example of Miskawayh allows him to define a humanist tradition of thought shared by a significant portion of Arab philosophers, which he explores through sophisticated perspectives such as discourse analysis, structuralism, semiotics, and the historical, anthropological, and sociological approach of the Annales school. In his first major academic publication, Arkoun not only employed an original mix of new methodologies but also established his long-term goal of using cultural anthropology to articulate a serious criticism of Islamic Studies. Thanks to his work, Miskawayh's importance was recognized and the debate about Arab humanism opened. In 1969 Arkoun left the Sorbonne to become a professor for the History of Islamic Thought at the University of Lyon (Lyon II). He held the same position at the University of Vincennes (Paris VIII) from 1971 to 1980, before he returned to the Sorbonne.

In his subsequent work Arkoun pursued his original approach to research in Islamic studies, finding the traditional historical-philological method dominant since the nineteenth century too restrictive. The reactions to his transgression of the borders of his field among his French colleagues were mixed. Representatives of traditional Islamic Studies or orientalism thought their "Muslim" colleague a rebel and did not adopt his methods. Opinions about the value of Arkoun's contribution among French orientalists remain divided.

Only three of the ten essays included in *Essais sur la pensée islamique* (1973, Essays on Islamic Thought) were written after *L'humanisme arabe au IVe/Xe siècle*. Although the volume appears heterogeneous at first glance, a thematic and methodological homogeneity can be discerned that corresponds to the general focus of Arkoun's interest: a critique of Islamic reason in the context of applied Islamic studies. *Essais sur la pensée islamique* is indispensable for the understanding of Arkoun's approaches, because it lays out fundamental parts of his research perspectives, methodology, and hypotheses, especially the need he sees for a meta-level discussion of philosophical-historical subjects. Arkoun's originality consists in his ability to integrate disparate approaches, but he has been criticized for not systematizing his ideas. Even in this early volume it is necessary to be familiar with the context of Arkoun's thinking to appreciate his insights. In *La pensée arabe* (1975, Arab Thought), a small volume that is addressed to a wider public, Arkoun sets out further details about his perspective regarding the Qur'an and introduces the concepts *qur'anic* and *islamic fact/event* in his discussions of the written word and liturgical speech. These concepts set up the analytical framework necessary for approaching the Qur'an beyond theological and orthodox postulates, differentiating between a linguistic event (qur'anic fact) and the consolidation of the new religion (islamic fact). They are useful in describing the historical process of the coming into being of a new religion, effected and supported by social, political, and cultural factors.

In 1980 Arkoun took a position at the Sorbonne Nouvelle (Paris III), where he served as director of the department of Arabic and History of Islamic Thought and editor of the journal *Arabica. Lectures du Coran* (1982, Readings of the Qur'an), the first of several volumes of essays published during his years at the Sorbonne, is probably his most challenging collection, which the author in retrospect regards as part of a necessary academic phase in his development. He explains in detail his central concepts and dedicates an entire essay to what he calls *societies of the Book/book*. His perspective respects the transcendent character of the Qur'an as a Revelation (The Book) as well as its character as a historical and literary document with its literary, social, and political meanings (the book).

Arkoun's fundamental project, to examine the cognitive principles dominating Islamic thought through the meta-analysis of anthropology and sociology, is expressed clearly in *Pour une critique de la raison islamique* (1984, For a Critique of Islamic Reason). Through his approach to Islam–which he terms *applied islamology* and to which he devotes an entire chapter– Arkoun seeks a deeper understanding of religion as an anthropological phenomenon. His methodology allows for the traditional limitations of the so-called Book religions (Judaism, Christianity, Islam) to be transgressed and permits an integrative view of Judeo-Christo-Islamic civilization. A core question, formulated in the introduction—"Under which circumstances does the idea of Truth take shape to the point of shaping an individual fate or a collective history?"—is addressed in one way or another in all of the essays. A further leitmotif, already touched upon in the title, is the concept of an Islamic reason, closely bound up with that of Islamic thought and consciousness. *Essais sur la pensée islamique, Lectures du Coran,* and *Pour une critique de la raison islamique* must be studied in connection with each other as they are complementary parts allowing deeper insight into Arkoun's thoughts and conceptions.

Ouvertures sur l'islam (1989, Openings to Islam; translated as *Rethinking Islam: Common Questions, Uncommon Answers,* 1994)—which Arkoun revised and enlarged in 1993, 1997, and 2007—is written in a question-and-answer format, treating twenty-one fundamental subjects of Islam. These topics, which include the Qur'an, exegesis, Muhammad, and mysticism, are complemented by an interview with the author and three essays on human rights, ethics, and Mediterranean civilization. In this volume, the first and so far only one of his works to be translated into English, Arkoun seeks to reach a wider public outside academic circles, while remaining true to his project by using "the trans-historical, cultural yet at the same time historical, sociological and anthropological approach to the phenomenon of religion using Islam as our example." *Ouvertures sur l'islam* not only is an interesting and rather unusual introduction to the central concepts of Islam but also offers a good entry point to Arkoun's thought.

In the late 1980s Arkoun began receiving fellowships and invitations for visiting professorships in Europe and the United States. He held fellowships at the Wissenschaftskolleg zu Berlin (1986–1987 and again in 1990) and at the Institute for Advanced Studies at Princeton (1992–1993). He was visiting professor inter alia at Temple University (1988–1990) and at New York University (March–April 2001 and 2002) and held a chair for Islam at Vreije Universteit Amsterdam (1988–1992). He also gave the Gifford Lectures at Edinburgh University in November 2001.

Since 1993 Arkoun's main position has been professor emeritus and visiting professor at the Institute of Ismaili Studies in London. He has also been a member of the Conseil National d'Ethique pour les sciences de la vie et de la santé (National Committee on Ethics in Life and Health Sciences, 1990–1998), the Haut Conseil de la Famille et de la Population (High Council on

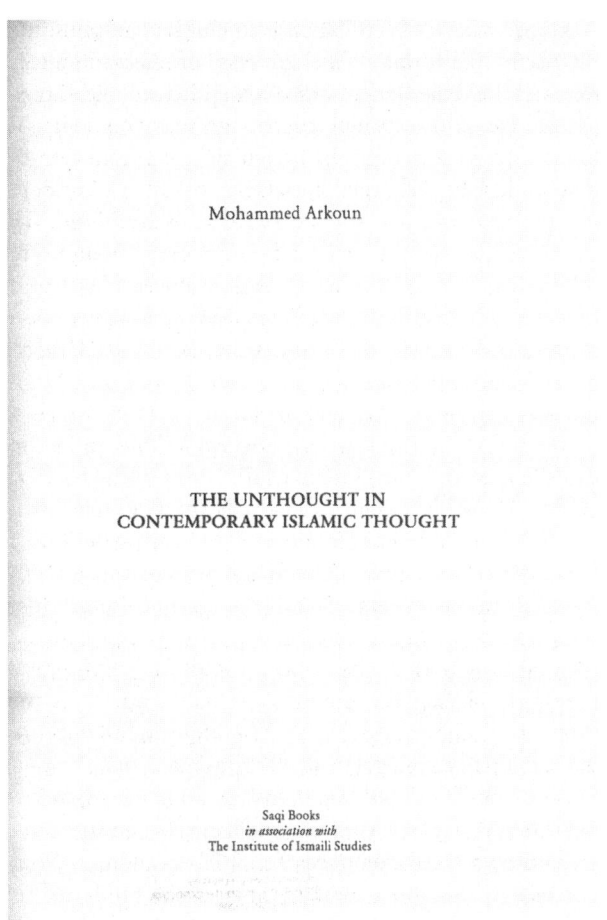

Title page for a 2002 book Arkoun prepared as an introduction to his concepts for English readers (Thomas Cooper Library, University of South Carolina)

the Family and Population, 1995–1998) as well as serving on the jury of the Prix Agha Khan d'Architecture (Agha Khan Award for Architecture, 1995–1998) and the board of Governors of the Institute of Ismaili Studies. The French state appointed him Commandeur de la légion d'honneur (2004–) and Officier des Palmes académiques (1998–).

Arkoun has remained a prolific and productive writer, publishing three further books between 2002 and 2005. *The Unthought in Contemporary Islamic Thought* (2002)—whose second edition, including a new preface, was published in 2006 as a paperback titled *Islam: To Reform or to Subvert?*—is a condensation of his thought and concepts made accessible to an English-language readership. Arkoun seeks to break open the boundaries of *cloture dogmatique* (dogmatic enclosure) that define the orthodoxy of Islamic reason, Islamic thought, and Islamic discourse and to bring the *unthought* and *unthinkable* to the light. In the preface of the second edition,

Arkoun writes, "my ambition is to embrace in the same intellectual gesture a radical criticism of reason in all its productions, methodologies and epistemological postures." He also explains the change from his original title: "The idea behind the earlier title, far from redundant, is in fact subsumed into its successor. For, to identify the *unthought* and the *unthinkable,* it is necessarily to *subvert.* This effect is secured by employing new methodologies, by problematizing unquestioned ideas, and by achieving a shift of paradigms." Written in response to the terror attacks of 11 September 2001, *De Manhattan à Bagdad: Au-delà du bien et du mal* (2003, From Manhattan to Baghdad: Beyond the Good and the Bad) is a conversation in three parts between Arkoun and the Middle East specialist Joseph Maïla, dean of the Faculty of Social and Economic Sciences of the Catholic Institute in Paris, that makes a plea for a new reading of Islam. In *Humanisme et Islam: Combats et propositions* (2005, Humanism in Islam: Combats and Propositions) Arkoun calls for the exploring of new horizons by reactivating the philosophical position of the Enlightenment, exposing the mytho-historical constructs of dogmatism and promoting *ijtihad*–independent, individual judgment in a legal or theological question.

Mohammad Arkoun in his work has attempted to open new avenues out of the intellectual one-way street created by a dualistic opposition of Islam and the West, but critics have been slow to open their minds to his approach. Even after thirty years of teaching at the Sorbonne and other European and American universities, he is still regarded in the West as a "moderate Muslim." Algerian or Arab critics, however, often focus on the perceived "Western" quality of his work, citing Arkoun's lack of genuine Muslim or Arab qualities. Both perspectives share the construct of a divide between the West and Islam and thus are unable to see the central point of Arkoun's criticism, which addresses precisely this polarizing view. Neither side can escape the charge or Euro- or Arabocentrism and the attendant exclusion of the "other." Through his holistic, integrative approach, Arkoun aims for nothing less than a union of the theological claims of the faithful, the philological demands of the historian, the explicatory perspective of the anthropologist, and the critical scrutiny of the philosopher in one vision of a unified anthropology of religious and philosophical theology. It remains to be seen if his voice will find the response it merits.

Interviews:

Yves Lacoste, "L'Islam et les islams; Entretien avec Mohammed Arkoun," *Hérodote,* 35 (1984): 19–34;

Philippe Barbulesco, "Mohammed Arkoun," in *L'Islam en questions: Vingt-quatre écrivains arabes répondent,* edited by Barbulesco (Paris: Grasset, 1986), pp. 175–183;

Michael Lüders, "Für eine Kritik der islamischen Vernunft; Ein Gespräch mit Mohammed Arkoun," *Die Zeit* (Hamburg), 10 July 1987, p. 32;

Paul Balta, "Mohamed Arkoun: Passer au crible de la pensée islamique," *Arabies,* 13 (January 1988): 68–73;

Lüders, "Wider das Dogma; Ein Gespräch über Fundamentalismus und Moderne im arabischen Geistesleben," *Frankfurter Rundschau* (14 July 1990);

"Demagogen haben die Macht über das Volk," *Zeitmagazin,* 5, no. 4, 1991, p. 22;

"Qui est dangereux, l'Islam ou l'Occident?" *Alternatives Non Violentes,* no. 83 (Summer 1992): 19–27;

"Der Islam? Gefahr für die Welt?" *Die Zeit* (Hamburg), 2 April 1993, pp. 9, 24, 38;

"Mener la critique de la raison islamique," *La Croix* (Paris), 1 June 1993, p. 24;

"Qui a peur de Mohammed Arkoun? Entretien réalisé par Hachem Saleh," *Arabies,* 81 (September 1993): 50–55;

"Plenary Debate: Humanism Toward the Third Millenium," *Forum 2001 Symposium: Humanism Toward the Third Millennium,* edited by Fons Elders (Amsterdam & Brussels: VUB Press, 1993), pp. 83–103.

Jean-Pierre Chagnollaud, Bassma Kodmani-Darwish, and Abderrahim Lamchici, "Le fait islamique: Vers un nouvel espace d'intelligibilité," *Confluences Méditerranée,* 12 (1994): 13–31;

Henri Tincq, "Entre l'islam et l'Occident, tout se passe désormais dans un imaginaire qui nourrit une exclusion réciproque," *Les Grands Entretiens du Monde,* 2 (May 1994): 77–80;

"Der Koran ist keine Waffe" *Die Zeit* (Hamburg), 23 December 1994, p. 30;

Hassan Arfaoui, "Entretien avec Mohammed Arkoun," *M.A.R.S.: Le Monde Arabe dans la Recherche Scientifique,* 5 (1995): 7–32;

Sophie Bessis, "Entretien avec Mohammed Arkoun," *Les Cahiers de l'Orient,* 36/37 (1995): 231–243;

"Le cheminement d'une critique. Entretien," *Revue Intersignes,* 10 (1995): 217–227;

"Wir brauchen Visionäre," *Die Tageszeitung* (Berlin), 6 February 1996, pp. 14–15;

Laurent Marchand, "Histoires tronquées ou les origines d'un malentendu dans le labyrinthe de l'idéologie: Entretien avec Mohammed Arkoun," *Rive: Revue de Politique et de Culture Méditerranéennes,* 3 (Summer 1997): 53–56;

"Wann begreifen die Europäer, daß Muslime keine Wilden sind?" *Die Welt* (Berlin), 16 November 1998, p. 8;

"Islam und Christentum müssen ihre gemeinsamen Wurzeln erkennen; Adelbert Reif im Gespräch mit Mohammed Arkoun," *Universitas: Zeitschrift für interdisziplinäre Wissenschaft,* 53, no. 630 (December 1998): 1202–1212;

Spielgelbild Barbarisches, "Wie der Gegensatz zwischen Islam und Okzident überwunden werden kann," *Süddeutsche Zeitung,* 30 June 1999, p. 16.

References:

Mohammed el-Ayadi, "Mohammed Arkoun ou l'ambition d'une modernité intellectuelle," in *Penseurs Maghrébins Contemporains,* edited by Collectif (Casablanca: Cérès-Editions, 1993), pp. 43–71;

Farid Esack, "Mohammed Arkoun: Dekonstructing Revelation," in his *Qur'an, Liberation & Pluralism. An Islamic Perspective of Interreligious Solidarity against Oppression* (Oxford: One World Press, 1997), pp. 68–73;

Ursula Günther, *Mohammed Arkoun: Ein moderner Kritiker der islamischen Vernunft* (Würzburg: Ergon, 2004);

Günther, "Mohammed Arkoun: Towards a Radical Rethinking of Islamic Thought," in *Modern and Postmodern Approaches to the Qur'an,* edited by Suha Taji-Farouki (London: Oxford University Press in association with The Institute of Ismaili Studies, 2004), pp. 125–167;

Günther, "Weder Modernismus noch Fundamentalismus: Karl-Jaspers-Vorlesungen zu Fragen der Zeit an der Universität Oldenburg vom 9.11. bis 19.11.1994," *Verfassung und Recht in Übersee,* 28, no. 4 (1995): 550–558;

Günther, "Zum Potenzial von Mohammed Arkouns Dialogkonzepten," in *Theologie–Pädagogik–Kontext. Zukunftsperspektiven der Religionspädagogik,* edited by Günther and others (Münster: Waxmann, 2005), pp. 209–222;

Ron Haleber and P. S. van Koningsveld, *Islam en humanisme. De wereld van (Mohammed) Arkoun* (Amsterdam: VU Uitgeverij, 1991);

Robert D. Lee, "Arkoun and Authenticity," *Peuples Méditerranéens,* 50 (January–March 1990): 75–106;

Lee, "Foreword," in *Rethinking Islam: Common Questions, Uncommon Answers,* by Arkoun (Boulder, San Francisco & Oxford: Westview Press, 1994), pp. vii–xiii;

Christine Souriau, "La conscience islamique dans quelques oeuvres récentes d'intellectuels du Maghreb," *Revue de l'Occident Musulman et de la Méditerranée,* 29 (1980): 69–107;

W. Montgomery Watt, "A Contemporary Muslim Thinker," *Scottish Journal of Religious Studies,* 6, no. 1 (1985): 5–10.

Sadik Jalal al-Azm
(7 November 1934 –   )

Sebastian Maisel
Grand Valley State University

BOOKS: *Dirasat fi al-falsafah al-gharbiyah al-hadithah* (Beirut: Manshurat al-Jami'a al-'Arabiyyah, 1966);

Kant's Theory of Time (New York: Philosophical Library, 1967);

Naqd al-fikr al-dini (Beirut: Dar al-Tali'ah, 1967);

Fi al-hubb wa al-hubb al-'Udhri (Beirut: Manshurat Nizar Qabbani, 1968);

Al-Naqd al-dhati ba'da al-hazimah (Beirut: Dar al-Tali'ah, 1968);

The Origins of Kant's Arguments in the Antinomies (Oxford: Clarendon Press, 1972);

Dirasah naqdiyyah li fikr al-muqawamah al-Filastiniyyah (Beirut: Dar al-'Awdah, 1973);

Al-Sahyuniyyah wa al-sira' al-tabaqi (Beirut: Dar al-'Awdah, 1975);

Ziyarat al-Sadat wa bu's al-salam al-'adil (Beirut: Dar al-Tali'ah li al-Tiba'ah wa al-Nashr, 1978);

Al-Istishraq wa al-istishraq ma'kusan (Beirut: Dar al-Hadathah, 1981);

Thalath muhawarat falsafiyyah difa'an 'an al-maddiyah wa al-Tarikh (Beirut: Dar al-Fikr al-Jadid, 1990);

Athar al-thawrah al-Faransiyyah fi fikr al-nahdah (Tunis: Al-'Arabiyah Muhammad 'Ali al-Hami, 1991);

Dhihniyat al-tahrim (London: Riyad al-Rayyis, 1992);

Unbehagen in der Moderne: Aufklärung im Islam, edited by Kai-Henning Gerlach (Frankfurt: Fischer Taschenbuch Verlag, 1993);

Al-Usuliyyah al-Islamiyyah (Cairo: Markaz al-Dirasat wa al-Ma'lumat al-Qanuniyyah li Huquq al-Insan, 1997);

Al-'Ilmaniyyah wa al-mujtama' al-madani (Cairo: Markaz al-Dirasat wa al-Ma'lumat al-Qanuniyyah li Huquq al-Insan, 1998);

Al-Sira' al-Filastini al-Isra'ili: Ila Ayn? (Beirut: Dar Ibn Rushd, 1998);

Hiwarat fi al-wataniyyah al-Suriyyah (Damascus: Batra li al-Nashr wa al-Tawzi', 2003);

Sadik Jalal al-Azm (Erasmus Prize Foundation)

Ma ba'da dhihniyyat al-tahrim: qira'at "al-ayat al-shaytaniyah": radd wa ta'qib (Damascus: Dar al-Mada, 2004);

Islam und Säkularer Humanismus, bilingual edition, English translation by Alexandra Riebe, edited by Eilert Herms (Tübingen: Mohr Siebeck, 2005).

OTHER: "Is Islam Secularizable?" in *Civil Society, Democracy, and the Muslim Middle East: Papers Read at a Conference Held at the Swedish Research Institute in Istanbul 28–30 October, 1996,* edited by Elisabeth Ozdalga and Sune Persson (Istanbul: Swedish Research Institute, 1997), pp. 17–22;

"Politischer Islam im 20. Jahrhundert," in *Islam und Politik,* edited by Albrecht Metzger (Bonn: Bundeszentrale für Politische Bildung, 2002);

"Western Historical Thinking from an Arabian Perspective," in *Western Historical Thinking: An Intercultural*

Debate, edited by Jörn Rüsen (New York: Berghahn Books, 2002), pp. 119–127.

SELECTED PERIODICAL PUBLICATIONS–
UNCOLLECTED: "Orientalism and Orientalism in Reverse," *Khamsin,* no. 8 (1981): 5–26;

"Palestinian Parallels: The Zionist Analogy," *Nation,* 233 (5 December 1981): 605–611;

"Palestinian Zionism," *Die Welt des Islams,* 28 (1988): 90–98;

"The Importance of Being Earnest about Salman Rushdie," *Die Welt des Islams,* 31 (1991): 1–49;

"Owning the Future: Modern Arabs and Hamlet," *ISIM Newsletter,* May 2000, p. 11;

"The Satanic Verses Post-Festum: The Global, The Local, The Literary," *Comparative Studies of South Asia, Africa and the Middle East,* 20, nos. 1 and 2 (2000): 44–66;

"The View from Damascus," *New York Review of Books,* 47, no. 10 (15 June 2000);

"Time Out of Joint: Western Dominance, Islamist Terror, and the Arab Imagination," *Boston Review,* (October/November 2004);

"Islam, Terrorism, and the West," *Comparative Studies of South Asia, Africa and the Middle East,* 25, no. 1 (2005): 6–16;

Although it is the general impression that Islamic thought dominates the wider political and philosophical discourse in the Arab world, some powerful voices of secularism are continually heard. One prominent voice is that of Sadik Jalal al-Azm, professor of modern European Philosophy at the University of Damascus and restless advocate of self-criticism in the analysis of current philosophical debates between the Arab-Islamic world and the West. He is considered one of the most important philosophers in the Arab world. Beginning in the late 1960s with the "Azm Affair," he became a symbol for an uncompromising stand for the separation of religion and the state as well as for social enlightenment and pluralism. Since his retirement from the university in 1999, he continues to propagate his vision of democracy and civil justice in the Middle East. Owing to his contrarian position, his works have earned him the title "heretic from Damascus," and in 2004 he was named one of the recipients of the prestigious Erasmus Prize, the most important cultural award in the European Union.

Sadik Jalal al-Azm was born on 7 November 1934 in Damascus but grew up in Lebanon. He comes from an old, politically influential family in Syria. His grandfather was a senior civil servant in the Ottoman Empire, and his father a great admirer of Kamal Atatürk, who separated religion and state in Turkey. He studied at the American University of Beirut (AUB) and went on to study philosophy in the United States, receiving his Ph.D. in 1961 from Yale University with a dissertation on Henri Bergson. Al-Azm returned to Beirut and was appointed his first professorship in philosophy at AUB in 1963. While at AUB, he finished and published his first book, *Dirasat fi al-falsafah al-gharbiyah al-hadithah* (1966, Studies in Modern Western Philosophy), a work that addresses trends in Western philosophy.

After he had been at AUB for four years, the Middle East experienced the crisis of the 1967 Six-Day War. Although Lebanon was not directly involved in the conflict, al-Azm, like most Arabs, was dismayed at the outcome for the Palestinian people, and the experience had a significant influence on his thought. The shock and disillusionment following Israel's humiliating defeat of Egypt, Jordan, and Syria brought to the fore the old question about the relationship between the Arab world and the West. As a philosopher, al-Azm naturally considers the current political, cultural, and social circumstances of the time and place in which he lives. Al-Azm contributed to this debate over the relationship between the Arab world and the West, starting with *Naqd al-fikr al-dini* (1967, Critique of Religious Thought), a book that along with *al-Naqd al-dhati ba'da al-hazimah* (1968, Self-Criticism after the Defeat) made him one of the most controversial intellectuals in the Arab world. Many of al-Azm's critical remarks caused a scandal and enraged the religious establishment in the Arab world, particularly the Mufti of Lebanon. During this same period, al-Azm in *Kant's Theory of Time* (1967), a work he wrote in English, put forward the Western philosopher Immanuel Kant as an example of the triumph of reason and rationality over superstition. All along, al-Azm advocated the centrality of questioning and discussing taboo—an approach that creates controversy but also helps to bring change. He found encouragement in comparing the Arab world to Europe in the eighteenth and nineteenth centuries, as he believed in the example of European history, which showed that social and political development is possible when religious belief does not hinder progress.

In *al-Naqd al-dhati ba'da al-hazimah,* al-Azm analyzed why the Arabs succumbed to the Israelis. He was harsh in his conclusions, arguing that the Arabs lost because they did not question religious traditions and doctrines, respect the individual, or take responsibility for their situation and actions. He also criticized the Arab inclination to fatalism, which he believed led to the acceptance of their victimhood to the great powers. This analysis cost him his professorship at AUB. He was banned from lecturing and for a while was not even allowed to enter the campus. Indeed, the publication of *Naqd al-fikr al-dini* and *al-Naqd al-dhati ba'da al-hazimah* caused him even more trouble, as he was jailed and prosecuted by the Lebanese government in 1969. However, minister of interior Kamal Junblat invited him to an intellectual discussion, and the charges were eventually dismissed. The court came to the conclusion that al-Azm's writings were a scholarly philosophical critique and not a call to sectarian violence. The scandal became known as the "Azm Affair." Ultimately, his trial paved the way for greater freedom of expression in Lebanon. Since that time his statements, publications, and remarks on current events have polarized the Arab public.

After leaving AUB, al-Azm in 1969 became the editor in chief of the Beirut journal *Arabic Studies* and continued his writing career. *The Origins of Kant's Arguments in the Antinomies* (1972) was followed by another book on the issue of Palestinian resistance to the Israeli occupation, *Dirasah naqdiyyah li fikr al-muqawamah al-Filastiniyyah* (1973, Critical Studies of Palestinian Resistance). This latter book is an analysis of the Palestinian involvement in the events of Black September in Jordan of 1970—the beginning of a bitter power struggle between the fedayeen and the Jordanian government. Al-Azm depicts the Palestinian Liberation Organization (PLO) and its main component, Fatah, in the same negative light he does the traditional Jordanian conservative ruling class—neither of which he saw as effectively able to respond to contemporary problems. He argues that their similarity was one of the reasons for their disastrous conflict, which in the long run he sees as comparable to the defeat of 1967 in its ramifications. In *al-Sahyuniyyah wa al-sira' al-tabaqi* (1975, Zionism and Class Struggle), al-Azm discusses the origins of Jewish emigration to Palestine as a product of Western capitalism. He argues that the interest of the Jewish intellectual and financial elite in the Zionist movement stemmed from the prevailing imperialistic ambitions in countries such as Great Britain and France.

Besides looking at philosophical trends and changes in the West and the East and the Palestinian case, al-Azm continually engaged in current political debates. An example is his response to the Egyptian president Anwar Sadat's visit to Jerusalem in 1978, a step that surprised most of the Arab world. In his book *Ziyarat al-Sadat wa bu's al-salam al-'adil* (1978, The Visit of Sadat and the Misery of a Just Peace), he places the sudden move into a larger historical and political framework. He examines the Arab, the Palestinian, and the international reaction to the visit, citing conservative forces and regimes in the Arab world as real hindrances to a final solution for the conflict. The book was written with a sad and angered undertone, showing disappointment over a fragmented and divided Arab world unable to deal effectively with the Palestinian question.

In the 1980s al-Azm devoted most of his writing energy not to books but to shorter works; however, his choice of topics remained the same. In his 5 December

Title page for al-Azm's 1968 book al-Naqd al-dhati ba'da al-hazimah, *in which he analyzed the Arab defeat in the Six-Day War (University of Chicago Library)*

1981 article in *The Nation*, "Palestinian Parallels: The Zionist Analogy," he continues his analysis of the leadership of the Palestinian movement, drawing remarkable connections between the strategy of the PLO and the politics of the Zionist movement. He finds an Israeli equivalent for the most prominent Palestinian leaders, such as Yasir Arafat (Chaim Weizmann), George Habbash (Zeev Jabotinsky), and Nayef Hawatmeh (David Ben-Gurion). In his article "Palestinian Zionism" in the German journal *Die Welt des Islams* (1988, The World of Islam), he comes back to the Palestinian questions right after the outbreak of the Intifadah in 1987. As in his first book on the Palestinian situation, he analyzes the leadership of the resistance movement of the PLO and draws an even more pessimistic picture of their incompetence. He focuses in particular on the personality of Yasir Arafat, whom he sees as a sheer copy of the prototypical nineteenth-century Zionist. In general, he considers the Palestinian leaders to be carbon copies of their Jewish counterparts. In 1988 al-Azm returned to

Damascus to teach at the university until 1999, taking several opportunities to work internationally.

In the late 1980s and early 1990s al-Azm became embroiled in the controversy surrounding Salman Rushdie's *The Satanic Verses* (1988), which outraged the Islamic world for what was supposed to be Rushdie's blasphemous treatment of the Qur'an and the Prophet Muhammad and led Ayatollah Khomeini in 1989 to proclaim a *fatwa* sentencing Rushdie to death. Al-Azm openly supported Rushdie and received death threats. As a staunch proponent of secularism and the freedom of discussing taboos, he publicly called Islam a "backward" religion during a televised debate in 1997 on al-Jazeera, stirring great controversy like Rushdie before him. He was defended by many liberal intellectuals throughout the Middle East, who compared him to Naguib Mahfouz, Faruq Foda, and Rushdie. Like Rushdie, al-Azm deliberately criticizes religion, living conditions, and political circumstances. While both contribute significantly to an Islamic enlightenment, the difference between the two is that al-Azm is a political activist and radical philosopher, while Rushdie is a postmodern novelist.

In his 1991 essay "The Importance of Being Earnest about Salman Rushdie" in *Die Welt des Islams,* al-Azm addressed the Rushdie controversy at length. Al-Azm's essay is summarized as an important contribution to the debate about the novel in Arne Ruth's retrospective lecture "The Outsider as Insider: Speaking Earnestly about the Rushdie Case" (14 August 2000):

> Throughout the *fatwa* decade, starting in his 1990 essay *The Importance of Being Earnest About Salman Rushdie,* Al-Azm held that the main reason why *The Satanic Verses* caused such violent reactions was its literary sophistication in treating its theme. Al-Azm reminds us that James Joyce's *Ulysses* was prosecuted for blasphemy, obscenity and subversion, and was banned in the United States until 1933, and in Britain until 1936. He makes the case for a universal definition of aesthetic modernism as an integral part of the Enlightenment project.
>
> By using religious mythology as elements in a powerful piece of fiction, appropriating a canonical Muslim story for his own creative, artistic and literary purposes, Rushdie started a process of literary emancipation in the Muslim world. He pointed to a door opened a century ago by literary modernists in the West, but up until now largely inaccessible in Muslim countries. In Al-Azm's view, this modernist avenue will never be closed again, regardless of the fatwa.

Arne later points out that "By using the title of an Oscar Wilde play as a metaphor for Western double standards, al-Azm points to the potentially liberating role of the outsider among us."

The role of Western scholars in the field of Arabic, Islamic, and Oriental Studies sparked a debate about the role and influence of French and British academics in fostering the colonial hegemony of the West over the Middle East. Al-Azm participated in the evolving debate by writing a commentary on Edward W. Said's famous book *Orientalism* (1978) in *Dhihniyat al-tahrim* (1992, The Mental Taboo), which also includes a chapter defending Rushdie. Al-Azm interprets *Orientalism* as a philosophical treatise, noting that Said does not refer to important Western influences on his work such as Michel Foucault or Antonio Gramsci. His harshest criticism pertains to Said's short section on Karl Marx, which al-Azm calls a "travesty," because he, unlike Said, agrees with Marx's analysis of class distinction in Western societies. Al-Azm also criticizes other less-radical intellectuals and writers, for example the poet Adonis, for reducing the Arab-Islamic world to essential elements and thus neglecting its deep-rooted pluralism and diversity in the same way as Bernard Lewis and other orientalists did. Al-Azm criticizes Said for endorsing powerful Western elites, a charge that Said challenged as being incorrect. Al-Azm warns that the Arab academic and intellectual elite might fall in the trap of following the same narrow approach in their studies of the West as they believe Westerners do in the study of the East. His critique led to the estrangement of the formerly close friendship. No less polemical than Said in *Orientalism,* al-Azm argues that Arab-Muslim authors orientalize themselves when they claim a frame of reference different from those of the rest of humanity. In al-Azm's view, this is Orientalism in reverse.

Al-Azm's controversial ideas spread rapidly throughout intellectual circles, universities, and the general media, especially as his work became available through translations into different languages. With *Unbehagen in der Moderne: Aufklärung im Islam* (1993, Discomfort in Modernity: Enlightenment in Islam)—a work in which he collaborated with a German translator—al-Azm reached out to a new philosophical, historical, and political sphere. The book includes translations of two previously published essays—"The Importance of Being Earnest about Salman Rushdie" and "Satan's Tragedy"—together with a new essay, "Islamischer Fundamentalismus–Neubewertet" (Islamic Fundamentalism–Reevaluated). In this last essay—which was part of the opening up the debate among Arab and Muslim scholars over the issue of enlightenment in Islam—al-Azm writes in opposition to both Catholic antimodernism and Islamic fundamentalism. In an article published in 1997 titled "Is Islam Secularizable?" he elaborated his critique of Islamic fundamentalism, arguing that "the Arab liberation movement considered the cultural superstructure worthy of respect and veneration. It surrounded retarded mental habits, Bedouin and feudal values, backward human relations, and obscurantist, quietist world views with an aura of sacredness which put them outside the pale of scientific and historical analysis."

With the advent of the new millennium al-Azm returned to the political debate over the Arab-Israeli conflict by examining the position of his home country, Syria, in "The View from Damascus," a feature article for *The New York Review of Books* (15 June 2000). He asks if the current Syrian state is ready for peace with Israel and no longer clings to the conflict as a source of legitimization of the government and regime. His answer is a cautious and qualified "yes," but the future peace he imagines would not be an achievement of bravery and political determination but the peace of the weary and exhausted people of the region.

Even though the divine Qur'anic guidelines are considered infallible, al-Azm argues in his 2002 article "Politischer Islam im 20. Jahrhundert" (Political Islam in the Twentieth Century) that they need human interpretation if they are to be used in daily life. He illustrates his position with an example: According to the Qur'anic scriptures, amputating the right hand punishes theft. The meaning of this statement is clear and obvious; however, al-Azm explains, that at the time of the prophet Muhammad, the Islamic community was small and homogenous, and questions were not as complex as they have become in the modern world. Nowadays such a punishment would not be so easily and clearly applied. What does one do to a thief who steals $1 versus one who steals $2 million? What if a Muslim steals a pig that belongs to a Christian? Shall his hand be cut off, even though it was a Christian infidel, and the pig is considered taboo? He further maintained that the imperative precondition for meeting the challenges posed by an encounter with the West is an unconditional embracing of the reality that is manifested in history. He thus argues for an historical approach in studying Islam and the Qur'an, which he asserts should be read in the same historical context as the ancient Greek texts.

Another important line of argument in "Politischer Islam im 20. Jahrhundert" is al-Azm's attack on Samuel Huntington's controversial theory in international relations of "the clash of civilizations," which states that different cultural and religious identities will be the main cause for conflicts in the twenty-first century. Al-Azm described Huntington as a pupil of the radical Islamists and disparaged Iranian president Mohammed Khatami's call for the dialogue of civilizations, seeing it as a political ploy, more amusing than serious. Al-Azm's assertion that "Islam is not a civilization" was quickly attacked by his critics in a string of articles, books, and debates.

Al-Azm again criticized the "class of civilizations" theory in "Time Out of Joint: Western Dominance, Islamist Terror, and the Arab Imagination," an article published in the *Boston Review* (October/November 2004):

> The two supposedly clashing sides are so unequal in power, military might, productive capacity, efficiency, effective institutions, wealth, social organization, science, and technology that the clash can only be of the inconsequential sort. As one literary metaphor says, if a stone falls on an egg, the egg breaks; and if an egg falls on an egg, the egg breaks too. From the Arab Muslim side of the divide, the West seems so powerful, so efficient, so successful, and so unstoppable, that the very idea of an ultimate "clash" is fanciful.

Al-Azm also questions the reason for a clash, as he believes that politics and vital interests are stronger catalysts than purely spiritual ideals.

On 7 April 2004 al-Azm, together with Fatima Mernissi and Abdulkarim Soroush, was awarded the Erasmus Prize because each has "helped reconcile processes of modernisation and cultures that are shaped by religion." In an interview with Matrina Sabra, al-Azm, who was then teaching in Antwerp, Belgium, said he was surprised to receive the award: "I am very interested in Renaissance thinking and I naturally knew a little about Erasmus. To be linked to him in this way is very gratifying for me." In the interview, al-Azm zealously argues for the modernization of Islamic doctrine and law:

> Al-Azm explains that it was never personally important for him to reform Islam from the inside out. However, he goes on to say that it is hugely important to him to modernise Islamic theology and Islamic law. "There are Islamic theologians who still claim that the world is flat. Such convictions are simply not compatible with modernity," says Al-Azm, shaking his head.
>
> "The same applies to specific principles in Islamic law: active and passive religious freedom must be guaranteed, as must the freedom from bodily harm and equal rights for women. This means: no accusations of apostasy, no corporal punishment, and no enforced wearing of the veil. If the corresponding passages from the Koran are not cancelled for all time, and if Islamic legal regulations are not annulled, Islam cannot become the foundation on which a modern state apparatus is built, like in Iraq, for example."

In the same year, al-Azm was awarded the Dr. Leopold Lucas Prize honoring his efforts for promoting Western philosophy's orientation toward the Arab world, his advocacy for the ability to modernize Arabic culture, and his fearless critique of any kind of fundamentalism in the Middle East.

In analyzing current conflicts between the West and Islam, al-Azm believes that the influence of religious fundamentalism has no long-term prospects, and he predicts that current violence will be the prelude to the dissipation and final demise of militant Islamism in general. Al-Azm sees the mosque, the public symbol of Islam, as a servant of the state and notes that in key countries such as Egypt, Syria, and Turkey hardly anything runs according to Islamic precepts. In a 23 January 2005 article in the *Washington Post* titled "Religious Surge Alarms Secular Syrians" al-Azm was cited for his insight on his own country:

> Sadiq Azm, a leading Syrian writer who has criticized Arab nationalism and political Islam for decades, said religion will inevitably exert more influence here as pressure builds for the government to reform a largely stagnant economy and closed political institutions. But Syria's Islamic community is fractured, he said, with opinions ranging from militant to "good-for-business Islam" that takes into account the rights of religious minorities.
>
> "This is an evolution that Syria will go through," Azm said. "The question is, what role will it play? And will it be the moderate middle-class version?"

Al-Azm argues that Turkey, the first Islamic society that completed the separation of religion and state, could become a model for the entire Middle East.

In his book *Islam und Säkularer Humanismus* (2005, Islam and Secular Humanism), a bilingual edition with English translations of al-Azm's German text, al-Azm discusses why the West was surprised by the rise of Islamic fundamentalism and the Islamic renaissance. He compares origins of the rise of fundamentalism in the West with those of the Middle East. He concludes that neither by coincidence nor arbitrarily can we apply the same principles that originated in the fundamental dispute over Christian understandings of modernity to the development of modern Islamism. In the same book he discusses the development of human rights in Islam and explains how freedom of conscience and religious tolerance can grow from its traditions.

Fluent in Arabic and several Western languages, Sadik Jalal al-Azm in his life and works has sought to bring the Arabic and Western worlds together, as he believes that neither dialogue nor appreciation can occur without deliberate, sometimes difficult effort. In his career he has shown the cultural and intellectual limitations of both sides when it comes to the basic question of what each knows about the other. In particular, has noted the ignorance of Western scholars, philosophers, intellectuals, and politicians of Islamic texts and Arab history, demonstrating that the West is as blind as the East in its cultural self-centeredness. Al-Azm continues to make the argument that both sides need to avoid two main, tragic misconceptions: from the Middle Eastern perspective, that the West is still pursuing its colonial quest for hegemony; and from the Western viewpoint, that the Arabs understand nothing but the language of violence.

Interviews:

Ghada Talhami, "An Interview with Sadik Al-Azm," *Arab Studies Quarterly,* 19, no. 3 (1997): 113–126;

"Trends in Arab Thought: An Interview with Sadek Jalal al-'Azm," *Journal of Palestine Studies,* 27, no. 2 (Winter 1998): 68–80;

Andrea Nüsse, "Islamisten in der Krise: Der syrische Philosoph Sadiq al-Azm zu Folgen des 11. September," *Der Tagesspiegel* (9 September 2002) <http://www.tagesspiegel.de/politik/;art771,2093169> (accessed 26 August 2008);

Larissa Bender and Mona Naggar, "Hoffnungsschimmer in der arabischen Welt," *Qantara.de* (September 2003) <http://qantara.de/webcom/show_article.php/_c-468/_nr-1/_p-2/i.html?PHPSESSID=faf0b92f38e3f563c0a2a46e7dc7d085> (accessed 26 August 2008);

'Abd al-Karim al-Afnan, *Al-Thaqafah* (10 November 2003) <http://www.al-jazirah.com.sa/culture/10112003/hauar68.htm> (accessed 29 August 2008);

Mona Sarkis, "Islamstaat sucht Untertanen," *Telepolis* (28 February 2005) <http://www.heise.de/tp/r4/artikel/19/19551/1.html> (accessed 29 August 2008);

Christian Meier, "Der arabischen Welt fehlt die kritische Masse," *NZZ* [Neue Zürcher Zeitung] *Online* (23 August 2005) <http://www.nzz.ch/2005/08/23/fe/articleCWO8L.html> (accessed 29 August 2008).

References:

Anouar Abdallah and others, *For Rushdie: Essays by Arab and Muslim Writers in Defense of Free Speech* (New York: George Brazilier, 1994);

Tony Bey, "Importing Democracy," *Across the Bay* (23 July 2004) <http://beirut2bayside.blogspot.com/2004/07/importing-democracy.html> (accessed 26 August 2006);

John Donohue and John Esposito, eds., *Islam in Transition: Muslim Perspectives* (New York & Oxford: Oxford University Press, 1982);

Arne Ruth, "The Outsider as Insider: Speaking Earnestly about the Rushdie Case," Lecture given at the 66th IFLA General Conference, 14 August 2000, Jerusalem <http://www.ifla.org/faife/papers/guest/ruth.htm>;

Martina Sabra, "Important Figures from the Islamic World Awarded," translated from German by Aingeal Flanagan, *Qantara.de* (20 April 2004) <http://qantara.de/webcom/show_article.php/_c-478/_nr-101/i.html> (accessed 26 August 2008);

Scott Wilson, "Religious Surge Alarms Secular Syrians: Islam's Clout Among Frustrated Youth Challenging Governments Across The Mideast," *Washington Post,* 23 January 2005, p. A21.

Liana Badr

(6 September 1952 –   )

Angela Saliba Bajalieh
Grand Valley State University

BOOKS: *Busalah min ajl 'abbad al-shams* (Beirut: Dar Ibn Rushd, 1979); translated by Catherine Cobham as *A Compass for the Sunflower* (London: Women's Press, 1989);

Nafidhah 'ala al-fakahani (Beirut, 1983); translated by Peter Clark and Christopher Tingley as *A Balcony over the Fakihani* (New York: Interline, 1993);

Qisas al-hub wa al-mulahaqa (Aden, Yemen: Dar el Hamadani, 1983);

Ana urid al-nahar (Acre: Dar al-Aswar, 1986);

'Ayn al-mir'at (Casablanca: Dar Tubqal, 1991); translated by Samira Kawar as *The Eye of the Mirror* (London: Garnet, 1996);

Nujum Ariha (Cairo: Dar el Hilal, 1993); selections translated by Seema Attala as *The Stars over Jericho* in *Modern Arabic Fiction,* edited by Salma Khadra Jayyusi (New York: Columbia University Press, 2005);

Fadwa Tuqan: Zilal al-kalimat al-mahkiyya (Cairo: Dar al-Fata al-'Arabi, 1996).

Edition: *Nafidha 'ala al-Fakahani* (Damascus: Dar el Alam, 1990).

OTHER: "The Story of a Novel or Reflections of Details in the Mirror: Between Awareness and Madness," in *In the House of Silence: Autobiographical Essays by Arab Women Writers,* edited by Fadia Faqir, translated by Faqir and Shirley Eber (Reading, U.K.: Garnet, 1998), pp. 27–32.

PRODUCED SCRIPTS: *Fadwa: A Tale of a Palestinian Poetess,* motion picture, Palestine, 1999;

Zeitounat, motion picture, Palestine, 2000;

Al-Tayr al-akhdar, Palestinian Ministry of Information, Department of Women and Children, 2002;

Al-Quds fi yaym akhar (also known as *Rana's Wedding*), Augustus Film, 2002.

Liana Badr is an influential Palestinian author whose fiction often depicts the struggles of Palestinians after the establishment of the state of Israel. For more than twenty years she has been producing fiction and screenplays that give voice to Palestinians both in the diaspora and those living within Israel and the occupied territories. Tremendously influenced by her exposure to political struggles and violence from a young age, Badr's writings, which are often based on her own experiences, deal with difficult issues, including sexism, women's struggles against oppression, and the importance of creating a sense of community through the use of memory. Her work has been translated into many languages, and her screenplays have been lauded internationally.

Liana Badr was born on 6 September 1952 in Palestinian Jerusalem, to parents Dr. 'Abd al-Rahim Badr, a well-known writer in science and literature, and Hayat, a teacher, political activist and intellectual. Her parents' political activities came at a price: her father spent some time in prison, and both parents spent some time avoiding authorities. As a result of this instability, Badr was sent to the Jerusalem boarding school Dar al-Tifl when she was about five years old. At Dar al-Tifl, which had originally been established as an orphanage for children after the 1948 Arab-Israeli War, Badr learned about the lives of loss and despair suffered by the orphans and refugees from the Palestinian-Israeli conflict. These early experiences proved formative, and she returned to some of these memories in writing her fiction.

Growing up in an active intellectual family, Badr was constantly surrounded by books. Culture and the arts were central pillars of her family's interests. During more-stable times, the family often hosted poetry recitals and discussions by other Palestinian intellectuals. At the age of eleven, Badr was given a translation of Margaret Mitchell's *Gone With the Wind* (1936). The book left an impression on her, and for the first time she began to think about the way authors create the characters of their novels. As a child and young adolescent, she was also exposed to the cinema and attended movies with her family in Jerusalem. She came to love the cinema and began to read any information about it that she could obtain.

Cover for Liana Badr's first book, Busalah min ajl 'abbad al-shams (1979) with the title page for the 1989 English translation (left, Burke Library, Columbia University; right, Jean and Alexander Heard Library, Vanderbilt University)

In the aftermath of the June 1967 Six-Day War, Badr and her father left Palestine for Jordan. In Amman, Badr began her studies at the University of Jordan, planning to major in sociology and psychology. In 1970, however, her studies were cut short by the events of Black September, when clashes erupted between Palestinian groups and the Jordanian monarchy. The Palestinian Liberation Organization (PLO) was expelled from the country, and many Palestinians chose to leave because of the level of violence. Badr became a refugee once again, traveling to Beirut. She was able to continue her studies at the Beirut Arab University, studying philosophy and psychology, and began to take the prospect of becoming an author seriously. In 1979 she completed what would become her most well-known work, *Busalah min ajl 'abbad al-shams* (1979; translated as *A Compass for the Sunflower*, 1989). The novel, which was set in Palestine during the few years after the Six-Day War, draws on many of the experiences Badr had in her childhood, including her father's political activities and the instability this brought to the family. The disconnected narrative tracks the lives of the protagonist Jinan, along with her friends Shahd and Thurayya, Jinan's love Shaher, and her cousin Amer. The position of women in the Palestinian struggle is a central theme in the novel, as each character deals with the war and exile in varying ways. Jinan, confident and independent, defies many of the cultural norms by continuing to involve herself in activism, volunteer work, and fighting.

While living in Lebanon, Badr met and married Yasser Abd Raboo, a well-known Palestinian politician, with whom she would have two children. After completing her B.A., she began to study for a master's degree in English literature. War interrupted her studies again, however, and in 1982 Badr fled Beirut during the Israeli bombardment of the city. She went first to Syria for five years, and from there to Tunisia for another seven. While her husband was helping to establish diplomatic ties and design new strategies to bring the Palestinian people back to Palestine, Badr used her time to read and write more.

In 1983 Badr published a short-story collection, *Qisas al-hub wa al-mulahaqa* (Stories of Love and Pursuit), as well as a series of three important novellas that focused on the early years of the Lebanese Civil War (1975–1990): *Ard min hajar wa za'tar* (translated as *A Land of Rock and Thyme*, 1993), *Shurfah 'ala al-fakihani* (translated as *A Balcony Over the Fakihani*, 1993), and *al-kanari wa al-bahr* (translated as *The Canary and the Sea*, 1993), all of which were collected as *Nafidha 'ala al-fakahani* (1990; translated as *A Balcony over the Fakihani*, 1993). Each of the three novellas featured its own theme regarding the exile and suffering of the Palestinian people. The first novella, *Ard min hajar wa za'tar*, treats the idea of maintaining a collective memory. Yusra, the main character, is forced to deal with her father's death, which symbolized the ill-fated Palestinian history. Water, difficult to obtain and extremely valuable, is used to represent memories, for it is a "fluid, unifying element that connects scattered images and broken lives, an image of life and death, of landlessness."

The theme of the title novella of the collection, *Nafidha 'ala al-fakahani*, is the solidarity of the Palestinian people, shown by the compassion between men and women. The balcony, which was one of the headquarters of the resistance movement before it was destroyed on 17 July 1981 by Israeli bombardment (an attack that reportedly resulted in 350 civilian deaths), symbolizes that solidarity. The shifting perspectives of the three main characters, Su'ad, her husband, 'Umar, and their friend Jinan (the same character, though less significant, as in *Busalah min ajl 'abbad al-Shams*) provide the narrative for this story. The relationship between the husband and wife is shaped by the conditions of their suffering, exile, and commitment to the resistance.

The final novella, *al-kanari wa al-bahr*, is told through the experiences of Abu Husayn during the years following the establishment of Israel in 1948 up to the Israeli invasion of Lebanon in 1982. Husayn tells his family's story and chronicles the hardships he experienced growing up in refugee camps in Lebanon. He relates the lack of symmetry between the Lebanese and Israeli armies: while the Israelis were dropping tens of thousands of bombs on the city of Beirut each day, the Lebanese army was not able to draw upon anywhere near the same kind of resources. Badr again uses images of water—in this case the tumult of the sea that suggests the ceaseless roiling of the nation—to signify the intangible idea of Palestine. Each story depicts Palestinian people adrift from their homeland, tossed by the turbulence of landlessness.

In her 1980 interview with Matteo Bellinelli and Sahar Khalifah, Badr recalls "I hate Beirut. I hate that life full of bombardment, of shelling, of all the time trying to hide with the children. Weeping of women, loss, killing of children." However, for her there was also the other side of Beirut, the side that taught her the meaning of solidarity between people. She discovered how the ordinary Palestinian women coped with the demands of their difficult lives generously and without asking for anything in return. She also realized the meaning of religious discrimination, which was later referenced in her novel *'Ayn al-mira'at* (1991, translated as *The Eye of the Mirror*, 1996).

In 1984 Badr began her meticulous study of the story of Tal al-Za'tar (the Hill of Thyme), the site of the 1975–1976 massacre of Palestinians by Maronite militiamen that took place during the Lebanese Civil War. Her interviews with women who were part of the Tal al-Za'tar refugee camp were the basis for *'Ayn al-mira'at*. In part, this novel deals with discrimination resulting from religious differences. Badr begins her narrative with the reporting of a Beirut journalist, like herself, leading the readers into the story.

The story is primarily told through the eyes of a young Palestinian woman, Aisha, who was working as a maid in a convent school in return for schooling. After a bus is bombed by a Christian militia in April 1975, Aisha's family takes her back to her home at the Tal al-Za'tar camp. Back at home, the young girl faces the difficulties of a mother who does not understand her, an alcoholic and controlling father, and two mischievous siblings. Her father forces her to renounce the Christianity that she had picked up at the convent school and return to the Muslim faith. She lives a hard and imprisoned life back at the camp, but despite this fact she falls in love with a family friend, George, a fighter. However, a marriage to another man is arranged for her. She suffers the agony of a voice unheard and a life decided for her. Before she is able to get accustomed to her life as a married woman, severe shellings and attacks disrupt the lives of everyone in the camp. What follows are detailed horrors of what happened to the many people and fighters of Tal al-Za'tar that Aisha and her family experience. Aisha and another character, Hana, an outspoken worker on the resistance, represent two different models of women that allow Badr to explore the theme of personal responsibility. She holds women responsible for their own liberation, decisions, and feminine identity.

Aisha finds a mirror in the midst of war rubble. The image in the mirror is used by Badr to symbolize Aisha's self-discovery and to suggest the importance of each individual's role in the collective struggle of the society. At various points in the novel Badr changes from a third-person perspective to a first-person perspective, giving the character of the moment a voice. One such moment in the story depicts Aisha's own struggles:

> At that moment, a Lebanese fighter wearing the badge of the Guardians of the Cedars came forward. He was carrying things he had gathered from breaking into a Palestinian shop. It seemed that our passing had interrupted him as he gathered them. He motioned the long procession to follow him. He took us. He led us through the lentil factory. We sank into the piles of lentils up to our knees. Lentils slipped over my feet soft and cool. The grains spread a gentle powder over the perspiring feet that had stepped through burning fires. The lentils. Piles upon pile. As we pass through the thick mounds, I stop crying and am cheered as I remember Ibtissam and Husam. Where are they, my God? Will my mother be able to take care of them and save them?

In 1993, a year before her return to Palestine, Badr published her acclaimed novel *Nujum Ariha* (selec-

Cover for the DVD of a 2002 dramatic comedy from a script by Badr and Ihab Lamey, in which a seventeen-year-old Palestinian must defy her father to marry the man she loves (Richland County Public Library)

tions translated as *The Stars over Jericho*, 2005), which she wrote in response to the First Gulf War in 1991. Badr brings to the novel her search for her own sense of identity as a Palestinian and as a citizen of the larger Arab world. Using autobiographical details, she documents a history that is defined by the 1967 and 1991 wars.

Following the Israeli-Palestinian peace accord in 1993, Badr finally returned to the West Bank after twenty-seven years away from home. In her 1980 interview with Bellinelli and Khalifah, Badr commented, "It was easier to go to the moon than to get back to Palestine." After her return, she began to read the memoir of the poet Fadwa Tuqan, whose work seemed to Badr to express the experience of all Palestinian women. In *Fadwa Tuqan: Zilal al-kalimat al-mahkiyyah* (1996, Shadows of Narrated Words), Badr presented the poet as a symbol for what she believed was a new female generation. Badr regarded this new generation as under fear and stress after the intifada and understood that many young women were trying to protect themselves and their bodies. Badr noted that Tuqan allowed women to think about why they behaved the way they did and to consider why they do not have the chance to be themselves. Badr particularly admired Tuqan as a creative woman who refused to be simply a victim all the time.

In addition to her novels and stories, Badr has published five children's books (1980–1991) and a collection of poetry (1997). She currently runs the Cinema and Audiovisual Department in Ramallah, Palestine, and is creating documentaries related to her work as a journalist. She is also the founding editor of *Dafatir Thaqafiyyah* (Cultural Notebooks), the ministry's periodical. Badr continues to write and to explore the concept of memory as a crucial aspect of identity. She has directed and written several films, including *Al Quds Fi Yaym Akhar* (Rana's Wedding), which had its world premiere during the 2002 Semaine Internationale de la Critique in Cannes. Her 2000 film *Zeitounat* won many awards, including the best film for Women in Arab Countries and the golden medal from Florence Municipality at the International Women's Festival in 2001. Badr has fulfilled several of her lifelong dreams, including returning to her homeland and working with films. With each new movie, novel, and poem, Badr immortalizes Palestinian history and the struggles for their past and future.

Interviews:
Matteo Bellinelli and Sahar Khalifah, videorecorded interview with Badr, 1980 (New York: Filmmakers Library, 2000);

Angela Bajalieh, e-mail interview with Badr, 26 June 2006.

References:
"Liana Badr," *Arab World Books* <http://www.arabworldbooks.com/authors/liana_badr.html> (accessed 2 September 2008);

"Liana Badr," *Khalil Sakakini Cultural Centre* <http://www.sakakini.org/literature/novelists.htm> (accessed 2 September 2008);

Therese Saliba, "A Country Beyond Reach," in *Intersections: Gender, Nation, and Community in Arab Women's Novels,* edited by Lisa Suhair Majaj, Paula W. Sunderman, and Therese Saliba (New York: Syracuse University Press, 2002), pp. 132–161;

Joseph T. Zeidan, "Liyanah Badr: A Compass for the Sunflower," in his *Arab Women Novelists: The Formative Years and Beyond* (New York: State University of New York Press, 1995), pp. 186–191.

Halim Barakat

(4 December 1936 –   )

Jared Reene

BOOKS: *Al-Qimam al-khadra'* (Beirut: Al-Mu'asasah al-Ahliyyah, 1955);

Al-Samt wa al-matar (Beirut: Dar Majallat Shi'r, 1958);

Sitat ayam (Beirut: Dar Majallat Shi'r, 1961); translated by Bassem Frangieh and Scott McGehee as *Six Days* (Boulder, Colo.: Lynne Rienner, 1990);

'Awdat al-ta'ir ila al-bahr (Beirut: Dar al-Nahar, 1969); translated by Trevor Le Gassick as *Days of Dust* (Wilmette, Ill.: Medina University Press International, 1974);

River without Bridges: A Study of the Exodus of the 1967 Palestinian Arab Refugees, by Barakat and Peter Dodd (Beirut: Institute of Palestine Studies, 1969);

Lebanon in Strife: Student Preludes to the Civil War (Austin: University of Texas Press, 1977);

Visions of Social Reality in the Contemporary Arab Novel (Washington, D.C.: Institute of Arab Development, Center for Contemporary Arab Studies, Georgetown University, 1977);

Al-Rahil bayna al-sahm wa al-watar (Beirut: Al-Mu'assasah al-'Arabiyyah li al-Dirasat wa al-Nashr, 1979);

Ta'ir al-hawm (Casablanca: Dar Tubqal, 1988); translated by Bassam Frangieh and Roger Allen as *The Crane* (Cairo & New York: American University in Cairo Press, 2008);

Harb al-Khalij: Khutut fi al-raml wa al-zaman (Beirut: Markaz Dirasat al-Wahdah al-'Arabiyyah, 1992);

The Arab World: Society, Culture, and State (Berkeley: University of California Press, 1993);

Inanah wa al-nahr (Beirut: Dar al-Adab, 1995);

Al-Dimuqratiyyah wa al-'adala al-ijtima'iyyah fi sabil ighna' al-tajribah al-'Arabiyyah (Ramallah: MUWATIN-The Palestinian Institute for the Study of Democracy, 1995);

Al-Mujtama' al-'Arabi fi al-qarn al-'ishrin: Bahth fi taghayyur al-ahwal wa al-'alaqat (Beirut: Markaz Dirasat al-Wahdah al-'Arabiyyah, 2000).

OTHER: *Al-Mujtama' al-'Arabi al-mu'asir,* edited by Barakat (Beirut: Center for Arab Studies, 1984);

Halim Barakat (from Days of Dust, *translated by Trevor Le Gassick, 1974; Thomas Cooper Library, University of South Carolina*)

Contemporary North Africa: Issues of Development and Integration, edited by Barakat (Washington, D.C.: Center for Contemporary Arab Studies, 1985; London: Croom Helm, 1985);

Toward a Viable Lebanon, edited by Barakat (Washington, D.C.: Center for Contemporary Arab Studies, 1988; London: Croom Helm, 1988).

SELECTED PERIODICAL PUBLICATIONS–UNCOLLECTED: "Alienation: A Process of Encounter between Utopia and Reality," *British Journal of Sociology,* 20, no. 1 (1969): 1-10;

Halim Barakat

Title page for 'Awdat al-ta'ir ila al-bahr *(1969; translated as* Days of Dust, *1974), Barakat's novel about the June 1967 Six-Day War (Widener Library, Harvard University)*

"Social Factors Influencing Attitudes of University Students in Lebanon towards the Palestinian Resistance Movement," *Journal of Palestinian Studies*, 1 (Autumn 1971): 87–112;

"The Palestinian Refugees: An Uprooted Community Seeking Reparation," *International Migration Review*, 7 (Summer 1973): 147–161;

"The Wild Beast that Zionism Created: Self-Destruction," *Al-Hayat* (London), 11 April 2002.

The sociologist and fiction writer Halim Barakat has been an influential voice in Arab and Middle Eastern studies since the mid 1950s. A leftist advocate of radical pan-Arab reformation and a critic of the effects of Western imperialism on the Middle East, Barakat has used a combination of literary prose and sociological and anthropological analysis to address issues ranging from the Palestinian refugee crisis to the role of women in Arab society and the adjustment of that society to modernity. In his fiction Barakat depicts the Arab world in fresh and poetically striking ways.

The fifth of seven children, Halim Isber Barakat was born on 12 December 1936 in the village of Kafrun, Syria, on the Mediterranean coast near the Lebanese border. His parents were Greek Orthodox, and his father was a farmer. The four older siblings died before Barakat's tenth birthday, and their father, who was only in his mid thirties, died soon afterward. Unable to maintain the farm on her own, their mother moved to Beirut to find a job; after establishing herself as a baker, she sent for the children. Accompanied by their uncle Jamil, Barakat and his brother and sister walked through the mountains to Tripoli, Lebanon. From there, the children took a bus to Beirut. Barakat completed his B.A. in sociology at the American University in Beirut in 1955. Shortly after his graduation, his first novel, *al-Qimam al-khadra'* (1955, Green Summits) was published. It received the Al-Mudarris Award as the best Syrian novel in 1956.

Barakat remained at the American University in Beirut for his master's degree in sociology. He published a collection of short stories, *al-Samt wa al-mattar* (Silence and Rain), in 1958. He received his M.A. in 1960 and went to the University of Michigan to pursue a Ph.D. in social psychology. His second novel, *Sitat ayam* (translated as *Six Days*, 1990), appeared in 1961. The novel is set in a small city, Dayr al-Bahr, which is intended to represent Palestine. A besieging army has given the citizens six days to surrender; otherwise, Dayr al-Bahr will be destroyed. *Sitat ayam* is divided into six parts, each depicting a day. The central character, Suhayl, is a reluctant leader of the city's resistance. His love for Nahida is forbidden because she is a Muslim and he is a Christian; and his love of Dayr al-Bahr is complicated by feelings of shame and embarrassment for the city's traditional ways and stagnation. Observing the countryside from a hilltop, he thinks: "The city is like a ship from the land of Canaan, plowing the sea for the first time, defying certain death. A thick fog is rolling in, surrounding Dayr al-Bahr, separating it from the rest of the world. . . . The ship challenges death, without oars. No matter, it challenges." He is captured by the invaders at the beginning of the siege and tortured for information about the city's defenses but refuses ro betray his fellow citizens. The residents of Dayr al-Bahr, who have drastically underestimated the force that is poised against them, reject surrender and choose to fight; the decision results in their complete destruction. Suhayl's captors lead him to a peak overlooking the smoldering city: "Something snaps inside him. Foam covers the world. It is Dayr al-Bahr. It is ablaze. The fire stretches in a long line, bending along the shoreline, and rising toward the white peaks. The smoke rises, changing from red to black to gray. It doesn't disappear.... Six days without boredom. What to do tomorrow? The clouds and the ashes."

While working on his doctorate, Barakat served as assistant study director of the Institute of Social Research at the University of Michigan. He received his Ph.D. in 1966 with the dissertation "Alienation from the School System: Its Dynamics and Structure" and returned to the American University of Beirut as an assistant professor of sociology.

The title of Barakat's second novel proved to be prophetic when Israel defeated Egypt, Syria, and Jordan in the Six-Day War of 5 to 10 June 1967 and seized a sizable amount of land from them. Barakat's third novel, 'Awdat al-ta'ir ila al-bahr (1969, The Return of The Flying Dutchmen to the Sea; translated as *Days of Dust,* 1974), which is widely regarded as his crowning literary achievement, is set during the Six-Day War. *'Awdat al-ta'ir ila al-bahr* combines dramatic imagery, references to the Bible's Book of Genesis, firsthand accounts of the experiences of Palestinians, and paraphrases of speeches and war updates broadcast on radio stations in Beirut and Amman. Barakat paints a chilling portrait of the mixture of excitement, hope, optimistic nationalism, misjudgment, and, finally, horror that dominated the Arab world as the war unfolded. Through a mixture of short and long sentences, he gives the reader an impression of the alternation of frantic action with those dreadful moments when time seems to stand still. Constantly reassured by their leaders, the Arabs hold fast to their belief in victory until they are painfully stripped of their illusions at the war's end. The protagonist, Ramzy, views the chaos in Amman as Palestinian refugees pour into the city:

The world changed into water, and darkness covered all. The sun was extinguished, and the moon did not yet exist.... The Arab was not made in the likeness of God, so the fish of the sea, the birds of the air, and the creatures of the land had dominion over him. And the Arab saw all he had done and, behold, it was very bad.

The reader is left with a sense of shock and displacement at the close of the novel that parallel—albeit weakly—the feelings of the Arab world as the war came to an end. The fate of the displaced Palestinians is symbolized in the recurrent theme of the Flying Dutchman, who is doomed to roam without a homeland for the remainder of his existence. Barakat writes:

On the seventh day the Arab did not rest. And he did not know how long this seventh day would last. He sensed that there were to be many days of dust and cries of children from beneath tents in the desert. His seventh day would be months, perhaps years. The Arab was not made in the likeness of God, so the fish of the sea, the birds of the air, and the creatures of the land had dominion over him. All the Arab had created in the first six days was dust, and now the tempests were revealing the nature of his creations. There was nothing but the future left for him now, but he still reached back for the past.

Barakat began to make an impact in the field of sociology with his early writings, most notably his article "Alienation: A Process of Encounter between Utopia and Reality" (1969). In this piece Barakat combines the notions of alienation found in the German idealistic philosophy of Georg Wilhelm Friedrich Hegel, the materialism of Karl Marx, the sociology of Emile Durkheim, and the existentialism of Søren Kierkegaard, Friedrich Nietzsche, and Jean-Paul Sartre in an attempt to understand deviant social behavior.

In 1969 Barakat and Peter Dodd published *River without Bridges: A Study of the Exodus of the 1967 Palestinian Arab Refugees,* about the expulsion of Palestinians from the territories annexed by Israel after the Six-Day War. The authors describe the eviction of people from their homes, the destruction of villages, and mass detentions of male civilians for the purpose of applying pressure on the remaining residents.

In his 1971 article "Social Factors Influencing Attitudes of University Students in Lebanon towards the Palestinian Resistance Movement" Barakat analyzes the relationship between class and upbringing, on the one hand, and the tendency of Lebanese students to become agents of social and political change, on the other hand. He finds that students' political preferences tend to be determined by their religious and regional rather than their class background. Those who support armed struggle to resolve the Palestinian problem generally hold to a socialistic, democratic, and secular ideology, while those who favor a diplomatic solution show tendencies toward capitalism, conservatism, and religious traditionalism.

In 1972 Barakat received a one-year research fellowship at Harvard University. In his 1973 article "The Palestinian Refugees: An Uprooted Community Seeking Reparation" he argues that the exodus from Palestine between 1948 and 1967 created a people who had lost the social ties that provided the source of their psychological security and balance.

After completing his fellowship Barakat became vice president of academic affairs at Harvard's Center for Educational Research and Development. In 1975 he was named visiting professor of sociology at the University of Texas. The following year he took a position as research professor at Georgetown University's Center for Contemporary Arab Studies. In 1977 he published *Lebanon in Strife: Student Preludes to the Civil War,* in

Title page for Barakat's 1993 work of comparative sociology, in which he provides a new theoretical framework for understanding Arabs' place in the modern era (Thomas Cooper Library, University of South Carolina)

which he points out that the Lebanese student movement emerged as the struggle for independence started to take shape throughout the Third World in the second quarter of the twentieth century. He notes that the students took part in strikes and public demonstrations, some of which were met with a violent response by French mandate troops.

In Barakat's third novel, *al-Rahil bayna al-sahm wa al-watar* (1979, A Journey between the Arrow and the Cord), two women have affairs while attending a conference on the future of the Arab world in Alexandria in the 1970s. The novel asks whether Arab women can be liberated by a political revolution or whether they will continue to be victims of their culture. In 1988 Barakat published *Ta'ir al-hawm* (translated as *The Crane*, 2008), a novel in which the protagonist grows up in Syria and attends a university in the United States during the turbulent 1960s. It was followed in 1992 by the nonfiction work *Harb al-Khalij: Khutut fi al-raml wa al-zaman* (Gulf War: Lines in Sand and Time), in which he argues that the 1991 Gulf War undid the gains made in the twentieth century and returned the Middle East to foreign domination.

Hailed as an instant classic and an essential part of any Arab studies or comparative-sociology course, Barakat's *The Arab World: Society, Culture, and State* (1993) combines his previous research into a streamlined and coherent work that provides a new theoretical framework for understanding Arabs and their place in the modern era. Barakat rejects the Western Orientalist notion of Arabs as a "mosaic" society and calls for an Arab *nahda* (reformation). He traces the evolution of Arab identity through common characteristics such as family orientation, shared economics, and language. Bringing his analysis up to the Gulf War, he writes:

> These historical events at the beginning of the last decade of the twentieth century signal the end of one era and the beginning of a new one for the whole world. Such drastic changes may finally dare Arabs to free themselves from their deeply rooted skepticism about the possibility of remaking society. Despite Arab apprehensiveness that the current upheavals may reinforce the Western sense of self-righteousness, and consequently the uncontested dominance of the capitalist world system over Arabs and other peoples of developing societies, Arabs share a growing awareness that a new era is in the making.

Writing while "the fires in Kuwait are still smoldering," Barakat concludes the work by stating that the Arab world "is living one of the darkest moments of its modern history."

In the spring of 2002 Barakat received widespread criticism for an article in the London-based Arabic newspaper *al-Hayat* titled "The Wild Beast that Zionism Created: Self-Destruction," in which he set out to analyze and resolve two issues that had plagued him throughout his professional career: the mutation of Arab states from representative governments into instruments of repression, and how Zionism, a movement that emerged in the nineteenth century in reaction to European anti-Semitism, could have resulted in a state that persecutes the Palestinian people. The second issue was immediately picked up by the Washington, D.C.–based Middle East Media Research Institute (MEMRI), which placed an article on its website headlined "Georgetown University Professor, Halim Barakat: 'The Jews Have Lost Their Humanity,' 'They Do Not Raise Their Children to Be Weak.'" Replacing Barakat's word "Zionists" with "Jews" and phrase "Zionist Leadership" with "Israeli Jews," the institute charged Barakat with being an anti-Semite who lumps Judaism and Zionism together. The public outcry that erupted was joined by some of his colleagues at Georgetown University. Barakat issued statements denying the claims made by MEMRI and distinguishing between Judaism as a religion and Zionism as a movement. Although he dismisses the criticism he experienced as a public intimidation campaign against all who criticize the actions of the Israeli government, he continues to be labeled by some as an anti-Semite. He retired from the Center for Contemporary Arab Studies in 2002.

Halim Barakat's writings have both criticized and encouraged the Arab world, while always pushing for its improvement. His politically charged fiction and critical social analyses will continue to influence Arab literature and sociology in the twenty-first century.

References:

Roger Allen, *The Arabic Novel: An Historical and Critical Introduction,* second edition (Syracuse, N.Y.: Syracuse University Press, 1995), pp. 153–158;

M. M. Badawi, *A Short History of Modern Arabic Literature* (Oxford: Clarendon Press / New York: Oxford University Press, 1993), pp. 201, 217, 219–221, 324;

Elizabeth Warnock Fernea, *Remembering Childhood in the Middle East: Memoirs from a Century of Change* (Austin: University of Texas Press, 2002), pp. 127–132;

Fernea, ed., *Women and the Family in the Middle East: New Voices of Change* (Austin: University of Texas Press, 1984), pp. 27–48.

Rachid Boudjedra

(5 September 1941 –)

Boutheina Khaldi
Yale University

BOOKS: *Pour ne plus rêver* (Algiers: Editions nationales algériennes, 1965);

La répudiation (Paris: Denoël, 1969); translated by Golda Lambrova as *The Repudiation,* introduction by Hédi Abdel Jaouad (Colorado Springs, Colo.: Three Continents Press, 1995);

La vie quotidienne en Algérie (Paris: Hachette, 1971);

Naissance du cinéma algérien (Paris: F. Maspéro, 1971);

Journal palestinien (Paris: Hachette, 1972);

L'insolation (Paris: Denoël, 1972); translated by Boudjedra as *al-Ra'n* (Algiers: Al-Mu'assasah al-Wataniyah lil-Kitab, 1984);

Topographie idéale pour une agression caractérisée: Roman (Paris: Denoël, 1975);

L'escargot entêté: Roman (Paris: Denoël, 1977);

Les 1001 années de la nostalgie (Paris: Denoël, 1979);

Le vainqueur de coupe: Roman (Paris: Denoël, 1981);

Al-Tafakkuk (Algiers: Al-Sharikah al-Wataniyyah li al-Nashr wa al-Tawzi', 1982); translated by Boudjedra as *Le Démantèlement* (Paris: Denoël, 1982);

Al-Marth (Algiers: Al-Mu'assasah al-Wataniyyah li al-Kitab, 1984); translated by Boudjedra and Antoine Moussali as *La macération* (Paris: Denoël, 1984);

Greffe (Paris: Denoël, 1985);

Layliyyat imra'ah ariq (Algiers: Al-Mu'assasah al-Wataniyyah li al-Kitab, 1985); translated by Boudjedra and Moussali as *La pluie* (Paris: Denoël, 1987); translated by Angela M. Brewer as *Rain (Diary of an Insomniac)* (New York: Les Mains Secrètes, 2002);

Ma'rakat al-zuqaq (Algiers: Al-Mu'assasah al-Wataniyyah li al-Kitab, 1986); translated by Boudjedra and Moussali as *La prise de Gibraltar* (Paris: Denoël, 1987);

Fawda al-ashya' (Algiers: Dar Bushan li al-Nashr, 1991); translated by Boudjedra and Moussali as *Le désordre des choses* (Paris: Denoël, 1991);

FIS de la haine (Paris: Denoël, 1992);

Rachid Boudjedra (<http://www.restena.lu/clae/salon.du.livre.et.des.cultures/5e.salon2005/rachid.boudjedra.jpg>)

Timimoun (Algiers: Dar al-Ijtihad, 1994); translated into French by Boudjedra as *Timimoun* (Paris: Denoël, 1994);

Mines de rien: Le retable du nord et du sud: Théâtre (Paris: Denoël, 1995);

Lettres algériennes (Paris: Bernard Grasset, 1995);

Peindre l'orient (Cadeilhan, France: Zulma, 1996);
La vie à l'endroit: Roman (Paris: Bernard Grasset, 1997);
Fascination (Paris: Bernard Grasset, 2000);
Cinq fragments du désert (La Tour d'Aigues: Editions de l'Aube, 2002);
Les funérailles (Paris: Bernard Grasset, 2003);
Hôtel Saint-Georges (Oran: Dar el-Gharb, 2007).

Rachid Boudjedra is an innovative Algerian writers and the first outspoken critic of postindependence Algeria. The best-known bilingual writer in North Africa, he started his literary career in the late 1960s as a Francophone poet and then novelist, essayist, and playwright. He wrote in French rather than Arabic not only to escape Algerian censorship but also to be widely read, and he acknowledges that without the fame he achieved in France his works would not have been as well received in Algeria as they have been. In 1981, after publishing six novels in French, he began to write in Arabic; he has rendered some of his Arabic novels into French, sometimes in collaboration with his Lebanese mentor, Antoine Moussali. Boudjedra's fiction is subversive, nonconformist, and provocative and has been translated into seventeen languages. Unlike other Algerian fiction writers, Boudjedra does not deal explicitly with colonialism but denounces conformity and treats themes such as religion, rape, sexuality, women, and hypocrisy. His intricate and complex style is frequently compared to that of William Faulkner.

Boudjedra was born into a wealthy family on 5 September 1941 in Ain Beida, near Constantine in eastern Algeria. His father repudiated Boudjedra's mother and took other wives; including Rachid, the father has thirty-seven sons and daughters.

Boudjedra spent part of his early childhood in *al-kuttab* (Qur'anic school). He started his secular education in Ain Beida and pursued it in Tunis at the prestigious bilingual Sadiqi boarding school. In 1959 he joined the resistance against the French; after being wounded, he traveled to Communist Eastern Europe and to Spain as a representative of the Front de Liberation Nationale (National Liberation Front [FLN]). After Algeria won independence from France in 1962, Boudjedra attended the École Normale Supérieure (College of Higher Education) in Algiers. In 1965 he earned a bachelor's degree in philosophy at the Sorbonne in Paris, where he did research on the nineteenth-century French novelist Louis-Ferdinand Céline and married a Frenchwoman. He returned to Algeria and taught philosophy at the Lycée des Jeunes Filles (School for Young Girls) in Blida and published a collection of poems, *Pour ne plus rêver* (1965, To Dream No Longer). He left Algeria for France when Houari Boumédienne took power in 1965. There he wrote his first novel, *La répudiation* (1969; translated as *The Repudiation*, 1995). The narrator, Rachid, tells the story to his French lover, Céline, between bouts of lovemaking and periods of confinement in a psychiatric ward. A large part of the novel is devoted to his childhood in the Casbah in Algiers. When Rachid's fifty-year-old father, Si Zoubir, becomes bored with Rachid's thirty-year-old mother, Ma, he repudiates her and marries fifteen-year-old Zoubida, whom he has "purchased." Repudiation is different from divorce: it is an irrevocable public oath of refusal to sleep with one's wife. Si Zoubir thus keeps his wife but deprives her of satisfaction of her sexual needs. He not only makes Ma accept his marriage to a younger woman but even orders her to organize the wedding ceremony. Ma displays no sign of rebellion; she considers it normal for a man to exercise his rights. Rachid and his brother, Zahir, are offended by their father's abandonment of their mother. To avenge her humiliation, Rachid enters into an incestuous relationship with his stepmother, Zoubida. He also takes revenge on his clan by satisfying the sexual needs of its wives and daughters. Ma, Zahir, and Rachid's sister Yasmina die; his other sister, Saida, marries and drifts away; and Rachid enters the asylum. Meanwhile, Si Zoubir takes a third wife and also continues to enjoy his many mistresses.

Rape and other forms of violence abound in the novel. Women's menstrual periods and the blood of virgins' ruptured hymens are associated in Rachid's mind with the ritual slaughter of animals on 'Id al-Adha (the Festival of the Sacrifice). Women are thus viewed as the sacrificial victims of inevitable violence. Boudjedra also establishes a parallel between the rape of women and the "rape" of Algeria by the French colonizers. Finally, he condemns the rising postindependence Algerian middle class, of which Si Zoubir is a member, as no better than the French colonizers. *La répudiation* was banned in Algeria for seven years because of its depictions of sex, rape, violence, and incest, as well as for its explicit language and its assault on Muslim traditionalism.

In 1972 Boudjedra left France to teach at Rabat University in Morocco. His second novel, *L'insolation* (1972, Sunstroke; translated by Boudjedra as *al-Ra'n*, 1984), was written there. It opens with the Marxist philosophy teacher Mehdi in the hospital suffering from sunstroke after a night of drinking and lovemaking. He tells his nurse, Nadia, how his student Samia decided to break the shackles imposed on her by her patriarchal family and go to the beach with him the day before. Samia was "heureuse d'avoir rompu les amarres avec son feodal père" (happy to have cut off ties with her feudal father), and Mehdi rejoiced at "l'avais coupée du clan auquel elle été rattachée depuis toujours, j'avais

Front cover for Boudjedra's first novel (1969; translated as The Repudiation, 1995), in which the narrator's father repudiates the narrator's mother and marries a fifteen-year-old girl (Jean and Alexander Heard Library, Vanderbilt University)

tranché le fil de l'honneur" (having cut her off from the clan which she was always tied to, I have severed the thread of honor). His deflowering of Samia is juxtaposed with a sacrifice performed by a black man who has been spying on the couple; by superimposing the sacrificial victim on the deflowered Samia, the defloration becomes identified with rape. Seized with regret, Samia denounced Mehdi to the police and returned to the control of her father. Mehdi is confined to a mental asylum by his political adversaries.

Mehdi's "rape" of Samia was prefigured by the rape of his mother, Selma, by his father, Si Omar, a rich landowner and businessman who completed the hajj (pilgrimage to Mecca) three times and was legally married to Selma's sister Malika. Si Omar forced another man to marry Selma on paper by threatening to report his political affiliation to the authorities if he did not do so. Selma's rape, like Samia's, is juxtaposed with sacrifice: Mehdi says that the "viol de ma mère . . . par terre" (rape of my mother . . . on the floor) was "à la manière des moutons de mon enfance que j'avais vu tuer" (like the way sheep in my childhood were slaughtered). The scene of Selma's sacrifice is interspersed with descriptions of the brutality of the conquest of Algeria. Here, as in *La répudiation,* Boudjedra equates the rape of the protagonist's mother with the rape of the motherland, Algeria, by the colonizers.

L'insolation also expresses Boudjedra's disenchantment with the governments of Ahmed Ben Bella, who served as president from 1963 to 1965, and Houari Boumédienne, who deposed Ben Bella in 1965 and ruled until his death in December 1978. In Boudjedra's view, the two presidents betrayed the 1954–1962 revolution that had liberated the nation from the French and promised the building of a socialist Muslim society: according to Boudjedra, they allowed the emergence of the bourgeoisie represented in the novel by Si Omar. Boudjedra argues that the bourgeoisie misuses religion to serve its interests: "cette démagogie faite autour de la religion des ancêtres . . . n'arrangeait rien dans les affaires des masses, mais que certains utilisent pour détourner l'attention et profiter tant qu'ils peuvent" (this demagogy constructed around the religion of the ancestors . . . does not help people in their affairs. Some, however, use it to avert the attention and benefit as much as they can).

While in Morocco, Boudjedra also wrote *Topographie idéale pour une agression caractérisée* (1975, Ideal Topography for a Characteristic Aggression). An illiterate Algerian Berber peasant, whose name is never given in the novel, immigrates to France in search of a job. Carrying a heavy suitcase in one hand and a piece of paper with the address of a countryman in the other, he gets lost in the Paris Métro (subway). The novel is divided into five chapters; the title of each chapter is the number of a subway line taken by the immigrant. Boudjedra's detailed explanations of the technical workings of the subway system help to convey the immigrant's irritation and anxiety. He approaches a group of men and shows them the paper with the address. Unbeknownst to him, they are racists; instead of helping him find his destination, they kill him. The story is told by an omniscient narrator who relates the immigrant's point of view and that of a biased French police inspector who investigates the crime. The novel was inspired by the murders of Algerian immigrants in the streets of Paris,

Marseilles, and Lyon in 1972, following Boumédienne's February 1971 nationalization of French oil companies in Algeria.

In 1975 Boudjedra returned to Algeria and became an adviser to the Ministry of Information and Culture. Two years later, he published *L'escargot entêté* (1977, The Stubborn Snail), a fable that exposes the mediocre values in postrevolutionary Algeria. It is told in the form of a journal kept by a fifty-year-old civil servant closed up in his room over a period of six days.

In 1979 Boudjedra published *Les 1001 années de la nostalgie* (The Thousand and One Years of Nostalgia). The novel is set in the Sahara village of Manama, which was built in the ninth century by a rich trader. The narrator, Mohammad S.N.P., is the only single child in a family of nine sets of twins. He has inherited from his grandfather a keen interest in history; his quest to find out where in the village the fourteenth-century historian Ibn Khaldun wrote his most important books alienates him from the other inhabitants of Manama, who have no idea who Ibn Khaldun was or why he came to their village. The governor of Manama, Bendar Chah (a Persian name similar to those of sultans and princes in *The Arabian Nights*), and his entourage live luxurious lives on the revenues from the oil they sell to foreign consuls; the cost of the wedding of Bendar Chah's daughter, Leila, equals the ten-year budgets of some poor countries. The foreign consuls come in disguise so as not to be recognized by the exploited and poverty-stricken people of Manama. One day an American movie company arrives in the town to film a new version of *The Arabian Nights*. They have been sent by Leila's husband "pour montrer à l'univers à quel degré de raffinement la civilisation musulmane était arrivé dans le passé" (to show to the world the degree of refinement the Islamic civilization reached in the past). The presence of the foreigners destabilizes the village and leads to violence that provides footage for the movie. Boudjedra's narrator demythologizes the American film company's, and hence the Occident's, notion of *The Arabian Nights* by asserting that it is all "du sexe. . . . Mais rien sur la misère des masses" (about sexuality. . . . But there is nothing on the misery of the populace). The American moviemakers' invasion of Manama, like the American Banana company's invasion of Macondo in Gabriel García Márquez's novel *Cien años de soledad* (1967; translated as *One Hundred Years of Solitude*, 1970), symbolizes twentieth-century Western imperialism.

Since 1981 Boudjedra has taught at the Institut des Sciences Politiques (Political Science Institute) in Algiers and served as a reader and adviser for the national publishing house, Enterprise Nationale Algérienne du Livre (Algerian National Enterprise of the Book). In 1983 he was sentenced to death in a *fatwa* by

Front cover for Boudjedra's 1972 novel, about a philosophy teacher who has a one-night affair with a student. Boudjedra translated the novel from French into Arabic in 1984 (Tulane University Library).

the fundamentalist Front Islamique du Salut (Islamic Salvation Front [FIS]) for writing in *La répudiation* that Islam is incompatible with a modern state. The death threat has forced him to lead a semiclandestine existence, frequently changing apartments.

Unlike Boudjedra's other novels, *Layliyat imra'ah ariq* (1985; translated by Boudjedra and Moussali as *La pluie*, 1987; translated as *Rain (Diary of an Insomniac)*, 2002) has a female narrator. The structure mirrors that of *L'escargot entêté*: a doctor is closed up in her room during her menstrual period, writing in her journal over a period of six nights. The novel opens with the narrator's melancholy experience of her first menstruation and her entrance into womanhood; this opening is reminiscent of Nawal El Sadaawi's *Mudhakkirat tabibah* (1958; translated as *Memoirs of a Woman Doctor*, 1988), in which the female narrator associates menses with death. Boudjedra's narrator was brought up not to speak about the intimate parts of her body: her now-deceased father instilled in her the idea that the female body is taboo, and her younger brother slaps her when she asks him if he menstruates. Through his female narrator Boudjedra denounces a patriarchal society dominated by archaic values that sentence women to silence. The novel was adapted as a play by Antoine Caubet and staged at Institut du monde Arabe in Paris on 3 October 2003. It was adapted again by Eddy Pallaro and staged in February 2008 in Le Théâtre du Lierre in Paris.

In 1987 Boudjedra founded the Ligue Algérienne des Droits de l'Homme (Algerian League for Human Rights), of which he served as secretary-general. The following year he and some other Algerian intellectuals founded the Comité contre la Torture (Committee against Torture).

In 1992 the FIS, which aimed to establish Islamic law in Algeria, was set to win the first free legislative elections since the country won its independence in 1962; the ruling FLN canceled the elections. Boudjedra welcomed the move, which he saw as the salvation of the country, in a polemic titled *FIS de la haine* (1992, The Hateful FIS). The book attacks not only the FIS and Islamists in general but also Western governments and media, the postindependence Algerian regimes, and the Algerian people for encouraging the ascent of the Islamists. Boudjedra condemns Ben Bella for making Islam the official state religion; Boumédienne for surrendering Algerian schools to "instituteurs de la Haute-Egypte, semi-analphabètes, ayant appris un peu de Coran" (semiliterate Egyptian fundamentalist teachers with little knowledge of the Qur'an); and Boumédienne's successor, Chadli Bendjedid, who ruled from February 1979 until January 1992, for dismantling state enterprises and importing luxury goods and other unnecessary commodities that led to the emergence of an elite class and the impoverishment of many Algerians.

In *Hôtel Saint-Georges* (2007) the protagonist, Jean, is called on by the French government during the Algerian War of Liberation to make coffins for the repatriation of the remains of soldiers who "died for France." Seeing the decomposition of the bodies, he discovers the horrors of war. To drown his horror and his disgust for the colonial occupation, he frequents the bar at the Saint-Georges (now the al Djaza'ir) Hotel, where he meets Nabila, a student and waitress who works for the Algerian revolution. Years later, Jean returns to France but cannot forget his life in Algiers. On his deathbed he asks his daughter, Jeanne, to visit Algeria.

Rachid Boudjedra continued to defend the FLN in the 1992–1999 civil war between the FLN and the FIS, notwithstanding growing evidence of torture and extrajudicial executions committed by government security forces and state-armed militias. On 25 May 2006 he was honored by the Union des Écrivains Algériens (Union of Algerian Writers) at the fourteenth annual Journées Littéraires (Literary Days) held at the Djillali-Mebarek cultural center in El Eulma in Sétif province. On 27 April 2007 he was invited by the Department of Modern Languages and Literatures at Swarthmore College to give a lecture in Arabic on his writing in Arabic and French and in French on the influence of William Faulkner on Maghrebian literature. In November 2007 he won the Prix des Librairies for his outspoken and controversial books.

References:

Kagni Alemdjrodo, *Rachid Boudjedra: La passion de l'intertexte* (Bordeaux: Presses Universitaires de Bordeaux, 2001);

Hafid Gafaiti, *Boudjedra ou la passion de la modernité* (Paris: Denokl, 1987);

Benaouda Lebdaï, *Post-Independence African Literature: Case Study, Boudjedra/Ngugi* (Algiers: Office des Publications Universitaires, 1992);

Yahia H. Zoubir, "*FIS de la haine:* De la barbarie en général et de l'intégrisme en particulier," *Journal of Modern African Studies,* 31 (December 1993): 709–713.

Slaheddine Boujah

(3 February 1956 –)

Hager Ben Driss
University of Tunis

BOOKS: *Mudawanat al-i'tirafat wa al-asrar* (Tunis: Demeter, 1985);
Al-Taj wa al-khinjar wa al-jasad (Cairo: Dar Su'ad al-Subah, 1992);
Al-Jawhar wa al-'ard fi al-riwayah al-waqi'iyyah (Beirut: Al-Mu'assasah al-Jami'iyyah li al-Nashr, 1993);
Al-Ramz wa al-usturah (Beirut: Al-Mu'assasah al-Jami'iyyah li al-Nashr, 1994);
Maqalah fi al-riwayah (Beirut: Al-Mu'assasah al-Jami'iyyah li al-Nashr, 1995);
Al-Nakhkhas (Tunis: Dar al-Janub li al-Nashr, 1995);
Radya wa al-sirk (Beirut: Dar al-Adab, 1997); republished as *Al-Sirk* (Tunis: Al-Sharikah al-Tunisiyyah li al-Nashr, 2001);
Sahl al-Ghuraba' (Cairo: Al-Hay'a al-'Amma li kusur al-Thaqafah, 1999);
La shay'a yahduthu al-an (Tunis: Al-Sharika al-Tunusiyyah li al-Nashr, 2001);
Fi al-ulfah wa al-ikhtilaf (Tunis: Dar al-Janub li al-Nashr, 2004);
Lawn al-ruh (Tunis: Dar al-Janub li al-Nashr, 2008).

Slaheddine Boujah (<http://www.asslivre.com>)

SELECTED PERIODICAL PUBLICATION–
UNCOLLECTED: "Ecrire l'eau . . . Réécrire l'imaginaire," *Ifriquiya: Littérature de Tunisie*, 1 (1997): 75–82.

Slaheddine Boujah (also transliterated as Salah al-Din Bugah) writes within an experimental tradition that has flourished in Tunisia since the 1960s. Highly influenced by preceding Tunisian writers who paved the way for a revolution in narrative techniques and content, Boujah adopts subversive strategies such as deliberately tampering with language, challenging the sacred, and exploding taboos. He uses the stream-of-consciousness technique as a liberating mode of narration in which the text is transformed into a fluid space, free of order or any type of restraining hierarchy. A bold blending between opposite worlds characterizes Boujah's writing, for his novels accommodate the classic and the modern, the real and the imaginary, logic as well as magic. His works deliberately disappoint the reader who looks for a story, for traditional narrative in his novels and is replaced by a Chinese box–like text in which fragmented tales invite readers to participate in the game of creativity.

The fourth child of Hasan Boujah and Shedlia Bint Said, Boujah was born on 3 February 1956 in Sidi Farhat, the site of the mausoleum of an ancestor of that name; his father's family had changed their name from Farhat in 1910. Sidi Farhat is about eighteen miles from Kairouan, the northern Tunisian city famous for its Islamic shrines. Boujah spent his childhood and early youth in Humat al-Jami', the mosque quarter of Kairouan, where the mosque built in 671 by the *Sahabi* (Prophet's Companion) 'Uqbah ibn Nafi' still stands. His father had studied at the al-Zaytuna Mosque, a prestigious educational and religious institution in Tunis, and had received the certificate al-Tahsil, the highest degree offered by the Qur'anic school. The father's education accounts for Boujah's mastery of the Arabic language, as well as his deep knowledge of classic Arabic literature.

During his primary education from 1962 to 1967 Boujah stood out among his fellow students. Shy and aloof, he raised the anxiety of a teacher in his first year at school. "Your son will be either very brilliant or a complete failure," a teacher told his father. Fortunately for the absent-minded child, the first part of the prophecy proved true. At the age of eleven Boujah proudly showed his father his first attempts at writing stories. When he was seventeen, he published his first poems and short stories in *Majallat al-Fikr* (Intellectual Journal). His shyness continued into his literary career. "My writing activities," Boujah told Majid al-Samirra'i in a 2003 interview, "definitely stem from the great amount of fear, timidity and aloofness I internalize."

In 1974 Boujah moved to Tunis for his higher education. He attended Tunis University, where he earned a B.A. in Arabic language and literature in 1978. He continued studying while working as a secondary-school teacher, and in 1984 he received his Certificat d'Aptitude a la Recherche. A year later, he joined the University of Kairouan as a teacher in the Arabic department. In 1987 he earned the Diplôme de Recherches Approfondis. In 1993 he was appointed a dean (the equivalent of a professor) at the University of Kairouan. His political interests took him away from teaching in 1994, when he was elected to Parliament; he served until 2004. Boujah continued working on his Doctorat d'Etat in Tunisian literature, which he completed in May 2004.

In many interviews Boujah speaks with love and pride about the importance of his father's huge collection of books, his first source of reading, in shaping his mind and has often referred to it in his semiautobiographical narratives. His early reading of the Arabic classic texts of poetry, theology and history had a significant influence on his style and language. Later, Boujah's personal library became another source of inspiration. Besides an extensive reading of Arabic novels, he devoured French classic prose and verse, including the works of Honoré de Balzac, Emile Zola, Arthur Rimbaud, Charles Baudelaire, and Paul Verlaine. He was also attracted to French translations of other world literature, such as the works of Fyodor Dostoevsky and Franz Kafka. Boujah's first encounter with the fictional world of Kafka was through *Die Verwandlung* (1915; translated as *The Metamorphosis*, 1937) a narrative that transformed his vision of life and inspired his first novel.

Mudawanat al-i'tirafat wa al-asrar (The Book of Confessions and Secrets, 1985) was the first published work that brought Boujah, then twenty-nine, real literary recognition. In his 2003 interview he described it as "a beginning characterized by freedom, unrestraint and the naivety of youth." The novel narrates the story of Abu 'Umran Sa'id, a young man who becomes invisible. He is able to see everything and everybody without being seen. When he wrote the book, Boujah had in mind Kafka's *Die Verwandlung,* in which a young man wakes up one morning to find himself transformed into a cockroach. Though different in plot, the two stories share the same spirit, for each protagonist suffers because of others' egoism and ignorance. Like Kafka's protagonist, who is shunned by his family and dies alone, Boujah's protagonist becomes transparent, alienated from ordinary life, suggesting that the fate of human beings is to be ostracized, muted, and buried in oblivion. Boujah in his interview commented on his identification with his protagonist: "I came to think that I became, with my Tunisian and Arab generation, inexistent gelatinous beings."

Boujah's *Mudawanat al-i'tirafat wa al-asrar* deals with a generation characterized by loss and lack of faith. Portrayed as alienated individuals living a spiritual and existential crisis, his characters confess their religious doubts and political anxieties. Because their firm certainties are that they do not belong to their age and no longer believe in the idea of a homeland, they are in a perpetual search for identity. The vacillation of the characters between a dead past and a dubious present is evident in the form Boujah has given his novel, as he imitates an old Arabic form by dividing the pages of the narratives into a body *(matn)* and a margin or footnotes *(hashiya)*. The events are narrated in two different ways.

Mudawanat al-i'tirafat wa al-asrar was received rather cautiously and somewhat coldly in Tunisa but has since achieved acclaim in the wider Arab critical world as one of the most important novels of the mid 1980s because of the serious questions it raises concerning literary genres and techniques of writing. Looking back on his novel in *al-Zaman* (8 March 1999), Boujah confessed that his exaggerated focus on language and his fixation on embellishing the style marred his book. He declared that his "critical knowledge has more spoiled his fiction writing than it has benefitted it." He calls *Mudawanat al-i'tirafat wa al-asrar* "a laboratory novel" in which he experimentally mixed his knowledge of classic Arabic texts and contemporary European schools of criticism. The outcome, he asserted, "lacks basic stylistic smoothness necessary to render it palatable for the Tunisian readers' taste."

Boujah continued experimenting in his second novel, *al-Taj wa al-khinjar wa al-jasad* (1992, The Crown, the Sword, and the Body), in which his ostensible subject is the history of his mystic ancestor, Sidi Farhat al-

'Amiri. He dedicates his narrative first "to Sidi Farhat" and second "to our house: the courtyard, the storing room, the roof, my father's books, the mulberry, the well and the memory of grandfather, 'Ali." The writer adopts the grandiloquent style of epical narratives. "I will sculpt you O homeland history," the narrator states, "and make of you the epic of the coming generations." This sentence becomes a leitmotiv repeated in different parts of the text with slight changes in the second part as "and make of you the tune of the coming generations" or "and make of you my epic and the Iliad of the coming generations." The narrative invokes aspects of the political life in Tunisia during the Husayni reign in the eighteenth century. Sidi Farhat, "a rebellious Sufi, a dervish and a restless traveler," managed to rally his followers and disciples against the despotic regime of the king. He refuses bribes and will not be co-opted by the king, who offers alluring propositions.

Boujah always claims that his works are void of political ideologies. In his 2003 interview he insisted that writing for him "is essentially an existential experience." Taken from this perspective, then, *al-Taj wa al-khinjar wa al-jasad* may be read as an aesthetic recreation of the political game based on the rulers' despotism and the populations' victimization and potential upheavals. But in a larger sense the novel treats political struggle as a dynamic force in shaping the history of civilizations. Boujah's explanation of the title of his novel suggests a universal dimension: "This is the game of the crown, the sword and the body: the King protects himself through deceit and hypocrisy; the commander of the army is proudly safe with his sword and soldiers; meanwhile, the body of population—the common people—is sometimes disarmed and sometimes violent."

The story of Sidi Farhat, however, is not Boujah's central interest, for his novel is much more concerned with the anxieties of creativity and writing than with tracing historical events. The Chinese box–like narrative is divided into two stories: the first deals with the rebellion of Sidi Farhat against despotism, and the second is about the narrator's struggle to produce a work of art. The two stories converge in the hazy figure of the narrator. The point of view is so blurred between two main narrating voices that it is difficult at times to differentiate between them. The omniscient narrator tells the story or comments on the writing of a second narrator called Sahib al-Makhtut (The Manuscript Owner). The latter narrates his own story, which is the history of his family and his ancestor Sidi Farhat. In some places of the text, the two voices are deliberately fused and confused, as when Boujah writes "he said, or I said, no he rather said."

The metanarrative—in which the writer/narrator self-consciously discusses his strategies of writing and questions his own text—becomes a technique of narration in the novel. Readers are also involved in the act of writing as they witness the birth of a text with all that it entails—labor, suffering, doubt and frustration. The text becomes the mirror of itself; it reflects its own tactics of narration.

One of the artistic anxieties raised in *al-Taj wa al-khinjar wa al-jasad* is the audience reception. For whom the writer is writing and whether he should strive to please his readers or to follow his artistic inclinations are thorny questions that the book raises but fails to resolve. Sahib al-Makhtut is portrayed in a perpetual anxiety at what people can think of his writings: "Sahib al-Makhtut was lost in meditations about people's reaction to what he writes and what he says. He wondered: if mere approval is impossible to reach, then what's the use of embarrassing my pen when it wakes up?" This type of internal monologue occupies a great space of the narrative. It has the function of not only bringing the writer to the fore but also of involving the reader in the game of creativity.

The narrative challenges the reader who would passively consume the story as an entertainment with an ironic invitation to stop resistance and surrender to the text: "What's the use of resistance and interrogation? I suggest you surrender to the pleasure of the novel and the lullaby of the tale." But the narrator Sahib al-Makhtut does not allow the reader to be passive: he interrupts, disrupts, and spoils the pleasure of following the progression of a story. The narrative structure is based on discontinuity and rupture as there is no linear plot. The omniscient narrator, who confesses ironically "Here I am unmasking the secrets of his narrative game and I hope you keep the secret," also comments on Sahib al-Makhtut's self-contradictory invitation: "This Sahib al-Makhtut is quite strange! He invites you to listen to him and then he exhausts you by confusing time and space, inside and outside, what is accessible and what is looked for. He should either change his strategies or perhaps you'd better leave him alone." The omniscient narrator, in this instance, works as an ironic observer or a potential reader. The text mirrors itself by making the narrator a resisting reader, allowing the narrative to be reflected on by a proxy reader within the text.

This anxiety about reception is shared by Boujah, who knows his experimental, postmodern style is not popular and in his novel may be said to have anticipated its failure to attract critical interest in Tunisia. In *al-Taj wa al-khinjar wa al-jasad,* as well as in other novels, Boujah is primarily concerned with the question of creativity as an abstract concept. He adopts what he calls *muʿabathah* (flirting) with received ideas, the sacred and the established. His writing is a "flirtation" with both reader and text. Aware that his work will disappoint the reader seeking simple entertainment, Boujah writes for a small audience—a circumstance that does not satisfy a writer's pride and feeds the anxiety over reception.

While uncertain whether he should continue writing or give up the whole enterprise, Sahib al-Makhtut insists on the importance of the written word in the formation of his identity. "But I'm addicted to the word," he claims; "there I exist in a perfect harmony with myself." Embodying the text creates a type of symbiotic relationship between text and writer or creation and creator. The act of writing is often considered within a mystical context of Genesis or world creation: "Sahib al-Makhtut thought of the beginning of creation, he felt that dizziness which accompanies a moment of epiphany."

Sahib al-Makhtut's moment of celebrating the self through the written word gives way to his anxiety of artistic impotence. Boujah suggests that creativity can only function within a fertile linguistic or emotional milieu by linking fertility to artistic production through sexual metaphors. The opening sentence of the novel uses such a metaphor to describe the writer's relationship with his work: "Sahib al-Makhtut went back to his papers after long abandon. . . . He went back the way a stallion returns to his sweet and tender female." He goes on describing his text/manuscript as female, adopting a highly erotic style: "Here is the female's veil like a lush thicket and here are the exciting and inciting meanders of the manuscript inviting for biting, reproaching, and justifying."

As the text is presented as a sensual woman ready for sexual pleasure, the act of writing is eroticized. It is not surprising, then, that the artistic crisis is articulated through images of impotence or sterility. In a moment combining impotence and agony, Sahib al-Makhtut presents himself as an embodiment of impotence: "I am impotence," he declares, "the impotence of discovering a virgin word able to beget."

Sahib al-Makhtut is able to cope with this anxiety by finding a new story to tell. Leaving the history of his Sufi ancestor, he enters into his own narrative in the way Alice enters the mirror in Lewis Carroll's *Through the Looking-Glass, and What Alice Found There* (1871), and becomes a character in a world of dreams and fantasies. Invited by the Sultan of Ifriqiyyah (the old name of Tunisia), who wants to know about the manuscript concerning Sidi Farhat and the history of Kairouan, where the revolt started, he finds himself in a luxurious palace surrounded by beautiful women. As Sahib al-Makhtut is not sure whether he is really a guest in the sultan's palace or a prisoner, he begins to doubt the sincerity of the sultan's interest in his work.

Through Sahib al-Makhtut's situation, Boujah raises the question of the intellectual's integrity. Writing has to be completely free, outside the influence or the custody of any ruling power, otherwise it becomes a type of intellectual prostitution. Bartering one's intellectual favors for money or any form of material benefit is expressed in terms of slavery: "when Sahib al-Makhtut considered discussing with the new despot his project of recording the history of his ancestors, he was really in a strange state . . . Where is the difference between him and any woman in the harem he saw in the locales of the Great Ruler?"

Boujah wrote three critical studies—*al-Jawhar wa al-ard fi al-riwayah al-waqiʿiyyah* (1993; The Center and the Margin in the Realistic Novel), *al-Ramz wa al-usturah* (1994; The Symbol and the Myth), and *Maqalah fi al-riwayah* (1995; A Dissertation on the Novel)—before his third novel, *al-Nakhkhas* (1995, The Slaver) was published. He again pursued his own inclinations as a writer in producing a novel that is highly fragmented and not easily accessible. Although interested in how his work is received by readers, Boujah's two main reasons for writing are first, a desire of intellectual knowledge, and second, a desire for sensory knowledge. In his interview in *al-Zaman,* he claims that *al-Nakhkhas* manages to portray this longing for the exploration of the "unknown," both intellectual and sensory.

Al-Nakhkhas continues Boujah's exploration of the dark recesses of the creative mind. The narrative blurs the boundaries between the real and the imaginary, the intellectual and the sensual, and the concrete and the abstract. In his 1997 article "Ecrire l'eau . . . Réécrire l'imaginaire" (Writing Water . . . Rewriting the Imaginary), he commented on his work: "Ce roman se veut comme la scène d'un tourbillon de sens et parfois de non-sens, ou rien ne se perd, rien ne se crée, tout se transforme!" (This novel presents itself as the site of a whirl of senses, sometimes of nonsense, where nothing is lost, nothing is created, everything is transformed!") Like all Boujah's narratives, *al-Nakhkhas* does not lend itself to an easy summary. Purposely lacking order and unity, it also mocks storytelling in its traditional sense. The novel is based on several intertwined stories, none of which has a clear or definite end.

The central character is Taj al-Din Farhat, a writer from Kairouan who has always cherished the dream of becoming a famous literary figure. One day, he receives a phone call from the Italian Embassy in Tunis telling him that he is nominated for a literary prize and that he is invited to visit Italy. He decides to go to Genoa on the ship *La Capo Bella,* which has seven rooms containing the secrets, the writings, and the food and spices of different Mediterranean countries. His fellow voyagers belong to different nationalities and cultures—a Mediterranean melting pot.

Taj al-Din finds the ship a fertile site of inspiration. As he believes that the act of writing is primarily an act of *talassus* (spying or voyeurism), he spends his time observing the activities of the voyagers and exploring the secret corridors of the ship. He loses his old leather bag containing all his papers, including his manuscript, while he stealthily examines the kitchen of the ship.

The captain of the ship, Gabriello Cavinalia, who commits suicide toward the end of the novel, is one of the mysterious characters of the narrative. His daughter, Laura, with whom Taj al-Din has a sexual experience, is equally enigmatic. Taj al-Din's sensual side is also gratified with an erotic encounter with the Moroccan dancer, Lola. The passengers include many other sensual women who engage in a striptease orgy that is stopped only by the discovery of a corpse, which turns out to be a smuggled Egyptian mummy. There are also male characters from Algeria and Palestine and a trader, called 'Abdun, who gives up much of his silk to hear stories from Taj Eddine. The narrative ends with the mysterious disappearance of the protagonist and subsequent reports saying that he was seen in Egypt carrying an old bag full of his manuscripts. Boujah draws on the Qur'anic version of Jesus Christ's crucifixion, adopting the same divine words used in describing Jesus Christ's seeming death. The Islamic version states that Jesus is not killed; he is rather *rufi'a* (uplifted) by God.

A line Boujah quotes from the French poet Rimbaud—"Je finis par trouver sacré le désordre de mon esprit" (I came to realize that the disorder of my spirit is sacred)—is the best way to describe the nub of the novel. Boujah uses disorder as a technique to mirror the work of the mind in its natural functioning. A highly deceptive text, *al-Nakhkhas* presents events as happening on the board of a ship while in fact everything happens in the mind of the narrator. The narrative abounds with flashbacks, memories of childhood, historical events, descriptions of smells, and even old recipes of traditional dishes.

Boujah makes it clear that Taj al-Din Farhat is his alter ego. The novel is dedicated "to Taj al-Din Farhat, the creature who emerges out of my fingers and whose presence almost terrifies me!" The novel is based on exploring the deep corridors of the self and unveiling secret fantasies. In his 2003 interview Boujah himself describes his work as removing the mask of his everyday life: "it raises a question around my secret madness hiding behind the mantle of the teacher, the Parliament member, the husband and the father."

Memory in *al-Nakhkhas* goes beyond the personal to embrace origins, as Boujah presents a mosaic of cultures and ethnicities. In the prologue he quotes a short excerpt taken from the introduction of *al-Fihrist* (The Index or The Catalogue) by the tenth-century historian Ibn al-Nadim: "This is the Fihrist (Index) of all nations: Arabs and Persians. . . ." Aboard *La Capo Bella,* which accommodates all the nationalities of the Mediterranean, colonial encounters are parodied. The episode in which the Captain Gabriello and Taj al-Din look at each other with a mixed feeling of attraction and repulsion suggests the ambivalent relationship between East and West or Europe and its colonized Other. The discovery of the smuggled mummy is a historical testimony of the way the riches of colonized lands were pillaged "and sent to the North."

"Al-Nakhkhas," an often repeated word, is fully explained only at the end of the novel when the narrator cites the etymology of the verb "nakhasa" from *Lisan al-'Arab* (The Arab's Tongue), a dictionary compiled by Ibn Mandur. The two major meanings are "animal trader" and "slaver." Not satisfied with these definitions, the narrator provides his own, saying that "the essence of al-nakhasa" is found in any type of transgressive or subversive act. Taj al-Din links the concept to creativity, which he describes as "the desire to spy on, uncover and penetrate the lives of the others." The identification of the writer with an *a akhkhas* is clear from the beginning of the novel: Taj al-Din is represented as "a thief of images, scenes and emotions! He has become a *nakhkhas,* a collector of slaves, pictures and many small things he does not know." The closing scene presents a portrait of a writer in agony: "Taj al-Din is an eternal nakhkhas writer. He is a creeping snail . . . carrying the shell of his suffering on his back."

The anxiety over reception and artistic sterility, much brooded upon in *al-Taj wa al-khinjar wa al-jasad,* is not really addressed in *al-Nakhkhas,* for Boujah in the later novel is interested in exploring the pursuit of creativity as an act of pleasure. Muhsin Jasim al-Musawi notes Boujah's "understanding of literature as a pleasurable experience, divorced from . . . socio-political concerns." He explains the writer's reference to old manuscripts as a "celebration of embellished and profusely decorated manuscripts within a tradition that had been alive once in Muslim Spain and the Arab west." In his analysis "Une sonde éblouissante de la mémoire Méditerranéenne" (Dazzling Soundings of the Mediterranean Memory) Tunisian academic Hedi Khalil calls the novel "an infinite eulogy of words." Being more powerful that other means of communication, such as painting, photography, or the cinematographic image, the word, insists Khalil, "is much more pliable to fantasy because more volatile and connotative."

The pleasure of writing and the celebration of the written word are articulated within an erotic discourse. The Egyptian novelist Jamal al-Ghitani has described *al-Nakhkhas* as "an erotic novel *par excellence*." Al-Musawi traces back this sexual discourse to the Tunisian Erotica tradition of the thirteenth century. Writing of his novel in "Ecrire l'eau," Boujah qualifies the word "erotic" while linking it exclusively to the act of writing: "I would like to moderate it ['erotic'] by underlining rather its essential playful aspect. We witness here the preludes which make of the writing scene a slippery terrain immersed in a double game of languorous stripping, essentially linked to the writing game."

Contrary to his two previous novels, *al-Nakhkhas* has enjoyed a good critical reception. In his 2003 interview Boujah declared: "I believe that *al-Nakhkhas* is my basic work so far." Although he was pleased with the laudatory reviews of his novel, he was critical of the tenor of Tunisian criticism in his interview in *al-Zaman*: "When Tunisian criticism is unable to grasp a new literary trend, it tries to contain it within laws and frames; this has a negative effect on literary creativity." He went so far as to accuse "the recent critical visions in Tunisia" of having "no legitimacy in discussing new creativity." He described the Tunisian critical scene as divided between academic criticism, only interested in established forms, and the "friendly" criticism provided by newspapers, only based on personal relationships. He called for a middle terrain accommodating "serious academic criticism (which hardly exists) and the common lively criticism (which is hardly serious)."

In his preface to *al-Nakhkhas* the Tunisian academic and poet Muncif al-Whaybi praises the novel in highly laudatory terms: "After al-Mis'adi, whom I believe the father of the modern Tunisian novel, I hardly know any Tunisian novelist who masters both language and narration other than Slaheddine Boujah." Khalil, however, believes that al-Whaybi's preface pours into the same stream of "the excessive, and consequently dubious, enthusiasm with which the novel has been received either by academic criticism or journalistic one." Khalil concludes his exploration of the novel, in which he tries to locate the text within an indigenous literary tradition, by asking whether *al-Nakhkhas* "does not run the risk of looking as a body clad in baggy clothes–a body of writing which is young and euphoric, yet old and frozen." Al-Musawi claims that the evocation of Tunisian heritage in Kairouan "saves the novel from a 'Western' sense of exhaustion."

Interviewed by Karim al-Sharif in October 1996, Boujah announced the completion of his fourth novel–a work dedicated to the city of his birth. In the interview he discussed the title of the new novel, which he called *al-Qa'* (The Bottom): "The original title of *al-Qa',*" he declared, "was 'Qa' al-Madinah' (The Bottom of the City), but I finally opted for *al-Qa'*." In an interview in *al-Adab* (October 2003) he expressed his dissatisfaction with *Radya wa al-sirk* (1997, Radya and the Circus), the title that was imposed by the publisher, Suhayl Idriss. Boujah prefers the title given to the Tunisian edition of the novel, *al-Sirk* (2001, The Circus).

Boujah's concern in *al-Sirk* is quite different from the anxieties he has raised in his two preceding novels. His attempts at exploring the hidden work of the mind change into an attempt at uncovering the secret underworld of Kairouan. The novel presents the dark heart of this sacred city by unveiling its social intrigues, political conspiracies, and sexual revelries. Contrary to his other narratives, there is a clear story in *al-Sirk,* at least in the five first chapters. The reader is able to distinguish between characters and voices, and to follow the threads of a unified plot.

One of the central characters, Radya al-Jammali, keeps a brothel visited by businessmen and distinguished figures in society. She offers wild nights in her big traditional house where all the senses are gratified. Her visitors enjoy food, wine, drugs, dance, and sex. The hedonism of the brothel attracts the poet, Hasan, who falls in love with Maryam, Radya's sister. He gets married to her, but soon realizes that what he once felt for Maryam was enhanced by the sensual atmosphere of the brothel. Once in their own house, she becomes an ordinary woman unable to satisfy his poetic vision of life.

While Hasan is enticed by the artistic side of Radya's house, Maymun al-Najjar, a police inspector, is interested in the amount of information he can obtain there to further his dream of controlling the whole city of Kairouan. He transforms criminals, beggars, and poor workers into informants, creating a huge network to support his ambition. Radya's brothel, a place where all types of deals are concluded, is key to his effort. Maymun's relationship with Radya changes from rivalry to partnership. They even become physically and emotionally intimate.

The plot undergoes a drastic change in the three last chapters of the novel, for while the characters remain the same, clear and recognizable, setting and events become hazy and blurred. In chapter 6 Maymun rallies marginalized groups–prostitutes, criminals, and intellectuals such as Hasan–and leads a disordered march that takes quarters in a cemetery. Maymun is called "the Commander of chaos." Chapter 7 describes the end of the chaos and the establishment of order: Radya is imprisoned (her crime not mentioned); Hasan is banished; and Maymun is suspended from work. Chapter 8 focuses on the creation of a circus where all the major characters present spectacles.

The eight chapters of *al-Sirk* are titled after the various parts of a traditional Tunisian house: "al-zqaq" (the alley), "al-sqifa al-ula" (the first portico), "al-sqifa al-thania" (the second portico), "wasat al-dar" (the courtyard), "al-majlis al-kabir" (a room to meet guests), "al-maqsura" (a rather dark room without windows), "al-mistraq" (a small room to store unused objects), and "al-khukha" (a small door carved in a big gate). While associating the structure of the novel with house architecture, Boujah suggests the metaphorical nature of the house and the novel by the fact that the titles attributed to chapters do not directly correspond to their settings or contents. For instance, chapter 7, "al-Maqsura," does not deal with a dark room without windows but with Maymun's disordered march. In that chapter the sexual chaos reaches its apogee: "Everything is upside down: men and women in a forlorn cemetery. Some of them are drunk, some are intoxicated by drugs, and some are dizzy with the pleasure of the unknown."

In addition to his novels and critical studies, Slaheddine Boujah has published two volumes of short stories—*Sahl al-ghuraba'* (1999, The Valley of Strangers) and *La shaya yahduthu al-an* (2001, Nothing Happens Now). Whether he sets his texts in the liquid world of the Mediterranean, traditional Tunisian houses, or the dark recesses of the mind, Kairouan remains central in Boujah's novels. He can be truly called the writer of Kairouan not only because it is the city of his birth but also because he celebrates it in all his works. More than just a physical setting, Kairouan is Boujah's muse—an originator of stories. Even though Boujah adopts occidental techniques of narration, his writings remain Tunisian at the core as he uses the names of streets, rituals, songs, and culinary recipes to give his works with an indigenous flavor. His novels so claim their Tunisian identity that it is even difficult to place his work under the umbrella of Arabic literature.

Interviews:

Karim al-Sharif, "Hiwar ma'a S. Boujah," *al-Shahid,* 134 (October 1996): 12–15;

Al-Sharif, "Hiwar ma'a S. Boujah," *al-Zaman,* 2 (8 March 1999): 9–12;

Majid al-Samirrai, "Hiwar ma'a S. Boujah," *al-Adab,* 9 October 2003, pp. 13–16.

References:

Khalil Hedi, "Une sonde éblouissante de la mémoire Méditerranéenne," *Ifriquiya: Littérature de Tunisie,* 1 (1997): 83–102;

Muhsin Jasim al-Musawi, *The Postcolonial Arabic Novel: Debating Ambivalence* (Leiden & Boston: Brill, 2003), pp. 372–373.

Assia Djebar
(Fatima-Zohra Imalayène)
(30 June 1936 -)

Boutheina Khaldi
Yale University

BOOKS: *La soif: Roman* (Paris: René Julliard, 1957); translated by Frances Frenaye as *The Mischief* (London: Elek, 1958; New York: Simon & Schuster, 1958);
Les impatients: Roman (Paris: René Julliard, 1958);
Les enfants du nouveau monde (Paris: René Julliard, 1962); translated by Marjolijn de Jager as *Children of the New World* (New York: Feminist Press at the City University of New York, 2005);
Les alouettes naïves (Paris: René Julliard, 1967);
Poèmes pour l'Algérie heureuse (Algiers: SNED, 1969);
Rouge l'aube: Pièce en 4 actes et 10 tableaux, by Djebar and Walid Carn (Algiers: SNED, 1969);
Femmes d'Alger dans leur appartement (Paris: Des Femmes, 1980); translated by Jager as *Women of Algiers in Their Apartment,* afterword by Clarisse Zimra (Charlottesville: University Press of Virginia, 1992);
L'amour, la fantasia (Paris: J.-C. Lattès, 1985); translated by Dorothy S. Blair as *Fantasia: An Algerian Cavalcade* (London: Quartet, 1989);
Ombre sultane (Paris: J.-C. Lattès, 1987); translated by Blair as *A Sister to Scheherazade* (London: Quartet, 1988);
Loin de Médine (Paris: Albin Michel, 1991); translated by Blair as *Far from Madina* (London: Quartet, 1994);
Chronique d'un eté Algerien (Paris: Éditions Plume, 1993);
Vaste est la prison (Paris: Albin Michel, 1995); translated by Betsy Wing as *So Vast the Prison* (New York: Seven Stories Press, 1999);
Le blanc de l'Algérie (Paris: Albin Michel, 1995); translated by Jager and David Kelley as *Algerian White* (New York: Seven Stories Press, 2000);
Oran, langue morte (Arles: Actes Sud, 1997);
Les nuits de Strasbourg (Arles: Actes Sud, 1997);
Ces voix qui m'assiègent (Paris: Albin Michel, 1999);
La femme sans sépulture (Paris: Albin Michel, 2002);

Assia Djebar (from the dust jacket for Algerian White, *2000; Richland County Public Library)*

La disparition de la langue française (Paris: Albin Michel, 2003).

PRODUCED SCRIPTS: *Noubat Nisa' Djebal Chenoua,* motion picture, Women Make Movies, 1979;
La zerda ou les chants de l'oubli, motion picture, Radio Télévision Algérienne, 1982.

Assia Djebar is the most prolific and internationally acclaimed Algerian woman novelist. She is also a screenwriter, playwright, and poet. Djebar's works express her concern with the sociopolitical issues of her time. In her largely autobiographical novels she depicts the struggle of Algerian women to rebel against the stifling lives imposed on them by a patriarchal society.

Fatima-Zohra Imalayène was born on 30 June 1936 in Cherchell, a coastal town west of Algiers, to Tahar Imalhayène, an Algerian Arab, and Bahia Sahraoui, a Berber. As was usual for girls her age, she attended *al-kuttab* (Qur'anic school) from 1937 to 1946; she also attended the French primary school in Mouzaiville in Mitidja where her father taught. From 1946 to 1953 she pursued her secondary studies in Blida and then in Algiers, where she received a baccalaureate in Latin, Greek, and philosophy. In 1954 she enrolled at the Fénelon School in Paris; on 1 November of that year the Algerian war of independence broke out. In 1955 Imalayène became the first Algerian woman to enter the École Normale Supérieure (College of Higher Education) in Sèvres, where she studied history.

Imalayène wrote her first novel, *La soif* (Thirst), in two months in 1956. The half-French, half-Algerian protagonist, Nadia, is an emancipated Westernized girl who tries to seduce her friend's husband to arouse her boyfriend's jealousy. Imalayène was afraid that her father would disapprove of a story about erotic self-indulgence, and in the taxi on the way to the Julliard publishing house she asked her fiancé, Ahmad Ouled-Rouis, to repeat the ninety-nine ritual appeals to Allah so that she could choose one of them as a nom de plume. She selected *djabbar* (omnipotent), but, being in a hurry, she misspelled it on her manuscript as *Djebar* (healer); Assia is a family name. The novel was published in 1957, the year Djebar was expelled from the École Normale Supérieure for joining a student strike for Algerian independence in Paris. Algerian reviewers criticized the novel for its slight plot and for not reflecting the actual political situation or the realities of the Algerian war. Translated into English in 1958 as *The Mischief*, however, the novel was acclaimed by Jean Campbell Jones in *The New York Times* (12 October 1958). Djebar was hailed in France as an Algerian Françoise Sagan; Sagan's novel of teenage rebellion, *Bonjour tristesse* (1954; translated, 1955), had become a best-seller.

Djebar and Ouled-Rouis were married in 1958 and left France for Switzerland and then Tunis. In Tunis, Djebar worked in collaboration with Franz Fanon as a journalist for *al-Moujahid* (The Militant), the newspaper of the Front de Liberation Nationale (National Liberation Front [FLN]) of Algeria. In the summer of 1959 Djebar accompanied the Red Cross on a visit to Algerian refugee camps on the Tunisian border. During this period she studied the history of miracles and, under the supervision of the prominent French historian Louis Massignon, prepared an M.A. thesis on the twelfth-century Tunisian saints 'Aisha and Manoubia.

In September 1959 Djebar began teaching history at the Institute of Literatures in Rabat, Morocco. In the summer of 1960 she wrote the novel *Les enfants du nouveau monde* (1962; translated as *Children of the New World*, 2005); it was mostly inspired by episodes in the war of independence in Blida that Djebar's mother and mother–in-law related to her on a visit to Rabat. The protagonist, Lila, joins her cousin, Bachir, in the fight for independence; she is arrested and tortured by the French, and Bachir is shot for setting a farm on fire.

Djebar returned to Algeria on 1 July 1962 to report for the magazine *L'Express* on the first days of independence. In September she was appointed professor of history at the University of Algiers, but she returned to France in 1965 because the Algerian government had decreed that history was to be taught only in Arabic. Djebar opposed Arabization on the grounds that classical Arabic is an authoritarian language, a language of men. In October 1966, on a visit to her parents in Algiers, she adopted a thirteen-month-old girl named Djalila.

Djebar's novel *Les alouettes naïves* (Innocent Larks) was published in 1967. Nfissa and Rachid, a married couple living in exile in Tunis, are prototypes of the emerging generation that is trying to destroy the stereotypes imposed by patriarchy. When the war for independence breaks out, Rachid leaves the pregnant Nfissa and returns to Algeria to take part. By the end of the novel Nfissa is no longer the *alouette naïve* that Rachid used to call her. She and her heroic sister, Nadjia, are fully involved in the struggle for change.

In 1969 Djebar published *Poèmes pour l'Algérie heureuse* (Poems to the Happy Algeria) and a play, *Rouge l'aube* (Red Is the Dawn), coauthored with Walid Carn, which was performed that same year at the Panafrican Cultural Festival in Algiers. She also adapted and directed many other plays, including Tom Eyen's *The White Whore and the Bit Player* (1968), for her husband's experimental L'Arlequin Theater in Paris. In January 1974 she returned to Algiers to teach French literature and cinema in the French Department of the University of Algiers. She and Ouled-Rouis were divorced in October 1975.

The movie *Noubat nisa' jabal Chenoua* (The Nouba of the Women of Mount Chenoua) was released in 1979 (the *Nouba* is a traditional Algerian song in five movements); a blend of documentary and narrative, it was written, directed, and produced by Djebar in Algerian Arabic. Lila, an expatriate obsessed by memories of the Algerian war for independence, returns to the country fifteen years after the war. There she hears the stories of female Algerian revolutionaries and reflects

Front covers for the 1995 French original and the 1999 English translation of Djebar's novel, narrated by a historian and filmmaker who grew up during the Algerian war of independence (left, Thomas Cooper Library, University of South Carolina; right, Richland County Public Library)

on the little-known but vital role these women played in the war. *Noubat nisa' jabal Chenoua* won the International Critics' Prize at the 1979 Venice Film Festival.

In 1980 Djebar published a collection of short stories, *Femmes d'Alger dans leur appartement* (translated as *Women of Algiers in Their Apartment*, 1992); the title is taken from Eugène Delacroix's 1834 painting of the harem, executed after his visit to Algiers in 1832. In an interview with Clarisse Zimra that is included in an afterword to the English translation, Djebar says that the collection, which includes a wide range of female perspectives, experiences, and dialects, is her first response to the Arabization policy. The stories relate the experiences of peasant and educated Algerian women who participated alongside the men in the struggle against France but were denied access to public life when the war was over. Two of the pieces—the title story and "Les morts parlent" (translated as "The Dead Speak")—are new; the rest are taken from previous works, some of which go back to her Tunisian exile of 1959, and "Nostalgie de la horde" (translated as "Nostalgia of the Horde") is the third part of *Les alouettes naïves*. Djebar told Zimra that mixing new and old material was an attempt "to bring the past in dialogue with the present." Some of the stories are autobiographical: "The Dead Speak" recalls the death of Djebar's grandmother eight days after Algerian independence was declared on 1 July 1962, and "Nostalgia of the Horde" was inspired by Djebar's mother-in-law.

In 1981 Djebar married Malek Alloula, an Algerian poet living in Paris. The following year the film company Pathé-Gaumont asked her to examine, in her capacity as a historian, some old reels stored in a warehouse; they turned out to be newsreels about France's colonies. Out of these newsreels Djebar, in collaboration with the musician Hamed Essayad, wove her second film: *La zerda ou les chants de l'oubli* (1982, The Celebration; or, The Songs of Forgetting). The movie is a celebration of the retrieval of these pieces of the past to the collective memory. It won a special prize as best historical film at the 1982 Berlin Film Festival.

Djebar again made use of her historical training to sift through documents, memoirs, letters, and newspaper articles about the French colonization of Algeria in 1830. The research resulted in her novel *L'amour, la fantasia* (1985; translated by Dorothy S. Blair as *Fantasia: An Algerian Cavalcade*, 1989), which interweaves the history of the French conquest, her memories of the Algerian war for independence, and her own life story. The historical documents begin by describing Algiers as it appears to the invading French fleet; Djebar answers the French accounts by engaging Algerians in a dialogue with the colonizers. The history of the French conquest is interspersed with autobiographical material from Djebar's childhood that holds the text together. The narrator, a girl going to school for the first time, joins her voice with other Algerian women to weave a collective autobiography.

L'amour, la fantasia was followed by *Ombre Sultane* (1987, Sultana's Shadow; translated as *A Sister to Scheherazade*, 1988). To free herself from her passionate love for her husband, whose name is never given in the novel, Isma, the modern, educated narrator, decides to act as matchmaker for him. She chooses Hajila, a traditional cloistered woman, as his second wife and rents and furnishes an apartment for the newlyweds. After her marriage, Hajila becomes fed up with her cloistered life and uncaring husband; she goes outdoors unveiled and unescorted to explore the public gardens and squares of her neighborhood. Through Hajila's mother, Touma, and Isma's aunt, Djebar criticizes the matriarchs who uphold the traditions bequeathed to them by the patriarchy. When Hajila tells Touma that she frequently goes out, Touma says: "Oh bad girl! I'll stay here and keep you shut up at home and keep the Devil away!" When Isma's aunt is informed that Isma will attend a boarding school, she says: "Is she a man? . . . Alas! Everything is changing nowadays, everything is upside down." Through Isma, Djebar condemns the matriarchs, who "From time immemorial have tried to teach us to stifle our voices. 'Keep silent,' they used to recommend, 'and never admit to anything.'" Isma and Hajila do not meet until the end of the novel, when they establish a sense of sisterly solidarity. Isma chooses the *hammam* (Turkish bath) for their meeting, because it is "the only temporary reprieve from the harem." It "offers a secret consolation to sequestered women. . . . This surrogate cocoon providing an escape from the hot house of cloistration."

In the prologue and epilogue Djebar reconfigures the legendary complicity of the heroine of *The Arabian Nights*, Scheherazade, and her sister, Dinarzade, in the relationship between Isma and Hajila by comparing Isma to "a shadow behind the sultan's bride" and Hajila to the sultan's bride. At Scheherazade's request, Dinarzade sleeps in the bridal chamber and wakens Scheherazade every day one hour before daybreak to spin her tales for the sultan and thereby save her own life and the life of her sister. The dual presence of Scheherazade and Dinarzade in the bridal chamber symbolizes the relationship of Isma and Hajila. Isma takes Scheherazade's role, helping Hajila rebel against patriarchy and escape confinement.

In 1991 Djebar published *Loin de Médine* (translated as *Far from Madina*, 1994), a collection of stories about women known for their eloquence, discretion, and fierceness on the battlefield who were given cursory treatment by the seventh- to tenth-century chroniclers Ibn Hisham, Ibn Sa'd, and al-Tabari: the Prophet's wives, his daughter Fatima, the wives of his companions, the Yemenite queen, Umm Hakim, Umm Kulthum, Salma, Sajah, and many others. Djebar rejects the view that men alone create history and build civilizations and shows that politics is not the exclusive preserve of men.

In 1994 Djebar went to Strasbourg on a three-month scholarship and also served as a visiting scholar at the University of California at Berkeley, where she wrote *Vaste est la prison* (1995; translated as *So Vast the Prison*, 1999). The title of the novel is taken from the French translation of an old Berber song: "Vaste est la prison qui m'écrase / D'ou me viendras-tu, délivrance?" (So vast the prison crushing me / Release, where will you come from?). The narrator is Isma, the character from *Ombre Sultane;* she is a historian and filmmaker who grew up during the Algerian war of independence. The novel is divided into three sections. In the first section, set in the 1970s, Isma falls in love with a young musicologist she calls "the Beloved." When she tells her husband, Leo, he beats her, and she flees. In the second section Isma recounts a series of anecdotes about the attempts made over several centuries to decipher a bilingual inscription on a stele at Dougga concerning the history of Carthage. The third section alternates between chapters describing Isma's semidocumentary film project, *Arable Woman,* and chapters describing her family history: Isma's grandmother was married at an early age to a rich old man; in early childhood Isma played with the daughters of a traditional Algerian chief; and her brother was imprisoned by the French during the war of independence.

Front covers for the 1995 French original and the 2000 English translation of Djebar's novel about the atrocities committed during the civil war that broke out in Algeria in 1992 (left, Thomas Cooper Library, University of South Carolina; right, Richland County Public Library)

Le blanc de l'Algérie (translated as *Algerian White*, 2000) was published in the same year as *Vaste est la prison*. In this novel and her next, *Oran, langue morte* (1997, Oran, Dead Language), Djebar examines the atrocities of the civil war that broke out in Algeria in 1992.

Between 1996 and 2002 Djebar received many awards and honors, among them the 1996 Neustadt International Prize for Contributions to World Literature for *L'amour, la fantasia*. In 1997 she received the Marguerite Yourcenar Prize in Boston and the International Prize of Palmi in Italy. That same year she was appointed director of the center of French and Francophone Studies at Louisiana State University.

In *Les nuits de Strasbourg* (1997, Strasbourg Nights) Djebar reacts indirectly to the situation in Algeria through the love story of Thelja and François.

In her talk "Writing in Europe," given on 28 November 1998 at the House of World Cultures in Berlin, she said:

> It will not surprise you that I wrote this novel in 1997 in Louisiana on hearing from a great distance of the massacres of villagers in my land. After two books about death, *Le blanc de l'Algérie* and *Oran, langue morte,* my first reaction to the bloody present was to write in more detail about those nine imaginary nights of love in Strasburg. To be frank, my *"Fantaisie"* was in a sense pure therapy.

In 1999 Djebar was inducted into the Académie Royale de Langue et de Littérature Françaises de Belgique (Royal Academy of French Language and Literature of Belgium). On 28 October 2000 she won the prestigious Peace Prize of the German Book Trade. In

2002 she was awarded an honorary doctorate by Concordia University in Montreal. Also that year she published the novel *La femme sans sépulture* (The Woman without a Sepulcher), a mixture of fact and fiction about Zoulika, a heroine of the Algerian resistance. In preparation for writing the work Djebar interviewed Zoulika's daughter and many of her friends. It was followed a year later by the novel *La disparition de la langue française* (The Disappearance of the French Language), a novel about a man who returns to Algeria after twenty years in France to find it torn by civil war.

Since 2002 Assia Djebar has been Silver Chair Professor of French and Francophone Studies at New York University. In 2005 she became a member of the French Academy and received the Naples Pablo Neruda Prize. In January 2006 she won the Turin Grinzane Cavour Prize, and on 22 June the French Academy held a ceremony in her honor. Djebar is frequently mentioned as a candidate for the Nobel Prize in literature.

References:

"Assia Djebar," *culturebase.net: The international artist database* <http://www.culturebase.net/artist.php?436> (accessed 5 September 2008);

Mary Jean Green, "Dismantling the Colonizing Text: Anne Herbert's *Kamouraska* and Assia Djebar's *l'Amour, la Fantasia*," *French Review,* 66 (May 1993): 959–966;

Rafika Merini, "Djebar's *Les enfants du nouveau monde* and *Les alouettes naives:* At Last, Liberation, Peace, and Growth," in her *Two Major Francophone Women Writers, Assia Djébar and Leila Sebbar: A Thematic Study of Their Works* (New York: Peter Lang, 1999), pp. 87–115;

Priscilla Ringrose, *Assia Djebar: In Dialogue with Feminisms* (Amsterdam & New York: Rodopi, 2006).

Gamal al-Ghitani
(9 May 1945 –   )

Ayman A. El-Desouky
School of Oriental and African Studies, University of London

BOOKS: *Awraq shabb 'asha mundhu alf 'am* (Cairo: Dar al-Tali'a, 1969);

Ard–ard (Cairo: Al-Hay'ah al-Misriyyah al-'Ammah li al-Kitab, 1972);

Al-Misriyyun wa al-harb (Cairo: Ruz al-Yusuf, 1974);

Al-Zayni Barakat (Damascus: Wazarat al-Thaqafah wa al-Irshad al-Qawmi, 1974); translated by Farouk Abdel Wahab as *Zayni Barakat* (London: Viking, 1988);

Al-hisar min thalath jihat (Damascus: Ittihad al-Kuttab al-'Arab, 1975);

Hurras al-bawwabah al-sharqiyyah (Cairo: Maktabat Madbuli, 1975);

Al-Zuwayl (Baghdad: Wazarat al-I'lam, 1975);

Waqa'i' harat al-Za'farani (Cairo: Dar al-Thaqafah al-Jadidah, 1976); translated by Peter O'Daniel as *Incidents in Zafrani Alley* (Cairo: General Egyptian Book Organization, 1986);

Hikayat al-gharib (Cairo: Dar Majallat al-Ida'a wa al-Tilifizyun, 1976);

Al-Rifa'i (Cairo: Al-Hay'ah al-Misriyyah al-'Ammah li al-Kitab, 1977);

Dhikr ma jara (Cairo: Maktabat Madbuli, 1978);

Khitat al-Ghitani (Beirut: Dar al-Masira, 1980);

Mustafa Amin yatadhakkar (Cairo: Maktabat Madbuli, 1980);

Naguib Mahfouz yatadhakkar (Beirut: Dar al-Masira, 1980)–includes sections translated by Mona N. Mikhail as "From Naguib Mahfouz Remembers," in *Naguib Mahfouz, from Regional Fame to Global Recognition*, edited by Michael Beard and Adnan Haydar (Syracuse, N.Y.: Syracuse University Press, 1993), pp. 37–52;

Kitab al-tajalliyat, 3 volumes (Cairo: Dar al-Mustaqbal al-'Arabi, 1983–1987);

Malamih al-Qahira fi alf sana (Cairo: Dar al-Hilal, 1983);

Muntasaf layl al-ghurbah (Cairo: Al-Hay'ah al-Misriyyah al-'Ammah li al-Kitab, 1984);

Qahiriyyat: Asbilat al-Qahira (Cairo: Maktabat Madbuli, 1984);

Ahrash al-madina (Cairo: Mu'assasat Akhbar al-Yawm, 1985);

Ithaf al-zaman bi hikayat Jalabi al-sultan (Cairo: Dar al-Mustaqbal al-'Arabi, 1985)–includes "Al-Mahsul," translated by Mohammed Shaheen as "The Crop," in *Sardines and Oranges: Short Stories from North Africa,* edited by Margaret Obank (London: Banipal Books, 2005);

Risalah fi al-saba wa al-wajd (Cairo: Dar al-Hilal, 1987);

Thimar al-waqt (Cairo: Dar al-Hilal, 1989);

Risalat al-basa'ir fi al-masa'ir (Cairo: Dar al-Hilal, 1989);

Shath al-madinah (Cairo: Dar al-Hilal, 1990);

Asfar al-asfar (Kuwait: Dar Su'ad Al-Sabbah, 1992);

Asfar al-mushtaq: mutataliyat fi al-makan wa al-zaman (Kuwait: Dar Su'ad Al-Sabbah, 1992);

Hatif al-maghib (Cairo: Dar al-Hilal, 1992);

Min daftar al-'ishq wa al-ghurbah (Cairo: Al-Hay'ah al-Misriyyah al-'Ammah li al-Kitab, 1993);

Nafthat masdur (Kuwait: Dar Su'ad Al-Sabbah, 1993);

Mutun al-Ahram (Cairo: Dar Sharqiyyat, 1994); translated by Humphrey Davies as *Pyramid Texts* (Cairo: American University in Cairo Press, 2007);

Khulsat al-kara: Dafatir al-tadwin: Al-Daftar al-Awwal (Cairo: Dar Sharqiyyat, 1996);

Shatf al-nar (Cairo: Al-Hay'ah al-'Ammah li Qusur al-Thaqafah, 1996);

Hikayat al-mu'assasah (Beirut: Mu'assasat al-Intishar al-'Arabi, 1997);

Al-Khutut al-fasila: Yawmiyyat al-qalb al-maftuh (Cairo: Al-Dar al-Misriyyah al-Lubnaniyyah, 1997);

Muntaha al-talab ila turath al-'Arab: Dirasat fi al-turath (Cairo: Dar al-Shuruq, 1997);

Mutribat al-ghurub (Giza: Markaz al-Hadarah al-'Arabiyyah, 1997);

Sifr al-bunyan (Cairo: Dar al-Hilal, 1998);

Afaq al-dhakirah (Cairo: Nahdat Misr, 1998);

Dana fa-tadalla: Dafatir al-tadwin: Al-Daftar al-thani (Cairo: Markaz al-Hadarah al-'Arabiyyah, 1998);

Qut al-'uyun (Cairo: Nahdat Misr, 1998);

Yawmiyyat al-hajj (Cairo: Nahdat Misr, 1998);

Masarrat al-ruh (Cairo: Nahdat Misr, 1999);
Al-tariq ila al-jihat al-asliyyah (Cairo: Nahdat Misr, 1999);
The Cairo of Naguib Mahfouz, photographs by Britta Le Va, foreword by Naguib Mahfouz (Cairo: American University in Cairo Press, 1999);
Ibra' al-dhimmah (Cairo: Dar al-Shuruq, 2000);
Muqarabat al-abad (Cairo: Nahdat Misr, 2000);
Hikayat al-khabi'a (Cairo: Dar al-Shuruq, 2002);
Rashahat al-Hamra': Dafatir al-tadwin: Al-Daftar al-thalith (Cairo: Dar al-Shuruq, 2003);
Nawafidh al-nawafidh: Dafatir al-tadwin: Al-Daftar al-rabi' (Cairo: Dar al-Hilal, 2004);
Nithar al-mahwu: Dafatir al-tadwin: Al-Daftar al-khamis (Cairo: Dar al-Shuruq, 2006);
Al-majalis al-mahfuziyyah (Cairo: Dar al-Shuruq, 2006);
Rinn: Dafatir al-tadwin: Al-Daftar al-sadis (Cairo: Dar al-Shuruq, 2008).

Collection: *Al-A'mal al-qasasiyyah al-kamilah,* 6 volumes (Cairo: Al-Hay'ah al-Misriyyah al-'Ammah li al-Kitab, 1990–1996).

Editions in English: "Buzzing," translated by Amira Nowaira, in *Egyptian Tales and Short Stories of the 1970s and 1980s,* edited by William M. Hutchins (Cairo: American University in Cairo Press, 1987), pp. 151–157;
A Distress Call: Short Stories by Gamal al-Ghitani, translated by Soad Naguib (Cairo: State Publishing House, 1997);
"An Invitation," in *Under the Naked Sky: Short Stories from the Arab World,* edited and translated by Denys Johnson-Davies (Cairo: American University in Cairo Press, 2000), pp. 46–56;
"An Enlightenment to the People of this World," in *Modern Arabic Fiction: An Anthology,* edited by Salma Khadra Jayyusi (New York: Columbia University Press, 2005), pp. 318–326.

OTHER: Mustafa Mahmud, *Al'ab al-sirk al-siyasi,* edited by al-Ghitani (Cairo: Mu'assasat Akhbar al-Yawm, 1991);
Abu Hayyan al-Tawhidi, *Khulasat al-Tawhidi: Mukhtarat min nathr Abu Hayyan al-Tawhidi,* edited by al-Ghitani (Cairo: Al-Majlis al-A'la li al-Thaqafah, 1995);
Al-qisas al-fa'izah fi musabaqat adab al-harb, edited by al-Ghitani (Cairo: Al-Hay'ah al-Misriyyah al-'Ammah li al-Kitab, 1996).

SELECTED PERIODICAL PUBLICATIONS– UNCOLLECTED: *Hikayat muwazaf kabir, al-Muharrir* (1965);
Hikayat muwazaf saghir, al-Jumhur al-Jadid (1965);
"Ba'd mukawwinat 'alami al-riwa'i," *al-Adab,* 2–3 (February–March 1980): 113–114;

"Mushkilat al-ibda' al-riwa'i 'inda jil al-sittiniyyat wa al-sab'iniyyat," by al-Ghitani, Sabri Musa, Sonallah Ibrahim, Yusuf al-Qa'id, I'tidal 'Uthman, and Muhammad Mustafa Badawi, *Fusul,* 2, no. 2 (1982): 208–214;
"Isharat . . . Ila ma'rifat al-bidayat," *al-Adab,* 4–6 (April–June 1990): 80–97.

The development of Gamal al-Ghitani's theory of the novel was inspired by his formative years growing up in old Cairo. His ambition to grasp the procession of historical time in a single, bounded space has led to his acclaim as one of the most prominent contemporary Arab writers. He is generally credited with creating a new type of narrative discourse that is uniquely Arabic and Islamic, which he called "fann al-qass al-Islami" (the art of Islamic narration). In al-Ghitani's view, the temporality of narrative movement is the essential feature of Islamic narration, and it is most obvious in the basic order of words *(mythos)* and the mixing of classical and modern registers. Even the spatial relation in Islamic art is seen in terms of temporal movement: the relation of part to whole as the movement of that part's fulfilment in the whole, which endows it with its meaning. Time, in personal experience as in narrative, moves forward with the act of pursuing one's own destiny, the relationship to which is seen as one of part to whole. This crucial relation of part to whole is ultimately seen by al-Ghitani as the grounding aesthetic vision which the Qur'anic verse offers to all Arabo-Islamic arts, including the art of prose.

The remarkable persistence with which he has pursued his project has won him wide acclaim and severe criticism. Al-Ghitani was also one of the founding members of the radical and highly politicized movement famously known as Gallery 68, spearheaded by a group of Egyptian writers and intellectuals in the 1960s, the crucial decade of revolutionary ideals, nationalism, and pan-Arabism. Since then he has been active on the Arab and Egyptian literary and intellectual scenes. Al-Ghitani is perhaps best known outside of Egypt for his most successful experiment with the art of the novel *al-Zayni Barakat* (1974; translated as *Zayni Barakat,* 1988). He has represented Egypt in many literary conferences and symposia held in Italy, Mexico, France, Iraq, Morocco, the Netherlands, Tunisia, Algeria, Russia, Poland, and the United States. His works have been translated into French, German, Russian, Chinese, Spanish, Italian, Dutch, Hungarian, Polish, and English. He has been awarded many prizes, including the Egyptian State Prize for the Novel (1980), the State Medal for the Arts and Sciences of the First Degree (1987), the prestigious French Chevalier de l'Ordre des Arts et des Lettres (1987), the French Prix de l'amitié

Title page for the 1988 English translation of Gamal al-Ghitani's 1974 novel, al-Zayni Barakat, his most celebrated achievement (Emory University Library)

franco-arabe (2005), and the Egyptian State Prize for Literature (2007). In 1985 he began his career as a literary journalist, having become head of the cultural section of the daily al-Akhbar (News of the Day), with his own column, and, soon after, chief editor of the paper's book monthly, Kitab al-Yawm (Book of the Day). Since 1993 he has been chief editor of the influential weekly literary review Akhbar al-Adab (Literature News).

Gamal Ahmad al-Ghitani 'Ali was born on 9 May 1945 in Juhaina, a village in the Governorate of Souhag, Upper Egypt. Pursuing a job as a civil servant, his father moved the family to Cairo, and his mother continued as homemaker. The details of his parents' move to Cairo, his childhood, education, and intellectual and artistic maturation (up to the age of forty) are interspersed in his three-volume, highly nuanced, semi-autobiographical novel, Kitab al-tajalliyat (1983–1987,

The Book of Revelations). He grew up in Old Cairo, and for thirty years he lived in al-Gamaliyyah—a part of town made famous by the novels of Naguib Mahfouz, the 1988 Nobel laureate.

lAl-Ghitani received his education in public schools in Old Cairo: Abd al-Rahman Katkhuda Elementary, al-Gamaliyyah Elementary, and Muhammad 'Ali. In 1959 he entered al-Abbasiyyah Secondary School, where he served an apprenticeship in the arts of oriental carpets and graduated with a diploma in the art of carpet painting in 1962. As a teenager he developed an interest in reading and writing. He wrote a short story, "Nihayat al-sikkir" (The Drunkard Meets His End), as early as 1959, but it was never published. In 1961 he put together his first collection of short stories, which he titled "al-Masakin" (Poor People) after Fyodor Dostoevsky's novel Bednye liudi (1846; translated as Poor Folk, 1887). He submitted the collection to the Egyptian Organization for Authorship and Publications, but it was not published.

At sixteen al-Ghitani met Mahfouz, already a renowned writer in Egypt, and the two formed a strong relationship based on mentorship, friendship, and a common love of Cairo. Al-Ghitani and Mahfouz shared the habit of visiting their old haunts, most notably the Husayn Mosque area. Al-Ghitani's intimate knowledge of Old Cairo, his ceaseless peregrinations in its vicinity, and his subsequent interest in the arts prepared al-Ghitani for his career as a writer and novelist. His literary sensibilities were shaped by his fascination with Arabo-Islamic history, decorative and graphic arts, and classical narratives.

Despite his initial setback with publishing, al-Ghitani persevered and started to publish short stories in Egyptian and Arab newspapers as early as July 1963. In 1965 he published two serialized novels in Lebanese newspapers: Hikayat muwazaf kabir (Tales of a Senior Civil Servant) in al-Muharrir (The Editor) and Hikayat muwazaf saghir (Tales of a Junior Civil Servant) in al-Jumhur al-Jadid (The New Jumhur). He also wrote three novels between 1963 and 1969 that were never published: "Dhahab al-kharif al-damawi" (Departure of the Bloody Autumn), "Mahkamat al-ayam" (The Days' Court) and "Habs ghiyabi" (Sentenced in Absentia). Two of the novels, still in manuscript form, were lost when he was arrested in 1966 for his Marxist leanings and underground political activities. He was released six months later, but the experience of detention and torture seems to have left strong marks on him. Ultimately, only one story written before 1967 was published in book form, "al-Maghul" (The Moguls), which appeared in his second short-story collection, Ard–ard (1972, Land–Land). In 1969 al-Ghitani published his first book, Awraq shabb 'asha mundhu alf 'am (Papers of a

Young Man from a Thousand Years Ago). In this short-story collection he turns to history, partly to escape the present, partly as a way to address present concerns while circumventing the censor. He writes against the backdrop of 1967, when frustration and disillusionment pervaded the Arab world, then reeling from the Israeli defeat of Arab forces in the Six-Day War. One of the first significant fruits of the experience was his story "Hidayat ahl al-wara li ba'd mimma jara fi al-miqshara" (Enlightening the People with Regard to Some of What Transpired inside the Miqshara), included in his first collection *Awraq shabb 'asha mundhu alf 'am*. The story presents excerpts from an old scroll found in one of the mosques in the old quarters of al-Gamaliyyah that includes the memoirs of the overseer of the Miqshara prison, a notorious establishment in the time of the Mamluks, perhaps toward the end of their rule in Egypt in the sixteenth century. The story was submitted to the Egyptian daily *al-Masa'* (Evening Post) and, according to al-Ghitani, apparently passed the censor because it was taken as an authentic discovery. The title of the story, which rhymes in the style of premodern Arabic works, together with its language and narrative techniques all emulate the style of medieval Arabic chronicles and works of historiography. In particular, the story, and others like it in the collection, was inspired by the work of the historian Muhammad Ibn Iyas, who witnessed the fall of Mamluk Egypt to the Ottomans in 1517 and chronicled the events in his *Bada'i' al-zuhur fi waqa'i' al-duhur* (The Best Accounts of the Events of the Times).

Al-Ghitani found in Ibn Iyas's work and times a historical precedent to the oppressive 1960s, but more crucially he was attracted to Iyas's language, varying style of description, and his coupling of patriotic sentiment with a cool, observant eye. The inspiration of Ibn Iyas led him to other medieval chronicles and works from the classical genres of historiography, geography and *khitat* literature, travel literature, Sufi works, and the various medieval compendia of *'aja'ib* (Marvelous Occurrences), *ukhrawiyyat* (Apocalyptic) and *adab* (mannerist) literature, as well as traditional popular genres such as the Arabian Nights and medieval oral epics. The success of the experiment and favorable reception by critics also led him to the composition of more stories in similar style to "al-Maghul" and "Hidayat ahl al-wara li ba'd mimma jara fi al-miqshara." Mahmud Amin al-'Alim—a prominent Egyptian writer, Marxian literary critic, and editor of the Egyptian daily *Akhbar al-Yawm* (News of the Day)—took notice of al-Ghitani's first story collection. He invited the author to work as a journalist at *Akhbar al-Yawm*, shortly after he read the book, in 1969.

Although al-Ghitani continued writing in the 1970s, with several short-story collections and novels appearing throughout the decade, he did not lose his connection with his first career as a carpet painter, serving as Secretary for the Egyptian Cooperative of Manufacturers and Artists of *Khan al-Khalili* in 1972. In 1974 he published what many consider his masterpiece, *al-Zayni Barakat,* his single most translated work, in which he achieves an intertextual narrative style and a mature vision of history in a fully fledged Arabic novel, beyond traditional social realism or the experimental novel. The novel is based on the historical figure of al-Zayni Barakat, whose career is summed up in a few enigmatic lines in Ibn Iyas's *Bada'i' al-zuhur fi waqa'i' al-duhur*. Barakat rises to power in the last days of the final Mamluk sultan, al-Ghuri, before his defeat at the hands of the Ottomans in the battle of Marj Dabiq in 1516–1517, which also forms the temporal focus of the novel. After the defeat of the sultan, Barakat continued to rise in prominence, leading al-Ghitani to regard him as the archetype of the political opportunist.

Al-Ghitani clearly encourages an allegorical reading of his novel by incorporating into his depiction of fifteenth-century political turmoil such features as the office of the chief-of-spies and a closely knit network of secret service and spying agents, who belong to post-1967 Egypt. And critics and general readers received *al-Zayni Barakat* as a symbolic treatment of the era dominated by the Egyptian leader Gamal Abdel Nasser. The correspondence between the two historical moments—as between al-Ghitani and Ibn Iyas as narrators who share affinities despite historical distance—is fully utilized by al-Ghitani. The character al-Zayni Barakat appears in only one scene; but the novel is structured through reports about him that also vividly re-create a turbulent period in Egyptian history.

Al-Zayni Barakat is formally divided into six sections, with each given the title of *suradiq* (a traditional canopy or makeshift pavilion); each section references historical or fictitious sources and parodies a whole range of styles and genres, varying or mixing them in the reports and accounts of the different characters. The narrative is framed with the firsthand accounts of a Venetian traveler, Viasconti Gianti, who offers the only instances of first-person narrative, and one of whose notable friends is Ibn Iyas, who grants Gianti the permission to quote from his accounts.

Al-Zayni Barakat is perhaps the only work by al-Ghitani that can be considered a historical novel, for it has a consistently medieval setting and historical figures. And even then, when the novel is compared to other historical novels proper—for example, Moroccan Bin Salim Himmish's *Majnun al-hukm* (1990, Power Crazed) or Mahfouz's early novels on Ancient Egypt,

Front cover for the 1986 English translation of al-Ghitani's 1976 novel Waqa'i' harat al-Za'farani, which the translator calls an "anti-epic" work because it focuses on "the ignominious behaviour of anti-heroes" (Thomas Cooper Library, University of South Carolina)

'Abath al-aqdar (1939; translated as Khufu's Wisdom, 2003), Radubis (1943; translated as Rhadopis of Nubia, 2003) and Kifah Tibah (1944; translated as Thebes at War, 2003)–al-Ghitani clearly subverts the conventions of the historical novel through his deployment of various genres and narrative techniques and the fact that the main character only appears once in the novel. Al-Ghitani's subsequent novels break away from the traditions of the historical novel in many ways.

In the 1970s al-Ghitani published wartime studies, interviews, and narrative accounts, notably Ard–ard in 1972 and al-Misriyyun wa al-harb (1974, Egyptians and the War), as well as novels and short-story collections. The stories and novels of the 1970s, including the collection al-Hisar min thalath jihat (1975, Under Siege in Three Directions), the novel al-Zuwayl (1975), the collection Hikayat al-gharib (1976, Tales of al-Gharib), the novel al-Rifa'i (1977), and the collection Dhikr ma jara (1978, Chronicles of Transpired Events), set a pattern that characterizes much of al-Ghitani's career, as he has tended to alternate between narratives in the realist mode, delivered in a highly charged language and a variety of narrative techniques reminiscent of classical historiographical or mystical discourses, and actual pseudo-historical narratives almost entirely in the style of medieval sources. Some of the short stories inspired later novels. "Waqa'i' harat al-Tabalawi" (Incidents in Al-Tabalawi's Alley), for instance, was developed into the novel Waqa'i' Harat al-Za'farani (1976; translated as Incidents in Zafrani Alley, 1986), which was written in the style of medieval chronicles. The collection Dhikr ma jara introduced material explored again in the novel Khitat al-Ghitani (1980, The Khitat of al-Ghitani). Both works were modeled after the medieval khitat, exemplified by the Khitat of al-Maqrizi (d. 1422), a purely Arabic genre that anticipates sociological novels such as 'Ali Mubarak's al-Khitat al-Tawfiqiyya (1887–1889) and Muhammad Kurd 'Ali's Khitat al-Sham (1925–1928).

After the death of his father around 1980, al-Ghitani began a period of intense soul-searching, and his writing is marked by the invocation as well as interrogation of figures of authority in his life, especially Gamal Abdel Nasser. In 1983 al-Ghitani published the first of three volumes of his semiautobiographical novel, Kitab al-tajalliyat (1983, 1985, 1987, The Book of Revelations). The three volumes are called asfar, the term reserved for the books of the Torah and also used in mystical treatises. The first sifr (the singular form of asfar) offers meditations and revelatory fragments on death and metaphors of parting, travels, and exile. The narrative is delivered in the first person, and the speaking "I" is eventually addressed and named Gamal. The second sifr is arranged into maqamat or sufi stations of spiritual attainment, while the third sifr is arranged into ahwal or existential sufi states. The novel does not treat events in any chronological order, nor does it document events in the life of the author. Rather, strong moments and key references, recognizable in the context of al-Ghitani's life, are offered in the texture of dense and suggestive accounts of emotions and personal meditations. Visions of Nasser occur in the novel alongside many strong demiurgic figures for Gamal, the young main character. The character Gamal has no ambitions to emulate Nasser; rather, he identifies the euphoric periods of Nasser's Egypt in the 1960s with strong moments in his life and his relations with his father. The demiurgic impulse leads Gamal to meditate on strong human types and historical figures, all of whom serve as reflections of the figure of the father.

Kitab al-tajalliyat, which al-Ghitani began partly in response to his father's death, also reveals his increasing interest in the richness of the Arabic language, particularly as it is used in Sufi or Islamic mystical discourses. Al-Ghitani was particularly impressed by the works of

Muhiyi al-Din ibn 'Arabi (1165–1240), whose influence can be detected in many of his works but in particular in *Kitab al-tajalliyat*, where Ibn 'Arabi appears as the personal guide to the protagonist. The title of the novel, with its evocation of the biblical Book of Revelations, is appropriate for a work that has historiographical, mythical, and metaphorical dimensions. Emphasizing the mysteries of personal and human destiny, the novel offers long meditations on the body, death and exile, time (biographical and historical) and space (real and imagined). Personal experiences merge with historical events as al-Ghitani creates a narrative notable for his protagonist's intense personal ambition and self-probing, firm conviction in the continuities in history, impossible desire to overcome time and its discontents, and belief in the power of language.

A key exchange in *Kitab al-tajalliyat* occurs between Jamal and Sayyidah Zaynab, the sister of Iman al-Husayn. Sayyidah Zaynab and Imam al-Husayn, the children of Imam 'Ali, are revered by Shiite Muslims, as well as by Sunni Egyptians. The mosques and shrines of the sister and brother are the most visited in Egypt, and Egyptians appeal to them in times of need. In the Egyptian popular imagination Sayyidah Zaynab and Iman al-Husayn preside over a tribunal, not unlike the Osiris and Isis of ancient Egyptian myth, which al-Ghitani often cites as one of the main examples of continuities in Egyptian culture and history. Jamal appeals to Sayyidah Zaynab as *ra'isat al-diwan* (She-Who-Presides-over-the-Tribunal):

> ... I heard my name summoned from an unknown direction, I pulled myself together and stood in awe, quiet and expectant.
> What is your wish? I said: I seek the presence of *ra'isat al-diwan*.
> What is your wish? I said: My burden is unbearable, but I shall briefly state my wish: My wish is to retrieve what has irretrievably transpired. It was then said to me: your wish is difficult to grant.
> What have you left behind you, Jamal? I said: mortal existence and a desire for immortality. What perplexes you? I said: impermanence. And what else? She asked. I said: that which disintegrates, vanishes. And what else? She asked. I said: No faith remains unshaken. And what else? She persisted. I said: Having consecrated myself ever to be wishful only to witness the passing of time before wishes ever came true. She paused. I withdrew and kept silent.
> *Ra'isat al-diwan* then broke the silence and said: Because you have shown initiative and attempted, because you have sought and stood fast therein, there shall be revealed to you "part of the part" and not "whole from the whole". . . . (Translated by Ayman A. El-Desouky)

This exchange is composed in the manner of mystical discourses and revelations, particularly those of Muhammad Ibn 'Abd al-Jabbar al-Niffari in the tenth century. Al-Ghitani makes use of the historical layering of sensibilities embedded in the language itself. Although he culls from ancient sources, he is always focused on the living legacy, on popular lore or surviving cultural practices. By recasting personal or historical concerns in classical forms of expression, he encourages his reader to ponder rather than to argue or rationalize.

Among al-Ghitani's most notable works in the 1980s is his series of studies on the historical monuments of Cairo, inspired by his readings in traditional sources and his preparations for his literary compositions, which came out in two volumes, *Malamih al-Qahira fi alf sana* (1983, Features of Cairo over a Thousand Years) and *Qahiriyyat: Asbilat al-Qahira* (1984, Cairine Features: Medieval Fountainheads). In 1985 he published the short-story collection *Ithaf al-zaman bi hikayat Jalabi al-sultan* (1985, Astonishing Signs of the Ages in the Tale of Sultan Jalabi), which presents personal destinies in contemporary Egypt in classical registers. In 1987 he published *Risalah fi al-saba wa al-wajd* (A Treatise on Love and Passion), which recasts the details of an amorous encounter abroad in the style of medieval treatises on love, mystical love poetry, and the *ghazal* (a short lyric poem, usually amatory, written in couplets using a single rhyme). His final work of the decade, *Risalat al-basa'ir fi al-masa'ir* (1989, A Treatise on the Insights Obtained into Human Destinies), again treats the fates of contemporary Egyptians in parodic styles, drawing on a variety of classical discursive practices.

In his article "Isharat . . . Ila ma'rifat al-bidayat" (1990, Intimations . . . Toward the Knowledge of Beginnings) al-Ghitani singles out *Shath al-madinah* (1990, The Wiles of the City) and the then not-yet-published *Hatif al-maghib* (1992, The Call at Sunset) as the turning point in his relationship to language, for he believed that in these works he achieved linguistic mastery over the different narrative styles with which he had long been experimenting and was able to appropriately vary his style according to the demands of each work. *Shath al-madinah* follows the adventures and misadventures of a man attending a conference in an unspecified European college town. The theme of personal quest is heightened by his loss of his documents of identification. *Hatif al-maghib,* on the other hand, presents the account of a medieval journey in quest of knowledge, of self-knowledge, rendered in the manner of *'aja'ib,* or journey-to-fantastic-lands literature. Other notable volumes by al-Ghitani in the 1990s include two travel memoirs with medieval rhyming titles, best described as personal meditations written in the manner of medieval travelers: *Asfar al-asfar* (1992, Travel Biblia) and *Asfar al-mushtaq: mutataliyat fi al-makan wa al-zaman* (1992, Wanderings of the Passionate: Narrative Sequences in Space and in Time). Al-Ghitani's views on continuities in history and on classical Arabic sources are outlined in his study *Muntaha al-talab ila turath al-'Arab: Dirasat fi al-turath* (1997, The Ultimate Quest for the Traditions of the Arabs: Studies in the Sources of the Tradition).

Since the 1990s al-Ghitani's novels have been marked by a strong and consistent, if somewhat anomalous, literary ambition, for while working within a non-Arabic or Western genre, he insists on the importance and necessity of drawing on traditional Arabic prose and narrative genres. Moreover, he does so in a conscious effort to endow the Arabic novel with a cultural specificity that sets it apart from the forms of the novel in other cultures. Two of al-Ghitani's most successful books, which explore the same theme and deal with ancient Egypt and are thoroughly Arab and Arabic in their ethos and style, are *Mutun al-Ahram* (1994; translated as *Pyramid Texts*, 2007) and *Sifr al-bunyan* (1998, The Book of Raising Edifices). In both books the stories of ancient Egypt become ways for al-Ghitani to explore the idea of monumentality—that which survives both in time and in space. The marrying of word and architectural form—both in the language scripts and in monumental inscriptions and the arrangement of word and image in mortuary complexes, temples and commemorative stelae and murals—is one of the hallmarks of ancient Egyptian cultural achievement. Al-Ghitani's ambition for a uniquely Arabic art of prose and his fascination with architecture naturally led him to ancient Egypt, and particularly to the Pyramids, as the ultimate trope.

In *Mutun al-Ahram* al-Ghitani follows in the footsteps of earlier figures, such as Abu Ja'far Muhammad al-Idrisi (d. 1251) and Ahmad Ibn 'Ali al-Maqrizi (d. 1422) and, indeed, all Arab scholars and historians until Rifa'ah Rafi' al-Tahtawi (1801–1874) by Arabizing and Islamizing the history of the Pyramids and their abiding symbolism. He relies exclusively on pre–Modern Arabic sources for his accounts of the Pyramids and the web of personal destinies woven in and around them. In *Sifr al-bunyan* al-Ghitani offers a series of narratives, each of which deals with a different kind of architectural form or edifice, but his approach to his material is the same as for *Mutun al-Ahram*. In his exploration of monumentality al-Ghitani creates his own style by creatively engaging the works of historians, travelers, geographers, mannerists, commentators and compilers. He does not seek simply to reconstruct, appropriate, adapt, or allegorize his historical subjects—the conventional techniques of the historical novelist—but instead seeks what he describes as *yuhawiurhum ibda'iyyan* (creative dialogue).

Mutun al-Ahram is arranged episodically into *mutun*, texts or, as in the original Pyramid Texts, utterances. Just as al-Ghitani views the individual Qur'anic verse as a complete narrative unit, each *matn*, or utterance in the novel is a complete and independent narrative unit, or so it appears at first reading. The Arabic term *matn* also suggests the body of a text, as opposed to marginal commentaries. Each *matn* therefore awaits its commentary, just as the mummy, its body enshrined and its destiny inscribed, awaits its resurrection. Each text introduces and follows the threads of one or more characters whose lives and destinies are mysteriously and powerfully linked to one or more of the Pyramids. These characters, it should be noted, belong to different historical periods and hail from different regions. What unites them across time and space, history and geography, are their common but diverging destinies, which converge on the shape of the Pyramid, its physical properties and spiritual powers. The tenth text, which marks the end of narrative proper, offers the utterance that unites them: "It is as if they were gathered to a known appointment, even if time had sundered their lives" (translated by El-Desouky). In the last four *mutun* (11–14) the utterances become more pointed and proclamatory in tone.

There are a total of fourteen texts or utterances of varying length, arranged according to an obvious architectural plan. The texts become shorter and shorter until the last utterance, which is simply the repetition three times of the word *la shay'* (nothing). The fourteen texts thus evoke the shape of the Great Pyramid, primarily through the relation of part to whole, beginning with the grand base and rising to the top, which cannot be seen when one stands at the base of the monument.

A virtually limitless repertoire of idioms and narrative techniques continue to inspire al-Ghitani's literary compositions. His later works include a series of short narratives published so far as a work in six parts: *Khulsat al-kara: Dafatir al-tadwin: Al-Daftar al-'awwal* (1996, Archival Works I: Stolen Periods of Repose), *Dana fa-tadalla: Dafatir al-tadwin: Al-Daftar al-thani* (1998, Archival Works II: Ever so Nearer), *Rashahat al-Hamra': Dafatir al-tadwin: Al-Daftar al-Thalith* (2003, Archival Works III: Al-Hamra Percolations), *Nawafidh al-nawafidh: Dafatir al-tadwin: Al-Daftar al-rabi'* (2004, Archival Works IV: Windows/Penetrating Visions), *Nithar al-mahwu: Dafatir al-tadwin: Al-Daftar al-khamis* (2006, Archival Works V: Scattered Traces of Erasure) and *Rinn: Dafatir al-tadwin: Al-Daftar al-sadis* (2008, Archival Works VI: Rann). The narratives in each of these collections seem to embody or expound on the meaning of a classical concept, a strikingly suggestive word or

Front covers for the three volumes of al-Ghitani's semiautobiographical novel, Kitab al-tajalliyat (The Book of Revelations), published in 1983, 1985, and 1987 (Sterling Memorial Library, Yale University)

expression that provides the unifying insight into the lives and events portrayed. His later novels, such as *Hikayat al-mu'assasah* (1997, Tales of the Establishment) and *Hikayat al-khabi'ah* (2002, Tales of Hiddenness), follow the style of earlier pastiche works in handling contemporary themes and events. The prolific al-Ghitani has also continued to publish memoirs, diaries, travel accounts, and short stories, all of which are composed in his signature style. One of his most interesting works is *al-Majalis al-Mahfuziyyah* (2006, Mahfouzian Sessions), a record of al-Ghitani's meetings with Naguib Mahfouz over the years, but particularly since the Egyptian icon was stabbed in 1994–an incident al-Ghitani considers not only for the changes it forced on Mahfouz's regular weekly meetings and other public appearances and routines but also for its ramifications for the larger intellectual scene.

Gamal al-Ghitani still resides in Cairo and since 1993 has served as the editor in chief of *Akhbar al-Adab* (Literary News), an important weekly cultural magazine. His work represents the belief that tradition–"that which has survived over certain or extended stretches of time"–can provide the source of inspiration for "articulating our present powerfully." As an artist, al-Ghitani is most influenced by Arabic historiographical and Sufi discourses. He understands history not in the conventional terms of periodization but in terms of the perishable historical moment and its fragile present–one of the crucial Sufi insights into our relation with time. Indeed, the highly self-reflective moments, personal or historical, with which al-Ghitani's works abound, bring to a single focus the nature of his creative impulse. His impulse is often autobiographical but is reworked in different contexts, mostly through his emulation of medieval Arabic prose genres. The moment itself is, however, placed on a trajectory of personal destiny, the mysterious course of an individual's fate. In addition, al-Ghitani's persistent appeal to architecture, to Arabo-Islamic graphic arts, and to the arts of Arabic prose narratives are major keys to his literary achievements.

Interview:

"Jadaliyyat al-Tanas: An Interview," *Alif: A Journal of Comparative Poetics,* no. 4 (1984): 71–82.

References:

'Afaf 'Abd al-Mu'ti, "Gamal al-Ghitani fi *Hikayat al-khabi'ah*," *Nizwa,* 33 (January 2003): 78–82;

Aminah 'Adwan, *Qira'at naqdiyyah* (Amman: Dar al-Karmal, 1993);

Mahmud Amin al-'Alim, *Arba'un 'aman min al-naqd al-tatbiqi: Al-Binyah wa al-dilalah fi al-qissah wa al-ruwayah al-'Arabiyyah al-mu'asirah* (Cairo: Dar al-Mustaqbal al-'Arabi, 1994);

Al-'Alim, "Al-Tarikh wa al-fann wa al-dilala fi thalathat riwayat misriyyah," *Fusul,* 2, no. 2 (1982): 15–28;

Roger Allen, *The Arabic Novel: An Historical and Critical Introduction* (Syracuse, N.Y.: Syracuse University Press, 1982);

Allen, "The Novella in Arabic: A Study in Fictional Genres," *International Journal of Middle East Studies,* 18 (November 1986): 473–484;

Samiya As'ad, "'Indama yaktub al-riwa'i al-tarikh," *Fusul,* 2, no. 2 (1982): 67–74;

Muhammad Mustafa Badawi, "Mughamarat al-shakl 'inda riwa'iyyi al-sittiniyyat: Madkhal li ijtima'iyyat al-shakl al-ruwa'i," *Fusul,* 2, no. 3 (1982): 125–142;

Faisal Darraj, "Al-Intaj al-riwa'i wa al-tali'ah al-'Adabiyyah," *al-Karmal,* 1 (Winter 1981): 134–137;

Darraj, *Nadhariyyat al-ruwaya wa al-ruwaya al-'arabiyya* (Beirut: Al-Markaz al-Thaqafi al-'Arabi, 1999);

Ayman A. El-Desouky, "Al-Qass wa al-iqtisas bayna qadim al-lahza wa jadid al-tarikh: Qira'ah fi riwayat *Mutun al-Ahram* li al-Ghitani," *Alif: A Journal of Comparative Poetics,* 24 (2004): 119–152;

C. K. Draz, "In Quest of New Narrative Forms: Irony in the Works of Four Egyptian Writers (1967–1979): al-Ghitani, Yahya T. 'Abdallah, M. Tubya, Sun'allah Ibrahim," *Journal of Arab Literature,* 12 (1981): 137–144;

Sabry Hafez, "The Transformation of Reality and the Arabic Novel's Aesthetic Response," *Bulletin of the School of Oriental and African Studies, University of London,* 57, no. 1 (1994): 93–112;

Walid Hamarneh, "Some Narrators and Narrative Modes in the Contemporary Arabic Novel," in *The Arabic Novel since 1950,* edited by Issa J. Boullata, Mundus Arabicus, volume 5 (Cambridge, Mass.: Dar Mahjar, 1992), pp. 205–236;

'Abd al-Salam Kakli, *Al-Zaman al-riwa'i: Jadaliyyat al-madi wa al-hadir 'inda Gamal al-Ghitani min khilal al-Zayni Barakat wa Kitab al-tajalliyyat* (Cairo: Maktabat Madbuli, 1992);

Richard van Leeuwen, "The Enchantment of Space: Two Novels of Gamal Ghitani and Huda Barakat," in *La poétique de l'espace dans la littérature arabe moderne,* edited by Boutros Hallaq, Robin Ostle, and Stefan Wild (Saint Étienne: Presses Sorbonne Nouvelle, 2002), pp. 153–171;

Samia Mehrez, "Re-Writing the City: The Case of *Khitat al-Ghitani*," and "*Al-Zayni Barakat*: Narrative as History," in *Egyptian Writers between History and Fiction* (Cairo: American University in Cairo Press, 1994), pp. 58–77, 96–118;

Mehrez, "Al-Zayni Barakat: Narrative Strategy," *Arab Studies Quarterly,* 8 (Spring 1986): 120–142;

Walid Munir, "Hawla tawzif al-'unsur al-usturi: Al-Ruwaya al-misriyya al-mu'asira," *Fusul,* 2, no. 2 (1982): 31–38;

Bashir Qamri, *Shi'riyyat al-nass al-riwa'i: Qira'a tanassiyya fi Kitab al-tajalliyyat* (Rabat: Sharikat al-Baydar li al-Nashr wa al-Tawzi', 1991);

Thana' Anas al-Wujud Rabi', "Ruwayat *al-Tajalliyat* li al-Ghitani: Baina al-tamahi al-sufi wa tashabuk al-fada'at al-hika'iyya," *Fusul,* 2, no. 2 (1982): 297–320;

Mahmoud Tarshuna, "Madrasat tawzif al-turath fi al-ruwaya al-'arabiyya al-mu'asira," *Fusul,* 2, no. 2 (1982): 27–39;

Sa'id Yaqtin, *Infitah al-nass al-riwa'i* (Beirut: Al-Markaz al-Thaqafi al-'Arabi, 1989);

Yaqtin, *Al-Ruwaya wa al-turath al-sardi: Min ajl wa'iy jadid bi al-turath* (Beirut: Al-Markaz al-Thaqafi al-'Arabi, 1992);

Yusuf Zaidan, "Al-Hurriyya wa al-jabr fi adab al-Ghitani: Qira'a fi *Risalat al-Basa'ir,*" *Fusul,* 11, no. 1 (1992): 300–309.

Kahlil Gibran

(6 January 1883 – 10 April 1931)

John Walbridge
Indiana University

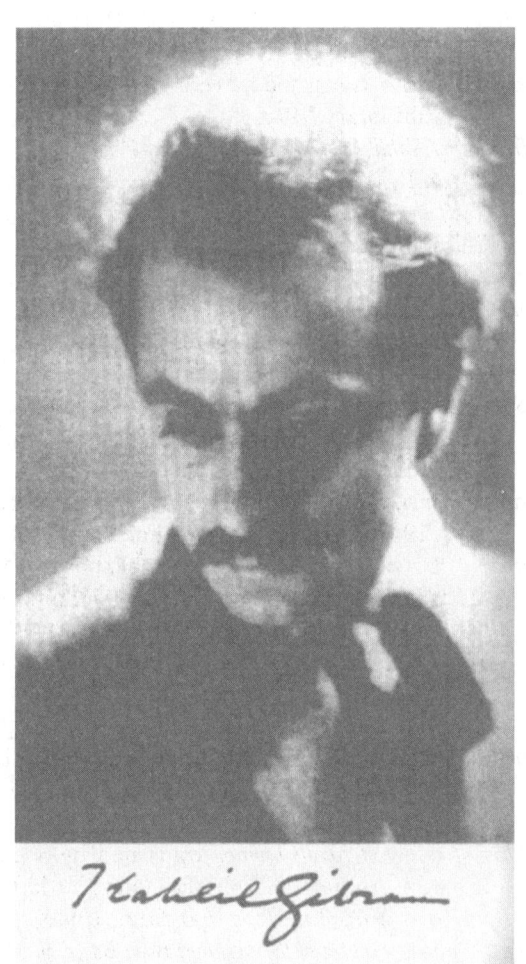

Photograph by Barbara Young (from Suheil Bushrui and Joe Jenkins, Kahlil Gibran, Man and Poet: A New Biography, *1998;* Thomas Cooper Library, University of South Carolina)

BOOKS: *Al-Musiqa* (New York: Al-Mohajer, 1905);

'Ara'is al-Muruj (New York: Al-Mohajer, 1906); translated by H. M. Nahmad as *Nymphs of the Valley* (New York: Knopf, 1948; London: Heinemann, 1948);

Al-Arwah al-mutamarridah (New York: Al-Mohajer, 1908); translated by Nahmad as *Spirits Rebellious* (New York: Knopf, 1948; London: Heinemann, 1948);

Al-Ajniha al-mutakassirah (New York: Mir'at al-Gharb, 1912); translated by Anthony R. Ferris as *The Broken Wings* (New York: Citadel Press, 1957; London: Heinemann, 1966);

Dam'a wa ibtisamah (New York: Atlantic, 1914); translated by Nahmad as *A Tear and a Smile* (New York: Knopf, 1950; London: Heinemann, 1950);

The Madman: His Parables and Poems (New York: Knopf, 1918; London: Hutchinson, 1919);

Al-Mawakib (New York: Mir'at al-Gharb, 1919); translated by M. F. Kheirallah as *The Procession* (New York: Arab-American Press, 1947);

Twenty Drawings (New York: Knopf, 1919);

Al-'Awasif (Cairo: al-Hilal, 1920);

The Forerunner: His Parables and Poems (New York: Knopf, 1920; London: Heinemann, 1963);

Al-Bada'i' wa al-tara'if (Cairo: Yusuf Bustani, 1923);

The Prophet (New York: Knopf, 1923; London: Heinemann, 1926);

Sand and Foam (New York: Knopf, 1926);

Kalimat Jubran (Cairo: Yusuf Bustani, 1927); translated by Ferris as *Spiritual Sayings* (New York: Citadel Press, 1962; London: Heinemann, 1962);

Jesus, the Son of Man: His Words and His Deeds as Told and Recorded by Those Who Knew Him (New York: Knopf, 1928; London: Heinemann, 1928);

Al-Sanabil (New York: Al-Sa'ih', 1929);

The Earth Gods (New York: Knopf, 1931; London: Heinemann, 1931);

The Wanderer: His Parables and His Sayings (New York: Knopf, 1932; London: Heinemann, 1965);

The Garden of the Prophet, by Gibran and Barbara Young (New York: Knopf, 1933; London: Heinemann, 1935);

Lazarus and His Beloved: A One-Act Play (Greenwich, Conn.: New York Graphic Society, 1973; London: Heinemann, 1973);

Dramas of Life (Philadelphia: Westminster Press, 1981)—comprises *Lazarus and His Beloved* and *The Blind*;

Paintings and Drawings 1905–1930 (New York: Vrej Baghoomian, 1989).

Collection: *Al-Majmu'a al-kamilah li mu'allafat Jubran Khalil Jubran,* 2 volumes, edited by Mikha'il Nu'aymi, Arabic translations of English works by Antuniyus Bashir and 'Abd al-Latif Sharara (Beirut: Dar al-Sadir, 1964).

Editions in English: *Prose Poems,* translated by Anthony Ghareeb (New York: Knopf, 1934; London: Heinemann, 1954);

Secrets of the Heart, translated by Anthony R. Ferris (New York: Philosophical Library, 1947);

Tears and Laughter, translated by Ferris (New York: Philosophical Library, 1947);

A Treasury of Kahlil Gibran, translated by Ferris, edited by Martin L. Wolf (New York: Citadel Press, 1951);

The Voice of the Master, translated by Ferris (New York: Philosophical Library, 1958; London: Heinemann, 1960);

Thoughts and Meditations, translated by Ferris (London: Heinemann, 1960; New York: Philosophical Library, 1961);

A Second Treasury of Kahlil Gibran, translated by Ferris (New York: Citadel Press, 1962; London: Mandarin, 1992);

Spiritual Sayings, translated by Ferris (New York: Citadel Press, 1962; London: Heinemann, 1962);

Mirrors of the Soul, translated by Joseph Sheban (New York: Philosophical Library, 1965; London: Mandarin, 1993);

The Wisdom of Gibran: Aphorisms and Maxims, translated by Sheban (New York: Philosophical Library, 1966; London: Mandarin, 1993);

Between Night and Morn, translated by Ferris (New York: Philosophical Library, 1972; New Delhi & London: UBSPD, 1996);

A Third Treasury of Kahlil Gibran, translated by Sheban, edited by Andrew Dib Sherfan (New York: Citadel Press, 1975; London: Mandarin, 1993);

Kahlil Gibran: A Prophet in the Making: Book Based on Manuscript Pages of The Madman, The Forerunner, The Prophet, and The Earth Gods, Including Four Hitherto Unpublished Manuscripts, Lullaby, The Last Guest, Untitled, Poverty and Sundry Aphorisms. Included Is a Biographical Introduction, edited by William Shehadi (Beirut: American University of Beirut, 1991);

Spirit Brides, translated by Juan R. I. Cole (Santa Cruz, Cal.: White Cloud Press, 1993; London: Arkana Penguin, 1998);

The Storm: Stories and Prose Poems, translated by John Walbridge (Ashland, Ore.: White Cloud Press, 1993; London: Arkana Penguin, 1997);

The Beloved: Reflections on the Path of the Heart, translated by Walbridge (Ashland, Ore.: White Cloud Press, 1994; London: Arkana Penguin, 1997);

The Vision: Reflections on the Way of the Soul, translated by Cole (Ashland, Ore.: White Cloud Press, 1994);

The Broken Wings, translated by Cole (Ashland, Ore.: White Cloud Press, 1998; London & New York: Penguin, 1998).

Though he considered himself to be mainly a painter, lived most of his life in the United States, and wrote his best-known works in English, Kahlil Gibran was the key figure in a Romantic movement that transformed Arabic literature in the first half of the twentieth century. Educated in Beirut, Boston, and Paris, Gibran was influenced by the European modernists of the late nineteenth century. His early works were sketches, short stories, poems, and prose poems written in simple language for Arabic newspapers in the United States. These pieces spoke to the experiences and loneliness of Syrian immigrants in the New World. For Arab readers accustomed to the rich but difficult and rigid tradition of Arabic poetry and literary prose, many of the forms and conventions of which went back to pre-Islamic Bedouin poetry, Gibran's simple and direct style was a revelation and an inspiration. His themes of alienation, disruption, and lost rural beauty and security in a modernizing world also resonated with the experiences of his readers. He quickly found admirers and imitators among Arabic writers, and his reputation as a central figure of Arabic literary modernism has never been challenged.

Gibran's reputation in the English-speaking world, on the other hand, has been mixed. His works have been hugely popular, making him the best-selling American poet of the twentieth century, but that enthusiasm has not been shared by critics. His paintings and drawings of sinuous idealized nudes belong to symbolism and art nouveau and are, thus, a survival of a tradition rejected both by American realists and European abstractionists. His English books—most notably, *The Prophet* (1923), with its earnest didactic romanticism—found no favor with critics whose models were the cool intellectualism of James Joyce and T. S. Eliot or the gritty realism of Ernest Hemingway. As a result, Gibran has been dismissed as a popular sentimentalist by American critics and historians of art and of literature. There are signs that this situation is changing, at least on the literary side, as critics become more sensitive to the characteristics of immigrant writing.

Jubran Khalil Jubran was born on 6 January 1883 to Kamila Jubran and her second husband, Khalil Sa'd Jubran, in the village of Bisharri in what is now northern Lebanon but was then Ottoman Syria. He had a

Pencil drawing by Gibran of his friend, patron, and editor Mary Haskell, 1910 (from Suheil Bushrui and Joe Jenkins, Kahlil Gibran, Man and Poet: A New Biography, *1998; Thomas Cooper Library, University of South Carolina)*

half brother, Butrus (also known as Peter) Rahma, and two younger sisters, Sultana and Marianna. The family were Maronite Christians, and Kamila Jubran was the daughter of a Maronite priest. The father seems to have been a violent drinker and a gambler; rather than tend the walnut grove he owned, he was a collector of taxes for the village headman, a job that was not considered reputable. In 1891 he was convicted of some irregularity, and his property was confiscated. Gibran later described his father to his women friends as a descendant of cavaliers, a romantic figure, who got into trouble with the law for refusing to compromise with corrupt village authorities.

Similarly, Gibran later portrayed his life in Lebanon as idyllic, stressing his precocious artistic and literary talents and his mother's efforts to educate him; some of these stories were obviously tall tales meant to impress his American patrons. His education in a school run by the local priest would have been erratic; since Bisharri was a Maronite village, the new education offered by the Protestant missionaries was not available to him. A local doctor, Salim Dahir, seems to have played a role in Gibran's education. He claimed that his interest in art was inspired in part by a book of Leonardo da Vinci's drawings that his mother gave him. He absorbed a good deal of Lebanese folk culture that appears in his writings. His sensitivity to natural beauty owed much to the magnificent setting of impoverished Bisharri above the Qadisha Valley on the slopes of Mount Lebanon.

Kamila left her husband in 1895 and took the children to the United States; they were part of the large wave of Syrian immigration that took place in the three decades before World War I. They arrived in New York on 17 June and went on to Boston, where they settled in the teeming immigrant slums of the South End. Kamila, as was common for Syrian immigrants, became a peddler; soon she had saved enough money to open a shop with her son Butrus. Khalil went to school, while his sisters helped in the shop. The school gave him the American form and spelling of his last name, Gibran. He began in an ungraded class for immigrants who knew no English; he learned the language quickly, though his written English, especially the spelling, remained erratic. The school was across the street from Denison House, a settlement house, and one of Gibran's teachers referred him to the drawing classes there.

In November 1896 Gibran was introduced to Fred Holland Day, the eccentric leader of a Boston avant-garde group who called themselves the Visionists. They were imitators of the British decadents and Pre-Raphaelites; though their artistic achievements did not equal those of their British models, they established two of the first "little magazines" of poetry and art in America and a distinguished art press, Copeland and Day, that published a hundred highly regarded volumes in five years. A pioneering art photographer, Day was partial to exotic and orientalist themes and produced elegant homoerotic photographs of young men. Day became Gibran's friend and patron, using the boy as a model (a few photographs survive of Gibran in Arab costume), introducing him to Romantic literature, and helping him with his drawing. For a time Gibran was a pet of Day's fashionable bohemian set. His drawing progressed, and he published at least one book cover. Day read to him from English literature and, as Gibran's English improved, lent him books and directed him to the new Boston Public Library. Romantics such as the Italian poet, novelist, and short-story writer Gabriele D'Annunzio and the Belgian essayist Maurice Maeterlinck influenced Gibran most deeply. No one who reads

Gibran's works and knows Day's tastes can doubt the depth of the latter's influence on Gibran. Perhaps more important, Day and Day's friends convinced Gibran that he had a special artistic calling.

At an exhibit of Day's photographs in 1898 Gibran met a Cambridge poet, Josephine Prescott Peabody, who was nine years older than he. He sketched a portrait of her from memory and gave it to Day to pass on to her. Peabody was charmed by the sketch, and she and Gibran exchanged a few letters.

Shortly afterward, Gibran's mother sent him back to Lebanon to continue his education; she may have been concerned about the influence of his new friends, and Gibran later said that he lost his virginity to an older married woman around this time. He attended the Maronite high school Madrasat al-Hikma in Beirut, where he was allowed to study independently; he read widely in Arabic and French literature, started a school poetry magazine, and won a poetry contest. He visited Bisharri during vacations, but his relationship with his father was strained. Several of Gibran's works of fiction—including the novella *al-Ajniha al-mutakassira* (1912; translated as *The Broken Wings*, 1957), with its story of a doomed love affair—are set in Beirut and other parts of Lebanon around this time, leading to speculation that they may be autobiographical; but nothing can be determined with certainty, especially given Gibran's habit of embroidering his past.

Gibran left Beirut in 1901 and wandered around Europe; Paris was among the places he visited. In April 1902 he received news that his sister Sultana had died of glandular tuberculosis; he hurried home, arriving two weeks after her death. Butrus also had tuberculosis and left for Cuba that winter in search of a more healthful climate. Soon afterward, their mother was diagnosed with cancer.

In November 1902 Gibran wrote to Peabody, and she invited him to a party held at her house two weeks later. An intense platonic relationship resulted, though Gibran seems to have wanted it to progress to a sexual one. He visited her regularly; they went to musical and artistic events together; they wrote to each other often; and she encouraged his writing and his art. She gave him the nickname that he later used as the title of his most famous book: "the Prophet." The relationship must have been a comfort to Gibran during the harrowing months when his brother and mother were dying. Butrus died on 12 March 1903. In May, Peabody helped to arrange to have Gibran's work included in an art exhibition at Wellesley College. Kamila died on 28 June, leaving Gibran responsible for Marianna and the debt-ridden family shop. He ran the business long enough to pay off the debts, then allowed Marianna to support the two of them on her earnings as a seamstress. In October 1903 Gibran wrote something in a letter to Peabody that angered her, and their relationship cooled.

In April 1904 Day held an exhibit of Gibran's work at his studio. It was favorably reviewed, and some of the pictures were sold. At the show Gibran met a woman who became his most important patron: Mary Haskell was from a wealthy South Carolina family and ran a private Boston girls' school. Unlike Peabody and the other women who drifted in and out of Gibran's life, she was a hardheaded businesswoman. She seems to have concluded that Gibran was the most important person she would ever meet and that it was her responsibility to encourage him and to document his intellectual and artistic life. She recorded their conversations and preserved his sketches and other ephemera in extremely detailed journals. She supported him intellectually, financially, and emotionally, with, it seems, a clear understanding of the financial and emotional costs that would be involved. They considered marriage, but their relationship never became sexual. Haskell's role in Gibran's life did not become known until some of their correspondence was published in the 1970s. Their letters and her journals are now seen as a significant aspect of Gibran's literary legacy.

Day's studio burned in the winter of 1904, destroying Gibran's entire portfolio. Around that time Ameen Guraieb, the editor of the New York Arabic newspaper *al-Mohajer* (The Emigrant), hired Gibran to write a weekly column; he paid Gibran $2.00 for each piece. In the first, "Ru'ya" (The Vision), Gibran describes a birdcage in a field at the edge of a brook. Inside the cage is a sparrow that has died of hunger and thirst, despite being within sight of water and food. The cage dissolves into a skeleton containing a human heart dripping blood. The heart speaks, declaring that it has died from being imprisoned by human laws that bind the emotions.

In 1905 Guraieb published Gibran's first book, *al-Musiqa* (On Music); it is really just a pamphlet and occupies only eleven pages in his collected works (1964). Inspired by concerts Gibran attended with Day and his other intellectual friends, it is a Romantic paean to music. Gibran begins by comparing music to the speech of his beloved, goes on to discuss how music was worshiped by civilizations of the past, and concludes with short poetic descriptions of four modes of Middle Eastern music. The piece is passionate, unspecific, and immature, but it points to Gibran's future work.

By 1906 Gibran's columns in *al-Mohajer*, which had come to be titled "Dam'a wa'btisama" (Tears and Laughter), were becoming popular because of their difference from conventional Arabic literature. Arabic writers were expected to have mastered the rigid poetic

Gibran in an Arab cloak, circa 1918 (from Suheil Bushrui and Joe Jenkins, Kahlil Gibran, Man and Poet: A New Biography, *1998; Thomas Cooper Library, University of South Carolina)*

forms and vocabulary of the pre-Islamic period and the first centuries of Islam; having absorbed this rich literary heritage, they could not escape its overwhelming influence. Gibran, however, did not have the training to imitate the old masters of Arabic literature: his education had been haphazard and was as much in English as in Arabic, and there is little evidence of the influence of classical Arabic literature in his works. Instead, his Arabic style was influenced by the Romantic writers of late-nineteenth-century Europe and shows obvious traces of English syntax. His allegorical sketches of exile, oppression, and loneliness spoke to the experiences of Syrian immigrants and had none of the rhetorical decoration that made high Arabic literature difficult for ordinary readers.

The newspaper-column format determined the form of Gibran's Arabic writings, most of which are collections of short pieces with little thematic unity. Even the novella *al-Ajniha al-mutakassira* and the later English works tend to be short units strung together rather than sustained narratives or exposition. His written works also exhibit an underlying painterly aesthetic in which the basic unit is the exposition of a single vivid image.

In 1906 Gibran published *'Ara'is al-muruj* (Spirit Brides; translated as *Nymphs of the Valley,* 1948), a collection of three short stories. "Rimal al-ajyal wa al-nar al-khalidah" (The Ash of Centuries and the Immortal Flame) is a story of reincarnation. Nathan, the son of the priest of Astarte in Baalbek, loses his lover to disease. Despite her promise that they will meet again, he is maddened by grief and wanders lost in the desert. Ages pass, and a Bedouin shepherd, 'Ali al-Husayni, falls asleep in the ruins of the temple and dreams of love. Seeing a girl by a stream, he recognizes himself as Nathan and her as his long-lost lover. It is noteworthy that the main part of the story is set in the Phoenician, not the Islamic, Lebanese past. The other two stories deal with social oppression. In "Marta al-baniya" an orphan is kidnaped from her village by a man from the city, who rapes her and keeps her as his mistress. She becomes pregnant, and he throws her out. When she dies, the priests refuse to bury her in consecrated ground. In "Yuhanna al-majnum" (Yuhanna the Madman) a poor cowherd's cattle stray onto monastery land while he is reading his Bible, and the monks refuse to return them. When Yuhanna preaches against the monks at the Easter service, they arrest him; he is freed only after his father testifies that he is a madman.

Gibran's relationship with Peabody ended completely with her marriage in 1906. He then began a secret affair with a pianist, Gertrude Barrie, who, like Peabody, was several years his senior. During this period Haskell introduced him to an aspiring French actress, Émilie Michel, who taught French at Haskell's school, and the two fell in love. In 1908 Michel suffered an ectopic pregnancy and had an abortion. The relationship waned and ultimately ended, a victim of Michel's ambitions for a career on the stage.

Gibran's *al-Arwah al-mutamarrida* (translated as *Spirits Rebellious,* 1948), a collection of four stories, appeared in 1908. The title character of "Warda al-Hani" is a young woman in an arranged marriage with a kindly older man whom she does not love. She leaves him for a younger lover, disgraced in the eyes of the world but honest in love. In "Surakk al-qubur" (The Cry of the Graves) the emir sentences three criminals to death: a young man who murdered an official, a woman caught by her husband in adultery, and an old man who stole precious ornaments from a church. The narrator approves of the emir's stern justice, but the day after the executions he learns the truth: the young man was defending a girl the official wanted to rape; the woman loved a young man but had been married against her will; and the old man rented land from the monastery, but the monks left him with so little that his family was starving. In "Madja' al-'arus" (The Bridal Bed), which Gibran claims is a true story, a girl is tricked into marrying a man she does not love; she kills her true love and herself on her wedding day. In "Khalil al-kafir" (Khalil the Heretic), the most ambitious story in the collection, the young monk Khalil denounces other monks for violating the teachings of Christ. He is beaten and brought to trial, where his eloquence wins over the villagers. They demand that he be made headman, but Khalil knows that power corrupts. He refuses the position and lives quietly with his lover.

In 1908 Haskell paid for Gibran travel to Paris to study art. There he improved his skill with pastels and oils and was impressed by the symbolist paintings of Eugene Carrière. He also discovered the art of William Blake after finding a book of Blake's poetry. Gibran's painting *Autumn,* a female nude, was accepted for an exhibition by the Société Nationale des Beaux-Arts, and he was invited to contribute six paintings to another prestigious show. He made a series of pencil portraits of major artists, of which that of Auguste Rodin is the best known. He later stressed Rodin's influence on him; but although he certainly met Rodin, he did not have a personal relationship with the sculptor. In Paris he also encountered the works of the German philosopher Friedrich Nietzsche, who became a major influence on his writing. He met several Syrian political exiles and the Lebanese American writer Amin Rihani, who became his friend and literary ally. Eventually his money ran out, and he returned to the United States in October 1910.

In 1912 Gibran published *al-Ajniha al-mutakassira,* which he seems to have written several years earlier. The novella, which occupies sixty-five pages in the standard Arabic edition, is Gibran's only attempt at a sustained narrative. When he was eighteen, the narrator fell in love in Beirut with Salma Karama. Forced by her father to marry an archbishop's nephew, Salma was able to meet her lover occasionally until they were discovered together. Salma was then confined to her home and eventually died in childbirth. Reviews in the Arabic press were strongly positive, though there were some reservations about the character of Salma and Gibran's views on the position of Arab women. The book led to a correspondence with the Syrian writer May Ziyada that evolved into an epistolary love affair.

After Paris, Gibran found Boston provincial and stifling. Haskell arranged for him to visit New York in April 1911; he moved there in September, using $5,000 that Haskell gave him to rent an apartment in Greenwich Village. He immediately acquired a circle of admirers that included the Swiss psychiatrist and psychologist Carl Gustav Jung and several Baha'is; the latter introduced him to the visiting Baha'i leader 'Abd al-Baha', whose portrait he drew. New York was the center of the Arabic literary scene in America; Rihani was there, and Gibran met many literary and artistic figures who lived in or passed through the city, including the Irish poet and dramatist William Butler Yeats. He grew more politically active, supporting the idea of revolution to gain Syrian independence from the Ottoman Empire.

Though Gibran initially had some success as an artist in New York, artistic currents were moving rapidly in other directions. In the spring of 1913 he visited the International Exhibition of Modern Art–the "Armory Show"–which introduced European modern art to America. He approved of the show as a "declaration of independence" from tradition, but he did not think most of the paintings were beautiful and did not care for the artistic ideologies behind movements such as cubism. The reviews of an exhibition of his own work in December 1914 were mixed. He devoted most of his time to painting for the next eighteen years but remained loyal to the symbolism of his youth and became an isolated figure on the New York art scene.

Gibran's literary career, however, was blossoming. *Al-Funun* (The Arts), an Arabic newspaper founded in New York in 1913, provided a new vehicle for his writings, some of which were openly political. The editor of *al-Funun* published a collection of fifty-six of Gibran's early newspaper columns as *Dam'a wa ibtisamah* (1914; translated as *A Tear and a Smile,* 1950); most are a page or two long, and the volume as a whole comprises about a hundred pages. For the most part they are prose poems: painterly expositions of a vivid image or story fragments. The themes are love, spirituality, beauty, nature, and alienation and homecoming. Typical are "Hayat al-hubb" (The Life of Love), portraying the seasons of love of a man and a woman from the spring of youth to the winter of old age, and "Amama 'arsh al-jamal" (Before the Throne of Beauty), in which the goddess of nature tells the poet how she was worshiped by his ancestors and counsels him to commune with nature in wild places. Gibran feigned reluctance to republish these pieces on the grounds that he had moved beyond them. They are not especially deep, but they have a freshness and the moral and aesthetic earnestness that was always Gibran's strength in his writing and his art. The collection was dedicated to Haskell using her initials, "M.E.H."

During World War I, Gibran was active in Syrian nationalist circles and in efforts to bring relief to the starving people of his homeland. He was unable to accept the pacifism that was popular among his American intellectual friends. Along with such eminent writers as the poet Robert Frost and the critic Van Wyck Brooks, Gibran was a member of the advisory board of the prominent literary magazine *The Seven Arts,* which was founded in 1916. The magazine published some of Gibran's work, as well as a laudatory article, "The Art of Kahlil Gibran," by Alice Raphael. Gibran's association with the magazine established him as a significant literary figure and made him popular on the poetry-

The members of the literary/political group Arrabitah in New York, 7 September 1920: Naseeb Arida, Gibran, Abdul Massih Haddad, and Mikhail Naimy (from Suheil Bushrui and Joe Jenkins, Kahlil Gibran, Man and Poet: A New Biography, *1998; Thomas Cooper Library, University of South Carolina)*

reading circuit. The magazine's pacifist editorial policy became politically unacceptable after the United States entered the war in the spring of 1917, and it ceased publication.

Gibran's first book in English, *The Madman: His Parables and Poems,* was completed in 1917; it was brought out in 1918 by the young literary publisher Alfred A. Knopf, who went on to publish all of Gibran's English works. An introduction, in which the narrator tells how he became a madman when a thief stole his masks and he ran maskless through the streets, is followed by a series of pieces that were written, and sometimes published, separately. Most were composed in Arabic and translated into English by Gibran with Haskell's editorial assistance. New here are a sardonic or bitter tone and a move from prose poem to parable as Gibran's major mode of expression. The pieces include "The Two Cages," in which a caged sparrow greets a caged lion each morning as "brother," and "The Three Ants," in which the insects meet on the nose of a sleeping man. The first two remark on the barren nature of this strange land; the third insists that they are on the nose of the Supreme Ant. The other ants laugh at his strange preaching; at that moment the man awakes, scratches his nose, and crushes the ants. Reviews were mixed but mostly positive. Ziyada, however, told Gibran that the "cruelty" and "dark caverns" in the work made her nervous. Several of the poems were anthologized in poetry collections.

In 1919 Gibran published *al-Mawakib* (translated as *The Procession,* 1947). He had written it during summer vacations in Cohasset, Massachusetts, in 1917 and 1918 but wanted to bring it out in an elegant illustrated edition on heavy stock that was unavailable in wartime. It is a two-hundred-line poem in traditional rhyme and meter comprising a dialogue between an old man and a youth on the edge of a forest. The old man is rooted in the world of civilization and the city; the youth is a creature of the forest and represents nature and wholeness. The old man expresses a gloomy philosophy to which the carefree youth gives optimistic responses. Some critics noted the irregularities in the Arabic; Gibran's haphazard education meant that his Arabic, like his English, was never perfect. Conservative reviewers objected to the poem's solecisms, but Ziyada dismissed them as expressions of the poet's independence. The work immediately became popular, especially as a piece to be sung. It is one of the great examples of *mahjari* (immigrant) poetry and pioneered a new form of verse in Arabic.

Also in 1919 Knopf published a collection of Gibran's art works as *Twenty Drawings,* with Raphael's essay as an introduction. The pictures are not his best work; the book did not draw much attention, and the one review was ambivalent. It is Gibran's only book published in the West that has gone out of print.

A fourth collection of Gibran's Arabic stories and prose poems, *al-'Awasif* (The Storms), came out in Cairo in 1920. The contents dated from 1912 to 1918 and had been published in *al-Funun* and *Mir'at al-gharb* (Mirror of the West), an immigrant newspaper. It consists of thirty-one pieces that are generally harsher in tone than the sketches and stories of the three earlier collections. In the title story the narrator is curious about Yusuf al-Fakhri, a hermit who abandoned society in his thirtieth year to live alone on Mount Lebanon. Driven to the hermit's cell by a storm, he is surprised to find such comforts as cigarettes and wine. The hermit tells the narrator that he did not flee the world to be a contemplative but to escape the corruption of society. In "'Ala bab al-haykal" (At the Gate of the Temple) a man asks passersby about the nature of love. The powerful "al-'Ubudiya" (Slavery) catalogues the forms of human bondage throughout history. In "al-Shaytan" (Satan) a priest finds the devil dying by the side of the road; Satan persuades the priest that he is necessary to the well-being of the world, and the clergyman takes him home to nurse him back to health. Several other stories deal with the political themes that had concerned Gibran during the war.

Also in 1920 Knopf published *The Forerunner: His Parables and Poems*. It begins with a prologue in which the narrator says that each person is his or her own forerunner. Among the twenty-three parables are one in which a king abandons his kingdom for the forest; another in which a saint meets a brigand and confesses to committing the same sins as the bandit; and a third in which a weathercock complains because the wind always blows in his face. The volume closes with a speech, "The Last Watch," presumably by the Forerunner, addressing the people of a sleeping city. The bitterness of the wartime writings of the years is largely gone, replaced by an ethereal love and pity for humanity that foreshadows Gibran's later work.

Al-Funun had collapsed in 1919; in April 1920 Gibran and some friends who had been associated with the paper formed al-Rabitah al-Qalamiyyah (the Pen-Bond), or Arrabitah, as they called it when writing in English. The group elected Gibran president and Mikhail Naimy secretary and met regularly until Gibran's death eleven years later. The goals of the group were a mixture of the literary and the political; Gibran and some other members were fervent nationalists with misty ideas of liberation through literature. The group published a journal, *al-Sa'ih* (The Traveler), edited by 'Abd al-Masih Haddad. The works of the Arrabitah members were eagerly read in the Arab world, where literature was only beginning to break free from a stale and rigid traditionalism.

In 1923 the financially and emotionally exhausted Haskell moved to Savannah, Georgia, and became the companion of an elderly widower, Colonel Jacob Florence Minis. But her faith in Gibran's literary and artistic importance never wavered, and she continued to edit his English manuscripts—discreetly, since Minis did not approve of Gibran.

Al-Bada'i' wa al-tara'if (Best Things and Masterpieces), a collection of thirty-five of Gibran's pieces, was published in Cairo in 1923. The works had been selected by the publisher, and the collection is uneven and miscellaneous. It includes several short articles on major Arab thinkers, illustrated with portraits drawn from Gibran's imagination, and prose poems and sketches of the sort familiar from his earlier collections. Two pieces are of more interest than the others. "Safinat al-dubab" (A Ship in the Mist) is a strange romantic short story. A lonely young man dreams of a woman who visits him continually in his sleep and is his wife in spirit. When he is sent to Venice, he finds her; but she has just died. *Iram, dhat al-'imad* (Iram, City of Lofty Pillars) is a one-act play set in a city mentioned in the Qur'an. A young scholar, Najib Rahma, comes to the mysterious city seeking a prophetess, Amina al-'Alawiya, who is said to have visited there. He first meets her disciple, the dervish Zayn al-'Abidin; then Amina al-'Alawiya appears and expounds a monistic mystical philosophy.

Gibran's masterpiece, *The Prophet,* was published in September 1923. The earliest references to a mysterious prophet counseling his people before returning to his island home can be found in Haskell's journal from 1912. Gibran worked on it from time to time and had finished much of it by 1919. He seems to have written it in Arabic and then translated it into English. As with most of his English books, Haskell acted as his editor, correcting Gibran's chronically defective spelling and punctuation but also suggesting improvements in the wording. The work begins with the prophet Almustafa preparing to leave the city of Orphalese, where he has lived for twelve years, to return to the island of his birth. The people of the city gather and beg him not to leave, but the seeress Almitra, knowing that his ship has come for him, asks him instead to tell them his truths. The people ask him about the great themes of human life: love, marriage, children, giving, eating and drinking, and many others, concluding with death. Almus-

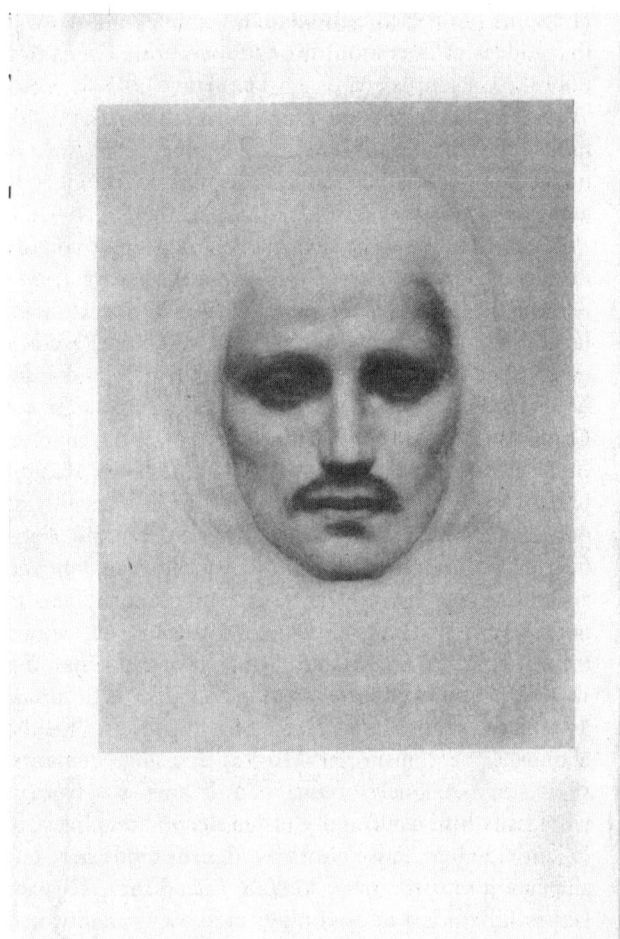

Frontispiece and title page for an edition of Gibran's best-known work, originally published in 1923 (Thomas Cooper Library, University of South Carolina)

tafa speaks of each of the themes in sober, sonorous aphorisms grouped into twenty-six short chapters. As in earlier books, Gibran illustrated *The Prophet* with his own drawings, adding to the power of the work.

The Prophet received tepid reviews in *Poetry* and *The Bookman,* an enthusiastic review in the *Chicago Evening Post,* and little else. On the other hand, the public reception was intense. It began with a trickle of grateful letters; the first edition sold out in two months; 13,000 copies a year were sold during the Great Depression, 60,000 in 1944, and 1,000,000 by 1957. Many millions of copies were sold in the following decades, making Gibran the best-selling American poet of the twentieth century. It is clear that the book deeply moved many people. When critics finally noticed it, they were baffled by the public response; they dismissed the work as sentimental, overwritten, artificial, and affected. Neither *The Prophet* nor Gibran's work in general are mentioned in standard accounts of twentieth-century American literature, though Gibran is universally considered a major figure in Arabic literature. Part of the critical puzzlement stems from a failure to appreciate an Arabic aesthetic: *The Prophet* is a Middle Eastern work that stands closer to eastern didactic classics such as the Book of Job and the works of the twelfth- and thirteenth-century Persian poets Rumi and Sa'di than to anything in the modern American canon. Gibran knew that he would never surpass *The Prophet,* and for the most part his later works do not come close to measuring up to it. The book made him a celebrity, and his monastic lifestyle added to his mystique.

In 1925 the poet Barbara Young (pseudonym of Henrietta Breckenridge Boughton) became Gibran's secretary. She remained with Gibran for the rest of his life and played a major role in events after his death.

In 1926 and 1927, respectively, Gibran published *Sand and Foam* in English and *Kalimat Jubran* (Spiritual Sayings) in Arabic. Each comprises about three hundred aphorisms of two to a dozen lines, generally written in the style of *The Prophet*. *Sand and Foam* is decorated with Gibran's drawings, and the aphorisms are separated by floral dingbats also drawn by Gibran. Most critics did not like the book, but, like all of his English works except *Twenty Drawings,* it has remained in print since its publication.

Around this time Gibran also wrote two one-act plays in English. *Lazarus and His Beloved* is set in Bethany the day after the Resurrection. Lazarus has become a sort of Gibranian mystic wandering the hills. When he hears the news of Jesus' resurrection, he leaves to join his beloved in martyrdom. A madman comments on the proceedings. In *The Blind,* David, a musician, gains wisdom through his blindness. The madman again appears as commentator. *Lazarus and His Beloved* was first published in 1973; the two plays were published together in 1981.

In 1928 Gibran published his longest book, *Jesus, the Son of Man: His Words and His Deeds as Told and Recorded by Those Who Knew Him.* Jesus had appeared in Gibran's writings and art in various forms; he told Haskell that he had recurring dreams of Jesus and mentioned wanting to write a life of Jesus in a 1909 letter to her. The book was written in a little over a year in 1926–1927. Haskell, who had married Minis in 1926, edited the manuscript. Seventy-eight people who knew Jesus—some real, some imaginary; some sympathetic, others hostile—tell of him from their own points of view. Anna is puzzled by the worship of the Magi. An orator is impressed by Jesus' rhetoric. A merchant sees the parable of the talents as the essence of commerce and cannot understand why Jesus' followers insist that he is a god. Pontius Pilate discusses the political factors leading to his decision to execute Jesus. Barabbas is tormented by the knowledge that he is alive only because Jesus died in his place. It was the most lavishly produced of Gibran's books, with some of the illustrations in color. For once, the reviews were strongly and uniformly favorable, and the book has remained the most popular of his works next to *The Prophet.*

The last of Gibran's Arabic books was published in 1929. *Al-Sanabil* (Heads of Grain) is a commemorative anthology of his works that was presented to him at an Arrabitah banquet.

Gibran's final work to be published in his lifetime was *The Earth Gods* (1931). He had mentioned it to Haskell in 1915 as the prologue to a play in English; it seems to have been largely completed the following year and thus belongs to the period just before *al-Mawakib*. It is a debate among three gods: the first speaks for pessimism; the second defends the potential for transcendence of the human world; and the third reconciles the positions of the other two.

Around the end of March 1931 Gibran sent the manuscript for *The Wanderer: His Parables and His Sayings* (1932) to Haskell for editing. The form of the work is that of *The Madman* and *The Forerunner:* the unnamed narrator tells of meeting a traveler at the crossroads "with but a cloak and staff, and a veil of pain upon his face." The fifty short pieces are reminiscent of those in the two earlier works.

At his death Gibran was working on *The Garden of the Prophet* (1933), which was to be the second volume in a trilogy begun by *The Prophet*. It is the story of Almustafa's return to his native island and deals with humanity's relationship with nature. Of the third volume, "The Death of the Prophet," only one sentence was written: "And he shall return to the City of Orphalese . . . and they shall stone him in the marketplace, even unto death; and he shall call every stone a blessed name."

Gibran died on 10 April 1931 of cirrhosis of the liver. He was an alcoholic and had been in poor health since the early 1920s. His body was taken to Boston, and despite his family's fears that he would be denied Catholic rites, his friend Monsignor Stephen El-Douaihy conducted a funeral mass. Hundreds attended—far too many for all of them to get into the church. Several memorial services were conducted during the following weeks. Gibran had wanted to be buried in his native village, and his coffin was sent to Lebanon in July. Since Gibran was a major Arabic literary figure, the procession to Bisharri and the associated ceremonies were elaborate to the edge of absurdity.

Gibran's death set off a series of sordid conflicts that have clouded his reputation. His will left money and real estate to his sister (Marianna Jubran never married and died in Boston in 1972) and his papers and the contents of his studio to Haskell, with a request that she send any materials she did not want to Bisharri; he also left the royalties from his copyrights to the village. At the studio Haskell found her own correspondence with Gibran, his other correspondence, her notebooks, and Gibran's manuscripts; she locked them in two large suitcases and sealed the studio. Haskell, however, had to return to her husband and relied on Young to handle affairs in New York. Young was immediately jealous of Haskell, whose existence she had only discovered after Gibran's death. She wanted to destroy Gibran's letters, especially the correspondence with Haskell; while Haskell was able to prevent her from doing so, Young did destroy or return letters from others. There is little question that she was trying to protect Gibran's reputation from any taint of normal humanity.

The most serious problem concerned Young's handling of Gibran's unpublished manuscripts. Haskell had finished editing *The Wanderer* after Gibran's death and sent it to Young, who undid the editing and published it with the original "words of the blessed one."

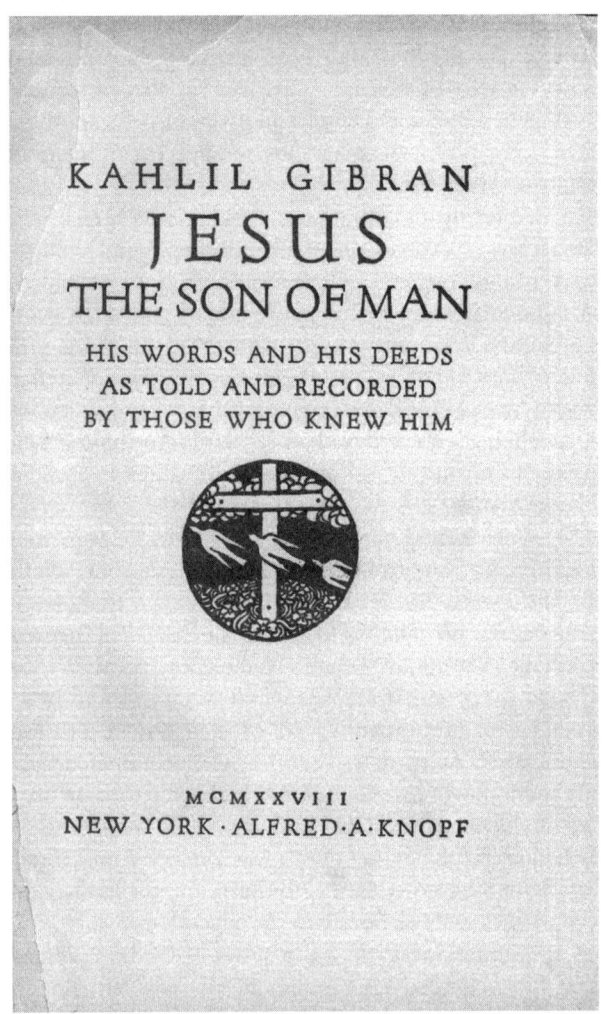

Title page for Gibran's longest work, a fictionalized biography of Jesus (Thomas Cooper Library, University of South Carolina)

The infuriated Haskell demanded that all of the English manuscripts be sent to her immediately. When they arrived, those for *The Wanderer* and *The Garden of the Prophet* were missing. Young explained that she had destroyed the manuscript for *The Wanderer* that Haskell had edited; as for *The Garden of the Prophet*, she later wrote that the urge to complete the book came to her "in the deep of night" and that "his glowing words came into being as if he were indeed supplying the need." Finally, her 1945 biography of Gibran, an adulatory work full of misinformation–much of which may have come from Gibran himself–continues to create confusion even after the publication of several excellent biographies.

The other major difficulty concerned Gibran's bequest of his royalties to his native village. By the time the copyrights came up for renewal, sales of Gibran's works were substantial; his sister contested the will, which was not properly drafted. The village won, but at the cost of giving 25 percent of the royalties to its lawyer and, later, his heirs. The unearned wealth wrought havoc in Bisharri, dividing families and leading to at least two murders. The Lebanese government finally had to step in to restore peace and deal with the corruption that was dissipating the funds. The feud among the copyright holders has prevented the publication of Haskell's journals, creating an impediment to Gibran studies. The journals are also a literary loss in themselves.

Kahlil Gibran occupies a curious place in literary history. As one of the writers who broke with the old and rigid conventions of Arabic poetry and literary prose, he is among the great figures in the twentieth-century revival of Arabic literature. His Arabic works are read, admired, and taught, and they are published and sold among the classics of Arabic literature. In English, on the other hand, a chasm remains between his popularity and the lack of critical respect for his work. Although in the 1910s his writings were published by Knopf alongside those of such authors as Eliot and Frost, he quickly ceased to be considered an important writer by critics. He has generally been dismissed as sentimental and mawkishly mystical. Nevertheless, his works are widely read and are regarded as serious literature by people who do not often read such literature. The unconventional beauty of his language and the moral earnestness of his ideas allow him to speak to a broad audience as only a handful of other twentieth-century American poets have. Virtually all of his English works have been in print since they were first published. His literary and artistic models were the Romantics of the late nineteenth century to whom he was introduced as a teenager by his avant-garde friends in Boston, and Gibran's continuing popularity as a writer testifies to the lasting power of the Romantic tradition.

Letters:

Kahlil Gibran: A Self-Portrait, translated by Anthony R. Ferris (New York: Citadel Press, 1959; London: Heinemann, 1960);

The Letters of Kahlil Gibran and Mary Haskell, edited by Annie Salem Otto (Houston: Otto, 1970);

Beloved Prophet: The Love Letters of Kahlil Gibran and Mary Haskell and Her Private Journal, edited by Virginia Hilu (New York: Knopf, 1972);

Unpublished Gibran Letters to Ameen Rihani, edited and translated by Suheil Bushrui and Salma Kuzbari (Beirut: Rihani House, 1972);

Blue Flame: The Love Letters of Kahlil Gibran to May Ziadah, edited and translated by Bushrui and Kuzbari (Harlow, U.K.: Longman, 1983); revised as *Gibran: Love Letters* (Oxford: One World, 1995).

Bibliography:

Suheil Bushrui, *Kahlil Gibran: A Bibliography* (Beirut: Centenary Publications, 1983).

Biographies:

Mikhail Naimy, *Jubran Khalil Jubran: Hayatuhu, Mawtuhu, Adabuhu, Fannuhu* (Beirut: Dar Sadir, 1934); translated by Naimy as *Kahlil Gibran: His Life and His Works* (Beirut: Khayyat, 1964);

Barbara Young, *This Man from Lebanon* (New York: Knopf, 1945);

Naimy, *Kahlil Gibran: A Biography* (New York: Philosophical Library, 1950);

Jean Gibran and Kahlil Gibran, *Kahlil Gibran: His Life and World* (New York: Interlink, 1974; revised, 1991);

Suheil Bushrui and Joe Jenkins, *Kahlil Gibran, Man and Poet: A New Biography* (Oxford: One World, 1998);

Robin Waterfield, *Prophet: The Life and Times of Kahlil Gibran* (New York: St. Martin's Press, 1998).

References:

Suheil Bushrui, ed., *An Introduction to Kahlil Gibran* (Beirut: Dar el-Mashreq, 1970);

Bushrui and Paul Gotch, eds., *Gibran of Lebanon: New Papers* (Beirut: Librairie du Liban, 1975);

Bushrui and Albert Mutlak, eds., *In Memory of Kahlil Gibran: The First Colloquium on Gibran Studies* (Beirut: Librairie du Liban, 1981);

Khalil S. Hawi, *Kahlil Gibran: His Background, Character, and Works* (Beirut: American University of Beirut, 1963);

Wahib Kayrouz, *'Alam Jubran al-fikri*, 2 volumes (Beirut: Bishariya, 1984);

Kayrouz, *'Alam Jubran al-rassam* (Beirut: Gibran National Committee, 1982);

Habib Mas'ud, ed., *Jubran hayyan wa mayyitan* (São Paulo, 1932).

Papers:

Kahlil Gibran's correspondence with Mary Haskell, her notebooks and papers, and English materials from Gibran's studios are in the Southern Historical Collection, University of North Carolina at Chapel Hill; Arabic materials and many of Gibran's art works are in the Gibran Museum in Bisharri, Lebanon. Other manuscripts and papers are in the Gibran family's private collection in Boston.

Emile Habiby
(29 August 1922 – 2 May 1996)

Kamal Abdel-Malek
American University of Sharjah

BOOKS: *Sudasiyyat al-ayyam al-sittah* (Haifa: Matba'at al-Itihad al-Ta'awuniyyah, 1969);

Al-Waqa'i' al-gharibah fi ikhtifa' abi al-Nahs Sa'id al-Mutasha'il (Haifa: Dar Arabesque, 1974); translated by Salma K. Jayyusi and Trevor Le Gassick as *The Secret Life of Saeed, the Ill-Fated Pessoptomist: A Palestinian Who Became a Citizen of Israel* (New York: Vantage, 1982; London: Zed, 1985);

Kafr Qasim (Haifa: Dar Arabesque, 1976);

Liki' ibn Liki' (Beirut: Dar al-Farabi, 1980);

Ikhtiyyeh (Cyprus: Ittihad al-Kuttab wa al-Sahafiyyin al-Filastiniyyin, 1985);

Khurafiyyat saraya bint al-ghul (Haifa: Dar Arabesque, 1991; London: Riad el-Rayyes, 1992);

Nahwa 'alam bila aqfas (Shafa Amr: Dar al-Mashriq, 1993).

Politician, novelist, short-story writer, dramatist, and journalist Emile Habiby was one of the most eminent Arab authors in Israel. He was highly regarded throughout the Arab world both for his creative work and for his political activity.

Emile Shukri Habiby was born in Haifa, Palestine, on 29 August 1922 to a family of Protestant Christians who were originally from nearby Shafa 'Amr. He worked in Haifa's oil refinery as a young man and joined the Palestine Communist Party in 1940. From 1941 to 1943 he worked as a radio announcer. In 1943 he was a leader in the founding of the National Liberation League.

After the creation of the State of Israel in 1948, Habiby remained in Haifa. He helped to establish the Israeli Communist Party (ICP) and represented it in the Israeli parliament, the Knesset, from 1952 to 1965; he then represented the Reshima Komunistit Hadashah (New Communist List), or RAKAH, which seceded from the ICP over ideological differences, from 1965 to 1972. He observed that while journalists were frequently arrested or attacked, he had immunity as a member of the Knesset. Nonetheless, he was detained

Emile Habiby (State of Israel, National Photo Collection)

on many occasions by police who pretended not to know that he was a member of parliament. He was also editor in chief of the RAKAH Arabic newspaper, *al-Ittihad* (The Union), in the 1950s.

In a 1982 interview Habiby said about Palestinian literature written by Arabs in Israel after the Arab defeat in the June 1967 Six-Day War:

Samih al-Qasim wrote a poem about the effects of the 1967 war, and spoke of a "shattering of idols." He, and other poets, told the Palestinians outside about us, and said to them, "Don't think that before 1967 we were idle and that our struggle started only in 1967." They discovered us because, it seems, they needed us. Necessity, as the saying goes, was the mother of invention.

Often we ask ourselves what the difference is between our Palestinian literature and other Palestinian literature, or "refugee" literature. The answer is that, from Israel's appearance in 1948, we have been confronted with a challenge: to be or not to be. There was an official policy of "cleansing" the country of Palestinians, and to a certain extent this policy is still continuing. There were schemes, at various times, for the expulsion of Palestinians. We were the candidates for this expulsion. We remember Ghassan Kanafani's novel, *Men in the Sun*, written after ten years of the tragedy: you have to knock on the walls of the tank if you want to live. We had to fight, from the very beginning, for our survival. We could not wait. There were some writers who hoped for a knight on a white horse who would come and rescue us; but these were few—most had a daily struggle for bread and work and survival.

For Habiby the solution to the Arab-Jewish conflict always lay in peaceful coexistence. "What is the alternative?" he asks, observing that "the Israeli leaders have other alternatives—more occupation, another war. Our solution—which the world community is presenting—is the only possible solution. It is not only Arabs who will suffer from further conflict; Jews too will suffer. Peace is in everyone's interest."

Habiby started writing short stories in the early 1950s. One of his earliest pieces, "Bawwabat Mandilbum" (1954, Mandelbaum Gate), depicts a heart-wrenching goodbye between an Arab girl and her grandmother at the Mandelbaum Gate, which before 1967 stood at the border between Israel and Jordan. The Arab girl ran through the gate:

> From afar we saw the man with the Arab headdress lower his head and with my sharp eyes I saw him examine the ground with his foot. The soldier with the bare head, who was with us he too was lowering his head, examining the ground with his foot. The policeman who was standing in front of his office, folding his arms against his chest, I saw him enter his office. And the Customs official looked as though he suddenly remembered something he had forgotten and began to look for it in his pocket.

The soldier, the policeman, and the customs official are presented as human beings with tender emotions. They do not prevent the Arab girl from seeing her grandmother off. Rather than arresting the girl when she

Front cover for Habiby's novel al-Waqa'i' al-gharibah fi ikhtifa' abi al-Nahs Sa'id al-Mutasha'il, *1974 (Widener Library, Harvard University)*

runs through the gate, a violation of security regulations, they all pretend that they do not see her.

In 1969 Habiby published *Sudasiyyat al-ayyam al-sittah* (Six Stories for the Six-Day War). Critics differ on whether to call the work a novella or a collection of short stories, literary tableaux, or nonfiction pieces depicting the lives of Palestinians after the war. In the first piece, "Hina sa'ida Mas'ud bi ibni 'ammihi" (When Mas'ud Felt Delighted to See His Cousin), young Mas'ud, who lives inside Israel proper, discovers his identity through the visit of his cousins from the West Bank—a visit made possible because Israel has occupied the West Bank and opened its pre-1967 borders (the so-called Green Line) with the Occupied Territories. The unity of Palestine is thus achieved, paradoxically, by an act of foreign occupation. Mas'ud's joy is mingled with worry: "Would I, once the Israelis withdrew become without cousins, again?" In "Akhiran nawwar al-lawz" (Finally the Almond Trees Blossomed)

Title page for the 1982 English translation of al-Waqa'i' al-gharibah fi ikhtifa' abi al-Nahs Sa'id al-Mutasha'il
(Emory University Libraries)

Mr. M. goes back to his native town, which is now part of Israel, twenty years after his exile from it. He reminisces about his life and his plan to write "A Tale of Two Cities—Haifa and Nazareth," which was disrupted by the war. His return stirs up the memory of an old love, and he set out to look for her. In "Umm al-rubabikiyyah" (Odds and Ends Woman) the title character keeps in her chest love letters of twenty years ago and other memories that time cannot erase. The tale is open-ended, and therein lies the hope for a better future. The other stories depict a Palestinian family reunion under occupation; the return of Jabina, a mythical creature during whose absence water wells dried up but now flow abundantly, as in the Palestinian folktale; and the reunion of another Palestinian family, this one taking place in a Jerusalem prison cell.

In 1974 Habiby published his masterpiece, *al-Waqa'i' al-gharibah fi ikhtifa' abi al-Nahs Sa'id al-Mutasha'il* (translated as *The Secret Life of Saeed, the Ill-Fated Pessoptimist: A Palestinian Who Became a Citizen of Israel,* 1982), an epistolary novel that has appeared in many Arabic editions and been translated into fifteen languages, including Hebrew and English. In a series of letters sent by Sa'id al-Mutasha'il (*sa'id* is Arabic for "happy"; *mutasha'il* was coined by Habiby as a combination of *mutasha'im* [pessimist] and *mutafa'il* [optimist]) to an unidentified recipient, Habiby combines comedy and tragedy to portray the strange life of a Palestinian citizen of Israel. Sa'id claims that he was rescued from being impaled on a stake by compassionate space aliens and is sending his letters from the sanctuary of their home planet. Toward the end of the novel it is revealed that his letters bear the return address of a mental hospital in Acre.

Sa'id sits astride two worlds, Arab and Jewish, and two languages, Arabic and Hebrew, and he wavers between sanity and madness. The novel begins shortly after the end of the 1948 War, which ended with the establishment of the State of Israel. Sa'id sneaks into Israel, leaving his mother and sister behind in Lebanon, turns himself in to the Jewish military authorities, and requests sanctuary in the name of an Israeli official with whom his father collaborated. He is kept as a prisoner overnight; in the morning he is taken to his native Haifa, where an Israeli soldier welcomes him in Arabic: "Ahlan wa sahlan fi medinat yisra'il!" (Welcome to the *medinah* of Israel!). Sa'id misinterprets the phrase to mean that the Israelis have changed the name of Haifa to Israel; later, he realizes that while *medinah* means "city" in Arabic, with a slight difference in stress it means "state" in Hebrew. Lital Levy points out that Sa'id's confusion shows "the irony of an Israeli using standard Arabic greetings *(ahlan wa sahlan)* to 'welcome' a Palestinian refugee to his own, now occupied city." This error is one of many examples in the novel of false cognates, mispronunciations, and double entendres that reflect the misunderstandings that abound in Arab-Jewish relations. At the end of the June 1967 Six-Day War, Sa'id hears an announcer on the Arabic language station of Radio Israel calling on the "defeated Arabs" to display white flags of surrender. Sa'id does not know whether the reference is to Arabs defeated in the Six-Day War or to those defeated in the 1948 War, so, to be on the safe side and to show his patriotism, he ties a sheet to a broomstick and flies it from the roof of his home. The order was, in fact, directed to the Arabs in the newly occupied West Bank; Sa'id's flying of the flag from his home in Haifa, in the heart of Israel proper, indicates to the authorities that he considers that city to be under occupation and desires its liberation. Consequently, he is arrested and thrown into the Shatta prison, where he is beaten.

Habiby inserts into the novel a story about the Ashkenazi, the European Jews who form the ruling elite in Israel. The elders of the community of Zikhron Yaqub disagree as to whether it is lawful for a man to sleep with his wife on the Sabbath. Some think the act is a form of work and, therefore, not lawful. The elders go to the rabbi for an answer. The rabbi declares that sexual relations are not work but pleasure and explains: "If I had ruled it to be work, you would have given it to the Arabs of the nearby town to perform!" The humor of Habiby's story is based on the reality that Israeli Jews rely on Arab laborers to perform tasks that the Jews consider unacceptable.

Habiby's novel reflects the dilemma of Palestinians who have remained in Israel after 1948, discriminated against by the Jewish state and mistrusted by Arab regimes. Yasin Ahmad Fa'ur interprets Sa'id's deliverance by aliens called *fada'iyyin,* a word akin to the Arabic *fida'iyyin* (freedom fighters), as a suggestion that Habiby advocates armed struggle. Peter Heath points to Habiby's use of what Roland Barthes calls "narrative codes": pseudo-autobiography (the foolish antihero narrates the story of his life of exile with no heroic return to the tribe), romance (Sa'id loses a beloved at the conclusion of each of the three books into which the novel is divided), symbol and allegory (two characters named Yu'ad, representing two generations of Palestinians in exile), the fantastic (Sa'id joins creatures from outer space), intertextuality (the novel imitates medieval Arabic narratives such as the *maqamah* but also includes many references to Arab and Islamic history), absurdist parody (the use of comedic anecdotes to reflect harsh truths), and creative harmony (the dissonance of the combination of symbolic and allegorical elements with the realistic details of mundane events).

Habiby published *Liki' ibn Liki'* (Liki' Son of Liki') in 1980. The structure of this satirical play is modeled on the peep show employed in Arab folk tradition to address the common people. Habiby depicts the Palestinian as a victim facing his Israeli executioner:

> Young man: Sheath your sword.
> Executioner: And what to do with my sword, then?
> Young man: We turn it into a ploughshare.
> Executioner: And my tank?
> Young man: Change it back to a tractor.
> Executioner: And my fighter plane?
> Young man: Use it to dust insecticides.
> Executioner: What to do then with my American ally?
> Young man: We screw him together.

At the same time as he criticizes Zionism and its cruel treatment of Palestinians, Habiby condemns Palestinian helplessness.

In 1985 Habiby's novella *Ikhtiyyeh* (Pity) appeared in the review *al-Karmel* and afterward in book form. He received the Jerusalem Medal from the Palestine Liberation Organization in 1990. In 1991 he established the Arabesque Publishing Company in Haifa. In 1992 he received the Israel Prize, the State of Israel's most prestigious cultural award. Widely criticized by Arabs for accepting the award, he donated the $8,000 monetary prize to a charity for child victims of the *intifada*. In 1995 he founded the monthly journal *Masharif,* which he edited until his death.

Emile Habiby died in Haifa on 2 May 1996. At his request, his tombstone reads, "Emile Habiby– Remained in Haifa."

Interview:

Roger Hardy, "Palestinian Writers in Israel," *Boston Review,* 7 (1982).

References:

Kamal Abdel-Malek, *The Rhetoric of Violence: Arab-Jewish Encounters in Palestinian Literature and Film* (New York: Palgrave Macmillan, 2005);

Abdel-Malek and David Jacobson, eds., *Israeli and Palestinian Identities in History and Literature* (New York: St. Martin's Press, 1999);

Roger Allen, *The Arabic Novel: An Historical and Critical Introduction* (Syracuse, N.Y.: Syracuse University Press, 1982);

Yasin Ahmad Fa'ur, *Al-Sukhriyah fi adab Emile Habiby* (Tunis: Dar al-Ma'arif, 1993);

Peter Heath, "Creativity in the Novels of Emile Habiby, with Special Reference to *Sa'id the Pessoptimist,*" in *Tradition, Modernity, and Postmodernity,* edited by Abdel-Malek and Wael Hallaq (Leiden: Brill, 2000), pp. 158–172;

Lital Levy, "Exchanging Words: Thematization of Translation in Arabic Writing from Israel," *Comparative Studies of South Asia, Africa and the Middle East,* 23, nos. 1–2 (2003): 106–127;

Faruq Wadi, *Thalath 'alamat fi al-riwayah al-filastiniyyah* (Beirut: Al-Muassasa al-'Arabiyyah li al-Dirasat wa al-Nashr, 1981), pp. 93–140.

Sonallah Ibrahim
(1937-)

Mara Naaman
Williams College

BOOKS: *Tilka al-ra'ihah* (Cairo: Maktab Yuliu, 1966; expurgated edition, introduction by Yusuf Idris, Cairo: Dar al-Thaqafah al-Jadidah, 1969; unexpurgated edition, Casablanca, 1986);

Insan al-Sad al-'Aly, by Ibrahim, Kamal al-Qilish, and Ru'uf Mus'ad (Cairo: Dar al-Kaatib al-'Arabi, 1967);

Najmat Aghustus: Riwayah (Damascus: Itihad al-Kutab al-'Arabi, 1974);

Al-Lajnah (Beirut: Dar al-Kalima, 1981); translated by Mary St. Germain and Charlene Constable as *The Committee,* afterword by Roger Allen (Syracuse, N.Y.: Syracuse University Press, 2001);

Bayrut Bayrut (Cairo: Dar al-Mustaqbal al-'Arabi, 1984);

Dhat (Cairo: Dar al-Mustaqbal al-'Arabi, 1992); translated by Anthony Calderbank as *Zaat* (Cairo: American University in Cairo Press, 2001);

Sharaf (Cairo: Dar al-Hilal, 1997); translated into French by Richard Jacquemond as *Charaf, ou, L'honneur* (Arles: Actes sud, 2004);

Cairo from Edge to Edge, photographs by Jean Pierre Ribiere (Cairo: American University in Cairo Press, 1998);

Wardah (Cairo: Dar al-Mustaqbal al-'Arabi, 2000);

Amrikanli (Cairo: Dar al-Mustaqbal al-'Arabi, 2003);

Muthakarat Sijin al-Wahat: Sirra Thatiya (Cairo: Dar al-Mustaqbal al-'Arabi, 2006);

Al-Talassus (Cairo: Dar al-Mustaqbal al-'Arabi, 2007);

Al-'Amama wa al-Quba'a (Cairo: Dar al-Mustaqbal al-'Arabi, 2008).

Edition in English: *The Smell of It and Other Stories,* translated by Denys Johnson-Davies (London: Heinemann Educational, 1971).

TRANSLATIONS: Günter de Bruyn, *Al-Himar* (Beirut: Dar Ibn Rushd, 1983);

Al-Tajribah al-unthawiyyah (Cairo: Dar al-Thaqafah al-Jadidah, 1994).

Sonallah Ibrahim (photograph by Youssef Rakha; from al-Ahram Weekly Online: <http://weekly.ahram.org.eg/2003/666/_cu1.htm>)

SELECTED PERIODICAL PUBLICATION–
UNCOLLECTED: "Shahaddah," *Fusul,* 11 (Autumn 1992): 176–180.

One of the best-known members of the 1960s generation of Egyptian authors, Sonallah Ibrahim has emerged as a bold voice of dissent in the Arab world. His polemical novels have critiqued the hypocrisy and contradictions underwriting Arab regimes. In these minimalist and often ironic works he has called attention to the geopolitical effects of global capitalism and its localized marks on the psyches of middle-class Arabs. In 2003, as an act of protest against Egyptian domestic and foreign policy, Ibrahim rejected a prestigious writing award from the Supreme Council of Culture; the gesture won praise from fellow intellectuals, writers, and activists.

At the age of sixty Ibrahim's father, a respected civil servant, had fallen in love with the eighteen-year-old private nurse who was attending to his wife. They were married in secret, and Ibrahim was born to them in 1937 in Cairo. He spent his early youth in the middle-class district of 'Abbasiyah. His mother fled the family after six years of marriage and was eventually hospitalized for mental illness. Not long after she left, Ibrahim's father was forced to retire from his civil-service position and began selling radios to supplement his pension. Ibrahim and his father moved to a less-expensive neighborhood surrounding the Bab al-Futuh (Gate of the Conquests), the eleventh-century Fatimid gate that marks the entrance to one of Cairo's oldest districts. In *Cairo from Edge to Edge* (1998) Ibrahim recalls,

> I grew used to discovering—upon my return from school—that a piece of furniture was missing, until the day when all the living room furniture disappeared. That was where the maid used to sleep, and I sometimes with her, listening to the stories of Ummina al-Ghula and al-Shatir Hasan [the names of two popular fairytales]. In this living room I had invented my first games on the designs of the carpet with simple props, no more than match boxes and newspapers: with the first I would make trains and cars and with the second boats, ships, and armadas.

Ibrahim's father married a Turkish woman, with whom they lived briefly in a two-story home in Sayyidah Zeinab in central Cairo. There Ibrahim saw his first Egyptian and foreign movies at the open-air theater near the main square. Aside from these films, his father's natural ability as a storyteller and their abundant collection of books, particularly novels, had the greatest effect on Ibrahim's writing.

In July 1952 the Free Officers led by Gamal Abdel Nasser seized power in a military coup and sent King Farouk into exile. That fall Ibrahim entered Cairo University to study law, supporting himself with writing for newspapers and doing translation work. During this period he began what he calls "my life's mission": involvement with the Egyptian Marxist group al-Haraka al-Dimuqratiyya li al-Taharrur al-Watani (The Democratic Party for the Liberation of the Homeland), or Haditu, also known as the Democratic Movement for National Liberation (DMNL), which had helped to bring down the monarchy and initially supported Nasser's revolutionary council. The regime's suppression of a factory workers' strike at Kafr al-Dawwar in 1953 led Haditu to withdraw its support from Nasser.

Having become a publicly declared opposition party, they were forced to go underground. Owing to his political activities, Ibrahim neglected his university studies and never graduated.

Ibrahim was arrested and released several times for his political activities and writings. In 1959 he was arrested, along with hundreds of intellectuals and leftists, including many other members of Haditu, charged with conspiring to overthrow the regime, and sentenced to seven years in prison. During his time in prison he decided to become a writer. His recollections of this period formed the basis for his first—and what many call his best—work, the novella *Tilka al-ra'ihah* (1966; translated as "The Smell of It," 1971). In a 2003 interview with Youssef Rakha he recalled:

> Prison at the age of 21 or 22 was a cruel but rich experience, and it was directly after my release—when *Tilka al-ra'ihah* was written—that I began to feel the need to tell. Once again I resolved that certain things must be communicated and expressed. Maybe it was isolation within the prison precincts, which is imposed on you as part of the torture. To ease the passing of time you automatically exercise your imagination. Day dreams. Fantasies. Plus what you're seeing all around you: people's stories and how they lived outside, their methods of adjusting to prison life. And then there were instances of heroism or cowardice, of people standing up to persecution of people dying of torture—representative, telling instances that I wanted to capture in some form. At the time I would write a new novel every day—in my head.

Ibrahim's imprisonment seems to have generated many of the themes of his oeuvre: the tyranny and bureaucracy of the state, the existential struggle of the individual to act, and sexual impotence as a manifestation of political and psychological paralysis. Ibrahim has called prison a university and a rite of passage for an entire generation of writers and activists during Nasser's regime.

Ibrahim was exonerated and released in 1964. He worked at a bookstore, then as an editor for the Egyptian government's wire service, the Middle East News Agency.

Tilka al-ra'ihah was published in Cairo in 1966 and immediately banned: a committee of government officials condemned the work on the basis of its language and its political and explicit sexual content. A second edition, in which passages were censored without Ibrahim's permission, was published in 1969. Expurgated versions also appeared in Cairo in 1971 and in the Lebanese literary journal *Sh'ir* in 1968. The complete version was translated into English in 1971, and an unexpurgated Arabic text was finally published in Morocco in 1986.

Front cover for a 1971 collection of English translations of Ibrahim's short stories (Thomas Cooper Library, University of South Carolina)

In the introduction to the 1969 edition the writer Yusuf Idris calls *Tilka al-ra'ihah* not "just a story" but "a revolution, the beginning of which is the artist's rebellion against himself." *Tilka al-ra'ihah* offers a semiautobiographical portrait of Ibrahim's prison experience, release, and attempt to adjust to a life without political struggle. The unnamed narrator struggles to write in the face of his sense of disorientation at the bourgeois values his family and friends have adopted. The bulk of the narrative describes the details of his days under the watchful eye of his parole officer. These scenes are written in in prose that borrows stylistically from Ernest Hemingway and became Ibrahim's signature voice: the sentences are short and stripped of all literary flourish and figurative language. But when the narrator's thoughts drift in stream-of-consciousness fashion to memories of his childhood, his romantic relationships, and his time in prison, the style becomes lyrical and expresses longing and deep loss. In his 1992 article "Shahaddah" (A Testimony) Ibrahim notes that he was particularly influenced by the work of Virginia Woolf and by Naguib Mahfouz's Cairo Trilogy (1956–1957).

In the summer of 1966 Ibrahim and the writers Kamal al-Qilish and Ru'uf Mus'ad traveled to the south of Egypt to visit the Aswan High Dam. The project had been conceived in 1952; work had begun in 1960, and the dam was completed in 1965. As a result of the massive propaganda campaign surrounding the dam and the years Egyptians had waited in anticipation of its completion, the dam, as the Arabic literary scholar Céza Kassem-Draz notes in a 1982 article, had come to symbolize many things—first and foremost, the will and self-determination of the people. Ibrahim and his colleagues published their observations in 1967 as *Insan al-Sad al-'Aly* (The Man of the High Dam). For the next several years Ibrahim was obsessed with the idea of writing a novel about the building of the dam. He writes in "Shahaddah,"

> this immense engineering project . . . brought together all of the contradictions of reality. Because it was born in the fierce confrontation with colonialism, old and new, the process itself contained an important moral: that of changing the course of the Nile whose course hadn't been altered for a thousand years. Likewise, it required the introduction of new tools and techniques, and was completed with the zeal of the people in the shadow of a military administration. Taking part in it were representatives of all classes, yet it carried in it features of the next class to rule, namely the class of contractors, entrepreneurs, and the agents of foreign companies. In addition to that, the work on the project was divided into two phases: the first phase consisted of simple, clear work—merely digging and filling up the ground with earth to a large extent; in the second phase the work became more artistic, [performed] at a high technical level using tools that were more complex.

In 1967 Ibrahim completed an autobiographical novel similar to *Tilka al-ra'ihah,* but he took a position as a correspondent in the Arabic bureau of the press agency of the German Democratic Republic in East Berlin and was unable to look for a publisher for it. It was finally published in 2006 as *Muthakarat Sijin al-Wahat: Sirra Thatiya* (Memoirs of the Oasis Prison: An Autobiography).

The Aswan High Dam was officially inaugurated by President Anwar Sadat in 1970. That same year Ibraham received a grant to study cinematography in Moscow. He returned to Cairo in 1974 and went to work for the publishing house Dar al-Thaqafah al-Jadidah. That same year he published his novel about the High Dam, *Najmat Aghustus* (The Star of August). The unnamed narrator visits the dam site and compares the official announcements about the construction process with the reality as he observes it. Ibrahim's narration, written in the same sparse prose style as in *Tilka al-ra'ihah*, is interspersed with excerpts from publications of the Egyptian Ministry of Culture, the High Dam administration, and the Arab Contractors Company, and sources related to Ancient Egypt. In her 1982 analysis of the work Kassem-Draz argues that the discrepancy between the official propaganda about the construction and the daily reality for the workers and Nubians of the area deflates the myth of the High Dam and, with it, the promises of the 1952 Free Officer's Revolution to transform Egypt.

In 1975 Ibrahim married and devoted himself to writing full-time. He and his wife settled in the district of Heliopolis in Cairo, where they still live.

In "Shahaddah" Ibrahim describes the 1970s as a period of confusion. The struggle for independence from the British had been won; but the project of modernization had failed miserably, multinational corporations had replaced British imperial hegemony, and many workers lost their gains and fell back to the standard of living of the 1950s. In this climate Ibrahim returned to a piece of paper on which, many years earlier, he had recorded an account of an individual confronting a committee of examiners who require him to respond to a series of vague questions for the sole purpose of debasing and humiliating him. Incorporating his own experience of being interrogated by the committee that had banned *Tilka al-ra'ihah*, he produced one of his most significant works. *Al-Lajnah* (1981; translated as *The Committee*, 2001) is a critique of totalitarian bureaucracy reminiscent of Franz Kafka's *Der Prozeß* (1925; translated as *The Trial*, 1937) and the first Arabic novel to expose the role of multinational corporations and the consequences of President Sadat's Open Door Policy. The unnamed narrator is brought before a committee, presumably to defend himself against charges of a crime of which he has no knowledge; instead, the committee assigns him to report back to it on the person he considers "the greatest contemporary Arab luminary." After researching the possibilities at length, the narrator presents to the committee a report on a man known only as "the Doctor": an elite businessman and politician who has opportunistically used the Open Door Policy for his private gain. As Roger Allen notes in the afterword to the English translation of the novel, the report is a "stinging indictment of the values of an entire class in Egypt that has chosen to enrich itself at the expense of its fellow citizens." The narrator's monologues in response to the committee's questions offer an abbreviated catalogue of twentieth-century cultural, commercial, and political history. Ibrahim traces the global migration of a bottle of Coca-Cola and considers the interrelatedness of various market phenomena from Egyptian cigarettes and the price of petroleum to the ways in which the Doctor's decisions influence Egyptian foreign policy.

In 1983 Ibrahim translated the novel *Brudians Esel* (1968, Brudian's Donkey), by the German author Günter de Bruyn. The following year he turned to the civil war in Lebanon in his novel *Bayrut Bayrut* (1984, Beirut Beirut). In "Shahaddah" he suggests that just as the High Dam project served in *Najmat Aghustu* as a portal for understanding the experience of a generation of Egyptians, the fifteen-year Lebanese civil war functioned as a focal point for considering the political and religious factionalism that shook the Arab world in the 1980s. The narrator is a young writer who comes to Beirut in the fall of 1980 hoping that his manuscript, which has been rejected in Egypt, can be published in the freer intellectual environment of Lebanon. On his arrival a friend asks him to write the narration for a documentary film on the history of the civil war. His transcriptions of his viewing sessions, excerpts from articles he is reading on Lebanon, and his discussions with Lebanese friends and acquaintances provide the reader with information about the complex political and social circumstances that have given rise to the war. The narrator's conversations with several Lebanese publishers reveal that the industry is just as corrupt and state-controlled there as it is in Egypt. Samia Mehrez argues in *Egyptian Writers between History and Fiction: Essays on Naguib Mahfouz, Sonallah Ibrahim and Gamal al-Ghitani* (1994) that *Bayrut Bayrut*, like *Tilka al-ra'ihah* and *al-Lajnah*, is an attempt to "recount the fate of the book" as one and the same as the fate of the writer: both are taken seriously as moral and political threats to the nation and, at the same time, trivialized.

Ibrahim's best-received work to date, *Dhat* (1992; translated as *Zaat*, 2001), is the product of extensive archival research and is his first novel with a female narrator. The Arabic word *Dhat* can be translated as "self" or "essence," but some critics have speculated that Ibrahim uses it to refer to the courageous princess who is the title character of the Arabic *sirah* (popular epic) *Dhat al-himmah*. Ibrahim later said that he initially wanted to construct a protagonist of mythic proportions but that in the process of composition the character evolved in a more tragic direction.

Departing from the short, clipped sentences of his earlier works, Ibrahim writes *Dhat* in a verbose style that resembles the novels of American writers such as Thomas Pynchon and David Foster Wallace. The work takes the form of a long monologue filled with qualifiers and parenthetical clauses, interjections from the author mocking and deconstructing the artifice of his own novel, and extensive excerpts from Egyptian newspapers of the 1970s and 1980s—a method he calls "contextualization" rather than "documentation." (He told

Front cover for the 2001 English translation of Ibrahim's 1992 novel, Dhat, *about a modern professional woman—a Cairo newspaper editor—who decides to wear the veil and send her son to a religious school (Thomas Cooper Library, University of South Carolina)*

Rakha in 2003, "Documentation would imply backing up certain truths or ideas with evidence, facts that can be checked and verified. The kind of contextualization that I practice does not serve that purpose. There are no proper references, for example. The insertions merely act to surround the text with a relevant discourse, and there are no factual arguments as such.")

The inundation of detail thrusts the reader into the mind of Dhat, whose ever-pressing concerns as a young wife and middle-class professional prove humorous as they are set against a sea of headlines that outline the corruption and hypocrisy of President Hosni Mubarak's regime in the 1980s. As Dhat, an editor at a Cairo paper, strives to keep up with the trends and styles set by her neighbors in modern Cairo—household renovations, new appliances, fashions, and social causes—the headlines suggest an unprecedented level of corruption, propaganda, and political whitewashing. Dhat's personal triumphs and struggles are understood as the struggles of a generation only in the context of the historical and political discourse surrounding them. The tender and often humorous portrayal of Dhat's relationship with her husband, 'Abdel Maguid, is an attempt to demystify, from a woman's point of view, the romance of modern-day marriage in Egypt. Her decisions to wear the *hijab* (veil) and to send her son to a religious school are juxtaposed with headlines that report the increasing visibility of Shaykh Muhammad Sharawi and his militant Islamist group, Gama'at Islamiyyah. Sharawi's popularity and Dhat's decision to wear the veil symbolize the shift in consciousness in middle-class Egyptian communities to a less secular worldview. Her quest for redress for being sold a can of olives on which the expiration date was changed by the grocer leads her down the labyrinthine halls of Egyptian administrative offices, where she learns that "justice" is an illusion perpetuated by professional bureaucrats. The realization of the futility of her pursuit and the bankruptcy of the state apparatus is the last straw for Dhat; her decision to abandon her grievance is the moment in which she turns her back on the promise of Egypt.

Ibrahim received the Ghalib Halasa Award from the Jordanian Author's Union in 1992 and the Sultan Eleweiss Prize of the United Arab Emirates—one of the most prestigious literary awards in the Arab world—in 1994. Also in 1994 he translated a collection of prose by Western authors as *al-Tajribah al-unthawiyyah* (The Female Experience).

Ibrahim returned to a prison setting in the novel *Sharaf* (1997, Honor). Sharaf, a twenty-year-old middle-class Egyptian, innocently strikes up a friendship with a blond foreigner named John outside a Cairo movie theater. After the film, John invites Sharaf to his apartment in the wealthy Zamalek district for a drink. After giving Sharaf a necklace he had admired, John makes a sexual advance that quickly becomes aggressive. Attempting to repel the attack, Sharaf hits John over the head with a bottle of whiskey and accidentally kills him. In prison, with the help of his fellow inmates, Sharaf comes to realizes the shallowness of his materialistic values. A Coptic pharmacist, Dr. Ramzi Boutros Nassif, details for Sharaf his attempts to expose the corruption undergirding a multinational pharmaceutical corporation. Like *al-Lajnah* and *Dhat*, *Sharaf* includes excerpts from newspapers, magazines, and journals. The documents chronicle the pharmaceutical company's financial rise and reveal the awesome reach of global capitalism, particularly as it has affected Arab countries. In this respect *Sharaf* picks up where *al-Lajnah* left off, elucidating in greater detail what Amina Elbendary terms the "Cocacolisation of the Middle East." Ibrahim indicts not only corporate interests in the Third World but also the ruling elites who work with exploitative foreign companies instead of developing sound economies in their own countries. *Sharaf* received rave reviews in Egypt and was awarded the Naguib Mahfouz Prize as best Egyptian novel by the American University in Cairo in 1998. In an act of protest against the university, Ibrahim refused the prize. A 2004 French translation by the Arabic literary scholar Richard Jacquemond, *Charaf, ou, L'honneur* (Charaf; or, Honor) was widely praised in the French press.

In 1998 Ibrahim accepted a visiting professorship at the University of California at Berkeley. During his seven months in the United States he worked on his longest novel to date, *Wardah* (2000). The product of five years of extensive research and interviewing, *Wardah*, like *Bayrut Bayrut*, seeks to understand the geopolitical situation in the Middle East by focusing on a single country. A Communist writer, Rushdie, travels to Oman in the 1960s to look for an old friend he has not seen in thirty years. In the course of his search he is entrusted with the diaries of his friend's sister, Wardah, a leader of the Dhufar liberation movement. The bulk of the novel is the story of Wardah's passage from young idealist to impassioned radical and leader of the movement against the British and the Omani sultanate. Ibrahim incorporates into Wardah's diaries newspaper extracts, portions of political speeches, and passages from books. The novel is a highly charged polemic that criticizes the British and the Americans, who, with the help of Iran, curtailed and eventually dismantled the Dhufar movement.

In California, Ibrahim had kept a journal of his observations and experiences and had clipped articles from American newspapers. He used some of these materials in his next novel, *Amrikanli* (2003), about an Egyptian named Shukri who is spending a year as a visiting professor of history at a fictional university in the San Francisco Bay Area. With the exception of Shukri, the characters are not well developed but represent various political positions. Shukri lectures on the history of Egypt from pharaonic times to the present and on the imperial history of the United States from its occupation of Native American territory in the eighteenth century to its current involvement in the Middle East. He compares American military and economic hegemony to the history of past empires, such as the Roman and Ottoman, and argues that America, through its neglect of its own people and its bombastic foreign policy, has sown the seeds of its own demise: it is only a matter of time before the American empire, like others before it, will collapse from within. While Shukri has an encyclopedic knowledge of history, he is ignorant about class stratification in contemporary America. Through his colleagues at the university and the diverse backgrounds of his students, he comes to understand the complex social fabric of the United States and the plight of the American underclass.

The title of the novel puzzled some reviewers. The Egyptian writer and translator Mona El-Ghobashy contended in her review in the literary magazine *al-Jadid* (2004): "The title, *Amrikanli*, is a creative, ambiguous play on words: it can either be read as Amri-kan-li (the idea credited to Ali Muhammad Ali on the inside front cover), meaning, 'I was my own master,' or it can be read as an echo of *Osmanli*, the disparaging Egyptian slang for the externally powerful, internally rotting Ottoman Empire that ruled the Middle East for centuries." Others suggested that *Amrikanli* may mean "American-like" or "Americanish."

The publication of *Amrikanli* was overshadowed in the press by Ibrahim's rejection of the Supreme Council for Culture's 2003 Novelist of the Year Award, which carried a monetary prize of 100,000 Egyptian pounds ($17,000). When his name was announced at the Novelist's Assembly in Cairo on 22 October, he made a speech in which he gave his reasons for refusing the prize: the suffering of the Palestinians, Egypt's relationship with the United States, and the Egyptian government's failure to provide adequate support for education and the arts. He concluded: "I publicly decline the prize because it is awarded by a government that in my opinion, lacks the credibility of bestowing it." Minister of Culture Farouq Hosni accused Ibrahim of hypocrisy for refusing this award while accepting others, but Ibrahim's willingness to take a public stand against the government was widely praised.

One year later, the German-based Ibn Rushd Foundation awarded Ibrahim its sixth annual Freedom of Thought Prize, noting that he had "enriched modern engaged literature with outstanding writing." In his acceptance speech he recalled that in prison in 1964 he had read a statement by Mahfouz: "The only basic commitment one must have in art is honesty." He quoted a passage from the Indian writer Arundhati Roy's novel *The God of Small Things* (1996) in which she decries the exploitation of poorer countries by wealthy nations and multinational corporations and makes an impassioned plea that the leaders of these nations recognize their accountability to their own people and thus not blur the lines between democracy and fascism. Paraphrasing Roy, Ibrahim emphasized that resistance to such exploitation should not be branded terrorism but an act of war. He ended his speech by saying of Roy's novel, "This, too, is a form of honesty."

From his first novella, *Tilka al-ra'ihah*, Sonallah Ibrahim has offered his works as literary testaments to the experience of a region undergoing vast transformation. In his writing he has sought to make sense of the conflicts and injustices that have plagued the Arab world by showing how corrupt regimes and global capitalism have chipped away at the regions's sense of collective agency. In spite of, and perhaps because of, his notoriety, Ibrahim has proven to be one of the most prolific and internationally recognized authors of the 1960s generation in Egypt. His work, with its raw candor, challenges his readers to examine critically the political and economic forces shaping the world around them.

Interview:

Youssef Rakha, "The Smell of Dissent," *al-Ahram Weekly On-line,* 666 (27 November–3 December 2003) <http://weekly.ahram.org.eg/2003/666/cu1.htm> (accessed 23 September 2008).

References:

Firas 'Abid, *Al-Insan al-maqhur fi adab Sonallah Ibrahim: Ru'yyah sociolojiyyah nasiyyah* (Acre, Israel: Mu'assasat al-Aswar, 2001);

Catherine Bédarida, "Sonallah Ibrahim, L'Utopie par les Femmes," *Le Monde,* 4 November 2002;

Amina Elbendary, "East, West and in Between," *Al-Ahram Weekly On-line,* 507 (9-15 November 2000) <http://weekly.ahram.org.eg/2000/507/cu4.htm> (accessed 23 September 2008);

Mona El-Ghobashy, "Restoration or Ruin? Sonallah Ibrahim Rejects Arab Novel Award," *Al-Jadid Magazine: A Review and Record of Arab Culture and Arts,* nos. 46-47 (2004): 4-6;

Sabry Hafez, The Egyptian Novel in the Sixties," in *Critical Perspectives on Modern Arabic Literature: 1945-1980,* edited by Issa J. Boullata (Washington, D.C.: Three Continents Press, 1980), pp. 171-187;

Abdalla F. Hassan, "Black Humor in Dark Times," *Worldpress.org,* (19 June 2003) <http://www.worldpress.org/Mideast/1205.cfm> (accessed 23 September 2008);

Céza Kassem-Draz, "In Quest of New Narrative Forms: Irony in the Works of Four Egyptian Writers (1967-1979): Al-Ghitani, Yahya T. Abdallah, Tubya, Sonallah Ibrahim," *Journal of Arabic Literature,* 12 (1981): 137-159;

Kassem-Draz, "Opaque and Transparent Discourse: A Contrastive Analysis of the 'Star of August' and 'The Man of the High Dam' by Sonallah Ibrahim," *Alif: Journal of Comparative Poetics,* 2 (Spring 1982): 32-50;

Charles Levinson, "Outside the Barn," *Cairo Times Magazine,* 30 October–5 November 2003, p. 9;

Samia Mehrez, *Egyptian Writers between History and Fiction: Essays on Naguib Mahfouz, Sonallah Ibrahim and Gamal al-Ghitani* (Cairo: American University in Cairo Press, 1994);

Mehrez, "The Value of Freedom," *al-Ahram Weekly On-line,* 662 (30 October–5 November 2003) <http://weekly.ahram.org.eg/print/2003/662/cu6.htm>; (accessed 23 September 2008);

Youssef Rakha, "An Odd Assortment," *al-Ahram Weekly On-line,* 487 (22–28 June 2000) <http://weekly.ahram.org.eg/2000/487/cu2.htm> (accessed 23 September 2008);

Hamdi Sakkut, *The Arabic Novel: Bibliography and Critical Introduction: 1865-1995,* translated by Roger Monroe, volume 1 (Cairo: American University in Cairo Press, 2000), pp. 17-57.

Yusuf Idris
(19 May 1927 – 1 August 1991)

Wyoma vanDuinkerken
Texas A&M University

BOOKS: *Arkhas layali* (Cairo: Dar Ruz al-Yusuf, 1954); translated by Wadida Wassef as *The Cheapest Nights and Other Stories* (Washington, D.C.: Three Continents Press, 1978);

Jumhuriyyat Farahat (Cairo: Dar Ruz al-Yusuf, 1956);

Malik al-Qutn (Cairo: Al-Mu'assasah al-Qawmiyyah li al-Nashr, 1956);

Al-Batal (Cairo: Dar al-Fikr, 1957);

Alaysa kadhalika (Cairo: Markaz Kutub al-Sharq al-Aswat, 1957);

Hadithat sharaf (Beirut: Lebanon: Dar al-Adab, 1958);

Al-Lahzah al-harijah (Cairo: Al-Kitab al-Fiddi, al-Sharikah al-'Arabiyyah li al-Tiba'ah, 1958);

Al-Haram (Cairo: Al-Sharikah al-'Arabiyyah li-al-Tiba'ah, 1959); translated by Kristin Peterson-Ishaq as *The Sinners* (Washington: Three Continents Press, 1984);

Akhir al dunya (Cairo: Mu'assasat Ruz al-Yusuf, 1961);

Al-'Askari al-Aswad (Cairo: Dar al-Ma'rifah, 1962);

Al-'Ayb (Cairo: Mu'assasat Ruz al-Yusuf, 1962);

Rijal wa thiran (Cairo: Al-Mu'assasah al-Misriyyah al-'Ammah li al-Ta'lif, 1964);

Qa' al-Madina (Cairo: Sharikat Markaz Kutub al-Sharq al-Awsat, 1964);

Al-Farafir (Cairo: Dar al-Tahrir, 1964);

Al-Mahzalah al-Ardiyyah (Cairo: Majallat al-Masrah, 1965);

Lughat al-ay ay (Cairo: Mu'assasat Ruz al-Yusuf, 1966); translated by Nawal Nagib as *The Language of Pain and Other Stories* (Cairo: General Egyptian Book Organization, 1990);

Qissat Hubb (Cairo: Dar al-Kitab al-'Arabi, 1967); translated by R. Neil Hewison as *City of Love and Ashes* (Cairo: American University of Cairo Press, 1999);

An-Nadahah (Cairo: Mu'assasat Dar al-Hilal, 1969);

Al-Mukhatatin (Cairo: Majallat al-Masrah, 1969);

Mashuq al-Hams (Beirut: Dar al-Tali'ah li al-Tiba'ah wa al-Nashr, 1970);

Al-Bayda' (Beirut: Dar al-Tali'ah, 1970);

Al-Jins al-thalith (Cairo: 'Alam al-Kutub, 1971);

Yusuf Idris (from P. M. Kurpershoek, The Short Stories of Yusuf Idris: A Modern Egyptian Author, *1981; Tulane University Library)*

Bayt min lahm (Cairo: 'Alam al-Kutub, 1971);

Al-Sayyidah Fiyyina (Beirut: Dar al-'Awdah, 1977);

Ana sultan qanun al-wujud (Cairo: Maktabat Gharib, 1978);

Nyu-Yurk 80 (Cairo: Maktabat Misr, 1981);

Uqtulha (Cairo: Maktabat Misr, 1982);

Al-Bahlawan (Cairo: Maktabat Misr, 1983);

Al-'Atab 'ala al-nazar (Cairo: Markaz al-Ahram li al-Tarjamah wa al-Nashr, Mu'assasat al-Ahram, 1987).

Editions in English: *Modern Egyptian Short Stories*, translated by Sa'd al-Gabalawy (Fredericton, N.B.: York Press, 1977)–includes "The Wallet," "Farahat's Republic," and "Sultan, the Law of Existence";

In the Eye of the Beholder: Tales of Egyptian Life, edited by Roger Allen (Minneapolis: Bibliotheca Islamica, 1978)—comprises "A Stare," "The Wallet," "City Dregs," "Playing House," "The Omitted Letter," "The Aorta," "The Concave Mattress," "The Greatest Sin of All," "The Little Bird on the Telephone Wire," "The Chair Carrier," "The Chapter on the Cow," "Lily, Did you have to put the light on?," "In Cellophane Wrapping," and "A House of Flesh";

Rings of Burnished Brass, translated by Catherine Cobham (London: Heinemann, 1984; Washington, D.C.: Three Continents Press, 1984)—includes "Rings of Burnished Brass," "The Stranger," "The Black Policeman," and "The Siren";

A Leader of Men, translated by Saad Elkhadem (Fredericton, N.B.: York Press, 1988);

Selected Stories, translated and introduced by Dalya Cohen (Exeter, U.K.: Ithaca, 1991);

Three Egyptian Short Stories, translated by Sa'd al-Gabalawy (Fredericton, N.B.: York Press, 1991)—includes "Farahat's Republic," "The Wallet," and "Abu Sayyid";

The Piper Dies and Other Short Stories, translated and introduced by Dalya Cohen-Mor (Potomac, Md.: Sheba Press, 1992)—comprises "Egyptian Mona Lisa," "The Point," "Swan Song," "The Game," "Caught Red-Handed," "Innocence," "19502," "The Sunken Mattress," "Kill Her," "She," "The Man and the Ant," and "The Piper Dies."

Yusuf Idris was an Egyptian short-story writer, novelist, and playwright whose work recorded the images of a changing society from the 1950s into the 1990s. He achieved his goal of drawing attention to important social, economic, and political concerns by realistically portraying the lives of ordinary people. Idris's keen eye for detail helped to introduce realism to Arabic fiction as he explored such topics as political and social freedom, Egypt's soaring population, loss of innocence, homosexuality, love, repression of civil liberties, alienation, poverty, traditional Egyptian customs, and religious fundamentalism.

On 19 May 1927 'Ali Yusuf Sayyid Yusuf (Idris) was born into a middle-class farming family in the small Egyptian village of al-Bayrum in the province of Sharqiyyah. His father, Idris 'Ali, was a successful cultivator of arid land and became known as a "Ma'mour," the name given to senior officials who administrated both a large area of land and the people who inhabited the area. As the eldest son in a family of six children, Idris benefited from his father's position for the first five years of his life and was treated like a prince by all the people who lived in the area his father managed. Idris's mother came from a poor family in al-Bayrum and was stingy with money. She was much younger than Idris's father, and according to Idris, as quoted in Roger Allen's *Critical Perspectives on Yusuf Idris* (1994), "she was and perhaps still is one of the most aggressive characters I have ever known."

When Idris reached school age, the comfortable world he had known came crashing down. He lived in a remote area where there was no school or town, so when he was six, his parents sent him to live with his mother's family in al-Bayrum. His grandmother was a hard woman with a dreadful temper who yelled at her grandson for the slightest reason. He was the only child in a house of more than twenty-five adults, and she expected him to behave like the adults. The one comfort in his mother's ancestral home was his great-grandmother's stories. Idris sat on her lap as she told him tales of her childhood and relayed old Egyptian folktales. These stories had a lasting effect on Idris's imagination.

On school days Idris had to leave at 5:00 A.M. to make the two-hour walk to the town of Faqqus, the site of the closest primary school. Here too Idris felt out of place as he was the youngest student in a group of adolescents. Both in his great-grandmother's home and in his school Idris felt isolated, and to combat his loneliness he used his imagination to escape his unhappy existence. When Idris completed his elementary education, his parents sent him to continue his education in Damietta, where he lived with his uncle 'Abd al-Salim. Although Idris was forced to live a quiet life because of his uncle's poor health, they were by no means hermits. Idris's uncle earned a living as a tailor, and this job brought many women into Idris's world. These women gossiped with their dressmaker, and the stories they told help foster Idris's imagination and love for storytelling.

With the outbreak of World War II Idris was once again uprooted from his home and was forced to return to live with his family of three brothers and two sisters. As the family moved many times in order to live close to his father's work, Idris attended a chain of secondary schools in Mansaral, Zaqaziq, and Tanta. The end of the war coincided with the end of Idris's secondary education, and in 1945 he was able to enroll in the medical school of Cairo University with a full scholarship. At the university Idris became an active member of the student's nationalist movement, which played a key role in the political turmoil in Egypt prior to the Revolution of 1952. His political actions led to his arrest and spending two months in prison in 1949.

Idris's political activism led to his becoming the executive secretary of the anti-British student nationalist movement. His main role as secretary was to write leaflets and pamphlets that supported the revolutionary cause, which contributed to his realization of his love for writing. He had been writing stories for his own amusement throughout his university career, but it was not until 1950 when his story "Unshudat al-ghuraba" (The Strangers' Song) was published in the magazine *al-Qissah* that his writing career truly began to flourish. Gradually, he started to write short stories for *al Masri*, a well-known Cairo newspaper, as well as *Rose al-Yusuf*, a weekly magazine.

In 1951 Idris was imprisoned again for his participation in the student demonstrations and spent three months in prison before being released. That same year he graduated from medical school and began an internship at Qasr el-Aini Hospital. He soon opened his own clinic in Cairo and also began working as a medical inspector for the Department of Health. His experiences visiting some of the poorest neighborhoods in Cairo provided material for his stories. Idris's first collection of short stories, *Arkhas layali* (1954; translated as *The Cheapest Nights and Other Stories*, 1978), was introduced by the celebrated Egyptian writer Taha Husayn, who saluted Idris as an outstanding writer with immense talent. The stories included in this volume are some of the most prominent examples of Idris's realism.

Drawing on his childhood experiences, medical knowledge, and political beliefs, Idris gives his readers a vivid picture of how Egyptian people endured difficult social conditions such as poverty and oppression. He typically does this by introducing his characters, such as 'Abd al-Karim, the main character of the title story "Arkhas Layali" (The Cheapest Nights), in their everyday, often rural, surroundings. 'Abd al-Karim's story begins as he is leaving his local mosque after evening prayer and encounters a street filled with children who are begging for food. Irritated because he has not slept well for some time and angered by his own impoverished condition, he curses the children and their existence. Further frustrated by the fact that he cannot find any of his friends to talk to at this late hour, he is forced to return to his home. When he arrives home, he must climb over his six children (reminiscent of the street children) to reach his wife. Once he reaches her, they make love. The story quickly moves into the future, and 'Abd al-Karim is once again being congratulated on the birth of another son. A central theme of this story is the accelerating population rate of Egypt at the time and how this population boom affects the economic condition of the poorer classes.

Unlike other writers who mask the topic of poverty and its effect on Egyptian society with philosophi-

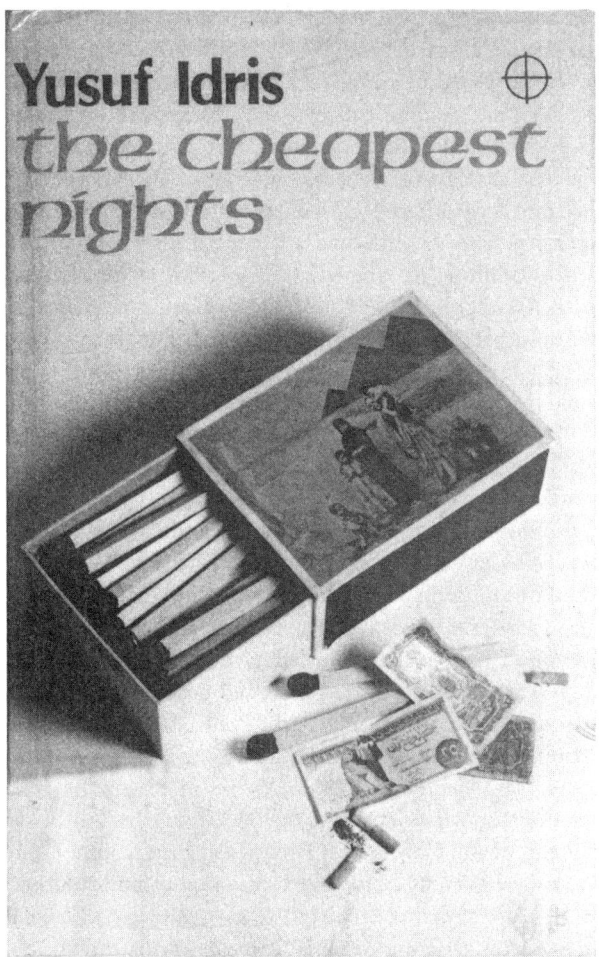

Front cover for the translation of Arkhas layali, *a 1954 collection of Idris's stories that depicts life in the poorest sections of Cairo (Thomas Cooper Library, University of South Carolina)*

cal commentary, Idris uses colloquial language to directly depict the lives of the poor. Never judging his characters, he describes their poverty-stricken surroundings as a way of having the reader relate to the characters and their fight against their fate and circumstance. Because Idris is committed to powerful, unflinching realism, he seldom offers his reader a happy ending: his characters rarely appear better off at the end of the story than they were at the start.

Idris's attention to the problems of poverty in Egyptian society is also clear in "Shughlana" (Hard Up) in *Arkhas layali*. This story follows the downward progression of 'Abduh, who starts out as a cook but gradually works down the career ladder to jobs as doorman and waiter. He ends up at a blood bank selling his blood to support his family. The day that 'Abduh goes to the blood bank and is informed that he has anemia—meaning he can no longer sell his blood to feed, clothe, and house his family—the attendant tells him that they do not want to "exploit" him. Idris has his character ask sarcastically how he is *not* being exploited.

Idris's concern for rural folk, especially peasants, is clear in his first collection of stories. At the time, Eygpt's farmland was managed by large landowners who used peasants to work their land. When workers became too old or feeble, they were replaced by new farmers. The discarded peasants were left with nothing and little hope for the future. Egyptian leader Gamal Abdel-Nasser originally promoted agrarian reform that was intended to improve the lot of peasants. Idris, however, believed that Nasser was being pressured by the wealthy landlords to squash the farmer's dreams of financial stability. Idris's dream of Egypt becoming an idyllic state under Nasser began to vanish as he watched not only the disintegration of the agrarian reform policy but also Nasser's compromise with Britain, allowing the foreign power to withdraw gradually rather than immediately from the Suez Canal.

Upset at what he believed to be a betrayal of the Egyptian people, Idris started writing articles in local papers that criticized the Nasser-led government. Eventually, Nasser began imprisoning all who opposed his administration, and Idris was incarcerated from August 1954 until September 1955. While in prison he met communist prisoners who belonged to the Author's Bureau of the Communist Party. Idris briefly joined the Communist Party but left in 1956 because he could not fully support their beliefs.

After severing ties with the party Idris took a job writing for the newspaper *al-Jumhuriyyah,* where he met Anwar al-Sadat, who was then the editor. Learning that Idris had limited time to write, Sadat arranged for the author to hold a position in the Ministry of National Guidance so that he could focus more time on his writing. When Sadat became the Secretary-General of the Egyptian National Union in 1957, he appointed Idris as his aide-de-camp–a position that did not last long because Nasser, who was unsure of Idris's allegiance to the revolution, told Sadat not to rely on Idris. Idris was subsequently dismissed from the Ministry of National Guidance and the Ministry of Health. At *al-Jumhuriyyah* Idris began writing a weekly column called "Yawmiyyat" (Diaries) that ran until 1969 in which he commented on social and political issues. His position allowed him to travel extensively throughout the Middle East, and he witnessed social injustices in other nations.

In 1956 Idris released his second short-story collection, *Jumhuriyyat Farahat* (Farahat's Republic), again focused on the difficult lives of workers, as well as the play *Malik al-qutn* (The Cotton King). The collection established Idris as a master of the short story and became one of his most famous works, translated into many languages. The title story, the best-known tale in the collection, features an unnamed narrator in dialogue with Farahat, a sergeant who works the front desk at the Cairene Police Station processing victims' complaints and incoming prisoners. When the narrator enters the station, Farahat recognizes him as being from a higher social class than his own. The sergeant assumes that the gentleman is not a detainee and strikes up a conversation, though in fact the narrator has been arrested for his political activity and has come to the police station to be processed for questioning. Farahat tells the narrator how he once made a utopian film about an Egypt for Egyptians, free from foreign pressure or control–a theme that indirectly indicates Idris's own dissatisfaction with what he regarded as Nasser's accommodating spirit with Britain. When Farahat discovers that the man he is talking to has been arrested for political reasons, his demeanor immediately changes. As in his previous stories, Idris effectively uses colloquial language, allowing the reader to vividly imagine the police officer and to show how in a moment of disgust and anger the disappointed Farahat is once again brought back to the unhappy reality of his life, hiding his dreams for the future of his country behind a veil.

Despite Idris's contribution to the development of the short story, his use of colloquial Arabic was criticized throughout his career. Indeed, Husayn, who had praised Idris in introducing *Arkhas Layali,* recommended in the introduction he wrote for *Jumhuriyyat Farahat* that the young author change his style and write in modern standard Arabic rather than in the language used by ordinary Arabs. Despite this call for change, Idris adapted the story "Jumhuriyyat Farahat" as a play, and continued to write colloquial Arabic. In *Critical Perspectives on Yusif Idris,* Idris asserted that his choice of language was integral to his writing process:

> I personally regard the language problem as a burden to me. But I'm very content when writing in Egyptian Colloquial.... Personally, I cannot write in the classical written language *(fusha).* I can do it and it may turn out fine, but at the crucial moment of composition I am not in a position to choose between what is suitable and what is not. The writing is almost dictated to me. I am the means, not the writer himself. Introducing the force of will here impairs the entire process. Perhaps it is better to interfere later with a conscious mind and through the author himself.

Idris's devoted readers would no doubt agree with the author that it is not possible to realistically portray characters without hearing the language they use.

Idris's political ideals, mainly an Egypt free of foreign occupation, are also highlighted in "Qissat Hubb"

(A Love Story), first appearing in the *Jumhuriyyat Farahat* collection, then published separately as the novel *Qissat Hubb* (1967; translated as *City of Love and Ashes,* 1999). Set in Cairo prior to the Egyptian Revolution, *Qissat Hubb* features as its main character Hamza, a man who dreams of a free Egyptian state. He is given the task of organizing a training camp to fight for Egyptian independence. Fawziya, the heroine of the story, is a teacher in Munira School who helps Hamza with his work. Fawziya becomes the secretary of the Women Teachers' National Resistance Committee, a group that raises funds to support the cause of Egyptian freedom. As Cairo is engulfed in the nationwide struggle for freedom, Hamza and Fawziya discover their love for one another, though they fight their mutual desire as they see love as secondary to the greater good of freedom. In this novel, Idris creatively uses language, changing the language patterns to suit the character's dialogue–at the time an innovative technique in Arabic literature. He uses classical Arabic terminology for the narrator, and moves to the colloquial Egyptian when Fawziya speaks. Idris takes his colloquial Arabic style further by also capturing the diction of other characters from different regions and social classes.

Idris married in 1957. He and his wife, Raja', raised three children, but she took care that family life did not interfere with his writing. In the year of their marriage Idris published two more collections, *al-Batal* (The Hero) and *Alaysa kadhalika* (Isn't That So), which focus on the lack of civil liberties among the poor. The stories in *Al-Batal* portray anti-British sentiment within Egyptian society. An example of this xenophobia can be found in "It Is a Game?" a story that begins with a father coming home to find his wife in shock because their son had been badly beaten. The father eventually learns that the culprit was his son's friend, the son of their neighbor. The friends had been caught up in playing a game in which a group of boys had divided themselves into two teams: Egyptians versus British. The Egyptian team became so enthralled with defeating the British that they lost all sense of reality and gave vent to their suppressed emotion through physical violence.

In *Alaysa kadhalika* Idris examines the oppression of the poor by wealthier members of society. In the title story the reader is introduced to a judge, "Maître" Abdallah, a man who makes life-and-death court rulings every day in his courtroom. When he discovers the loss of his watch, however, the judge seems to believe that he has lost the order and control of his whole world. At the end of the first section of the story, Idris shows that little distinguishes the judge from any other Egyptian man:

> Now he was a judge. He is not married yet. Nevertheless his flat is magnificently furnished, and his life is full of numbers: 3445, 299876, 10031, 66, 8345–these are the numbers of his car, of his refrigerator, of his life insurance policy, of his apartment, of his bank account. . . Let no one rush to the conclusion that Maître Abdallah is outrageously rich. He is a man of average circumstances. Indeed it can almost be said that he is average in everything. He is not tall, but neither can it be said that he is short. Similarly he is neither thin nor stout, neither fair-skinned nor dark. In brief, if we were to take a hundred men from all parts of the world and work out their average in height, weight and complexion, we should find Maître Abdallah before us. (Translated by Roger Allen)

At the beginning of the second section of the story, Abdallah concludes that Shuhrat, his servant and former mistress, has stolen his watch. Through Abdallah and his pursuit of Shuhrat, Idris suggests by implication that many, while realizing the fact of oppression of the poor, close their eyes to such conditions unless they actually feel its effects. Abdallah meets with Shuhrat in an impoverished part of Cairo, where she admits that she stole the watch. The consequences of Shuhrat's actions lead her to lose her job and become a prostitute. At the end of the story, the reader is left with the realization that the judge who has exploited Shuhrat for his own pleasure is only affected by their relationship when he is forced to look upon poverty firsthand.

In the story "al-Mahraza" (translated as "The Wallet" in *Modern Egyptian Short Stories,* 1997), also from the collection *Alaysa kadhalika,* Idris uses Sami, a poor young boy who wants to see a movie with his classmates, to show the effects of poverty on an Egyptian family. Sami cannot believe that his parents do not have the five piasters for a ticket because he thinks his father is invincible. Idris vividly describes Sami's disbelief:

> What was the matter with them? Not once had they given him any money when he had asked. Always it was: "Honest to God, we haven't any!" Even his father, for all his size and stature, his soft belly and his thick fingers. Imposing as he was, his father thought it no sin to swear the greatest oaths that he had not a penny on him. Did that make sense? Could anyone believe that his father was as broke as he tried to make out? Never! (Translated by Roger Allen)

At night while his parents are sleeping, Sami sneaks into their room to steal the money from his father's wallet, only to find a ten-piaster note plus a two-piaster piece. At first he cannot fathom the idea that his parents were telling him the truth and did not have the money for him to attend the movies. He becomes resentful and wonders where they hid their money or what they spent it on. As Sami's eyes rest on his father's slumber-

Front cover for a translation of Idris's 1959 novel al-Haram, about class prejudice on an Egyptian cotton estate in the 1950s (Thomas Cooper Library, University of South Carolina)

ing body, however, his feelings of anger turn to pity as he realizes that his father is not all powerful. Consequently, he decides that he should help support the family by getting a job and giving his wages to his father. Idris shows his readers how Sami's enlightenment arouses in him a sense of responsibility.

In his 1958 drama *al-Lahzah al-harijah* (The Critical Moment), Idris explores the Egyptian nationalist and anti-imperialist sentiment that reached its height after Nasser nationalized the Suez Canal. The play tells the story of an Egyptian family that endures hardship during the 1957 crisis, and it glorifies the Egyptian people's struggle against an imperialist aggressor. But the play was also critical of the government, and the expression of such sentiments by Egypt's intellectuals led to the Egyptian government cracking down on the country's publishers.

To avoid censors, Idris published his next short-story collection *Hadithat sharaf* (1958, The Shame) in Lebanon. The title story calls attention to the plight of women in Egypt by addressing the double standards that exist for the two sexes. When it is learned that Fatima, the most beautiful girl in her community, was seen in a field alone with Gharib, a young man who has a reputation of being a ladies' man, the two become the talk of their neighbors, who assume that she has lost her virtue. While Gharib, unable to handle the scrutiny of the community, flees the area, Fatima must remain behind to face her neighbors' suspicions. The only way Fatima can convince her community of her innocence is to subject herself to a humiliating physical examination. When it is announced that she is indeed still a virgin, everyone rejoices that she has not been violated by Gharib. But the experience changes Fatima, who becomes defiant and remains unmarried because she was presumed guilty of an impropriety solely because she is a woman while the man is not held accountable for his promiscuous ways.

In 1959 Idris published the short novel *al-Haram* (The Sinners), in which he shows how class discrimination affects perceptions of sin. Set on a cotton estate in the Nile Delta in the early 1950s, the story revolves around 'Azizah, a poor migrant worker who comes to a cotton estate and in secret gives birth to a baby. The story opens with the discovery of the baby's dead body by an estate guard. The guard notices marks on the baby's body and states that it has been murdered by its mother. As suspicion mounts around the mother's identity, a deepening conflict develops between the two social classes on the estate: the residents who live on the farm year round and the migrant workers. The estate residents treat the migrant workers like second-class citizens who must be tolerated only because the residents need their help with the cotton crop. The migrant workers feel they must endure this hostile situation because they need a job to feed themselves and their families.

The residents of the estate and the estate's chief administrative officer Fikri Afendi believe without proof that the sinner is a migrant worker because they imagine that poor people must have a lower standard of morals. Idris shows how judging others based on economic standing in the community happens and how such misjudgements increase distrust in society. When Afendi and the residents of the estate find that 'Azizah was the victim of rape, they reflect upon their own moral behavior. Idris counterposes the divided adult community with his description of the farmer's children playing with the migrant worker's children. The youngest children from both groups play together on equal footing with no other object than having fun. The description suggests that discrimination is learned behavior, that only when the children become older do they have the prejudices of society forced upon them.

In 1960 Idris gave up medicine to concentrate on writing full-time. In the late 1950s and in the early 1960s he was also beginning to change his approach to his material. Readers began to note a transformation in Idris's writing style as he gradually shifted away from the realistic depiction of domestic Egyptian life in rural society and the poor quarters of Cairo toward a more universal and complex style of short-story writing. He began to broaden his range of settings and characters and to go beyond straightforward descriptions of ethical and political subjects to present more symbolic tales. It was also in 1960 that the Egyptian Higher Council for Arts and Literature voted to exclude plays using the vernacular language from a theater competition. In response, Idris wrote a vehement criticism of the council in his column in *al-Jumhuriyyah*. The following year the council excluded vernacular short stories from another competition.

In 1961 Idris left Egypt for Algeria to cover the war of independence for *al-Jumhuriyyah* but ended up joining the resistance movement against the French. After six months he was wounded and returned to Egypt and a position at *al-Jumhuriyyah*. He continued to write about the lack of civil liberties of the poor in his short-story collection *Akhir al-dunya* (1961, The End of the World). One of the most powerful stories from this collection is the "Alif al-Ahrar" (Omitted Letter)—a symbolic look at a man's dehumanization in an administrative bureaucracy. Narrated with satirical humor, the story concerns Ahmad Rashwan, a graduate from the University of Cairo with a degree in commerce, who is troubled by his boss's apparent belief that he and his typewriter are the same. Ahmad cannot understand why his boss wants him to type letters exactly as they are written, regardless of spelling or grammar mistakes. Ahmad wants to fix the spelling and grammar mistakes as he types up the letters, but such initiative goes beyond his place in the bureaucracy.

The crisis arises when Ahmad refuses to copy a mistake and misspell the word "ahrar" (free) with a final "an" incorrectly added (ahrar*an*). When Ahmad brings the corrected letter to his boss, he is told to retype the letter with the word misspelled. Ahmad's defiant refusal is reported to the Director-General, who tells Ahmad that even he, the Director-General, is a machine in the organization and must do what he is told by his boss. For Ahmad, though, the argument has become a matter of principle and honor. He remains defiant, which leads to his dismissal. When Ahmad returns to his desk to clear it out, he finds that the two keys "a" and "n" do not work on his typewriter. Consequently, he rushes to his boss's office to inform him that he must fire the typewriter as well because it too will not type "an": "'Just look boss!' he blurted out, 'come and take a look. The machine's refusing to type 'an', see for yourself! You must fire it at once, boss, on the spot!!' 'My boy,' the boss commented with a cough, 'machines are not fired when they refuse to type, they're repaired. Consign it to the workshop and have it put right.'"

In 1962 Idris published a novel and a story collection. In his novel *al-'Ayb* (Shame) he shows how traditional values are being affected by a changing society as he examines the idea of women working outside the home from the perspectives first of women and then of men. The three long stories Idris collected under the title *al-'Askari al-aswad* (The Black Policeman)—the title story, "al-Sayyidah Fiyyina" (Lady Vienna), and "Rijal wa thiran" (Men and Bulls)—were each republished individually as novels.

In "al-'Askari al-aswad," a powerful story that shows the author's continuing advocacy of Egyptian personal liberty, Idris provides a vivid example of the emotional effects of unjust imprisonment and torture. The hero of the story is a physician named Shawqi who while attending medical school in the 1940s was a vocal member of an antigovernment student organization that fought for civil liberties. Prior to graduation Shawqi was imprisoned and tortured by a member of the Egyptian secret police known as the "Black Policeman." The story revolves around the narrator's attempt to understand how Shawqi's experience changed his outlook on life. When at the climax of the story Shawqi travels to the home of the former policeman who was his torturer, the memories of his cruel treatment overwhelm him and he reveals his anger, frustration, and distrust for all people. The narrator realizes that all his hypothesizing about Shawqi's mental state was wrong and that Shawqi had not recovered from the experience even after the many years that had passed: Shawqi befriended people as a way of hiding among society; he married as a way of not calling attention to why he was not married; he avoided making decisions that he feared would call attention to his existence. The outspoken caring young gentleman had become a fearful and suspicious man who had lost all trust in his fellow human beings. Shawqi had lived his life hiding in fear of being discovered by society. Through Shawqi, Idris shows how the inhumanity of authority figures can have lasting effects that undermine the freedom of the people.

In the 1960s Idris began to take a greater interest in the theater and to publish more plays. In 1963 he wrote a series of articles in the literary magazine *al-Kitab* that called for a shift away from foreign plays and toward Egyptian material. Unlike most plays produced during the early 1960s, Idris's plays illustrated the social and political changes occurring in Egypt. With his shift in interest toward the theater, Idris wrote fewer stories and never again published more than one collection of stories in a single year. His use of colloquial language was a natural fit for the theater, and his work and ideas began reaching broader audiences. His most famous play was *al-Farafir* (The Flutterbugs), a two-act satire about the relationship between a servant, Farfur, and his master. Performed and published in 1964, *al-Farafir* caused a sensation in Egypt, prompting a lively discussion among critics.

In 1965 Idris was awarded the Hiwar International Literary prize by the Lebanese journal *Hiwar* (Dialogue) for his literary achievements. He did not accept the award, however, because he was dissuaded by critics who claimed the journal was financially backed by the Central Intelligence Agency of the United States. The same year he released the play *al-Mahzalah al-Ardiyyah* (The Farce of the World) and the collection *Lughat al-ay ay* (The Language of Screams), comprised of twelve stories written between 1957 and 1965. Like his other works, the stories in the collection address critical issues within Egyptian society. One of most striking stories, "al-Aurti" (The Aorta), relates the tragic fate of 'Abduh, a man suspected of stealing money who is confronted by his accuser in public. The crowd that gathers around the two characters believes that 'Abduh has the money on him and begins a zealous search for the money. The accused pleads that he did not take the money and that he just had an operation that replaced his aorta. Refusing to believe 'Abduh, the mob places him on a butcher's hook and begins to strip him. Once he is naked they see that his heart is covered with bandages, but they still refuse to believe his story and begin removing the dressing. Only when the bandages are fully removed, revealing 'Abduh's new aorta, does the crowd realize that he is telling the truth. But it is too late, and 'Abduh dies, the victim of the mob's frenzy. Writing in *Critical Perspectives on Yusuf Idris*, Roger Allen calls "al-Aurti" one of the most impressive of Idris's short stories of this period. Allen suggests that the treatment of human cruelty in this period before the 1967 War was "prophetic." The theme of cruelty became common in Arabic literature after the war.

Like all intellectuals in the Arab world, Idris was shaken by the Six-Day War in 1967, during which Israel occupied more territory of Egypt, Syria, Jordan, and historic Palestine. Although Idris became subject to increased bouts of depression, he continued to write. His 1969 collection *al-Nadahah* (The Siren) includes stories written between 1965 and 1969. A highlight of the volume is "al-Martabah al-muqa'arah" (The Concave Mattress). This symbolic, surrealistic tale, one of Idris's shortest short stories, depicts a newly married couple who waste their lives sleeping while they wait for the world to change. Periodically the couple wakes to check for change in the world, but when they see that things are the same, they go back to sleep. When one day the husband dies, his body has sunken so far into the mattress that it is now acting as his coffin. For Idris, the couple represents the passivity of the Egyptian people who do nothing to force social change; he regards such inactivity as the foremost obstruction to progress.

Idris's dissatisfaction with Nasser's regime was again demonstrated in the controversial play *al-Mukhatatin* (The Stripped Ones, 1969), which was immediately banned. In 1969 he became the literary editor for the Cairo daily paper *al-Ahram*. In 1970 he published *al-Bayda'* (The White Woman), a novel which he originally wrote in 1955 and serialized in *al-Jumhuriyyah* in 1959. In 1971 Idris also released the play *al-Jins al-thalith* (The Supermen) and the collection *Bayt min Lahm* (The House of Flesh), which contained stories written in 1970 and 1971.

In the title story (translated as "The House of Flesh," 1978), Idris shows how Egyptian society views sex inside and outside of marriage while at the same time giving an insightful glimpse into the difficult conditions that unmarried women face. The story features a poor widow and three unmarried daughters who live in a one-room house. The three daughters fear they are doomed to remain single because there is no man in their home to meet possible suitors. Consequently, they devise a plan to have their mother marry the blind Korean man who comes to their house to pray for their deceased father. But after their mother marries, suitors still do not present themselves to their new father, and the daughters become envious of their mother. Eventually, the mother discovers that one of her daughters, pretending to be her, has been sleeping with her new husband. Although angry, she pities her daughters and allows each of her daughters to share the pleasures of her husband's bed. Idris describes this as the ring game: "The ring is lying beside the lamp. Silence prevails, and ears grow blind. In silence the finger whose turn comes gropes stealthily for the ring and turns off the light. Darkness reigns, and in darkness eyes grow blind." Each daughter in turn puts on their mother's wedding ring and pretends to be their stepfather's wife. The husband, whose knowledge of the arrangement is uncertain, leaves the morality of the situation to those who can see. He states, "They alone have the blessing of certainty, since they are able to make distinctions"(translated by Allen). What is interesting about *Bayt min Lahm* is that Idris's usual theme of poverty plays only a small role in the story. Rather, the story focuses on the importance of sex and how this primal need surpasses societal beliefs and customs.

The title story of Idris's 1978 collection *Ana sultan qanun al-wujud* (I Am the Lord of the Law of Existence) focuses on Muhammad El-Helou, a lion trainer in a circus, and his defiant lion named Sultan. During a performance the trainer shows signs of hesitation that the lion perceives as weakness. The lion takes the opportunity to kill the trainer. Idris may well have intended the story to be read as a fable about standing up to tyrants, for oppressed people, like the lion, have the power to act: they just need to suppress their fear and stand up against tyranny.

Although Idris was a successful writer in the 1960s and 1970s, he wrote much less in these two decades than he did in the 1950s. Part of this decrease in output was the result of periods of depression that at times left him unable to write. In order to push himself to work he began taking amphetamines, which led to a drug habit that he was unable to recover from until 1975 when he was forced to undergo a heart operation.

Despite his deteriorating health, in 1981 Idris published *Nyu-Yurk 80* (New York 80), a novel set in the United States that examines the cultural differences between the East and the West. The West in the novel is represented by a prostitute who is proud of her profession, and the East is represented by a professional writer. Narrating the story, the writer tells the tale of how the prostitute continually chases him though he constantly refuses her advances. The more he refuses, the more she persists, until she eventually offers him money to sleep with her. Repulsed by the idea of trading sex for money, the narrator, despite his obvious attraction to the woman, once again refuses her. Through his depiction of the relationship between the writer and the prostitute, Idris clearly proposes a rejection of materialism and calls for his readers to reexamine their personal priorities.

In the story "19502," which appeared in his 1982 short-story collection *Uqtulha* (Kill Her), Idris returns to the 1952 Egyptian revolution. His anger at the outcome of the event is evident in his relation of the tale of 'Abduh, whose gradual loss of identity begins with his realization that no one can see or hear him. 'Abduh slowly loses all hope and eventually commits suicide. His identity is still unknown after his death as the district attorney files the death under "Anonymous" with the file number 19502. The story has an explicitly political message: when people are not allowed to speak, they cannot be heard by their government officials, who therefore lack the understanding necessary to solve society's problems. Citizens lose their sense of identity as they fruitlessly struggle to be heard. The number "19502" is an allusion to the year of the revolution with an added zero. Neither 'Abduh nor the revolution was successful: 'Abduh's suicide did not give him back his identity, and the revolution did not achieve its goals.

CITY OF LOVE AND ASHES

Yusuf Idris

Translated by
R. Neil Hewison

THE AMERICAN UNIVERSITY IN CAIRO PRESS

Title page for a translation of Idris's 1967 novel, Qissat Hubb, *set in Cairo as Egypt moves toward revolution in the 1950s (Thomas Cooper Library, University of South Carolina)*

The following year Idris published the play *al-Bahlawan* (The Clown), which takes a humorous look at the deterioration of Egyptian society, a deterioration Idris links to Sadat's *infitah* (open door) policy that was intended to encourage private foreign investment. *Al-'Atab 'ala al-nazar* (1987, Sight Is to Blame), Idris's last short-story collection published before his death, includes the notable "Abu al-rijal" (translated as *The Leader of Men,* 1988). Originally published in the Egyptian magazine *October* on 1 November 1987, "Abu al-rijal" is the story of a sultan who faces his homosexuality after years of repression. As he has throughout his career, Idris calls into question societal beliefs that cause individuals suffering and hardship and encourages the oppressed to stand up for themselves.

On 1 August 1991 Yusuf Idris died in London. Through his novels, short stories, journalism, and plays he was able to give his readers insight into the day-to-day life of ordinary Egyptians. He wrote not only to document his native land but also to call on its people to actively seek to solve Egypt's social, economic, and political problems. Even when his writing underwent a significant change as he shifted from realistic stories to more symbolic or surreal tales, Idris's fiction never failed to represent, challenge, and criticize the people of Egypt. He entertained and enlightened the Arab world as well as those who have read his work in translation, leaving an indelible mark on the history of Arab literature.

References:

M. Akif Kirecci, "Political Criticism in the Short Stories of Yusuf Idris: 'Innocence' and '19502,'" *Massachusetts Review,* 42 (Winter 2001): 672–688;

Roger Allen, *Critical Perspectives on Yusuf Idris* (Colorado Springs: Three Continents Press, 1994);

Dalya Cohen, "'Innocence' by Yusuf Idris," *Journal of Arabic Literature,* 19, no. 1 (1988): 68–78;

Dalya Cohen-Mor, *Yusuf Idris: Changing Visions* (Potomac, Md.: Sheba Press, 1992);

Rasheed El-Enany, "The Western Encounter in the Works of Yusuf Idris," *Research in African Literatures,* 28 (Fall 1997): 33–55;

Sabry Hafez, "Yusuf Idris: 1927–1991," in *African Writers,* edited by C. Brian Cox (New York: Simon & Schuster Prentice Hall International, 1997), pp. 345–365;

Hilary Kilpatrick, *The Modern Egyptian Novel: A Study in Social Criticism* (London: Ithaca, 1974), pp. 113–127;

P. M. Kurpershoek, *The Short Stories of Yusuf Idris: A Modern Egyptian Author* (Leiden: Brill, 1981);

Salti Ramzi, "A Different Leader of Men," *World Literature Today,* 75 (Spring 2001): 246–257;

Dorota Rudnicka-Kassem, *Egyptian Drama and Social Change: A Study of Thematic and Artistic Development in Yïsuf Idrÿs's Plays* (Montreal: Enigma Press, 1993);

Sasson Somekh, "The Function of Sound in the Stories of Yusuf Idris," in *Critical Perspectives on Yusuf Idris,* edited by Roger Allen (Colorado Springs: Three Continents Press, 1994), pp. 97–104;

Somekh, "Structure of Silence: A Reading in Yusuf Idris's 'Bayt min Lahm' (House of Flesh)," in *Writer, Culture, Text: Studies in Modern Arabic Literature,* edited by Ami Elad (Fredericton, N.B.: York Press, 1993), pp. 56–61.

Isma'il Fahd Isma'il
(1940-)

Sebastian Maisel
Grand Valley State University

BOOKS: *Al-Buq'ah al-dakinah* (Beirut: Dar al-'Awdah, 1965);

Kanat al-sama' zarqa' (Beirut: Dar al-'Awdah, 1970);

Al-Mustanqa'at al-daw'iyyah (Beirut: Dar al-'Awdah, 1971);

Al-Habl (Beirut: Dar al-'Awdah, 1972);

Al-Difaf al-ukhra (Beirut: Dar al-'Awdah, 1973);

Malaff al-hadithah 67 (Beirut: Dar al-'Awdah, 1974);

Al-Aqfas wa al-lughah al-mushtarakah (Beirut: Dar al-'Awdah, 1975);

Al-Shayyah (Beirut: Dar al-'Awdah, 1976);

Al-Qissah al-'Arabiyyah fi al-Kuwayt (Beirut: Dar al-'Awdah, 1980);

Al-Nass (Beirut: Dar al-'Awdah, 1980);

Khutwah fi al-hulm (Beirut: Dar al-'Awdah, 1980);

Al-Tuyur wa'l-asdiqa (Beirut: Dar al-'Awdah, 1981);

Al-Kalimah–al-fi'l fi masrah Sa'd Allah Wannus (Beirut: Dar al-Adab, 1981);

Al-Nil yajri shamalan (Beirut: Dar al-'Awdah, 1981);

Al-Nawatir (Beirut: Dar al-'Awdah, 1982);

Al-Nil: al-Ta'm wa al-ra'ihah (Beirut: Dar al-Adab, 1988);

Ihdathiyat zaman al-uzlah (N.p., 1996);

Yahduthu ams (Damascus: Dar al-Mada li al-Thaqafah wa-al-Nashr, 1997);

Ba'idan . . . ila huna (Cairo: Dar Sharqiyat li al-Nashr wa-al-Tawzi', 1998);

Al-Ka'in al-zill (Cairo: Dar al-Hilal, 1999);

Sama' na' iyah (Damascus: Dar al-Mada li al-Thaqafah wa al-Nashr, 2000);

Ali al-Sabti–sha'ir fi al-hawa' al-talq (Damascus, 2002);

Mubdi'un mughayirun: Kitabat mughamarah: maqarabat (Cairo: Dar Sharqiyat, 2004);

Al-Tarikh . . . kitabat mughayirah (N.p., 2004);

Li al-hadath baqiyatun (Kuwait: Dar Masa, 2008).

Isma'il Fahd Isma'il is recognized as the spiritual father of the Kuwaiti novel and as one of the most important contemporary Arab writers in the genre. He has published twenty-four novels as well as ten collections of short stories, plays, and two literary studies. Although he was born in Iraq and set his early novels in that country, he is regarded as–and considers himself to be–a Kuwaiti. To those who argue he is not really a Kuwaiti writer, Isma'il has responded: "I am one of those who believe that any dramatic event in any part of the Arab world will affect the other. Yes, I was born in Basra, but my father was a Kuwaiti citizen, and in 1966 I moved to Kuwait. Today I live in Kuwait and have Kuwaiti citizenship. It is right to say this: as a man, I am a Kuwaiti, but as a novelist I am an Arab." In his early works he dealt with issues affecting Iraqi society in the 1960s but he has since treated such subjects as the always-present Palestinian question, terrorism, Kuwaiti society, Egyptian history, and Arab intellectuals–all of which underlines his pan-Arab identification as a writer.

Isma'il was born in Basra, Iraq, in 1940. His father was a Kuwaiti who had moved to Basra when he was young, and his mother was an Iraqi. The eldest of ten siblings, Isma'il grew up in monarchist Iraq, reading everything from newspapers to classical Arabic poetry and the stories of Arabian Nights to his blind father. At school he distinguished himself by writing poetry. After finishing high school in 1957, Isma'il immediately took a teaching job. He was excited by the 14 July 1958 revolution in which the Iraqi monarchy was overthrown by military officers and joined the crowds in the streets of Baghdad, but his enthusiasm vanished when he realized the revolution had evolved into a power struggle between two men, Brigadier 'Abd al-Karim Qasim and Colonel 'Abd al-Salam 'Arif, and their constituencies.

In the late 1950s Isma'il married for the first time, but he divorced his wife after two years; he has since married and divorced four times. In 1966 Isma'il left Iraq to work temporarily as a teacher in Kuwait. Three years later, he moved for six months to Cairo, mainly to study administration but also to develop friendships with important writers and literary figures such as Salah 'Abd al-Sabur and Yusuf Idris. After his return, he worked for the Kuwaiti Ministry of Education and received a degree in dramatic criticism from the High Institute of Theatre in 1976. In 1987 he retired from

Front cover for Kanat al-sama' zarqa' (*The Sky Was Blue*), 1970 (Duke University Libraries)

governmental work and joined his brothers in managing a construction and food distribution company.

Isma'il began writing the novels that were published in the early 1970s in the two-year period between 1965 and the Six-Day War of 1967. According to Mursel al-'Ajmi, Isma'il's early work was characterized by his openness to political opinions. He was drawn to the ideals of existentialism, nationalism, and socialism through popular journals such as *al-Adab*, edited by Suhayl Idris, which included translations of the work of Fyodor Dostoevsky, Jean-Paul Sartre, and Albert Camus. He was also influenced by the Palestinian writer and politician Ghassan Kanafani, with whom he developed a close personal relationship. After the defeat of 1967 Kanafani introduced Isma'il to Marxism, which contributed to his development as a writer. Although Isma'il came to consider himself a Marxist, he did not join any communist party.

In his formative period Isma'il wrote three novels: *Kanat al-sama' zarqa'* (1970, The Sky Was Blue), *al-Mustanqa'at al-daw'iyyah* (1971, The Light Swamps), and *al-Habl* (1972, The Rope). The main characters in all three novels are not named. Roger Allen observes that this device forces the narrative to proceed on an impersonal and anonymous level, which contributes to the generally sinister and aggressive atmosphere.

Kanat al-sama' zarqa' depicts the conflict between two men stuck together in a small hut during their attempt to escape from Iraq to Iran after the 1958 revolution. One is a former police officer who fled because the new Iraqi regime under Qasim did not trust him. During the escape he killed three soldiers but was seriously wounded himself. The second man is an intellectual and writer who still struggles with the question of his escape. He remembers his relationships with two women: his wife, whom his father had chosen for him, and a socialistic and philosophical woman, who was infatuated with him, the famous writer. Being stuck together for three days, the two men become closer, and each begins to understand the reasons for the other's escape. The realistic and critical depiction of the relation in its historical context led Kuwaiti authorities to ban the distribution of the novel.

Al-Mustanqa'at al-daw'iyyah deals with traditional customs and their implications on the modernizing Iraqi society of the 1960s. The fate of an ordinary man—married, a successful writer and political activist—turns when he witnesses an honor killing, two men executing their sister as an alleged prostitute. In his attempts to intervene, he himself is attacked and forced to kill the two men. Having become a murderer, the protagonist is subsequently imprisoned for life. In his early years in prison, he remains politically active, but when his wife leaves him for his best friend he becomes disengaged. He does not even take up the unexpected chance to escape from prison because the outside world no longer has meaning for him.

Al-Habl continues Isma'il's social and political exploration of Iraq in the 1960s. Because of a single poem he wrote, the protagonist, a revolutionist and poet, is arrested on his wedding night. He becomes a professional thief upon his release because he lost his ability to write in prison. In several flashbacks, the past is revealed depicting his childhood, marriage, and life in prison, his release, and job-loss. Although cleared and freed, he no longer can leave the country because he is considered a dangerous political extremist. The "habl" (rope) of the title, which the protagonist used in his robberies, more importantly represents the connection to normal life and his wife, who wants the rope used to dry the laundry in the wind. In an optimistic ending, the thief is overwhelmed by his childhood memories and decides to give up his profession. He donates the rope to his wife.

After the *hazimah,* the ultimate defeat of the Arab armies by Israel's military in the Six-Day War of 1967, Isma'il became more involved in politics and his sympathy with Marxism is evident in his subsequent novels. In *al-Difaf al-ukhra* (1973, Other Shores) he continues the story of characters whom he introduced in previous books: a girl from *Kanat al-sama' zarqa',* the hero of *al-Habl,* and the warden of the prison from *al-Mustanqa'at al-daw'iyyah.* The setting of the story is a machine factory where the workers are about to go on strike. The four main characters, all workers, and their role in the strike make up the framework of the story and reveal their political and personal development. Interestingly, it is only the girl, Fatimah, who shows a positive development, when she is able to stand up to her passive husband and challenge his authority.

In his following novel, *Malaff al-hadithah 67* (1974, The File of Case 67)–which was written in 1971, shortly after the Jordanian civil war involving exiled Palestinians–Isma'il examines the position of the Palestinian cause in the Arab world through the plight of a Palestinian baker who accidentally comes across a murder victim. In his attempt to quickly call the police, the baker is arrested because he is seen fleeing the scene. In the end, the interrogator's vicious zeal makes the baker confess to the crime, even though the real killer was found. The struggle between the baker and the interrogator may be read as symbolizing the struggle between the Palestinian movement and the Arab regimes, where the interests of the Palestinian people were placed second behind the political interests of Jordanian government. The novel suggests that Isma'il was pessimistic about the ultimate success and mobilization of the Palestinian movement. In 1999 Zamil Burhan Shawi made a film titled *Dhat Masa'* based on the novel.

A close observer of conflicts within the Arab world, Isma'il traveled to Beirut when the Lebanese civil war broke out in 1975. During the war, he lived in the city and visited some of the areas that saw heavy fighting at the beginning of the fifteen-year conflict. In *al-Shayyah* (1976, The Sheik), set in a Shiite neighborhood in Beirut, Isma'il depicts the impact of the war on the people and examines the causes for the war. He does not believe it was a simple conflict along sectarian lines between Muslims and Christians; rather, he suggests that the real origins lie in the economic hierarchy of rich and poor, as well as in the influence of the Palestinian refugees and militia. His leftist attitude is clearly seen in his sympathy for the besieged poor, both Lebanese and Palestinian, and his portrayal of the ongoing class struggle and war. The lives and fates of the main characters–a Palestinian journalist, a Christian Lebanese woman and her son, a former policeman, and a Palestinian driver with his family–are determined by

Title page for al-Nil yajri shamalan *(The Nile Flows North), 1981 (Emory University Libraries)*

their decision to work together to overcome the threats posed by an outside sniper. Drastic changes happen to all of them, as some die while others grow emotionally and politically. *Al-Shayyah* was adopted as a theater production by the Iraqi playwright Fadil Khalil.

Perhaps, as al-'Ajmi suggests, in some measure to counter criticism that he lacked "local color" in his fiction, Isma'il in 1980 wrote two novels that treat Kuwaiti society. In *Khutwah fi al-hulm* (1980, A Step in the Dream) and *al-Tuyur wa al-asdiqa'* (1981, The Bird and the Friends) he includes many autobiographical experiences–particularly when he writes about divorce and the contrast between fictional and real life. The books depict some of the conflicts within Kuwaiti society, especially between traditional tribal customs and the capitalistic economic system. Isma'il's Marxist viewpoint is clear in his examination of the realities of the market economy in daily Kuwaiti life. The main character in *Khutwah fi al-hulm* lives with his disloyal wife but is in love with another woman. The story line follows his attempts to step into freedom and leave behind a past that is filled with social injustice. Al-'Ajmi suggests that

Front cover for al-Nil: al-Ta'm wa al-ra'ihah *(The Nile: Taste and Smell)*, 1988 *(Sterling Memorial Library, Yale University)*

the wife symbolizes established, capitalistic society, while the woman the protagonist loves represents the dream of an ideal, socialistic society. Similarly, in *al-Tuyur wa al-asdiqa'* the protagonist is caught between his past ambitions and his present life. He attends a concert of a famous singer in an expensive hotel with his girlfriend. As the night goes on, the thoughts and memories of the past become overwhelming, and he, too, needs to free himself.

The next period of Isma'il's work is influenced by his interest in the history of Egypt, in particular the era of the Mamluks and the French invasion of 1798. In the late 1970s Isma'il spent half a year in Upper Egypt to study the life and customs of the *fellahin* (villagers), and he also consulted historical sources such as 'Abd al-Rahman al-Jabarti's *'Aja'ib al-Athar fi al-tarajim wa al-akhbar* (The Miracles of History in Translations and News), from which he extensively quotes in the beginning of *al-Nil yajri shamalan* (1981, The Nile Flows North). The plot of the story centers around the Mamluk ruler Murad Bey and his difficult relations with the local population. It is told from the perspective of 'Atiyyah, the illegitimate daughter of Murad Bey. Her misfortunes at the hand of her father, who destroys her family and the life of other villagers, symbolize the divided society of Egypt, split between the Mamluks, selfish foreign rulers, and the *fellahin,* who are portrayed as the only legitimate representatives of Egypt. While the lower-class *fellahin* stand up against the French invasion, the Mamluk representative worries only about himself and his political future, ignoring the serious threat to his power. Even though the resistance of the people of Alexandria is quickly broken, they are not completely destroyed and continue to resist the invaders. Isma'il thus shows the history of the region: how for the last two hundred years the people have endured the poor representation of alien regimes and corrupt rulers. In Isma'il's political ideology—based on Marxism, Arab nationalism, and the struggle between traditions and modernity—social justice will prevail only when the people overcome the forces arrayed against them.

Sulayman al-Halabi, the protagonist of *al-Nil: al-Ta'm wa al-ra'ihah* (1988, The Nile: Taste and Smell), is named after the man who assassinated the French general Jean-Baptiste Kléber in June 1800. Al-Halabi is a young Palestinian who grew up in Gaza, fled to Amman, joined Fath (the leading resistance movement within the PLO), and became politically active in Beirut. A series of emotional and political failures lead him to look for meaning through the inspiration of his historical namesake, and he decides to assassinate the president of Egypt. Isma'il describes the assassination plot in detail as well as the events and incidents that prevent al-Halabi from carrying out his plan. His relationship with Shirin, a young Egyptian woman, forces him to reevaluate his decisions as he contemplates the possibility of a new life with her. Although he finally decides to carry out his plot, he yet hopes for a miracle to change his fate. When it seems as though the lateness of the president for a speech will deny al-Halabi the opportunity to put his plan into action, he is ready to give up. But chance or fate brings him into the presence of the president and he must face his defining moment.

Isma'il briefly retired from writing in order to join his brothers in a business venture in the late 1980s. In 1991 he left Kuwait, with its oil fields still burning from the First Gulf War, for the Philippines to find a safe and quiet place to write. After six years of research and writing he finished a seven-part novel, *Ihdathiyat zaman al-uzlah* (1996, Coordinates of the Time of Isolation), which treats the months of the Kuwaiti occupation by Iraqi forces 1990–1991, describing in detail their aggressive raids and their humiliation of the local population. In parts 6 and 7 he narrates the killing of Abu

Ziyad Qabalawi, a senior Palestinian representative in Kuwait during an air strike, as well as the case of the famous Palestinian leader Salah Khalaf "Abu Iyad," who was assassinated in Tunis, perhaps because of his opposition to the Iraqi invasion. A documentary film about the Iraqi aggression was based on Isma'il's novel.

Isma'il's work includes a study of the well-known Kuwaiti poet 'Ali al-Sabti, *Ali al-Sabti–Sha'ir fi al-hawa' al-talq* (2002, Ali al-Sabti–a Poet in Open Air). Isma'il followed the literary works of al-Sabti for more than half a century, introducing the reader to the biography of the poet and providing an analysis of his works. He also points to artistic features in his lyrics, which help to better appreciate the *qasidah* (Arabic poem).

Isma'il Fahd Isma'il was awarded the Kuwaiti Prize for Recognition and Encouragement for Literary Critique in 2002 and for Literature in 2004. His work is often compared to, and is said to have been significantly influenced by, the writings of French writer Albert Camus. This influence can be found particularly in his depiction of protagonists, his intellectual vision, and to a degree in his topics and style. Al-Rashed Bushair notes Isma'il's emulation in his 2004 article "The Influence of Albert Camus on the Narrative of Isma'il Fahad Ismail," but argues that Isma'il's achievement does not match that of Camus. Isma'il continues to work on novels and is also producing television documentaries on other writers and intellectuals, such as Khalid Nafisi. He is an active influence on young writers, hosting a weekly literary salon in his home.

Interview:

Jamal Shubaybi, "Interview with the Novelist Ismail Fahd Ismail," *Al-Mada* <http://www.almadapaper.com/sub/09-479/p13.htm#5> (accessed 22 October 2008).

References:

Roger Allen, *The Arabic Novel: An Historical and Critical Introduction* (Syracuse, N.Y.: Syracuse University Press, 1995);

Mursel F. S. al-'Ajmi, "Isma'il Fahd Isma'il: A Thematic Study of his Novels," dissertation, University of Michigan, 1990;

Al-'Ajmi, "The Narrative Discourse in 'Time of Solitude,'" *Journal for Studies of the Gulf and the Arabian Peninsula,* 26, no. 97 (2000);

Al-Rashed Bushair, "The Influence of Albert Camus on the Narrative of Ismail Fahad Ismail," *Arabic Journal for the Arts,* 1, no. 1 (2004): 1–19;

'Umar Subhi Jabir, *Al-Bunyah wa al-dalalah fi riwayat Isma'il Fahd Isma'il* (Beirut: Al-Mu'assasa al-'Arabiyyah li al-Dirasat wa al-Nashr, 2002).

Jabra Ibrahim Jabra

(28 August 1920 – 12 December 1994)

Kamal Abdel-Malek
American University of Sharjah

BOOKS: *Surakh fi layl tawil* (Beirut: Matba'at al-Ani, 1955);

Araq wa qisas ukhra (Beirut: al-Mu'assasah al-Ahliyyah, 1956);

Tammuz fi al-madinah (Beirut: Dar Majallat Shi'r, 1959);

Al-Huriyyah wa al-tufan (Beirut: Dar Majallat Shi'r, 1960);

Hunters in a Narrow Street (London: Heinemann, 1960);

Art in Iraq Today (London: Iraqi Embassy, 1961);

Al-Madar al-mughlaq (Beirut: Al-Mu'assasah al-Wataniyyah, 1964);

Al-Rihlah al-thaminah: Dirasah naqdiyyah (Beirut: Dar al-Maktaba al-'Asriyyah, 1967);

Al-Safinah (Beirut: Dar al-Nahar, 1970); translated by Adnan Haydar and Roger Allen as *The Ship* (Washington, D.C.: Three Continents Press, 1985);

Harakat al-rasm al-mu'asir fi al-'Iraq (Baghdad: Wizarat al-Thaqafah wa al-I'lam, 1972);

Jawad Salim wa nasb al-huriyyah (Baghdad: Wizarat al-Thaqafah wa al-I'lam, 1974);

Al-Nar wa al-jawhar (Beirut: Dar al-Quds, 1975);

Law'at al-shams (Baghdad: Mu'assasat Ramzi, 1978);

Al-Bahth 'an Walid Mas'ud (Beirut: Dar al-Adab, 1978); translated by Allen and Haydar as *In Search of Walid Masoud* (Syracuse, N.Y.: Syracuse University Press, 2000);

Yanabi' al-ru'yah (Beirut: Al-Mu'assasah al-'Arabiyyah li al-Dirasat wa al-Nashr, 1979);

Al-Fann al-'Iraqi (Baghdad: Al-Dar al-'Arabiyyah li al-Tiba'a wa al-Nashr, 1980);

'Araq wa bidayah min harf al-ya' (Beirut: Dar al-Adab, 1981);

'Alam bila khara'it, by Jabra and Abdelrahman Munif (Beirut: Al-Mu'assasah al-'Arabiyyah li al-Dirasat wa al-Nashr, 1982);

The Grass Roots of Iraqi Art (St. Helier, U.K.: Wasit, 1983);

Al-Fann wa al-hulm wa al-fi'l (Baghdad: Dar al-Shu'un al-Thaqafiyyah, 1985);

Al-Ghuraf al-ukhra (Beirut: Al-Mu'assasah al-'Arabiyyah li al-Dirasat wa al-Nashr, 1986);

Al-Malik al-shams (Baghdad: Dar al-Shu'un al-Thaqafiyyah, 1986);

Baghdad bayn al-ams wa al-yawm, by Jabra and Ihsan Fathi (Baghdad, 1986);

Al-Bi'r al-ula (Beirut: Al-Mu'assassah al-'Arabiyyah li al-Dirasat wa al-Nashr, 1987); translated by Issa J. Boullata as *The First Well: A Bethlehem Boyhood* (Fayetteville: University of Arkansas Press, 1995);

Tamjid al-hayat (Beirut: Al-Mu'assassah al-'Arabiyyah li al-Dirasat wa al-Nashr, 1987);

A Celebration of Life: Essays on Literature and Art (Baghdad: Dar al-Ma'mun, 1988);

Ta'ammulat fi bunyan marmari (Beirut: Riyad al-Rayyis li al-Kutub wa al-Nashir, 1989);

Al-Majmu'at al-shi'riyyah al-kamilah (London: Riyad al-Rayyis, 1990);

Aqni'at al-haqiqah wa aqni'at al-khyal (Beirut: Al-Mu'assassah al-'Arabiyyah li al-Dirasat wa al-Nashr, 1992);

Mu'ayashat al-nimrah (Beirut: Al-Mu'assassah al-'Arabiyyah li al-Dirasat wa al-Nashr, 1992);

Yawmiyyat Sarab 'Affan (Beirut: Dar al-Adab, 1992);

Shari' al-amirat: Fusul min sirah dhatiyyah (Beirut: Al-Mu'assassah al-'Arabiyyah li al-Dirasat wa al-Nashr, 1994); translated by Boullata as *Princesses' Street* (Fayetteville: University of Arkansas Press, 2005);

Ara kitaban jamilan: Rasa'il Jabra Ibrahim Jabra ila Mahir al-Kayyali, 1981–1994 (Beirut: Al-Mu'assassah al-'Arabiyyah li al-Dirasat wa al-Nashr, 1994);

Mutawaliyat shi'riyyah: Ba'duha li al-tayf wa ba'duha li al-jasad, edited by 'Abd al-Wahid Lu'lu'a (Beirut: Al-Mu'assassah al-'Arabiyyah li al-Dirasat wa al-Nashr, 1996);

Al-Tajribah al-jamilah: Rasa'il Jabra Ibrahim Jabra ila 'Isa Bullatah, 1966–1994 (Beirut: Al-Mu'assassah al-'Arabiyyah li al-Dirasat wa al-Nashr, 2001).

TRANSLATIONS: Sir James Frazer, *Adunis aw Tammuz* (Beirut: Dar al-Sira' al-Fikri, 1957);

William Shakespeare, *Hamlit* (Beirut: Dar Majallat Shi'r, 1960);

Henry Frankfort and others, *Ma-qabl al-falsafah* (Beirut: Dar Maktabat al-Haya, 1960);

William Faulkner, *Al-Sakhab wa al-'unf* (Beirut: Al-Maktabah al-Ahliyyah, 1961);

Alexander Eliot, *Afaq al-fann* (Beirut: Dar al-Kitab al-'Arabi, 1964).

Noted Palestinian-in-exile writer Jabra Ibrahim Jabra was a prolific author who over the course of fifty years published works of literary criticism, fiction, autobiography, and translation. Though his mother tongue was Arabic, in which he wrote most of his work, Jabra came to love the English language. He is one of the first writers to translate classics from English and American literature into Arabic, making these works available to Arabic readers for the first time. His writing style was a modern influence on Arabic writing. His fiction is set against the background of real historical events and is often hauntingly nostalgic.

Jabra was born 28 August 1920 in Bethlehem, which at the time was part of Mandate Palestine. His Orthodox Christian family was poor, and the memory of his childhood poverty stayed with him even through his successful years. Although his parents were illiterate, they nourished the young Jabra on orally transmitted tales and songs from the Palestinian and Arab past. Some of these tales were derived from the stories of *The Arabian Nights*. Others were tales of great love, such as the Turkish tale of the star-crossed lovers Mammu and Zayn. Thanks to this early introduction to the power of words, Jabra developed a love of poetry and stories that determined his future calling as an author.

When Jabra was still a young boy his parents moved the family to Jerusalem so that he might continue his schooling there. He graduated from the Arab College in Jerusalem in 1937, after which he attended the University of Exeter and Cambridge University in England on a scholarship. He completed his bachelor's degree in 1943 and his master's degree in 1948, both in English literature. Upon completion of his education in England, Jabra returned to Jerusalem to teach at the Rashidiyya Secondary School until he was uprooted by the *Nakbah* (Catastrophe), the Israeli war for statehood. Homeless and stateless, Jabra traveled to Baghdad, the city that became his adopted home for the rest of his life. He took a position teaching English literature at the University of Baghdad until 1952. He met, and in 1952 married, Lami'a, who was an Iraqi college professor. That same year Jabra left Baghdad for a two-year research fellowship at Harvard University in the United States. On his return to Baghdad in 1954, Jabra took a position with the Iraq Petroleum Company as a director of its publicity department.

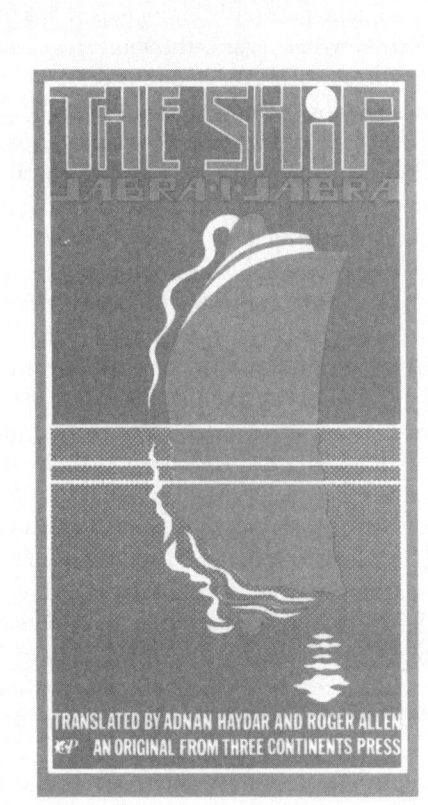

Front cover for the 1985 English translation of Jabra's 1970 novel, al-Safinah *(Thomas Cooper Library, University of South Carolina)*

Jabra began his first novel, *Surakh fi layl tawil* (Screaming in a Long Night) before the war, while he was still living in Jerusalem, but publication was delayed until 1955. The novel treats a day in the life of the narrator, Amin Samma', a journalist who is sick with grief over the death of his wife of two years. Much of the story is told through memories. Despite his sadness, Samma' is eventually able to recover himself sufficiently, even to the extent that he can fathom life without attaching himself to a woman. One cannot say that Samma' lives "happily ever after," but at least he has moved away from his dark personal crisis. Though it was his first novel, *Surakh fi layl tawil* already had some of what became "trademark Jabra" qualities, such as intellectual conversations and a nostalgic tone.

In 1956 Jabra published *Araq wa qisas ukhra* (Arrack and Other Stories). The short story for him was an easy art; in later years he devoted his energy to novels, which were more difficult to create. He once observed that the writing of short fiction in the Arab world was not taken seriously enough, perhaps because the Arab fiction writer regards the short story as a transition from the classical Arabic ode *(qasida)* and dreads the longer and more complex novelistic art. In Jabra's first poetry collection, *Tammuz fi al-madinah* (1959, Tammuz in the City), the city he presents through the poems suffers from a spiritual emptiness and is in need of some kind of redemption.

Jabra's next two important books were written in English. Despite being accessible to English readers, his novel *Hunters in a Narrow Street* (1960), which he had started writing during his short stay at Harvard, is not Jabra's best-known work, even to western readers. The protagonist of this novel—which was later translated into Arabic—is an educated Palestinian man, Jameel Farran, who fled Palestine in the terrible circumstances of the war of 1948. Having lost his home and his fiancée, he seeks a life of exile in Iraq. Jameel settles in Baghdad, starts a teaching career, and meets a native young woman, Sulafa, whom he later marries. But Palestine and its tragedy still haunt him, and he lives life not completely in the present. He meets people from different walks of life, including women with whom he develops love affairs. Some of the individuals he meets are basking in wealth and pleasures, others are committed to class struggle, and others appear totally lost. In 1961 Jabra published *Art in Iraq Today,* a work that shows he had developed from his early love of art into an accomplished observer and art critic.

Jabra's poetry volume *al-Madar al-mughlaq* (1964, Closed Circuit) includes some poems that became well known in the Arab world. In "Halq al-bi'r" (The Mouth of the Well) he compares the massacre at Dayr Yasin to Golgotha, suggesting that both are places of crucifixion but also of resurrection. "Bawadi al-nafy" (Deserts of Exile) treats the Palestinian wanderings in exile. The tone of *al-Madar al-mughlaq,* like that of *Tammuz fi al-madinah,* is both sad and hopeful, for in each the vicious grip of oppression does not rule out the possibility for release.

Al-Safinah (1970; translated as *The Ship,* 1985) became one of Jabra's most famous novels and is considered an important contribution to Arab literature. Using two narrators, Jabra plots out a complicated tapestry of love and politics. The narrators are 'Isam Salman, an architect, and Wadi 'Assaf, a Palestinian businessman who had been living in Kuwait. The two men are aboard a ship, the *Hercules,* which is leaving Beirut to cross the Mediterranean and dock in Italy. 'Assaf and Salman are both preoccupied with problems that they have left behind on land. 'Assaf is in pursuit of land he "owns" in Jerusalem but is unable to possess because of the political situation in Israel. Salman is lovesick, having become involved in a hopeless relationship with the niece of a man his father had murdered years before. She in fact marries another man, whom she does not love, and remains hopeful that she can at least be with Salman on the ship.

The plot of *al-Safinah* is rife with love affairs, flashbacks, and drama, as well as many details Jabra drew from his own life. Certainly, Jabra's sophistication is evident in his characters, who have lengthy discussions about philosophy, existential literature, and Sufi poets. Although it appears at first that the main characters have met on the ship by accident, it is revealed slowly that almost all of them have arranged to be on the cruise in order to meet with their lovers. Suicide is a theme in the novel as one of the European passengers attempts to kill himself, and Falih, the man who married Salman's true love, carries out the act.

Al-Safinah in its original language and its English translation was praised by both Arab and Western critics. Some critics have suggested that Jabra's novel was influenced by William Faulkner's *The Sound and the Fury* (1929), which Jabra translated into Arabic in 1961 as *al-Sakhab wa al-'unf.* Jabra responded to such observations at times by saying that he wished those who made such claims could point to specific examples. He also has asserted that in the world of art significant new techniques have a way of forcing themselves on artists who cannot afford to ignore them. When perspective in painting was discovered in the early Renaissance period, no artist could afford to ignore so significant a development, and perspective formed an integral part of every artistic work. The novelistic techniques of Faulkner, according to Jabra, may be said to reflect the influence of James Joyce and Virginia Woolf, but Faulkner went beyond his predecessors to create his own novelistic style. Jabra observed that he was the first Arab critic to introduce Faulkner to the Arab reader through his critical writing in the Beirut literary magazine *al-Adab* and later through his Arabic translation of *The Sound and Fury. Al-Safinah,* he said, went beyond earlier experiments and certainly set a precedent in Arabic literature. Novelistic techniques belong to all writers; the question that should be asked is not what novelistic techniques a writer appropriates but to what end and in what particular way the writer contributes to its potential.

Between 1974 and 1978 Jabra continued writing and publishing and was appointed cultural counselor at the Iraqi Ministry of Culture and Information, a position he retained until his retirement in 1984. Like his previous two poetry collections, his 1978 volume, *Law'at al-shams* (The Anguish of the Sun) is critical of city life but offers of hope for escape through love.

Jabra's novel *al-Bahth 'an Walid Mas'ud* (1978; translated as *In Search of Walid Masoud*, 2000) is generally recognized as one of his most important works. Walid Mas'ud, a Palestinian intellectual and successful businessman, has disappeared from the home in Baghdad where he had lived since the Arab-Israeli War of 1948. Because Mas'ud is a member of an organization engaged in the armed struggle against Israel, the suspicion arises that he has gone underground for political reasons. His brother had been killed by Zionists, and his son Marwan was killed in a vigilante attack on an Israeli village in occupied Palestine. The only clue that Mas'ud leaves behind is a lengthy but disconnected tape recording of garbled utterances—mainly reminiscences of love affairs and childhood—which Jabra artfully uses as the basis of the narration. The main setting is a dinner party in Baghdad, where a group of intellectuals has gathered to listen to Mas'ud's tape. Jabra employs the voices of several characters, all of whom must confront the situation of Mas'ud's disappearance. Jabra transforms the transcription of the tape by each of Mas'ud's comrades into a study of character, as each participant becomes a narrator.

Jabra turns Mas'ud's memories into a study of memory itself, as is suggested by the masterful opening of the novel:

> "If only there were an elixir for the memory, something that could bring events back in the order they happened, one by one, then turn them into words that would cascade out onto paper!" Perhaps I might, at this point, resort to these words Walid Masoud so often repeated in his last months. However much we fight against it, we remain playthings of our memories. We are, at one and the same time, their products and their victims. Rightly or wrongly, they obsess us, sweetening the bitterness, deluding us and consuming our soul with sighs. How are we to capture these inverted dreams that both freeze the past and release it—theme images scattered, at times, like clouds over the expanses of the mind, like precious diamonds compressed within the folds of the soul?

Before he became a memory to his friends, Mas'ud concerned himself with memory.

The memory theme is further played out because even though Mas'ud's memories are recorded in words, they remain problematic. His last words on the tape are: "no no no that's not what I wanted to say even though I did want to say some of it when everything I've already said is merely marginal and the main text is missing so let me try again." As Jabra unwinds the story, the reader comes to see that these words could have been uttered by any of the characters who are "searching" for Mas'ud. Each character has his or her own chapter in which he or she recounts memories and reactions. All of them move

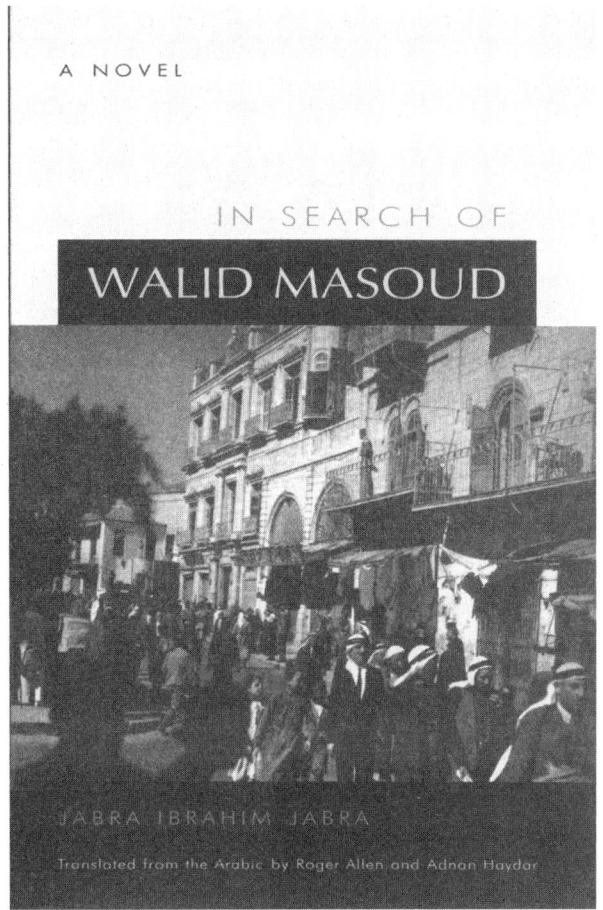

Dust jacket for the 2000 English translation of Jabra's 1978 novel al-Bahth'an Walid Mas'ud *(Richland County Public Library)*

through a process of self-examination and self-scrutiny that is more noteworthy for what it fails to reveal rather than any actual self-discovery. All of the characters are searching for a different man; Mas'ud was known to each of them in different ways, and these different ways of knowing Mas'ud add up to some sort of complete life of the man. The book ends with Mas'ud's whereabouts still unknown.

Al-Bahth 'an Walid Mas'ud, like *al-Safinah*, treats highly educated characters from the elite of society, who bring thoughtfulness and intellectuality to the story. The narrators discuss the misperceptions between Western and Islamic cultures and the necessity of political commitment. One narrator, Mas'ud's recent lover Wisal, is convinced that he has joined the freedom fighters in Palestine and leaves to join him there. The narrator's monologues reveal the recurring concerns of the lost homeland and the tragedy of exile—themes that were personal to Jabra. The novel is noteworthy also for its style of weaving the different narrative voices

Title page for the English translation of Jabra's 1987 novel al-Bi'r al-ula (Thomas Cooper Library, University of South Carolina)

together, something which until that time had not been seen in Arabic fiction.

In his next major project Jabra collaborated with the Saudi writer Abdelrahman Munif on the novel 'Alam bila khara'it (1982, Mapless World). The plot, which unfolds in the imaginary Arab city named 'Ammuriyya, begins when Najwa al-'Amiri is found murdered. The narrator, 'Ala' al-Din Najib, had been having a love affair with Najwa. Although by the end of the novel the reader has probably absolved 'Ala' al-Din Najib and some other primary suspects of the crime, the murder of Najwa is not solved, and there is no sense of closure.

In 1983 Jabra published *The Grass Roots of Iraqi Art,* which he wrote in English to reach non-Arabic readers. Scholars have noted that Jabra in his art criticism aims to promote Arab culture without sacrificing its roots and identity.

In 1987 Jabra published the first of his two autobiographical works, *al-Bi'r al-ula* (translated as *The First Well: A Bethlehem Boyhood,* 1995), a moving account of his childhood memories of Bethlehem and Jerusalem. He begins with his awareness of his familial and environmental surroundings: "First I became aware. . . ." For Jabra, awareness is the equivalent of the word in the beginning of the Gospel of John–"In the beginning there was the Word . . ."–for it is a creative force that transforms the inner being and shapes events throughout one's life. The narrative takes the reader through events in Jabra's life into 1932, when he turned twelve years old. Jabra illustrates how childhood memories are at times the well from which the mature adult draws sustenance and how such memories can have a profound effect on the individual.

The well is the major metaphor and organizing principle of this work, having psychological, social, and religious meanings. The first well of childhood is the origin of life and its creative power, the fountain of primordial motivations, of pain, fears, and joyfulness of life. The social meaning of the metaphor is clear in the author's observations that the first thing that Palestinian peasants inquire about upon moving to a different dwelling is the well: Is it deep enough? Is it in good shape? Is its water drinkable? The well, too, is an indicator of social standing of the Palestinian family: the better the well, the higher the social status of the family. When the fortunes of Jabra's family were down, they had to dwell in a well-less house. As a religious metaphor, the well figures in the Bible stories about Joseph and Daniel. The well in which Joseph's jealous brothers threw him is the crucial beginning of his rise to prominence, for from the bottom of the well Joseph is lifted by God up to the highest position in the land of Egypt. Likewise, Daniel was thrown into the pit with ferocious lions unleashed to tear him apart. But the Lord saved Daniel from the pit, showing that those who fear the Lord will eventually be saved.

Several events left an indelible effect on the young Jabra. He relates in *al-Bi'r al-ula* that as a child he got into trouble and was punished by his mother, whose presence in the narrative is pervasive. Jabra's father, on the other hand, is a marginal figure. His effect on young Jabra was manifested more by his conspicuous absence, whether due to his father's preoccupations or long bouts of illness. Jabra singles out Jesus as the person with whom he greatly identified as a child, and like Jesus, his life was shaped by his mother.

Jabra's fiction includes references to the early years of his life in Palestine, his mother and grandmother, and his playmates and relatives. The first well of childhood pervades his world of fiction. The sea he longed for as a child haunts his imagination as he records in his autobiography:

> The idea of a vast body of surging water fascinated me, but Bethlehem had no water, not even a stream, other than the piped spring water or Ayn al-Qanat, as it was called. I used to hear about Solomon's Pools, but they were far away, and admission to them was forbidden. My friends and I had no alternative but to make a sea, if we wanted a sea. Making a sea occupied us for a long time. We decided to dig a sea where ships could sail in one of the green plots. Each of us brought a pickax or an adz, and we began to dig.

Jabra also recounts how he used to dream of the impossible and the distant—his only escape from the harsh life of the present. He remarks that the inventor of the idea of the flying carpet in *The Arabian Nights* probably was stuck in the crowded and smelly streets of Cairo or Baghdad: his imagined flying carpet was a way to escape the suffocating reality of his sordid neighborhood. Jabra's disparagements of the city in *al-Bi'r al-ula* are familiar to readers who have followed his criticisms of urban life throughout his fiction and poetry.

Jabra's career through the late 1980s and early 1990s was quite productive. During this time he published approximately a book a year, including *al-Majmu'at al-shi'riyyah al-kamilah* (1990, Complete Poetry Works) and some literary criticism. In 1994 Jabra published *Shari' al-amirat: Fusul min sirah dhatiyyah* (translated as *Princesses' Street*, 2005), a continuation of his autobiography that picks up in his adult years. Readers are given a glimpse at Baghdad before World War II and in its aftermath. It was the last book he published before his death in Iraq on 12 December 1994. Both of Jabra's autobiographies have been popular with English readers, who appreciate his detailed descriptions of such places as Bethlehem, Jerusalem, and Baghdad.

Looking over the characters of Jabra's novels, one notices the recurring theme of middle- or upper-class educated people facing difficult times. His characters most often are Arab, many times Palestinians who, like Jabra, lost their land and homes in the 1948 War. The themes of exile and the search for identity recur frequently. Jabra found his style early and spent nearly half a century refining it, and his works have appealed to pleasure readers and scholars alike. In 1990 Jabra was the recipient of two literary prizes: the Sultan Uweis Prize for Literary Criticism and the Jerusalem medal for literary achievement.

Did Jabra Ibrahim Jabra's diverse talents as a poet, fiction writer, critic, painter, and translator cause him to branch out in different directions, or did his talents converge in a unified artistic vision of the world? In an interview with Alaa Elgibali and Barbara Harlow in 1981 Jabra explained that what he called his "lust for creation" had led him to find different forms for expression. The different arts helped him to express different aspects of himself. What he could not express as a painter, he said, he tried to express as a poet or a fiction writer.

Interview:

Alaa Elgibali and Barbara Harlow, "Jabra's Interpoetics: An Interview with Jabra Ibrahim Jabra," *Alif: Journal of Comparative Poetics*, no. 1 (Spring 1981).

References:

Roger Allen, *The Arabic Novel: A Historical and Critical Introduction* (Syracuse, N.Y.: Syracuse University Press, 1995);

Muhammad Mustafa Badawi, *A Short History of Modern Arabic Literature* (Oxford: Clarendon Press, 1993);

Al-Qalaq wa tamjid al-hayat: Kitab takrim Jabra Ibrahim Jabra (Beirut: Al-Mu'assasah al-'Arabiyyah li al-Dirasat wa al-Nashr, 1995).

Mohammed 'Abed al-Jabri
(27 December 1935 -   )

Mohamed Ourya
University of Sherbrooke

BOOKS: *Durus al-falsafah,* by al-Jabri and others (Morocco, 1966);

Al-Fikr al-Islami wa dirasat al-mu'allafat, by al-Jabri and others (Morocco, 1967);

Al-'Asabiyyah wa al-dawlah: Ma'alim nazariyyah Khalduniyyah fi al-tarikh al-Islami (Casablanca: Dar al-Nashr al-Maghribiyyah, 1971);

Adwa' 'ala mushkil al-ta'lim bi al-Maghrib (Casablanca: Dar al-Nashr al-Maghribiyyah, 1973);

Madkhal ila falsafat al-'ulum, 2 volumes (Casablanca: Dar Annachr al-Maghribia, 1976)—comprises *Tatawwur al-fikr al-riyadi wa al-'aqlaniyyah al-mu'asirah* and *Al-Minhaj al-tajribi wa tatawwur al fikr al-'ilmi;*

Min ajli ru'yah taqaddumiyyah li badi mashakilina al-fikriyyah wa al-tarbawiyyah (Casablanca: Dar al-Nashr al-Maghribiyyah, 1977);

Nahnu wa al-turath: Qira'at mu'asira fi turathina al-falsafi (Beirut: Dar al-Tali'ah, 1980);

Al-Khitab al-'Arabi al-mu'asir: Dirasah tahliliyyah naqdiyyah (Beirut: Dar al-Tali'a li al-Tiba'ah wa al-Nashr, 1982);

Naqd al-'aql al-'Arabi: Takwin al-'aql al-'Arabi (Beirut & Casablanca: Al-Markaz al-Thaqafi al-'Arabi, 1984);

Naqd al-'aql al-'Arabi: Binyat al-'aql al-'Arabi: Dirasah tahliliyyah naqdiyyah li nuzum al-ma'rifah fi al-thaqafah al-'Arabiyyah (Beirut & Casablanca: Al-Markaz al-Thaqafi al-'Arabi, 1986);

Ishkaliyyat al-fikr al-'Arabi al-mu'asir (Casablanca: Mu'assasat Banshara li al-Tiba'ah wa al-Nashr, 1988);

Al-Syiasat al-ta'limiyyah fi al-Maghrib al-'Arabi (Casablanca: Dar al-Nashr al-Maghribiyyah, 1988);

Al-Maghrib al-mu'assir: Al-Khususiyyah wa al-huwiyyah . . . al-Hadatha wa al-tanmyiah (Casablanca: Mu'assasat Banshara li al-Tiba'ah wa al-Nashr, 1988);

Hiwar al-Mashriq wa al-Maghrib: Hiwar ma'a Hassan Hanafi (Cairo: Maktabat Madbouly, 1990);

Naqd al-'aql al-'Arabi: Al-'aql al-siyasi al-'Arabi: Muhaddidatuh wa fajalliyatuh (Beirut & Casablanca: Al Markaz al-Thaqafi al-'Arabi, 1990);

Mohammed 'Abed al-Jabri (<http://www.islamonline.net/arabic/arts/2004/10/article09.shtml>)

Al-Turath wa al-hadatha (Beirut: Al-Markaz at-Thaqafi al-'Arabi, 1991);

Wijhat Nazar: Nahwa i'adat bina' qadaya al-fikr al-'Arabi al-mu'asir (Beirut: Al-Markaz al-Thaqafi al-'Arabi, 1992);

Al Mas'alah al-thaqafiyyah (Beirut: Al-Markaz al-Thaqafi al-'Arabi, 1994);

Introduction à la critique de la raison arabe (Paris: Editions La Découverte, 1994); translated by Aziz Abbassi as *Arab-Islamic Philosophy: A Contemporary Critique* (Austin, Tex.: Center for Middle Eastern Studies, 1999);

Al Muthaqqafun fi al-hadarah al-'Arabiyyah: Mihnat Ibn Hanbal wa nakbat Ibn Rushd (Beirut: Markaz Dirasat al-Wahdah al-'Arabiyyah, 1995);

Mas'alat al-huwiyyah: Al-'Urubah wa al Islam . . . wa al-Gharb (Beirut: Markaz Dirasat al-Wahdah al-'Arabiyyah, 1995);

Al-Din wa al-dawlah wa tatbiq al-Shari'ah (Beirut: Markaz Dirasat al-Wahdah al-'Arabiyyah, 1996);

Al-Mashru' al-nahdawi al-'Arabi (Beirut: Markaz Dirasat al-Wahdah al-'Arabiyyah, 1996);

Al-Dimuqratiyyah wa huquq al-insan (Beirut: Markaz Dirasat al-Wahdah al-'Arabiyyah, 1997);

Hafriyyat fi al-dhakirah (Beirut: Markaz Dirasat al-Wahdah al-'Arabiyyah, 1997);

Al-Tanmiyah al-bashariyyah wa al-khususiya al-susyulujiyyah: al-'alam al-'Arabi namudhajan (New York: United Nations Publications, 1997);

Qadaya fi al-fikr al-mu'asir (Beirut: Markaz Dirasat al-Wahdah al-'Arabiyyah, 1997);

Ibn Rushd: Sirah wa fikr (Beirut: Markaz Dirasat al-Wahdah al-'Arabiyyah, 1998);

Naqd al-'aql al-'Arabi: Al-'Aql al-akhlaqi al-'Arabi: Dirasah tahliliyyah naqdiyyah li nuzum al-qiyam fi al-thaqafah al-'Arabiyyah (Beirut & Casablanca: Al-Markaz al-Thaqafi al-'Arabi, 2001);

Fi naqd al-hajah ila al-islah (Beirut: Markaz Dirasat al-Wahdah al-'Arabiyyah, 2005).

Mohammed 'Abed al-Jabri is among the most notable contemporary Arab intellectuals. His monumental four-volume critique of Arab reason, begun in 1984 and completed in 2001, made this Moroccan philosopher one of the most powerful representatives of Arabic-Islamic thought in the twentieth century. Al-Jabri's work is known by scholars of philosophy and political science throughout the Muslim world. However, he is not just an intellectual for the academy. His respected journal articles are also read by much of the public at large in the Arab world, particularly in his native Morocco and in North Africa. Al-Jabri's works have been translated into many languages, and his theories have exerted a decisive influence on students and scholars of Arab intellectual history and become required reading for those wishing to understand the genesis and mechanisms of Arabic thought.

Al-Jabri was born in Figuig, Morocco, on 27 December 1935. He was the only child of parents who divorced just prior to his birth. His father was a businessman who traveled frequently, in addition to owning a small boulangerie (bakery) in Figuig. Al-Jabri lived with his mother in her parents' house. After completing his early preliminary education, he continued his studies so that he could become a schoolteacher. In 1957 he began work as a teacher, but he continued to study philosophy. He also became a contributor to several Moroccan newspapers. In 1961 he completed his studies for his bachelor's degree in philosophy.

In 1962 al-Jabri began what was to be a rather short political career by becoming a member on the council of the Union Nationale des Forces Populaires (National Union of Popular Forces, UNFP), one of the largest political parties in Morocco at the time. The following year, al-Jabri, along with the leaders of the party, was charged by the government with compromising national security and imprisoned. He was released after two months. In the mid 1960s al-Jabri participated in establishing several journals and newspapers in the social sciences, including the newspapers *Aqlam* (Pens), *al-Ahdaf* (Goals), and *al-Moharrir* (The Editor), which was founded in 1964. At the time, these newspapers were known for their leftist-socialist editorials, to which al-Jabri subscribed. *Al-Moharrir,* for example, later became the official newspaper of the Union Socialiste des Forces Populaires (USFP), the main opposition party to the government, which played a decisive role in the politics of the country.

Al-Jabri was imprisoned for a second time in 1965 after March riots in Casablanca, the result of political discontent aggravated by economic difficulties. The authorities' severe repression of the riots led to violence and the arrest of several hundred people. After his release from prison, al-Jabri participated in founding the National Teachers Union. He collaborated on two works for bachelor's students in philosophy: *Durus al-falsafah* (1966, Lessons of Philosophy) and *al-Fikr al-Islami wa dirasat al-mu'allafat* (1967, The Islamic Thought and the Study of Its Texts). These two books were accepted by Morocco's Ministry of Education and had a considerable influence on the teaching of philosophy in Morocco, explaining the progress of philosophy from the ancient Greek philosophers until the contemporary era, including the contributions of Arab and Islamic thinkers.

In 1967 al-Jabri received his master's degree in philosophy from the University Mohamed V in Rabat and joined the faculty of literature at the school as an assistant professor. The following year he was named the Inspector of National Education for the discipline of philosophy in high schools. After successfully defending his dissertation in 1970, al-Jabri was able to begin his career as professor of philosophy at the University of Rabat in 1971. In his dissertation, which was published in 1971 as *al-'Asabiyyah wa al-dawlah: Ma'alim nazariyyah Khalduniyyah fi al-tarikh al-Islami* (Militancy and the State: Principles of Ibn Khaldoun's Theory in Islamic History), al-Jabri examined the work of the fourteenth-century intellectual.

In the 1970s al-Jabri continued to be involved in politics in the USFP, a party that derived from the UNFP after a schism in 1975, while also beginning to develop his project for a grand criticism of Arab reason, which would occupy much of his writing career. During these early years, however, his project on Arab reason was in an embryonic stage and did not result in any

Title page for the first book of al-Jabri's four-volume critique of Arab reason, Naqd al-'aql al-'Arabi: Takwin al-'aql al-'Arabi, *1984 (University of Pennsylvania Libraries)*

publications. Al-Jabri was also interested in the philosophy of science and published his work on the subject as *Madkhal ila falsafat al-'ulum* (Introduction to the Philosophy of Science) in 1976. What became his principal ideas, however, began to be developed through his works criticizing Abdallah Laroui, a Moroccan thinker and influential intellectual historian who was extremely well known in the Arab world. Laroui was a colleague of al-Jabri's at the University Mohamed V in Rabat; his basic historical and intellectual orientation was the European Enlightenment.

In 1980 al-Jabri published *Nahnu wa al-turath: Qira'at mu'asirah fi turathina al-falsafi* (Us and Our Tradition: Contemporary Reading of Our Philosophical Tradition), a work he began as a response to Laroui's thesis about Arab tradition but that turned out to be something of a prelude to his later critique of Arab reason. Both men were concerned with the question of how to respond to contemporary problems without betraying their culture to the West. Al-Jabri considered Laroui's argument, which called for a complete break with the Arab-Muslim tradition, to be a problematic ideological project. Arguing that the "glorious past" of the Arabs should not even be mentioned, Lauroui opposed any temptation to reconcile the past—no matter how glorious—and the present. Al-Jabri believed that Laroui provided no philosophical basis for such a break and insisted that Laroui's thesis, which called for an Arab integration into the Western paradigm of modernism, neglected the real problems associated with the present. Al-Jabri's critique of Laroui's thesis focuses on the emptiness of Laroui's insistence that Arabs not appeal to a past rooted in the Muslim-Arab collective imagination.

In criticizing Laroui, al-Jabri asserted that only by confronting their tradition could the Arab world be successful in catching up with the Occident. For al-Jabri, ruptures with the past cannot be imposed externally. The Arab world cannot just "adopt" modernity from the Occident, for it is not as if there is just one modernity that can be applied everywhere. In part, al-Jabri's ideas involve a rejection of secularism, and in part they involve a call for serious self-determination on the part of the Arabs—they must create their own modernity by consciously transcending their complicated past. Each attempt to overcome the tradition one wishes to leave behind must itself be analyzed. In any endeavor to overthrow tradition, one must be constantly vigilant of the methods and tools that are used. The project necessitates a critical analysis of itself. As al-Jabri worked through these ideas in this early work, he concluded that what was needed was a deconstruction of the mechanisms of Arab thought from its inception.

During the 1980s al-Jabri's theoretical efforts evident in his dissertation and his early writings were elaborated in his critique of Arab reason. Owing to health reasons and in order to devote himself to his critique of Arab reason, al-Jabri resigned from the political office of the USFP in April 1981. But though he divorced himself from politics, al-Jabri did not lose interest in the boundary between his cultural and political endeavors. He later said that he had no difficulty in marrying politics and science in his intellectual works, because he believed the two fields are complementary and complete each other: a philosopher must use both of them to better comprehend and assimilate the past with the present.

To overcome what he regarded as the deadlock in the political, economic, and social thinking of the Arab world, al-Jabri in articles and interviews beginning in 1982 proposed the notion of "historical block," which he borrowed from the Italian philosopher Antonio Gramsci (1891–1937). Al-Jabri makes an analogy between the Italian society led by Benito Mussolini in the mid 1920s and the Arabic societies of the 1980s. He proposes a regrouping, or blocking together, of effective forces from all different ideologies—including Marxism, liberalism (the understanding that there are universal human values and a notion of human liberty that can be found through reason), and Islam—to achieve the single objective of liberating the culture from the aftermath of colonization, and the political, economic, and cultural imperialist hegemony of the West. He believed that cultural liberation had to be enacted with balanced social relations, assuring an equitable distribution of goods and uninterrupted progress in research. Al-Jabri considered this "block" to be a historical necessity, although he did not explain at all how heterogeneous ideologies could be united in one purpose. He saw the problem of development in the Arab world as being connected substantially to the question of an "Arab unity," and with his idea of the "historical block" al-Jabri aligned himself with the Arabic unionist and nationalist movement in all its theorizing, its programs, and its struggles.

In 1984 al-Jabri published the first volume of what became his comprehensive critique of Arab reason. All four volumes have the general title *Naqd al-'aql al-'Arabi* (Critique of Arab Reason), which precedes a more specific subtitle. *Naqd al-'aql al-'Arabi: Takwin al-'aql al-'Arabi* (Critique of Arab Reason: The Genesis of Arab Reason) was followed in 1986 by *Naqd al-'aql al-'Arabi: Binyat al-'aql al-'Arabi: Dirasah tahliliyyah naqdiyyah li nuzum al-ma'rifah fi al-thaqafah al-'Arabiyyah* (Critique of Arab Reason: The Structure of Arab Reason: Analytical and Critical Studies of the Cognitive Level of Order in the Arab Culture). The third volume, *Naqd al-'aql al-'Arabi: Al-'aql al-siyasi al-'Arabi: Muhaddidatuh wa tajalliyatuh* (Critique of Arab Reason: The Arabic Political Reason: Determination and Manifestation) appeared in 1990. The fourth and final volume, *Naqd al-'aql al-'Arabi: Al-'aql al-akhlaqi al-'Arabi: Dirasah tahliliyyah naqdiyyah li nuzum al-qiyam fi al-thaqafah al-'Arabiyyah* (Critique of Arab Reason: Ethical Arab Reason: Analytic and Critical Studies of the Ethical Order in the Arab Culture), was published in 2001. Al-Jabri's monumental project proved influential in contemporary Arabic thought in part because his ideas were controversial, and his writings contained stinging critiques of some of his contemporaries. His work was also important because it had a mass appeal among Arab readers. Although the theoretical debates described in his books treat historical subjects, al-Jabri manages to link such debates to contemporary problems of the Arab world.

In the first two volumes of the tetralogy al-Jabri argued that the current of modernity was evident in Arabic-Muslim history itself and that the past held answers as to how Arabs must wrestle with the present and the future. He holds up the twelfth-century Arabic philosopher Averroës, also called Ibn Rushd, as an example of a modern thinker. By reconceiving how philosophy and religion are related—regarding each as a way of looking at the truth—Averroës opened an avenue to secularism. Al-Jabri thus recognizes the ideological continuity of the past and the present and argues that modernity can and must be conceived without a total break from tradition.

Al-Jabri asserts that there are three cognitive orders that emerged to define Arabic-Muslim knowledge the time of the Codification (*'asr al-tadwin*) in the early days of Islam during the eighth and ninth centuries. By this period almost all of the foundations for Arabic sciences had been cast, perfected, and transcribed. He labels these cognitive orders as "al-Bayan" (Indication), "al-'Irfan" (Gnosis), and "al-Burhan" (Demonstration).

The Indication sciences include linguistics (*'ilm al-lughah*), law (*al-fiqh*), and dialectical theology (*al-kalam*), disciplines that get their foundations from the Qur'anic texts and the Hadith. They are aligned with the sacred text, which is accepted without dispute, and are devoted to its interpretation. Al-Jabri emphasizes the central place of the *fiqh* foundations in Arabic reason and suggests that its place is similar to the one occupied by mathematics in Western civilization. These sciences provided the means of understanding the sacred text in all its epistemological dimensions during the time of the Prophet and his companions. Al-Jabri believes that Arabic reason excelled in these fields, and he considers them part of what he calls the "Arab miracle." Al-Jabri argues that once the period of codification was over, these disciplines entered a phase of stagnation and repetition that has lasted until the present. The same ideas and principles have been reiterated, without taking historical evolution into account. In the first volume of his study he explains:

> . . . these sciences have reached their highest degree of their evolution, and they have completed themselves when they were at their beginnings, the Arab reason which produced them added nothing to them. Nothing could be added to what was formulated during the period of codification. Arab reason has remained a prisoner of the intellectual production of that period. (Translated by Mohamed Ourya and Coeli Fitzpatrick)

Because of the early advancement of these disciplines, traditional understandings weigh heavily on contemporary Arabic thought, contributing to difficulty of breaking with, or even reconciling with, the past.

Al-Jabri's second cognitive order, gnosis, is based in hermetic theosophy. Gnostic interpretations, which extract from the sacred text a "hidden meaning" (*batin*), provide the foundation for the Sufi and the "chii" culture in Islam. According to al-Jabri, gnosis is an episte-

Front cover for the 1999 English translation of Introduction à la critique de la raison arabe, *which al-Jabri published in 1994 as an introduction to his thought for Western readers (Thomas Cooper Library, University of South Carolina)*

mological system of knowledge acquisition, a vision of the world, and also represents a position taken in relation to the world. The origin of this order is from Arabic cultures of the pre-Islamic period, especially those present in lands now known as Egypt, Syria, Palestine and Iraq. Al-Jabri argues that gnosis affirms the beliefs of ancient cultures wherein magic and supernatural forces, not science, are relied upon to explain the world. He regards gnosticism as an irrational position, one which divides the world and makes of the gnostic "self" and "knower" the only existing reality. The gnostic believes knowledge comes directly from God and thus transcends both time and space. Al-Jabri argues that gnosticism, which has remained influential for centuries in erudite Arabic culture, was detrimental to thought and to all Arabic-Muslim civilization, which entered into a state of hibernation as the result of the work of famous gnostics such as al-Ghazali (1058–1111). According to al-Jabri, Arabic-Muslim thought can only progress through a complete negation of gnosis and the irrational elements in the culture.

In both of his critiques, al-Jabri argues that the "Arabic sciences of demonstration"–logical demonstration, proceeding from premises to conclusions–were born with the philosopher al-Farabi and afterward developed in the philosophical schools of Baghdad. This order was then transmitted to Morocco and Andalusia by Avempace (1095–1139), Averroës, and Ibn Khaldoun (1331–1406). Al-Jabri excludes the Muslim philosopher and physician Avicenna (980–1037) from the rational sphere of the order of "demonstration." He considers Avicenna to be the precursor of the lethargy in Arabic thinking and charges him with contributing to the instauration of an incurable irrationality of Arabic-Muslim thought.

Al-Jabri's elaboration of these three orders led him to conclusions that were contested by other contemporary Arab thinkers. Al-Jabri argued that if Greek civilization is philosophical and Western civilization is scientific and technological, then Arabic-Muslim civilization is a *fiqh* civilization. His thesis was most controversial in its critique of Arabic reason, for he finds an epistemological break between the Arab East, which he associates with gnosticsm because of the influence of Avicenna and al-Ghazali, and the Maghreb, or Arab West, which he associates with rationality because of the influence of Averroës and Andalusian philosophy. Critics of al-Jabri's analysis have accused him of chauvinism and of having an ideological agenda. The notable Arab thinkers Georges Tarabichi and Hassan Hanafi discussed their objections to al-Jabri's ideas in their *Dialogue de l'Orient et de l'Occident: Dialogue avec Hassan Hanafi* (Dialogue on the Orient and the Occident: Dialogue with Hassan Hanafi, 1990).

In the third volume of his critique, al-Jabri proposed another reading of the political history of Islam. Stipulating that political practice was not completely shaped by religion, he argued that other factors also conditioned the development of politics in Arabic-Muslim history. He suggests that political realities in the Arab world since the inception of Islam have obeyed three essential determinants: the tribe, war booty, and dogma.

While acknowledging that the Prophet Muhammad formed his community of the faithful on the basis of a singular dogma and that Islam originated in the new principles he preached in his Quraysh tribe, al-Jabri forcefully argues that Muhammad's membership in the tribe played an important role (whether positive or negative) in political practice. Muhammad benefited from the tribal support of some of the Quraysh to form his state after several years of fighting against the tribe as a whole. Al-Jabri is certain that the spirit of the clan was a powerful force in Muhammad's formation of alliances in the quest for power. Even establishment of the caliphates several years after the death of the prophet did not escape the tribal determinant. There was always a tension between Muslims from tribes in Mecca and those in Medina, and these tensions were the cause of grave political problems for the early caliphs. Tribalism is therefore considered by al-Jabri as the basic unity of all the social and political games in the Arab world. Thanks to tribalism, the term "individual" in Islam is not really meaningful.

By "profit" al-Jabri refers to several ideas, including the distribution of goods won after a holy war, money collected as alms, and the tribute that the conqueror imposes on the vanquished after war. Profit is the only material link that guarantees that a tribe belongs to Islam, and profit serves as a tribe's guarantee of security. Al-Jabri reminds his readers that to continue its expansion and to prosper in the international system of the time, Islam needed a state, and that a state could not survive merely from the religious determinant (dogma). He cites as an example the Caliph Mu'awiya Ibn Abi Soufiane, the founder of the Umayyad dynasty who, thanks to wise management, built a Muslim state that became one of the most powerful of its time. Therefore, al-Jabri argues, power in Islam is far from being purely religious, and all attempts to exclude the tribe and profit in the development of Islam and its nation states are problematic.

Because of his desire to renew Arabic political reason, al-Jabri proposes that the determinants of tribe, profit, and dogma be newly understood so as to make them better fit with the paradigm of Western modernity. According to him, the tribe must disappear from contemporary Arabic societies to give place to a civil and political system where parties, syndication, and other institutions coexist. For profit, tributary economy must become productive. As for dogma, faith in a doctrine ought to become simple opinion. In other words, fundamentalism must disappear and give way to freedom of thought and of religion.

In 1994 al-Jabri published *Introduction à la critique de la raison arabe* (translated as *Arab-Islamic Philosophy: A Contemporary Critique*, 1999), a book that in its original French and its English translation introduced Western readers who could not read Arabic to al-Jabri's ideas. An extremely abridged version of his large project, it treated questions of interest to Occidental readers, such as how contemporary Arab intellectuals conceived of their relation in the world vis-à-vis the West and "modernity." As if he were still in dialogue with Laroui, al-Jabri writes:

> Modernity, therefore, is not to refute tradition or break with the past, but rather to upgrade the manner in which we assume our relationship to tradition at the level of what we call "contemporaneity," which, for us, means catching up with the great strides that are being made worldwide. True, modernity must find the substantiation of its species within its own discourse, the discourse of contemporaneity, but must not be a "fundamentalism" that clings to some inspiring sources/foundations. Alas, modernity in contemporary Arab thought has not gone that far yet. It remains limited/in the conception of its species/to getting its inspiration from European modernity, from which it draws the rational and the "foundations" to its discourse.

In order to be "authentic" to one's society and one's tradition, al-Jabri concluded, one must not embrace that tradition uncritically, but rather take from tradition what can still resonate true for us in the contemporary world. It is not a matter of simply choosing what "fits in" with Western thought, but rather choosing those ideas which are still viable despite their age.

Al-Jabri enjoys considerable respect in the Arab community, but he is also criticized by Arab thinkers for his use of "Western" concepts. Al-Jabri's reading of the past is acknowledged as rigorous, but it leaves unanswered questions, and he has been criticized for leaving out any analysis of Qur'anic texts. In a review of the third volume of al-Jabri's project published in the March 1994 edition of *Contemporary Sociology,* Mahmoud Dhaouadi writes that al-Jabri is too tempted by his vision for reform in the Arab world to see the impossibility of disentangling the political from the religious. In the West, al-Jabri's *Arab-Islamic Philosophy* is seen as a welcome addition to intellectual writings available in translation. Ibrahim M. Abu-Rabi' includes a discussion of al-Jabri's work in his *Contemporary Arab Thought: Studies in Post-1967 Arab Intellectual History* (2004), presenting al-Jabri's thesis in an even more abridged form.

Al Jabri's fourth and final contribution to the critique of Arab reason, *Naqd al-'aql al-'Arabi: Al-'aql al-akhlaqi al-'Arabi: Dirasah tahliliyyah naqdiyyah li nuzum al-qiyam fi al-thaqafah al-'Arabiyyah* is a study of the values in Arab culture and their roots in the Persians, Greeks, Sufism, and Islam. One criticism of the book was that it omits the Christian heritage as influential on Arab culture.

Mohamed 'Abed al-Jabri retired from teaching in 2002 but continues his research into the relationship of the Arab world to the West. He has also written about democracy, human rights, and the wars in Iraq. On his Internet site he lists his current articles, which are directed toward a general audience. His most recent work treats the notion of Arab collective imagination. He directs the Moroccan journal *Fikr wa naqd* (Thought and Critique) and continues to reside in Rabat.

References:

Kamal 'Abd al-Latif, *Naqd al-'aql am 'aql al-tawafuq?* (Latakia, Syria: Dar al-Hiwar, 2002);

Ibrahim M. Abu-Rabi', "Towards a Critical Arab Reason: The Contributions of Muhammad 'Abid al-Jabiri," in his *Contemporary Arab Thought: Studies in Post-1967 Arab Intellectual History* (London: Pluto Press, 2004), pp. 256–295;

Georges Tarabichi, *Naqd naqd al-'aql al-Arabi,* 4 volumes (Beirut: Dar As-saqi, 1996–2004)—comprises *Nazariyyat al-'aql al-'Arabi* (1996), *Ishkaliyyat al-'aql al-'Arabi* (1998), *Wahdat al-'aql al-'Arabi al-Islami* (2002), and *Aal aql al moustaqil en islam* (2004).

'Aziz al-Sayyid Jasim

(1941–1991?)

Hager Ben Driss
University of Tunis

BOOKS: *Al-Munadil* (Beirut: Dar al-Tali'ah, 1972);

Haqq al-mar'ah bayna mushkilat al-takhalluf al-ijtima'i wa mutatallabat al-hayah al-jadidah: Ru'yah thaqafiyyah, ijtima'iyah, jinsiyyah (Beirut: Al-Mu'assasah al-'Arabiyyah, 1980);

Dirasat naqdiyyah fi al-adab al-hadith (Cairo: GEBO, 1980);

Dialiktik al-'alaqa al-mu'aqqadah bayna al-madiyyah wa al-mithaliyyah (Baghdad: Dar al-Nahar, 1982);

Al-Ightirab fi hayat wa shi'r al-Sharif al-Radi (Baghdad: Dar al-Andalus, 1986);

Ta'ammulat fi al-hadarah wa al-ightirab (Baghdad: Dar al-Andalus, 1987);

Iqa' Babili: Shi'r Hamid Sa'id (Baghdad: Dar al-Shuruq, 1987);

'Ali ibn Abi Talib: Sultat al-haqq (Beirut: Dar al-Adab, 1988);

Al-Zahr al-shaqi (Cairo: GEBO, 1988);

Al-Tasawwuf wa al-iltizam fi Shi'r 'Abd al-Wahab al-Bayyati (Baghdad: Dar al-Shuruq, 1989);

Mutasawifat Baghdad (Baghdad, 1990);

Al-Maftun (Beirut: Al-Mu'assasah al-'Arabiyyah li al-Dirasat wa al-Nashr, 2003).

'Aziz al-Sayyid Jasim's three novels are somewhat eclipsed by his other writings on literary criticism, the history of Islam, and class and gender issues. To locate his novels in Arabic literature, one needs to understand his position in the Iraqi intellectual scene. Jasim was deliberately marginalized by the regime of Saddam Hussein, and as a result many of his works sank into oblivion. The significance of his narratives, however, resides in his ability to link a subtle autobiographical stand to political and cultural movements in Iraq. More than those of other novelists, Jasim's writings demonstrate his intellectual involvement in the political scene in Iraq since the 1950s. He opted, in Robert Frost's words, for the "less traveled" road, for throughout his career he remained faithful to his Marxist orientation even as he appropriated nationalism and Sufism into his deeply grounded leftist thought.

'Aziz al-Sayyid Jasim, also called Abu Khawla, was born in 1941 in al-Nasiriyyah, a province of southern Iraq. He was the fourth child of a large family composed of four daughters and four sons. His parents, al-Sayyid Jasim 'Ali and Maliqa al-Sayyid Haydar, were reportedly from a noble family that traces its ancestry to Islam's prophet, Muhammad. He grew up in al-Nasr, a town in the province, where he attended elementary school between 1946 and 1951. At an early age, he showed signs of intellectual distinction as well as of independence and, to an extent, defiance. For example, when he learned to write, he chose to write his name as "'Aziz al-Sayyid Jasim," despite regulations that required he sign his name "Jasim 'Ali." He continued to use "Jasim" as his last name. In 1951 he moved to the city of al-Nasiriyyah, where he continued his secondary education until 1955, followed by two years in the Teachers' Training School. Precocious and gifted, Jasim never sat for any exam. His teachers acknowledged his learning, and he was exempted from all types of examinations.

At fourteen, Jasim experienced the death of his father. Despite this tragedy, he continued to go school, though he carried a heavy responsibility to take care of his family, being the oldest of his brothers. While a secondary-school student, Jasim went through another traumatic experience when he was shot in the leg during a demonstration that he led against the British, French, and Israeli attack on Egypt in 1956. He recovered after being secretly nursed by his mother, whose courage and perseverance as a young widowed woman inspired his portraits of mothers in his fiction. Despite his injury, he continued his political activity in Iraq, joining the Communist Party in 1957. In 1958 he was appointed as a primary-school teacher in al-Nasr, but he was fired two months later following an argument with the inspector over teaching methodologies.

Jasim was imprisoned in 1960 and the following year severed his ties with the Communist Party. The Baath (Resurrection) Party came to power briefly in 1963 and carried out a major campaign against the

Front cover for 'Aziz al-Sayyid Jasim's first novel, al-Munadil *(The Militant), 1972 (Harlan Hatcher Library, University of Michigan)*

Communist Party and anyone who had been associated with it. Jasim was jailed for three months on accusations of being a communist, though he was no longer a party member. After the Baath Party was replaced through a military coup, Jasim was imprisoned again in 1964 and put on trial before a martial court. His speech in his own defense was reported to be so powerful and cogent that the attorney general ordered his immediate release. In 1968 the Baath Party returned to power. 'Abd al-Khaliq al-Samirra'i, who was in charge of the Cultural Bureau within the party, knew Jasim and his conjoining of Marxism and nationalism. In 1969 he invited Jasim to join the bureau, and a year later the party offered Jasim an honorary membership to legitimize his intellectual views within the party. It is important to note, however, that Jasim was never a militant member of the Baath Party.

In the early 1970s Jasim turned to writing as a way of expressing some of his experiences, publishing his first book, *al-Munadil* (1972, The Militant); like all of his novels, it was published outside Iraq, mainly through the agency of his brother, Muhsin Jassim al-Musawi, a writer and literary critic. Jasim had always been an avid reader and the influences on his writing were many. His library included books of the most prominent Egyptian writers, works of leading figures of the existentialist, nationalist, and Marxist thought, as well as an interesting collection of translated foreign texts. George Orwell's *Nineteen Eighty-Four* (1949) was one of his favorite novels and clearly colored his subtle satirical portraits of Iraqi political life. The existentialist mood permeating Jasim's narratives is inspired by Albert Camus and Jean-Paul Sartre. He intended *al-Munadil* to be the first part of a trilogy, though the subsequent novels were never published, and there is no evidence that Jasim wrote them.

Al-Munadil is set in Iraq during the late 1950s and the early 1960s. Jasim draws heavily on his own experiences, including first and foremost his disillusionment with the Iraqi government, but he also exposes the Communist Party and its progressive transformation into a totalitarian organization. Babil, the main character, finds himself caught between the government's persecution and his own party's betrayal. Babil is given the directive to lead a students' demonstration asking for the liberation of their comrades. Upon realizing that their scheme has been discovered by the police and that venturing a march is a suicidal mission, he improvises a sit-in inside the school. The following day Babil is arrested and the Communist Party freezes his membership, as he has not followed orders to the letter. Like Jasim, Babil refuses to become a conformist or a blind disciplined partisan of the Communist Party.

The major part of *al-Munadil* takes place in prison, and the novel, with its descriptions of the physical and psychological torture of political prisoners, is considered a prominent example of *adab al-sujun* (literature of prison). The experience of the jail reveals the hidden psychologies and souls of the prisoners. The reader soon realizes the skin-deep political convictions and commitments of some prisoners who quickly ally with a nonpolitical prisoner, a landowner–the symbol of political and economic evil they are supposed to fight. The reason for their admiration of this criminal is his open boasting of his homosexual practices, which they shamefully hide. Later in the narrative, Husayn, a communist militant, is ferociously attacked by the landowner's admirers because he announces his homosexuality. While the landowner's act of raping a boy is regarded by the prisoners as a demonstration of his "virility," Husayn's admitting his genuine love for a young man is seen as aberrant. The confinement of prison is ironically portrayed as liberating, as it accommodates all types of fantasies and inhibited sexual practices. The easy corruption of the political prisoners, who quickly forget their ideals and commitments, allows Jasim to demystify conceited discourses of engagement and self-sacrifice in a powerful political satire.

Among its many voices, stories, and subplots, *al-Munadil* traces the lives of three comrades, Babil, Husayn, and Sharaf, who belong to the Communist Party. Babil is the major protagonist, as he is present almost throughout the narrative. A disciplined activist who accepts no compromises, Babil dedicates all his energy and thoughts to his work, stifling his sexual drive and withdrawing "from all types of pleasure with the hope to belong exclusively to his political cause." Yet, he is attracted to Dalal, one of several strong women who figure in Jasim's novels and short stories. She is a revolutionary activist who leads the female section of the Communist Party. The few passionate moments they share together do not lead to any sexual fulfillment. Dalal's marriage to another man coincides with Babil's failure to accommodate to his party's deviations. His feeling of loss is doubled, for he considers Dalal's decision as a betrayal added to that of the Communist Party.

Husayn shares Babil's disappointment and frustration caused by the machinations and conspiracies within the party. When he decides to withdraw from the organization, he becomes the target of ferocious attacks and defamation. The story of Husayn and his life after leaving the party is presented to the reader through two letters he writes to Babil. In the first letter he speaks about torture in prison and his illness, which he faces alone as party members refuse to support him. Husayn presents another facet of the militant. While as strong-willed as Babil, he shows a wise and calm character. He represents the Sufi warrior, often depicted in Jasim's novels. "The militant needs isolation," he writes to Babil, "It is purification and a sign of courage. Isolation is the inaugurating phase of one's dissolution in the universe . . . it sweeps temptation and engages a sharp trial of the self." In his second letter, Husayn confesses his homosexuality and describes his love of a young man. Like all of Jasim's important characters, Husayn is a person who is always questioning himself. The party's progressive movement toward conformity is paralleled by the muting of his own sexual drives. His rebellion against his Communist Party is paralleled to his rebellion against his inhibited sexuality. Husayn, then, announces openly his homosexuality the day he decides to withdraw from his party. In his process of self-assessment, he interrogates both his party and his body. Like Babil, however, he fails to have a satisfactory emotional relationship. The narrative ends with him in a brothel, attempting to convert to heterosexuality.

If Babil represents the stern side and Husayn the wise one, Sharaf affords the "clownish" facet of the militant. His comic attitude is in reality a strategy of survival. Before leaving the Communist Party, Sharaf used to be an activist in the countryside. His role was to educate the farmers and rally them against the feudal system. When he tried to take political initiative, he was fired from the party and his membership was frozen. It is in jail that Sharaf learns to survive through comedy. His rapid socialization with other prisoners is a way to escape "the stifling depression" he feels inside the prison, which leads him to think seriously of committing suicide. Oscillating between considering suicide a courageous act or a cowardly deed, he ends up by adopting a "third understanding," something in-between that "goes beyond the logic and the official." He becomes an actor because, as he says, "things are tasteless without simulation." Simulating an epileptic spell, he manages to get deported to a hospital. Later in the narrative, he reappears disguised as a fortune-teller. Behind this mask, he continues his political activities.

The trio, Babil, Husayn, and Sharaf, share the same political aspirations and dreams of democracy. "You, Sharaf and myself," writes Husayn to Babil, "dedicated our lives to our nation; we had no other fate but the one we chose, and we made the right choice." The trio, however, witness the collapse of their dreams as they are caught between governmental oppression and their party's rigid regulations and intrigues.

Front cover for Jasim's novel al-Maftun (The Bewitched), 2003 (Widener Library, Harvard University)

By presenting different facets of the militant, *al-Munadil* offers a miniature of the political scene during the 1960s. The prison gathers all political allegiances and orientations: "Communists, Baathists, Democratic Nationalists and independents." Babil believes that heated discussions verging on vituperation show immature political thinking "hindering any attempt at a national unity." Basim 'Abd al-Hamid Hamudi takes Jasim as an example of some Iraqi novelists "who dedicated their fictional writings to monitor an age in which the secondary oppositions between national and liberal forces overpowered the major oppositions between these forces and both colonization and Zionism."

By 1973 Jasim's relationship with the Baath Party had started to sour. Although he had cherished a conviction that the party could make Iraq a leading country in democracy, social development, and Arab nationalism, he decided to withdraw from the Cultural Bureau, disgusted by the internal machinations of a party veering toward dictatorship. His intellectual commitment to the party, which he bitterly regretted later, caused him a great deal of damage. Other Marxists, especially those of the Diaspora, never forgave him and did not try to understand Jasim's attempts to influence the party from within. The Baath Party, on the other hand, considered his withdrawal as a betrayal. In 1977 his honorary membership was withdrawn, and his books, deemed to be against the mainstream of the Baath Party, were banned. Jasim was caught between two opposite forces that combined to marginalize him.

The 1980s proved to be Jasim's most prolific decade, though he turned more toward scholarly and literary critical studies than to fiction. The study that is most germane to his fiction, in which he depicts strong female characters, is *Haqq al-mar'ah bayna mushkilat al-takhalluf al-ijtima'i wa mutatallabat al-hayah al-jadidah: Ru'yah thaqafiyyah, ijtima'iyyah, jinsiyyah* (1980, Women's Rights between the Problem of Social Backwardness and the Demands of Modern Life: A Cultural, Social, and Gender Vision). In this book Jasim analyzes the social, cultural, economic, political, and historical causes that make women oppressed beings, alienated from the power of production. His Marxist orientation is clear in this and his other studies, as it also is in his narratives.

From 1980 to 1988 Jasim published several more books, addressing a variety of topics, including the status of women, modern literature, Arabic poetry, exile, and the relationship between materialism and idealism. After the publication of his *'Ali ibn Abi Talib: Sultat al-Haq* (1988, Ali: The Authority of Righteousness), Jasim was imprisoned for six months by the government of Saddam Hussein. Jasim's book was accused of promoting Shiism because of its admiring treatment of the life and thought of Imam 'Ali, revered by Shiites.

Now regarded as Jasim's most important contribution in the 1980s, *al-Zahr al-shaqi* (1988, The Suffering Primrose), his second novel, came out in Egypt after he had been arrested and jailed. The novel was first serialized in *Jaridat al-'Iraq* (Iraq Daily), a weekly Kurdish newspaper. While taking as a background the June 1967 Israeli surprise attack and defeat of Arab armies, the narrative re-creates the corrupt political life in Iraq during the 1980s. More episodic than linear, the structure of *al-Zahr al-shaqi* draws on the stream-of-consciousness technique wherein the main character, Wa'il, a marginalized artist and intellectual, confesses his political anxieties, spiritual meditations, and sexual fantasies. The small job he has in a governmental office, where his gift as a painter is buried, is a punishment for his dead father's Marxist allegiances. Wa'il declares himself an independent intellectual, Jasim's own stand. But Wa'il withdraws from political life, and over time he identifies with Sufis (Muslim mystics).

Wa'il exemplifies Jasim's creation of restless protagonists who are projections of his own search for a meaningful political and spiritual identity. His fiction is full of people who are in a perpetual search for identity. His narratives are stamped by Jasim's ongoing desire to regenerate aesthetic, political, and social values. Wa'il expresses such feelings when he compares his static present to an active past that he seeks to resurrect and improve: "Is there any meaning to my present life, if meaning is only present in the past? I am terrified by this huge void crushing me. I am not myself . . . this person lurking in the shadow, drowned in oblivion, is ash-colored. This is not my real self. I have surrendered myself to putrefaction." Like all Jasim's fictional protagonists, Wa'il questions everything, including his own convictions and stands. Wa'il swings between Marxism and Sufism, trying to find equilibrium between the body, the intellect and the soul. The major anxieties manifest in this novel—sex, politics, and mysticism—permeate his other fiction as well.

In *al-Zahr al-shaqi* sexuality is connected to the corrupt political life. Wa'il links his own sexual degeneration to political repression under a totalitarian regime. He wonders:

> Is this the weapon of triviality? Is it the fear of meditation, or the fear of the rebellion against the self? Why do we hide behind this revelry? Is it a captivation of virility, or a castration in life, and then we try to substitute things with sexual bravura? Or is it revenging us against ourselves? Is it the proof of our interior wrath?

Wa'il is saved from self-destruction by his mystical love for Muna. Their asexual relationship, based on what he calls "sanctified love," provides him with courage to enter the political arena again. Toward the end of the novel, he becomes an activist militant.

Muna is the best example of a strong-willed woman in Jasim's novels, which are notable for such characters. In *The Postcolonial Arabic Novel* (2003) al-Musawi reads her imposing presence in the narrative as "a heroic role, which is denied to women in many male narratives." Indeed, Muna is portrayed as a Marxist intellectual militant with a strong personality. The image of the passive woman permeating the majority of Arab male-authored texts is destroyed in Jasim's narratives. His female protagonists are outspoken, challenging women with an acute political awareness, sometimes superior to that of the male characters.

Jasim's life witnessed a drastic metamorphosis after the 1988 imprisonment. His inclination toward withdrawal and loneliness prepared him for the Sufi phase in his life. During the last years of the 1980s, he insisted on wearing modest, dark blue clothes, "the Sufis' attire," his brother Muhsin al-Musawi comments, "as they perceive life ephemeral and treacherous." His interest in living as a Sufi was evident in his writings. In 1989 Jasim published *al-Tasawwuf wa al-iltizam fi shi'r 'Abd al-Wahab al-Bayyati* (Sufism and Commitment in the Poetry of 'Abd al-Wahab al-Bayyati), a study of one of Iraq's most important contemporary poets. His *Mutasawifat Baghdad* (1999, The Sufis of Baghdad) is interesting for the connections Jasim makes between Sufism and politics.

Jasim withdrew from political life to become a shopkeeper. At forty-seven he was a father to seven children, and his major concern was to take care of his family and not to provide the government with any reason to imprison him again. But Jasim's wish to fall into oblivion was never realized. On 15 April 1991 he was arrested by the special security office with the personal authorization of President Saddam Hussein. He was accused of showing opposition to the invasion of Kuwait, sympathizing with the popular uprising against Saddam in 1991, and refusing to write on behalf of the regime. Considered as three deadly sins, these charges resulted in him becoming one of "the disappeared"—prisoners who were taken to jail and never seen again.

Jasim's last published novel, *al-Maftun* (The Bewitched), which he wrote in 1987, came out in Beruit in 2003. Although it was supposed to be published by the Cairo-based General Egyptian Book Office (GEBO), the manuscript was lost for years in Egypt before it was recovered by his brother. Deftly hiding political issues behind psychological concerns, *al-Maftun* has as one of its key settings a clinic that—like the prison in *al-Munadil*—allows Jasim to examine the inner worlds of his characters. The focus of the novel is Yusuf, a handsome young man who is transformed under torture into a half-virile, half-castrated person. He enjoys six months of sexual fertility followed by six months of impotence. Harun is a psychiatrist solicited by Yusuf to help him get outside the vicious circle of exterior violence and interior self-destruction in which he is trapped. Yusuf's sadistic relationship with Najwa, a girl bewitched by his love, turns out to be a means of revenge against her father, who tormented him in the prison. While trying to probe the complex personality of Yusuf, Harun strives to keep silent about his hidden political activities. The closing scene of the novel shows Harun arrested in a police station.

Jasim's three novels show that he is not averse to shocking his audience. He combines the crude language of revolutionaries with the highly poetical oratory of mystics. In *al-Munadil*, for instance, he concentrates on the sexual activities of the prisoners. He speaks about homosexuality and masturbation and parallels them to political impotence and hypocrisy. In an episode of *al-Zahr al-shaqi,* he treats women's sexual pleasure. Wa'il and his friends pay a visit to a Gypsy camp where they can meet prostitutes. Mu'izz, who turns out later to be impotent, accompanies a girl to her tent. What happens there is reported to the reader through the voyeuristic eye of another character. Unable to make a full sexual act, Mu'izz promises the girl to satisfy her in a different way, something he does with success. The girl reports later that his touches have provided her with a pleasure never experienced before. The episode is followed by other stories about lesbian women.

Jasim's career offers an outstanding case of dissidence and creativity. The outcome of his ongoing interrogation of the self is a set of semiautobiographical characters who resist static ideologies. His protagonists articulate his own open dissent—an attitude that shaped his life and made him an easy target for persecution.

Jasim was never seen again after his arrest in 1991, despite the interventions of Amnesty International in 1992, PEN International in 1993, and other organizations on his behalf. Unconfirmed reports began to appear about his deportations to different prisons or hospitals as well as his possible execution. His death was only confirmed in April 2003 after the invasion of Iraq by the U.S. and British troops and the fall of Baghdad. However, all attempts at muting 'Aziz al-Sayyid Jasim's voice have failed. His narratives will remain important documents for any serious student of Iraqi literature, culture, and history.

References:

Basim 'Abd al-Hamid Hamudi, *Al-Waqi' al-jama'i wa al-ijtima'i fi al-riwayah al-'Iraqiyyah al-mu'asirah* (Baghdad, 1980);

Muhsin Jassim al-Musawi, *The Postcolonial Arabic Novel: Debating Ambivalence* (Leiden & Boston: Brill, 2003);

'Umran Rachid, "Mufakkir Hurr fi Masir Majhul," *Azzaman Daily,* 1 May 2004.

Ghassan Kanafani
(9 April 1936 – 8 July 1972)

Kamal Abdel-Malek
American University of Sharjah

BOOKS: *Mawt sarir raqam 12 wa qisas ukhra* (Beirut: Maktabat Manaymanah, 1961); title story translated by Denys Johnson-Davies as "The Death of Bed Number 12," in *Modern Arabic Short Stories* (London: Heinemann, 1976);

Ard al-burtuqal al-hazin: Majmu'at qisas (Beirut: Al-Ittihad al-'Amm li Talabat Filastin, 1963);

Rijal fi al-Shams (Beirut: Dar al-Tali'ah, 1963);

Alam laysa lana (Beirut: Dar al-Tali'ah, 1965);

Ma Tabaqqa Lakum (Beirut: Dar al-Tali'ah, 1966);

Fi al-adab al-sihyuni (Beirut: Munazamat al-Tahrir al-Filastiniyya, 1967);

'An al-rijal wa al-banadiq (Beirut: Dar al-Udaba', 1968);

Al-Adab al-Filastini al-muqawim tahta al-ihtilal, 1948–1968 (Beirut: Mu'assasat al-Dirasat al-Filastiniyyah, 1968);

Umm Sa'd: Qisas Filastiniyyah (Beirut: Dar al-'Awdah, 1969);

'A'id ila Hayfa (Beirut: Dar al-'Awdah, 1969);

The 1936–1939 Revolution in Palestine (N.p.: Committee for Democratic Palestine, 1972);

Al-Athar al-kamilah, 7 volumes (Beirut: Dar al-Tali'ah, 1972);

Al-Qindil al-Saghir (Damascus: Dar al-Mada li al-Thaqafah wa-al-Nashr, 2005).

Editions in English: *Men in the Sun and Other Palestinian Stories,* translated by Hilary Kilpatrick (Washington, D.C.: Three Continents Press, 1978)—comprises "Men in the Sun," "The Land of Sad Oranges," "If You Were a Horse," "A Hand in the Grave," "Umm Saad," "The Falcon," and "Letter from Gaza";

All That's Left to You: A Novella and Short Stories, translated by May Jayyusi and Jeremy Reed (Austin: Center for Middle Eastern Studies, the University of Texas at Austin, 1990)—comprises "All that's Left to You," "In My Funeral," "Kafr Al-manjam," "The Shore," "The Viper's Thirst," "The Cake Vendor," "The Cat," "Pearls in the Street," "A Concise Principle," "Eight Minutes," and "Death of Bed 12";

"The Slave Fort," in *Arabic Short Stories,* translated by Denys Johnson-Davies (Berkeley: University of California Press, 1994);

Palestine's Children: Returning to Haifa and Other Stories, translated by Barbara Harlow and Karen E. Riley (Boulder, Colo.: Lynne Rienner, 2000)—comprises "The Slope," "Paper from Ramleh," "A Present for the Holiday," "The Child Borrows His Uncle's Gun and Goes East to Safad," "Doctor Qassim Talks to Eva about Mansur Who Has Arrived in Safad," "Abu al-Hassan Ambushes an English Car," "The Child, His Father, and the Gun Go to the Citadel in Jaddin," "The Child Goes to Camp," "The Child Discovers That the Key Looks like an Axe," "Suliman's Friend Learns Many Things in One Night," "Hamid Stops Listening to the Uncles' Stories," "Guns in the Camp," "He Was a Child That Day," "Six Eagles and a Child," and "Returning to Haifa."

Ghassan Kanafani was a Palestinian novelist, dramatist, and short-story writer; he was also a revolutionary journalist who served as the official spokesman for the Popular Front for the Liberation of Palestine (PFLP). He was born in Acre in Palestine on 9 April 1936 to a middle-class Muslim family and received his early education in French missionary schools until the family was forced into exile during the 1948 Arab-Israeli War. They stayed briefly in Lebanon, then moved to Damascus, where Kanafani finished his secondary-school education and went on to obtain a teaching certificate. In 1952 he enrolled at the University of Damascus to study Arabic literature. He was expelled in 1955 because of his involvement with the Movement of Arab Nationalists (MAN) and took a teaching position in Kuwait. He later became the editor of the MAN newspaper, *al-Ra'y*. In 1960 he moved to Beirut to join the editorial staff of the MAN official organ, *al-Hurriyyah* (Liberty). In 1961 he married a Danish activist, Anni Hoover; their son, Fayiz, was born the following year. In 1962 Kanafani had to go underground for

Ghassan Kanafani (<www.ghassankanafani.com>)

about a year because he lacked official papers. In 1963 Kanafani became editor in chief of the pro-Gamal Abdel Nasser newspaper *al-Muharrir* (The Liberator) and its weekly supplement, *Filastin* (Palestine).

Also in 1963 Kanafani published two of his most important works of fiction: the short story "Ard al-burtuqal al-hazin" (translated as "The Land of Sad Oranges," 1978) and the novella *Rijal fi al-shams* (translated as "Men in the Sun," 1978). "Ard al-burtuqal al-hazin" is the story of the flight of a Palestinian family from their land during the Arab-Israeli war of 1948. The father laments the loss of the orange trees he left behind; the narrator says that the oranges, "according to a peasant who used to cultivate them until he left, would shrivel up if a change occurred and they were watered by a strange hand." The violence of war and occupation keeps nature from taking its habitual course; the father violates the natural instinct of keeping one's offspring safe by trying to shoot his own children and himself in a moment of horrific despair. The uncle barges into the house of a Jewish Lebanese family and yells, "Go to Palestine!" One violation breeds another.

In *Rijal fi al-shams* three Palestinian refugees are smuggled from Iraq into Kuwait inside an empty water-tanker truck. The elderly Abu Qays hopes to find work in Kuwait and send money back to his poverty-stricken family. The novella opens with Abu Qays waiting to be picked up by the truck; he becomes aware that he is near where the Tigris and Euphrates Rivers meet and recalls the voice of his geography teacher in a Palestinian school going over a lesson about the Tigris and the Euphrates joining to form one river. Edward W. Said observes in *The Question of Palestine* (1980) that Abu Qay's present "is an amalgam of disjointed memory with the gathering force to seek employment in a country whose blinding sun signifies the universal indifference to his fate." Abu Qay's fellow refugee As'ad is wanted by the Israeli authorities for his political activities. He has been helped to flee by his uncle, who hopes to marry him off to his cousin, Nada; but As'ad does not want to marry her. As As'ad puts it, the uncle wants to buy him for his daughter as one would buy a sack of manure for a field. Sixteen-year-old Marwan is the youngest of the refugees. His older brother, Zakariyya, had gone to Kuwait years before and had sent money back to the family but no longer does so. Marwan is determined to send every penny he earns to his mother and young siblings in the refugee camp where they live. Abu al-Khayzuran is the truck driver who smuggles people into Kuwait in exchange for money. He served in the British army during the Palestine mandate, and in a battle with Zionist forces he was hit between the thighs and became impotent. Thus, in the war he lost both his manhood and his home.

The truck travels through the scorching heat of the desert, where "the sun was pouring its inferno down on them without any respite." Abu al-Khayzuran thinks of the road as the *sirat*, "the path which God in the Qur'an promised his creatures they must cross before being directed either to Paradise or to Hell. If anyone falls he goes to Hell, and if anyone crosses safely he reaches Paradise. Here the angels are the frontier guards."

Left in the tank as Abu al-Khayzuran negotiates with the border inspection, the three refugees die of suffocation. At the end of the novel, Abu al-Khayzuran takes the corpses out of the tank and throws them onto a municipal waste dump. As he climbs into the cab of his truck, he shouts, "Why didn't you knock on the sides of the tank? Why didn't you say anything? Why?" The desert echoes back his questions.

Muhammad Siddiq argues that the three characters' plunge into the empty tank symbolizes the descent into Hades of mythical heroes. Far from gaining rebirth or immortality as is expected of such heroes, however, the Palestinians silently suffocate and die. Siddiq contends that Abu al-Khayzuran stands for the failed leadership of the Arab leaders who misled their people into believing that they could do battle with the enemy. He also notes that as the three Palestinians are suffocating, the officials, unaware that Abu al-Khayzuran is castrated, are quizzing him about his supposed sexual adventures. A further irony, according to Siddiq, is that the only survivor of the journey, Abu al-Khayzuran, is "incapable of perpetuating the Palestinian species."

The novella was made into a film, al-Makhdu'un (The Dupes), directed by Tawfik Saleh, in 1972. Saleh found the original ending too depressing, so in the movie the characters attempt to knock on the sides of the tank; the last scene in the film shows the corpses with their arms raised and their fists closed. The film was banned in several Arab countries for pointing an accusing finger at their treatment of the Palestinian refugees.

Kanafani's daughter, Layla, was born in 1965. That same year he visited China and India and published a collection of short stories 'Alam laysa lana (1965, A World Not for Us), which includes "al-Arus" (The Bride). The story is in a form of a letter sent by the narrator to a friend about a strange tall, strong Palestinian who is roaming the world in search of his "bride," his term of endearment for the Czech rifle that he took from a dead Israeli soldier during the 1948 War. An Arab officer confiscated the rifle, saying that he wanted to send it to headquarters in Damascus to alert his superiors to the new weapons Israelis were receiving during the war; he promised to return the rifle but never did. The Palestinian finally finds it in the hands of an old man, who says that he bought it for an outrageously high price from a retreating Arab officer. But the Palestinian has gone mad and continues his search. The story ends with the narrator asking his friend to look for the mad Palestinian, because he has some news about the rifle. According to Siddiq, the story symbolizes the Palestinians' shift from being defenders of their homeland in 1948 to fighters with a passionate desire to do battle with the enemy.

Front cover for a 1978 collection of English translations of Kanafani's short fiction. The title piece is his best-known work, the 1963 novella Rijal fi al-Shams (Thomas Cooper Library, University of South Carolina).

In 1966 Kanafani published his highly acclaimed novella Ma tabaqqa lakum (translated as "All That's Left to You," 1990), one of the earliest and most successful modernist experiments in Arabic literature. Hamid travels from Gaza to visit his mother in the West Bank. Crossing Israel at night, he encounters an Israeli soldier. The two do not know each other's native language and are unable to communicate. The Israeli is armed with a gun, but Hamid pins him on the ground with a knife pressed against his throat. Other Israeli soldiers are in the vicinity, searching for their comrade with lights and dogs; Hamid seems to stand no chance of survival. Meanwhile, in Gaza, Hamid's sister Maryam's husband, not wanting a "child of sin," is trying to force her to abort the baby that was conceived when they had premarital sexual relations, and she stabs him with a knife just as her brother is confronting the Israeli with a knife. The reader is left unsure whether the Israeli soldier is killed or not; Siddiq notes that Kanafani spares

Front cover for a 1990 collection of English translations of Kanafani's short fiction. The title piece is his novella Ma Tabaqqa Lakum, 1966 (Thomas Cooper Library, University of South Carolina).

Hamid "the cheap victory that would have been utterly inconsistent with the actual balance of power between Palestinians and Israelis." Hamid's struggle with the soldier symbolizes the fact that to confront the Israeli enemy, Palestinians need to recognize it; one cannot fight an apparition, a nameless entity. The novella won Kanafani Lebanon's Literature Prize in 1966 and, posthumously, the Afro-Asian Writers' Conference Lotus Prize in 1975.

In 1967 Kanafani joined the editorial board of the Nasirite newspaper *al-Anwar* (Light) and became editor in chief of its weekly magazine. That same year he became a member of the Popular Front for the Liberation of Palestine (PFLP), a radical Marxist offshoot of the MAN.

In 1968 Kanafani published the short-story collection *'An al-rijal wa al-banadiq* (Of Men and Guns; translated as *Palestine's Children*, 1984). The stories present Palestinian characters of various ages with various views on how to confront the Zionist enemy. The boy Mansur is looking for a rifle and a way to join the resistance fighters who are fending off Zionist attacks on Palestinian villages in Upper Galilee. Lured away from the struggle by Eva, a beautiful Jewish woman, Dr. Qasim opens his clinic in the city of Haifa rather than in his village, where it is desperately needed. The wealthy landowner Hajj 'Abbas rents arms to the resistance, and the poor peasant Abu Qasim is willing to give all he owns to procure a rifle. The stories, which are set in 1936, 1948, 1967, and 1968, deal not only with nationalist struggle but also with class division.

In 1969 Kanafani became the official spokesman for the PFLP. He resigned from *al-Anwar* to establish and edit the weekly organ of the PFLP, *al-Hadaf* (The Target). That same year he published the novella *'A'id ila Hayfa* (translated as "Returning to Haifa," 2000), in which he presents his most sustained account of an encounter between Arab and Jewish characters. During the 1948 War, Sa'id and his wife, Safiyyah, flee from Haifa to Ramallah in the West Bank; in the chaos they leave behind their five-month-old son, Khaldun. After the Six-Day War in 1967, the borders between Israel proper and the newly occupied Palestinian territories are opened, and it becomes possible for the couple to return to Haifa. They find an Israeli woman, Miriam, living in their old house; she and her late husband, Ephrat, refugees of the Nazi Holocaust, adopted their baby, renamed him Dov, and raised him as a Jew. He is now an officer in the Israeli army. In a painful meeting, Khaldun/Dov berates the Arab couple: how could they leave him behind for twenty years, making no attempt to retrieve him? They are weak and helpless people who have lost their right to their progeny. Sa'id tells Dov that his first battle will be with a freedom fighter named Khalid, Sa'id and Safiyyah's other son. He goes on to say that the reason they named him Khalid and not Khaldun was that they always hoped that one day they would locate their lost son. Said and Safiyya return to Ramallah, dejected, but with a new awareness that leads them to drop their objections to their other son, Khalid's, joining the Palestinian guerrillas.

As Joseph Zeidan remarks, while Dov criticizes the Palestinians for their weakness and helplessness, "Miriam, on the other hand, symbolizes the humanistic camp among the Israelis: she admits the historical facts (from the Palestinian point of view) and shows readiness to talk. She is an Israeli, not a Zionist, and her Israeli identity is depicted through symbolism, albeit rather flat." As examples of such symbolism Zeidan cites references to Miriam's "blue dress with white polka dots" and the curtains with "long blue stripes"; both are allusions to the Israeli flag. For Miriam, the Zionist dream turned into a nightmare: when she saw the Haganah fighters toss the corpse of an Arab boy as though it were a piece of wood, she was reminded of her brother, who was killed by the Nazis at Auschwitz, and felt like fleeing back to Europe. Through the character of Miriam, Kanafani links the tragic experiences of the European Jews and the Palestinian Arabs.

Siddiq observes that the novella suffers from several shortcomings in technique. The tone is didactic as the work points to the necessity of armed struggle to regain the lost homeland. Kanafani also inserts a parallel story of a Palestinian family who moved into the abandoned house of fellow Palestinians who fled Haifa in 1948; the story is narrated by Sa'id to Safiyyah in their former house in Haifa, and the reader is left with no indication of Miriam's whereabouts during the conversation. Nor does Kanafani specify the language—Arabic, English, or Hebrew—in which the exchange between the Arab and Jewish characters is conducted.

On 30 May 1972 three Japanese Red Army gunmen killed twenty-six people in a terrorist attack at Lod Airport in Tel Aviv. The PFLP claimed responsibility for the massacre. On 8 July, Kanafani and his sixteen-year-old niece were killed by a bomb that had been planted in his car. In 1973 *The Jerusalem Post* reported that the assassination was carried out by the Mossad, the Israeli intelligence service.

Kanafani left behind seven novels, three of them unfinished; five collections of short stories; two plays; and studies on Palestinian history, including *The 1936–1939 Revolution in Palestine*, which was published shortly after his death. His collected works were published in seven volumes in 1972. Roger Allen observes that no modern Arab novelist has been able to project the tragedy of the Palestinian people in fiction with greater impact than Ghassan Kanafani, who devoted his life to the service of his people and to the development of a distinguished style of Arabic fiction.

Biography:
Stefan Wild, *Ghassan Kanafani: Life of a Palestinian* (Wiesbaden: Harrassowitz, 1975).

References:
Kamal Abdel-Malek, "Living on Border Lines: War and Exile in Selected Works by Ghassan Kanafani, Fawaz Turki, and Mahmud Darwish," in *Israeli and Palestinian Identities in History and Literature,* edited by Abdel-Malek and David Jacobson (New York: St. Martin's Press, 1999), pp. 179–193;

Abdel-Malek, *The Rhetoric of Violence: Arab-Jewish Encounters in Palestinian Literature and Film* (New York: Palgrave-Macmillan, 2005);

S. Abraham, "The Jew and the Israeli in Modern Arabic Literature," *Jerusalem Quarterly,* 2 (1977): 119–136;

Mohammed Abu-Nimer, *Dialogue, Conflict Resolution, and Change: Arab-Jewish Encounters in Israel* (New York: State University of New York Press, 1999);

Ammiel Alcalay, *After Jews and Arabs: Remaking Levantine Culture* (Minneapolis: University of Minnesota Press, 1993);

Roger Allen, *The Arabic Novel: An Historical and Critical Introduction,* second edition (Syracuse, N.Y.: Syracuse University Press, 1995);

Salih Altoma, "The Image of the Jew in Modern Arabic Literature 1900–1947," *Al-Arabiyya,* 2 (1978): 60–73;

Altoma, *Palestinian Themes in Modern Arabic Literature, 1917–1970* (Cairo: Anglo-Egyptian Bookshop, 1972);

Mohmmad Alwan, "Jews in Arabic Literature 1830–1914," *Al-Arabiyya,* 2 (1978): 46–59;

Hanan Mikhail Ashrawi, *Contemporary Palestinian Literature under Occupation* (Ramallah: Beir Zeit University, 1976);

Ashrawi, "The Contemporary Palestinian Poetry of Occupation," *Journal of Palestine Studies,* 7 (1978): 77–101;

Ehud Ben Ezer, "War and Siege in Hebrew Literature after 1967," *Jerusalem Quarterly,* 9 (Fall 1978): 20–37;

Ben Ezer, "War and Siege in Israeli Literature (1948–1967)," *Jerusalem Quarterly,* 2 (Winter 1977): 94–112;

Pierre Cachia, "Themes Related to Christianity and Judaism in Modern Egyptian Drama and Fiction," *Journal of Arabic Literature,* 2 (1971): 178–194;

Risa Domb, *The Arab in Hebrew Prose 1911–1948* (London, 1982);

Abdelwahab M. El-Messiri, "The Palestinian Wedding: Major Themes of Palestinian Resistance Poetry," *Journal of Palestine Studies,* 10 (Spring 1981): 77–99;

Ami Elad-Bouskila, *Modern Palestinian Literature and Culture* (London: Frank Cass, 1999);

Werner Ende, "The Palestine Conflict as Reflected in Contemporary Arabic Literature," in *The Contemporary Middle Eastern Scene,* edited by Gustav Stein and Udo Steinbach (Opladen: Leske & Budrich, 1979), pp. 154–167;

Bassam K. Frangieh, "The Theme of Alienation in the Novel of Palestine," dissertation, Georgetown University, 1986;

Jacqueline S. Ismail, "The Alienation of Palestine in Palestinian Poetry," *Arab Studies Quarterly,* 3 (1981): 43–55;

Hilary Kilpatrick, "Tradition and Innovation in the Fiction of Ghassan Kanafani," *Journal of Arabic Literature,* 12 (1976): 53–64;

Trevor Le Gassick, "The Image of the Jew in Post World War II Arabic Literature," *Al-Arabiyya,* 2 (1978): 74–89;

Barbara MacKean Parmenter, *Giving Voice to Stones: Place and Identity in Palestinian Literature* (Austin: University of Texas Press, 1994);

Wielandt Rotraud, *Das Bild der Europaer in der modernen arabischen Erzahl- und Theaterliteratur* (Beirut: Orient-Inst. d. Dt. Morgenländ. Ges. / Wiesbaden: Steiner in Komm, 1980);

Howard Douglas Rowland, "The Arab-Israeli Conflict as Represented in Arabic Fictional Literature," dissertation, University of Michigan, 1971;

Edward W. Said, *The Question of Palestine* (New York: Vintage, 1980), p. 151;

Muhammad Siddiq, *Man Is a Cause: Political Consciousness and the Fiction of Ghassan Kanafani* (Seattle: University of Washington Press, 1984);

Joseph Zeidan, "The Image of the Jew in the Arabic Novel, 1920–1973," *Shofar,* 7 (Spring 1989): 58–82.

Sahar Khalifeh
(1941 -   )

Ahmad al-Mallah
Indiana University

BOOKS: *Lam na'ud jawari lakum* (Cairo: Dar al-Ma'arif, 1974);

Al-Subbar (Jerusalem: Galileo, 1976); translated by Trevor Le Gassick and Elizabeth Fernea as *Wild Thorns* (London: Al-Saqi, 1985; New York: Olive Branch Press, 1985);

'Abbad al-shams (Jerusalem: Dar al-Kitab, 1980);

Mudhakkirat imra'ah ghayr waqi'iyyah (Beirut: Dar al-Adab, 1986);

Bab al-sahah (Beirut: Dar al-Adab, 1990);

Al-Mirath (Beirut: Dar al-Adab: 1997); translated by Aida Bamia as *The Inheritance* (Cairo: American University in Cairo Press, 2005);

Surah wa ayqunah wa-'ahd qadim (Beirut: Dar al-Adab, 2002); translated by Aida Bamia as *The Image, the Icon, and the Covenant* (Northampton, Mass.: Interlink, 2008);

Rabi' har: Rihlat al-sabr wa al-subbar (Beirut: Dar al-Adab, 2004); translated by Pamela Haydar as *The End of Spring* (Northampton, Mass.: Interlink, 2008).

SELECTED PERIODICAL PUBLICATION–UNCOLLECTED: "My Life, Myself, and the World," translated by Musa al-Halool and Katia Sakka, *Al Jadid*, 8, no. 39 (2002).

Sahar Khalifeh (<http://www.unionsverlag.com>)

Known for her active involvement in women's issues and her open feminist stand, Sahar Khalifeh is considered a leading Palestinian novelist. She is the first feminist novelist to write about women's issues in the occupied West Bank and Gaza Strip. Her work achieved wide recognition in the Arab world and internationally with the publication of her most acclaimed novel *al-Subbar*, 1976; translated as *Wild Thorns*, 1985. She is also the most translated Palestinian writer after Mahmoud Darwish. Many of her novels have been translated from Arabic, including translations into English, Hebrew, French, German, Dutch, Spanish, Malay, and Russian.

Born in 1941 into a traditional family in the Palestinian city of Nablus, Khalifeh was the fifth child of a family of eight girls and a boy. Because her parents were desperately waiting for a son to bear the family's name, her birth was received with disappointment. Khalifeh recalls in her autobiographical essay "My Life, Myself, and the World" (2002) in the magazine *al Jadid* that from early childhood she came to view herself as belonging to a "miserable, useless, worthless sex," and as a means of escaping her family's depressing environment she occupied herself with reading, writing poetry, and even painting. Khalifeh received her elementary education in

Nablus, but because of differences with her family, especially with her mother, she was enrolled in a boarding school. She graduated from Rosary College in Amman at the age of eighteen. Soon after her graduation, her family arranged for her to be married.

Khalifeh's marriage was a source of unhappiness and fierce confrontations with her husband. "It was a miserable, devastating marriage," she recalled in her autobiograhical essay. Despite the many problems with her husband, she remained with him for thirteen years, during which she gave birth to two daughters. But tensions with her husband increased, especially after the Arab defeat of 1967 when Khalifeh started working on her first novel. The aftermath of the 1967 War was a turning point for her in terms of increasing personal and political awareness. Writing, however, was not easy under the circumstances of her troubled household. As she explains, "I was married then and living in Libya. The tensions in my marriage had stifled my creativity . . . marriage consumed all my creative energies and left me feeling powerless to direct the course of my life." Nevertheless, Khalifeh was keen on reading, and during that time she encountered such feminist thinkers as Simone de Beauvoir, whose writings influenced her deeply.

During Khalifeh's marriage her brother was paralyzed in a car accident. What affected her most, as she recalls in her 1998 interview with Suha Sabbagh, was her father's reaction to the accident. After many weeks of depression, he "felt compelled to remarry in order to have a son who would carry on the name of the family." In her autobiographical essay for *al-Jadid* she reflects upon how her father's decision and the disheartening condition of her mother, especially after his death, made her come to the realization "that my mother . . . like me, like all women, like my sisters and all the sisters" was a mere victim. "In her tragedy and mine, I saw the tragedy of all women regardless of traditions, laws, or cultures. That is how I became a feminist."

Khalifeh divorced her husband in 1972 and found work as a secretary, saving the necessary money to go back to Palestine. Immediately after her divorce was finalized, she returned with her two daughters, carrying the only copy of her first novel *Ba'da al-hazimah* (After the Defeat). When she was crossing the Israeli borders to the West Bank, the Israeli authorities confiscated the only draft of this novel as they were searching her belongings: "No specific reason was given then, and all my efforts to recover the manuscript were futile," she told Sabbagh. Khalifeh never attempted to rewrite her novel, but the title suggests that its primary concern was the Arab defeat in the 1967 war with Israel rather than her feminist perspectives.

Upon Khalifeh's return to the West Bank she enrolled in Birzeit University in Ramallah where she attained her B.A. in English literature. While there, she submitted the manuscript for her first published novel, *Lam na'ud jawari lakum* (1974, We Are Not Your Slave Girls Anymore), to one of the largest Arabic publishers, Dar al-Ma'arif in Cairo. As she puts it in "My Life, Myself, and the World," "Salvation came in the form of a letter from Hilmy Murad, one of the editors of the Kitabi series published by Dar al-Ma'arif. . . . In his letter, Hilmy Murad said that he saw in me the signs of a great novelist."

Murad wrote an introduction to the novel, praising the book and predicting "the birth" of a promising novelist. The events of the novel take place in the West Bank city of Ramallah. The plot concerns the lives of a group of people from different backgrounds in Palestinian society, all of whom are educated middle-class or higher. Two of the main characters are Samya and her sister Nisrin, who, after the death of Samya's husband in the United States, go back to the West Bank to open a library in Ramallah. Most of the characters are frequent visitors of this library, and the novel reports literary and social discussions that take place there. Khalifeh's female characters—whether traditional, moderate, artistic, or radical—all voice criticism of patriarchal traditions in Palestinian society. The novel, as Salma Khadra Jayyusi observes, "made quite an impact because of its advocacy of feminist freedom." It was the basis for a radio and television series in 1977.

Many critics agree that the novel was unsuccessful on different levels, especially artistically. Khalifeh admits in "My Life, Myself, and the World" that her feelings at the time she was writing were of being "an outcast and an outsider, a victim, a lost soul unable to find a safe haven." Many of these feelings seeped into the work, where she presents a set of characters locked in and consumed by their personal problems, unable to free themselves from the suffocating surroundings of their environment. Roger Allen describes the novel as "somewhat strident and its construction diffuse." Muhammad Siddiq called it "more a project for a novel than an accomplished work."

During her years at Birzeit University, Khalifeh worked on her most important work, *al-Subbar*. After falling deeply in love with one of her professors, she was again disappointed in her relationship with a man. She wrote in "My Life, Myself, and the World," "One day I woke up from my dreams, looked at myself in the mirror, and whispered: 'You are stupid; he's not a god but a man.'" The broken affair motivated her to leave her studies for two semesters to concentrate on completing *al-Subbar*. Khalifeh submitted her novel in the place of a senior seminar project at Birzeit University.

The manuscript caused instant controversy among the seminar's committee. As a result, the book was rejected, primarily for Khalifeh's use of colloquial Arabic. However, with the support and encouragement of Dr. Hanan Mikhail Ashrawi, the novel was finally accepted by the committee and was soon published in Jerusalem.

Al-Subbar is the story of a Palestinian family named al-Karmi. Contradictions and disagreements within the family provide a microcosm of Palestinian society. The traditional father wants his daughter, Nuwar, to marry a man she does not love. 'Adil is the elder son who seems passive about almost everything and most of the time is unable to act without becoming entangled in reluctance and confusion. Nuwar remains a passive character, as well. But, with the encouragement of her younger brother, Basil, who is involved in armed Palestinian resistance, Nuwar defies her father's wish to marry any person except her imprisoned lover, Salih. At the center is Usama, a relative. After working in the Arabian Gulf, he is now on his journey back to the city of Nablus with the sole goal of blowing up the buses that carry Palestinian laborers into Israel. He refuses to comprehend the Palestinian workers' need to work for their oppressors to make a living. Many more characters get involved, including Zuhdi, who was forced to seek a job in Israel due to his financial difficulties and Lina, a strong and rebellious woman who works closely with Usama and Basil on their destructive mission. Tragic events unfold and others get involved in what seems to be a cycle of violence, suffering, and death.

Soon after its first publication, *al-Subbar* was translated into Hebrew. It attracted immediate attention among both Palestinians and Israelis, probably because of its focus on the suffering of the Palestinian labor force in Israeli factories. Leftist Palestinian novelist Emile Habibi was quick to criticize Khalifeh for focusing on Palestinian laborers rather than the effects of the Israeli occupation that compels these workers to seek jobs in Israel. However, the novel remained relatively unknown to the Arab world for many years. It was only after its French translation appeared that a publisher in Lebanon was willing to reprint it in 1990. It is now available in German, English, Spanish, Malay, Russian, and other languages. This novel brought Khalifeh international recognition; Allen calls it "a major contribution to Palestinian literature." In her interview with Sabbagh, Khalifeh believes, though, that the book enjoyed such popularity and recognition "because it is about a problem facing men rather than women."

After four years of continued success, Khalifeh came back to *al-Subbar* in a sequel. She picks up where the previous novel ends to write *'Abbad al-shams* (1980, The Sunflower). Despite the use of some characters from the previous novel, *'Abbad al-shams* has an entirely different focus and several new faces. Khalifeh regards this novel as her first serious attempt to write a feminist narrative. It deals with the Palestinian labor force in Israel, but this time she focuses on women laborers in the Israeli clothing industry. As she explains to Sabbagh, "I did not mean to reinforce the segregation of the sexes by creating in two consecutive novels a woman's world and a man's world. This was simply the outcome of my late arrival to feminism."

'Abbad al-shams tells the stories of Sa'diyyah, Rafif, and 'Adil. Sa'diyyah is the widow whose husband was killed in the previous novel. Forced to support her family, she takes a job in an Israeli tailoring company. 'Adil, a factory worker at the conclusion of *al-Subbar*, is now working on the editorial board for a local newspaper. After the Israeli authorities find out his brother's involvement with the resistance they blow up the house. Working with him at the newspaper is Rafif, who is torn apart between her affection for 'Adil and her feminist views. Finally, fed up with 'Adil's inability to respond to her gestures, she overcomes her love for him.

Khalifeh's clear message in this novel is her attempt to show how women suffer twice as much oppression as men in the occupied West Bank and Gaza Strip. Women are oppressed by both the Israeli forces and the patriarchal society. The novel is full of subplots, but Sa'diyyah's story illustrates this notion the best. She is presented at the beginning of the novel as a traditional character who abides by the rules of the authorities and traditional society. But when she is forced to go out of the house to work in Israel, people start talking about her untraditional look and manners, and eventually they start questioning her values. In one scene she defends a fellow worker, Khardrah, an outspoken prostitute, against the abuse of women in the town. After defending Khardrah, Sa'diyyah becomes more uncomfortable with her town. She works hard to buy a piece of land on the outskirts of the city to build a house, but her land is confiscated by the Israeli authorities to build a settlement.

This novel is a turning point in Khalifeh's writing because she tries to argue that feminist consciousness and political struggle for freedom cannot be looked upon as two separate issues. Not only is the liberation of women important for securing their freedom in Palestinian society, it is also important for the political struggle of all Palestinians and their liberation. Henceforward, as she told Sabbagh, Khalifeh's work emphasized that, "the liberation of women impacts in a very direct way on the liberation of the land."

Cover for the 1985 English translation of Khalifeh's 1976 novel, al-Subbar *(Thomas Cooper Library, University of South Carolina)*

As in the case of her previous novel, *'Abbad al-shams* gained Khalifeh a wide audience and was translated into several languages. The Palestinian Liberation Organization bought the rights to both *al-Subbar* and *'Abbad al-shams* in 1980 to produce a television series based on the events of the two novels. That same year Khalifeh was awarded a Fulbright scholarship to study in the United States, where she gained her M.A. in English literature from the University of North Carolina, Chapel Hill. She went on to obtain a Ph.D. in women's studies from the University of Iowa. However, despite the exceptional success of *al-Subbar* and *'Abbad al-shams,* Khalifeh was emotionally and physically exhausted. Controversies attached to her work arose from all throughout the political spectrum in Palestine, and she endured another failed love affair with a married man. At work on her next novel, *Mudhakkirat imra'ah ghayr waqi'iyyah* (1986, Memoirs of an Unrealistic Woman), she felt in need of a change. Her trip to the United States became the escape that she was looking for, and as she puts it in "My Life, Myself, and the World," "Nature and the shopping malls soothed my nerves and hypnotized my mind." Focusing on her studies, Khalifeh did not write novels after *Mudhakkirat imra'ah ghayr waqi'iyyah* for the duration of her stay in the United States.

Khalifeh admits that *Mudhakkiraat imra'ah ghayr waqi'iyyah* was her most autobiographical novel. In this work she recounts some of what she calls her "bitter childhood memories" and her life as an alienated housewife. She also voices her disappointment and frustration with marriage by portraying the marital life of her main character, 'Afaf, as one devoid of personal growth or fulfillment. Unlike her previous novels, this work concentrates on the life and thoughts of a woman from childhood to maturity. 'Afaf is an unsatisfied housewife, but she is reluctant to divorce her husband because she fears being unable to support herself. She constantly reflects upon her past and complains about her inability to change the direction of her life. Along 'Afaf's side is the strong-willed Nawal, who encourages her friend to stop complaining and start acting. And as critic Aida A. Bamia pointed out, Nawal speaks on many occasions for the fearful 'Afaf, carrying with her words the true voice and message of Sahar Khalifeh to all women. Bamia quotes from the novel, "'Afaf is part of the Palestinian woman revolution and the Palestinian woman revolution is part of the Palestinian revolution and the Palestinian revolution is part of the world revolution." The novel clearly shows, what Muhsin Jassim al-Musawi called, "feminist willfulness and affirmation."

After finishing her studies in the United States, Khalifeh returned to Palestine in 1988. She had two new projects ahead of her: establishing a center for women's issues and eventually writing her next novel, *Bab al-sahah* (1990, The Courtyard's Gate). In 1989 she opened the Women's Affairs Center in Nablus (previously called Women's Resource Center). The center's primary purpose is to collect information related to women's participation in the Intifada (Resistance). Many of these studies are being published by the center's journal *Shu'un al-Mar'ah* (Women's Affairs). The Women's Affairs Center opened two branches: one in Gaza (1991) and the other in the capital of Jordan, Amman (1994).

Two years after her return to Palestine from the United States, Khalifeh published her sixth novel. *Bab al-sahah* reflects Khalifeh's new concern, manifested in opening the women's center. The novel is specifically written to record the role of women in the first Palestinian uprising. As Bamia notes, there are many female characters like Zakiyyah and Samar, who seem to emphasize "the role of the woman-mother and the woman-sister rather than the woman-wife." But Khalifeh's real heroine is a prostitute. Her actions have a great impact on the lives of people who had initially rejected her because of her profession. She is dedicated in her fight to defend her country, but because of her questionable morality, she is accused of collaborating with the Israeli authorities. She has no problem when people call her a prostitute, because that is how she makes a living; but she does not allow anyone to call her a collaborator. Even Ahmad, her brother, who is part of the resistance, is convinced of her treason and plans at one point to kill her with his friend Husam. Despite this treatment, Nazha does not hesitate to take care of Husam when he is wounded by Israeli bullets, after which Ahmad and Husam suspend their plan to murder her.

In the overdramatic nature of most of Khalifeh's work, the story shifts suddenly when the Israeli authorities kill Nazha's brother. At once, she is no longer regarded as a prostitute, but as the sister of a martyr who seeks revenge for her brother's death. She participates in the national struggle, although she claims that her fight against occupation is only for the sake of her brother. Followed by many women who previously rejected her, Nazha leads a crowd and eventually succeeds in burning the Israeli flag. The novel concludes romantically when the characters of the novel end up accepting her, even viewing her in a heroic lens, showing gratitude and admiration.

Criticism of Khalifeh's novel touched upon her tendency to romanticize her female characters in what seem for the most part to be realistic settings. Joseph T. Zeidan points out that some of her novels fail to support their progressive message by overlooking how her heroines aspire to feel and become like men. The author's keenness to expose the oppression of women is engaging, but it often leads Khalifeh's narrative to a stylistic dead end. Also, within the realistic atmosphere of her novels, portrayals of women who stunningly succeed in breaking out of traditional values, without any obvious explanation of how, seem to overshadow their actual tragedy rather than exposing it. But as Nejd Yaziji explains, the drawback of Khalifeh's employment of realism in her work "does not merely explore contradictory dynamics in the colonial situation; rather, its narrative as a whole is affected by their consequences."

Seven years passed and many political events and changes took place before Khalifeh attempted another novel. The Oslo Accords led Israelis and Palestinians to sign a peace agreement in 1993. Palestinians immediately crowded the streets with their flags and their hopes for a state, celebrating the peace agreement they learned about on their radios and television sets. After the Palestinian Authority took the limited control it was given over a few Palestinian cities, people started to realize a different reality than they expected. Khalifeh's *al-Mirath* (1997; translated as *The Inheritance,* 2005) registers Palestinians' disappointment and her own in the results of the peace process.

Al-Mirath begins just after the Oslo Accords with the main character's first visit to the West Bank after the establishment of the Palestinian Authority. Upon receiving a letter from her uncle saying that her father was dying and that she should "Hurry up to collect the inheritance," Zaynab rushes to see her father. She, called Zayna, had been living in the United States. She separated from her father after she got pregnant and ran away to her American grandmother, Debra.

Back in a village called Wadi al-Rayhan, Zayna gets entangled in the realities of people in the early years of the Palestinian Authority. Her father, she finds out, has a wife almost the same age as she, named Fitna. Wanting to secure her share of the inheritance, the young wife goes through a medical procedure to get herself pregnant with a boy who will inherit his father's wealth. Among the many subplots of the novel is the story of Mazen. He has been an active member of the resistance, but finding nothing to do after the peace agreements he occupies his time organizing a cultural event. The dramatic tone of the novel suddenly elevates to convey death and tragedy. The chaos caused by the cultural event happens at the same time Fitna is dying at an Israeli checkpoint while giving birth to a sick boy.

Khalifeh wrote two more novels in which she sets the main events after the outbreak of the second Intifada. The first is *Surah wa ayqunah wa 'ahd qadim* (2002; translated as *The Image, the Icon, and the Covenant,* 2008). For the first time in Khalifeh's work, the narrator is a man, the elderly Ibrahim. He tells the story of three different stages in his life, starting with the 1967 war with Israel and ending in 2000. The second novel, *Rabi' Har: Rihlat al-sabr wa al-subbar* (2004; translated as *The End of Spring,* 2008), is set at the time of the later Palestinian-Israeli conflict when the Israeli military reoccupied the Palestinian territories, confining President Yasir Arafat to his compound in Ramallah.

Despite the dramatic and political realities in which her novels take place, in all her work Khalifeh has not abandoned her feminist critique of Palestinian society, though many critics question the success of her efforts. She identifies her task as seeking to free women from "an image imposed on them by male writers." Providing a new and different image of women, she proclaims, has been the major project of all her novels. To her this is the first step in the process of liberating women. Her task, as she puts it, is that "of a doctor that must first undress and then examine the patient before arriving at a cure." Living between her hometown of Nablus and the Jordanian capital, Amman, Sahar Khalifeh describes her life to Sabbagh as one divided "between my work with women in the Women's Center and writing about women's issues."

Interview:

Suha Sabbagh, "An Interview with Sahar Khalifeh, Feminist Novelist," in *Palestinian Women of Gaza and the West Bank,* edited by Sabbagh (Bloomington & Indianapolis: Indiana University Press, 1998), pp. 136–144.

References:

Roger Allen, *The Arabic Novel: An Historical and Critical Introduction* (Syracuse, N.Y.: Syracuse University Press, 1995), pp. 74–75, 77;

Amal Amireh, "Between Complicity and Subversion: Body Politics in Palestinian National Narrative," *South Atlantic Quarterly,* 102 (2003): 747–772;

Aida A. Bamia, "Feminism in Revolution: The Case of Sahar Khalifeh," in *Tradition, Modernity, and Postmodernity in Arabic Literature: Essays in Honor of Professor Issa J. Boullata,* edited by Kamal Abdel-Malek and Wael Hallaq (Leiden & Boston: Brill, 2000), pp. 173–185;

Salma Khadra Jayyusi, ed., *Anthology of Modern Palestinian Literature* (New York: Columbia University Press, 1992), p. 598;

Muhsin Jassim al-Musawi, *The Postcolonial Arab Novel: Debating Ambivalence* (Leiden & Boston: Brill, 2003), pp. 37, 50, 281;

Mattityahu Peled, "Sahar Khalifeh's *'Abbad al-Shams:* A Feminist Challenge," in *Writer, Culture, Text: Studies in Modern Arabic Literature,* edited by Ami Elad (Fredericton, N.B.: York Press, 1993), pp. 37–46;

Muhammad Siddiq, "The Fiction of Sahar Khalifeh: Between Defiance and Deliverance," *Arab Studies Quarterly,* 8, no. 2 (1987): 143–160;

Nejd Yaziji, "Exile and Politics of (Self-)Representation: The Narrative of Bounded Space and Action in Sahar Khalifeh's *Wild Thorns,*" in *Cross-Addressing: Resistance Literature and Cultural Borders,* edited by John C. Hawley (Albany: State University of New York Press, 1996), pp. 87–105;

Joseph T. Zeidan, *Arab Women Novelists: The Formative Years and Beyond* (Albany: State University of New York Press, 1995), pp. 178–186, 200, 227, 234, 236.

Raif Khuri
(1913 – 2 November 1967)

Malakeh Khoury
American University of Beirut

and

Goetz Nordbruch
Humboldt University of Berlin

BOOKS: *Imru' al-Qays: Naqd wa tahlil* (Beirut: Matba'at Sadir, 1934);

Habbat al-rumman wa qisas 'Arabiyyah ukhra (Beirut: Al-Maktabah al-Ahliyyah, 1935);

Jihad Filastin: Kifah al-'Arab fi sabil al-huriyyah wa al-Istiqlal. Al-Thawrat al-Filastiniyyah fi mukhtalaf marahiliha, as al-Fata al-'Arabi (Damascus, 1936);

Thawrat Baydaba (Beirut: Rawdat al-Funun, 1936);

Huquq al-insan (Damascus: Ibn Zaydun, 1938);

Majusi fi al-jannah (Beirut: Dar al-Makshuf, 1938);

Al-Naqd wa al-dirasat al-adabiyyah (Beirut: Dar al-Makshuf, 1939);

Wa hal yakhfa al-qamar: 'Umar ibn Abi Rabi'ah (Beirut: Dar al-Makshuf, 1939);

Ma'alim al-wa'y al-qawmi (Beirut: Dar al-Makshuf, 1941);

Hurriyatuna bi-hurriyat al-'Alam: Zikra 14 Tamuz (Damascus, 1941);

Ma'a al-'Arab fi al-tarikh wa al-usturah (Beirut: Dar al-Makshuf, 1942);

Al-Turath al-qawmi al-'Arabi (Beirut: Manshurat Majallat al-Tariq, 1942);

Suhun mulawana (Beirut: Dar al-Makshuf, 1947);

Amin al-Rihani fi haqiqat al-dimuqratiyyah al-Amirikiyyah (Beirut: Dar al-Qari' al-'Arabi, 1948);

Al-Thawrah al-Rusiyyah: Qisat Mawlid Hadarah Jadidah (Beirut, 1948);

Dik al-Jinn al-Hubb al-muftaris (Beirut: Dar al-Makshuf, 1948);

Al-Hubb aqwa (Beirut: Dar al-Makshuf, 1950);

Nusus al-ta'rif fi al-adab al-'Arabi: 'Asr al-ihya' wa al-nahda 1850–1950 (Beirut: Dar al-Makshuf, 1957);

Al-Ta'arif fi al-adab al-'Arabi (Beirut: Dar al-Makshuf, 1960);

Al-Adab al-mas'ul (Beirut: Dar al-Adab, 1968);

Thawrat al-fata al-'Arabi: A'mal mukhtara min Turath Raif Khuri, edited by Ilyas Shakir (Beirut: Dar al-Farabi, 1984).

TRANSLATIONS: Morris Kamil, *Al-Dimuqratiyyah al-jadidah tubna* (Beirut: Dar al-Qari' al-'Arabi, 1948);

John Carne, *Rihlah fi Lubnan fi al-thuluth al-awwal min al-qarn al-tasi'a 'ashar* (Beirut: Dar al-Makshuf, 1948).

OTHER: *Al-Fikr al-'Arabi al-hadith: Athar al-thawra al-Faransiyyah fi tawjihihi al-siyasi wa al-ijtima'i,* edited by Khuri (Beirut: Dar al-Makshuf, 1943); revised and edited by Charles Issawi, translated by Ihsan 'Abbas as *Modern Arab Thought: Channels of the French Revolution to the Arab East* (Princeton: Kingston Press, 1983);

Ahmad al-Safi Al-Najafi, *Hasad al-Sujun: Qasa'id Mukhtarah,* introduction by Khuri (Beirut: Dar al-Makshuf, 1951);

Nicolas al-Tawil, *Al-Talqa al-thaniya,* introduction by Khuri (Beirut: Al-Najah, 1959);

Elias Abu Shabaka, *Al-Alhan,* introduction by Khuri (Beirut: Dar al-Makshuf, 1962).

Charles Issawi, the editor of an English translation of one of the Lebanese writer Raif Khuri's works, calls Khuri "one of the last representatives of the Arab liberal age." A Marxist who was deeply influenced by the ideals of the French Revolution, Khuri contributed to the intellectual controversies that raged during the last decade of the French mandates in Lebanon and Syria. He was actively involved in local and regional struggles for political rights, individual liberties, and national independence.

Raif Najm Najeeb Khuri was born in 1913 in Nabay, a village in Mount Lebanon. He was the first

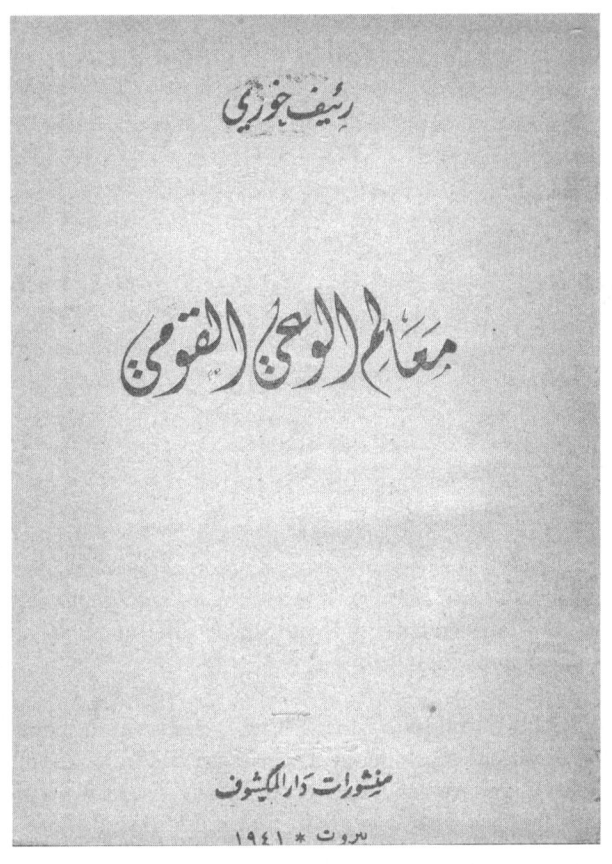

Title page for Raif Khuri's Ma'alim al-wa'y al-qawmi
*(Characteristics of National Consciousness), 1941
(Herman B. Wells Library, Indiana University)*

child of Najm Najeeb al-Khuri, a landowner and merchant who composed poetry and knew classical Arabic literature, poetry, and tales of poets' lives by heart, and Malakeh Haddad. His brother, Mickael, was born in 1919, and his sister, Farideh, was born in 1924. Khuri's parents taught him Arabic and English and read with him the works of Arabic poets and prose writers. He graduated from Brummana High School, run by a British Quaker missionary, in 1928. At fifteen he was technically too young to enroll at the American University of Beirut (AUB), but he was admitted as an exceptional case on a recommendation by the high school vouching for his academic excellence. When his mother died during his freshman year, Khuri composed an elegy for her patterned after al-Mutanabbi's elegy on the death of his grandmother. Life in modern Beirut distracted the village boy from his studies, and he failed all of his courses. Faced with the prospect of returning to the life of a farmer on his family's lands, he took make-up examinations and passed them.

Khuri began publishing in the literary and political magazine *al-Ma'rid* in 1929. His work also appeared in the literary weekly *al-Barq*, edited by the well-known poet Bishara al-Khoury. In 1932 he received a B.A. in Arabic history and literature, with a thesis on the ninth-century theologian and writer al-Jahiz prepared under the supervision of Constantine Zurayk, and became a journalist with *al-Riyad* magazine. He left in 1933 to teach Arabic literature at al-Sharq College in the Syrian coastal town of Tartus.

In 1934 Khuri published his first book, *Imru' al-Qays: Naqd wa tahlil* (Imru' al-Qays: Analysis and Critique), about the fifth-century Arabic poet. The following year he brought out a collection of Arab popular tales under the title *Habbat al-rumman* (A Pomegranate Grain).

In 1935 Khuri moved to Jerusalem, where he taught Arabic literature, the history of Eastern literature, and translation at Bishop Gobat School and witnessed the tense and highly politicized atmosphere on the eve of the Arab-Jewish-British clashes. He began writing for the progressive *al-Tali'a* magazine, edited by the Lebanese intellectual Raja Hourani. His first major political pamphlet, *Jihad Filastin: Kifah al-'Arab fi sabil al-huriyyah wa al-Istiqlal. Al-Thawra al-Filastiniyyah fi mukhtalaf marahiliha* (Jihad of Palestine: The Arab Struggle for Freedom and Independence. The Palestinian Revolution in Its Different Phases), was published during the regional turmoil of 1936 under the pseudonym al-Fata al-'Arabi, which means "the young Arab" or "the Arab youth"; *al-Fata* carries nuances of dignity, heroic bravery, and gallantry. Khuri defends the Arab-Palestinian general strike against the British Mandate and its escalation into an armed revolt; he also refutes claims by the British authorities of Italian or German government involvement in the popular protests.

Khuri takes a literary approach to the subject of political rights and national independence in his seven-act verse play *Thawrat Baydaba* (1936, Baydaba's Rebellion). It is set in India in the last part of the fourth century B.C.E., following Alexander the Great's conquest of the country, and features King Baydaba and the philosopher Dapshaleem.

Written in late 1937 and published in early 1938, Khuri's *Huquq al-insan* (Human Rights) offers a detailed historical account of the struggle for political, civil, and social rights; it was the first comprehensive work in Arabic on the subject. Alluding to the rise of the National Socialists in Germany and the Fascists in Italy, Khuri writes: "The reader must know that we are at a turning point of history. This moment forces us to fight two Jihads for the sake of human rights: a Jihad to guard the rights of bourgeois democracy; and another Jihad to extend these rights into socialist rights. Each of these Jihads completes the other." He considers the French Revolution the most important step in the history of liberation but argues that political rights lack substance if the individual is denied the economic basis for their exercise. He concludes that the Russian Revolution of 1917 and the establishment of the Soviet Union will overcome the limitations of liberal democracy and complete the process of emancipation: "If the human being is political and civil by nature, as Ibn Khaldun has said, he is also economic, as reality has proven."

Khuri was a delegate to the Second International Youth Conference, held in New York on 8 August 1938. His presentation of the Arab viewpoint on recent events in Palestine and the proposed division into a Jewish and an Arab state triggered intense reactions in American newspapers. On his return to the Middle East he was prevented by the British authorities from entering Palestine and was forced to go to Beirut; later that year, he settled in Damascus. He was a central figure in the League against Nazism and Fascism in Syria and Lebanon, an organization that had emerged in 1935 among socialist and liberal-progressive circles. In May 1939 the league held an antifascist conference in Beirut in which more than two hundred representatives of unions and cultural and political associations participated. Also in 1939 Khuri published *Wa hal yakhfa al-qamar* (Could the Moon Hide), a historical novel about the Umayyad poet Umar Ibn Abi Rabi'a that was later made into a drama that was broadcast by Lebanese radio.

In 1939 the French authorities in Syria and Lebanon imposed administrative restrictions on political activities and instituted censorship of publications. Remaining freedoms were suspended after the fall of France to the Germans in June 1940 and the establishment of the Vichy regime in July. Khuri experienced these repressions personally when the newspaper *al-Difa'*, which he had started that summer, was banned after its sixth issue. He returned to Tartus to teach at Al-Sharq College, which was then being managed by a French missionary, and began writing steadily for *al-Makshuf* magazine. His contacts with the Dar al-Makshuf publishing house offered him the opportunity to make the acquaintance of the Lebanese and Syrian writers Ilyas Abu Shabaka, Maroun Abboud, Amin al-Rihani, and Umar Fakhuri.

In *Ma'alim al-wa'y al-qawmi* (1941, Characteristics of National Consciousness) Khuri provides a detailed critique of his former teacher Zurayk's *al-wa'y al-qawmi* (1939, The Nationalist Conscience), a work that was considered a landmark of liberal Arab thought. In an often ironic tone Khuri rejects Zurayk's "romantic" and "idealist" conception of nationalism that assigns distinctive features to the Arab "nation": "The Arabs don't want to have railways, because they are increasingly used in America. If they would use railways, it would

Front cover for al-Adab al-mas'ul (*Engaged Literature*), 1968 (Yale University Libraries)

not be of their 'distinct Arab nationalist' civilization." Khuri emphasizes the universality of values and the goals shared by all human beings. He further elaborates on this issue in the pamphlet *al-Turath al-qawmi al-'Arabi* (Arab National Heritage), published in September 1942 and based on a speech he had given at a rally of the League against Nazism and Fascism in Syria and Lebanon. He argues that one of the most important features of Arab history, the struggle against oppression, is part of the universal human longing for liberation and that the Arab nation is a natural ally of the democracies led by Britain and the United States and of the Free French forces who were fighting against the Vichy regime in German-occupied France: "The flame of the struggle against ignorance, tyranny, submission, and against everything that is distorting the humanity of man, this is our tradition which we do not give up, this is our great Arab heritage whose flag we proudly raise."

In the introduction to his extensive collection of Arab reflections on the French Revolution, *al-Fikr al-*

'Arabi al-hadith: Athar al-thawra al-Faransiyyah fi tawjihihih al-siyasi wa al-ijtima'i (1943; translated as *Modern Arab Thought: Channels of the French Revolution to the Arab East*, 1983), Khuri points out that supporters and critics of the revolution are to be found not only in Europe but also in the Arab world. The admirers of the revolution studied the course of history and "were inspired by what would direct them towards freedom and resistance to oppression. They would open their minds and hearts to the French Revolution and its doctrines, and to principles of modern democratic rule."

In addition to writing for the magazine *al-Tariq*, which had been founded at the end of 1941 as the voice of the League against Nazism and Fascism in Syria and Lebanon, Khuri contributed to the cultural magazine *al-Adib*. In 1943 he began working as a news interpreter and broadcaster for the Information and Publicity Bureau, which was supervised by the French authorities, alongside the well-known Lebanese writers and journalists Abu Shabaka, Abboud, Fakhuri, and Nasib Al-Matni. After the achievement of Lebanese independence later that year, he taught at various colleges, among them the Collège Laïc Français. He stopped writing for *al-Tariq* and started publishing steadily in *al-Tayar* and *al-Taligraf*. In 1954 he played a leading role at the first conference of Arab writers in Beit Meri, a mountain town overlooking Beirut.

In 1955 Khuri publicly debated the eminent Egyptian author Taha Hussein in the UNESCO Hall in Beirut on the topic "For Whom Does the Writer Write? For the Elite or for the Laypeople?" Khuri defended the second position, calling for literature on topics that interest most people and is written in an artistic style. He rejected art for the sake of art, absurdist literature, and pessimistic writing that expresses only dejection and despair. Khuri contended that literature must not destroy all traditional values but should elevate human beings from feelings of insignificance to an awareness that they are the center of the universe. A summary of the debate was published in the literary journal *al-Adab* and collected with Khuri's other articles from that journal in *al-Adab al-mas'ul* (1968, Engaged Literature).

Khuri participated in the conference of Afro-Asian Solidarity held in Cairo in 1957 and in the Third Conference of African and Asian Writers in Beirut in 1967. In the summer of the latter year he was diagnosed with a malignant brain tumor. On 12 October the comatose writer was given the President of the Republic Award for his contributions to literature and culture. He died on 2 November.

Raif Khuri's writing style reflects his personality and the influence of his work as a journalist: it is simple, clear, bold, lively, and humorous. It is often conversational, mixing the vernacular with standard Arabic if the situation calls for it. Sometimes his tone becomes didactic, and he tends to repeat himself to ensure clarity. At other times he deviates from the subject at hand to have an aside with the reader or to tell a joke. A Marxist but not a member of the Communist Party, and a nationalist but highly critical of common visions of the Arab nation, Khuri did not fit into the dominant intellectual currents of his time. There may be no better way to characterize Khuri than to quote his own description, in a 1965 article in *al-Adab*, of the Lebanese writer Amin al-Rihani: "great literature could never be without a great personality behind its creation, and this great literature is rarely as great as the personality that created it."

References:

'Abd al-Razzaq 'Id, *Madkhal ila fikr Raif Khuri* (Nicosia: IBAL, 1990);

Muhammad Dakrub, "Min Masirat Raif Khuri," *al-Tariq* (February 1989): 135–147;

Samah Idris, *Raif Khuri wa turath al-'Arab* (Beirut: Dar al-Adab, 1986);

Hussein Muruwa, "Al-Udaba' wa al-mufakkirun al-Lubnaniyyun fi al-nidal didd al-fashiyyah wa min ajli al-sadaqa ma' al-ittihad al-Sufyiti," *al-Tariq* (September 1985): 165–178;

Götz Nordbruch, "Defending the French Revolution during World War II: Raif Khoury and the Intellectual Challenge of Nazism in the Levant," *Mediterranean Historical Review*, 21 (December 2006): 219–238;

"Raif Khoury–al-Katib wa al-qadiyyah," *al-Tariq* (February 1989);

Mtanious Tawuq, "Raif Khuri: Siratuhu wa Adabuhu," thesis, Lebanese University of Beirut, 1971;

Ahmad 'Ulabi, "Raif Khuri (1913–1967): Masirat adib mukafih," *al-Mashriq* (August–December 2005): 353-377; (January–June 2006): 77–94.

Abdallah Laroui
(1933 -)

Mohamed Ourya
University of Sherbrooke

BOOKS: *L'idéologie arabe contemporaine* (Paris: Maspero, 1967);

L'histoire du Maghreb (Paris: Maspero, 1970); translated by Ralph Manheim as *The History of the Maghrib: An Interpretive Essay* (Princeton: Princeton University Press, 1977);

Al-Ghurbah (Casablanca: Centre Culturel Arabe, 1971); translated into French by Catherine Charruau as *L'exil* (Arles: Sindbad, Actes sud, 1999);

Al-'Arab wa al-fikr al-tarikhi (Beirut: Al-Haqiqah, 1973);

La crise des intellectuels arabes: Traditionalisme ou historicisme (Paris: Maspero, 1974); translated by Diarmid Cammell as *The Crisis of the Arab Intellectual: Traditionalism or Historicism?* (Berkeley: University of California Press, 1976);

L'Algerie et le Sahara marocain (Casablanca: Seror, 1976);

Les origines sociales et culturelles du nationalisme marocain, 1830–1912 (Paris: Maspero, 1977);

Al-Yatim (Casablanca: Al-Markaz al-Thaqafi al-'Arabi, 1978);

Mafhum al-hurriyyah (Beirut: Al-Markaz al-Thaqafi al-'Arabi, 1980);

Mafhum al-dawlah (Beirut: Al-Markaz al-Thaqafi al-'Arabi, 1981);

Mafhum al-idyulugiyyah (Beirut: Al-Markaz al-Thaqafi al-'Arabi, 1981);

Al-Fariq (Casablanca: Al-Markaz al-Thaqafi al-'Arabi, 1986);

Islam et modernité (Paris: La Découverte, 1987);

Awraq (Beirut: Al-Markaz al-Thaqafi al-'Arabi, 1989);

Ibn Khaldun wa Makyavilli (London: Dar al-Saqi, 1990);

Thaqafatuna fi daw' al-tarikh (Beirut: Al-Markaz al-Thaqafi al-'Arabi, 1992);

Mafhum al-tarikh (Beirut: Al-Markaz al-Thaqafi al-'Arabi, 1992);

Esquisses historiques (Casablanca: Centre Culturel Arabe, 1992);

Mafhum al-'aql (Beirut: Centre Culturel Arabe, 1996);

Islamisme, modernisme, libéralisme: Equisses critiques (Casablanca: Centre Culturel Arabe, 1997);

Ghilah (Casablanca: Al-Markaz al-Thaqafi al-'Arabi, 1998);

Islam et histoire (Paris: Bibliothèque Albin Michel Idées, 1999);

Khawatir Assabah, Journal de Abdalla Laroui (Casablanca: Centre Culturel Arabe, 2005);

Le Maroc et Hassan II: Un témoignage (Quebec: Presses Inter Universitaires, 2005).

The thought of Moroccan historian and political theorist Abdallah Laroui has profoundly influenced the contemporary Arab world. A pillar of Arab intellectual life for over four decades, Laroui is the author of more than thirty books, including works of philosophy, history, analyses of Arab culture, four novels, and an autobiography. It is impossible to conceive of a responsible study of contemporary Arab thought that does not treat his work. Steeped in rationalism and an ardent defender of modernity, Laroui seeks to radically change the Arab world by bringing it up-to-date with the Western world. His breadth of knowledge is impressive: he has written complex comparative studies of different thinkers and intellectual paradigms, and he reads history with a philosopher's understanding, bringing new terminology to bear upon old ideas. The essential problem continually posed by Laroui is the question of objectivity in science and the social sciences. Laroui's primary methodology is one of comparison–putting Arab traditions beside those of the Occident to gain a better understanding of how they differ.

Laroui was born in Azemmour, Morocco, in 1933 to a family of nobility from Makhzen, the administrative center of Morocco before the institution of the French protectorate in the kingdom. Laroui's mother died when he was two years old. His father was secrétaire du Qaïd (similar to a police officer in the country) who later opened a shoe store. He became very attached to his father, a benevolent dictator, who pushed his son hard in school, sending him off to Rabat to study in the Lycée Moulay Youssef. In the 1950s Laroui traveled to Paris to continue his studies, first at

Abdallah Laroui (<www.uam.es/otroscentros/TEIM/Revista/reim%202/Bernabe_Lopez_ent.htm>)

the Institut d'Études Politiques (Institute of Political Studies) and then at the Sorbonne. In 1958 he completed his master's degree in history with a thesis on the commercial relations between Morocco and Europe in the Middle Ages. He was a participant in the Moroccan nationalist movement, and a founding member of the Union Nationale des Forces Populaires (National Union of Popular Forces), a major Moroccan political party. Laroui relocated to Egypt, where in 1960 he became the cultural adviser to the Moroccan ambassador to Cairo. In 1961 Laroui obtained a master's degree in Arab literature. He continued to be active during the 1960s in the socialist politics of the day, and worked with Mahdi Ben Barka, the Moroccan icon of the Left, on his work "L'option révolutionnaire" (The Revolutionary Option), a text that became the foundation of the ideological movement of the Moroccan Left. In 1962 Laroui became the cultural adviser to the Moroccan Ambassador to Paris as well as the Moroccan representative for UNESCO (United Nations Educational, Scientific and Cultural Organization). In 1963 he returned to Morocco to start his career as an assistant professor of history at the faculty of arts at the University Mohamed V in Rabat.

All of Laroui's work, beginning with his earliest books, manifests his belief that the essence of society is best understood through the shaping forces of ideology and history. A harsh and acerbic critic of contemporary Arab ideology, Laroui looks at the philosophical and political choices that have allowed the Arabs to grasp the foundations of modernity. Faced with the growing potential of the Occidental world (particularly after Napoleon's invasion of Egypt in 1798), the Arab elites began to question the causes of corruption of their world. The thinkers of the *Nahda* (Arab Renaissance) during the nineteenth century were preoccupied with the examination of the reasons for the "cultural retardation" of the Arabs. The problem of underdevelopment in Arab countries and what he saw as the necessity of Arab integration with modernity is summed up by Laroui in the question: "How does one break with the past?"

In an effort to respond to this question, Laroui's career took shape, beginning with *L'idéologie arabe contemporaine* (1967, Contemporary Arab Ideology), a radical critique of what he sees as the dominant intellectual current in the Arab Middle East. Recognizing the intellectual and political problems facing the Arabs, Laroui suggests that new conditions must be achieved to bring about another renaissance. He proposes an alternative way of thinking about these problems, first by outlining what he sees as three typical intellectual types: the clerics, who dominated in the colonial state and found legitimacy and value only in the sacralized authority of the past; the liberal, a figure saturated in Occidental culture who dominates the state after independence; and the technophile, who adopts the technological ideals of the West at the expense of his own cultural ideals. Laroui argues that Arab society must overcome the weaknesses of these types and assure that they do not dominate the culture. Critics disparaged *L'idéologie arabe contemporaine* for being too critical of Arab intellectuals and too uncritical of the West.

In the late 1960s Laroui took a position as a visiting professor of North African history at UCLA, where he taught courses on the history of the Maghreb (1968–1971) as well working on other projects. He returned to Morocco in 1971 to work on his doctorate. As he continued to reflect on the crisis of the contemporary Arab world, Laroui theorized that Arab intellectuals had not been able to become the instruments for needed change because they had not developed new ideological tools. This "misery" of the intellectuals became the subject of Laroui's novels, which he began writing in the early 1970s with *al-Ghurbah* (1971, The Exile), which was translated into French as *L'exil* in 1999.

With *al 'Arab wa al-fikr al-tarikhi* (1973, The Arabs and Historical Thought) and *La crise des intellectuels arabes: Traditionalisme ou historicisme* (1974; translated as *The Crisis of the Arab Intellectual: Traditionalism or Historicism?* 1976) Laroui emerged as an imposing force on the Arab intellectual scene. In these two works Laroui contends that conditions in the Arab world have delayed its acceptance of progress in many areas. He argues that this "delay" affects all parts of the society but that it is the failure of intellectuals that is the most crippling to Arab culture. One of the few Arab critics to continue to take seriously the notion of Arab "delay"–a idea others had dismissed–Laroui calls for intellectuals to undergo a radical self-criticism in order to be able to truly understand the problems that plague the Arab world. It is generally held that these works, owing to their richness and depth, surpass previous contemporary Arab analyses. Tunisian thinker Hicham Djait in his work *L'Europe et l'Islam* (1978, Europe and Islam) highly praises Laroui's works, particularly referring to these earlier ones.

As he had done in his previous work, in *al-'Arab wa al-fikr al-tarikhi* Laroui classifies Arab intellectuals by taking into consideration ideology and religion, this time positing only two types: a majority with a *"Salafist"* logic (a reference to the first generation of the companions of the Prophet Muhammad) and a minority with a "liberal" logic. The Salafists are conservative, ideological fundamentalists who call for a return to religious sources. The liberals, on the other hand, are a less coherent group, not always deeply committed to the ideals of liberalism such as commitment to universal natural rights and the ability of reason to discover them," which Laroui says they have never examined other than on a superficial level. According to Laroui, neither of these two models of Arab intellectuals is capable of producing a cultural program that could

Front cover for Laroui's first book, 1967, a critique of Arab intellectuals (Thomas Cooper Library, University of South Carolina)

overcome the historical delay and create a new Arab renaissance.

Laroui argues that the current clerical class, who are most representative of contemporary Salafism, reiterate the same thesis that has been elaborated by the thinkers of this conservative current since the *Nahda*, that is, a rejection of Occidental ideas and a return to the "glorious" past of Islam. In glorifying a notion of truth that was to be found only in the past, the Salafists neglected the elemental principles of historical thought. Laroui contends that for the Salafist intellectual, science becomes merely an interpretation of theses between competing scientists. For them, therefore, all scientific history is merely a repetition of the past, with no new discoveries or creations. On the other hand, what lib-

Title page for the first edition of Laroui's 1974 call for self-criticism among Arab intellectuals (Thomas Cooper Library, University of South Carolina)

eral intellectuals bring to Arab thought, in Laroui's critique, is more negative. The liberals follow the Occidental cultural movement superficially and uncritically. Laroui suggests that the liberal intellectual is a victim of his adoration for an Occident that he imagines. European liberalism then becomes sacred and untouchable in the Arab liberal's view, despite the fact that European liberals themselves are constantly subjecting their ideas to harsh criticism. After illustrating these two models and pointing out their flaws, Laroui suggests the construction of another model–a cultural revolution in which intellectual discourse would be based on rationalism and the understanding of the forces of history. Radically, this new intellectual model is based culturally and ideologically on historicism, the idea that all human sciences are shaped by historical forces. It is in this fashion that history is considered as the only cause of, and as the foundation for, all existence.

Laroui's blaming the failure of Arab intellectuals for all the faults in the Arab world was not a sentiment shared by his contemporaries, especially the Moroccan philosopher Mohammed 'Abed al-Jabri, who published several long articles criticizing Laroui in 1974 in the Moroccan journal *al'muharrir* (The Editor). Al-Jabri argued that Laroui's dismissal of Salafisim was unhistorical and inappropriately devalued the rich legacy of the most influential tradition of Arab thinkers. In asking why the present should completely break with the past, al-Jabri and other critics also argued that Salafist thought was not as homogenous as Laroui portrayed it to be. They pointed out that the tradition contains divers movements, from the most radical, which do not accept other viewpoints, especially those of the West, to the most moderate, which are ready to accept Western modernity.

In 1976 Laroui defended his dissertation at the Sorbonne; the dissertation was published in 1977 as *Les origines sociales et culturelles du nationalisme marocain, 1830–1912* (The Social and Cultural Origins of Moroccan Nationalism, 1830–1912). In this work Laroui analyzes the sociopolitical structure of precolonial Morocco and argues that an understanding of nationalism is necessary to explain Moroccan society.

Laroui's involvement with politics during the 1980s brought negative attention from the Moroccan monarchy, and in 1984 he was briefly deprived of his university post in Rabat. The state reappointed him to Casablanca shortly thereafter without any serious consequences having occurred. Indeed, Laroui later wrote a positive portrayal of the Moroccan monarch.

In his 1989 novel *Awraq* (Papers) Laroui draws upon real-life contemporary intellectuals, both in Morocco and the Arab world in general, to explore the kinds of dilemmas such people had to confront in Morocco during the 1950s and 1960s. Idris, the protagonist of the novel, is torn between his attraction to the Occidental world and his own Arab-Muslim culture. Choosing to leave Morocco to study in France on a scholarship, Idris in Paris discovers the gap between his own culture and that of the Occident. At the same time he realizes his own cowardice because he has left his own people to fight the French colonizers. Knowing that on his return to Morocco he will have an important bureaucratic career waiting for him, Idris applies himself to his studies and distances himself from the anticolonial politics of many of the Moroccan students in Paris.

At the point of his early death at age forty, seemingly brought about by his grief over his inability to make the right decisions, Idris looks back on his life and his return to Morocco with bitterness and shame. Laroui portrays such hesitation as characteristic of Arab intellectuals. The suffering of Idris comes from his comprehension of Occidental thought, as if he were himself in the Occident, living their philosophy. In one passage Idris comments on conflicted Moroccan intellectuals, students who lived in France at the time of the French protectorate:

> Anarchists who live objectively in a state of schizophrenia. They are opposed to the protectorate, and at the same time they benefit from its system. . . . they make apparent their attachment to the Moroccan tradition through their dress, their décor, their culinary habits, nevertheless their hearts (and their heads) are full of what they have learned from their foreign professors in their French schools (in Morocco) from where they took their degrees.

Throughout the novel Idris is burdened by feelings of dishonesty and treason and by his incapacity to elaborate a clear vision of the world. He lives with two points of reference that are diametrically opposed to each other: the West, which is open to the future, and his Arab-Muslim heritage, by which he is still transfixed to the past.

In 1996 Laroui published *Mafhum al-'aql* (The Concept of Reason), in which he criticizes those intellectuals with traditional dogmatic tendencies who prefer to escape to the past rather than come to terms with modernity. This escape, Laroui argues, represents today a psychological mechanism of compensation, a nostalgic romanticism for all that has been lost from the greatness of Arab-Muslim civilization. His criticism is focused on two intellectual giants of Arab thought: Ibn Khaldun (1332–1406) and Muhammad 'Abduh (1849–1905). According to Laroui, the Salafist thought of 'Abduh is the expression of traditional tendencies in contemporary Arab thought. 'Abduh's Salafism is evident in his positions vis-à-vis the Occident, and it represents a paradoxical phase in Arab thought. 'Abduh, who stipulated that "Islam is a religion of science, compatible with the spirit of the age," was trying to reconcile the past with the present. But he could not understand the epistemological and historical bridges that existed between traditional reason and contemporary rationalism. Laroui argues that 'Abduh attacks the West and its pursuit of modernity with a theological mind-set that recalls the first centuries of Islam. Reason, for 'Abduh, resides in the Text–the Qur'an and Hadith–and is absolute. The paradox of 'Abduh rests in his denial of the temporal dimension of history. Colonialism ruptured the continuity between the Arab past and the present, and 'Abduh's tools, derived only from the past, proved incapable of handling this new Arab situation.

Front cover for the 1999 French translation of al-Ghurbah, *Laroui's 1971 novel (Michigan State University Libraries)*

In his review of the work of the Arab historian Khaldun, who is frequently referenced in the works of contemporary Arab intellectuals, Laroui keeps to his thesis that the epistemology of the great Arab-Muslim civilizations is no longer relevant while acknowledging Khaldun's achievement. Laroui puts Khaldun back into his own era, treating his studies of history within the context of his own time. Rather than seeing Khaldun as a "meta-historian" who can pass judgment on all history, Laroui argues that each epoch has its own proper cognitive system and proper philosophy of history. He asserts that Arab social and economic situations cannot improve without a new reading of the problems and concepts of history, a rethinking of the scientific domain on the basis of modern Europe.

Throughout Laroui's career, critics have argued that he has not sufficiently appreciated the legacy of Islamic thought. One of the main criticisms of Laroui is that he neglects to analyze the Qur'an and the corpus of the Sunna (the words and acts of the prophet of Islam), the fundamental benchmark of the Salafist thought. Critics charge that he has paid attention to the thinking that has arisen from reading the sacred text but not to the text itself. In any event, Laroui's critics find it a fundamental flaw that Laroui, a critic of the foundation of Islamic thought, has managed to ignore the texts sacred to that thought.

Laroui has positioned himself as an ideological critic as well as a formulator of concepts with which to study the contemporary problems of the Arab world. His discourse is directed to the intellectual Arab elite as well as against them. This degree of conceptualization transcends and necessarily ignores specific social, political, and economic problems of the Arab peoples. In fact, the real battle for the Arabs, as al-Jabri affirms, has never been between Reason and the Text, nor between religion and philosophy (irrational and the rational) but rather between the nondemocratic political system (always sustained by the Western democracies) and of the people themselves, who lack the resources to implement meaningful change. Such a situation can breed fanaticism from many sides. To combat such fanaticism, Laroui in his 1997 work *Islamisme, modernisme, libéralisme: Esquisses critiques* (Islamism, Modernism, Liberalism: Critical Sketches) seeks to bring the debate back to the reality Arabs currently face.

Laroui continued as professor of history at the University Mohamed V until his retirement in 2000. Over the course of his long career he has won many prestigious prizes, including Le Prix International de Catalogne (The Catalonia International Prize) in 2000. He continues to publish. In his 2005 work *Le Maroc et Hassan II: Un témoignage* (The Morocco of Hassan II: A Testimony) Laroui discusses his relationship with King Hassan II (1929–1999) and the Moroccan political system:

> Each time I had the occasion to see him tête-à-tête and to observe from close-up his method of thinking and making decisions, I would leave the interview always asking the same question: Was it him who had created the system under which we are living, which we critique often but which we end up accepting? Or is it Morocco, if it is true that it exists, which has produced it, and that he was, like the rest of us, the consenting victim? The problem that we are confronting for more than forty years that none of us could really understand, is getting clearer—though in different ways depending on how we perceive it—is Hassan II the innovator or a proponent of the status quo?

Abdallah Laroui's works have been translated into many languages. His influence is particularly apparent in many Arab universities throughout North Africa.

References:

Ibrahim M. Abu-Rabi', "Abdallah Laroui: From Objective Marxism to Liberal Etatism," in his *Contemporary Arab Thought: Studies in Post-1967 Arab Intellectual History* (London: Pluto Press, 2003);

Yousseff M. Choueiri, "The Panacea of Historicism: Abdallah Laroui and Morocco's Cultural Retardation," in his *Arab History and the Nation State: A Study in Modern Arab Historiography 1820–1980* (London & New York: Routledge, 1989), pp. 165–188;

W. Fritschy, "The King, the Nation and the Gap with the West: Recent Studies on Moroccan History," *Tijdschrift Voor Geschiedenis,* 117, no. 1 (2004): 86–95.

Mohammed 'Abed al-Jabri, *Nahnu wa al-turath: Qira'at mu'asira fi turathina al-falsafi* (Beirut: Dar al-Tali'ah, 1980).

Amin Maalouf
(25 February 1949 –   )

Coeli Fitzpatrick
Grand Valley State University

BOOKS: *Les Croisades vues par les Arabs* (Paris: Jean-Claude Lattés, 1983); translated by Jon Rothschild as *The Crusades through Arab Eyes* (London: Saqi, 1984; New York: Schocken, 1985);

Léon l'Africain (Paris: Jean-Claude Lattés, 1986); translated by Peter Sluglett as *Leo the African* (London: Quartet, 1988); translation republished as *Leo Africanus* (New York: Norton, 1989);

Samarcande (Paris: Jean-Claude Lattés, 1988); translated by Russell Harris as *Samarkand* (London: Quartet, 1992);

Les jardins de lumière (Paris: Jean-Claude Lattés, 1991); translated by Dorothy S. Blair as *The Gardens of Light* (London: Quartet, 1996; New York: Interlink, 1999);

Le premier siècle après Béatrice (Paris: Bernard Grasset, 1992); translated by Blair as *The First Century after Beatrice* (London: Abacus, 1994; New York: Braziller, 1995);

Le rocher de Tanios (Paris: Bernard Grasset, 1993); translated by Blair as *The Rock of Tanios* (London: Quartet, 1994; New York: Braziller, 1994);

Les échelles du Levant (Paris: Bernard Grasset, 1996); translated by Alberto Manguel as *Ports of Call* (London: Harvill Press, 1999);

Les identités meurtrières (Paris: Bernard Grasset, 1998); translated by Barbara Bray as *On Identity* (London: Harvill Press, 2000); translation republished as *In the Name of Identity: Violence and the Need to Belong* (New York: Arcade, 2001);

Le périple de Baldassare (Paris: Grasset & Fasquelle, 2000); translated by Bray as *Balthasar's Odyssey* (New York: Arcade, 2003);

L'amour de loin, music by Kaija Saariaho (Salzburg: Salzburger Festspiele, 2000; Paris: Grasset & Fasquelle, 2001);

Origines (Paris: Grasset & Fasquelle, 2004); translated by Catherine Temerson as *Origins: A Memoir* (London: Picador, 2008; New York: Farrar, Straus & Giroux, 2008);

Amin Maalouf (from the dust jacket for The Rock of Tanios: A Novel, *1994; Richland County Public Library)*

Adriana Mater: An Opera in Seven Scenes, translated by Bray, music by Saariaho (Santa Fe, N.Mex.: Santa Fe Opera, 2008).

The Lebanon-born writer of fiction, philosophy, and opera librettos Amin Maalouf is renowned for his poetic style and lyrical storytelling. His works have been translated into more than thirty languages and are best-sellers in his adopted home, France. His fiction is notable for its historical basis and its often playful depiction of characters who find themselves wandering through various lands and cultures, and his nonfiction

The Crusades Through Arab Eyes

Translated by Jon Rothschild

Title page for the 1984 English translation of Maalouf's first book, Les Croisades vues par les Arabs, *1983 (Thomas Cooper Library, University of South Carolina)*

is known for its honest and personal evaluation of such difficult subjects as identity and exile.

A great-great-great-nephew of the first translator of the works of Molière into Arabic, Maalouf was born in Beirut on 25 February 1949. He was the second of four children of the well-known journalist Ruchdi Maalouf and Odette Ghossein Maalouf. The father was a Protestant and the mother a Maronite Catholic; the children were raised as Catholics and attended French Catholic schools rather than the American-run Protestant ones. At the time of Maalouf's birth the family lived in a quarter of Beirut known as "Caracas" after a supermarket in the area owned by a Venezuelan immigrant. It was a cosmopolitan neighborhood, where Christians and Muslims lived side by side. When Maalouf was thirteen, they moved to a larger, more sumptuous apartment in an exclusively Christian part of the city. After this move, Maalouf began to feel the effects of being a member of a minority—his family were Melkite Christians; the majority were Maronites—and became profoundly aware of discrimination. This feeling was heightened when he was seventeen by a visit to the Maalouf home by Oliver Tambo, a leader of the then-banned South African black nationalist organization, the African National Congress. For Maalouf, Tambo became the living symbol of the struggle against racism—a theme of most of the writing Maalouf produced in the future.

Like most Lebanese Christians, Maalouf was fluent in French and Arabic. His education at the Pères Jesuites school was conducted in French, but Arabic was the language his family spoke at home and that he used in the street. The first novels he read were translated from English or French into Arabic, but he kept his diaries in French and later referred to it as the "shadow language" he used to record his secret thoughts. He gradually became dissatisfied with Arabic translations and began to read books in their original languages, reserving Arabic for works on Middle Eastern history.

As a sociology student at the French University of Beirut, Maalouf became associated with leftist students who were inspired by the May 1968 student demonstrations in Paris. In 1971 he married Andrée, a teacher at an institute for deaf children, and took a job as a reporter for the newspaper *al-Nahar*. He covered the independence of Bangladesh that year; traveled to Ethiopia, Somalia, and Algeria; and witnessed the events that led to the fall of Saigon in 1975.

On 13 April 1975 a Palestinian gunman fired at a group of mourners gathered outside a church for a funeral in a Christian suburb of Beirut. Several hours later, Christians ambushed a bus full of Palestinians. That same day Maalouf, his wife, and one of their sons witnessed a gunfight in the street outside their house; the family moved to Maalouf's parents' home in a safer part of the city. These events were the beginning of the fifteen-year Lebanese civil war. Determined not to get caught up in the conflict, Maalouf sailed on 16 June 1976 from the port at Jounieh to Cyprus, then flew on to Paris and went to work for the magazine *Jeune Afrique* (Young Africa). His wife, who was eight months pregnant, remained in Lebanon with their sons, Ruchdi and Tarek; after the baby—another son, Ziad—was born, the family joined Maalouf in Paris. In 1979 Maalouf became director of *Al-Nahar Arabe et International*, a Paris-based weekly edition of the Lebanese newspaper. In 1982 he returned to *Jeune Afrique*.

A friend who was fascinated by the Crusades suggested that Maalouf write a nonfiction book on the subject; the result was *Les Croisades vues par les Arabs* (1983, translated as *The Crusades through Arab Eyes,* 1984). The work covers the years 1096 to 1291 and is based almost exclusively on the testimonies of Arab eyewitnesses, chroniclers, and historians; recording historical events through the eyes of the losing side became a trademark of Maalouf's fiction. In the foreword Maalouf explains: "Rather than offer yet another history book, I have sought to write, from a hitherto neglected point of view, what might be called the 'true-life novel' of the Crusades, of those two centuries of turmoil that shaped the West and the Arab world alike, and that affect relations between them even today." Maalouf traces the path of the Crusaders, called the "Franj" by the Arabs, through what is now Turkey southward into the Levant, Jerusalem, and Egypt. He notes that although the early Crusaders were Europeans, many of the later ones were born in the East. He quotes Saladin's admiring comments about the Crusaders: "Regard the Franj! Behold with what obstinacy they fight for their religion, while we, the Muslims, show no enthusiasm for waging holy war." In general, however, the Muslims had contempt for the Franj, whom they considered uncivilized and barbaric. Maalouf quotes the chronicler Usamah, who recounts with horror how the Crusaders determined guilt for a crime:

> A large cask had been set up and filled with water. The young man who was the object of suspicion was pinioned, suspended from a rope by his shoulder-blades, and plunged into the cask. If he was innocent, they said, he would sink into the water, and they would pull him out by the rope. If he was guilty, it would be impossible for him to sink into the water. When he was thrown into the cask, the unfortunate man made every effort to descend to the bottom, but he could not manage it, and thus had to submit to the rigours of their law, may God's curse be upon them! He was then blinded by a red-hot silver awl.

Maalouf also brings to light the curious alliances, based on the self-interest of various rulers, that were formed during the Crusades. For example, al-Afdal Shahinshah, vizier of Cairo in 1097, was pleased with the Western onslaught on Asia Minor because of his dislike of the Turks and Sunni Muslims. Maalouf cites a Syrian proverb dating from the time of the Crusades: "Kiss any arm you cannot break, and pray to God to break it." He shows that it was not unusual for two armies to face each other, each composed of a hodgepodge of Western Christians, Eastern Christians, and Muslims. He traces the origins of the Assassins, a Shia sect founded in 1090 by the Persian thinker Hasan Ibn al-Sabbah that gained a reputation for carrying out daring murders and was at one point allied with the Franj.

Maalouf concludes the book by noting that the Crusades have retained an importance in the Arab world that has long been lost in the West. He points out that Mehmet Ali Hagca, the would-be assassin of Pope

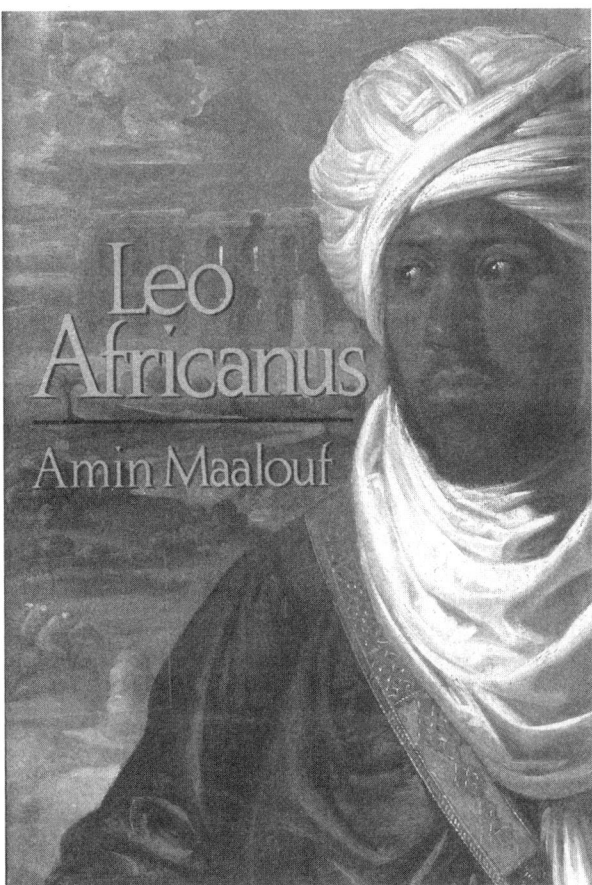

Title page for the first American edition, 1989, of the English translation of Maalouf's second book, Léon l'Africain, *1986 (Richland County Public Library)*

John Paul II in 1981, wrote in a letter: "I have decided to kill John Paul II, supreme commander of the Crusades." Modern Arab leaders refer in speeches to the Crusades and their Muslim heroes, such as Saladin, to inspire the masses with confidence that they can prevail against the West.

For the most part *Les Croisades vues par les Arabs* received praise from the critics. Some reviewers, however, asserted that Maalouf was simply telling the story as it had been taught to him in Lebanon, ignoring the fact that in the Jesuit school that he attended the Crusades were presented from a Catholic perspective that viewed the Crusaders as heroes. In *TLS: The Times Literary Supplement* (16 November 1984) Robert Irwin called the book "partisan for the Muslim side" but welcomed its offsetting of traditional narratives drawn from European sources. He also praised Maalouf for introducing the Arab, Turkish, and Kurdish participants in the Crusades to Western readers, most of whom would only recognize the name of Saladin.

Maalouf resigned from *Jeune Afrique* in 1985 to devote himself to writing full-time. In 1986 he published *Léon l'Africain* (translated as *Leo the African*, 1988). The novel established a pattern that is seen in most of Maalouf's novels: a lone narrator is forced by circumstances into a life of wandering from place to place and from adventure to adventure. *Léon l'Africain* is narrated by Hasan, a character based on the sixteenth-century traveler Hasan al-Wazzan, or Leo Africanus, and takes the form of a chronicle written for Hasan's son to read when he is older. It begins:

> I, Hasan the son of Muhammad the weigh-master, I, Jean-Leon de Medici, circumcised at the hand of a barber and baptized at the hand of a pope, I am now called the African, but I am not from Africa, nor from Europe, nor from Arabia. I am also called the Granadan, the Fassi, the Zayyati, but I come from no country, from no city, no tribe. I am the son of the road, my country is the caravan, my life the most unexpected of voyages.

After the capture of Granada by the Christians in 1492, Hasan's family chooses exile over conversion and moves to Fez. Hasan's maternal uncle takes him along on a diplomatic mission to Africa; the uncle dies of fever, leaving Hasan with the responsibility of leading the caravan. His success in the endeavor opens the way to his later adventures: he becomes head of another caravan, is forced into exile, experiences plague in Egypt, is kidnapped by pirates and taken to Rome, is baptized and renamed by Pope Leo X, and becomes an emissary from the Vatican to Africa, where he converts back to Islam. Meeting his oldest friend and brother-in-law, who has become a delegate to the Ottoman sultan, Hasan asks: "Wouldn't it be wonderful if Christians and Muslims all around the Mediterranean could live and trade together without war or piracy, if I could go from Alexandria to Tunis with my family without being kidnapped by some Sicilian?" Hasan ends his chronicle with advice to his son:

> Wherever you are, some will want to ask questions about your skin or your prayers. Beware of gratifying their instincts, my son, beware of bending before the multitude! Muslim, Jew or Christian, they must take you as you are, or lose you. When men's minds seem narrow to you, tell yourself that the land of God is broad; broad His hands and broad His heart. Never hesitate to go far away, beyond all seas, all frontiers, all countries, all beliefs.

Léon l'Africain was a huge success. Maalouf followed it with *Samarcande* (1988; translated as *Samarkand*, 1992), a novel about the twelfth-century Persian poet Omar Khayyam and a manuscript of his that is rediscovered in the early twentieth century and lost in the sinking of the *Titanic*; it was awarded the Prix des Maisons de la Press in 1988. The central figure of *Les jardins de lumière* (1991; translated as *The Gardens of Light*, 1996) is Mani, the third-century Persian founder of Manichaeanism. *Le premier siècle après Béatrice* (1992; translated as *The First Century after Beatrice*, 1994) is set in the twenty-first century: a drug is developed from beans to reduce Third World populations; it guarantees the birth of male children, and the resulting shortage of women leads to violence by men, the sale of women on the black market, economic collapse, and wars. The narrator, a French entomologist, is trying to eradicate the drug.

Maalouf wrote *Le rocher de Tanios* (1993; translated as *The Rock of Tanios*, 1994) in his newly acquired home in the Channel Islands. The novel is set in the nineteenth century. Tanios is nominally the son of Gerios, the major domo of Sheikh Francis, the Christian Arab ruler of the mountain village of Kfaryabda, but it is rumored that his mother, Lamia, was raped by the sheikh and that Tanios is the result of the affair. When the village patriarch takes Tanios's beloved for his nephew, Gerios murders the prelate. Father and son flee to Cyprus, but they are found by a spy who has been sent to search for them. Gerios is lured back to the village and hanged. Tanios remains in Cyprus and plots against his enemies in Lebanon with the aid of the French and British, who have designs on the region. He returns to Kfaryabda and is declared the new sheikh by acclamation. The rock of the title is an oddly shaped stone formation where Tanios is last seen before he mysteriously vanishes forever. The narrator reflects on the disappearance:

> One could even list the reasons which could have encouraged him to leave, and the ones which, on the contrary, ought to have made him stay. . . . What would be the use? That is not the way a decision to depart is made. You don't evaluate, you don't draw up a list of advantages and disadvantages. You alternate, from one moment to the next, now this way, now that. Towards another life, towards another death. Towards glory or oblivion. Who can ever tell because of what look, what word, what sneer, a man suddenly finds himself an outsider in the midst of his own people? So that he feels this sudden, urgent need to go far away, or disappear. . . . My Mountains are like that. Attachment to the soil and aspiration towards departure. Place of refuge, place of passage. Land of milk and honey and of blood. Neither paradise nor hell. Purgatory.

Maalouf portrays the villagers as provincial, proud, and stubborn. Anyone from outside Kfaryabda is mocked for his or her strangeness of accent and manner. The villagers take malicious delight in discussing the affairs of the sheikh but have no sympathy for his wife, who returned to her father's village after being humiliated by her husband's unfaithfulness beyond her ability to endure. When she dies, the village is unmoved: "What the 'Sheikha of the Locusts' had suffered at her husband's hands during the short years they had been together was, according to the folk on the *Blata,* nothing but her just deserts. And at the very moment of her funeral, the only comment certain village-women could make was the terrible curse, 'May God bury her even deeper!'" (Blata means "rock" and refers here to the people who live around the stone formation from which Tanios disappeared. The residents of the sheikha's paternal village, Jord, were known as "the locusts" because to the inhabitants of Kfaryabda their accent was ugly and grating, like the chirping of the insects.) The novel won the Goncourt Prize, the most prestigious literary award in France; the announcement caused jubilation in Lebanon.

Maalouf mentions the Lebanese civil war for the first time in his next novel, *Les échelles du Levant* (1996; translated as *Ports of Call,* 1999); it does not play a large role in the story, however. Ossyane Ketabdar, a Muslim of mixed aristocratic Ottoman and humble Armenian origins, travels from Lebanon to Montpellier in the late 1930s to study medicine and to avoid getting caught up in his father's revolutionary ambitions. During World War II he joins the French Resistance, where he meets Clara, a Jewish woman. They marry and return to the Middle East; they are separated by the Arab-Israeli War, and Ossyane temporarily goes insane, but they are eventually reunited.

In 1997 Maalouf was invited by Gérard Mortier, the director of the Salzburg Music Festival, to write a libretto for an opera by the Finnish composer Kaija Saariaho. *L'amour de loin* (Love from Afar) premiered in Salzburg in August 2000 and was produced at the Châtelet Theater in Paris in November 2001. It is set during the Crusades and tells of the prince of Aquitaine and troubadour Jaufré Rudel's pining for his idealized distant love, Countess Clémence of Tripoli, whom he has never met. Anthony Tommasini in *The New York Times* (17 August 2000) called it one of the best operas in years.

Les identités meurtrières (1998, Murderous Identities; translated as *On Identity,* 2000) marks Maalouf's return to nonfiction after more than ten years. His first book written in the first person, it begins with his reflections on a question he is often asked: whether he feels "more French" or "more Lebanese." His reply is "both!" The question troubles him because it assumes that everyone should have just one national, ethnic, or religious affiliation. He notes that the twentieth century is rife with examples of how this attitude leads to violence, including the Holocaust, the genocide in Rwanda in 1993,

Front cover for the American edition, 1994, of the English translation of Maalouf's 1993 novel, Le rocher de Tanios *(Richland County Public Library)*

ethnic cleansing in the Balkans in the 1990s, and the Lebanese civil war. That century brought resurgence of religion as a major component of identity for many people, and Maalouf suggests that it is necessary to "leave religious allegiance behind" if a more humane world is to be achieved:

> I dream not of a world where religion no longer has any place but of one where the need for spirituality will no longer be associated with the need to belong. A world in which a man, while remaining attached to his beliefs, to a faith, or to moral values that may or may not be inspired by scripture, will no longer feel the need to enroll himself among his co-religionists. A world in which religion will no longer serve to bind together warring ethnic groups. It is not enough now to separate Church and State: what has to do with religion must be kept apart from what has to do with identity. And if we want that amalgam to stop feeding fanaticism, terror and ethnic wars, we must find other ways of satisfying the need for identity.

One way to satisfy that need is to move toward what Maalouf calls "universality": "the basic postulate of universality is that there exist inherent rights to human dignity that no one may deny to his fellow creatures, whether on the grounds of religion, colour, nationality or sex, or on any other consideration."

Maalouf's novel *Le périple de Baldassare* (2000; translated as *Balthasar's Odyssey*, 2003) was a best-seller in France. It is the tale of yet another wanderer, a seventeenth-century merchant in search of a book known as the "One Hundreth Name" that is rumored to hold the secret name of God that is not mentioned in the Qur'an. In *The Independent* (London) for 12 October 2002 the French novelist Michèle Roberts described the book as a "meditation on the need for Christianity, Muslims and Jews to tolerate each other and a fantastic travelogue."

Shortly after the terrorist attacks of 11 September 2001, the English translation of *Identités meurtrières* was republished in the United States as *In the Name of Identity: Violence and the Need to Belong*. Critics applauded the work for offering insight into the rift between the West and the Arab world. Ian Buruma suggested in *The New York Review of Books* (11 April 2002) that Maalouf's belief that multiple identities will prevent fanaticism was too optimistic, but he called Maalouf a "rare voice of sanity in this murderous discord" and found that the book addressed many of the causes of crimes perpetuated in the name of identity. Jonathan Lear wrote in *The New York Times Book Review* (25 November 2001), "In the aftermath of September 11, we want to know more facts, we need political analyses, but we are also hungry for general reflection on what human beings are like. *In the Name of Identity* bridges theses concerns."

In May 2004 A website devoted to Maalouf (<http://www.aminmaalouf.org/>) was launched by Alex Barrière with the author's cooperation. Maalouf's *Origines* (translated as *Origins: A Memoir*, 2008) was published that spring. It concerns Maalouf's great-uncle Gebrayel, who immigrated to Cuba, and his grandfather Boutros, who opened the first coeducational school in Lebanon. Called a "historical investigation," the book is based on letters from Gebrayel to Boutros that Maalouf discovered. It received the Prix Méditerranée in June 2004.

Maalouf and Saariaho collaborated on a second opera, *Adriana Mater*, which premiered in Paris in 2006. In a civil-war torn Eastern European country a fellow villager breaks into Adriana's house and rapes her; she gives birth to a son, Yonas, who vows revenge on his father when he learns the truth years later but ultimately forgives the man.

Amin Maalouf has received several honorary degrees, including a doctorate from the American University in Beirut. He will likely continue to occupy a prominent place in Arab intellectual history well into the twenty-first century.

Interview:

Carole Corm, "Amin Maalouf Talks about His Latest Book, 'Origins,'" *Al Jadid Magazine*, 10 (Winter–Spring 2004).

Naguib Mahfouz
(11 December 1911 – 30 August 2006)

Majd Yaser Al-Mallah
Grand Valley State University

See also the Mahfūz (Mahfouz) entries in *DLB 331: Nobel Prize Laureates in Literature, Part 3: Lagerkvist–Pontoppidan* and *DLB Yearbook: 1988.*

BOOKS: *Hams al-junun* (Cairo: Maktabat Misr, 1939);
'Abath al-aqdar (Cairo: Maktabat Misr, 1939); translated by Raymond Stock as *Khufu's Wisdom* (Cairo: American University in Cairo Press, 2003);
Radubis (Cairo: Maktabat Misr, 1943); translated by Anthony Calderbank as *Rhadopis of Nubia* (Cairo: American University in Cairo Press, 2003);
Kifah Tibah (Cairo: Maktabat Misr, 1944); translated by Humphrey Davies as *Thebes at War* (Cairo: American University in Cairo Press, 2003);
Khan al-Khalili (Cairo: Maktabat Misr, 1945);
Al-Qahirah al-jadidah (Cairo: Maktabat Misr, 1946);
Zuqaq al-Midaqq (Cairo: Maktabat Misr, 1947); translated by Trevor Le Gassick as *Midaq Alley* (Beirut: Khayyat, 1966);
Al-Sarab (Cairo: Maktabat Misr, 1948);
Bidayah wa nihayah (Cairo: Maktabat Misr, 1949); translated by Ramses Awad as *The Beginning and the End* (New York: Doubleday, 1989);
Bayn al-qasrayn (Cairo: Maktabat Misr, 1956); translated by William M. Hutchins and Olive E. Kenny as *Palace Walk* (New York: Doubleday, 1991);
Qasr al-shawq (Cairo: Maktabat Misr, 1957); translated by Hutchins, Lorne M. Kenny, and Olive E. Kenny as *Palace of Desire* (New York: Doubleday, 1991);
Al-Sukkariyyah (Cairo: Maktabat Misr, 1957); translated by Hutchins and Angele Botros Samaan as *Sugar Street* (New York: Doubleday, 1992);
Al-Liss wa al-kilab (Cairo: Maktabat Misr, 1961); translated by Le Gassick and Mustafa Badawi and revised by John Rodenbeck as *The Thief and the Dogs* (New York: Doubleday, 1989);
Al-Summan wa al-kharif (Cairo: Maktabat Misr, 1962); translated by Roger Allen as *Autumn Quail* (Cairo: American University in Cairo Press, 1985);
Dunya Allah (Cairo: Maktabat Misr, 1962);

Naguib Mahfouz (from the dust jacket for The Dreams, *2004; Richland County Public Library)*

Al-Tariq (Cairo: Maktabat Misr, 1964); translated by Muhammad Islam as *The Search* (Cairo: American University in Cairo Press, 1987);
Bayt sayyi' al-sum'ah (Cairo: Maktabat Misr, 1965);
Al-Shahhadh (Cairo: Maktabat Misr, 1965); translated by Kristin Walker Henry as *The Beggar* (Cairo: American University in Cairo Press, 1986);
Thartharah fawqa al-Nil (Cairo: Maktabat Misr, 1966);
Awlad haratina (Beirut: Dar al-Adab, 1967); translated by Philip Stewart as *Children of Gebelawi* (London: Heinemann; Washington, D.C.: Three Continents Press, 1981);

Miramar (Cairo: Maktabat Misr, 1967); translated by Fatma Moussa-Mahmoud as *Miramar* (London: Heinemann, 1978);

Khammarat al-qitt al-aswad (Cairo: Maktabat Misr, 1969);

Tahta al-mizallah (Cairo: Maktabat Misr, 1969);

Hikayah bi la bidayah wa la nihayah (Cairo: Maktabat Misr, 1971);

Shahr al-'asal (Cairo: Maktabat Misr, 1971);

Al-Maraya (Cairo: Maktabat Misr, 1972); translated by Allen as *Mirror* (Minneapolis: Bibliotheca Islamica, 1977);

Al-Hubb tahta al-matar (Cairo: Maktabat Misr, 1973);

Al-Jarimah (Cairo: Maktabat Misr, 1973);

Al-Karnak (Cairo: Maktabat Misr, 1974); translated by Saad El-Gabalawy in *Three Contemporary Egyptian Novels* (New Brunswick: York Press, 1984);

Hadrat al-muhtaram (Cairo: Maktabat Misr, 1975); translated by Rashid El-Enany as *Respected Sir* (London: Quartet, 1986);

Hikayat haratina (Cairo: Maktabat Misr, 1975); translated by Soad Sobhy, Essam Fattouh, and James Kenneson as *Fountain and Tomb* (Washington, D.C.: Three Continents Press, 1988);

Qalb al-layl (Cairo: Maktabat Misr, 1975);

Malhamat al-harafish (Cairo: Maktabat Misr, 1977); translated by Catherine Cobham as *The Harafish* (New York: Doubleday, 1994);

Al-Hubb fawqa hadbat al-haram (Cairo: Maktabat Misr, 1979);

Al-Shaytan ya'iz (Cairo: Maktabat Misr, 1979);

'Asr al-hubb (Cairo: Maktabat Misr, 1980);

Afrah al-qubbah (Cairo: Maktabat Misr, 1981); translated by Olive Kenny as *Wedding Song* (New York: Doubleday, 1989);

Al-Baqi mina al-zaman sa'ah (Cairo: Maktabat Misr, 1982);

Layali alf laylah (Cairo: Maktabat Misr, 1982); translated by Denys Johnson-Davies as *Arabian Nights and Days* (New York: Doubleday, 1995);

Ra'aytu fi ma yara al-na'im (Cairo: Maktabat Misr, 1982);

Amam al-'arsh: Hiwar ma'a rijal Misr min Mina hatta Anwar al-Sadat (Cairo: Maktabat Misr, 1983);

Rihlat Ibn Fattumah (Cairo: Maktabat Misr, 1983); translated by Johnson-Davies as *The Journey of Ibn Fattouma* (London: Doubleday, 1992);

Al-Tanzim al-sirri (Cairo: Maktabat Misr, 1984);

Al-'Aysh fi al-haqiqah (Cairo: Maktabat Misr, 1985); translated by Tagreid Abu Hassabo as *Akhenaten: Dweller in Truth* (Anchor, 2000);

Yawma qutila al-za'im (Cairo: Maktabat Misr, 1985); translated by Malak Hashim as *The Day the Leader Was Killed* (Cairo: General Egyptian Book Organization, 1989);

Hadith al-sabah wa al-masa' (Cairo: Maktabat Misr, 1987);

Sabah al-ward (Cairo: Maktabat Misr, 1987);

Al-Fajr al-kadhib (Cairo: Maktabat Misr, 1989);

Qushtumur (Cairo: Maktabat Misr, 1989);

Hawla al-din wa al-dimuqratiyya (Cairo: Al-Dar al-Misriyyah al-Lubnaniyyah, 1990);

Hawla al-thaqafah wa al-ta'lim (Cairo: Al-Dar al-Misriyyah al-Lubnaniyyah, 1990);

Hawla al-shabab wa al-huriyyah (Cairo: Al-Dar al-Misriyyah al-Lubnaniyyah, 1990);

Asda' al-sira al-dhatiyyah (Cairo: Maktabat Misr, 1995); translated by Johnson-Davies as *Echoes of an Autobiography* (New York: Doubleday, 1997);

Al-Qarar al-akhir (Cairo: Maktabat Misr, 1996);

Naguib Mahfouz at Sidi Gaber: Reflections of a Nobel Laureate, 1994–2001, by Mahfouz and Mohamed Salmawy (Cairo & New York: American University in Cairo Press, 2001).

Editions in English: *God's World,* translated by Akef Abadir and Roger Allen (Minneapolis: Bibliotheca Islamica, 1973);

Naguib Mahfouz, One-Act Plays, translated by Nehad Selaiha (Cairo: General Egyptian Book Organization, 1989);

The Time and the Place and Other Stories, translated by Denys Johnson-Davies (New York: Doubleday, 1991);

Children of the Alley, translated by Peter Theroux (New York: Doubleday, 1996);

The Cairo Trilogy, translated by William M. Hutchins, Lorne M. Kenny, Olive E. Kenny, and Angele Botros Samaan (New York: Knopf, 2001)—comprises *Palace Walk, Palace of Desire,* and *Sugar Street;*

Voices from the Other World: Ancient Egyptian Tales, translated by Raymond Stock (Cairo: American University in Cairo Press, 2002).

The Dreams, translated by Stock (Cairo: American University in Cairo Press, 2004);

The Seventh Heaven: Stories of the Supernatural, translated by Stock (Cairo & New York: American University in Cairo Press, 2005).

OTHER: James Baikie, *Misr al-qadima,* translated by Mahfouz (Cairo: Al-Majallah al-Jadidah, 1932).

In October 1988, Naguib Mahfouz received the Nobel Prize for literature, affirming his status as the leading writer of fiction in Egypt and, to many, the Arab world at large. Indeed, he is the only Arab writer to receive this prestigious recognition. But Mahfouz enjoyed respect and acknowledgment in the Arab world long before the Nobel Prize was awarded. More than any other writer, he is credited with making Arabic fiction a mature literary form that rivals poetry, which for centuries was the dominant literary genre. Mahfouz's renown in Egypt and the Arab world began in the 1950s, following the publication of his most famous, and probably one of his most important works: the novels known in the English world as the Cairo Trilogy. Although he published several novels and short stories prior to the Cairo Trilogy, his art clearly matured with the publication of these novels, which were published in Arabic in 1956 and 1957. The most telling testament to Mahfouz's significance and centrality in the Arabic art of fiction is the breadth of his body of work, which spans more than sixty years.

Born 11 December 1911, Mahfouz was the youngest child of a traditional middle-class family in the city of Cairo. His father, 'Abd al-'Aziz al-Sibilji, was reportedly an accountant in the civil service, though he retired early to work for a friend as a business manager. Mahfouz recalls that his mother had a fascination for ancient Egyptian monuments and often took him to the pyramids and the Museum of Antiquities. Unlike the character Amina in the Cairo Trilogy, she enjoyed the freedom to leave the house and visit different areas and monuments as she pleased. His mother, following a difficult and dangerous labor, is also known for having named her son Naguib Mahfouz after the doctor who delivered him. He had four sisters and two brothers, but because of the age difference between him and his siblings (a ten-year gap between him and his youngest brother), Mahfouz does not remember his brothers and sisters as playing important roles in his childhood. He mainly recalls his family home with just himself and his parents, as his siblings left the house in his early years because of marriage or job relocations. This age difference caused Mahfouz to feel that he lacked a real relationship with his siblings, an emotional distance that is perhaps detectible in character relationships in some of his works of fiction, such as *Khan al-Khalili* (1945), a novel titled after a Cairo neighborhood, and the Cairo Trilogy.

Mahfouz's family, as he recalled in one of his interviews, was religious. From his family, he learned faith and visited the revered al-Husayn mosque. In school, Mahfouz read the work of Charles Darwin and, as he grew intellectually, came to abandon some of his religious upbringing. Although Mahfouz does not reveal much about his own "religious crisis," in the Cairo Trilogy he depicts Kamal—a character Mahfouz has acknowledged as being the nearest he comes to having a fictional alter ego—as experiencing a crisis that leads eventually to a total abandonment of religion. Though his family cared about religion, they were not a particularly cultured family. Mahfouz recalls only one book that his father owned, *Hadith 'Isa Ibn Hisham* (1907, The Conversation of 'Isa Ibn Hisham), which he kept, apparently, because the author, Muhammad al-Muwaylihi, was a friend of his father.

Malfouz grew up in the traditional Cairo neighborhood of Jamaliyyah (Gamaliyyah, according to Egyptian pronunciation), where the important religious shrine of al-Husayn, grandson of the Prophet Muhammad, and the Khan al-Khalili *suq* (bazaar) are located. His parents sent him to the local *kuttab* schools, which were widespread prior to the establishment of modern public and private schools. There, the children learned the Qur'an and other religious materials under a shaykh (teacher) with knowledge in the Islamic religion. Mahfouz does not have fond memories of this period, for he mentions in one of his interviews that the other children in the *kuttab* used to take advantage of his physical weakness to steal his food. After the *kuttab,* he attended al-Husayniyyah elementary school and Fu'ad al-Awal (Fu'ad the First) secondary school. Although Mahfouz was an excellent student in sciences and Arabic writing, he did not do as well in English and other topics in the humanities. In elementary school, Mahfouz discovered his love for reading when he borrowed a detective novel from one of his friends, leading him to search for other such stories. Mahfouz remembers rewriting the detective stories with minor adjustments to the narratives, then adding his name as the author and even creating an imaginary publisher for his new creation.

In 1919 Mahfouz experienced, along with the rest of the country, the revolution against the British, an event that played a central role in shaping Mahfouz, his nationalist feelings, and later, important fictional works such as the Cairo Trilogy. However much the 1919 revolution affected Mahfouz as a young boy, it did not directly cause personal tragedy in his family. He remembers a normal childhood under the wings of two parents who lived together lovingly and created a stable, comfortable environment despite the generally tense atmosphere that engulfed the country. At ten years of age, Mahfouz was diagnosed with a neurological illness, at the time said to be epilepsy. Despite having to stay at home and not go to school for one year, the illness did not apparently affect Mahfouz's development in any serious way, either physically or mentally.

After twelve years of living in the traditional neighborhood of Jamaliyyah, Mahfouz's family decided to move to the modern neighborhood of Eastern 'Abbasiyyah, a middle-class area, distinct from Western 'Abbasiyyah, where the upper classes resided. Despite the move, Mahfouz continued to visit Jamaliyyah, and his place of birth with its various small neighborhoods became the center of many of his novels and stories. Mahfouz had fond memories of 'Abbasiyyah as well as

Front cover for Mahfouz's 1956 novel Bayn al-qasrayn, *which was translated as* Palace Walk *(Thomas Cooper Library, University of South Carolina)*

Jamaliyyah, forming friendships in both that continued into adulthood and contributed to his creation of memorable characters. Mahfouz's fascination with Jamaliyyah is clear in his frequent re-creation of the beloved *harah* (small neighborhood) and his particular interest in *futuwwas* (thugs). He recalls as a boy seeing the *futuwwas* participate in neighborhood events, even playing a role in the 1919 revolution against the British.

In 'Abbasiyyah, Mahfouz began to notice the differences between the middle and upper classes. Mahfouz recalls political as well as financial differences, namely the middle-class support for the Wafd nationalist party (with its famous leader Sa'd Zaghlul) and the upper-class support for the Liberal Constitutionalist Party. This class distinction became even more significant when Mahfouz, at about the age of thirteen, fell in love with an older girl from a wealthy part of the 'Abbasiyyah neighborhood. In interviews Mahfouz points out that he had no contact with this girl because of the age and class differences, though he affirms that the experience had a profound impact on him and his perception of love and beauty. In the second book of the Cairo Trilogy Mahfouz depicts in vivid details the teenaged Kamal's one-sided infatuation for an older girl. In addition to falling in love while in 'Abbasiyyah, Mahfouz recalls it as a place where he enjoyed playing soccer with friends. His friend Adham Rajab reports that Mahfouz was an excellent player.

In secondary school, Mahfouz's infatuation with reading expanded beyond detective stories to historical novels and to his discovery of writers such as Mustafa Lutfi al-Manfaluti (1876–1924). Initially, he considered reading fiction a hobby and was more interested in philosophical and intellectual writings. In *Naguib Mahfouz yatadhakkar* (1987, Naguib Mahfouz Remembers), Gamal al-Ghitani records that Mahfouz reports being deeply influenced by 'Abbas Mahmoud al-'Aqqad (1889–1964) and Taha Husayn (1889–1973). Mahfouz's interests led him to pursue a degree in philosophy from King Fu'ad I University between 1930 and 1934. Mahfouz's father, who had expected his son to study medicine or engineering, was deeply annoyed by his decision, and his teachers were also surprised because the humanities were not regarded as his strongest subject. But Mahfouz hoped studying philosophy would answer some of the questions, such as the secret of existence, that "agonized" him. Although he immersed himself in philosophy and published essays in magazines and journals, Mahfouz began to doubt his course of study could really answer his difficult questions. As he neared the completion of his undergraduate degree in 1934, he began to turn more toward literature. The internal conflict reached a peak when he was writing his master's thesis in philosophy, and in 1936 he made the decision to go in the direction of writing outside of academia rather than continuing his philosophy thesis.

Mahfouz, who in 1934 had received a secretary position at the university, in 1938 took a government position in the ministry of Awqaf (religious endowments). He was later able to work at Qubbat al-Ghuri, an old building that had an excellent library and that was close to the public library, which gave him the opportunity to read widely. He had a pressing sense of lack of time, as he felt the need to be better read and more disciplined to succeed as a writer. He embarked on a program of reading literature from around the world. He studied the classical writers of the Arabic tradition such as al-Jahiz, al-Ma'arri, and al-Mutanabbi, and turned to the great writers of the West, including William Shakespeare, Charles Dickens, George Bernard Shaw, Herman Melville, Ernest Hemingway, and William Faulkner as well as Fyodor Dostoevsky, Leo Tolstoy, and Henrik Ibsen. He read Western works in English and in Arabic translations, preferring those languages, though he knew some French. Mahfouz loved

Shakespeare and Shaw but did not like Dickens. He enjoyed the Russian authors, especially Dostoevsky. He was not particularly impressed with Faulkner, whom he called too complicated; he liked *The Old Man and the Sea* (1952) but none of Hemingway's other work. In one of his interviews he said that Melville's *Moby-Dick* (1851) was probably one of the greatest novels ever written. Had Mahfouz not organized his few precious leisure hours he could not have progressed as a writer. He usually worked on his writing at dusk for two or three hours at a time but certainly not more than that. He also contended with eye allergies that prevented him from doing any writing during the summer months.

Mahfouz began publishing short stories in obscure magazines and journals. His main love was novels, but at the beginning of his career no publishing house would even consider his longer works. His first published book was *Misr al-qadima* (1932), a translation of James Baikie's *Ancient Egypt* (1912), which he sent to *al-Majallah al-Jadidah* (The New Magazine), thinking that it would be serialized. He was surprised when one day, he answered a knock at the door and was presented with a published copy of the book, which had been produced as a special issue of the magazine. Mahfouz did not intend to be a translator but had taken on the job to strengthen his English. He was clearly interested in the history of Egypt as a subject, though, as the first three novels that he published take place in ancient Egypt. Mahfouz recalls that he studied with the intention of writing his country's full history through novels. However, as he developed as a writer, his interests turned in a different direction.

In Mahfouz's first novel, *'Abath al-aqdar* (1939; The Absurdity of Fates; translated as *Khufu's Wisdom*, 2003), the ancient Egyptian king Khufu (Cheops) asks his fortune-teller to predict the future for him and his family. To the king's dismay, the fortune-teller informs him that none of his sons will take the throne after him, and that a boy born to a priest of the god Ra' will succeed him to the throne. In his attempt to avert the prophecy by slaughtering the boy, the king not only kills the wrong boy but also unwittingly raises up his eventual successor. Although not highly acclaimed by critics, the novel reveals that Mahfouz from the beginning of his career was interested in the absurdity of the unexpected and human impotence in the face of other higher powers that determine the course of life. In this work, as well as later ones, this higher power is not necessarily defined specifically as divine. As Rasheed El-Enany points out in *Naguib Mahfouz: The Pursuit of Meaning* (1993), Mahfouz's fascination is with the power of "fate, accident, chance, coincidence, time or death," which "will always have the same effect—to upset man's plans and shake the foundation of his rational calculations for his life and the world."

In his second novel, *Radubis* (1943; translated as *Rhadopis of Nubia,* 2003), Mahfouz continues his exploration of ancient Egypt through the story of Mirinra', pharaoh of Egypt, who at the beginning of the novel appears to be on a confrontation course with the priests in his kingdom over the issue of their massive landownership. By sheer coincidence, Mirinra' meets Radubis and falls in love with her instantly; he then abandons his wife and decides to move in with his new lover. The priests are able to manipulate this situation to their advantage by staging an uprising, and the pharaoh, who bravely confronts the crowd, is injured by an arrow and requests to die by the hand of his beloved. Radubis also commits suicide by taking poison. As in his previous novel, Mahfouz is still honing his art, depending on coincidence and chance to advance his plot.

Submitted before its publication to the Fuad I Academy contest, *Kifah Tibah* (1944; The Struggle of Thebes; translated as *Thebes at War,* 2003) won Mahfouz third place and a minor prize. His third novel dealing with ancient Egypt, *Kifah Tibah* tells the story of the struggle of the Pharaonic family against the Hyksus' foreign rule over Egypt in the sixteenth century B.C.E. Ahmas emerges as the novel's hero when he leads the Egyptians to defeat the Hyksus and restores power to the pharaoh and his family. In the course of his battles, he meets Aminridis, the daughter of the Hyksus' king. Despite their mutual romantic attraction, Ahmas and Aminridis cannot overcome the scars of war that, in the end, separate them. *Kifah Tibah* was the last novel in what critics later called the "historical period" or the "Romantic period" in Mahfouz's literary career. These early novels, while not highly acclaimed, launched his career and made it easier for him to publish subsequent work.

After *Kifah Tibah,* Mahfouz turned to writing novels that dealt with Egyptian society in the twentieth century. Critics call this period the author's realistic or social period because of his interest in exploring in fiction the social issues that Egypt was struggling with at the time. Mahfouz was aware that the realistic novel was viewed as passé by experimental, modernist writers in the West who were reacting against already established literary traditions of realism and naturalism, but he believed that the issues he wanted to address had not been dealt with in the Arabic literary tradition.

A clear departure from his historical novels, *Khan al-Khalili* tells the story of an Egyptian family that moves to the ancient neighborhood of Khan al-Khalili following air raids on Cairo in 1941. Upon taking residence in their new home, Ahmad 'Akif, a forty-year-old government employee of modest means, falls in love with his young, beautiful neighbor, Nawal. But while she is open to his advances, Ahmad is too shy to ask for her hand in marriage or even to talk to her. When Ahmad's younger brother Rushdi is transferred to a new position in Cairo and moves to live with his family in Khan al-Khalili, he is not aware of Ahmad's feelings and flirts with Nawal. Although Nawal eventually falls in love with Rushdi, their relationship is severed by her family when Rushdi is diagnosed with a deadly lung illness. Ahmad's family prepares to leave Khan al-Khalili after Rushdi's death. In this novel Mahfouz treats the life and struggles of Ahmad's family with sympathy and honesty, but as an artist he is clearly still experimenting with narrative in general and realism in particular.

Khan al-Khalili proved to be an important novel for Mahfouz because of the way it was publicized and distributed. The publisher produced fifteen thousand copies in the first edition, in contrast with a limited printing of only two thousand copies for previous books. For the first time, Mahfouz remembers, there was a major advertising campaign for this novel, one that resulted in selling out all fifteen thousand copies in the first week alone. It was a major stepping-stone for the new and relatively unknown novelist.

Mahfouz published four novels between 1946 and 1950, all dealing with current social issues in the framework of realism. *Al-Qahirah al-jadidah* (1946, New Cairo) focuses on three Egyptians—'Ali, Ma'mun, and Mahjub—studying philosophy at the university in Cairo. After graduation, 'Ali finds a job in the library; Ma'mun receives a scholarship to study abroad; but Mahjub, who comes from a poor family, finds himself jobless. Mahjub, whose family desperately needs him to work since his father was paralyzed after having a stroke, is finally able to attain a job when he marries a woman who is having a secret affair with a high government official, the Bey, thus providing cover for the relationship. When the affair is discovered, the Bey resigns his high position, and Mahjoub is transferred to another district. The novel was well received by the critics of the time, notably by Sayyid Qutb, who became a champion of Mahfouz's career. In his positive reviews of Mahfouz's Cairo novels, Qutb suggested that the novelist was breaking new ground in the Arabic literary tradition by treating mature themes in his fiction.

In *Zuqaq al-Midaqq* (1947; translated as *Midaq Alley*, 1966)—which owns the distinction of being the first Mahfouz novel to be translated into English—the author explores how the traditional inhabitants of Midaq Alley respond to changing times in the early 1940s. By this point in his career, Mahfouz was able to publish his novels easily and on a regular basis, though neither *Zuqaq al-Midaqq* nor the two novels that followed—*al-Sarab* (1948, The Mirage) and *Bidayah wa nihayah* (1949; translated as *The Beginning and the End*, 1989)—added much to his literary reputation. Critic Anwar Ma'addawi did praise *Bidayah wa nihayah* as an excellent work of art.

In the early 1950s, Mahfouz stopped publishing for a few years as the new decade brought national and personal changes and challenges that slowed his production. Egypt in 1952 went through a military coup, led by Gamal Abdel Nasser, that brought about an end to the Egyptian monarchy and a new beginning to a modern republic. At the end of the 1940s Mahfouz had started working as a screenwriter, initially with the well-known director Salah Abu Seif. In addition, Mahfouz got married in 1954. Although he had feared that marriage and children might interfere with his work, his wife tended to their two daughters so he could devote himself to his writing. He adjusted his writing schedule to fit his family life, taking Friday mornings, for example, to spend with his family while continuing to write daily.

In 1956 Mahfouz published the first volume of his ambitious Cairo Trilogy, *Bayn al-qasrayn* (translated as *Palace Walk*, 1991), the popular success of which led to the quick publication of the subsequent novels, *Qasr al-shawq* (1957; translated as *Palace of Desire*, 1991) and *al-Sukkariyyah* (1957; translated as *Sugar Street*, 1992). According to al-Ghitani account's in *Naguib Mahfouz yatadhakkar*, the publication of what many regard as Mahfouz's greatest work was not certain at first. When Mahfouz initially presented his work to his publisher as one long novel (approximately one thousand pages) titled *Bayn al-qasrayn*, it was rejected as "impossible." The disheartened Mahfouz could not comprehend not being able to publish his "dearest" work yet. It was only after the work began to attract notice when it was serialized in a new magazine edited by Yusuf al-Siba'i, titled *al-Risalah al-jadidah* (The New Message), that the publisher suggested its publication as a trilogy.

The idea of the Cairo Trilogy, according to Mahfouz, came as a result of his reading on the art of the novel. Intrigued by novels that dealt with generations within the same family, he decided to write a similar kind of work. He read extensively, specifically in preparation for such a work, which he had not done for any of his previous novels. His study of precedents included Tolstoy's *War and Peace* (translated 1886), John Galsworthy's *Forsyte Saga* (1922), and Thomas Mann's *Buddenbrooks* (translated 1924).

Mahfouz's trilogy tells the story of a middle-class family in Cairo, beginning around the time of World War I and ending in the mid 1940s. *Bayn al-qasrayn* focuses on al-Sayyid Ahmad 'Abd Al-Jawwad and his wife, Amina, as they raise their five children in a traditional neighborhood. Beginning with a memorable scene in which Amina awakens in the middle of the night to wait for her husband to return from his nightly outing, the novel examines the daily lives and minds of all the members of the family. Al-Sayyid Ahmad is portrayed as a man who enjoys the pleasures of life, including drinking, flirting, having affairs with women, and going to parties with friends during the night hours. At such parties, he is always the center of attention, with a sense of humor and unlimited zeal for enjoying life and having a good time. At home, however, he is a different person, stern with his wife and his children, pious and serious to the extreme. No one in the family dares to defy his will or argue with him. Amina, on the other hand, holds the family together with her immense love for her children and her good-hearted nature. Having lived with al-Sayyid Ahmad for more than a quarter of a century, she has learned how to adjust to his demands and feels blessed to have a family that she loves.

Bayn al-qasrayn also introduces the children of the family. Yasin, al-Sayyid Ahmad's eldest son from a previous marriage, is a government employee who is consumed with seeking pleasures anywhere he can find them. Mostly he spends his time drinking alone in a bar and chasing an entertainer named Zanubah. Al-Sayyid and Amina have two sons: Fahmi, a law student at the university, and Kamal, a student in elementary school. They also have two daughters: Khadijah and 'A'ishah, who stay at home to help their mother while the men leave each morning either to go to work or school. After a careful presentation of each of these characters, Mahfouz's plot intensifies when Amina's children convince her to go visit al-Husayn's mosque while al-Sayyid Ahmad is on a business trip outside Cairo. Upon contact with the outside, a car hits Amina, and once she recovers, al-Sayyid Ahmad banishes her from the home as a punishment for defying his orders. Eventually, Amina returns and both Khadijah and 'A'ishah marry the sons of Mrs. Shawkat and move to a different neighborhood. The novel ends with Fahmi's death, when he defies his father and participates in a demonstration in support of the 1919 revolution against the British forces.

Qasr al-shawq begins five years after the death of Fahmi, whose death has aged al-Sayyid Ahmad and Amina beyond their years. Al-Sayyid, who had abandoned his nightly outings, allows friends to convince him to go back to drinking and attending parties. He also returns to his extramarital affairs, including a relationship with Zanubah, who was Yasin's lover in *Bayn al-qasrayn*. Zanubah realizes al-Sayyid's weakness as an old man and tries to take advantage of him by demanding large amounts of money and even marriage. Al-Sayyid does not marry her and leaves her when he realizes that she is having an affair with Yasin. Another major plot involves Kamal, now a teenager who just graduated from high school and entered college to become a teacher. Kamal's story revolves around his love for 'Aydah, a sister of his friend from an aristocratic family, his interest in becoming a writer, and his loss of faith as a result of learning about scientific theories such as Darwin's theory of evolution. Yasin's story of bringing shame to his father and family does not stop. He marries Maryam, their neighbor and Fahmi's old flame, then marries Zanubah after divorcing his second wife. Khadijah and 'A'ishah live in the same house with their families; Khadijah has two sons, while 'A'ishah has a daughter and two sons. The novel ends with a tragedy for 'A'ishah, who loses her husband and two sons to typhoid.

Al-Sukkariyyah begins approximately eight years after the end of *Qasr al-shawq*. Although this novel provides a conclusion to al-Sayyid's story, who dies following one of the raids on Cairo during World War II, its main focus is actually the third generation, the grandsons and daughters of al-Sayyid and Amina. Mahfouz also continues the stories of Kamal and Yasin. Kamal is unhappy in his life as a teacher and writer, but he gets a glimpse of hope when he meets Budur, 'Aydah's young sister, who is attending college. Because Kamal is stiff and slow in his advances, Budur soon marries someone else. The important third-generation characters of *al-Sukkariyyah* are Radwan, Yasin's eldest son; Abd al-Muh'im and Ahmad, Khadija's sons; and Na'imah and Karima, daughters of 'A'ishah and Yasin, respectively. Radwan, who is living with his father while attending college, becomes a political activist. Driven mainly by self-interest and high ambition, he becomes well-connected in the government through engaging in homosexual relationships with high-level politicians. 'Abd al-Muh'im and Ahmad are also involved in political activism, the former joining the Muslim Brothers and the latter becoming a communist, but their political activity, unlike that of Radwan, leads them to jail at the end of the novel. Na'imah marries 'Abd al-Mu'im and dies while giving birth, which devastates and drives 'A'ishah to the verge of madness. The novel ends with Amina on her deathbed.

Critics hailed the Cairo Trilogy, and because of it Mahfouz won the prestigious state award for literature in 1957. In *The Early Novels of Naguib Mahfouz: Images of Modern Egypt* (1994), Matti Moosa calls it the "crowning glory of Mahfouz's literary career, undoubtedly his most important work." Mahfouz, as Sasson Somekh reports in *The Changing Rhythm: A Study of Najib Mahfouz's Novels* (1973), was "now unanimously acclaimed as the foremost novelist of modern Egypt." The Cairo Trilogy broke ground in many areas. Critics and pleasure read-

Dust jackets for the English editions of Mahfouz's Cairo Trilogy (Richland County Public Library)

ers alike find it one of the most enjoyable narratives in modern Arabic fiction. While certainly easy to read, it is at the same time complex and sophisticated in its treatment of issues and characters, depicting the trials of Egypt and Egyptians from the turn of the twentieth century to the waning days of World War II.

Awlad haratina (translated as *Children of Gebelawi,* 1981), which was serialized in 1959 in the newspaper *al-Ahram* (Pyramids) but was not published as a book until 1967, marks a departure from realism for Mahfouz. An allegorical novel that draws on incidents in the history of Judaism, Christianity, and Islam, *Awlad haratina* anticipates Mahfouz's move into new modes of narrative and experimentation that he carried on throughout the 1960s. Though Mahfouz returned to his exploration of social and political issues, especially those that confronted the country after the 1952 revolution, he did not do so in the style of the Cairo Trilogy. In his new phase, Mahfouz wrote relatively short novels without, as El-Enany observes, the "multi-threaded plots, the immense variety of characters and omniscient author's freedom to move at will among their consciousness." Mahfouz's novels in the 1960s generally present a veiled–sometimes direct–critique of the revolution and its impact on Egypt. Mahfouz became disillusioned with Nasser's reign, which he saw as marred by the suppression of dissent and the creation of a new class of corrupt elite that replaced the old corrupt elite of the monarchy.

Al-Liss wa al-kilab (1961; translated as *The Thief and the Dogs,* 1989), a representative novel of Mahfouz's new phase, tells the story of a sympathetic thief, Sa'id Mahan who just left prison after serving a four-year sentence. He is determined to take revenge on his wife, Nabawiyyah, and 'Ilish, a man who used to work with him, because it was their betrayal that led to his being imprisoned. His only hope for a new life is his daughter Sana', now five years old, but she does not even recognize him. Finding no solace when he turns to a Sufi shaykh, the desperate Sa'id remembers his mentor Ra'uf 'Ilwan, who used to be a radical leftist calling for social justice and justifying to Sa'id his work as a thief. However, Ra'uf 'Ilwan is no longer the "revolutionary" he knew, but rather a rich and well-connected journalist, living in a luxurious home in one of the nice neighborhoods of Cairo. Sa'id fails in his attempts to assassinate 'Ilish, his wife, and Ra'uf 'Ilwan: he becomes a fugitive, who hides with Nur, a prostitute who helps him survive for a while, but he is eventually shot dead by the police.

Al-Liss wa al-kilab is a dark and, in many ways, depressing look at Egyptian society in the aftermath of the revolution. Sa'id is trapped in a web of betrayal and disappointment, symbolic of the Egyptian people's dilemma as they became disillusioned with the revolution and its ideals. Another important character, in many ways symbolic of the new regime, is Ra'uf 'Ilwan. His transformation from a revolutionary leftist to a rich journalist indicates that is he now part of the establishment and the newly emerging elite that is disconnected from ordinary people and their plights.

Miramar (1967; translated, 1978) provides another critical look at Egyptian society under Nasser. The story centers on residents of a pension, Miramar, in the city of Alexandria and is narrated by four characters: 'Amir Wajdi, Husni 'Allam, Sarhan al-Buhayri, and Mansur Bahi. The novel begins with the decision of Wajdi, a retired journalist, to move to Miramar. With no family and old age taking a toll, Wajdi finds comfort in the fact that the pension is owned by his old friend, Mariana. Other characters begin to arrive at the pension, including Tulbah, an old aristocrat who lost most of his wealth as a result of Nasser's land reforms; al-Buhayri, a government official and part of the new Egyptian elite; 'Allam, a young landowner who spends his time chasing women and driving fast cars; and Bahi, a young man who works in broadcasting. The focus of attention for the main characters is Zohra, a young peasant woman works as a servant. Mahfouz depicts the male characters as corrupt or weak, not fit to lead Egypt and its people. Sarhan al-Buhayri, for example, is depicted as a corrupt and opportunist character. Zohra, who ran away from her family to escape being forced into a marriage that she did not want, is probably the most positive character in the novel, as she only wants to make a better life for herself through hard work and education.

Although Nasser's revolution is not depicted in positive light in many of Mahfouz's works, Mahfouz has said in some of his interviews that he was never against the revolution and its ideals of political and social justice. However, his belief that Nasser's government did not take Egypt in the right direction is evident in his novels and stories. After the Arab defeat in the 1967 Six-Day War with Israel, Mahfouz wrote symbolic short stories that revealed his "sense of questioning challenge, and recrimination which were so characteristic of this period," as Roger Allen observes in *The Arabic Novel: An Historical and Critical Introduction* (1995).

One of Mahfouz's most notable works in the 1970s, a decade in which he published five short-story collections and seven novels, was *al-Maraya* (1972; translated as *Mirror,* 1977)–a semiautobiographical narrative that is unified by the persona the author adopts as its narrator and main character. Although it comprises fifty-five "semi-independent stories," Mahfouz considers it a novel. Basing some of the diverse characters he creates on people he personally knew, Malfouz uses his narrator to comment, as Allen notes, "with extreme frankness about politics, including the Egyptian revolution itself, international relations, and the continuing dilemma regarding the fate of the Palestinian people in their struggle with Israel." Mahfouz continued to criticize oppression and the "police state" in other novels during the 1970s and through the 1980s that, according to Allen, "make it abundantly clear that the values of the Egyptian society and its leadership have given Mahfouz much to be angry about."

Malhamat al-harafish (1977; translated as *The Harafish*, 1994), another significant novel of the 1970s, tells the symbolic story of 'Ashur and his family, who are forced to leave their neighborhood in old Cairo as a result of the plague. Six months later, 'Ashur returns to the neighborhood with his family only to find out that they were the only survivors (thus the name of the family becomes al-Naji–survivor). 'Ashur, an honest and hardworking man, rules the neighborhood with compassion and justice, and his son follows in his footsteps. After his son dies, however, chaos, violence, and greed erupt, and the ordinary people (the *harafish*) are abused by local leaders and the rich. The oppression continues until a descendant of 'Ashur, who also bears his name, leads the *harafish* in a rebellion that brings justice and prosperity. Structurally, *Malhamat al-harafish* is similar to *al-Maraya*–both use, as Menahem Milson remarks in *Najib Mahfuz: The Novelist-Philosopher of Cairo* (1998), an "episodic composition" that is distinct from his approach in the Cairo Trilogy. Thematically, the novel suggests that through unity people can act effectively against political oppression and private corruption. Milson also compares *Malhamat al-harafish* to *Awlad haratina*, with its "semi-mythological setting," though he sees that the later novel differs because it "does not attempt to illustrate any particular era, and focuses primarily on personal desires and fears: sex, greed, the various forms of love, the inevitability of death and the yearning for the infinite."

In the 1980s, the decade in which he won the Nobel Prize, Mahfouz continued to write prolifically, publishing ten novels and four short-story collections. In *al-Baqi mina al-zaman sa'ah* (1982, Only One Hour Remains), he uses the story of a family to survey the development of Egyptian political life from the 1930s until the post–Camp David agreements, signed between Egypt and Israel in 1978. The same year he brought out *Layali alf laylah* (1982; translated as *Arabian Nights and Days*, 1995) a novel that serves as a sequel to the great classic of Arabic literature *Alf laylah wa laylah* (A Thousand and One Nights). Malfouz's novel picks up the story at the point that the original work ends: After he grants Shahrazad life and security, King Shahryar begins a personal quest to seek truth and knowledge, learning from one of the famous characters of the classical work, Sindibad, who reveals to the king his wisdom after many years of travel. At the end of the novel, King Shahryar decides to leave his position as king, choosing to live a simple life. Mahfouz continued to evoke the classical tradition in *Rihlat Ibn Fattumah* (1983; translated as *The Journey of Ibn Fattumah*, 1992), which recalls the travels of Ibn Battutah (died 1377) as preserved in the treatise *Tuhfat al-nuzar fi ghara'ib al-amsar was 'aja'ib al-asfar* (The Jewel of the Observers in the Oddities of Countries and Travels). While Ibn Battutah travels in search of adventure and knowledge, Ibn Fattumah travels in search of a perfect society. Unhappy about his life in his country, *dar al-Islam* (the land of Islam), he travels in search of another society but is disappointed with all of those that he encounters along the way. The ambiguous ending does not clearly reveal whether Ibn Fattumah is able to find a perfect society. Mahfouz may be suggesting that such a society is yet to be realized.

In *Yawma qutila al-za'im* (1985; translated as *The Day the Leader Was Killed*, 1989), Mahfouz takes a critical look at Egypt in the wake of President Anwar Sadat and his policies of *infitah* (economic liberalization), which Mahfouz believed only benefited a small segment of society while hurting the majority of Egyptians. The novel, which tells the story of a young couple who are unable to marry because of the economic downturn, was understood to indicate not only Mahfouz's discontent with Sadat's economic policies but also his repression of activists and intellectuals toward the end of his tenure. Mahfouz, however, supported Sadat's controversial decision to sign a peace agreement with Israel at Camp David. In his final novel published in the 1980s, *Qushtumur* (1989), Mahfouz examines the lives of five friends who grew up in 'Abbasiyyah, the neighborhood where he came of age and lived for many years.

In the 1990s Mahfouz's publications included three nonfiction books on issues of public interest: *Hawla al-din wa al-dimuqratiyya* (1990, On Religion and Democracy), *Hawla al-thaqafah wa al-ta'lim* (1990, On Culture and Education), and *Hawla al-shabab wa al-huriyyah* (1990, On Youth and Freedom). He was almost killed by an assassin on a Friday evening in October 1994. As Mahfouz was entering a friend's car, a man attacked him with a knife, stabbing him in the the neck. As a result of his wound Mahfouz lost the ability to use his right hand, though he regained its use to a great degree with physical therapy and great persistence. He eventually learned to write again on a limited scale and continued to compose short pieces, though he attempted no more novels. He contributed a weekly column for *al-Ahram* with the aid of his friend Mohamed Salmawy, who met regularly with him from 1994 through 2001 and edited their conversations for the newspaper. In celebration of Mahfouz's ninetieth birthday, these columns were collected and translated as *Naguib Mahfouz at Sidi Gaber: Reflections of a Nobel Laureate, 1994–2001* (2001). The first piece in the book comes from a conversation in December of 2000, in which Mahfouz speaks about his life as he approaches his ninetieth birthday:

> The journey of life–well, . . . I feel I am passing the penultimate station, Sidi Gaber station, as it were. When I went to Alexandria by train, I would always get off at Mahattat Masr, the last station on the line. So when I passed Sidi Gaber station I could afford the comfort of knowing that I wasn't getting off quite yet. But I also knew that I was edging closer and closer to Mahattat Masr, that it wouldn't be long before I had to pack my luggage and get ready to exit the train. This is what my birthday feels like this year: It is like passing Sidi Gaber station on the train.

Mahfouz died on 30 August 2006 in a Cairo hospital after suffering from internal bleeding, leaving behind a literary legacy that will never pass away.

References:

Roger Allen, *The Arabic Novel: An Historical and Critical Introduction,* second edition (Syracuse: Syracuse University Press, 1995);

Rasheed El-Enany, *Naguib Mahfouz: The Pursuit of Meaning* (London & New York: Routledge, 1993);

Samir Farid, *Najib Mahfouz wa al-sinama* (Cairo: Kitab al-Thaqafah al-Jadidah, 1990);

Jamal al-Ghitani, *Najib Mahfouz yatadhakkar* (Cairo: Mu'assasat Akhbar al-Yawm, 1987);

Menahem Milson, *Najib Mahfuz: The Novelist-Philosopher of Cairo* (New York: St. Martin's Press, 1998).

Matti Moosa, *The Early Novels of Naguib Mahfouz: Images of Modern Egypt* (Gainesville: University Press of Florida, 1994).

Mohamed Salmawy, ed., *Naguib Mahfouz at Sidi Gaber: Reflections of a Nobel Laureate 1994–2001* (Cairo: American University Press, 2001);

Sasson Somekh, *The Changing Rhythm: A Study of Najib Mahfouz's Novels* (Leiden: Brill, 1973).

Fatima Mernissi
(1940 –)

Azza Basarudin
University of California, Los Angeles

BOOKS: *Beyond the Veil: Male-Female Dynamics in Modern Muslim Society* (Cambridge, Mass.: Schenkman, 1975; revised edition, Bloomington: Indiana University Press, 1987);

Country Reports on Women in North Africa: Libya, Morocco, Tunisia (Addis Ababa: African Training and Research Center for Women, United Nations Economic Commission for Africa, 1978);

Historical Insights for New Population Strategies: Women in Pre-Colonial Morocco, Changes and Continuities (Lahore: Simorgh Women's Resource and Publication Centre, 1978);

The Effects of Modernization on the Male-Female Dynamics in a Muslim Society: Morocco (Ann Arbor, Mich.: University Microfilms International, 1978);

Développement capitaliste et perceptions des femmes dans la société arabo-musulmane: Une illustration des paysannes du Gharb, Maroc (Geneva: Organisation International du Travail, 1981);

Al-Suluk al-jinsi fi mujtama' in Islami taba'i (Beirut: Dar al-Hadatha, 1982);

Al-Hubb fi hadaratina al-Islamiyah (Beirut: Al-Dar al-'Alamiyyah, 1983);

Women in Muslim Paradise (New Delhi: Kali for Women, 1986);

Le harem politique: Le Prophète et les femmes (Paris: Albin Michel, 1987); translated by Mary Jo Lakeland as *The Veil and the Male Elite: A Feminist Interpretation of Women's Rights in Islam* (New York: Basic Books, 1991); translation republished as *Women and Islam: An Historical and Theological Enquiry* (Oxford: Blackwell, 1991);

The Fundamentalist Obsession with Women: A Current Articulation of Class Conflict in Modern Muslim Societies (Lahore: Simorgh Women's Resource and Publication Centre, 1987);

Women, Saints and Sanctuaries (Lahore: Simorgh Women's Resource and Publication Centre, 1987);

Women in Muslim History: Traditional Perspectives and New Strategies (Lahore: Simorgh Women's Resource and Publication Centre, 1989);

Sultanes Oubliées: Femmes chefs d'état en Islam (Paris: Albin Michel, 1990); translated by Lakeland as *The Forgotten Queens of Islam* (Cambridge: Polity Press, 1993; Minneapolis: University of Minnesota Press, 1997);

Chahrazad n'est pas Marocaine: Autrement, elle serait salariée! (Casablanca: Le Fennec, 1991);

Can We Women Head a Muslim State? (Lahore: Simorgh Women's Resource and Publication Centre, 1991);

La peur–modernité: Conflit Islam démocratie (Paris: Albin Michel, 1992); translated by Lakeland as *Islam and Democracy: Fear of the Modern World* (Reading, Mass.: Addison-Wesley, 1992);

Dreams of Trespass: Tales of a Harem Girlhood (Reading, Mass.: Addison-Wesley, 1994);

The Harem Within (London: Doubleday, 1994);

Women's Rebellion and Islamic Memory (London & Atlantic Highlands, N.J.: Zed, 1996);

Les ait-débrouille du haut-atlas (Morocco: Le Fennec, 1997);

Scheherazade Goes West: Different Cultures, Different Harems (New York: Washington Square Press, 2001);

Les Sindbads marocains: Voyage dans le Maroc civique (Rabat: Marsam, 2004).

SELECTED PERIODICAL PUBLICATIONS–UNCOLLECTED: "Unearthing the Present: Women's Rights and Muslim Laws," *Ms. Magazine,* 1 (November–December 1990): 74–76;

"Veil of Tears: Arab Hopes for Democracy, Raised by the Collapse of the Berlin Wall, Were Brutally Crushed by the Gulf War," *New Statesman and Society,* 7 (29 April 1994): 26–29;

"Cyber-Islam Time Zone," *Weltwoche* (Summer 2002);

"The Satellite, the Prince and Scheherazade," *Transnational Broadcasting Studies,* 12 (Spring–Summer 2004).

OTHER: *Le Maroc raconté par ses femmes,* edited by Mernissi (Paris: Société Marocaine des Editeurs Réunis, 1984); translated by Mary Jo Lakeland as

Doing Daily Battles: Interviews with Moroccan Women (London: Women's Press, 1988; New Brunswick, N.J.: Rutgers University Press, 1989).

Fatima Mernissi is a Moroccan sociologist, feminist, and writer who is fluent in English, French, and Arabic. Mernissi has written extensively on the social, political, economic, and religious conditions of women in the Muslim world; her works question religious authoritarianism, deep-seated cultural traditions, and entrenched gender-power dynamics. She has a clear, creative, persuasive, and engaging style; her works have been translated into more than twenty languages, including English, Chinese, German, Indonesian, Turkish, Italian, Urdu, Dutch, Finnish, Greek, and Hungarian. She frequently begins her books by relating her personal experiences in her native Morocco or in her travels abroad. Ann Louise Bardach, who interviewed her in 1993, calls Mernissi the "pre-eminent Koranic scholar of our time." She is a member of various national, regional, and international organizations devoted to the advancement of women's rights in the Muslim world. Maggie Huff-Rousselle quotes Naguib Mahfouz, recipient of the 1988 Nobel Prize in literature, calling Mernissi "the most influential intellectual of the Arab world."

Mernissi was born in 1940 in one of the last remaining harems in Fez. Fez was a stronghold of nationalist struggle against French colonial rule; the nationalists expanded educational opportunities to include girls and women, who were traditionally segregated and secluded. Mernissi thus escaped illiteracy and went on to study political science and sociology at Mohamed V University in Rabat, the Sorbonne in Paris, and Brandeis University in Waltham, Massachusetts. She received her doctorate in sociology from Brandeis in 1974 and became a professor at Mohamed V University.

Mernissi's groundbreaking *Beyond the Veil: Male-Female Dynamics in Modern Muslim Society* (1975) is based on her doctoral dissertation. Combining sociological data from her own interviews with Moroccan "urban petite bourgeoisie" with historical material, Mernissi explores how the Islamic family-law code and local customs relegate women to second-class citizenship. She contrasts the views on female sexuality of the eleventh-century Muslim philosopher al-Ghazali and the twentieth-century Austrian founder of psychoanalysis, Sigmund Freud: while Freud viewed women as frigid and sexually passive, al-Ghazali regarded them as sexually active. Mernissi quotes al-Ghazali: "The virtue of the woman is a man's duty. And the man should increase or decrease sexual intercourse with the woman according to her needs so as to secure her virtue." In Muslim societies female sexuality is considered a source of *fitna* (chaos) that must be restricted by the institution of polygamy and the customs of veiling, seclusion, and sexual segregation. In the modern world, however, high unemployment among men and the expansion of employment opportunities for urban women have facilitated women's entry into male-dominated fields, destabilizing the conventional family structure. Mernissi argues that the regulation of female sexuality is aimed at controlling access to public spaces, reestablishing patriarchal rule, and maintaining social structures and hierarchies. In *Contemporary Sociology* (May 1977) Janet Abu-Lughod called *Beyond the Veil* a "powerful and seminal book whose theoretical insights deserve a careful reading and much further testing," while Suad Joseph argued in *American Anthropologist* (June 1977) that Mernissi "treats Islam outside of historical context, comparing 7th, 10th, and 20th century Islamic scholars with modern Western theorists, thereby producing a monolithic notion of Islam, the Middle East, Middle Eastern women, and the West." Juan Cole and Nikki Keddie question Mernissi's focus on al-Ghazali and Freud: "taking a single thinker to represent each of two huge and changing cultures is a procedure of doubtful validity." Lamia Ben Youssef Zayzafoon contends that Mernissi's interpretation of al-Ghazali contributes to the "cultural mummification" of Moroccan and Muslim societies. Despite such limitations, *Beyond the Veil* paved the way for more-rigorous research into the lives of Muslim women and the challenges confronting Muslim societies in a rapidly changing world.

In the late 1970s and the 1980s Mernissi was a consultant on the North African region and on Moroccan women for the United Nations Educational, Scientific and Cultural Organization (UNESCO), the International Labor Organization (ILO), and the United Nations Population Fund (UNFPA) and wrote several country-report monographs and papers. In her *Country Reports on Women in North Africa: Libya, Morocco, Tunisia* (1978) she shows that the *Muduwana* (Moroccan Family Law), which was supposed to protect citizens regardless of gender, actually supports patriarchal rule; that the penal code deals leniently with men who injure or murder their wives or the wives' lovers in cases of adultery; and that wives must obtain their husbands' permission to apply for passports. In 1982 she published *al-Suluk al-jinsi fi mujtama' Islami taba'i* (Sexual Behavior in Islamic Societies), a collection of articles that had appeared in the Moroccan magazine *Lamalif*. It is widely speculated in Western academic circles that she wrote *La femme dans l'inconscient musulman: Désir et pouvoir* (1982; translated as *Women in the Muslim Unconscious*, 1984), about Muslim women's sexuality, under the pseudonym Fatna Aït Sabbah. In 1983 and 1984,

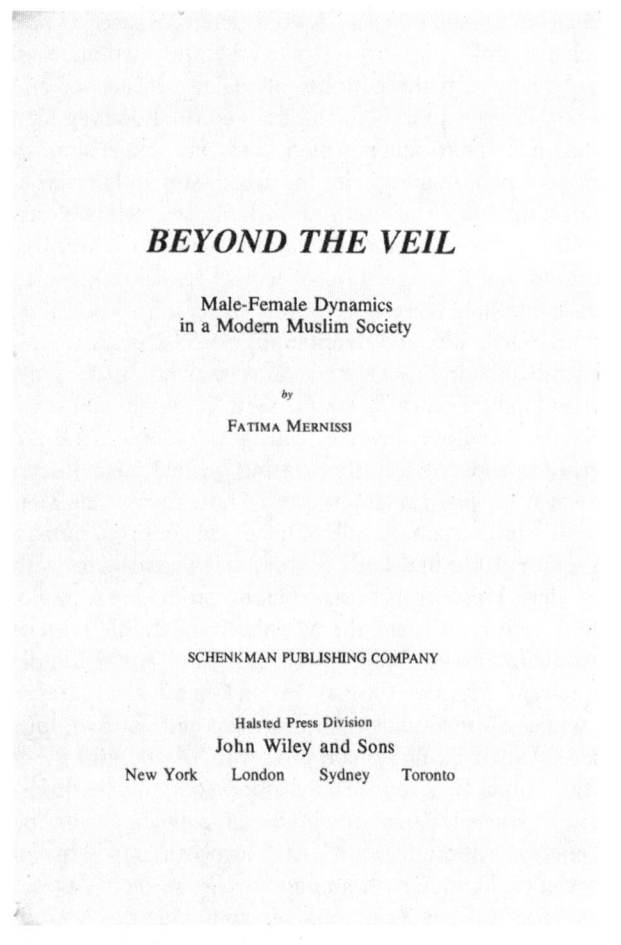

Title page for Fatima Mernissi's first book, 1975 (Thomas Cooper Library, University of South Carolina)

respectively, she published *al-Hubb fi hadaratina al-Islamiyah* (Love in Our Muslim Civilization) and *Le Maroc raconté par ses femmes* (translated as *Doing Daily Battles: Interviews with Moroccan Women*, 1988).

Le Maroc raconté par ses femmes presents life in Morocco through women's eyes. Powerful narratives of struggle and survival emerge from Mernissi's interviews with young and old, literate and illiterate, educated and uneducated, and urban and rural women on issues of family, childcare, employment, poverty, health, education, sexuality, social programs, and religion. The subjects worked in the fields and in factories and as housemaids, teachers, and psychics. Mernissi cautions that the "pervasive male discourse" that projects women as dependent on men for economic security excludes half of the population and obscures women's roles as agents of social transformation. Far from bemoaning their status, the women Mernissi interviewed perceive themselves as "a race of giants doing daily battle against the destructive monsters of unemployment, poverty, and degrading jobs." This book is noteworthy not only for allowing Moroccan women to speak for themselves but also for questioning the notion of objectivity in social science:

> How and according to what rules did I conduct these interviews? I began by violating Rule No. 1 that I learned at the Sorbonne and at the American University where I was trained in "research technique": to maintain objectivity toward the person being interviewed. I cannot be objective towards an illiterate woman, because I have a very special affective relationship to her: I identify with her. I was born in 1940, and very few Moroccan women of that generation had access to writing and still fewer to an advanced education.

Mernissi's monograph *Women in Muslim Paradise* (1986) was inspired by a television program on religion broadcast on the eve of Ramadan that described the unlimited number of eternally youthful, extremely beautiful houris awaiting men after death as a reward for their piety and morality: "By the end of the programme my male university colleague was so excited about the manifold pleasures and delights that were promised to him in paradise that he upset his glass of tea all over his clothes. But I found that I could not share his excitement, since whatever made *him* happy about paradise made *me* suspicious of my chances of achieving happiness there." Mernissi attributes this popular belief to patriarchal Qur'anic hermeneutics and exegesis and counters it with a feminist vision of paradise as "a place where I and everyone else is free from earthly bondage." The monograph includes extensive miniature Persian illustrations and calligraphies of verses from the Qur'an and the *ahadith* (sayings of the Prophet Muhammad).

In 1987 Mernissi published *Le harem politique: Le Prophète et les femmes* (The Political Harem: The Prophet and Women; translated as *The Veil and The Male Elite: A Feminist Interpretation of Women's Rights in Islam*, 1991). The book opens with a description of Mernissi's experience at a grocery stand in Morocco: she asked the grocer, considered a "barometer of public opinion," whether a woman could be a leader of Muslims; his shock and the unfavorable comments of other customers, particularly the usage of a "fatal" *hadith* (the singular of *ahadith*)— "Those who entrust their affairs to women will never know prosperity"—provoked Mernissi to research the methods of authenticating *ahadith*. Drawing on textual analysis and archival research, and assisted by a religious scholar and an expert in Islamic philosophy, Mernissi discovered that the process of *hadith* translation is fraught with power struggles, forgery, and corruption. She notes that the collector of *ahadith* has to establish *isnad* (the chain of trustworthy people who transmitted them from their sources: the companions of the Prophet who heard his speech). She argues that the Prophet Muhammad experimented with ideas of democracy, individual autonomy, and gender justice in his own household but that the best-known narrator of *ahadith,* Abu Hurayra, contaminated the *ahadith* he transmitted with his own patriarchal beliefs. She concludes that "if women's rights are a problem for some modern Muslim men, it is neither because of the Koran nor the Prophet, nor the Islamic tradition, but simply because those rights conflict with the interests of a male elite." Widely cited in publications by Muslim feminists, *Le harem politique* remains one of Mernissi's most influential publications.

Also in 1987 Mernissi published a revised edition of *Beyond the Veil* in which she adds extensive analysis of the social changes that have occurred in Muslim societies, including the rise of fundamentalism, since 1975. That same year she brought out *The Fundamentalist Obsession with Women: A Current Articulation of Class Conflict in Modern Muslim Societies,* in which she argues that fundamentalists are a product of modernity—that is, of confusion and anxiety resulting from unequal access to rapid urbanization and educational opportunities—and asks what motivates those who ascribe to this ideology to be obsessed with controlling women's morality and sexuality. In a fourth 1987 publication, *Women, Saints and Sanctuaries,* she interviews Moroccan women about the local saints and sanctuaries on which they depend to cope with the challenges of their daily lives. She suggests that the practice serves as an alternative to organized religion, which excludes women; but she also notes that worship of saints serves the state by assuaging women's discontent within authoritarian structures and defusing potential organized rebellion.

In *Women in Muslim History: Traditional Perspectives and New Strategies* (1989) Mernissi proposes that the "low image of Muslim women in their own society and in the world at large" has resulted from a selective interpretation of Islamic history. In a review of medieval Muslim literature Mernissi uncovers documentation of women's vigorous social and political lives: women were integral to the first Muslim *ummah* (community); the Prophet Muhammad's wife Khadija was the first person he consulted after receiving his revelation and the one who convinced him of its divine origin; and many *ahadith* are attributed to 'Aisha, the Prophet's favorite wife, who was also involved in political decision-making and led Muslim troops in battle. Mernissi stresses the need to continue excavating and disseminating contributions of women in Islamic history to legitimize contemporary struggles of Muslim women for rights and self-representation.

Title page for Mernissi's 1987 book, translated in 1991 as The Veil and the Male Elite: A Feminist Interpretation of Women's Rights in Islam *(Thomas Cooper Library, University of South Carolina)*

Mernissi begins *Sultanes oubliées: Femmes chefs d'état en islam* (1990, Forgotten Sultanas: Female Heads of State in Islam; translated as *The Forgotten Queens of Islam,* 1993) by addressing the 1988 election of Benazir Bhutto as prime minister of Pakistan. The opposition party declared Bhutto's election a "blasphemy," claiming that "no woman had ever governed a Muslim state between 622 and 1988." Turning to Islam's religious texts and historical documents, Mernissi discovers fifteen female rulers, including Sultana Radiyya; Balqis, the Queen of Sheba; Shajarat al-Durr; Taj al-'Alam; and Turkan Khatun. Some of these women, she notes, even had their names recited in sermons during Friday prayers. In the *International Journal of Middle East Studies* (August 1999) Mary Ann Fay recommended the book "with reservation," pointing out that Mernissi's "lack of training as a historian is evident in her mishandling of historical events and chronology, her ahistoricism, and her superficial reading of the relevant secondary sources of her topic and of women's history in general." Mernissi followed *Sultanes oubliées* with *Can We Women Head a Muslim State?* (1991), in which she combines biographies of women who have headed Muslim countries with Qur'anic exegesis on the subject to refute the popular belief that Muslim women do not have the ability to rule.

In *La peur–modernité: Conflit islam démocratie* (1992; translated as *Islam and Democracy: Fear of the Modern World*, 1992) Mernissi makes use of history, sociology, and Islamic theology to give an affirmative answer to the question "Is Islam compatible with democracy?" Arguing that nothing is more false than the conception of Islam "as a bastion of fanatical despotism in which reason has no place," she distinguishes two strands of Islamic thought: the first requires obedience and order, limits freedom of expression, and places the utmost importance on communal cohesion; the second encourages freedom of opinion and the exercise of reason. For Islam to thrive, she maintains, Muslims must emphasize the second strand in their governments and social systems. She urges Muslims to understand that democracy and human rights are not foreign to Islam and that embracing those concepts does not compromise their faith. The key is to find a balance: "Islam doesn't reject anything; it manages all things. Its ideal schema is equilibrium." Miriam Cooke in the *International Journal of Middle East Studies* (May 1994) applauded Mernissi's analysis but noted, "It is not always clear whom Mernissi is addressing. Sometimes it seems that she is targeting Arabs, then all Muslims, and sometimes even a Western audience. . . . With whom does she identify? Or, does she feel herself to be sufficiently distanced that she can choose the perspective she wants depending on the rhetorical goal?" Other critics fault her call for the West to use "its power to instill democracy in the Arab world" as naive.

Mernissi's *Dreams of Trespass: Tales of a Harem Girlhood* (1994) has become a textbook for courses in women's and gender studies and anthropology, as well as in Middle East studies. She told Public Broadcasting System host Charlie Rose in 1994 that "Westerners have a different harem in mind. Mine is about an extended family and growing up in a household of 30 people, but for the Westerners it is a sexual space." She explained that *Dreams of Trespass* is centered on "powerlessness, of how women make change out of powerlessness." Mernissi paints a picture of resilient, resourceful, and imaginative women who defy Orientalist images of harem life, pointing to her rebellious mother's insistence that her birth be celebrated in a similar fashion to that of a male child and her grandmother's defiance of conventional female roles by riding horses and refashioning clothing for freedom of movement. Within this protective environment Mernissi–whose father was supportive of her mother's rebellion and need for occasional privacy in a large household–learned about the power of knowledge and creative imagination, beauty rituals and secrets, sex and sexuality, the French occupation and World War II, and Arabic music and movies. Her aunt Habiba cautioned her against underestimating the importance of dreams: "The main thing for the powerless is to have a dream. True, a dream alone, without the bargaining power to go with it, does not transform the world or make the walls vanish, but it does help you keep a hold of dignity." One of the most salient lessons in *Dreams of Trespass* concerns the frontiers–unwritten and invisible rules, as well as explicit ones–that are marked out by masculine culture and customs; trespassing across the frontiers "leads only to sorrow and unhappiness. But women dream of trespassing all the time."

Although the book is classified, marketed, and widely understood as a memoir, Mernissi told Rose that much of the content is fictional, including the character of Aunt Habiba. Interviewer Maggie Huff-Rousselle characterizes the book as a "necklace of fairytale vignettes strung out like semi-precious gemstones," while Mary Ellen Sullivan wrote in *Booklist* (June 1994) that it reads as "part fairy tale, part feminist manifesto." Patricia Jeffrey in *Contemporary Sociology* (May 1995) warns that readers who are looking for a link between Mernissi's career and her early life will be disappointed.

Six of the chapters in *Women's Rebellion and Islamic Memory* (1996) were previously published as monographs or in journals or anthologies; the other four are new. In the first chapter, "Writing Is Better than a Face-lift," Mernissi extols writing as "the best remedy for all kinds of crises, all types of wrinkles . . . a miracle the equal of all the revitalizing creams and energizing treatments." Other essays deal with power and knowledge, authoritarian political structures, education and employment of women, population planning, Islamic history, and Qur'anic exegesis on women's rights and sexuality.

Traveling to Western cities to promote *Dreams of Trespass,* Mernissi discovered that her audiences–particularly men–were intrigued by the idea of the harem. While for Mernissi *harem* is another word for "family," for Westerners it is, she told Rose, an "orgiastic feast where men benefited from a true miracle: receiving sexual pleasure without resistance or trouble from the women they had reduced to slaves." *Scheherazade Goes West: Different Cultures, Different Harems* (2001) juxtaposes Eastern and Western portrayals of the harem in history, literature, and art–including paintings by Jean-Auguste-Dominique Ingres, Henri Matisse, and Eugène Dela-

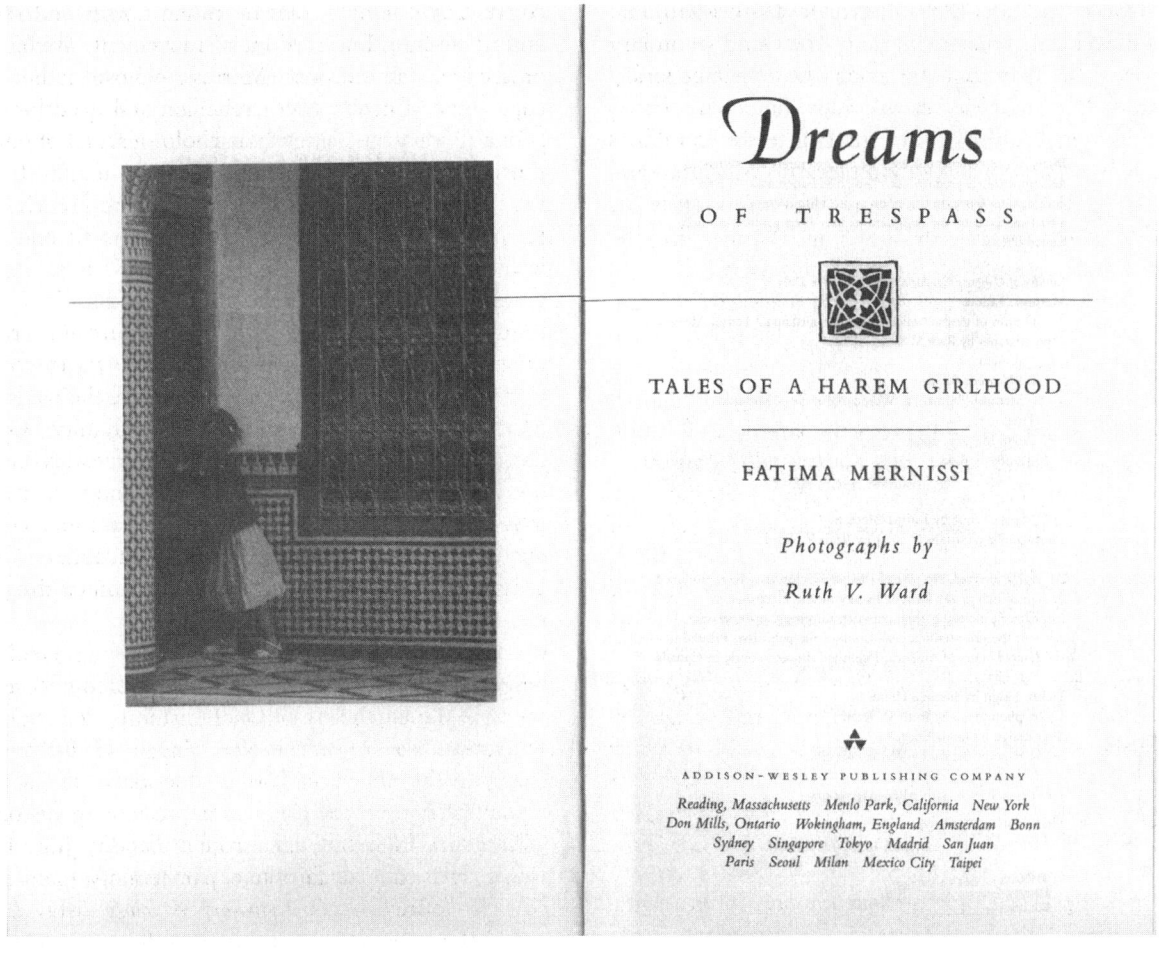

Frontispiece and title page for Mernissi's 1994 book about "how women make change out of powerlessness" (Thomas Cooper Library, University of South Carolina)

croix—to show the erroneousness of the Western view of harem women as passive sexual objects. She includes a personal anecdote about going to a department store to purchase a skirt. Informed by the salesperson that the norm is size 4 or 6, Mernissi realizes that

> maybe size 6 is a more violent restriction imposed on women than is the Muslim veil. . . . I have finally found the answer to my harem enigma. Unlike Muslim men, who use time and space to establish male dominance by excluding women from the public arena, Western men manipulate time and light. He declares that in order to be beautiful, a woman must look fourteen years old. Framing youth as beauty and condemning maturity is the weapon used against women in the West just as limiting access to public space is the weapon used in the East. The objective remains identical in both cultures: to make women feel unwelcome, inadequate, and ugly.

In fact, Mernissi generally designs her own wardrobe, which Huff-Rousselle describes as a combination of Moroccan vest and hip-length caftans that are "gauzy and fragile like a butterfly's wings, and then are fastened together and bordered with heavier, hand-woven, silk tapestry." Huff-Rousselle also characterizes Mernissi as the "modern-day Scheherazade of the Arab world," who combines "creativity with shrewdest intelligence" in her writings as Scheherazade does in her storytelling in *The Thousand and One Nights' Entertainments*.

In 2003 Mernissi shared the Príncipe de Asturias Award for Letters with Susan Sontag. Mernissi was recognized for her scholarship that approaches Muslim women's issues with a profound vision of social transformation and for her emphasis on the necessity of cross-cultural dialogues. She told Huff-Rousselle that the award "gives me hope and vibrancy. It gives me hope for the Arab world, for civil society." In 2004 Mernissi shared the Erasmus Prize with the Syrian philosopher Sadiq Jalal al-Azm and the Iranian religious scholar Abdulkarim Soroush. Mernissi was honored for her writings on modernization and Muslim societies.

Since the late 1980s Mernissi has collaborated with the German-born American artist and photographer Ruth V. Ward on a series of verbal/visual projects dealing with "women's status and identity," such as "The Harem Within: Fear of the Difference," "Vanishing Orient: Papa's Harem Is Shifting to Mama's Civil Society," and "Portraits of Women Weaving Magic Carpets," that have been exhibited in Europe and the United States and are also available on Mernissi's website: <http://www.mernissi.net>. For instance, in "Vanishing Orient" Ward's photograph of two women watching television is accompanied by Mernissi's caption: "The funny part of the story is that while oil-rich Emirs invest furiously in luxurious harems their wives travel luggage-free daily, riding high on satellite TV."

On her website Mernissi discourages her admirers from offering last-minute invitations for her to participate in or speak at events. She notes that "most of the letters from those who contact me reveal that they have no idea about my current research focus: the impact of the satellite on the Arab world" and points out that she practices "tadbir (long-term self-governance planning), a discipline I was taught in my Koranic school in Fez developed by Ibn Baja, known in the West as Avempace (a 12th century Andalusian scholar who was born in the Spanish city of Saragossa and died in Fez in 533 of the Hijra/1138 A.D.). And tadbir implies that you never embark on last minute opportunistic adventures." She suggests that those who are interested in her work should instead "connect with the 'Synergie Civique' network, a group of friends and colleagues who help me clarify whether the futuristic trends of a digitally-induced Arab renaissance I have noticed, are sheer imagination or glimpses of an unexpected reality."

As she notes on her website, Mernissi's current research project is the "digital *ummah*"; she concentrates on "the new sexual and political game produced by the new communication technology's demolition of frontiers." She believes that the future of Arab and Muslim societies lies in their finding creative ways to use information technology to their advantage. In a 2002 interview with Carin Norberg she explained that "information technology increases the youths' self-confidence by strengthening their individual autonomy via self-expression" and that "the translation and publication of many modern works, presently only available in Arabic, would increase the West's knowledge and understanding of problems and development in the Arab world."

Mernissi's generalizations about "Muslim women," "Muslim men," "Arab society," "Islamic practices," "Eastern cultures," and "Western cultures" have been criticized as simplistic; she has been accused of reducing the multiplicity of Muslim experiences, cultures, and communities and of obscuring the fact that the ways in which Islam is interpreted, debated, and legislated are dependent on local contexts. Such oversimplification is troubling for scholars and activists who are laboring to counter stereotypical Eurocentric views of a monolithic Islam. Critics suggest that her work would benefit from more extensive empirical research. Nevertheless, critics and admirers alike acknowledge Mernissi's profound respect for her culture, religion, and country even as she calls for Muslim women to struggle against patriarchy and become active interpreters of their religion. Arguing that Islam, as a faith and a way of life, is compatible with the challenges of globalization, Mernissi identifies illiteracy and authoritarianism as barriers to self-determination for both women and men in postcolonial Muslim societies. She also challenges readers to recognize that women are not passive acceptors of their condition even when they are complicit in their own subjugation. The women Mernissi presents in her scholarship are creative and resourceful agents as they negotiate the dynamics of their faith, personal relationships, communities, and cultures. Fatima Mernissi has been a visiting professor at the University of California at Berkeley, Tulane University, the Massachusetts Institute of Technology, Cornell University, and Harvard University, and a research scholar at the Institut Universitaire de Recherche Scientifique (University Institute for Scientific Research) in Rabat. Her courage and her commitment to improving Muslim women's–and men's–lives continue to inspire other writers, academics, and activists.

Interviews:

Ann Louise Bardach, "Tearing off the Veil: Islamic Fundamentalism's War against Women," *Vanity Fair* (August 1993): 123–127, 154–158;

Charlie Rose, "A Conversation with Fatima Mernissi," *The Charlie Rose Show* (14 September 1994) <http://www.charlierose.com/guests/fatima-mernissi> (accessed 3 October 2008);

Carin Norberg, "I Have Two Lives: Interview with Fatima Mernissi," *News from the Nordic Africa Institute,* 3 (2002): 16–18;

Maggie Huff-Rousselle, "Sheherazade without Borders," *Cairo Times,* 7 (22–28 May 2003): 16–17.

References:

Juan Cole and Nikki Keddie, eds., *Shi'ism and Social Protest* (New Haven: Yale University Press, 1986), pp. 109–111;

Lamia Ben Youssef Zayzafoon, *The Production of the Muslim Woman* (New York: Rowman & Littlefield, 2005), pp. 23–26.

Hanna Mina

(9 March 1924 -   )

Toufoul Abou-Hodeib
University of Chicago

BOOKS: *Al-Masabih al-zurq* (Beirut: Dar al-Fikr al-Jadid, 1954);

Al-Shira' wa al-'Asifah (Beirut: Dar Antun, 1966);

Al-Thalj ya'ti min al-nafidhah (Damascus: Wizarat al-Thaqafah, 1969);

Nazim Hikmat wa-qadaya adabiyyah wa-fikriyah (Damascus: Wizarat al-Thaqafah, 1971);

Al-Shams fi yawm gha'im (Damascus: Wizarat al-Thaqafah, 1973); translated by Bassam Frangieh and Clementina Brown as *Sun on a Cloudy Day* (Pueblo, Colo.: Passeggiata Press, 1997);

Man yadhkuru tilka al-ayyam? by Mina and Najah al-'Attar (Damascus: Wizarat al-Thaqafah, 1974);

Al-Yatir (Damascus: Wizarat al-Thaqafah, 1975);

Baqaya suwar (Damascus: Wizarat al-Thaqafah, 1975); translated by Olive Kenny and Lorne Kenny as *Fragments of Memory: A Story of a Syrian Family* (Austin: Center for Middle Eastern Studies at the University of Texas, 1993);

Al-Abnusah al-bayda' (Damascus: Ittihad al-Kuttab al-'Arab, 1976);

Adab al-harb, by Mina and Najah al-'Attar (Damascus: Wizarat al-Thaqafah, 1976);

Al-Mustanqa' (Damascus: Wizarat al-Thaqafah, 1977);

Nazim Hikmat: Al-Sijn, al-mar'ah, al-hayah (Beirut: Dar al-Adab, 1978);

Al-Marsad (Beirut: Dar al-Adab, 1980);

Nazim Hikmat Tha'iran (Beirut: Dar al-Adab, 1980);

Hikayat Bahhar (Beirut: Dar al-Adab, 1981);

Al-Daqal (Beirut: Dar al-Adab, 1982);

Hawajis fi al-tajribah al-riwa'iyyah (Beirut: Dar al-Adab, 1982);

Al-Marfa' al-ba'id (Beirut: Dar al-Adab, 1983);

Al-Rabi' wa al-kharif (Beirut: Dar al-Adab, 1984);

Ma'sat Dimitriyu (Beirut: Dar al-Adab, 1985);

Kayfa hamaltu al-qalam (Beirut: Dar al-Adab, 1986);

Al-Qitaf (Beirut: Dar al-Adab, 1986);

Hamamah zarqa' fi al-suhub (Beirut: Dar al-Adab, 1988);

Nihayat rajul shuja' (Beirut: Dar al-Adab, 1989);

Al-Walla'ah (Beirut: Dar al-Adab, 1990);

Fawqa al-jabal wa tahta al-thalj (Beirut: Dar al-Adab, 1991);

Al-Rahil 'inda al-ghurub (Beirut: Dar al-Adab, 1992);

Al-Nujum tuhakim al-qamar (Beirut: Dar al-Adab, 1993);

Al-Qamar fi al-mahaq (Beirut: Dar al-Adab, 1994);

Hadatha fi Bitakhu (Beirut: Dar al-Adab, 1995);

'Arus al-mawjah al-sawda' (Beirut: Dar al-Adab, 1996);

Al-Mar'ah dhata al-thawb al-aswad (Beirut: Dar al-Adab, 1996);

Al-Mughamarah al-akhirah (Beirut: Dar al-Adab, 1997);

Al-Rajul al-ladhi yakrahu nafsahu (Beirut: Dar al-Adab, 1998);

Al-Famm al-karazi (Beirut: Dar al-Adab, 1999);

Al-Qissah wa-al-dalalah al-fikriyyah (Riyad: Mu'ssasat al-Yamamah al-Sahafiyyah, [1999]);

Harat al-shahhadin (Beirut: Dar al-Adab, 2000);

Sira' imra'atayn (Beirut: Dar al-Adab, 2001);

Al-Bahr wa al-safinah . . . wa hiyah (Beirut: Dar al-Adab, 2002);

Hina mata al-nahd (Beirut: Dar al-Adab, 2003);

Sharaf qati' tariq (Beirut: Dar al-Adab, 2004);

Al-Riwayah wa al-riwa'i (Damascus: Dar al-Ba'th, 2004);

Al-Dhi'b al-aswad (Beirut: Dar al-Adab, 2005);

Al-Arqash wa al-ghajariyyah (Beirut: Dar al-Adab, 2006);

Al-Nar bayna asabi' imra'ah (Beirut: Dar al-Adab, 2007);

'Ahirah wa nisf majnun (Beirut: Dar al-Adab, 2008).

Hanna Mina's work draws heavily on his life during a turbulent period in Syria's history. He grew up under the French mandate in the poverty that pervaded the country under the control of colonial managers. He was a young activist in the opposition to the oppressive mandate, and as an adult became politically and intellectually involved in the Syrian and Arab literary movement struggling to build a more equitable Syrian state after independence. This rich experience forms the basis for most of his writing, providing valuable historical insight into a sparsely documented era. Mina's use of literature to press for social change has produced a corpus that reflects the everyday struggles of twentieth-century Syrians. Blurring the line between reality and

Front cover for the 1993 English translation of Mina's 1975 novel, Baqaya suwar *(Thomas Cooper Library, University of South Carolina)*

fiction, his writing brings to life characters who are at once historic in their symbolism and familiar in their vividness. He excels at portraying a panoply of faces from his impoverished past, ranging from sailors and dockworkers to farmers and shopkeepers, from lowly drunks to haughty employers.

Hanna Mina was born 9 March 1924 to a poor family in Latakia, Syria's main port on the Mediterranean at the time. His mother, Miryana Mikha'il Zakkur, who was relieved at bearing a boy after three girls, was fraught with fear over the health of her thin and frail child. As she told him later, she would look at him pitifully and wonder: "Could this boy ever become a man and make a living for himself?" His mother and three sisters worked as maids while his father, Salim Hanna Mina, shifted among various jobs, working as a porter, traveling merchant, cobbler, construction worker, silkworm raiser, and sweets vendor. With a weakness for alcohol and women, he often disappeared, leaving the family to fend for itself. When Salim Hanna Mina fell ill, the family went north to the Iskenderun province. They moved several times before settling in the city of Iskenderun, where Mina received his primary and only education at a French school. Even after publishing his first novel, his primary-school degree still hung on the wall of his apartment out of respect to his mother, who regarded it as the highest degree attainable in Syria.

On completing his primary education in 1936 at the age of twelve, Mina started working in the docks to help support his family. For his first job he pushed loaded trolleys between the docked ships and depot at the Iskenderun harbor. Because of his frail frame, he did not last long and was moved to the warehouses where he labeled sacks. In 1939 the province of Iskenderun was annexed to Turkey by the French. Mina and his family returned to Latakia, where he opened a barbershop. Until he established himself as a novelist in his forties, Mina spent his life, like his father before him, shifting among jobs. He worked in a grocery store, in a bike repair shop, as an assistant to a pharmacist, and as a barber. Throughout that time, he read widely. He returned frequently to the Jesuit edition of *A Thousand and One Nights,* which introduced him to a world of adventure and sea life that later influenced his writings. A teacher at the Evangelical school regularly lent him issues of *al-Makshuf* (The Revealed), the Lebanese literary magazine. *Al-Makshuf* was Mina's first window into contemporary literary production in Arabic.

His literary development went hand in hand with his political involvement. Following World War I and the dismantling of the Ottoman Empire, Syria and Lebanon came under French mandate. With the advent of World War II, the people expressed their opposition to the French occupation through demonstrations for independence. Mina participated in these demonstrations, sold progressive newspapers at his shop, and acted as the voice and pen of the illiterate workers in his neighborhood who were petitioning the government for employment rights, food, and education. His activism resulted in several terms in prison. He spoke his experience to Sa'id Huraniyah, who quoted Mina in the introduction he wrote for a 1999 edition of *al-Shira' wa al-'Asifah:* "Prison was my first teacher. I read many books there and I shivered in the face of each new word. A well educated prisoner used to explain difficult words to me and I would cry for joy."

While working as a barber Mina published short stories in Lebanese and Damascene newspapers and literary magazines. Believing that culture was the basis of politics, he used his work as a vehicle to address society's problems. He portrayed the extreme poverty of the Syrian countryside in his first published short story,

"Tiflah li al-bay'" (1945, "A Child for Sale"). An impoverished peasant from the mountains of Latakia, faced with the possibility of seeing his children starve to death, goes to the city to rent out his daughter as a maid. As with his later work, Mina drew on personal experience, in this case his sisters' work as maids, to present a dramatized portrayal of the ailments of Syrian society. "Tiflah li al-bay'" and others of his early short stories were published in the Lebanese newspaper *al-Tariq* (The Path), which he often referred to later as his university.

Mina opposed both the French occupation and Nazism. He volunteered to join the Allied Forces to fight Erwin Rommel in North Africa but was refused because of his frailty. One day in 1946, Mina told Huraniyah, an old man stood at the door of his barbershop looking at him intently: "You are still here.... Don't you remember me? I shaved here right before I left and roamed the world. I volunteered in the Allied army and fought everywhere. I won the battle of Al-'Alamayn against Rommel.... Ah, the things I have seen. And here I return and there you still are: standing the same way, holding the scissors and comb." Mina watched the man walk away, closed down his shop, packed his belongings, and left for Beirut. While this is the story that Mina likes to tell about his departure, in fact his repeated arrests by the French were driving customers away.

Mina spent a few months in Beirut, where he translated one of Maxim Gor'ky's short stories and published his own stories in various literary magazines. Gor'ky's belief in ordinary man and his innate ability to shed the yoke of tradition in order to change for the better had an enormous influence on Mina. Like him, Mina avoided flowery language and sought to write for and about a broad section of people. In Beirut Mina worked as a correspondent for one of the Damascene newspapers, *al-Insha'* (The Composition). In less than a year, he was called to work in Damascus as a literary editor and a specialist in foreign affairs. He later became editor of *al-Insha'* and of literary sections in several other newspapers. He married Miryam Dimyan Sim'an, with whom he had five children. After Husni al-Za'im's military coup of March 1949, Mina fled to Beirut for fear of the new regime's crackdown on intellectuals and social activists. The regime proved to be short-lived, however, and Mina returned to Damascus in August of the same year.

His work in journalism introduced him to active young writers, such as Shawqi Baghdadi, Mawahib al-Kayyali, Sa'id Huraniyah, Liyan Dirani, Shihadah al-Khuri, Salah Dahni, and Hasib Kayyali, with whom he formed the Syrian Writers' Union in 1951. In its literary manifesto, the Union declared its commitment to struggle for the nation, the people, progress, and just peace. Mina participated in the first conference of 1954 when the Syrian Writers' Union became the Arab Writers' Union. The conference was first of its kind in bringing together leading figures in modern Arabic literature including Marun 'Abbud and Husayn Muruwwah from Lebanon, Yusaf Idris from Egypt, 'Abd al-Wahhab al-Bayati from Iraq, 'Abd al-Rahman Shuqayr from Jordan, and Nasir Abu Haymad from Bahrain.

The same year, Mina published his first novel, *al-Masabih al-zurq* (1954, Blue Lanterns), referring to the inhabitants of Latakia who used to paint their lanterns blue during World War II to discourage air raids. While not the subject of the novel, the war provides the setting for the story of the sixteen-year-old Faris and his poor Latakia neighborhood. Faris, who loses his job when his employer is called to serve in the military, finds difficulty dealing with the emptiness that ensues and the cramped living conditions in his quarter. The emptiness is displaced when Faris falls in love with his neighbor, Randa, who works with Faris's mother for the French tobacco monopoly. Faris decides to join the Allied forces in order to earn enough money to get married. While he is away, Randa dies of tuberculosis, and Faris is later killed fighting in Libya. Mina's vivid depiction of secondary characters and everyday life in the shadow of war is related in a trite plot that was a source of much criticism. The novel is richest in its description of life in Latakia, from the clashes with French authorities to Café Shawqi, where the inhabitants of the quarter go to gamble and drink. Through the juxtaposition of the political coming-of-age of the protagonist and the awakening of a neighborhood, Mina presents his vision of a people rising against the injustices of history and fighting for their independence.

Many critics object to the ideological encumberances of *al-Masabih al-zurq*. As Mina later admitted, his political preaching disturbed the sequence of events and dominated the presentation of the characters. Nevertheless, along with Naguib Mahfouz's *Zuqaq al-Midaqq* (1947; translated as *Midaq Alley,* 1966) and 'Abd al-Rahman al-Sharqawi's *al-Ard* (1954; translated as *Egyptian Earth,* 1962), literary critics consider *al-Masabih al-zurq* one of the first novels to embrace social realism in modern Arabic literature. Social realism, an artistic movement which developed toward the end of the nineteenth century, values unsparing, accurate representations of the psychological and material realities of life. The Arab intellectuals adopted social realism and the notion of political commitment in the wake of World War II. Those ideals were espoused by both the Syrian Writers' Union and the Arab Writers' Union in its first conference in 1954. *Al-Masabih al-zurq* indelibly linked Mina's work to that movement.

In 1956 Mina started working on his second novel, which was a response to the Suez Canal conflict and the legendary stories of the heroism of Arab sailors during that war. This work came to a halt with the formation of the United Arab Republic in 1958, when Mina went into voluntary exile after the newly formed government accused him of being a communist. His wife and children accompanied him for eight years on most of his peregrinations from Beirut to Japan, China, the Soviet Union, and several European cities. This period remains relatively obscure in Mina's life and devoid of any writing. He taught Arabic conversation and literary syntax at the University of Beijing. He also presented literary programs on the Arab radio station in Budapest. A year before his return from exile, Mina published his second novel, *al-Shira' wa al-'asifah* (1966, The Sail and the Storm). The novel explores the character of Abu Zahdi al-Turusi, whose struggle with the sea is intertwined with the conflict between the classes and the struggle of the Syrian people against French occupation. Mina says he meant for this work to portray an odyssey of man's confrontation with history, represented symbolically through his struggle with nature.

After al-Turusi loses his ship in a wild storm, his attention turns to a small popular café that he has carved out of the cliffs facing the sea, turning it into a meeting place for fishermen, sailors, and their friends from all walks of life. As in *al-Masabih al-zurq*, World War II is the backdrop. The outbreak of the war brings news of the struggle against French rule. The café becomes a focus of activity for the local nationalist group, and al-Turusi even smuggles arms for the resistance. His fame increases when he saves another sailor from his sinking boat during a storm, turning him into a local hero. He incites the workers to form a union in order to safeguard their rights in their struggle against the local employers and their thugs. His engagement, however, remains without political motives. He watches political events pass him by and believes politics to be nothing but abstract discussions and theory: "Why do they get so excited about politics? Whose side am I on? I am not on anyone's side, neither do I stand against anyone. I am a nationalist who lacks any philosophy."

Throughout, al-Turusi expresses his wish to go back to the sea, but circumstances thwart him. In the end, he decides to sell his café and set sail with a partner, affirming that he can maintain his independence while continuing to struggle with life. Al-Turusi's situation is paralleled by the Syrian people's confrontation with the French mandate and their return to clamoring for their independence after the end of World War II. According to Mina, al-Turusi's return to sea with a communist partner signifies a change in the character of the protagonist and his willingness to engage in collaborative effort. The uncomplicated narrative sequence of *al-Shira' wa al-'asifah* is presented in the form of a heroic saga. The affirmation of man's capability to surmount all obstacles has led many critics to compare Mina's novel to Ernest Hemingway's *The Old Man and the Sea* (1952).

Though Mina's first two novels were published twelve years apart, he had completed the bulk of his second novel two years after the first, before leaving Syria. Critics noted the aesthetic difference between the two works. Mina abandoned the traditional narrative form that crippled his first novel for a more poetic language and a more accomplished literary aesthetic. *Al-Shira' wa al-'asifah* brought Mina immediate recognition in the Arab world and won him the Syrian State's Encouragement Award in 1967. Nevertheless, when he returned to Latakia he could not find a job. Already forty-four years of age, he was unable to find even a position as a barber's assistant. About to start his own barbershop in a converted garage, he was called by a friend in Damascus to write programs in colloquial Arabic for radio.

Al-Thalj ya'ti min al-nafidhah (1969, Snow Comes in Through the Window) represents another shift in Mina's writing into a more symbolic narrative. He started the book in China and Budapest, but it was completed only after his return to Syria. Drawing on his experience in politics and exile, it explores the life of a political activist and his encounter with injustice in society. The novel is set in the early 1950s, when the euphoria of the newly acquired independence of Lebanon and Syria had worn off, and the complications of the political and social realities began to emerge. Fayyad, a Syrian writer and university professor involved in politics, escapes oppression in Syria, finding refuge with an impoverished friend in Beirut. The narrative concerns Fayyad's quest for inner peace as he restlessly moves between friends' homes and from job to job. He becomes familiar with the economic difficulties his friends have to deal with and their constant struggle for social justice. In the various jobs he undertakes he is also exposed to the life of luxury and extravagance that other people lead in Beirut and to their greed and exploitation of the poor.

Fayyad, who never had to do manual work, begins to realize the importance of alloying political activism with intellect, an attempt Mina articulates using Christian metaphors. He refers to Fayyad as the "chief cornerstone" rejected by builders and to his struggle as a "cross to bear." Toward the end of the novel, Fayyad is sent to prison after the secret printing press he had used to print revolutionary pamphlets is discovered. When he is released six months later, Fayyad returns to Damascus to confront his pursuers.

Mina wrote this novel during the rise of the petite bourgeoisie in Syria, to which the protagonist belonged. Again, Mina grounds his fiction in his personal experience as a political activist and in the environment he knew to portray a social reality and its attendant problems.

Mina's first three novels established his reputation as a leading Arabic literary figure. In 1969 he secured a job with the Ministry of Culture and National Guidance as an adviser on publication and translations. After this first sign of stability, Mina published a collection of short stories, *al-Abnusah al-bayda'* (1976, White Ebony), and a series of three novels: *Al-Shams fi yawm gha'im* (1973; translated as *Sun on a Cloudy Day*, 1997); *Al-Yatir* (1975, The Anchor); and *Baqaya suwar* (1975; translated as *Fragments of Memory: A Story of a Syrian Family*, 1993). Whereas Mina's first three novels focused on struggle against oppression, his new works dealt with the theme of liberation from within. The theme of class struggle and the parallel search for the self, previously alluded to in *al-Thalj ya'ti min al-nafidhah*, reappears in *al-Shams fi yawm gha'im*. This work also relies on the superimposition of two contrasting modes of existence, misery and luxury, to express the reality of social injustice. In addition to these recurrent themes, Mina proposes that the liberation of the human soul from the shackles of outmoded concepts and traditions is a prerequisite to national liberation.

Al-Shams fi yawm gha'im is set in the 1920s, during the French mandate in Syria. The protagonist, whose name is never revealed, is a bourgeois, intellectual youth who sympathizes with the cause of the working class and believes that his father's business with the French contributes to their oppression. The novel uses symbolism to elucidate the tensions in the narrative. The most acclaimed example of Mina's mastery of this form is the climactic scene of the "dagger dance." The protagonist seeks the help of a tailor to learn the traditional dance, which, for him, is an expression of belonging and an attempt to move from his father's exploitative feudalism to the world of the destitute. Symbolizing the failure of this endeavor, the protagonist's father reappropriates the dagger, a family heirloom, and uses it to murder the tailor, the protagonist's mentor and friend. The abundance of ideas, allusions, and symbols in this work have elicited mixed reactions from critics. Some criticized them as a hindrance to the reader's ability to focus on a single topic in the novel. Others perceived this ambiguity not only as Mina's way of broadening his message, but also as a way for him to subtly criticize the contemporary political regime in Syria.

This exploration of the self is continued in *al-Yatir*, where the half-man, half-beast character of Zakariya al-

Front cover for the 1997 English translation of Mina's 1973 novel al-Shams fi yawm gha'im *(Thomas Cooper Library, University of South Carolina)*

Mirsanli is only able to find himself after losing his way. When a whale shows up in the city of Iskenderun, threatening to destroy the port, al-Mirsanli dives under the creature, ties it up, and kills it. He then sells its entrails to Zakhriyadis, the Greek owner of the inn where al-Mirsanli habitually gets drunk. Al-Mirsanli is later led to believe that the whale was stuffed with diamonds and gold, so he kills (or believes he has killed) Zakhriyadis, who refused to return the treasures. Al-Mirsanli escapes to the forest, angry at the city that had turned its back on him. The natural existence of the forest replaces his city life of sex, alcohol, tobacco, and coffee. He then meets the shepherdess Shakibah, who tames him and nurses him until one day the whale returns. Al-Mirsanli conquers his anger and his feeling of injustice and heads back to the city, where the fishermen join him in the fight against their common enemy, the whale.

After the mythological novels *al-Shams fi yawm gha'im* and *al-Yatir,* Mina wrote a thinly disguised autobiography, *Baqaya suwar,* an honest portrayal of family life and its social environment in Latakia during the 1920s. Dedicated to his mother, the narrative unfolds through the eyes of a child between the ages of three and eight. It follows the family of six as they wander from city to countryside and back struggling for survival. Critics have rightfully pointed out the subtle interplay between the narrators in this work. The "I" refers at one and the same time to a first-person Mina, the protagonist, and a third-person Mina, the author. This device allows the narrative to move outside the perspective of a child, recollecting childhood from the point of view of an adult. The protagonist in the novel is continuously inhabiting other people's subjectivities, knowledgeable of their thoughts, and seeing the world through their points of view.

Although at the surface the novel is not blatantly political and lacks the overladen symbolism of his previous sea novels, *al-Shira' wa al-'asifah* and *al-Yatir,* Mina continues to take up the cause of the underprivileged class. This time he delves into the ignorance and poverty pervading peasant communities that subsist by raising silkworms and the havoc wreaked upon their lives by the introduction of synthetic silk. The interplay between first and third persons turns the novel into more than a purely personal history, it becomes also a story of a prototypical Syrian family and its social environment in the first half of this century. In that respect, his autobiography has been regarded as a historical account of the epoch that followed the collapse of the Ottoman Empire and the French mandate, bringing the conflict between the peasants and landowners and the ensuing peasant revolution into the canon of recorded Syrian history. *Baqaya suwar* closes with the family traveling in a ramshackle carriage drawn by a single horse. The mother covers her children with a blanket: "Sleep my little ones....We are going to the city."

Al-Mustanqa' (1977, The Swamp), written two years later, begins when that family arrives in the city. This sequel traces the family's life in Iskenderun until around 1939 and the outbreak of World War II. As in the first part, *al-Mustanqa'* goes beyond the lives of the narrator and his family by exploring the impact of the international economic crisis on the city of Iskenderun. The name of the work refers to the Saz neighborhood where the whole city dumped its garbage. Mina describes the poverty of the neighborhood and its inhabitants, the strife of the dockworkers and the railway workers of the city, and the struggles that marked the beginning of the formation of workers' unions in Syria. With the publication of these two works, Mina established himself as a master of the autobiographical novel.

From that point on, Mina's literary production continued at the rate of a novel a year. Following his semiautobiographical work, Mina returned to the world of the sea and wrote the trilogy: *Hikayat bahhar* (1981, A Sailor's Yarn), *al-Daqal* (1982, The Mainmast), and *al-Marfa' al-ba'id* (1983, The Far Haven) which, along with *al-Shira' wa al-'asifah* and *al-Yatir,* won him the title of "the novelist of the sea." A recurrent device in his sea novels is the model of the traditional epic hero who stands up with the weak against the tyranny of the rich and powerful elite. Such was the character of al-Turusi in *al-Shira' wa al-'asifah* and of al-Mirsanli in *al-Yatir.* Sa'id Hazzum's father, a courageous sailor feared and admired by everyone, disappears during a pursuit by the French mandate forces. The sea trilogy is an odyssey of Hazzum's quest to find his father, and it constitutes Mina's longest work.

As old age forces Sa'id Hazzum to leave his work at sea, he reminisces about his life and the paternal heritage he has felt compelled to follow. His father started his maritime career in Anatolian Turkey on a riverboat, which he had left after a heroic rescue in a storm on the river. He returns to his Arab neighborhood in Iskenderun where his heroism is enhanced when he defends it against attacks from other neighborhoods and against Turkish authorities. When he disappears without a trace, the story develops into a son's search for the lost father, which is paralleled by a quest for the self. On Iskenderun's annexation by Turkey, Sa'id sails to Latakia with his family where he further complicates his life by embroiling himself in an affair with Katrin, his employer's wife and his father's former mistress. Although her husband dies while at sea, Katrin marries another man, who also employs Sa'id. Even after this second husband dies, she spurns Sa'id for a Greek sailor with whom she departs on a search for Sa'id's father. In jobless despair, Sa'id sails after them, hoping to find both his father and Katrin. On a seemingly endless quest, his adventures in Latakia unappreciated, Sa'id nears the end of his life at the verge of madness, his fate unresolved and the search unsettled. The trilogy is about the search for the father and the permanent struggle of exile.

Mina elaborates on the theme of exile in *al-Rabi' wa al-kharif* (1984, Spring and Autumn). The life of Karam, the protagonist of this work, parallels Mina's experience in Beijing and Budapest. The novel was not received as well as his previous work and has been criticized for its flatness and the dominance of the narrator's personality at the expense of the other characters in the novel. The third part of his autobiography, *al-Qitaf* (1986, The Harvest), suffered a similar fate at the hands of the critics. *Al-Qitaf* deals with the last part of the fifteen years covered by the autobiographic trilogy when Mina was working at the docks and in various other jobs to help support his family. The most significant work of Mina's profuse production after the publication of *Hikayat bahhar* in 1981 is the novel *Nihayat rajul shuja'* (1989, End of a Brave Man). Mina has characterized it as a return to the sea and the world of the harbor. The novel, set in the 1950s, addresses port life and its conflicts through the character of "Wild Mufid," a young man who struggles against the French mandate and against the overlords of the harbor. In spite of his many personal victories, he refuses to collaborate with the other workers in their demands for rights and unions and consequently suffers a tragic end.

In 1993 *Nihayat rajul shuja'* was turned into a popular television series in Syria directed by Najdat Isma'il Anzur. The prominent Syrian filmmaker Muhammad Shahin directed *al-Shams fi yawm gha'im* (1985) and *Ah, ya bahr* (1994), based on *al-Daqal*. Nabil al-Malih, another prominent filmmaker, based his *Baqaya suwar* (1979) on Mina's novel of the same name. Iraqi Qays al-Zubaydi's *al-Yazirli* (1974), which was banned in Syria, is loosely based on one of Mina's short stories—"'Ala al-akyas" (1976, On the Sacks).

Hanna Mina is regarded by many as one of the most prominent writers in the Arab world, and his works have been translated into English, French, Russian, Chinese, and Spanish. In 1990, he was awarded the Sultan 'Uways Award, one of the most prestigious literary awards in the Arab world. Even though Mina's early work suffered from its overemphasis on political and ideological messages, he was able later to blend his messages into his fiction artistically so that the dialectics of fear and courage, of weakness and strength, of failure and achievement are presented in a manner that portrays the complexity of human nature. Mina's literary corpus, based on his personal experience, faithfully portrays a sparsely documented part of Syrian history. For him, the importance of the past lies in the possibility of change for the future. He was able to bridge what is viewed as a gap between literary and colloquial Arabic, the former commonly perceived as intellectual and the latter the spoken language of the people. He was able through historical narratives to express his calls for social justice to a broad audience. Despite his fame, Mina in the 13 May 2001 issue of *al-Bayan* said of himself: "I had not imagined, even when I was forty, that I would become a famous writer. I was born by mistake, raised by mistake, even wrote by mistake."

Interview:

Hiwarat wa ahadith (Beirut: Dar al-Fikr al-Jadid, 1992).

References:

Roger Allen, *The Arabic Novel: An Historical and Critical Introduction* (Syracuse, N.Y.: Syracuse University Press, 1995), pp. 83–85;

Allen, ed., *Modern Arabic Literature* (New York: Ungar, 1987), pp. 219–224;

Muhammad al-Baridi, *Hanna Minah: Katib al-kifah wa al-farah* (Beirut: Dar al-Adab, 1993);

Muhammad Dakrub, ed., *Hanna Minah: Hiwarat wa-ahadith fi al-hayah wa al-kitabah al-riwa'iyyah* (Beirut: Dar al-Fikr al-Jadid, 1992);

Murad Kasuhah, *Al-Manfa al-siyasi fi al-riwayah al-'Arabiyyah* (Damascus: Dar al-Hasad, 2000);

Muhammad Kamil al-Khatib, *'Alam Hanna Minah al-riwa'i* (Beirut: Dar al-Adab, 1979);

Hamdi Sakkut, *The Arabic Novel: Bibliography and Critical Introduction, 1865–1995* (Cairo & New York: The American University in Cairo Press, 2000), pp. 74–77;

Firyal Kamil Samahah, *Rasm al-shakhsiyyah fi riwayat Hanna Minah* (Beirut: Al-Mu'assasah al-'Arabiyyah li al-Dirasat wa al-Nashr, 1999);

Faysal Sammaq, *Al-Riwayah al-Suriyyah: Nash'atuha wa-tatawwuruha, madhahibuha* (Damascus, 1984);

Sammaq, *Al-Waqi'iyyah fi al-riwayah al-Suriyyah* (Damascus: Dar al-Ba'th al-Jadidah, 1979);

Jamal Shihayyid and Heidi Toëlle, eds., *Al-Riwayah al-Suriyyah al-mu'asirah* (Damascus: French Institute of Arabic Studies, 2001);

Élisabeth Vauthier, *Le roman Syrien de 1967 à nos jours* (Paris: L'Harmattan, 2002), pp. 119–122, 172–175.

Abdelrahman Munif
(29 May 1933 – 24 January 2004)

Sebastian Maisel
Grand Valley State University

BOOKS: *Al-Ashjar wa ightiyal Marzuq* (Beirut: Al-Mu'assasah al-'Arabiyyah li al-Dirasat wa al-Nashr, 1973);

Qissat hubb Majusiyyah (Beirut: Al-Mu'assasah al-'Arabiyyah li al-Dirasat wa al-Nashr, 1974);

Sharq al-Mutawassit (Beirut: Dar al-Tali'ah, 1975);

Sibaq al-masafa al-tawilah (Beirut: Al-Mu'assasah al-'Arabiyyah li al-Dirasat wa al-Nashr, 1976);

Al-Nihayat (Beirut: Al-Mu'assasah al-'Arabiyyah li al-Dirasat wa al-Nashr, 1977); translated by Roger Allen as *Endings* (London: Quartet, 1989);

Hina tarakna al-jisr (Beirut: Dar al-'Awdah, 1979);

'Alam bi la khara'it, by Munif and Jabra Ibrahim Jabra (Beirut: Al-Mu'assasah al-'Arabiyyah li al-Dirasat wa al-Nashr, 1982);

Mudun al-milh: Al-Tih (Beirut: Al-Mu'assasah al-'Arabiyyah li al-Dirasat wa al-Nashr, 1984); translated by Peter Theroux as *Cities of Salt* (New York: Random House, 1987);

Mudun al-milh: Al-Ukhdud (Beirut: Al-Mu'assasah al-'Arabiyyah li al-Dirasat wa al-Nashr, 1985); translated by Theroux as *The Trench* (New York: Pantheon, 1991);

Mudun al-milh: taqasim al-layl wa al-nahar (Beirut: Al-Mu'assasah al-'Arabiyyah li al-Dirasat wa al-Nashr, 1989); translated by Theroux as *Variations on Night and Day* (New York: Pantheon, 1993);

Mudun al-milh: Al-Munbat (Beirut: Al-Mu'assasah al-'Arabiyyah li al-Dirasat wa al-Nashr, 1989);

Mudun al-milh: Badiyat al-zulumat (Beirut: Al-Mu'assasah al-'Arabiyyah li al-Dirasat wa al-Nashr, 1989);

Al-An huna aw sharq al-Mutawassit marratan ukhra (Beirut: Al-Mu'assasah al-'Arabiyyah li al-Dirasat wa al-Nashr, 1991);

Al-Dimuqratiyyah awalan, al-dimuqratiyyah da'iman (Beirut: Al-Mu'assasah al-'Arabiyyah li al-Dirasat wa al-Nashr, 1991);

Sirat madinah (Damascus: Al-Mu'assasah al-'Arabiyyah li al-Dirasat wa al-Nashr, 1994); translated by Samira Kawar as *Story of a City: A Childhood in Amman* (London: Quartet, 1998);

Abdelrahman Munif (from the dust jacket for The Trench, *1991 (Thomas Cooper Library, University of South Carolina)*

Marwan Qassab Bashi: Rihlat al-fan wa al-hayat (Beirut: Al-Markaz al-Thaqafi al-Arabi, 1996);

'Urwat al-zaman al-bahi (Beirut: Bisan li al-Nashr wa al-Tawzi', 1997);

Ard al-sawad (Beirut: Al-Mu'assasah al-'Arabiyyah li al-Dirasat wa al-Nashr, 1999);

Rihlat du' (Beirut: Al-Mu'assasah al-'Arabiyyah li al-Dirasat wa al-Nashr, 2001);

Al-'Iraq: Hawamish min al-tarikh wa al-muqawamah (Casablanca: Al-Markaz al-Thaqafi al-'Arabi li al-Nashr wa al-Tawzi', 2003).

SELECTED PERIODICAL PUBLICATIONS–
UNCOLLECTED: "Other Voices–Saudi Bomb Attack an Act of Despair," *Jinn Magazine* (2 July 1996) <http://www.pacificnews.org/jinn/stories/2.14/960702-bomb.html (accessed 20 October 2008);

"Fateh al-Moudarres, Syrian Artist Who Fought for Justice with Brush, Pen," *al-Jadid*, 5, no. 29 (Fall 1999);

"Al-Tarikh dhakira idhafiyna li'l-insan," *al-Karmel*, 63 (Spring 2000): 86–104;

"Longing for Baghdad," *al-Ahram Weekly*, no. 634 (17–23 April 2003);

"The Novel: A Homeland and a Passion," *al-Ahram Weekly*, no. 678 (19–24 February 2004).

Abdelrahman Munif was one of the most prominent Arab novelists of the modern era. The jury's citation for the 1998 Cairo Award for Novels recognized his wide appeal: "It seems that Munif writes at the same time about each individual Arab country as well as all Arab countries together." Often considered a Saudi Arabian writer, he could also be called an Iraqi writer, or a Jordanian, a Syrian, or even a Palestinian. Although he had roots in several states of the Arab East, he belonged to the entire Arab world. As Tariq Ali suggested in his 1 February 2004 tribute in *Counterpunch*, Munif was a patriarch of Arab literature.

Born 29 May 1933 in Amman, Jordan, to an Iraqi mother and a Saudi Arabian father from Najd, Munif spent his childhood and adolescent years in the Jordanian capital. He drew on memories of this time for his autobiographical novel *Sirat madinah* (1994; translated as *Story of a City: A Childhood in Amman*, 1998). His father was a trader who often traveled to distant places in the neighboring countries, exposing his son to a variety of different Arab and non-Arab cultures in the area. During summer vacations, which Munif spent mostly in Saudi Arabia, he heard stories of the Bedouins, farmers, and merchants, and learned about the importance of roots, tradition, and identity. He lived for periods in Amman, Qasim, and Baghdad, his mother's native city. In *Sirat madinah* he wrote of missing Baghdad: "although we were separated from Baghdad by a great distance and different accent, Baghdad was very close."

After high school, Munif left for Iraq in 1952 to study law. Because of his political activities and involvement with the Baath (Resurrection) Party, which was associated with Arab nationalism and unity, he and other Arab students were expelled after two years. He continued his education at Cairo University, where Gamal Abdel Nasser's Pan-Arabism and the revolutionary movement led him to become a secular socialist militant. In 1958 he moved to Yugoslavia to finish his studies, earning his Ph.D. in economic sciences from the University of Belgrade in 1961.

In the following years Munif worked in the oil sector in Syria for the Syrian Oil Company, resuming his political activism as a member of the Baath Party, which resulted in the revocation of his Saudi citizenship in 1963. With his realization of the failing of the Pan-Arab movement, particularly the tristate union of Egypt, Syria, and Iraq, the increasing internal divisions between the Syrian and the Iraqi factions of the Baath Party, as well as the defeat of the leading Arab nations in the 1967 Six-Day War, Munif became disillusioned with politics. He moved to Lebanon in 1973 where he started to write for the Lebanese newspaper *al-Balagh* (The Report).

In his first novel, *al-Ashjar wa ightiyal marzuq* (1973, The Trees and the Killing of Marzuq), Munif portrays two men who begin to confront the difficult realities of their lives. It begins with a casual meeting between the men, Elias Nahle and Mansur. Elias, a restless man who often changes jobs, is always looking for a partner for life, having suffered the death of his wife, Hannah. He wonders why people cut down trees, because he sees a resemblance between trees and women. He believes that Hannah was the only tree in his life, symbolizing everything growing, continuing, and real. If a tree is cut down, he feels, things begin to lose their meanings, their coherency. Elias represents people who deal and cope with daily life while always feeling the burden of reality. On the other hand, Mansur represents the intellectual who is pessimistic, adrift, always complaining. He studies in the West and returns as a professor. Soon afterward, he is drafted into the army and experiences the defeat of the Six-Day War. Like many others, he criticizes the failures of the Arab regimes and governments, and as a result, he loses his job. Thus, he reaches a point where he is unable to maintain relationships with other people.

Over the next decade Munif continued write as well as to work in the oil industry. In 1975, at the time of the creation of the Progressive Front between the Iraqi Baath Party and the Iraqi Communist Party, he moved back to Baghdad, where he became the editor of the monthly journal *an-Naft wa't-tanmiya* (Oil and Development), a magazine published by the Iraqi Ministry of Oil. His enchantment with the new political trends did not last long and by 1978 he was quoted as saying that the Iraqi system was no better than that of Saudi Arabia. During the mid to late 1970s he increasingly concentrated on his writing, producing several works.

One of Munif's most celebrated novels, *Sharq al-Mutawassit* (1975, East of the Mediterranean), deals with an all too common pattern of political life in the Middle East: captivity, exile, and return to the home-

Front cover for the 1987 English translation of al-Tih (1984), the first volume in Munif's five-volume masterwork, Mudun al-milh (Thomas Cooper Library, University of South Carolina)

land. Ragab, the main character, experiences the harsh reaction of the state to his political beliefs, and even more important, the beliefs of his friends. He is arrested and taken to an unidentified Arab prison. Munif describes in detail the torture and humiliation that occurs in prisons throughout the Arab world. Later, Ragab decides to write about his encounters, even though he realizes that words are no longer useful. The book he writes has neither logic nor context. His aim is to create a text in which all the characters talk to each other at the same time without listening, because "a human being in the lands east of the Mediterranean is cheaper than anything and a cigarette stub has more value to him."

Munif's deep knowledge of the oil business, politics, and social conditions served him well in his novel *Sibaq al-masafa al-tawilah* (1976, The Long-Distance Race) which treats the machinations of Western powers for oil and the 1953 coup engineered against the popularly elected Iranian prime minister Mohammad Mosaddeq, which restored Shah Mohammad Reza Pahlavi to the throne. The story is told from the viewpoint of a British officer who falls in love with Shirin, an Iranian woman.

Munif's concern for the environment is evident in *al-Nihayat* (1977; translated as *Endings*, 1989), a collection of short stories centered on a small community at the edge of the desert, al-Tiba, which faces great distress because of an ongoing drought. As supplies are short, all the hopes of the desperate people lie in the building of a dam. To eke out their marginal existence, the men of the village go off to hunt in the desert, sometimes serving as guides for people from the city. One of these trips, which is headed by the main character Assaf, the outsider of the community and guardian of wildlife, results in his death. The book ends with several stories that contribute to the portrayal of the admirable Assaf and the mourning of his death starts a healing process in the village. The people become encouraged and motivated to demand the dam as a positive step for the whole community. Through these stories, Munif shows a society that has lost the proper balance between humans and the environment. But he still wants to report about this world of the past. His sympathy is clearly on the side of the vanishing world, allowing him to narrate their tales convincingly.

One of the last works Munif worked on before he left Baghdad was a collaboration with the renowned Palestinian-born author Jabra Ibrahim Jabra, *'Alam bi la khara'it* (1982, Mapless World). A long, complex novel set in the imaginary city of 'Ammuriyya, *'Alam bi la khara'it* is ostensibly centered on the murder of a young woman, but ranges backward and forward in time in its examination of the uncertainty of truth. By 1981 Munif, like many other Arab intellectuals living in Iraq under the reign of Saddam Hussein, went into exile in France. For five years he resided in Boulogne, devoting his time entirely to writing fiction.

The first two volumes of Munif's monumental five-volume novel *Mudun al-milh* (Cities of Salt)—*al-Tih* (1984, The Labyrinth; translated as *Cities of Salt,* 1987) and *al-Ukhdud* (1985; translated as *The Trench,* 1991)—were published while he was living in France. *Mudun al-milh,* which was originally planned as a trilogy, gives a portrait of the traditional society the imaginary Sultanate of Mooran, tracing its transformation from the Bedouin culture of the 1930s as a result of the discovery of oil and "modernization." While the books were banned in Saudi Arabia and his passport was confiscated, Munif has always insisted that what he wrote was fiction, though it is clearly fiction inspired by the history of the Kingdom of Saudi Arabia. Munif's style is oriented to oral speech and rarely leaves the perspective of the suffering people who oppose the changes in the lifestyles they inherited from their ancestors. In the mid 1990s, Munif gave an explanation for the title of his major work to Tariq Ali, who recalled it in his tribute to the author in *Counterpunch:* "Cities of Salt means cities that offer no sustainable existence. When the water comes in, the first waves will dissolve the salt and reduce these great glass cities to dust. In antiquity, many cities simply disappeared. It is possible to foresee the downfall of cities that are inhuman. With no means of livelihood they won't survive. Look at us now how the West sees us. The twentieth century is almost over, but when the West looks at us, all they see is oil and petrodollars."

Al-Tih is about the life of two communities, a small town on the edge of the desert and a fishing village at the gulf, and the sudden intrusion of foreigners when oil is discovered. The local population experienced how first the palm trees and then they themselves were uprooted. Munif created an imaginary desert town of Wadi al-Uyoun (Valley of the Wells), where rain, prayer and the occasional arrival of caravans dictate the rhythm of life: "For caravans, Wadi al-Uyoun was a phenomenon, something of a miracle, unbelievable to those who saw it for the first time and unforgettable forever after. The wadi's name was repeated at all stages of a journey, in setting out and returning: 'How much longer to Wadi al-Uyoun?' 'If we make it to Wadi al-Uyoun, we'll rest up for a few days before going on,' and 'Where are you, Wadi al-Uyoun, earthly paradise?'" Some of its inhabitants occasionally join the caravans to travel and return after several years with new ideas and stories, but the villagers are unprepared for the sudden appearance of Western strangers who disturb their centuries-old rhythm of life. Some are excited, others confused, and a few worried. But all of them are one day expelled from their homeland, and their orchards and palm trees are cut down. From one day to the next their world is turned upside down. What used to be right is now wrong, and traditions no longer are respected. The ones who collaborate with the new system profit and prosper from the destruction of their traditional society. The villagers move to Harran, the small fishing community on the coast of the gulf, which turns into an artificial city based on profit and oil, where the values of the civilized are no longer honored. The locals have to deal with various new components to their society: the Americans, the new ruling class, the noveau riche, and the laborers.

For a while, the Arab laborers are blinded by the prospects of money and the possibility that they might be able to have relations with unattainable white women. To live close to the American compound becomes a privilege of the rich, while the poor laborers are almost paralyzed and awestruck. But, the gap between the business and those who rely on technology and the tribal way of thinking widens every day and with every arrival of new ships and clients. An old Bedouin, for example, does not understand why he was denied his traditional right to carry out blood revenge against the company after his nephew dies as the result of a work accident. The local healer of Harran is killed as a tramp by the newly established police force. Frequent conflicts culminate in a revolt and strike against the oil company. Munif's illustration and elaboration of the class system, which allows some people to share the wealth and gives many nothing, resonates for many readers.

The second volume of Munif's work, *al-Ukhdud,* is set in the 1950s and focuses on the establishment of the city of Mooran as a regional power and its accumu-

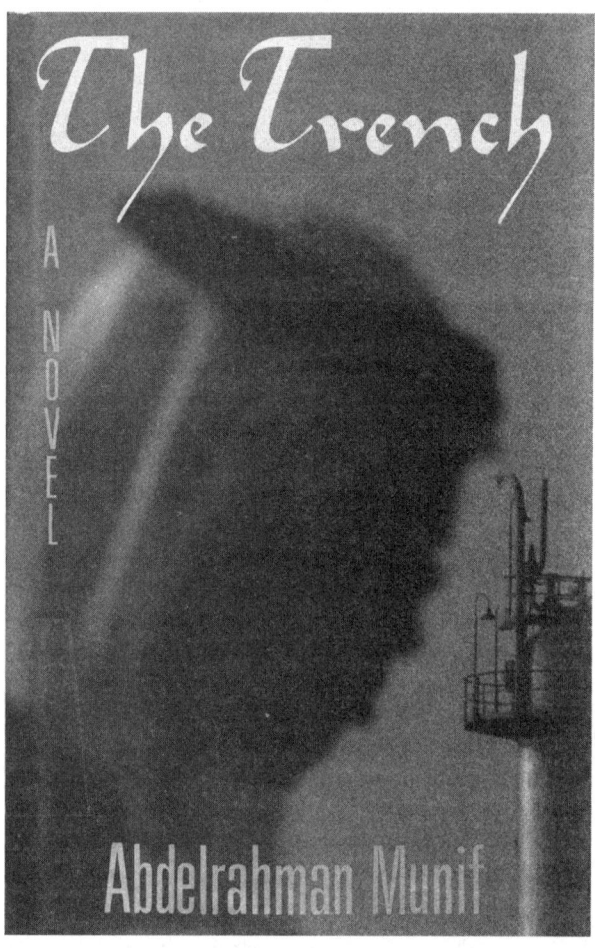

Dust jacket for 1991 English translation of al-Ukhdud (1985), the second volume of Mudun al-milh (Thomas Cooper Library, University of South Carolina)

lation of oil wealth that attracts much stronger outside powers. The main characters include the inexperienced Sultan Khazel and his chief adviser, the treacherous Subhi Mahmilji as well as such strong, complex women as Mahmilji's wife and the ancient Sheikha. The flavor of the novel is well captured by Francine Prose in her 27 October 1991 *New York Times* review of the English translation: "As the novel progresses, seismic social and economic changes open chasms so wide that Mr. Munif's characters are always scrambling to keep from tumbling in. Their fates suggest the convolutions of a Victorian novel transcribed into Arabic calligraphy, or perhaps 'The Arabian Nights' as retold by Stendhal—with Sinbad driving a white Rolls-Royce and the Grand Vizier jetting off to Atlanta for counterintelligence training."

With the success of the first two volumes of *Mudun al-milh,* Munif during his years in exile achieved a reputation as a well-respected and prolific novelist. In 1986 he returned to the Middle East, settling in Damascus, Syria, the homeland of his wife, Soad Qawadhri, where he lived the rest of his life. He continued to pursue vigorously his career as a novelist and also edited a cultural journal with Syrian writer Sadallah Wanus and the Palestinian critic Faisal Darraj. In 1989 Munif brought out the final three volumes of the *Mudun al-Milh* series, the last two of which have not been translated into English: *Taqasim al-layl wa al-nahar* (translated as *Variations on Night and Day,* 1993), *al-Munbat* (The Rootless), and *Badiyat al-Zulumat* (Desert of Darkness). Munif takes his story back in time in *Taqasim al-layl wa al-nahar,* to explore the beginnings of the Sultanate of Mooran in the first decades of then twentieth century and the collaboration of Sultan Khureybit with the British surveyor Hamilton. *Al-Munbat* continues the story of Sultan Khazel, who lives in exile in Germany. The final volume in the series, *Badiyat al-Zulumat* goes back in time and follows the career of Khazael's brother and replacement, King Fanar, who is later assassinated.

Mudun al-milh shows how oil, the Americans, and local despots dominate life in a gulf state. The form of the work—with its lack of concern about a straightforward chronology, lengthy digressions, and its presentation of multiple versions of the same events—pays tribute to the traditions of Arabic narrative. Beyond his protagonists, Munif creates a vast number of named characters, most of whom appear briefly, sometimes described with only a few words. His intent is to take an approach that differs from a traditional historical account, for his most important focus is the common people who were betrayed and expelled.

In 1991 Munif published two new works: *al-An, huna aw sharq al-Mutawassit marratan ukhra* (Now, Here, and East of the Mediterranean Again), a sequel to his 1975 novel *Sharq al-Mutawassit,* in which he deepens his analysis of the system that persecutes Ragab, and the nonfiction *al-Dimuqratiyyah awalan, al-dimuqratiyyah da'iman* (Democracy First, Democracy Always). Munif found his way into writing through politics, because he had been dissatisfied with methods of political expression and subsequently started to search for a new means to manifest his concerns. As his career progressed, he became more concerned with suggesting possible solutions to the problems of Arab governance, though he was careful not to allow his novels to become political tracts.

In *al-Dimuqratiyyah awalan, al-dimuqratiyyah da'iman* Munif articulates the necessary requirements and conditions that contemporary Arab states need to consider to adjust to the international community and to become countries for citizens rather than for rulers. Munif believes that "democracy is a pre-condition for any successful transformation in the Middle East. Achieving economic development, building civil societies, and establishing modern states cannot be accomplished if democracy is missing." But as long as totalitarian regimes are pampered and protected by outside forces, a change toward democracy is hard to imagine. He indicts the nature of this connection, such as the one between Saudi Arabia and the United States. Democracy, as defined by Munif, is not a prescription for solving political problems but rather a means to deal with them effectively. While Munif warns that democracy does not offer magical solutions, he stresses that it is the correct basis upon which to build society: "Democracy is not merely a legal form or a temporary condition. It is also not a gift or a grant from anyone, but rather a fundamental right of all human beings." He further asserts that once democracy is established, it should be maintained to serve the interests of minorities and majorities in the society. Munif calls for the combined effort of all Arabs to work toward the establishment of democracy: "Maybe our generation will not be lucky enough to live to see the fruits of a better world where democracy flourishes, but actions are urgently needed to guarantee that our children will not suffer as we did."

In his 1994 novel based on his childhood years, *Sirat madinah,* Munif describes how Amman was seen from the perspective of a child in the 1940s. Particularly interesting is the multicultural atmosphere of Amman, the various educational systems, and the many quotes and sayings of famous contemporaries. He uses his childhood memories to shed light on the general ideas and conceptions of that time period. Some of the most memorable passages concern Munif's maternal relatives, especially his grandmother. During her stay in Amman, she continued to wear her Baghdadi dress and did not cover her face, much to the distress of the community, explaining, "Yes, I am an Iraqi from Baghdad, from the Karkh side of the river, from the al-Dahdawanah quarter. Is that enough, or do you need to know anything else?"

In the latter half of the 1990s Munif wrote about art and continued to speak out about politics. His interest in fine arts, especially modern Arab art, and his desire to share this appreciation led him to write about three major Arab artists: Marwan Qassab Basha, Fateh al-Mudarris, and Diya al-Azzawi in *Marwan Qassab Bashi: Rihlat al-fan wa al-hayat* (1996, Marwan Qassab Bashi: The Journey of Light) and such articles as "Fateh al-Moudarres, Syrian Artist Who Fought for Justice with Brush-Pen," which was published in the fall 1999 issue of *al-Jadid*. Not only did Munif collect their artwork but while doing so he established close relationships with them. He complained about factions in the Arab artistic world, that each form of expression existed isolated from the other, resulting in the weakening of the art scene in general.

Munif's political insights were acute. In an article that appeared in 1996 on the website *Jinn,* "Other Voices–Saudi Bomb Attack an Act of Despair," Munif reacted to an attack on U.S. soldiers in Dhahran with a warning about Islamic fundamentalism:

> I speak as a novelist who follows events, and tries to understand them. I have no way of dealing with them other than with words. In my book "Cities of Salt," I wrote about the dangerous relationship between America and the countries of the Arabian Peninsula. Now it appears that what I imagined and expected–that the salt would dissolve in water–has begun.
>
> The spread of fundamentalism, especially its violent aspect, results from an accumulation of errors. The people behind the movement's current hard line were recruited as youths, then nurtured in Afghanistan, and ultimately sent on to Bosnia, all with the enthusiastic support of the United States and Saudi Arabia. He who sows the wind, as the saying goes, will reap the whirlwind.
>
> Fundamentalism will spread in the Gulf region and possibly turn more violent because no political movement or party offers a formula for acknowledging ordinary people and engaging them in the political process.

In an interview with the French magazine *L'Orient Express* in 1999 he stated that "the (current) crisis is a trilogy: oil, political Islam and dictatorship. This trilogy is the factor that led to the collapse, confusion, and consequently the suffering lived by Arab societies in their search for the road to modernity."

Munif returned to fiction in his last novel, *Ard al-sawad* (1999, Land of Darkness), a three-volume work set in the nineteenth century Ottoman province of Iraq that warns against corrupt regimes and governments who urge imperialistic wars. *Ard al-sawad* explores the relationships between the different segments of Iraqi society, particularly between the urban and rural classes. The Ottoman occupation of Iraq is represented in the character of Dawud Pasha, the Wali (governor) of Baghdad, a Georgia-born military slave who rose to power. As a historical person, Dawud Pasha, who ruled Iraq between 1817 and 1831, is well documented. His life coincides with the continual decrease of Ottoman central authority and the rising to power of local dynasties, in this case the Mamluks, who only nominally recognized the sultan's authority. In addition, the European powers increased their influence in the region. Munif picked a four-year period (1817–1821) filled with dramatic political and social events as the focus for his novel.

Although the main rivals of the story, Dawud and the British consul Ritch, are considered the main characters, Munif also carefully depicts the ordinary people. That is how the book may be best understood: the stories of the Iraqi people and the unique environment in which they live. Munif dedicated the book to his mother, and it is written in her Arabic dialect of Baghdad. The Karkh side of the river, where Munif's maternal grandmother was from, is one of the main settings. Again, Munif introduces a variety of characters and the contrasts between them giving even minor characters the chance to narrate his story. Munif considered this book "a love-song to the people of Iraq and their struggle against all hazards."

In the final years of his life Abdelrahman Munif began to write about political issues related to the American occupation of Iraq and resistance movement, which culminated in the publication of *al-Iraq–Hawamish min al-Tarikh wa'l-Muqawamah* (2003, Iraq–Footnotes on History and Resistance). He died on 24 January 2004 in Damascus. Many Arab critics consider Munif and the Egyptian novelist Naguib Mahfouz to be the two masters of Arab literature. When Mahfouz was awarded the Nobel Prize in 1988, some believed it should have gone to Munif. The following year Munif received the Sultan al-Uwais Prize for Arabic Literature and Criticism, the Arab equivalent, as well as the Cairo Award for Novels in 1998.

References:

Faruq Abdel-Qadir, "The Barber of Baghdad," *al-Ahram Weekly*, no. 464 (13–19 January 2000);

Fouad Ajami, "A Yellow Wind in the Desert," *New York Times*, 5 September 1993;

Tariq Ali, "Farewell to Munif–a Patriarch of Arab Literature," *Counterpunch* (1 February 2004);

Ludwig Ammann, "Der Fluch des Schwarzen Goldes," *Neue Zürcher Zeitung*, 4 March 2004;

Mona Anis, "Arab Citizen par Excellence," *al-Ahram Weekly*, no. 678 (19–24 February 2004);

M. M. Badawi, "Two Novelists from Iraq: Jabra and Munif," *Journal of Arabic Literature*, 23 (1992): 141–154;

Iskandar Habash, "Crisis in the Arab World–Oil, Political Islam, and Dictatorship," *al-Jadid*, 9, no. 45 (2003);

Abdul-Hadi Jiad, "Abdul-Rahman Mounif," *Guardian*, 5 February 2004;

Francine Prose, "Sinbad in a White Rolls-Royce," *New York Times*, 27 October 1991.

Muhsin al-Musawi
(23 April 1945 –)

Hager Ben Driss
University of Tunis

BOOKS: *Scheherazade in England: A Study of Nineteenth-Century English Criticism of the* Arabian Nights (Washington, D.C.: Three Continents Press, 1981);

Naz'at al-hadathah fi al-qissah al-'Iraqiyyah fi al-khamsinat (Beirut: MADN, 1984);

Al-Wuqu' fi da'irat al-sihr: Alf laylah wa laylah fi nazariyyat al-adab al-Ingilizi (Cairo: GEBO, 1986);

Al-Riwayah al-'Arabiyyah: Al-Nashat wa al-tahawul (Baghdad, 1986);

'Asr al-riwayah (Cairo: GEBO, 1986);

Adab al-harb al-qasasi fi al-'Iraq (Baghdad: Al-Thaqafiyyah, 1986);

Al-'Uqdah (Baghdad: Maktabat al-Tahrir, 1989);

Darb al-Za'faran (Cairo: Dar al-Shuruq, 1990);

Awtar al-qasab (Baghdad: Al-Ma'rifah li al-Nashr wa al-Tawzi', 1990);

Tharat Shahrazad (Beirut: Dar al-Adab, 1993);

Al-Istishraq fi al-fikr al-'Arabi (Beirut: Al-Mu'assasah al-'Arabiyyah li al-Dirasat, 1993):

Sardiyyat al-'asr al-'Arabi al-wasit (Beirut: Al-Markaz al-Thaqafi al-'Arabi, 1997);

Al-Nukhbah wa al-inshiqaq: Tawaludat al-nass min al-nahda ila al-'isyan (Cairo: Al-Sahafa, 1998);

Duna sa'iri al-nas: Infi'alat al-raqm 46 (Beirut: Al-Markaz al-Thaqafi al-'Arabi, 1999);

Anglo-Orient: Easterners in Textual Camps (Tunis: Centre de Publication Universitaire, 2000);

Mujtama' Alf laylah wa laylaj (Tunis: Centre de Publication Universitaire, 2000);

The Postcolonial Arabic Novel: Debating Ambivalence (Leiden: Brill, 2003).

SELECTED PERIODICAL PUBLICATIONS–UNCOLLECTED: "Writing in Exile: Which Sense of Be-Longing?" *English Studies in Canada,* 27, no. 4 (2001): 481–508;

"Shahadah," in *'Abd al-Ilah 'Abd al-Qadir: Al-Fa'izun bi Ja'izah* (Al-Fujayrah: Mu'assasat Sultan bin 'Ali al-Owais, 2002), pp. 137–179.

The Iraqi critic and writer Muhsin al-Musawi has published on Arabic fiction and poetry since the late 1960s. His concentration on criticism may have hindered his creative impulse, but his four novels cannot be severed from his many critical studies in Arabic and English. Indeed, his easy faring between creativity and criticism is so distinctive that any serious reader must consider each in light of the other.

To appreciate al-Musawi's importance both as a critic and a novelist, one must understand the state of the Iraqi literary scene before the end of the Iraq-Iran War in 1988. The culture had a weak novelistic tradition. Despite the fact that Iraqis have been among the best short-story writers, few of their novels had received good critical response. Most of these were social narratives with uneven emphasis on psychological dimensions. The novels dealing with the war were too documentary or imitative to deserve special attention. Al-Musawi himself wrote negatively about them in *Adab al-harb al-qasasi fi al-'Iraq* (1986, War Narratives in Iraq). As a novelist, al-Musawi attempted to infuse into fiction new visions and orientations.

Because of his academic training and knowledge of the major trends of Arabic culture in general and the Iraqi context in particular, it is not surprising that al-Musawi's expertise as a critical scholar affected his creative side. However, al-Musawi takes the novel into the lives of intellectuals without overburdening it with his own career. He avoids falling in the trap of self-reflective writing and ideological digressions that characterized the works of some novelists of the 1960s, such as Ghanim al-Dabbagh in his novel *Dajjah fi al-Zuqaq*. As al-Musawi devoted a good part of his life to studying the compilation of classic Arabic stories known as *Alf laylah wa laylah* (The Thousand and One Nights), all his narratives are tinged with the dreamy world of these folk tales. Building his narratives with anecdotal material, parody, and pastiche, al-Musawi proves himself a gifted *bricoleur* (handyman). He succeeds in bringing

Muhsin al-Musawi (Columbia University)

into the Iraqi novel a smooth postmodern navigation between tradition and modernity.

Muhsin al-Musawi was born on 23 April 1945 in al-Nasr, a village in southern Iraq. In his 2002 essay "Shahadah" (Testimony), he describes his childhood world on the shores of the Gharraf River as "very quiet; it wakes at the voice of the Muezzin Shaykh Murtada bin Muhammad Haraj al-Waili calling for the first dawn prayer and goes back to sleep at his voice calling for the last one." He was the sixth child of al-Sayyid Jasim 'Ali, from an Ashraf family (descendent of the Prophet). His mother, Malikah al-Sayyid Haydar, a charismatic 'Alawiyat (descendent of Imam 'Ali, the cousin of the Prophet), took care of her eight children after the death of their father–al-Musawi was only ten years old at the time. Of his father, a trader who was often absent from home, he can remember only his returns loaded with books for his elder brother, 'Aziz al-Sayyid Jasim, who supported the family after his father's death and became a notable author. 'Aziz also took the image of the father in al-Musawi's narratives. 'Aziz's intellectual influence on his younger brother, especially in his formative years, is undeniable. Al-Musawi claims that his "biography without 'Aziz's role is incomplete, fake and mutilated."

After primary school in al-Ghaziyah (1950–1959), al-Musawi moved to the secondary school in the nearby town, al-Rifa'i, where his developing literary gifts attracted his teachers' attention. He explains his good command of Arabic language at an early age by his reading of the Qur'an. He also learned by heart the marginal remarks and notes 'Aziz used to write on his books or on his pocket notebooks. In 1963 he left his secluded village to go to Baghdad where he attended the university and earned a B.A. in English language and literature. After graduating in 1966, he was appointed a secondary-school teacher in the city. While teaching, he continued his literary activities, publishing literary criticism in Iraqi journals and editing the literary page of *Abna' al-Nur* (1964–1965, Sons of Light) and *al-Anwar Daily* (1966).

Al-Musawi's stay in Baghdad opened new horizons of knowledge and led to encounters with intellectuals. He spent his time in cafés where he discussed literary cultural issues and became acquainted with new and different ways of thinking. Baghdad also offered a profusion of literary journals and books in all fields of knowledge, including many translations of Western works. He describes the Baghdad of the second half of the 1960s, before it became subject to the censor, as "a wonderful cultural city."

Al-Musawi opted for comparative literature as his field of his postgraduate studies. As a child, he read books of adventure stories. In his early youth, he devoured the works of Yahya Haqqi, Ibrahim al-Mazini, and Taha Husayn. He also read the translated works of Ernest Hemingway, Charles Dickens, Franz Kafka, and existentialist writers such as Jean-Paul Sartre and Albert Camus, all of which shaped al-Musawi's comparative critical mind. His journey to Canada in 1973, where he earned his M.A. and Ph.D. in comparative literature at Dalhousi University, strengthened his concern with cultural interaction through literature. He met Cantle Smith, a specialist in comparative religions, and he worked on his dissertation with the Canadian scholar Malcolm Ross. In 1978 he went back home with a Ph.D., having earned his degree with a dissertation on the critical reception of the English translation of *Alf laylah wa laylah,* which became his first published book, *Scheherazade in England: A Study of Nineteenth-Century Criticism of the* Arabian Nights (1981).

Taking a post as professor at the University of Baghdad, al-Musawi became an active member of al-Mirbad, the annual poetry festival. It was a huge gathering, named after Basra Mirbad and aimed at reviving the old Arabic tradition of poetry markets. Besides teaching, he occupied the prestigious position of Director of Culture (1983–1990), responsible for translation and cultural publications projects. In 1983 al-Musawi was elected to preside over the Iraqi Critics' Association and to be president of the critical session of al-Mirbad, which was attended by scholars from all over the world. This position lasted until 1988, a year that marked a turning point in al-Musawi's life.

In July 1988 al-Musawi was arrested and then imprisoned for three months. He was suspected of helping his brother 'Aziz—a Marxist intellectual who had often been persecuted by authorities—to publish his book *'Ali ibn Abi Talib: Sultat al-Haq* (Ali the Authority of Righteousness) in Beirut. Al-Musawi, though, was only sympathetic with nationalism and leftist ideology without ever being a partisan for any specific group. As it happened, prison liberated al-Musawi's creative side. He wrote his first novel, *al-'Uqdah* (1989, The Knot), while incarcerated. The prison experience compelled him to explore his gift for narrative; previously, with his busy life of teaching, writing criticism, and editing, he had not made a concerted effort to write fiction.

The circumstances of the writing and publication of *al-'Uqdah* were extraordinary and touched by Kafkaesque absurdity. While detained, al-Musawi was reassured that he was the government's "guest" and in some ways was treated as such. By allowing al-Musawi to write while in prison, the authorities were able to claim that they were not really persecuting him as an intellectual. When al-Musawi completed his manuscript, it was scrutinized by the security office of the prison and released for publication. Al-Musawi reports that the officer who read the manuscript nevertheless felt the need to say, "I hope there's nothing against us in the novel!" Thus, while al-Musawi remained in prison, his novel was acquitted.

The prison officer's remark was gratuitous but necessary for the official game that was being played—a game in which al-Musawi himself was able to cleverly participate in his short preface to *al-'Uqdah*:

> This novel has lived in my mind for years. I wrote its general outlines and then left it. But it clung to me in such a way . . . that I could not escape writing it. And then I got the opportunity to write. It may look close to reality, but it is not the case. . . .

Such a preface could pass without being noticed were it written by any other writer in more comfortable surroundings. Claiming that events and characters are imaginary is a common narrative practice. But al-Musawi's sarcasm is deftly hidden behind this literary convention. His use of specific words and phrases fill in the gaps of the pact of silence enforced by the official game. With phrases such as "I could not escape" (*la mafarra*) and "I got the opportunity" (*tayassarat al-fursatu*) he alludes to his forced status as the government's guest whose long delayed "opportunity" is actually imprisonment. *Al-'Uqdah* was initially published and circulated in Baghdad by Maktabat al-Tahrir (Al-Tahrir Bookshop) as weekly illustrated installments in *Majallat al-Iza'a wa al-Tilfiziun* (Magazine of Cairo Radio and TV), edited by the story writer Sukaynah Fu'ad. The novel won acclaim as being new and experimental.

Under psychological pressure and within a stifling atmosphere of doubt and ambiguity, al-Musawi created a work that expressed his anxiety. He channeled his frustration at being imprisoned without a valid charge or a trial into a frenzy of writing, finishing the text in a few weeks. His protagonist, Mr. S., like Kafka's K. in *The Trial* (1937), lives a psychological siege. Mr. S. becomes a vehicle for repressed identity, and it is worth noting that the letter *s* (*sin* in Arabic) usually stands for ambiguity or anonymity.

A brooding character, Mr. S. is a type of a Romantic, Byronic hero, who spends his time reading, writing, and meditating in silent seclusion. His relationship with the beautiful Layl is ambiguous and knotty. Although he loves her, he resists any type of emotional or sexual fulfillment. Layl tries hard, though in vain, to penetrate his closed world. "He entices me and I strive to understand him," she states, "both enigmatic and clear, he slips away the moment I believe I have caught him." Desperate and unable to fathom Mr. S., Layl leaves him. Mr. S. is left alone recollecting his sad and secret memories of his dead wife, Wisal, in anxious

Title page for al-Musawi's first book (1981), based on his dissertation at Dalhousie University (Thomas Cooper Library, University of South Carolina)

tranquility. He is unable to betray the memory of his young bride whose shadow often visits him to warn "don't substitute me with another wife; I haven't enjoyed life with you yet."

Mr. S. anticipates the reader's interpretation of his dead wife's apparition and refuses to compare her to Rochester's wife in Charlotte Brontë's *Jane Eyre* (1847) or Heathcliff's Kathy in Emily Brontë's *Wuthering Heights* (1847). The academic side of al-Musawi is evident in the narrative as he deviates into an analysis of the two female characters. Such deviations recur in many parts of the narrative, as in the lengthy discussions about the psychology of big cities or John Barth's novel *The End of the Road* (1958). Such discussions do not preclude the text, however, from being heavily tinted by Romanticism, al-Musawi's focus of critical attention.

The narrative recalls Edgar Allan Poe's morbid poems that are characterized by the dialogue of the mind with itself, verging sometimes on madness. Wisal is another appellation of Poe's dead young Annabel Lee or Lenore. Like Poe's poems, al-Musawi's novel makes the case that the death of a beautiful woman is the most poetical topic in the world. The beautiful Wisal dies leaving her bereaved husband haunted by her ghost. All his attempts to escape her memory are doomed to failure. Even his passionate embraces of Layl are interrupted by the sudden appearance of his dead wife's shadow. Like Poe's male personae, Mr. S. Is imprisoned in memory. *Al-'Uqdah* moves in a closed, claustrophobic setting of his house, recalling the prison. Mr. S. is never seen outside in the open air. He is either inside a room or enclosed in his thoughts.

Mr. S. becomes a figure who while serving as a stand-in for al-Musawi's fears and uncertainties also seems to represent his desire to retain or regain his faith. While Mr. S. states, "I live my terror every night. . . . I feel my exile, affliction and tragedy," he is also described as someone who "carries his suffering within himself without allowing it to overwhelm him or to keep him away from joining the others' anxieties and joys." Mr. S's real knot is an aspiration to release himself from the burdening memory of his dead wife. Al-Musawi's knot was to untangle himself from the political game in which he was unwillingly trapped. The knot was also suggestive of the deteriorating political life in Iraq during the 1980s, which was veering irremediably towards totalitarianism, as well as the exhausting Iraq-Iran War that was reaching its end at the time the novel was written.

In September 1988 the government released al-Musawi from prison. No explanation was given to him or to his family, and his release seemed as mysterious as his initial arrest. An officer drove him directly to his Director of Culture office. Taking him to the office instead of to his home was in keeping with the rules of the government's game. The three months he spent in prison were to be immediately forgotten and never mentioned again. To show the world that Iraqi intellectuals were free, al-Musawi was soon sent to Tunis to participate in a conference about Afro-Asian writers. Yet, to play the game is one thing, but to actually forget is something else. The three months al-Musawi spent in prison left a deep impression upon him. A sense of disappointment and distrust thereafter shaped his vision of the future. Merely to be an intellectual was a potential crime, enough to keep one under suspicion. Al-Musawi came to realize that it was not safe even to be a liberal intellectual without political commitment. He knew he could be detained and questioned at any moment.

Al-Musawi's sense of disillusion verging on disgust was fully expressed in his second novel, *Darb al-Za'faran* (1990, Za'faran Alley). The first draft of this novel was also written during his enforced sojourn in prison and within the same frenzy of exorcizing his anxiety. The Gothic atmosphere of *Darb al-Za'faran* captures the dark heart of Baghdad. The narrative explores the climate of political intrigues, conspiracies, failure of love, and degradation of human relations. It starts with the narrator hastening to attend the funeral of his neighbor Jalal al-Din al-Amin and ends with his pressing feeling to leave the site of death and hasten to meet the woman he loves, Sahar. The narrative flows between these two moments of arrival and departure. The stream-of-consciousness technique allows al-Musawi to combine fragmented memories and stories.

While watching Jalal al-Din al-Amin's corpse, ready for burial, Wahhab narrates the story of Za'faran Street where he lives. The rich, beautiful, calm façade of the street hides an ugly world of intrigues and corruption. Wahhab, a painter, reluctantly enters the secret life of his beloved street. While trying to keep neutral, he listens to Thiqab, his mistress, unveiling the dangerous scandals of the city. He learns that Zaydan, the postmaster, is involved in base blackmail, using the discomforting information he finds in the letters of the rich to press them for money. Jalal al-Din al-Amin was one of his victims. Zaydan had discovered his love affair with a woman living in Beirut and had threatened to destroy his family life.

While Wahhab's flashbacks are interrupted by short returns to the funeral he is attending, the real setting and names are intricately enmeshed with imaginary ones. Wahhab explains his fascination with the street by the fact that its name takes him back to the fourth century of the Islamic calendar (10th century B.C.E.), to the Za'faran alley of *Alf laylah wa laylah*. Al-Musawi employs two characters from Scheherazade's tales, Jamilah bint Abi al-Layth al-'Amid and her cousin, Abu al-Qasim al-Sandalani, the painter, who failed to attract her attention. They function as shadow characters in an imaginary space where he escapes from the intrigues of his city. "The alley is the life and history I'm living," Wahhab says, "I may be the prolongation of a single person or a dynasty or much more than an individual, an identity and a hobby. For I am the painter, the amateur, the bookseller, the lover, the prince, the merchant and the bewitched. All of them lived in and were haunted by the Alley."

The sense of mystery and darkness permeating *Darb al-Za'faran* corresponds to the corrupt Iraqi political scene. In his "Shahadah," al-Musawi states that he "was observing with affliction the ordeal of Iraq, the waste of energies and people's competence with continuous despotic manipulations, national struggles and suspect political interests." The hideous figure of Zaydan, poking into people's lives and secrets, is a mocking rendition of the intelligence director Fadil al-Barrak, who was apparently behind the imprisonment of al-Musawi and 'Aziz. The writer draws on the medieval Islamic state to forge the figure of the postmaster, who held a key position, especially in the Abbasid period.

Al-Musawi's first two novels paved the way toward a more refined style and narrative techniques in his third novel, *Awtar al-qasab* (1990, Reed Strings). The Romanticism, the dialogue with the self, and the morbidity of the mind, which permeate the two first novels, almost disappear. In *Awtar al-qasab,* al-Musawi seems to have escaped his prison and tried to go back to life. He wrote the novel during his sojourn in Tunis in 1989. The feeling of freedom he experienced, combined with the beautiful woody space of Radis, a southern suburb, inspired one of his most acclaimed novels.

Awtar al-qasab offers an interesting array of experimental narrative techniques. It is divided into a center and a margin or footnotes. The center is about the love story between Salma and Shaykh Ghalib, who narrates this part. The footnotes are written by three different readers of the central text. They provide comments on the events of the story, explanations of names of fauna and flora, and information about the excerpts of poetry cited and allusions used. According to critic Fadil Thamir, writing in 11 September 1991 issue of *Al-Qadisiyyay,* the fact that al-Musawi has called his work a "Nath riwai" (narrative text) "is a deliberate way to inscribe his work within a specific literary genre": "He seems keen to include his novel in the new narrative trend called 'metafiction' or what al-Musawi himself calls 'riwayat al-nass'" (literally, "the story of a text"). But while al-Musawi's experiments with the shape of narrative might be termed postmodern, his text remains fluid and accessible.

Taking as a background the colonial history of Iraq during the British occupation, *Awtar al-qasab* presents a narrative of rebellion and dissent. While the grandfather, Shaykh Badr, ferociously struggles against colonization, the grandson, Shaykh Ghalib, stubbornly opposes customs and traditions. Chained by his family's high origins, Ghalib is forced to behave according to the norms of his social class. His strong love for Salma, a girl belonging to the Sabian religious minority, mars his relationship with his grandfather. The Sabians adhere to a pre-Islamic religious sect connected to John the Baptist and believe in purification, cleanliness, and righteousness. They live on the banks of rivers and marshes, the major setting of the novel. Ghalib breaks the law of his family by marrying Salma and moving to the city. Away from water, her natural surrounding, Salma withers away. The narrative ends with her death.

Besides its sophisticated language and style, part of the significance of *Awtar al-qasab* lies in the fact that it is the first Iraqi novel that deals with the marshes, a region dried up and poisoned by the government in

Front cover for al-'Uqdah *(The Knot)*, 1989
(Sterling Memorial Library, Yale University)

1992. Details about its fauna, flora, colors, and smells create a vivid impression of the marshes. Al-Musawi, who had never visited the marshes even though his hometown was near them, was able through his reading and research to create strikingly authentic descriptions.

Al-Musawi intended his novel to celebrate rebellion, perseverance, and regeneration. The tragic ending is balanced by the humorous comments in the footnotes, which are not only about the central story but also about the footnotes themselves. The third and second readers, for instance, make funny comments on the observations of Mr. Rahim, Ghalib's teacher and first reader. "He is a teacher brought up in the countryside and never left the marshes," the second reader says about Mr. Rahim, "this man hinders my readings with his comments, but I should be patient . . . (I shouldn't forget to sweep this comment!)." Humor is also a strategy of survival and perseverance. The grandfather's closing sentence reveals the gist of the whole novel: "Be happy, for life is a continuous hardship. Good seagulls never get tired. They keep patient without anguish, and perseverant without reluctance."

The advice of the grandfather, a character modeled on the strong personality of al-Musawi's brother 'Aziz, turned out to be appropriate for the author's near future. In 1991 al-Musawi needed all his patience and perseverance to face the successive blows destabilizing his life. The First Gulf War affected him deeply as an intellectual. He saw Saddam Hussein's invasion of Kuwait in August 1990 as a reckless act and the war on Iraq in January 1991 as a collective punishment of a helpless population. The imprisonment of 'Aziz on 15 April 1991 was another strong emotional blow. While trying to recover his intellectual and emotional balance within a chaotic country, he was forced into early retirement by the end of April 1991, with no official explanation given for this action. Being an intellectual and the brother of a political prisoner were evidently sufficient reasons to eliminate him from public and academic life. At the age of forty-six and father to four children, al-Musawi had to find a solution to his precarious situation.

In August 1991 he went alone to Jordan, where he joined Amman University. After four months he was obliged to leave Amman after a top official in the Iraqi embassy informed him that the Iraqi government did not want him to stay in Amman because he was a public figure. Al-Musawi left Amman in secret and went to teach in San'a' University in Yemen, where his family joined him in 1992. He later decided to move to a more secure place. As he has always been interested in the Tunisian cultural and intellectual environment, he opted to settle down in Tunisia, where he was warmly welcomed by important academics. He was given the post of professor in comparative literature at the University of Manouba, one of Tunisia's major universities. His family joined him by the end of 1993.

Al-Musawi wrote his fourth novel, *Duna sa'iri al-nas: Infi'alat al-raqm 46* (1999, Of All People Alone: Emotions of Size 46), in Tunis. He completed the manuscript in 1994, two years after he moved to Tunisia. Blending the grotesque with sardonic humor, the novel is an interesting example of magical realism, combining realism and fantasy in a way that blurs the boundaries between the marvelous and the ordinary. *Duna sa'iri al-nas* is notable for its use of black humor as a way of dealing with an oppressive reality—a strategy al-Musawi tentatively used in his previous novel, *Awtar al-qasab*.

"The story started in 1988," the narrator states, "I had an evening walk with Shakir Nuri in the Champs Elisee. We were laughing and backbiting the slippers of Ahmad al-Madini." Shakir Nuri, an Iraqi artist who studied cinema, is the inspiration for al-Musawi's major character in the novel, Jallu, a student of cinema who ends up as a shoemaker. Ahmad al-Madini is a Moroccan novelist whose old traditional slippers become one of the funniest voices of the narrative, called Balghat Ahamad (Ahmad's slippers). Laughter, however, is more a tactical maneuver to hide suffering than an inclination towards entertaining. The novel transports the reader into the heart of horror—a world inspired by George Orwell's *Animal Farm* (1945) though exceeding it in terror. The horse-leather shoes, one of the animal voices, reports that "the animal farm is nothing compared to the Commander's farm."

The postmodern techniques al-Musawi uses in *Duna sa'iri al-nas*—pastiche, polyphony, and fragmentation—make it difficult for the reader to follow story lines or even to identify a central plot. The narrative is an ensemble of intertwined and deferred stories that, like all of al-Musawi's works, owes something to *Arabian Nights*. Yet, the basic textual background is *Kalilah wa dimnah* by Ibn al-Muqaffa'. This work was a political satire based on a Persian collection of stories taken from Indian folklore. It is composed of tales narrated and acted by animals and, according to critic Hanna al-Fakhuri in *Al-Jami' fi al-Adab al-'Arabi* (1986, Survey of Arabic Literature,) is considered "a treasure of Oriental wisdom."

Al-Musawi's narrative is based on conversations between Jallu and animal voices. Jallu, whose origin is based on biblical and Qur'anic versions of Jesus' birth, began to speak in the cradle. Presented as the descendant of mythic and religious figures, the shoemaker is surrounded with different speaking animal skins. Al-Musawi's text is so tightly enmeshed with al-Muqaffa''s that it is difficult sometimes to separate the one from the other. Full excerpts are literally quoted, and the animal skins and shoes surrounding Jallu act the parts of animal characters in *Kalilah wa dimnah,* creating a confusion crucial to the writer's strategy of camouflage. Al-Musawi not only hides his political critique behind speaking animal skins and shoes, he also makes of *Kalilah wa dimnah* another protecting shield. Al-Muqaffa' wrote his book to criticize, in a covert way, the despotic Abbasid kings, especially Abu Ja'far al-Mansur. Likewise, al-Musawi's novel is a political satire denouncing the Iraqi totalitarian regime during Saddam Hussein's reign. While distancing takes place through Arabic scriptory tradition (al-warraqin), the veiled narrative takes as its lineage writers who underwent persecution such as al-Muqaffa' and the poet Bashshar Ibn Burd (714–784), both of whom were executed during the Abbasid period.

The humor of *Duna Sa'iri al-nas* resides mainly in the grotesque figure of the Commander, a hilarious caricature of Saddam Hussein. The despotic Commander, who transforms the city into a farm where people are slaughtered, is represented as a sexually impotent man. His lust for torture and killing is a way to camouflage his impotence. The Commander is also obsessed by his size forty-six boots—hence the subtitle, *Infi'alat al-raqm 46*. Proud of his big size, he is in a continuous search for comfortable boots. The boots, used by the Commander to trample people, are the symbol of dictatorship and despotism. The narrative ends with the rebellion of the boots, which destroy the Commander. The proud military man is reduced to a mutilated bundle that "passersby piss on." A character in the novel comments on this scene: "Homeland, my friend, is neither a piece of land nor a number of walls; it is people. Humiliating people is humiliating the homeland, and deceiving them is a betrayal of life. A greedy ruler is doomed to loss and ruin."

Whether he begins in pain or in laughter, al-Musawi strives to end his narratives in wisdom. His novels oscillate between morbidity and humor. In fact, they translate his cultural background as a Shiite Muslim as well as his personal character as a man hiding his suffering behind irony and laughter. The climate of pain permeating all his texts is traceable back to the Shiite tradition of suffering and redemption. The Shiites' celebration of the death of Husayn, Imam 'Ali's son, killed by the Umayyad, is a ritual indicating a passage to redemption. The same idea of suffering leading to regeneration is found in the Babylonian and Sumerian legend of death and rebirth. The resurrection of Tammuz (Adonis) can happen only through the descent of Astarte. Al-Musawi, then, draws on religion and mythology to recreate a deep sense of redemptive suffering in his novels.

Like the Shiite tradition and Babylonian mythology, suffering in these novels is not gratuitous or vain. It is rather the gateway to wisdom. The concluding sentences of al-Musawi's third and fourth novels show a wise acceptance and understanding of life. While *Awtar al-qasab* ends with a Sufi-like question, "Do I own anything more than my body?" *Duna sa'iri al-nas* closes with a maxim-like statement: "Danger has a shadow which can materialize when consciousness is absent and memory is lost, and then another Commander will appear." Such a fear of forgetfulness is one of the reasons al-Musawi struggled to revive the memory of 'Aziz. Cherishing the hope that 'Aziz was still alive, he started in 1992 discreet contacts with Amnesty International and PEN International to make his case known. In November 2002 he organized a panel at the annual meeting of the Middle Eastern Studies Association (MESA), dedicated to the works of 'Aziz al-Sayyid Jasim.

Biography, allegory, and space (physical and psychological settings) are three major elements in al-Musawi's

Front cover for al-Musawi's novel Duna sa'iri al-nas: Infi'alat al-raqm 46 (Of All People Alone: Emotions of Size 46), 1999 (Olin Library, Cornell University)

novels. Sometimes they are difficult to separate, as is the case in *al-'Uqdah*, in which the author's experience is apparent in the closed setting of the narrative, which stands for the prison in which he wrote the work. Space, states al-Musawi in *The Postcolonial Arabic Novel: Debating Ambivalence* (2003), "is in constant dialogue with the creative mind." This observation accounts for his tendency to blur the demarcating lines between physical settings and mental ones. The dialectical relationship between the inner and outer worlds yields a space where the boundaries between reality and imagination are oblique.

The settings in al-Musawi's four novels translate an anxious desire to escape. In *Duna sa'iri al-nas*, for instance, Jallu, an incarnation of Ma'ruf al-Iskafi, a character in the *The Arabian Nights*, lives in a mental space inhabited by animal skins and shoes and is visited by famous Arab literary figures of the Middle Ages. His imaginary city, built in the geography of the mind, is juxtaposed to the real "dying" city of Baghdad "eaten up by the Commander's farm." Jallu finds some release in the smart speaking shoes, which are identified with contemporary as well as classical poetry. Such conversations create an alternative world completely opposed to the world of horror ruled by chaos. The same strategy of escaping to a substitute space is used in *Darb al-Za'faran* and *Al-'Uqdah*. While Wahhab in *Darb al-Za'faran* recreates an aesthetic space based on the Za'faran alley of *The Arabian Nights*, Mr. S. in *al-'Uqdah* "only finds solace in books," a space of philosophers and fictional characters.

Space, in the fiction as well as the personal life of al-Musawi, is linked to exile. Starting from the poetry of Adonis, al-Musawi in "Writing in Exile: Which Sense of Be-Longing?" (2001) defines three aspects of exile:

> There is exile from homeland whenever it turns into a repressive state; there is exile from oneself whenever the poet suffers alienation in its many ramifications; and there is also exile from one's culture whenever it is made into a dominant structure of restrictions and prohibitions.

Al-Musawi has experienced these three facets of exile. While his emotional and intellectual alienation at home began with his imprisonment in 1988, his physical exile from homeland started in 1991, the first time he left Iraq. Jordan (1991), Yemen (1991), Tunisia (1992), United Arab Emirates (2000), and the USA (2002) are all spaces of exile. The academic recognition he received abroad, however, did not sweep the feeling of bitterness and guilt accompanying exile. Neither the Owais Prize in literary criticism (2002), the most prestigious nongovernmental award in the Arab world, nor his position as a tenured professor at Columbia University (2003) can assuage his sense of "sorrow and guilt." "For writers-in-exile," states al-Musawi, "recognize the fact that prisoners and martyrs have been more courageous." Comparing his choice of leaving Iraq to the resistance of his brother, 'Aziz, at home, he confesses his guilt as he feels he has not been "able to live up to his ['Aziz's] expectations of intellectual defiance."

Muhsin al-Musawi's four novels can be considered a rebellion against exile, either intellectual or physical. Each of his narratives is a testimony of struggle and perseverance. While trying to exorcize his anxieties through writing, al-Musawi has created texts that are interesting records of the social and political life in Iraq during the two last decades of the twentieth century.

Reference:

Hanna Al-Fakhuri, *Al-Jami' fi al-Adab al-'Arabi* (Beirut: Dar al-Jil, 1986).

Emily Nasrallah
(6 July 1931 -)

Pennie Johnson

BOOKS: *Tuyur Aylul* (Beirut: Dar Nawfal, 1962);
Shajarat al-difla (Beirut: Dar Nawfal, 1968);
Jazirat al-wahm (Beirut: Bayt al-Hikmah, 1973);
Al-Rahinah (Beirut: Dar Nawfal, 1974);
Al-Bahirah (Beirut: Dar Nawfal, 1975);
Shadi al-saghir, with Nafissa al-Rifai (Beirut: Dar Nawfal, 1977);
Al-Yunbu' (Beirut: Dar Nawfal, 1978);
Tilka al-dhikrayat (Beirut: Dar Nawfal, 1980);
Al-Iqla' aks al-zaman (Beirut: Dar Nawfal, 1981); translated by Issa J. Boullata as *Flight against Time* (Charlottetown, P.E.I.: Ragweed Press, 1987);
Al-Mara'ah fi 17 qissah (Beirut: Dar Nawfal, 1983);
Al-Tahunah al-da'i'ah (Beirut: Dar Nawfal, 1984);
Nisa' ra'idat, 6 volumes (Beirut: Dar al-Kutub al-Hadithah, 1986);
Khubzuna al-yawmi (Beirut: Dar Nawfal, 1990); translated by Thuraya Khalil-Khouri as *A House Not Her Own* (Charlottetown, P.E.I.: Gynergy, 1992; Austin: Center for Middle Eastern Studies, University of Texas, 1997);
Al Jamr al-ghafi (Beirut: Dar Nawfal, 1995);
Fantastic Strokes of Imagination, Bilingual Edition, translated by Rebecca Porteous (Cairo: Elias Modern Publishing House, 1995);
Mahattat al-rahil (Beirut: Dar Nawfal, 1996);
Rawat li al-ayyam (Beirut: Dar al-Ibda', 1997);
Yawmiyyat hirr (Beirut: Dar al-Kitab al-'Alami, 1997); translated by Denys Johnson-Davies as *What Happened to Zeeko* (Cairo: Hoopoe, 2000);
Al-Layali al-ghajariyyah (Beirut: Dar Nawfal, 1998);
'Ala bissat al-thalj (Beirut: Dar al-Ibda', 2000);
Anda al-khawta (Beirut: Dar al-Ibda', 2000);
Fi al-bal (Beirut: Dar Nawfal, 2000);
Awraq mansiyyah (Beirut: Dar al-Ibda', 2001);
Aswad wa abyad (Beirut: Dar al-Kutub al-Hadithah, 2001);
Riyah janubiyyah (Beirut: Dar Nawfal, 2005);

Emily Nasrallah (from Nelda LaTeef, Women of Lebanon: Interviews with Champions for Peace, *1997)*

Ma Hadatha fi jourzour tamaya (Beruit: Dar Nawfal, 2006).

Known as the Village Poet, Emily Nasrallah has focused much of her work on the depiction of life in traditional Lebanese villages, a topic not often explored before her debut. She is also cited for her articulation of the complexities that both traditional and modern conventions inflict on Arabic women and for her expression of the multifaceted effects of emigration on the Lebanese people. Her later works are known for their exposition of the tragic effects of war, particularly on women and children. Nasrallah is

Front cover for Nasrallah's novel Shajarat al-difla (The Oleander Tree), 1968 (Princeton University Library)

sometimes referred to as existentialist; her writings often focus fatalistically on the personal choices and responsibilities facing her characters.

Emily Abi Rashed was born on 6 July 1931 in the Kfeir al-Zait (Village of Oil), a village located in Southern Lebanon. She was the first of six children born to Daoud Abi Rashed and Lutfa Abou Nasser. She started her formal education in the village elementary public school, which then provided schooling through only the third grade. Because of financial restrictions and cultural constraints on women leaving their village, the continuance of education for village girls such as Abi Rashed was an exceptional event. To continue attending school, she repeated the final third-grade class for several years before her uncle, Ayoub Abou Nasser, suggested she ask the advice of another uncle, Toufic Abou Nasser, concerning how she might continue her education. Toufic Abou Nasser had immigrated to Huntington, West Virginia, and since had become a successful businessman. He suggested that her parents send her to Shoueifat National College, a boarding school near Beirut, for four years of formal secondary education. Thus she became one of the first women of her generation to leave her village to further her education.

After finishing the four-year program at Shoueifat, Abi Rashed had the credentials to be a teacher. She taught at Shoueifat for two years before again facing the traditional constraints of her culture against education, this time for her desire to attend a university in Beirut. Her parents agreed to her departure in 1953 on the condition that she attend a boarding school. For the next three years she lived and worked in the Ahliya School, teaching Arabic for room and board, meanwhile securing other jobs in journalism and translation to pay for her tuition. During this time she wrote articles for the Beirut weekly al-Sayyad (The Hunter), monthly articles for Sawt al-Mar-at (Voice of Woman Magazine), and once a month spoke on a radio program for women hosted by pioneer journalist Edvic Shaiboub. Through these jobs Abi Rashed was able to attend Beirut University College and later the American University of Beirut.

In her third year at the university Abi Rashed met chemist Philip Nasrallah, whom she married in 1957. After her marriage, she was able to quit teaching at Ahliya School and focus on her journalism and studies. In 1958 Emily Nasrallah had her first child, an event that resulted in her having to delay her exams. Her exams were further delayed by the first Lebanese Civil War, which erupted in July of 1958. In October she was finally able to sit for her finals and earn a bachelor of arts degree in education with minors in Arabic and English literature.

In her attempt to balance the competing roles of mother, wife, journalist, and writer, Nasrallah decided to focus on her journalism and writing rather than continue her education, and she wrote her first and perhaps best-known book, Tuyur Aylul (1962, Birds of September). The novel was well received by both the Lebanese and international literary communities and has been published in several languages, though not English. It received several prestigious literary awards, including the Laureate Best Novel award, the Poet Said Akl Prize, and the Friends of the Book Prize. Tuyur Aylul is standard reading in Lebanese public secondary schools.

Emigration was a common aspect of Lebanese life at the time Nasrallah began writing. Many citizens left the country in pursuit of educational and professional opportunities unattainable in Lebanon, though the period between the mid 1950s and 1975 was considered one of great prosperity for Lebanon, particularly in comparison with the rest of the Arabic world. The title of her novel suggests that the seasonal migration of birds away from Lebanon mirrors the emigration of Lebanese people from the village to the city and to foreign countries. Intertwined with the theme of emigration is that of alienation resulting from the cultural dissonance of the conflict between tradition and modernity. Described as a fictionalized autobiography, *Touyour Ayloul* tells the story of Mona, a Lebanese village girl who leaves home to attend school and establish a career. Her move to the city is traumatic and estranging, so Mona attempts to return to her village only to discover that both she and her village have changed, and as a result she is ostracized. In Nasrallah's account, Mona's experience ties together three dramatic love stories that elaborate on the complexities of the evolving Lebanese culture and the effects of the mass departure of the Lebanese people. Miriam Cooke notes that Nasrallah captures the sense of abandonment as the village girls reflect on their feeling of desertion while watching the flight of migrating birds.

Six years passed between the publication of *Tuyur Aylul* and *Shajarat al-difla* (1968, The Oleander Tree). Nasrallah's second book continued her examination of conflicting generational values and practices introduced in *Tuyur Aylul*. The setting is similar to the strictly traditional village of *Tuyur Aylul,* and both involve a young heroine whose defiance of convention leads to tragedy. The heroine of *Shajarat al-difla* is Rayya, an unconventional girl who has been traumatized by her parents' disappointment that she is not a boy and by a sexual assault in her early childhood. Like Mona of *Tuyur Aylul,* Rayya dreams of escaping to the city. As a young woman, Rayya defies convention at a wedding by performing a wild dance, which her village looks upon as obscene. In an attempt to repair Rayya's damaged reputation, her mother arranges for her to be married. Rayya defies tradition by convincing the man to whom she is betrothed to elope in a nearby village. She and her husband return to her home, but unhappy in her marriage, she defies her husband. The novel ends with Rayya taking her own life.

Some critics claim that Rayya's suicide reinforces rather than undermines the strict tradition Nasrallah attempts to challenge. Joseph T. Zeiden states that a thread of fatalism underlies *Shajarat al-difla,* expressed by Rayya when she states, "I do not have the ability to object. It was not up to me to raise objections about my birth. . . . I am a puff of air. No, I am a drop of water which tried to flow against the current." Thus the social conservatism that Nasrallah criticizes seems more of an inevitable, immutable power than a force one can fight. Cooke suggests that Rayya's suicide is a final act of independence and of insubordination, forcing the people of her village to acknowledge the psychological effect of arranged marriages and oppression of women.

While working on her first two books Nasrallah maintained the responsibilities of raising a family, simul-

Title page for Nasrallah's novel Tilka al-dhikrayat (Those Memories), 1980 (Widener Library, Harvard University)

taneously working as a journalist and writing short stories. In 1970 she quit her position as a journalist at *al-Sayyad* magazine to concentrate on her fiction. Three years later in 1973 she published her third book, *Jazirat al-wahm* (The Island of Illusion), a collection of short stories. In 1974 Nasrallah became a United Nations delegate, representing the Economic Commission for Western Asia (ECWA) at the United Nations Women's Forum on Population.

In 1974 Nasrallah published her third novel, *al-Rahinah* (The Bonded), which returns to the topic of arranged marriage, examining the complexities women's liberation presents to the women of Lebanon. The heroine, Raniah, is a peasant woman who has been engaged to a wealthy man, Namrod, since her birth. Although Namrod is controlling of Raniah, he sends her to Beirut to go to school. While in Beirut Raniah falls in love with a classmate, and she has the opportunity to escape from her betrothal to Namrod. Instead of choosing escape, however, Raniah rejects the student

Front cover for Nasrallah's al-Iqla' aks al-zaman *(translated as* Flight Against Time, *1987), 1981 (Georgetown University Library)*

and returns to her village. *Al-Rahinah* ends without revealing the results of her choice. Evelyne Accad and Rose Ghurayyib suggest that Nasrallah wants to demonstrate that the choice of liberation is a complex intersection of the forces of tradition, respect for one's family, and the freedom of modernity. When confronted with such a choice, some women would rather accept their fate than determine it themselves.

In the years following the publication of *al-Rahinah,* Nasrallah published her first children's books, *al-Bahirah* (1975, The Resplendent Flower) and *Shadi al-saghir* (1977, Little Shadi), the latter book co-authored with teacher Nafissa al-Rifai. These years marked the outbreak of civil war in Lebanon, an event that had a profound impact on Nasrallah's life and work. Though the war persisted for seventeen years, she remained in west Beirut. During this time she wrote primarily short stories and children's books. Nasrallah said that she stopped writing novels to write these stories for her own children as a way to distract them from the war.

Most of her writing from this period was accomplished under shelling. In a 1997 interview with Nelda LaTeef, Nasrallah said, "I was trying to survive by doing something that would take my mind off the fighting and keep me mentally alert."

A year after the publication of *Shadi al-saghir* Nasrallah completed a volume of stories, *al-Yunbu'* (1978, The Source). Though it was published after the war, *al-Yunbu'* only briefly touches on the conflict itself. Nearly all of the short stories in the book were written between 1961 and June of 1975 and concerned Nasrallah's home village. Only one story, "The Miracle," about a person who survives an explosion simply because she happened to be asleep, is set during the war.

Tilka al-dhikrayat (1980, Those Memories) draws on the Lebanese Civil War for a new setting and a further source of tragedy for her characters. The familiar theme of emigration remains, although it, too, is altered by the war. In this novel she expresses the feelings of those left behind in the hostile land Lebanon had become. For the first two years of the war, Nasrallah told LaTeef, "only one class of people emigrated: the rich class. . . . Those of us who remained were very angry." Those who stayed did so out of a sense of duty, and they resented those who left voluntarily. Nasrallah articulates these feelings through her characters in *Tilka al-dhikrayat,* particularly the characters Maha and Hanan. Maha remains during the war, and Hanan leaves for an extended stay in London. When Hanan returns, she accepts Maha's invitation to stay with her and confronts the realization that Lebanon and those who stayed during the war have changed. Cooke describes Hanan's recognition that she has not "suffered pain on [Lebanon's] behalf" and questions whether she deserves to remain there.

Not all emigration after the start of the war, however, was cause for animosity. Nasrallah states that as the war progressed so too did the threat of being kidnapped by the aggressors, often because of religion. Furthermore, opportunity for education and work was still scarce. Nasrallah's first novel to be translated into English, *al-Iqla' aks al-zaman* (1981; translated as *Flight against Time,* 1987), concerns the anxiety of emigrants as they attempt to assimilate to the cultures of their new countries and their fear for those who remained in the war-torn country. Again the complications of the conflict between tradition and modernity arise, but this time the emphasis is on the elderly attempting to accommodate modernity.

Nasrallah sometimes refers to *al-Iqla' aks al-zaman* as a sequel to *Tuyor Aylul,* published nineteen years earlier. The later novel is based on the experience of Nasrallah and her parents while visiting her four brothers and her sister, who had immigrated to Canada in the 1950s and 1960s. *Al-Iqla' aks al-zaman* brings into relief Nasrallah's frequent themes of dissonance between tradition and modernity, village and city life, and old and new generations. The comparatively peaceful period of 1980–1981, when the war subsided in Beirut, afforded Nasrallah the time to shape her years of research and reflection into a novel.

The central character of *al-Iqla' aks al-zaman* is Radwan, a seventy-year-old peasant from Jurat al-Sidyan, a village in the south of Lebanon. Radwan and his wife, Umm Nabil, have never traveled beyond Beirut, though all four of their children gradually immigrated to Canada. Midway through 1975, Radwan's children send their parents money to pay for their trip to Canada under the guise of a vacation but with the intent of removing their parents before the civil war fully erupted. Most of the book takes place in Canada as Radwan and Umm Nabil attempt to adjust to their temporary home, emphasizing the psychological and emotional effects of exile as the potential for return to Lebanon becomes less likely. Throughout the novel, Nasrallah describes the general confusion of both Radwan and Umm Nabil concerning the political climate of Lebanon. The novel ends with Radwan insisting on returning home, ending his stay in Canada early, and days later being tortured and murdered in Lebanon.

The calm during which *al-Iqla' aks al-zaman* was completed was violently disrupted in June 1982 with the Israeli invasion of Lebanon. Nasrallah's home in west Beirut was burned, destroying more than twenty years' worth of unpublished manuscripts. Nasrallah and her family rebuilt their home over a two-year period, only to have it hit again by rockets in 1984 and 1985. Despite the turmoil, Nasrallah managed to complete another collection of short stories, *al-Mara'ah fi 17 qissah* (1983, The Woman in Seventeen Stories), inspired by the lives of women, followed by a compilation of biographies written over a period of six years. From 1981 to 1987 Nasrallah worked both as an editor and as a writer for the women's magazine *Fayruz*, contributing a monthly profile in the series "Women Who Have Succeeded." Subjects included Helen Keller, Susan B. Anthony, and Ibitihaj Qaddura (a prominent figure in the Lebanese woman's movement). In 1986 these biographies were published in six volumes as *Nisa' ra'idat* (Biographies of Pioneer Women from East and West). The first three volumes are about women from the East, and the second three about women from the West.

The Lebanese Civil War ended in 1990, the year that Nasrallah's *Khubzuna al-yawmi* (Our Daily Bread; translated as *A House Not Her Own*, 1992) was published; it was her second work to be translated into English. This collection emphasizes the mundane realities of civilian life in an environment marked by continuous violence. In the English introduction Nasrallah writes of her stories, "they are a living testimony, rising from the core of fire and destruction." All of the stories are based on the experiences of either Nasrallah herself or people close to her.

Through the 1990s and into the next century, Nasrallah published another novel focusing on the effects of emigration, *al-Jamr al-ghafi* (1995, Sleeping Ember), seven more collections of short stories, and six new children's books. Two of these works were translated into English. *Fantastic Strokes of Imagination* (1995) is a collection of stories that focus on assorted forms of self-transformation, and *Yawmiyyat hirr* (1997, A Cat's Diary; translated as *What Happened to Zeeko*, 2000) is a children's book that tells the story of the effect of the war on a young girl from the perspective of her cat. In 2005 Nasrallah published a collection of short stories, *Riyah janubiyyah* (Southern Winds).

In the introduction to *Khubzuna al-yawmi* Emily Nasrallah considers the effect of writing about war: "if the word still possesses the power to champion right does it still possess the strength to carry the cries of the destitute and oppressed?" Though the cries she refers to here are those of war victims, the sentiment can be extended to the variety of voices Nasrallah brings awareness to through her writings. Her compulsion to bring about such awareness has taken many literary forms, but from children's books to biographies her writing develops the same related themes. Some critics claim that her writing, like that of many women from countries with evolving women's liberation movements, lacks diversity. One might also add, however, that Nasrallah's repeated themes result from her desire to give voice to the people in the country that she loves that are too often silenced.

Interview:

Nelda LaTeef, "Emily Nasrallah, Novelist," *Women of Lebanon: Interviews with Champions for Peace* (Jefferson, N.C.: McFarland, 1997), pp. 57–66.

References:

Evelyne Accad and Rose Ghurayyib, *Contemporary Arab Women Writers and Poets* (Beirut: Institute for Women's Studies in the Arab World, Beirut University College, 1985), pp. 64–70;

Miriam Cooke, "Flight against Time," in *War's Other Voices* (New York: Cambridge University Press, 1987), pp. 144–163;

Joseph T. Zeidan, "Emily Nasrallah: Village Novelist," *Arab Women Novelists: The Formative Years and Beyond* (Albany: State University of New York Press, 1995), pp. 119–124, 220–225.

'Abd al-Hakim Qasim

(1935 – 13 November 1990)

Christina Phillips
School of Oriental and African Studies, University of London

BOOKS: *Ayyam al-insan al-sab'ah* (Cairo: Dar al-Kitab al-'Arabi, 1968); translated by Joseph Norment Bell as *The Seven Days of Man* (Cairo: General Egyptian Book Organization, 1989; Evanston, Ill.: Hydra/Northwestern University Press, 1996);

Muhawalah li al-khuruj (Beirut: Dar al-Haqa'iq, 1980);

Qadar al-ghuraf al-muqbidah (Cairo: Matbu'at al-Qahira, 1982);

Al-Ukht li ab wa sutur min daftar al-ahwal (Beirut: Dar al-Tanwir, 1983);

Al-Mahdi wa Turaf min khabar al-akhirah: Riwayatan (Beirut: Dar al-Tanwir, 1984); translated by Peter Theroux as *Rites of Assent: Two Novellas,* introduction by Samia Mehrez (Philadelphia: Temple University Press, 1995);

Al-Ashwaq wa al-asa (Cairo: Al-Hay'ah al-Misriyyah al-'Ammah li al-Kitab, 1984);

Al-Zunun wa al-ru'a (Cairo: Dar al-Mustaqbal al-'Arabi, 1986);

Al-Hijrah ila ghayr al-ma'luf (Cairo: Dar al-Fikr li al-Dirasat wa al-Nashr wa al-Tawzi', 1986);

Diwan al-mulhaqat (Cairo: Al-Hay'ah al-Misriyyah al-'Ammah li al-Kitab, 1990);

Al-Diwan al-akhir (Cairo: Dar al-Sharqiyat, 1991).

'Abd al-Hakim Qasim was a member of a group of Egyptian writers generally referred to as the "generation of the sixties," who reacted against social realism and articulated the dreams and frustrations of the nation around the time of and following Gamal Abdel Nasser's Revolution of 1952 and the declaration of the Egyptian Republic in 1953. Qasim was not prolific, but his contribution to modern Arabic literature, in particular his treatment of the Egyptian village, qualifies him as an important twentieth-century Arab writer.

Born in 1935 in the village of al-Bandara in the Nile Delta province of Gharbiyyah, Qasim lived with his grandparents from the age of eight to thirteen in Mit Ghamr, where he attended the local Coptic primary school. He went to secondary school in the provincial capital Tanta then moved to Cairo, and for the next three years he took odd jobs to support his family before entering Alexandria University in 1955 to begin a law degree. The move to the city opened up new avenues for Qasim in terms of intellectual growth and the opportunity to get involved in political activities. It also caused him to revise his view of village culture, with its popular religion, rituals, and traditions. The resulting inner conflict, like his later incarceration and exile, had a profound effect on his writing, where the village often provides the setting and where themes relating to the struggle between traditional and modern values, the clash of urban and rural mind-sets, the mixed benefits of education and religion, as well as the experience of suffering, oppression, and alienation often recur. Qasim did not study for his degree uninterruptedly, for in the late 1950s he went to work in the post office in Cairo to support his family. In December 1960 he was arrested for having links with clandestine leftist organizations, and in 1962 he was sentenced by a military court to five years' imprisonment. He was released early in 1964, having used his years of incarceration to write short stories and the first draft of his novel *Ayyam al-insan al-sab'ah* (1968; translated as *The Seven Days of Man,* 1989).

This first novel laid the foundations of Qasim's artistic vision. The story has autobiographical elements, as the protagonist's education matches the author's own, and the protagonist's conflict, which arises from his encounter with life outside the village, is precisely the one suffered by Qasim as a young man. The narrative follows a group of dervishes through the various stages of the annual pilgrimage from their village in the northern delta to the shrine of al-Sayyid Badawi, a popular Muslim saint, in Tanta. Each of the seven days referred to by the title represents one of the seven stages of the pilgrimage, beginning with preparations in the village through to the journey to Tanta, the sojourn in a hostel there, the mosque visit, and the return home. These are spread over several years so that besides an account of the pilgrimage the narrative also follows the journey from childhood to young adulthood of its protagonist, 'Abd al-'Aziz, and the changes in the dervish group and village over time. At each stage of the journey 'Abd al-'Aziz is a little older, and as his schooling progresses and he becomes acquainted with urban life, he begins to find himself repulsed by certain aspects of village life while at the same time remaining emotionally attached to it. The novel is then the story of a child's initiation into the world and of the passage from a traditional mind-set to a more liberal one, with all the suffering this entails. The process is mapped out by changes in 'Abd al-'Aziz's attitude toward village rituals; the breakdown of his relationship with his father, Hajj Karim, who is the leader of the village dervishes and is well respected; and 'Abd al-'Aziz's own increasing inner turmoil.

When the novel opens, 'Abd al-'Aziz is a young child, in awe of his father and the world around him. By the time the Sufis set out from the village in the third chapter, "The Journey," however, 'Abd al-'Aziz no longer sleeps with the rest of his family. In the following chapter 'Abd al-'Aziz is ashamed of his father and his Sufi comrades when they meet him in Tanta, where the boy is now in school, and the atmosphere between him and the villagers on this trip is awkward. The tension comes to a head in the fifth chapter, "The Big Night," when 'Abd al-'Aziz unleashes a stream of abuse at the group as they are gathered in a hostel on the eve of the pilgrimage. By the final visit to the mosque in chapter 6 'Abd al-'Aziz appears to be more or less alienated from the group. In the seventh and final chapter, however, he returns to the village on the occasion of his father's death and undergoes a kind of awakening. The village, it becomes clear, has itself undergone considerable change, and 'Abd al-'Aziz is suddenly able to see the things that unite him with the villagers rather than only the differences. The novel thus ends with a plea for reconciliation and understanding in a society suffering under the pressures of modernization and the growing gap between different classes and social groups.

The theme of change and the clash of ideologies, two concerns that have characterized the Arabic novel since its inception, are central to *Ayyam al-insan al-sab'ha*. The novel is conventional in comparison to some of the more adventurous experiments in modern Arabic fiction of the time, but it nevertheless represents a departure insofar as Qasim's treatment of the village goes beyond the sentimental portrayals of rural life found in the work of the previous generation of Arab writers. Space is not simply a setting here but a means of charting the hero's inner struggle; hence, 'Abd al-'Aziz begins the narrative sleeping in the same room as his family, then moves to the roof, then to Tanta and Alexandria. Similarly, when he leaves the hostel after his outburst in chapter 5, his steps lead him towards the mosque, demonstrating the hold his father still has over him. The sections of narra-

Dust jacket for the American edition (1996) of the English translation of 'Abd al-Hakim Qasim's first novel, Ayyam al-insan al-sab'ah, *1968 (Richland County Public Library)*

tive set in the provincial capital, on the other hand, provide the opportunity to contrast modern urban life with traditional rural existence. Presented like all of Qasim's cities from the perspective of the outsider, Tanta, with its busy but cleaner streets, crowded with cars and other symbols of modern technology, is the complete antithesis of mundane life in rural Egypt as depicted in the early chapters of the book. Village life is portrayed as a cycle of hot days filled with toil followed by cool, relaxing evenings, a time for talk, storytelling, and Sufi rituals. It is a harsh existence, partly because nature dictates it to be so but also because of the injustices mankind creates for himself, as demonstrated in Hajj Karim's gradually diminishing land next to al-Mitwalli Sarukh's increasing wealth and in the butcher's attempt to avoid paying a fair price for the meat of the buffalo belonging to Hajj Karim's family when the animal is no longer good for work.

The theme of oppression runs through all of Qasim's work but does not necessarily make his stories dark and pessimistic. The human spirit shines through in the abundance of love and friendship found in his villages, and characters are seen to have found happiness in Sufism. For instance, in *Ayyam al-insan al-sab'ha* the cohesive function mystical Islam plays in the village is clear. Some of Qasim's Sufis, however, fail to rise to the occasion to combat evil, as is the case in "Al-Mahdi" (1984; translated as "The Mahdi," 1995), and the author's overall attitude toward religion, like education, is rather ambivalent. Religion can bring solace to the individual and the community, but it can also be exploited and used as an instrument of repression. Similarly, education can bring enlightenment and help individuals out of oppressive situations by opening doors to them and facilitating upward social mobility, but it is also a painful process which leads to ruptures in the family and inner conflict in the individual, whose knowledge and expanded intellectual horizons become a barrier between him and his people.

The picture of rural Egypt that emerges from Qasim's first novel and the stories that followed, as a place where friendship and mysticism flourish under harsh physical and economic conditions, is far from the romantic depictions of the Egyptian village found in the work of some of his predecessors. Modern Arabic prose before the 1960s was characterized by polarities, such as city/village, science/religion, modernity/tradition, and West/East, and the treatment of them could be simplistic. Modernity was often seen as desirable, and many Egyptian writers looked to a future based on science and reason. Yet, traditional life was still cherished and not easily abandoned, even if reform seemed to demand as much. This sentimental attitude to traditional Egyptian life comes across clearly in the novels and short stories of the first half of the twentieth century, where scenes from the countryside are infused with nostalgia. The 1960s, however, brought a sea change and marked a turning point in modern Arabic literature. The shattering Arab defeat by Israel in the Six-Day War of 1967 along with growing disillusionment with the path of modernization raised questions about the future and caused Egyptian writers and intellectuals to reconsider some of the principles on which they had based their artistic vision. Many Arab writers and intellectuals began to turn back to indigenous culture and tradition to search for alternative solutions to current problems and to forge a future grounded more firmly in local history and norms. This move meant washing away the sentimentality that had characterized attitudes to the past for the previous half century and reexamining Arab heritage with a critical eye. Qasim's village in *Ayyam al-insan al-sab'ah* is among the first examples of such a critical approach. The same sophisticated attitude is found in the portrayal of Sufi characters in his work. The otherworldly social recluse or mad-religious representative familiar in the literature of earlier generations is replaced by individuals who form an essential part of the social fabric and are active participants in village life. They have their faults, as any authentically represented human character would, but they are considerably closer to their counterparts in real life.

In 1965, one year after his release from prison, Qasim completed his law degree and went to work for the Department of Insurance and Pensions. Over the next nine years he published short stories in the newspapers *al-Adab* and *al-Majallah,* but, like many of his contemporaries, he felt increasingly ill at ease as President Anwar Sadat's regime perpetuated and escalated the authoritarian practices of Nasser. The situation came to a head in 1973 when the measures taken by Sadat against liberals and leftists who had sided with the student movement in 1972 forced several writers and critics to flee the country. Qasim followed them into exile a year later when he chose not to return home from Berlin after delivering a lecture series on Egyptian literature at the invitation of the Evangelical Academy and the Institute of Islamic Studies of the Free University. Qasim remained in Berlin with his wife and two children until 1982, taking modest jobs, such as a night-guard post, and working on a doctoral dissertation on either modern Arabic literature or the 1960s underground movement in Egypt, which he never completed. Qasim's period in exile–his experience of Europe coupled with a profound yearning for the village of his childhood–energized him to write, and during this time he produced some of his most important work.

The village of the northern delta and the character of 'Abd al-'Aziz in *Ayyam al-Insan al-Sab'a* are carried on into the stories written in exile and beyond and can be seen as the center of Qasim's world. Qasim also expanded his fictional world, however, to take in the Egyptian cities of Alexandria and Cairo, Fez in Morocco, and the European metropolis Berlin, each with its own special attributes. Like Tanta in *Ayyam al-insan al-sab'ah,* Cairo, with its historical monuments and learning institutions, is filled with novelty and excitement for the peasant outsider. But the sense of wonderment is mediated by the alienation and anxiety Qasim's villager suffers in the Egyptian capital, where he can afford only cheap, dirty accommodation and remains on the margins of the vibrant city life. The situation is worse in Berlin, where the outsider does not suffer so much from the aggressiveness of the locals but from the way they ignore him and render him invisible.

Alexandria and Fez, on the other hand, are more amenable cityscapes. The former, where the writer attended university, with its cool climate and sea views, embodies a kind of urban harmony while the latter, a city that Qasim visited only briefly, is surrounded by an almost mythical aura. All these places are approached from the perspective of the outsider, which enables the author to describe and comment on them afresh.

Naturally, themes of freedom and oppression assume particular significance in the work of an exiled writer, and a yearning for home is to be expected. Yet, Qasim's approach to the Egyptian village, which he treats as a symbol of broader human reality, is consistently unsentimental, and his fiction does not betray a personal or political agenda, even though he held strong political views and was involved with political groups at different times. His novella *al-Mahdi*, written in Berlin in 1977, demonstrates well the writer's nonpartisan approach and rejection of artificial, black-and-white renderings of complex issues. It is also prophetic, for it warned of the dangerous rise of fundamentalism long before the movement was perceived as a threat. *Al-Mahdi* is the story of the forced conversion of 'Awdallah, a Copt umbrella maker. No longer able to afford lodgings in Tanta, 'Awdallah and his family set out for the countryside, where the cost of living is cheaper. After a time they come to the village of Mahallat al-Jiyad, where a local Sufi, a man of standing named 'Ali Effendi, insists on extending his hospitality to the family and brings them into his house. With seemingly good intentions 'Ali Effendi takes 'Awdallah's case to the leader of the Muslim Brotherhood in the village in the hope that they will extend some of their charity to him. According to 'Ali Effendi's exposition in the opening pages, the Muslim Brothers have gained influence in the village and, in his analysis, have been a positive influence; hence he has no qualms about entrusting 'Awdallah to their care. The Muslim Brothers, for their part, seize the opportunity, find a place for 'Awdallah to live that is, significantly, close to the mosque and mission, and begin preparations for a ceremony in which the Copt is to convert to Islam. 'Awdallah and his wife, Fulla, are uneasy about the gushing reception and the charity they receive in Mahallat al-Jiyad, and their anxiety increases as the story proceeds. The ceremony turns into a frenzy, with a delirious crowd fighting to get close to 'Awdallah, whom they hail as the *Mahdi* (Saviour), while the Muslim Brothers resolutely lead him to the mosque. 'Awdallah's health has been deteriorating since he arrived in the village, and he never actually makes it into the mosque. He collapses at the gate and dies in the arms of his wife as she prays and makes the sign of the cross over him. Meanwhile, the local sheikh and the mayor privately deplore the way 'Awdallah is being

Dust jacket for the English translation, 1995, of Qasim's al-Mahdi wa Turaf min khabar al-akhirah: Riwayatan, *1984 (Thomas Cooper Library, University of South Carolina)*

treated, but neither does anything to stop it. The village mayor, symbolizing the impotence of the state, is preoccupied with his own sexual gratification, and the sheikh opts to take refuge in prayer.

The treatment of 'Awdallah is clearly condemnable, but Qasim is careful not to simplify the matter by assigning sole blame to the Muslim Brothers. The novella is not the plea for religious tolerance it might appear to be at first glance but rather a measured exploration of a real historical situation–the growing influence of radical Islam in the Egyptian countryside–and a probing of man's motivations and actions. No single individual or group is portrayed as wholly responsible for 'Awdallah's death; instead, the responsibility is collective, and there are various mitigating factors to consider. The Muslim Brothers are themselves disillusioned individuals who have turned to fundamental religion in order to recover a lost sense of identity and belonging, while 'Ali Effendi's intentions are sincere, even if handing 'Awdallah over to the Brothers seals the Copt's fate. The sheikh and mayor, who perceive coercion from the outset, take no steps to thwart the process, so they can hardly be regarded as morally superior to those who actively participate in the evil. Even 'Awdallah himself puts up no resistance other than a few weak protests that are easily mistaken for modesty.

The theme of responsibility is also important in "Turaf min khabar al-akhirah" (translated as "Good News from the Afterlife"), a novella written in Berlin in 1981 and published with *al-Mahdi* in 1984. "Turaf min Khabar al-akhirah" stands out in modern Arabic literature as a rare attempt to depict death and the afterlife in detail. The narrative opens in a remote village in the Egyptian countryside and follows the movements of a young boy, "the grandson." On the occasion of a villager's death, the grandson follows him into the afterlife in a dream, after falling asleep on his grave. In the afterlife the deceased is confronted with the two angels of death, Naker and Nakeer, who proceed to consider and judge his life, though on different terms than the traditional Muslim representation of death has led the dead man to expect: the angels are not concerned with adherence to the principles of Islamic law but with whether the individual has remained true to himself and acted on his conscience. Over the course of a long dialogue it becomes clear that the dead man wasted many opportunities and allowed his fears and prejudices to guide him away from what the angels judge to have been the right path for him. Here again Qasim conveys the message that to avoid evil is not enough; the individual must follow his inner voice and act. An interesting feature of the narrative is the extended account it offers of the funerary rites and burial, which is unusual in modern Arabic writing; and the reworking of the scene of judgment is a courageous attempt to examine some commonly held religious beliefs.

When Qasim returned to Egypt in 1982 he found work as a freelance journalist and for a time wrote a weekly column for the Labour Party newspaper *al-Sha'b*. The short stories he published in the 1980s reflect a continued sense of geographical and existential dislocation and the archetypal village continues to provide the setting for many of the stories in *Diwan al-mulhaqat* (1990, The Collected Appendices) and *al-Diwan al-akhir* (1991, The Last Collection). Back in Egypt, Qasim also engaged in political activity and stood for election as a candidate for the leftist opposition party al-Tajammu' in 1987. He was defeated, and his health deteriorated after a stroke. He continued to work until he died on 13 November 1990, leaving behind a small but important body of fiction, whose themes of oppression and alienation remain pertinent to Arab society to this day.

The last thirty years of Qasim's life were a particularly difficult period in Egyptian history. Nasser's revolution in 1952 raised the nation's hopes after years of ineffective government under King Farouk but failed to deliver on its promises. The regime's corruption and excess created a feeling of unease and disillusionment, which reached a climax in June 1967 when Israel inflicted a devastating defeat on the Arabs. The soul-searching and questions about the future continued through the 1970s, as Sadat's policy of *infitah* (opening up the Egyptian market to intentional capitalism) widened the gap between rich and poor and the new president cracked down on the Muslim Brotherhood and other opponents of government.

'Abd al-Hakim Qasim was one of many who faced the choice of silence, exile, or imprisonment. Yet, despite the bleak political outlook, exciting developments were taking place in the realm of literature, and Qasim was at the heart of them. As a member of the "generation of the sixties" he participated in one of the most important literary movements in modern Arabic literature, a movement that brought fresh energy to the Arabic novel and short story and whose members dedicated themselves to matters of form and experimentation with impressive results. Qasim's contribution was quantitatively small (three novels and seven story collections, including his five novellas and a play) and has received less attention from critics than other members of the group, but he is nevertheless significant, not least because he succeeded in resurrecting the Egyptian village from some of the static representations of his predecessors and transforming it into a conduit of theme and meaning and a microcosm of universal patterns of behavior.

Interview:

"Hakadha yatakallamunu al-udaba' al-shabab," *al-Tali'ah*, 5 (September 1969): 20–22.

References:

Roger Allen, "*Ayyam al-insan al-sab'ah:* 'Abd al-Hakim Qasim," in his *The Arabic Novel: An Historical and Critical Introduction,* second edition (Syracuse, N.Y.: Syracuse University Press, 1995), pp. 167–177;

Hilary Kilpatrick, "'Abd al-Hakim Qasim and the Search for Liberation," *Journal of Arabic Literature,* 26 (March–June 1995): 50–66;

Kilpatrick, "'Abd al-Hakim Qasim and the Seven Days of Man," in her *The Modern Egyptian Novel: A Study in Social Criticism* (London: Ithaca, 1974), pp. 140–148;

Sabry Hafez, *The Quest for Identities: The Development of the Modern Arabic Short Story* (London: Saqi, 2007), pp. 337–381;

Samah Selim, "The Exiled Son," in her *The Novel and the Rural Imaginary in Egypt, 1880–1985* (New York & London: RoutledgeCurzon, 2004).

Sayyid Qutb
(9 October 1906 – 19 August 1966)

Ovamir Anjum
University of Wisconsin–Madison

BOOKS: *Muhimmat al-Sha'ir fi al-hayah* (Cairo, 1932);

Al-Shati al-majhul (Cairo, 1935);

Naqd kitab: Mustaqbal al-thaqafah fi Misr (Cairo, 1939);

Al-Taswir al-fanni fi al-Qur'an (Cairo: Dar al-Ma'arif, 1945);

Al-Atyaf al-arba'ah (Cairo: Lajnat al-Nashr li al-Jami'iyyin, 1945);

Tifl min al-qaryah (Cairo, 1946); translated and edited by John Calvert and William E. Shepard as *A Child from the Village* (Syracuse, N.Y.: Syracuse University Press, 2004);

Kutub wa shakhsiyyat (Cairo, 1946);

Mashahid al-qiyamah fi al-Qur'an (Cairo, 1947);

Al-Naqd al-Adabi: Usuluhu wa manahijuhu (Cairo: Dar al-Fikr al-'Arabi, 1947);

Ashwak (Cairo: Dar Sa'd Misr, 1947);

Al-'Adalah al-ijtima'iyyah fi al-Islam (Cairo: Lajnat al-Nashr li al-Jami'iyyin, 1949); translated by John B. Hardie as *Social Justice in Islam* (Washington, D.C.: American Council of Learned Societies, 1953); translation revised by Hamid Algar (Oneonta, N.Y.: Islamic Publications International, 2000);

Al-Salam al-'alami wa al-Islam (Cairo: Maktabat Wahbah, 1951); translated as *Islam and Universal Peace* (Indianapolis: American Trust Publications, 1977);

Ma'rakat al-Islam wa al-Ra'smaliyyah (Cairo: Dar al-Ikhwan li al-Sahafah wa al-Tiba'ah, 1951);

Fi zilal al-Qur'an, 20 volumes (Cairo: Dar Ihya' al-Kutub al-'Arabiyyah, 1952–1959); translated by M. A. Salahi and A. A. Shamis as *In the Shade of the Quran* (London: MWH, 1979);

Hadha al-din (Cairo: Dar al-Qalam, 1962); translated as *This Religion of Islam* (Delhi: Markazi Maktaba Islami, 1974);

Al-Mustaqbal li hadha al-din (Cairo: Maktabat Wahbah, 1962); translated as *Islam: The Religion of the Future* (Kuwait: I.I.F.S.O., 1971);

Al-Islam wa mushkilat al-hadara (Cairo: Dar Ihya' al-Kutub al-'Arabiyyah, 1962);

Khasa'is al-tasawwur al-Islami wa muqawwimatuhu (Cairo: 'Isa al-Babi al-Halabi, 1962); translated by

Sayyid Qutb in an Egyptian prison (<http://speakingoffaith.publicradio.org/programs/britishradical/particulars.shtml>)

Mohammed Moinuddin Siddiqui as *The Islamic Concept and Its Characteristics* (Indianapolis: American Trust Publications, 1991);

Ma'alim fi al-tariq (Cairo: Maktabat Wahbah, 1964); translated by Badar ul-Hasan as *Milestones* (Karachi: International Islamic Publishers, 1981);

Muqawwimat al-tasawwur al-Islami (N.p., 1986); translated by Rami David as *Basic Principles of the Islamic Worldview* (North Haledon, N.J.: Islamic Publications International, 2006);

The Sayyid Qutb Reader: Selected Writings on Politics, Religion, and Society, edited by Albert J. Bergesen (London: Routledge, 2007; New York: Routledge, 2008).

Sayyid Qutb was one of the most influential Arab writers of the twentieth century. Critics have described him as "the ideologue of the modern Islamic movement," "the father of radical Islam," and "the John

Locke of the Muslim world." His life was devoted to the struggle against inequality in his native Egypt and the domination of the country by the imperialist West and to the search for a just, egalitarian, and spiritually fulfilling society. He found his answer in the Islam preached in the Qur'an—not the one practiced in his age, which he ruthlessly criticized. He embraced many values that may be identified as modern, such as the censure of unthinking tradition and despotism and dedication to egalitarianism, social justice, and freedom of conscience. In the introduction to his revised translation of Qutb's *Social Justice in Islam* (2000) Hamid Algar observes that Qutb's early writings reveal a "Western-tinged outlook on cultural and literary questions"; yet, his attacks on Western materialism and imperialism were scathing.

Qutb's intense writings gripped his Arab readers, and their poetic ambiguity left much room for interpretation. The ambiguity and imbalance of his writings was increased by the fact that during the last fifteen years of his life he composed them while under almost continuous imprisonment. A variety of subsequent movements in the Arab-Muslim world, from progressive to puritanical and from quietist to violent, have embraced his ideas. His execution in 1966 has made him a martyr for many and has contributed to his continued popularity.

Quite a bit is known about Qutb's childhood from his autobiography, *Tifl min al-qaryah* (1946; translated as *A Child from the Village,* 2004). He was born on 9 October 1906 in the village of Mosha in the Asyut district of Upper Egypt, the first of five children of Ibrahim Qutb, a farmer, and Fatima Husain Usman. His brother, Muhammad, continued to publish widely influential books in a style and with a content similar to Qutb's for decades after Sayyid's death, and two of his sisters, Hamida and Amina, also became known for their Islamic writings and dedication to the cause of Islamic revival.

As is traditional in religious Muslim families, Sayyid and his siblings had memorized the Qur'an by the time they reached the age of ten. Qutb attended a modern primary school from age six to twelve. In 1921 he was sent to live with an uncle in a Cairo suburb and enrolled in a preliminary teachers' training school in the city. He published his first article in a literary journal in 1924. In 1928 he attended the preparatory high school for the Dar al-'Ulum, a prestigious teachers' training college that later became Cairo University; he entered the Dar al-'Ulum the following year. His first book, *Muhimmat al-Sha'ir fi al-hayah* (The Task of a Poet in Life), appeared in 1932. He graduated from the Dar al-'Ulum in 1933 with a B.A. in Arabic language and literature and a diploma in education and taught at various schools for the next seven years. He became an active member of the Wafd, a nationalist party founded by Sa'd Zaghlul; on Zaghlul's death in 1938 Qutb joined the breakaway Sa'dist party, which claimed a higher degree of loyalty to the founder's ideas. He also became involved with al-Hizb al-Watani (The Patriotic Party) and Hizb Misr al-Fata (The Young Egypt Party).

Also in 1938 Qutb published two articles arguing for the superiority of the Egyptian language to classical Arabic and the Islamic culture it represented. In doing so he was taking the modernist side in a quarrel between traditionalist and modernist scholars of Arabic language and literature. The traditionalists, led by Mustafa Sadiq al-Rafa'i, defended the superiority of classical Arabic on the basis that God must have chosen the best language to reveal his final message. Qutb, influenced by his modernist mentors 'Abbas al-'Aqqad and Taha Husayn, contends that the traditionalist school failed to respond to the changing world: "language is a living organism adaptable to the environment of its speakers, and it parallels the progress of ideas and science, and is influenced by politics, economics and society"; it "evolves and grows." He maintains that "We should not be hesitant to proclaim that this language is not our native tongue, but that of another nation (the Arabs) that differed from our own in its mores, traditions, thoughts, environment, political and economic conditions—in the same way that any two nations differ from each other." He derides the traditionalists as "shallow in feeling, primitive in consciousness and ill-equipped psychologically and experientially, as compared to the expansive world of feeling of the modernist school and its rich psychological ammunition and existential experience."

Qutb was, however, shaken by the publication later in 1938 of Husayn's *Mustaqbal al-thaqafa fi Misr* (translated as *The Future of Culture in Egypt,* 1975), which argued that Egypt could only prosper by imitating the West. Reinterpreting history to discount a millennium-long Arab-Islamic presence at the deepest levels of Egyptian society, Husayn contended that Egypt had been part of the West at least since the period of its colonization by Rome and perhaps even earlier, when the great Egyptian civilization interacted as an equal or superior with its Greek counterpart. Qutb felt compelled to write a refutation of Husayn's thesis; the work marked the beginning of a new intellectual direction for his critique. *Naqd kitab:* Mustaqbal al-thaqafa fi Misr (1939, Critique of a Book: *The Future of Culture in Egypt*) appeared the year after Husayn's work. One reason Qutb gives for being uncomfortable with the idea of Egypt as a long-lost part of Western civilization is that the Roman period was an oppressive colonialism supported by "the pharaohs who were hated by the people." He was no doubt implicitly comparing it to the contemporary British colonialism that he despised. Second, he points out that while Islam and Arabic have penetrated all levels of Egyptian society, contacts with the Greeks were limited to the elite. In sharp contrast to the position he took in his two antitraditionalist articles, Qutb here argues for a fundamental difference between the Egyptian and European minds and civilizations.

In 1940 Qutb became a school inspector for the Egyptian Ministry of Education. During World War II he wrote two books, *al-Taswir al-fanni fi al-Qur'an* (1945) and *al-Atyaf al-arba'ah* (1945), in which he treats the Qur'an as literature. Around 1945 he became disgusted with contemporary politics and renounced activism. In 1945 or 1946 he wrote his autobiography, *Tifl min al-qaryah*. In the work he paints a sympathetic picture of the Egyptian peasantry, which was exploited by the dominant classes and ridden with a superstitious popular culture.

By 1947 Qutb had published ten books, including a volume of poetry; a collection of his articles about current writers; a book on literary theory; and the novel *Ashwak* (1947, Thorns). That year he became editor in chief of two journals, *al-'Alam al-'Arabi* (The Arab World) and *al-Fikr al-Jadid* (New Thought); the latter sought to present a model of an Islamic society free of corruption, tyranny, and foreign domination. Both journals were short-lived; *al-Fikr al-Jadid* was shut down by the government.

Qutb's turn toward Islam was inaugurated by his reading of the works of Muslim reformist scholars of the Indian subcontinent: the Pakistani theologian Abul A'la Maududi; the Indian Arabist, litterateur, and historian Abul Hasan Ali Nadwi; and the charismatic Austrian Jew Leopold Weiss, who had converted to Islam, taken the name Muhammad Asad, and settled in Pakistan. Qutb was also aware of Western critics of the West and is thought to have been particularly impressed by a philosophical work, *L'Homme, cet inconnu* (1935; translated as *Man, the Unknown*, 1935), by Alexis Carrel, a Nobel prize–winning French medical scientist. Maududi's thought was, however, the greatest influence on Qutb. Maududi held that Islam is a self-contained system of life, an ideology incommensurate with any foreign ideologies such as capitalism or communism.

Qutb's first Islamist work, *al-'Adalah al-ijtima'iyyah fi al-Islam* (translated as *Social Justice in Islam*, 1953), appeared in 1949 and became one of his most widely read books. It presents a humanistic interpretation of Islam; censures feudalism, capitalism, and communism; and decries the incompetence, shortsightedness, and self-centeredness of the "men of religion," his name for traditional religious scholars.

In an attempt to reverse Qutb's Islamic leanings, the Ministry of Education sent him to study in the United States in November 1948. The effect of the trip was almost the opposite: Qutb deplored American materialism, racism, and sexual permissiveness and became convinced that the

A CHILD FROM THE VILLAGE

Sayyid Qutb

Edited, Translated, and with an Introduction by
John Calvert *and* William Shepard

SYRACUSE UNIVERSITY PRESS

Title page for the 2004 English translation of Qutb's 1946 autobiography, Tifl min al-qaryah *(Thomas Cooper Library, University of South Carolina)*

West was leading humanity toward spiritual, social, and even physical destruction. In 1949, while Qutb was in the United States, the charismatic founder of the increasingly popular Islamic reformist party al-Ikhwan al-Muslimun (The Muslim Brotherhood [or Brethren]), Hasan al-Banna, was assassinated in Egypt; Qutb noticed that many American observers rejoiced at the murder. He studied at Wilson Teachers College in Washington, D.C., and obtained a master's degree in education at Colorado State Teachers College (now the University of Northern Colorado) in Greeley. As soon as he returned from America in August 1950, he made contact with the Muslim Brotherhood, whose leaders were already admirers of *al-'Adala al-ijtima'iyyah fi al-Islam* and his critique of Husayn's book.

By 1951 *al-'Adala al-ijtima'iyyah fi al-Islam* had gone through four editions. That year Qutb published two shorter books, *al-Salam al-'alami wa al-Islam* (translated as *Islam and Universal Peace*, 1977) and *Ma'rakat al-Islam wa al ra'smaliyyah* (Islam's Battle with Capitalism). He had also

Title page for the first English translation of Qutb's first Islamist work, Al'Adalah al-ijtima 'iyyah fi al-Islam, published four years earlier (Thomas Cooper Library, University of South Carolina)

begun his multivolume commentary on the Qur'an, *Fi Zilal al-Qur'an* (1952–1959; translated as *In the Shade of the Quran*, 1979), on which he continued to work for the rest of his life. Also in 1951 Qutb resigned from the Ministry of Education and began writing for the Muslim Brotherhood periodicals *al-Risala* (The Message), *al-Da'wa* (The Summons), and *al-Liwa' al-Jadid* (The New Banner).

On 23 July 1952 Egypt's King Farouk, a British puppet, was overthrown by nine soldiers who styled themselves "al-Dubbat al-Ahrar" (the Free Officers). They were nominally led by General Muhammad Naguib, but the real force behind the group was the ambitious Lieutenant Colonel Gamal Abdel Nasser. The Free Officers sought the cooperation of the Muslim Brotherhood, which by then was two decades old and was rapidly becoming the most popular organization in Egypt. Qutb, who had formally joined the Brotherhood that year, seems to have impressed the officers—or, perhaps, they found the power of his pen useful in realizing their ambitions. A close associate of Qutb's, Salah al-Khalidi, wrote in 1981 that Qutb had been visited by Nasser four days before the coup. A month after the coup Qutb delivered a lecture at the Officers' Club in Cairo on intellectual and spiritual liberation in Islam. He was appointed cultural adviser to the governing Revolutionary Council, which consisted of the nine officers who had staged the coup; he was the only civilian allowed to attend their meetings.

The collaboration soon collapsed, however. Confident of its popular support, the Muslim Brotherhood wanted to implement Islamic law in Egypt through democratic means; but its call for a return to civilian rule based on elections or a constitutional referendum was ignored by the Revolutionary Council. Algar contends that the Free Officers had never been sincere in their overtures to the Brotherhood:

> As a prelude to eliminating the Brethren as an autonomous force capable of challenging him, 'Abd al-Nasir [Nasser] sought first to coopt the organization by offering cabinet posts to some of its leading members. It was thus intimated to Qutb that the Ministry of Education was his for the asking. He was also invited to become director of the *Hay'at al-Tahrir* (Liberation Rally), the newly established government party, and to draw up its programs and statutes. Qutb refused all such offers, and most of his colleagues in the Brethren also had the good sense to resist full-scale absorption into the emerging structures of the Nasserist state.

In 1953 Qutb was made editor in chief of *al-Ikhwan al-Muslimun*, the official journal of the Brotherhood. In January 1954 the Revolutionary Council decreed the dissolution of the Muslim Brotherhood and banned the journal. Naguib tried to intercede on the Brotherhood's behalf, but Nasser ousted his old comrade and then staged an attempt on Naguib's life as an excuse to crack down on the Brotherhood more harshly. Seven of the most prominent members were sentenced to death. Qutb, who was suffering a severe illness, was arrested and tortured; at his trial in July 1955 he was sentenced to fifteen years' imprisonment. Qutb's thought became further radicalized in prison, especially after guards killed twenty-one members of the Muslim Brotherhood and injured many others in June 1957. The savagery Qutb and his fellow inmates suffered led him to conclude that a regime unprecedented in its ruthlessness was governing Egypt; the problem was no longer foreign rule or the absence of social justice but the usurpation of power by native forces hostile to Islam and given to self-aggrandizement at any cost. This new *jahiliyyah* (ignorance of divine guidance), he believed, was fostered and protected by the coercive apparatus of a modern authoritarian state and could be remedied only by a radical long-term program of ideological and organizational work carried out by a vanguard of sincere believers who would bring true Islam to the society. He developed these ideas in dialogues with fellow inmates from the Brotherhood and wrote them down in letters to his siblings. They came to the attention of members of the Brotherhood who were dissatisfied with the uncertain leadership of Hasan al-Hudaybi, and a group of more than two hundred was formed among those who were persuaded by Qutb's arguments.

In prison Qutb produced his most important writings—above all, his exegesis of the Qur'an; such a work is the highest intellectual attainment to which a traditional Muslim scholar can aspire. Qutb's primary concerns in his commentary are to draw out the practical instructions contained in the Qur'an and to demonstrate the coherent structure that underlies the apparent diversity of the text.

Qutb's *Ma'alim fi al-tariq* (translated as *Milestones*, 1981) was published in 1964. It is a slim volume of thirteen essays, mainly selections from his exegesis and some of the letters he sent from prison. In the work Qutb describes his turn to the Qur'an:

> The person writing these lines has spent forty years of his life readings books and researching almost all aspects of human knowledge. Then he turned to the fountainhead of his religion and doctrine. He discovered that whatever he had read so far was indeed minute in comparison with the colossal monument (the Qur'an). He does not, however, regret spending forty years of his life in the pursuit of these sciences. He became cognizant of the nature, perversity, pettiness, conceit and noise of *jahiliyyah*. He now realizes that no Muslim should combine these two sources—divine and *jahili*—in his education.

His condemnation of his society as *jahili* (un-Islamic) is uncompromising:

> We are also surrounded by *jahiliyyah* today, which is of the same nature as it was during the first period of Islam, perhaps a little deeper. Our whole environment—people's beliefs and ideas, habits and art, rules and laws—is *jahili*, so much so that what we consider to be Islamic culture, Islamic sources, Islamic philosophy, and Islamic thought, are also constructs of *jahiliyyah*.

Qutb was released from prison shortly after the publication of *Ma'alim fi al-tariq*. In the first six months of 1965 the book went through five further editions and became one of founding documents of the modern Islamic movement. Qutb was rearrested on 9 August 1965 and charged with participating in a Muslim Brotherhood plot to assassinate Nasser. He was tried, convicted, tortured, and, on 19 August 1966, executed by hanging.

Robert Lee notes that "Although Qutb never explicitly called for violent attack on his own or other governments that he deemed negligent of Islamic law, his arguments provide a rationale for others to do so." Qutb's writings influenced the founders of radical Islamic groups, including al Qaeda. How he would have reacted to Islamist terrorism had he lived to see it cannot be known for certain, but it seems unlikely that he would have approved of it.

Sayyid Qutb's thought emerged from his passionate search for authenticity, humanity, and meaning in a time of tremendous upheaval and change. He saw Europe weakened by its ideology-driven wars and forced to relinquish its colonies; yet, he found that the elites who inherited power in those countries were often enamored of the West and subscribed to the same ideologies that had brought ruin to Europe. Qutb's desire to improve the welfare of the Egyptian people led him to Islamism, and he became its most eloquent and radical spokesperson. His oeuvre reveals a single-minded pursuit of social justice through submission to God.

References:

Yusuf Al'Azm, *Ra'id al-fikr al-Islami, al-shahid Sayyid Qutb* (Damascus: Dar al-Qalam, 1980);

Ibrahim Abu-Rabi', *Intellectual Origins of Islamic Resurgence in the Modern Arab World* (Albany: State University of New York Press, 1996);

Yvonne Y. Haddad, "Sayyid Qutb: Ideologue of Islamic Revival," in *Voices of Resurgent Islam,* edited by John Esposito (New York: Oxford University Press, 1983);

Badrul Hasan, *Syed Qutb Shaheed* (Karachi: International Islamic Publishers, 1980);

Gilles Kepel, *Muslim Extremism in Egypt: The Prophet and Pharaoh* (Berkeley: University of California Press, 1985);

Salah Al-Khalidi, *Sayyid Qutb, al-shahid al-hayy* (Amman: Maktabat al-Aqsa, 1981);

Robert Lee, *Overcoming Tradition and Modernity: The Search for Islamic Authenticity* (Boulder, Colo.: Westview Press, 1997);

Ahmad S. Moussalli, *Radical Islamic Fundamentalism: The Ideological and Political Discourses of Sayyid Qutb* (Beirut: American University of Beirut Press, 1992);

Adnan A. Musallam, *From Secularism to Jihad: Sayyid Qutb and the Foundations of Radical Islamism* (Westport, Conn.: Praeger, 2005);

Muhammad Qutb, *Sayyid Qutb, al-Shahid al-Azali* (Cairo: Al-Mukhtar al-Islami, 1974);

William E. Shepard, *Sayyid Qutb and Islamic Activism: A Translation and Critical Analysis of "Social Justice in Islam"* (Leiden & New York: Brill, 1996).

Nawal El Saadawi

(27 October 1931 –)

Coeli Fitzpatrick
Grand Valley State University

BOOKS: *Ta'allamat al-hubb* (Cairo: Maktabat al-Nahda al-Misriyyah, 1957);

Mudhakkirat tabibah (Cairo: Dar al-Ma'arif, 1958); translated by Catherine Cobham as *Memoirs of a Woman Doctor* (London: Saqi, 1988; San Francisco: City Lights, 1989);

Lahzat sidq (Cairo: Dar Roze al-Yusuf, 1959);

Hanan qalil (Cairo: Dar Roze al-Yusuf, 1960);

Al-Gha'ib (Cairo: Hay'at al-Kitab, 1969); translated by Shirley Eber as *Searching* (London: Zed, 1991);

Imra'atan fi imara'ah (Cairo: Hay'at al-Kitab, 1971); translated by Osman Nusairi and Jana Gough as *Two Women in One* (London: Saqi, 1985);

Al-Khayt wa-'ayn al-hayat (Cairo: Maktabat Madbuli, 1972); translated by Sherif Hetata as *The Well of Life and the Thread* (London: Lime Tree, 1993);

Imra'ah 'inda nuqtat al-sifr (Beirut: Dar al-Adab, 1973); translated by Hetata as *Women at Point Zero* (London: Zed, 1983);

Al-Mar'ah wa al-jins (Cairo: Maktabat Madbuli, 1974);

Al-Untha hiya al-asl (Beirut: Al-Mu'assasah al-'Arabiyyah li al-Dirasat wa al-Nashr, 1974);

Mawt al-rajul al-wahid 'ala al-ard (Beirut: Dar al-Adab, 1975); translated by Hetata as *God Dies by the Nile* (London: Zed, 1985);

Al-Rajul wa al-jins (Beirut: Al-Mu'assasah al-'Arabiyyah li al-Dirasat wa al-Nashr, 1976);

Al-Mar'a wa al-sira' al-nafsi (Beirut: Al-Mu'assasah al-'Arabiyyah li al-Dirasat, 1976);

Ughniyat al-atfal al-da'iriyyah (Beirut: Dar al-Adab, 1976); translated by Marilyn Booth as *The Circling Song* (London: Zed, 1989);

Al-Wajh al-'ari li al-mar'ah al-'Arabiyyah (Beirut: Al-Mu'assasah al-'Arabiyya li al-Dirasat wa al-Nashr, 1977); translated by Hetata as *The Hidden Face of Eve: Women in the Arab World* (Boston: Beacon Press, 1982);

'An al-mar'ah (Cairo: Dar al-Mustaqbal al-'Arabi, 1977);

Kanat hiya al-ad'af (Cairo: Maktabat Madbuli, 1979); translated by Eber as *She Has No Place in Paradise* (London: Minerva, 1989);

Nawal El Saadawi in a women's prison near Cairo (from A Daughter of Isis: The Autobiography of Nawal El Saadawi, *1999)*

Mawt ma'ali al-wazir sabiqan (Cairo: Maktabat Madbuli, 1980); translated by Eber as *Death of an Ex-Minister* (London: Methuen, 1987);

Mudhakkirati fi Sijn al-Nisa' (Cairo: Dar al-Mustaqbal al'Arabi, 1983); translated by Booth as *Memoirs from the Women's Prison* (London: Women's Press, 1986; Berkeley & Los Angeles: University of California Press, 1994);

Ithnay 'ashar imra'ah fi zinzanah wahidah (Cairo: Maktabat Madbuli, 1984);

Izis (Cairo: Dar al-Mustaqbal al-'Arabi, 1985);

Rihlati fi al-'alam (Cairo: Dar Nashr Tadamun al-Mar'ah al-'Arabiyyah, 1987); translated by Eber as *My Travels around the World* (London: Methuen, 1991);

Suqut al-imam (Cairo: Dar al-Mustaqbal al-'Arabi, 1987); translated by Hetata as *The Fall of the Imam* (London: Methuen, 1988);

Mudhakkirat tiflah ismuha Su'ad (Cairo: Manshurat Dar Tadamun al-Mar'ah al-'Arabiyyah, 1990);

Jannat wa Iblis (Beirut: Dar al-Adab, 1992); translated by Hetata as *The Innocence of the Devil* (Los Angeles: University of California Press, 1994);

Ma'rakah jadidah fi qadiyyat al-mar'ah (Cairo: Sina li al-Nashr, 1992);

Al-Hubb fi zaman al-naft (Cairo: Maktabat Madbuli, 1993); translated by Basil Hatim and Malcolm Williams as *Love in the Kingdom of Oil* (London: Al-Saqi, 2001);

Awraq hayati: Aljuz' al-awal (Cairo: Dar al-Hilal, 1995); translated by Hetata as *A Daughter of Isis: The Autobiography of Nawal El Saadawi* (London: Zed, 1999);

The Nawal El Sadaawi Reader (London: Zed, 1997);

Al-Mar'ah wa al-ghurbah (Cairo: Dar al-Ma'arif, 1997);

Awraq hayati: Al-Juz' al-thani (Cairo: Dar al-Mustaqbal al-'Arabi, 1998); translated by Hetata as *Walking through Fire* (London: Zed, 2002);

Taw'am al-sultah wa al-jins (Cairo: Dar al-Mustaqbal al-'Arabi, 1999);

Adab am qillat adab (Alexandria: Dar al-Mustaqbal, 2000);

Awraq hayati: Al-Juz' al-thalith (Beirut: Dar al-Adab, 2001);

Qadaya al-mar'ah wa al-fikr wa al-siyasah (Cairo: Dar Mabduli, 2002);

Qasr al-hudud (Cairo: Dar Mabduli, 2004);

Al-Riwayah (Cairo: Dar al-Hilal, 2005).

OTHER: "Growing up Female in Egypt," translated by Fedwa Malti-Douglas, in *Women and the Family in the Middle East: New Voices of Change*, edited by Elizabeth Warnock Fernea (Austin: University of Texas Press, 1985), pp. 111–120;

"Reply," in *Woman against Her Sex: A Critique of Nawal El Saadawi*, by Georges Tarabishi, translated by Basil Hatim and Elisabeth Orsini (London: Saqi, 1988), pp. 189–211;

"The Political Challenges Facing Arab Women at the End of the 20th Century," in *Women of the Arab World: The Coming Challenge*, edited by Nahid Toubia, translated by Marilyn Booth (Atlantic Highlands, N.J.: Zed, 1988), pp. 8–26;

"An Overview of My Life," translated by Antoinette Tuma, in *Contemporary Authors Autobiography Series*, volume 2, edited by Mark Zadrozny (Detroit: Gale Research, 1990), pp. 61–72;

"Women's Resistance in the Arab World and in Egypt," in *Women in the Middle East: Perceptions, Realities and Struggles for Liberation*, edited by Haleh Afshar (New York: St. Martin's Press, 1993), pp. 139–145.

SELECTED PERIODICAL PUBLICATION–UNCOLLECTED: "A New Battle for the Women's Movement in Egypt," translated by Seemi Ghazi, in *Comparative Studies of South Asia, Africa and the Middle East*, 15, no. 2 (1995): 90–98.

The Arab world's foremost feminist, Nawal El Saadawi is a physician, a novelist, an activist, and an outspoken opponent of racism, oppression, and exploitation. Since she began publishing her fiction in the late 1950s, El Saadawi has been a thorn in the side of Egyptian authorities and conservative Islamists everywhere. Daring in her choice of words and topics, she was the first Arab woman to address taboo subjects such as sex and female circumcision. She writes in Arabic, but almost all of her works have been translated into Western languages.

The second of nine children, Nawal al-Sayed Habash El Saadawi was born on 27 October 1931 in the village of Kafr Tahla, Egypt, to El Sayed and Zeinab El Saadawi, née Shoukry. Her father was a school inspector for the Ministry of Education. When El Saadawi was still quite young, the family moved to Alexandria, where she attended the Muharram Bey School for Girls. Like most Egyptian girls, both Muslim and Coptic Christian, El Saadawi was circumcised at age six. The following year her father was transferred to the village of Menouf; the family remained there for ten years. She excelled at the school in Menouf, surpassing her elder brother, Tala'at; her parents expressed no joy at her grades, however, merely disappointment in Tala'at.

When El Saadawi was ten years old, she attended the wedding of her slightly older cousin Zaynab in Kafr Tahla; the marriage was arranged by Zaynab's family. El Saadawi noted that as the bride sat surrounded by her wedding party, she had tears of sadness in her eyes: the marriage meant the end of her dream of becoming a teacher. The night of the wedding El Saadawi overheard her aunts saying that it was time for her, too, to get married. The family had already found a husband for her–a man El Saadawi had only glimpsed from afar. She decided that rather than surrender to an arranged marriage, she would resist in any way she could. When the prospective bridegroom arrived at her home for a visit, she blackened her teeth with eggplant and "accidentally" spilled the coffee tray all over him. The man disappeared–the first in a long line of suitors who were chased away by her apparent clumsiness.

When El Saadawi finished school in Menouf, her father considered keeping her at home to help her mother with the housework and the other children. But her mother had noticed El Saadawi's performance at school and wanted her to continue her education. Her parents sent her to Cairo, where she lodged with relatives for a few years before moving into a girls' boarding school. In Cairo she participated in some of the

Title page for the 1988 English translation of El Saadawi's first novel, Mudhakkirat tabibah, *1958 (Thomas Cooper Library, University of South Carolina)*

frequent street demonstrations against the British occupation of Egypt.

In the fall of 1948 El Saadawi was admitted to the medical school at Fouad Al-Awal University in Giza. Her sense of justice led her to stand up for herself in daring ways. For example, on hearing that students with good connections were exempt from tuition, she burst into the dean's office and successfully demanded the same privilege because of the excellent grades on her transcript. She received her M.D. in 1955.

In September 1955 El Saadawi married Ahmed Helmi, a freedom fighter she had met at one of the student demonstrations, who had also become a physician. They had a daughter, Mona. The marriage was unhappy, and in 1956 El Saadawi returned to Kafr Tahla to work in the village clinic; she and Helmi were divorced the following year.

After her mother's death in 1957, El Saadawi looked into the Qur'an and the *hadith* (records of the sayings of the Prophet Muhammad) to see what Muslim women could expect in Paradise. Apparently, the woman was to wait for her husband to die and hope that he would choose to spend eternity with her rather than the seventy-two virgins promised to him; should he reject her, the absence from the texts of any alternative indicated that she would have to spend eternity alone. That same year El Saadawi published her first book, the short-story collection *Ta'allamat al-Hubb* (She Learned Love).

In *Awraq hayati: Aljuz' al-awal* (1995, Papers of My Life: Volume 1; translated as *A Daughter of Isis: The Autobiography of Nawal El Saadawi,* 1999) El Saadawi says that some of her fondest memories are of caring for the villagers, some of whose lives she saved. But she also encountered the darker side of village life: botched male and female circumcisions and infections caused by attempts to deflower virgins surgically. El Saadawi tried to teach the villagers hygiene and to call into question their customs, but she was fighting against deeply entrenched traditions and also threatening the livelihoods of the village barbers who performed the operations. The Supreme Council of Combined Health Units in Cairo received complaints that she had shown contempt for the moral values of the villagers and caused some of the women of Kafr Tahla to lose respect for the laws of Islam. In 1958 she was reassigned to the Hospital for Chest Diseases in a Cairo suburb.

El Saadawi's first novel, *Mudhakkirat tabibah* (1958; translated as *Memoirs of a Woman Doctor,* 1988), was serialized in the magazine *Ruz al-Yusuf* before being published in book form. The narrator defies her family's wishes that she marry and enters medical school. By becoming a doctor she will gain the power and respect that are typically denied women in Arab societies; she also wants to prove to her mother that she is more intelligent than her brother. El Saadawi published two more novels in the next two years: *Lahzat sidq* (1959, A Moment of Truth) and *Hanan qalil* (1960, Little Tenderness); neither is considered particularly important. In 1960 she married a judge; his name is not known. They had a son, Atef. The date of their divorce is not known.

In December 1964 El Saadawi married the physician and writer Sherif Hetata. During the June 1967 Six-Day War with Israel she volunteered as a doctor in the Suez Canal Zone; on the way to the hospital in Isma'ileya, the truck in which she was riding was hit by Israeli shells. The driver was killed, and a doctor traveling with El Saadawi was wounded. El Saadawi then went to Jordan to work in the Palestinian refugee camps.

In 1969 El Saadawi published the novel *al-Gha'ib* (translated as *Searching,* 1991). It was followed in 1971 by *Imra'atan fi-imara'ah* (translated as *Two Women in One,* 1985). Bahiah Shaheen is an eighteen-year-old medical student; she is considered a respectable, obedient daughter, but inside her lurks another woman longing to escape:

> Some hidden insistent feeling told her that her future did not lie in those long, boring lectures, nor in getting a medical degree and hanging a shingle in the square saying "Dr. Bahiah Shaheen," nor in settling her ass in a comfortable seat behind the wheel of a car. Something told her that this was all meaningless, like a blank sheet of paper or a dark night without a single star, as if the whole world had become black or white, it really didn't matter which, so long as it was all one colour.

Bahiah falls in love with Saleem, but their affair is cut short when they are arrested for participating in anti-British demonstrations and for having communist associations. Diana Royer notes that "the theme of repression that runs though the novel makes readers aware that all members of Egyptian society are suffering under the current structure."

In 1972 El Saadawi was dismissed from her position as director general of public health education because of her outspokenness and progressive publications. That year she published the short-story collection *al-Khayt wa-'ayn al-hayat* (translated as *The Well of Life and the Thread*, 1993); some of the pieces draw on her experiences in the war and her friendship with Umm al-Fida'iyyin, a woman named she met in one of the refugee camps. In 1973 she entered 'Ain Shams University in Cairo to study psychiatry and published the novel *Imra'ah 'inda nuqtat al-sifr* (translated as *Women at Point Zero*, 1983), inspired by a prostitute El Saadawi had met who was sentenced to death for killing a man. It was followed in 1974 by two nonfiction books, *al-Mar'ah wa al-jins* (Woman and Gender) and *al-Untha hiya al-asl* (The Female Is the Origin).

El Saadawi returned to fiction in 1975 with the novel *Mawt al-rajul al-wahid 'ala al-ard* (The Death of the Only Man on Earth; translated as *God Dies by the Nile*, 1985). Zakiyyah is a poor peasant whose niece runs away from the village of Kafr El Ten after being raped and impregnated by the mayor; the mayor then frames the father of Zeinab, another of Zakiyyah's nieces, for murder so that he can rape her, as well. The mayor is all-powerful in the village; one resident says to another, "These people are unbelievers, Fatheya. They don't have faith in God nor do they worry their heads about what will happen either in this world, or in the next. In their hearts they don't fear God. What they really fear is the Mayor. He holds their daily bread in his hands and if he wants, he can deprive them of it." God does not answer the prayers of the citizens of Kafr El Ten; in that sense his death is a daily occurrence in this village on the banks of the Nile. At the end of the novel Zak-

Title page for the English translation, 1985, of El Saadawi's 1975 novel, Mawt al-rajul al-wahid 'ala al-ard *(Thomas Cooper Library, University of South Carolina)*

iyyah, beaten down and left with nothing—perhaps not even a full awareness of her actions—kills the mayor with a hoe and goes to prison. She mutters to herself in her cell during the night:

> "I know who it is." And the woman asked her curiously, "Who is it, my dear?" And Zakeya answered, "I know it's Allah, my child." "Where is He?" sighed her companion. "If He were here, we could pray Him to have mercy on women like us." "He's over there, my child. I buried him there on the bank of the Nile."

Royer argues that *God Dies by the Nile* "holds nothing back in its indictment of an immoral and hypocritical government figure and his lackeys who feel no sense of responsibility for the land or the people who work it. It is also a novel that offers no relief in the suffering of its just characters."

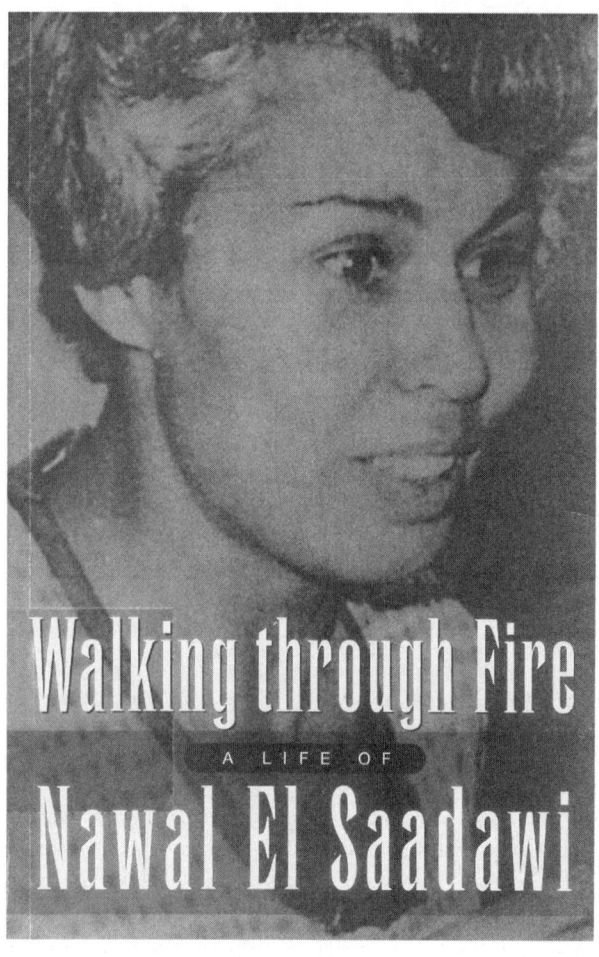

Front cover for the English translation, 2002, of El Saadawi's 1998 autobiography, Awraq hayati: Al-Juz' al-thani (Richland County Public Library)

In 1976 El Saadawi published the novel *Ughniyat al-atfal al-da'iriyyah* (translated as *The Circling Song*, 1989) and two books on gender issues: *al-Mar'a wa al-sira' al-nafsi* (Women and Psychological Struggle) and *al-Rajul wa al-jins* (Man and Gender). Two more nonfiction works appeared the following year: *'An al-mar'ah* (About Women) and the controversial *al-Wajh al-'ari li al-mar'ah al-'Arabiyyah* (translated as *The Hidden Face of Eve: Women in the Arab World*, 1982), an account of the history of patriarchy and religion and their effects on women from pharaonic times to the present. She shows that ancient Egypt moved from a culture supportive of and reverent to women to a patriarchy that was hostile and often violent to them. She traces the origins of practices such as segregation and veiling of women and female circumcision and analyzes the justifications that are given for them.

El Saadawi's short-story collection *Kanat hiya al-ad'af* (1979; translated as *She Has No Place in Paradise*, 1989) includes a dark tale in which a young man is obsessed with his fingernail, with which he will one day "open the way" of his bride. When the time comes, however, he is unable to bring himself to tear his wife's hymen. Humiliated by his weakness, he throws the unbloodied handkerchief in her father's face. The evidence that his daughter was not a virgin on her wedding night is a blow to the father's honor. The girl has no way to establish the truth of what happened, and the society closes in on her; being accused of premarital sexual relations is essentially a death sentence for a woman in Egypt.

In September 1981 El Saadawi was arrested for alleged crimes against the state and put in the women's prison in al-Kanatir, outside of Cairo. She was not officially charged and was released when the political situation changed about a month later with the assassination of President Anwar Sadat by an Islamist gunman. While in prison she wrote *Mudhakkirati fi Sijn al-Nisa'* (1983; translated as *Memoirs from the Women's Prison*, 1986) on toilet paper with a pen.

In 1982 El Saadawi and 119 other women founded the Arab Women's Solidarity Association (AWSA) to promote participation by Arab women in social, economic, cultural, and political life and to increase their awareness of the link between women's liberation and the liberation of other oppressed groups in society. El Saadawi was elected president.

In 1984 Georges Tarabishi published *Untha didda al-unuthah: Dirasah fi adab Nawal al-Sa'dawi 'ala daw' al-tahlil al-nafsi* (1984; translated as *Woman against Her Sex: A Critique of Nawal El Saadawi*, 1988), in which he subjected El Saadawi's work to a Freudian analysis and concluded that she rejects her femininity owing to a neurosis. El Saadawi's response was included in the English translation of Tarabishi's book.

By 1985 AWSA had three thousand members in several countries and became the first pan-Arab society to be granted the status of a nongovernmental organization (NGO) by the Economic and Social Council of the United Nations. In 1991 the authorities shut down the Egyptian branch of the association and also banned El Saadawi's magazine, *Noon*, which she had started that year. In her essay "The Enigmatic South," included in *The Nawal El Saadawi Reader* (1997), El Saadawi notes that

> there is no doubt that the orientation of AWSA, its unveiling of the relationships between gender discrimination and the socioeconomic structure of society, was the main reason for closing it down. Such a conception inevitably meant highlighting the need for deep changes in the structures of Arab society and in all aspects of life starting from the family and extending nationally to the state and including education, culture, religion, and social and economic activity.

El Saadawi and her husband, Sherif Hetata, 1989 (from A Daughter of Isis, *1999; Thomas Cooper Library, University of South Carolina)*

El Saadawi's novel *Jannat wa Iblis* (1992; translated as *The Innocence of the Devil*, 1994) is a complex work in which reality, fantasy, and passages from Islamic texts are mixed and characters blend together. The protagonists are two women in a mental hospital, one of whom has been placed there for failing a test of virginity on her wedding night. *Al-Hubb fi zaman al-naft* (1993; translated as *Love in the Kingdom of Oil*, 2001) also uses a complex narrative form. A young woman in the "Kingdom of Oil" suddenly disappears without a trace; the novel was inspired by the kingdom of Saudi Arabia, where women are forbidden to travel unaccompanied by a male relative.

On 8 January 1993 El Saadawi and her husband left Egypt for the United States; they were weary of constant government surveillance, and their names were on a fundamentalist death list. El Saadawi took a position as a visiting professor at Duke University in Durham, North Carolina. In 1995 El Saadawi published *Awraq hayati: Aljuz' al-awal;* it covers her life from childhood through 1995.

In 1997 El Saadawi and her husband returned to Cairo. That year El Saadawi published *The Nawal El Saadawi Reader,* a collection of essays and recorded talks. In one essay she notes the change in terminology used by First World nations to discuss their involvement with Third World countries—involvement that usually results in increased wealth for the former and increased poverty for the latter. She cites the 1914 British occupation of Egypt, which was called a "protectorate." The term suggests a parent protecting a child, but the occupation actually served Britain's needs rather than those of the Egyptians; for example, Egyptian agriculture shifted from crops to feed Egyptians to cotton to support the British textile industry. In the 1970s the term "developing countries" came to be applied to nations such as Egypt, and many programs were instituted to "help" those countries to "catch up" with their Western counterparts. El Saadawi describes these programs as "a disguised form of economic genocide, more pernicious than military genocide because they killed more people but were not as visible as blood shed in war." When the "developing countries" euphemism wore out its welcome, the phrase "structural adjustment" came into vogue. El Saadawi does not claim that Third World governments are innocent; on the contrary, she says, much of the problem lies with corrupt leaders who become richer and more powerful by cooperating with Western neocolonial programs. The poor are betrayed both by their own governments and by the Western governments and corporations that support them.

In the essay "Dissidence and Creativity" El Saadawi criticizes intellectuals who present research papers discussing the problems of the Third World but have no sincere interest in improving the lives of the citizens of those countries:

> A philosopher who is not an activist in a struggle ends up as an empty shell: as a shelf of books in academia. S/he struggles in closed rooms, using words to fence with other users of words. S/he has a love-hate relation-

ship with poor oppressed women and men who are struggling to live. S/he worships them, calls them "subaltern," glorifies their authentic identity or culture, but at the same time looks down on them, considers them as docile or struggling bodies unable to produce philosophy or as local activists but not global thinkers.

These intellectuals include "dissidents" from the Orient who have spent most of their lives in the West. To them the Orient is little more than a means of furthering their careers.

In the essay "Gendering South-North Politics" El Saadawi argues that capitalist media promote a notion of normality based on consumption. When people resist this "global culture" and try to assert their own identities, they often fall into religious fundamentalism, racism, or sexism. The protest against globalization "very often takes on reactionary, retrograde, anti-women, and anti-progressive characteristics thus leading to division and discord; it thus serves the purpose of capitalist globalization because it divides the people who are resisting it." El Saadawi points out that Islam does not have a monopoly on fundamentalism; any religion can fall prey to believing that its "fundamentals" must be imposed on others.

El Saadawi's essays are notable in that, unlike most contemporary scholars, she does not engage in literary criticism or commentary on other thinkers' ideas. Everything she writes is taken directly from her experiences growing up in Egypt, practicing medicine, being imprisoned, attending conferences, or teaching. She does not engage in theory for its own sake; her writing is an attempt to change the world.

In 1998 El Saadawi published another autobiography, *Awraq hayati: Al-Juz' al-thani* (1998, Papers of My Life: Volume 2; translated as *Walking through Fire*, 2002). The English title was inspired by what her mother would say when other relatives–particularly her father–worried about allowing El Saadawi to do something such as going off to Cairo on her own to attend school: "Throw Nawal into the midst of fire and she'll come out unscathed." *Awraq hayati: Al-Juz' al-thani* is a highly intimate book: El Saadawi discusses her marriages, her pregnancies, and how she responded to events and people around her. In a moving passage about her first husband, who had gone to fight the British in the Suez Canal Zone, she writes:

> His enemies had been the British, the King and those who ruled in the King's name. He shouldered his gun and went off, his heart full of faith in God, in his country, in the power of love. But he came back defeated, broken. All he had learned as a freedom fighter was how to kill. His beliefs had drained away step by step, and been shaken every time one of his comrades shed his blood, for there was treason in the air. So when he came back he took to drugs, injected himself with poison, let it rise up to his head, so that now he saw treason in everything, felt betrayed by the very things he had believed in and fought for: God, his country, and love. But he could not revenge himself on God, or his country. His hands could not reach out to strangle them. They had no body, no neck to throttle with his fingers. When he looked around all he could see now was the woman he loved. Her neck was there to strangle, even though she had given him love.

Such personal writing led critics to call *Awraq hayati: Al-Juz' al-thani* an unforgettable memoir. In the *API Review of Books* (July 2006) Maggie Tankin praised the book as having "much to teach Western feminists about the priorities of Arab women." El Saadawi herself has criticized Western feminists for their failure to consider what Arab women are fighting against and that Arab women know better than Westerners what their priorities are. In 2001 El Saadawi published a third autobiography, *Awraq hayati: Al-Juz' al-thalith* (Papers of My Life: Volume 3).

In the introduction to *Jannat wa Iblis* Fedwa Malti-Douglas notes that Nawal El Saadawi has "the dubious honor of supposedly being the only woman whose name has been placed on Islamist death lists." Her outspokenness has earned her the ire of many others, including the Egyptian government. But El Saadawi refuses to be cowed into silence. She has received many honors, including the 2003 International Writer of the Year Award and the American Biographical Institute's Great Minds of the 21st Century Award, also in 2003, and holds honorary degrees from universities around the world. She and her husband Hetata, who has translated several of her works into English, live in Cairo.

References:

Nawar al-Hassan Golley, *Reading Arab Women's Autobiographies* (Austin: University of Texas Press, 2003), pp. 131–180;

Fedwa Malti-Douglas, *Men, Women, and God(s): Nawal El Saadawi and Arab Feminist Poetics* (Berkeley: University of California Press, 1995);

Diana Royer, *A Critical Study of the Works of Nawal El Saadawi, Egyptian Writer and Activist* (Lewiston, N.Y.: Edwin Mellen Press, 2001);

Georges Tarabishi (Jurj Tarabishi), *Untha didda al-unuthah: Dirasah fi adab Nawal al-Sa'dawi 'ala daw' al-tahlil al-nafsi* (Beirut: Dar al-Tali'ah, 1984); translated by Basil Hatim and Elisabeth Orsini as *Woman against Her Sex: A Critique of Nawal El Saadawi* (London: Saqi, 1988).

Muhammad Baqir al-Sadr

(1 March? 1935 – 8 April 1980)

John Walbridge
Indiana University

BOOKS: *Fadak fi al-tarikh* (Najaf: Al-Matba'ah al-Haydariyyah, 1955); revised by Abdul-Jabbar Sharara, translated by Abdullah al-Shahin as *Fadak in History* (Qom: Ansariyan, 2002);

Falsafatuna (Najaf: Matba'at al-Adab, 1959); translated by Shams C. Inati as *Our Philosophy* (London & New York: Muhammadi Trust, 1987);

Iqtisaduna, 2 volumes (Najaf: Matabi' al-Nu'man, 1961, 1964); translated as *Our Economics,* 4 volumes (Tehran: World Organization for Islamic Services, 1982–1984);

Madha ta'rifu 'an al-iqtisad al-Islami (Najaf: Matba'at al-Nu'man, 1964); translated by Yasin T. al-Jibouri as *What Do You Know about Islamic Economics?* (Lanham, Md.: Imamia Center, 1990);

Al-Insan al-mu'asir wa al-mushkilah al-ijtima'iyyah (Najaf: Matba'at al-Nu'man, 1964); translated by al-Jibouri as *Contemporary Man and the Social Problem* (Tehran: World Organization for Islamic Services, 1980);

Al-Ma'alim al-jadidah li al-usul (Najaf: Matba'at al-Nu'man, 1964);

Ahl al-bayt, tanawwu' adwar wa wahdat hadaf (Beirut: Dar al-Ta'aruf, 1968);

Al-Bank al-laribawi fi al-Islam (Kuwait: Maktabat Jami' al-Naqa al-'Ammah, 1969);

Mujaz fi usul al-din (Beirut: Dar al-Zahra', 1970);

Buhuth fi sharh al-'urwa al-wuthqa, 4 volumes (Najaf: Matba'at al-Adab, 1971);

Al-Usus al-mantiqiyyah li al-istiqra' (Beirut: Dar al-Fikr, 1972);

Al-Madrasah al-Islamiyyah (Beirut: Dar al-Zahra', 1973); translated by Mustajab A. Ansari as *Islam and Schools of Economics* (Karachi: Islamic Seminary Pakistan, 1980; Albany, Cal.: Muslim Students' Association [Persian Speaking Group], 1981);

Al-Tashayyu' wa al-Islam (Beirut: Dar al-Ghadir, 1973);

Ikhtarna laka buhath Islamiyyah wa mawadi' ukhra (Beirut, 1975);

Al-Fatawa al-wadihah wafqan li madhhab ahl al-bayt (Najaf: Matba'at al-Najaf al-Ashraf, 1976);

Muhammad Baqir al-Sadr

Al-Ta'liq 'ala minhaj al-salihin, 3 volumes (Najaf: Matba'at al-Adab, 1976–1980);

Bahth hawla al-Mahdi (Beirut: Dar al-Ta'aruf, 1977);

Bahth hawla al-Walaya (Kuwait: Dar al-Tawhid, 1977);

Nazra 'amma fi al-'ibadat (Beirut: Dar al-Ta'aruf, 1977);

Al-Tashayyu': Zahirah tabi'iyyah fi ithar al-da'wa al-Islamiyyah (Cairo: Al-Khanji, 1977);

Al-Siyam fi shahr Ramadan: Falsafatuhu wa ahkamuhu (Beirut: Dar al-Ta'aruf, 1977);

Durus fi 'ilm al-usul, 3 volumes (Cairo: Dar al-Kitab al-Misri, 1978–1980); volume 1 translated by Roy Parviz Mottahedeh as *Lessons in Islamic Jurisprudence* (Oxford: One World, 2003); excerpts translated by Arif Abdul Hussain, Hamid Algar, and Sa'eed Bahmanpour as *Principles of Islamic Jurisprudence according to Shi'a Law* (London: ICAS, 2003);

Al-Mursil, al-rasul, al-risalah (Beirut: Dar al-Ta'aruf, 1978); translated as *He, His Messenger and His Message* (Karachi: Islamic Seminary Pakistan, 1980); revised edition, edited by Raza H. Rizwani (Accra & New York: Islamic Seminary, 1982);

The Awaited Saviour, translated by Ansari (Karachi: Islamic Seminary Pakistan, 1979);

Manabi' al-qudrah fi al-dawla al-Islamiyyah (Beirut: Dar al-Ta'aruf, 1979);

Khilafat al-insan wa shahadat al-anbiya' (Beirut: Dar al-Ta'aruf, 1979);

Sura 'an iqtisad al-mujtama' al-Islami (Beirut: Dar al-Ta'aruf, 1979);

Al-Usus al-'ammah li al-bank fi al-mujtama' al-Islami (Beirut: Dar al-Ta'aruf, 1979);

Dawr al-a'immah fi al-hayah al-Islamiya (Tehran: Al-Maktaba al-Islamiyyah al-Kubra, 1980);

Al-Madrasa al-Qur'aniya (Beirut: Dar al-Ta'aruf, 1980);

Al-Islam yaqudu al-hayat (Beirut: Dar al-Ta'aruf, 1980);

Ghayat al-fikr fi usul al-fiqh: Mabahith al-Ishtighal (Qom: Manshurat al-Hashimi, 1984);

Al-Nubuwwah al-khatimah (Beirut, 1985);

Al-Sunan al-tarikhiyyah fi al-Qur'an (Beirut: Dar al-Ta'aruf, 1989);

Buhuth wa-Hiwara Qur'aniya (Beirut: Al-Dar al-'Aulamiya, 1994); translated as *Lectures on Trends of History in Qur'an* (London: Cultural and Guidance Section, Al-Khoei Foundation, 1991);

Buhuth fi 'ilm al-usul, 7 volumes, by al-Sadr and Mahmud Hashimi (Qom: Mu'assasat Da'irat Ma'arif al-Fiqh al-Islami, 1996–1997).

Muhammad Baqir al-Sadr was the most important ideologist of the Shiite revival in Iraq between the fall of the monarchy in 1958 and the outbreak of the Iran-Iraq War in 1980. He was convinced that Islam was gravely endangered by Communism, nationalism, and Western secularism; as a member of the first generation of Shiite clerics to receive a modern education in addition to the traditional religious one, he was able to engage those ideologies on their own terms and to restate religious doctrines and practices in a language that reached both young people and modern intellectuals. He is best known for *Falsafatunu* (1959; translated as *Our Philosophy,* 1987), a critique of the major Western ideologies, particularly Marxism, and *Iqtisaduna* (1961, 1964; translated as *Our Economics,* 1982–1984), in which he attempts to create a basis for a distinctively Islamic economic system. To establish himself as a Shiite religious scholar he also wrote on Islamic law; these works are unusual in that they abandon much of the complexity of traditional Islamic legal scholarship in favor of a more accessible style. Finally, he published many popular articles and pamphlets. He was executed by Saddam Hussein in 1980, when it appeared that the Iranian revolution might spread to the Shiite areas of Iraq.

Al-Sayyid Muhammad Baqir al-Sadr was born in the Baghdad suburb of Kazimiya, the site of two important Shiite shrines, probably on 1 March 1935 (sources disagree on the date) to Haydar al-Sadr and the daughter of the cleric Shaykh 'Abdu al-Husayn al-Yasin. The al-Sadr family had immigrated to Iraq and Iran from southern Lebanon in the eighteenth century; it produced many notable clerics, of whom the best known outside the Shiite community are Musa al-Sadr, the religious leader of Lebanese Shiites until his disappearance in 1978, and Muhammad Baqir al-Sadr's son-in-law, Muqtada al-Sadr, the charismatic militia leader and opponent of the American occupation of Iraq. (Muhammad Baqir al-Sadr is known to have had three daughters who married sons of Ayatollah Muhammad Sadiq al-Sadr, a distant relative who was assassinated in 1999). The title *Sayyid* indicates that one is descended from the Prophet, an informal requirement for high religious leadership in Shiism.

Al-Sadr's father died when al-Sadr was an infant. In 1945 the family moved to Najaf, the most important Shiite holy city in Iraq and the seat of the most prominent clerical leaders, the *maraji' al-taqlid* (sources of emulation).

Education in the Shiite seminaries of Iraq and Iran is informal but rigorous. Students begin, usually between the ages of ten and fourteen, with the *muqaddimat* (introductory studies): logic, Arabic grammar, and law, along with some other subjects for better students; all are taught from traditional textbooks. As part of his studies the eleven-year-old al-Sadr wrote a treatise on logic. The *muqaddimat* is followed by *sutuh* (superficial studies): the principles of the deduction of Islamic law. The first two levels take about ten years. The final level, *bahth al-kharij* (outside research), consists of a critical study of the Islamic legal sciences and their bases. The student who completes the entire course of study becomes a *mujtahid* (one qualified to exercise independent judgment in matters of Islamic law), roughly equivalent to a Ph.D. According to the dominant interpretation of Shiite law, every believer must either be a *mujtahid* or follow the legal judgments of one—preferably of the most learned and pious of the living *mujtahids*. A *mujtahid* who is followed by a significant number of ordinary believers is a *marji' al-taqlid* and is entitled to receive religious taxes from his followers. At any given time there are likely to be half a dozen such individuals, including several in Najaf. The leading *marji' al-taqlid* in Najaf is considered the leader of the Shiite religious establishment worldwide, except in Iran. To become a *marji' al-taqlid* it is necessary to make a reputation for scholarship by writing extensively in the traditional style on Islamic law. Much of al-Sadr's effort was devoted to modernizing this institution and making it more relevant to the needs of the Shiite community.

Al-Sadr's first published work, *Fadak fi al-tarikh* (1955; translated as *Fadak in History,* 2002), deals with historical issues that are at the foundation of Shiite religious authority. Fadak was a village captured from the Jews, the revenues of which were Muhammad's personal property. Muhammad's daughter Fatima claimed it after his death, but the claim was rejected by Abu Bakr, the first caliph. The dispute festered for generations and provided part of the basis for the Shiite religious taxes received by the *marji' al-taqlid*.

In 1957 al-Sadr was a founder or early member of the Islamic Dawa (Call) Party, formed to promote Islamic values and ethics. Two years later he published *Falsafatunu,* his exposition of the flaws of the major Western philosophies. The work is organized around a series of dichotomies: rationalism versus empiricism, realism versus idealism, logic versus dialectic, and theology versus metaphysics; al-Sadr supports the first member of each pair. The danger of empiricism to religion is obvious: empiricism grounds all knowledge in experience, but God and the spiritual are not known through experience. Al-Sadr critiques empiricism first by pointing out that while it can explain the origin of the concept of red, which is encountered in experience, and of a golden mountain, which is a combination of ideas that are derived from experience, the idea of cause-and-effect as a necessary connection between events is not found in experience. Yet, this idea is somehow acquired in childhood and is essential to science. Second, empiricism cannot account for knowledge of universal and necessary propositions such as the principle of noncontradiction and the truths of mathematics. Only rationalism, which grounds knowledge in reason, provides a satisfactory epistemology. In the debate between realism and idealism al-Sadr lumps together as "idealists" all philosophers who cast doubt on the possibility of objective knowledge of the external world: Hegelians, Marxists (who would have vehemently denied the label "idealist"), Freudians, and behaviorists contend that the content of consciousness is shaped, respectively, by history, economic forces, the unconscious, or psychological conditioning. But, al-Sadr asks, how can such theories assert without self-contradiction that they themselves are objectively true? Dialectic, al-

Title page for the 1987 English translation of al-Sadr's best-known work, Falsufatunu, 1959 (Thomas Cooper Library, University of South Carolina)

Sadr asserts, is based on the misunderstanding that a contradiction results if something is true under some conditions but not under others. Finally, the distinction between theology and metaphysics turns on the question of whether matter can be the cause of the universe. Al-Sadr attempts to show that modern atomism does not necessarily imply the rejection of the traditional Aristotelian concepts of matter and form: even in subatomic particles, matter and form are philosophically distinct; thus, their combination requires some other cause, which must be God. He also tries to refute scientific theories—especially evolution, which is widely rejected by Muslims—on the basis of philosophical and theological arguments. He concludes by citing the Islamic epistemological notion of "knowledge by presence" to show that knowledge implies an immaterial subject to possess the knowledge; he claims that the problem of the relationship of mind and body that is raised by such a dualistic position has been solved by Islamic philosophers, particularly Mulla Sadra. The

Front cover for a partial English translation, 2003, of Durus fi 'ilm al-usul, al-Sadr's last major work on law, 1978–1980 (Widener Library, Harvard University)

book ends with the argument that if there is a nonmaterial component to human beings, then their consciousness cannot be entirely determined by their material conditions.

Al-Sadr's membership in the Dawa Party was controversial among his peers. The leading Shiite clerics had always been reluctant to become involved in politics; such was the case with the two *marji' al-taqlid* who then dominated Najaf, Muhsin al-Hakim and Abu al-Qasim al-Kha'i. To advance his career as an Islamic scholar, al-Sadr resigned from the party in 1961.

In 1961 and 1964 al-Sadr published the two volumes, comprising more than seven hundred pages, of his most important work, *Iqtisaduna*. Critical analyses of Marxism and capitalism occupy more than a third of the book. Marxism is treated in considerably more detail: in the late 1950s, when al-Sadr was working on the book, socialism dominated nationalist debates in the Arab world, and Communist literature was widely available in Arabic translation. His discussion of capitalism takes up barely forty pages, and the fact that he consistently deals with the West in terms of capitalism rather than liberal democracy indicates that the terms of reference are being set by Marxism. The remainder of *Iqtisaduna* is devoted to the construction of an Islamic economic system based on principles drawn mostly from the Islamic legal tradition; that tradition includes a highly developed system of contract law developed in the wealthy mercantile culture of medieval Islam. Islamic economics, al-Sadr says, does not claim to be a science; it is, rather, a *madhhab* (school of thought) characterized by realism, in contrast to Marxism, and by ethical values, in contrast to capitalism. The three fundamental features of Islamic economics are a classification of property more diverse than those of capitalism and Marxism; limitations on economic freedom, such as the prohibition of usury; and social justice. Natural resources are sufficient to satisfy human needs; the problem is distribution. The work closes with an analysis of the role of the state in production and distribution. Al-Sadr summarizes the themes of *Iqtisaduna* in *Madha ta'rifu 'an al-iqtisad al-Islami* (translated as *What Do You Know about Islamic Economics?* 1990) and expands on them in *al-Insan al-mu'asir wa al-mushkilah al-ijtima'iyyah* (translated as *Contemporary Man and the Social Problem*, 1980), both published in the same year as the second volume of *Iqtisaduna*.

While al-Sadr's works on contemporary issues established him as a major ideologist of political Islam, they were not the kinds of books that would win him the status of *marji' al-taqlid*. His first significant work on Islamic law in the narrower sense was *al-Ma'alim al-jadidah li al-usul* (1964, New Outlooks on the Principles of Jurisprudence), an introductory textbook on *usal al-fiqh* (the logic of Islamic law). Since the Qur'an and the traditions about the Prophet do not directly address many legal issues, Islamic law is an elaborate tissue of inferences from the these materials; *usal al-fiqh* sets the rules for making such inferences. It is a discipline one must master to become a *mujtahid*, and only the more promising students go on to study it.

Al-Sadr's final major work on economic and social issues was *al-Bank al-laribawi fi al-Islam* (1969, The Nonusurious Bank in Islam), which was occasioned by a query from the Kuwaiti Ministry of Religious Endowments. A major difficulty in "Islamic economics" is the prohibition in Islamic law of giving and taking interest. Medieval lawyers dealt with the problem through a combination of loopholes and prohibitions of various disguised forms of interest, but it reemerged in the nineteenth century with the arrival in the Middle East of European-style banks and colonial legal codes. For Shiites the issue became urgent in the 1960s, when oil wealth began to accumulate. Al-Sadr says that an Islamic bank dealing with non-Islamic institutions may give and take interest; this position is justified by practical considerations and by exceptions in classical Islamic law for dealings with non-Muslims. The basis of Islamic banking is *mudarabah* (partnership): the depositor becomes an investor in the enterprises supported by the bank's loans, sharing both the risks and the profits; there is no fixed rate of return, as in Western interest payments. Al-Sadr works out in detail the various sorts of transactions, such as checks and fees, in which the bank may legitimately engage. The book is a pioneering study in what has since become a flourishing field.

Al-Sadr also wrote two long works on *fiqh* (the content of Islamic law). The first was *Buhuth fi sharh al'urwa al-wuthqa* (1971, Investigations in Commentary on *The Firm Cord*), a commentary on a standard summary of Shiite law by Muhammad Kazim al-Tabataba'i al-Yazdi, who died in 1919.

In 1972 al-Sadr returned to his early epistemological interests with *al-Usus al-mantiqiyyah li al-istiqra'* (The Logical Foundations of Induction). The book is a remarkable turn away from traditional Islamic philosophy. Rather than the rationalism taught in Islamic seminaries and defended in his own earlier *Falsufatunu*, he bases his ideas mainly on the British empiricists and develops a theory of probability drawn from Bertrand Russell to support a new proof of the existence of God. The book impressed but puzzled his peers.

In 1976 al-Sadr published *al-Fatawa al-wadiha wafqan li-madhhab ahl al-bayt* (Clear Rulings in Accordance with the School of the Family of the Prophet), a *risalah 'amaliyyah* (simple, topically organized manual of Islamic law for the guidance of Shiites who are not *mujtahids*). Since about the beginning of the twentieth century the publication of such a work has been taken as a sign that a Shiite cleric wants to be accepted as a *marji' al-taqlid*. Al-Sadr's book is conventional in content, but the organization differs noticeably from the traditional format. The work remained unfinished; only the first part, dealing with ritual, was ever published.

Al-Sadr's second long work on *fiqh* was *al-Ta'liq 'ala minhaj al-salihin* (1976–1980, Notes on *The Path of the Righteous*). It is a series of glosses on another summary of Shiite law, al-Hakim's *Minhaj al-Salihin* (1949, The Path of the Righteous). Neither *Buhuth fi sharh al-'urwa al-wuthqa* nor *al-Ta'liq 'ala minhaj al-salihin* is particularly innovative, but they clearly represent an attempt by al-Sadr to establish his credentials as a religious authority.

Al-Sadr's final major work on law, *Durus fi 'ilm al-usul* (1978–1980; translated in part as *Lessons in Islamic Jurisprudence*, 2003), is a textbook for students beginning more advanced studies. More approachable than the traditional texts, it represents a tentative step toward the modernization of a core Islamic discipline.

Al-Sadr also wrote a large number of lesser works on similar themes, ranging from newspaper articles to short books. Most are addressed to a general readership, though some, including works compiled from his lectures by his students, are technical in nature. His early education in secular schools enabled him to write for laymen, and he had a knack for making religious ideas and figures come alive for modern Iraqis by showing their contemporary political relevance. His greatest importance was in combating Communist influence and making Islamic ideas relevant to Shiite Iraqis who were becoming disillusioned with the socialism and Arab nationalism dominant in the 1950s and 1960s.

On 11 February 1979 a revolution in Iran brought to power a Shiite clerical government led by Ayatollah Ruhollah Khomeini, a friend of al-Sadr's who had spent fourteen years in exile in Najaf. On 16 July 1979 Saddam Hussein, who had been the real power in the ruling Iraqi Baath Party, replaced the figurehead president Ahmed Hassan al-Baker. Khomeini hated Saddam for expelling him from Iraq in 1978 and retaliated by beaming propaganda broadcasts into Iraq calling for Shiites to rise up in support of a pan-Islamic revolution. When the broadcasts identified al-Sadr as the natural leader of the revolution, Saddam ordered al-Sadr and his sister Amina, a Dawa Party activist known as Bint al-Huda, arrested on 5 April 1980. After being tortured, al-Sadr was executed on 8 April; his sister's fate was not disclosed by the regime, but there is no doubt that she was executed, as well.

Muhammad Baqir al-Sadr was only forty-five at the time of his death, rather young for a cleric of his rank. Some of his best-known books, such as *Falsufatunu*, show evidence of his youth, while much of his mature work remained incomplete. His ideological polemics have not aged well: he knew no Western languages, and his targets, especially Communism, are less important today than they were in his time. But as a charismatic martyr in a branch of Islam founded on martyrdom, he is an iconic figure for Shiites. And his notion of Islam as a complete ideological system has become fundamental to modern Islamic thought. Almost all of his works have been republished frequently, and many have been translated into the major Islamic and European languages.

References:

Talib Aziz, "Baqir al-Sadr's Quest for the *Marji'iya*," in *The Most Learned of the Shi'a: The Institution of the Marja' Taqlid*, edited by Linda S. Walbridge (New York: Oxford University Press, 2001), pp. 140–148;

Aziz, "The Islamic Political Theory of Muhammad Baqir Sadr of Iraq," dissertation, University of Utah, 1991;

Aziz, "The Political Theory of Muhammad Baqir Sadr," in *Ayatollahs, Sufis and Ideologues: State, Religion and Social Movements in Iraq*, edited by Faleh Abdul-Jabar (London: Al-Saqi, 2002), pp. 231–244;

Aziz, "The Role of Muhammad Baqir al-Sadr in Shi'i Political Activism in Iraq from 1958–1980," *International Journal of Middle East Studies*, 25 (1993): 207–222;

Chibli Mallat, *The Renewal of Islamic Law: Muhammad Baqer as-Sadr, Najaf and the Shii International* (Cambridge: Cambridge University Press, 1993);

John Walbridge, "Muhammad Baqir al-Sadr: The Search for New Foundations," in *The Most Learned of the Shi'a*, pp. 131–139.

Edward W. Said
(1 November 1935 – 25 September 2003)

Matthew Abraham
DePaul University

See also the Said entry in *DLB 67: Modern American Critics Since 1955*.

BOOKS: *Conrad and the Fiction of Autobiography* (Cambridge, Mass.: Harvard University Press, 1966);

Beginnings: Intention and Method (New York: Basic Books, 1975);

Orientalism (New York: Pantheon, 1978; London: Routledge & Kegan Paul, 1979);

The Question of Palestine (New York: New York Times Books, 1979; London: Routledge & Kegan Paul, 1980);

The Palestine Question and the American Context (Beirut: Institute for Palestine Studies, 1979);

Covering Islam: How the Media and the Experts Determine How We See the Rest of the World (New York: Pantheon Books, 1981; London: Routledge & Kegan Paul, 1981; revised edition, with new introduction, New York: Vintage, 1997);

The World, the Text, and the Critic (Cambridge, Mass.: Harvard University Press, 1983);

After the Last Sky: Palestinian Lives, photographs by Jean Mohr (New York: Columbia University Press: 1986);

Musical Elaborations (New York: Columbia University Press, 1991);

Culture and Imperialism (New York: Knopf, 1993);

The Politics of Dispossession: The Struggle for Palestinian Self-Determination (New York: Pantheon, 1994);

Representations of the Intellectual: The 1993 Reith Lectures (New York: Pantheon, 1994);

The Pen and the Sword: Conversations with David Barsamian (Monroe, Me.: Common Courage Press, 1994);

Peace and Its Discontents: Essays on Palestine in the Middle East Peace Process (New York: Vintage, 1995);

Entre guerre et paix (Paris: Arlea, 1997);

Out of Place: A Memoir (New York: Knopf, 1999);

Acts of Aggression: Policing Rogue States, by Said, Noam Chomsky, and Ramsey Clark (New York: Seven Stories Press, 1999);

Edward W. Said (Brown University)

The End of the Peace Process: Oslo and After (New York: Pantheon Books, 2000);

Reflections on Exile and Other Essays (Cambridge, Mass.: Harvard University Press, 2000);

Parallels and Paradoxes: Explorations in Music and Society, by Said and Daniel Barenboim (New York: Pantheon Books, 2002);

Freud and the Non-European (London: Verso, 2003);

From Oslo to Iraq and the Road Map (New York: Vintage, 2004);

Humanism and Democratic Criticism (New York: Columbia University Press, 2004);

On Late Style: Music and Literature against the Grain (New York: Pantheon, 2006).

Collection: *The Edward Said Reader,* edited by Moustafa Bayoumi and Andrew Rubin (New York: Vintage, 2000).

OTHER: "Conrad, Nostromo Record and Reality," in *Approaches to the Twentieth Century Novel,* edited by John Unterecker (New York: Crowell, 1965), pp. 108–152;

Halim Barakat, *Days of Dust,* introduction by Said (Wilmette, Ill.: Medina University Press International, 1974);

Literature and Society: Selected Papers from the English Institute, 1978, edited by Said (Baltimore & London: Johns Hopkins University Press, 1980);

Blaming the Victims: Spurious Scholarship and the Question of Palestine, edited by Said and Christopher Hitchens (London: Verso, 1988);

Henry James: Complete Stories 1864–1874, edited by Said, Denis Donoghue, John Hollander, and others (New York: Penguin, 1999);

Mourid Barghouti, *I Saw Ramallah,* introduction by Said (Cairo: American University in Cairo Press, 2000).

SELECTED PERIODICAL PUBLICATIONS– UNCOLLECTED: "Swift's Tory Anarchy," *Eighteenth-Century Studies,* 3 (Autumn 1969): 48–66;

"The Palestine Question and the American Context," *Arab Studies Quarterly,* 29 (Spring 1980): 127–149;

"The Satanic Verses and Democratic Freedoms," *Black Scholar,* 20 (March–April 1989): 17–18;

"The Desertion of Arafat," *New Left Review,* 11 (September–October 2001): 23–31;

"Clash of Ignorance," *Nation,* 273 (22 October 2001): 11.

Literary critic, political activist, skilled polemicist, recognized founder of postcolonial studies, concert pianist, music critic, and public intellectual, Edward W. Said defied easy categorization–intellectually and biographically–throughout much of his life. He literally and figuratively crossed and blurred boundaries that prevent human understanding and perpetuate global conflict. Said is the world's most well-known Palestinian intellectual; for more than thirty years he read and wrote prolifically, forever changing the way we think about the so-called divide between East and West. His death in 2003, just two years after the terrorist attacks of 9/11, was a great loss to the people whose rights he tirelessly championed and to the international dialogue about the Middle East.

Born on 1 November 1935 in Jerusalem, Edward William Said began his life in a region of the world to which he devoted much of his later life analyzing. Said grew up in Cairo, where he attended St. George's School, the American School, and Victoria College. He was expelled from Victoria College in 1951 for being a troublemaker. Later his parents decided to send him to Mount Hermon School in Massachusetts for his secondary education. As the eldest son of a Palestinian businessman named Wadie Said, Edward found himself surrounded by the trappings of the upper class during his youth and adulthood. Said frequently referred to the tremendous advantages he had been given throughout his life and the privileges he had the good fortune to enjoy. After completing his bachelor's degree at Princeton University, Said began his doctoral work in English at Harvard University, studying under R. P. Blackmur. After completing a dissertation, "Joseph Conrad and the Fiction of Autobiography," a work devoted to an analysis of how Conrad's corpus had been influenced by actual events in his life, Said became an assistant professor of English at Columbia University in New York in 1963. In the long course of his career at Columbia, Said held the Parr (1977–1989), Old Dominion (1989–1991), and University Professorships (1992–2002). Among many prestigious awards, he won the Trilling Prize for *Beginnings: Intention and Method* in 1976 and the René Wellek Prize of the American Comparative Literature Association for *The World, the Text, and the Critic* in 1984. Said was a frequent contributor to *The Nation,* the *London Review of Books, Al Ahram,* and *The Guardian.*

Said's dissertation became his first book, *Conrad and the Fiction of Autobiography* (1966). His next book, *Beginnings: Intention and Method* (1975), demonstrated the full range of Said's critical capacities as it surveyed the critical scene as it existed then, demonstrating a deep understanding of the work of Claude Lévi-Strauss, Sigmund Freud, Michel Foucault, Jacques Derrida, and a whole host of other structuralist and poststructuralist thinkers, as well as a complete mastery of such writers as Conrad, Honoré de Balzac, Charles Dickens, Gustave Flaubert, and Marcel Proust. The book represented what Abdirahman Hussein calls "a ground-clearing exercise," a sweeping examination of the various eddies of structuralist and poststructuralist theory that opened the way for Said's political work.

Said's central concern in *Beginnings* may be summed up in two questions: what does it mean to begin and what takes place when one begins? A writer seeks to clear a space for an expression of his or her agency, point of view, or perspective through a beginning, which is also a stocktaking, a measuring up of the critical scene in an attempt to figure out where to place one's voice in a conversation that has been long running. Discourse, as it is structured by power and knowledge, enables only certain people to speak and only at certain times. Concepts such as authority, molestation, and origins occupy Said throughout *Beginnings,* as he seeks to understand why the notion of a beginning is so important within the intellectual history of the West, structuring the very conditions of possibility of the bounds of the thinkable. How have the ideas generated by philosophers and critics connected to the need for territorial acquisition of imperial countries as these have sought to accumulate land, people, and the economic advantage of the colonial relation for the promotion of self-idealizing and self-occulting images? Said provided answers to this question throughout his political corpus.

Said's political conscience was stirred by the Arab-Israeli Wars of 1967 and 1973. Before then he had restricted his professional writing to literary criticism. After the Six-Day War of June 1967, Said became overtly political in his writing, taking up such issues as the Palestinian-Israeli conflict, the role that intellectuals should play in society, and the effects and traces of imperialism that continue to taint the relationship between the Occident and the Orient.

As a Palestinian exile, Said was forced to reconcile his loss of home in Palestine because of Israel's creation in 1948–which some consider a form of settler colonialism–with his Western education that placed him among an academic elite. His education created a tension within and put him at odds with himself. In the institution of Western academia, with its knowledge-making quest to categorize and describe the "Other," Said was an outsider who had become a knowledge-insider. Said was a postcolonial subject, whose education and family wealth helped make him what he would term a "secular border intellectual," someone who could use his specific position to understand how the West constructs and perceives its ethnic others.

Said attempted to understand the extremely complicated dynamic between Western and non-Western cultures, which became a central theme in his work. Exile, the feeling that accompanies someone who is unattached to a specific cultural or physical home, brings with it a heightened sense of how and why cultural difference often produces strong clashes sometimes resulting in state violence, forced migration, and the dispossession of indigenous populations. For Said, the forced expulsion of nearly 800,000 Palestinians in 1947 and 1948 from what is now Israel created the Palestinian Question just as the Jewish Question seemingly reached its conclusion. That the tragedy of the Palestinian people began through the creation of a Jewish state at the hands of a people, the Jews, who themselves had suffered so much, stood as one of the most profound ironies of the twentieth century.

In the background of all of Said's various writings on imperialism and colonialism stands the abiding and

Dust jacket for Said's controversial 1978 volume arguing that Western ideas of the East are imposed by the "imperial ego" (Richland County Public Library)

persistent question of all his work: The Question of Palestine. One can trace through all of Said's work a return to this question, particularly as it shaped his formation as an intellectual and his personal identity. In 1978 he published his groundbreaking criticism of how the Orient was "created and discovered" by the Occident. In *Orientalism,* one can sense Said's lingering feelings of discomfort and angst about being a Palestinian in the West:

> Much of the personal investment in this study derives from my awareness of being an "Oriental" as a child growing up in two British colonies. All of my education, in those colonies (Palestine and Egypt) and in the United States, has been Western, and yet that deep early awareness has persisted. In many ways my study of Orientalism has been an attempt to inventory the traces upon me, the Oriental subject, of the culture whose domination has been so powerful a factor in the life of all Orientals.

The distinct sense of not quite belonging to his surroundings, being out of place despite his well-heeled upbringing and education, pervades almost all of Said's work as he weaves aspects of his biography together with contemporary political circumstances. Said writes that "the history of Orientalism has both an internal consistency and a highly articulated set of relationships to the dominant culture surrounding it." His goal is to "to show the field's shape and internal organization, its pioneers, patriarchal authorities, canonical texts, doxological ideas, exemplary figures, its followers, elaborators, and new authorities; I try also to explain how Orientalism borrowed and was frequently informed by 'strong' ideas, doctrines, and trends ruling the culture." Orientalism then, is a way of seeing, a way of coming to terms with the Orient—always as something set apart and distinguished from the Occident by its otherness, its "exotic-ness." The difference the West saw in the Orient permitted its imperial "civilizing" missions, in the name of which anything was acceptable.

Orientalism relays how the West's will to power subjugated the East through a sort of willed projection: "Description of the Orient is obliterated by the designs and patterns foisted upon it by the imperial ego, which makes no secret of its powers." The West, in some sense, had to create the East in order to create itself. The necessity of this Other is carefully laid out in three densely argued chapters that survey the vast number of writers influenced by Orientalist ideas: Flaubert, François-René de Chateaubriand, Louis Massignon, Gérard de Nerval, Alphonse de Lamartine, D. H. Lawrence, Karl Marx, Benjamin Disraeli, and Sir Richard Francis Burton. The noted French writer Chateaubriand, for example, "found in the Orient a locale sympathetic to [his] private myths, obsessions, and requirements" and "brought a very heavy load of personal objectives and suppositions to the Orient, unloaded them there, and proceeded thereafter to push people, places, and ideas around in the Orient as if nothing could resist his imperious imagination." Said notes: "Here we notice how all the pilgrims, but especially the French ones, exploit the Orient in their work so as in some urgent way to justify their existential vocation." Said contends that Orientalism, as a distinct set of ideas and as a style, continues to pervade Western thinking. To argue the point he draws upon the writings of Henry Kissinger and other leading late-1970s statesmen of American foreign policy in the Middle East.

According to Said, academic disciplines such as anthropology, sociology, history, and geography created a web of discourse that shaped the belittling Western "understanding" of a huge swath of territory (generally known as the East) and its peoples. These disciplines contributed to an understanding of the East which posited that Orientals are lazy, morally degenerate, emotional, incapable of reason, and unskilled in creating and maintaining civilizational order. In addition, the Orient, what Chateaubriand had described as "a decrepit canvas awaiting his restorative efforts" is represented as a place of mystery, licentiousness, and wanton sexuality, a place in need of being tamed and controlled by Western rationality and measured judgment. Through this lens, the Arab is seen as a "civilized man fallen again into a savage state." He is portrayed as a creature ruled by the base passions, someone who does not understand that the world goes on outside his head, indicating his incapacity for comprehending the laws of science. This portrayal of the "typical Oriental" stood in sharp contrast to the Westerner's commitments to reason, order, rationality, and evenhandedness.

As a discourse—indeed, *the* discourse of the West—Orientalism established a relationship between texts that asserted a consistent picture of the Orient. Even if not true, this picture created an almost incontestable set of stereotypes about Orientals that, in some sense, helped the West define itself. As Said writes of Chateaubriand, "We will have understood that his egoistic Oriental memoirs supply us with a constantly demonstrated, an indefatigably performed experience of self" as he "would make everything he said about the Orient wholly dependent on his ego." Said argues that the Orientalist's ego-informed analysis of the East evolved into an institutional discourse:

> During the nineteenth and twentieth centuries the Orientalists became a more serious quantity, because by then the reaches of imaginative and actual geography had shrunk, because the Oriental-European relationship was determined by an unstoppable European expansion in search of markets, resources, and colonies, and finally, because Orientalism had accomplished its self-metamorphosis from a scholarly discourse to an imperial institution.

The attitude of Orientalism circulated in and through texts and reinforced a set of images that—while not grounded in direct experience of the East—were accepted as real.

The grip Orientalism held over Western thinking was so powerful that for centuries it justified Europeans in their subordination of millions of Orientals. Orientalism, as a sort of closed system of representations about the people of the Middle East and the far East, made it nearly impossible for people to think about, much less talk and write about, the Orient without trafficking in the orientalist stereotypes Said describes. These stereotypes are codified in the conditions of possibility for thinking itself. Colonialism, and the politics of empire, depended upon the discursive power of Orientalism as it provided a rationale for conquest that required little or no explication because the East existed simply as something to be tamed and analyzed for Western consumption and understanding. The politics of conquest and the Orientalist outlook facilitated the elevation of the West to the entity doing the seeing, while the East could simply be seen. The overwhelming weight of this discourse, and its close connections to colonial violence, wiped out alternative perspectives that questioned the sharp binary structuring of West versus East.

Said sought to introduce a new sequence of thought and analysis to replace the thought-stopping fury that resulted in collective passion rather than genuine understanding and disclosure. He called his approach humanism, by which he meant the attempt to dissolve what poet William Blake called "mind-forged manacles" and to open the mind for humane, rational reflection. Because humanism is sustained by a sense of community of one thinker with another across culture and time, there is, strictly speaking, no such thing as an isolated humanist.

Said argued that texts must be read in what he called "worldly ways," meaning that the reader must become aware of underlying ideas, especially those that reveal power relationships of domination and subjugation. In *Orientalism,* Said demonstrated that the insinuations and imbrications of power are present in even the most recondite studies. For Said, humanism is the last and final resistance we have against the injustices and inhuman practices that disfigure human history. He hoped his book would gain a small place in the long and often interrupted road to human freedom.

Orientalism—a book with both ardent supporters and vicious critics—set off an intense, continuous discussion that has not lessened in the years since its publication. In his December 1980 review in *International Journal of Middle East Studies,* Malcolm Kerr—who was wholly sympathetic to the conclusions Said drew—was disappointed with how he had carried out his project. Kerr asserted that Said, whom he called "overzealous," had assumed points that needed further development and wished that the book had been better written. His criticism echoed a common perception of scholars who found the book difficult to read but at the same time praised its message as extremely necessary. The intensity of those opposed to Said's message is well represented by Robert Irwin, who in *The Lust of Knowing: The Orientalists and Their Enemies* (2006), published nearly three decades after Said's work, called it "a work of malignant charlatanry in which it is hard to distinguish honest mistakes from willful misrepresentation."

Said wrote his next work, *The Question of Palestine* (1979), to help Americans better understand the plight

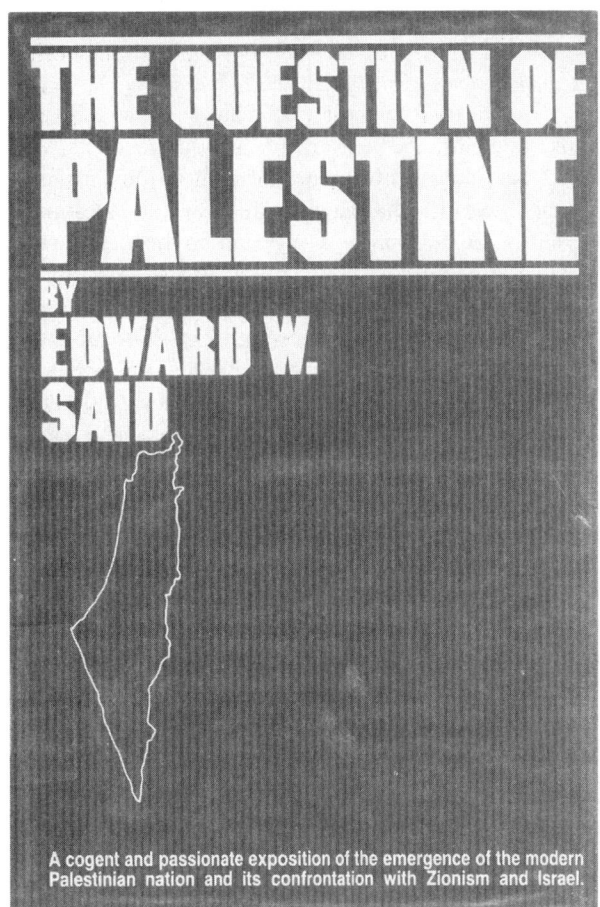

Dust jacket for Said's 1979 volume written to explain the situation in Palestine to Americans (Richland County Public Library)

of the Palestinian refugees in Gaza and the West Bank. In his inquiry into the history of the conflict, he argues that Zionism was able to connect to the imperial adventures of the British by offering the possibility of a state in the Middle East favorable to Western interests that would stem the rise of Arab nationalism in the region. Zionism as a movement long predated the Holocaust, perhaps having its start in the late nineteenth century, as Theodor Herzl, Vladimir Jabotinsky, Chaim Weizmann, and many others sought to gain the cooperation of the imperial powers in securing a Jewish national home. Of the Palestinian cause since the creation of Israel, Said writes:

> Partly because of its cultural, religious, and historical depth, partly because it abuts on so many interests, both local and international, the cause of Palestine has remained for two decades the one un-cooptable, undomesticated, and fierce national and anti-colonial cause still alive—to its adherents a source of unrealized hope and somewhat tarnished idealism, to its enemies a goad

and a perdurable political alter ego that will neither go away nor settle into amiable nonentity.

In one of the most compelling chapters in this book, titled "Zionism from the Standpoint of its Victims," Said conveys his understanding of the epistemological categories that have made the Arab-Palestinian an entity to be erased, a problem to be dealt with, within the Zionist weltanschauung. He asserts that in establishing Israel, the presence of the indigenous population was literally erased through expulsion and the razing of villages and land. Said notes that this behavior of the Zionists illustrates the primary difference between "classical" imperialism and Zionism. Although the Zionists depended on the groundwork that imperialism had already laid—the idea that the "native peoples" of the Orient were disposable and exploitable—Zionism "was a colonial vision unlike that of most other nineteenth-century European powers, for whom the natives of outlying territories were *included* in the redemptive *mission civilisatrice*" (civilizing mission). In other words, the Zionists needed the notion that natives were expendable in order to take the land, and the creation of Israel required that the natives be removed from the land altogether.

Said reminds his readers that imperial visions, whether British or Zionist, "belong fundamentally to the ethos of this European *mission civilisatrice*—nineteenth-century, colonialist, racist even—built on notions about the inequality of men, races, and civilizations, an inequality allowing the most extreme forms of self-aggrandizing projections, and the most extreme forms of punitive discipline toward the unfortunate natives whose existence, paradoxically, was denied." As a movement to create a Jewish national state, Zionism sought for nearly a hundred years to establish a piece of territory somewhere in the world for the sole development of the Jewish people, presumably to safeguard against the ravages of anti-Semitism. While East Africa and South America were presented as possible locations for the Jewish state, Palestine became the logical choice.

Said argues that as a national movement, Zionism launched a continuing onslaught against the Palestinian people, their cultural symbols, and institutions. He notes that the display of the Palestinian flag can lead to detention and the simple attempt to attend a Palestinian school in the West Bank can result in blacklisting and defamation. The preservation of the Palestine of the past, he contends, has been rendered all but nearly impossible as Israeli Defense Forces have frequently raided, vandalized, and razed Palestinian cultural museums and archives. The erasure of the Palestine reality—the view of Zionism "from the standpoint of its victims"—in events such as the expulsion of 750,000 Palestinians to clear the way for the creation of Israel, clashes with the way that this reality has been interpreted by Zionism itself: that repetition of the image of the Arab terrorist being put forward in the Western press, while eliding the image of the educated Palestinian who is a doctor, lawyer, educator, or politician.

Said views the Israel-Palestine conflict as a test case for the future because it involves various types of ethnic and religious conflicts that if not directly addressed will lead to larger and larger scales of violence within the world. Ultimately, Said asks: How do we understand differences between groups without the polarizing forces of violence and exclusion and how have these forces conditioned our ability to think about difference? In other words, have not the categories through which we understand the world—the conditions of possibility for thinking itself—been conditioned or honed by violence? He returned to these questions throughout his career.

Said devoted himself to exposing the web of Western images and stereotypes about Arabs and Muslims, revealing a long history of anti-Arab and anti-Muslim bias that reduces nearly three hundred million people to one seething mass of fanaticism and terrorism. In an attempt to complicate these one-dimensional images, as well as to expose the diversity within Islam, Said brought the insights broached in *Orientalism* to larger projects such as *Covering Islam: How the Media and the Experts Determine How We See the Rest of the World* (1981), a book that covers in great detail the 1979 Iranian hostage crisis when fifty Americans were held hostage for more than a year inside the U.S. embassy in Tehran. Said shows how the media "covered Islam" by producing reports that not only treated the hostage situation but that also obscured larger issues, such as the fact that the vast majority of Muslims are not terrorist hostage-takers. The images projected around the world of swarthy Iranian men displaying weapons and blindfolded Americans cemented within the United States (and the West in general) the image of Arabs as devoted to violence. Said, however, reminds his readers that there are many "Islams," as well as many "Arabs" (noting that Iranians are not even Arabs). He argues that it is a grave mistake to decontextualize specific terrorist events in order to then tie them together and create a mistaken impression of having adequately understood Arab or Islamic terror.

In addition to the poor work of journalists covering events in the Middle East, Said criticizes a parade of so-called experts who have emerged within U.S. cultural discourse. He argues that Steve Emerson, Judith Miller, Fouad Ajami, Thomas Friedman, and many other commentators on the Middle East and Islamic terrorism have driven home a consistent message representing Islam as an ideology of extremism that shares nothing with the major world religions because of its ties to violence and jihad. Such commentators have capitalized upon anti-Arab racism and gross caricatures and misunderstandings about Islam to produce jejune and offensive constructions as stand-ins for the Orient and Islam.

Said's aim in *Covering Islam* is ultimately to change how the West thinks about Islam and the Middle East. He argues that the complex ways in which government interests, academic knowledge, and social-political exigencies have seemingly conspired against Islam, particularly with respect to the Israeli government's treatment of the Palestinians, suggest that more extensive work needs to be done on how academic expertise easily blends into media punditry–producing a continual stream of propaganda that is presented as objective, fair, and balanced. He recognizes the great challenge of countering the presentation of the Orient and Islam in the media as well as in academia, which has been so totalizing, unreflective, and biased that it has produced a seeming orthodoxy the public has consumed unreflectively as objective and factual. The legitimation of such suspect representations of Islam and the Orient, Said notes, has dovetailed nicely with the needs of the Western powers (primarily the United States and Britain) and their client states (primarily Israel, Saudi Arabia, Egypt, and Iraq) as Western, Judeo-Christian values and material interests are camouflaged in the language of "security" and "the vital need to contain Arab nationalism." From the standpoint of U.S. regional planners, Gamal Abdel Nasser's seizure of power in Egypt in 1952 necessitated an on-going containment policy because charismatic Arab leaders forwarding a nationalist agenda have been viewed as in league with the Soviets.

With the publication of such obviously political works as *Orientalism* and *Covering Islam,* Said found himself isolated from the main critical currents of poststructuralism, then reaching its zenith. In *The World, the Text, and the Critic* (1983) Said seeks to rouse fellow intellectuals and humanists out of their fascination with theory so as to move them into the world of politics and negotiation, areas seemingly long ago abandoned by the leading lights of postmodern criticism. In this collection of essays that celebrates figures such as Jonathan Swift, György Lukács, and Nina Auerbach, Said exposes what he sees as the taming of the critical temperament by the bounds of professionalism and decorum, which he regards as death knells for the intellectual activist. He argues that the rise of poststructural theory had led to such a preoccupation with the puzzles and implications of texts that intellectuals had become unable or

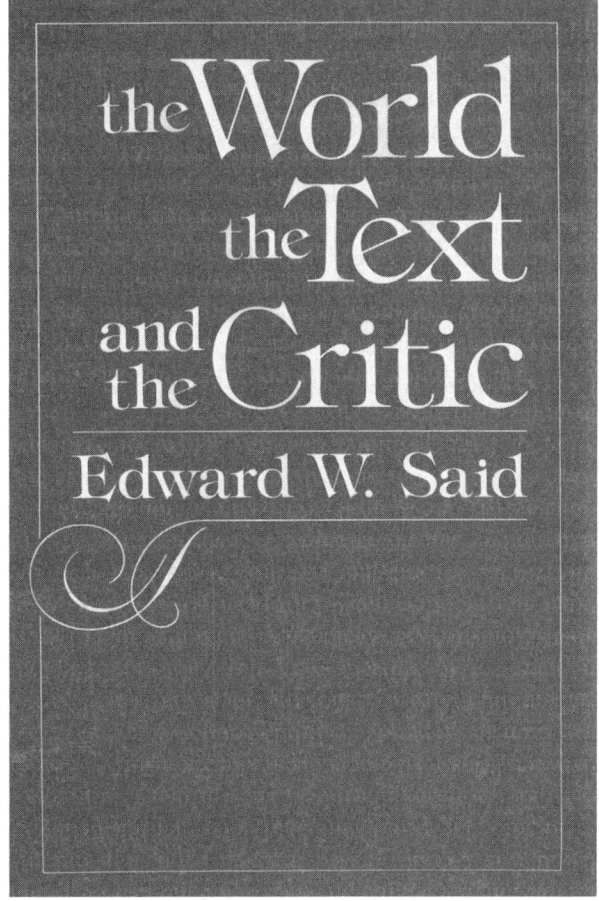

Dust jacket for Said's 1983 collection of critical essays that attempt to move intellectuals from fascination with poststructuralist theory to an engagement with world events (Richland County Public Library)

perhaps unwilling to connect to the wider world and the political struggles therein.

Said advocates the reinvigoration of literary criticism as it is practiced in the United States by defining "worldliness" as a legitimate object of critical inquiry. According to Said, the literary theorist should move beyond a mere analysis of texts to investigate how texts connect to events in the world. He notes that in the 1960s political events were central to the work of such cultural critics as Noam Chomsky, Howard Zinn, and Richard Ohmann, whose work held implications for millions of people throughout the world. For critics to remain important, Said argues they must interrogate how literary works connect to the promotion of state doctrine and cultural values.

In the introduction to *The World, the Text, and the Critic* Said tells a story of how during the height of the Vietnam War an old college friend had told him about seeing a copy of Lawrence Durrell's *Alexandria Quartet* (1957–1960) on the desk of the Secretary of Defense.

For Said, his friend's observation raised an important question: How could the secretary, a man who was ordering the dropping of millions of pounds of munitions over Southeast Asia resulting in the deaths of countless Vietnamese, also appreciate Durrell's novel, a product of high culture and learning? Said tells this story to suggest how a distinct separation between professions and the specializations within those professions enables the development of a cult of expertise, authorizing individuals to speak on certain topics while prohibiting others from speaking because of a lack of credentials. Such separation allows the secretary his amateur interest in literature while keeping the literary critic from criticizing public policy. In his essay titled "Between Culture and System" Said demonstrates how the literary critic has been forced to write criticism "between" the demands of a national culture and the professional parameters of the guild system, leading to a tamed critical sense that deliberately avoids difficult questions about domestic and foreign policy and the intellectual's place in either exposing or legitimating the interests that support them.

There is a palpable sense of anger in these essays, as Said encourages the literary-theory establishment to take stock of how far it has drifted from the social involvement of intellectuals such as Jean-Paul Sartre. Said is particularly disturbed by the cults that had sprung up around the work of Derrida and Foucault by the early 1980s because he saw their followers becoming obsessed with issues in literary texts that are unconnected to the pressing public issues. Said believed intellectuals could play a meaningful role in helping to resolve ethnic and religious conflicts, and he sought to reclaim this lost ideal of the activist intellectual. Leaving the world to politicians and demagogues, who offer only clichés and demonizing images as appeals to their followers, stands as the ultimate *trahison des clercs* (betrayal of the intellectuals), in Said's estimation. Worldliness, the capacity to see how texts connect to events and representations in the field of action, along with secular criticism, must be—in the final analysis—the task of the responsible intellectual, who should provide the means for understandings that transcend the binary divisions of various competing nationalisms, which offer only the bleak prospect of further suffering and destruction.

Said sought to understand, throughout all of his work, how societies in their attempts to make the strange familiar, interact with those who are different from themselves, the cultural Others. He recognized that the process leads to societies that are technologically or militarily superior assuming the superiority of their own culture or civilization. Conrad's famous quote from *Heart of Darkness* (1902) captures Said's understanding of the implications of this process perfectly: "The conquest of the earth, which mostly means the taking it away from those who have a different complexion or slightly flatter noses than ourselves, is not a pretty thing when you look into it too much."

In *After the Last Sky: Palestinian Lives* (1986) Said worked with photographer Jean Mohr to reveal the Palestinian plight in words and pictures. Said argues that the Palestinians have not been given "permission to narrate" in the West because they have been placed in direct competition with the story of the Holocaust, which is honored in American culture. In Said's view, the Palestinians, in being denied the fundamental right to choose their own representatives in negotiations with Israel, must rely upon the United States as an unfair broker in what has been deceptively called the "peace process"—a reference to the newspeak that encapsulates the treaties and language used to mask the ethnic cleansing of Palestinians from the occupied territories through Israeli land appropriation and illegal settlement.

Said's frequent ventures into the public sphere often made him a target for harsh criticism. His support for the Palestinians in the Israel-Palestine conflict was a distinctly minority opinion in the United States, where mainstream opinion favored Israel. In "The Professor of Terror," an article published in the August 1989 issue of the conservative Jewish periodical *Commentary*, Edward Alexander argued that Said harbored a secret admiration for the terrorist bomber in the Conrad novel *The Secret Agent: A Simple Tale* (1907).

In early September 1991, nearly forty years after Said had left the Middle East for the United States, he was diagnosed with chronic lymphocytic leukemia—a rare form of leukemia that attacks certain white blood cells. He writes of the experience in his memoir *Out of Place: A Memoir* (1999): "It took me another month to understand how thoroughly I was shaken by this 'sword of Damocles,' as one volubly callous doctor called it, hanging over me." While it is impossible to estimate the far-reaching implications of this diagnosis for Said's personal life, as he sought to spend more time with friends and family in what he believed would be his last year or two of life, the implications for his scholarly and political commitments became readily clear as he completed pressing projects after receiving what can rightly be called "a death sentence." That Said lived nearly twelve years beyond the date of the original diagnosis, while continuing to write as a critic and impassioned activist, stands as a testament to his commitment to human liberation. In 1992 Said traveled to Palestine with his wife, Miriam, and two children for the first time in forty-five years. He could hardly recognize the Palestine of his childhood.

In *Culture and Imperialism* (1993), which can be seen as a continuation of some of the themes and questions he raised in *Orientalism*, Said is particularly interested in how British cultural domination structured literary narratives about the colonial period. He develops terms that are useful in examining how an overwhelmingly dominant culture contains and shapes the foreign culture it inhabits, and in turn creates the perceptual modes through which "reality" is apprehended. The first of these terms, "structures of attitude and reference," refers to how social space relates to and is oriented by colonial dominance–that is, how characters, even within novels, are seemingly unaware of how strong a role imperialism plays in structuring social space and political economies. For example, Said devotes an extended discussion to an analysis of Jane Austen's *Mansfield Park* (1814), noting how Fanny Price only once throughout the novel remarks upon her uncle Sir Thomas Bertram's slaves, who harvest the sugar crops in Antigua and make the wealth of the estate possible. Fanny Price's "structure of attitude and reference," that of a well-to-do English woman, suggests she is relatively ignorant of the state of affairs–people of a "lower order" doing manual labor–that contributes to her luxurious lifestyle. The second concept that Said develops is "contrapuntal," a specialized term in music that refers to how the whole consists of many interacting and dynamic parts. According to Said, how a culture operates is best understood by examining its constitutive parts, noting the nature and intensity of interactions between, say, a society's civil institutions and mass culture or between the media and popular culture. Reading a novel contrapuntally, for instance, entails situating the work within a larger framework, such as the historical and cultural milieu of the author, that allows for a fuller understanding of the context that produced the theme or problematic attitudes to be studied. Through these major concepts Said examines a whole range of literary and musical works that were developed within and in response to the politics of empire, including William Makepeace Thackeray's *Vanity Fair* (1847–1848), George Eliot's *Daniel Deronda* (1874–1876), and Conrad's *Nostromo* (1904).

In 1993 Said was invited to deliver the Reith Lectures on the BBC. The lectures, published as *Representations of the Intellectual: The 1993 Reith Lectures* (1994), brought together Said's thoughts on the state of contemporary intellectual culture. In the spirit of Julien Benda's *La trahison des clercs* (1927; translated as *The Treasons of the Intellectuals*, 1928), Said traces the collusive elements within the intellectual community that often reduce the most vocal critics to mere state functionaries. He cites a crippling conformism among university intellectuals who seek the promise of a big prize and position. Criticizing

Dust jacket for Said's 1993 study of the effect of British colonialism on literature (Richland County Public Library)

commentators such as Walter Lippman, Said identifies three general rules that those aspiring to be cultural pundits should never violate: never be too controversial; never upset people with your ideas; and speak in the accepted lingua franca of the day. Said, who violated these rules throughout his career, points to such examples as Voltaire, Emile Zola, Benda, and Chomsky, and calls for a reclamation of the ideals that animate the life and career of a committed intellectual: telling the truth while exposing lies. Said believes it is particularly necessary to speak the truth to power in cynical times. While the material costs of being a truth teller are high–often involving the loss of employment, popularity, and friends–Said believes there will always be individuals who will dedicate their lives and careers to exposing the corruption of organizations and governments.

In "Intellectual Exile: Expatriates and Marginals," a short essay from the Reith series, Said draws a distinction between two general ways of living in exile: the way of assimilating and aligning with the centers of power and the way of willingly and deliberately choosing to remain on the margins. Henry Kissinger is an example of the first type of exile; Theodor W. Adorno represents the second. Said, who as a stateless Palestinian did not choose exile deliberately, argues that "writing from the margins" is the only way to truly be a constructive critic, a modern gadfly, to one's home. He believes that it is a moral necessity for the intellectual to cultivate the sense of exile even if one is not actually an exile:

> A condition of marginality, which might seem irresponsible or flippant, frees you from having always to proceed with caution, afraid to overturn the applecart, anxious about upsetting fellow members of the same corporation . . . I am saying, however, that to be as marginal and as undomesticated as someone who is in real exile is for an intellectual to be unusually responsive to the traveler rather than to the potentate, and to the provisional and risky rather than to the habitual, to innovation and experiment rather than the authoritatively given *status quo*.

Said's memoir *Out of Place* primarily focuses on his childhood and the beginning of his teaching career in the United States; it concludes with his diagnosis of leukemia. After its publication Justus Reid Weiner attempted to undermine Said's credibility as a Palestinian in his September 1999 article in *Commentary* titled "'My Beautiful Old House' and other Fabrications by Edward Said." Weiner alleged that Said was not nearly as Palestinian as he claimed to be. He pointed out that Said's family owned a home in Egypt, where Said spent most of his childhood and early adulthood. The gist of Weiner's attack was that Said had rearranged the facts of his life to present himself as a Palestinian refugee in the United States. Said, however, never claimed to be a political refugee. What he claimed was that he could never return to the area of his birth, which is present-day Israel, because of Israel's law of return, which allows any Jew anywhere to settle and live in Israel. Said, who was born there, merely pointed out that he was denied the same right.

In 1999 Said became president of the Modern Language Association. In this position he encouraged language specialists to return to the rigorous historical study of literature, instead of allowing the field to devolve into an untenable landscape where graduate students could choose specialties, such as postmodernism, as if they were selecting items off a menu. The demands of professionalism, he maintained, require that literary critics commit themselves to the demands of their work without worrying about the political implications of the external behavior of their nation-states. Political dissenters within U.S. political culture, as Said repeatedly stated, face—and ultimately resist the strong pressure to conform to—the extraordinary demands of the dominant culture.

Said again visited Palestine in 1999. In 2000, while on a visit to the newly liberated south Lebanon, Said was photographed throwing a stone in the direction of the Israeli border. The picture produced a firestorm of criticism in the United States, with many people, including some of his colleagues at Columbia University, calling for Said's dismissal. The university supported Said, and he addressed the issue in a March 2001 essay in *Counterpunch* titled "Freud, Zionism & Vienna" saying that the act was symbolic and that it was a form of protected speech. It was not long after this incident that Said's health began to deteriorate rapidly.

Said was invited to deliver the 2001 Freud Memorial Lecture in Vienna, but the invitation was cancelled because of what the organizers called the "political conflict in the Middle East." Critics, primarily in the United States, had argued that it was inappropriate for him to deliver the lecture. The Freud Museum in London responded by inviting Said to give the lecture there. The talk was published in 2003, with an accompanying response by Jacqueline Rose, as *Freud and the Non-European*. In the lecture, in which he also reflects on some of the anticolonialist writings of Frantz Fanon, Said discusses how Freud adamantly insisted that Moses, the founder of the Jewish religion, was not a European. This "non-European" identity put Moses in the unique position of being "inside-outside." He was outside of the European identity, but yet thoroughly assimilated into that identity by the European. Said believes that Freud's *Moses and Monotheism* (1939) speaks to people over generations without becoming stale. He writes: "Reading the treatise, we feel that Freud wishes us to understand that there are other issues at stake here—other, more pressing problems to expose than ones whose solution might be comforting, or provide a sort of resting-place." Once again Said urges the intellectual to resist the temptation to offer simple and comforting solutions to political problems.

Said died of complications of leukemia on 25 September 2003. In his commitment to developing a critical consciousness for the unmasking of state apologetics for illegitimate forms of violence, Said made few friends in the corridors of power. Although he occupied a prestigious university professorship at Columbia, he was not spared the kind of verbal and press abuse those choosing to engage the field of political struggle so often face. He made his peace with this inconvenience, as he elaborates in the foreword to the revised version of Chomsky's *The Fateful Triangle: The United States, Israel, and the Palestinians* (1999): "It is a lonely condition, yes, but it is always a better one than a gregarious tolerance for the way things are."

Throughout his life and career Edward W. Said chose to be a lone voice in the wilderness hoping to trouble the conscience of enough fellow-citizens to spark a revolution in thought and action. Yet, Said was also an eternal optimist: he never gave up on the idea of justice as a true possibility. He was fond of quoting the Italian philosopher Antonio Gramsci's statement, "pessimism of the intellect, optimism of the will." The sheer volume of his writings is a testament to this optimism.

Interviews:

Tahar Ben Jelloun, "Edward Said," in *Entretiens avec "Le Monde," Vol. 4, Civilisations* (Paris: La Decouverte/Le Monde, 1984), pp. 230–236;

Matthew Stevenson, "Edward Said: An Exile's Exile," *Progressive* (February 1987): 30–34;

"Orientalism and After: An Interview with Edward Said," *Radical Philosophy* (Spring 1993): 22–32;

Power, Politics, and Culture: Interviews with Edward W. Said, edited by Gauri Viswanathan (New York: Pantheon, 2001).

References:

Edward Alexander, "The Professor of Terror," *Commentary*, 88 (August 1989): 49–50;

Bill Ashcropt and Pal Ahluwalia, *Edward Said: The Paradox of Identity* (London & New York: Routledge, 1999);

Paul A. Bove, ed., *Edward Said and the Work of the Critic: Speaking Truth to Power* (Durham, N.C.: Duke University Press, 2000);

William D. Hart, *Edward Said and the Religious Effects of Culture* (New York: Cambridge University Press, 2000);

Abdirahman Hussein, *Edward Said: Criticism and Society* (London: Verso, 2004);

Mark Krupnik, "Edward Said and the Discourse of Palestinian Rage," *Tikkun*, 4 (November-December 1989): 21–24;

Mustapha Marrouchi, *Edward Said at the Limits* (Albany: State University of New York Press, 2004);

Michael Sprinker, ed., *Edward Said: A Critical Reader* (Oxford & Cambridge, Mass.: Blackwell, 1992);

Asha Varadharajan, *Exotic Parodies: Subjectivity in Adorno, Said and Spivak* (Minneapolis: University of Minnesota Press, 1995);

Michael Walzer, "An Exchange: Michael Walzer and Edward Said," *Grand Street*, 5, no. 4 (1986);

Justus Reid Weiner, "'My Beautiful Old House' and Other Fabrications by Edward Said," *Commentary*, 108 (September 1999): 23–31.

Tayeb Salih
(1929 -)

Majd Yaser Al-Mallah
Grand Valley State University

BOOKS: *Dawmat Wad Hamid: Sab' qisas* (Beirut: Dar al-'Awdah, 1962);

'Urs al-Zayn (Beirut: Dar al-'Awdah, 1962); translated by Denys Johnson-Davies as *The Wedding of Zein and Other Stories* (London: Heinemann, 1969; Washington, D.C.: Three Continents Press, 1985);

Mawsim al-hijrah ila al-shamal (Beirut: Dar al-'Awdah, 1967); translated by Johnson-Davies as *Season of Migration to the North* (London: Heinemann, 1969; corrected edition, 1978);

Bandar Shah: Daw al-Bayt (Beirut: Dar al-'Awdah, 1971);

Maryud: Al-Juz' al-thani min Bandar Shah (Beirut: Dar al-'Awdah, 1976); translated by Johnson-Davies as *Bandarshah* (London: Unesco, 1996).

OTHER: "Al-Rajul al-Qubrusii," *Majallat al-Dawlah* (1973);

"Yawm mubarak 'ala shati' Umm Bab," in *Mukhtarat min al-qisas al-qasirah fi 18 baladan 'Arabiyyan* (Cairo: Markaz al-Ahram li al-Tarjamah wa al-Nashr, 1993).

Tayeb Salih (al-Ahram Weekly)

A recipient of the prestigious Cairo Prize for Creativity in the Arabic Novel (2005), Tayeb Salih is regarded as one the most important fiction writers in the Arab world. Widely recognized for his innovations, Salih gained fame in the West as well as the Arab world after the publication of his acclaimed novel *Mawsim al-hijrah ila al-shamal* (1969; translated as *Season of Migration to the North,* 1969). Although Salih has not been a prolific writer, his few works have drawn considerable critical attention. Books, dissertations, and articles have been written on Salih and his complex fiction.

Tayeb Salih, born in 1929, grew up in al-Dabbah, one of the main villages in the Marwi district located in central northern Sudan, a thriving region for farming because of the Nile. His father, Muhammad Salih Ahmad, and his mother, 'Aisha Ahmad Zakariyya, came from the Shaygiyyah tribe, one of the major tribes in that area of Sudan. In interviews, Salih describes his family and people as "religious people"; they belonged to Rikabiyyah, a group that was influential in spreading Islam in the areas south of Sudan's capital, Khartoum.

Salih enjoyed life in the village, where people grew crops and raised animals to fulfill their everyday needs of survival. Despite the simplicity of the life, Salih remembers a rich culture, for after working in the field during the day, the people gathered in the evening for conversations and social activities, regularly listening to poets reciting and singing their poetry. Salih described the enduring importance of the village to him in a conversation with Talhah Jibril: "I see it [the village] in my imagination, wherever I turn, I sometimes remember it during the summer months in London; at a raindrop, I smell the fragrance of that far away village!" To Salih, the village "was the only world that [he] loved without any reservations," the only place he experienced "complete and total happiness." The village plays a central role in the setting of all of his stories.

Salih went to the Qur'anic schools, known in Sudan as *khalwah* (and in other Arab countries as *kuttab*), where he learned the basics of religion as well as to read and write. He then attended elementary public schools in his village, at the time newly installed by the British authorities that ruled Sudan. Since his village did not have schools beyond the elementary level, he moved to the city of Port Sudan, where he finished middle school. His enrollment in middle school in itself indicates that Salih was a distinguished student, for the handful of such schools in the country were reserved for only the very best students. During his years in middle school, Salih learned English. He recalls that a British administrator visited his school and selected him, because of his good English language skills, to greet the governor, who intended to visit the school shortly thereafter. Salih, who did not then understand the British role as colonizers, cried out "Long live the governor."

After graduating from middle school, Salih attended Wadi Sidna School, one of only two secondary schools for the entire country, which the British had built on the outskirts of the city of Umm Durman. The students and teachers lived in the school, with the students allowed weekly visits to their families. Salih enjoyed cultural activities at Wadi Sidna School and wrote for the school paper. He was given his first experience of Western literature as he read works by such authors as William Shakespeare and Charles Dickens. He also remembers Umm Durman fondly, as a city with a "village feel." Although the school's principal, Mr. Lang, was prepared to help Salih get a scholarship to study at Cambridge or Oxford, Salih's family did not want to send him abroad, so he continued his studies at the college in Khartoum (which after independence in 1956 became the University of Khartoum).

Despite his interest in literature and desire to study the humanities, Salih enrolled as a science student, mainly because he believed that such studies would open the most practical way for him to help in the development of his country. He had the "romantic" notion that he would become an "agriculture inspector." But he did not enjoy science and spent a great deal of time attending literature classes. Mr. Hart, an English professor who had confronted Salih for participating in his class without being his student, tried to convince him to drop science and go into the humanities. In 1951, conflicted over his passion for literature and lack of interest in science, Salih decided to leave the college altogether. He taught briefly at a private school in the city of Rifa'ah, but he left that post to enroll in Bakht al-Rida institute for training teachers. In 1952 he applied for a position with the British Broadcasting Corporation (BBC) and in the winter of the following year left Sudan for Britain.

Salih's experience in Britain did not begin well, and he almost decided to return home soon after his arrival. He had difficulty adjusting to cold weather, small rooms, and food that was too "plain." During this trying time, he wrote his first story, "Nakhla 'ala al-jadwal" (A Palm Tree on the Stream), which was first published in 1953. In his story about a rich merchant trying to buy a palm tree from a poor farmer, Salih clearly is sympathetic to, even identifies with, the poor man. Salih's decision to persevere and stay in London was made easier when he found a Sudanese friend, Salah Ahmad Salih, with whom he worked to establish a small Sudanese community. Initially, the two men rented adjacent rooms but later found a house that they shared together. The house turned into a hosting home to people who visited from Sudan, a place that they called the House of Sudan. This sense of community in London not only made Salih feel more comfortable in his new world but also provided a strong, continual connection back to his beloved country.

Salih's early years in Britain were formative to his development as a writer. As well as working for the BBC, Salih also studied political science at the University of London. The BBC work environment was vastly different from anything that he had experienced before, as his fellow employees came from various backgrounds across the globe, including Arabs from countries other than Sudan. At age twenty-nine Salih was named the head of the Arabic drama department of the corporation. Working at the BBC required him to write in modern standard Arabic, which allowed him to reach a broader Arabic audience. In addition to a broader perspective on news, Salih's BBC experience exposed him to rich programming that dealt with cultural issues, including interviews with writers and authors from different parts of the Arab world.

Salih immersed himself in British culture, joining a social and cultural club and frequently attending the theater. While in London he saw as many plays as possible, including every play by Shakespeare he could. He enjoyed the theater even more than reading novels, but he also read British and American novels on a regular basis, enjoying in particular the works of Joseph Conrad and William Faulkner. Salih also was an avid reader of Arabic literature, particularly the Abbasid poet Abu Nuwas.

After his friend Salah Ahmad Salih left London to go back to Sudan, Salih shared an apartment with an Egyptian friend, 'Abd al-Rahim al-Rifa'i, who also worked at the Arabic section of the BBC. Following the 1956 War, in which Britain, France, and Israel attacked Egypt after the Egyptian president Gamal Abdel Nasser declared the nationalization of the Suez Canal, al-Rifa'i resigned from the BBC. Salih, however, decided to stay.

Front cover for the 1978 English translation of Salih's first novella, 'Urs al-Zayn, 1962 (Thomas Cooper Library, University of South Carolina)

As a correspondent, he traveled to several countries to cover events and work at the regional offices. In 1960 he fell ill on a trip to Beirut and had to be hospitalized for three months. Following his recovery, he married a British woman, Julie. Salih and his wife would have three daughters, Zaynab, Sarah, and Samirah.

Salih's career as a writer really began with the 1960 publication of his short story "Dawmat Wad Hamid." The story was first published in *Aswaat* (Voices), a magazine whose founder and editor, Denys Johnson-Davies, was a close friend and supporter of Salih and his work. The following year, the story was collected in *Dawmat Wad Hamid: Sab'qisas* (1962; The Doum Tree of Wad Hamid: Seven Stories) and Johnson-Davies published a translation of it as "The Doum Tree of Wad Hamid" in *The Encounter,* a prestigious London magazine, bringing early recognition and appreciation of Salih's writing.

"Dawmat Wad Hamid" is set in the village of Wad Hamid, which is used often in Salih's fiction. Although Salih intended the village to be fictional, he later discovered that a small village by that name did exist near al-Dabba, his birth village. A good example of Salih's innovative style that does not rely on a central plot, the story focuses on an extended conversation in which an old man tells a young man the story of the village and its revered doum tree. As the old man describes village life, he shows that he is fully aware of the difficulty and suffering that villagers must endure and the modern comforts city dwellers enjoy. While he and other villagers value their way of life, the old man realizes that outsiders have a negative view of the village and the villagers. He reveals that the central government has had an obsession with "helping" the village. He recalls how a preacher—a man who had little respect or appreciation for the village or its traditions—was sent to lead the villagers in prayer. Shortly after the preacher fell ill and left the village, the government began various initiatives to "modernize" the village and the villagers by installing a station for a steamship, a task that can only be accomplished, in the eyes of the government planners, by cutting down the doum tree to put the steamer in its place.

In this story Salih explores the dialectics of change, through several dichotomies, including old versus young, tree versus steamer, village versus city, and tradition versus modernity. He shows great sensitivity toward the villagers and their way of life while the advantages of modernity are also appreciated. Salih's message is one of tolerance and deep understanding of belief systems and the complexities change entails. Salih ends the story with the old man telling the young man: "There will not be the least necessity for cutting down the doum tree. There is not the slightest reason for the tomb to be removed. What all these people have overlooked is that there's plenty of room for all these things: the doum tree, the tomb, the water-pump, and the steamer's stopping-place."

In 1962 Salih's novella *'Urs al-Zayn,* was published in a volume with seven of his short stories (translated as *The Wedding of Zein and Other Stories,* 1969). Like "Dawmat Wad Hamid," *'Urs al-Zayn* is set in a Sudanese village and features an old man. The main character is not handsome or wealthy or from a respected family, but he has a good heart and a sense of humor. The story is about the triumph of an unlikely underdog who would not ordinarily have a place in society. Zayn uses the strategy of playing the fool in order to gain acceptance. He goes around, for example, screaming the names of any woman that he likes, declaring his love for her. The mothers seeking marriage for their daughters come to believe that he has a power, for the women whose names Zayn calls out seem guaranteed to find a husband almost immediately. Salih sympathetically employs the villager's beliefs in the miraculous in his resolution of the story, in which Zayn marries Ni'mah, the most beautiful girl in the community. Salih discusses his use of the miraculous in interviews, claiming that though he may not necessarily believe in miracles, he does not discount the beliefs of the villagers: "I cannot state positively that there are not metaphysical forces in the world. So, if some of the characters in the novel believe in these metaphysical beliefs, it is not my job as a writer to reject these beliefs and to claim that they are myths." 'Urs al-Zayn was made into a feature film in 1976 by Kuwaiti director Khalid al-Sadiq.

In 1967 Salih published his most acclaimed novel, Mawsim al-hijrah ila al-shamal (translated as Season of Migration to the North, 1969), the story of two Sudanese men who have experienced the West. Salih began workng on this novel shortly after he finished 'Urs al-Zayn, while on vacation in southern France. He wrote a third of it in France, then stopped writing for almost four years. During these years he read about the major setting for the novel, the historical period between World War I and World War II in England. When he returned to the work, he finished the remaining part in about one month; thus, the writing itself took him about two months with a four-year period of formulation and research.

The story unfolds with the return of the narrator, who remains unnamed, to his home village in Sudan after having earned a Ph.D. in English literature from a university in Britain. When the villagers inquire about the people in Britain, the narrator emphasizes the common experience of all human beings:

> They were surprised when I told them that Europeans were, with minor differences, exactly like them, marrying and bringing up their children in accordance with principles and traditions, that they had good morals and were in general good people.
> "Are there any farmers among them?" Mahjoub asked me.
> "Yes, there are some farmers among them. They've got everything–workers and doctors and farmers and teachers, just like us."

Soon after his arrival, the narrator notices Mustafa Sa'id, a man he knows is not native to the village. The narrator learns that Mustafa had come to the village five years ago, began farming, and married a local woman. At a party the narrator hears Mustafa, who drinks heavily that night, accurately reciting English poetry with excellent pronunciation.

Salih then shifts the narrative to Mustafa, who reveals his story to the narrator. Mustafa turns out to have been one of the first Sudanese to migrate to London, where he received an education that allowed him to lecture at a university in Britain. Aside from his academic success, Mustafa speaks of his difficult adjustment to a new culture that saw him as an Arab, a stereotype rather than as an individual. At first, Mustafa is puzzled by certain things that he hears or encounters upon meeting people from Britain. While taking the train from Sudan to Cairo to pursue his education, Mustafa has a conversation with a British priest, who tells him, "You speak English with astonishing fluency." Mustafa only was able to understand the meaning of this statement much later in his life, after he had lived in Britain and understood the superior British attitude that regarded him as an exotic being, essentially uncivilized, and thus incapable of speaking English with such fluency.

Mustafa's crisis of identity is depicted through his relationship with British women. Throughout his stay in London, Mustafa engaged in relationships with many women, but most importantly Anne Hammond, Sheila Greenwood, Isabella Seymour, and Jean Morris. His relationship with the first three is founded on illusions and lies, dominated by his quest for sexual gratification and theirs for an "exotic" experience. Mustafa claims that each of these women died tragically because of him–though he did not kill them directly. The last one, Jean Morris, he killed with his own hands. Unlike the other women, Morris humiliated and manipulated Mustafa, serving as a catalyst for him to reach a deeper understanding of his relationships and his own identity: "Everything which happened before my meeting her was a premonition; everything I did after I killed her was an apology, not for killing her, but for the lie that was my life." After serving a prison sentence, Mustafa returned to live in Sudan, marry, and father two children.

The story then shifts back to the narrator, who becomes the guardian of Mustafa's children following the latter's mysterious disappearance and suspected death. The focus of the novel becomes the narrator's developing relationship with Mustafa's wife, Husna. Although the narrator is attracted to Husna, he is unable to reveal his feelings to her or marry her, since he is already married. Influenced by Western ideas, he cannot think of marrying more than one wife. To further complicate matters, Wad Rayyis, a local man, proposes marriage to Husna. When her family forces the unwilling Husna to marry Rayyis, she swears not to allow him to touch her and kills him when he tries to rape her. The narrator, shocked and confused by these events, looks for answers to his questions by searching Mustafa's private room and going through his belongings. Becoming even more confused, the narrator jumps

Front cover for the corrected 1978 translation of Salih's 1967 novel, Mawsim al-hijrah ila al-shamal *(Thomas Cooper Library, University of South Carolina)*

in the river and starts swimming, in a possible attempt to commit suicide. However, once he reaches the middle of the river, he decides to call for help and not allow himself to drown.

Mawsim al-hijrah ila al-shamal encountered some obstacles upon its first publication in the Arab world. The publication of *al-Hiwar* (Dialogue), the magazine that first serialized the novel, was halted temporarily in Kuwait because of what was considered the novel's risqué material and language. Since its publication in book form, the novel has been banned in some Arab universities and even in Salih's native Sudan. Nonetheless, critics in the Arab world and the West alike have hailed it as a classic of modern Arabic fiction, one of the most important works to deal with the complex issue of cross-cultural identity. Edward W. Said lists it "among the six finest novels to be written in modern Arabic literature." Roger Allen calls it "the most accomplished among several works of Arabic literature that deal with cultures in contact."

Salih's next novel appeared in two volumes, *Bandarshah: Daw al-Bayt* (1971, Bandarshaw: Daw al-Bayt) and *Maryud: Al-Juz' al-thani min Bandarshah* (1976, Maryud: Part Two of Bandarshaw), which were translated into English as *Bandarshah* (1996). In *Bandarshah: Daw al-Bayt*, set in the village of Wad Hamid, the reader is immersed into the life and everyday occurrences of the village. But Salih mixes the real and the ordinary with the imaginary and myths of the village in a complex, non-linear narrative. Narrated by Meheimeed, who comes back to the village to retire after working in the city all his life, the story begins with a scene depicting the loss of the village leadership role by Mahjub, a character who was introduced in *'Urs al-Zayn*. Having grown old, Mahjub is no longer a commanding personality and is supplanted by Sa'id (Asha al-Baitat) and Mahjub's nephew Turayfi. Asha al-Baitat, the treasurer in the village cooperative, suddenly becomes rich and marries the daughter of the headmaster–an event described as seeming even less likely than the marriage of Zayn. In addition to the village characters, the narrative also introduces Bandarshah and his grandson Maryud. In a perplexing story, Bandarshah is portrayed observing with pleasure as Maryud tortures Bandarshah's eleven sons/slaves. In the end, however, the eleven sons rebel, killing Bandarshah and Maryud.

As the reader almost loses hope of finding the reason for the book's subtitle, *Daw al-Bayt*, the answer comes near the end of the volume when the story of a white stranger with green eyes is related. Wounded and suffering from amnesia, the man recovers from his injuries and is taken in and given a new name, Daw al-Bayt ("The Light of the House"). He works in the fields and eventually marries a villager. Daw al-Bayt died soon after his marriage, leaving behind a son, 'Isa, who is known as Bandarshah. The story leaves the reader wondering about Bandarshah and his grandson Maryud, the subject of the next volume.

Maryud: Al-Juz' al-thani min Bandarshah begins with a scene in which Meheimeed is looking at the river, preoccupied and "resisting an overpowering desire to cry." He remembers his days of childhood, the "smell of talh flowers," and his grip on a stick reminds him of his lost love Maryam, Mahjub's sister: "That voice. That time of youth, That dream." Although the reader may expect a continuation of the story of Daw al-Bayt, introduced at the end of the previous volume, he encounters instead a new maze of confusion, reality mixed with illusion, and no clear plot progression. Throughout the narrative, one feels a heavy sense of nostalgia and an emphasis on memory–the last chapters affording some of the most touching passages of the narrative. The source of nostalgia in the novel is undoubtedly Meheimeed's memory of Maryam. Although he fell in love with her and wanted to marry her, his grandfather refused to allow the union. With his return to the village, the memories of his relationship with Maryam come back to haunt him, especially when he goes to her funeral. He remembers how they used to play together and how Maryam showed great resolve to learn and go to school, how she even argued that she had the right to an education just like boys. Meheimeed is full of regrets for the life he might have lived had he chosen his own course and not allowed his grandfather to define his life. As Wail Hassan observes in *Tayeb Salih: Ideology and the Craft of Fiction* (2003), "For Meheimeed, who yearns for stability and abhors change, these transformations accentuate his nostalgia for a world that has disappeared. By the end he is submerged in the bitter regret that old age casts over the memory of missed opportunities and lost love."

Since *Maryud: Al-Juz' al-thani min Bandarshah* Salih has published only a single story, "Yawm mubarak 'ala shat Umm Bab" (1993, A blessed Day on the Shores of Umm Bab), and his two-volume novel is probably his last significant work. Hassan calls it "one of the most ambitious experiments in Arabic literature since Mahfouz's *Trilogy*." Although Salih in some of his interviews alluded to writing a completion to *Maryud,* until the present, he has not produced a "third part" of what he believes is his most important achievement.

Interviews:

Tayeb Salih Speaks: Four Interviews with the Sudanese Novelist, translated and edited by Constance Berkley and Osman Hassan Ahmad (Washington, D.C.: Office of Cultural Council of Sudan, 1982).

References:

Roger Allen, *The Arabic Novel: An Historical and Critical Introduction,* second edition (Syracuse, N.Y.: Syracuse University Press, 1995);

Mona Amyuni, *Season of Migration to the North by Tayeb Saleh: A Casebook,* edited by Amyuni (Beirut: American University of Beirut, 1985);

Ahmad Muhammad Al-Badawi, *Al-Tayyib Salih: Sirat katib wa nass* (Cairo: Al-Dar al-Thaqafiyyah li al-Nashr, 2000);

Wail Hassan, *Tayeb Salih: Ideology and the Craft of Fiction* (Syracuse, N.Y.: Syracuse University Press, 2003);

Talha Jibril, *'Ala al-darb ma'a al-Tayyib Salih: Malamih min al-sirah al-dhatiyyah* (Ribat & Cairo: Markaz al-Dirasat al-Sudaniyyah, 1997);

Barbra Diane Peters, "Power Relations and Conflict in Selected Works of Tayeb Salih: Implications for a New History," dissertation, University of Wisconsin, 1989.

Anton Shammas
(1950 –   )

Mahmoud Kayyal
Tel Aviv University

BOOKS: *Asir yaqzati wa-nawmi: Qasa'id* (Jerusalem: Al-Sharq, 1974);

Krikha Qashah (Tel Aviv: Sefriat Poalim, 1974);

Shetah Hefqir (Tel Aviv: Ha-Qiboutz ha-Meuhad, 1979);

Ha-shaqran ha-Khi Gadoul ba-'Olam (Jerusalem: Keter, 1982);

'Arabesqot (Tel Aviv: Am Oved, 1986); translated by Vivian Eden as *Arabesques* (London: Viking, 1988; Berkeley: University of California Press, 2001).

PLAY PRODUCTIONS: *Ta'ah bi al-hayt,* Haifa, Haifa Theater, 1978;

Samuel Beckett, *Natrin Gudu,* translated by Shammas, Haifa, Haifa Theater, 1984;

Stuffed Ducks, Woodstock, River Arts, 1989;

Ghassil wijjak ya qamar, Haifa, Arab Theater, 1997.

TRANSLATIONS: Miriam Yalan-Schtekilis, *Al-Safrah ila jazirat yumkin* (Jerusalem: Al-Sharq, 1972);

Bi sawt muzdawaj, edited and translated by Shammas (Haifa: Bait al-Karmah, 1974);

Ka-Tzetnik 135633 (Yehiel Dinur), *Kawkab al-ramad* (Jerusalem: Dogma, 1975);

David Rokeah, *Min sayf ila sayf* (Jerusalem: Al-Sharq, 1977);

David Avidan, *Idha'ah min qamar istina'i* (Tel Aviv: Al-Qarn al-Thalathun, 1982);

Sayd al-ghazalah: 12 qissah min al-adab al-'Ibri al-hadith, edited and translated by Shammas (Tel Aviv: Tel Aviv University Press, 1984);

Emile Habiby, *Ha-Opsimist* (Jerusalem: Mifras, 1984);

Habiby, *Ikhtayyeh* (Tel Aviv: Am Oved, 1988);

Athol Fugard, *Ha'ei* (Ramat Gan: Beit Zvi, 1990);

Habiby, *Saraya bat ha-Shed ha-Ra'* (Tel Aviv: Ha-Qiboutz ha-Meuhad, 1993);

Taha Muhammad 'Ali, *Shirim = Qasaid* (Tel Aviv: Andalus, 2006).

Anton Shammas (from the dust jacket for Arabesques, *1988; Richland County Public Library)*

SELECTED PERIODICAL PUBLICATIONS–
UNCOLLECTED: "Metahat li-'Ets, Metahat li-Qorat Gag, Yoman Qriah," *Iton 77,* 20 (March–April 1980): 8–11;

"'Al Yamin vi-Smoul ba-Tirgum," *Iton 77,* 64–65 (May–June 1985): 18–19;

"'Al Galut vi-Sifrut," *Agra,* 2 (1986): 67–70;

"Ashmat ha-Baboshka," *Politiqa,* 5–6 (1986): 44–45;

"Your Worst Nightmare," *Jewish Frontier,* 51 (July–August 1989): 8–10;

"Amérka, Amérka," *Harper's Magazine,* 282 (February 1991): 55–61;

"'Aziva–ha-Shanah ha-Marah mi-Kulan," *Ha'artez,* 15 September 1993, p. B3.

Anton Shammas is a novelist, poet, playwright, translator, and essayist who has written most of his works in two languages: Arabic and Hebrew. In his article "Ashmat ha-Baboshka" (1986) he says, "I feel like an exile in Arabic, which is the language of my blood, and I feel like an exile in Hebrew, which is my stepmother-tongue." This sense of exile stemmed from his feelings that the two cultures, currently engaged in an antagonistic relationship, were alienating him despite—or perhaps because of—his efforts to mediate between them. Paradoxically, the obsessive treatment of his fragmented identity as an Arab in a Jewish state finds its expression in his Hebrew writings. Shammas demonstrates an excellent command of the intricacies of Hebrew and at the same time presents polemical arguments regarding Israel's character and the status of Palestinian Arabs within it; therefore, his place in Hebrew literature has provoked heated debates among Jewish intellectuals. Meanwhile, his authentic and impressive description of the Palestinian society, especially in his novel *'Arabesqot* (1986; translated as *Arabesques,* 1988), aroused the interest of Arab intellectuals in his works.

Shammas was born in 1950 in the Arab village of Fassuta in Galilee. His father was the village cobbler and barber, "a man of extremities—head and feet," as Shammas calls him in "Metahat li-'Ets, Metahat li-Qorat Gag, Yoman Qriah" (1980). Shammas attended the village primary school until his family relocated to Haifa in 1962. There he attended a high school with separate classes for the Jewish and Arab children. In 1968 he moved to Jerusalem to study at the Hebrew University. In 1970, while still a student, he became editor of *al-Sharq* (The Orient), a journal sponsored by the government newspaper *al-Anba'* (The News), in which he published several Arabic translations of contemporary Hebrew literature. He completed his B.A. in English and Arabic literature and art history in 1972. That year he translated a children's book by Miriam Yalan-Schtekilis. In 1974 he edited and translated an anthology of Hebrew literature. In "'al Galut vi-Sifrut" (1986) Shammas expresses dissatisfaction with these translations: most of which seemed to him "like an inverted transparency," since modern Hebrew has "lost its Semitic lineage" and is "being increasingly exposed to sublinguistic trends with conflicting directions." He goes on to say:

> The joy that accompanied the translations I did in the early 1970s has faded, and has been replaced with an outward sense of ingratitude and an inward sense of self-coercion. The practice of translating from Arabic into Hebrew resembles the solitude of walking down a one-way street: authors with whom I was in contact in the course of the translations did not understand a single word of the new language in which their works were clad.

Also in 1974 Shammas published two collections of his own poetry: *Asir yaqzati wa-nawmi* (Walking in My Awakening and Slumber) in Arabic and *Krikha Qashah* (Hard Cover) in Hebrew. The former was received coolly by Arab reviewers, while Israeli critics praised the Hebrew volume. These divergent reactions encouraged Shammas gradually to abandon writing in Arabic and direct his energies toward writing in Hebrew.

In 1975 Shammas left his position at *al-Sharq* and translated a novel about the Holocaust by Yehiel Dinur. He translated a volume of poetry by David Rokeah in 1977.

In the 1970s and 1980s Shammas published poems, political essays, and translations of modern Arabic literature in Hebrew literary journals, such as *Iton 77* (Magazine 77), *Keshet* (Rainbow), and *Moznayim* (Scales). He also published original works in Hebrew and translations and adaptations into Hebrew from Arabic and English. His young-adults' play *Ta'ah bi al-hayt* (A Hole in the Wall), staged at the Haifa Theater in 1978–1979, was written in Arabic and Hebrew versions. In his own collection of Hebrew poems, *Shetah Hefqir* (1979, No Man's Land), the influence of the Israeli poets Yehuda Amichai and Natan Zach is evident, and the two are mentioned in the volume. The work contributed to Shammas's being awarded the prestigious Levi Eshkol Prime Minister's Prize for Literature in 1980. He participated in the International Writing Program at the University of Iowa in 1981.

Shammas's children's book *Ha-shaqran ha-Khi Gadoul ba-'Olam* (1982, The Biggest Liar in the World) is a Hebrew adaptation of a well-known Arabic folktale. The youngest of three brothers tells a complex and outrageous tale in a successful bid to marry a princess. Shammas preserves the structure and plot of the original but introduces a humorous tone. Also in 1982 he translated a volume of poetry by David Avidan. In 1984 he edited and translated another anthology of Hebrew literature and translated Emile Habiby's novel *al-Waqa'i' al-gharibah fi ikhtifa' Abi al-Nahs Sa'id al-Mutasha'il* (1974; translated as *The Secret Life of Saeed, the Ill-Fated Pessoptomist: A Palestinian Who Became a Citizen of Israel,* 1982) into Hebrew as *Ha-Opsimist* (1984, The Optimist).

Shammas's bilingual adaptation of Samuel Beckett's *En attendant Godot* (1953; translated as *Waiting for Godot,* 1955), *Natrin Gudu,* was staged in Hebrew and Arabic at the Haifa Theater in 1984. In "'al Galut vi-Sifrut" he says that "the Hebrew version is closer to the spirit of the source, to the tragicomedy that Beckett wrote from left to right, than its Semitic sister."

Front cover for Shammas's Hebrew children's book Ha-shaqran ha-Khi Gadoul ba-'Olam *(The Biggest Liar in the World), 1982 (Widener Library, Harvard University)*

In 1985 Shammas was attacked in print by the author A. B. Yehoshua for holding that Palestinian Arabs should be given equal citizenship with Jews in a unified Israeli nation. Yehoshua, who refuses to relinquish Israel's Jewish character, and whose opinions seem to represent those of the majority of the Israeli Jewish public, told Shammas: "If you want your full identity, if you want to live in a country that has an independent Palestinian character, an original Palestinian culture, get up, gather your belongings, and move a hundred meters to the east, to the Palestinian state that will be established adjacent to Israel."

The following year Shammas published his most notable work, the semiautobiographical novel *'Arabesqot*. The complex plot is so densely woven that the thread connecting the characters, events, and places gradually disappears. The style is replete with intertextual references, allegorical allusions, history combined with fiction, and abrupt transitions between stories, narrators, times, and places. Shammas seems to be trying to examine his fragmented identity as a Christian, a Palestinian Arab, and an Israeli. These components of his identity contain contradictions and deep tensions that are difficult to bridge. So, on the one hand, he emphasizes Palestinian unity despite the division of the Palestinian population after the 1948 war into those living in Israel, in the West Bank and Gaza, and in the Diaspora. On the other hand, he contends that the Palestinian Arabs must be equal citizens in Israel and that the Israeli identity is not purely Jewish, as many Israelis believe.

The principal narrator, Anton Shammas, is named after a dead cousin. He discovers that the cousin is not dead but was fraudulently adopted by the wealthy Abyad family, who named him Michel. The Abyads, fearing blackmail and embarrassment should anyone learn of the adoption, sent Michel to the United States, where he has lived since he was twenty. Anton decides to find out what has become of his lost cousin, and the opportunity to do so presents itself when he attends the International Writers' Conference in Iowa City. Michel tells Anton that Almazah, Anton's uncle's wife, who worked as a servant in the home of his adoptive parents and lost her son, is not his biological mother, but he regards her as his mother. Michel asks Anton to edit the manuscript for his autobiography, in which Anton appears as the dead child. Thus, Shammas creates confusion regarding the identity of the narrator, especially when he quotes Jorge Luis Borges: "I do not know which of us wrote this book."

One of the participants in the writers' conference is Yehoshua Bar-On; the character is apparently based on A. B. Yehoshua. Bar-On wants to write a novel in which Anton will be one of the main characters, but their relationship deteriorates because Bar-On is an arrogant man who has stereotypical opinions about Arabs and is unprepared to accept them as Israeli citizens with equal rights with Jews. Bar-On maintains that Anton is not an authentic Palestinian, calling him "My Jew."

Another character whose destiny is tied to the Shammas family is Laila Khoury, who was taken by Anton's father from an orphanage in Nazareth and transported to Lebanon to work as a servant. Laila endured a succession of agonies and humiliations. Her love for the man now known as Michel Abyad was the one bright spot in her life, but they were forced apart when he was sent to the United States. Before they parted, he gave her a half-amulet that he had worn around his neck since he was a baby. After the 1948 war, Laila's sister brought her back to Israel; but the Israeli authorities deported her to the West Bank, at that time under Jordanian rule, with other Palestinian refugees. In the truck that transported them into exile she met the son of Abdullah al-Asbah, one of the leaders of the pre-1948 Palestinian rebellion. They were married; she converted to Islam, changed her name to

Suraya Sa'id, and gave birth to deaf-mute twins. After Israel's occupation of the West Bank in 1967, the Israeli army arrested her husband.

The residents of Anton's village believe that if Suraya's part of the amulet is joined with the other half, the restored amulet will open a cave adjacent to the home of Anton's family where a treasure from Crusader times is buried and guarded by a mythical cockerel. The other half was passed down to another leader of the Palestinian rebellion, Mahmoud al-Ibrahim, who gave it to a man who lives in the village. The man promises to turn over his half of the amulet to Anton if Anton finds the other half.

A newspaper photograph of the blond Christian woman who converted to Islam catches the attention of Anton, who has heard Laila's story from his relatives, and he visits her. She sees in him the image of her beloved Anton (now Michel), and they have an intimate encounter. She invites him to take the amulet from between her breasts, but he is unable to do so.

Although Shammas gives his characters realistic qualities, it is difficult to ignore their representative function. For example, the relationship between the Palestinian Diaspora and the Palestinians who remained in Israel is represented by the complex relationship between Anton Shammas, on one hand, and Laila and Michel, on the other hand. The relationship between Palestinians who are Israeli citizens and the Jewish citizens of Israel is symbolized by the hostile relationship between the narrator and Yehoshua Bar-On.

'Arabesqot was a best-seller in Israel. Many Israeli critics praised the novel, including Ameil Alkalai in Apirion: "It is indisputably a true literary gem." It was translated into English, French, Spanish, German, Italian, and Portuguese; The New York Times Book Review named the English version one of the seven best works of fiction of 1988. It has never been translated into Arabic, even though the major characters are Palestinian Arabs; Shammas has explained that he does not want to embarrass the relatives on whom some of those characters are based.

Many reviews of Shammas's novel raised the issue of why he and other Arab authors, including Atallah Mansour, Naim Araidi, and Sayyid Kashua, have chosen to write some, or even most, of their works in Hebrew. The discussions included speculations about the motives of these authors; the significance of their choice and its implications for relations between Jews and Arabs and between majority and minority populations in general; the status of these works in Hebrew culture, toward which they are oriented, and in Arab culture, to which their authors belong; and the effect of these writings on the unique character of Hebrew as the holy language and the

Dust jacket for the first American edition of the English translation of Shammas's semiautobiographical novel 'Arabesqot, 1986 (Richland County Public Library)

language of the national rebirth of the Jewish people. Mansour, whose Hebrew novel bi-Or Hadash (In a New Light) was published in 1966, maintains that the bilingualism of Arabs living in Israel does not detract from their identity as Arabs. In his opinion, a Hebrew work by an Arab author can promote Jewish understanding of Arabs' condition; it also underscores Israel's binational and bicultural character, a character to which the Jewish population objects. Mansour also claims that many Jewish critics feel a degree of pride in these works, since it shows that their language, which has been viewed as moribund for hundreds of years, is useful even to non-Jewish authors.

Shammas's Hebrew writing drew ambivalent reactions from Jewish critics and intellectuals in Israel. In the journal Muznaim Nilli Carmel-Flomin expressed admiration for his "command of the mysteries of the Hebrew language, its strata, idiomatics, and internal rhythm." The critics were divided with regard to his call for de-Judification and de-Zionization of the Hebrew language, which for them symbolized the national rebirth of the Jewish people in Israel. Some maintained that Shammas had opened a door to a reexamination of Israeli identity and the connection between Judaism and Hebrew. Others viewed his work as a transient and inconsequential phenomenon that does not pose a threat to the connection between Judaism and Hebrew. Reuven Snir claims that even if Shammas and his colleagues were to demonstrate astounding literary skill in Hebrew, the lines separating them from Jewish authors would always remain.

Most Arab critics have ignored these authors' Hebrew writings because the critics do not have a command of Hebrew and because they consider Hebrew literature undeserving of attention. Many Arab intellectuals regard Hebrew as the moribund language of a transient neocolonial entity; to them, an Arab who writes in Hebrew is denying the rich cultural, literary, and linguistic heritage that constitutes a central component of Arab national identity. Some go so far as to consider an Arab's use of Hebrew as groveling and treacherous. But the widespread publicity accorded to *'Arabesqot*, especially after it was translated into English and French, and its sophisticated handling of the questions of Palestinian national identity and the identity of Palestinian citizens of Israel, encouraged critics in the Arab world to discuss the work and the issue of its language. The Lebanese critic Yumna al-'Id identified many signs of the influence of Arabic in the novel, which were apparently preserved in the French translation she read. In her opinion, Shammas's use of Hebrew indicates a worldview that is manifested at the end of the novel. A Jewish sapper helps to lay the foundations for the new home of one of the Shammas family's grandchildren. 'Id claims that this ending points to Shammas's desire for peace with the Jews, which is founded on admission of their technological and cultural superiority.

The Palestinian critic Muhammad Siddiq, who read the novel in its original language, maintains that criticism of Shammas for his use of Hebrew ignores the fact that Palestinian protest poets such as Mahmoud Darwish, Samih al-Qasem, and Rashid Hussein studied and were influenced by classical and modern Hebrew literature. Siddiq expresses admiration for the novel's rich language, which apparently stems from the author's awareness that he is "requisitioning" the language of the "other" and using it to get to know himself artistically. He is unconvinced by Shammas's claim that the use of Hebrew was intended to avoid offending family members. According to Siddiq, it is impossible to distinguish form and content, style and significance, or aesthetic endeavor and the language that represents it; hence, it is hard to imagine the novel being written in any other language. The Palestinian critic Husam al-Khatib calls *'Arabesquot* one of the most notable Palestinian novels, one that "has attained high standards, in which life experience and artistic experience merge to present an elaborate, contemplative, and perturbing ideological and artistic outlook, one that successfully transforms the Palestinian issue into something human and mature, rather than being declaratory and tawdry."

Shammas himself is aware, as he says in "Metahat li-'Ets, Metahat li-Qorat Gag, Yoman Qriah," that writing in Hebrew is "likened to cultural trespass." He has repeatedly attempted to explain why he chose to write in this language. In "'al Galut vi-Sifrut" he points to the state of confusion in which Arabs in Israel find themselves: "For me, the language of grace [Hebrew] is the only language capable of expressing my confusion and drawing a filament of grace over my bewilderment. As for bewilderment, I belong to the Arab minority that lives within the Jewish minority that lives within the Arab majority in the Middle East." Shammas also raises arguments of a more practical nature: for example, that a mother tongue mandates the use of hackneyed clichés and linguistic structures, whereas writing in another language releases the author from these constraints. He also says that he wanted to demonstrate his linguistic skill in the language used of one of the most beautiful texts in history: the Bible.

In 1987 Shammas moved to the United States. The following year he translated Habiby's *Ikhtiyyeh* (1985, Pity) into Hebrew as *Ikhtayyeh*. His translations of Habiby's works were widely praised; Sasson Somekh calls them a "linguistic miracle." According to Somekh, Shammas overcame enormous translational difficulties with great resourcefulness and facility: Habiby's language excels in linguistic acrobatics, frequently exploiting the multiple meanings of words and collocations. Shammas's translations were instrumental in Habiby's winning the 1992 Israel Prize for Literature. Habiby was so pleased with Shammas's renderings that he wrote in his novel *Khurafiyyat Saraya Bint al-Ghoul* (1991, The Tale of Saraya the Daughter of the Ghoul): "I present Anton Shammas with the challenge of translating these collocations and homonyms into any language, close or distant." Shammas's translation, *Saraya bat ha-Shed ha-Ra'* (Saraya the Devil's Daughter), appeared in 1993.

Anton Shammas's essay "Amérka, Amérka," published in *Harper's Magazine* in February 1991, was chosen by the editors of *The Best American Essays 1992* as one of the Notable Essays of 1991. He won the Whiting Writer's Award, 1991–1992, and the Lila Wallace-*Reader's Digest* Writers' Award, 1993–1996. In the article "'Aziva–ha-Shanah ha-Marah mi-Kulan" (1993) he declared: "I, who for many years attempted to examine the boundaries of Israeli identity and the boundaries of its tolerance, now wash my weary hands of the whole affair." He is a professor of Middle Eastern literature at the University of Michigan.

References:

Rachel Feldhay Brenner, "In Search of Identity: The Israeli Arab Artist in Anton Shammas's *Arabesques*," *PMLA,* 108 (May 1993): 431–445;

Emile Habiby, *Saraya, Bint al-Ghoul* (Haifa: Dar Arabesque, 1991);

Hanan Hever, "Hebrew in Israeli Arab Hand: Six Miniatures on Anton Shammas's *Arabesques*," *Cultural Critique,* 7 (1987): 47–76;

Yumna al-'Id, "Mithal tahlili li riwayat Arabisk," in her *Taqaniyyat al-sard al-riwa'i fi du' al-manhaj al-Bunyawi* (Beirut: Dar al-Farabi, 1990), pp. 123–160;

Husam al-Khatib, "Al-Riwayah al-Filastiniyyah: Al-Sawt wa al-sada," *Al-'Arabi,* 379 (June 1990): 110–115;

Atallah Mansour, "'Arab yaktubun bi al-'Ibriyyah: Al-Wusul ila al-Jar,"*Bulletin of the Israeli Academic Center in Cairo,* 16 (1992): 63–66;

Gerald Marzorati, "An Arab Voice in Israel," *New York Times Magazine,* 18 September 1988, pp. 54, 100–101, 106, 108–109;

Cynthia Ozick, "Unforgiveable, Indefensible, Uninnocent," *Jewish Frontier,* 56 (July–August 1989): 11–13;

Muhammad Siddiq, "Al-Kitabah bi al-'Ibriyyah, al-Fusha: Taqdim Riwayat 'Arabisk wa hiwar ma' Anton Shammas," *Alif: Journal of Comparative Poetics,* 20 (2000): 155–167;

Reuven Snir, "Maqour vi-Tirgum 'al Qav Hatifir," in *Tirgoum bi-Tzidi Hadirkh: 'Eyunim bi-Tirgoumim min ha-Sifrut ha-'Aravit li-'Evrit bi-Yaminu,* edited by Sasson Somekh (Tel Aviv: Tel Aviv University Press, 1993), pp. 21–39;

Snir, "Ma'galim Nihtakhim bin ha-Sifrut ha-'Evrit li-Bin ha-Sifrut ha-'Aravit," in *Bin 'Ever li-'Arav: Ha-Maga'im bin ha-Sifrut ha-'Aravit li-Bin ha-Sifrut ha-Yehudit bi-Yami ha-Binayim oba-Zman ha-Hadash,* edited by Yosef Tobi (Tel Aviv: Afiqim, 1998), pp. 177–210;

Christian Szyska, "Geographies of the Self: Text and Space in Anton Shammas's *Arabesques*," in *Erzählter Raum in literaturen der Islamischen Welt / Narrated Space in Literature of the Islamic World,* edited by Szyska and Roxane Haag-Higuchi (Wiesbaden: Harrassowitz, 2001), pp. 217–232;

A. B. Yehoshua, "Ashmat ha-Smoul," *Politiqa,* 4 (1985): 8–13.

Hanan al-Shaykh
(12 November 1945 –   )

Wyoma vanDuinkerken
Texas A&M University

BOOKS: *Intihar rajul mayyit* (Beirut: Dar al-Dahar li al-Nashr, 1970);

Faras al-shaytan (Beirut: Dar al-Dahar li al-Nashr, 1971);

Hikayat Zahrah (Beirut: Hanan al-Shaykh & N. Tahar, 1980); translated by Peter Ford as *The Story of Zahra* (London: Quartet, 1986);

'Usfur al-hynna (Beirut: Dar al-Fata al-'arabi, 1981);

Wardat al-sahra' (Beirut: Al-Mu'assasah al-Jami'iyya li al-Dirasat wa al-Nashr wa al-Tawzi', 1982);

Misk al-ghazal (Beirut: Dar al-Adab, 1988); translated by Catherine Cobham as *Women of Sand and Myrrh* (London: Quartet, 1989);

Barid Bayrut (Cairo: Dar al-Hilal, 1992); translated by Cobham as *Beirut Blues* (New York: Anchor, 1995);

Ukannis al-shams 'an al-sutuh (St. Leonards, Australia: Allen & Unwin, 1994); translated by Cobham as *I Sweep the Sun off Rooftops* (New York: Doubleday, 1998);

Innaha Landan ya 'azizi: Riwayah (Beirut: Dar al-Adab, 2001); translated by Cobham as *Only in London* (New York: Pantheon, 2001);

Imra'atan 'alá shati al-bahr: riwayah (Beirut: Dar al-Adab, 2003).

PLAY PRODUCTIONS: *A Dark Afternoon Tea,* London, Hampstead Theatre, February 1995;

The Paper Husband, London, Hampstead Theatre, January 1996.

OTHER: "Angels Sharpened My Pen," in *The Writer and Religion,* edited by William H. Gass and Lorin Cuoco (Carbondale: Southern Illinois University Press, 2000).

Hanan al-Shaykh is a Lebanese novelist, short-story writer, and playwright who is seen as a leading figure in Arab feminist literature. Her stories highlight women's roles in male-dominated societies, the institution of marriage, civil war, and the influence of Western ideals on traditional Arab life. Al-Shaykh examines controversial topics such as women's sexuality, spousal abuse, rape, divorce, and polygamy to criticize Arab patriarchal ideas about women. Her female characters are usually shown as victims in a male authoritarian society where they are powerless both financially and politically to change their condition. Al-Shaykh shows how they struggle to make a place for themselves within society and how when they attempt to take their lives into their own hands they are ostracized by their family and friends as well as by the wider society. Al-Shaykh continues to publish her work in Arabic, but several of her books and short stories have been translated into many different languages. These translations have helped to open the door for her work to the West, where there is growing interest in her career.

Hanan al-Shaykh (from the dust jacket for Beirut Blues, *1995; Richland County Public Library)*

Al-Shaykh was born on 12 November 1945 in al-Nabatiyyah in southern Lebanon into a strict Shiite Muslim family; she had three brothers from her father's previous marriage and one sister. Her father, Mohammad, was a pious man who always consulted the Qur'an when making decisions. He wanted his daughter to follow accepted practices, such as wearing the veil. She refused at first but later submitted to his request.

When al-Shaykh was five years old, her parents divorced. Her mother, Kamila, married a man that she had been having an affair with, leaving al-Shaykh to be raised by her father. Al-Shaykh grew up in an area known as Ras al-Naba'a, a conservative part of West Beirut. The end of their street became the no-man's-land between the warring Muslim West and Christian East of the city. The lasting effect of the constant danger she experienced is evident in works such as *Hikayat Zahrah* (1980; translated as *The Story of Zahra*, 1986) and *Barid Bayrut* (1992; translated as *Beirut Blues*, 1995).

Growing up, al-Shaykh always felt like an outsider. She grew up on a street surrounded by native Beirut families, and since her parents were divorced and her family was from the south of Lebanon, she felt out of place and isolated. In a 1992 interview with Paula W. Sunderman she said that she did not feel comfortable either in the south of Lebanon or in Beirut, and this insecurity made her more sensitive and more observant to her surroundings. Al-Shaykh went to school at a local traditional Muslim primary school for girls called al-'Amiliyyah. Later she attended al-Ahliyyah school, a modern secular secondary school, where she was introduced to new ideals.

Al-Shaykh started to write as a means of releasing her anger and frustration toward her father because he restricted her freedom. At sixteen she was publishing articles in the Beirut newspaper *al-Nahar* about freedom, boredom, and infidelity. In 1963 al-Shaykh moved to Cairo to study at the American College for Girls. She loved living in Cairo, since it gave her a sense of relief from the constant pressure of her father and brothers. She was free to experience new things and reinvent her life.

During the three years she spent in Egypt, al-Shaykh wrote her first novel, *Intihar rajul mayyit* (1970, Suicide of a Dead Man). The narrator is an unnamed forty-four-year-old married man who becomes obsessed with Danya, a seventeen-year-old girl dreaming of becoming a great painter. Prior to meeting Danya, the narrator was in complete control of his life, but everything changes for him when Danya refuses his advances; he slowly slips into a depression that eventually leads to his death. Through the narrator's controlling nature and uncontrollable desire for the young girl, the author analyzes the power struggle between men and women. The outcome of this story is a metaphor of man's inability to deal with the liberated woman. In the interview with Sunderman, al-Shaykh expressed her dissatisfaction with her first work: "I wasn't true to myself when I wrote it. I was camouflaging events by creating and being concerned with description and a beautiful style and sentences which sometimes didn't fit the novel."

In 1966 al-Shaykh returned to Beirut to work for two years as a journalist for *al-Hasna'*, an innovative women's magazine. In 1967 she also began writing for *al-Nahar Newspaper Supplement,* a job she held until 1975. During her career as a journalist al-Shaykh began writing a series of articles about well known Lebanese women titled "The Portrayal of Women." She developed a fascination with these powerful women and in particular how they defied traditional customs. In the interview with Sunderman al-Shaykh stated that being a journalist taught her "the patience to ask questions and to get involved in drawing characters. It sharpened my eyes and sense of observation and enabled me to point a pen at the important aspects of life."

At a party in Beirut, al-Shaykh met Fouad Malouf, an engineer who had received his education in the United States. As Malouf was raised Greek Orthodox, the couple's elopement in 1968 caused a scandal. Her marrying outside of her religion devastated her father, who reportedly cried for days after he learned of his daughter's marriage. The couple moved to Saudi Arabia, where they began a family and al-Shaykh completed her second novel, *Faras al-shaytan* (1971, Satan's She-Horse).

Faras al-shaytan treats the moral and psychological development of a liberated woman from southern Lebanon, Sarah, who struggles to resolve past issues related to her strict religious upbringing as she searches for independence and success. The story is narrated by Sarah's two inner voices that switch back and forth. The first voice examines Sarah as an individual, providing the reader with insight into how she feels about her life. The second narrative voice examines Sarah's past, where she came from, the family traditions and tragedies she endured—all of which help to explain her rationale for the way she behaves. The story touches on aspects of al-Shaykh's religious upbringing, as well as her past relationships and marriage. In Maya Jaggi's profile for *Guardian Unlimited,* al-Shaykh admits that she wrote her second novel "to make peace with the way I rebelled against my father." She is pleased that *Faras al-shaytan* has never been translated, because, as she told Pascale Ghazzaleh in *al-Ahram Weekly Online,* "It would be used against Islam. It's not meant as an attack on religion." In her 1992 interview with Sunderman she asserted that "Muslim women are oppressed not by the teachings of the Koran but by the arrogance of men."

Dust jacket for the 1995 English translation of al-Shaykh's 1992 novel Barid Bayrut *(Richland County Public Library)*

In 1975, after al-Shaykh and her two children returned to live in Beirut, a civil war broke out in Lebanon, prompting her the following year to flee with her children to Saudi Arabia, where her husband was working. In 1982 the family settled in London, where they have lived ever since. Al-Shaykh told Jaggi, "The fear of the war stimulated old fears from my childhood, as though war is an x-ray showing us who we are."

Al-Shaykh vividly portrays the Lebanese Civil War in her 1980 novel, *Hikayat Zahrah*. The novel tells the story of Zahrah, a Shiite woman growing up in southern Lebanon during the war. In the first part of the novel, "The Scars of Peace," Zahrah suffers from low self-esteem and depression because of the searing experiences of her young life. Physically abused by her father, Zahrah was also sexually molested by her cousin and as a teenager was repeatedly raped by a family friend, which caused her to have two abortions. Having been further traumatized by witnessing her mother's affairs, Zahrah can not even turn to her for help.

Al-Shaykh drew on her own experience in depicting the relationship between Zahrah and her mother, for she remembers that when she was a child her mother used to take her along on her visits to her lover.

When Zahrah is sent to South Africa to live with her uncle Hashem, she enters into a loveless marriage with her uncle's associate, Majed, as a way of avoiding her uncle's sexual advances. At this juncture al-Saykh temporarily shifts the point of view from Zahrah to Hashem and Majed, using their voices to reveal insights, unknown by Zahrah, about the psyches of her uncle and husband. An important similarity between the male viewpoints is that both see Zahrah as representing their homeland of Lebanon. The reader learns that Hashem never got over being forced to leave Lebanon and sees Zahrah as being a link back to all that he loved in his native land. Majed on the other hand sees her as a property to be acquired and immediately condemns her because she was not a virgin on their wedding night.

Zahrah escapes her oppressive life in Africa by returning to Beirut during the height of the civil war. In the second part of the novel, "The Torrents of War," she falls in love for the first time. When she informs her lover, a sniper named Sami, that she is pregnant with his child, he tells her to get an abortion. But he changes his mind and declares that he will marry her. As she is walking in the street after this encounter that seems to end so well, Zahrah is shot by her lover.

Nine publishing houses in Beirut initially refused *Hikayat Zahrah*, citing as reasons its sexual imagery and depiction of such subjects as child abuse, adultery, rape, and murder. In many Arab countries these topics were then taboo, especially when treated with such openness and graphic details. Determined to publish the novel, al-Shaykh used her own money and with the help of her friend Najah Taher, a Lebanese artist, put her work into print. According to al-Shaykh, publishers only came around after *Hikayat Zahrah* received good reviews and enjoyed healthy sales. Although *Hikayat Zahrah* was banned in several Arab countries, its English translation earned a following in the West. Al-Shaykh received international praise for her description of a woman's attempt to find peace and happiness in a male-dominated society.

In 1981 al-Shaykh published her first children's book, *'Usfur al-hynna* (The Bird of Henna), about a Bedouin girl named Nawf, who asks her mother to paint with henna a bird that has alighted on her hand. When the bird dries, it flies away in the middle of the night and is caught by a woman who wants the bird tied to her dress. The bird escapes the woman's dress and returns to the kindness of Nawf's hand. The central theme of the story is freedom and how some freedoms can quickly become cages.

Al-Shaykh's first collection of short stories, *Wardat al-sahra'* (1982, The Rose of the Desert), is comprised of twenty-two stories that focus primarily on the roles of women in patriarchal Arab societies. Through these tales the author shows the effects of marriage, divorce, abuse, and polygamy on women in Middle Eastern countries where Islamic fundamentalists hold sway as well as in more secularized societies. Al-Shaykh's stories reveal tension between women who recognize their abused state but feel they can do nothing to change it and those women who struggle to improve their situations. This tension can at times lead to hostility and treachery, especially against those who struggle for change. While al-Shaykh sometimes, especially in her early stories, does treat women who have done well for themselves through education, careers, or family life, her greater focus here is on poor, uneducated women.

In stories such as "Lulu" and "Wardat al-sahra'" al-Shaykh shows how women sometimes blame themselves or other women rather than the patriarchal society in which they live for their husband's polygamous acts. In "Lulu" the title character is so upset that her husband has married a second wife, Salama, that she strikes out against Salama by concocting a plan to find her husband a third wife. Lulu's plan is to find a replacement for Salama in her husband's life, thereby placing Salama in the same situation in which Lulu finds herself. On the other hand, in "Wardat al-sahra'," Mahyouba blames herself for her husband's polygamous behavior rather than blaming the system that allowed her husband, Nayef, to marry his second wife, Rouheyya. Mahyouba feels compelled to submit to Nayef's wishes when he abandons her to live with Rouheyya. She suffers in silence and frustration for two years before she confronts her husband, and even then she accepts her fate of being deprived of a companion for the remaining years of her life. Although Lulu and Mahyouba deal with their situations differently, neither rebels against the patriarchal system that allows polygamy and neither considers divorce as an option. For al-Shaykh, these women are part of the problem, not part of the solution.

In "A Girl Called Apple" al-Shaykh turns her attention to the topic of arranged marriages and demonstrates how young women are affected by the pressure placed on them by parents and society to marry before they are deemed too old. In the story, set in an oasis village, age is represented by the color of the wedding flag placed on the roof of every home where a woman desires marriage: red represents women under twenty years old; blue, between twenty and thirty; and yellow, women thirty and older. The story shows how unmarried women in the oasis, such as Apple, spend their lives anxiously awaiting husbands, fearful of the next change of color for their flag. The people of the oasis do not understand why Apple does not want to place a flag on her roof, particularly when they know that it is the only way that she will be able to find a husband. They only feel sorry for her and her family. At no time do the women consider an alternative to marriage, nor does anyone acknowledge Apple's potential for being anything but a wife and mother.

Drawing from her childhood, al-Shaykh wrote "The Persian Carpet" to show how a divorce can be devastating to children. The story is narrated by a young girl who recounts a secret visit she and her sister took to see her mother for the first time after her parents' divorce and her mother's remarriage. When she enters her mother's new home the young girl notices a Persian carpet—the same carpet that had disappeared from their family home months before her mother left her father. At the time her mother had accused an old blind man named Ilya of stealing the carpet. The young girl's realization of her mother's lie changes their relationship forever. She goes from being excited at the prospect of a reunion to wishing she had never seen her mother again.

Al-Shaykh's next novel, *Misk al-ghazal* (1988; translated as *Women of Sand and Myrrh,* 1989), is set in an anonymous oil-rich Arab country and is told through the experiences of four women: Suha, Nur, Tamr, and Suzanne. Al-Shaykh gives these four women, each from a different social and cultural background, a voice in a land where women are not usually heard. What binds them together is the struggle they face to make lives for themselves in this society. Two of the women, Nur and Tamr, are natives, one rich and the other poor; the other two are outsiders, as Suha is from Lebanon and Suzanne is from the United States. Al-Shaykh weaves their stories so that they sometimes intersect and yet has each narrate her own experience. She thus allows the reader to see different perspectives and to understand how each woman is individually affected.

Suha is an educated woman who has a degree in management studies from the American University in Beirut. She and her husband and child escaped the Lebanese Civil War, but once she arrives in her new home she soon longs for the freedoms she had in Beirut. She can not understand why she can not walk outside without her husband or why she is forbidden to drive. Her questioning of her identity as a wife and mother within the oppressive society is further complicated when she begins a lesbian affair with Nur.

The daughter of a wealthy Bedouin, Nur challenges social rules and reacts against her sheltered existence by acting like a spoiled, self-indulgent child. Her reason for

Suzanne is a blond-haired, blue-eyed, middle-aged woman from America who moves to the country with her son and estranged husband. While Suzanne recognizes the oppressiveness of this foreign land, she generally ignores its effects because of the male attention she receives. She becomes obsessed with the desire for wealth and sexual gratification from her multiple affairs, which she mistakes for love. Suzanne is frightened of the day when her husband's job is complete and she must return home to Texas. In her new surroundings she is seen by men as exotic, and she fears that when she returns home, she will no longer be desired.

Al-Shaykh's 1992 novel *Barid Bayrut* is a first-person narrative told through a series of ten letters by a woman named Asmahan, whose family had moved to Beruit from southern Lebanon. Revealing the devastating effects of the Lebanese Civil War on the city and its people in the 1980s, the ten unanswered letters are written to people who live within and outside the war-torn country, to geographical locations such as the city of Beirut, and to the war itself. The reader can see the depths of the narrator's inner turmoil in the letter she writes to Jill Morrell, the girlfriend of John McCarthy, a British hostage. In showing that she, too, is being held hostage, kept away from all she loves, Asmahan explains the uniqueness of her own situation: "For I'm still in my own place but separated from it in a painful way: this is my city and I don't recognize it." Despite the departure of her friends, family, and lovers from Beirut, Asmahan remains in her desperate situation, refusing to leave the city despite food shortages and electricity cuts. Under the constant threat of snipers, she remains optimistic, sure that things will turn out for the best.

Al-Shaykh dedicated *Barid Bayrut* to her friend Najah Taher, who had remained in Beirut throughout the civil war. In 1997 Taher told Sunderman that al-Shaykh's experience of writing the novel was "cleansing for Hanan, for the guilt of leaving Lebanon." Al-Shaykh admitted that in writing Asmahan's letters, particularly the one to the city of Beirut, she was perhaps subconsciously saying goodbye to that painful period in her life. Coming to grips with this part of her life enabled al-Shaykh to write about her new home, London. She did so when she completed two plays for Hampstead Theatre: *A Dark Afternoon Tea* (produced 1995) and *The Paper Husband* (produced 1996).

In 1994, al-Shaykh completed her second collection, *Ukannis al-shams 'an al-sutuh* (translated as *I Sweep the Sun off Rooftops*, 1998). The primary focus of the seventeen stories is to show how traditional Arabs, living in a variety of countries, struggle to adapt to modern western ideals such as premarital sex, divorce, and female independence. In the story translated as "An Unreal

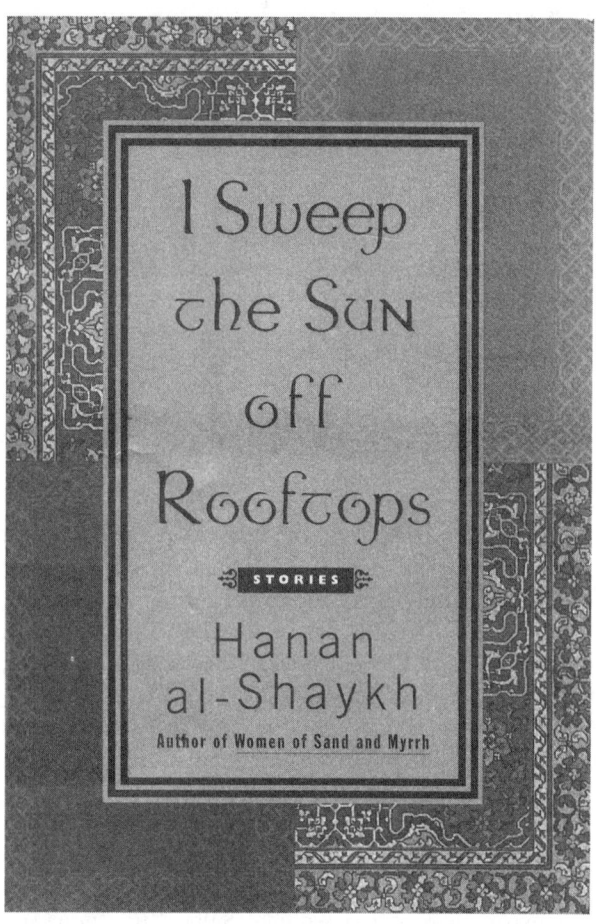

Front cover for the 1998 English translation of al-Shaykh's 1994 collection of seventeen stories, Ukannis al-shams 'an al-sutuh *(Richland County Public Library)*

demanding an abortion is that a pregnancy would prevent her from wearing her fashionable western wardrobe. Becoming increasingly unhappy with her lack of freedom and trapped by her own boredom, Nur longs to travel, but her western-educated, would-be-reformer husband keeps her passport from her. Her constant search for entertainment blinds her to the consequences of her actions and leads to destruction.

Tamr's story revolves around her relationships with her family. She gives the reader insight into the patriarchal society in which she lives through the stories of the arranged marriages of her mother and aunt, relating them to her own marriage at the age of twelve. Tamr fights for her right to be educated and threatens to starve herself if she is not given the opportunity to learn to read. She is allowed to attend the Gulf Institute for Women and Girls, where Suha teaches. Later, encouraged by Suha, she divorces her husband and opens a beauty shop. But she is constantly worried that her shop will be shut down by those who resent her independence.

Life," for example, the narrator, Samr, is married to a Westerner, but she remains caught between two cultures. Although she loves her homeland and immerses herself in her culture, she does not like the patriarchal society in which she lived in as a child and is drawn to western freedoms. This theme, like many other al-Shaykh stories, arises to some extent from the author's life.

Another story rooted in al-Shaykh's experience is translated as "The Scratching of Angels' Pens." While attending the funeral of her second husband, who had died in a car accident, Shadiah is confronted by an aunt who asks her to repent and return to her first husband:

> "Naturally, the angels' pens will cross your bad deed off the slate if you return to your first husband . . . Repent so that you can go to heaven and see 'the ground gleaming white like silver and pearls, the earth made of musk, the saffron plants, the trees with alternative leaves of silver and gold.'"

Shadiah, who divorced her first husband to marry the man she loved, rejects her aunt's suggestion. Shadiah is then surprised when her aunt begins yelling at her in front of everyone, telling her that she has cursed herself and God is punishing her. Like Shadiah, al-Shaykh's mother did not return to al-Shaykh's father after her second husband was killed in a car accident. In a 1999 profile by Pascale Ghazaleh, al-Shaykh commented: "Everyone said his death was my father's revenge."

Al-Shaykh further explores the theme of modern Western ideals mixing with traditional Eastern ways in *Innaha Landan ya 'azizi* (2001; translated as *Only in London*, 2001), a humorous, touching story that contrasts the Arab and British cultures. When Jaggi asked why it took her twenty-five years to write a novel set outside the Arab world, al-Shaykh replied: "I used to feel I was still living in the Arab world; my thoughts were in Lebanon; I was following the war from day to day, eating tabbouleh with other Lebanese, asking, 'are we going back?' It's as if you're in a train station, in transit." When the Lebanese Civil War ended, she decided to remain in London. She told Jaggi, "You leave the cocoon and want to experience the city. Writing about London rooted me; I became real here. Every day something makes me feel more at home."

The novel opens on a flight from Dubai to London's Heathrow Airport. When the aircraft hits turbulence, the lives of four people begin to entwine: an Englishman, Nicholas; and three Arabs: Samir, Amirah, and Lamis. The novel follows these characters after this initial encounter as their lives slowly intermingle while they search for their dreams of love, happiness, and fortune in London.

Dust jacket for the English translation of al-Shaykh's 2001 novel, Innaha Landan ya 'azizi *(Richland County Public Library)*

Samir is a closet transvestite and homosexual from Lebanon, who is trying to smuggle a monkey into England for £1,000. His intent is to deliver the monkey and then return to his wife and five children in Lebanon the following day. He soon learns, however, that what he really is delivering is the diamonds the monkey ingested before leaving the Middle East. Samir becomes saddled with the monkey, and his plan to return to Lebanon dissipates as he moves in with Amirah in London. Samir's desire is to be himself, and love who he wishes regardless of gender. He becomes obsessed with finding a man, but the monkey somehow always seems to get in the way. After three months, his wife and children come to London and he finds himself being pulled between the life he once lived in Lebanon and the life he desires in London.

Amirah is a thirty-eight-year-old Moroccan prostitute whose real name is Habibah Mustanaimi. She grew up in a home where she was ignored and abused by her parents because she was born a girl and was molested by her uncle. In order to escape the terrible situation at home she moves to London with dreams of a better life, but instead becomes a prostitute. Inspired by seeing an Arab princess, Amirah decides to pose as a princess herself to scam rich Arab men. Once she is discovered as a fraud, however, she is beaten by a prince of the royal family of which she has been pretending to be a member. In the end her humor comes to her rescue and she becomes a storyteller, telling people tales of the princess's adventures.

Lamis is an Iraqi who as a twelve-year-old was forced to move to London and marry a man twice her age. Her husband saw her as nothing more than a trophy and ignored her most of the time. Now divorced, Lamis falls in love with Nicholas, whom she loves so deeply that she tries to change herself to please him. To fit in, she tries to talk and act as English as possible; but she cannot change who she is and where she came from. Her struggle to change is symbolized in her failed attempts to pronounce the English letter *r*. As the East-West cultural differences surface, the couple breaks apart. Only then does Lamis accept her situation, get a job in a flower shop, and decide to go to college. When she eventually reunites with Nicholas in Oman, she promises herself that she will be true to who she is and not try to be someone she is not.

Nicholas, an expert in Islamic daggers, works for Sotheby's in London and has a fascination for all things Arab. Although he thinks he understands Arab culture, Nicholas continually pushes Lamis into situations that make her feel uncomfortable. He does not understand why she will not move in with him or why she does not introduce him to her son, Khalid. He is not sensitive to Lamis's past life and does not understand that she is constantly frightened that her former husband and mother-in-law will take away her newfound independence and force her to return to her old home. Nicholas must come to a deeper understanding of his cultural differences with Lamis before the couple can reunite.

Al-Shaykh sees the novel *Innaha Landan ya 'azizi* as a turning point for her writing. She stated in a 2001 interview with Pat Lancaster: "When I wrote the *Story of Zahra* I was writing about the agony of civil war. In *Women of Sand and Myrrh* I examined some of the problems with oppressed women, but now after living in London for 18 years, I have opened up the other side of my personality in this book, the humorous side."

In *Imra'atan 'alá shati al-bahr* (2003, Two Women on the Beach) al-Shaykh returns to Lebanon as a setting while continuing to explore the struggles of women who must reconcile traditional Arab values with modern Western ideals. The novel, set in the city of Beirut during the summer months, revolves around two women, Huda and Evon, who fled Lebanon during the civil war. Huda is a Muslim who immigrated to Canada, and Evon is a Christian who immigrated to London. In their new countries, both women embrace western culture and their new freedoms, but when they return to Lebanon to visit their families they are once again faced with their traditions of their families.

The conflict escalates when the women wear Western swimsuits on a visit to the beach in Beirut. Both women's parents see their daughters' swimwear as inappropriate and confront their daughters. Huda's father, a Muslim leader, sees his daughter's actions as his own personal failure. He believes that because Huda dresses the way she does she is not a practicing Muslim. He feels that if he can not help her come back to the faith, then he can not help others live as devout Muslims. He fears that he can not face God if Huda dies without coming back to the faith. Huda's mother handles her anger and disappointment by ostracizing Huda, refusing to speak to her. Evon's mother, on the other hand, confronts Huda head on, by accusing her of being selfish. She praises her three sons and blames Evon's behavior for the poverty they are enduring.

Although Hanan al-Shaykh continues to live in London, she remains committed to exploring social issues in her native land of Lebanon and providing a voice for women in the Arab world. In a 1995 interview with Richard Swift, she stated that there were two types of war in Lebanon: "One is the civil war" and "the other is the war against the old customs and taboos." Her fiction has helped to highlight the difficulties women face in patriarchal societies and reveal how traditional customs affect all women regardless of their class standing.

Interviews:

Paula W. Sunderman, "An Interview with Hanan al-Shaykh," *Michigan Quarterly Review,* 31 (Fall 1992): 625–636;

Richard Swift, "Hanan al-Shaykh," *New Internationalist,* 274 (December 1995): 31;

Sunderman, "Between Two Worlds: An Interview with Hanan al-Shaykh," *Literary Review,* 40 (Winter 1997): 297–308;

Pat Lancaster, "Only in London," *Middle East,* 314 (July/August 2001): 42–44;

Christiane Scholte, "An Interview with Hanan al-Shaykh," *Literary London: Interdisciplinary Studies in the Representation of London,* 1, no. 2 (September 2003) <http://homepages.gold.ac.uk/london-journal/september2003/Schlote.html#1A> (accessed 22 October 2008).

References:

Evelyne Accad, "Hanan al-Shaykh: Despair, Resignation, Masochism, and Madness," *Sexuality and War: Literary Masks of the Middle East* (New York & London: New York University Press, 1990), pp. 43–63;

Anne Marie Adams, "Writing Self, Writing Nation: Imagined Geographies in the Fiction of Hanan Al-Shaykh," *Tulsa Studies in Women's Literature*, 20 (Fall 2001): 201–217;

Samira Aghacy, "Lebanese Women's Fiction: Urban Identity and the Tyranny of the Past," *International Journal of Middle Eastern Studies*, 33 (2001): 503–523;

Catherine Cobham, "The Poetics of Space in Two Stories by Hanan Al-Shaykh," in *La poétique de l'espace: dans la literature arabe moderne*, edited by Boutros Hallaq, Robin Ostle, and Stefan Wild (Paris: Presses Sorbonne Nouvelle, 2002), pp. 131–142;

Miriam Cooke, "The Story of Zahra," in *World Literature and Its Times: Profiles of Notable Literary Works and the Historical Events that Influenced Them*, volume 6, edited by Joyce Moss (Detroit: Thomson Gale, 2004), pp. 527–533;

Samar Farah, "Muse, Not Politics, Inspires Novelist," *Christian Science Monitor*, 27 December 1994, p. 14;

Susan Alice Fischer, "Women Writers, Global Migration, and the City: Joan Riley's 'Waiting in the Twilight' and Hanan al-Shaykh's 'Only in London,'" *Tulsa Studies in Women's Literature*, 23 (Spring 2004): 107–121;

Sabah Ghandour, "Hanan al-Shaykh's 'Hikayat Zahra': A Counter-Narrative and a Counter-History," in *Intersections: Gender, Nation, and Community in Arab Women's Novels*, edited by Lisa Suhair Majaj, Paula W. Sunderman, and Therese Saliba (Syracuse, N.Y.: Syracuse University Press, 2002), pp. 231–249;

Pascale Ghazaleh, "Hanan al-Shaykh: From the Rooftops," *Al-Ahram Weekly Online* (11–17 November 1999) <http://weekly.ahram.org.eg/1999/455/profile.htm> (accessed 22 October 2008);

Sabry Hafez, "London Calling," *Al-Ahram Weekly Online* (10–16 January 2002) <http://weekly.ahram.org.eg/2002/568/bo7.htm> (accessed 22 October 2008);

Barbara Harlow, "City of Flight," *Nation*, 260 (19 June 1995): 894–896;

Maya Jaggi, "Conflict Unveiled," *Guardian Unlimited* (7 July 2001) <http://www.guardian.co.uk/Archive/Article/0,4273,4217303,00.html> (accessed 22 October 2008);

Charles R. Larson, "The Fiction of Hanan al-Shaykh, Reluctant Feminist," *World Literature Today*, 65 (Winter 1991): 14–18;

Elise Manganaro, "Lebanon Mythologized or Lebanon Deconstructed: Two Narratives of National Consciousness," in *Women and War in Lebanon*, edited by Lamia Rustum Shehadeh (Gainesville: University Press of Florida, 1999), pp. 112–128;

Roberta Rubenstien and Charles R. Larson, "Hanan al-Shaykh," *Worlds of Fiction* (New York: Macmillan, 1993), pp. 64–66;

Renate Wise, "A Bubble of Their Own: The Heroines in the Short Stories of Hanan al-Shaykh," *Critique: Journal of Critical Studies of Iran and the Middle East*, 5 (1994): 53–65;

Joseph T. Zeidan, "Hanan al-Shaykh and *The Story of Zahara*," *Arab Women Novelists: The Formative Years and Beyond* (Albany: State University of New York Press, 1995), pp. 205–217.

Bahaa' Taher
(13 January 1935 -   )

Ayman A. El-Desouky
School of Oriental and African Studies, University of London

BOOKS: *Bila Rajul* (Cairo, 1957);

Kana (Cairo, 1962);

Al-Khutubah wa qisas ukhra (Cairo: Al-Hay'ah al-Misriyyah al-'Ammah li al-Kitab, 1972)–includes "Al-Khutuba," translated by Faris Glubb and Christopher Tingley as "The Engagement," in *Modern Arabic Fiction: An Anthology,* edited by Samla Khadra Jayyusi (New York: Columbia University Press, 2005), pp. 711–721; and "Al-Matar faj'a," translated as "Suddenly It Rained," in *Egyptian Short Stories,* edited and translated by Denys Johnson-Davies (Washington, D.C.: Three Continents Press, 1978), pp. 40–42;

Bi al-ams halumtu bika (Cairo: Al-Hay'ah al-Misriyyah al-'Ammah li al-Kitab, 1984)–includes "Bi al-ams halumtu Bika," translated by W. M. Hutchins as "Last Night I Dreamt of You," in *Egyptian Tales and Short Stories of the 1970s and 1980s,* edited by Hutchins (Cairo: American University in Cairo Press, 1987); and "Nasiha min shabb 'aqil," translated as "Advice from a Sensible Young Man," in *Arabic Short Stories,* edited and translated by Johnson-Davies (London & New York: Quartet, 1983), pp. 40–45;

Ana al-malik ji'tu (Cairo: Al-Hay'ah al-Misriyyah al-'Ammah li al-Kitab, 1985);

'Ashr masrahiyyat Misriyyah: 'Ard wa naqd (Cairo: Dar al-Hilal, 1985);

Sharq al-nakhil, Law namut ma'an: Qissah tawilah (Cairo: Dar al-Mustaqbal al-'Arabi, 1985);

Qalat Duha: Riwayah (Cairo: Dar al-Hilal, 1985);

Abna' Rifa'ah: Al-Thaqafah wa al-hurriyyah (Cairo: Dar al-Hilal, 1987);

Khalati Safiyyah wa al-dayr (Cairo: Dar al-Hilal, 1991); translated by Barbara Romaine as *Aunt Safiyya and the Monastery* (Berkeley: University of California Press, 1996);

Al-Hubb fi al-manfa: Riwayah (Cairo: Dar al-Hilal, 1995); translated by Farouk Abdel Wahab as *Love in Exile* (Cairo & New York: American University in Cairo Press, 2001);

Bahaa' Taher (<http://auxarcspublications.wordpress.com>)

Dhahabtu ila shallal (Cairo: Maktabat Madbuli, 1998);

Nuqtat al-nur (Cairo: Dar al-Hilal, 2001);

Fi madih al-riwayah: Qira'ah li riwayat wa riwa'iyyin (Al-Minya, Egypt: Dar al-Huda, 2004);

Wahat al-ghurub (Cairo: Dar al-Hilal, 2006).

Collection: *Majmu'at a'mal: Al-Khutubah, Bi al-ams halumtu bika, Ana al-malik ji'tu, Sharq al-nakhil, Qalat Duha* (Cairo: Dar al-Hilal, 1992).

TRANSLATIONS: Eugene O'Neill, *Fasil gharib [Strange Interlude]* (Cairo: Dar al-Katib, 1970);

Paulo Coelho, *Sahir al-sahara'* [*L'alchemiste*] (Cairo: Dar al-Hilal, 1996).

OTHER: Fawzia Assad, *Hatshepsuut, al-Mar'ah al-fir'awn,* translated by Mahir Guweigati, preface by Taher (Cairo: Al-Majlis al-A'la li al-Thaqafah, 2003).

The novelist, short-story writer, and journalist Bahaa' Taher is one of the few uncompromising veterans of the Egyptian leftist literary "Generation of the 1960s." One of eight children, Taher was born in Giza on 13 January 1935; his father was a religious scholar and schoolteacher. His parents had moved to Giza from the village of Karnak in Upper Egypt; his mother told him many stories about the village and their extended family there, and it figures prominently in his works. He attended school in Cairo and was admitted to Cairo University in 1952; his father died that same year. He graduated with a degree in history in 1956 and became a producer and program host on Radio 2, the cultural channel of Cairo Radio, in 1957. That year he published his first book, the play *Bila rajul* (Without a Man). He contributed regularly to periodicals such as *al-Masrah* (Theater) and *al-Katib* (The Writer). By 1962, when he published a second play, *Kana* (There Was), he was editor of the theater section of *al-Katib* and a member of the executive committee of the National Theater. In 1968 he became co-director of Radio 2.

Taher's first short-story collection, *al-Khutubah wa qisas ukhra* (The Engagement and Other Stories), appeared in 1972. The title story (translated as "The Engagement," 2005) was written in 1968 in the atmosphere of disillusionment following Egypt's defeat in the 1967 Six-Day War with Israel and reveals the social and moral anarchy behind the facade of middle-class stability in Cairo. The unnamed narrator, a young bank clerk, prepares carefully for a prearranged formal visit to meet the family of his coworker Layla and to ask her father for her hand in marriage. He is ushered into the living room not by the head of the household but by Layla's eleven-year-old sister—an inauspicious beginning. The family's status-consciousness and bourgeois ambitions are indicated by the first object to catch the young man's eye on entering the room: a painting of a Venetian gondola that is obviously a cheap imitation. The father enters, purposely underdressed for the occasion, and offers a hand that is cold to the touch. The conversation quickly becomes an interrogation that reveals the father's meticulously gathered knowledge of potential scandals in the young man's family, such as his uncle's attempted suicide, and of his precarious situation at work. He offers the young man a more promising position in exchange for dropping the marriage proposal. The young man acquiesces and hurries out,

Front cover for Taher's al-Khutubah wa qisas ukhra *(The Engagement and Other Stories), 1972 (Widener Library, Harvard University)*

falls down the stairs, and staggers across the road. The ending of the story is left open as he decides to retrace his steps to Layla's home. The stories in the collection expose many of the social and political realities of Egyptian society in the 1960s; while they are generally set in middle-class Cairo, most of the characters are young, revolutionary, secular idealists from rural Egypt.

In 1975 Taher was transferred to the Foreign Service of Radio Cairo because of what the newly appointed minister of culture, the writer Yusuf al-Siba'i, called his "left-wing sympathies." Two years later, he began working as a translator for the United Nations Educational, Scientific, and Cultural Organization (UNESCO) in Cairo, and in 1981 he escaped the repressive atmosphere of Egypt by moving to the United Nations Office at Geneva. His second collection of short stories, *Bi al-ams halumtu bika* (Last Night I Dreamt of You), appeared in 1984. The unnamed narrator of the title story (translated as "Last Night I Dreamt of You," 1987) is an Egyptian living abroad in an unnamed northern city where snow is continually falling. He meets Ann Marie, a mysterious young woman, a native of the city, who lives with her mother. She is tormented by memories of lost love and nightmares about a menacing falcon that she identifies with the narrator, as she confesses when she describes the dream to him. She finally commits suicide. The story concludes with the narrator's vision of the falcon, which is the hieroglyph for the Egyptian god Horus:

> Had I been sleeping or awake when those wings started fluttering in the room? Have I seen a real falcon or was it only a dream? I reached out with my hands. I was listening intently to the sound of fluttering as I reached out with my hands. And then all kinds of majestic lights and colours, incomparably beautiful, spread all around me, as did the fluttering, and so I reached out with my hands. I was crying but without sound or tears, reaching out with my hands.

In 1985 Taher published his third short-story collection, *Ana al-malik ji'tu* (I, the King, Have Hailed Hither). The title piece takes place in the 1930s. While studying medicine abroad, Farid loses his love to an abrupt, inexplicable death. In his despair he goes into the desert in search of meaning and ends up at the ruins of a temple near the Siwa oasis. He abandons himself to the spirit of the place, which must deliver the answer–if there is one. The gradual dawning of recognition is dispersed over repeated attempts, each slightly more successful, to decipher the hieroglyphic inscriptions on the inner walls of the temple that begin with the phrase "I, the King, have hailed hither":

> and when those around me have disbanded and I came upon myself in my aloneness, I gathered in my folds and was perfect as whole. And as You are my Lord and I am Your chosen one, as You are the Light and I am but Your luminous reflection . . . far from others and all otherness, I have come hither so that we may become one, You and I. And now that time has transpired and exhausted itself and only Eternity remains, now I whisper unto You, and You, You recognize me. I inscribe my own secret, hidden away from all seeing, that only Your eyes may gaze upon it and You recognize me. . . . I fix my gaze upon Your bright disc that oversees all from high above, and I chisel my secret in the rock: I AM SAD. . . .

The story "Muhakamat al-kahin Kay-nin" (The Trial of the Priest Kay-nin) is set in ancient Egypt but reflects the repressive atmosphere of the 1980s. Kay-nin, a follower of the heretical monotheist pharaoh Ikhnaton, is put on trial after the worship of Amun is reestablished by corrupt priests and officials; the trial is presided over by a sympathetic though befuddled high priest.

Taher's *Sharq al-nakhil, Law namut ma'an: Qissah tawilah* (East of the Palm Orchards, Should We Perish Together: A Novella) also appeared in 1985; he had written it around 1979 but was banned from publishing in Egypt at that time. The unnamed narrator, a university student in Cairo, is torn between his political ambitions and the traditional values of his rural background; the conflict is brought to a crisis by a family dispute in his home village, and he falls into a state of emotional paralysis. But he displays a certain resilience, an almost instinctive impulse not to give up entirely. This sort of resilience in the face of adversity marks many of Taher's characters, despite the charge of passivity leveled at them by some critics.

Qalat Duha (1985, Duha Says), Taher's second novel, was written while he was working on *Ana al-malik ji'tu;* it is a modern adaptation of the myth of Isis and Osiris. In 1987 he published a collection of cultural essays titled *Abna' rifa'ah* (Disciples of Rifa'a); Rifa'ah Rafi' al-Tahtawi was one of the leaders of the nineteenth-century Egyptian *nahdah* (enlightenment).

Taher's third novel, *Khalati Safiyyah wa al-dayr* (1991; translated as *Aunt Safiyya and the Monastery,* 1996), is set in Karnak. Harbi is in love with his cousin Safiyyah, but she marries his uncle, who amassed a fortune and was given the title of consul-bey in the days of the monarchy; the bey is three times Safiyyah's age. Harbi would have been the heir to his uncle's fortune, but Safiyyah bears her husband a son. When a malicious rumor is spread that Harbi plans to kill the baby, the bey and his guards go to Harbi's shack and torture him. Harbi offers no resistance at first but finally frees himself and shoots and kills the bey. While Harbi is in prison, Safiyyah becomes obsessed with exacting revenge on him for the killing of her husband and raises her son to carry it out. On his release Harbi is given sanctuary by Brother Bishay, the gatekeeper of the historic Coptic Christian monastery near the village.

Taher took almost ten years to write his novel *al-Hubb fi al-manfa* (1995; translated as *Love in Exile,* 2001). The unnamed narrator, a disillusioned Egyptian journalist living in self-imposed exile in an unidentified European city in 1982, has an affair with Brigitte, an equally disillusioned Austrian woman who is much younger than he. Their happy interlude is ended when they are run out of the city by a treacherous Arab prince who wanted the narrator to start a newspaper, supposedly to promote pan-Arab and revolutionary ideals but actually to further the prince's political ambitions. Brigitte's attempt to swerve their car into an abyss fails; the journalist is unwilling to die before he settles scores with the prince; doing so will be the first step toward settling scores with all the failures in his life. News of the Israeli invasion of Lebanon and the massacres in the Sabra and Shatila refugee camps revives the narrator's ideological passions after a brief interlude in a hospital and abstinence from politics and strong emo-

Front cover for the 1996 English translation of Taher's third novel, Khalati Safiyyah wa al-dayr, 1991 (William T. Young Library, University of Kentucky)

tions on his doctor's orders. The novel ends on a note of defeat: in the final chapter, "Su'ud al-jabal" (Climbing up the Mountain), the protagonist attempts to settle scores with the corrupt prince but fails even to get past the gates to the prince's private mansion on the mountaintop.

Taher retired from his position at the UN and returned to Cairo in 1996. Of the stories in his 1998 collection, *Dhahabtu ila shallal* (A Visit to the Waterfalls), only the title piece and "Atlal al-bahr" (Revisiting Sea Memories) were written in Egypt; the rest were composed in Geneva. "Usturat hubb" (The Legend of a Love Affair) is an experiment in language, suffused with poetic imagery and mythical references.

Taher's novel *Nuqtat al-nur* (2001, The Point of Light) is presented through the points of view of three characters: the university student Salim; his fellow student and lover, Lubna; and Salim's grandfather, a retired *bashkatib* (head scribe in a government department), the patriarch of an extended family that lives in an old house that the *bashkatib*'s son wants to demolish and replace with an upscale apartment building. Salim and Lubna both suffer nervous breakdowns but are brought together in the end by the wisdom of the *bashkatib*.

Taher's 2006 novel, *Wahat al-ghurub*, takes place a few years after the British occupation of Egypt in 1882. Mahmud Afandy is an Egyptian police officer who is torn between his loyalties to his country and to his British superiors. Suspected by the British of sympathizing with the failed 1881 revolt by Colonel Ahmad 'Urabi against European influence in Egypt, he is sent from Cairo to collect taxes in the remote Siwa oasis near the Libyan border–an assignment that resulted in the death of his predecessor at the hands of the inhabitants. His Irish wife, Catherine, is fascinated by the archaeology of the area, which was visited by Alexander the Great and is rumored to be the site of his tomb. Her interest is shared by Wasfi, Mahmud's ambitious deputy. The locals resent the heavy taxes levied by the British and suspect that Catherine and Wasfi are actually searching for buried treasure in the ancient temple where they believe Alexander is buried. In the end Mahmud places explosives in the temple. Saying, "The temple must be completely destroyed. We must end all past stories in order for the grandchildren to wake up from the illusions of greatness and false solace," he sets off the explosives, blowing up the temple and himself.

For Bahaa' Taher history, whether ancient or contemporary, is a living, continuous and uninterrupted process. He has received several prestigious prizes and awards, including the Prize for Best Novel for *al-Hubb fi al-manfa* in 1995; the State's Award of Merit in Literature, one of the highest literary prizes awarded by the Egyptian cultural establishment, in 1998; the 2000 Italian Giuseppi Acerbi Prize for *Khalati Safiyya wa al-dayr;* the 2004 Naguib Mahfouz Prize; and the first International Prize for Arabic Fiction, a $50,000 award modeled on the British Man Booker Prize, for *Wahat Al-Ghurub* in 2008.

References:

Mahmud Amin Al-'Alim, *Arba'un 'Aman min al-naqd al-tatbiqi: Al-Binya wa al-dilalah fi al-qissah wa al-riwayah al-'Arabiyyah al-mu'asirah* (Cairo: Dar al-Mustaqbal al-'Arabi, 1994);

Roger Allen, "The Novella in Arabic: A Study in Fictional Genres," in *International Journal of Middle East Studies,* 18 (November 1986): 473–484;

Sabry Hafez, "The Modern Arabic Short Story," in *Modern Arabic Literature,* edited by Muhammad M. Badawi (Cambridge & New York: Cambridge University Press, 1992), pp. 270–328;

Hafez, "The Transformation of Reality and the Arabic Novel's Aesthetic Response," *Bulletin of the School of Oriental and African Studies, University of London,* 57, no. 1 (1994): 93–112;

Al-Baha Husayn, *Qariban min Bahaa' Taher: Muhawarat wa malamih* (Cairo: Al-Majlis al-A'la li al-Thaqafah, 2004).

Fuad al-Takarli

(August 1927 – 11 February 2008)

Imed Nsiri
American University of Sharjah

BOOKS: *Al-Wajh al-akhar* (Baghdad: Manshurat Wizarat al-Thaqafah wa al-I'lam, 1960);

Al-Raj' al-ba'id (Beirut: Dar Ibn Rushd, 1980); translated by Catherine Cobham as *The Long Way Back* (New York: AUC Press, 2001);

Al-Sakhrah (Baghdad: Dar al-Shu'un al-Thaqafiyyah, 1986);

Maw'id al-nar (Tunis: Dar al-Janub li al-Nashr, 1991);

Khatam al-raml (Beirut: Dar al-Adab, 1995);

Al-Kaff (Tunis: Dar Sihr li al-Nashr, 1995);

Al-Masarrat wa al-awja' (Damascus: Dar al-Mada, 1998);

Ghuraba' (Al-Haram: Wakalat al-Sahafah al-'Arabiyyah, 1999);

Basqah fi wajh al-hayat (Cologne: Al-Jamal, 2000);

Khazin al-lamar'iyat: Aqasis (Damascus: Dar al-Mada, 2004);

Al-lasual wa al-lajawab: Riwayah (Damascus: Dar al-Mada, 2007);

Hadith al-ashjar: Qissas wa hiwarat (Damascus: Dar al-Mada, 2007).

Collection: *Al-A'mal al-kamilah*, 6 volumes (Damascus: Dar al-Mada li al-Thaqafah wa al-Nashr, 2002).

In 1999 Fuad al-Takarli was chosen as the winner of the prestigious Sultan Bin Al Owais Cultural Foundation Prize for the short story, the novel, and drama. This award from Dubai, United Arab Emirates, recognized al-Takarli as a leading voice in the field of literature, not only in Iraq but throughout the Arab world. In the wake of the award the Syrian-based publishing house al-Mada published *al-A'mal al-kamilah* (2002), his complete works, and his books have been translated into several languages, including French, Spanish, and English. This recognition has triggered broad critical interest in al-Takarli.

Al-Takarli was born in Baghdad in August 1927. He grew up in a relatively well-off family in the neighborhood of Bab al-Shaykh. In his memoirs he recalls a time when he turned five and the family was about to leave the old deteriorating family house in Bab al-Shaykh. Al-Takarli had a sense that his seventy-year-old father and the house were one, and the end of an era was looming. He mentions in the sixth volume of *al-A'mal al-kamilah* that an old pomegranate tree reminded him of his "father's protruding blue veins." Since then," he says, "I held fast to people and things." He recalls that at the age of six "I used to love walking around the mosque of Shaykh 'Abd al-Qadir al-Kilani (1077–1165) . . . and I was in reality, storing up images in my memory for the coming writing phase." His family had been the custodian of the mosque. No surprise then that Bab al Shaykh is a key presence in al-Takarli's works.

Al-Takarli gained his education in Baghdad, going through school, then attending Baghdad University to pursue a law degree. While al-Takarli was in his third year at the university, his father died, leaving him and his family to endure the hardship and humiliation of poverty. The same year brought the defeat of Arab armies in the War of 1948 and creation of the state of Israel. Upon graduation with a law degree in 1949, al-Takarli worked in the Iraqi ministry of justice for thirty-five years, but he also pursued his interest in writing, meeting regularly with fellow writers and intellectuals. Indeed, in the late 1940s and the early 1950s, al-Takarli had a very good literary support group. He and his older brother Nihad, 'Abd al-Malik Nuri, and the famous poet 'Abd al-Wahhab al-Bayyati often met to discuss intellectual matters and comment on each others' work. Al-Takarli's knowledge of Western literature was, at least partially, due to his brother's influence. Wiebke Walther reflects the observations of several critics in his "Studies in Human Psyche and Human Behavior Under Political and Social Pressure: The Recent Literary Works of Fuad al-Takarli" when he writes that al-Takarli "often depicts characters who identify with French existentialism portrayed in works of such authors as Camus and Sartre." Al-Takarli believes that any development in Iraqi and Arabic fiction must necessarily benefit from Western achievement. He was also very much driven by the search for literary forms and techniques that would preserve his

Front cover for Fuad al-Takarli's collection al-Wajh al-akhar (The Other Face), 1960 (Widener Library, Harvard University)

cultural heritage in his works. On several occasions al-Takarli expressed his concern that critics seemed to limit the scope of his work to existentialism.

In 1952, while working at the civil court in Baqubah, al-Takarli published his first story, "al-'Uyun al-khudr" (The Green Eyes), in *al-Usbu'* magazine; the story was later included in his first collection *al-Wajh al-akhar* (1960, The Other Face). "Al-'Uyun al-khudr," which attracted the attention of Iraqi intellectuals, is narrated by a prostitute, an unusual protagonist in Iraqi as well as Arabic literature. Salimah, the main character, is traveling by train from Baghdad to Baqubah. A flashback reveals her miserable life before and after she became a prostitute. The only bright spot in her life is a man who used to come with his friends to the brothel. His friends had sex with her, but he did not. Instead, he would sit with her to talk. Although she liked him and enjoyed his company, she was puzzled by his behavior and ended up hurting his feelings by suggesting that he was no better than a pimp. The story juxtaposes two worlds; the outside world is as chaotic as the prostitute's internal world. The story is a critique of the inaction of intellectuals and of the indifference of society to individuals.

In 1956 al-Takarli was appointed a judge, and the job gave him firsthand experience of the lives of ordinary Iraqis. From the start of his writing career, al-Takarli's attention to technical and philosophical concerns were well balanced by his treatment of the everyday problems of common people. Al-Takarli is a pioneer not only in form but also in content. In his short stories and novels, as well as plays, the reader often has the opportunity of seeing the characters as psychological beings in a dialectical relationship with their surroundings.

In 1960 he published *al-Wajh al-akhar,* comprising six short stories and a novella that bears the same title as the collection. Written between 1956 and 1957, the novella focuses on the internal malaise of the protagonist confronted with the reality around him. The main character, Muhammad Ja'far, feels happy with himself and thinks that he has a noble nature. However, when his "noble self" is faced with the first test, he fails to act properly. As he is waiting for a bus, he is approached by a sick young man who asks him for help. Instead of taking him to the hospital, Muhammad Ja'far catches the next bus and leaves the young man behind. The image of the young man dying haunts Muhammad Ja'far and foreshadows events in the life of Muhammad Ja'far himself. His wife is pregnant and her due date is approaching, but he does not have the money to pay the hospital bill. He is further frustrated because he is not supposed to have sex with her. Lack of money and sex seem to be two problems in his life, and concern about them sometimes triggers his thoughts about the meaning of life and the universe. He borrows money from his neighbor, Sayyid Hashim, who charges him too much interest and takes his wife's gold as collateral. The baby is born dead, and his wife loses her sight after fever brought on by childbirth. He then becomes attracted to Salimah, the fifteen-year-old daughter of his landlady. Salimah had reluctantly just married the old Sayyid Hashim, and she helps Muhammad Ja'far defer the hospital bill. Bored with his wife and completely frustrated with life, he takes his wife back to her family and eventually divorces her. Unable to tell her about the divorce because he is afraid of her reaction, he recognizes that she is also a victim; nonetheless, he leaves her to rot like a dying horse that he sees on the way back from taking her to her family.

Despite the intellectual analysis that he makes of himself and the world around him and the high hope he has for his "noble self," Muhammad Ja'far always fails to act according to the values that he thinks set him apart from the people around him. The reader sees the other face of Muhammad Ja'far, but there is never a condemnation of him by the omniscient narrator. In fact, Muhammad Ja'far himself seems quite often at the mercy of a higher being and the left-to-die horse could as well represent him.

Al-Takarli studied law in France from 1964 to 1966. Before he left, he met an acquaintance who told him about a serious relationship that he had had with a primary school teacher; they were planning to get married when he discovered that she was not a virgin. She tearfully explained that her nephew deflowered her when she had visited the family a month earlier. This incident triggered al-Takarli's novel *al-Raj' al-ba'id* (1980; translated as *The Long Way Back,* 2001), which took him eleven years to complete. When al-Takarli attempted to publish *al-Raj' al-ba'id* at the beginning of 1979, he had to go through the Iraqi political censorship for approval. The censor declared that one of the characters, 'Adnan, represented a negative portrayal of the Baath party, the ruling party in Iraq. The censor lectured al-Takarli on the historical significance of the events of 1963 and compared the people who participated in the events to angels. He wanted 'Adnan taken out of the novel, which al-Takarli refused to do. As a result, the novel could not be published in Iraq, and it was instead published in Beirut in 1980. *Al-Raj' al-ba'id* was translated into French in 1985 and reprinted in 1993 in a revised edition in which al-Takarli reworked the Iraqi dialect dialogue for non-Iraqi Arab readers. *Al-Raj' al-ba'id* is considered al-Takarli's masterpiece. Muhammad Mustafa Badawi calls it "the most impressive Iraqi novel to date."

The novel achieves a multiplicity of perspectives. The title is taken from a verse in the Qur'an in which the disbelievers question resurrection and rhetorically ask "When we are dead and have become dust (can there be resurrection?) That is a far return" *(Surat Qaf,* 50: 3). From the start, the novel delineates the scope of the story that puts together three generations living in the same traditional house. The novel opens with the grandmother, Nuriyyah, coming home in Bab al-Shaykh with her granddaughter, Sana', carrying groceries. As they approach the house, the grandmother sees a character, who is presented later in the novel from a different perspective, whom she recognizes as her son-in-law, and she tries to prevent her granddaughter from seeing him. The character is Husayn, Sana''s father, who was supposed to be working in Kuwait and who does not have the usual nickname "Abu" (father of). Sana' and her sister Suha live in the old house with their mother, Madihah, because Husayn is an alcoholic who forsook his family. Madihah is not surprised that he came back, because the political situation in Kuwait made it uncomfortable for Iraqis. Al-Takarli subtly suggests that the destiny and turmoil of this family is intertwined with the chaotic politics of the country. An Iraqi reader would recognize the reference to 'Abd al-Karim Qasim and his worsened relations with Kuwait, setting the time of the action in the early 1960s, just before his assassination. By 1963 Qasim, who became the head of the Republic of Iraq after he overthrew the Iraqi monarchy in 1958, had become unpopular, owing in part to his refusal to consider any sort of federation with the newly formed United Arab Republic between Egypt and Syria. His previous supporter 'Abd al-Salam 'Arif overthrew him in February 1963. The events of the novel take place toward the end of Qasim's regime, and this political chaos provides the background for the internal and personal turmoil of the house in Bab al-Shaykh.

Karim is a young man at the university and his internal malaise seems to have been triggered by witnessing a friend's tragic death. His seems to suffer from existential angst or, as Wiebke says, "unusual psychic conditions." Karim's inertia affects everybody in the family, including the old ladies, Aunt Safiyyah (Abu Midhat's aunt) and Umm Hasa (Sana''s great-grandmother), who cannot wait to see Karim go back to school to get them the pastries they dream of. Their lives, at their end, are contrasted with the other characters' lives, at their beginning. The old ladies' hunger for life is a reminder of how short life is and makes Karim's dark view of life seem wasteful. Nevertheless, a new addition to the household at Bab al-Shaykh gives Karim a new hope. His cousin Munirah, a young teacher, and her mother, Karim's paternal aunt, come to live in the household. Munirah, transferred from Baqubah to Baghdad, draws the interest of Karim and two other young men: Midhat, Karim's older brother, and 'Adnan, Munirah's nephew. Midhat proposes to Munirah, but she is reluctant to accept, to her mother's surprise, because 'Adnan had raped her, and she is worried that Midhat will not understand.

After deliberation Munirah accepts Midhat's offer, and they marry. When he learns that she is not a virgin, he leaves her without a word, never to return. He goes into soul searching and spends more time with his brother-in-law, Husayn, who becomes a link of sorts between Midhat and his family. When Midhat comes to terms with his emotional trauma and decides to go back to his wife, he is shot dead in the streets of Baghdad during the violence that led eventually to the assassination of Qasim.

Critics who portray al-Takarli as an existentialist writer divorced from the problems of his society are

Dust jacket for the English translation, 2001, of al-Takarli's 1980 novel, al-Raj' al-ba'id, written over a period of eleven years (Thomas Cooper Library, University of South Carolina)

often confronted by other critics who refute such claims, giving *al-Raj' al-ba'id* as an example. Al-Takarli's defenders argue that he is concerned with the individual, but the psychological aspect of the individual is intertwined with the political, economic, and social woes of the people. Al-Takarli himself, in the sixth volume of *al-A'mal al-kamilah,* says he decided to use the technique of multiple points of view because "that is what I needed in order to present, as much as I could, a complete image of the Iraqi society in the beginning of the Sixties."

With the publication of *al-Raj' al-ba'id,* al-Takarli's target audience started to shift toward the general Arab reader. He dropped the use of Iraqi dialect altogether and wrote solely in standard Arabic. He also broadened the content of his art.

In 1986 al-Takarli moved to Tunisia, where he started working on new projects. The first was a short-story collection, *Maw'id al-nar* (1991, An Appointment by Fire). The notion of exile is an important theme in this collection. His short story "Dhaka al-nida" (That Call), finished in 1985, is narrated by a wretched homeless Iraqi emigrant lost in Paris. After finding a fifty-franc banknote in the streets of Paris, he reflects on his life and what to do with the money. Instead of using the money for survival, he decides to have a nice meal that would cost most of the money. When he finally chooses the restaurant and the meal, he is joined by an American couple who start a conversation with him. They discover that he originally came to France for a short period of time but has been living in Paris for several years. He lost all his money and was eventually evicted because he would not leave his apartment, as he was waiting for a call from his wife which never came. When the tourist couple discovers that his wife is dead, they depart, leaving their meal behind.

Though some critics have criticized al-Takarli for his lack of production—or what some call a "silence"—for fifteen years, from the publication of his first novel in 1980 to his second novel in 1995, they have overlooked his other publications, including his short stories and plays. While in Tunis, al-Takarli published his second and last play, *al-Kaff* (1995, The Palm of the Hand). However, the most important work he produced while living in Tunisia is his novel *Khatam al-raml* (1995, The Ring of Sand) published in Beirut.

Critics argue that it is of paramount importance that *Khatam al-raml* continues the author's emphasis on exile and alienation, even though the story is set in Baghdad. As a matter of fact there is an insistence on the re-creation of Baghdad through detailed description of the place. In *Khatam al-raml* there is no Iraqi dialect, and no historical background is needed to understand the novel. Nevertheless, the setting is Baghdad of the 1970s, as if al-Takarli wanted to create a mental picture of the Baghdad that he knew before it was lost. *Khatam al-raml* deals with Hashim's psychic inability to deal with the death of his mother when he was nine. On the day of his wedding, he finds himself bound to his mother's grave. He misses his wedding ceremony and ends up sick for a couple of weeks. His psychic dilemma prevents him from taking any action, such as leaving his fiancée, Amal, even though she does not mean anything to him and he knows that refusing to leave her might cause him physical harm. Amal's cousin, Salma, tries to persuade him to give Amal the much-needed release, as she wants to be engaged to someone else. Hashim becomes sexually attracted to Salma, who seems to have feelings for him as well, and who is sympathetic, especially after she talks to his uncle Ra'uf and recognizes the similarities between his psychological dilemmas and those of his mother.

Hashim refuses to listen to anybody and ends up murdered because he refuses to grant Amal her release.

Some critics see *Khatam al-Raml* as among the many other works by al-Takarli that are divorced from their own culture. Wiebke argues that this novel "deals with psychosocial problems rather than with political ones." In his review in the Baghdad newspaper *al-Thawrah* (Revolution) 'Ali Jawad al-Tahir characterizes it as "a non-Iraqi or non-Arabic novel." Wiebke rightly recognized that the novel is grounded in its culture, but besides the treatment of psychological problems, it also deals with sociopolitical issues that are always at the background of al-Takarli's work.

Al-Takarli's next novel, *al-Masarrat wa al-awja'* (1998, The Joys and the Sorrows) is, unlike *Khatam al-raml*, a long work that is structured in four parts. *Al-Masarrat wa al-awja'* was written right after *Khatam al-raml* as if the latter was an artistic exercise that prepared him and set him free to write the longer work. The novel is the history of an Iraqi family from the beginning of the twentieth century until the Iraq-Iran war. Through this family and the main character, Tawfiq Lam, al-Takarli traces the history of modern Iraq. The extended family of Tawfiq Lam have strange facial appearances—they resemble monkeys—but Tawfiq is blessed with great looks and a promising future, though he grows up to have his share of sorrow.

The first part of the book is narrated in the third person and traces the history of this strange family of carpenters that moved from the margins of society to occupy an important place in the furniture business. Thanks to Tawfiq's mother, the family grows richer. Tawfiq, unlike his older brother, pursues his education. He becomes interested in reading novels and is more and more alienated from his family. Tawfiq, as several critics have noticed, resembles the earlier protagonists of al-Takarli's works. He is an avid reader, he is interested in writing, and he has the characteristics of the existential hero. These traits are often intertwined with problematic relationships with the opposite sex. His first love is Adele, but he ends up marrying Camilla, his brother's sister-in-law. She had been pursuing him since she was nine. Soon Camilla is disappointed that she has not conceived, and the chapter ends with her starting to turn against him.

In the second part al-Takarli tells the story through the eyes of the first-person narrator writing in his personal diary, so the reader gets to know Tawfiq's inner thoughts—the way he sees himself, the events, and the people around him. The chain of events is a chronological continuation of the first part. The sex scenes are multiplied and Tawfiq's weakness in the face of sexual temptation is confirmed. He seems to have inherited this trait from his family, as his uncle was lynched because he raped a Polish female soldier. While his first forbidden relationship with a married woman was initiated by Adele, in this second chapter he is pursuing Anwar, the wife of his relative. Although Anwar's husband helps Tawfiq in several occasions, Tawfiq continues his endeavor to have sex with Anwar. This part of the novel also records the effect of politics on people like Tawfiq who are not interested in politics. Because of his political connections, Tawfiq's co-worker Sulayman Fathallah keeps being promoted to positions that he does not deserve, and Tawfiq loses his job and the ability to work again because of him. With the loss of his job, Tawfiq also loses his wife and finds out that he has no place to live, as his mother has given everything to his older brother.

In the third part al-Takarli reverts to the third-person narration. Tawfiq is now living in a rented room in a poor area of Baghdad that belongs to Fathiyyah, the young widowed daughter of the janitor at the office where he used to work. Tawfiq, alienated and marginalized, both mentally and physically, moves to work for Anwar's husband in Khanaqin, where his family started their fortune. Yet, politics and sex draw him back to Baghdad. His politically influential cousin, Mumtaz al-Lami, husband of his niece, warns Tawfiq that his life is in danger. Like Tawfiq, Mumtaz is attracted to his cousin's wife, Anwar, and seems to consider Tawfiq a rival.

The final part reverts to first-person narration, but not in the form of a diary. Tawfiq narrates the love story between his ex-lover, Fathiyyah, and Ghassan, a boy from his neighborhood, whom Tawfiq used to pity. Ghassan suffers from the psychological effect of having been left behind by his mother who fled with a lover. Ghassan is now an army officer and has inherited a lot of money from his mother. Yet his life was in shambles until he met Fathiyyah. Tawfiq plays the father figure for the two young lovers and feels responsible for Fathiyyah after she gets pregnant and Ghassan is unable to fulfill his promise of marriage because of the war. Ghassan is killed in the war, and Tawfiq finds out that Ghassan left him a fortune. Tawfiq understands he needs to use the fortune to support Fathiyyah and her unborn baby. Seemingly changed, Tawfiq attempts to leave his cocoon, take control of his life, and become actively engaged in the lives of those who matter to him.

In 1999 al-Takarli returned to the short story, publishing a collection titled *Ghuraba'* (Strangers), and a year later, he published his novella, *Basqah fi wajh al-hayat* (Spit in the Face of Life). Although this novella was published in 2000, he had written it in the summer of 1948. In "An Introduction to a Cursed Text" in the third volume of *al-A'mal al-kamilah*, he recalls his first

Front cover for al-Takarli's novel, al-Masarrat wa al-awja' (The Joys and the Sorrows), 1998 (R. W. Woodruff Library, Emory University)

attempt at writing when he was only twenty-one and a third-year-student at the Iraqi School of Law. He had tried writing before and found that it was not as easy as he had thought. When it proved to be difficult, he got into the habit of keeping a journal and that made the transition easier. His vivid and detailed memory of the time leading to the writing of the text is indicative of the personal significance of this novella. The text seems to have acted a catharsis for the disturbed self of the author at the time: "It was for me a work of regaining my balance and rebuilding what had been destroyed in my personality because of circumstances that surrounded me and repeatedly beat my existential self in particular." Some of these circumstances seem to be both political and personal. On the impersonal level there was the "division of Palestine," as the author puts it, as well as the violence that emerged in Iraq after the strikes against the government during the early part of 1948. On the personal level there was the malaise that al-Takarli felt throughout the years. The death of his father and his ensuing poverty, especially in comparison with the rich students at the university, made writing a necessity. The fact that he felt uprooted from the old family house at Bab al-Shaykh seems to have contributed to the importance of the place in his writings. Bab al-Shaykh, Baqubah, and Baghdad in general are common settings in al-Takarli's writings. In a 2003 interview he discussed again his reason for waiting more than fifty years before publishing Basqah fi wajh al-hayat. He points out that he considered it technically not mature enough and the content of the story too taboo for that time. In his opinion, one of the redeeming aspects of this text is that it acted, as he wrote in the introduction, as "a healthy way out" of his complex psychological crisis. He says that the novel made him strong enough to graduate from law school, while also giving him the confidence that afterwards enabled him to write fiction.

This novella is made of what looks like journal entries and was a transition from his habitual journal entries to fiction-writing. Despite the fact that it is not technically as sophisticated as his other works, it still has the same thematic concerns that some critics identify as his main interest, namely existential malaise and sexual and sexually taboo relationships, such as incest. Also the main character often has an interest in literature.

The narrator is a retired police officer who develops a sexual attraction to his daughter Fatimah. He has been retired for five years and is now saddened by his daughters' shameful work that is financially supporting the needs of the family. Nevertheless, he reminds himself that their work is not more shameful than the bribes he used to take before he retired. The father's infatuation with his daughter makes him act strangely in several attempts to deal with this fatal attraction, and in the end he kills her and then waits for the police to come.

Al-Takarli left Tunisia in August 2003 and moved to Damascus, Syria. In 2004 he published a short-story collection, Khazin al-lamar'iyat: Aqasis (Storage of the Invisible). In 2005 al-Takarli moved to Amman, Jordan. His novel al-Lasual wa al-lajawab (2007, The Non-Question and the Non-Answer) traces the changes that occur in an Iraqi family and to the country in the 1980s and 1990s. His final work was Hadith al-ashjar: Qissas wa hiwarat (2007, Talk of the Trees: Stories and Conversations). Al-Takarli died on 11 February 2008.

Fuad al-Takarli attempted to change the perception of narrative in the Arab world. Although the short story and the novel in Iraq cannot compare with modern Arabic poetry in terms of the respect they attract, al-Takarli thought that they should. The prizes he was awarded and the respect accorded translations of his books have gone far toward elevating the regard for Arabic prose fiction both locally and internationally.

References:

Muhammad Mustafa Badawi, *A Short History of Modern Arabic Literature* (Oxford: Oxford University Press, 1993);

Fabio Caiani, "Polyphony and Narrative Voice in Fu'ad al-Takarli's *Al-Raj' al-ba'id*," *Journal of Arabic Literature*, 35, no. 1 (2004): 45–70;

Catherine Cobham, "The Long Way Back: Possibilities for Survival and Renewal in *al-Raj' al-ba'id* by Fu'ad al-Takarli," *Middle Eastern Literatures*, 5, no. 2 (July 2002): 181–194;

Cobham, "Reading and Writing in *Al-Masarrat wa al-awja'* by Fu'ad al-Takarli," *Journal of Arabic Literature*, 35, no. 1 (2004): 25–44;

Salman Kasid, *'Alam al-nass: Dirasah binyawiyyah fi al-adab al-qisasi Fu'ad al-Takarli Namudhajan* (Irbid: Dar al-Kindi, 2003);

Muhsin al-Musawi, *Naz'at al-hadathah fi al-qissah al-'Iraqiyyah* (Baghdad: Al-Maktabah al-'Alamiyah, 1984);

Al-Musawi, "Al-Insan wa al-zaman fi riwayat *Al-Raj' al-ba'id* li Fuad al-Takarli," in his *al-Riwayah al-Arabiyyah: Al-Nash'ah wa al-Tahawwul* (Beirut: Dar al-Adab, 1988), pp. 245–267;

Wiebke Walther, "Distant Echoes of Love in the Narrative Works of Fuad al-Tikirl," in *Love and Sexuality in Modern Arabic Literature,* edited by Roger Allen, Hilary Kilpatrick, and Ed de Moor (London: Saqi, 1995);

Walther, "Studies in Human Psyche and Human Behavior under Political and Social Pressure: the Recent Literary Works of Fuad al-Takarli," *Arab Studies Quarterly* (Fall 1997): 21–36.

Zakaria Tamer
(1931 -)

Mahmoud Kayyal
Tel Aviv University

BOOKS: *Sahil al-jawad al-abyad* (Beirut: Dar Majallat Shi'ir, 1960);

Rabi' fi al-ramad (Damascus: Wizarat al-Thaqafah, 1963);

Al-Ra'd (Damascus: Itihad al-Kuttab al-'Arab, 1970);

Dimashq al-hara'iq (Damascus: Itihad al-Kuttab al-'Arab, 1973);

Limadha sakata al-nahr (Damascus: Wizarat al-Thaqafah, 1973);

Qalat al-wardah li al-sununu (Damascus: Itihad al-Kuttab al-'Arab, 1977);

Al-Numur fi al-yawm al-'ashir (Beirut: Dar al-Adab, 1978); translated by Denys Johnson-Davies as *Tigers on the Tenth Day and Other Stories* (London: Quartet, 1985);

Amjad ya 'Arab amjad (Ramallah: Al-Yarmuk li al-Thaqafah wa al-'Ilm, 1986);

Nida' Nuh (Beirut: Riyad al-Rayyis, 1994);

Sanadhak (Beirut: Riyad al-Rayyis, 1998);

Al-Husrum (Beirut: Riyad al-Rayyis, 2000);

Taksir rukab (Beirut: Riyad al-Rayyis, 2002);

Al-Qatil Yahju Qatilah (Beirut: Riyad al-Rayyis, 2003);

Al-Qunfudh (Beirut: Riyad al-Rayyis, 2005).

Zakaria Tamer is widely regarded as one of the finest short-story writers in the Arab world; Sabry Hafez calls him "the poet of the short story *par excellence*." Some critics go so far as to contend that his unique style and the fictional world he has created make him a one-man literary movement, although a few are put off by what they see as his distorted, pessimistic, and elitist worldview. His stories have been translated into many languages, including English, French, Spanish, Serbian, German, and Italian. He has also published satirical articles and children's books.

Tamer was born in Damascus in 1931. He left school at thirteen to help support his family by working as a blacksmith in a scale factory while continuing to study independently. Some sources claim that he joined the underground Communist Party in the mid 1950s but was expelled for revealing the existence of the organization under police interrogation.

In 1957 Tamer began publishing stories in journals such as *al-Nuqqad* (Critics) and *al-Thaqafah* (Culture). His first collection, *Sahil al-jawad al-abyad* (The Neighing of the White Steed), appeared in 1960. The protagonists in most of these expressionistic pieces are variants of what Emma Westney calls the "café man": a simple factory worker who finds escape from the loneliness and alienation of the city in daydreams and sex. The female characters are sex objects and the subjects of male fantasies. In the Lebanese literary journal *al-Aadab* (Literature) in November 1960 Muhyi al-Din Muhammad expressed appreciation for Tamir's representation of characters who suffer from Western materialism and Eastern social problems.

In 1960 Tamer left his blacksmith job and took a position in the Department of Creativity, Translation, and Publication of the Syrian Ministry of Culture. He found his distinctive voice in his second collection of stories, *Rabi' fi al-ramad* (1963, Spring in the Ashes). His writing is characterized by lyrical language, allegories, metaphors, irony, black humor, and grotesque descriptions; he defies conventions of narrative structure, introduces absurd incidents, and gives his characters mythical qualities. Blurring the boundaries between the real and the imaginary, the rational and the irrational, and present and past, he creates an imaginary world that criticizes the real one by exaggerating aspects of it to an extreme. The volume includes the story "al-Nahr" (The River): 'Umar al-Sa'di (his surname suggests Sa'di Square, a traditional Damascus neighborhood that is mentioned frequently in Tamer's stories) is in prison; he finds escape from his dreary surroundings in a fantasy about a woman who has the attributes of nature:

> He felt that his blood was a weeping infant at the moment when he heard the guard's boots thudding on the floor of the paved corridor, and began to forget the

river and his home, and the sun did not shine from his forehead. Once he saw in his sleep a pale-faced woman with dark hair and green eyes emerging from the river dripping with water, and she was very sweet, and her hair was redolent of dried wheat.

The stories in the collection deal with social and political problems: poverty, hunger, sexual repression, exploitation of women, and denial of freedom of expression. A mood of alienation, loss, and impotence predominates; male protagonists are powerless, obsequious, lacking in freedom and dignity; they respond docilely to humiliation. The women are even more downtrodden than the men: they are timid, subservient, and subject to both verbal and physical violence. Tamer shocks the reader with scenes of gang rape, dismemberment of bodies, and necrophilia. His writing is filled with ironic derision of Arab rulers, the corrupt elites that surround them, religious people, and the older generation. The only hopeful note in the depressing world Tamer constructs is the possibility that the younger generation will challenge conservatism, patriarchy, and oppression.

Between 1963 and 1965 Tamer edited the weekly *al-Mawqif al-'Arabi* (The Arabic Position). In 1967 he became an inspector in the Ministry of Communication and director of the manuscript section of Syrian Television. He began writing children's stories in 1968. In 1969 he was one of the founders of the Syrian Writers' Union; he was elected to the union's governing council and put in charge of the publications section. He edited the monthly children's magazine *Rafi'* in 1969–1970 and began editing another, *Usamah*, in 1970.

Tamer's third short-story collection, *al-Ra'd* (The Thunder), appeared in 1970. In the story "al-'Urs al-sharqi" (The Oriental Wedding) he heaps scorn on arranged marriages and the degrading attitude they display toward women. A student looking for help with his mathematics homework asks his parents to arrange a marriage for him with their neighbors' beautiful and educated sixteen-year-old daughter. The negotiation over the dowry calls to mind merchants and customers dickering over wares in the marketplace. The girl's price is mainly determined by her weight; her beauty and education affect it only slightly.

In 1973 Tamer became deputy chairman of the Syrian Writers' Union; he left *Usamah* and took over the editorship of the union journal, *al-Mawqif al-Adabi* (The Literary Position). That same year 1973 he published his fourth short-story collection, *Dimashq al-hara'iq* (Damascus Fires), in which he introduces two archetypal characters: the policeman and the historical personage. The policeman is a symbol of evil and

Dust jacket for the first English edition, 1985, of Tamer's fifth collection of stories for adults, 1978 (Thomas Cooper Library, University of South Carolina)

dominance; he not only torments innocent and helpless citizens but also possesses supernatural powers that he uses for cruel and pitiless oppression: he is capable of holding sway over the natural order of the universe and the fate of the dead. The historical characters are resuscitated in the stories but lose the glory that surrounds them: they are so humiliated and depressed that they deny their past. The two archetypes appear together in "al-Istighathah" (The Call for Help). A call for assistance from a conquered land–probably Palestine–goes unheeded by the lethargic inhabitants of Damascus but brings to life a statue of the Syrian military hero Yusuf al-'Azamah, who died in battle against the French colonizers in 1920. As he wanders the streets of Damascus he is arrested because he is wearing a sword. At the police station he is interrogated, treated with scorn and derision, and finally taken to a mental hospital. In his

Front cover for Limadha sakata al-nahr (Why Did the River Become Silent?), 1973 (Widener Library, Harvard University)

locked room he hears another call for help but cannot escape to answer it; he collapses and calls for help himself, but both calls fade away in the night.

Also in 1973 Tamer published his first collection of children's stories, *Limadha sakata al-nahr* (Why Did the River Become Silent?). In the title story a talking river plays with cats, birds, and children and gives water to them and to the flowers and trees. One day a man with a gloomy face and a sword appears; he does not allow the animals or children to drink unless they give him gold. Some cry, others leave, and still others die. The river becomes angry and stops talking. Some other men, who love cats, birds, children, flowers, and trees, drive off the man with the sword; the river is happy and gives the men drinks. But the river never talks again, because it is afraid that the man with the sword will return.

Tamer became the head of the private producers' scenario committee of the Institution for Film Arts in 1976. He published another volume of children's stories, *Qalat al-wardah li al-sununu* (The Rose Said to the Swallow), in 1977. In his fifth collection of stories for adults, *al-Numur fi al-yawm al-'ashir* (1978, translated as *Tigers on the Tenth Day and Other Stories*, 1985), he criticizes tradition and oppression even more sharply and sarcastically than in his earlier works. He also increases the fragmentation of his narratives: every story includes several plots, each of which constitutes a story of its own, but all of which combine to make up a tale of a crushed and fragmented world. The title story is an allegory about Arab rulers who use hunger and poverty to oppress their citizens. An animal trainer is teaching his pupils how to train a wild tiger. He starves the animal for nine days, demanding obedience before giving it a morsel of food. Every day his demands become more extreme: on the first day the tiger has to declare that it is hungry to get its food; by the eighth day it has to clap its paws after the trainer delivers a speech filled with the hollow slogans of Arab politics. When the tiger says that it could not understand a word of the speech, it is accused of hypocrisy and given no food. On the ninth day it is given only weeds to eat. On the tenth day the tiger becomes a citizen, and the cage becomes a city.

In 1978 Tamer began editing the periodical *al-Ma'rifah* (Knowledge), published by the Ministry of Culture. Fired in 1980 for printing excerpts from 'Abd al-Rahman al-Kawakibi's *Taba'i' al-Istibdad* (1900, The Characteristics of Despotism), he moved to London. There he edited the weekly *al-Dustur* (The Constitution) for the publishing house Dar Riyad el-Rayyis, the cultural section of the weekly magazine *al-Tadamun* (Solidarity), and the journal *al-Naqid* (The Critic); and joined the editorial board of the newspaper *al-Quds al-Arabi* (Arab Jerusalem). He also wrote satirical columns for various newspapers and magazines, such as "Khawatir tasurr al-khatir" (Reflections to Make the Heart Rejoice) for *al-Doha* magazine and "Qal al-malik li-wazirih" (The King Said to His Wazir) in *al-Naqid*. These columns include sharp criticism of despotic Arab regimes; many of them were collected in *Amjad ya 'Arab amjad* (1986, Glories, O Arabs, Glories).

In 1994 Tamer published his sixth short-story collection, *Nida' Nuh* (Noah's Summons). It contains the seeds of stylistic changes that become more pronounced in his subsequent collections *Sanadhak* (1998, We shall Laugh) and *al-Husrum* (2000, Sour Grape). The stories in these books tend to be short and condensed and to contain a pronounced element of surprise. Simplistic dichotomies such as rulers versus ruled and good versus evil are replaced by a many-sided reality. The characters' inner worlds are no longer one-dimensional but are complex and tinged with neurosis.

The story "al-Sariq wa al-masruq" (The Stealer and the Stolen) in *Sanadhak* exemplifies many of the characteristics of Tamer's later work. On a stormy night an aging burglar chooses a suitable house to rob, breaks in, and starts searching for valuables. He notices a familiar picture on the wall and realizes that he is burglarizing his own home. He sits on one of his chairs and thinks about how he will soon be eligible for retirement benefits.

Tamer's later collections also break taboos concerning sexual relationships. In contrast to the patriarchal society Tamer described in his earlier works, women are now dominant, sexually aggressive, and dynamic. They express their sexual desires without regard to moral norms, and their encounters are daring and varied. For example, the opening of "al-Tatliq" (The Divorcée) in *al-Husrum* resembles the rape scenes in Tamer's early stories: a man armed with a knife is assaulting a seemingly defenseless woman in a deserted cemetery. But the "victim's" only fear is that he will tear her clothes; she calms down when the man assures her that he will only rip her underwear. She cooperates with the "rapist" and takes pleasure in the act, which takes place next to the tomb of the woman's husband. The husband "witnesses" the events from the beyond and calls on his widow to resist the "rapist" even at the cost of her life. Finally, betrayed and hurt, he divorces her—a meaningless gesture, since he is dead. For the widow, her own sexual pleasure takes precedence over her dead husband's honor. The sexual freedom Tamer allows women in his later stories is influenced by his residency in the more liberal atmosphere of Britain and reflects his desire to shake the foundations of traditional Arab society.

In 2002 Tamer received the prestigious Sultan Bin Ali Al Owais Foundation Cultural Award from the United Arab Emirates. According to the decision of the General Secretariat, Tamer

> is one of the most important Arab story writers and novelists whose works criticise society and politics. The criticism might take a symbolic or open form. His style is a mixture of bitter sarcasm and violent attack, without neglecting style that has no pretension at all. In his works, he tackles Arab events with the causes behind them.
>
> Tamer is capable of transforming the normal and familiar aspects of everyday life into something extremely exceptional.

After winning the award, Tamer visited Damascus. He was welcomed by leading personalities in Syria, and fes-

Front cover for al-Husrum *(Sour Grape), 2000 (R. W. Woodruff Library, Emory University)*

tivals were arranged in his honor. Syrian Television presented a series of thirty dramas based on his works.

Another volume of Tamer's satirical newspaper columns, *al-Qatil yahju qatilih* (The Victim's Satire of His Killer), appeared in 2003, followed in 2005 by the short-story collection *al-Qunfudh* (The Hedgehog). This latter is atypical for Tamer since all the stories describe the childhood experiences of the narrator. Some critics have treated it as an autobiographical novel.

Zakaria Tamer lives in Oxford with his wife, Nadia, and their two children. He continues to write satirical articles and short stories.

References:
'Abd al-Razzaq 'Id, *Al-'Alam al-qasasi li Zakaria Tamer* (Beirut: Dar al-Farabi, 1989);

Sabry Hafez, "The Modern Arabic Short Story," in *Modern Arabic Literature,* edited by Muhammad

Mustafa Badawi (Cambridge & New York: Cambridge University Press, 1992), pp. 270–328;

Mahmoud Kayyal, "Damascene Sharahzad: The Images of Women in Zakarriya Tamir's Short Stories," *Hawwa*, 4, no. 1 (2006): 93–113;

Husam al-Khateeb, "A Modern Syrian Short Story," *Journal of Arabic Literature*, 3 (1972): 96–105;

Yasin Kittani, "Tatawur mabna al-nass fi qisas Zakaria Tamer," M.A. thesis, Tel Aviv University, 1986;

Al-Mawqif al-adabi, special Tamer issue, 352 (2000);

Muhyi al-Din Muhammad, "Al-Jawad al-abyad wa zaman al-mararah," *al-Adab*, 11 (November 1960);

Al-Naqid, special Tamer issue, 82 (1995);

Al-Usbu' al-adabi, special Tamer issue, 766 (7 July 2001);

Baian Rayhanova, "Mythological and Folkloric Motifs in Syrian Prose: The Short Stories of Zakariyya Tamir," *Journal of Arabic and Islamic Studies*, 5 (2003): 1–12;

Imtinan al-Samadi, *Zakaria Tamer wa al-qissah al-qasirah* (Beirut: Al-Mu'asasah al-'Arabiyyah, 1995);

Emma Westney, "Individuation and Literature: Zakariyya Tamir and His Café Man," in *Marginal Voices in Literature and Society: Individual and Society in the Mediterranean Muslim World,* edited by Robin Ostle (Strasbourg: European Science Foundation, 2000), pp. 189–199.

Hasan al-Turabi
(1932 -)

Carol Bargeron
Central State University

BOOKS: *Al-Salah 'imad al-din* (Jadda: Al-Dar al-Sa'udiyyah li al-Nashr wa al-Tawzi', 1971);

Hawla wad' al-mar'ah fi al-Islam wa fi al-mujtama' al-Islami (N.p., 1973); translated as "On the Position of Women in Islam and Islamic Society," *Islam for Today* <www.islamfortoday.com/turabi01.htm> (accessed 17 October 2008);

Al-Iman: Atharuhu fi hayat al-insan (Kuwait City: Dar al-Qalam, 1974);

Mushkilat tatbiq al-Shari'ah al-Islamiyyah (Khartoum, 1978);

Al-Din wa al-tajdid (Tunisia: Dar al-Rayah, 1980);

Al-Harakah al-Islamiyyah wa al-tahdith, by al-Turabi and Rashid al-Ghanoushi (Beirut: Dar al-Jil / Khartoum: Maktabat dar al-Fikr, 1980);

Tajdid usul al-fiqh al-Islami (Beirut: Dar al-Jil / Khartoum: Maktabat dar al-Fikr, 1980);

Khitab al-ummah al-Islamiyyah al-Sudaniyyah ila ahl al-milal al-ukhra (Khartoum: Khartoum University Press, 1981);

Al-Muslim bayn al-wujdan wa al-sultan (Khartoum, 1981);

Qadaya al-hurriyyah wa al-wahdah; al-shura wa al-dimuqratiyyah; al-din wa al-fann (Jadda: Al-Dar al-Sa'udiyyah li al-Nashr wa al-Tawzi', 1987);

Qadaya al-tajdid: Nahwa manhaj usuli (Cairo: Al-Sharikah al-'Alamiyyah li Khidmat al-'Ilm, 1989);

Al-Harakah al-Islamiyyah fi al-Sudan: Al-Tatawwur wa al-kasb wa al-manhaj (Cairo: Al-Qari' al-'Arabi, 1991);

Tajdid al-fikr al-Islami (Rabat: Dar al-Qarafi li al-Nashr wa al-Tawzi', 1993);

Al-Mashru al-Islami al-Sudani (Khartoum: Ma'had al-Buhuth wa al-Dirasat al-Ijtima'iyyah, 1995);

Islam, avenir du monde: Entretiens avec Alain Chevalérias (Paris: J.-C. Lattès, 1997);

Al-Tafsir al-tawhidi (Khartoum: Hay'at al-A'mal al-Fikriyyah, 1998);

Al-Mar'ah bayna al-usul wa al-taqalid (Khartoum: Markaz Dirasat al-Mar'ah, 2000);

Al-Mustalahat al-siyasiyyah fi al-Islam (Beirut: Dar al-Saqi, 2000);

Al-Shura wa al-dimuqratiyyah (Khartoum: Alam al-Alamiyya, 2000);

Hasan al-Turabi (al-Ahram Weekly)

Al-Islamiyun wa al-mas'alah al-siyasiyyah (Beirut: Markaz Dirasat al-Wahdah al-'Arabiyyah, 2003);

Al-Siyasah wa al-Hukm: Al-Nuzum al-sultaniyyah bayna al-usul wa sunan al-waqi' (Beirut: Dar al-Saqi, 2003).

OTHER: "The Islamic State," in *Voices of Resurgent Islam,* edited by John L. Esposito (New York: Oxford University Press, 1983), pp. 241–252;

"Al-Bu'd al-alami li al-harakah al-Islamiyyah: Al-Tajruba al-Sudaniyyah," in *al-Harakah al-Islamiyyah: Ru'yah mustaqbaliyyah,* edited by Abdalla al-Nafisi (Cairo: Maktabat Madbuli, 1989).

SELECTED PERIODICAL PUBLICATIONS–
UNCOLLECTED: "Principles of Governance, Freedom, and Responsibility in Islam," *American Journal of Islamic Social Science,* 4, no. 1 (1987): 1–11;

"Hiwar m'a Hasan al-Turabi," *Qira'at siyasiyyah,* 2, no. 3 (1992): 5–32;

"Islam, Democracy, the State and the West," *Middle East Policy,* 1, no. 3 (1992): 49–61;

"The Case of Islamic Populism," *New Perspective Quarterly,* 10, no. 3 (1993): 42–51.

Hasan al-Turabi is one of the most charismatic intellectuals of the modern Muslim world. In Sudan, however, he is the second most important political and religious figure after Muhammad Ahmad al-Mahdi, the leader of the Mahdiyya uprising and the independent Sudanese state that it produced and that lasted until 1898. Since the middle of the twentieth century al-Turabi has propounded and worked to implement his vision of a just, egalitarian, and spiritually fulfilling society in Sudan and, in the wider Muslim world, a society that is free of the secularism and materialism of the modern West. His detractors are as repelled by that vision as his admirers are drawn to it. Widely traveled, broadly educated, literate in several languages, and conversant with world history, al-Turabi is an urbane and cosmopolitan Islamist thinker and activist whose ideas and activities have thrust him into high-level political positions, as well as into prison.

Hasan Abdallah Dafaallah al-Turabi was born in 1932 in Kassala, the capital of the eastern Sudanese state of the same name. His ancestors since the seventeenth century had been prominent in popular Sufism, law, and academia. As a *qadi* (religious-law court judge) and an expert in the study and application of the principles of Islamic jurisprudence *(faqih),* al-Turabi's father emphasized to his son the importance of studying Islam. Al-Turabi thus received a thorough traditional Islamic education before enrolling at Khartoum University, where he assisted in establishing al-Ikhwan al-Muslimin (the [Unified Sudanese] Muslim Brotherhood) in August 1954. He earned his law degree in 1955. After completing an M.A. in law at the University of London in 1957, he took a position as an assistant lecturer in the Faculty of Law at Khartoum University. In 1959 he began doctoral studies in law at the Sorbonne. During this period he traveled to the United States, where, he later maintained, "the natives never showed any interest in what I had to say. I would speak only to students of Arab, African, or Asian origin, whom I was always happy to meet." He completed his doctorate in law in 1964 with a dissertation on emergency powers in a constitutional democracy. Al-Turabi's education exemplifies a model that had become familiar in European colonies in the Islamic world since the early nineteenth century: the sons of well-placed families were given both a traditional and a "modern" education, so that they would be able to retain their families' leadership roles under either ruling system. Al-Turabi's admirers and critics have emphasized that his influence stems in part from his familiarity with both Islamic and Western traditions.

Al-Turabi became dean of the Faculty of Law at Khartoum University in 1964 but left the school the following year. In a 1994 interview he told Mohamed E. Hamdi: "the reason for retiring from university work might have been purely Sudanese considerations, but I should not have done so were my work to be limited to the Sudan. I was aware from the beginning that my interests would be both inside and outside the Sudan." That year he became the head of the Islamic Charter Front (ICF), an Islamist student group.

In his first book, *al-Salah 'imad al-din* (1971, Prayer: The Mainstay of Religion), al-Turabi argues that the separation of Islam from the state and its restriction to the realm of private faith enfeebles the abilities of Muslims to meet the *ibtila'* (challenges) of modern life. The state is so crucial to every aspect of individual and corporate life that its organization and functioning must not be left to secularists. Al-Turabi maintains that Muslims can understand the indispensable relationship between society and the state by seeing the *salah* (prayer) as a metaphor for the workings of government. Muslims must not retreat from government but must participate in it and shape it to serve the needs of a modernizing Muslim society.

In 1973 al-Turabi published the seminal *Hawla wad' al-mar'ah fi al-Islam wa fi al-mujtama' al-Islami* (translated as "On the Position of Women in Islam and Islamic Society," n.d.). In this pamphlet, which was widely disseminated in scholarly as well as in public circles, he observes that the inferior status of women in Muslim countries results from traditions that are alien or even hostile to the true model of Islam contained in the Qur'an and the *Sunna* (reports of the deeds of the Prophet). He argues that "segregation and isolation may well protect a woman from temptation, but it essentially denies her the benefits of the communal life of Muslims. It denies and abrogates her legitimate role in the social process of cooperation in the promotion of knowledge and good work." Patriarchal beliefs and actions not only distort the egalitarian message of Islam but also weaken the energies of Muslim men and women and thereby retard the growth of Muslim societies. According to al-Turabi, the unjust treatment of women is owed to many factors, among them men's lukewarm religious commitment and male ignobility, vanity, arrogance, and jealousy. Men use the "fantasy" of female incapacity "as an excuse to ban women from active participation in the broad spectrum of human life and to deprive them of experience and training–thereby devitalizing and debilitating them–and finding reason for further ill-treatment and prejudice." Often, juridical rules and stratagems were adopted to mold the *Sharia* (Islamic law) to suit un-Islamic customs and mores. Al-Turabi notes that "another tricky approach is to read liberally and to broaden the scope of rules granting authority to men, while reading literally and strictly those imposing limitations on women." The old values are "merely a legacy received from historical custom" that now serves as a yoke around the necks of Muslims, who must take up the challenge of revising and reinvigorating Islamic society. Islamists are urged by their own ideals to reform the traditional society and close the gap between historical reality and the model of ideal Islam.

In *al-Iman: Atharuhu fi hayat al-insan* (1974, Faith and Its Influence in Human Life) al-Turabi argues that the physical conduct of the prayer easily translates to matters of governance. For example, worshipers standing shoulder to shoulder symbolize a unified community that can defend itself against aggression, and the free choice and acceptance of the imam by the congregation signifies the election of political leaders, the duty to follow them, and the freedom to correct them should they make a mistake. When understood correctly, the model of prayer inculcates an egalitarian and democratic obligation to resist autocratic rule and to stand united in the face of attack.

Mushkilat tatbiq al-Shari'ah al-Islamiyyah (1978, The Challenge of Implementing Islamic Law) explores another central theme in al-Turabi's thinking about *tajdid wa islah* (renewal and reform) in Islam. By the early twelfth century the divorce of Islam from the state had left the traditional scholarly class, particularly the jurists, with little role to play in temporal governance; in the modern era colonialism restricted their activities to private family law. Neither the traditional religious elites nor the "effendis"–al-Turabi's term for secular leaders who had received a modern education–are able to meet the *ibtila'* of modern civilization. These *ibtila'* require collective efforts that, in turn, demand a broad distribution of knowledge and power. In *Mushkilat tatbiq al-Shari'ah al-Islamiyyah* he maintains that separation of the religious law courts and judges from the modern secular schools and the "effendis" they produce benefits both classes of elites. This dualism must be abolished in favor of an integrated state capable of grappling with the problems of contemporary Muslim societies.

As a result of al-Turabi's 1977 détente with the government of Sudanese president Jafar Numeiri, who had come to power in a coup d'état in 1969, the ICF emerged as the only legal political party in Sudan. It expanded geographically, its membership increased, and its adherents occupied significant positions in critical state institutions; al-Turabi became attorney general in 1979.

In three books published in 1980 al-Turabi revisited themes he had explored in his writings of the 1970s–not from his previous point of view, which had highlighted where Muslims had gone wrong, but from the perspective of the pragmatic reorientation of Islam toward the state. He laid out a fairly detailed vision of how an Islamic state should be organized, governed, and operated and, most critically, why one was needed. In *al-Din wa al-tajdid* (Religion and Renewal) he argues that since religion is a potent force for societal change, it must be renewed and revitalized. Governance requires innovative responses to modern *ibtila'*. The solutions, however, cannot come from those who are mired in religious conservatism and envision a return to "Pristine Medina." In *al-Haraka al-Islamiyyah wa al-tahdith* (The Islamic Movement and Modernization) he accuses those who believe in the inevitable degradation of Islam from the ideal age of the Prophet and the Rashidun caliphate–an era that ended in 661–of using their veneration of the past as an excuse to avoid the *ibtila'* of the present. Repetition of the past is a "backward-looking" strategy that leaves the current generation of Muslims leaderless and voiceless. In an increasingly globalized world Islamists must take the initiative in guiding reform before alien trends are assimilated. Al-Turabi elaborates on the theme of "authentication" in "al-Islam wa nizam al-Hukm" (Islam and the Ordering of Governance), an essay included in *al-Haraka al-Islamiyya wa al-tahdith*, in which he notes that political liberalism and modern political parties are an "ordained failure" and that the "prevalent nonreligious traditions of Western rule" account for this lack of success. Interpretive extension of traditional Islamic concepts will enhance the ability of Muslims to govern themselves. Islam is thus eminently consonant with democracy. Finally, in *Tajdid usul al-fiqh al-Islami* (Renewal of the Fundamental Principles of Islamic Jurisprudence) al-Turabi argues that Muslims cannot simply cling to the decisions of medieval jurists:

> the science of the classical origins [of the Law] through which we seek to find guidance is no longer suitable to satisfy our contemporary needs on a full scale. The reason is that it is a science influenced by the impact of the historical circumstances in which it had grown up, even more so by the nature of the juristic problems encountered in the jurisprudence of the time.... The jurists were not tackling, for the most part, problems of the public life. Thus the public life evolved away from them.... Therefore, the fundamentals of jurisprudence moved to a concern with rituals, marriage, and divorce. The questions of the comprehensive legal policy were issues in which the responsible leaders were not inter-

ested. These included the processes of production, distribution, importation, exportation, and the treatment of a high cost of living or depressing it. Nor did the leaders seek the advice of jurists to provide them with the necessary jurisprudence on these matters. Likewise, the questions of the public economy and political conditions were equally ignored.

In *Tajdid usul al-fiqh al-Islami* al-Turabi deals in only the most general terms with the situation of non-Muslims within an Islamic constitutional framework. He does suggest autonomous rule for the Christians and animists in southern Sudan "to preserve for them the type of governance for which they have long yearned" and says that their religious, cultural, and political freedoms must be fully guaranteed.

In *al-Muslim bayn al-wujdan wa al-sultan* (1981, The Muslim between Consciousness and Power) al-Turabi explains his alliance with the Numeiri regime as a policy of "positive engagement" with the state. His *Khitab al-ummah al-Islamiyyah al-Sudaniyyah ila ahl al-milal al-ukhra* (1981, The Sudanese Muslim Community and the People of Other Sects) explores several procedural implications and difficulties attached to religion-based governance in a plural state.

In "The Islamic State" (1983) al-Turabi again argues that Islam must not try to separate religion from the state. He points out that by lacking access to the state, Muslims have lost the most powerful means for facilitating societal change. Properly educated and possessing modern skills, Muslims must engage in every legitimate type of activity, and each must be done with the proper Muslim religious intention, which, in summary form, enjoins "commanding the right and forbidding the wrong." This obligation is a communal one; it is not exclusive to the "men of religion."

Government-sponsored Islamization of Sudan began in September 1983, when traditional *Sharia* penalties were incorporated into the penal code; the policy provoked civil warfare that continued for twenty-one years. For al-Turabi, the revival and reinterpretation of authentic Islamic concepts—such as *shura*, *ijtihad* (interpretive initiative), *ijma* (consensus), *bay'* (contract), *ikhtilafat* (the right of interpretation), *dhimma* (minorities), and *hisba* (commanding the right and forbidding evil)—as well as of Bedouin tribal practices that foster an indigenous form of "democracy" are critically important if participatory government and societal openness are to take root in a non-Western intellectual soil. *Din* (religion) and *tadayn* (religiosity) must be distinguished from one another, so that the present generations of Muslims may practice *ijtihad* of the *usul al-fiqh* (principles of Islamic jurisprudence). Without that ability, Islam and its practitioners are left defenseless in the new age. The idea of *ijtihad* as a tool for reshaping the traditions of Islam by rethinking its fundamentals did not originate with al-Turabi; it was first employed by Jamal al-din al-Afghani and his successor, Sheikh Muhammad 'Abduh, in the nineteenth century. Al-Turabi, however, broadens the community of those who possess the right to exercise *ijtihad;* he told Hamdi, "I believe that *ijtihad* is open to every Muslim, no matter how ignorant or illiterate he or she might be. Everyone can exercise *ijtihad*, even if only to make a small contribution." Thus, Islamism's abiding goal, the establishment of *hakimiyyat Allah* (God's governance), does not necessarily lead to totalitarian rule. Ahmed S. Moussalli maintains that according to al-Turabi, any government that operates according to Islamic principles is intrinsically *dimuqrati* (democratic) because the ruler acknowledges his responsibility and accountability to the people when he accepts the *bay'* the representatives of the people offer him; the *bay'* functions as a contract between ruler and ruled. Moreover, the ruler must consult with and accept advice from others: the duty of *shura* is designed to restrict authoritarian governance.

The National Islamic Front (NIF) emerged in 1985 from a reorganization of the ICF. A military coup ousted Numeiri and dissolved his Sudan Socialist Union in April 1986. In elections that year a coalition of Islamist groups, including the NIF and several southern parties, came to power, and Sadiq al-Mahdi, al-Turabi's brother-in-law, became prime minister.

Al-Turabi has devoted several texts to a comparative examination of Islamic and Western ideas of popular participation. He argues in *Qadaya al-hurriyyah wa al-wahdah; al-shura wa al-dimuqratiyyah; al-din wa al-fann* (1987, The Way to Freedom and Reawakening; Consultation and Democracy; Religion and Discipline) that Islam democratically binds leaders to "the people" and naturally opposes despotism. Equality, freedom, and justice are cardinal Islamic virtues; during the history of Islam, however, these virtues have been variously formulated and suffered many abuses. Muslims must reinterpret the source texts of Islam and extend the meanings of basic concepts to show that the *Sharia* is capable of comprehending and encompassing ideas such as human rights, pluralism, and democracy.

In his article "Principles of Governance, Freedom, and Responsibility in Islam" (1987) al-Turabi notes that "the problem of non-Muslim minorities within a Muslim state is nothing new." A guiding precept from the *umma*'s early history is that non-Muslims have a guaranteed right to many freedoms, including the professing and defense of their religious convictions and "even to criticize Islam and engage in a dialogue with Muslims. . . . They also have the right to regulate their private life, education and family life by adopting their own family laws." Al-Turabi asserts that non-Muslims have the right to claim the incompatibility of any rule within the *Sharia* with their religion and can be absolved from obeying it. As a corollary of the rights of non-Muslims, Muslims are required to relate positively to those who are not their co-religionists: "it is more than a matter of toleration and legal immunity. Muslims have a moral obligation to be fair and friendly in their person-to-person conduct toward non-Muslim citizens, and will be answerable to Allah for that. They must treat them with trust, beneficence, and equity."

Al-Turabi's NIF turned against al-Mahdi and supported a coup at the end of June 1989 that brought a military junta to power with Omar Hasan al-Bashir as president, chief of state, prime minister, and commander in chief of the armed forces. A civilian cabinet assisted the junta. Al-Bashir widened the application of the policy of state Islamization that Numeiri had implemented.

While many of his Islamist colleagues wanted to replace the state as an "un-Islamic entity," al-Turabi sought to guide the powers of the state toward the achievement of Muslim objectives. He argues in *al-Haraka al-Islamiyyah fi al-sudan: al-Tatawwur wa al-kasb wa al-manhaj* (1991, The Islamic Movement in Sudan: Conceptualization, Achievement, Curricular Program) that his alliance with Numeiri illustrates the same shrewd pragmatism—working with the state while simultaneously opposing it—that is exemplified by Joseph in Sura 12 of the Qur'an. The comparison struck some critics as prideful arrogance bordering on megalomania. In *al-Haraka al-Islamiyya fi al-Sudan* al-Turabi also emphasizes the importance of an education not only in the *Sharia* but also in modern physical, technological, and social science. Education cannot serve only the purpose of enhancing personal piety; all professions and forms of knowledge must interact with and reinforce each other to meet the challenges of the modern age. Al-Turabi has been harshly criticized for advocating the democratization of knowledge and the abolition of the monopoly held by the men of religion over the production of the *fiqh*. In *Tajdid al-fikr al-Islami* (1993, Renewal of Islamic Speculative Thought) al-Turabi calls for the creation of a popular *fiqh* (jurisprudence) in which the members of the *umma* (Muslim community) provide legal legitimacy by exercising their legislative rights in *shura* (consultation) bodies.

The National Congress Party was founded in 1998 by former members of the NIF and some other politicians, and al-Turabi was elected secretary general. The Islamist-military alliance had been unraveling for several years, and on 12 December 1999 al-Bashir declared a state of emergency, suspended the Constitution, and sent troops to intimidate the National Assembly. Al-Turabi was imprisoned, losing the influence he had exerted over the Sudanese government as speaker of Parliament and constitutional successor in case of the president's demise or incapacitation. In late January 2000 a reconciliation was reached between al-Turabi and al-Bashir, and their powers and responsibilities were divided. In early May, however, al-Turabi and his supporters were ousted from their positions, and he was briefly placed under arrest. In August he left the NCP to form the Popular National Congress (PNC). On 20 February 2001 the PNC signed a "memorandum of understanding" with John Garang de Mabior, head of the Sudan People's Liberation Movement. During periods of imprisonment and house arrest al-Turabi produced five books on women, Islamic political acculturation, the compatibility of *shura* and democracy, Islamism and the common good, and politics and governance that were published between 2000 and 2003; each expands on or qualifies positions he formulated in earlier works.

Al-Turabi has not yet laid out a precisely delineated theory of the Islamic state, with detailed descriptions of the roles and functions to be allotted to various groups. To some extent, his personal charisma has papered over the delicate problems of institutionalizing an Islamic government in a religiously and culturally diverse nation. His forceful and charming personality and single-mindedness have also prompted criticism that a self-cultivated "cult of personality" surrounds him and that, contrary to his deprecation of the title "Sheikh," he enjoys the sort of reverence that accompanies the title. Reflecting these criticisms, the Islamist movement in Sudan has been referred to as "harakat al-Turabi" (al-Turabi's movement).

Hasan al-Turabi has devoted his life to a reconstruction and revivification of Islam and a new Islamist polity that will lead to an orderly, egalitarian, prosperous, participatory, and godly society. By elaborating what Abdullahi Ali Ibrahim calls a "theology of modernity," he has endeavored to lay out a path along which Muslims and non-Muslims may walk together. He is committed to rethinking not the spirit but the traditionally received legacy of his faith so that a flexible and modernized Islam may meet contemporary internal and global challenges.

Interviews:

Mohamed E. Hamdi, *The Making of an Islamic Political Leader: Conversations with Hasan al-Turabi,* translated by Asher A. Shamis (Boulder, Colo.: Westview Press, 1998).

References:

Abdullahi Ali Ibrahim, "A Theology of Modernity: Hasan al-Turabi and Islamic Renewal in Sudan," *Africa Today,* 46 (June 1999): 52–63;

Ahmad S. Moussalli, "Hasan al-Turabi's Islamist Discourse on Democracy and Shura," *Middle Eastern Studies,* 30 (January 1994): 194–222.

Latifa al-Zayyat

(8 August 1923 – 10 September 1996)

Ellen McLarney
Duke University

BOOKS: *Al-Bab al-maftuh* (Cairo: Al-Hay'ah al-Misriyyah al-'Ammah li al-Kitab, 1960); translated by Marilyn Booth as *The Open Door* (Cairo & New York: American University in Cairo Press, 2000);

Al-Shaykhukhah wa-qisas ukhra (Cairo: Dar al-Mustaqbal al-'Arabi, 1986);

Min suwar al-mar'ah fi al-qisas wa-al-riwayat al-'Arabiyyah (Cairo: Dar al-Thaqafah al-Jadidah, 1989);

Najib Mahfuz, al-surah wa-al-mithal: Maqalat naqdiyyah (Cairo: Majallat al-Ahali, 1989);

Hamlat taftish: Awraq shakhsiyyah (Cairo: Dar al-Hilal, 1992); translated by Sophie Bennett as *The Search: Personal Papers* (London: Quartet, 1996);

Bay'wa-shira': Masrahiyyah fi thalath fusul (Cairo: Al-Hay'ah al-Misriyyah al-'Ammah li al-Kitab, 1994);

Sahib al-bayt (Cairo: Dar al-Hilal, 1994); translated by Bennett as *The Owner of the House* (London: Quartet, 1997);

Adwa': Dirasat naqdiyah (Cairo: Al-Hay'ah al-Misriyyah al-'Ammah li al-Kitab, 1995);

Al-Rajul al-ladhi 'arafa tuhmatah (Cairo: Dar al-Sharqiyat li al-Nashr wa-al-Tawzi', 1995);

Ford Madox Ford wa al-hadathah (Cairo: Al-Hay'ah al-Misriyyah al-'Ammah li al-Kitab, 1996).

OTHER: T. S. Eliot, *Maqalat naqdiyyah,* translated by al-Zayyat (Cairo: Maktabat al-Anglo, 1962);

Kull hadha al-sawt al-jamil: Mukhtarat qisasiyyah li katibat 'Arabiyyat, edited by al-Zayyat (Cairo: Dar al-Mar'ah al-'Arabiyyah, 1994);

"On Political Commitment and Feminist Writing," in *The View from Within: Writers and Critics on Contemporary Arabic Literature,* edited by Ferial J. Ghazoul and Barbara Harlow (Cairo: American University in Cairo Press, 1994), pp. 246–260;

Karl Marx, *Hawl al-fann, ru'yah markisiyyah, tarjamah wa ta'liq,* translated, with commentary, by al-Zayyat (Cairo: Markaz al-Buhuth al-'Arabiyyah, 1995).

Latifa al-Zayyat's first novel, *al-Bab al-maftuh* (1960; translated as *The Open Door,* 2000), opens on 21 February 1946, the day the National Committee of Students and Workers organized a massive strike and demonstration against the British occupation of Egypt. The British had withdrawn from Cairo and the Nile Delta area in 1923 but had retained control over the Suez Canal, one of Egypt's crucial economic and strategic resources. The protestors marched across Cairo to deliver their resolutions at the palace. As the general secretary of the National Committee of Students and Workers, al-Zayyat had helped orchestrate these events. Joel Beinin and Zachary Lockman call "Evacuation Day," as the protest is known, "the climax of the nationalist agitation" that laid the groundwork for the Free Officers' Revolution of July 1952 that toppled the Egyptian monarchy. In the novel al-Zayyat synthesizes Marxism, feminism, and nationalism and writes of her own struggle for self-determination in terms of the era's political battles.

Al-Zayyat was born on 8 August 1923 in the Nile Delta town of Damietta into what had been a family of wealthy merchants. Her paternal grandfather had inherited six ships that traded with the Levant, while her grandmother's family owned a textile factory and large tracts of agricultural land. Al-Zayyat's father left his engineering studies to join the shipping business when he was sixteen; but as ship after ship foundered in the shallow port of Damietta, the family's wealth declined and was ultimately wiped out. Al-Zayyat's father left the business and became a civil servant.

In her memoirs, *Hamlat taftish: Awraq shakhsiyyah* (1992; translated as *The Search: Personal Papers,* 1996), al-Zayyat describes the plunge in the family's status through the changing architecture of their home in Damietta. She knew of the past glories of the house from her grandmother's tales of crystal chandeliers, mirrors imported from Belgium, Persian carpets, marble tables, and furniture inlaid with mother-of-pearl. By the time al-Zayyat was born, the house had become crowded with relatives, and additions had been constructed to accommodate them; the garden was filled with snakes, weeds, and barren fruit trees, and wildflowers were breaking down its walls. Al-Zayyat describes the house as "a tombstone of an era that had come to an end." Like the garden, the roof features prominently in al-Zayyat's descriptions of the house. Because she was forbidden to go there, it became, in her imagination, a treasured place—a site of freedom where she could burst into laughter, sing, and skip and jump. The family moved to Mansoura when al-Zayyat was six, but she returned to the "old house" during the summers.

Like the roof of the old house in Damietta, the roof of the family's new home in Mansoura was a place the child was forbidden to go; her grandmother paced "like a sentry" in front of the entrance to the roof, but al-Zayyat occasionally managed to sneak up to it. The young poet Muhammad 'Abd al-Mu'ti al-Hamshari inhabited a small room constructed on the roof, and al-Zayyat remembers sitting in the corner of the room, admiring the poet for hours on end as he worked at his desk. In the translator's introduction to *The Open Door* Marilyn Booth interprets this scene in the memoirs as symbolic of the elevated place of writing, of the freedom it affords, and of the position of the male writer: "Sitting above her," Booth writes, "he is the sign of centrality, of 'high' literature, the scion of a longstanding tradition of poetic composition." The girl sits in the corner of the room, at the edges of this world, looking in.

In her memoirs al-Zayyat attributes her political awakening to a demonstration she witnessed in Mansoura at age eleven. The demonstrators were rallying around the visit of Mustafa al-Nahhas, leader of the nationalist Wafd party; from the balcony of her home she watched the police open fire on them, killing twenty-four: "I abandon the child in me and the girl comes of age before her time, weighed down with a knowledge wider than the limits of the house, a knowledge that includes the entire nation."

Al-Zayyat's father died when she was twelve, and she moved to Cairo with her mother; her younger sister, Safiyyah; and her older brothers, 'Abd al-Fattah and Muhammad. As a student at Fu'ad I University from 1942 to 1946 al-Zayyat became the general secretary of the National Committee of Students and Workers. Referring to herself in the third person, al-Zayyat describes in her memoirs "the way this girl developed.... She stood up to deliver speeches, her voice ringing out on the steps of the university's administrative building, on the doorstep of the Faculty of Law, in the corridor of the Great Hall . . . from the girl who bore her womanly body as if it were a sin into that tough, liberated young woman, so full of vigorous protest." She also joined the communist Iskra Party, of which her first husband (his name, the date of their marriage, and the date of their divorce do not appear in biographical sources) was a

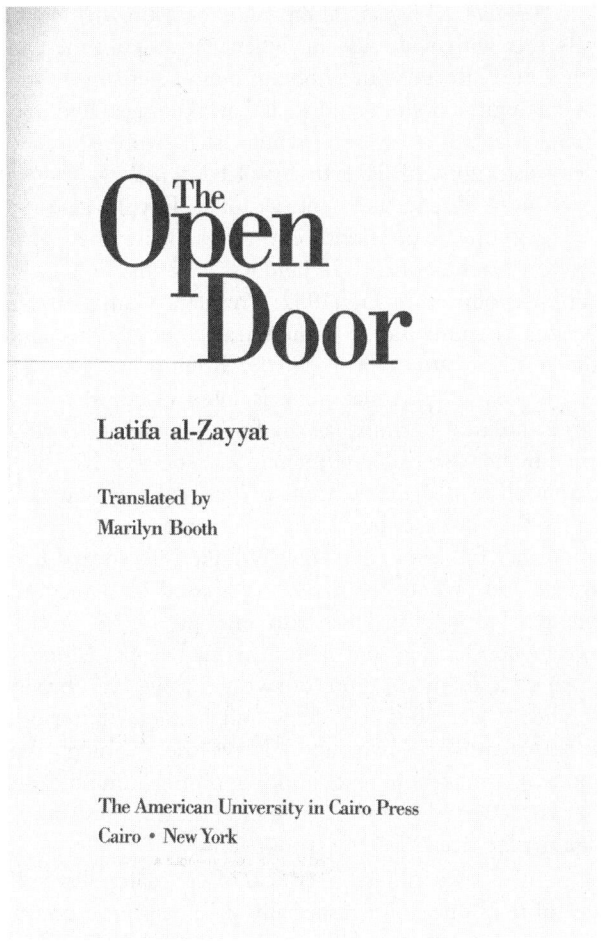

Title page for the English translation, 2000, of Latifa al-Zayyat's first novel, al-Bab al-maftuh, published in 1960 (Thomas Cooper Library, University of South Carolina)

member of the group. Selma Botman quotes al-Zayyat as explaining that "What appealed to me very much in Marxism . . . was the ethics . . . the absence of discrimination in religion, race, and sex." Al-Zayyat's husband was arrested in 1948 under the martial law imposed after the war in Palestine. He escaped, and he and al-Zayyat were fugitives until they were caught by the military police in 1949. Al-Zayyat was sentenced to three years in prison but released after six months of solitary confinement; her husband was sentenced to seven years.

In 1952 al-Zayyat married Rashad Rushdi, the first Egyptian to head the English department at Cairo University; he was a prolific literary critic, playwright, and short-story writer and a conservative ideologue. Al-Zayyat completed a doctorate in English literature at the university in 1957 and took a position as professor of English at the Girls' School of 'Ain Shams University in Cairo; a few years later she became chairperson of the English department.

Al-Bab al-maftuh, al-Zayyat's best-known work, was met with wide acclaim when it was published in 1960. It is infused with autobiographical elements, combining a girl's political and sexual awakenings. The heroine, Layla, is eleven when she witnesses the demonstrations of 21 February 1946. *Al-Bab al-maftuh* goes on to chart a turbulent decade in Egypt's history: the resistance to the British in the canal zone; the Cairo Fire on Black Saturday, 26 January 1952; the Free Officers' Revolution in July 1952; President Gamal Abdel Nasser's nationalization of the Suez Canal in 1956; and the resulting attack on Egypt by Britain, France, and Israel. Layla's personal story is intertwined with this larger political narrative as she finds her passion awakened by her dedication to the nationalist cause. Her participation in a demonstration is unmistakably sensual, as al-Zayyat describes Layla's "embarrassed shyness about her full body. . . . The rhythmic yells surged like waves and abated, the first wave chased by a second, the pair coming together into one swell . . . bodies everywhere, rising and falling in mad leaps. Mouths open wide to shout, drops of sweat glinting on a broad forehead, feet pounding, flags and banners fluttering, tears streaming down, and always the pushing, the pushing, on and on." Her budding desire culminates in her attraction to Husayn, a soldier in the Suez resistance against the British.

Al-Zayyat is harshly critical of the materialist values of the bourgeoisie, especially with respect to courtship. The negative example of Layla's cousin Gamilah consumes a large part of the narrative: Gamilah is seduced into marriage by promises of a generous dowry, an automobile, a diamond ring, a refrigerator, a butane gas stove, pink lace, and a villa near the Pyramids; when she wavers, her mother mentions a girl "who'd married for love but then had failed in her marriage, because after all, material security was the foundation of every successful union." The prospective groom is fat and vulgar, but the mother says that "a man's only shame is his pocket." Layla fumes that girls are being sold like slaves at a market, dressed up to attract the highest bidder. Moreover, it is a market saturated with foreign commodities and values, expressed by foreign words such as *chiffon, dentelle* (lace), *villa, Ford, solitaire,* and *Frigidaire.* The novel closes with Layla and Husayn fighting side by side in Port Said after Nasser's nationalization of the canal.

Al-Bab al-maftuh represents the culmination of the "nationalist romance" genre that emerged when Egyptians began clamoring for independence at the turn of the twentieth century. In these works allegorical love scenarios symbolize a love/hate relationship with modernity and Western influence. Al-Zayyat's novel is distinguished from those of her predecessors by her frank depiction of female desire and awakening sexuality.

Al-Bab al-maftuh was published, however, at a time when critical currents were running against romanticism: with the professed socialism of the Nasser era, realism became the favored literary trend; romanticism was condemned as mere entertainment for the bourgeoisie. Al-Zayyat uses two main techniques to inject the novel with a sense of realism: vivid accounts of historical events and lifelike dialogue that makes liberal use of Egyptian dialect.

Al-Zayyat dedicates the semiautobiographical *al-Bab al-maftuh* to Rushdi, "my teacher"; perhaps significantly, Layla's teacher is one of the most unsympathetic characters in the novel. Cold, supercilious, and traditional, he disdains her political activities and treats her condescendingly.

Al-Zayyat published a translation of T. S. Eliot's literary criticism in 1962. She divorced Rushdi in 1965. In her memoirs she writes about her pain at his unfaithfulness, although she claims that their final separation resulted from "deeper and more complicated" causes than his infidelities. Their highly publicized divorce led one journalist to remark that while al-Zayyat held a doctorate, she had failed elementary school in being a wife. Another journalist, with leftist leanings, said that she understood why al-Zayyat divorced the conservative Rushdi but not why she had married him. Al-Zayyat's answer was "sex." She writes in her memoirs, "He was the first man to awaken the woman in me."

After *al-Bab al-maftuh,* al-Zayat did not publish another literary work for twenty-six years. She was head of the Department of Dramatic Criticism at the Higher Institute of the Arts, director of the Egyptian Academy of the Arts, and a member of the Union of Egyptian Writers; served on committees to grant state prizes for novels and short stories; and worked in broadcasting, publishing, and journalism, writing a column for the women's journal *Hawa'* in the late 1960s. She was also a member of the Union of Palestinian Writers and Egypt's representative to the Palestine National Council. In the wake of the 1979 Camp David Peace Accords between Egypt and Israel she became head of the Committee for the Defense of National Culture, which challenged Sadat's policies.

In 1981 President Anwar Sadat rounded up intellectuals of all ideological stripes who criticized his government and, especially, the normalization of relations with Israel. Al-Zayyat was incarcerated in Qanatir prison with some of the most celebrated women of the Egyptian intelligentsia, including the feminist writer Nawal El Saadawi, the Islamist Safinaz Kazim, professor of French literature Aminah Rashid, the journalist 'Awatif 'Abd al-Rahman, and the Nasserist Shahinda

Maqlad. The prisoners were released later that year, after Sadat was assassinated and Hosni Mubarak succeeded him as president.

The title piece of al-Zayyat's collection *al-Shaykhukhah wa-qisas ukhra* (1986, Old Age and Other Stories) is a meditation on the difficulties of writing in the form of a diary. The narrator is a novelist in her fifties who is suffering from writer's block:

> I am striving for a perfection for which I don't have the ability, or a perfection that doesn't exist in this world. I leave one work and strive for another, with the hope that it will be better. Beginnings proliferate, beginnings after beginnings, not one written for completion. I am working against myself, not for myself.

The narrator dreams of a desk stuffed with sheaves of papers. Is it the past weighing her down, she wonders, or the future works she will compose? In the end she concludes that she will fill the white papers "to reclaim the terms of my language."

In 1989 al-Zayyat published a collection of essays, *Min suwar al-mar'ah fi al-qisas wa-al-riwayat al-'Arabiyyah* (From Images of Woman in Arabic Stories and Novels), and *Najib Mahfuz, al-surah wa al-mithal: Maqalat naqdiyyah* (Naguib Mahfouz, Image and Ideal: Critical Essays), treating the works of the Nobel laureate. Al-Zayyat's memoirs, *Hamlat taftish*, appeared in 1992. It is a loose amalgam of unfinished pieces; the subtitle, *Awraq shakhsiyyah* (Personal Papers), accurately reflects the sense the book conveys of being an archive of fragments rather than a completed work. The memoirs begin in March 1973 as her brother 'Abd al-Fattah is dying of an illness: "I push away death as I sit writing what seems to be an autobiography not destined to be completed." Al-Zayyat launches into a lengthy reflection on her family history, childhood, and first home; the narrative thread then suddenly jumps to the 1967 Arab defeat by the Israelis, linking this national disappointment to a personal one, her divorce from her second husband. The second part of *Hamlat taftish* begins with al-Zayyat's arrest and confinement in Qanatir Prison in 1981. She scoffs at the charade of a fifty-eight-year-old woman being escorted to jail, surrounded by police "armed to the teeth"; even the policemen laugh at the absurdity of the scenario. She describes the experience as a flourishing, using the metaphor of a tree blossoming within and beyond the prison walls. Thought, she asserts, cannot be imprisoned.

After her divorce in 1965, al-Zayyat had composed a play, *Bay' wa-shira'* (Buying and Selling), but she did not publish it until 1994. As a man lies dying in the hospital, the members of his wealthy family obsess about their shares of the inheritance. Meanwhile, he is

Dust jacket for the English translation, 1996, of al-Zayyat's 1992 memoir, Hamlat taftish: Awraq shakhsiyyah *(University of California Libraries)*

cut off from the daughter who truly loves him; she is disdained by the other family members, who will not allow the father to see her. The play has been interpreted as a veiled critique of Nasser, who became estranged from his "true love," the masses, toward the end of his career and became too weak to defy the demands of the middle class.

Sahib al-bayt (1994; translated as *The Owner of the House*, 1997), al-Zayyat's only novel other than *al-Bab al-maftuh*, fictionalizes her life in hiding with her first husband in 1949. After the narrator's husband escapes from prison, the two assume false identities and move into a cramped apartment with a friend. The three live in a state of paranoia, evading the probing eye of the landlord, the "owner of the house," who constantly reminds them of his watchful eye. "All day and all night, I see you," he says. In the courtyard of the house is a tower with round openings; it is a dove coop, but the narrator sees it as an observation tower with "eyes

. . . drilling into my back." The sense of surveillance oppresses the inhabitants of the house, turning it into a kind of prison. The novel symbolically criticizes the censorship and repression of the Egyptian intelligentsia, a situation that did not end with the 1952 revolution.

The sense of oppression that pervades *Sahib al-bayt* is existential as well as political. The narrator constantly experiences feelings of entrapment, helplessness, and paralysis. She asks, "Who am I?" as the cracked mirror no longer reflects her image, her clothes no longer fit, and she assumes the false identity. "Everyone who came into this house, apparently, must play a role, the role assigned him by the owner of the house," she says. Her relationship with her husband has deteriorated into a playing of roles devoid of passion. She continually asks, "Why am I here?" since the men have no use for her presence.

The theme of imprisonment resurfaces frequently in al-Zayyat's writing. "Kalimat al-sirr" (The Secret Word), one of the pieces in her final work of fiction, the 1995 short-story collection *Al-Rajul al-ladhi 'arafa tuhmatah* (The Man Who Knew His Accusation), uses a prison door as its central metaphor. In her memoirs al-Zayyat writes that she has always been interested in showing that "the most cruel prison is the one in which the individual imprisons himself, and that the most cruel form of oppression is that which is self-imposed." Also in 1995 al-Zayyat published a translation of Karl Marx's essays on art and *Adwa': Dirasat naqdiyyah* (Lights: Critical Studies), in which she discusses leading "lights" of Egyptian literature such as Mahfouz, Selwa Bakr, Muhammad al-Bisati, Sun'allah Ibrahim, 'Abd al-Rahman al-Sharqawi, and Tawfiq Hakim. In 1996 she published *Ford Madox Ford wa al-hadathah* (Ford Madox Ford and Modernism). She was awarded the State Prize for Literature shortly before her death on 10 September of that year.

Latifa al-Zayyat is a pioneering figure in Egyptian literature because of her stylistic experimentation, expansion of women's roles, and unwavering political commitment and activism. She began as a shy girl, unsure of herself and ashamed of her body, but transformed herself into a leader of literary, political, and cultural movements.

Interviews:

"Latifa al-Zayyat, al-katib wa al-hurriyah," *Fusul,* 10 (Fall 1992): 237–239;

"Latifa al-Zayyat fi mir'at Latifa al-Zayyat," *Ibda',* 1 (January 1993): 54–58.

References:

Al-Adab wa-al-Naqd, special al-Zayyat issue, 106 (June 1994);

Amal Amireh, "Remembering Latifa al-Zayyat," *Al-Jadid: A Review and Record of Arab Culture and Arts,* 2 (October 1996);

Sayyid al-Bahrawi and others, *Latifa al-Zayyat: Al-adab wa al-watan* (Cairo: Dar al-Mara'ah al-'Arabiyyah li al-Nashr, 1997);

Joel Beinin and Zachary Lockman, *Workers on the Nile: Nationalism, Communism, Islam, and the Egyptian Working Class: 1882–1954* (Princeton: Princeton University Press, 1987), pp. 340–362, 412–417;

Selma Botman, *Engendering Citizenship in Egypt* (New York: Columbia University Press, 1999), pp. 42–47;

Ferial Jaburi Ghazoul, "Idiyulujiyat binyat al-qass, Latifa al-Zayyat namudhaj," *Fusul,* 12 (Spring 1993): 108–119;

Safinaz Kazim, *Al-Kitabah: Ru'a wa dhat* (Cairo: Al-Hay'ah al-Misriyyah al-'Ammah li al-Kitab, 2003), pp. 145–156;

Ilyas Khoury, "Al-Shahid al-Shahid, tahiyah ila Latifa al-Zayyat," *Al-Tariq* (November–December 1995);

Magda al-Nowaihi, "Resisting Silence in Arab Women's Autobiographies," *International Journal of Middle East Studies,* 33 (2001): 477–502;

Joseph T. Zeidan, *Arab Women Novelists: The Formative Years and Beyond* (New York: State University of New York Press, 1995), pp. 165–170.

Constantine K. Zurayk

(18 April 1909 – 12 August 2000)

Noomane Raboudi
University of Ottawa

BOOKS: *Al-Yazidiyyah qadiman wa hadithan* (Beirut: Al-Matba'ah al-Kathulikiyyah, 1934);

Al-Wa'y al-qawmi (Beirut: Dar al-Makshuf, 1939);

Ma'na al-nakbah (Beirut: Dar al-'Ilm li al-Malayin, 1948); translated by R. Bayly Winder as *The Meaning of the Disaster* (Beirut: Khayat's College Book Cooperative, 1956);

Ayyu ghadin (Beirut: Dar al-'Ilm li al-Malayin, 1957);

Nahnu wa al-tarikh (Beirut: Dar al-'Ilm li al-Malayin, 1959);

Hadha al-'asr al-mutafajjir (Beirut: Dar al-'Ilm li al-Malayin, 1963);

Fi m'rakat al-hadarah (Beirut: Dar al-'Ilm li al-Malayin, 1964);

Ma'na al-nakbah mujadadan (Beirut: Dar al-'Ilm li al-Malayin, 1967);

Nahnu wa al-mustaqbal (Beirut: Dar al-'Ilm li al-Malayin, 1977);

Tensions in Islamic Civilization (Washington, D.C.: Center for Contemporary Arab Studies, Georgetown University, 1978);

Matalib al-mustaqbal al-'Arabi (Beirut: Dar al-'Ilm li al-Malayin, 1983);

Al-A'mal al fikriyyah al-'ammah li al-ductur Constantine Zurayk, 4 volumes (Beirut: Markaz Dirasat al-Wihda al-'Arabiyyah, 1994).

TRANSLATION: Ahmad ibn-Muhammad Miskawayh, *The Refinement of Character: A Translation from the Arabic of Ahmad ibn-Muhammad Miskawayh's* Tahdhib al-Akhlaq (Beirut: American University of Beirut, 1968).

Constantine K. Zurayk (from Hisham Nashabe, ed., Studia Palaestina: Studies in Honor of Constantine K. Zurayk, *1988; Thomas Cooper Library, University of South Carolina)*

Constantine K. Zurayk was one of the central intellectual figures of the contemporary Arab nationalist movement. He had many titles, including educator, reformer, diplomat, and administrator, as he divided his time between the Middle East and the West throughout his long and influential career. His double specialization in history and philosophy provided him with the tools to determine the historical origins, dimensions, and dangers of the political, economic, and cultural doldrums into which the Arab world has been plunged for several centuries. He was one of the first to call attention to the glorification of the past that is symptomatic of many contemporary voices in the Arab world, and he argued that the psychological weight of this heritage evidences itself in the work of many Muslim Arab reformers. One of the most ardent defenders of the idea of progress in contemporary Arab culture, Zurayk critiqued the cultural foundations of Arab-Muslim civilization in works that have been translated into many languages and continue to exert an influence on scholars.

Zurayk argued that the basis of the Israeli-Palestinian conflict was a confrontation between the assertion of two opposed rights: on the one hand, the legitimate rights of the Palestinians, which were betrayed by the powerlessness, decadence, and underdevelopment of the Arab world, and, on the other, the fictitious and illegitimate rights claimed by the Israelis, which gained credence through a powerful military reinforced by unlimited support from the Western powers. He contended that Zionism is a colonial ideology that cannot survive except by maintaining a weak and divided Arab world; consequently, the Zionists have implemented a strategy of balkanization of the Middle East into small states and ethnic or tribal societies. Unfortunately, he argued, this strategy has been aided and abetted by Islamic fundamentalism, which has opposed Arab unification of society. In spite of his strong criticisms of Israel and Zionism, Zurayk never took an anti-Semitic position: in sixty years of reflection and writing he never stigmatized Judaism as a religion or ethnicity. His attacks were directed at the political philosophy of Zionism and its enactment by the State of Israel.

Constantine Kaisar Zurayk was born into an Orthodox Christian family in Damascus, Syria, on 18 April 1909. After completing a B.A. in literature at the American University in Beirut (AUB) in 1928, he traveled to the United States to earn a master's degree in history at the University of Chicago in 1929 and a Ph.D. in philosophy at Princeton University in 1930. He then returned to the AUB as assistant professor of history.

In 1939 Zurayk published *Al-wa'y al-qawmi* (The Nationalist Conscience), a history and analysis of the various Arab nationalist movements. In 1945–1946 he served as first counselor at the Syrian legation in Washington, D.C., and in 1946–1947 as plenipotentiary Syrian minister to the United States and also as a delegate to the United Nations. He returned to the AUB as a vice president in 1947.

Almost immediately after the establishment of the State of Israel in 1948, Zurayk published *Ma'na al-nakbah* (translated as *The Meaning of the Disaster*, 1956). In this book he argues that the European colonial powers exploited the "Jewish problem" and exported it to the Arab world. Since the publication of the work, the term *Nakbah* (Disaster or Catastrophe) has been used by Palestinians to refer to the 1948 Arab-Israeli War.

In 1949 Zurayk was named rector of the University of Damascus. In 1952 he returned to the AUB as a vice president. He served as interim president of the university from 1954 to 1957.

Zurayk's *Ayyu ghadin* (1957, Which Tomorrow) is a study of the future of Arab society. In *Nahnu wa al-tarikh* (1959, Us and History) Zurayk argues that history can either be a burden to a society or propel it toward improvement and change. How Arabs read their history, therefore, is extremely important. If a society conceives of its history not as it was but as it would like to imagine that it was, it falls into the trap of "self-congratulatory" history. Instead of being a tool for self-criticism, history then becomes a psychological refuge for a people. The society escapes the present and falsely represents itself both to itself and to others. Self-congratulatory history, Zurayk argues, is the cultural source of the religious fervor that encourages militants. He was a proponent of secularism and believed that religion was a private matter and should not be brought into government affairs.

In *Hadha al-'asr al-mutafajjir* (1963, This Explosive Century) Zurayk situates the crisis of the Arab world in the context of a global crisis. He argues that modern human life has been shaken by three explosions: of science and knowledge, of desires and needs, and of population. A minority profits from the advantages of these explosions, and the rest of the world submits to their negative effects. He maintains that the Arab world needs a "renaissance" that must be consciously developed by Arab intellectuals. It might be true that Israel and the West advanced at the expense of others, but this issue is secondary to the fact that the Arabs have failed to modernize themselves.

In 1963 Zurayk and some colleagues founded the Institute for Palestinian Studies to try to find a peaceful solution to the Arab-Israeli conflict. Zurayk was president of the board of trustees of the institute from 1963 until 1984 and honorary president from 1984 until his death.

In 1964 Zurayk published *Fi m'arakat al-hadarah* (In the Battle for Culture), in which he argues that the crisis of the Arab world is at bottom a cultural one that, in turn, engenders the political, economic, social, and scientific crises. He contends that only a dynamic and rational society that believes in science and technological progress and respects democracy, freedom, religious differences, and equality of opportunity can survive. Such a society, he argues, must be constructed deliberately; it is the result of will and effort, not destiny.

Zurayk served as president of the International Association of Universities from 1965 to 1970. A few months after Israel's victory over Jordan, Egypt, Syria, and the Palestinians in the June 1967 Six-Day War, he published *Ma'na al-nakbah mujadadan* (Revisiting the

Meaning of the Disaster). In this work he examines the factors that contributed to the defeat of the Arab nations. He acknowledges that Western aid played a decisive role in the defeat of the Arabs, but he contends that the impotence of modern Arab civilization is, above all, the result of its own weaknesses. A large part of *Ma'na al-nakbah mujadadan* is taken up with examples of these weaknesses. If the Arab world wishes to save itself from the kinds of colonization it has experienced at the hands of the West and the Israelis, Zurayk concludes, it must adopt the scientific and philosophical advancements made by the West.

Zurayk retired from the AUB in 1977. In 1983 he published *Matalib al-mustaqbal al-'Arabi* (The Necessities of the Arab Future), in which he argues that the persistence of certain ideological tendencies has had a devastating effect on Arab societies. In particular, the Arab notion of community is contradicted by modern philosophical and political theories that separate national politics from religious politics. Such an ideology is incapable of contributing to the political and economic flourishing of Arab society. Zurayk's collected works were published in four volumes by the Center for the Study of Arab Unity in Beirut in 1994.

Constantine K. Zurayk died on 12 August 2000. He was survived by his wife, Najla Cortas Zurayk, and their daughters, Elham, Huda, Afaf, and Hanan. He had published ten original books, a translation, eighty-three articles in Arabic, and thirteen in English. His works exhibit a remarkable continuity of thought. His lifelong ambition was to equalize the forces in the Middle East. Zurayk saw such an equilibrium as the sine qua non for finding an equitable solution to the Arab-Israeli conflict and bringing about a just peace that guarantees the rights of Arabs in historical Palestine. Scores of scholars continue to reflect on and draw inspiration from his work; Ibrahim Abu-Rabi' wrote in 2004 that "One must take Zurayk seriously." Zurayk believed that Arab history was in a period of awakening that would eventually bring about reform and unity. If so, his voice is an important part of this awakening.

References:

Ibrahim M. Abu-Rabi', *Contemporary Arab Thought: Studies in Post-1967 Arab Intellectual History* (Sterling, Va.: Pluto Press, 2004), pp. 296–317;

Samir Karam, *Al-Waqi' al-'Arabi wa tajawuzuhu bayna Manzuri al-'ulum wa al-akhlaq: Naqd li kitab Constantine Zurayk Nahnu wa al-mustaqbal, Majallat al-Mustakbal al-'Arabi, al-adab al-awal Mayu 1978* (Beirut: Markaz Dirasat al-Wihdah al-'Arabi, 1978);

Elizabeth Suzanne Kassab, "An Arab Neo-Kantian Philosophy of Culture: Constantine Zurayk on Culture, Reason and Ethics," *Philosophy East and West*, 49 (October 1999): 494–512;

Muhamad Salah al-Marakishi, *Qira'at fi al-fikr al-'Arabi al-hadith wa al-mu'asir* (Tunis: Dar al-Tunisiyyah li al-Nashr, 1992);

Philip Mattar, "In Memoriam: Constantine Zurayk," *Middle East Studies Association Bulletin* (August 2000): 303–304;

Hisham Nashshaba, ed., *Studia Palaestinia: Studies in Honour of Constantine K. Zurayk* (Beirut: Institute for Palestine Studies, 1988).

Books for Further Reading

Abu-Rabi', Ibrahim M. *Contemporary Arab Thought: Studies in Post-1967 Arab Intellectual History.* London & Sterling, Va.: Pluto Press, 2004.

Al-Alim, Muhammad Amin. *Al-Riwayah al-'Arabiyyah bayna al-waqi' wa al-idyulujiyyah.* Latakia, Syria: Dar al-Hiwar, 1986.

Allen, Roger. *The Arabic Novel: An Historical and Critical Introduction,* second edition. Syracuse, N.Y.: Syracuse University Press, 1995.

Allen. *An Introduction to Arabic Literature.* New York: Cambridge University Press, 2000.

Allen, Hilary Kilpatrick, and Ed de Moor. *Love and Sexuality in Modern Arabic Literature.* London: Saqi, 1995.

Altoma, Salih J. *Modern Arabic Literature in Translation: A Companion.* London: Saqi, 2005.

Arkoun, Mohammed. *The Unthought in Contemporary Islamic Thought.* London: Saqi, 2002.

Badawi, Muhammad Mustafa. *A Short History of Modern Arabic Literature.* Oxford: Clarendon Press / New York: Oxford University Press, 1993.

Badawi, ed. *Modern Arabic Literature.* Cambridge & New York: Cambridge University Press, 1992.

Badran, Margot, and Miriam Cooke, eds. *Opening the Gates: A Century of Arab Feminist Writing.* Bloomington: Indiana University Press, 1990. Revised and enlarged as *Opening the Gates: An Anthology of Arab Feminist Writing.* Bloomington: Indiana University Press, 2004.

Bahrawi, Hasan. *Bunyat al-shakl al-riwa'i.* Casablanca: Al-Markaz al-Thaqafi al-'Arabi, 1990.

Barradah, Muhammad. *Al-Riwayah al-'Arabiyyah.* Beirut: Dar Ibn Rushd, 1981.

Boullata, Issa. *Trends and Issues in Contemporary Arab Thought.* Albany: State University of New York Press, 1990.

Brown, Daniel. *Rethinking Tradition in Modern Islamic Thought.* Cambridge & New York: Cambridge University Press, 1996.

Cachia, Pierre. *Arabic Literature: An Overview.* London & New York: RoutledgeCurzon, 2002.

Chomsky, Noam. *The Fateful Triangle: The United States, Israel and the Palestinians.* Boston: South End Press, 1983.

Cooper, John, Ronald Nettler, and Mohamed Mahmoud, eds. *Islam and Modernity: Muslim Intellectuals Respond.* London: I. B. Tarus, 1998.

Donohue, John J., and John L. Esposito, eds. *Islam in Transition: Muslim Perspectives,* second edition. New York & Oxford: Oxford University Press, 2006.

Books for Further Reading

Eickelman, Dale F., and James Piscatori. *Muslim Politics*. Princeton: Princeton University Press, 1996.

El Fadl, Khaled Abou. *Speaking in God's Name: Islamic Law, Authority and Women*. Oxford: Oneworld, 2001.

Esack, Farid. *Qur'an, Liberation and Pluralism: An Islamic Perspective of Interreligious Solidarity against Oppression*. Oxford: Oneworld, 1997.

Esposito, John L., ed., *The Oxford History of Islam*. Oxford & New York: Oxford University Press, 1999.

Esposito and John O. Voll. *Makers of Contemporary Islam*. Oxford & New York: Oxford University Press, 1999.

Fernea, Elizabeth, and Bassima Bezirgan. *Middle Eastern Muslim Women Speak*. Austin: University of Texas Press, 1977.

Frangieh, Bassam K. *Anthology of Modern Arabic Literature, Culture, and Thought from Pre-Islamic Times to the Present*. New Haven: Yale University Press, 2005.

Gibb, Sir H. A. R. *Arabic Literature: An Introduction*, revised edition. Oxford: Clarendon Press, 1963.

Hafez, Sabri. *The Genesis of Arabic Narrative Discourse: A Study in the Sociology of Modern Arabic Literature*. London: Saqi, 1993.

Hefner, Robert W., ed. *Remaking Muslim Politics: Pluralism, Contestation, Democratization*. Princeton: Princeton University Press, 2005.

Hodgson, Marshall G. S. *Rethinking World History: Essays on Europe, Islam, and World History*, edited by Edmund Burke III. Cambridge & New York: Cambridge University Press, 1993.

Hourani, Albert. *Arabic Thought in the Liberal Age: 1798–1939*. Oxford: Oxford University Press, 1962.

Jayyusi, Salma Khadra, ed. *Anthology of Modern Palestinian Literature*. New York: Columbia University Press, 1992.

Jayyusi, ed. *The Literature of Modern Arabia: An Anthology*. Austin: University of Texas Press, 1989.

Johnson-Davies, Denys, ed. *The Anchor Book of Modern Arabic Fiction*. New York: Anchor, 2006.

Juergensmeyer, Mark. *Terror in the Mind of God: The Global Rise of Religious Violence*. Berkeley: University of California Press, 2000.

Kepel, Gilles. *The War for Muslim Minds: Islam and the West*. Cambridge, Mass.: Belknap Press of Harvard University Press, 2004.

Kurzman, Charles, ed. *Liberal Islam: A Sourcebook*. Oxford: Oxford University Press, 1998.

Kurzman, ed. *Modernist Islam, 1840–1940: A Sourcebook*. Oxford: Oxford University Press, 2002.

Lawrence, Bruce B. *Shattering the Myth: Islam beyond Violence*. Princeton: Princeton University Press, 1998.

Lockman, Zachary. *Contending Visions of the Middle East: The History and Politics of Orientalism*. Cambridge & New York: Cambridge University Press, 2004.

Mikhail, Mona. *Seen and Heard: A Century of Arab Women in Literature and Culture*. Northampton, Mass.: Olive Branch Press, 2004.

Mondal, Anshuman A. *Nationalism and Post-Colonial Identity: Culture and Ideology in India and Egypt.* London & New York: RoutledgeCurzon, 2003.

Rahman, Fazlur. *Islam and Modernity: Transformation of an Intellectual Tradition.* Chicago: University of Chicago Press, 1982.

Rahman. *Revival and Reform in Islam: A Study of Islamic Fundamentalism,* edited by Ebrahim Moosa. Oxford: Oneworld, 2000.

Ramadan, Tariq. *Islam, the West and the Challenges of Modernity,* translated by Saïd Amghar. Leicester, U.K.: Islamic Foundation, 2001.

Safi, Omid, ed. *Progressive Muslims: On Justice, Gender and Pluralism.* Oxford: Oneworld, 2003.

Starkey, Paul. *Modern Arabic Literature.* Washington, D.C.: Georgetown University Press, 2006.

Tresilian, David. *A Brief Introduction to Modern Arabic Literature.* San Francisco & London: Saqi, 2008.

Zeidan, Joseph T. *Arab Women Novelists: The Formative Years and Beyond.* Albany: State University of New York Press, 1995.

Contributors

Kamal Abdel-Malek . . . . *American University of Sharjah*
Toufoul Abou-Hodeib . . . . *University of Chicago*
Matthew Abraham . . . . *DePaul University*
Yasir Ibrahim Almallah . . . . *Al-Quds Open University*
Ovamir Anjum . . . . *University of Wisconsin–Madison*
Angela Saliba Bajalieh . . . . *Grand Valley State University*
Carol Bargeron . . . . *Central State University*
Azza Basarudin . . . . *University of California, Los Angeles*
Ayman A. El-Desouky . . . . *School of Oriental and African Studies, University of London*
Hager Ben Driss . . . . *University of Tunis*
Coeli Fitzpatrick . . . . *Grand Valley State University*
Ursula Günther . . . . *University of Hamburg*
Pennie Johnson . . . . *Grand Rapids, Michigan*
Mahmoud Kayyal . . . . *Tel Aviv University*
Boutheina Khaldi . . . . *Yale University*
Malakeh Khoury . . . . *American University of Beirut*
Sebastian Maisel . . . . *Grand Valley State University*
Ahmad al-Mallah . . . . *Indiana University*
Majd Yaser Al-Mallah . . . . *Grand Valley State University*
Ellen McLarney . . . . *Duke University*
Mara Naaman . . . . *Williams College*
Imed Nsiri . . . . *American University of Sharjah*
Goetz Nordbruch . . . . *Humboldt University of Berlin*
Mohamed Ourya . . . . *University of Sherbrooke*
Christina Phillips . . . . *School of Oriental and African Studies, University of London*
Noomane Raboudi . . . . *University of Ottawa*
Jared Reene . . . . *Custer, Michigan*
Wyoma vanDuinkerken . . . . *Texas A&M University*
John Walbridge . . . . *Indiana University*

Cumulative Index

Dictionary of Literary Biography, Volumes 1-346
Dictionary of Literary Biography Yearbook, 1980-2002
Dictionary of Literary Biography Documentary Series, Volumes 1-19
Concise Dictionary of American Literary Biography, Volumes 1-7
Concise Dictionary of British Literary Biography, Volumes 1-8
Concise Dictionary of World Literary Biography, Volumes 1-4

Cumulative Index

DLB before number: *Dictionary of Literary Biography,* Volumes 1-346
Y before number: *Dictionary of Literary Biography Yearbook,* 1980-2002
DS before number: *Dictionary of Literary Biography Documentary Series,* Volumes 1-19
CDALB before number: *Concise Dictionary of American Literary Biography,* Volumes 1-7
CDBLB before number: *Concise Dictionary of British Literary Biography,* Volumes 1-8
CDWLB before number: *Concise Dictionary of World Literary Biography,* Volumes 1-4

A

Aakjær, Jeppe 1866-1930 .... DLB-214
Aarestrup, Emil 1800-1856 .... DLB-300
Abbey, Edward 1927-1989 .... DLB-256, 275
Abbey, Edwin Austin 1852-1911 .... DLB-188
Abbey, Maj. J. R. 1894-1969 .... DLB-201
Abbey Press DLB-49
The Abbey Theatre and Irish Drama,
  1900-1945 .... DLB-10
Abbot, Willis J. 1863-1934 .... DLB-29
Abbott, Edwin A. 1838-1926 .... DLB-178
Abbott, Jacob 1803-1879 .... DLB-1, 42, 243
Abbott, Lee K. 1947- DLB-130
Abbott, Leonard 1878-1953 .... DLB-345
Abbott, Lyman 1835-1922 .... DLB-79
Abbott, Robert S. 1868-1940 .... DLB-29, 91
'Abd al-Hamid al-Katib
  circa 689-750 .... DLB-311
'Abduh, Muhammad 1849-1905 .... DLB-346
à Beckett, Gilbert Abbott 1811-1856 ..... DLB-344
Abe Kōbō 1924-1993 .... DLB-182
Abelaira, Augusto 1926- DLB-287
Abelard, Peter circa 1079-1142? DLB-115, 208
Abelard-Schuman DLB-46
Abell, Arunah S. 1806-1888 .... DLB-43
Abell, Kjeld 1901-1961 .... DLB-214
Abercrombie, Lascelles 1881-1938 .... DLB-19
  The Friends of the Dymock Poets Y-00
Aberdeen University Press Limited DLB-106
Abish, Walter 1931- DLB-130, 227
Ablesimov, Aleksandr Onisimovich
  1742-1783 .... DLB-150
Aboubakr, Mas'udah 1954- DLB-346
Abraham à Sancta Clara 1644-1709 ...... DLB-168
Abrahams, Peter
  1919- DLB-117, 225; CDWLB-3
Abramov, Fedor Aleksandrovich
  1920-1983 .... DLB-302
Abrams, M. H. 1912- DLB-67

Abramson, Jesse 1904-1979 .... DLB-241
Abrogans circa 790-800 .... DLB-148
Abschatz, Hans Aßmann von
  1646-1699 .... DLB-168
Abse, Dannie 1923- DLB-27, 245
Abu al-'Atahiyah 748-825? DLB-311
Abu Nuwas circa 757-814 or 815 ...... DLB-311
Abu Tammam circa 805-845 .... DLB-311
Abutsu-ni 1221-1283 .... DLB-203
Academy Chicago Publishers DLB-46
Accius circa 170 B.C.-circa 80 B.C. DLB-211
"An account of the death of the Chevalier de La
  Barre," Voltaire DLB-314
Accrocca, Elio Filippo 1923-1996 .... DLB-128
Ace Books DLB-46
Achebe, Chinua 1930- DLB-117; CDWLB-3
Achillini, Claudio 1574-1640 .... DLB-339
Achtenberg, Herbert 1938- DLB-124
Ackerman, Diane 1948- DLB-120
Ackroyd, Peter 1949- DLB-155, 231
Acorn, Milton 1923-1986 .... DLB-53
Acosta, José de 1540-1600 .... DLB-318
Acosta, Oscar Zeta 1935?-1974? DLB-82
Acosta Torres, José 1925- DLB-209
Actors Theatre of Louisville DLB-7
Adair, Gilbert 1944- DLB-194
Adair, James 1709?-1783? DLB-30
Aðalsteinn Kristmundsson (see Steinn Steinarr)
Adam, Graeme Mercer 1839-1912 .... DLB-99
Adam, Robert Borthwick, II
  1863-1940 .... DLB-187
Adame, Leonard 1947- DLB-82
Adameșteanu, Gabriel 1942- DLB-232
Adamic, Louis 1898-1951 .... DLB-9
Adamov, Arthur Surenovitch
  1908-1970 .... DLB-321
Adamovich, Georgii 1894-1972 .... DLB-317
Adams, Abigail 1744-1818 .... DLB-183, 200
Adams, Alice 1926-1999 .... DLB-234; Y-86

Adams, Bertha Leith (Mrs. Leith Adams,
  Mrs. R. S. de Courcy Laffan)
  1837?-1912 .... DLB-240
Adams, Brooks 1848-1927 .... DLB-47
Adams, Charles Francis, Jr. 1835-1915 .... DLB-47
Adams, Douglas 1952-2001 .... DLB-261; Y-83
Adams, Franklin P. 1881-1960 .... DLB-29
Adams, Glenda 1939- DLB-325
Adams, Hannah 1755-1832 .... DLB-200
Adams, Henry 1838-1918 .... DLB-12, 47, 189
Adams, Herbert Baxter 1850-1901 .... DLB-47
Adams, James Truslow
  1878-1949 .... DLB-17; DS-17
Adams, John 1735-1826 .... DLB-31, 183
Adams, John Quincy 1767-1848 .... DLB-37
Adams, Léonie 1899-1988 .... DLB-48
Adams, Levi 1802-1832 .... DLB-99
Adams, Richard 1920- DLB-261
Adams, Samuel 1722-1803 .... DLB-31, 43
Adams, Sarah Fuller Flower
  1805-1848 .... DLB-199
Adams, Thomas 1582/1583-1652 .... DLB-151
Adams, William Taylor 1822-1897 .... DLB-42
J. S. and C. Adams [publishing house] DLB-49
Adamson, Harold 1906-1980 .... DLB-265
Adamson, Sir John 1867-1950 .... DLB-98
Adamson, Robert 1943- DLB-289
Adcock, Arthur St. John
  1864-1930 .... DLB-135
Adcock, Betty 1938- DLB-105
  "Certain Gifts" DLB-105
  Tribute to James Dickey Y-97
Adcock, Fleur 1934- DLB-40
Addams, Jane 1860-1935 .... DLB-303
Addison, Joseph
  1672-1719 .... DLB-101; CDBLB-2
Ade, George 1866-1944 .... DLB-11, 25
Adeler, Max (see Clark, Charles Heber)
Adlard, Mark 1932- DLB-261
Adler, Richard 1921- DLB-265

291

Adonias Filho
(Adonias Aguiar Filho)
1915-1990............... DLB-145, 307

Adorno, Theodor W. 1903-1969 .... DLB-242

Adoum, Jorge Enrique 1926- DLB-283

Advance Publishing Company DLB-49

Adventures of Huckleberry Finn (Documentary)
.... DLB-343

Ady, Endre 1877-1919...... DLB-215; CDWLB-4

AE 1867-1935 .... DLB-19; CDBLB-5

Ælfric circa 955-circa 1010 .... DLB-146

Aeschines circa 390 B.C.-circa 320 B.C. DLB-176

Aeschylus 525-524 B.C.-456-455 B.C.
.... DLB-176; CDWLB-1

Aesthetic Papers DLB-1

Aesthetics
   Eighteenth-Century Aesthetic
    Theories DLB-31

African Literature
   Letter from Khartoum............. Y-90

African American
   Afro-American Literary Critics:
    An Introduction............... DLB-33

   The Black Aesthetic: Background DS-8

   The Black Arts Movement,
    by Larry Neal DLB-38

   Black Theaters and Theater Organizations
   in America, 1961-1982:
    A Research List............... DLB-38

   Black Theatre: A Forum [excerpts] ... DLB-38

   Callaloo [journal]................... Y-87

   Community and Commentators:
    Black Theatre and Its Critics...... DLB-38

   The Emergence of Black
    Women Writers DS-8

   The Hatch-Billops Collection........ DLB-76

   A Look at the Contemporary Black
    Theatre Movement DLB-38

   The Moorland-Spingarn Research
    Center DLB-76

   "The Negro as a Writer," by
    G. M. McClellan DLB-50

   "Negro Poets and Their Poetry," by
    Wallace Thurman DLB-50

   Olaudah Equiano and Unfinished Journeys:
   The Slave-Narrative Tradition and
   Twentieth-Century Continuities, by
   Paul Edwards and Pauline T.
   Wangman DLB-117

   PHYLON (Fourth Quarter, 1950),
   The Negro in Literature:
    The Current Scene DLB-76

   The Schomburg Center for Research
    in Black Culture DLB-76

   Three Documents [poets], by John
    Edward Bruce DLB-50

After Dinner Opera Company Y-92

Agassiz, Elizabeth Cary 1822-1907...... DLB-189

Agassiz, Louis 1807-1873 .... DLB-1, 235

Agee, James
1909-1955 .... DLB-2, 26, 152; CDALB-1

The Agee Legacy: A Conference at
the University of Tennessee
at Knoxville Y-89

Agnon, Shmuel Yosef 1887-1970 .... DLB-329

Aguilera Malta, Demetrio 1909-1981 .... DLB-145

Aguirre, Isidora 1919- DLB-305

Agustini, Delmira 1886-1914 .... DLB-290

Ahlin, Lars 1915-1997 .... DLB-257

Ai 1947- DLB-120

Ai Wu 1904-1992.................... DLB-328

Aichinger, Ilse 1921- DLB-85, 299

Aickman, Robert 1914-1981........... DLB-261

Aidoo, Ama Ata 1942- DLB-117; CDWLB-3

Aiken, Conrad
1889-1973........ DLB-9, 45, 102; CDALB-5

Aiken, Joan 1924-2004 .... DLB-161

Aikin, John 1747-1822................ DLB-336

Aikin, Lucy 1781-1864 .... DLB-144, 163

Ainsworth, William Harrison
1805-1882 .... DLB-21

Aïssé, Charlotte-Elizabeth 1694?-1733 ... DLB-313

Aistis, Jonas 1904-1973..... DLB-220; CDWLB-4

Aitken, Adam 1960- DLB-325

Aitken, George A. 1860-1917 .... DLB-149

Robert Aitken [publishing house]........ DLB-49

Aitmatov, Chingiz 1928- DLB-302

Akenside, Mark 1721-1770 .... DLB-109

Akhmatova, Anna Andreevna
1889-1966 .... DLB-295

Akins, Zoë 1886-1958................. DLB-26

Aksakov, Ivan Sergeevich 1823-1826 .....DLB-277

Aksakov, Sergei Timofeevich
1791-1859 .... DLB-198

Aksyonov, Vassily 1932- DLB-302

Akunin, Boris (Grigorii Shalvovich Chkhartishvili)
1956- DLB-285

Akutagawa Ryūnsuke 1892-1927 .... DLB-180

Alabaster, William 1568-1640.......... DLB-132

Alain de Lille circa 1116-1202/1203 ..... DLB-208

Alain-Fournier 1886-1914............. DLB-65

Alanus de Insulis (see Alain de Lille)

Alarcón, Francisco X. 1954- DLB-122

Alarcón, Justo S. 1930- DLB-209

Alba, Nanina 1915-1968............... DLB-41

Albee, Edward 1928- ... DLB-7, 266; CDALB-1

Albert, Octavia 1853-ca. 1889 .... DLB-221

Albert the Great circa 1200-1280 .... DLB-115

Alberti, Rafael 1902-1999............. DLB-108

Albertinus, Aegidius circa 1560-1620.... DLB-164

Alcaeus born circa 620 B.C. DLB-176

Alcoforado, Mariana, the Portuguese Nun
1640-1723.................... DLB-287

Alcott, Amos Bronson
1799-1888............... DLB-1, 223; DS-5

Alcott, Louisa May 1832-1888
...DLB-1, 42, 79, 223, 239; DS-14; CDALB-3

Alcott, William Andrus 1798-1859.... DLB-1, 243

Alcuin circa 732-804................. DLB-148

Aldana, Francisco de 1537-1578 .... DLB-318

Aldanov, Mark (Mark Landau)
1886-1957 ....DLB-317

Alden, Henry Mills 1836-1919.......... DLB-79

Alden, Isabella 1841-1930 .... DLB-42

John B. Alden [publishing house]........ DLB-49

Alden, Beardsley, and Company DLB-49

Aldington, Richard
1892-1962 ....DLB-20, 36, 100, 149

Aldis, Dorothy 1896-1966 .... DLB-22

Aldis, H. G. 1863-1919................ DLB-184

Aldiss, Brian W. 1925- DLB-14, 261, 271

Aldrich, Thomas Bailey
1836-1907 ....DLB-42, 71, 74, 79

Alegría, Ciro 1909-1967 .... DLB-113

Alegría, Claribel 1924- DLB-145, 283

Aleixandre, Vicente 1898-1984..... DLB-108, 329

Aleksandravičius, Jonas (see Aistis, Jonas)

Aleksandrov, Aleksandr Andreevich
(see Durova, Nadezhda Andreevna)

Alekseeva, Marina Anatol'evna
(see Marinina, Aleksandra)

d'Alembert, Jean Le Rond 1717-1783 .... DLB-313

Alencar, José de 1829-1877............ DLB-307

Aleramo, Sibilla (Rena Pierangeli Faccio)
1876-1960.................. DLB-114, 264

Aleshkovsky, Petr Markovich 1957- ... DLB-285

Aleshkovsky, Yuz 1929- DLB-317

Alexander, Cecil Frances 1818-1895..... DLB-199

Alexander, Charles 1868-1923 .... DLB-91

Charles Wesley Alexander
[publishing house] DLB-49

Alexander, James 1691-1756............ DLB-24

Alexander, Lloyd 1924- DLB-52

Alexander, Meena 1951- DLB-323

Alexander, Sir William, Earl of Stirling
1577?-1640.................... DLB-121

Alexie, Sherman 1966- DLB-175, 206, 278

Alexis, Willibald 1798-1871 .... DLB-133

Alf laylah wa laylah
ninth century onward DLB-311

Alfonso X 1221-1284................. DLB-337

Alfonsine Legal Codes DLB-337

Alfred, King 849-899 .... DLB-146

Alger, Horatio, Jr. 1832-1899 .... DLB-42

Algonquin Books of Chapel Hill DLB-46

Algren, Nelson
1909-1981 ....DLB-9; Y-81, 82; CDALB-1

Nelson Algren: An International Symposium ... Y-00
Ali, Agha Shahid 1949-2001 ... DLB-323
Ali, Ahmed 1908-1994 ... DLB-323
Ali, Monica 1967- ... DLB-323
'Ali ibn Abi Talib circa 600-661 ... DLB-311
Alinsky, Saul 1909-1972 ... DLB-345
Aljamiado Literature ... DLB-286
Allan, Andrew 1907-1974 ... DLB-88
Allan, Ted 1916-1995 ... DLB-68
Allbeury, Ted 1917-2005 ... DLB-87
Alldritt, Keith 1935- ... DLB-14
Allen, Dick 1939- ... DLB-282
Allen, Ethan 1738-1789 ... DLB-31
Allen, Frederick Lewis 1890-1954 ... DLB-137
Allen, Gay Wilson 1903-1995 ... DLB-103; Y-95
Allen, George 1808-1876 ... DLB-59
Allen, Grant 1848-1899 ... DLB-70, 92, 178
Allen, Henry W. 1912-1991 ... Y-85
Allen, Hervey 1889-1949 ... DLB-9, 45, 316
Allen, James 1739-1808 ... DLB-31
Allen, James Lane 1849-1925 ... DLB-71
Allen, Jay Presson 1922- ... DLB-26
John Allen and Company ... DLB-49
Allen, Paula Gunn 1939- ... DLB-175
Allen, Samuel W. 1917- ... DLB-41
Allen, Woody 1935- ... DLB-44
George Allen [publishing house] ... DLB-106
George Allen and Unwin Limited ... DLB-112
Allende, Isabel 1942- ... DLB-145; CDWLB-3
Alline, Henry 1748-1784 ... DLB-99
Allingham, Margery 1904-1966 ... DLB-77
    The Margery Allingham Society ... Y-98
Allingham, William 1824-1889 ... DLB-35
W. L. Allison [publishing house] ... DLB-49
The *Alliterative Morte Arthure* and the Stanzaic *Morte Arthur* circa 1350-1400 ... DLB-146
Allott, Kenneth 1912-1973 ... DLB-20
Allston, Washington 1779-1843 ... DLB-1, 235
Almeida, Manuel Antônio de 1831-1861 ... DLB-307
John Almon [publishing house] ... DLB-154
Alonzo, Dámaso 1898-1990 ... DLB-108
Alsop, George 1636-post 1673 ... DLB-24
Alsop, Richard 1761-1815 ... DLB-37
Henry Altemus and Company ... DLB-49
Altenberg, Peter 1885-1919 ... DLB-81
Althusser, Louis 1918-1990 ... DLB-242
Altolaguirre, Manuel 1905-1959 ... DLB-108
Aluko, T. M. 1918- ... DLB-117
Alurista 1947- ... DLB-82

Alvarez, A. 1929- ... DLB-14, 40
Alvarez, Julia 1950- ... DLB-282
Alvaro, Corrado 1895-1956 ... DLB-264
Alver, Betti 1906-1989 ... DLB-220; CDWLB-4
Amadi, Elechi 1934- ... DLB-117
Amado, Jorge 1912-2001 ... DLB-113
Amalrik, Andrei 1938-1980 ... DLB-302
Ambler, Eric 1909-1998 ... DLB-77
The Library of America ... DLB-46
The Library of America: An Assessment After Two Decades ... Y-02
America: or, A Poem on the Settlement of the British Colonies, by Timothy Dwight ... DLB-37
American Bible Society
    Department of Library, Archives, and Institutional Research ... Y-97
American Conservatory Theatre ... DLB-7
American Culture
    American Proletarian Culture: The Twenties and Thirties ... DS-11
Studies in American Jewish Literature ... Y-02
The American Library in Paris ... Y-93
American Literature
    The Literary Scene and Situation and ... (Who Besides Oprah) Really Runs American Literature? ... Y-99
    Who Owns American Literature, by Henry Taylor ... Y-94
    Who Runs American Literature? ... Y-94
American News Company ... DLB-49
A Century of Poetry, a Lifetime of Collecting: J. M. Edelstein's Collection of Twentieth-Century American Poetry ... Y-02
The American Poets' Corner: The First Three Years (1983-1986) ... Y-86
American Publishing Company ... DLB-49
American Spectator
    [Editorial] Rationale From the Initial Issue of the American Spectator (November 1932) ... DLB-137
American Stationers' Company ... DLB-49
The American Studies Association of Norway ... Y-00
American Sunday-School Union ... DLB-49
American Temperance Union ... DLB-49
American Tract Society ... DLB-49
The American Trust for the British Library ... Y-96
American Writers' Congress 25-27 April 1935 ... DLB-303
American Writers Congress
    The American Writers Congress (9-12 October 1981) ... Y-81
    The American Writers Congress: A Report on Continuing Business ... Y-81
Ames, Fisher 1758-1808 ... DLB-37
Ames, Mary Clemmer 1831-1884 ... DLB-23
Ames, William 1576-1633 ... DLB-281
Amfiteatrov, Aleksandr 1862-1938 ... DLB-317

Amiel, Henri-Frédéric 1821-1881 ... DLB-217
Amini, Johari M. 1935- ... DLB-41
Amis, Kingsley 1922-1995
    ... DLB-15, 27, 100, 139, 326; Y-96; CDBLB-7
Amis, Martin 1949- ... DLB-14, 194
Ammianus Marcellinus circa A.D. 330-A.D. 395 ... DLB-211
Ammons, A. R. 1926-2001 ... DLB-5, 165, 342
Amory, Thomas 1691?-1788 ... DLB-39
Amsterdam, 1998 Booker Prize winner, Ian McEwan ... DLB-326
Amyot, Jacques 1513-1593 ... DLB-327
Anand, Mulk Raj 1905-2004 ... DLB-323
Anania, Michael 1939- ... DLB-193
Anaya, Rudolfo A. 1937- ... DLB-82, 206, 278
Ancrene Riwle circa 1200-1225 ... DLB-146
Andersch, Alfred 1914-1980 ... DLB-69
Andersen, Benny 1929- ... DLB-214
Andersen, Hans Christian 1805-1875 ... DLB-300
Anderson, Alexander 1775-1870 ... DLB-188
Anderson, David 1929- ... DLB-241
Anderson, Frederick Irving 1877-1947 ... DLB-202
Anderson, Jessica 1916- ... DLB-325
Anderson, Margaret 1886-1973 ... DLB-4, 91
Anderson, Maxwell 1888-1959 ... DLB-7, 228
Anderson, Patrick 1915-1979 ... DLB-68
Anderson, Paul Y. 1893-1938 ... DLB-29
Anderson, Poul 1926-2001 ... DLB-8
    Tribute to Isaac Asimov ... Y-92
Anderson, Robert 1750-1830 ... DLB-142
Anderson, Robert 1917- ... DLB-7
Anderson, Sherwood 1876-1941
    ... DLB-4, 9, 86; DS-1; CDALB-4
Andrade, Jorge (Aluísio Jorge Andrade Franco) 1922-1984 ... DLB-307
Andrade, Mario de 1893-1945 ... DLB-307
Andrade, Oswald de (José Oswald de Sousa Andrade) 1890-1954 ... DLB-307
Andreae, Johann Valentin 1586-1654 ... DLB-164
Andreas Capellanus fl. circa 1185 ... DLB-208
Andreas-Salomé, Lou 1861-1937 ... DLB-66
Andreev, Leonid Nikolaevich 1871-1919 ... DLB-295
Andres, Stefan 1906-1970 ... DLB-69
Andresen, Sophia de Mello Breyner 1919-2004 ... DLB-287
Andreu, Blanca 1959- ... DLB-134
Andrewes, Lancelot 1555-1626 ... DLB-151, 172
Andrews, Charles M. 1863-1943 ... DLB-17
Andrews, Miles Peter ?-1814 ... DLB-89
Andrews, Stephen Pearl 1812-1886 ... DLB-250
Andrian, Leopold von 1875-1951 ... DLB-81

Andrić, Ivo 1892-1975...DLB-147, 329; CDWLB-4

Andreini, Francesco
before 1548?-1624 .... DLB-339

Andreini, Giovan Battista 1576-1654 .... DLB-339

Andreini, Isabella 1562-1604 .... DLB-339

Andrieux, Louis (see Aragon, Louis)

Andrus, Silas, and Son DLB-49

Andrzejewski, Jerzy 1909-1983......... DLB-215

Angell, James Burrill 1829-1916 .... DLB-64

Angell, Roger 1920- DLB-171, 185

Angelou, Maya 1928- DLB-38; CDALB-7

Tribute to Julian Mayfield Y-84

Anger, Jane fl. 1589................. DLB-136

Angers, Félicité (see Conan, Laure)

The Anglo-Saxon Chronicle
circa 890-1154 .... DLB-146

Angus and Robertson (UK) Limited DLB-112

Anhalt, Edward 1914-2000............. DLB-26

Anissimov, Myriam 1943- DLB-299

Anker, Nini Roll 1873-1942 .... DLB-297

Annenkov, Pavel Vasil'evich
1813?-1887.................... DLB-277

Annensky, Innokentii Fedorovich
1855-1909 .... DLB-295

Henry F. Anners [publishing house]..... DLB-49

Annolied between 1077 and 1081 .... DLB-148

Anouilh, Jean 1910-1987.............. DLB-321

Anscombe, G. E. M. 1919-2001 .... DLB-262

Anselm of Canterbury 1033-1109....... DLB-115

Ansky, S. (Sh. An-Ski; Solomon Zainwil [Shloyme-Zanvl] Rapoport) 1863-1920 .... DLB-333

Anstey, F. 1856-1934 ....DLB-141, 178

'Antarah ('Antar ibn Shaddad al-'Absi)
?-early seventh century?........... DLB-311

Anthologizing New Formalism DLB-282

Anthony, Michael 1932- DLB-125

Anthony, Piers 1934- DLB-8

Anthony, Susanna 1726-1791 .... DLB-200

Antin, David 1932- DLB-169

Antin, Mary 1881-1949 ....DLB-221; Y-84

Anton Ulrich, Duke of Brunswick-Lüneburg
1633-1714..................... DLB-168

Antschel, Paul (see Celan, Paul)

Antunes, António Lobo 1942- DLB-287

Anyidoho, Kofi 1947- DLB-157

Anzaldúa, Gloria 1942- DLB-122

Anzengruber, Ludwig 1839-1889 .... DLB-129

Apess, William 1798-1839..........DLB-175, 243

Apodaca, Rudy S. 1939- DLB-82

Apollinaire, Guillaume
1880-1918.................. DLB-258, 321

Apollonius Rhodius third century B.C..... DLB-176

Appeal to Reason, The 1895-1922 .... DLB-345

Appelfeld, Aharon 1932- DLB-299

Apple, Max 1941- DLB-130

D. Appleton and Company DLB-49

Appleton-Century-Crofts DLB-46

Applewhite, James 1935- DLB-105

Tribute to James Dickey................ Y-97

Apple-wood Books DLB-46

April, Jean-Pierre 1948- DLB-251

Apukhtin, Aleksei Nikolaevich
1840-1893 .... DLB-277

Apuleius circa A.D. 125-post A.D. 164
.... DLB-211; CDWLB-1

Aquin, Hubert 1929-1977.............. DLB-53

Aquinas, Thomas 1224/1225-1274...... DLB-115

Aragon, Louis 1897-1982 .... DLB-72, 258

Aragon, Vernacular Translations in the
Crowns of Castile and 1352-1515 ... DLB-286

Aralica, Ivan 1930- DLB-181

Aratus of Soli
circa 315 B.C.-circa 239 B.C. DLB-176

Arbasino, Alberto 1930- DLB-196

Arbor House Publishing Company DLB-46

Arbuthnot, John 1667-1735............ DLB-101

Arcadia House DLB-46

Arce, Julio G. (see Ulica, Jorge)

Archer, William 1856-1924............. DLB-10

Archilochhus
mid seventh century B.C.E..........DLB-176

The Archpoet circa 1130?-? DLB-148

Archpriest Avvakum (Petrovich)
1620?-1682.................... DLB-150

Arden, John 1930- DLB-13, 245

Arden of Faversham DLB-62

Ardis Publishers Y-89

Ardizzone, Edward 1900-1979 .... DLB-160

Arellano, Juan Estevan 1947- DLB-122

The Arena Publishing Company DLB-49

Arena Stage........................... DLB-7

Arenas, Reinaldo 1943-1990........... DLB-145

Arendt, Hannah 1906-1975 .... DLB-242

Arensberg, Ann 1937- Y-82

Arghezi, Tudor 1880-1967 ... DLB-220; CDWLB-4

Arguedas, José María 1911-1969 .... DLB-113

Argüelles, Hugo 1932-2003 .... DLB-305

Argueta, Manlio 1936- DLB-145

'Arib al-Ma'muniyah 797-890 .... DLB-311

Arias, Ron 1941- DLB-82

Arishima Takeo 1878-1923 .... DLB-180

Aristophanes circa 446 B.C.-circa 386 B.C.
.... DLB-176; CDWLB-1

Aristotle 384 B.C.-322 B.C.
.... DLB-176; CDWLB-1

Ariyoshi Sawako 1931-1984 .... DLB-182

Arkoun, Mohammed 1928- DLB-346

Arland, Marcel 1899-1986 .... DLB-72

Arlen, Michael 1895-1956 ....DLB-36, 77, 162

Arlt, Roberto 1900-1942............. DLB-305

Armah, Ayi Kwei 1939- ...DLB-117; CDWLB-3

Armantrout, Rae 1947- DLB-193

Der arme Hartmann ?-after 1150 .... DLB-148

Armed Services Editions................ DLB-46

Armitage, G. E. (Robert Edric) 1956- .. DLB-267

Armstrong, Jeanette 1948- DLB-334

Armstrong, Martin Donisthorpe
1882-1974.....................DLB-197

Armstrong, Richard 1903-1986 .... DLB-160

Armstrong, Terence Ian Fytton (see Gawsworth, John)

Arnauld, Antoine 1612-1694 ....DLB-268

Arndt, Ernst Moritz 1769-1860......... DLB-90

Arnim, Achim von 1781-1831 .... DLB-90

Arnim, Bettina von 1785-1859 .... DLB-90

Arnim, Elizabeth von (Countess Mary Annette
Beauchamp Russell) 1866-1941 .....DLB-197

Arno Press DLB-46

Arnold, Edwin 1832-1904 .... DLB-35

Arnold, Edwin L. 1857-1935 ....DLB-178

Arnold, Matthew
1822-1888 .... DLB-32, 57; CDBLB-4

Preface to *Poems* (1853) DLB-32

Arnold, Thomas 1795-1842 .... DLB-55

Edward Arnold [publishing house]...... DLB-112

Arnott, Peter 1962- DLB-233

Arnow, Harriette Simpson 1908-1986 ..... DLB-6

Arp, Bill (see Smith, Charles Henry)

Arpino, Giovanni 1927-1987...........DLB-177

Arrabal, Fernando 1932- DLB-321

Arrebo, Anders 1587-1637 .... DLB-300

Arreola, Juan José 1918-2001 .... DLB-113

Arrian circa 89-circa 155...............DLB-176

J. W. Arrowsmith [publishing house] DLB-106

Arrufat, Antón 1935- DLB-305

Art
John Dos Passos: Artist Y-99

The First Post-Impressionist
Exhibition....................DS-5

The Omega Workshops..............DS-10

The Second Post-Impressionist
Exhibition....................DS-5

Artale, Giuseppi 1628-1679 .... DLB-339

Artaud, Antonin 1896-1948 .... DLB-258, 321

Artel, Jorge 1909-1994 .... DLB-283

Arthur, Timothy Shay
1809-1885 ....DLB-3, 42, 79, 250; DS-13

Artmann, H. C. 1921-2000............. DLB-85

Artsybashev, Mikhail Petrovich 1878-1927 ... DLB-295

Arvin, Newton 1900-1963 ... DLB-103

Asch, Nathan 1902-1964 ... DLB-4, 28

    Nathan Asch Remembers Ford Madox Ford, Sam Roth, and Hart Crane ... Y-02

Asch, Sholem 1880-1957 ... DLB-333

Ascham, Roger 1515/1516-1568 ... DLB-236

Aseev, Nikolai Nikolaevich 1889-1963 ... DLB-295

Ash, John 1948- ... DLB-40

Ashbery, John 1927- ... DLB-5, 165; Y-81

Ashbridge, Elizabeth 1713-1755 ... DLB-200

Ashburnham, Bertram Lord 1797-1878 ... DLB-184

Ashendene Press ... DLB-112

Asher, Sandy 1942- ... Y-83

Ashton, Winifred (see Dane, Clemence)

Asimov, Isaac 1920-1992 ... DLB-8; Y-92

    Tribute to John Ciardi ... Y-86

Askew, Anne circa 1521-1546 ... DLB-136

Aspazija 1865-1943 ... DLB-220; CDWLB-4

Asselin, Olivar 1874-1937 ... DLB-92

The Association of American Publishers ... Y-99

The Association for Documentary Editing ... Y-00

The Association for the Study of Literature and Environment (ASLE) ... Y-99

Astell, Mary 1666-1731 ... DLB-252, 336

Astley, Thea 1925- ... DLB-289

Astley, William (see Warung, Price)

Asturias, Miguel Ángel 1899-1974 ... DLB-113, 290, 329; CDWLB-3

Atava, S. (see Terpigorev, Sergei Nikolaevich)

Atheneum Publishers ... DLB-46

Atherton, Gertrude 1857-1948 ... DLB-9, 78, 186

Athlone Press ... DLB-112

Atkins, Josiah circa 1755-1781 ... DLB-31

Atkins, Russell 1926- ... DLB-41

Atkinson, Kate 1951- ... DLB-267

Atkinson, Louisa 1834-1872 ... DLB-230

The Atlantic Monthly Press ... DLB-46

Attaway, William 1911-1986 ... DLB-76

Atwood, Margaret 1939- ... DLB-53, 251, 326

Aubert, Alvin 1930- ... DLB-41

Aub, Max 1903-1972 ... DLB-322

Aubert de Gaspé, Phillipe-Ignace-François 1814-1841 ... DLB-99

Aubert de Gaspé, Phillipe-Joseph 1786-1871 ... DLB-99

Aubigné, Théodore Agrippa d' 1552-1630 ... DLB-327

Aubin, Napoléon 1812-1890 ... DLB-99

Aubin, Penelope 1685-circa 1731 ... DLB-39

    Preface to *The Life of Charlotta du Pont* (1723) ... DLB-39

Aubrey-Fletcher, Henry Lancelot (see Wade, Henry)

Auchincloss, Louis 1917- ... DLB-2, 244; Y-80

Auden, W. H. 1907-1973 ... DLB-10, 20; CDBLB-6

Audiberti, Jacques 1899-1965 ... DLB-321

Audio Art in America: A Personal Memoir ... Y-85

Audubon, John James 1785-1851 ... DLB-248

Audubon, John Woodhouse 1812-1862 ... DLB-183

Auerbach, Berthold 1812-1882 ... DLB-133

Auernheimer, Raoul 1876-1948 ... DLB-81

Augier, Emile 1820-1889 ... DLB-192

Augustine 354-430 ... DLB-115

Aulnoy, Marie-Catherine Le Jumel de Barneville, comtesse d' 1650/1651-1705 ... DLB-268

Aulus Gellius circa A.D. 125-circa A.D. 180? ... DLB-211

Austen, Jane 1775-1817 ... DLB-116; CDBLB-3

Auster, Paul 1947- ... DLB-227

Austin, Alfred 1835-1913 ... DLB-35

Austin, J. L. 1911-1960 ... DLB-262

Austin, Jane Goodwin 1831-1894 ... DLB-202

Austin, John 1790-1859 ... DLB-262

Austin, Mary Hunter 1868-1934 ... DLB-9, 78, 206, 221, 275

Austin, William 1778-1841 ... DLB-74

Australie (Emily Manning) 1845-1890 ... DLB-230

Authors and Newspapers Association ... DLB-46

Authors' Publishing Company ... DLB-49

Avallone, Michael 1924-1999 ... DLB-306; Y-99

    Tribute to John D. MacDonald ... Y-86

    Tribute to Kenneth Millar ... Y-83

    Tribute to Raymond Chandler ... Y-88

Avalon Books ... DLB-46

Avancini, Nicolaus 1611-1686 ... DLB-164

Avendaño, Fausto 1941- ... DLB-82

Averroës 1126-1198 ... DLB-115

Avery, Gillian 1926- ... DLB-161

Avicenna 980-1037 ... DLB-115

Ávila Jiménez, Antonio 1898-1965 ... DLB-283

Avison, Margaret 1918-1987 ... DLB-53

Avon Books ... DLB-46

Avyžius, Jonas 1922-1999 ... DLB-220

Awdry, Wilbert Vere 1911-1997 ... DLB-160

Awoonor, Kofi 1935- ... DLB-117

Ayala, Francisco 1906- ... DLB-322

Ayckbourn, Alan 1939- ... DLB-13, 245

Ayer, A. J. 1910-1989 ... DLB-262

Aymé, Marcel 1902-1967 ... DLB-72

Aytoun, Sir Robert 1570-1638 ... DLB-121

Aytoun, William Edmondstoune 1813-1865 ... DLB-32, 159

Azevedo, Aluísio 1857-1913 ... DLB-307

Azevedo, Manuel Antônio Álvares de 1831-1852 ... DLB-307

al-Azm, Sadik Jalal 1934- ... DLB-346

Azorín (José Martínez Ruiz) 1873-1967 ... DLB-322

B

B.V. (see Thomson, James)

Ba Jin 1904-2005 ... DLB-328

Babbitt, Irving 1865-1933 ... DLB-63

Babbitt, Natalie 1932- ... DLB-52

John Babcock [publishing house] ... DLB-49

Babel, Isaak Emmanuilovich 1894-1940 ... DLB-272

Babits, Mihály 1883-1941 ... DLB-215; CDWLB-4

Babrius circa 150-200 ... DLB-176

Babson, Marian 1929- ... DLB-276

Baca, Jimmy Santiago 1952- ... DLB-122

Bacchelli, Riccardo 1891-1985 ... DLB-264

Bache, Benjamin Franklin 1769-1798 ... DLB-43

Bachelard, Gaston 1884-1962 ... DLB-296

Bacheller, Irving 1859-1950 ... DLB-202

Bachmann, Ingeborg 1926-1973 ... DLB-85

Bačinskaitė-Bučienė, Salomėja (see Nėris, Salomėja)

Bacon, Delia 1811-1859 ... DLB-1, 243

Bacon, Francis 1561-1626 ... DLB-151, 236, 252; CDBLB-1

Bacon, Sir Nicholas circa 1510-1579 ... DLB-132

Bacon, Roger circa 1214/1220-1292 ... DLB-115

Bacon, Thomas circa 1700-1768 ... DLB-31

Bacovia, George 1881-1957 ... DLB-220; CDWLB-4

Richard G. Badger and Company ... DLB-49

Badr, Liana 1952- ... DLB-346

Bagaduce Music Lending Library ... Y-00

Bage, Robert 1728-1801 ... DLB-39

Bagehot, Walter 1826-1877 ... DLB-55

Baggesen, Jens 1764-1826 ... DLB-300

Bagley, Desmond 1923-1983 ... DLB-87

Bagley, Sarah G. 1806-1848? ... DLB-239

Bagnold, Enid 1889-1981 ... DLB-13, 160, 191, 245

Bagryana, Elisaveta 1893-1991 ... DLB-147; CDWLB-4

Bahr, Hermann 1863-1934 ... DLB-81, 118

Baïf, Jean-Antoine de 1532-1589 ... DLB-327

Bail, Murray 1941- ... DLB-325

Bailey, Abigail Abbot 1746-1815 ... DLB-200

Bailey, Alfred Goldsworthy 1905-1997 ... DLB-68

Cumulative Index

Bailey, H. C. 1878-1961 .... DLB-77
Bailey, Jacob 1731-1808 .... DLB-99
Bailey, Paul 1937- DLB-14, 271
Bailey, Philip James 1816-1902 .... DLB-32
Francis Bailey [publishing house] DLB-49
Baillargeon, Pierre 1916-1967 .... DLB-88
Baillie, Hugh 1890-1966 .... DLB-29
Baillie, Joanna 1762-1851 .... DLB-93, 344
Bailyn, Bernard 1922- DLB-17
Bain, Alexander
   English Composition and Rhetoric (1866)
   [excerpt].................... DLB-57
Bainbridge, Beryl 1933- DLB-14, 231
Baird, Irene 1901-1981 .... DLB-68
Baker, Alison 1953- DLB-335
Baker, Augustine 1575-1641 .... DLB-151
Baker, Carlos 1909-1987............... DLB-103
Baker, David 1954- DLB-120
Baker, George Pierce 1866-1935........ DLB-266
Baker, Herschel C. 1914-1990 .... DLB-111
Baker, Houston A., Jr. 1943- DLB-67
Baker, Howard
   Tribute to Caroline Gordon............ Y-81
   Tribute to Katherine Anne Porter Y-80
Baker, Nicholson 1957- DLB-227; Y-00
   Review of Nicholson Baker's *Double Fold:
   Libraries and the Assault on Paper* Y-00
Baker, Ray Stannard (David Grayson)
   1870-1946................................. DLB-345
Baker, Samuel White 1821-1893........ DLB-166
Baker, Thomas 1656-1740 .... DLB-213
Walter H. Baker Company
   ("Baker's Plays") DLB-49
The Baker and Taylor Company DLB-49
Bakhtin, Mikhail Mikhailovich
   1895-1975..................... DLB-242
Bakunin, Mikhail Aleksandrovich
   1814-1876.................... DLB-277
Balaban, John 1943- DLB-120
Bald, Wambly 1902-1990............... DLB-4
Balde, Jacob 1604-1668................ DLB-164
Balderston, John 1889-1954 .... DLB-26
Baldwin, James 1924-1987
   ...... DLB-2, 7, 33, 249, 278; Y-87; CDALB-1
Baldwin, Joseph Glover
   1815-1864................. DLB-3, 11, 248
Baldwin, Louisa (Mrs. Alfred Baldwin)
   1845-1925 .... DLB-240
Baldwin, Roger 1884-1981 .... DLB-345
Baldwin, William circa 1515-1563 ...... DLB-132
Richard and Anne Baldwin
   [publishing house] DLB-170
Bale, John 1495-1563 .... DLB-132
Balestrini, Nanni 1935- DLB-128, 196
Balfour, Sir Andrew 1630-1694 .... DLB-213

Balfour, Arthur James 1848-1930 .... DLB-190
Balfour, Sir James 1600-1657 .... DLB-213
Ballantine Books..................... DLB-46
Ballantyne, R. M. 1825-1894 .... DLB-163
Ballard, J. G. 1930- DLB-14, 207, 261, 319
Ballard, Martha Moore 1735-1812 ...... DLB-200
Ballerini, Luigi 1940- DLB-128
Ballou, Maturin Murray (Lieutenant Murray)
   1820-1895 ....DLB-79, 189
Robert O. Ballou [publishing house] DLB-46
Bal'mont, Konstantin Dmitrievich
   1867-1942 .... DLB-295
Balzac, Guez de 1597?-1654............DLB-268
Balzac, Honoré de 1799-1855 .... DLB-119
Bambara, Toni Cade
   1939-1995 .... DLB-38, 218; CDALB-7
Bamford, Samuel 1788-1872 .... DLB-190
A. L. Bancroft and Company DLB-49
Bancroft, George 1800-1891 ... DLB-1, 30, 59, 243
Bancroft, Hubert Howe 1832-1918.....DLB-47, 140
Bandeira, Manuel 1886-1968 .... DLB-307
Bandelier, Adolph F. 1840-1914 .... DLB-186
Bang, Herman 1857-1912 .... DLB-300
Bangs, John Kendrick 1862-1922 ......DLB-11, 79
Banim, John 1798-1842.........DLB-116, 158, 159
Banim, Michael 1796-1874 .... DLB-158, 159
Banks, Iain (M.) 1954- DLB-194, 261
Banks, John circa 1653-1706........... DLB-80
Banks, Russell 1940- DLB-130, 278
Bannerman, Helen 1862-1946 .... DLB-141
Bantam Books DLB-46
Banti, Anna 1895-1985.................DLB-177
Banville, John 1945- DLB-14, 271, 326
Banville, Théodore de 1823-1891....... DLB-217
Bao Tianxiao 1876-1973 .... DLB-328
Baraka, Amiri
   1934- DLB-5, 7, 16, 38; DS-8; CDALB-1
Barakat, Halim 1936- DLB-346
Barańczak, Stanisław 1946- DLB-232
Baranskaia, Natal'ia Vladimirovna
   1908- DLB-302
Baratynsky, Evgenii Abramovich
   1800-1844 .... DLB-205
Barba-Jacob, Porfirio 1883-1942....... DLB-283
Barbauld, Anna Laetitia
   1743-1825....... DLB-107, 109, 142, 158, 336
Barbeau, Marius 1883-1969 .... DLB-92
Barber, John Warner 1798-1885 .... DLB-30
Bàrberi Squarotti, Giorgio 1929- DLB-128
Barbey d'Aurevilly, Jules-Amédée
   1808-1889 .... DLB-119
Barbier, Auguste 1805-1882 .... DLB-217
Barbieri, Nicolò 1576-1641 .... DLB-339

Barbilian, Dan (see Barbu, Ion)
Barbour, Douglas 1940- DLB-334
Barbour, John circa 1316-1395 .... DLB-146
Barbour, Ralph Henry 1870-1944........ DLB-22
Barbu, Ion 1895-1961...... DLB-220; CDWLB-4
Barbusse, Henri 1873-1935............ DLB-65
Barclay, Alexander circa 1475-1552 ..... DLB-132
E. E. Barclay and Company DLB-49
C. W. Bardeen [publishing house] DLB-49
Barham, Richard Harris 1788-1845 ..... DLB-159
Barich, Bill 1943- DLB-185
Baring, Maurice 1874-1945............ DLB-34
Baring-Gould, Sabine 1834-1924 ... DLB-156, 190
Barker, A. L. 1918-2002 .... DLB-14, 139
Barker, Clive 1952- DLB-261
Barker, Dudley (see Black, Lionel)
Barker, George 1913-1991 .... DLB-20
Barker, Harley Granville 1877-1946 ..... DLB-10
Barker, Howard 1946- DLB-13, 233
Barker, James Nelson 1784-1858......... DLB-37
Barker, Jane 1652-1727 .... DLB-39, 131
Barker, Lady Mary Anne 1831-1911 .... DLB-166
Barker, Pat 1943- DLB-271, 326
Barker, William circa 1520-after 1576.... DLB-132
Arthur Barker Limited DLB-112
Barkov, Ivan Semenovich 1732-1768..... DLB-150
Barks, Coleman 1937- DLB-5
Barlach, Ernst 1870-1938 .... DLB-56, 118
Barlow, Joel 1754-1812 .... DLB-37
   The Prospect of Peace (1778) DLB-37
Barnard, John 1681-1770 .... DLB-24
Barnard, Marjorie (M. Barnard Eldershaw)
   1897-1987..................... DLB-260
Barnard, Robert 1936- DLB-276
Barne, Kitty (Mary Catherine Barne)
   1883-1957 .... DLB-160
Barnes, Barnabe 1571-1609 .... DLB-132
Barnes, Djuna 1892-1982 .... DLB-4, 9, 45; DS-15
Barnes, Jim 1933- DLB-175
Barnes, Julian 1946- DLB-194; Y-93
   Notes for a Checklist of Publications Y-01
Barnes, Margaret Ayer 1886-1967 .... DLB-9
Barnes, Peter 1931- DLB-13, 233
Barnes, William 1801-1886 .... DLB-32
A. S. Barnes and Company DLB-49
Barnes and Noble Books DLB-46
Barnet, Miguel 1940- DLB-145
Barney, Natalie 1876-1972 .... DLB-4; DS-15
Barnfield, Richard 1574-1627 ....DLB-172
Baroja, Pío 1872-1956................. DLB-322
Richard W. Baron [publishing house]..... DLB-46

Barr, Amelia Edith Huddleston 1831-1919 ..... DLB-202, 221

Barr, Robert 1850-1912 ..... DLB-70, 92

Barral, Carlos 1928-1989 ..... DLB-134

Barrax, Gerald William 1933- DLB-41, 120

Barreno, Maria Isabel (see The Three Marias: A Landmark Case in Portuguese Literary History)

Barrès, Maurice 1862-1923 ..... DLB-123

Barrett, Andrea 1954- DLB-335

Barrett, Eaton Stannard 1786-1820 ..... DLB-116

Barrie, J. M. 1860-1937 ..... DLB-10, 141, 156; CDBLB-5

Barrie and Jenkins DLB-112

Barrio, Raymond 1921- DLB-82

Barrios, Gregg 1945- DLB-122

Barry, Philip 1896-1949 ..... DLB-7, 228

Barry, Robertine (see Françoise)

Barry, Sebastian 1955- DLB-245

Barse and Hopkins DLB-46

Barstow, Stan 1928- DLB-14, 139, 207

Tribute to John Braine Y-86

Barth, John 1930- DLB-2, 227

Barthelme, Donald 1931-1989 ..... DLB-2, 234; Y-80, 89

Barthelme, Frederick 1943- DLB-244; Y-85

Barthes, Roland 1915-1980 ..... DLB-296

Bartholomew, Frank 1898-1985 ..... DLB-127

Bartlett, John 1820-1905 ..... DLB-1, 235

Bartol, Cyrus Augustus 1813-1900 ..... DLB-1, 235

Barton, Bernard 1784-1849 ..... DLB-96

Barton, John ca. 1610-1675 ..... DLB-236

Barton, Thomas Pennant 1803-1869 ..... DLB-140

Bartram, John 1699-1777 ..... DLB-31

Bartram, William 1739-1823 ..... DLB-37

Barykova, Anna Pavlovna 1839-1893 ..... DLB-277

Bashshar ibn Burd circa 714-circa 784 ..... DLB-311

Basic Books DLB-46

Basille, Theodore (see Becon, Thomas)

Bass, Rick 1958- DLB-212, 275

Bass, T. J. 1932- Y-81

Bassani, Giorgio 1916-2000 ..... DLB-128, 177, 299

Basse, William circa 1583-1653 ..... DLB-121

Bassett, John Spencer 1867-1928 ..... DLB-17

Bassler, Thomas Joseph (see Bass, T. J.)

Bate, Walter Jackson 1918-1999 ..... DLB-67, 103

Bateman, Stephen circa 1510-1584 ..... DLB-136

Christopher Bateman [publishing house] DLB-170

Bates, H. E. 1905-1974 ..... DLB-162, 191

Bates, Katharine Lee 1859-1929 ..... DLB-71

Batiushkov, Konstantin Nikolaevich 1787-1855 ..... DLB-205

B. T. Batsford [publishing house] DLB-106

Batteux, Charles 1713-1780 ..... DLB-313

Battiscombe, Georgina 1905-2006 ..... DLB-155

The Battle of Maldon circa 1000 ..... DLB-146

Baudelaire, Charles 1821-1867 ..... DLB-217

Baudrillard, Jean 1929- DLB-296

Bauer, Bruno 1809-1882 ..... DLB-133

Bauer, Wolfgang 1941- DLB-124

Baum, L. Frank 1856-1919 ..... DLB-22

Baum, Vicki 1888-1960 ..... DLB-85

Baumbach, Jonathan 1933- Y-80

Bausch, Richard 1945- DLB-130

Tribute to James Dickey Y-97

Tribute to Peter Taylor Y-94

Bausch, Robert 1945- DLB-218

Bawden, Nina 1925- DLB-14, 161, 207

Bax, Clifford 1886-1962 ..... DLB-10, 100

Baxter, Charles 1947- DLB-130

Bayer, Eleanor (see Perry, Eleanor)

Bayer, Konrad 1932-1964 ..... DLB-85

Bayle, Pierre 1647-1706 ..... DLB-268, 313

Bayley, Barrington J. 1937- DLB-261

Bayly, Thomas Haynes (Q. in the Corner) 1797-1839 ..... DLB-344

Baynes, Pauline 1922- DLB-160

Baynton, Barbara 1857-1929 ..... DLB-230

Bazin, Hervé (Jean Pierre Marie Hervé-Bazin) 1911-1996 ..... DLB-83

Bazzani Cavazzoni, Virginia 1669-1720? DLB-339

The BBC Four Samuel Johnson Prize for Non-fiction Y-02

Beach, Sylvia 1887-1962 ..... DLB-4; DS-15

Beacon Press DLB-49

Beadle and Adams DLB-49

Beagle, Peter S. 1939- Y-80

Beal, M. F. 1937- Y-81

Beale, Howard K. 1899-1959 ..... DLB-17

Beard, Charles A. 1874-1948 ..... DLB-17

Beat Generation (Beats)
  As I See It, by Carolyn Cassady DLB-16

  A Beat Chronology: The First Twenty-five Years, 1944-1969 ..... DLB-16

  The Commercialization of the Image of Revolt, by Kenneth Rexroth DLB-16

  Four Essays on the Beat Generation DLB-16

  in New York City DLB-237

  in the West DLB-237

  Outlaw Days DLB-16

  Periodicals of DLB-16

Beattie, Ann 1947- DLB-218, 278; Y-82

Beattie, James 1735-1803 ..... DLB-109

Beatty, Chester 1875-1968 ..... DLB-201

Beauchemin, Nérée 1850-1931 ..... DLB-92

Beauchemin, Yves 1941- DLB-60

Beaugrand, Honoré 1848-1906 ..... DLB-99

Beaulieu, Victor-Lévy 1945- DLB-53

Beaumarchais, Pierre-Augustin Caron de 1732-1799 ..... DLB-313

Beaumer, Mme de ?-1766 ..... DLB-313

Beaumont, Francis circa 1584-1616 and Fletcher, John 1579-1625 ..... DLB-58; CDBLB-1

Beaumont, Sir John 1583?-1627 ..... DLB-121

Beaumont, Joseph 1616-1699 ..... DLB-126

Beauvoir, Simone de 1908-1986 ..... DLB-72; Y-86

Personal Tribute to Simone de Beauvoir Y-86

Beaver, Bruce 1928- DLB-289

Bechdel, Alison 1960- DLB-345

Becher, Ulrich 1910-1990 ..... DLB-69

Beck, Warren 1896-1986 ..... DLB-335

Becker, Carl 1873-1945 ..... DLB-17

Becker, Jurek 1937-1997 ..... DLB-75, 299

Becker, Jurgen 1932- DLB-75

Beckett, Mary 1926- DLB-319

Beckett, Samuel 1906-1989 ..... DLB-13, 15, 233, 319, 321, 329; Y-90; CDBLB-7

Beckford, William 1760-1844 ..... DLB-39, 213

Beckham, Barry 1944- DLB-33

Bećković, Matija 1939- DLB-181

Becon, Thomas circa 1512-1567 ..... DLB-136

Becque, Henry 1837-1899 ..... DLB-192

Beddoes, Thomas 1760-1808 ..... DLB-158

Beddoes, Thomas Lovell 1803-1849 ..... DLB-96

Bede circa 673-735 ..... DLB-146

Bedford-Jones, H. 1887-1949 ..... DLB-251

Bedregal, Yolanda 1913-1999 ..... DLB-283

Beebe, William 1877-1962 ..... DLB-275

Beecher, Catharine Esther 1800-1878 ..... DLB-1, 243

Beecher, Henry Ward 1813-1887 ..... DLB-3, 43, 250

Beer, George L. 1872-1920 ..... DLB-47

Beer, Johann 1655-1700 ..... DLB-168

Beer, Patricia 1919-1999 ..... DLB-40

Beerbohm, Max 1872-1956 ..... DLB-34, 100

Beer-Hofmann, Richard 1866-1945 ..... DLB-81

Beers, Henry A. 1847-1926 ..... DLB-71

S. O. Beeton [publishing house] DLB-106

Begley, Louis 1933- DLB-299

Bégon, Elisabeth 1696-1755 ..... DLB-99

Behan, Brendan 1923-1964 ..... DLB-13, 233; CDBLB-7

Behn, Aphra 1640?-1689 ..... DLB-39, 80, 131

Behn, Harry 1898-1973 ..... DLB-61

Behrman, S. N. 1893-1973 ..... DLB-7, 44

Beklemishev, Iurii Solomonvich
(see Krymov, Iurii Solomonovich)

Belaney, Archibald Stansfeld (see Grey Owl)

Belasco, David 1853-1931 .... DLB-7

Clarke Belford and Company.......... DLB-49

Belgian Luxembourg American Studies
Association....................... Y-01

Belinsky, Vissarion Grigor'evich
1811-1848..................... DLB-198

Belitt, Ben 1911-2003 .... DLB-5

Belknap, Jeremy 1744-1798.......... DLB-30, 37

Bell, Adrian 1901-1980................ DLB-191

Bell, Clive 1881-1964 ....DS-10

Bell, Daniel 1919- DLB-246

Bell, Gertrude Margaret Lowthian
1868-1926 .... DLB-174

Bell, James Madison 1826-1902 .... DLB-50

Bell, Madison Smartt 1957- DLB-218, 278

    Tribute to Andrew Nelson Lytle Y-95

    Tribute to Peter Taylor................ Y-94

Bell, Marvin 1937- DLB-5

Bell, Millicent 1919- DLB-111

Bell, Quentin 1910-1996................ DLB-155

Bell, Vanessa 1879-1961 ....DS-10

George Bell and Sons DLB-106

Robert Bell [publishing house] DLB-49

Bellamy, Edward 1850-1898............ DLB-12

Bellamy, Joseph 1719-1790 .... DLB-31

John Bellamy [publishing house]........ DLB-170

La Belle Assemblée 1806-1837 .... DLB-110

Bellezza, Dario 1944-1996 .... DLB-128

Belli, Carlos Germán 1927- DLB-290

Belli, Gioconda 1948- DLB-290

Belloc, Hilaire 1870-1953 .... DLB-19, 100, 141, 174

Belloc, Madame (see Parkes, Bessie Rayner)

Bellonci, Maria 1902-1986 .... DLB-196

Bellow, Saul 1915-2005
.... DLB-2, 28, 299, 329; Y-82;
                        DS-3; CDALB-1

    Tribute to Isaac Bashevis Singer......... Y-91

Belmont Productions DLB-46

Belov, Vasilii Ivanovich 1932- DLB-302

Bels, Alberts 1938- DLB-232

Belševica, Vizma 1931- ... DLB-232; CDWLB-4

Bely, Andrei 1880-1934 .... DLB-295

Bemelmans, Ludwig 1898-1962 .... DLB-22

Bemis, Samuel Flagg 1891-1973 .... DLB-17

William Bemrose [publishing house] DLB-106

Ben no Naishi 1228?-1271?........... DLB-203

Benavente, Jacinto 1866-1954.......... DLB-329

Benchley, Robert 1889-1945............ DLB-11

Bencúr, Matej (see Kukučin, Martin)

Benedetti, Mario 1920- DLB-113

Benedict, Pinckney 1964- DLB-244

Benedict, Ruth 1887-1948............ DLB-246

Benedictus, David 1938- DLB-14

Benedikt Gröndal 1826-1907 .... DLB-293

Benedikt, Michael 1935- DLB-5

Benediktov, Vladimir Grigor'evich
1807-1873 .... DLB-205

Benét, Stephen Vincent
1898-1943 .... DLB-4, 48, 102, 249

    Stephen Vincent Benét Centenary Y-97

Benét, William Rose 1886-1950 .... DLB-45

Benford, Gregory 1941- Y-82

Benítez, Sandra 1941- DLB-292

Benjamin, Park 1809-1864 ..... DLB-3, 59, 73, 250

Benjamin, Peter (see Cunningham, Peter)

Benjamin, S. G. W. 1837-1914 .... DLB-189

Benjamin, Walter 1892-1940 .... DLB-242

Benlowes, Edward 1602-1676.......... DLB-126

Benn, Gottfried 1886-1956............ DLB-56

Benn Brothers Limited DLB-106

Bennett, Alan 1934- DLB-310

Bennett, Arnold
1867-1931.... DLB-10, 34, 98, 135; CDBLB-5

    The Arnold Bennett Society............ Y-98

Bennett, Charles 1899-1995 .... DLB-44

Bennett, Emerson 1822-1905 .... DLB-202

Bennett, Gwendolyn 1902-1981 .... DLB-51

Bennett, Hal 1930- DLB-33

Bennett, James Gordon 1795-1872 .... DLB-43

Bennett, James Gordon, Jr. 1841-1918 .... DLB-23

Bennett, John 1865-1956 .... DLB-42

Bennett, Louise 1919-2006...DLB-117; CDWLB-3

Benni, Stefano 1947- DLB-196

Benoist, Françoise-Albine Puzin de
La Martinière 1731-1809 .... DLB-313

Benoit, Jacques 1941- DLB-60

Benrimo, J. Harry 1874-1942 .... DLB-341

Benson, A. C. 1862-1925 .... DLB-98

Benson, E. F. 1867-1940 .... DLB-135, 153

    The E. F. Benson Society............. Y-98

    The Tilling Society.................. Y-98

Benson, Jackson J. 1930- DLB-111

Benson, Robert Hugh 1871-1914 ...... DLB-153

Benson, Stella 1892-1933 .... DLB-36, 162

Bent, James Theodore 1852-1897........DLB-174

Bent, Mabel Virginia Anna ?-?..........DLB-174

Bentham, Jeremy 1748-1832....DLB-107, 158, 252

Bentley, E. C. 1875-1956............. DLB-70

Bentley, Phyllis 1894-1977 .... DLB-191

Bentley, Richard 1662-1742 .... DLB-252

Richard Bentley [publishing house] DLB-106

Benton, Robert 1932- DLB-44

Benziger Brothers DLB-49

Beowulf circa 900-1000 or 790-825
.... DLB-146; CDBLB-1

Berberova, Nina 1901-1993 ....DLB-317

Berent, Wacław 1873-1940............ DLB-215

Beresford, Anne 1929- DLB-40

Beresford, John Davys
1873-1947............DLB-162, 178, 197

    "Experiment in the Novel" (1929)
[excerpt]...................... DLB-36

Beresford-Howe, Constance 1922- DLB-88

R. G. Berford Company................ DLB-49

Berg, Elizabeth 1948- DLB-292

Berg, Stephen 1934- DLB-5

Bergelson, David (Dovid Bergelson)
1884-1952 .... DLB-333

Bergengruen, Werner 1892-1964 .... DLB-56

Berger, John 1926- DLB-14, 207, 319, 326

Berger, Meyer 1898-1959 .... DLB-29

Berger, Thomas 1924- DLB-2; Y-80

    A Statement by Thomas Berger......... Y-80

Bergman, Hjalmar 1883-1931 .... DLB-259

Bergman, Ingmar 1918-2007 .... DLB-257

Bergson, Henri 1859-1941 .... DLB-329

Berkeley, Anthony 1893-1971........... DLB-77

Berkeley, George 1685-1753 .....DLB-31, 101, 252

The Berkley Publishing Corporation DLB-46

Berkman, Alexander 1870-1936 .... DLB-303

Berlin, Irving 1888-1989.............. DLB-265

Berlin, Lucia 1936- DLB-130

Berman, Marshall 1940- DLB-246

Berman, Sabina 1955- DLB-305

Bernal, Vicente J. 1888-1915 .... DLB-82

Bernanos, Georges 1888-1948 .... DLB-72

Bernard, Catherine 1663?-1712 ....DLB-268

Bernard, Harry 1898-1979 .... DLB-92

Bernard, John 1756-1828 .... DLB-37

Bernard of Chartres circa 1060-1124? ... DLB-115

Bernard of Clairvaux 1090-1153 .... DLB-208

Bernard, Richard 1568-1641/1642 ...... DLB-281

Bernard Silvestris
fl. circa 1130-1160 .... DLB-208

Bernardin de Saint-Pierre 1737-1814..... DLB-313

Bernari, Carlo 1909-1992.............DLB-177

Bernhard, Thomas
1931-1989 ....DLB-85, 124; CDWLB-2

Berniéres, Louis de 1954- DLB-271

Bernstein, Charles 1950- DLB-169

Béroalde de Verville, François
1556-1626 .... DLB-327

Berriault, Gina 1926-1999 .... DLB-130

Berrigan, Daniel 1921- DLB-5

Berrigan, Ted 1934-1983 . . . . DLB-5, 169

Berry, Wendell 1934- . . . DLB-5, 6, 234, 275, 342

Berryman, John 1914-1972 . . . . DLB-48; CDALB-1

Bersianik, Louky 1930- DLB-60

Berssenbrugge, Mei-mei 1947- DLB-312

Thomas Berthelet [publishing house] DLB-170

Berto, Giuseppe 1914-1978 . . . . DLB-177

Bertocci, Peter Anthony 1910-1989 . . . . . . DLB-279

Bertolucci, Attilio 1911-2000 . . . . DLB-128

Berton, Pierre 1920-2004 . . . . DLB-68

Bertrand, Louis "Aloysius" 1807-1841 . . . . DLB-217

Besant, Sir Walter 1836-1901 . . . . DLB-135, 190

Bessa-Luís, Agustina 1922- DLB-287

Bessette, Gerard 1920-2005 . . . . DLB-53

Bessie, Alvah 1904-1985 . . . . DLB-26

Bester, Alfred 1913-1987 . . . . DLB-8

Besterman, Theodore 1904-1976 . . . . DLB-201

Beston, Henry (Henry Beston Sheahan)
  1888-1968 . . . . DLB-275

Best-Seller Lists
  An Assessment Y-84
  What's Really Wrong With
    Bestseller Lists Y-84

Bestuzhev, Aleksandr Aleksandrovich
  (Marlinsky) 1797-1837 . . . . DLB-198

Bestuzhev, Nikolai Aleksandrovich
  1791-1855 . . . . DLB-198

Betham-Edwards, Matilda Barbara
  (see Edwards, Matilda Barbara Betham-)

Bethune, Mary McLeod 1875-1955 . . . . . . DLB-345

Betjeman, John
  1906-1984 . . . . DLB-20; Y-84; CDBLB-7

Betocchi, Carlo 1899-1986 . . . . DLB-128

Bettarini, Mariella 1942- DLB-128

Betts, Doris 1932- DLB-218; Y-82

Beveridge, Albert J. 1862-1927 . . . . DLB-17

Beveridge, Judith 1956- DLB-325

Beverley, Robert circa 1673-1722 . . . . . . DLB-24, 30

Bevilacqua, Alberto 1934- DLB-196

Bevington, Louisa Sarah 1845-1895 . . . . . DLB-199

Beyle, Marie-Henri (see Stendhal)

Bèze, Théodore de (Theodore Beza)
  1519-1605 . . . . DLB-327

Bhatt, Sujata 1956- DLB-323

Białoszewski, Miron 1922-1983 . . . . DLB-232

Bianco, Margery Williams 1881-1944 . . . . DLB-160

Bibaud, Adèle 1854-1941 . . . . DLB-92

Bibaud, Michel 1782-1857 . . . . DLB-99

Bibliography
  Bibliographical and Textual Scholarship
    Since World War II Y-89
  Center for Bibliographical Studies and
    Research at the University of
    California, Riverside Y-91

The Great Bibliographers Series Y-93
  Primary Bibliography: A Retrospective Y-95

Bichsel, Peter 1935- DLB-75

Bickerstaff, Isaac John 1733-circa 1808 . . . . DLB-89

Drexel Biddle [publishing house] DLB-49

Bidermann, Jacob
  1577 or 1578-1639 . . . . DLB-164

Bidwell, Walter Hilliard 1798-1881 . . . . . . DLB-79

Biehl, Charlotta Dorothea 1731-1788 . . . . . DLB-300

Bienek, Horst 1930-1990 . . . . DLB-75

Bierbaum, Otto Julius 1865-1910 . . . . DLB-66

Bierce, Ambrose 1842-1914?
  . . . . . . DLB-11, 12, 23, 71, 74, 186; CDALB-3

Bigelow, William F. 1879-1966 . . . . DLB-91

Biggers, Earl Derr 1884-1933 . . . . DLB-306

Biggle, Lloyd, Jr. 1923-2002 . . . . DLB-8

Bigiaretti, Libero 1905-1993 . . . . DLB-177

Bigland, Eileen 1898-1970 . . . . DLB-195

Biglow, Hosea (see Lowell, James Russell)

Bigongiari, Piero 1914-1997 . . . . DLB-128

Bilac, Olavo 1865-1918 . . . . DLB-307

Bilenchi, Romano 1909-1989 . . . . DLB-264

Billinger, Richard 1890-1965 . . . . DLB-124

Billings, Hammatt 1818-1874 . . . . DLB-188

Billings, John Shaw 1898-1975 . . . . DLB-137

Billings, Josh (see Shaw, Henry Wheeler)

Binchy, Maeve 1940- DLB-319

Binding, Rudolf G. 1867-1938 . . . . DLB-66

Bing Xin 1900-1999 . . . . DLB-328

Bingay, Malcolm 1884-1953 . . . . DLB-241

Bingham, Caleb 1757-1817 . . . . DLB-42

Bingham, George Barry 1906-1988 . . . . . . DLB-127

Bingham, Sallie 1937- DLB-234

William Bingley [publishing house] DLB-154

Binyon, Laurence 1869-1943 . . . . DLB-19

Biographia Brittanica DLB-142

Biography
  Biographical Documents Y-84, 85
  A Celebration of Literary Biography Y-98
  Conference on Modern Biography Y-85
  The Cult of Biography
    Excerpts from the Second Folio Debate:
    "Biographies are generally a disease of
    English Literature" Y-86
  New Approaches to Biography: Challenges
    from Critical Theory, USC Conference
    on Literary Studies, 1990 . . . . Y-90
  "The New Biography," by Virginia Woolf,
    New York Herald Tribune,
    30 October 1927 . . . . DLB-149
  "The Practice of Biography," in *The English
    Sense of Humour and Other Essays*, by
    Harold Nicolson DLB-149
  "Principles of Biography," in *Elizabethan
    and Other Essays*, by Sidney Lee . . . DLB-149

Remarks at the Opening of "The Biographical
  Part of Literature" Exhibition, by
  William R. Cagle Y-98
Survey of Literary Biographies Y-00
A Transit of Poets and Others: American
  Biography in 1982 . . . . Y-82
The Year in Literary
  Biography Y-83–01

Biography, The Practice of:
  An Interview with B. L. Reid Y-83
  An Interview with David Herbert Donald . . Y-87
  An Interview with Humphrey Carpenter . . . Y-84
  An Interview with Joan Mellen Y-94
  An Interview with John Caldwell Guilds . . . Y-92
  An Interview with William Manchester . . . Y-85

John Bioren [publishing house] DLB-49

Bioy Casares, Adolfo 1914-1999 . . . . DLB-113

Birch, Thomas 1705-1766 . . . . DLB-336

Bird, Isabella Lucy 1831-1904 . . . . DLB-166

Bird, Robert Montgomery 1806-1854 . . . . DLB-202

Bird, William 1888-1963 . . . . DLB-4; DS-15

  The Cost of the *Cantos*: William Bird
    to Ezra Pound Y-01

Birdsell, Sandra 1942- DLB-334

Birken, Sigmund von 1626-1681 . . . . DLB-164

Birney, Earle 1904-1995 . . . . DLB-88

Birrell, Augustine 1850-1933 . . . . DLB-98

Bisher, Furman 1918- DLB-171

Bishop, Elizabeth
  1911-1979 . . . . DLB-5, 169; CDALB-6
  The Elizabeth Bishop Society Y-01

Bishop, John Peale 1892-1944 . . . . DLB-4, 9, 45

Bismarck, Otto von 1815-1898 . . . . DLB-129

Bisset, Robert 1759-1805 . . . . DLB-142

Bissett, Bill 1939- DLB-53

Bitov, Andrei Georgievich 1937- DLB-302

Bitzius, Albert (see Gotthelf, Jeremias)

Bjørnboe, Jens 1920-1976 . . . . DLB-297

Bjørnson, Bjørnstjerne 1832-1910 . . . . . . DLB-329

Bjørnvig, Thorkild 1918-2004 . . . . DLB-214

Black, David (D. M.) 1941- DLB-40

Black, Gavin (Oswald Morris Wynd)
  1913-1998 . . . . DLB-276

Black, Lionel (Dudley Barker)
  1910-1980 . . . . DLB-276

Black, Winifred 1863-1936 . . . . DLB-25

Walter J. Black [publishing house] DLB-46

Blackamore, Arthur 1679-? DLB-24, 39

Blackburn, Alexander L. 1929- Y-85

Blackburn, John 1923-1993 . . . . DLB-261

Blackburn, Paul 1926-1971 . . . . DLB-16; Y-81

Blackburn, Thomas 1916-1977 . . . . DLB-27

Blacker, Terence 1948- DLB-271

Blackmore, R. D. 1825-1900 . . . . DLB-18

Blackmore, Sir Richard 1654-1729 ...... DLB-131

Blackmur, R. P. 1904-1965 .... DLB-63

Blackwell, Alice Stone 1857-1950 ...... DLB-303

Basil Blackwell, Publisher DLB-106

Blackstone, William 1723-1780 .... DLB-336

Blackwood, Algernon Henry
  1869-1951 .... DLB-153, 156, 178

Blackwood, Caroline 1931-1996 ..... DLB-14, 207

William Blackwood and Sons, Ltd. DLB-154

Blackwood's Edinburgh Magazine
  1817-1980 .... DLB-110

Blades, William 1824-1890 .... DLB-184

Blaga, Lucian 1895-1961 .... DLB-220

Blagden, Isabella 1817?-1873 .... DLB-199

Blair, Eric Arthur (see Orwell, George)

Blair, Francis Preston 1791-1876 .... DLB-43

Blair, Hugh
  Lectures on Rhetoric and Belles Lettres (1783),
  [excerpts] DLB-31

Blair, James circa 1655-1743 .... DLB-24

Blair, John Durburrow 1759-1823 .... DLB-37

Blais, Marie-Claire 1939- DLB-53

Blaise, Clark 1940- DLB-53

Blake, George 1893-1961 .... DLB-191

Blake, Lillie Devereux 1833-1913 .... DLB-202, 221

Blake, Nicholas (C. Day Lewis)
  1904-1972 .... DLB-77

Blake, William
  1757-1827 ...... DLB-93, 154, 163; CDBLB-3

The Blakiston Company DLB-49

Blanchard, Stephen 1950- DLB-267

Blanchot, Maurice 1907-2003 .... DLB-72, 296

Blanckenburg, Christian Friedrich von
  1744-1796 .... DLB-94

Blandiana, Ana 1942- DLB-232; CDWLB-4

Blanshard, Brand 1892-1987 .... DLB-279

Blasco Ibáñez, Vicente 1867-1928 .... DLB-322

Blaser, Robin 1925- DLB-165

Blaumanis, Rudolfs 1863-1908 .... DLB-220

Bleasdale, Alan 1946- DLB-245

Bledsoe, Albert Taylor
  1809-1877 .... DLB-3, 79, 248

Bleecker, Ann Eliza 1752-1783 .... DLB-200

Blelock and Company DLB-49

Blennerhassett, Margaret Agnew
  1773-1842 .... DLB-99

Geoffrey Bles [publishing house] DLB-112

Blessington, Marguerite, Countess of
  1789-1849 .... DLB-166

Blew, Mary Clearman 1939- DLB-256

Blicher, Steen Steensen 1782-1848 ...... DLB-300

The Blickling Homilies circa 971 .... DLB-146

Blind, Mathilde 1841-1896 .... DLB-199

The Blind Assassin, 2000 Booker Prize winner,
  Margaret Atwood DLB-326

Blish, James 1921-1975 .... DLB-8

E. Bliss and E. White
  [publishing house] DLB-49

Bliven, Bruce 1889-1977 .... DLB-137

Blixen, Karen 1885-1962 .... DLB-214

Bloch, Ernst 1885-1977 .... DLB-296

Bloch, Robert 1917-1994 .... DLB-44
  Tribute to John D. MacDonald Y-86

Block, Lawrence 1938- DLB-226

Block, Rudolph (see Lessing, Bruno)

Blok, Aleksandr Aleksandrovich
  1880-1921 .... DLB-295

Blondal, Patricia 1926-1959 .... DLB-88

Bloom, Harold 1930- DLB-67

Bloomer, Amelia 1818-1894 .... DLB-79

Bloomfield, Robert 1766-1823 .... DLB-93

Bloomsbury Group DS-10
  The *Dreadnought* Hoax DS-10

Bloor, Ella Reeve 1862-1951 .... DLB-303

Blotner, Joseph 1923- DLB-111

Blount, Thomas 1618?-1679 .... DLB-236

Bloy, Léon 1846-1917 .... DLB-123

Blue Cloud, Peter (Aroniawenrate)
  1933- DLB-342

Blume, Judy 1938- DLB-52
  Tribute to Theodor Seuss Geisel Y-91

Blunck, Hans Friedrich 1888-1961 ...... DLB-66

Blunden, Edmund 1896-1974 .... DLB-20, 100, 155

Blundeville, Thomas 1522?-1606 .... DLB-236

Blunt, Lady Anne Isabella Noel
  1837-1917 .... DLB-174

Blunt, Wilfrid Scawen 1840-1922 ..... DLB-19, 174

Bly, Carol 1930- DLB-335

Bly, Nellie (see Cochrane, Elizabeth)

Bly, Robert 1926- DLB-5, 342

Blyton, Enid 1897-1968 .... DLB-160

Boaden, James 1762-1839 .... DLB-89

Boal, Augusto 1931- DLB-307

Boas, Frederick S. 1862-1957 .... DLB-149

The Bobbs-Merrill Company DLB-46, 291

The Bobbs-Merrill Archive at the
  Lilly Library, Indiana University Y-90

Boborykin, Petr Dmitrievich
  1836-1921 .... DLB-238

Bobrov, Semen Sergeevich
  1763?-1810 .... DLB-150

Bobrowski, Johannes 1917-1965 .... DLB-75

Bocage, Manuel Maria Barbosa du
  1765-1805 .... DLB-287

Bodenheim, Maxwell 1892-1954 ...... DLB-9, 45

Bodenstedt, Friedrich von 1819-1892 .... DLB-129

Bodini, Vittorio 1914-1970 .... DLB-128

Bodkin, M. McDonnell 1850-1933 .... DLB-70

Bodley, Sir Thomas 1545-1613 .... DLB-213

Bodley Head DLB-112

Bodmer, Johann Jakob 1698-1783 .... DLB-97

Bodmershof, Imma von 1895-1982 ...... DLB-85

Bodsworth, Fred 1918- DLB-68

Böðvar Guðmundsson 1939- DLB-293

Boehm, Sydney 1908-1990 .... DLB-44

Boer, Charles 1939- DLB-5

Boethius circa 480-circa 524 .... DLB-115

Boethius of Dacia circa 1240-? DLB-115

Bogan, Louise 1897-1970 .... DLB-45, 169

Bogarde, Dirk 1921-1999 .... DLB-14

Bogdanov, Aleksandr Aleksandrovich
  1873-1928 .... DLB-295

Bogdanovich, Ippolit Fedorovich
  circa 1743-1803 .... DLB-150

Bogosian, Eric 1953- DLB-341

David Bogue [publishing house] DLB-106

Bohjalian, Chris 1960- DLB-292

Böhme, Jakob 1575-1624 .... DLB-164

H. G. Bohn [publishing house] DLB-106

Bohse, August 1661-1742 .... DLB-168

Boie, Heinrich Christian 1744-1806 ...... DLB-94

Boileau-Despréaux, Nicolas 1636-1711 .... DLB-268

Bojunga, Lygia 1932- DLB-307

Bok, Edward W. 1863-1930 ...... DLB-91; DS-16

Boland, Eavan 1944- DLB-40

Boldrewood, Rolf (Thomas Alexander Browne)
  1826?-1915 .... DLB-230

Bolingbroke, Henry St. John, Viscount
  1678-1751 .... DLB-101, 336

Böll, Heinrich
  1917-1985 ..... DLB-69, 329; Y-85; CDWLB-2

Bolling, Robert 1738-1775 .... DLB-31

Bolotov, Andrei Timofeevich
  1738-1833 .... DLB-150

Bolt, Carol 1941- DLB-60

Bolt, Robert 1924-1995 .... DLB-13, 233

Bolton, Herbert E. 1870-1953 .... DLB-17

Bonarelli, Guidubaldo 1563-1608 ...... DLB-339

Bonaventura DLB-90

Bonaventure circa 1217-1274 .... DLB-115

Bonaviri, Giuseppe 1924- DLB-177

Bond, Edward 1934- DLB-13, 310

Bond, Michael 1926- DLB-161

Bondarev, Iurii Vasil'evich 1924- DLB-302

The Bone People, 1985 Booker Prize winner,
  Keri Hulme DLB-326

Albert and Charles Boni
  [publishing house] DLB-46

Boni and Liveright DLB-46

Bonnefoy, Yves 1923- DLB-258

Bonner, Marita 1899-1971 . . . . DLB-228

Bonner, Paul Hyde 1893-1968 . . . . DS-17

Bonner, Sherwood (see McDowell, Katharine Sherwood Bonner)

Robert Bonner's Sons DLB-49

Bonnin, Gertrude Simmons (see Zitkala-Ša)

Bonsanti, Alessandro 1904-1984 . . . . DLB-177

Bontempelli, Massimo 1878-1960 . . . . DLB-264

Bontemps, Arna 1902-1973 . . . . DLB-48, 51

The Book Buyer (1867-1880, 1884-1918, 1935-1938) DS-13

The Book League of America DLB-46

Book Reviewing
    The American Book Review: A Sketch. . . . Y-92

    Book Reviewing and the Literary Scene Y-96, 97

    Book Reviewing in America Y-87–94

    Book Reviewing in America and the Literary Scene Y-95

    Book Reviewing in Texas Y-94

    Book Reviews in Glossy Magazines Y-95

    Do They or Don't They? Writers Reading Book Reviews Y-01

    The Most Powerful Book Review in America [*New York Times Book Review*] Y-82

    Some Surprises and Universal Truths Y-92

    The Year in Book Reviewing and the Literary Situation Y-98

Book Supply Company DLB-49

The Book Trade History Group Y-93

Bookchin, Murray 1921-2006 . . . . DLB-345

The Booker Prize Y-96–98

    Address by Anthony Thwaite, Chairman of the Booker Prize Judges Comments from Former Booker Prize Winners Y-86

Boorde, Andrew circa 1490-1549 . . . . DLB-136

Boorstin, Daniel J. 1914-2004 . . . . DLB-17

    Tribute to Archibald MacLeish Y-82

    Tribute to Charles Scribner Jr. Y-95

Booth, Franklin 1874-1948 . . . . DLB-188

Booth, Mary L. 1831-1889 . . . . DLB-79

Booth, Philip 1925-2007 . . . . Y-82

Booth, Wayne C. 1921-2005 . . . . DLB-67

Booth, William 1829-1912 . . . . DLB-190

Bor, Josef 1906-1979 . . . . DLB-299

Borchardt, Rudolf 1877-1945 . . . . DLB-66

Borchert, Wolfgang 1921-1947 . . . . . . DLB-69, 124

Bording, Anders 1619-1677 . . . . DLB-300

Borel, Pétrus 1809-1859 . . . . DLB-119

Borgen, Johan 1902-1979 . . . . DLB-297

Borges, Jorge Luis 1899-1986 . . . DLB-113, 283; Y-86; CDWLB-3

    The Poetry of Jorge Luis Borges Y-86

    A Personal Tribute Y-86

Borgese, Giuseppe Antonio 1882-1952 . . . DLB-264

Börne, Ludwig 1786-1837 . . . . DLB-90

Bornstein, Miriam 1950- DLB-209

Borowski, Tadeusz 1922-1951 . . . . DLB-215; CDWLB-4

Borrow, George 1803-1881 . . . . . . DLB-21, 55, 166

Bosanquet, Bernard 1848-1923 . . . . DLB-262

Boscán, Juan circa 1490-1542 . . . . DLB-318

Bosch, Juan 1909-2001 . . . . DLB-145

Bosco, Henri 1888-1976 . . . . DLB-72

Bosco, Monique 1927- DLB-53

Bosman, Herman Charles 1905-1951 . . . . DLB-225

Bossuet, Jacques-Bénigne 1627-1704 . . . . . DLB-268

Bostic, Joe 1908-1988 . . . . DLB-241

Boston, Lucy M. 1892-1990 . . . . DLB-161

Boston Quarterly Review DLB-1

Boston University
    Editorial Institute at Boston University Y-00

    Special Collections at Boston University . . . Y-99

Boswell, James 1740-1795 . . . . DLB-104, 142; CDBLB-2

Boswell, Robert 1953- DLB-234

Bosworth, David Y-82

    Excerpt from "Excerpts from a Report of the Commission," in *The Death of Descartes* Y-82

Bote, Hermann circa 1460-circa 1520 . . . . DLB-179

Botev, Khristo 1847-1876 . . . . DLB-147

Botkin, Vasilii Petrovich 1811-1869 . . . . . DLB-277

Botta, Anne C. Lynch 1815-1891 . . . . . DLB-3, 250

Botto, Ján (see Krasko, Ivan)

Bottome, Phyllis 1882-1963 . . . . DLB-197

Bottomley, Gordon 1874-1948 . . . . DLB-10

Bottoms, David 1949- DLB-120; Y-83

    Tribute to James Dickey Y-97

Bottrall, Ronald 1906-1959 . . . . DLB-20

Bouchardy, Joseph 1810-1870 . . . . DLB-192

Boucher, Anthony 1911-1968 . . . . DLB-8

Boucher, Jonathan 1738-1804 . . . . DLB-31

Boucher de Boucherville, Georges 1814-1894 . . . . DLB-99

Boucicault, Dion (Dionysius Boursiquot, Dion Bourcicault, Lee Moreton) 1820-1890 . . . . DLB-344

Boudreau, Daniel (see Coste, Donat)

Bouhours, Dominique 1628-1702 . . . . DLB-268

Boudjedra, Rachid 1941- DLB-346

Boujah, Slaheddine 1956- DLB-346

Bourassa, Napoléon 1827-1916 . . . . DLB-99

Bourget, Paul 1852-1935 . . . . DLB-123

Bourinot, John George 1837-1902 . . . . DLB-99

Bourjaily, Vance 1922- DLB-2, 143

Bourne, Edward Gaylord 1860-1908 . . . . . . DLB-47

Bourne, Randolph 1886-1918 . . . . DLB-63

Bousoño, Carlos 1923- DLB-108

Bousquet, Joë 1897-1950 . . . . DLB-72

Bova, Ben 1932- Y-81

Bovard, Oliver K. 1872-1945 . . . . DLB-25

Bove, Emmanuel 1898-1945 . . . . DLB-72

Bowen, Elizabeth 1899-1973 . . . . DLB-15, 162; CDBLB-7

Bowen, Francis 1811-1890 . . . . DLB-1, 59, 235

Bowen, John 1924- DLB-13

Bowen, Marjorie 1886-1952 . . . . DLB-153

Bowen-Merrill Company DLB-49

Bowering, George 1935- DLB-53

Bowering, Marilyn 1949- DLB-334

Bowers, Bathsheba 1671-1718 . . . . DLB-200

Bowers, Claude G. 1878-1958 . . . . DLB-17

Bowers, Edgar 1924-2000 . . . . DLB-5

Bowers, Fredson Thayer 1905-1991 . . . . DLB-140; Y-91

    The Editorial Style of Fredson Bowers Y-91

    Fredson Bowers and Studies in Bibliography Y-91

    Fredson Bowers and the Cambridge Beaumont and Fletcher Y-91

    Fredson Bowers as Critic of Renaissance Dramatic Literature Y-91

    Fredson Bowers as Music Critic Y-91

    Fredson Bowers, Master Teacher Y-91

    An Interview [on Nabokov] Y-80

    Working with Fredson Bowers Y-91

Bowles, Paul 1910-1999 . . . . . . DLB-5, 6, 218; Y-99

Bowles, Samuel, III 1826-1878 . . . . DLB-43

Bowles, William Lisle 1762-1850 . . . . DLB-93

Bowling, Tim 1964- DLB-334

Bowman, Louise Morey 1882-1944 . . . . DLB-68

Bowne, Borden Parker 1847-1919 . . . . DLB-270

Boyd, James 1888-1944 . . . . DLB-9; DS-16

Boyd, John 1912-2002 . . . . DLB-310

Boyd, John 1919- DLB-8

Boyd, Martin 1893-1972 . . . . DLB-260

Boyd, Thomas 1898-1935 . . . . DLB-9, 316; DS-16

Boyd, William 1952- DLB-231

Boye, Karin 1900-1941 . . . . DLB-259

Boyesen, Hjalmar Hjorth 1848-1895 . . . . DLB-12, 71; DS-13

Boylan, Clare 1948- DLB-267

Boyle, Kay 1902-1992 . . . . DLB-4, 9, 48, 86; DS-15; Y-93

Boyle, Roger, Earl of Orrery 1621-1679 . . . DLB-80

Boyle, T. Coraghessan 1948- DLB-218, 278; Y-86

Božić, Mirko 1919- DLB-181

Bracciolini, Francesco 1566-1645 . . . . DLB-339

Brackenbury, Alison 1953- DLB-40

Cumulative Index

Brackenridge, Hugh Henry
1748-1816................... DLB-11, 37
   The Rising Glory of America....... DLB-37

Brackett, Charles 1892-1969............ DLB-26

Brackett, Leigh 1915-1978 .... DLB-8, 26

John Bradburn [publishing house] DLB-49

Bradbury, Malcolm 1932-2000...... DLB-14, 207

Bradbury, Ray 1920- DLB-2, 8; CDALB-6

Bradbury and Evans................. DLB-106

Braddon, Mary Elizabeth
1835-1915..................DLB-18, 70, 156

Bradford, Andrew 1686-1742........ DLB-43, 73

Bradford, Gamaliel 1863-1932........... DLB-17

Bradford, John 1749-1830............... DLB-43

Bradford, Roark 1896-1948............. DLB-86

Bradford, William 1590-1657 .... DLB-24, 30

Bradford, William, III 1719-1791 ...... DLB-43, 73

Bradlaugh, Charles 1833-1891.......... DLB-57

Bradley, David 1950- DLB-33

Bradley, F. H. 1846-1924 .... DLB-262

Bradley, Katherine Harris (see Field, Michael)

Bradley, Marion Zimmer 1930-1999 ...... DLB-8

Bradley, William Aspenwall 1878-1939 .... DLB-4

Ira Bradley and Company DLB-49

J. W. Bradley and Company............ DLB-49

Bradshaw, Henry 1831-1886 .... DLB-184

Bradstreet, Anne
1612 or 1613-1672 .... DLB-24; CDALB-2

Bradūnas, Kazys 1917- DLB-220

Bradwardine, Thomas circa 1295-1349 .. DLB-115

Brady, Frank 1924-1986 .... DLB-111

Frederic A. Brady [publishing house] DLB-49

Braga, Rubem 1913-1990 .... DLB-307

Bragg, Melvyn 1939- DLB-14, 271

Brahe, Tycho 1546-1601............... DLB-300

Charles H. Brainard [publishing house] ... DLB-49

Braine, John 1922-1986 . DLB-15; Y-86; CDBLB-7

Braithwait, Richard 1588-1673 .... DLB-151

Braithwaite, William Stanley
1878-1962................... DLB-50, 54

Bräker, Ulrich 1735-1798 .... DLB-94

Bramah, Ernest 1868-1942 .... DLB-70

Branagan, Thomas 1774-1843 .... DLB-37

Brancati, Vitaliano 1907-1954............ DLB-264

Branch, William Blackwell 1927- DLB-76

Brand, Christianna 1907-1988 .... DLB-276

Brand, Dionne 1953- DLB-334

Brand, Max (see Faust, Frederick Schiller)

Brandão, Raul 1867-1930............. DLB-287

Branden Press..................... DLB-46

Brandes, Georg 1842-1927 .... DLB-300

Branner, H.C. 1903-1966 .... DLB-214

Brant, Sebastian 1457-1521 ....DLB-179

Brantôme (Pierre de Bourdeille)
1540?-1614..................... DLB-327

Brassey, Lady Annie (Allnutt)
1839-1887..................... DLB-166

Brathwaite, Edward Kamau
1930- DLB-125; CDWLB-3

Brault, Jacques 1933- DLB-53

Braun, Matt 1932- DLB-212

Braun, Volker 1939- DLB-75, 124

Brautigan, Richard
1935-1984 ....DLB-2, 5, 206; Y-80, 84

Braverman, Kate 1950- DLB-335

Braxton, Joanne M. 1950- DLB-41

Bray, Anne Eliza 1790-1883 .... DLB-116

Bray, Thomas 1656-1730 .... DLB-24

Brazdžionis, Bernardas 1907-2002 ...... DLB-220

George Braziller [publishing house] DLB-46

The Bread Loaf Writers' Conference 1983 ... Y-84

Breasted, James Henry 1865-1935 .... DLB-47

Brecht, Bertolt
1898-1956 ....DLB-56, 124; CDWLB-2

Bredel, Willi 1901-1964 .... DLB-56

Bregendahl, Marie 1867-1940........... DLB-214

Breitinger, Johann Jakob 1701-1776....... DLB-97

Brekke, Paal 1923-1993 .... DLB-297

Bremser, Bonnie 1939- DLB-16

Bremser, Ray 1934-1998............... DLB-16

Brennan, Christopher 1870-1932 .... DLB-230

Brentano, Bernard von 1901-1964 .... DLB-56

Brentano, Clemens 1778-1842 .... DLB-90

Brentano, Franz 1838-1917............. DLB-296

Brentano's........................ DLB-49

Brenton, Howard 1942- DLB-13

Breslin, Jimmy 1929-1996............. DLB-185

Breton, André 1896-1966 .... DLB-65, 258

Breton, Nicholas circa 1555-circa 1626... DLB-136

The Breton Lays
1300-early fifteenth century DLB-146

Brett, Lily 1946- DLB-325

Brett, Simon 1945- DLB-276

Brewer, Gil 1922-1983 .... DLB-306

Brewer, Luther A. 1858-1933 .... DLB-187

Brewer, Warren and Putnam DLB-46

Brewster, Elizabeth 1922- DLB-60

Breytenbach, Breyten 1939- DLB-225

Bridge, Ann (Lady Mary Dolling Sanders O'Malley)
1889-1974..................... DLB-191

Bridge, Horatio 1806-1893 .... DLB-183

Bridgers, Sue Ellen 1942- DLB-52

Bridges, Robert
1844-1930 .... DLB-19, 98; CDBLB-5

The Bridgewater Library DLB-213

Bridie, James 1888-1951 .... DLB-10

Brieux, Eugene 1858-1932 .... DLB-192

Brigadere, Anna
1861-1933 .... DLB-220; CDWLB-4

Briggs, Charles Frederick
1804-1877................... DLB-3, 250

Brighouse, Harold 1882-1958........... DLB-10

Bright, Mary Chavelita Dunne
(see Egerton, George)

Brightman, Edgar Sheffield 1884-1953....DLB-270

B. J. Brimmer Company............... DLB-46

Brines, Francisco 1932- DLB-134

Brink, André 1935- DLB-225

Brinley, George, Jr. 1817-1875.......... DLB-140

Brinnin, John Malcolm 1916-1998 .... DLB-48

Brisbane, Albert 1809-1890 .... DLB-3, 250

Brisbane, Arthur 1864-1936 .... DLB-25

British Academy..................... DLB-112

The British Critic 1793-1843 .... DLB-110

British Library
   The American Trust for the
     British Library................... Y-96
   The British Library and the Regular
     Readers' Group.................. Y-91
   Building the New British Library
     at St Pancras Y-94

British Literary Prizes............. DLB-207; Y-98

British Literature
   The "Angry Young Men"........... DLB-15
   Author-Printers, 1476-1599 .... DLB-167
   The Comic Tradition Continued..... DLB-15
   Documents on Sixteenth-Century
     Literature................ DLB-167, 172
   Eikon Basilike 1649 .... DLB-151
   Letter from London.................. Y-96
   A Mirror for Magistrates DLB-167
   "Modern English Prose" (1876),
     by George Saintsbury DLB-57
   Sex, Class, Politics, and Religion [in the
     British Novel, 1930-1959] DLB-15
   Victorians on Rhetoric and Prose
     Style........................ DLB-57
   The Year in British Fiction.......... Y-99–01
   "You've Never Had It So Good," Gusted
     by "Winds of Change": British
     Fiction in the 1950s, 1960s,
     and After.................... DLB-14

British Literature, Old and Middle English
   Anglo-Norman Literature in the
     Development of Middle English
     Literature.................... DLB-146
   The *Alliterative Morte Arthure and the
     Stanzaic Morte Arthur*
     circa 1350-1400 .... DLB-146
   Ancrene Riwle circa 1200-1225 .... DLB-146
   The Anglo-Saxon Chronicle circa
     890-1154 .... DLB-146
   The Battle of Maldon circa 1000 ...... DLB-146

Beowulf circa 900-1000 or
   790-825 . . . . DLB-146; CDBLB-1

The Blickling Homilies circa 971 . . . . . DLB-146

The Breton Lays
   1300-early fifteenth century DLB-146

The Castle of Perserverance
   circa 1400-1425 . . . . DLB-146

The Celtic Background to Medieval
   English Literature DLB-146

The Chester Plays circa 1505-1532;
   revisions until 1575 . . . . DLB-146

Cursor Mundi circa 1300 . . . . DLB-146

The English Language: 410
   to 1500 . . . . DLB-146

The Germanic Epic and Old English
   Heroic Poetry: *Widsith, Waldere,*
   and *The Fight at Finnsburg* DLB-146

Judith circa 930 . . . . DLB-146

The Matter of England 1240-1400 . . . DLB-146

The Matter of Rome early twelfth to
   late fifteenth centuries DLB-146

Middle English Literature:
   An Introduction DLB-146

The Middle English Lyric DLB-146

Morality Plays: *Mankind* circa 1450-1500
   and *Everyman* circa 1500 . . . . DLB-146

N-Town Plays circa 1468 to early
   sixteenth century DLB-146

Old English Literature:
   An Introduction DLB-146

Old English Riddles
   eighth to tenth centuries DLB-146

The Owl and the Nightingale
   circa 1189-1199 . . . . DLB-146

The Paston Letters 1422-1509 . . . . DLB-146

The Seafarer circa 970 . . . . DLB-146

The *South English Legendary* circa
   thirteenth to fifteenth centuries DLB-146

*The British Review and London Critical
   Journal* 1811-1825 . . . . DLB-110

Brito, Aristeo 1942- DLB-122

Brittain, Vera 1893-1970 . . . . DLB-191

Briusov, Valerii Iakovlevich
   1873-1924 . . . . DLB-295

Brizeux, Auguste 1803-1858 . . . . DLB-217

Broadway Publishing Company DLB-46

Broch, Hermann
   1886-1951 . . . . DLB-85, 124; CDWLB-2

Brochu, André 1942- DLB-53

Brock, Edwin 1927-1997 . . . . DLB-40

Brockes, Barthold Heinrich
   1680-1747 . . . . DLB-168

Brod, Max 1884-1968 . . . . DLB-81

Brodber, Erna 1940- DLB-157

Brodhead, John R. 1814-1873 . . . . DLB-30

Brodkey, Harold 1930-1996 . . . . DLB-130

Brodsky, Joseph (Iosif Aleksandrovich Brodsky)
   1940-1996 . . . . DLB-285, 329; Y-87

   Nobel Lecture 1987 . . . . Y-87

Brodsky, Michael 1948- DLB-244

Broeg, Bob 1918-2005 . . . . DLB-171

Brøgger, Suzanne 1944- DLB-214

Brome, Richard circa 1590-1652 . . . . DLB-58

Brome, Vincent 1910-2004 . . . . DLB-155

Bromfield, Louis 1896-1956 . . . . DLB-4, 9, 86

Bromige, David 1933- DLB-193

Broner, E. M. 1930- DLB-28

   Tribute to Bernard Malamud Y-86

Bronk, William 1918-1999 . . . . DLB-165

Bronnen, Arnolt 1895-1959 . . . . DLB-124

Brontë, Anne 1820-1849 . . . . . . DLB-21, 199, 340

Brontë, Branwell 1817-1848 . . . . DLB-340

Brontë, Charlotte
   1816-1855 . . DLB-21, 159, 199, 340; CDBLB-4

Brontë, Emily
   1818-1848 . . DLB-21, 32, 199, 340; CDBLB-4

The Brontë Society Y-98

Brook, Stephen 1947- DLB-204

Brook Farm 1841-1847 . . . . DLB-1; 223; DS-5

Brooke, Frances 1724-1789 . . . . DLB-39, 99

Brooke, Henry 1703?-1783 . . . . DLB-39

Brooke, L. Leslie 1862-1940 . . . . DLB-141

Brooke, Margaret, Ranee of Sarawak
   1849-1936 . . . . DLB-174

Brooke, Rupert
   1887-1915 . . . . DLB-19, 216; CDBLB-6

   The Friends of the Dymock Poets Y-00

Brooker, Bertram 1888-1955 . . . . DLB-88

Brooke-Rose, Christine 1923- DLB-14, 231

Brookner, Anita 1928- DLB-194, 326; Y-87

Brooks, Charles Timothy 1813-1883 . . . DLB-1, 243

Brooks, Cleanth 1906-1994 . . . . DLB-63; Y-94

   Tribute to Katherine Anne Porter Y-80

   Tribute to Walker Percy Y-90

Brooks, Gwendolyn
   1917-2000 . . . . DLB-5, 76, 165; CDALB-1

   Tribute to Julian Mayfield Y-84

Brooks, Jeremy 1926-1994 . . . . DLB-14

Brooks, Mel 1926- DLB-26

Brooks, Noah 1830-1903 . . . . DLB-42; DS-13

Brooks, Richard 1912-1992 . . . . DLB-44

Brooks, Van Wyck 1886-1963 . . . . DLB-45, 63, 103

Brophy, Brigid 1929-1995 . . . . . . DLB-14, 70, 271

Brophy, John 1899-1965 . . . . DLB-191

Brorson, Hans Adolph 1694-1764 . . . . . . DLB-300

Brossard, Chandler 1922-1993 . . . . DLB-16

Brossard, Nicole 1943- DLB-53

Broster, Dorothy Kathleen 1877-1950 . . . DLB-160

Brother Antoninus (see Everson, William)

Brotherton, Lord 1856-1930 . . . . DLB-184

Brougham, John 1810-1880 . . . . DLB-11

Brougham and Vaux, Henry Peter
   Brougham, Baron 1778-1868 . . . . DLB-110, 158

Broughton, James 1913-1999 . . . . DLB-5

Broughton, Rhoda 1840-1920 . . . . DLB-18

Broun, Heywood 1888-1939 . . . . DLB-29, 171

Browder, Earl 1891-1973 . . . . DLB-303

Brown, Alice 1856-1948 . . . . DLB-78

Brown, Bob 1886-1959 . . . . DLB-4, 45; DS-15

Brown, Cecil 1943- DLB-33

Brown, Charles Brockden
   1771-1810 . . . . DLB-37, 59, 73; CDALB-2

Brown, Christy 1932-1981 . . . . DLB-14

Brown, Dee 1908-2002 . . . . Y-80

Brown, Frank London 1927-1962 . . . . DLB-76

Brown, Fredric 1906-1972 . . . . DLB-8

Brown, George Mackay
   1921-1996 . . . . DLB-14, 27, 139, 271

Brown, Harry 1917-1986 . . . . DLB-26

Brown, Ian 1945- DLB-310

Brown, Larry 1951- DLB-234, 292

Brown, Lew 1893-1958 . . . . DLB-265

Brown, Marcia 1918- DLB-61

Brown, Margaret Wise 1910-1952 . . . . . . DLB-22

Brown, Morna Doris (see Ferrars, Elizabeth)

Brown, Oliver Madox 1855-1874 . . . . DLB-21

Brown, Sterling 1901-1989 . . . . DLB-48, 51, 63

Brown, T. E. 1830-1897 . . . . DLB-35

Brown, Thomas Alexander (see Boldrewood, Rolf)

Brown, Warren 1894-1978 . . . . DLB-241

Brown, William Hill 1765-1793 . . . . DLB-37

Brown, William Wells
   1815-1884 . . . . DLB-3, 50, 183, 248

Brown University
   The Festival of Vanguard Narrative Y-93

Browne, Charles Farrar 1834-1867 . . . . . . DLB-11

Browne, Frances 1816-1879 . . . . DLB-199

Browne, Francis Fisher 1843-1913 . . . . DLB-79

Browne, Howard 1908-1999 . . . . DLB-226

Browne, J. Ross 1821-1875 . . . . DLB-202

Browne, Michael Dennis 1940- DLB-40

Browne, Sir Thomas 1605-1682 . . . . DLB-151

Browne, William, of Tavistock
   1590-1645 . . . . DLB-121

Browne, Wynyard 1911-1964 . . . . . . DLB-13, 233

Browne and Nolan DLB-106

Brownell, W. C. 1851-1928 . . . . DLB-71

Browning, Elizabeth Barrett
   1806-1861 . . . . DLB-32, 199; CDBLB-4

Browning, Robert
   1812-1889 . . . . DLB-32, 163; CDBLB-4

   Essay on Chatterton DLB-32

   Introductory Essay: *Letters of Percy
   Bysshe Shelley* (1852) DLB-32

   "The Novel in [Robert Browning's]
   'The Ring and the Book'" (1912),
   by Henry James DLB-32

Brownjohn, Allan 1931- DLB-40
 Tribute to John Betjeman Y-84
Brownson, Orestes Augustus
 1803-1876 .... DLB-1, 59, 73, 243; DS-5
Bruccoli, Matthew J. 1931-2008 .... DLB-103
 Joseph [Heller] and George [V. Higgins] Y-99
 Response [to Busch on Fitzgerald] Y-96
 Tribute to Albert Erskine Y-93
 Tribute to Charles E. Feinberg Y-88
 Working with Fredson Bowers Y-91
Bruce, Charles 1906-1971 .... DLB-68
Bruce, John Edward 1856-1924
 Three Documents [African American
  poets] DLB-50
Bruce, Leo 1903-1979 .... DLB-77
Bruce, Mary Grant 1878-1958 .... DLB-230
Bruce, Philip Alexander 1856-1933 ...... DLB-47
Bruce-Novoa, Juan 1944- DLB-82
Bruchac, Joseph 1942- DLB-342
Bruckman, Clyde 1894-1955 .... DLB-26
Bruckner, Ferdinand 1891-1958 .... DLB-118
Brundage, John Herbert (see Herbert, John)
Brunner, John 1934-1995 .... DLB-261
 Tribute to Theodore Sturgeon Y-85
Brutus, Dennis
 1924- DLB-117, 225; CDWLB-3
Bryan, C. D. B. 1936- DLB-185
Bryan, William Jennings 1860-1925 ..... DLB-303
Bryant, Arthur 1899-1985 .... DLB-149
Bryant, William Cullen 1794-1878
 .... DLB-3, 43, 59, 189, 250; CDALB-2
Bryce, James 1838-1922 .... DLB-166, 190
Bryce Echenique, Alfredo
 1939- DLB-145; CDWLB-3
Bryden, Bill 1942- DLB-233
Brydges, Sir Samuel Egerton
 1762-1837 .... DLB-107, 142
Bryskett, Lodowick 1546?-1612 .... DLB-167
Buchan, John 1875-1940 .... DLB-34, 70, 156
Buchanan, George 1506-1582 .... DLB-132
Buchanan, Robert 1841-1901 .... DLB-18, 35
 "The Fleshly School of Poetry and
  Other Phenomena of the Day"
  (1872) DLB-35
 "The Fleshly School of Poetry:
  Mr. D. G. Rossetti" (1871),
  by Thomas Maitland DLB-35
Buchler, Justus 1914-1991 .... DLB-279
Buchman, Sidney 1902-1975 .... DLB-26
Buchner, Augustus 1591-1661 .... DLB-164
Büchner, Georg
 1813-1837 .... DLB-133; CDWLB-2
Bucholtz, Andreas Heinrich 1607-1671 .... DLB-168
Buck, Pearl S.
 1892-1973 ...... DLB-9, 102, 329; CDALB-7

Bucke, Charles 1781-1846 .... DLB-110
Bucke, Richard Maurice 1837-1902 ...... DLB-99
Buckingham, Edwin 1810-1833 .... DLB-73
Buckingham, Joseph Tinker 1779-1861 ... DLB-73
Buckler, Ernest 1908-1984 .... DLB-68
Buckley, Vincent 1925-1988 .... DLB-289
Buckley, William F., Jr.
 1925-2008 .... DLB-137; Y-80
 Publisher's Statement From the
  Initial Issue of *National Review*
  (19 November 1955) DLB-137
Buckminster, Joseph Stevens
 1784-1812 .... DLB-37
Buckner, Robert 1906-1989 .... DLB-26
Buckstone, John Baldwin 1802-1879 ..... DLB-344
Budd, Thomas ?-1698 .... DLB-24
Budé, Guillaume 1468-1540 .... DLB-327
Budrys, A. J. 1931- DLB-8
Buechner, Frederick 1926- Y-80
Buell, John 1927- DLB-53
Buenaventura, Enrique 1925-2003 ...... DLB-305
Bufalino, Gesualdo 1920-1996 .... DLB-196
Buffon, Georges-Louis Leclerc de
 1707-1788 .... DLB-313
 "Le Discours sur le style" DLB-314
Job Buffum [publishing house] DLB-49
Bugnet, Georges 1879-1981 .... DLB-92
al-Buhturi 821-897 .... DLB-311
Buies, Arthur 1840-1901 .... DLB-99
Bukiet, Melvin Jules 1953- DLB-299
Bukowski, Charles 1920-1994 ... DLB-5, 130, 169
Bulatović, Miodrag
 1930-1991 .... DLB-181; CDWLB-4
Bulgakov, Mikhail Afanas'evich
 1891-1940 .... DLB-272
Bulgarin, Faddei Venediktovich
 1789-1859 .... DLB-198
Bulger, Bozeman 1877-1932 .... DLB-171
Bull, Olaf 1883-1933 .... DLB-297
Bullein, William
 between 1520 and 1530-1576 .... DLB-167
Bullins, Ed 1935- DLB-7, 38, 249
Bulosan, Carlos 1911-1956 .... DLB-312
Bulwer, John 1606-1656 .... DLB-236
Bulwer-Lytton, Edward (also Edward
 Bulwer) 1803-1873 .... DLB-21
 "On Art in Fiction" (1838) DLB-21
Bumpus, Jerry 1937- Y-81
Bunce and Brother DLB-49
Bunin, Ivan 1870-1953 .... DLB-317, 329
Bunner, H. C. 1855-1896 .... DLB-78, 79
Bunting, Basil 1900-1985 .... DLB-20
Buntline, Ned (Edward Zane Carroll
 Judson) 1821-1886 .... DLB-186

Bunyan, John 1628-1688 ..... DLB-39; CDBLB-2
 The Author's Apology for
  His Book DLB-39
Buonarroti *il Giovane,* Michelangelo
 1568-1646 .... DLB-339
Burch, Robert 1925- DLB-52
Burciaga, José Antonio 1940- DLB-82
Burdekin, Katharine (Murray Constantine)
 1896-1963 .... DLB-255
Bürger, Gottfried August 1747-1794 ...... DLB-94
Burgess, Anthony (John Anthony Burgess Wilson)
 1917-1993 ..... DLB-14, 194, 261; CDBLB-8
 The Anthony Burgess Archive at
  the Harry Ransom Humanities
  Research Center Y-98
 Anthony Burgess's *99 Novels*:
  An Opinion Poll Y-84
Burgess, Gelett 1866-1951 .... DLB-11
Burgess, John W. 1844-1931 .... DLB-47
Burgess, Thornton W. 1874-1965 .... DLB-22
Burgess, Stringer and Company DLB-49
Burgos, Julia de 1914-1953 .... DLB-290
Burick, Si 1909-1986 .... DLB-171
Burk, John Daly circa 1772-1808 .... DLB-37
Burk, Ronnie 1955- DLB-209
Burke, Edmund 1729?-1797 .... DLB-104, 252, 336
Burke, James Lee 1936- DLB-226
Burke, Johnny 1908-1964 .... DLB-265
Burke, Kenneth 1897-1993 .... DLB-45, 63
Burke, Thomas 1886-1945 .... DLB-197
Burley, Dan 1907-1962 .... DLB-241
Burley, W. J. 1914-2002 .... DLB-276
Burlingame, Edward Livermore
 1848-1922 .... DLB-79
Burliuk, David 1882-1967 .... DLB-317
Burman, Carina 1960- DLB-257
Burnard, Bonnie 1945- DLB-334
Burnet, Gilbert 1643-1715 .... DLB-101
Burnett, Frances Hodgson
 1849-1924 .... DLB-42, 141; DS-13, 14
Burnett, W. R. 1899-1982 .... DLB-9, 226
Burnett, Whit 1899-1973 .... DLB-137
Burney, Charles 1726-1814 .... DLB-336
Burney, Fanny 1752-1840 .... DLB-39
 Dedication, *The Wanderer* (1814) DLB-39
 Preface to *Evelina* (1778) DLB-39
Burns, Alan 1929- DLB-14, 194
Burns, Joanne 1945- DLB-289
Burns, John Horne 1916-1953 .... Y-85
Burns, Robert 1759-1796 ..... DLB-109; CDBLB-3
Burns and Oates DLB-106
Burnshaw, Stanley 1906-2005 .... DLB-48; Y-97
 James Dickey and Stanley Burnshaw
  Correspondence Y-02

Review of Stanley Burnshaw: The Collected Poems and Selected Prose..................Y-02

Tribute to Robert Penn Warren.........Y-89

Burr, C. Chauncey 1815?-1883.........DLB-79

Burr, Esther Edwards 1732-1758.......DLB-200

Burroughs, Edgar Rice 1875-1950.......DLB-8

The Burroughs Bibliophiles............Y-98

Burroughs, John 1837-1921........DLB-64, 275

Burroughs, Margaret T. G. 1917-.......DLB-41

Burroughs, William S., Jr. 1947-1981....DLB-16

Burroughs, William Seward 1914-1997
...........DLB-2, 8, 16, 152, 237; Y-81, 97

Burroway, Janet 1936-.................DLB-6

Burt, Maxwell Struthers 1882-1954..............DLB-86; DS-16

A. L. Burt and Company................DLB-49

Burton, Hester 1913-2000.............DLB-161

Burton, Isabel Arundell 1831-1896.....DLB-166

Burton, Miles (see Rhode, John)

Burton, Richard Francis 1821-1890..............DLB-55, 166, 184

Burton, Robert 1577-1640.............DLB-151

Burton, Virginia Lee 1909-1968........DLB-22

Burton, William Evans 1804-1860.......DLB-73

Burwell, Adam Hood 1790-1849.........DLB-99

Bury, Lady Charlotte 1775-1861.......DLB-116

Busch, Charles 1954-.................DLB-341

Busch, Frederick 1941-2006........DLB-6, 218

Excerpts from Frederick Busch's USC Remarks [on F. Scott Fitzgerald]......Y-96

Tribute to James Laughlin.............Y-97

Tribute to Raymond Carver.............Y-88

Busch, Niven 1903-1991................DLB-44

Busenello, Gian Francesco 1598-1659....DLB-339

Bushnell, Horace 1802-1876.............DS-13

Business & Literature
The Claims of Business and Literature: An Undergraduate Essay by Maxwell Perkins..................Y-01

Bussières, Arthur de 1877-1913........DLB-92

Butler, Charles circa 1560-1647......DLB-236

Butler, Guy 1918-2001................DLB-225

Butler, Joseph 1692-1752.............DLB-252

Butler, Josephine Elizabeth 1828-1906....DLB-190

Butler, Juan 1942-1981................DLB-53

Butler, Judith 1956-..................DLB-246

Butler, Octavia E. 1947-2006..........DLB-33

Butler, Pierce 1884-1953.............DLB-187

Butler, Robert Olen 1945-........DLB-173, 335

Butler, Samuel 1613-1680.........DLB-101, 126

Butler, Samuel 1835-1902......DLB-18, 57, 174; CDBLB-5

Butler, William Francis 1838-1910....DLB-166

E. H. Butler and Company..............DLB-49

Butor, Michel 1926-...................DLB-83

Nathaniel Butter [publishing house]................DLB-170

Butterworth, Hezekiah 1839-1905.......DLB-42

Buttitta, Ignazio 1899-1997..........DLB-114

Butts, Mary 1890-1937................DLB-240

Buzo, Alex 1944-.....................DLB-289

Buzzati, Dino 1906-1972..............DLB-177

Byars, Betsy 1928-....................DLB-52

Byatt, A. S. 1936-........DLB-14, 194, 319, 326

Byles, Mather 1707-1788...............DLB-24

Henry Bynneman [publishing house]................DLB-170

Bynner, Witter 1881-1968..............DLB-54

Byrd, William circa 1543-1623........DLB-172

Byrd, William, II 1674-1744........DLB-24, 140

Byrne, John Keyes (see Leonard, Hugh)

Byron, George Gordon, Lord 1788-1824..........DLB-96, 110; CDBLB-3

The Byron Society of America..........Y-00

Byron, Henry J. 1834-1884............DLB-344

Byron, Robert 1905-1941..............DLB-195

Byzantine Novel, The Spanish.........DLB-318

C

Caballero Bonald, José Manuel 1926-........................DLB-108

Cabañero, Eladio 1930-2000...........DLB-134

Cabell, James Branch 1879-1958.......DLB-9, 78

Cabeza de Baca, Manuel 1853-1915....DLB-122

Cabeza de Baca Gilbert, Fabiola 1898-1993.......................DLB-122

Cable, George Washington 1844-1925..............DLB-12, 74; DS-13

Cable, Mildred 1878-1952.............DLB-195

Cabral, Manuel del 1907-1999.........DLB-283

Cabral de Melo Neto, João 1920-1999........................DLB-307

Cabrera, Lydia 1900-1991.............DLB-145

Cabrera Infante, Guillermo 1929-..............DLB-113; CDWLB-3

Cabrujas, José Ignacio 1937-1995.....DLB-305

Cadell [publishing house]............DLB-154

Cady, Edwin H. 1917-.................DLB-103

Caedmon fl. 658-680..................DLB-146

Caedmon School circa 660-899.........DLB-146

Caesar, Irving 1895-1996.............DLB-265

Cafés, Brasseries, and Bistros........DS-15

Cage, John 1912-1992.................DLB-193

Cahan, Abraham 1860-1951........DLB-9, 25, 28

Cahn, Sammy 1913-1993................DLB-265

Cain, George 1943-....................DLB-33

Cain, James M. 1892-1977.............DLB-226

Cain, Paul (Peter Ruric, George Sims) 1902-1966......................DLB-306

Caird, Edward 1835-1908..............DLB-262

Caird, Mona 1854-1932................DLB-197

Čaks, Aleksandrs 1901-1950..............DLB-220; CDWLB-4

Caldecott, Randolph 1846-1886........DLB-163

John Calder Limited [Publishing house]..............DLB-112

Calderón de la Barca, Fanny 1804-1882......................DLB-183

Caldwell, Ben 1937-...................DLB-38

Caldwell, Erskine 1903-1987........DLB-9, 86

H. M. Caldwell Company................DLB-49

Caldwell, Taylor 1900-1985............DS-17

Calhoun, John C. 1782-1850........DLB-3, 248

Călinescu, George 1899-1965..........DLB-220

Calisher, Hortense 1911-...........DLB-2, 218

Calkins, Mary Whiton 1863-1930.......DLB-270

Callaghan, Mary Rose 1944-..........DLB-207

Callaghan, Morley 1903-1990.....DLB-68; DS-15

Callahan, S. Alice 1868-1894......DLB-175, 221

Callaloo [journal].....................Y-87

Callimachus circa 305 B.C.-240 B.C....DLB-176

Calmer, Edgar 1907-1986................DLB-4

Calverley, C. S. 1831-1884............DLB-35

Calvert, George Henry 1803-1889..............DLB-1, 64, 248

Calverton, V. F. (George Goetz) 1900-1940......................DLB-303

Calvin, Jean 1509-1564...............DLB-327

Calvino, Italo 1923-1985.............DLB-196

Cambridge, Ada 1844-1926.............DLB-230

Cambridge Press......................DLB-49

Cambridge Songs (Carmina Cantabrigensia) circa 1050........................DLB-148

Cambridge University Cambridge and the Apostles.........DS-5

Cambridge University Press..........DLB-170

Camden, William 1551-1623............DLB-172

Camden House: An Interview with James Hardin.....................Y-92

Cameron, Eleanor 1912-2000............DLB-52

Cameron, George Frederick 1854-1885.......................DLB-99

Cameron, Lucy Lyttelton 1781-1858....DLB-163

Cameron, Peter 1959-.................DLB-234

Cameron, William Bleasdell 1862-1951....DLB-99

Camm, John 1718-1778..................DLB-31

Camões, Luís de 1524-1580............DLB-287

Camon, Ferdinando 1935-..............DLB-196

Camp, Walter 1859-1925...............DLB-241

Campana, Dino 1885-1932..............DLB-114

Campbell, Bebe Moore 1950-2006 ...... DLB-227
Campbell, David 1915-1979 .... DLB-260
Campbell, Gabrielle Margaret Vere
   (see Shearing, Joseph, and Bowen, Marjorie)
Campbell, James Dykes 1838-1895 ..... DLB-144
Campbell, James Edwin 1867-1896 .... DLB-50
Campbell, John 1653-1728 .... DLB-43
Campbell, John W., Jr. 1910-1971 .... DLB-8
Campbell, Ramsey 1946- DLB-261
Campbell, Robert 1927-2000 .... DLB-306
Campbell, Roy 1901-1957 .... DLB-20, 225
Campbell, Thomas 1777-1844 ...... DLB-93, 144
Campbell, William Edward (see March, William)
Campbell, William Wilfred 1858-1918 .... DLB-92
Campion, Edmund 1539-1581 .... DLB-167
Campion, Thomas
   1567-1620 .... DLB-58, 172; CDBLB-1
Campo, Rafael 1964- DLB-282
Campton, David 1924-2006 .... DLB-245
Camus, Albert 1913-1960 ...... DLB-72, 321, 329
Camus, Jean-Pierre 1584-1652 .... DLB-268
The Canadian Publishers' Records Database ... Y-96
Canby, Henry Seidel 1878-1961 .... DLB-91
Cancioneros DLB-286
Candelaria, Cordelia 1943- DLB-82
Candelaria, Nash 1928- DLB-82
Candide, Voltaire DLB-314
Canetti, Elias
   1905-1994 ..... DLB-85, 124, 329; CDWLB-2
Canham, Erwin Dain 1904-1982 .... DLB-127
Canin, Ethan 1960- DLB-335
Canitz, Friedrich Rudolph Ludwig von
   1654-1699 .... DLB-168
Cankar, Ivan 1876-1918 ..... DLB-147; CDWLB-4
Cannan, Gilbert 1884-1955 .... DLB-10, 197
Cannan, Joanna 1896-1961 .... DLB-191
Cannell, Kathleen 1891-1974 .... DLB-4
Cannell, Skipwith 1887-1957 .... DLB-45
Canning, George 1770-1827 .... DLB-158
Cannon, Jimmy 1910-1973 .... DLB-171
Cano, Daniel 1947- DLB-209
   Old Dogs / New Tricks? New
      Technologies, the Canon, and the
      Structure of the Profession Y-02
Cantar de mio Cid circa 1200 .... DLB-337
Cantigas in the Galician-Portuguese
   Cancioneiros DLB-337
Cantú, Norma Elia 1947- DLB-209
Cantwell, Robert 1908-1978 .... DLB-9
Jonathan Cape and Harrison Smith
   [publishing house] DLB-46
Jonathan Cape Limited DLB-112
Čapek, Karel 1890-1938 .... DLB-215; CDWLB-4

Capen, Joseph 1658-1725 .... DLB-24
Capes, Bernard 1854-1918 .... DLB-156
Caponegro, Mary 1956- DLB-335
Capote, Truman 1924-1984
   .... DLB-2, 185, 227; Y-80, 84; CDALB-1
Capps, Benjamin 1922- DLB-256
Caproni, Giorgio 1912-1990 .... DLB-128
Caragiale, Mateiu Ioan 1885-1936 ...... DLB-220
Carballido, Emilio 1925- DLB-305
Cardarelli, Vincenzo 1887-1959 .... DLB-114
Cardenal, Ernesto 1925- DLB-290
Cárdenas, Reyes 1948- DLB-122
Cardinal, Marie 1929-2001 .... DLB-83
Cardoza y Aragón, Luis 1901-1992 ..... DLB-290
Carducci, Giosuè 1835-1907 .... DLB-329
Carew, Jan 1920- DLB-157
Carew, Thomas 1594 or 1595-1640 .... DLB-126
Carey, Henry circa 1687-1689-1743 ...... DLB-84
Carey, Mathew 1760-1839 .... DLB-37, 73
M. Carey and Company DLB-49
Carey, Peter 1943- DLB-289, 326
Carey and Hart DLB-49
Carlell, Lodowick 1602-1675 .... DLB-58
Carleton, William 1794-1869 .... DLB-159
G. W. Carleton [publishing house] DLB-49
Carlile, Richard 1790-1843 .... DLB-110, 158
Carlson, Ron 1947- DLB-244
Carlyle, Jane Welsh 1801-1866 .... DLB-55
Carlyle, Thomas
   1795-1881 ...... DLB-55, 144, 338; CDBLB-3
   "The Hero as Man of Letters:
      Johnson, Rousseau, Burns"
      (1841) [excerpt] DLB-57
   The Hero as Poet. Dante; Shakspeare
      (1841) DLB-32
Carman, Bliss 1861-1929 .... DLB-92
Carmina Burana circa 1230 .... DLB-138
Carnap, Rudolf 1891-1970 .... DLB-270
Carnero, Guillermo 1947- DLB-108
Carossa, Hans 1878-1956 .... DLB-66
Carpenter, Humphrey
   1946-2005 .... DLB-155; Y-84, 99
Carpenter, Stephen Cullen ?-1820? DLB-73
Carpentier, Alejo
   1904-1980 .... DLB-113; CDWLB-3
Carr, Emily 1871-1945 .... DLB-68
Carr, John Dickson 1906-1977 .... DLB-306
Carr, Marina 1964- DLB-245
Carr, Virginia Spencer 1929- DLB-111; Y-00
Carrera Andrade, Jorge 1903-1978 ..... DLB-283
Carrier, Roch 1937- DLB-53
Carrillo, Adolfo 1855-1926 .... DLB-122
Carroll, Gladys Hasty 1904-1999 .... DLB-9

Carroll, John 1735-1815 .... DLB-37
Carroll, John 1809-1884 .... DLB-99
Carroll, Lewis
   1832-1898 ...... DLB-18, 163, 178; CDBLB-4
   The Lewis Carroll Centenary Y-98
   The Lewis Carroll Society
      of North America Y-00
Carroll, Paul 1927-1996 .... DLB-16
Carroll, Paul Vincent 1900-1968 .... DLB-10
Carroll and Graf Publishers DLB-46
Carruth, Hayden 1921- DLB-5, 165
   Tribute to James Dickey Y-97
   Tribute to Raymond Carver Y-88
Carryl, Charles E. 1841-1920 .... DLB-42
Carson, Anne 1950- DLB-193
Carson, Rachel 1907-1964 .... DLB-275
Carswell, Catherine 1879-1946 .... DLB-36
Cartagena, Alfonso de circa 1384-1456 .. DLB-286
Cartagena, Teresa de 1425?-? DLB-286
Cărtărescu, Mirea 1956- DLB-232
Carte, Thomas 1686-1754 .... DLB-336
Carter, Angela
   1940-1992 .... DLB-14, 207, 261, 319
Carter, Elizabeth 1717-1806 .... DLB-109
Carter, Henry (see Leslie, Frank)
Carter, Hodding, Jr. 1907-1972 .... DLB-127
Carter, Jared 1939- DLB-282
Carter, John 1905-1975 .... DLB-201
Carter, Landon 1710-1778 .... DLB-31
Carter, Lin 1930-1988 .... Y-81
Carter, Martin 1927-1997 .... DLB-117; CDWLB-3
Carter, Robert, and Brothers DLB-49
Carter and Hendee DLB-49
Cartwright, Jim 1958- DLB-245
Cartwright, John 1740-1824 .... DLB-158
Cartwright, William circa 1611-1643 .... DLB-126
Caruthers, William Alexander
   1802-1846 .... DLB-3, 248
Carver, Jonathan 1710-1780 .... DLB-31
Carver, Raymond 1938-1988 ... DLB-130; Y-83, 88
   First Strauss "Livings" Awarded to Cynthia
      Ozick and Raymond Carver
      An Interview with Raymond Carver Y-83
Carvic, Heron 1917?-1980 .... DLB-276
Cary, Alice 1820-1871 .... DLB-202
Cary, Joyce 1888-1957 ... DLB-15, 100; CDBLB-6
Cary, Patrick 1623?-1657 .... DLB-131
Casal, Julián del 1863-1893 .... DLB-283
Case, John 1540-1600 .... DLB-281
Casey, Gavin 1907-1964 .... DLB-260
Casey, Juanita 1925- DLB-14
Casey, Michael 1947- DLB-5
Cassady, Carolyn 1923- DLB-16

"As I See It".....................DLB-16

Cassady, Neal 1926-1968..........DLB-16, 237

Cassell and Company DLB-106

Cassell Publishing Company DLB-49

Cassill, R. V. 1919-2002........ DLB-6, 218; Y-02

 Tribute to James Dickey Y-97

Cassity, Turner 1929- DLB-105; Y-02

Cassius Dio circa 155/164-post 229 ......DLB-176

Cassola, Carlo 1917-1987..............DLB-177

Castellano, Olivia 1944- DLB-122

Castellanos, Rosario
 1925-1974 .... DLB-113, 290; CDWLB-3

Castelo Branco, Camilo 1825-1890......DLB-287

Castile, Protest Poetry in DLB-286

Castile and Aragon, Vernacular Translations
 in Crowns of 1352-1515 ....DLB-286

Castillejo, Cristóbal de 1490?-1550 ......DLB-318

Castillo, Ana 1953- DLB-122, 227

Castillo, Rafael C. 1950- DLB-209

The Castle of Perserverance
 circa 1400-1425..................DLB-146

Castlemon, Harry (see Fosdick, Charles Austin)

Castro, Brian 1950- DLB-325

Castro, Consuelo de 1946- DLB-307

Castro Alves, Antônio de 1847-1871 .....DLB-307

Čašule, Kole 1921- DLB-181

Caswall, Edward 1814-1878.............DLB-32

Catacalos, Rosemary 1944- DLB-122

Cather, Willa 1873-1947
 .... DLB-9, 54, 78, 256; DS-1; CDALB-3

 The Willa Cather Pioneer Memorial
  and Education Foundation Y-00

Catherine II (Ekaterina Alekseevna), "The Great,"
 Empress of Russia 1729-1796 ....DLB-150

Catherwood, Mary Hartwell 1847-1902 ...DLB-78

Catledge, Turner 1901-1983 ....DLB-127

Catlin, George 1796-1872..........DLB-186, 189

Cato the Elder 234 B.C.-149 B.C.........DLB-211

Cattafi, Bartolo 1922-1979 ....DLB-128

Catton, Bruce 1899-1978 ....DLB-17

Catullus circa 84 B.C.-54 B.C.
 ....DLB-211; CDWLB-1

Causley, Charles 1917-2003.............DLB-27

Caute, David 1936- DLB-14, 231

Cavendish, Duchess of Newcastle,
 Margaret Lucas
 1623?-1673 ....DLB-131, 252, 281

Cawein, Madison 1865-1914............DLB-54

William Caxton [publishing house] DLB-170

The Caxton Printers, Limited DLB-46

Caylor, O. P. 1849-1897...............DLB-241

Caylus, Marthe-Marguerite de
 1671-1729 ....DLB-313

Cayrol, Jean 1911-2005 ....DLB-83

Cecil, Lord David 1902-1986 ....DLB-155

Cela, Camilo José
 1916-2002 .... DLB-322, 329; Y-89

 Nobel Lecture 1989..................Y-89

Celan, Paul 1920-1970 ......DLB-69; CDWLB-2

Celati, Gianni 1937- DLB-196

Celaya, Gabriel 1911-1991..............DLB-108

Céline, Louis-Ferdinand 1894-1961.......DLB-72

Celtis, Conrad 1459-1508 ....DLB-179

Cendrars, Blaise 1887-1961 ....DLB-258

 The Steinbeck Centennial Y-02

Censorship
 The Island Trees Case: A Symposium on
  School Library Censorship..........Y-82

Center for Bibliographical Studies and
 Research at the University of
 California, Riverside Y-91

Center for Book Research Y-84

The Center for the Book in the Library
 of Congress........................Y-93

 A New Voice: The Center for the
  Book's First Five Years Y-83

Centlivre, Susanna 1669?-1723 ....DLB-84

The Centre for Writing, Publishing and
 Printing History at the University
 of Reading........................Y-00

The Century Company DLB-49

A Century of Poetry, a Lifetime of Collecting:
 J. M. Edelstein's Collection of
 Twentieth-Century American Poetry Y-02

Cernuda, Luis 1902-1963 ....DLB-134

Cerruto, Oscar 1912-1981 ....DLB-283

Cervantes, Lorna Dee 1954- DLB-82

Césaire, Aimé 1913- DLB-321

de Céspedes, Alba 1911-1997 ....DLB-264

Cetina, Gutierre de 1514-17?-1556 ......DLB-318

Ch., T. (see Marchenko, Anastasiia Iakovlevna)

Cha, Theresa Hak Kyung 1951-1982 ....DLB-312

Chaadaev, Petr Iakovlevich
 1794-1856 ....DLB-198

Chabon, Michael 1963- DLB-278

Chacel, Rosa 1898-1994 ....DLB-134, 322

Chacón, Eusebio 1869-1948 ....DLB-82

Chacón, Felipe Maximiliano 1873-?.......DLB-82

Chadwick, Henry 1824-1908...........DLB-241

Chadwyck-Healey's Full-Text Literary Databases:
 Editing Commercial Databases of
 Primary Literary Texts Y-95

Challans, Eileen Mary (see Renault, Mary)

Chalmers, George 1742-1825.............DLB-30

Chaloner, Sir Thomas 1520-1565 ....DLB-167

Chamberlain, Samuel S. 1851-1916.......DLB-25

Chamberland, Paul 1939- DLB-60

Chamberlin, William Henry 1897-1969....DLB-29

Chambers, Charles Haddon 1860-1921 ... DLB-10

Chambers, María Cristina (see Mena, María Cristina)

Chambers, Robert W. 1865-1933 ....DLB-202

W. and R. Chambers
 [publishing house] DLB-106

Chambers, Whittaker 1901-1961 ....DLB-303

Chamfort, Sébastien-Roch Nicolas de
 1740?-1794.....................DLB-313

Chamisso, Adelbert von 1781-1838.......DLB-90

Champfleury 1821-1889 ....DLB-119

Champier, Symphorien 1472?-1539?.....DLB-327

Chan, Jeffery Paul 1942- DLB-312

Chandler, Harry 1864-1944............DLB-29

Chandler, Norman 1899-1973 ....DLB-127

Chandler, Otis 1927-2006 ....DLB-127

Chandler, Raymond
 1888-1959 ....DLB-226, 253; DS-6; CDALB-5

 Raymond Chandler Centenary..........Y-88

Chang, Diana 1934- DLB-312

Channing, Edward 1856-1931..........DLB-17

Channing, Edward Tyrrell
 1790-1856 ....DLB-1, 59, 235

Channing, William Ellery
 1780-1842 ....DLB-1, 59, 235

Channing, William Ellery, II
 1817-1901 ....DLB-1, 223

Channing, William Henry
 1810-1884 ....DLB-1, 59, 243

Chapelain, Jean 1595-1674 ....DLB-268

Chaplin, Charlie 1889-1977.............DLB-44

Chaplin, Ralph 1887-1961 ....DLB-345

Chapman, George
 1559 or 1560-1634 ....DLB-62, 121

Chapman, Olive Murray 1892-1977 .....DLB-195

Chapman, R. W. 1881-1960 ....DLB-201

Chapman, William 1850-1917...........DLB-99

John Chapman [publishing house].......DLB-106

Chapman and Hall [publishing house] ...DLB-106

Chappell, Fred 1936- DLB-6, 105

 "A Detail in a Poem"................DLB-105

 Tribute to Peter Taylor Y-94

Chappell, William 1582-1649 ....DLB-236

Char, René 1907-1988 ....DLB-258

Charbonneau, Jean 1875-1960...........DLB-92

Charbonneau, Robert 1911-1967 ....DLB-68

Charles, Gerda 1914-1996 ....DLB-14

William Charles [publishing house].......DLB-49

Charles d'Orléans 1394-1465 ....DLB-208

Charley (see Mann, Charles)

Charrière, Isabelle de 1740-1805 ....DLB-313

Charskaia, Lidiia 1875-1937............DLB-295

Charteris, Leslie 1907-1993 ....DLB-77

Chartier, Alain circa 1385-1430 ....DLB-208

Charyn, Jerome 1937- Y-83

Cumulative Index

Chase, Borden 1900-1971 . . . . DLB-26
Chase, Edna Woolman 1877-1957 . . . . DLB-91
Chase, James Hadley (René Raymond)
   1906-1985 . . . . DLB-276
Chase, Mary Coyle 1907-1981 . . . . DLB-228
Chase-Riboud, Barbara 1936- DLB-33
Chateaubriand, François-René de
   1768-1848 . . . . DLB-119
Châtelet, Gabrielle-Emilie Du
   1706-1749 . . . . DLB-313
Chatterjee, Upamanyu 1959- DLB-323
Chatterton, Thomas 1752-1770 . . . . DLB-109
   Essay on Chatterton (1842), by
      Robert Browning DLB-32
Chatto and Windus DLB-106
Chatwin, Bruce 1940-1989 . . . . DLB-194, 204
Chaucer, Geoffrey
   1340?-1400 . . . . DLB-146; CDBLB-1
   New Chaucer Society Y-00
Chaudhuri, Amit 1962- DLB-267, 323
Chaudhuri, Nirad C. 1897-1999 . . . . DLB-323
Chauncy, Charles 1705-1787 . . . . DLB-24
Chauveau, Pierre-Joseph-Olivier
   1820-1890 . . . . DLB-99
Chávez, Denise 1948- DLB-122
Chávez, Fray Angélico 1910-1996 . . . . DLB-82
Chayefsky, Paddy 1923-1981 . . . . . DLB-7, 44; Y-81
Cheesman, Evelyn 1881-1969 . . . . DLB-195
Cheever, Ezekiel 1615-1708 . . . . DLB-24
Cheever, George Barrell 1807-1890 . . . . . . DLB-59
Cheever, John 1912-1982
   . . . . DLB-2, 102, 227; Y-80, 82; CDALB-1
Cheever, Susan 1943- Y-82
Cheke, Sir John 1514-1557 . . . . DLB-132
Chekhov, Anton Pavlovich 1860-1904 . . . . DLB-277
Chelsea House DLB-46
Chênedollé, Charles de 1769-1833 . . . . . . DLB-217
Cheney, Brainard
   Tribute to Caroline Gordon Y-81
Cheney, Ednah Dow 1824-1904 . . . . . . DLB-1, 223
Cheney, Harriet Vaughan 1796-1889 . . . . . DLB-99
Chénier, Marie-Joseph 1764-1811 . . . . DLB-192
Cheng Xiaoqing 1893-1976 . . . . DLB-328
Cherny, Sasha 1880-1932 . . . . DLB-317
Chernyshevsky, Nikolai Gavrilovich
   1828-1889 . . . . DLB-238
Cherry, Kelly 1940- DLB-335; Y-83
Cherryh, C. J. 1942- DLB-335; Y-80
Chesebro', Caroline 1825-1873 . . . . DLB-202
Chesney, Sir George Tomkyns
   1830-1895 . . . . DLB-190
Chesnut, Mary Boykin 1823-1886 . . . . . . DLB-239
Chesnutt, Charles Waddell
   1858-1932 . . . . DLB-12, 50, 78

Chesson, Mrs. Nora (see Hopper, Nora)
Chester, Alfred 1928-1971 . . . . DLB-130
Chester, George Randolph 1869-1924 . . . . DLB-78
The Chester Plays circa 1505-1532;
   revisions until 1575 . . . . DLB-146
Chesterfield, Philip Dormer Stanhope,
   Fourth Earl of 1694-1773 . . . . DLB-104
Chesterton, G. K. 1874-1936
   . . . DLB-10, 19, 34, 70, 98, 149, 178; CDBLB-6
   "The Ethics of Elfland" (1908) DLB-178
Chettle, Henry
   circa 1560-circa 1607 . . . . DLB-136
Cheuse, Alan 1940- DLB-244
Chew, Ada Nield 1870-1945 . . . . DLB-135
Cheyney, Edward P. 1861-1947 . . . . DLB-47
Chiabrera, Gabriello 1552-1638 . . . . DLB-339
Chiang Yee 1903-1977 . . . . DLB-312
Chiara, Piero 1913-1986 . . . . DLB-177
Chicanos
   Chicano History DLB-82
   Chicano Language DLB-82
   Chicano Literature: A Bibliography . . DLB-209
   A Contemporary Flourescence of Chicano
      Literature Y-84
   Literatura Chicanesca: The View From
      Without DLB-82
Child, Francis James 1825-1896 . . . DLB-1, 64, 235
Child, Lydia Maria 1802-1880 . . . . . DLB-1, 74, 243
Child, Philip 1898-1978 . . . . DLB-68
Childers, Erskine 1870-1922 . . . . DLB-70
Children's Literature
   Afterword: Propaganda, Namby-Pamby,
      and Some Books of Distinction . . . DLB-52
   Children's Book Awards and Prizes . . . DLB-61
   Children's Book Illustration in the
      Twentieth Century DLB-61
   Children's Illustrators, 1800-1880 . . . DLB-163
   The Harry Potter Phenomenon Y-99
   Pony Stories, Omnibus
      Essay on DLB-160
   The Reality of One Woman's Dream:
      The de Grummond Children's
      Literature Collection Y-99
   School Stories, 1914-1960 . . . . DLB-160
   The Year in Children's
      Books Y-92–96, 98–01
   The Year in Children's Literature Y-97
Childress, Alice 1916-1994 . . . . DLB-7, 38, 249
Childress, Mark 1957- DLB-292
Childs, George W. 1829-1894 . . . . DLB-23
Chilton Book Company DLB-46
Chin, Frank 1940- DLB-206, 312
Chin, Justin 1969- DLB-312
Chin, Marilyn 1955- DLB-312
Chinweizu 1943- DLB-157
Chinnov, Igor' 1909-1996 . . . . DLB-317

Chitham, Edward 1932- DLB-155
Chittenden, Hiram Martin 1858-1917 . . . . DLB-47
Chivers, Thomas Holley 1809-1858 . . DLB-3, 248
Chkhartishvili, Grigorii Shalvovich
   (see Akunin, Boris)
Chocano, José Santos 1875-1934 . . . . DLB-290
Cholmondeley, Mary 1859-1925 . . . . DLB-197
Chomsky, Noam 1928- DLB-246
Chopin, Kate 1850-1904 . . . DLB-12, 78; CDALB-3
Chopin, René 1885-1953 . . . . DLB-92
Choquette, Adrienne 1915-1973 . . . . DLB-68
Choquette, Robert 1905-1991 . . . . DLB-68
Choyce, Lesley 1951- DLB-251
Chrétien de Troyes
   circa 1140-circa 1190 . . . . DLB-208
Christensen, Inger 1935- DLB-214
Christensen, Lars Saabye 1953- DLB-297
The Christian Examiner DLB-1
The Christian Publishing Company DLB-49
Christie, Agatha
   1890-1976 . . . . DLB-13, 77, 245; CDBLB-6
Christine de Pizan
   circa 1365-circa 1431 . . . . DLB-208
Christopher, John (Sam Youd) 1922- . . DLB-255
Christus und die Samariterin circa 950 . . . . . . DLB-148
Christy, Howard Chandler 1873-1952 . . . DLB-188
Chu, Louis 1915-1970 . . . . DLB-312
Chukovskaia, Lidiia 1907-1996 . . . . DLB-302
Chulkov, Mikhail Dmitrievich
   1743?-1792 . . . . DLB-150
Church, Benjamin 1734-1778 . . . . DLB-31
Church, Francis Pharcellus 1839-1906 . . . . DLB-79
Church, Peggy Pond 1903-1986 . . . . DLB-212
Church, Richard 1893-1972 . . . . DLB-191
Church, William Conant 1836-1917 . . . . . DLB-79
Churchill, Caryl 1938- DLB-13, 310
Churchill, Charles 1731-1764 . . . . DLB-109
Churchill, Winston 1871-1947 . . . . DLB-202
Churchill, Sir Winston
   1874-1965 . . . DLB-100, 329; DS-16; CDBLB-5
Churchyard, Thomas 1520?-1604 . . . . . . DLB-132
E. Churton and Company DLB-106
Chute, Marchette 1909-1994 . . . . DLB-103
Ciampoli, Giovanni Battista
   1590-1643 . . . . DLB-339
Ciardi, John 1916-1986 . . . . DLB-5; Y-86
Cibber, Colley 1671-1757 . . . . DLB-84
Cicero 106 B.C.-43 B.C. DLB-211, CDWLB-1
Cicognini, Giacinto Andrea
   1606-1649 . . . . DLB-339
Cima, Annalisa 1941- DLB-128
Čingo, Živko 1935-1987 . . . . DLB-181
Cioran, E. M. 1911-1995 . . . . DLB-220

Čipkus, Alfonsas (see Nyka-Niliūnas, Alfonsas)

Cirese, Eugenio 1884-1955 .... DLB-114

Cīrulis, Jānis (see Bels, Alberts)

Cisneros, Antonio 1942- DLB-290

Cisneros, Sandra 1954- DLB-122, 152

City Lights Books DLB-46

Civil War (1861–1865)
    Battles and Leaders of the Civil War ... DLB-47
    Official Records of the Rebellion DLB-47
    Recording the Civil War DLB-47

Cixous, Hélène 1937- DLB-83, 242

Claire d'Albe, Sophie Cottin DLB-314

Clampitt, Amy 1920-1994 .... DLB-105
    Tribute to Alfred A. Knopf Y-84

Clancy, Tom 1947- DLB-227

Clapper, Raymond 1892-1944 .... DLB-29

Clare, John 1793-1864 .... DLB-55, 96

Clarendon, Edward Hyde, Earl of 1609-1674 .... DLB-101

Clark, Alfred Alexander Gordon (see Hare, Cyril)

Clark, Ann Nolan 1896-1995 .... DLB-52

Clark, C. E. Frazer, Jr. 1925-2001 .. DLB-187; Y-01
    C. E. Frazer Clark Jr. and Hawthorne Bibliography DLB-269
    The Publications of C. E. Frazer Clark Jr. DLB-269

Clark, Catherine Anthony 1892-1977 .... DLB-68

Clark, Charles Heber 1841-1915 .... DLB-11

Clark, Davis Wasgatt 1812-1871 .... DLB-79

Clark, Douglas 1919-1993 .... DLB-276

Clark, Eleanor 1913-1996 .... DLB-6

Clark, J. P. 1935- DLB-117; CDWLB-3

Clark, Lewis Gaylord 1808-1873 .... DLB-3, 64, 73, 250

Clark, Mary Higgins 1929- DLB-306

Clark, Walter Van Tilburg 1909-1971 .... DLB-9, 206

Clark, William 1770-1838 .... DLB-183, 186

Clark, William Andrews, Jr. 1877-1934 .... DLB-187

C. M. Clark Publishing Company DLB-46

Clarke, Sir Arthur C. 1917-2008 .... DLB-261
    Tribute to Theodore Sturgeon Y-85

Clarke, Austin 1896-1974 .... DLB-10, 20

Clarke, Austin C. 1934- DLB-53, 125

Clarke, George Elliott 1960- DLB-334

Clarke, Gillian 1937- DLB-40

Clarke, James Freeman 1810-1888 .... DLB-1, 59, 235; DS-5

Clarke, John circa 1596-1658 .... DLB-281

Clarke, Lindsay 1939- DLB-231

Clarke, Marcus 1846-1881 .... DLB-230

Clarke, Pauline 1921- DLB-161

Clarke, Rebecca Sophia 1833-1906 .... DLB-42

Clarke, Samuel 1675-1729 .... DLB-252

Robert Clarke and Company DLB-49

Clarkson, Thomas 1760-1846 .... DLB-158

Claudel, Paul 1868-1955 .... DLB-192, 258, 321

Claudius, Matthias 1740-1815 .... DLB-97

Clausen, Andy 1943- DLB-16

Claussen, Sophus 1865-1931 .... DLB-300

Clawson, John L. 1865-1933 .... DLB-187

Claxton, Remsen and Haffelfinger DLB-49

Clay, Cassius Marcellus 1810-1903 .... DLB-43

Clayton, Richard (see Haggard, William)

Cleage, Pearl 1948- DLB-228

Cleary, Beverly 1916- DLB-52

Cleary, Kate McPhelim 1863-1905 .... DLB-221

Cleaver, Vera 1919-1992 and Cleaver, Bill 1920-1981 .... DLB-52

Cleeve, Brian 1921-2003 .... DLB-276

Cleland, John 1710-1789 .... DLB-39

Clemens, Samuel Langhorne (Mark Twain) 1835-1910 .... DLB-11, 12, 23, 64, 74, 186, 189; CDALB-3
    Comments From Authors and Scholars on their First Reading of *Huck Finn* Y-85
    Huck at 100: How Old Is Huckleberry Finn? Y-85
    Mark Twain on Perpetual Copyright Y-92
    A New Edition of *Huck Finn* Y-85
    Mark Twain's *Adventures of Huckleberry Finn* (Documentary) DLB-343

Clement, Hal 1922-2003 .... DLB-8

Clemo, Jack 1916-1994 .... DLB-27

Clephane, Elizabeth Cecilia 1830-1869 ... DLB-199

Cleveland, John 1613-1658 .... DLB-126

Cliff, Michelle 1946- DLB-157; CDWLB-3

Clifford, Lady Anne 1590-1676 .... DLB-151

Clifford, James L. 1901-1978 .... DLB-103

Clifford, Lucy 1853?-1929 .... DLB-135, 141, 197

Clift, Charmian 1923-1969 .... DLB-260

Clifton, Lucille 1936- DLB-5, 41

Clines, Francis X. 1938- DLB-185

Clive, Caroline (V) 1801-1873 .... DLB-199

Edward J. Clode [publishing house] DLB-46

Clough, Arthur Hugh 1819-1861 .... DLB-32

Cloutier, Cécile 1930- DLB-60

Clouts, Sidney 1926-1982 .... DLB-225

Clutton-Brock, Arthur 1868-1924 .... DLB-98

Coates, Robert M. 1897-1973 .... DLB-4, 9, 102; DS-15

Coatsworth, Elizabeth 1893-1986 .... DLB-22

Cobb, Charles E., Jr. 1943- DLB-41

Cobb, Frank I. 1869-1923 .... DLB-25

Cobb, Irvin S. 1876-1944 .... DLB-11, 25, 86

Cobbe, Frances Power 1822-1904 .... DLB-190

Cobbett, William 1763-1835 .... DLB-43, 107, 158

Cobbledick, Gordon 1898-1969 .... DLB-171

Cochran, Thomas C. 1902-1999 .... DLB-17

Cochrane, Elizabeth 1867-1922 .... DLB-25, 189

Cockerell, Sir Sydney 1867-1962 .... DLB-201

Cockerill, John A. 1845-1896 .... DLB-23

Cocteau, Jean 1889-1963 .... DLB-65, 258, 321

Coderre, Emile (see Jean Narrache)

Cody, Liza 1944- DLB-276

Coe, Jonathan 1961- DLB-231

Coetzee, J. M. 1940- DLB-225, 326, 329

Coffee, Lenore J. 1900?-1984 .... DLB-44

Coffin, Robert P. Tristram 1892-1955 .... DLB-45

Coghill, Mrs. Harry (see Walker, Anna Louisa)

Cogswell, Fred 1917-2004 .... DLB-60

Cogswell, Mason Fitch 1761-1830 .... DLB-37

Cohan, George M. 1878-1942 .... DLB-249

Cohen, Arthur A. 1928-1986 .... DLB-28

Cohen, Leonard 1934- DLB-53

Cohen, Matt 1942- DLB-53

Cohen, Morris Raphael 1880-1947 .... DLB-270

Colasanti, Marina 1937- DLB-307

Colbeck, Norman 1903-1987 .... DLB-201

Colden, Cadwallader 1688-1776 .. DLB-24, 30, 270

Colden, Jane 1724-1766 .... DLB-200

Cole, Barry 1936- DLB-14

Cole, George Watson 1850-1939 .... DLB-140

Colegate, Isabel 1931- DLB-14, 231

Coleman, Emily Holmes 1899-1974 .... DLB-4

Coleman, Wanda 1946- DLB-130

Coleridge, Hartley 1796-1849 .... DLB-96

Coleridge, Mary 1861-1907 .... DLB-19, 98

Coleridge, Samuel Taylor 1772-1834 .... DLB-93, 107; CDBLB-3

Coleridge, Sara 1802-1852 .... DLB-199

Colet, John 1467-1519 .... DLB-132

Colette 1873-1954 .... DLB-65

Colette, Sidonie Gabrielle (see Colette)

Colinas, Antonio 1946- DLB-134

Coll, Joseph Clement 1881-1921 .... DLB-188

A Century of Poetry, a Lifetime of Collecting: J. M. Edelstein's Collection of Twentieth-Century American Poetry Y-02

Collier, John 1901-1980 .... DLB-77, 255

Collier, John Payne 1789-1883 .... DLB-184

Collier, Mary 1690-1762 .... DLB-95

Collier, Robert J. 1876-1918 .... DLB-91

P. F. Collier [publishing house] DLB-49

Collin and Small DLB-49

Collingwood, R. G. 1889-1943 .... DLB-262

Cumulative Index

Collingwood, W. G. 1854-1932 .... DLB-149

Collins, An floruit circa 1653 .... DLB-131

Collins, Anthony 1676-1729 .... DLB-252, 336

Collins, Arthur 1681?-1762............ DLB-336

Collins, Martha 1940- DLB-342

Collins, Merle 1950- DLB-157

Collins, Michael 1964- DLB-267

Collins, Michael (see Lynds, Dennis)

Collins, Mortimer 1827-1876 .... DLB-21, 35

Collins, Tom (see Furphy, Joseph)

Collins, Wilkie
   1824-1889 ...... DLB-18, 70, 159; CDBLB-4

   "The Unknown Public" (1858)
   [excerpt].................... DLB-57

   The Wilkie Collins Society Y-98

Collins, William 1721-1759............ DLB-109

Isaac Collins [publishing house] DLB-49

William Collins, Sons and Company DLB-154

Collis, Maurice 1889-1973 .... DLB-195

Collom, Jack 1931- DLB-342

Collyer, Mary 1716?-1763?............ DLB-39

Colman, Benjamin 1673-1747 .... DLB-24

Colman, George, the Elder 1732-1794 .... DLB-89

Colman, George, the Younger
   1762-1836..................... DLB-89

S. Colman [publishing house]........... DLB-49

Colombo, John Robert 1936- DLB-53

Colonial Literature DLB-307

Colquhoun, Patrick 1745-1820 .... DLB-158

Colter, Cyrus 1910-2002................ DLB-33

Colum, Padraic 1881-1972 .... DLB-19

The Columbia History of the American Novel
   A Symposium on Y-92

Columbus, Christopher 1451-1506 ..... DLB-318

Columella fl. first century A.D. DLB-211

Colvin, Sir Sidney 1845-1927 .... DLB-149

Colwin, Laurie 1944-1992 ....DLB-218; Y-80

Comden, Betty 1915- and
   Green, Adolph 1918-2002 ...... DLB-44, 265

Comi, Girolamo 1890-1968 .... DLB-114

Comisso, Giovanni 1895-1969 .... DLB-264

Commager, Henry Steele 1902-1998 ..... DLB-17

Commynes, Philippe de
   circa 1447-1511................. DLB-208

Compton, D. G. 1930- DLB-261

Compton-Burnett, Ivy 1884?-1969....... DLB-36

Conan, Laure (Félicité Angers)
   1845-1924 .... DLB-99

Concord, Massachusetts
   Concord History and Life DLB-223

   Concord: Literary History
   of a Town................... DLB-223

   The Old Manse, by Hawthorne..... DLB-223

   The Thoreauvian Pilgrimage: The
   Structure of an American Cult .. DLB-223

Concrete Poetry DLB-307

Conde, Carmen 1901-1996 .... DLB-108

Condillac, Etienne Bonnot de
   1714-1780 .... DLB-313

Condorcet, Marie-Jean-Antoine-Nicolas Caritat,
   marquis de 1743-1794............. DLB-313

   "The Tenth Stage" DLB-314

Congreve, William
   1670-1729........... DLB-39, 84; CDBLB-2

   Preface to *Incognita* (1692)........... DLB-39

W. B. Conkey Company DLB-49

Conlon, Evelyn 1952- DLB-319

Conn, Stewart 1936- DLB-233

Connell, Evan S., Jr. 1924- DLB-2, 335; Y-81

Connelly, Marc 1890-1980..........DLB-7; Y-80

Connolly, Cyril 1903-1974 .... DLB-98

Connolly, James B. 1868-1957 .... DLB-78

Connor, Ralph (Charles William Gordon)
   1860-1937..................... DLB-92

Connor, Tony 1930- DLB-40

Conquest, Robert 1917- DLB-27

Conrad, Joseph
   1857-1924.... DLB-10, 34, 98, 156; CDBLB-5

John Conrad and Company DLB-49

Conroy, Jack 1899-1990 .... Y-81

   A Tribute [to Nelson Algren] Y-81

Conroy, Pat 1945- DLB-6

The Conservationist, 1974 Booker Prize winner,
   Nadine Gordimer................. DLB-326

Considine, Bob 1906-1975 .... DLB-241

Consolo, Vincenzo 1933- DLB-196

Constable, Henry 1562-1613 .... DLB-136

Archibald Constable and Company DLB-154

Constable and Company Limited....... DLB-112

Constant, Benjamin 1767-1830 .... DLB-119

Constant de Rebecque, Henri-Benjamin de
   (see Constant, Benjamin)

Constantine, David 1944- DLB-40

Constantine, Murray (see Burdekin, Katharine)

Constantin-Weyer, Maurice 1881-1964.... DLB-92

Contempo (magazine)
   Contempo Caravan:
   Kites in a Windstorm Y-85

The Continental Publishing Company.... DLB-49

A Conversation between William Riggan
   and Janette Turner Hospital............ Y-02

Conversations with Editors Y-95

Conway, Anne 1631-1679.............. DLB-252

Conway, Moncure Daniel
   1832-1907.................... DLB-1, 223

Cook, Ebenezer circa 1667-circa 1732..... DLB-24

Cook, Edward Tyas 1857-1919 .... DLB-149

Cook, Eliza 1818-1889 .... DLB-199

Cook, George Cram 1873-1924 .... DLB-266

Cook, Michael 1933-1994 .... DLB-53

David C. Cook Publishing Company..... DLB-49

Cooke, George Willis 1848-1923 .... DLB-71

Cooke, John Esten 1830-1886 .... DLB-3, 248

Cooke, Philip Pendleton
   1816-1850 .... DLB-3, 59, 248

Cooke, Rose Terry 1827-1892 ....DLB-12, 74

Increase Cooke and Company DLB-49

Cook-Lynn, Elizabeth 1930- DLB-175

Coolbrith, Ina 1841-1928.......... DLB-54, 186

Cooley, Dennis 1944- DLB-334

Cooley, Peter 1940- DLB-105

   "Into the Mirror" DLB-105

Coolidge, Clark 1939- DLB-193

Coolidge, Susan
   (see Woolsey, Sarah Chauncy)

George Coolidge [publishing house]...... DLB-49

Coomaraswamy, Ananda 1877-1947..... DLB-323

Cooper, Anna Julia 1858-1964 .... DLB-221

Cooper, Edith Emma (see Field, Michael)

Cooper, Giles 1918-1966 .... DLB-13

Cooper, J. California 19??- DLB-212

Cooper, James Fenimore
   1789-1851....... DLB-3, 183, 250; CDALB-2

   The Bicentennial of James Fenimore Cooper:
   An International Celebration......... Y-89

   The James Fenimore Cooper Society..... Y-01

Cooper, Kent 1880-1965................ DLB-29

Cooper, Susan 1935- DLB-161, 261

Cooper, Susan Fenimore 1813-1894..... DLB-239

William Cooper [publishing house] DLB-170

J. Coote [publishing house]............ DLB-154

Coover, Robert 1932- DLB-2, 227; Y-81

   Tribute to Donald Barthelme........... Y-89

   Tribute to Theodor Seuss Geisel Y-91

Copeland and Day DLB-49

Ćopić, Branko 1915-1984.............. DLB-181

Copland, Robert 1470?-1548 .... DLB-136

Coppard, A. E. 1878-1957 .... DLB-162

Coppée, François 1842-1908 ....DLB-217

Coppel, Alfred 1921-2004 .... Y-83

   Tribute to Jessamyn West............. Y-84

Coppola, Francis Ford 1939- DLB-44

Copway, George (Kah-ge-ga-gah-bowh)
   1818-1869 ....DLB-175, 183

Copyright
   The Development of the Author's
   Copyright in Britain DLB-154

   The Digital Millennium Copyright Act:
   Expanding Copyright Protection in
   Cyberspace and Beyond Y-98

   Editorial: The Extension of Copyright ... Y-02

   Mark Twain on Perpetual Copyright..... Y-92

Public Domain and the Violation
    of Texts........................Y-97

The Question of American Copyright
    in the Nineteenth Century
    Preface, by George Haven Putnam
    The Evolution of Copyright, by
        Brander Matthews
    Summary of Copyright Legislation in
        the United States, by R. R. Bowker
    Analysis of the Provisions of the
        Copyright Law of 1891, by
        George Haven Putnam
    The Contest for International Copyright,
        by George Haven Putnam
    Cheap Books and Good Books,
        by Brander Matthews..........DLB-49

Writers and Their Copyright Holders:
    the WATCH Project..............Y-94

Corazzini, Sergio 1886-1907............DLB-114
Corbett, Richard 1582-1635.............DLB-121
Corbière, Tristan 1845-1875............DLB-217
Corcoran, Barbara 1911- DLB-52
Cordelli, Franco 1943- DLB-196
Corelli, Marie 1855-1924...........DLB-34, 156
Corle, Edwin 1906-1956.................Y-85
Corman, Cid 1924-2004..............DLB-5, 193
Cormier, Robert 1925-2000....DLB-52; CDALB-6
    Tribute to Theodor Seuss Geisel.....Y-91
Corn, Alfred 1943- DLB-120, 282; Y-80
Corneille, Pierre 1606-1684............DLB-268
Cornford, Frances 1886-1960...........DLB-240
Cornish, Sam 1935- DLB-41
Cornish, William
    circa 1465-circa 1524..............DLB-132
Cornwall, Barry (see Procter, Bryan Waller)
Cornwallis, Sir William, the Younger
    circa 1579-1614....................DLB-151
Cornwell, David John Moore (see le Carré, John)
Cornwell, Patricia 1956- DLB-306
Coronel Urtecho, José 1906-1994.......DLB-290
Corpi, Lucha 1945- DLB-82
Corrington, John William
    1932-1988.......................DLB-6, 244
Corriveau, Monique 1927-1976..........DLB-251
Corrothers, James D. 1869-1917........DLB-50
Corso, Gregory 1930-2001........DLB-5, 16, 237
Cortázar, Julio 1914-1984...DLB-113; CDWLB-3
Cortese, Giulio Cesare circa
    1570-1626?........................DLB-339
Cortéz, Carlos 1923-2005..............DLB-209
Cortez, Jayne 1936- DLB-41
Corvinus, Gottlieb Siegmund
    1677-1746.........................DLB-168
Corvo, Baron (see Rolfe, Frederick William)
Cory, Annie Sophie (see Cross, Victoria)
Cory, Desmond (Shaun Lloyd McCarthy)
    1928-2001.........................DLB-276
Cory, William Johnson 1823-1892........DLB-35

Coryate, Thomas 1577?-1617.......DLB-151, 172
Ćosić, Dobrica 1921- DLB-181; CDWLB-4
Cosin, John 1595-1672..............DLB-151, 213
Cosmopolitan Book Corporation.........DLB-46
Cossa, Roberto 1934- DLB-305
Costa, Margherita 1600/1610?-1657.....DLB-339
Costa, Maria Velho da (see The Three Marias:
    A Landmark Case in Portuguese
    Literary History)
Costain, Thomas B. 1885-1965............DLB-9
Coste, Donat (Daniel Boudreau)
    1912-1957..........................DLB-88
Costello, Louisa Stuart 1799-1870......DLB-166
Cota-Cárdenas, Margarita 1941- DLB-122
Côté, Denis 1954- DLB-251
Cotten, Bruce 1873-1954................DLB-187
Cotter, Joseph Seamon, Jr. 1895-1919....DLB-50
Cotter, Joseph Seamon, Sr. 1861-1949....DLB-50
Cottin, Sophie 1770-1807...............DLB-313
    Claire d'Albe......................DLB-314
Joseph Cottle [publishing house].......DLB-154
Cotton, Charles 1630-1687..............DLB-131
Cotton, John 1584-1652.................DLB-24
Cotton, Sir Robert Bruce 1571-1631.....DLB-213
Couani, Anna 1948- DLB-325
Coulter, John 1888-1980................DLB-68
Coupland, Douglas 1961- DLB-334
Cournos, John 1881-1966................DLB-54
Courteline, Georges 1858-1929..........DLB-192
Cousins, Margaret 1905-1996............DLB-137
Cousins, Norman 1915-1990..............DLB-137
Couvreur, Jessie (see Tasma)
Coventry, Francis 1725-1754............DLB-39
    Dedication, The History of Pompey
        the Little (1751)..............DLB-39
Coverdale, Miles 1487 or 1488-1569.....DLB-167
N. Coverly [publishing house]..........DLB-49
Covici-Friede..........................DLB-46
Cowan, Peter 1914-2002.................DLB-260
Coward, Noel
    1899-1973....................DLB-10, 245; CDBLB-6
Coward, McCann and Geoghegan..........DLB-46
Cowles, Gardner 1861-1946..............DLB-29
Cowles, Gardner "Mike", Jr.
    1903-1985......................DLB-127, 137
Cowley, Abraham 1618-1667..........DLB-131, 151
Cowley, Hannah 1743-1809...............DLB-89
Cowley, Malcolm
    1898-1989.......DLB-4, 48; DS-15; Y-81, 89
Cowper, Richard (John Middleton Murry Jr.)
    1926-2002.........................DLB-261
Cowper, William 1731-1800..........DLB-104, 109
Cox, A. B. (see Berkeley, Anthony)

Cox, James McMahon 1903-1974.........DLB-127
Cox, James Middleton 1870-1957........DLB-127
Cox, Leonard circa 1495-circa 1550....DLB-281
Cox, Palmer 1840-1924..................DLB-42
Coxe, Louis 1918-1993...................DLB-5
Coxe, Tench 1755-1824..................DLB-37
Coyne, Joseph Stirling 1803-1868......DLB-344
Cozzens, Frederick S. 1818-1869.......DLB-202
Cozzens, James Gould 1903-1978...............
    ....DLB-9, 294; Y-84; DS-2; CDALB-1
    Cozzens's Michael Scarlett..........Y-97
    Ernest Hemingway's Reaction to
        James Gould Cozzens............Y-98
    James Gould Cozzens—A View
        from Afar.......................Y-97
    James Gould Cozzens: How to
        Read Him........................Y-97
    James Gould Cozzens Symposium and
        Exhibition at the University of
        South Carolina, Columbia........Y-00
    Mens Rea (or Something).............Y-97
    Novels for Grown-Ups................Y-97
Crabbe, George 1754-1832...............DLB-93
Crace, Jim 1946- DLB-231
Crackanthorpe, Hubert 1870-1896........DLB-135
Craddock, Charles Egbert (see Murfree, Mary N.)
Cradock, Thomas 1718-1770..............DLB-31
Craig, Daniel H. 1811-1895.............DLB-43
Craik, Dinah Maria 1826-1887.......DLB-35, 163
Cramer, Richard Ben 1950- DLB-185
Cranch, Christopher Pearse
    1813-1892................DLB-1, 42, 243; DS-5
Crane, Hart 1899-1932.........DLB-4, 48; CDALB-4
    Nathan Asch Remembers Ford Madox
        Ford, Sam Roth, and Hart Crane..Y-02
Crane, R. S. 1886-1967.................DLB-63
Crane, Stephen
    1871-1900........DLB-12, 54, 78; CDALB-3
    Stephen Crane: A Revaluation, Virginia
        Tech Conference, 1989...........Y-89
    The Stephen Crane Society.........Y-98, 01
Crane, Walter 1845-1915................DLB-163
Cranmer, Thomas 1489-1556..........DLB-132, 213
Crapsey, Adelaide 1878-1914............DLB-54
Crashaw, Richard 1612/1613-1649........DLB-126
Crate, Joan 1953- DLB-334
Craven, Avery 1885-1980................DLB-17
Crawford, Charles 1752-circa 1815......DLB-31
Crawford, F. Marion 1854-1909..........DLB-71
Crawford, Isabel Valancy 1850-1887.....DLB-92
Crawley, Alan 1887-1975................DLB-68
Crayon, Geoffrey (see Irving, Washington)
Crayon, Porte (see Strother, David Hunter)
Creamer, Robert W. 1922- DLB-171

Creasey, John 1908-1973 . . . . DLB-77
Creative Age Press DLB-46
Creative Nonfiction Y-02
Crébillon, Claude-Prosper Jolyot de *fils*
   1707-1777 . . . . DLB-313
Crébillon, Claude-Prosper Jolyot de *père*
   1674-1762. DLB-313
William Creech [publishing house]. DLB-154
Thomas Creede [publishing house] DLB-170
Creel, George 1876-1953 . . . . DLB-25
Creeley, Robert 1926-2005
   . . . . .DLB-5, 16, 169; DS-17
Creelman, James
   1859-1915. . . . . DLB-23
Cregan, David 1931- DLB-13
Creighton, Donald 1902-1979. . . . . DLB-88
Crémazie, Octave 1827-1879. . . . . DLB-99
Crémer, Victoriano 1909?- DLB-108
Crenne, Helisenne de (Marguerite de Briet)
   1510?-1560?. DLB-327
Crescas, Hasdai circa 1340-1412?. DLB-115
Crespo, Angel 1926-1995 . . . . DLB-134
Cresset Press. DLB-112
Cresswell, Helen 1934- DLB-161
Crèvecoeur, Michel Guillaume Jean de
   1735-1813. . . . . DLB-37
Crewe, Candida 1964- DLB-207
Crews, Harry 1935- DLB-6, 143, 185
Crichton, Michael (John Lange, Jeffrey Hudson,
   Michael Douglas) 1942- DLB-292; Y-81
Crispin, Edmund (Robert Bruce Montgomery)
   1921-1978. . . . . DLB-87
Cristofer, Michael 1946- DLB-7
Criticism
   Afro-American Literary Critics:
     An Introduction. DLB-33
   The Consolidation of Opinion: Critical
     Responses to the Modernists. DLB-36
   "Criticism in Relation to Novels"
     (1863), by G. H. Lewes DLB-21
   The Limits of Pluralism DLB-67
   Modern Critical Terms, Schools, and
     Movements DLB-67
   "Panic Among the Philistines":
     A Postscript, An Interview
     with Bryan Griffin. Y-81
   The Recovery of Literature: Criticism
     in the 1990s: A Symposium. Y-91
   The Stealthy School of Criticism (1871),
     by Dante Gabriel Rossetti DLB-35
Crnjanski, Miloš
   1893-1977. . . . . .DLB-147; CDWLB-4
Crocker, Hannah Mather 1752-1829 . . . . DLB-200
Crockett, David (Davy)
   1786-1836. . . . . DLB-3, 11, 183, 248
Croft-Cooke, Rupert (see Bruce, Leo)
Crofts, Freeman Wills 1879-1957 . . . . DLB-77
Croker, John Wilson 1780-1857 . . . . DLB-110

Croly, George 1780-1860 . . . . DLB-159
Croly, Herbert 1869-1930 . . . . DLB-91
Croly, Jane Cunningham 1829-1901 . . . . . DLB-23
Crompton, Richmal 1890-1969 . . . . DLB-160
Cronin, A. J. 1896-1981 . . . . DLB-191
Cros, Charles 1842-1888 . . . . DLB-217
Crosby, Caresse 1892-1970 and
   Crosby, Harry 1898-1929 and . . DLB-4; DS-15
Crosby, Harry 1898-1929 . . . . DLB-48
Crosland, Camilla Toulmin (Mrs. Newton
   Crosland) 1812-1895 . . . . DLB-240
Cross, Amanda (Carolyn G. Heilbrun)
   1926-2003 . . . . DLB-306
Cross, Gillian 1945- DLB-161
Cross, Victoria 1868-1952 . . . . .DLB-135, 197
Crossley-Holland, Kevin 1941- DLB-40, 161
Crothers, Rachel 1870-1958 . . . . .DLB-7, 266
Thomas Y. Crowell Company DLB-49
Crowley, John 1942- Y-82
Crowley, Mart 1935- DLB-7, 266
Crown Publishers DLB-46
Crowne, John 1641-1712 . . . . DLB-80
Crowninshield, Edward Augustus
   1817-1859. . . . . DLB-140
Crowninshield, Frank 1872-1947 . . . . DLB-91
Croy, Homer 1883-1965. . . . . DLB-4
Crumley, James 1939-2008. . . . . . . .DLB-226; Y-84
Cruse, Mary Anne 1825?-1910 . . . . DLB-239
Cruz, Migdalia 1958- DLB-249
Cruz, Sor Juana Inés de la 1651-1695. . . . DLB-305
Cruz, Victor Hernández 1949- DLB-41
Cruz e Sousa, João 1861-1898 . . . . DLB-307
Csokor, Franz Theodor 1885-1969. . . . . . . DLB-81
Csoóri, Sándor 1930- DLB-232; CDWLB-4
Cuadra, Pablo Antonio 1912-2002. . . . . . DLB-290
Cuala Press. DLB-112
Cudworth, Ralph 1617-1688. . . . . DLB-252
Cueva, Juan de la 1543-1612 . . . . DLB-318
Cugoano, Quobna Ottabah 1797-?. Y-02
Cullen, Countee
   1903-1946 . . . . DLB-4, 48, 51; CDALB-4
Culler, Jonathan D. 1944- DLB-67, 246
Cullinan, Elizabeth 1933- DLB-234
Culverwel, Nathaniel 1619?-1651?. DLB-252
Cumberland, Richard 1732-1811 . . . . DLB-89
Cummings, Constance Gordon
   1837-1924. . . . . DLB-174
Cummings, E. E.
   1894-1962 . . . . DLB-4, 48; CDALB-5
   The E. E. Cummings Society. Y-01
Cummings, Ray 1887-1957 . . . . DLB-8
Cummings and Hilliard DLB-49
Cummins, Maria Susanna 1827-1866 . . . . . DLB-42

Cumpián, Carlos 1953- DLB-209
Cunard, Nancy 1896-1965. . . . . DLB-240
Joseph Cundall [publishing house] DLB-106
Cuney, Waring 1906-1976 . . . . DLB-51
Cuney-Hare, Maude 1874-1936 . . . . DLB-52
Cunha, Euclides da 1866-1909. . . . . DLB-307
Cunningham, Allan 1784-1842 . . . . .DLB-116, 144
Cunningham, J. V. 1911-1985 . . . . DLB-5
Cunningham, Michael 1952- DLB-292
Cunningham, Peter (Peter Lauder, Peter
   Benjamin) 1947- DLB-267
Peter F. Cunningham
   [publishing house] DLB-49
Cunqueiro, Alvaro 1911-1981 . . . . DLB-134
Cuomo, George 1929- Y-80
Cupples, Upham and Company. DLB-49
Cupples and Leon DLB-46
Cuppy, Will 1884-1949. . . . . DLB-11
Curiel, Barbara Brinson 1956- DLB-209
Curley, Daniel 1918-1988. . . . . DLB-335
Edmund Curll [publishing house] DLB-154
Currie, James 1756-1805. . . . . DLB-142
Currie, Mary Montgomerie Lamb Singleton,
   Lady Currie (see Fane, Violet)
Currie, Sheldon 1934- DLB-334
Cursor Mundi circa 1300. . . . . DLB-146
Curti, Merle E. 1897-1996 . . . . .DLB-17
Curtis, Anthony 1926- DLB-155
Curtis, Cyrus H. K. 1850-1933 . . . . DLB-91
Curtis, George William
   1824-1892 . . . . DLB-1, 43, 223
Curzon, Robert 1810-1873 . . . . DLB-166
Curzon, Sarah Anne 1833-1898 . . . . DLB-99
Cusack, Dymphna 1902-1981 . . . . DLB-260
Cushing, Eliza Lanesford 1794-1886 . . . . . DLB-99
Cushing, Harvey 1869-1939. . . . . .DLB-187
Custance, Olive (Lady Alfred Douglas)
   1874-1944. . . . . DLB-240
Cynewulf circa 770-840 . . . . DLB-146
Cyrano de Bergerac, Savinien de
   1619-1655 .DLB-268
Czepko, Daniel 1605-1660 . . . . DLB-164
Czerniawski, Adam 1934- DLB-232

D

Dabit, Eugène 1898-1936 . . . . DLB-65
Daborne, Robert circa 1580-1628 . . . . DLB-58
Dąbrowska, Maria
   1889-1965 . . . . .DLB-215; CDWLB-4
Dacey, Philip 1939- DLB-105
   "Eyes Across Centuries:
     Contemporary Poetry and 'That
     Vision Thing,'" DLB-105
Dach, Simon 1605-1659 . . . . DLB-164

Dacier, Anne Le Fèvre 1647-1720........DLB-313

Dagerman, Stig 1923-1954............DLB-259

Daggett, Rollin M. 1831-1901........DLB-79

D'Aguiar, Fred 1960-................DLB-157

Dahl, Roald 1916-1990..........DLB-139, 255

    Tribute to Alfred A. Knopf.............Y-84

Dahlberg, Edward 1900-1977..........DLB-48

Dahn, Felix 1834-1912...............DLB-129

The Daily Worker...................DLB-303

Dal', Vladimir Ivanovich (Kazak Vladimir Lugansky) 1801-1872.............DLB-198

Dale, Peter 1938-...................DLB-40

Daley, Arthur 1904-1974.............DLB-171

Dall, Caroline Healey 1822-1912.....DLB-1, 235

Dallas, E. S. 1828-1879.............DLB-55

    The Gay Science [excerpt](1866)........DLB-21

The Dallas Theater Center...........DLB-7

D'Alton, Louis 1900-1951............DLB-10

Dalton, Roque 1935-1975.............DLB-283

Daly, Carroll John 1889-1958........DLB-226

Daly, T. A. 1871-1948...............DLB-11

Damon, S. Foster 1893-1971..........DLB-45

William S. Damrell [publishing house].....DLB-49

Dana, Charles A. 1819-1897......DLB-3, 23, 250

Dana, Richard Henry, Jr. 1815-1882................DLB-1, 183, 235

Dandridge, Ray Garfield 1882-1930......DLB-51

Dane, Clemence 1887-1965........DLB-10, 197

Danforth, John 1660-1730............DLB-24

Danforth, Samuel, I 1626-1674.......DLB-24

Danforth, Samuel, II 1666-1727......DLB-24

Dangerous Acquaintances, Pierre-Ambroise-François Choderlos de Laclos.............DLB-314

Daniel, John M. 1825-1865...........DLB-43

Daniel, Samuel 1562 or 1563-1619.......DLB-62

Daniel Press.........................DLB-106

Daniel', Iulii 1925-1988............DLB-302

Daniells, Roy 1902-1979.............DLB-68

Daniels, Jim 1956-..................DLB-120

Daniels, Jonathan 1902-1981.........DLB-127

Daniels, Josephus 1862-1948.........DLB-29

Daniels, Sarah 1957-................DLB-245

Danilevsky, Grigorii Petrovich 1829-1890......................DLB-238

Dannay, Frederic 1905-1982..........DLB-137

Danner, Margaret Esse 1915-1984......DLB-41

John Danter [publishing house]......DLB-170

Dantin, Louis (Eugene Seers) 1865-1945.........................DLB-92

Danto, Arthur C. 1924-..............DLB-279

Danzig, Allison 1898-1987...........DLB-171

D'Arcy, Ella circa 1857-1937........DLB-135

Darío, Rubén 1867-1916..............DLB-290

Dark, Eleanor 1901-1985.............DLB-260

Darke, Nick 1948-...................DLB-233

Darley, Felix Octavious Carr 1822-1888.........................DLB-188

Darley, George 1795-1846............DLB-96

Darmesteter, Madame James (see Robinson, A. Mary F.)

Darrow, Clarence 1857-1938..........DLB-303

Darwin, Charles 1809-1882........DLB-57, 166

Darwin, Erasmus 1731-1802...........DLB-93

Daryush, Elizabeth 1887-1977........DLB-20

Das, Kamala 1934-...................DLB-323

Dashkova, Ekaterina Romanovna (née Vorontsova) 1743-1810.......DLB-150

Dashwood, Edmée Elizabeth Monica de la Pasture (see Delafield, E. M.)

Dattani, Mahesh 1958-...............DLB-323

Daudet, Alphonse 1840-1897..........DLB-123

d'Aulaire, Edgar Parin 1898-1986 and d'Aulaire, Ingri 1904-1980.......DLB-22

Davenant, Sir William 1606-1668....DLB-58, 126

Davenport, Guy 1927-2005............DLB-130

    Tribute to John Gardner..............Y-82

Davenport, Marcia 1903-1996..........DS-17

Davenport, Robert circa 17th century.....DLB-58

Daves, Delmer 1904-1977.............DLB-26

Davey, Frank 1940-..................DLB-53

Davidson, Avram 1923-1993...........DLB-8

Davidson, Donald 1893-1968..........DLB-45

Davidson, Donald 1917-2003..........DLB-279

Davidson, John 1857-1909............DLB-19

Davidson, Lionel 1922-..........DLB-14, 276

Davidson, Robyn 1950-...............DLB-204

Davidson, Sara 1943-................DLB-185

Davið Stefánsson frá Fagraskógi 1895-1964........................DLB-293

Davie, Donald 1922-1995.............DLB-27

Davie, Elspeth 1919-1995............DLB-139

Davies, Sir John 1569-1626..........DLB-172

Davies, John, of Hereford 1565?-1618....DLB-121

Davies, Rhys 1901-1978..........DLB-139, 191

Davies, Robertson 1913-1995.........DLB-68

Davies, Samuel 1723-1761............DLB-31

Davies, Thomas 1712?-1785.......DLB-142, 154

Davies, W. H. 1871-1940..........DLB-19, 174

Peter Davies Limited................DLB-112

Davin, Nicholas Flood 1840?-1901......DLB-99

Daviot, Gordon 1896?-1952...........DLB-10
(see also Tey, Josephine)

Davis, Arthur Hoey (see Rudd, Steele)

Davis, Benjamin J. 1903-1964........DLB-303

Davis, Charles A. (Major J. Downing) 1795-1867........................DLB-11

Davis, Clyde Brion 1894-1962........DLB-9

Davis, Dick 1945-................DLB-40, 282

Davis, Frank Marshall 1905-1987......DLB-51

Davis, H. L. 1894-1960............DLB-9, 206

Davis, Jack 1917-2000...............DLB-325

Davis, John 1774-1854...............DLB-37

Davis, Lydia 1947-..................DLB-130

Davis, Margaret Thomson 1926-.......DLB-14

Davis, Ossie 1917-2005..........DLB-7, 38, 249

Davis, Owen 1874-1956...............DLB-249

Davis, Paxton 1925-1994.............Y-89

Davis, Rebecca Harding 1831-1910...................DLB-74, 239

Davis, Richard Harding 1864-1916
..........DLB-12, 23, 78, 79, 189; DS-13

Davis, Samuel Cole 1764-1809........DLB-37

Davis, Samuel Post 1850-1918........DLB-202

Davison, Frank Dalby 1893-1970......DLB-260

Davison, Peter 1928-................DLB-5

Davydov, Denis Vasil'evich 1784-1839........................DLB-205

Davys, Mary 1674-1732...............DLB-39

    Preface to *The Works of Mrs. Davys* (1725).........................DLB-39

DAW Books..........................DLB-46

Dawe, Bruce 1930-...................DLB-289

Dawson, Ernest 1882-1947........DLB-140; Y-02

Dawson, Fielding 1930-2002..........DLB-130

Dawson, Sarah Morgan 1842-1909......DLB-239

Dawson, William 1704-1752...........DLB-31

Day, Angel fl. 1583-1599.........DLB-167, 236

Day, Benjamin Henry 1810-1889.......DLB-43

Day, Clarence 1874-1935.............DLB-11

Day, Dorothy 1897-1980..............DLB-29

Day, Frank Parker 1881-1950.........DLB-92

Day, John circa 1574-circa 1640.....DLB-62

Day, Marele 1947-...................DLB-325

Day, Thomas 1748-1789...............DLB-39

John Day [publishing house].........DLB-170

The John Day Company................DLB-46

Mahlon Day [publishing house].......DLB-49

Day Lewis, C. (see Blake, Nicholas)

Dazai Osamu 1909-1948...............DLB-182

Deacon, William Arthur 1890-1977....DLB-68

Deal, Borden 1922-1985..............DLB-6

de Angeli, Marguerite 1889-1987.....DLB-22

De Angelis, Milo 1951-..............DLB-128

Debord, Guy 1931-1994...............DLB-296

De Bow, J. D. B. 1820-1867.......DLB-3, 79, 248

Debs, Eugene V. 1855-1926...........DLB-303

de Bruyn, Günter 1926- ... DLB-75

de Camp, L. Sprague 1907-2000 ... DLB-8

De Carlo, Andrea 1952- ... DLB-196

De Casas, Celso A. 1944- ... DLB-209

Dechert, Robert 1895-1975 ... DLB-187

Declaration of the Rights of Man and of the Citizen ... DLB-314

Declaration of the Rights of Woman, Olympe de Gouges ... DLB-314

de Cleyre, Voltairine 1866-1912 ... DLB-345

Dedications, Inscriptions, and Annotations ... Y-01–02

De' Dottori, Carlo 1618-1686 ... DLB-339

Dee, John 1527-1608 or 1609 ... DLB-136, 213

Deeping, George Warwick 1877-1950 ... DLB-153

Deffand, Marie de Vichy-Chamrond, marquise Du 1696-1780 ... DLB-313

Defoe, Daniel 1660-1731 ... DLB-39, 95, 101, 336; CDBLB-2

    Preface to *Colonel Jack* (1722) ... DLB-39

    Preface to *The Farther Adventures of Robinson Crusoe* (1719) ... DLB-39

    Preface to *Moll Flanders* (1722) ... DLB-39

    Preface to *Robinson Crusoe* (1719) ... DLB-39

    Preface to *Roxana* (1724) ... DLB-39

de Fontaine, Felix Gregory 1834-1896 ... DLB-43

De Forest, John William 1826-1906 ... DLB-12, 189

DeFrees, Madeline 1919- ... DLB-105

    "The Poet's Kaleidoscope: The Element of Surprise in the Making of the Poem" ... DLB-105

DeGolyer, Everette Lee 1886-1956 ... DLB-187

de Graff, Robert 1895-1981 ... Y-81

de Graft, Joe 1924-1978 ... DLB-117

De Groen, Alma 1941- ... DLB-325

De Heinrico circa 980? ... DLB-148

Deighton, Len 1929- ... DLB-87; CDBLB-8

DeJong, Meindert 1906-1991 ... DLB-52

Dekker, Thomas circa 1572-1632 ... DLB-62, 172; CDBLB-1

Delacorte, George T., Jr. 1894-1991 ... DLB-91

Delafield, E. M. 1890-1943 ... DLB-34

Delahaye, Guy (Guillaume Lahaise) 1888-1969 ... DLB-92

de la Mare, Walter 1873-1956 ... DLB-19, 153, 162, 255; CDBLB-6

Deland, Margaret 1857-1945 ... DLB-78

Delaney, Shelagh 1939- ... DLB-13; CDBLB-8

Delano, Amasa 1763-1823 ... DLB-183

Delany, Martin Robinson 1812-1885 ... DLB-50

Delany, Samuel R. 1942- ... DLB-8, 33

de la Roche, Mazo 1879-1961 ... DLB-68

Delavigne, Jean François Casimir 1793-1843 ... DLB-192

Delbanco, Nicholas 1942- ... DLB-6, 234

Delblanc, Sven 1931-1992 ... DLB-257

Del Castillo, Ramón 1949- ... DLB-209

Deledda, Grazia 1871-1936 ... DLB-264, 329

De Lemene, Francesco 1634-1704 ... DLB-339

De Leon, Daniel 1852-1914 ... DLB-345

De León, Nephtal 1945- ... DLB-82

Deleuze, Gilles 1925-1995 ... DLB-296

Delfini, Antonio 1907-1963 ... DLB-264

Delfino, Giovanni 1617-1699 ... DLB-339

Delgado, Abelardo Barrientos 1931-2004 ... DLB-82

Del Giudice, Daniele 1949- ... DLB-196

De Libero, Libero 1906-1981 ... DLB-114

Delibes, Miguel 1920- ... DLB-322

Delicado, Francisco circa 1475-circa 1540? ... DLB-318

DeLillo, Don 1936- ... DLB-6, 173

de Lint, Charles 1951- ... DLB-251

de Lisser H. G. 1878-1944 ... DLB-117

Dell, Floyd 1887-1969 ... DLB-9

Dell Publishing Company ... DLB-46

Della Valle, Federico circa 1560-1628 ... DLB-339

delle Grazie, Marie Eugene 1864-1931 ... DLB-81

Deloney, Thomas died 1600 ... DLB-167

Deloria, Ella C. 1889-1971 ... DLB-175

Deloria, Vine, Jr. 1933-2005 ... DLB-175

del Rey, Lester 1915-1993 ... DLB-8

Del Vecchio, John M. 1947- ... DS-9

Del'vig, Anton Antonovich 1798-1831 ... DLB-205

de Man, Paul 1919-1983 ... DLB-67

DeMarinis, Rick 1934- ... DLB-218

Demby, William 1922- ... DLB-33

De Mille, James 1833-1880 ... DLB-99, 251

de Mille, William 1878-1955 ... DLB-266

Deming, Alison Hawthorne 1946- ... DLB-342

Deming, Barbara 1917-1984 ... DLB-345

Deming, Philander 1829-1915 ... DLB-74

Deml, Jakub 1878-1961 ... DLB-215

Demorest, William Jennings 1822-1895 ... DLB-79

De Morgan, William 1839-1917 ... DLB-153

Demosthenes 384 B.C.-322 B.C. ... DLB-176

Henry Denham [publishing house] ... DLB-170

Denham, Sir John 1615-1669 ... DLB-58, 126

Denison, Merrill 1893-1975 ... DLB-92

T. S. Denison and Company ... DLB-49

Dennery, Adolphe Philippe 1811-1899 ... DLB-192

Dennie, Joseph 1768-1812 ... DLB-37, 43, 59, 73

Dennis, C. J. 1876-1938 ... DLB-260

Dennis, John 1658-1734 ... DLB-101

Dennis, Nigel 1912-1989 ... DLB-13, 15, 233

Denslow, W. W. 1856-1915 ... DLB-188

Dent, J. M., and Sons ... DLB-112

Dent, Lester 1904-1959 ... DLB-306

Dent, Tom 1932-1998 ... DLB-38

Denton, Daniel circa 1626-1703 ... DLB-24

DePaola, Tomie 1934- ... DLB-61

De Quille, Dan 1829-1898 ... DLB-186

De Quincey, Thomas 1785-1859 ... DLB-110, 144; CDBLB-3

    "Rhetoric" (1828; revised, 1859) [excerpt] ... DLB-57

    "Style" (1840; revised, 1859) [excerpt] ... DLB-57

Derby, George Horatio 1823-1861 ... DLB-11

J. C. Derby and Company ... DLB-49

Derby and Miller ... DLB-49

De Ricci, Seymour 1881-1942 ... DLB-201

Derleth, August 1909-1971 ... DLB-9; DS-17

Derrida, Jacques 1930-2004 ... DLB-242

The Derrydale Press ... DLB-46

Derzhavin, Gavriil Romanovich 1743-1816 ... DLB-150

Desai, Anita 1937- ... DLB-271, 323

Desani, G. V. 1909-2000 ... DLB-323

Desaulniers, Gonzalve 1863-1934 ... DLB-92

Desbordes-Valmore, Marceline 1786-1859 ... DLB-217

Descartes, René 1596-1650 ... DLB-268

Deschamps, Emile 1791-1871 ... DLB-217

Deschamps, Eustache 1340?-1404 ... DLB-208

Desbiens, Jean-Paul 1927- ... DLB-53

des Forêts, Louis-Rene 1918-2001 ... DLB-83

Deshpande, Shashi 1938- ... DLB-323

Desiato, Luca 1941- ... DLB-196

Desjardins, Marie-Catherine (see Villedieu, Madame de)

Desnica, Vladan 1905-1967 ... DLB-181

Desnos, Robert 1900-1945 ... DLB-258

Des Périers, Bonaventure 1510?-1543? ... DLB-327

Desportes, Philippe 1546-1606 ... DLB-327

DesRochers, Alfred 1901-1978 ... DLB-68

Des Roches, Madeleine 1520?-1587? and Catherine des Roches 1542-1587? ... DLB-327

Des Roches, Madeleine 1520?-1587? ... DLB-327

Desrosiers, Léo-Paul 1896-1967 ... DLB-68

Dessaulles, Louis-Antoine 1819-1895 ... DLB-99

Dessì, Giuseppe 1909-1977 ... DLB-177

Destouches, Louis-Ferdinand (see Céline, Louis-Ferdinand)

Desvignes, Lucette 1926- ... DLB-321

DeSylva, Buddy 1895-1950 ... DLB-265

De Tabley, Lord 1835-1895 . . . . DLB-35

Deutsch, Babette 1895-1982 . . . . DLB-45

Deutsch, Niklaus Manuel
  (see Manuel, Niklaus)

André Deutsch Limited DLB-112

Devanny, Jean 1894-1962 . . . . DLB-260

Deveaux, Alexis 1948- DLB-38

De Vere, Aubrey 1814-1902. . . . . DLB-35

Devereux, second Earl of Essex, Robert
  1565-1601 . . . . DLB-136

The Devin-Adair Company. DLB-46

De Vinne, Theodore Low 1828-1914 . . . . DLB-187

Devlin, Anne 1951- DLB-245

DeVoto, Bernard 1897-1955. . . . . DLB-9, 256

De Vries, Peter 1910-1993 . . . . DLB-6; Y-82

  Tribute to Albert Erskine Y-93

Dewart, Edward Hartley 1828-1903 . . . . . . DLB-99

Dewdney, Christopher 1951- DLB-60

Dewdney, Selwyn 1909-1979 . . . . DLB-68

Dewey, John 1859-1952. . . . . DLB-246, 270

Dewey, Orville 1794-1882 . . . . DLB-243

Dewey, Thomas B. 1915-1981. . . . . DLB-226

DeWitt, Robert M., Publisher DLB-49

DeWolfe, Fiske and Company DLB-49

Dexter, Colin 1930- DLB-87

de Young, M. H. 1849-1925. . . . . DLB-25

Dhlomo, H. I. E. 1903-1956 . . . . . . DLB-157, 225

Dhu al-Rummah (Abu al-Harith Ghaylan ibn 'Uqbah)
  circa 696-circa 735 . . . . DLB-311

Dhuoda circa 803-after 843 . . . . DLB-148

The Dial 1840-1844 . . . . DLB-223

The Dial Press DLB-46

"Dialogue entre un prêtre et un moribond,"
  Marquis de Sade DLB-314

Diamond, I. A. L. 1920-1988. . . . . DLB-26

Dias Gomes, Alfredo 1922-1999 . . . . DLB-307

Díaz del Castillo, Bernal
  circa 1496-1584 . . . . DLB-318

Dibble, L. Grace 1902-1998. . . . . DLB-204

Dibdin, Charles the Younger
  1768-1833 . . . . DLB-344

Dibdin, Thomas 1771-1841 . . . . DLB-344

Dibdin, Thomas Frognall
  1776-1847. DLB-184

Di Cicco, Pier Giorgio 1949- DLB-60

Dick, Philip K. 1928-1982 . . . . DLB-8

Dick and Fitzgerald DLB-49

Dickens, Charles 1812-1870
  . . . DLB-21, 55, 70, 159, 166; DS-5; CDBLB-4

Dickey, Eric Jerome 1961- DLB-292

Dickey, James 1923-1997 . . . . . . DLB-5, 193, 342;
    Y-82, 93, 96, 97; DS-7, 19; CDALB-5

  James Dickey and Stanley Burnshaw
    Correspondence Y-02

  James Dickey at Seventy–A Tribute Y-93

  James Dickey, American Poet Y-96

  The James Dickey Society. Y-99

  The Life of James Dickey: A Lecture to
    the Friends of the Emory Libraries,
    by Henry Hart Y-98

  Tribute to Archibald MacLeish Y-82

  Tribute to Malcolm Cowley Y-89

  Tribute to Truman Capote Y-84

  Tributes [to Dickey]. Y-97

Dickey, William 1928-1994 . . . . DLB-5

Dickinson, Emily
  1830-1886 . . . . DLB-1, 243; CDALB-3

Dickinson, John 1732-1808 . . . . DLB-31

Dickinson, Jonathan 1688-1747 . . . . DLB-24

Dickinson, Patric 1914-1994 . . . . DLB-27

Dickinson, Peter 1927- DLB-87, 161, 276

John Dicks [publishing house] DLB-106

Dickson, Gordon R. 1923-2001. . . . . DLB-8

Dictionary of Literary Biography
  *Annual Awards for Dictionary of
    Literary Biography Editors and
    Contributors*. Y-98–02

*Dictionary of Literary Biography
  Yearbook Awards* Y-92–93, 97–02

The Dictionary of National Biography DLB-144

Diderot, Denis 1713-1784. . . . . DLB-313

  "The Encyclopedia" DLB-314

Didion, Joan 1934-
  . . . . . . DLB-2, 173, 185; Y-81, 86; CDALB-6

Di Donato, Pietro 1911-1992. . . . . DLB-9

Die Fürstliche Bibliothek Corvey. Y-96

Diego, Gerardo 1896-1987. . . . . DLB-134

Dietz, Howard 1896-1983 . . . . DLB-265

Díez, Luis Mateo 1942- DLB-322

Digby, Everard 1550?-1605 . . . . DLB-281

Digges, Thomas circa 1546-1595 . . . . DLB-136

The Digital Millennium Copyright Act:
  Expanding Copyright Protection in
  Cyberspace and Beyond Y-98

Diktonius, Elmer 1896-1961 . . . . DLB-259

Dillard, Annie 1945- DLB-275, 278; Y-80

Dillard, R. H. W. 1937- DLB-5, 244

Charles T. Dillingham Company. DLB-49

G. W. Dillingham Company. DLB-49

Edward and Charles Dilly
  [publishing house] DLB-154

Dilthey, Wilhelm 1833-1911 . . . . DLB-129

Dimitrova, Blaga 1922- . . . DLB-181; CDWLB-4

Dimov, Dimitr 1909-1966 . . . . DLB-181

Dimsdale, Thomas J. 1831?-1866 . . . . . . DLB-186

Dinescu, Mircea 1950- DLB-232

Dinesen, Isak (see Blixen, Karen)

Ding Ling 1904-1986. . . . . DLB-328

Dingelstedt, Franz von 1814-1881 . . . . . . DLB-133

Dinis, Júlio (Joaquim Guilherme
  Gomes Coelho) 1839-1871 . . . . DLB-287

Dintenfass, Mark 1941- Y-84

Diogenes, Jr. (see Brougham, John)

Diogenes Laertius circa 200. . . . . DLB-176

DiPrima, Diane 1934- DLB-5, 16

Disch, Thomas M. 1940-2008 . . . . DLB-8, 282

"Le Discours sur le style," Georges-Louis Leclerc
  de Buffon DLB-314

Disgrace, 1999 Booker Prize winner,
  J. M. Coetzee. DLB-326

Diski, Jenny 1947- DLB-271

Disney, Walt 1901-1966. . . . . DLB-22

Disraeli, Benjamin 1804-1881 . . . . DLB-21, 55

D'Israeli, Isaac 1766-1848 . . . . DLB-107

DLB Award for Distinguished
  Literary Criticism Y-02

Ditlevsen, Tove 1917-1976 . . . . DLB-214

Ditzen, Rudolf (see Fallada, Hans)

Divakaruni, Chitra Banerjee 1956- DLB-323

Dix, Dorothea Lynde 1802-1887 . . . . . . DLB-1, 235

Dix, Dorothy (see Gilmer, Elizabeth Meriwether)

Dix, Edwards and Company DLB-49

Dix, Gertrude circa 1874-? DLB-197

Dixie, Florence Douglas 1857-1905 . . . . . DLB-174

Dixon, Ella Hepworth
  1855 or 1857-1932. . . . . DLB-197

Dixon, Paige (see Corcoran, Barbara)

Dixon, Richard Watson 1833-1900 . . . . . . DLB-19

Dixon, Stephen 1936- DLB-130

Djebar, Assia (Fatima-Zohra Imalayène)
  1936- DLB-346

DLB Award for Distinguished
  Literary Criticism Y-02

Dmitriev, Andrei Viktorovich 1956- . . . DLB-285

Dmitriev, Ivan Ivanovich 1760-1837 . . . . . DLB-150

Dobell, Bertram 1842-1914 . . . . DLB-184

Dobell, Sydney 1824-1874 . . . . DLB-32

Dobie, J. Frank 1888-1964. . . . . DLB-212

Dobles Yzaguirre, Julieta 1943- DLB-283

Döblin, Alfred 1878-1957 . . . . . DLB-66; CDWLB-2

Dobroliubov, Nikolai Aleksandrovich
  1836-1861 . . . . DLB-277

Dobson, Austin 1840-1921 . . . . DLB-35, 144

Dobson, Rosemary 1920- DLB-260

Doctorow, E. L.
  1931- DLB-2, 28, 173; Y-80; CDALB-6

Dodd, Susan M. 1946- DLB-244

Dodd, William E. 1869-1940. . . . . DLB-17

Anne Dodd [publishing house] DLB-154

Dodd, Mead and Company. DLB-49

Doderer, Heimito von 1896-1966 . . . . DLB-85

B. W. Dodge and Company DLB-46

Cumulative Index

Dodge, Mary Abigail 1833-1896 .... DLB-221

Dodge, Mary Mapes
1831?-1905............. DLB-42, 79; DS-13

Dodge Publishing Company............ DLB-49

Dodgson, Charles Lutwidge (see Carroll, Lewis)

Dodsley, Robert 1703-1764.............. DLB-95

R. Dodsley [publishing house] DLB-154

Dodson, Owen 1914-1983 .... DLB-76

Dodwell, Christina 1951- DLB-204

Doesticks, Q. K. Philander, P. B.
(see Thomson, Mortimer)

Doheny, Carrie Estelle 1875-1958....... DLB-140

Doherty, John 1798?-1854 .... DLB-190

Doig, Ivan 1939- DLB-206

Doinaș, Ștefan Augustin 1922- DLB-232

Dolet, Etienne 1509-1546............. DLB-327

Domínguez, Sylvia Maida 1935- DLB-122

Donaghy, Michael 1954- DLB-282

Patrick Donahoe [publishing house]...... DLB-49

Donald, David H. 1920- DLB-17; Y-87

Donaldson, Scott 1928- DLB-111

La doncella Theodor late-thirteenth or fourteenth
century....................... DLB-337

Doni, Rodolfo 1919- DLB-177

Donleavy, J. P. 1926- DLB-6, 173

Donnadieu, Marguerite (see Duras, Marguerite)

Donne, John
1572-1631......... DLB-121, 151; CDBLB-1

Donnelly, Ignatius 1831-1901........... DLB-12

R. R. Donnelley and Sons Company DLB-49

Donoghue, Emma 1969- DLB-267

Donohue and Henneberry DLB-49

Donoso, José 1924-1996 .... DLB-113; CDWLB-3

M. Doolady [publishing house] DLB-49

Dooley, Ebon (see Ebon)

Doolittle, Hilda 1886-1961 ..... DLB-4, 45; DS-15

Doplicher, Fabio 1938- DLB-128

Dor, Milo 1923-2005 .... DLB-85

George H. Doran Company............ DLB-46

Dorat, Jean 1508-1588 .... DLB-327

Dorcey, Mary 1950- DLB-319

Dorgelès, Roland 1886-1973............ DLB-65

Dorn, Edward 1929-1999............... DLB-5

Dorr, Rheta Childe 1866-1948 .... DLB-25

Dorris, Michael 1945-1997 ....DLB-175

Dorset and Middlesex, Charles Sackville,
Lord Buckhurst, Earl of 1643-1706....DLB-131

Dorsey, Candas Jane 1952- DLB-251

Dorst, Tankred 1925- DLB-75, 124

Dos Passos, John 1896-1970
.... DLB-4, 9, 316; DS-1, 15; CDALB-5

John Dos Passos: A Centennial
Commemoration................ Y-96

John Dos Passos: Artist Y-99

John Dos Passos Newsletter........... Y-00

U.S.A. (Documentary) DLB-274

Dostoevsky, Fyodor 1821-1881 .... DLB-238

Doubiago, Sharon 1946- DLB-342

Doubleday and Company DLB-49

Doubrovsky, Serge 1928- DLB-299

Dougall, Lily 1858-1923............... DLB-92

Doughty, Charles M.
1843-1926 .... DLB-19, 57, 174

Douglas, Lady Alfred (see Custance, Olive)

Douglas, Ellen (Josephine Ayres Haxton)
1921- DLB-292

Douglas, Gavin 1476-1522 .... DLB-132

Douglas, Keith 1920-1944 .... DLB-27

Douglas, Norman 1868-1952 .... DLB-34, 195

Douglass, Frederick 1817-1895
.... DLB-1, 43, 50, 79, 243; CDALB-2

Frederick Douglass Creative Arts Center. Y-01

Douglass, William circa 1691-1752....... DLB-24

Dourado, Autran 1926- DLB-145, 307

Dove, Arthur G. 1880-1946 .... DLB-188

Dove, Rita 1952- DLB-120; CDALB-7

Dover Publications DLB-46

Doves Press....................... DLB-112

Dovlatov, Sergei Donatovich
1941-1990 .... DLB-285

Dowden, Edward 1843-1913 .... DLB-35, 149

Dowell, Coleman 1925-1985 .... DLB-130

Dowland, John 1563-1626 ....DLB-172

Downes, Gwladys 1915- DLB-88

Downing, J., Major (see Davis, Charles A.)

Downing, Major Jack (see Smith, Seba)

Dowriche, Anne
before 1560-after 1613 ....DLB-172

Dowson, Ernest 1867-1900......... DLB-19, 135

William Doxey [publishing house] DLB-49

Doyle, Sir Arthur Conan
1859-1930 ...DLB-18, 70, 156, 178; CDBLB-5

The Priory Scholars of New York Y-99

Doyle, Kirby 1932-2003 .... DLB-16

Doyle, Roddy 1958- DLB-194, 326

Drabble, Margaret
1939- DLB-14, 155, 231; CDBLB-8

Tribute to Graham Greene............ Y-91

Drach, Albert 1902-1995 .... DLB-85

Drachmann, Holger 1846-1908 .... DLB-300

Dracula (Documentary) DLB-304

Dragojević, Danijel 1934- DLB-181

Dragún, Osvaldo 1929-1999 .... DLB-305

Drake, Samuel Gardner 1798-1875....... DLB-187

Drama (*See* Theater)

The Dramatic Publishing Company...... DLB-49

Dramatists Play Service DLB-46

Drant, Thomas
early 1540s?-1578................. DLB-167

Draper, John W. 1811-1882 .... DLB-30

Draper, Lyman C. 1815-1891.......... DLB-30

Drayton, Michael 1563-1631 .... DLB-121

Dreiser, Theodore 1871-1945
........DLB-9, 12, 102, 137; DS-1; CDALB-3

The International Theodore Dreiser
Society......................... Y-01

Notes from the Underground
of *Sister Carrie*.................... Y-01

Dresser, Davis 1904-1977 .... DLB-226

Drew, Elizabeth A.
"A Note on Technique" [excerpt]
(1926) DLB-36

Drewe, Robert 1943- DLB-325

Drewitz, Ingeborg 1923-1986........... DLB-75

Drieu La Rochelle, Pierre 1893-1945 .... DLB-72

Drinker, Elizabeth 1735-1807 .... DLB-200

Drinkwater, John 1882-1937......DLB-10, 19, 149

The Friends of the Dymock Poets Y-00

Dropkin, Celia (Tsilye Dropkin)
1887-1956 .... DLB-333

Droste-Hülshoff, Annette von
1797-1848............DLB-133; CDWLB-2

The Drue Heinz Literature Prize
Excerpt from "Excerpts from a Report
of the Commission," in David
Bosworth's *The Death of Descartes*
An Interview with David Bosworth...... Y-82

Drummond, William, of Hawthornden
1585-1649 .... DLB-121, 213

Drummond, William Henry 1854-1907 ... DLB-92

Drummond de Andrade, Carlos
1902-1987 .... DLB-307

Druzhinin, Aleksandr Vasil'evich
1824-1864 .... DLB-238

Druzhnikov, Yuri 1933- DLB-317

Dryden, Charles 1860?-1931 ....DLB-171

Dryden, John
1631-1700...... DLB-80, 101, 131; CDBLB-2

Držić, Marin
circa 1508-1567 ....DLB-147; CDWLB-4

Duane, William 1760-1835............. DLB-43

Du Bartas, Guillaume 1544-1590 .... DLB-327

Dubé, Marcel 1930- DLB-53

Dubé, Rodolphe (see Hertel, François)

Du Bellay, Joachim 1522?-1560 .... DLB-327

Dubie, Norman 1945- DLB-120

Dubin, Al 1891-1945 .... DLB-265

Du Boccage, Anne-Marie 1710-1802..... DLB-313

Dubois, Silvia 1788 or 1789?-1889 ...... DLB-239

Du Bois, W. E. B.
1868-1963 ....DLB-47, 50, 91, 246; CDALB-3

Du Bois, William Pène 1916-1993 .... DLB-61

Dubrovina, Ekaterina Oskarovna 1846-1913 ... DLB-238

Dubus, Andre 1936-1999 ... DLB-130

   Tribute to Michael M. Rea ... Y-97

Dubus, Andre, III 1959- ... DLB-292

Ducange, Victor 1783-1833 ... DLB-192

Du Chaillu, Paul Belloni 1831?-1903 ... DLB-189

Ducharme, Réjean 1941- ... DLB-60

Dučić, Jovan 1871-1943 ... DLB-147; CDWLB-4

Duck, Stephen 1705?-1756 ... DLB-95

Gerald Duckworth and Company Limited ... DLB-112

Duclaux, Madame Mary (see Robinson, A. Mary F.)

Dudek, Louis 1918-2001 ... DLB-88

Dudintsev, Vladimir Dmitrievich 1918-1998 ... DLB-302

Dudley-Smith, Trevor (see Hall, Adam)

Duell, Sloan and Pearce ... DLB-46

Duerer, Albrecht 1471-1528 ... DLB-179

Duff Gordon, Lucie 1821-1869 ... DLB-166

Dufferin, Helen Lady, Countess of Gifford 1807-1867 ... DLB-199

Duffield and Green ... DLB-46

Duffy, Maureen 1933- ... DLB-14, 310

Dufief, Nicholas Gouin 1776-1834 ... DLB-187

Dufresne, John 1948- ... DLB-292

Dugan, Alan 1923-2003 ... DLB-5

Dugard, William 1606-1662 ... DLB-170, 281

William Dugard [publishing house] ... DLB-170

Dugas, Marcel 1883-1947 ... DLB-92

William Dugdale [publishing house] ... DLB-106

Du Guillet, Pernette 1520?-1545 ... DLB-327

Duhamel, Georges 1884-1966 ... DLB-65

Dujardin, Edouard 1861-1949 ... DLB-123

Dukes, Ashley 1885-1959 ... DLB-10

Dumas, Alexandre *fils* 1824-1895 ... DLB-192

Dumas, Alexandre *père* 1802-1870 ... DLB-119, 192

Dumas, Henry 1934-1968 ... DLB-41

du Maurier, Daphne 1907-1989 ... DLB-191

Du Maurier, George 1834-1896 ... DLB-153, 178

Dummett, Michael 1925- ... DLB-262

Dunbar, Paul Laurence 1872-1906 ... DLB-50, 54, 78; CDALB-3

   Introduction to *Lyrics of Lowly Life* (1896), by William Dean Howells ... DLB-50

Dunbar, William circa 1460-circa 1522 ... DLB-132, 146

Duncan, Dave 1933- ... DLB-251

Duncan, David James 1952- ... DLB-256

Duncan, Norman 1871-1916 ... DLB-92

Duncan, Quince 1940- ... DLB-145

Duncan, Robert 1919-1988 ... DLB-5, 16, 193

Duncan, Ronald 1914-1982 ... DLB-13

Duncan, Sara Jeannette 1861-1922 ... DLB-92

Dunigan, Edward, and Brother ... DLB-49

Dunlap, John 1747-1812 ... DLB-43

Dunlap, William 1766-1839 ... DLB-30, 37, 59

Dunlop, William "Tiger" 1792-1848 ... DLB-99

Dunmore, Helen 1952- ... DLB-267

Dunn, Douglas 1942- ... DLB-40

Dunn, Harvey Thomas 1884-1952 ... DLB-188

Dunn, Stephen 1939- ... DLB-105

   "The Good, The Not So Good" ... DLB-105

Dunne, Dominick 1925- ... DLB-306

Dunne, Finley Peter 1867-1936 ... DLB-11, 23

Dunne, John Gregory 1932- ... Y-80

Dunne, Philip 1908-1992 ... DLB-26

Dunning, Ralph Cheever 1878-1930 ... DLB-4

Dunning, William A. 1857-1922 ... DLB-17

Duns Scotus, John circa 1266-1308 ... DLB-115

Dunsany, Lord (Edward John Moreton Drax Plunkett, Baron Dunsany) 1878-1957 ... DLB-10, 77, 153, 156, 255

Dunton, W. Herbert 1878-1936 ... DLB-188

John Dunton [publishing house] ... DLB-170

Dupin, Amantine-Aurore-Lucile (see Sand, George)

Du Pont de Nemours, Pierre Samuel 1739-1817 ... DLB-313

Dupuy, Eliza Ann 1814-1880 ... DLB-248

Durack, Mary 1913-1994 ... DLB-260

Durand, Lucile (see Bersianik, Louky)

Duranti, Francesca 1935- ... DLB-196

Duranty, Walter 1884-1957 ... DLB-29

Duras, Marguerite (Marguerite Donnadieu) 1914-1996 ... DLB-83, 321

Durfey, Thomas 1653-1723 ... DLB-80

Durova, Nadezhda Andreevna (Aleksandr Andreevich Aleksandrov) 1783-1866 ... DLB-198

Durrell, Lawrence 1912-1990 ... DLB-15, 27, 204; Y-90; CDBLB-7

William Durrell [publishing house] ... DLB-49

Dürrenmatt, Friedrich 1921-1990 ... DLB-69, 124; CDWLB-2

Duston, Hannah 1657-1737 ... DLB-200

Dutt, Toru 1856-1877 ... DLB-240

E. P. Dutton and Company ... DLB-49

Duun, Olav 1876-1939 ... DLB-297

Duvoisin, Roger 1904-1980 ... DLB-61

Duyckinck, Evert Augustus 1816-1878 ... DLB-3, 64, 250

Duyckinck, George L. 1823-1863 ... DLB-3, 250

Duyckinck and Company ... DLB-49

Dwight, John Sullivan 1813-1893 ... DLB-1, 235

Dwight, Timothy 1752-1817 ... DLB-37

America: or, A Poem on the Settlement of the British Colonies, by Timothy Dwight ... DLB-37

Dybek, Stuart 1942- ... DLB-130

   Tribute to Michael M. Rea ... Y-97

Dyer, Charles 1928- ... DLB-13

Dyer, Sir Edward 1543-1607 ... DLB-136

Dyer, George 1755-1841 ... DLB-93

Dyer, John 1699-1757 ... DLB-95

Dyk, Viktor 1877-1931 ... DLB-215

Dylan, Bob 1941- ... DLB-16

E

Eager, Edward 1911-1964 ... DLB-22

Eagleton, Terry 1943- ... DLB-242

Eames, Wilberforce 1855-1937 ... DLB-140

Earle, Alice Morse 1853-1911 ... DLB-221

Earle, John 1600 or 1601-1665 ... DLB-151

James H. Earle and Company ... DLB-49

Early Medieval Spanish Theater ... DLB-337

East Europe
   Independence and Destruction, 1918-1941 ... DLB-220

   Social Theory and Ethnography: Language and Ethnicity in Western versus Eastern Man ... DLB-220

Eastlake, William 1917-1997 ... DLB-6, 206

Eastman, Carol ?- ... DLB-44

Eastman, Charles A. (Ohiyesa) 1858-1939 ... DLB-175

Eastman, Crystal 1881-1928 ... DLB-345

Eastman, Max 1883-1969 ... DLB-91

Eaton, Daniel Isaac 1753-1814 ... DLB-158

Eaton, Edith Maude 1865-1914 ... DLB-221, 312

Eaton, Winnifred 1875-1954 ... DLB-221, 312

Eberhart, Richard 1904-2005 ... DLB-48; CDALB-1

   Tribute to Robert Penn Warren ... Y-89

Ebner, Jeannie 1918-2004 ... DLB-85

Ebner-Eschenbach, Marie von 1830-1916 ... DLB-81

Ebon 1942- ... DLB-41

E-Books' Second Act in Libraries ... Y-02

Ecbasis Captivi circa 1045 ... DLB-148

Ecco Press ... DLB-46

Echard, Laurence 1670?-1730 ... DLB-336

Echegaray, José 1832-1916 ... DLB-329

Eckhart, Meister circa 1260-circa 1328 ... DLB-115

The Eclectic Review 1805-1868 ... DLB-110

Eco, Umberto 1932- ... DLB-196, 242

Eddison, E. R. 1882-1945 ... DLB-255

Edel, Leon 1907-1997 ... DLB-103

Edelfeldt, Inger 1956- ... DLB-257

J. M. Edelstein's Collection of Twentieth-
  Century American Poetry (A Century of Poetry,
  a Lifetime of Collecting)............... Y-02
Edes, Benjamin 1732-1803 .... DLB-43
Edgar, David 1948- DLB-13, 233
  Viewpoint: Politics and
    Performance.................. DLB-13
Edgerton, Clyde 1944- DLB-278
Edgeworth, Maria
  1768-1849...............DLB-116, 159, 163
The Edinburgh Review 1802-1929 .... DLB-110
Edinburgh University Press DLB-112
Editing
  Conversations with Editors Y-95
  Editorial Statements DLB-137
  The Editorial Style of Fredson Bowers.... Y-91
  Editorial: The Extension of Copyright.... Y-02
  We See the Editor at Work............. Y-97
  Whose *Ulysses*? The Function of Editing .. Y-97
The Editor Publishing Company DLB-49
Editorial Institute at Boston University Y-00
Edmonds, Helen Woods Ferguson
  (see Kavan, Anna)
Edmonds, Randolph 1900-1983 .... DLB-51
Edmonds, Walter D. 1903-1998 .... DLB-9
Edric, Robert (see Armitage, G. E.)
Edschmid, Kasimir 1890-1966 .... DLB-56
Edson, Margaret 1961- DLB-266
Edson, Russell 1935- DLB-244
Edwards, Amelia Anne Blandford
  1831-1892 ....DLB-174
Edwards, Dic 1953- DLB-245
Edwards, Edward 1812-1886 .... DLB-184
Edwards, Jonathan 1703-1758........DLB-24, 270
Edwards, Jonathan, Jr. 1745-1801 .... DLB-37
Edwards, Junius 1929- DLB-33
Edwards, Matilda Barbara Betham
  1836-1919...................DLB-174
Edwards, Richard 1524-1566 .... DLB-62
Edwards, Sarah Pierpont 1710-1758 ..... DLB-200
James Edwards [publishing house] DLB-154
Effinger, George Alec 1947- DLB-8
Egerton, George 1859-1945 .... DLB-135
Eggleston, Edward 1837-1902............ DLB-12
Eggleston, Wilfred 1901-1986........... DLB-92
Eglītis, Anšlavs 1906-1993 .... DLB-220
Eguren, José María 1874-1942 .... DLB-290
Ehrenreich, Barbara 1941- DLB-246
Ehrenstein, Albert 1886-1950........... DLB-81
Ehrhart, W. D. 1948- DS-9
Ehrlich, Gretel 1946- DLB-212, 275
Eich, Günter 1907-1972............ DLB-69, 124
Eichelberger, Ethyl 1945-1990 .... DLB-341

Eichendorff, Joseph Freiherr von
  1788-1857..................... DLB-90
Eifukumon'in 1271-1342............. DLB-203
Eigner, Larry 1926-1996........... DLB-5, 193
Eikon Basilike 1649................. DLB-151
Eilhart von Oberge
  circa 1140-circa 1195 .... DLB-148
Einar Benediktsson 1864-1940......... DLB-293
Einar Kárason 1955- DLB-293
Einar Már Guðmundsson 1954- DLB-293
Einhard circa 770-840................ DLB-148
Eiseley, Loren 1907-1977.........DLB-275, DS-17
Eisenberg, Deborah 1945- DLB-244
Eisenreich, Herbert 1925-1986.......... DLB-85
Eisner, Kurt 1867-1919................ DLB-66
Ekelöf, Gunnar 1907-1968 .... DLB-259
Eklund, Gordon 1945- Y-83
Ekman, Kerstin 1933- DLB-257
Ekwensi, Cyprian
  1921-2007............DLB-117; CDWLB-3
Elaw, Zilpha circa 1790-? DLB-239
George Eld [publishing house] DLB-170
Elder, Lonne, III 1931- DLB-7, 38, 44
Paul Elder and Company DLB-49
Eldershaw, Flora (M. Barnard Eldershaw)
  1897-1956..................... DLB-260
Eldershaw, M. Barnard (see Barnard, Marjorie and
  Eldershaw, Flora)
The Elected Member, 1970 Booker Prize winner,
  Bernice Rubens DLB-326
The Electronic Text Center and the Electronic
  Archive of Early American Fiction at the
  University of Virginia Library Y-98
Eliade, Mircea 1907-1986 ... DLB-220; CDWLB-4
Elie, Robert 1915-1973 .... DLB-88
Elin Pelin 1877-1949 ....DLB-147; CDWLB-4
Eliot, George
  1819-1880 .... DLB-21, 35, 55; CDBLB-4
  The George Eliot Fellowship Y-99
Eliot, John 1604-1690................. DLB-24
Eliot, T. S. 1888-1965
  ....DLB-7, 10, 45, 63, 245, 329; CDALB-5
  T. S. Eliot Centennial: The Return
    of the Old Possum................ Y-88
  The T. S. Eliot Society: Celebration and
    Scholarship, 1980-1999 .... Y-99
Eliot's Court Press DLB-170
Elizabeth I 1533-1603................. DLB-136
Elizabeth von Nassau-Saarbrücken
  after 1393-1456 ....DLB-179
Elizondo, Salvador 1932- DLB-145
Elizondo, Sergio 1930- DLB-82
Elkin, Stanley
  1930-1995 .... DLB-2, 28, 218, 278; Y-80
Elles, Dora Amy (see Wentworth, Patricia)

Ellet, Elizabeth F. 1818?-1877.......... DLB-30
Ellin, Stanley 1916-1986......... DLB-306, 335
Elliot, Ebenezer 1781-1849........ DLB-96, 190
Elliot, Frances Minto (Dickinson)
  1820-1898 .... DLB-166
Elliott, Charlotte 1789-1871 .... DLB-199
Elliott, George 1923- DLB-68
Elliott, George P. 1918-1980............ DLB-244
Elliott, Janice 1931-1995............... DLB-14
Elliott, Sarah Barnwell 1848-1928 ...... DLB-221
Elliott, Sumner Locke 1917-1991 .... DLB-289
Elliott, Thomes and Talbot............. DLB-49
Elliott, William, III 1788-1863 .... DLB-3, 248
Ellis, Alice Thomas (Anna Margaret Haycraft)
  1932- DLB-194
Ellis, Bret Easton 1964- DLB-292
Ellis, Edward S. 1840-1916............. DLB-42
Frederick Staridge Ellis
  [publishing house] DLB-106
Ellis, George E.
  "The New Controversy Concerning
    Miracles......................DS-5
The George H. Ellis Company.......... DLB-49
Ellis, Havelock 1859-1939 .... DLB-190
Ellison, Harlan 1934- DLB-8, 335
  Tribute to Isaac Asimov............... Y-92
Ellison, Ralph
  1914-1994 ...DLB-2, 76, 227; Y-94; CDALB-1
Ellmann, Richard 1918-1987 ...... DLB-103; Y-87
Ellroy, James 1948- DLB-226; Y-91
  Tribute to John D. MacDonald Y-86
  Tribute to Raymond Chandler Y-88
Eluard, Paul 1895-1952 .... DLB-258
Elyot, Thomas 1490?-1546............. DLB-136
Elytis, Odysseus 1911-1996 .... DLB-329
Emanuel, James Andrew 1921- DLB-41
Emecheta, Buchi 1944- DLB-117; CDWLB-3
Emerson, Ralph Waldo
  1803-1882 ..... DLB-1, 59, 73, 183, 223, 270;
                                DS-5; CDALB-2
  Ralph Waldo Emerson in 1982 .... Y-82
  The Ralph Waldo Emerson Society...... Y-99
Emerson, William 1769-1811 .... DLB-37
Emerson, William R. 1923-1997............ Y-97
Emin, Fedor Aleksandrovich
  circa 1735-1770.................. DLB-150
Emmanuel, Pierre 1916-1984 .... DLB-258
Empedocles fifth century B.C...........DLB-176
Empson, William 1906-1984 .... DLB-20
Enchi Fumiko 1905-1986 .... DLB-182
"The Encyclopedia," Denis Diderot..... DLB-314
Ende, Michael 1929-1995............. DLB-75
Endō Shūsaku 1923-1996 .... DLB-182
Engel, Marian 1933-1985 .... DLB-53

Engel'gardt, Sof'ia Vladimirovna
1828-1894 .... DLB-277

Engels, Friedrich 1820-1895 .... DLB-129

Engels, John 1931- DLB-342

Engle, Paul 1908-1991 .... DLB-48

    Tribute to Robert Penn Warren Y-89

English, Thomas Dunn 1819-1902 ...... DLB-202

The English Patient, 1992 Booker Prize winner,
Michael Ondaatje DLB-326

Ennius 239 B.C.-169 B.C. DLB-211

Enquist, Per Olov 1934- DLB-257

Enright, Anne 1962- DLB-267

Enright, D. J. 1920-2002 .... DLB-27

Enright, Elizabeth 1909-1968 .... DLB-22, 335

Enright, Nick 1950-2003 .... DLB-325

Enslin, Theodore 1925- DLB-342

Epic, The Sixteenth-Century Spanish DLB-318

Epictetus circa 55-circa 125-130 .... DLB-176

Epicurus 342/341 B.C.-271/270 B.C. DLB-176

d'Epinay, Louise (Louise-Florence-Pétronille Tardieu
d'Esclavelles, marquise d'Epinay)
1726-1783 .... DLB-313

Epps, Bernard 1936- DLB-53

Epshtein, Mikhail Naumovich 1950- ... DLB-285

Epstein, Julius 1909-2000 and
Epstein, Philip 1909-1952 .... DLB-26

Epstein, Leslie 1938- DLB-299

Editors, Conversations with Y-95

Equiano, Olaudah
circa 1745-1797 ...... DLB-37, 50; CDWLB-3

    Olaudah Equiano and Unfinished
Journeys: The Slave-Narrative
Tradition and Twentieth-Century
Continuities DLB-117

Eragny Press DLB-112

Erasmus, Desiderius 1467-1536 .... DLB-136

Erba, Luciano 1922- DLB-128

Erdman, Nikolai Robertovich
1900-1970 .... DLB-272

Erdrich, Louise
1954- DLB-152, 175, 206; CDALB-7

Erenburg, Il'ia Grigor'evich 1891-1967 ... DLB-272

Erichsen-Brown, Gwethalyn Graham
(see Graham, Gwethalyn)

Eriugena, John Scottus circa 810-877 .... DLB-115

Ernst, Paul 1866-1933 .... DLB-66, 118

Erofeev, Venedikt Vasil'evich
1938-1990 .... DLB-285

Erofeev, Viktor Vladimirovich
1947- DLB-285

Ershov, Petr Pavlovich 1815-1869 ...... DLB-205

Erskine, Albert 1911-1993 .... Y-93

    At Home with Albert Erskine Y-00

Erskine, John 1879-1951 .... DLB-9, 102

Erskine, Mrs. Steuart ?-1948 .... DLB-195

Ertel', Aleksandr Ivanovich
1855-1908 .... DLB-238

Ervine, St. John Greer 1883-1971 .... DLB-10

Eschenburg, Johann Joachim
1743-1820 .... DLB-97

Escofet, Cristina 1945- DLB-305

Escoto, Julio 1944- DLB-145

Esdaile, Arundell 1880-1956 .... DLB-201

Esenin, Sergei Aleksandrovich
1895-1925 .... DLB-295

Eshleman, Clayton 1935- DLB-5

Espaillat, Rhina P. 1932- DLB-282

Espanca, Florbela 1894-1930 .... DLB-287

Espriu, Salvador 1913-1985 .... DLB-134

Ess Ess Publishing Company DLB-49

Essex House Press DLB-112

Esson, Louis 1878-1943 .... DLB-260

Essop, Ahmed 1931- DLB-225

Esterházy, Péter 1950- DLB-232; CDWLB-4

Estes, Eleanor 1906-1988 .... DLB-22

Estes and Lauriat DLB-49

Estienne, Henri II (Henricus Stephanus)
1531-1597 .... DLB-327

Estleman, Loren D. 1952- DLB-226

Eszterhas, Joe 1944- DLB-185

Etherege, George 1636-circa 1692 ...... DLB-80

Ethridge, Mark, Sr. 1896-1981 .... DLB-127

Ets, Marie Hall 1893-1984 .... DLB-22

Etter, David 1928- DLB-105

Ettner, Johann Christoph 1654-1724 ..... DLB-168

Etzioni, Amitai 1929- DLB-345

Eucken, Rudolf 1846-1926 .... DLB-329

Eudora Welty Remembered in
Two Exhibits Y-02

Eugene Gant's Projected Works Y-01

Eupolemius fl. circa 1095 .... DLB-148

Euripides circa 484 B.C.-407/406 B.C.
.... DLB-176; CDWLB-1

Evans, Augusta Jane 1835-1909 .... DLB-239

Evans, Caradoc 1878-1945 .... DLB-162

Evans, Charles 1850-1935 .... DLB-187

Evans, Donald 1884-1921 .... DLB-54

Evans, George Henry 1805-1856 .... DLB-43

Evans, Hubert 1892-1986 .... DLB-92

Evans, Mari 1923- DLB-41

Evans, Mary Ann (see Eliot, George)

Evans, Nathaniel 1742-1767 .... DLB-31

Evans, Sebastian 1830-1909 .... DLB-35

Evans, Ray 1915-2007 .... DLB-265

M. Evans and Company DLB-46

Evaristi, Marcella 1953- DLB-233

Evenson, Brian 1966- DLB-335

Everett, Alexander Hill 1790-1847 .... DLB-59

Everett, Edward 1794-1865 ...... DLB-1, 59, 235

Everson, R. G. 1903- DLB-88

Everson, William 1912-1994 ...... DLB-5, 16, 212

Evreinov, Nikolai 1879-1953 .... DLB-317

Ewald, Johannes 1743-1781 .... DLB-300

Ewart, Gavin 1916-1995 .... DLB-40

Ewing, Juliana Horatia 1841-1885 .... DLB-21, 163

The Examiner 1808-1881 .... DLB-110

Exley, Frederick 1929-1992 .... DLB-143; Y-81

Editorial: The Extension of Copyright Y-02

von Eyb, Albrecht 1420-1475 .... DLB-179

Eyre and Spottiswoode DLB-106

Ezekiel, Nissim 1924-2004 .... DLB-323

Ezera, Regīna 1930- DLB-232

Ezzo ?-after 1065 .... DLB-148

F

Faber, Frederick William 1814-1863 ..... DLB-32

Faber and Faber Limited DLB-112

Faccio, Rena (see Aleramo, Sibilla)

Facsimiles
    The Uses of Facsimile: A Symposium Y-90

Fadeev, Aleksandr Aleksandrovich
1901-1956 .... DLB-272

Fagundo, Ana María 1938- DLB-134

Fainzil'berg, Il'ia Arnol'dovich
(see Il'f, Il'ia and Petrov, Evgenii)

Fair, Ronald L. 1932- DLB-33

Fairfax, Beatrice (see Manning, Marie)

Fairlie, Gerard 1899-1983 .... DLB-77

Faldbakken, Knut 1941- DLB-297

Falkberget, Johan (Johan Petter Lillebakken)
1879-1967 .... DLB-297

Fallada, Hans 1893-1947 .... DLB-56

The Famished Road, 1991 Booker Prize winner,
Ben Okri DLB-326

Fancher, Betsy 1928- Y-83

Fane, Violet 1843-1905 .... DLB-35

Fanfrolico Press DLB-112

Fanning, Katherine 1927-2000 .... DLB-127

Fanon, Frantz 1925-1961 .... DLB-296

Fanshawe, Sir Richard 1608-1666 ...... DLB-126

Fantasy Press Publishers DLB-46

Fante, John 1909-1983 .... DLB-130; Y-83

Al-Farabi circa 870-950 .... DLB-115

Farabough, Laura 1949- DLB-228

Farah, Nuruddin 1945- ... DLB-125; CDWLB-3

Farber, Norma 1909-1984 .... DLB-61

A Farewell to Arms (Documentary) DLB-308

Fargue, Léon-Paul 1876-1947 .... DLB-258

Farigoule, Louis (see Romains, Jules)

Cumulative Index

Farjeon, Eleanor 1881-1965 . . . . DLB-160
Farley, Harriet 1812-1907 . . . . DLB-239
Farley, Walter 1920-1989 . . . . DLB-22
Farmborough, Florence 1887-1978 . . . . . . DLB-204
Farmer, Beverley 1941- DLB-325
Farmer, Penelope 1939- DLB-161
Farmer, Philip José 1918- DLB-8
Farnaby, Thomas 1575?-1647 . . . . DLB-236
Farnese, Isabella (Suor Francesca di Gesù Maria) 1593-1651 . . . . DLB-339
Farningham, Marianne (see Hearn, Mary Anne)
Farquhar, George circa 1677-1707 . . . . DLB-84
Farquharson, Martha (see Finley, Martha)
Farrar, Frederic William 1831-1903 . . . . . DLB-163
Farrar, Straus and Giroux DLB-46
Farrar and Rinehart DLB-46
Farrell, J. G. 1935-1979 . . . . DLB-14, 271, 326
Farrell, James T. 1904-1979 . . . . DLB-4, 9, 86; DS-2
Fast, Howard 1914-2003 . . . . DLB-9
Faulkner, William 1897-1962
 . . . . . . DLB-9, 11, 44, 102, 316, 330; DS-2; Y-86; CDALB-5
   Faulkner and Yoknapatawpha Conference, Oxford, Mississippi Y-97
   Faulkner Centennial Addresses Y-97
   "Faulkner 100–Celebrating the Work," University of South Carolina, Columbia Y-97
   Impressions of William Faulkner Y-97
   William Faulkner and the People-to-People Program Y-86
   William Faulkner Centenary Celebrations Y-97
   The William Faulkner Society Y-99
George Faulkner [publishing house] DLB-154
Faulks, Sebastian 1953- DLB-207
Fauset, Jessie Redmon 1882-1961 . . . . DLB-51
Faust, Frederick Schiller (Max Brand) 1892-1944 . . . . DLB-256
Faust, Irvin 1924- DLB-2, 28, 218, 278; Y-80, 00
   I Wake Up Screaming [Response to Ken Auletta] Y-97
   Tribute to Bernard Malamud Y-86
   Tribute to Isaac Bashevis Singer Y-91
   Tribute to Meyer Levin Y-81
Fawcett, Edgar 1847-1904 . . . . DLB-202
Fawcett, Millicent Garrett 1847-1929 . . . . . DLB-190
Fawcett Books DLB-46
Fay, Theodore Sedgwick 1807-1898 . . . . . DLB-202
Fearing, Kenneth 1902-1961 . . . . DLB-9
Federal Writers' Project DLB-46
Federman, Raymond 1928- Y-80
Fedin, Konstantin Aleksandrovich 1892-1977 . . . . DLB-272

Fedorov, Innokentii Vasil'evich (see Omulevsky, Innokentii Vasil'evich)
Fefer, Itzik (Itsik Fefer) 1900-1952 . . . . . . DLB-333
Feiffer, Jules 1929- DLB-7, 44
Feinberg, Charles E. 1899-1988 . . . . DLB-187; Y-88
Feind, Barthold 1678-1721 . . . . DLB-168
Feinstein, Elaine 1930- DLB-14, 40
Feirstein, Frederick 1940- DLB-282
Feiss, Paul Louis 1875-1952 . . . . DLB-187
Feldman, Irving 1928- DLB-169
Felipe, Carlos 1911-1975 . . . . DLB-305
Felipe, Léon 1884-1968 . . . . DLB-108
Fell, Frederick, Publishers DLB-46
Fellowship of Southern Writers Y-98
Felltham, Owen 1602?-1668 . . . . . . DLB-126, 151
Felman, Shoshana 1942- DLB-246
Fels, Ludwig 1946- DLB-75
Felton, Cornelius Conway 1807-1862 . . . . DLB-1, 235
Fel'zen, Iurii (Nikolai Berngardovich Freidenshtein) 1894?-1943 . . . . DLB-317
Mothe-Fénelon, François de Salignac de la 1651-1715 . . . . DLB-268
Fenn, Harry 1837-1911 . . . . DLB-188
Fennario, David 1947- DLB-60
Fenner, Dudley 1558?-1587? DLB-236
Fenno, Jenny 1765?-1803 . . . . DLB-200
Fenno, John 1751-1798 . . . . DLB-43
R. F. Fenno and Company DLB-49
Fenoglio, Beppe 1922-1963 . . . . DLB-177
Fenton, Geoffrey 1539?-1608 . . . . DLB-136
Fenton, James 1949- DLB-40
   The Hemingway/Fenton Correspondence Y-02
Ferber, Edna 1885-1968 . . . . . . DLB-9, 28, 86, 266
Ferdinand, Vallery, III (see Salaam, Kalamu ya)
Ferguson, Adam 1723-1816 . . . . DLB-336
Ferguson, Sir Samuel 1810-1886 . . . . DLB-32
Ferguson, William Scott 1875-1954 . . . . . . DLB-47
Fergusson, Robert 1750-1774 . . . . DLB-109
Ferland, Albert 1872-1943 . . . . DLB-92
Ferlinghetti, Lawrence 1919- DLB-5, 16; CDALB-1
   Tribute to Kenneth Rexroth Y-82
Fermor, Patrick Leigh 1915- DLB-204
Fern, Fanny (see Parton, Sara Payson Willis)
Fernández de Heredia, Juan circa 1310-1396 . . . . DLB-337
Ferrars, Elizabeth (Morna Doris Brown) 1907-1995 . . . . DLB-87
Ferré, Rosario 1942- DLB-145
Ferreira, Vergílio 1916-1996 . . . . DLB-287
E. Ferret and Company DLB-49

Ferrier, Susan 1782-1854 . . . . DLB-116
Ferril, Thomas Hornsby 1896-1988 . . . . . DLB-206
Ferrini, Vincent 1913-2007 . . . . DLB-48
Ferron, Jacques 1921-1985 . . . . DLB-60
Ferron, Madeleine 1922- DLB-53
Ferrucci, Franco 1936- DLB-196
Fet, Afanasii Afanas'evich 1820?-1892 . . . . DLB-277
Fetridge and Company DLB-49
Feuchtersleben, Ernst Freiherr von 1806-1849 . . . . DLB-133
Feuchtwanger, Lion 1884-1958 . . . . DLB-66
Feuerbach, Ludwig 1804-1872 . . . . DLB-133
Feuillet, Octave 1821-1890 . . . . DLB-192
Feydeau, Georges 1862-1921 . . . . DLB-192
Fibiger, Mathilde 1830-1872 . . . . DLB-300
Fichte, Johann Gottlieb 1762-1814 . . . . . . DLB-90
Ficke, Arthur Davison 1883-1945 . . . . DLB-54
Fiction
   American Fiction and the 1930s DLB-9
   Fiction Best-Sellers, 1910-1945 . . . . DLB-9
   Postmodern Holocaust Fiction DLB-299
   The Year in Fiction Y-84, 86, 89, 94–99
   The Year in Fiction: A Biased View Y-83
   The Year in U.S. Fiction Y-00, 01
   The Year's Work in Fiction: A Survey Y-82
Fiedler, Leslie A. 1917-2003 . . . . DLB-28, 67
   Tribute to Bernard Malamud Y-86
   Tribute to James Dickey Y-97
Field, Barron 1789-1846 . . . . DLB-230
Field, Edward 1924- DLB-105
Field, Eugene 1850-1895 . . . . DLB-23, 42, 140; DS-13
Field, John 1545?-1588 . . . . DLB-167
Field, Joseph M. 1810-1856 . . . . DLB-248
Field, Marshall, III 1893-1956 . . . . DLB-127
Field, Marshall, IV 1916-1965 . . . . DLB-127
Field, Marshall, V 1941- DLB-127
Field, Michael (Katherine Harris Bradley) 1846-1914 and (Edith Emma Cooper) 1862-1913 . . . . DLB-240, 344
   "The Poetry File" DLB-105
Field, Nathan 1587-1619 or 1620 . . . . DLB-58
Field, Rachel 1894-1942 . . . . DLB-9, 22
Fielding, Helen 1958- DLB-231
Fielding, Henry 1707-1754 . . . . DLB-39, 84, 101; CDBLB-2
   "Defense of *Amelia*" (1752) DLB-39
   The History of the Adventures of Joseph Andrews [excerpt] (1742) DLB-39
   Letter to [Samuel] Richardson on *Clarissa* (1748) DLB-39
   Preface to *Joseph Andrews* (1742) DLB-39
   Preface to Sarah Fielding's *Familiar Letters* (1747) [excerpt] DLB-39

Preface to Sarah Fielding's *The Adventures of David Simple* (1744) ...DLB-39
Review of *Clarissa* (1748) DLB-39
Tom Jones (1749) [excerpt] DLB-39
Fielding, Sarah 1710-1768.............DLB-39
Preface to *The Cry* (1754) DLB-39
Fields, Annie Adams 1834-1915 ....DLB-221
Fields, Dorothy 1905-1974............DLB-265
Fields, James T. 1817-1881.........DLB-1, 235
Fields, Julia 1938- DLB-41
Fields, Osgood and Company DLB-49
Fields, W. C. 1880-1946...............DLB-44
Fierstein, Harvey 1954- DLB-266
Figes, Eva 1932- DLB-14, 271
Figuera, Angela 1902-1984 ....DLB-108
Filiciaia, Vincenzo de 1642-1707 ....DLB-339
Filmer, Sir Robert 1586-1653..........DLB-151
Filson, John circa 1753-1788..........DLB-37
Finch, Anne, Countess of Winchilsea 1661-1720 ....DLB-95
Finch, Annie 1956- DLB-282
Finch, Robert 1900- DLB-88
Findley, Timothy 1930-2002 ....DLB-53
Finlay, Ian Hamilton 1925- DLB-40
Finley, Martha 1828-1909 ....DLB-42
Finn, Elizabeth Anne (McCaul) 1825-1921 ....DLB-166
Finnegan, Seamus 1949- DLB-245
Finney, Jack 1911-1995 ....DLB-8
Finney, Walter Braden (see Finney, Jack)
Fiorillo, Silvio 1560 or 1565?-1634? DLB-339
Firbank, Ronald 1886-1926...........DLB-36
Firmin, Giles 1615-1697.............DLB-24
First Edition Library/Collectors' Reprints, Inc......................Y-91
Fischart, Johann 1546 or 1547-1590 or 1591 ....DLB-179
Fischer, Karoline Auguste Fernandine 1764-1842 ....DLB-94
Fischer, Tibor 1959- DLB-231
Fish, Stanley 1938- DLB-67
Fishacre, Richard 1205-1248 ....DLB-115
Fisher, Clay (see Allen, Henry W.)
Fisher, Dorothy Canfield 1879-1958 ....DLB-9, 102
Fisher, Leonard Everett 1924- DLB-61
Fisher, Roy 1930- DLB-40
Fisher, Rudolph 1897-1934.........DLB-51, 102
Fisher, Steve 1913-1980 ....DLB-226
Fisher, Sydney George 1856-1927 ....DLB-47
Fisher, Vardis 1895-1968 ....DLB-9, 206
Fiske, John 1608-1677 ....DLB-24
Fiske, John 1842-1901 ....DLB-47, 64
Fitch, Thomas circa 1700-1774..........DLB-31
Fitch, William Clyde 1865-1909 ....DLB-7
Fitzball, Edward 1792-1873 ....DLB-344
FitzGerald, Edward 1809-1883 ....DLB-32

Fitzgerald, F. Scott 1896-1940
...................DLB-4, 9, 86; Y-81, 92; DS-1, 15, 16; CDALB-4
F. Scott Fitzgerald: A Descriptive Bibliography, Supplement (2001) Y-01
F. Scott Fitzgerald Centenary Celebrations Y-96
F. Scott Fitzgerald Inducted into the American Poets' Corner at St. John the Divine; Ezra Pound Banned Y-99
"F. Scott Fitzgerald: St. Paul's Native Son and Distinguished American Writer": University of Minnesota Conference, 29-31 October 1982 ....Y-82
First International F. Scott Fitzgerald Conference Y-92
The Great Gatsby (Documentary) DLB-219
Tender Is the Night (Documentary) DLB-273
Fitzgerald, Penelope 1916-2000 ....DLB-14, 194, 326
Fitzgerald, Robert 1910-1985...............Y-80
FitzGerald, Robert D. 1902-1987........DLB-260
Fitzgerald, Thomas 1819-1891..........DLB-23
Fitzgerald, Zelda Sayre 1900-1948 ....Y-84
Fitzhugh, Louise 1928-1974 ....DLB-52
Fitzhugh, William circa 1651-1701.......DLB-24
Flagg, James Montgomery 1877-1960 ....DLB-188
Flanagan, Thomas 1923-2002 ....Y-80
Flanner, Hildegarde 1899-1987 ....DLB-48
Flanner, Janet 1892-1978 ....DLB-4; DS-15
Flannery, Peter 1951- DLB-233
Flaubert, Gustave 1821-1880.......DLB-119, 301
Flavin, Martin 1883-1967................DLB-9
Fleck, Konrad (fl. circa 1220) DLB-138
Flecker, James Elroy 1884-1915 ....DLB-10, 19
Fleeson, Doris 1901-1970................DLB-29
Fleißer, Marieluise 1901-1974.......DLB-56, 124
Fleischer, Nat 1887-1972...............DLB-241
Fleming, Abraham 1552?-1607 ....DLB-236
Fleming, Ian 1908-1964 ...DLB-87, 201; CDBLB-7
Fleming, Joan 1908-1980 ....DLB-276
Fleming, May Agnes 1840-1880 ....DLB-99
Fleming, Paul 1609-1640 ....DLB-164
Fleming, Peter 1907-1971..............DLB-195
Fletcher, Andrew 1653-1716............DLB-336
Fletcher, Giles, the Elder 1546-1611 .....DLB-136
Fletcher, Giles, the Younger 1585 or 1586-1623 ....DLB-121
Fletcher, J. S. 1863-1935...............DLB-70
Fletcher, John 1579-1625 ....DLB-58
Fletcher, John Gould 1886-1950 ....DLB-4, 45
Fletcher, Phineas 1582-1650............DLB-121
Flieg, Helmut (see Heym, Stefan)
Flint, F. S. 1885-1960 ....DLB-19
Flint, Timothy 1780-1840............DLB-73, 186

Fløgstad, Kjartan 1944- DLB-297
Florensky, Pavel Aleksandrovich 1882-1937 ....DLB-295
Flores, Juan de fl. 1470-1500 ....DLB-286
Flores y Blancaflor circa 1375-1400 ......DLB-337
Flores-Williams, Jason 1969- DLB-209
Florio, John 1553?-1625................DLB-172
Flower, Benjamin Orange 1859-1918.....DLB-345
Fludd, Robert 1574-1637 ....DLB-281
Flynn, Elizabeth Gurley 1890-1964......DLB-303
Fo, Dario 1926- DLB-330; Y-97
Nobel Lecture 1997: Contra Jogulatores Obloquentes Y-97
Foden, Giles 1967- DLB-267
Fofanov, Konstantin Mikhailovich 1862-1911 ....DLB-277
Foix, J. V. 1893-1987 ....DLB-134
Foley, Martha 1897-1977 ....DLB-137
Folger, Henry Clay 1857-1930 ....DLB-140
Folio Society......................DLB-112
Follain, Jean 1903-1971 ....DLB-258
Follen, Charles 1796-1840 ....DLB-235
Follen, Eliza Lee (Cabot) 1787-1860....DLB-1, 235
Follett, Ken 1949- DLB-87; Y-81
Follett Publishing Company............DLB-46
John West Folsom [publishing house] DLB-49
Folz, Hans between 1435 and 1440-1513 ....DLB-179
Fonseca, Manuel da 1911-1993 ....DLB-287
Fonseca, Rubem 1925- DLB-307
Fontane, Theodor 1819-1898 ....DLB-129; CDWLB-2
Fontenelle, Bernard Le Bovier de 1657-1757 ....DLB-268, 313
Fontes, Montserrat 1940- DLB-209
Fonvisin, Denis Ivanovich 1744 or 1745-1792 ....DLB-150
Foote, Horton 1916- DLB-26, 266
Foote, Mary Hallock 1847-1938 ....DLB-186, 188, 202, 221
Foote, Samuel 1721-1777 ....DLB-89
Foote, Shelby 1916-2005 ....DLB-2, 17
Forbes, Calvin 1945- DLB-41
Forbes, Ester 1891-1967...............DLB-22
Forbes, John 1950-1998................DLB=325
Forbes, Rosita 1893?-1967............DLB-195
Forbes and Company DLB-49
Force, Peter 1790-1868................DLB-30
Forché, Carolyn 1950- DLB-5, 193
Ford, Charles Henri 1913-2002 ....DLB-4, 48
Ford, Corey 1902-1969 ....DLB-11
Ford, Ford Madox 1873-1939 ....DLB-34, 98, 162; CDBLB-6

Nathan Asch Remembers Ford Madox
  Ford, Sam Roth, and Hart Crane Y-02
J. B. Ford and Company................ DLB-49
Ford, Jesse Hill 1928-1996 .... DLB-6
Ford, John 1586-? DLB-58; CDBLB-1
Ford, R. A. D. 1915-1998 .... DLB-88
Ford, Richard 1944- DLB-227
Ford, Worthington C. 1858-1941 .... DLB-47
Fords, Howard, and Hulbert DLB-49
Foreman, Carl 1914-1984 .... DLB-26
Forester, C. S. 1899-1966 .... DLB-191
  The C. S. Forester Society Y-00
Forester, Frank (see Herbert, Henry William)
Formalism, New
  Anthologizing New Formalism...... DLB-282
  The Little Magazines of the
    New Formalism DLB-282
  The New Narrative Poetry......... DLB-282
  Presses of the New Formalism and
    the New Narrative............ DLB-282
  The Prosody of the New Formalism . DLB-282
  Younger Women Poets of the
    New Formalism DLB-282
Forman, Harry Buxton 1842-1917 ...... DLB-184
Fornés, María Irene 1930- DLB-7, 341
Forrest, Leon 1937-1997 .... DLB-33
Forsh, Ol'ga Dmitrievna 1873-1961 ..... DLB-272
Forster, E. M. 1879-1970
  ..DLB-34, 98, 162, 178, 195; DS-10; CDBLB-6
  "Fantasy," from *Aspects of the Novel*
    (1927) DLB-178
Forster, Georg 1754-1794 .... DLB-94
Forster, John 1812-1876............... DLB-144
Forster, Margaret 1938- DLB-155, 271
Forsyth, Frederick 1938- DLB-87
Forsyth, William
  "Literary Style" (1857) [excerpt] DLB-57
Forten, Charlotte L. 1837-1914...... DLB-50, 239
  Pages from Her Diary DLB-50
Fortini, Franco 1917-1994 .... DLB-128
Fortune, Mary ca. 1833-ca. 1910 ...... DLB-230
Fortune, T. Thomas 1856-1928 .... DLB-23
Fosdick, Charles Austin 1842-1915 ..... DLB-42
Fosse, Jon 1959- DLB-297
Foster, David 1944- DLB-289
Foster, Genevieve 1893-1979........... DLB-61
Foster, Hannah Webster
  1758-1840..................DLB-37, 200
Foster, John 1648-1681 .... DLB-24
Foster, Michael 1904-1956 .... DLB-9
Foster, Myles Birket 1825-1899........ DLB-184
Foster, William Z. 1881-1961 .... DLB-303
Foucault, Michel 1926-1984 .... DLB-242
Robert and Andrew Foulis
  [publishing house] DLB-154

Fouqué, Caroline de la Motte 1774-1831 ... DLB-90
Fouqué, Friedrich de la Motte
  1777-1843 .... DLB-90
Four Seas Company DLB-46
Four Winds Press DLB-46
Fournier, Henri Alban (see Alain-Fournier)
Fowler, Christopher 1953- DLB-267
Fowler, Connie May 1958- DLB-292
Fowler and Wells Company DLB-49
Fowles, John
  1926-2005 ..... DLB-14, 139, 207; CDBLB-8
Fox, John 1939- DLB-245
Fox, John, Jr. 1862 or 1863-1919 ... DLB-9; DS-13
Fox, Paula 1923- DLB-52
Fox, Richard Kyle 1846-1922 .... DLB-79
Fox, William Price 1926- DLB-2; Y-81
  Remembering Joe Heller Y-99
Richard K. Fox [publishing house] DLB-49
Foxe, John 1517-1587 .... DLB-132
Fraenkel, Michael 1896-1957 .... DLB-4
Frame, Ronald 1953- DLB-319
France, Anatole 1844-1924......... DLB-123, 330
France, Richard 1938- DLB-7
Francis, Convers 1795-1863 .... DLB-1, 235
Francis, Dick 1920- DLB-87; CDBLB-8
Francis, Sir Frank 1901-1988 .... DLB-201
Francis, H. E. 1924- DLB-335
Francis, Jeffrey, Lord 1773-1850 ....DLB-107
C. S. Francis [publishing house] DLB-49
Franck, Sebastian 1499-1542 ....DLB-179
Francke, Kuno 1855-1930 .... DLB-71
Françoise (Robertine Barry) 1863-1910 ... DLB-92
François, Louise von 1817-1893 .... DLB-129
Frank, Bruno 1887-1945.............. DLB-118
Frank, Leonhard 1882-1961 .... DLB-56, 118
Frank, Melvin 1913-1988 .... DLB-26
Frank, Waldo 1889-1967 .... DLB-9, 63
Franken, Rose 1895?-1988 ....DLB-228, Y-84
Franklin, Benjamin
  1706-1790 .... DLB-24, 43, 73, 183; CDALB-2
Franklin, James 1697-1735 .... DLB-43
Franklin, John 1786-1847 .... DLB-99
Franklin, Miles 1879-1954 .... DLB-230
Franklin Library..................... DLB-46
Frantz, Ralph Jules 1902-1979.......... DLB-4
Franzos, Karl Emil 1848-1904 .... DLB-129
Fraser, Antonia 1932- DLB-276
Fraser, G. S. 1915-1980............... DLB-27
Fraser, Kathleen 1935- DLB-169
Frattini, Alberto 1922- DLB-128
Frau Ava ?-1127 .... DLB-148

Fraunce, Abraham 1558?-1592 or 1593 .. DLB-236
Frayn, Michael 1933- DLB-13, 14, 194, 245
Frazier, Charles 1950- DLB-292
Fréchette, Louis-Honoré 1839-1908...... DLB-99
Frederic, Harold 1856-1898 ... DLB-12, 23; DS-13
Freed, Arthur 1894-1973.............. DLB-265
Freeling, Nicolas 1927-2003 .... DLB-87
  Tribute to Georges Simenon Y-89
Freeman, Douglas Southall
  1886-1953 ....DLB-17; DS-17
Freeman, Joseph 1897-1965 .... DLB-303
Freeman, Judith 1946- DLB-256
Freeman, Legh Richmond 1842-1915..... DLB-23
Freeman, Mary E. Wilkins
  1852-1930 ....DLB-12, 78, 221
Freeman, R. Austin 1862-1943.......... DLB-70
Freidank circa 1170-circa 1233 .... DLB-138
Freiligrath, Ferdinand 1810-1876 .... DLB-133
Fremlin, Celia 1914- DLB-276
Frémont, Jessie Benton 1834-1902 ...... DLB-183
Frémont, John Charles
  1813-1890 .... DLB-183, 186
French, Alice 1850-1934..........DLB-74; DS-13
French, David 1939- DLB-53
French, Evangeline 1869-1960 .... DLB-195
French, Francesca 1871-1960 .... DLB-195
James French [publishing house]......... DLB-49
Samuel French [publishing house] DLB-49
Samuel French, Limited DLB-106
French Literature
  Georges-Louis Leclerc de Buffon, "Le Discours
    sur le style" DLB-314
  Marie-Jean-Antoine-Nicolas Caritat, marquis de
    Condorcet, "The Tenth Stage" .. DLB-314
  Sophie Cottin, *Claire d'Albe*......... DLB-314
  Declaration of the Rights of Man and of
    the Citizen.................. DLB-314
  Denis Diderot, "The Encyclopedia".. DLB-314
  Epic and Beast Epic DLB-208
  French Arthurian Literature........ DLB-208
  Olympe de Gouges, *Declaration of the Rights
    of Woman*.................... DLB-314
  Françoise d'Issembourg de Graffigny, *Letters from
    a Peruvian Woman* DLB-314
  Claude-Adrien Helvétius, *The Spirit of
    Laws*...................... DLB-314
  Paul Henri Thiry, baron d'Holbach (writing as
    Jean-Baptiste de Mirabaud), *The System
    of Nature* DLB-314
  Pierre-Ambroise-François Choderlos de Laclos,
    Dangerous Acquaintances DLB-314
  Lyric Poetry DLB-268
  Louis-Sébastien Mercier, *Le Tableau
    de Paris*..................... DLB-314
  Charles-Louis de Secondat, baron de
    Montesquieu, *The Spirit of Laws* .. DLB-314
  Other Poets DLB-217

Poetry in Nineteenth-Century France: Cultural Background and Critical Commentary DLB-217

Roman de la Rose: Guillaume de Lorris 1200 to 1205-circa 1230, Jean de Meun 1235/1240-circa 1305 ..... DLB-208

Jean-Jacques Rousseau, *The Social Contract* DLB-314

Marquis de Sade, "Dialogue entre un prêtre et un moribond" DLB-314

Saints' Lives DLB-208

Troubadours, *Trobaíritz,* and Trouvères DLB-208

Anne-Robert-Jacques Turgot, baron de l'Aulne, "Memorandum on Local Government" DLB-314

Voltaire, "An account of the death of the chevalier de La Barre" DLB-314

Voltaire, *Candide* DLB-314

Voltaire, *Philosophical Dictionary* DLB-314

French Theater
  Medieval French Drama DLB-208
  Parisian Theater, Fall 1984: Toward a New Baroque Y-85

Freneau, Philip 1752-1832 .... DLB-37, 43
  The Rising Glory of America DLB-37

Freni, Melo 1934- DLB-128

Fréron, Elie Catherine 1718-1776 .... DLB-313

Freshfield, Douglas W. 1845-1934 ...... DLB-174

Freud, Sigmund 1856-1939 .... DLB-296

Freytag, Gustav 1816-1895 .... DLB-129

Frída Á. Sigurðardóttir 1940- DLB-293

Fridegård, Jan 1897-1968 .... DLB-259

Fried, Erich 1921-1988 .... DLB-85

Friedan, Betty 1921-2006 .... DLB-246

Friedman, Bruce Jay 1930- DLB-2, 28, 244

Friedman, Carl 1952- DLB-299

Friedman, Kinky 1944- DLB-292

Friedrich von Hausen circa 1171-1190 .... DLB-138

Friel, Brian 1929- DLB-13, 319

Friend, Krebs 1895?-1967? DLB-4

Fries, Fritz Rudolf 1935- DLB-75

Frisch, Max 1911-1991 .. DLB-69, 124; CDWLB-2

Frischlin, Nicodemus 1547-1590 .... DLB-179

Frischmuth, Barbara 1941- DLB-85

Fritz, Jean 1915- DLB-52

Froissart, Jean circa 1337-circa 1404 ..... DLB-208

Fromm, Erich 1900-1980 .... DLB-296

Fromentin, Eugene 1820-1876 .... DLB-123

Frontinus circa A.D. 35-A.D. 103/104 .... DLB-211

Frost, A. B. 1851-1928 .... DLB-188; DS-13

Frost, Carol 1948- DLB-342

Frost, Robert 1874-1963 ..... DLB-54, 342; DS-7; CDALB-4
  The Friends of the Dymock Poets Y-00

Frostenson, Katarina 1953- DLB-257

Frothingham, Octavius Brooks 1822-1895 .... DLB-1, 243

Froude, James Anthony 1818-1894 .... DLB-18, 57, 144

Fruitlands 1843-1844 .... DLB-1, 223; DS-5

Fry, Christopher 1907-2005 .... DLB-13
  Tribute to John Betjeman Y-84

Fry, Roger 1866-1934 .... DS-10

Fry, Stephen 1957- DLB-207

Frye, Northrop 1912-1991 ...... DLB-67, 68, 246

Fuchs, Daniel 1909-1993 ..... DLB-9, 26, 28; Y-93
  Tribute to Isaac Bashevis Singer Y-91

Fuentes, Carlos 1928- DLB-113; CDWLB-3

Fuertes, Gloria 1918-1998 .... DLB-108

Fugard, Athol 1932- DLB-225

The Fugitives and the Agrarians: The First Exhibition Y-85

Fujiwara no Shunzei 1114-1204 .... DLB-203

Fujiwara no Tameaki 1230s?-1290s? DLB-203

Fujiwara no Tameie 1198-1275 .... DLB-203

Fujiwara no Teika 1162-1241 .... DLB-203

Fuks, Ladislav 1923-1994 .... DLB-299

Fulbecke, William 1560-1603? DLB-172

Fuller, Charles 1939- DLB-38, 266

Fuller, Henry Blake 1857-1929 .... DLB-12

Fuller, John 1937- DLB-40

Fuller, Margaret (see Fuller, Sarah)

Fuller, Roy 1912-1991 .... DLB-15, 20
  Tribute to Christopher Isherwood Y-86

Fuller, Samuel 1912-1997 .... DLB-26

Fuller, Sarah 1810-1850 .... DLB-1, 59, 73, 183, 223, 239; DS-5; CDALB-2

Fuller, Thomas 1608-1661 .... DLB-151

Fullerton, Hugh 1873-1945 .... DLB-171

Fullwood, William fl. 1568 .... DLB-236

Fulton, Alice 1952- DLB-193

Fulton, Len 1934- Y-86

Fulton, Robin 1937- DLB-40

Funkhouser, Erica 1949- DLB-342

Furbank, P. N. 1920- DLB-155

Furetière, Antoine 1619-1688 .... DLB-268

Furman, Laura 1945- Y-86

Furmanov, Dmitrii Andreevich 1891-1926 .... DLB-272

Furness, Horace Howard 1833-1912 ...... DLB-64

Furness, William Henry 1802-1896 .... DLB-1, 235

Furnivall, Frederick James 1825-1910 .... DLB-184

Furphy, Joseph (Tom Collins) 1843-1912 .... DLB-230

Furthman, Jules 1888-1966 .... DLB-26
  Shakespeare and Montaigne: A Symposium by Jules Furthman Y-02

Furui Yoshikichi 1937- DLB-182

Fushimi, Emperor 1265-1317 .... DLB-203

Futabatei Shimei (Hasegawa Tatsunosuke) 1864-1909 .... DLB-180

Fyleman, Rose 1877-1957 .... DLB-160

G

G., 1972 Booker Prize winner, John Berger DLB-326

Gaarder, Jostein 1952- DLB-297

Gadallah, Leslie 1939- DLB-251

Gadamer, Hans-Georg 1900-2002 .... DLB-296

Gadda, Carlo Emilio 1893-1973 .... DLB-177

Gaddis, William 1922-1998 .... DLB-2, 278
  William Gaddis: A Tribute Y-99

Gág, Wanda 1893-1946 .... DLB-22

Gagarin, Ivan Sergeevich 1814-1882 ..... DLB-198

Gage, Matilda Joslyn 1826-1898 .... DLB-345

Gagnon, Madeleine 1938- DLB-60

Gaiman, Neil 1960- DLB-261

Gaine, Hugh 1726-1807 .... DLB-43

Hugh Gaine [publishing house] DLB-49

Gaines, Ernest J. 1933- DLB-2, 33, 152; Y-80; CDALB-6

Gaiser, Gerd 1908-1976 .... DLB-69

Gaitskill, Mary 1954- DLB-244

Galarza, Ernesto 1905-1984 .... DLB-122

Galaxy Science Fiction Novels DLB-46

Galbraith, Robert (or Caubraith) circa 1483-1544 .... DLB-281

Gale, Zona 1874-1938 .... DLB-9, 228, 78

Galen of Pergamon 129-after 210 .... DLB-176

Gales, Winifred Marshall 1761-1839 ..... DLB-200

Galich, Aleksandr 1918-1977 .... DLB-317

Medieval Galician-Portuguese Poetry DLB-287

Gall, Louise von 1815-1855 .... DLB-133

Gallagher, Tess 1943- DLB-120, 212, 244

Gallagher, Wes 1911-1997 .... DLB-127

Gallagher, William Davis 1808-1894 ...... DLB-73

Gallant, Mavis 1922- DLB-53

Gallegos, María Magdalena 1935- DLB-209

Gallico, Paul 1897-1976 .... DLB-9, 171

Gallop, Jane 1952- DLB-246

Galloway, Grace Growden 1727-1782 ..... DLB-200

Galloway, Janice 1956- DLB-319

Gallup, Donald 1913-2000 .... DLB-187

Galsworthy, John 1867-1933 .. DLB-10, 34, 98, 162, 330; DS-16; CDBLB-5

Galt, John 1779-1839 .... DLB-99, 116, 159

Galton, Sir Francis 1822-1911 .... DLB-166

Galvin, Brendan 1938- DLB-5

Gambaro, Griselda 1928- DLB-305

Cumulative Index

Gambit DLB-46

Gamboa, Reymundo 1948- DLB-122

Gammer Gurton's Needle DLB-62

Gan, Elena Andreevna (Zeneida R-va) 1814-1842 . . . . DLB-198

Gander, Forrest 1956- DLB-342

Gandhi, Mohandas Karamchand 1869-1948 . . . . DLB-323

Gandlevsky, Sergei Markovich 1952- DLB-285

Gannett, Frank E. 1876-1957 . . . . DLB-29

Gant, Eugene: Projected Works Y-01

Gao Xingjian 1940- DLB-330; Y-00

   Nobel Lecture 2000: "The Case for Literature" Y-00

Gaos, Vicente 1919-1980 . . . . DLB-134

García, Andrew 1854?-1943 . . . . DLB-209

García, Cristina 1958- DLB-292

García, Lionel G. 1935- DLB-82

García, Richard 1941- DLB-209

García, Santiago 1928- DLB-305

García Márquez, Gabriel 1927- DLB-113, 330; Y-82; CDWLB-3

   The Magical World of Macondo Y-82

   Nobel Lecture 1982: The Solitude of Latin America Y-82

   A Tribute to Gabriel García Márquez Y-82

García Marruz, Fina 1923- DLB-283

García-Camarillo, Cecilio 1943- DLB-209

Garcilaso de la Vega circa 1503-1536 . . . . DLB-318

Garcilaso de la Vega, Inca 1539-1616 . . . . DLB-318

Gardam, Jane 1928- DLB-14, 161, 231

Gardell, Jonas 1963- DLB-257

Garden, Alexander circa 1685-1756 . . . . . DLB-31

Gardiner, John Rolfe 1936- DLB-244

Gardiner, Margaret Power Farmer (see Blessington, Marguerite, Countess of)

Gardner, John 1933-1982 . . . . .DLB-2; Y-82; CDALB-7

Garfield, Leon 1921-1996 . . . . DLB-161

Garis, Howard R. 1873-1962 . . . . DLB-22

Garland, Hamlin 1860-1940 . . .DLB-12, 71, 78, 186

   The Hamlin Garland Society Y-01

Garneau, François-Xavier 1809-1866 . . . . . DLB-99

Garneau, Hector de Saint-Denys 1912-1943 . . . . DLB-88

Garneau, Michel 1939- DLB-53

Garner, Alan 1934- DLB-161, 261

Garner, Helen 1942- DLB-325

Garner, Hugh 1913-1979 . . . . DLB-68

Garnett, David 1892-1981 . . . . DLB-34

Garnett, Eve 1900-1991 . . . . DLB-160

Garnett, Richard 1835-1906 . . . . DLB-184

Garnier, Robert 1545?-1590 . . . . DLB-327

Garrard, Lewis H. 1829-1887 . . . . DLB-186

Garraty, John A. 1920-2007 . . . . DLB-17

Garrett, Almeida (João Baptista da Silva Leitão de Almeida Garrett) 1799-1854 . . . . DLB-287

Garrett, George 1929-2008 . . . . . . DLB-2, 5, 130, 152; Y-83

   Literary Prizes Y-00

   My Summer Reading Orgy: Reading for Fun and Games: One Reader's Report on the Summer of 2001 . . . . . . Y-01

   A Summing Up at Century's End Y-99

   Tribute to James Dickey Y-97

   Tribute to Michael M. Rea Y-97

   Tribute to Paxton Davis Y-94

   Tribute to Peter Taylor Y-94

   Tribute to William Goyen Y-83

   A Writer Talking: A Collage Y-00

Garrett, John Work 1872-1942 . . . . DLB-187

Garrick, David 1717-1779 . . . . DLB-84, 213

Garrison, William Lloyd 1805-1879 . . . . DLB-1, 43, 235; CDALB-2

Garro, Elena 1920-1998 . . . . DLB-145

Garshin, Vsevolod Mikhailovich 1855-1888 . . . . DLB-277

Garth, Samuel 1661-1719 . . . . DLB-95

Garve, Andrew 1908-2001 . . . . DLB-87

Garvey, Marcus 1887-1940 . . . . DLB-345

Gary, Romain 1914-1980 . . . . DLB-83, 299

Gascoigne, George 1539?-1577 . . . . DLB-136

Gascoyne, David 1916-2001 . . . . DLB-20

Gash, Jonathan (John Grant) 1933- DLB-276

Gaskell, Elizabeth Cleghorn 1810-1865 . . . . . DLB-21, 144, 159; CDBLB-4

   The Gaskell Society Y-98

Gaskell, Jane 1941- DLB-261

Gaspey, Thomas 1788-1871 . . . . DLB-116

Gass, William H. 1924- DLB-2, 227

Gates, Doris 1901-1987 . . . . DLB-22

Gates, Henry Louis, Jr. 1950- DLB-67

Gates, Lewis E. 1860-1924 . . . . DLB-71

Gatto, Alfonso 1909-1976 . . . . DLB-114

Gault, William Campbell 1910-1995 . . . . DLB-226

   Tribute to Kenneth Millar Y-83

Gaunt, Mary 1861-1942 . . . . .DLB-174, 230

Gautier, Théophile 1811-1872 . . . . DLB-119

Gautreaux, Tim 1947- DLB-292

Gauvreau, Claude 1925-1971 . . . . DLB-88

The *Gawain*-Poet fl. circa 1350-1400 . . . . DLB-146

Gawsworth, John (Terence Ian Fytton Armstrong) 1912-1970 . . . . DLB-255

Gay, Ebenezer 1696-1787 . . . . DLB-24

Gay, John 1685-1732 . . . . DLB-84, 95

Gayarré, Charles E. A. 1805-1895 . . . . . . DLB-30

Charles Gaylord [publishing house] DLB-49

Gaylord, Edward King 1873-1974 . . . . . . .DLB-127

Gaylord, Edward Lewis 1919-2003 . . . . . .DLB-127

Gazdanov, Gaito 1903-1971 . . . . .DLB-317

Gébler, Carlo 1954- DLB-271

Geda, Sigitas 1943- DLB-232

Geddes, Gary 1940- DLB-60

Geddes, Virgil 1897-1989 . . . . DLB-4

Gedeon (Georgii Andreevich Krinovsky) circa 1730-1763 . . . . DLB-150

Gee, Maggie 1948- DLB-207

Gee, Shirley 1932- DLB-245

Geibel, Emanuel 1815-1884 . . . . DLB-129

Geiogamah, Hanay 1945- DLB-175

Geis, Bernard, Associates DLB-46

Geisel, Theodor Seuss 1904-1991 . . .DLB-61; Y-91

Gelb, Arthur 1924- DLB-103

Gelb, Barbara 1926- DLB-103

Gelber, Jack 1932- DLB-7, 228

Gélinas, Gratien 1909-1999 . . . . DLB-88

Gellert, Christian Füerchtegott 1715-1769 . . . . DLB-97

Gellhorn, Martha 1908-1998 . . . . Y-82, 98

Gems, Pam 1925- DLB-13

Genet, Jean 1910-1986 . . . . .DLB-72, 321; Y-86

Genette, Gérard 1930- DLB-242

Genevoix, Maurice 1890-1980 . . . . DLB-65

Genis, Aleksandr Aleksandrovich 1953- DLB-285

Genlis, Stéphanie-Félicité Ducrest, comtesse de 1746-1830 . . . . DLB-313

Genovese, Eugene D. 1930- DLB-17

Gent, Peter 1942- Y-82

Geoffrey of Monmouth circa 1100-1155 . . . . DLB-146

George, Elizabeth 1949- DLB-306

George, Henry 1839-1897 . . . . DLB-23

George, Jean Craighead 1919- DLB-52

George, W. L. 1882-1926 . . . . .DLB-197

George III, King of Great Britain and Ireland 1738-1820 . . . . DLB-213

Georgslied 896? DLB-148

Gerber, Merrill Joan 1938- DLB-218

Gerhardie, William 1895-1977 . . . . DLB-36

Gerhardt, Paul 1607-1676 . . . . DLB-164

Gérin, Winifred 1901-1981 . . . . DLB-155

Gérin-Lajoie, Antoine 1824-1882 . . . . DLB-99

German Literature

   A Call to Letters and an Invitation to the Electric Chair DLB-75

   The Conversion of an Unpolitical Man DLB-66

   The German Radio Play DLB-124

The German Transformation from the
    Baroque to the Enlightenment DLB-97
Germanophilism DLB-66
A Letter from a New Germany.........Y-90
The Making of a People DLB-66
The Novel of Impressionism.........DLB-66
Pattern and Paradigm: History as
    Design......................DLB-75
Premisses........................DLB-66
The 'Twenties and Berlin DLB-66
Wolfram von Eschenbach's *Parzival*:
    Prologue and Book 3 ....DLB-138
Writers and Politics: 1871-1918.......DLB-66

German Literature, Middle Ages
    Abrogans circa 790-800 ....DLB-148
    Annolied between 1077 and 1081 .....DLB-148
    The Arthurian Tradition and
        Its European Context DLB-138
    Cambridge Songs (Carmina Cantabrigensia)
        circa 1050 ....DLB-148
    Christus und die Samariterin circa 950 ...DLB-148
    De Heinrico circa 980?...............DLB-148
    Ecbasis Captivi circa 1045 ....DLB-148
    Georgslied 896?....................DLB-148
    German Literature and Culture from
        Charlemagne to the Early Courtly
        Period..........DLB-148; CDWLB-2
    The Germanic Epic and Old English
        Heroic Poetry: *Widsith, Waldere,*
        and *The Fight at Finnsburg* DLB-146
    Graf Rudolf between circa
        1170 and circa 1185 ....DLB-148
    Heliand circa 850 ....DLB-148
    Das Hildesbrandslied
        circa 820 ....DLB-148; CDWLB-2
    Kaiserchronik circa 1147..............DLB-148
    The Legends of the Saints and a
        Medieval Christian
        Worldview DLB-148
    Ludus de Antichristo circa 1160........DLB-148
    Ludwigslied 881 or 882..............DLB-148
    Muspilli circa 790-circa 850..........DLB-148
    Old German Genesis and *Old German
        Exodus* circa 1050-circa 1130 .....DLB-148
    Old High German Charms
        and Blessings DLB-148; CDWLB-2
    The *Old High German Isidor*
        circa 790-800.................DLB-148
    Petruslied circa 854? DLB-148
    Physiologus circa 1070-circa 1150 ......DLB-148
    Ruodlieb circa 1050-1075 ....DLB-148
    "*Spielmannsepen*" (circa 1152
        circa 1500) DLB-148
    The Strasbourg Oaths 842 ....DLB-148
    Tatian circa 830 ....DLB-148
    Waltharius circa 825 ....DLB-148
    Wessobrunner Gebet circa 787-815 ....DLB-148

German Theater
    German Drama 800-1280 ....DLB-138
    German Drama from Naturalism
        to Fascism: 1889-1933 ....DLB-118

Gernsback, Hugo 1884-1967.........DLB-8, 137
Gerould, Katharine Fullerton
    1879-1944 ....DLB-78
Samuel Gerrish [publishing house] DLB-49
Gerrold, David 1944- DLB-8
Gersão, Teolinda 1940- DLB-287
Gershon, Karen 1923-1993 ....DLB-299
Gershwin, Ira 1896-1983............DLB-265
    The Ira Gershwin Centenary Y-96
Gerson, Jean 1363-1429.............DLB-208
Gersonides 1288-1344...............DLB-115
Gerstäcker, Friedrich 1816-1872.........DLB-129
Gertsen, Aleksandr Ivanovich
    (see Herzen, Alexander)
Gerstenberg, Heinrich Wilhelm von
    1737-1823.....................DLB-97
Gervinus, Georg Gottfried
    1805-1871 ....DLB-133
Gery, John 1953- DLB-282
Geßner, Solomon 1730-1788 ....DLB-97
Geston, Mark S. 1946-.................DLB-8
Al-Ghazali 1058-1111................DLB-115
Ghelderode, Michel de (Adolphe-Adhémar Martens)
    1898-1962 ....DLB-321
al-Ghitani, Gamal 1945- DLB-346
Ghose, Zulfikar 1935- DLB-323
Ghosh, Amitav 1956- DLB-323
The Ghost Road, 1995 Booker Prize winner,
    Pat Barker.....................DLB-326
Gibbings, Robert 1889-1958 ....DLB-195
Gibbon, Edward 1737-1794 ....DLB-104, 336
Gibbon, John Murray 1875-1952.........DLB-92
Gibbon, Lewis Grassic (see Mitchell, James Leslie)
Gibbons, Floyd 1887-1939..............DLB-25
Gibbons, Kaye 1960- DLB-292
Gibbons, Reginald 1947- DLB-120
Gibbons, William eighteenth century DLB-73
Gibran, Kahlil 1883-1931 ....DLB-346
Gibson, Charles Dana
    1867-1944 ....DLB-188; DS-13
Gibsão, Graeme 1934- DLB-53
Gibson, Margaret 1944- DLB-120
Gibson, Margaret Dunlop 1843-1920 ...DLB-174
Gibson, Wilfrid 1878-1962............DLB-19
    The Friends of the Dymock Poets........Y-00
Gibson, William 1914- DLB-7
Gibson, William 1948- DLB-251
Gide, André 1869-1951 ....DLB-65, 321, 330
Giguère, Diane 1937- DLB-53
Giguère, Roland 1929-2003............DLB-60
Gil de Biedma, Jaime 1929-1990 ....DLB-108
Gil-Albert, Juan 1906-1994 ....DLB-134
Gilbert, Anthony 1899-1973 ....DLB-77

Gilbert, Elizabeth 1969- DLB-292
Gilbert, Sir Humphrey 1537-1583 ....DLB-136
Gilbert, Michael 1912-2006............DLB-87
Gilbert, Sandra M. 1936- DLB-120, 246
Gilbert, W. S. 1836-1911 ....DLB-344
Gilchrist, Alexander 1828-1861.........DLB-144
Gilchrist, Ellen 1935- DLB-130
Gilder, Jeannette L. 1849-1916.........DLB-79
Gilder, Richard Watson 1844-1909 ....DLB-64, 79
Gildersleeve, Basil 1831-1924 ....DLB-71
Giles, Henry 1809-1882.................DLB-64
Giles of Rome circa 1243-1316 ....DLB-115
Gilfillan, George 1813-1878............DLB-144
Gilfillan, Merrill 1945- DLB-342
Gill, Eric 1882-1940...................DLB-98
Gill, Sarah Prince 1728-1771 ....DLB-200
William F. Gill Company................DLB-49
Gillespie, A. Lincoln, Jr. 1895-1950........DLB-4
Gillespie, Haven 1883-1975 ....DLB-265
Gilliam, Florence fl. twentieth century......DLB-4
Gilliatt, Penelope 1932-1993 ....DLB-14
Gillott, Jacky 1939-1980 ....DLB-14
Gilman, Caroline H. 1794-1888.........DLB-3, 73
Gilman, Charlotte Perkins 1860-1935 ....DLB-221
    The Charlotte Perkins Gilman Society Y-99
W. and J. Gilman [publishing house]......DLB-49
Gilmer, Elizabeth Meriwether
    1861-1951 ....DLB-29
Gilmer, Francis Walker 1790-1826.........DLB-37
Gilmore, Mary 1865-1962............DLB-260
Gilroy, Frank D. 1925-.................DLB-7
Gimferrer, Pere (Pedro) 1945- DLB-134
Ginger, Aleksandr S. 1897-1965.........DLB-317
Gingrich, Arnold 1903-1976 ....DLB-137
    Prospectus From the Initial Issue of
        Esquire (Autumn 1933) DLB-137
    "With the Editorial Ken," Prospectus
        From the Initial Issue of *Ken*
        (7 April 1938)................DLB-137
Ginibi, Ruby Langford 1934- DLB-325
Ginsberg, Allen
    1926-1997 ....DLB-5, 16, 169, 237; CDALB-1
Ginzburg, Evgeniian 1904-1977 ....DLB-302
Ginzburg, Lidiia Iakovlevna 1902-1990...DLB-302
Ginzburg, Natalia 1916-1991...........DLB-177
Ginzkey, Franz Karl 1871-1963 ....DLB-81
Gioia, Dana 1950- DLB-120, 282
Giono, Jean 1895-1970................DLB-72, 321
Giotti, Virgilio 1885-1957 ....DLB-114
Giovanni, Nikki 1943- DLB-5, 41; CDALB-7
Giovannitti, Arturo 1884-1959 ....DLB-303
Gipson, Lawrence Henry 1880-1971 ......DLB-17

Girard, Rodolphe 1879-1956 . . . . DLB-92

Giraudoux, Jean 1882-1944 . . . . DLB-65, 321

Girondo, Oliverio 1891-1967 . . . . DLB-283

Gissing, George 1857-1903 . . . . . DLB-18, 135, 184

    The Place of Realism in Fiction (1895) . . DLB-18

Giudici, Giovanni 1924- DLB-128

Giuliani, Alfredo 1924- DLB-128

Gjellerup, Karl 1857-1919 . . . . DLB-300, 330

Glackens, William J. 1870-1938 . . . . DLB-188

Gladilin, Anatolii Tikhonovich 1935- . . DLB-302

Gladkov, Fedor Vasil'evich 1883-1958 . . . DLB-272

Gladstone, William Ewart
    1809-1898 . . . . .DLB-57, 184

Glaeser, Ernst 1902-1963 . . . . DLB-69

Glancy, Diane 1941- DLB-175

Glanvill, Joseph 1636-1680. . . . . DLB-252

Glanville, Brian 1931- DLB-15, 139

Glapthorne, Henry 1610-1643? DLB-58

Glasgow, Ellen 1873-1945. . . . . DLB-9, 12

    The Ellen Glasgow Society Y-01

Glasier, Katharine Bruce 1867-1950 . . . . . DLB-190

Glaspell, Susan 1876-1948 . . . . . .DLB-7, 9, 78, 228

Glass, Montague 1877-1934 . . . . DLB-11

Glassco, John 1909-1981 . . . . DLB-68

Glatstein, Jacob (Yankev Glatshteyn)
    1896-1971. DLB-333

Glauser, Friedrich 1896-1938 . . . . DLB-56

Glavin, Anthony 1946- DLB-319

F. Gleason's Publishing Hall. DLB-49

Gleim, Johann Wilhelm Ludwig
    1719-1803. . . . . DLB-97

Glendinning, Robin 1938- DLB-310

Glendinning, Victoria 1937- DLB-155

Glidden, Frederick Dilley (Luke Short)
    1908-1975. DLB-256

Glinka, Fedor Nikolaevich 1786-1880. . . . DLB-205

Glover, Keith 1966- DLB-249

Glover, Richard 1712-1785 . . . . DLB-95

Glover, Sue 1943- DLB-310

Glück, Louise 1943- DLB-5

Glyn, Elinor 1864-1943 . . . . DLB-153

Gnedich, Nikolai Ivanovich 1784-1833. . . DLB-205

Gobineau, Joseph-Arthur de
    1816-1882. DLB-123

The God of Small Things, 1997 Booker Prize winner,
    Arundhati Roy DLB-326

Godber, John 1956- DLB-233

Godbout, Jacques 1933- DLB-53

Goddard, Morrill 1865-1937. . . . . DLB-25

Goddard, William 1740-1817 . . . . DLB-43

Godden, Rumer 1907-1998. . . . . DLB-161

Godey, Louis A. 1804-1878 . . . . DLB-73

Godey and McMichael. DLB-49

Godfrey, Dave 1938- DLB-60

Godfrey, Thomas 1736-1763. . . . . DLB-31

Godine, David R., Publisher. DLB-46

Godkin, E. L. 1831-1902 . . . . DLB-79

Godolphin, Sidney 1610-1643 . . . . DLB-126

Godwin, Gail 1937- DLB-6, 234

M. J. Godwin and Company DLB-154

Godwin, Mary Jane Clairmont
    1766-1841. DLB-163

Godwin, Parke 1816-1904 . . . . DLB-3, 64, 250

Godwin, William 1756-1836 . . . . . . .DLB-39, 104,
    142, 158, 163, 262, 336; CDBLB-3

    Preface to *St. Leon* (1799) DLB-39

Goering, Reinhard 1887-1936. . . . . DLB-118

Goes, Albrecht 1908- DLB-69

Goethe, Johann Wolfgang von
    1749-1832. . . . . DLB-94; CDWLB-2

Goetz, Curt 1888-1960. . . . . DLB-124

Goffe, Thomas circa 1592-1629 . . . . DLB-58

Goffstein, M. B. 1940- DLB-61

Gogarty, Oliver St. John 1878-1957 . . . DLB-15, 19

Gogol, Nikolai Vasil'evich 1809-1852. . . . DLB-198

Goines, Donald 1937-1974 . . . . DLB-33

Gold, Herbert 1924- DLB-2; Y-81

    Tribute to William Saroyan Y-81

Gold, Michael 1893-1967 . . . . DLB-9, 28

Goldbarth, Albert 1948- DLB-120

Goldberg, Dick 1947- DLB-7

Golden Cockerel Press DLB-112

Goldfaden, Abraham (Avrom Goldfadn)
    1840-1908 . . . . DLB-333

Golding, Arthur 1536-1606 . . . . DLB-136

Golding, Louis 1895-1958 . . . . DLB-195

Golding, William
    1911-1993 . . . . DLB-15, 100, 255, 326,
    330; Y-83; CDBLB-7

    Nobel Lecture 1993 . . . . Y-83

    The Stature of William Golding. Y-83

Goldman, Emma 1869-1940. . . . . DLB-221

Goldman, William 1931- DLB-44

Goldring, Douglas 1887-1960. . . . . DLB-197

Goldschmidt, Meir Aron 1819-1887. . . . . DLB-300

Goldsmith, Oliver 1730?-1774
    . . . DLB-39, 89, 104, 109, 142, 336; CDBLB-2

Goldsmith, Oliver 1794-1861 . . . . DLB-99

Goldsmith Publishing Company DLB-46

Goldstein, Richard 1944- DLB-185

Goldsworthy, Peter 1951- DLB-325

Gollancz, Sir Israel 1864-1930 . . . . DLB-201

Victor Gollancz Limited DLB-112

Gomberville, Marin Le Roy, sieur de
    1600?-1674 . . . . DLB-268

Gombrowicz, Witold
    1904-1969 . . . . .DLB-215; CDWLB-4

Gomez, Madeleine-Angélique Poisson de
    1684-1770. DLB-313

Gómez de Ciudad Real, Alvar (Alvar Gómez
    de Guadalajara) 1488-1538 . . . . DLB-318

Gómez-Quiñones, Juan 1942- DLB-122

Laurence James Gomme
    [publishing house] DLB-46

Gompers, Samuel 1850-1924 . . . . DLB-303

Gonçalves Dias, Antônio 1823-1864 . . . . DLB-307

Goncharov, Ivan Aleksandrovich
    1812-1891 . . . . DLB-238

Goncourt, Edmond de 1822-1896 . . . . . . DLB-123

Goncourt, Jules de 1830-1870. . . . . DLB-123

Gonzales, Rodolfo "Corky" 1928- DLB-122

Gonzales-Berry, Erlinda 1942- DLB-209

    "Chicano Language" DLB-82

González, Angel 1925- DLB-108

Gonzalez, Genaro 1949- DLB-122

Gonzalez, N. V. M. 1915-1999 . . . . DLB-312

González, Otto-Raúl 1921- DLB-290

Gonzalez, Ray 1952- DLB-122

González de Mireles, Jovita
    1899-1983 . . . . DLB-122

González Martínez, Enrique
    1871-1952. DLB-290

González-T., César A. 1931- DLB-82

Gonzalo de Berceo
    circa 1195-circa 1264 . . . . DLB-337

Goodis, David 1917-1967 . . . . DLB-226

Goodison, Lorna 1947- DLB-157

Goodman, Allegra 1967- DLB-244

Goodman, Nelson 1906-1998. . . . . .DLB-279

Goodman, Paul 1911-1972 . . . . DLB-130, 246

The Goodman Theatre DLB-7

Goodrich, Frances 1891-1984 and
    Hackett, Albert 1900-1995. . . . . DLB-26

Goodrich, Samuel Griswold
    1793-1860. . . . . .DLB-1, 42, 73, 243

S. G. Goodrich [publishing house] DLB-49

C. E. Goodspeed and Company. DLB-49

Goodwin, Stephen 1943- Y-82

Googe, Barnabe 1540-1594 . . . . DLB-132

Gookin, Daniel 1612-1687 . . . . DLB-24

Gopegui, Belén 1963- DLB-322

Goran, Lester 1928- DLB-244

Gordimer, Nadine
    1923- DLB-225, 326, 330; Y-91
    Nobel Lecture 1991 . . . . Y-91

Gordin, Jacob (Yankev Gordin)
    1853-1909 . . . . DLB-333

Gordon, Adam Lindsay 1833-1870. . . . . . DLB-230

Gordon, Caroline
    1895-1981 . . . . DLB-4, 9, 102; DS-17; Y-81

Gordon, Charles F. (see OyamO)

Gordon, Charles William (see Connor, Ralph)

Gordon, Giles 1940- DLB-14, 139, 207

Gordon, Helen Cameron, Lady Russell
1867-1949 ....DLB-195

Gordon, Lyndall 1941- DLB-155

Gordon, Mack 1904-1959 ....DLB-265

Gordon, Mary 1949- DLB-6; Y-81

Gordon, Thomas ca. 1692-1750.........DLB-336

Gordone, Charles 1925-1995............DLB-7

Gore, Catherine
1799 or 1800-1861............DLB-116, 344

Gore-Booth, Eva 1870-1926............DLB-240

Gores, Joe 1931- DLB-226; Y-02

Tribute to Kenneth Millar Y-83

Tribute to Raymond Chandler Y-88

Gorey, Edward 1925-2000..............DLB-61

Gorgias of Leontini
circa 485 B.C.-376 B.C. DLB-176

Gor'ky, Maksim 1868-1936...........DLB-295

Gorodetsky, Sergei Mitrofanovich
1884-1967 ....DLB-295

Gorostiza, José 1901-1979 ....DLB-290

Görres, Joseph 1776-1848..............DLB-90

Gosse, Edmund 1849-1928 .....DLB-57, 144, 184

Gosson, Stephen 1554-1624............DLB-172

The Schoole of Abuse (1579) DLB-172

Gotanda, Philip Kan 1951- DLB-266

Gotlieb, Phyllis 1926- DLB-88, 251

Go-Toba 1180-1239 ....DLB-203

Gottfried von Straßburg
died before 1230 ....DLB-138; CDWLB-2

Gotthelf, Jeremias 1797-1854 ....DLB-133

Gottschalk circa 804/808-869...........DLB-148

Gottsched, Johann Christoph
1700-1766......................DLB-97

Götz, Johann Nikolaus 1721-1781 ....DLB-97

Goudge, Elizabeth 1900-1984 ....DLB-191

Gouges, Olympe de 1748-1793 ....DLB-313

Declaration of the Rights of Woman DLB-314

Gough, John B. 1817-1886.............DLB-243

Gough, Richard 1735-1809 ....DLB-336

Gould, Wallace 1882-1940..............DLB-54

Gournay, Marie de 1565-1645..........DLB-327

Govoni, Corrado 1884-1965 ....DLB-114

Govrin, Michal 1950- DLB-299

Gower, John circa 1330-1408 ....DLB-146

Goyen, William 1915-1983 .....DLB-2, 218; Y-83

Goytisolo, José Augustín 1928- DLB-134

Goytisolo, Juan 1931- DLB-322

Goytisolo, Luis 1935- DLB-322

Gozzano, Guido 1883-1916 ....DLB-114

Grabbe, Christian Dietrich 1801-1836....DLB-133

Gracq, Julien (Louis Poirier) 1910-2007....DLB-83

Grade, Chaim (Khayim Grade)
1910-1982 ....DLB-333

Grady, Henry W. 1850-1889...........DLB-23

Graf, Oskar Maria 1894-1967 ....DLB-56

Graf Rudolf between circa 1170 and
circa 1185 ....DLB-148

Graff, Gerald 1937- DLB-246

Graffigny, Françoise d'Issembourg de
1695-1758 ....DLB-313

Letters from a Peruvian Woman DLB-314

Richard Grafton [publishing house]......DLB-170

Grafton, Sue 1940- DLB-226

Graham, Frank 1893-1965............DLB-241

Graham, George Rex 1813-1894.......DLB-73

Graham, Gwethalyn (Gwethalyn Graham
Erichsen-Brown) 1913-1965 ....DLB-88

Graham, Jorie 1951- DLB-120

Graham, Katharine 1917-2001.........DLB-127

Graham, Lorenz 1902-1989 ....DLB-76

Graham, Philip 1915-1963............DLB-127

Graham, R. B. Cunninghame
1852-1936 .... DLB-98, 135, 174

Graham, Shirley 1896-1977 ....DLB-76

Graham, Stephen 1884-1975 ....DLB-195

Graham, W. S. 1918-1986 ....DLB-20

William H. Graham [publishing house]....DLB-49

Graham, Winston 1910-2003............DLB-77

Grahame, Kenneth 1859-1932... DLB-34, 141, 178

Grainger, Martin Allerdale 1874-1941 .....DLB-92

Gramatky, Hardie 1907-1979 ....DLB-22

Gramcko, Ida 1924-1994..............DLB-290

Gramsci, Antonio 1891-1937 ....DLB-296

La gran conquista de Ultramar
thirteenth century ....DLB 337

Granada, Fray Luis de 1504-1588 ......DLB-318

Grand, Sarah 1854-1943 .... DLB-135, 197

Grandbois, Alain 1900-1975 ....DLB-92

Grandson, Oton de circa 1345-1397 .....DLB-208

Grange, John circa 1556-? DLB-136

Granger, Thomas 1578-1627 ....DLB-281

Granich, Irwin (see Gold, Michael)

Granin, Daniil 1918- DLB-302

Granovsky, Timofei Nikolaevich
1813-1855 ....DLB-198

Grant, Anne MacVicar 1755-1838.......DLB-200

Grant, Duncan 1885-1978 .... DS-10

Grant, George 1918-1988 ....DLB-88

Grant, George Monro 1835-1902 ....DLB-99

Grant, Harry J. 1881-1963.............DLB-29

Grant, James Edward 1905-1966 ....DLB-26

Grant, John (see Gash, Jonathan)

War of the Words (and Pictures): The Creation
of a Graphic Novel Y-02

Grass, Günter 1927- DLB-75, 124, 330; CDWLB-2

Nobel Lecture 1999:
"To Be Continued . . ." Y-99

Tribute to Helen Wolff Y-94

Grasty, Charles H. 1863-1924...........DLB-25

Grau, Shirley Ann 1929- DLB-2, 218

Graves, John 1920- Y-83

Graves, Richard 1715-1804 ....DLB-39

Graves, Robert 1895-1985
... DLB-20, 100, 191; DS-18; Y-85; CDBLB-6

The St. John's College
Robert Graves Trust...............Y-96

Gray, Alasdair 1934- DLB-194, 261, 319

Gray, Asa 1810-1888 ....DLB-1, 235

Gray, David 1838-1861 ....DLB-32

Gray, Simon 1936-2008 ....DLB-13

Gray, Robert 1945- DLB-325

Gray, Thomas 1716-1771 .....DLB-109; CDBLB-2

Grayson, Richard 1951- DLB-234

Grayson, William J. 1788-1863 ....DLB-3, 64, 248

The Great Bibliographers Series Y-93

The Great Gatsby (Documentary)..........DLB-219

"The Greatness of Southern Literature":
League of the South Institute for the
Study of Southern Culture and History
.................................Y-02

Grech, Nikolai Ivanovich 1787-1867 .....DLB-198

Greeley, Horace 1811-1872 ... DLB-3, 43, 189, 250

Green, Adolph 1915-2002 ....DLB-44, 265

Green, Anna Katharine
1846-1935 ....DLB-202, 221

Green, Duff 1791-1875..................DLB-43

Green, Elizabeth Shippen 1871-1954 .....DLB-188

Green, Gerald 1922-2006 ....DLB-28

Green, Henry 1905-1973 ....DLB-15

Green, Jonas 1712-1767 ....DLB-31

Green, Joseph 1706-1780 ....DLB-31

Green, Julien 1900-1998 ....DLB-4, 72

Green, Paul 1894-1981 ....DLB-7, 9, 249; Y-81

Green, T. H. 1836-1882 ....DLB-190, 262

Green, Terence M. 1947- DLB-251

T. and S. Green [publishing house] DLB-49

Green Tiger Press DLB-46

Timothy Green [publishing house] DLB-49

Greenaway, Kate 1846-1901 ....DLB-141

Greenberg, Joanne 1932- DLB-335

Greenberg: Publisher...................DLB-46

Greene, Asa 1789-1838 ....DLB-11

Greene, Belle da Costa 1883-1950.......DLB-187

Greene, Graham 1904-1991
.... DLB-13, 15, 77, 100, 162, 201, 204;
Y-85, 91; CDBLB-7

Cumulative Index

Tribute to Christopher Isherwood Y-86

Greene, Robert 1558-1592 . . . . DLB-62, 167

Greene, Robert Bernard (Bob), Jr. 1947- DLB-185

Benjamin H Greene [publishing house] . . . DLB-49

Greenfield, George 1917-2000 . . . . Y-91, 00

    Derek Robinson's Review of George Greenfield's *Rich Dust* Y-02

Greenhow, Robert 1800-1854 . . . . DLB-30

Greenlee, William B. 1872-1953 . . . . DLB-187

Greenough, Horatio 1805-1852 . . . . . . DLB-1, 235

Greenwell, Dora 1821-1882 . . . . DLB-35, 199

Greenwillow Books DLB-46

Greenwood, Grace (see Lippincott, Sara Jane Clarke)

Greenwood, Walter 1903-1974 . . . . . . DLB-10, 191

Greer, Ben 1948- DLB-6

Greflinger, Georg 1620?-1677 . . . . DLB-164

Greg, W. R. 1809-1881 . . . . DLB-55

Greg, W. W. 1875-1959 . . . . DLB-201

Gregg, Josiah 1806-1850 . . . . DLB-183, 186

Gregg Press DLB-46

Gregory, Horace 1898-1982 . . . . DLB-48

Gregory, Isabella Augusta Persse, Lady 1852-1932 . . . . DLB-10

Gregory of Rimini circa 1300-1358 . . . . . DLB-115

Gregynog Press DLB-112

Greiff, León de 1895-1976 . . . . DLB-283

Greiffenberg, Catharina Regina von 1633-1694 . . . . DLB-168

Greig, Noël 1944- DLB-245

Grekova, Irina (Elena Sergeevna Venttsel') 1907-2002 . . . . DLB-302

Grenfell, Wilfred Thomason 1865-1940 . . . . DLB-92

Grenier, Robert 1941- DLB-342

Grenville, Kate 1950- DLB-325

Gress, Elsa 1919-1988 . . . . DLB-214

Greve, Felix Paul (see Grove, Frederick Philip)

Greville, Fulke, First Lord Brooke 1554-1628 . . . . DLB-62, 172

Grey, Sir George, K.C.B. 1812-1898 . . . . DLB-184

Grey, Lady Jane 1537-1554 . . . . DLB-132

Grey, Zane 1872-1939 . . . . DLB-9, 212

    Zane Grey's West Society Y-00

Grey Owl (Archibald Stansfeld Belaney) 1888-1938 . . . . DLB-92; DS-17

Grey Walls Press DLB-112

Griboedov, Aleksandr Sergeevich 1795?-1829 . . . . DLB-205

Grice, Paul 1913-1988 . . . . DLB-279

Grier, Eldon 1917- DLB-88

Grieve, C. M. (see MacDiarmid, Hugh)

Griffin, Bartholomew fl. 1596 . . . . DLB-172

Griffin, Bryan

    "Panic Among the Philistines": A Postscript, An Interview with Bryan Griffin Y-81

Griffin, Gerald 1803-1840 . . . . DLB-159

The Griffin Poetry Prize Y-00

Griffith, Elizabeth 1727?-1793 . . . . DLB-39, 89

    Preface to *The Delicate Distress* (1769) . . . DLB-39

Griffith, George 1857-1906 . . . . DLB-178

Ralph Griffiths [publishing house] DLB-154

Griffiths, Trevor 1935- DLB-13, 245

S. C. Griggs and Company DLB-49

Griggs, Sutton Elbert 1872-1930 . . . . DLB-50

Grignon, Claude-Henri 1894-1976 . . . . . . DLB-68

Grigor'ev, Apollon Aleksandrovich 1822-1864 . . . . DLB-277

Grigorovich, Dmitrii Vasil'evich 1822-1899 . . . . DLB-238

Grigson, Geoffrey 1905-1985 . . . . DLB-27

Grillparzer, Franz 1791-1872 . . . . DLB-133; CDWLB-2

Grimald, Nicholas circa 1519-circa 1562 . . . . DLB-136

Grimké, Angelina Weld 1880-1958 . . . DLB-50, 54

Grimké, Sarah Moore 1792-1873 . . . . . . DLB-239

Grimm, Frédéric Melchior 1723-1807 . . . DLB-313

Grimm, Hans 1875-1959 . . . . DLB-66

Grimm, Jacob 1785-1863 . . . . DLB-90

Grimm, Wilhelm 1786-1859 . . . . DLB-90; CDWLB-2

Grimmelshausen, Johann Jacob Christoffel von 1621 or 1622-1676 . . . . . DLB-168; CDWLB-2

Grimshaw, Beatrice Ethel 1871-1953 . . . . DLB-174

Grímur Thomsen 1820-1896 . . . . DLB-293

Grin, Aleksandr Stepanovich 1880-1932 . . . . DLB-272

Grindal, Edmund 1519 or 1520-1583 . . . . DLB-132

Gripe, Maria (Kristina) 1923-2007 . . . . . . DLB-257

Griswold, Rufus Wilmot 1815-1857 . . . . DLB-3, 59, 250

Gronlund, Laurence 1846-1899 . . . . DLB-303

Grosart, Alexander Balloch 1827-1899 . . . DLB-184

Grosholz, Emily 1950- DLB-282

Gross, Milt 1895-1953 . . . . DLB-11

Grosset and Dunlap DLB-49

Grosseteste, Robert circa 1160-1253 . . . . . DLB-115

Grossman, Allen 1932- DLB-193

Grossman, David 1954- DLB-299

Grossman, Vasilii Semenovich 1905-1964 . . . . DLB-272

Grossman Publishers DLB-46

Grosvenor, Gilbert H. 1875-1966 . . . . DLB-91

Groth, Klaus 1819-1899 . . . . DLB-129

Groulx, Lionel 1878-1967 . . . . DLB-68

Grove, Frederick Philip (Felix Paul Greve) 1879-1948 . . . . DLB-92

Grove Press DLB-46

Groys, Boris Efimovich 1947- DLB-285

Grubb, Davis 1919-1980 . . . . DLB-6

Gruelle, Johnny 1880-1938 . . . . DLB-22

von Grumbach, Argula 1492-after 1563? DLB-179

Grundtvig, N. F. S. 1783-1872 . . . . DLB-300

Grundy, Sydney 1848-1914 . . . . DLB-344

Grymeston, Elizabeth before 1563-before 1604 . . . . DLB-136

Grynberg, Henryk 1936- DLB-299

Gryphius, Andreas 1616-1664 . . . . DLB-164; CDWLB-2

Gryphius, Christian 1649-1706 . . . . DLB-168

Guare, John 1938- DLB-7, 249

Guarini, Battista 1538-1612 . . . . DLB-339

Guarnieri, Gianfrancesco 1934- DLB-307

Guberman, Igor Mironovich 1936- DLB-285

Guðbergur Bergsson 1932- DLB-293

Guðmundur Böðvarsson 1904-1974 . . . . . DLB-293

Guðmundur Gíslason Hagalín 1898-1985 . . . . DLB-293

Guðmundur Magnússon (see Jón Trausti)

Guerra, Tonino 1920- DLB-128

Guest, Barbara 1920- DLB-5, 193

Guevara, Fray Antonio de 1480?-1545 . . . DLB-318

Guèvremont, Germaine 1893-1968 . . . . . . DLB-68

Guglielminetti, Amalia 1881-1941 . . . . . . DLB-264

Guidacci, Margherita 1921-1992 . . . . DLB-128

Guillén, Jorge 1893-1984 . . . . DLB-108

Guillén, Nicolás 1902-1989 . . . . DLB-283

Guilloux, Louis 1899-1980 . . . . DLB-72

Guilpin, Everard circa 1572-after 1608? DLB-136

Guiney, Louise Imogen 1861-1920 . . . . . . DLB-54

Guiterman, Arthur 1871-1943 . . . . DLB-11

Gul', Roman 1896-1986 . . . . DLB-317

Gumilev, Nikolai Stepanovich 1886-1921 . . . . DLB-295

Günderrode, Caroline von 1780-1806 . . . . DLB-90

Gundulić, Ivan 1589-1638 . . . DLB-147; CDWLB-4

Gunesekera, Romesh 1954- DLB-267, 323

Gunn, Bill 1934-1989 . . . . DLB-38

Gunn, James E. 1923- DLB-8

Gunn, Neil M. 1891-1973 . . . . DLB-15

Gunn, Thom 1929- DLB-27; CDBLB-8

Gunnar Gunnarsson 1889-1975 . . . . DLB-293

Gunnars, Kristjana 1948- DLB-60

Günther, Johann Christian 1695-1723 . . . DLB-168

Gupta, Sunetra 1965- DLB-323

Gurik, Robert 1932- DLB-60

Gurney, A. R. 1930- DLB-266

Gurney, Ivor 1890-1937..................Y-02

    The Ivor Gurney Society Y-98

Guro, Elena Genrikhovna 1877-1913.....DLB-295

Gustafson, Ralph 1909-1995 ....DLB-88

Gustafsson, Lars 1936- DLB-257

Gütersloh, Albert Paris 1887-1973 ....DLB-81

Guterson, David 1956- DLB-292

Guthrie, A. B., Jr. 1901-1991 ....DLB-6, 212

Guthrie, Ramon 1896-1973 ....DLB-4

Guthrie, Thomas Anstey (see Anstey, FC)

Guthrie, Woody 1912-1967 ....DLB-303

The Guthrie Theater DLB-7

Gutiérrez Nájera, Manuel 1859-1895.....DLB-290

Guttormur J. Guttormsson 1878-1966....DLB-293

Gutzkow, Karl 1811-1878..............DLB-133

Guy, Ray 1939- DLB-60

Guy, Rosa 1925- DLB-33

Guyot, Arnold 1807-1884 ....DS-13

Gwynn, R. S. 1948- DLB-282

Gwynne, Erskine 1898-1948 ....DLB-4

Gyles, John 1680-1755................DLB-99

Gyllembourg, Thomasine 1773-1856.....DLB-300

Gyllensten, Lars 1921- DLB-257

Gyrðir Elíasson 1961- DLB-293

Gysin, Brion 1916-1986...............DLB-16

H

H.D. (see Doolittle, Hilda)

Habiby, Emile 1922-1996..............DLB-346

Habermas, Jürgen 1929- DLB-242

Habington, William 1605-1654 ....DLB-126

Hacker, Marilyn 1942- DLB-120, 282

Hackett, Albert 1900-1995.............DLB-26

Hacks, Peter 1928- DLB-124

Hadas, Rachel 1948- DLB-120, 282

Hadden, Briton 1898-1929 ....DLB-91

Hagedorn, Friedrich von 1708-1754......DLB-168

Hagedorn, Jessica Tarahata 1949- DLB-312

Hagelstange, Rudolf 1912-1984.........DLB-69

Hagerup, Inger 1905-1985.............DLB-297

Haggard, H. Rider
    1856-1925 ....DLB-70, 156, 174, 178

Haggard, William (Richard Clayton)
    1907-1993 ....DLB-276; Y-93

Hagy, Alyson 1960- DLB-244

Hahn-Hahn, Ida Gräfin von 1805-1880...DLB-133

Haig-Brown, Roderick 1908-1976 ....DLB-88

Haight, Gordon S. 1901-1985 ....DLB-103

Hailey, Arthur 1920-2004 .... DLB-88; Y-82

Haines, John 1924- DLB-5, 212

Hake, Edward fl. 1566-1604 ....DLB-136

Hake, Thomas Gordon 1809-1895 ....DLB-32

Hakluyt, Richard 1552?-1616 ....DLB-136

Halas, František 1901-1949 ....DLB-215

Halbe, Max 1865-1944 ....DLB-118

Halberstam, David 1934-2007..........DLB-241

Haldane, Charlotte 1894-1969.........DLB-191

Haldane, J. B. S. 1892-1964..........DLB-160

Haldeman, Joe 1943- DLB-8

Haldeman-Julius Company DLB-46

Hale, E. J., and Son DLB-49

Hale, Edward Everett
    1822-1909 ....DLB-1, 42, 74, 235

Hale, Janet Campbell 1946- DLB-175

Hale, Kathleen 1898-2000 ....DLB-160

Hale, Leo Thomas (see Ebon)

Hale, Lucretia Peabody 1820-1900 ....DLB-42

Hale, Nancy
    1908-1988 .... DLB-86; DS-17; Y-80, 88

Hale, Sarah Josepha (Buell)
    1788-1879 ....DLB-1, 42, 73, 243

Hale, Susan 1833-1910 ....DLB-221

Hales, John 1584-1656................DLB-151

Halévy, Ludovic 1834-1908............DLB-192

Haley, Alex 1921-1992........DLB-38; CDALB-7

Haliburton, Thomas Chandler
    1796-1865 ....DLB-11, 99

Hall, Adam (Trevor Dudley-Smith)
    1920-1995 ....DLB-276

Hall, Anna Maria 1800-1881 ....DLB-159

Hall, Donald 1928- DLB-5, 342

Hall, Edward 1497-1547...............DLB-132

Hall, Halsey 1898-1977 ....DLB-241

Hall, James 1793-1868 .... DLB-73, 74

Hall, James B. 1918- DLB-335

Hall, Joseph 1574-1656 ....DLB-121, 151

Hall, Radclyffe 1880-1943 ....DLB-191

Hall, Rodney 1935- DLB-289

Hall, Sarah Ewing 1761-1830 ....DLB-200

Hall, Stuart 1932- DLB-242

Samuel Hall [publishing house] DLB-49

al-Hallaj 857-922 ....DLB-311

Hallam, Arthur Henry 1811-1833 ....DLB-32

    On Some of the Characteristics of
    Modern Poetry and On the
    Lyrical Poems of Alfred
    Tennyson (1831)................DLB-32

Halldór Laxness (Halldór Guðjónsson)
    1902-1998 ....DLB-293, 331

Halleck, Fitz-Greene 1790-1867 ......DLB-3, 250

Haller, Albrecht von 1708-1777 ....DLB-168

Halliday, Brett (see Dresser, Davis)

Halligan, Marion 1940- DLB-325

Halliwell-Phillipps, James Orchard
    1820-1889 ....DLB-184

Hallmann, Johann Christian
    1640-1704 or 1716?..............DLB-168

Hallmark Editions DLB-46

Halper, Albert 1904-1984 ....DLB-9

Halperin, John William 1941- DLB-111

Halpern, Moshe Leib (Moyshe Leyb Halpern)
    1886-1932.....................DLB-333

Halstead, Murat 1829-1908............DLB-23

Hamann, Johann Georg 1730-1788 ....DLB-97

Hamburger, Michael 1924- DLB-27

Hamilton, Alexander 1712-1756.........DLB-31

Hamilton, Alexander 1755?-1804 ....DLB-37

Hamilton, Cicely 1872-1952 .... DLB-10, 197

Hamilton, Edmond 1904-1977............DLB-8

Hamilton, Elizabeth 1758-1816 .....DLB-116, 158

Hamilton, Gail (see Corcoran, Barbara)

Hamilton, Gail (see Dodge, Mary Abigail)

Hamish Hamilton Limited.............DLB-112

Hamilton, Hugo 1953- DLB-267

Hamilton, Ian 1938-2001...........DLB-40, 155

Hamilton, Janet 1795-1873............DLB-199

Hamilton, Mary Agnes 1884-1962 ......DLB-197

Hamilton, Patrick 1904-1962........DLB-10, 191

Hamilton, Virginia 1936-2002... DLB-33, 52; Y-01

Hamilton, Sir William 1788-1856 ....DLB-262

Hamilton-Paterson, James 1941- DLB-267

Hammerstein, Oscar, 2nd 1895-1960 ... DLB-265

Hammett, Dashiell
    1894-1961........DLB-226; DS-6; CDALB-5

    An Appeal in TAC....................Y-91

    The Glass Key and Other Dashiell
    Hammett Mysteries Y-96

    Knopf to Hammett: The Editoral
    Correspondence.................Y-00

    The Maltese Falcon (Documentary) DLB-280

Hammon, Jupiter 1711-died between
    1790 and 1806.................DLB-31, 50

Hammond, John ?-1663................DLB-24

Hamner, Earl 1923- DLB-6

Hampson, John 1901-1955 ....DLB-191

Hampton, Christopher 1946- DLB-13

Hamsun, Knut 1859-1952 .... DLB-297, 330

Handel-Mazzetti, Enrica von 1871-1955 ...DLB-81

Handke, Peter 1942- DLB-85, 124

Handlin, Oscar 1915- DLB-17

Hankin, St. John 1869-1909............DLB-10

Hanley, Clifford 1922- DLB-14

Hanley, James 1901-1985..............DLB-191

Hannah, Barry 1942- DLB-6, 234

Hannay, James 1827-1873..............DLB-21

Cumulative Index

Hannes Hafstein 1861-1922 . . . . DLB-293

Hano, Arnold 1922- DLB-241

Hanrahan, Barbara 1939-1991 . . . . DLB-289

Hansberry, Lorraine
1930-1965 . . . . DLB-7, 38; CDALB-1

Hansen, Joseph 1923-2004 . . . . DLB-226

Hansen, Martin A. 1909-1955 . . . . DLB-214

Hansen, Thorkild 1927-1989 . . . . DLB-214

Hanson, Elizabeth 1684-1737 . . . . DLB-200

Hapgood, Norman 1868-1937 . . . . DLB-91

Happel, Eberhard Werner 1647-1690 . . . . DLB-168

Haq, Kaiser 1950- DLB-323

Harbach, Otto 1873-1963 . . . . DLB-265

The Harbinger 1845-1849 . . . . DLB-1, 223

Harburg, E. Y. "Yip" 1896-1981 . . . . DLB-265

Harcourt Brace Jovanovich DLB-46

Hardenberg, Friedrich von (see Novalis)

Harding, Walter 1917-1996 . . . . DLB-111

Hardwick, Elizabeth 1916- DLB-6

Hardy, Alexandre 1572?-1632 . . . . DLB-268

Hardy, Frank 1917-1994 . . . . DLB-260

Hardy, Thomas
1840-1928 . . . . . . DLB-18, 19, 135; CDBLB-5

"Candour in English Fiction" (1890). . . . DLB-18

Hare, Cyril 1900-1958 . . . . DLB-77

Hare, David 1947- DLB-13, 310

Hare, R. M. 1919-2002 . . . . DLB-262

Hargrove, Marion 1919-2003 . . . . DLB-11

Häring, Georg Wilhelm Heinrich
(see Alexis, Willibald)

Harington, Donald 1935- DLB-152

Harington, Sir John 1560-1612 . . . . DLB-136

Harjo, Joy 1951- DLB-120, 175, 342

Harkness, Margaret (John Law)
1854-1923 . . . . DLB-197

Harley, Edward, second Earl of Oxford
1689-1741 . . . . DLB-213

Harley, Robert, first Earl of Oxford
1661-1724 . . . . DLB-213

Harlow, Robert 1923- DLB-60

Harman, Moses 1830-1910 . . . . DLB-345

Harman, Thomas fl. 1566-1573 . . . . DLB-136

Harness, Charles L. 1915- DLB-8

Harnett, Cynthia 1893-1981 . . . . DLB-161

Harnick, Sheldon 1924- DLB-265

Tribute to Ira Gershwin Y-96

Tribute to Lorenz Hart Y-95

Harper, Edith Alice Mary (see Wickham, Anna)

Harper, Fletcher 1806-1877 . . . . DLB-79

Harper, Frances Ellen Watkins
1825-1911 . . . . DLB-50, 221

Harper, Michael S. 1938- DLB-41

Harper and Brothers DLB-49

Harpur, Charles 1813-1868 . . . . DLB-230

Harraden, Beatrice 1864-1943 . . . . DLB-153

George G. Harrap and Company
Limited DLB-112

Harriot, Thomas 1560-1621 . . . . DLB-136

Harris, Alexander 1805-1874 . . . . DLB-230

Harris, Benjamin ?-circa 1720 . . . . DLB-42, 43

Harris, Christie 1907-2002 . . . . DLB-88

Harris, Claire 1937- DLB-334

Harris, Errol E. 1908- DLB-279

Harris, Frank 1856-1931 . . . . DLB-156, 197

Harris, George Washington
1814-1869 . . . . DLB-3, 11, 248

Harris, Joanne 1964- DLB-271

Harris, Joel Chandler
1848-1908 . . . . DLB-11, 23, 42, 78, 91

The Joel Chandler Harris Association Y-99

Harris, Mark 1922-2007 . . . . DLB-2; Y-80

Tribute to Frederick A. Pottle Y-87

Harris, William 1720-1770 . . . . DLB-336

Harris, William Torrey 1835-1909 . . . . . . DLB-270

Harris, Wilson 1921- DLB-117; CDWLB-3

Harrison, Mrs. Burton
(see Harrison, Constance Cary)

Harrison, Charles Yale 1898-1954 . . . . . . DLB-68

Harrison, Constance Cary 1843-1920 . . . DLB-221

Harrison, Frederic 1831-1923 . . . . DLB-57, 190

"On Style in English Prose" (1898) . . . DLB-57

Harrison, Harry 1925- DLB-8

James P. Harrison Company DLB-49

Harrison, Jim 1937- Y-82

Harrison, M. John 1945- DLB-261

Harrison, Mary St. Leger Kingsley
(see Malet, Lucas)

Harrison, Paul Carter 1936- DLB-38

Harrison, Susan Frances 1859-1935 . . . . . DLB-99

Harrison, Tony 1937- DLB-40, 245

Harrison, William 1535-1593 . . . . DLB-136

Harrison, William 1933- DLB-234

Harrisse, Henry 1829-1910 . . . . DLB-47

Harry, J. S. 1939- DLB-325

The Harry Ransom Humanities Research Center
at the University of Texas at Austin Y-00

Harryman, Carla 1952- DLB-193

Harsdörffer, Georg Philipp 1607-1658 . . . DLB-164

Harsent, David 1942- DLB-40

Hart, Albert Bushnell 1854-1943 . . . . DLB-17

Hart, Anne 1768-1834 . . . . DLB-200

Hart, Elizabeth 1771-1833 . . . . DLB-200

Hart, Jonathan Locke 1956- DLB-334

Hart, Julia Catherine 1796-1867 . . . . DLB-99

Hart, Kevin 1954- DLB-325

Hart, Lorenz 1895-1943 . . . . DLB-265

Larry Hart: Still an Influence Y-95

Lorenz Hart: An American Lyricist Y-95

The Lorenz Hart Centenary Y-95

Hart, Moss 1904-1961 . . . . DLB-7, 266

Hart, Oliver 1723-1795 . . . . DLB-31

Rupert Hart-Davis Limited DLB-112

Harte, Bret 1836-1902
. . . . DLB-12, 64, 74, 79, 186; CDALB-3

Harte, Edward Holmead 1922- DLB-127

Harte, Houston Harriman 1927- DLB-127

Harte, Jack 1944- DLB-319

Hartlaub, Felix 1913-1945 . . . . DLB-56

Hartleben, Otto Erich 1864-1905 . . . . . . DLB-118

Hartley, David 1705-1757 . . . . DLB-252

Hartley, L. P. 1895-1972 . . . . DLB-15, 139

Hartley, Marsden 1877-1943 . . . . DLB-54

Hartling, Peter 1933- DLB-75

Hartman, Geoffrey H. 1929- DLB-67

Hartmann, Sadakichi 1867-1944 . . . . DLB-54

Hartmann von Aue
circa 1160-circa 1205 . . . . DLB-138; CDWLB-2

Hartshorne, Charles 1897-2000 . . . . DLB-270

Haruf, Kent 1943- DLB-292

Harvey, Gabriel 1550?-1631 . . . . DLB-167, 213, 281

Harvey, Jack (see Rankin, Ian)

Harvey, Jean-Charles 1891-1967 . . . . DLB-88

Harvill Press Limited DLB-112

Harwood, Gwen 1920-1995 . . . . DLB-289

Harwood, Lee 1939- DLB-40

Harwood, Ronald 1934- DLB-13

al-Hasan al-Basri 642-728 . . . . DLB-311

Hašek, Jaroslav 1883-1923 . . . DLB-215; CDWLB-4

Haskins, Charles Homer 1870-1937 . . . . . DLB-47

Haskins, Lola 1943- DLB-342

Haslam, Gerald 1937- DLB-212

Hass, Robert 1941- DLB-105, 206

Hasselstrom, Linda M. 1943- DLB-256

Hastings, Michael 1938- DLB-233

Hatar, Győző 1914- DLB-215

The Hatch-Billops Collection DLB-76

Hathaway, William 1944- DLB-120

Hatherly, Ana 1929- DLB-287

Hauch, Carsten 1790-1872 . . . . DLB-300

Hauff, Wilhelm 1802-1827 . . . . DLB-90

Hauge, Olav H. 1908-1994 . . . . DLB-297

Haugen, Paal-Helge 1945- DLB-297

Haugwitz, August Adolph von
1647-1706 . . . . DLB-168

Hauptmann, Carl 1858-1921 . . . . . . DLB-66, 118

Hauptmann, Gerhart
1862-1946 . . . . . DLB-66, 118, 330; CDWLB-2

Hauser, Marianne 1910-2006. . . . . .Y-83

Havel, Václav 1936- DLB-232; CDWLB-4

Haven, Alice B. Neal 1827-1863. . . . . .DLB-250

Havergal, Frances Ridley 1836-1879 . . . . .DLB-199

Hawes, Stephen 1475?-before 1529 . . . . . .DLB-132

Hawker, Robert Stephen 1803-1875. . . . . . .DLB-32

Hawkes, John
   1925-1998 . . . . DLB-2, 7, 227; Y-80, Y-98

   John Hawkes: A Tribute Y-98

   Tribute to Donald Barthelme Y-89

Hawkesworth, John 1720-1773. . . . . .DLB-142

Hawkins, Sir Anthony Hope (see Hope, Anthony)

Hawkins, Sir John 1719-1789 . . . DLB-104, 142, 336

Hawkins, Walter Everette 1883-?. DLB-50

Hawthorne, Nathaniel 1804-1864
   . . . DLB-1, 74, 183, 223, 269; DS-5; CDALB-2

   The Nathaniel Hawthorne Society Y-00

   The Old Manse. DLB-223

Hawthorne, Sophia Peabody
   1809-1871 . . . . .DLB-183, 239

Hay, John 1835-1905 . . . . DLB-12, 47, 189

Hay, John 1915- DLB-275

Hayashi Fumiko 1903-1951. . . . . .DLB-180

Haycox, Ernest 1899-1950. . . . . .DLB-206

Haycraft, Anna Margaret (see Ellis, Alice Thomas)

Hayden, Robert
   1913-1980 . . . . .DLB-5, 76; CDALB-1

Haydon, Benjamin Robert 1786-1846. . . .DLB-110

Hayes, John Michael 1919- DLB-26

Hayley, William 1745-1820 . . . . .DLB-93, 142

Haym, Rudolf 1821-1901 . . . . .DLB-129

Hayman, Robert 1575-1629. . . . . .DLB-99

Hayman, Ronald 1932- DLB-155

Hayne, Paul Hamilton
   1830-1886 . . . . DLB-3, 64, 79, 248

Hays, Mary 1760-1843. . . . . .DLB-142, 158

Hayslip, Le Ly 1949- DLB-312

Hayward, John 1905-1965. . . . . .DLB-201

Haywood, Eliza 1693?-1756. . . . . .DLB-39

   Dedication of *Lasselia* [excerpt]
   (1723) DLB-39

   Preface to *The Disguis'd Prince*
   [excerpt] (1723) DLB-39

   The Tea-Table [excerpt] DLB-39

Haywood, William D. 1869-1928 . . . . . . .DLB-303

Willis P. Hazard [publishing house]. DLB-49

Hazelton, George C., Jr. 1868-1921 . . . . . .DLB-341

Hazlewood, C. H. 1819-1875. . . . . .DLB-344

Hazlitt, William 1778-1830. . . . . .DLB-110, 158

Hazzard, Shirley 1931- DLB-289; Y-82

Head, Bessie
   1937-1986 . . . . DLB-117, 225; CDWLB-3

Headley, Joel T. 1813-1897 . . .DLB-30, 183; DS-13

Heaney, Seamus 1939- DLB-40, 330;
   Y-95; CDBLB-8

   Nobel Lecture 1994: Crediting Poetry Y-95

Heard, Nathan C. 1936- DLB-33

Hearn, Lafcadio 1850-1904 . . . . . . DLB-12, 78, 189

Hearn, Mary Anne (Marianne Farningham,
   Eva Hope) 1834-1909 . . . . .DLB-240

Hearne, John 1926- DLB-117

Hearne, Samuel 1745-1792. . . . . .DLB-99

Hearne, Thomas 1678?-1735. . . . . . .DLB-213, 336

Hearst, William Randolph 1863-1951 . . . . .DLB-25

Hearst, William Randolph, Jr.
   1908-1993 . . . . .DLB-127

Heartman, Charles Frederick
   1883-1953 . . . . .DLB-187

Heat and Dust, 1975 Booker Prize winner,
   Ruth Prawer Jhabvala DLB-326

Heath, Catherine 1924-1991 . . . . .DLB-14

Heath, James Ewell 1792-1862. . . . . .DLB-248

Heath, Roy A. K. 1926- DLB-117

Heath-Stubbs, John 1918- DLB-27

Heavysege, Charles 1816-1876 . . . . .DLB-99

Hebbel, Friedrich
   1813-1863 . . . . .DLB-129; CDWLB-2

Hebel, Johann Peter 1760-1826 . . . . .DLB-90

Heber, Richard 1774-1833 . . . . .DLB-184

Hébert, Anne 1916-2000 . . . . .DLB-68

Hébert, Jacques 1923-2007 . . . . .DLB-53

Hebreo, León circa 1460-1520. . . . . .DLB-318

Hecht, Anthony 1923-2004 . . . . .DLB-5, 169

Hecht, Ben 1894-1964 . . . . DLB-7, 9, 25, 26, 28, 86

Hecker, Isaac Thomas 1819-1888 . . . . DLB-1, 243

Hedge, Frederic Henry
   1805-1890 . . . . DLB-1, 59, 243; DS-5

Hefner, Hugh M. 1926- DLB-137

Hegel, Georg Wilhelm Friedrich
   1770-1831 . . . . .DLB-90

Heiberg, Johan Ludvig 1791-1860. . . . . . .DLB-300

Heiberg, Johanne Luise 1812-1890 . . . . . .DLB-300

Heide, Robert 1939- DLB-249

Heidegger, Martin 1889-1976. . . . . .DLB-296

Heidenstam, Verner von 1859-1940 . . . . .DLB-330

Heidish, Marcy 1947- Y-82

Heißenbüttel, Helmut 1921-1996 . . . . .DLB-75

Heike monogatari DLB-203

Hein, Christoph 1944- DLB-124; CDWLB-2

Hein, Piet 1905-1996. . . . . .DLB-214

Heine, Heinrich 1797-1856. . . .DLB-90; CDWLB-2

Heinemann, Larry 1944- DS-9

William Heinemann Limited DLB-112

Heinesen, William 1900-1991 . . . . .DLB-214

Heinlein, Robert A. 1907-1988 . . . . .DLB-8

Heinrich, Willi 1920-2005 . . . . .DLB-75

Heinrich Julius of Brunswick
   1564-1613 . . . . .DLB-164

Heinrich von dem Türlîn
   fl. circa 1230 . . . . .DLB-138

Heinrich von Melk
   fl. after 1160 .DLB-148

Heinrich von Veldeke
   circa 1145-circa 1190. . . . . .DLB-138

Heinse, Wilhelm 1746-1803. . . . . .DLB-94

Heinz, W. C. 1915-2008 . . . . .DLB-171

Heiskell, John 1872-1972 . . . . .DLB-127

Hejinian, Lyn 1941- DLB-165

Helder, Herberto 1930- DLB-287

Heliand circa 850 . . . . .DLB-148

Heller, Joseph
   1923-1999 . . . . . . DLB-2, 28, 227; Y-80, 99, 02

   Excerpts from Joseph Heller's
   USC Address, "The Literature
   of Despair". Y-96

   Remembering Joe Heller, by William
   Price Fox. Y-99

   A Tribute to Joseph Heller Y-99

Heller, Michael 1937- DLB-165

Hellman, Lillian 1906-1984 . . . . . DLB-7, 228; Y-84

Hellwig, Johann 1609-1674 . . . . .DLB-164

Helprin, Mark
   1947- DLB-335; Y-85; CDALB-7

Helvétius, Claude-Adrien 1715-1771 . . . . .DLB-313

   The Spirit of Laws DLB-314

Helwig, David 1938- DLB-60

Hemans, Felicia 1793-1835. . . . . .DLB-96

Hemenway, Abby Maria 1828-1890 . . . . .DLB-243

Hemingway, Ernest 1899-1961. . . . . . . DLB-4, 9, 102,
   210, 316, 330; Y-81, 87, 99; DS-1, 15, 16; CDALB-4

   A Centennial Celebration Y-99

   Come to Papa Y-99

   The Ernest Hemingway Collection at
   the John F. Kennedy Library Y-99

   Ernest Hemingway Declines to
   Introduce *War and Peace*. Y-01

   Ernest Hemingway's Reaction to
   James Gould Cozzens. Y-98

   Ernest Hemingway's Toronto Journalism
   Revisited: With Three Previously
   Unrecorded Stories. Y-92

   Falsifying Hemingway. Y-96

   A Farewell to Arms (Documentary) DLB-308

   Hemingway Centenary Celebration
   at the JFK Library Y-99

   The Hemingway/Fenton
   Correspondence Y-02

   Hemingway in the JFK Y-99

   The Hemingway Letters Project
   Finds an Editor. Y-02

   Hemingway Salesmen's Dummies Y-00

   Hemingway: Twenty-Five Years Later. Y-85

   A Literary Archaeologist Digs On:
   A Brief Interview with Michael
   Reynolds. Y-99

Not Immediately Discernible . . . but
 Eventually Quite Clear: The *First
 Light* and *Final Years* of
 Hemingway's Centenary Y-99

Packaging Papa: *The Garden of Eden* Y-86

Second International Hemingway
 Colloquium: Cuba. Y-98

Hémon, Louis 1880-1913 . . . . DLB-92

Hempel, Amy 1951- DLB-218

Hempel, Carl G. 1905-1997 . . . . DLB-279

Hemphill, Paul 1936- Y-87

Hénault, Gilles 1920-1996 . . . . DLB-88

Henchman, Daniel 1689-1761. . . . . DLB-24

Henderson, Alice Corbin 1881-1949 . . . . . DLB-54

Henderson, Archibald 1877-1963 . . . . DLB-103

Henderson, David 1942- DLB-41

Henderson, George Wylie 1904-1965 . . . . DLB-51

Henderson, Zenna 1917-1983 . . . . DLB-8

Henighan, Tom 1934- DLB-251

Henisch, Peter 1943- DLB-85

Henley, Beth 1952- Y-86

Henley, William Ernest 1849-1903 . . . . DLB-19

Henniker, Florence 1855-1923 . . . . DLB-135

Henning, Rachel 1826-1914 . . . . DLB-230

Henningsen, Agnes 1868-1962 . . . . DLB-214

Henry, Alexander 1739-1824 . . . . DLB-99

Henry, Buck 1930- DLB-26

Henry, Marguerite 1902-1997 . . . . DLB-22

Henry, O. (see Porter, William Sydney)

Henry, Robert Selph 1889-1970 . . . . DLB-17

Henry, Will (see Allen, Henry W.)

Henry VIII of England 1491-1547 . . . . . . DLB-132

Henry of Ghent
 circa 1217-1229 - 1293 . . . . DLB-115

Henryson, Robert
 1420s or 1430s-circa 1505 . . . . DLB-146

Henschke, Alfred (see Klabund)

Hensher, Philip 1965- DLB-267

Hensley, Sophie Almon 1866-1946 . . . . DLB-99

Henson, Lance 1944- DLB-175

Hentoff, Nat 1925- DLB-345

Hess, Karl 1923-1994 . . . . DLB-345

Henty, G. A. 1832-1902 . . . . DLB-18, 141

The Henty Society Y-98

Hentz, Caroline Lee 1800-1856 . . . . . . DLB-3, 248

Heraclitus fl. circa 500 B.C. DLB-176

Herbert, Agnes circa 1880-1960 . . . . DLB-174

Herbert, Alan Patrick 1890-1971 . . . . DLB-10, 191

Herbert, Edward, Lord, of Cherbury
 1582-1648 . . . . DLB-121, 151, 252

Herbert, Frank 1920-1986 . . . . . DLB-8; CDALB-7

Herbert, George 1593-1633 . . DLB-126; CDBLB-1

Herbert, Henry William 1807-1858 . . . . DLB-3, 73

Herbert, John 1926-2001 . . . . DLB-53

Herbert, Mary Sidney, Countess of Pembroke
 (see Sidney, Mary)

Herbert, Xavier 1901-1984 . . . . DLB-260

Herbert, Zbigniew
 1924-1998 . . . . DLB-232; CDWLB-4

Herbst, Josephine 1892-1969 . . . . DLB-9

Herburger, Gunter 1932- DLB-75, 124

Herculano, Alexandre 1810-1877 . . . . DLB-287

Hercules, Frank E. M. 1917-1996 . . . . DLB-33

Herder, Johann Gottfried 1744-1803 . . . . . DLB-97

B. Herder Book Company DLB-49

Heredia, José-María de 1842-1905 . . . . . . DLB-217

Herford, Charles Harold 1853-1931 . . . . . DLB-149

Hergesheimer, Joseph 1880-1954 . . . . . DLB-9, 102

Heritage Press DLB-46

Hermann the Lame 1013-1054 . . . . DLB-148

Hermes, Johann Timotheu 1738-1821 . . . . DLB-97

Hermlin, Stephan 1915-1997 . . . . DLB-69

Hernández, Alfonso C. 1938- DLB-122

Hernández, Inés 1947- DLB-122

Hernández, Miguel 1910-1942 . . . . DLB-134

Hernton, Calvin C. 1932- DLB-38

Herodotus circa 484 B.C.-circa 420 B.C.
 . . . . DLB-176; CDWLB-1

Héroët, Antoine 1490?-1567? DLB-327

Heron, Robert 1764-1807 . . . . DLB-142

Herr, Michael 1940- DLB-185

Herrera, Darío 1870-1914 . . . . DLB-290

Herrera, Fernando de 1534?-1597 . . . . . . DLB-318

Herrera, Juan Felipe 1948- DLB-122

E. R. Herrick and Company DLB-49

Herrick, Robert 1591-1674 . . . . DLB-126

Herrick, Robert 1868-1938. . . . . DLB-9, 12, 78

Herrick, William 1915-2004 . . . . Y-83

Herrmann, John 1900-1959 . . . . DLB-4

Hersey, John
 1914-1993 . . . DLB-6, 185, 278, 299; CDALB-7

Hertel, François 1905-1985 . . . . DLB-68

Hervé-Bazin, Jean Pierre Marie (see Bazin, Hervé)

Hervey, John, Lord 1696-1743 . . . . DLB-101

Herwig, Georg 1817-1875 . . . . DLB-133

Herzen, Alexander (Aleksandr Ivanovich
 Gersten) 1812-1870 . . . . DLB-277

Herzog, Emile Salomon Wilhelm
 (see Maurois, André)

Hesiod eighth century B.C. DLB-176

Hess, Karl 1923-1994 . . . . DLB-345

Hesse, Hermann
 1877-1962 . . . . DLB-66, 330; CDWLB-2

Hessus, Eobanus 1488-1540 . . . . DLB-179

Heureka! (see Kertész, Imre and Nobel Prize
 in Literature: 2002) Y-02

Hewat, Alexander circa 1743-circa 1824 . . . DLB-30

Hewett, Dorothy 1923-2002 . . . . DLB-289

Hewitt, John 1907-1987 . . . . DLB-27

Hewlett, Maurice 1861-1923 . . . . . . DLB-34, 156

Heyen, William 1940- DLB-5

Heyer, Georgette 1902-1974 . . . . DLB-77, 191

Heym, Stefan 1913-2001 . . . . DLB-69

Heyse, Paul 1830-1914 . . . . DLB-129, 330

Heytesbury, William
 circa 1310-1372 or 1373 . . . . DLB-115

Heyward, Dorothy 1890-1961 . . . . DLB-7, 249

Heyward, DuBose 1885-1940 . . . DLB-7, 9, 45, 249

Heywood, John 1497?-1580? DLB-136

Heywood, Thomas 1573 or 1574-1641 . . . . DLB-62

Hiaasen, Carl 1953- DLB-292

Hibberd, Jack 1940- DLB-289

Hibbs, Ben 1901-1975 . . . . DLB-137

"The Saturday Evening Post reaffirms
 a policy," Ben Hibb's Statement
 in *The Saturday Evening Post*
 (16 May 1942) DLB-137

Hichens, Robert S. 1864-1950 . . . . DLB-153

Hickey, Emily 1845-1924 . . . . DLB-199

Hickman, William Albert 1877-1957 . . . . . DLB-92

Hicks, Granville 1901-1982 . . . . DLB-246

Hidalgo, José Luis 1919-1947 . . . . DLB-108

Hiebert, Paul 1892-1987 . . . . DLB-68

Hieng, Andrej 1925- DLB-181

Hierro, José 1922-2002 . . . . DLB-108

Higgins, Aidan 1927- DLB-14

Higgins, Colin 1941-1988 . . . . DLB-26

Higgins, George V.
 1939-1999 . . . . DLB-2; Y-81, 98–99

Afterword [in response to Cozzen's
 Mens Rea (or Something)] Y-97

At End of Day: The Last George V.
 Higgins Novel Y-99

The Books of George V. Higgins:
 A Checklist of Editions
 and Printings Y-00

George V. Higgins in Class Y-02

Tribute to Alfred A. Knopf Y-84

Tributes to George V. Higgins Y-99

"What You Lose on the Swings You Make
 Up on the Merry-Go-Round" . . . Y-99

Higginson, Thomas Wentworth
 1823-1911 . . . . DLB-1, 64, 243

Highsmith, Patricia 1921-1995 . . . . DLB-306

Highwater, Jamake 1942?- DLB-52; Y-85

Highway, Tomson 1951- DLB-334

Hijuelos, Oscar 1951- DLB-145

Hildegard von Bingen 1098-1179 . . . . DLB-148

Das Hildesbrandslied
 circa 820 . . . . DLB-148; CDWLB-2

Hildesheimer, Wolfgang 1916-1991 . . DLB-69, 124

Hildreth, Richard 1807-1865 ...DLB-1, 30, 59, 235

Hill, Aaron 1685-1750 ....DLB-84

Hill, Geoffrey 1932- DLB-40; CDBLB-8

George M. Hill Company DLB-49

Hill, "Sir" John 1714?-1775................DLB-39

Lawrence Hill and Company, Publishers DLB-46

Hill, Joe 1879-1915..................DLB-303

Hill, Leslie 1880-1960 ....DLB-51

Hill, Reginald 1936- DLB-276

Hill, Susan 1942- DLB-14, 139

Hill, Walter 1942- DLB-44

Hill and Wang DLB-46

Hillberry, Conrad 1928- DLB-120

Hillerman, Tony 1925-2008........DLB-206, 306

Hilliard, Gray and Company...........DLB-49

Hills, Lee 1906-2000 ....DLB-127

Hillyer, Robert 1895-1961 ....DLB-54

Hilsenrath, Edgar 1926- DLB-299

Hilton, James 1900-1954 ....DLB-34, 77

Hilton, Walter died 1396 ....DLB-146

Hilton and Company..................DLB-49

Himes, Chester 1909-1984.... DLB-2, 76, 143, 226

Joseph Hindmarsh [publishing house] DLB-170

Hine, Daryl 1936- DLB-60

Hingley, Ronald 1920- DLB-155

Hinojosa-Smith, Rolando 1929- DLB-82

Hinton, S. E. 1948- CDALB-7

Hippel, Theodor Gottlieb von 1741-1796.....................DLB-97

Hippius, Zinaida Nikolaevna 1869-1945 ....DLB-295

Hippocrates of Cos fl. circa 425 B.C. DLB-176; CDWLB-1

Hirabayashi Taiko 1905-1972 ....DLB-180

Hirsch, E. D., Jr. 1928- DLB-67

Hirsch, Edward 1950- DLB-120

Hirschbein, Peretz (Perets Hirshbeyn) 1880-1948 ....DLB-333

Hirshfield, Jane 1953- DLB-342

"Historical Novel," The Holocaust DLB-299

Hoagland, Edward 1932- DLB-6

Hoagland, Everett H., III 1942- DLB-41

Hoban, Russell 1925- DLB-52; Y-90

Hobbes, Thomas 1588-1679 ...DLB-151, 252, 281

Hobby, Oveta 1905-1995 ....DLB-127

Hobby, William 1878-1964 ....DLB-127

Hobsbaum, Philip 1932- DLB-40

Hobsbawm, Eric (Francis Newton) 1917- DLB-296

Hobson, Laura Z. 1900-1986...........DLB-28

Hobson, Sarah 1947- DLB-204

Hoby, Thomas 1530-1566.............DLB-132

Hoccleve, Thomas circa 1368-circa 1437...............DLB-146

Hoch, Edward D. 1930- DLB-306

Hochhuth, Rolf 1931- DLB-124

Hochman, Sandra 1936- DLB-5

Hocken, Thomas Morland 1836-1910....DLB-184

Hocking, William Ernest 1873-1966 .....DLB-270

Hodder and Stoughton, Limited DLB-106

Hodgins, Jack 1938- DLB-60

Hodgman, Helen 1945- DLB-14

Hodgskin, Thomas 1787-1869 ....DLB-158

Hodgson, Ralph 1871-1962 ....DLB-19

Hodgson, William Hope 1877-1918 .... DLB-70, 153, 156, 178

Hoe, Robert, III 1839-1909 ....DLB-187

Hoeg, Peter 1957- DLB-214

Hoel, Sigurd 1890-1960 ....DLB-297

Hoem, Edvard 1949- DLB-297

Hoffenstein, Samuel 1890-1947 ....DLB-11

Hoffman, Alice 1952- DLB-292

Hoffman, Charles Fenno 1806-1884 ....DLB-3, 250

Hoffman, Daniel 1923- DLB-5

Tribute to Robert Graves Y-85

Hoffmann, E. T. A. 1776-1822.............DLB-90; CDWLB-2

Hoffman, Frank B. 1888-1958..........DLB-188

Hoffman, William 1925- DLB-234

Tribute to Paxton Davis Y-94

Hoffmanswaldau, Christian Hoffman von 1616-1679 ....DLB-168

Hofmann, Michael 1957- DLB-40

Hofmannsthal, Hugo von 1874-1929 .... DLB-81, 118; CDWLB-2

Hofmo, Gunvor 1921-1995 ....DLB-297

Hofstadter, Richard 1916-1970....... DLB-17, 246

Hofstein, David (Dovid Hofshteyn) 1889-1952 ....DLB-333

Hogan, Desmond 1950- DLB-14, 319

Hogan, Linda 1947- DLB-175

Hogan and Thompson DLB-49

Hogarth Press DLB-112; DS-10

Hogg, James 1770-1835 .... DLB-93, 116, 159

Hohberg, Wolfgang Helmhard Freiherr von 1612-1688 ....DLB-168

von Hohenheim, Philippus Aureolus Theophrastus Bombastus (see Paracelsus)

Hohl, Ludwig 1904-1980................DLB-56

Højholt, Per 1928- DLB-214

Holan, Vladimir 1905-1980............DLB-215

d'Holbach, Paul Henri Thiry, baron 1723-1789 ....DLB-313

The System of Nature (as Jean-Baptiste de Mirabaud)..................DLB-314

Holberg, Ludvig 1684-1754............DLB-300

Holbrook, David 1923- DLB-14, 40

Holcroft, Thomas 1745-1809......DLB-39, 89, 158

Preface to *Alwyn* (1780) DLB-39

Holden, Jonathan 1941- DLB-105

"Contemporary Verse Story-telling" ...DLB-105

Holden, Molly 1927-1981 ....DLB-40

Hölderlin, Friedrich 1770-1843 ....DLB-90; CDWLB-2

Holdstock, Robert 1948- DLB-261

Holiday, 1974 Booker Prize winner, Stanley Middleton.................DLB-326

Holiday House.......................DLB-46

Holinshed, Raphael died 1580.........DLB-167

Holland, J. G. 1819-1881................ DS-13

Holland, Norman N. 1927- DLB-67

Hollander, John 1929- DLB-5

Holley, Marietta 1836-1926.............DLB-11

Hollinghurst, Alan 1954- DLB-207, 326

Hollingshead, Greg 1947- DLB-334

Hollingsworth, Margaret 1940- DLB-60

Hollo, Anselm 1934- DLB-40

Holloway, Emory 1885-1977...........DLB-103

Holloway, John 1920- DLB-27

Holloway House Publishing Company DLB-46

Holme, Constance 1880-1955 ....DLB-34

Holmes, Abraham S. 1821?-1908 ....DLB-99

Holmes, John Clellon 1926-1988..... DLB-16, 237

"Four Essays on the Beat Generation" DLB-16

Holmes, Mary Jane 1825-1907 ..... DLB-202, 221

Holmes, Oliver Wendell 1809-1894.......DLB-1, 189, 235; CDALB-2

Holmes, Richard 1945- DLB-155

Holmes, Thomas James 1874-1959 ......DLB-187

The Holocaust "Historical Novel".......DLB-299

Holocaust Fiction, Postmodern DLB-299

Holocaust Novel, The "Second-Generation" DLB-299

Holroyd, Michael 1935- DLB-155; Y-99

Holst, Hermann E. von 1841-1904 ....DLB-47

Holt, John 1721-1784.................DLB-43

Henry Holt and Company DLB-49, 284

Holt, Rinehart and Winston DLB-46

Holtby, Winifred 1898-1935 ....DLB-191

Holthusen, Hans Egon 1913-1997........DLB-69

Hölty, Ludwig Christoph Heinrich 1748-1776.....................DLB-94

Holub, Miroslav 1923-1998............DLB-232; CDWLB-4

Holz, Arno 1863-1929.................DLB-118

Cumulative Index

Home, Henry, Lord Kames
(see Kames, Henry Home, Lord)

Home, John 1722-1808............ DLB-84, 336

Home, William Douglas 1912-1992...... DLB-13

Home Publishing Company............ DLB-49

Homer circa eighth-seventh centuries B.C.
.... DLB-176; CDWLB-1

Homer, Winslow 1836-1910........... DLB-188

Homes, Geoffrey (see Mainwaring, Daniel)

Honan, Park 1928- DLB-111

Hone, William 1780-1842......... DLB-110, 158

Hongo, Garrett Kaoru 1951-..... DLB-120, 312

Honig, Edwin 1919-................... DLB-5

Hood, Hugh 1928-2000............... DLB-53

Hood, Mary 1946-................... DLB-234

Hood, Thomas 1799-1845............. DLB-96

Hook, Sidney 1902-1989.............. DLB-279

Hook, Theodore 1788-1841............ DLB-116

Hooke, Nathaniel 1685?-1763......... DLB-336

Hooker, Jeremy 1941-................ DLB-40

Hooker, Richard 1554-1600........... DLB-132

Hooker, Thomas 1586-1647............ DLB-24

hooks, bell 1952-................... DLB-246

Hooper, Johnson Jones
1815-1862................ DLB-3, 11, 248

Hope, A. D. 1907-2000............... DLB-289

Hope, Anthony 1863-1933........ DLB-153, 156

Hope, Christopher 1944- DLB-225

Hope, Eva (see Hearn, Mary Anne)

Hope, Laurence (Adela Florence
Cory Nicolson) 1865-1904.......... DLB-240

Hopkins, Ellice 1836-1904............ DLB-190

Hopkins, Gerard Manley
1844-1889........... DLB-35, 57; CDBLB-5

Hopkins, John ?-1570................ DLB-132

Hopkins, John H., and Son............ DLB-46

Hopkins, Lemuel 1750-1801............ DLB-37

Hopkins, Pauline Elizabeth 1859-1930.... DLB-50

Hopkins, Samuel 1721-1803............ DLB-31

Hopkinson, Francis 1737-1791.......... DLB-31

Hopkinson, Nalo 1960-.............. DLB-251

Hopper, Nora (Mrs. Nora Chesson)
1871-1906....................... DLB-240

Hoppin, Augustus 1828-1896.......... DLB-188

Hora, Josef 1891-1945...... DLB-215; CDWLB-4

Horace 65 B.C.-8 B.C....... DLB-211; CDWLB-1

Horgan, Paul 1903-1995...... DLB-102, 212; Y-85

Tribute to Alfred A. Knopf............ Y-84

Horizon Press..................... DLB-46

Horkheimer, Max 1895-1973.......... DLB-296

Hornby, C. H. St. John 1867-1946...... DLB-201

Hornby, Nick 1957-................. DLB-207

Horne, Frank 1899-1974............... DLB-51

Horne, Richard Henry (Hengist)
1802 or 1803-1884................ DLB-32

Horne, Thomas 1608-1654............ DLB-281

Horney, Karen 1885-1952............ DLB-246

Hornung, E. W. 1866-1921............ DLB-70

Horovitz, Israel 1939- DLB-7, 341

Horta, Maria Teresa (see The Three Marias:
A Landmark Case in Portuguese
Literary History)

Horton, George Moses 1797?-1883?...... DLB-50

George Moses Horton Society.......... Y-99

Horváth, Ödön von 1901-1938..... DLB-85, 124

Horwood, Harold 1923- DLB-60

E. and E. Hosford [publishing house]..... DLB-49

Hoskens, Jane Fenn 1693-1770?........ DLB-200

Hoskyns, John circa 1566-1638.... DLB-121, 281

Hosokawa Yūsai 1535-1610............ DLB-203

Hospers, John 1918-................ DLB-279

Hospital, Janette Turner 1942-........ DLB-325

Hostovský, Egon 1908-1973........... DLB-215

Hotchkiss and Company DLB-49

Hotel du Lac, 1984 Booker Prize winner,
Anita Brookner DLB-326

Hough, Emerson 1857-1923......... DLB-9, 212

Houghton, Stanley 1881-1913........... DLB-10

Houghton Mifflin Company............ DLB-49

Hours at Home DS-13

Household, Geoffrey 1900-1988........ DLB-87

Housman, A. E. 1859-1936 ... DLB-19; CDBLB-5

Housman, Laurence 1865-1959......... DLB-10

Houston, Pam 1962-................ DLB-244

Houwald, Ernst von 1778-1845......... DLB-90

Hovey, Richard 1864-1900............. DLB-54

How Late It Was, How Late, 1994 Booker Prize winner,
James Kelman.................... DLB-326

Howard, Donald R. 1927-1987......... DLB-111

Howard, Maureen 1930-................ Y-83

Howard, Richard 1929-................ DLB-5

Howard, Roy W. 1883-1964............ DLB-29

Howard, Sidney 1891-1939 ....DLB-7, 26, 249

Howard, Thomas, second Earl of Arundel
1585-1646 .... DLB-213

Howe, E. W. 1853-1937 .... DLB-12, 25

Howe, Henry 1816-1893 .... DLB-30

Howe, Irving 1920-1993.............. DLB-67

Howe, Joseph 1804-1873............. DLB-99

Howe, Julia Ward 1819-1910 .... DLB-1, 189, 235

Howe, Percival Presland 1886-1944..... DLB-149

Howe, Susan 1937-................. DLB-120

Howe, Tina 1937-................. DLB-341

Howell, Clark, Sr. 1863-1936........... DLB-25

Howell, Evan P. 1839-1905 .... DLB-23

Howell, James 1594?-1666 .... DLB-151

Howell, Soskin and Company DLB-46

Howell, Warren Richardson 1912-1984.....DLB-140

Howells, William Dean 1837-1920
.... DLB-12, 64, 74, 79, 189; CDALB-3

Introduction to Paul Laurence
Dunbar's *Lyrics of Lowly Life*
(1896) DLB-50

The William Dean Howells Society...... Y-01

Howitt, Mary 1799-1888 .... DLB-110, 199

Howitt, William 1792-1879............ DLB-110

Hoyem, Andrew 1935-................ DLB-5

Hoyers, Anna Ovena 1584-1655 .... DLB-164

Hoyle, Fred 1915-2001.............. DLB-261

Hoyos, Angela de 1940-............. DLB-82

Henry Hoyt [publishing house] DLB-49

Hoyt, Palmer 1897-1979..............DLB-127

Hrabal, Bohumil 1914-1997 .... DLB-232

Hrabanus Maurus 776?-856 .... DLB-148

Hronský, Josef Cíger 1896-1960....... DLB-215

Hrotsvit of Gandersheim
circa 935-circa 1000 .... DLB-148

Hubbard, Elbert 1856-1915 .... DLB-91

Hubbard, Kin 1868-1930 .... DLB-11

Hubbard, William circa 1621-1704....... DLB-24

Huber, Therese 1764-1829 .... DLB-90

Huch, Friedrich 1873-1913 .... DLB-66

Huch, Ricarda 1864-1947............. DLB-66

Huddle, David 1942-................ DLB-130

Hudgins, Andrew 1951-........ DLB-120, 282

Hudson, Henry Norman 1814-1886 ..... DLB-64

Hudson, Stephen 1868?-1944..........DLB-197

Hudson, W. H. 1841-1922......DLB-98, 153, 174

Hudson and Goodwin DLB-49

Huebsch, B. W., oral history Y-99

B. W. Huebsch [publishing house] DLB-46

Hueffer, Oliver Madox 1876-1931 ....DLB-197

Huet, Pierre Daniel
Preface to *The History of Romances*
(1715).................... DLB-39

Hugh of St. Victor circa 1096-1141 ..... DLB-208

Hughes, David 1930- DLB-14

Hughes, Dusty 1947-................ DLB-233

Hughes, Hatcher 1881-1945........... DLB-249

Hughes, John 1677-1720.............. DLB-84

Hughes, Langston 1902-1967....... DLB-4, 7, 48,
51, 86, 228, 315; DS-15; CDALB-5

Hughes, Richard 1900-1976........ DLB-15, 161

Hughes, Ted 1930-1998........... DLB-40, 161

Hughes, Thomas 1822-1896 .... DLB-18, 163

Hugo, Richard 1923-1982 .... DLB-5, 206

Hugo, Victor 1802-1885.......DLB-119, 192, 217

Hugo Awards and Nebula Awards DLB-8

Huidobro, Vicente 1893-1948 . . . . DLB-283

Hull, Richard 1896-1973 . . . . DLB-77

Hulda (Unnur Benediktsdóttir Bjarklind)
1881-1946 . . . . DLB-293

Hulme, Keri 1947- DLB-326

Hulme, T. E. 1883-1917 . . . . DLB-19

Hulton, Anne ?-1779? DLB-200

Humanism, Sixteenth-Century
Spanish DLB-318

Humboldt, Alexander von 1769-1859 . . . . DLB-90

Humboldt, Wilhelm von 1767-1835 . . . . . . DLB-90

Hume, David 1711-1776 . . . . . . DLB-104, 252, 336

Hume, Fergus 1859-1932 . . . . DLB-70

Hume, Sophia 1702-1774 . . . . DLB-200

Hume-Rothery, Mary Catherine
1824-1885 . . . . DLB-240

Humishuma
(see Mourning Dove)

Hummer, T. R. 1950- DLB-120

Humor
American Humor: A Historical
Survey DLB-11

American Humor Studies Association Y-99

The Comic Tradition Continued
[in the British Novel] DLB-15

Humorous Book Illustration DLB-11

International Society for Humor Studies . . . Y-99

Newspaper Syndication of American
Humor DLB-11

Selected Humorous Magazines
(1820-1950) DLB-11

Bruce Humphries [publishing house] DLB-46

Humphrey, Duke of Gloucester
1391-1447 . . . . DLB-213

Humphrey, William
1924-1997 . . . . DLB-6, 212, 234, 278

Humphreys, David 1752-1818 . . . . DLB-37

Humphreys, Emyr 1919- DLB-15

Humphreys, Josephine 1945- DLB-292

Hunayn ibn Ishaq 809-873 or 877 . . . . DLB-311

Huncke, Herbert 1915-1996 . . . . DLB-16

Huneker, James Gibbons
1857-1921 . . . . DLB-71

Hunold, Christian Friedrich
1681-1721 . . . . DLB-168

Hunt, Irene 1907- DLB-52

Hunt, Leigh 1784-1859 . . . . DLB-96, 110, 144

Hunt, Violet 1862-1942 . . . . DLB-162, 197

Hunt, William Gibbes 1791-1833 . . . . DLB-73

Hunter, Evan (Ed McBain)
1926-2005 . . . . DLB-306; Y-82

Tribute to John D. MacDonald Y-86

Hunter, Jim 1939- DLB-14

Hunter, Kristin 1931- DLB-33

Tribute to Julian Mayfield Y-84

Hunter, Mollie 1922- DLB-161

Hunter, N. C. 1908-1971 . . . . DLB-10

Hunter-Duvar, John 1821-1899 . . . . DLB-99

Huntington, Henry E. 1850-1927 . . . . DLB-140

The Henry E. Huntington Library Y-92

Huntington, Susan Mansfield
1791-1823 . . . . DLB-200

Hurd and Houghton DLB-49

Hurst, Fannie 1889-1968 . . . . DLB-86

Hurst and Blackett DLB-106

Hurst and Company DLB-49

Hurston, Zora Neale
1901?-1960 . . . . DLB-51, 86; CDALB-7

Husserl, Edmund 1859-1938 . . . . DLB-296

Husson, Jules-François-Félix
(see Champfleury)

Huston, John 1906-1987 . . . . DLB-26

Hutcheson, Francis 1694-1746 . . . . DLB-31, 252

Hutchinson, Ron 1947- DLB-245

Hutchinson, R. C. 1907-1975 . . . . DLB-191

Hutchinson, Thomas 1711-1780 . . . . . . DLB-30, 31

Hutchinson and Company
(Publishers) Limited DLB-112

Huth, Angela 1938- DLB-271

Hutton, Richard Holt 1826-1897 . . . . DLB-57

von Hutten, Ulrich 1488-1523 . . . . DLB-179

Huxley, Aldous 1894-1963
. . . . . . DLB-36, 100, 162, 195, 255; CDBLB-6

Huxley, Elspeth Josceline
1907-1997 . . . . DLB-77, 204

Huxley, T. H. 1825-1895 . . . . DLB-57

Huyghue, Douglas Smith 1816-1891 . . . . . DLB-99

Huysmans, Joris-Karl 1848-1907 . . . . DLB-123

Hwang, David Henry
1957- DLB-212, 228, 312

Hyde, Donald 1909-1966 . . . . DLB-187

Hyde, Mary 1912-2003 . . . . DLB-187

Hyman, Trina Schart 1939- DLB-61

I

Iavorsky, Stefan 1658-1722 . . . . DLB-150

Iazykov, Nikolai Mikhailovich
1803-1846 . . . . DLB-205

Ibáñez, Armando P. 1949- DLB-209

Ibáñez, Sara de 1909-1971 . . . . DLB-290

Ibarbourou, Juana de 1892-1979 . . . . DLB-290

Ibn Abi Tahir Tayfur 820-893 . . . . DLB-311

Ibn Bajja circa 1077-1138 . . . . DLB-115

Ibn Gabirol, Solomon
circa 1021-circa 1058 . . . . DLB-115

Ibn al-Muqaffa' circa 723-759 . . . . DLB-311

Ibn al-Mu'tazz 861-908 . . . . DLB-311

Ibn Qutaybah 828-889 . . . . DLB-311

Ibn al-Rumi 836-896 . . . . DLB-311

Ibn Sa'd 784-845 . . . . DLB-311

Ibrahim al-Mawsili
742 or 743-803 or 804 . . . . DLB-311

Ibrahim, Sonallah 1937- DLB-346

Ibuse Masuji 1898-1993 . . . . DLB-180

Ichijō Kanera
(see Ichijō Kaneyoshi)

Ichijō Kaneyoshi (Ichijō Kanera)
1402-1481 . . . . DLB-203

Idris, Yusuf 1927-1991 . . . . DLB-346

Iffland, August Wilhelm
1759-1814 . . . . DLB-94

Iggulden, John 1917- DLB-289

Ignatieff, Michael 1947- DLB-267

Ignatow, David 1914-1997 . . . . DLB-5

Ike, Chukwuemeka 1931- DLB-157

Ikkyū Sōjun 1394-1481 . . . . DLB-203

Iles, Francis
(see Berkeley, Anthony)

Il'f, Il'ia (Il'ia Arnol'dovich Fainzil'berg)
1897-1937 . . . . DLB-272

Illich, Ivan 1926-2002 . . . . DLB-242

Illustration
Children's Book Illustration in the
Twentieth Century DLB-61

Children's Illustrators, 1800-1880 . . . . DLB-163

Early American Book Illustration DLB-49

The Iconography of Science-Fiction
Art DLB-8

The Illustration of Early German
Literary Manuscripts, circa
1150-circa 1300 . . . . DLB-148

Minor Illustrators, 1880-1914 . . . . DLB-141

Illyés, Gyula 1902-1983 . . . . . DLB-215; CDWLB-4

Imalayène, Fatima-Zohra (see Djebar, Assia)

Imbs, Bravig 1904-1946 . . . . DLB-4; DS-15

Imbuga, Francis D. 1947- DLB-157

Immermann, Karl 1796-1840 . . . . DLB-133

Imru' al-Qays circa 526-circa 565 . . . . DLB-311

In a Free State, 1971 Booker Prize winner,
V. S. Naipaul DLB-326

Inchbald, Elizabeth 1753-1821 . . . . DLB-39, 89

Indiana University Press Y-02

Industrial Workers of the World (IWW)
1905- DLB-345

Ingamells, Rex 1913-1955 . . . . DLB-260

Inge, William 1913-1973 . . . DLB-7, 249; CDALB-1

Ingelow, Jean 1820-1897 . . . . DLB-35, 163

Ingemann, B. S. 1789-1862 . . . . DLB-300

Ingersoll, Ralph 1900-1985 . . . . DLB-127

Ingersoll, Robert G. 1833-1899 . . . . DLB-345

The Ingersoll Prizes Y-84

Ingoldsby, Thomas (see Barham, Richard Harris)

Ingraham, Joseph Holt 1809-1860 . . . . . DLB-3, 248

Inman, John 1805-1850 . . . . DLB-73

Innerhofer, Franz 1944- DLB-85	Gores, Joe........................ Y-02	Schroeder, Patricia Y-99
Innes, Michael (J. I. M. Stewart) 1906-1994 .... DLB-276	Greenfield, George................. Y-91	Schulberg, Budd................. Y-81, 01
	Griffin, Bryan..................... Y-81	Scribner, Charles, III Y-94
Innis, Harold Adams 1894-1952......... DLB-88	Groom, Winston Y-01	Sipper, Ralph Y-94
Innis, Mary Quayle 1899-1972.......... DLB-88	Guilds, John Caldwell Y-92	Smith, Cork Y-95
Inō Sōgi 1421-1502................. DLB-203	Hamilton, Virginia................. Y-01	Staley, Thomas F................... Y-00
Inoue Yasushi 1907-1991.............. DLB-182	Hardin, James Y-92	Styron, William Y-80
"The Greatness of Southern Literature": League of the South Institute for the Study of Southern Culture and History Y-02	Harris, Mark Y-80	Talese, Nan Y-94
	Harrison, Jim Y-82	Thornton, John Y-94
	Hazzard, Shirley................... Y-82	Toth, Susan Allen.................. Y-86
	Herrick, William Y-01	Tyler, Anne Y-82
International Publishers Company DLB-46	Higgins, George V.................. Y-98	Vaughan, Samuel Y-97
Internet (publishing and commerce) Author Websites..................... Y-97	Hoban, Russell.................... Y-90	Von Ogtrop, Kristin Y-92
	Holroyd, Michael.................. Y-99	Wallenstein, Barry Y-92
The Book Trade and the Internet Y-00	Horowitz, Glen Y-90	Weintraub, Stanley................. Y-82
E-Books Turn the Corner Y-98	Iggulden, John Y-01	Williams, J. Chamberlain............. Y-84
The E-Researcher: Possibilities and Pitfalls..................... Y-00	Jakes, John Y-83	Into the Past: William Jovanovich's Reflections in Publishing Y-02
	Jenkinson, Edward B................ Y-82	
Interviews on E-publishing............ Y-00	Jenks, Tom Y-86	Ionesco, Eugène 1909-1994 .... DLB-321
John Updike on the Internet Y-97	Kaplan, Justin Y-86	Ireland, David 1927- DLB-289
LitCheck Website................... Y-01	King, Florence Y-85	The National Library of Ireland's New James Joyce Manuscripts Y-02
Virtual Books and Enemies of Books..... Y-00	Klopfer, Donald S.................. Y-97	
Interviews Adoff, Arnold..................... Y-01	Krug, Judith Y-82	Irigaray, Luce 1930- DLB-296
	Lamm, Donald.................... Y-95	Irving, John 1942- DLB-6, 278; Y-82
Aldridge, John W. Y-91	Laughlin, James Y-96	Irving, Washington 1783-1859 ..... DLB-3, 11, 30, 59, 73, 74, 183, 186, 250; CDALB-2
Anastas, Benjamin Y-98	Lawrence, Starling Y-95	
Baker, Nicholson Y-00	Lindsay, Jack Y-84	
Bank, Melissa Y-98	Mailer, Norman Y-97	Irwin, Grace 1907- DLB-68
Bass, T. J. Y-80	Manchester, William Y-85	Irwin, Will 1873-1948................ DLB-25
Bernstein, Harriet................... Y-82	Max, D. T. Y-94	Isaksson, Ulla 1916-2000 .... DLB-257
Betts, Doris....................... Y-82	McCormack, Thomas Y-98	Iser, Wolfgang 1926-2007 .... DLB-242
Bosworth, David Y-82	McNamara, Katherine Y-97	Isherwood, Christopher 1904-1986 .... DLB-15, 195; Y-86
Bottoms, David Y-83	Mellen, Joan...................... Y-94	
Bowers, Fredson.................... Y-80	Menaker, Daniel................... Y-97	The Christopher Isherwood Archive, The Huntington Library Y-99
Burnshaw, Stanley Y-97	Mooneyham, Lamarr................ Y-82	
Carpenter, Humphrey Y-84, 99	Murray, Les Y-01	Ishiguro, Kazuo 1954- DLB-194, 326
Carr, Virginia Spencer Y-00	Nosworth, David Y-82	Ishikawa Jun 1899-1987 .... DLB-182
Carver, Raymond................... Y-83	O'Connor, Patrick Y-84, 99	Iskander, Fazil' Abdulevich 1929- DLB-302
Cherry, Kelly Y-83	Ozick, Cynthia Y-83	
Conroy, Jack....................... Y-81	Penner, Jonathan Y-83	The Island Trees Case: A Symposium on School Library Censorship An Interview with Judith Krug An Interview with Phyllis Schlafly An Interview with Edward B. Jenkinson An Interview with Lamarr Mooneyham An Interview with Harriet Bernstein Y-82
Coppel, Alfred Y-83	Pennington, Lee Y-82	
Cowley, Malcolm Y-81	Penzler, Otto...................... Y-96	
Davis, Paxton..................... Y-89	Plimpton, George Y-99	
Devito, Carlo Y-94	Potok, Chaim Y-84	
De Vries, Peter Y-82	Powell, Padgett.................... Y-01	
Dickey, James..................... Y-82	Prescott, Peter S.................... Y-86	Islas, Arturo 1938-1991 .... DLB-122
Donald, David Herbert Y-87	Rabe, David Y-91	Isma'il, Isma'il Fahd 1940- DLB-346
Editors, Conversations with........... Y-95	Rechy, John Y-82	Issit, Debbie 1966- DLB-233
Ellroy, James Y-91	Reid, B. L. Y-83	Ivanišević, Drago 1907-1981........... DLB-181
Fancher, Betsy Y-83	Reynolds, Michael Y-95, 99	Ivanov, Georgii 1894-1954 ....DLB-317
Faust, Irvin....................... Y-00	Robinson, Derek Y-02	Ivanov, Viacheslav Ivanovich 1866-1949.........................DLB-295
Fulton, Len....................... Y-86	Rollyson, Carl Y-97	
Furst, Alan Y-01	Rosset, Barney Y-02	
Garrett, George Y-83		Ivanov, Vsevolod Viacheslavovich 1895-1963 ....DLB-272
Gelfman, Jane..................... Y-93	Schlafly, Phyllis Y-82	
Goldwater, Walter Y-93		

Ivask, Yuri 1907-1986....................DLB-317

Ivaska, Astrīde 1926- DLB-232

M. J. Ivers and Company...............DLB-49

Iwaniuk, Wacław 1915-2001............DLB-215

Iwano Hōmei 1873-1920................DLB-180

Iwaszkiewicz, Jarosław
 1894-1980........................DLB-215

Iyayi, Festus 1947- DLB-157

Izumi Kyōka 1873-1939................DLB-180

J

Jabra, Jabra Ibrahim 1920-1994........DLB-346

al-Jabri, Mohammed 'Abed 1935- DLB-346

Jackmon, Marvin E. (see Marvin X)

Jacks, L. P. 1860-1955..................DLB-135

Jackson, Angela 1951- DLB-41

Jackson, Charles 1903-1968............DLB-234

Jackson, Helen Hunt
 1830-1885............DLB-42, 47, 186, 189

Jackson, Holbrook 1874-1948..........DLB-98

Jackson, Laura Riding 1901-1991......DLB-48

Jackson, Shirley
 1916-1965...........DLB-6, 234; CDALB-1

Jacob, Max 1876-1944..................DLB-258

Jacob, Naomi 1884?-1964..............DLB-191

Jacob, Piers Anthony Dillingham
 (see Anthony, Piers)

Jacob, Violet 1863-1946................DLB-240

Jacobi, Friedrich Heinrich 1743-1819...DLB-94

Jacobi, Johann Georg 1740-1841.......DLB-97

George W. Jacobs and Company.......DLB-49

Jacobs, Harriet 1813-1897..............DLB-239

Jacobs, Joseph 1854-1916..............DLB-141

Jacobs, W. W. 1863-1943...............DLB-135

 The W. W. Jacobs Appreciation Society...Y-98

Jacobsen, J. P. 1847-1885..............DLB-300

Jacobsen, Jørgen-Frantz 1900-1938.....DLB-214

Jacobsen, Josephine 1908- DLB-244

Jacobsen, Rolf 1907-1994..............DLB-297

Jacobson, Dan 1929- DLB-14, 207, 225, 319

Jacobson, Howard 1942- DLB-207

Jacques de Vitry circa 1160/1170-1240...DLB-208

Jæger, Frank 1926-1977................DLB-214

Ja'far al-Sadiq circa 702-765............DLB-311

William Jaggard [publishing house]......DLB-170

Jahier, Piero 1884-1966...........DLB-114, 264

al-Jahiz circa 776-868 or 869............DLB-311

Jahnn, Hans Henny 1894-1959.....DLB-56, 124

Jaimes, Freyre, Ricardo 1866?-1933......DLB-283

Jakes, John 1932- DLB-278; Y-83

 Tribute to John Gardner................Y-82

 Tribute to John D. MacDonald.........Y-86

Jakobína Johnson (Jakobína Sigurbjarnardóttir)
 1883-1977........................DLB-293

Jakobson, Roman 1896-1982...........DLB-242

James, Alice 1848-1892................DLB-221

James, C. L. R. 1901-1989..............DLB-125

James, Clive 1939- DLB-325

James, George P. R. 1801-1860........DLB-116

James, Henry 1843-1916
 ......DLB-12, 71, 74, 189; DS-13; CDALB-3

 "The Future of the Novel" (1899).....DLB-18

 "The Novel in [Robert Browning's]
  'The Ring and the Book'"
  (1912).......................DLB-32

James, John circa 1633-1729............DLB-24

James, M. R. 1862-1936...........DLB-156, 201

James, Naomi 1949- DLB-204

James, P. D. (Phyllis Dorothy James White)
 1920- DLB-87, 276; DS-17; CDBLB-8

 Tribute to Charles Scribner Jr...........Y-95

James, Thomas 1572?-1629.............DLB-213

U. P. James [publishing house]..........DLB-49

James, Will 1892-1942................. DS-16

James, William 1842-1910.............DLB-270

James VI of Scotland, I of England
 1566-1625..................DLB-151, 172

 *Ane Schort Treatise Conteining Some Revlis
 and Cautelis to Be Observit and
 Eschewit in Scottis Poesi* (1584).....DLB-172

Jameson, Anna 1794-1860..........DLB-99, 166

Jameson, Fredric 1934- DLB-67

Jameson, J. Franklin 1859-1937.........DLB-17

Jameson, Storm 1891-1986..............DLB-36

Jančar, Drago 1948- DLB-181

Janés, Clara 1940- DLB-134

Janevski, Slavko
 1920-2000............DLB-181; CDWLB-4

Janowitz, Tama 1957- DLB-292

Jansson, Tove 1914-2001..............DLB-257

Janvier, Thomas 1849-1913............DLB-202

Japan
 "The Development of Meiji Japan"...DLB-180
 "Encounter with the West".........DLB-180

Japanese Literature
 Letter from Japan.................Y-94, 98
 Medieval Travel Diaries...........DLB-203
 Surveys: 1987-1995................DLB-182

Jaramillo, Cleofas M. 1878-1956........DLB-122

Jaramillo Levi, Enrique 1944- DLB-290

Jarir after 650-circa 730................DLB-311

Jarman, Mark 1952- DLB-120, 282

Jarrell, Randall
 1914-1965............DLB-48, 52; CDALB-1

Jarrold and Sons......................DLB-106

Jarry, Alfred 1873-1907............DLB-192, 258

Jarves, James Jackson 1818-1888........DLB-189

Jasim, 'Aziz al-Sayyid 1941-1991?.......DLB-346

Jasmin, Claude 1930- DLB-60

Jaunsudrabiņš, Jānis 1877-1962.........DLB-220

Jay, John 1745-1829....................DLB-31

Jean de Garlande (see John of Garland)

Jefferies, Richard 1848-1887........DLB-98, 141

 The Richard Jefferies Society..........Y-98

Jeffers, Lance 1919-1985................DLB-41

Jeffers, Robinson
 1887-1962......DLB-45, 212, 342; CDALB-4

Jefferson, Thomas
 1743-1826.........DLB-31, 183; CDALB-2

Jégé 1866-1940......................DLB-215

Jelinek, Elfriede 1946- DLB-85, 330

Jellicoe, Ann 1927- DLB-13, 233

Jemison, Mary circa 1742-1833.........DLB-239

Jen, Gish 1955- DLB-312

Jenkins, Dan 1929- DLB-241

Jenkins, Elizabeth 1905- DLB-155

Jenkins, Robin 1912-2005..........DLB-14, 271

Jenkins, William Fitzgerald (see Leinster, Murray)

Herbert Jenkins Limited...............DLB-112

Jennings, Elizabeth 1926-2001..........DLB-27

Jens, Walter 1923- DLB-69

Jensen, Axel 1932-2003................DLB-297

Jensen, Johannes V. 1873-1950.....DLB-214, 330

Jensen, Merrill 1905-1980...............DLB-17

Jensen, Thit 1876-1957................DLB-214

Jephson, Robert 1736-1803..............DLB-89

Jerome, Jerome K. 1859-1927....DLB-10, 34, 135

 The Jerome K. Jerome Society..........Y-98

Jerome, Judson 1927-1991.............DLB-105

 "Reflections: After a Tornado".......DLB-105

Jerrold, Douglas 1803-1857....DLB-158, 159, 344

Jersild, Per Christian 1935- DLB-257

Jesse, F. Tennyson 1888-1958............DLB-77

Jewel, John 1522-1571................DLB-236

John P. Jewett and Company............DLB-49

Jewett, Sarah Orne 1849-1909....DLB-12, 74, 221

Studies in American Jewish Literature........Y-02

Jewish Literature of Medieval Spain.....DLB-337

The Jewish Publication Society..........DLB-49

Jewitt, John Rodgers 1783-1821..........DLB-99

Jewsbury, Geraldine 1812-1880..........DLB-21

Jewsbury, Maria Jane 1800-1833........DLB-199

Jhabvala, Ruth Prawer
 1927- DLB-139, 194, 323, 326

Jiang Guangci 1901-1931...............DLB-328

Jiménez, Juan Ramón 1881-1958....DLB-134, 330

Jiménez de Rada, Rodrigo
  after 1170-1247 .... DLB-337
Jin, Ha 1956- DLB-244, 292
Joans, Ted 1928-2003 .... DLB-16, 41
Jodelle, Estienne 1532?-1573 .... DLB-327
Jōha 1525-1602 .... DLB-203
Jóhann Sigurjónsson 1880-1919 .... DLB-293
Jóhannes úr Kötlum 1899-1972 .... DLB-293
Johannis de Garlandia (see John of Garland)
John, Errol 1924-1988 .... DLB-233
John, Eugenie (see Marlitt, E.)
John of Dumbleton
  circa 1310-circa 1349 .... DLB-115
John of Garland (Jean de Garlande,
  Johannis de Garlandia)
  circa 1195-circa 1272 .... DLB-208
The John Reed Clubs DLB-303
Johns, Captain W. E. 1893-1968 .... DLB-160
Johnson, Mrs. A. E. ca. 1858-1922 ...... DLB-221
Johnson, Amelia (see Johnson, Mrs. A. E.)
Johnson, B. S. 1933-1973 .... DLB-14, 40
Johnson, Charles 1679-1748 .... DLB-84
Johnson, Charles 1948- DLB-33, 278
Johnson, Charles S. 1893-1956 .... DLB-51, 91
Johnson, Colin (Mudrooroo) 1938- ... DLB-289
Johnson, Denis 1949- DLB-120
Johnson, Diane 1934- Y-80
Johnson, Dorothy M. 1905–1984 .... DLB-206
Johnson, E. Pauline (Tekahionwake)
  1861-1913 .... DLB-175
Johnson, Edgar 1901-1995 .... DLB-103
Johnson, Edward 1598-1672 .... DLB-24
Johnson, Eyvind 1900-1976 .... DLB-259, 330
Johnson, Fenton 1888-1958 .... DLB-45, 50
Johnson, Georgia Douglas
  1877?-1966 .... DLB-51, 249
Johnson, Gerald W. 1890-1980 .... DLB-29
Johnson, Greg 1953- DLB-234
Johnson, Helene 1907-1995 .... DLB-51
Jacob Johnson and Company DLB-49
Johnson, James Weldon
  1871-1938 .... DLB-51; CDALB-4
Johnson, John H. 1918-2005 .... DLB-137
  "Backstage," Statement From the
    Initial Issue of *Ebony*
    (November 1945) DLB-137
Johnson, Joseph [publishing house] DLB-154
Johnson, Linton Kwesi 1952- DLB-157
Johnson, Lionel 1867-1902 .... DLB-19
Johnson, Nunnally 1897-1977 .... DLB-26
Johnson, Owen 1878-1952 .... Y-87
Johnson, Pamela Hansford 1912-1981 ..... DLB-15
Johnson, Pauline 1861-1913 .... DLB-92

Johnson, Ronald 1935-1998 .... DLB-169
Johnson, Samuel 1696-1772 ... DLB-24; CDBLB-2
Johnson, Samuel
  1709-1784 .... DLB-39, 95, 104, 142, 213
  Rambler, no. 4 (1750) [excerpt] DLB-39
The BBC Four Samuel Johnson Prize
  for Non-fiction Y-02
Johnson, Samuel 1822-1882 .... DLB-1, 243
Johnson, Susanna 1730-1810 .... DLB-200
Johnson, Terry 1955- DLB-233
Johnson, Uwe 1934-1984 ..... DLB-75; CDWLB-2
Benjamin Johnson [publishing house] DLB-49
Benjamin, Jacob, and Robert Johnson
  [publishing house] DLB-49
Johnston, Annie Fellows 1863-1931 ...... DLB-42
Johnston, Basil H. 1929- DLB-60
Johnston, David Claypole 1798?-1865 ... DLB-188
Johnston, Denis 1901-1984 .... DLB-10
Johnston, Ellen 1835-1873 .... DLB-199
Johnston, George 1912-1970 .... DLB-260
Johnston, George 1913-1970 .... DLB-88
Johnston, Sir Harry 1858-1927 .... DLB-174
Johnston, Jennifer 1930- DLB-14
Johnston, Mary 1870-1936 .... DLB-9
Johnston, Richard Malcolm 1822-1898 ... DLB-74
Johnston, Wayne 1958- DLB-334
Johnstone, Charles 1719?-1800? DLB-39
Johst, Hanns 1890-1978 .... DLB-124
Jökull Jakobsson 1933-1978 .... DLB-293
Jolas, Eugene 1894-1952 .... DLB-4, 45
Jolley, Elizabeth 1923-2007 .... DLB-325
Jón Stefán Sveinsson or Svensson (see Nonni)
Jón Trausti (Guðmundur Magnússon)
  1873-1918 .... DLB-293
Jón úr Vör (Jón Jónsson) 1917-2000 .... DLB-293
Jónas Hallgrímsson 1807-1845 .... DLB-293
Jones, Alice C. 1853-1933 .... DLB-92
Jones, Charles C., Jr. 1831-1893 .... DLB-30
Jones, D. G. 1929- DLB-53
Jones, David 1895-1974 .. DLB-20, 100; CDBLB-7
Jones, Diana Wynne 1934- DLB-161
Jones, Ebenezer 1820-1860 .... DLB-32
Jones, Ernest 1819-1868 .... DLB-32
Jones, Gayl 1949- DLB-33, 278
Jones, George 1800-1870 .... DLB-183
Jones, Glyn 1905-1995 .... DLB-15
Jones, Gwyn 1907-1999 .... DLB-15, 139
Jones, Henry Arthur 1851-1929 ..... DLB-10, 344
Jones, Hugh circa 1692-1760 .... DLB-24
Jones, James 1921-1977 .... DLB-2, 143; DS-17
  James Jones Papers in the Handy
    Writers' Colony Collection at

the University of Illinois at
  Springfield Y-98
The James Jones Society Y-92
Jones, Jenkin Lloyd 1911-2004 .... DLB-127
Jones, John Beauchamp 1810-1866 ...... DLB-202
Jones, Joseph, Major
  (see Thompson, William Tappan)
Jones, LeRoi (see Baraka, Amiri)
Jones, Lewis 1897-1939 .... DLB-15
Jones, Madison 1925- DLB-152
Jones, Marie 1951- DLB-233
Jones, Preston 1936-1979 .... DLB-7
Jones, Rodney 1950- DLB-120
Jones, Thom 1945- DLB-244
Jones, Sir William 1746-1794 .... DLB-109
Jones, William Alfred 1817-1900 .... DLB-59
Jones's Publishing House DLB-49
Jong, Erica 1942- DLB-2, 5, 28, 152
Jonke, Gert F. 1946- DLB-85
Jonson, Ben
  1572?-1637 .... DLB-62, 121; CDBLB-1
Jonsson, Tor 1916-1951 .... DLB-297
Jordan, June 1936- DLB-38
Jorgensen, Johannes 1866-1956 .... DLB-300
Jose, Nicholas 1952- DLB-325
Joseph, Jenny 1932- DLB-40
Joseph and George Y-99
Michael Joseph Limited DLB-112
Josephson, Matthew 1899-1978 .... DLB-4
Josephus, Flavius 37-100 .... DLB-176
Josephy, Alvin M., Jr.
  Tribute to Alfred A. Knopf Y-84
Josiah Allen's Wife (see Holley, Marietta)
Josipovici, Gabriel 1940- DLB-14, 319
Josselyn, John ?-1675 .... DLB-24
Joudry, Patricia 1921-2000 .... DLB-88
Jouve, Pierre Jean 1887-1976 .... DLB-258
Jovanovich, William 1920-2001 .... Y-01
  Into the Past: William Jovanovich's
    Reflections on Publishing Y-02
  [Response to Ken Auletta] Y-97
  The Temper of the West: William
    Jovanovich Y-02
  Tribute to Charles Scribner Jr. Y-95
Jovine, Francesco 1902-1950 .... DLB-264
Jovine, Giuseppe 1922-1998 .... DLB-128
Joyaux, Philippe (see Sollers, Philippe)
Joyce, Adrien (see Eastman, Carol)
Joyce, James 1882-1941
  .... DLB-10, 19, 36, 162, 247; CDBLB-6
  Danis Rose and the Rendering of *Ulysses*... Y-97
  James Joyce Centenary: Dublin, 1982 .... Y-82
  James Joyce Conference Y-85

A Joyce (Con)Text: Danis Rose and the
 Remaking of *Ulysses*. Y-97

The National Library of Ireland's
 New James Joyce Manuscripts Y-02

The New *Ulysses*. Y-84

Public Domain and the Violation of
 Texts Y-97

The Quinn Draft of James Joyce's
 Circe Manuscript Y-00

Stephen Joyce's Letter to the Editor of
 The Irish Times Y-97

Ulysses, Reader's Edition: First Reactions. . . Y-97

We See the Editor at Work Y-97

Whose *Ulysses*? The Function of Editing . . . Y-97

Jozsef, Attila 1905-1937 . . . . . DLB-215; CDWLB-4

San Juan de la Cruz 1542-1591 . . . . DLB-318

Juan Manuel 1282-1348 . . . . DLB-337

Juarroz, Roberto 1925-1995 . . . . DLB-283

Orange Judd Publishing Company DLB-49

Judd, Sylvester 1813-1853 . . . . DLB-1, 243

Judith circa 930 . . . . DLB-146

Juel-Hansen, Erna 1845-1922 . . . . DLB-300

Julian of Norwich 1342-circa 1420 . . . . . . DLB-1146

Julius Caesar
 100 B.C.-44 B.C. DLB-211; CDWLB-1

June, Jennie
 (see Croly, Jane Cunningham)

Jung, Carl Gustav 1875-1961 . . . . DLB-296

Jung, Franz 1888-1963 . . . . DLB-118

Jünger, Ernst 1895-1998 . . . . . . DLB-56; CDWLB-2

Der jüngere Titurel circa 1275 . . . . DLB-138

Jung-Stilling, Johann Heinrich
 1740-1817 . . . . DLB-94

Junqueiro, Abílio Manuel Guerra
 1850-1923 . . . . DLB-287

Just, Ward (Ward S. Just) 1935- DLB-335

Justice, Donald 1925-2004 . . . . Y-83

Juvenal circa A.D. 60-circa A.D. 130
 . . . . DLB-211; CDWLB-1

The Juvenile Library
 (see M. J. Godwin and Company)

K

Kacew, Romain (see Gary, Romain)

Kafka, Franz 1883-1924 . . . . . . DLB-81; CDWLB-2

Kahn, Gus 1886-1941 . . . . DLB-265

Kahn, Roger 1927- DLB-171

Kaikō Takeshi 1939-1989 . . . . DLB-182

Káinn (Kristján Níels Jónsson/Kristjan
 Niels Julius) 1860-1936 . . . . DLB-293

Kaiser, Georg 1878-1945 . . . . DLB-124; CDWLB-2

Kaiserchronik circa 1147 . . . . DLB-148

Kaleb, Vjekoslav 1905-1996 . . . . DLB-181

Kalechofsky, Roberta 1931- DLB-28

Kaler, James Otis 1848-1912 . . . . DLB-12, 42

Kalmar, Bert 1884-1947 . . . . DLB-265

Kamensky, Vasilii Vasil'evich
 1884-1961 . . . . DLB-295

Kames, Henry Home, Lord
 1696-1782 . . . . DLB-31, 104

Kamo no Chōmei (Kamo no Nagaakira)
 1153 or 1155-1216 . . . . DLB-203

Kamo no Nagaakira (see Kamo no Chōmei)

Kampmann, Christian 1939-1988 . . . . DLB-214

Kanafi, Ghassan 1936-1972 . . . . DLB-346

Kandel, Lenore 1932- DLB-16

Kane, Sarah 1971-1999 . . . . DLB-310

Kaneko, Lonny 1939- DLB-312

Kang, Younghill 1903-1972 . . . . DLB-312

Kanin, Garson 1912-1999 . . . . DLB-7

 A Tribute (to Marc Connelly) Y-80

Kaniuk, Yoram 1930- DLB-299

Kant, Hermann 1926- DLB-75

Kant, Immanuel 1724-1804 . . . . DLB-94

Kantemir, Antiokh Dmitrievich
 1708-1744 . . . . DLB-150

Kantor, MacKinlay 1904-1977 . . . . DLB-9, 102

Kanze Kōjirō Nobumitsu 1435-1516 . . . . . DLB-203

Kanze Motokiyo (see Zeimi)

Kaplan, Fred 1937- DLB-111

Kaplan, Johanna 1942- DLB-28

Kaplan, Justin 1925- DLB-111; Y-86

Kaplinski, Jaan 1941- DLB-232

Kapnist, Vasilii Vasilevich 1758?-1823 . . . . DLB-150

Karadžić, Vuk Stefanović
 1787-1864 . . . . DLB-147; CDWLB-4

Karamzin, Nikolai Mikhailovich
 1766-1826 . . . . DLB-150

Karinthy, Frigyes 1887-1938 . . . . DLB-215

Karlfeldt, Erik Axel 1864-1931 . . . . DLB-330

Karmel, Ilona 1925-2000 . . . . DLB-299

Karnad, Girish 1938- DLB-323

Karsch, Anna Louisa 1722-1791 . . . . DLB-97

Kasack, Hermann 1896-1966 . . . . DLB-69

Kasai Zenzō 1887-1927 . . . . DLB-180

Kaschnitz, Marie Luise 1901-1974 . . . . DLB-69

Kassák, Lajos 1887-1967 . . . . DLB-215

Kaštelan, Jure 1919-1990 . . . . DLB-147

Kästner, Erich 1899-1974 . . . . DLB-56

Kataev, Evgenii Petrovich
 (see Il'f, Il'ia and Petrov, Evgenii)

Kataev, Valentin Petrovich 1897-1986 . . . . DLB-272

Katenin, Pavel Aleksandrovich
 1792-1853 . . . . DLB-205

Kattan, Naim 1928- DLB-53

Katz, Steve 1935- Y-83

Ka-Tzetnik 135633 (Yehiel Dinur)
 1909-2001 . . . . DLB-299

Kauffman, Janet 1945- DLB-218; Y-86

Kauffmann, Samuel 1898-1971 . . . . DLB-127

Kaufman, Bob 1925-1986 . . . . DLB-16, 41

Kaufman, George S. 1889-1961 . . . . DLB-7

Kaufmann, Walter 1921-1980 . . . . DLB-279

Kavan, Anna (Helen Woods Ferguson
 Edmonds) 1901-1968 . . . . DLB-255

Kavanagh, P. J. 1931- DLB-40

Kavanagh, Patrick 1904-1967 . . . . DLB-15, 20

Kaverin, Veniamin Aleksandrovich
 (Veniamin Aleksandrovich Zil'ber)
 1902-1989 . . . . DLB-272

Kawabata Yasunari 1899-1972 . . . . . . DLB-180, 330

Kay, Guy Gavriel 1954- DLB-251

Kaye-Smith, Sheila 1887-1956 . . . . DLB-36

Kazakov, Iurii Pavlovich 1927-1982 . . . . . . DLB-302

Kazin, Alfred 1915-1998 . . . . DLB-67

Keane, John B. 1928-2002 . . . . DLB-13

Keary, Annie 1825-1879 . . . . DLB-163

Keary, Eliza 1827-1918 . . . . DLB-240

Keating, H. R. F. 1926- DLB-87

Keatley, Charlotte 1960- DLB-245

Keats, Ezra Jack 1916-1983 . . . . DLB-61

Keats, John 1795-1821 . . . . DLB-96, 110; CDBLB-3

Keble, John 1792-1866 . . . . DLB-32, 55

Keckley, Elizabeth 1818?-1907 . . . . DLB-239

Keeble, John 1944- Y-83

Keeffe, Barrie 1945- DLB-13, 245

Keeley, James 1867-1934 . . . . DLB-25

W. B. Keen, Cooke and Company DLB-49

The Mystery of Carolyn Keene Y-02

Kefala, Antigone 1935- DLB-289

Keillor, Garrison 1942- Y-87

Keith, Marian (Mary Esther MacGregor)
 1874?-1961 . . . . DLB-92

Keller, Gary D. 1943- DLB-82

Keller, Gottfried
 1819-1890 . . . . DLB-129; CDWLB-2

Keller, Helen 1880-1968 . . . . DLB-303

Kelley, Edith Summers 1884-1956 . . . . DLB-9

Kelley, Emma Dunham ?-? DLB-221

Kelley, Florence 1859-1932 . . . . DLB-303

Kelley, William Melvin 1937- DLB-33

Kellogg, Ansel Nash 1832-1886 . . . . DLB-23

Kellogg, Steven 1941- DLB-61

Kelly, George E. 1887-1974 . . . . DLB-7, 249

Kelly, Hugh 1739-1777 . . . . DLB-89

Kelly, Piet and Company DLB-49

Kelly, Robert 1935- DLB-5, 130, 165

Kelman, James 1946- DLB-194, 319, 326

Kelmscott Press DLB-112

Kelton, Elmer 1926- DLB-256

Cumulative Index

Kemble, Charles 1775-1854 . . . . DLB-344
Kemble, E. W. 1861-1933 . . . . DLB-188
Kemble, Fanny 1809-1893 . . . . DLB-32
Kemelman, Harry 1908-1996 . . . . DLB-28
Kempe, Margery circa 1373-1438 . . . . . . DLB-146
Kempinski, Tom 1938- DLB-310
Kempner, Friederike 1836-1904 . . . . . . DLB-129
Kempowski, Walter 1929-2007 . . . . DLB-75
Kenan, Randall 1963- DLB-292
Claude Kendall [publishing company] DLB-46
Kendall, Henry 1839-1882 . . . . DLB-230
Kendall, May 1861-1943 . . . . DLB-240
Kendell, George 1809-1867 . . . . DLB-43
Keneally, Thomas 1935- DLB-289, 299, 326
Kenedy, P. J., and Sons DLB-49
Kenkō circa 1283-circa 1352 . . . . DLB-203
Kenna, Peter 1930-1987 . . . . DLB-289
Kennan, George 1845-1924 . . . . DLB-189
Kennedy, A. L. 1965- DLB-271
Kennedy, Adrienne 1931- DLB-38, 341
Kennedy, John Pendleton 1795-1870 . . . DLB-3, 248
Kennedy, Leo 1907-2000 . . . . DLB-88
Kennedy, Margaret 1896-1967 . . . . DLB-36
Kennedy, Patrick 1801-1873 . . . . DLB-159
Kennedy, Richard S. 1920-2002 . . . . DLB-111; Y-02
Kennedy, William 1928- DLB-143; Y-85
Kennedy, X. J. 1929- DLB-5
  Tribute to John Ciardi Y-86
Kennelly, Brendan 1936- DLB-40
Kenner, Hugh 1923-2003 . . . . DLB-67
  Tribute to Cleanth Brooks Y-80
Mitchell Kennerley [publishing house] DLB-46
Kennett, White 1660-1728 . . . . DLB-336
Kenney, James 1780?-1849 . . . . DLB-344
Kenny, Maurice 1929- DLB-175
Kent, Frank R. 1877-1958 . . . . DLB-29
Kentfield, Calvin 1924-1975 . . . . DLB-335
Kenyon, Jane 1947-1995 . . . . DLB-120
Kenzheev, Bakhyt Shkurullaevich
  1950- DLB-285
Keough, Hugh Edmund 1864-1912 . . . . . .DLB-171
Keppler and Schwartzmann DLB-49
Ker, John, third Duke of Roxburghe
  1740-1804 . . . . DLB-213
Ker, N. R. 1908-1982 . . . . DLB-201
Keralio-Robert, Louise-Félicité de
  1758-1822 . . . . DLB-313
Kerlan, Irvin 1912-1963 . . . . DLB-187
Kermode, Frank 1919- DLB-242
Kern, Jerome 1885-1945 . . . . DLB-187
Kernaghan, Eileen 1939- DLB-251

Kerner, Justinus 1786-1862 . . . . DLB-90
Kerouac, Jack
  1922-1969 . . DLB-2, 16, 237; DS-3; CDALB-1
  Auction of Jack Kerouac's
    On the Road Scroll Y-01
  The Jack Kerouac Revival Y-95
  "Re-meeting of Old Friends":
    The Jack Kerouac Conference Y-82
  Statement of Correction to "The Jack
    Kerouac Revival" Y-96
Kerouac, Jan 1952-1996 . . . . DLB-16
Charles H. Kerr and Company DLB-49
Kerr, Orpheus C. (see Newell, Robert Henry)
Kersh, Gerald 1911-1968 . . . . DLB-255
Kertész, Imre DLB-299, 330; Y-02
Kesey, Ken 1935-2001 . DLB-2, 16, 206; CDALB-6
Kessel, Joseph 1898-1979 . . . . DLB-72
Kessel, Martin 1901-1990 . . . . DLB-56
Kesten, Hermann 1900-1996 . . . . DLB-56
Keun, Irmgard 1905-1982 . . . . DLB-69
Key, Ellen 1849-1926 . . . . DLB-259
Key and Biddle DLB-49
Keynes, Sir Geoffrey 1887-1982 . . . . DLB-201
Keynes, John Maynard 1883-1946 . . . . DS-10
Keyserling, Eduard von 1855-1918 . . . . . DLB-66
Khalifeh, Sahar 1941- DLB-346
al-Khalil ibn Ahmad circa 718-791 . . . . . DLB-311
Khan, Adib 1949- DLB-323
Khan, Ismith 1925-2002 . . . . DLB-125
al-Khansa' fl. late sixth-mid
  seventh centuries DLB-311
Kharik, Izi 1898-1937 . . . . DLB-333
Kharitonov, Evgenii Vladimirovich
  1941-1981 . . . . DLB-285
Kharitonov, Mark Sergeevich 1937- . . . DLB-285
Kharjas, The DLB-337
Khaytov, Nikolay 1919- DLB-181
Khemnitser, Ivan Ivanovich
  1745-1784 . . . . DLB-150
Kheraskov, Mikhail Matveevich
  1733-1807 . . . . DLB-150
Khlebnikov, Velimir 1885-1922 . . . . DLB-295
Khodasevich, Vladislav 1886-1939 . . . . . DLB-317
Khomiakov, Aleksei Stepanovich
  1804-1860 . . . . DLB-205
Khristov, Boris 1945- DLB-181
Khuri, Raif 1913-1967 . . . . DLB-346
Khvoshchinskaia, Nadezhda Dmitrievna
  1824-1889 . . . . DLB-238
Khvostov, Dmitrii Ivanovich
  1757-1835 . . . . DLB-150
Kibirov, Timur Iur'evich (Timur
  Iur'evich Zapoev) 1955- DLB-285
Kidd, Adam 1802?-1831 . . . . DLB-99
William Kidd [publishing house] DLB-106

Kidde, Harald 1878-1918 . . . . DLB-300
Kidder, Tracy 1945- DLB-185
Kiely, Benedict 1919-2007 . . . . DLB-15, 319
Kieran, John 1892-1981 . . . . .DLB-171
Kierkegaard, Søren 1813-1855 . . . . DLB-300
Kies, Marietta 1853-1899 . . . . .DLB-270
Kiggins and Kellogg DLB-49
Kiley, Jed 1889-1962 . . . . DLB-4
Kilgore, Bernard 1908-1967 . . . . .DLB-127
Kilian, Crawford 1941- DLB-251
Killens, John Oliver 1916-1987 . . . . DLB-33
  Tribute to Julian Mayfield Y-84
Killigrew, Anne 1660-1685 . . . . DLB-131
Killigrew, Thomas 1612-1683 . . . . DLB-58
Kilmer, Joyce 1886-1918 . . . . DLB-45
Kilroy, Thomas 1934- DLB-233
Kilwardby, Robert circa 1215-1279 . . . . . DLB-115
Kilworth, Garry 1941- DLB-261
Kim, Anatolii Andreevich 1939- DLB-285
Kimball, Richard Burleigh 1816-1892 . . . DLB-202
Kincaid, Jamaica 1949-
  . . . . DLB-157, 227; CDALB-7; CDWLB-3
Kinck, Hans Ernst 1865-1926 . . . . DLB-297
King, Charles 1844-1933 . . . . DLB-186
King, Clarence 1842-1901 . . . . DLB-12
King, Florence 1936- Y-85
King, Francis 1923- DLB-15, 139
King, Grace 1852-1932 . . . . .DLB-12, 78
King, Harriet Hamilton 1840-1920 . . . . . DLB-199
King, Henry 1592-1669 . . . . DLB-126
Solomon King [publishing house] DLB-49
King, Stephen 1947- DLB-143; Y-80
King, Susan Petigru 1824-1875 . . . . DLB-239
King, Thomas 1943- DLB-175, 334
King, Woodie, Jr. 1937- DLB-38
Kinglake, Alexander William
  1809-1891 . . . . DLB-55, 166
Kingo, Thomas 1634-1703 . . . . DLB-300
Kingsbury, Donald 1929- DLB-251
Kingsley, Charles
  1819-1875 . . . . DLB-21, 32, 163, 178, 190
Kingsley, Henry 1830-1876 . . . . DLB-21, 230
Kingsley, Mary Henrietta 1862-1900 . . . .DLB-174
Kingsley, Sidney 1906-1995 . . . . DLB-7
Kingsmill, Hugh 1889-1949 . . . . DLB-149
Kingsolver, Barbara
  1955- DLB-206; CDALB-7
Kingston, Maxine Hong
  1940- . . DLB-173, 212, 312; Y-80; CDALB-7
Kingston, William Henry Giles
  1814-1880 . . . . DLB-163
Kinnan, Mary Lewis 1763-1848 . . . . DLB-200

Kinnell, Galway 1927- DLB-5, 342; Y-87

Kinsella, John 1963- DLB-325

Kinsella, Thomas 1928- DLB-27

Kipling, Rudyard 1865-1936
......DLB-19, 34, 141, 156, 330; CDBLB-5

Kipphardt, Heinar 1922-1982 ....DLB-124

Kirby, William 1817-1906.............DLB-99

Kircher, Athanasius 1602-1680 ....DLB-164

Kireevsky, Ivan Vasil'evich 1806-1856....DLB-198

Kireevsky, Petr Vasil'evich 1808-1856...DLB-205

Kirk, Hans 1898-1962.................DLB-214

Kirk, John Foster 1824-1904 ....DLB-79

Kirkconnell, Watson 1895-1977.........DLB-68

Kirkland, Caroline M.
1801-1864 .... DLB-3, 73, 74, 250; DS-13

Kirkland, Joseph 1830-1893............DLB-12

Francis Kirkman [publishing house]......DLB-170

Kirkpatrick, Clayton 1915-2004........DLB-127

Kirkup, James 1918- DLB-27

Kirouac, Conrad (see Marie-Victorin, Frère)

Kirsch, Sarah 1935- DLB-75

Kirst, Hans Hellmut 1914-1989.........DLB-69

Kiš, Danilo 1935-1989......DLB-181; CDWLB-4

Kita Morio 1927- DLB-182

Kitcat, Mabel Greenhow 1859-1922 .....DLB-135

Kitchin, C. H. B. 1895-1967 ....DLB-77

Kittredge, William 1932- DLB-212, 244

Kiukhel'beker, Vil'gel'm Karlovich
1797-1846.........................DLB-205

Kizer, Carolyn 1925- DLB-5, 169

Kjaerstad, Jan 1953- DLB-297

Klabund 1890-1928.....................DLB-66

Klaj, Johann 1616-1656 ....DLB-164

Klappert, Peter 1942- DLB-5

Klass, Philip (see Tenn, William)

Klein, A. M. 1909-1972................DLB-68

Kleist, Ewald von 1715-1759 ....DLB-97

Kleist, Heinrich von
1777-1811.............DLB-90; CDWLB-2

Klíma, Ivan 1931- DLB-232; CDWLB-4

Klimentev, Andrei Platonovic
(see Platonov, Andrei Platonovich)

Klinger, Friedrich Maximilian
1752-1831 ....DLB-94

Kliuev, Nikolai Alekseevich 1884-1937...DLB-295

Kliushnikov, Viktor Petrovich
1841-1892.........................DLB-238

Klopfer, Donald S.
Impressions of William Faulkner.........Y-97
Oral History Interview with Donald
S. Klopfer Y-97
Tribute to Alfred A. Knopf Y-84

Klopstock, Friedrich Gottlieb
1724-1803 ....DLB-97

Klopstock, Meta 1728-1758 ....DLB-97

Kluge, Alexander 1932- DLB-75

Kluge, P. F. 1942- Y-02

Knapp, Joseph Palmer 1864-1951 ....DLB-91

Knapp, Samuel Lorenzo 1783-1838 ......DLB-59

J. J. and P. Knapton [publishing house]...DLB-154

Kniazhnin, Iakov Borisovich
1740-1791 ....DLB-150

Knickerbocker, Diedrich (see Irving, Washington)

Knigge, Adolph Franz Friedrich Ludwig,
Freiherr von 1752-1796 ....DLB-94

Charles Knight and Company..........DLB-106

Knight, Damon 1922-2002 ....DLB-8

Knight, Etheridge 1931-1992...........DLB-41

Knight, John S. 1894-1981.............DLB-29

Knight, Sarah Kemble 1666-1727.....DLB-24, 200

Knight-Bruce, G. W. H. 1852-1896 .....DLB-174

Knister, Raymond 1899-1932 ....DLB-68

Knoblock, Edward 1874-1945 ....DLB-10

Knopf, Alfred A. 1892-1984.............Y-84
Knopf to Hammett: The Editoral
Correspondence Y-00

Alfred A. Knopf [publishing house]......DLB-46

Knorr von Rosenroth, Christian
1636-1689 ....DLB-168

Knowles, James Sheridan 1784-1862 .....DLB-344

Knowles, John 1926-2001 ......DLB-6; CDALB-6

Knox, Frank 1874-1944 ....DLB-29

Knox, John circa 1514-1572............DLB-132

Knox, John Armoy 1850-1906...........DLB-23

Knox, Lucy 1845-1884 ....DLB-240

Knox, Ronald Arbuthnott 1888-1957 .....DLB-77

Knox, Thomas Wallace 1835-1896 ......DLB-189

Knudsen, Jakob 1858-1917 ....DLB-300

Knut, Dovid 1900-1955................DLB-317

Kobayashi Takiji 1903-1933............DLB-180

Kober, Arthur 1900-1975...............DLB-11

Kobiakova, Aleksandra Petrovna
1823-1892 ....DLB-238

Kocbek, Edvard 1904-1981 ...DLB-147; CDWLB-4

Koch, C. J. 1932- DLB-289

Koch, Howard 1902-1995 ....DLB-26

Koch, Kenneth 1925-2002 ....DLB-5

Kōda Rohan 1867-1947 ....DLB-180

Koehler, Ted 1894-1973 ....DLB-265

Koenigsberg, Moses 1879-1945 ....DLB-25

Koeppen, Wolfgang 1906-1996 ....DLB-69

Koertge, Ronald 1940- DLB-105

Koestler, Arthur 1905-1983 ......Y-83; CDBLB-7

Kogawa, Joy 1935- DLB-334

Kohn, John S. Van E. 1906-1976 ....DLB-187

Kokhanovskaia
(see Sokhanskaia, Nadezhda Stepanova)

Kokoschka, Oskar 1886-1980 ....DLB-124

Kolatkar, Arun 1932-2004.............DLB-323

Kolb, Annette 1870-1967 ....DLB-66

Kolbenheyer, Erwin Guido
1878-1962 ....DLB-66, 124

Kolleritsch, Alfred 1931- DLB-85

Kolodny, Annette 1941- DLB-67

Koltès, Bernard-Marie 1948-1989 ....DLB-321

Kol'tsov, Aleksei Vasil'evich
1809-1842 ....DLB-205

Komarov, Matvei circa 1730-1812 ......DLB-150

Komroff, Manuel 1890-1974 ....DLB-4

Komunyakaa, Yusef 1947- DLB-120

Kondoleon, Harry 1955-1994 ....DLB-266

Koneski, Blaže 1921-1993 ...DLB-181; CDWLB-4

Konigsburg, E. L. 1930- DLB-52

Konparu Zenchiku 1405-1468?.........DLB-203

Konrád, György 1933- DLB-232; CDWLB-4

Konrad von Würzburg
circa 1230-1287 ....DLB-138

Konstantinov, Aleko 1863-1897 ....DLB-147

Konwicki, Tadeusz 1926- DLB-232

Koontz, Dean 1945- DLB-292

Kooser, Ted 1939- DLB-105

Kopit, Arthur 1937- DLB-7

Kops, Bernard 1926?-..................DLB-13

Korn, Rachel (Rokhl Korn)
1898-1982 ....DLB-333

Kornbluth, C. M. 1923-1958............DLB-8

Körner, Theodor 1791-1813 ....DLB-90

Kornfeld, Paul 1889-1942 ....DLB-118

Korolenko, Vladimir Galaktionovich
1853-1921 ....DLB-277

Kosinski, Jerzy 1933-1991 ...... DLB-2, 299; Y-82

Kosmač, Ciril 1910-1980 ....DLB-181

Kosovel, Srečko 1904-1926 ....DLB-147

Kostrov, Ermil Ivanovich 1755-1796 ....DLB-150

Kotzebue, August von 1761-1819.........DLB-94

Kotzwinkle, William 1938- DLB-173

Kovačić, Ante 1854-1889..............DLB-147

Kovalevskaia, Sof'ia Vasil'evna
1850-1891 ....DLB-277

Kovič, Kajetan 1931- DLB-181

Kozlov, Ivan Ivanovich 1779-1840 ......DLB-205

Kracauer, Siegfried 1889-1966.........DLB-296

Kraf, Elaine 1946- Y-81

Kramer, Jane 1938- DLB-185

Kramer, Larry 1935- DLB-249

Kramer, Mark 1944- DLB-185

Kranjčević, Silvije Strahimir 1865-1908...DLB-147

Krasko, Ivan 1876-1958...............DLB-215

Krasna, Norman 1909-1984 .... DLB-26
Kraus, Hans Peter 1907-1988 .... DLB-187
Kraus, Karl 1874-1936 .... DLB-118
Krause, Herbert 1905-1976 .... DLB-256
Krauss, Ruth 1911-1993 .... DLB-52
Krauth, Nigel 1949- DLB-325
Kreisel, Henry 1922-1991 .... DLB-88
Krestovsky V.
   (see Khvoshchinskaia, Nadezhda Dmitrievna)
Krestovsky, Vsevolod Vladimirovich
   1839-1895 .... DLB-238
Kreuder, Ernst 1903-1972 .... DLB-69
Krėvė-Mickevičius, Vincas 1882-1954 ... DLB-220
Kreymborg, Alfred 1883-1966 .... DLB-4, 54
Krieger, Murray 1923-2000 .... DLB-67
Krim, Seymour 1922-1989 .... DLB-16
Kripke, Saul 1940- DLB-279
Kristensen, Tom 1893-1974 .... DLB-214
Kristeva, Julia 1941- DLB-242
Kristján Níels Jónsson/Kristjan Niels Julius
   (see Káinn)
Kritzer, Hyman W. 1918-2002 .... Y-02
Krivulin, Viktor Borisovich 1944-2001... DLB-285
Krleža, Miroslav
   1893-1981 .... DLB-147; CDWLB-4
Krock, Arthur 1886-1974 .... DLB-29
Kroetsch, Robert 1927- DLB-53
Kropotkin, Petr Alekseevich 1842-1921 ...DLB-277
Kross, Jaan 1920-2007 .... DLB-232
Kruchenykh, Aleksei Eliseevich
   1886-1968 .... DLB-295
Krúdy, Gyula 1878-1933 .... DLB-215
Krutch, Joseph Wood
   1893-1970 .... DLB-63, 206, 275
Krylov, Ivan Andreevich 1769-1844 ..... DLB-150
Krymov, Iurii Solomonovich
   (Iurii Solomonovich Beklemishev)
   1908-1941 .... DLB-272
Kubin, Alfred 1877-1959 .... DLB-81
Kubrick, Stanley 1928-1999 .... DLB-26
Kudrun circa 1230-1240 .... DLB-138
Kuffstein, Hans Ludwig von 1582-1656.. DLB-164
Kuhlmann, Quirinus 1651-1689 .... DLB-168
Kuhn, Thomas S. 1922-1996 .... DLB-279
Kuhnau, Johann 1660-1722 .... DLB-168
Kukol'nik, Nestor Vasil'evich
   1809-1868 .... DLB-205
Kukučín, Martin
   1860-1928 .... DLB-215; CDWLB-4
Kulbak, Moyshe 1896-1937 .... DLB-333
Kumin, Maxine 1925- DLB-5
Kuncewicz, Maria 1895-1989 .... DLB-215
Kundera, Milan 1929- DLB-232; CDWLB-4
Kunene, Mazisi 1930- DLB-117

al-Kuni, Ibrahim 1948- DLB-346
Kunikida Doppo 1869-1908 .... DLB-180
Kunitz, Stanley 1905-2006 .... DLB-48
Kunjufu, Johari M. (see Amini, Johari M.)
Kunnert, Gunter 1929- DLB-75
Kunze, Reiner 1933- DLB-75
Kuo, Helena 1911-1999 .... DLB-312
Kupferberg, Tuli 1923- DLB-16
Kuprin, Aleksandr Ivanovich
   1870-1938 .... DLB-295
Kuraev, Mikhail Nikolaevich 1939- ... DLB-285
Kurahashi Yumiko 1935- DLB-182
Kureishi, Hanif 1954- DLB-194, 245
Kürnberger, Ferdinand 1821-1879 ...... DLB-129
Kurz, Isolde 1853-1944 .... DLB-66
Kusenberg, Kurt 1904-1983 .... DLB-69
Kushchevsky, Ivan Afanas'evich
   1847-1876 .... DLB-238
Kushner, Tony 1956- DLB-228
Kuttner, Henry 1915-1958 .... DLB-8
Kuzmin, Mikhail Alekseevich
   1872-1936 .... DLB-295
Kuznetsov, Anatoli 1929-1979 ..... DLB-299, 302
Kvitko, Leib (Leyb Kvitko)
   1890-1952 .... DLB-333
Kyd, Thomas 1558-1594 .... DLB-62
Kyffin, Maurice circa 1560?-1598 ...... DLB-136
Kyger, Joanne 1934- DLB-16
Kyne, Peter B. 1880-1957 .... DLB-78
Kyōgoku Tamekane 1254-1332 .... DLB-203
Kyrklund, Willy 1921- DLB-257

L

L. E. L. (see Landon, Letitia Elizabeth)
Labé, Louise 1520?-1566 .... DLB-327
Laberge, Albert 1871-1960 .... DLB-68
Laberge, Marie 1950- DLB-60
Labiche, Eugène 1815-1888 .... DLB-192
Labrunie, Gerard (see Nerval, Gerard de)
La Bruyère, Jean de 1645-1696 .... DLB-268
La Calprenède 1609?-1663 .... DLB-268
Lacan, Jacques 1901-1981 .... DLB-296
La Capria, Raffaele 1922- DLB-196
La Ceppède, Jean de 1550?-1623 ...... DLB-327
La Chaussée, Pierre-Claude Nivelle de
   1692-1754 .... DLB-313
Laclos, Pierre-Ambroise-François Choderlos de
   1741-1803 .... DLB-313
   Dangerous Acquaintances DLB-314
Lacombe, Patrice
   (see Trullier-Lacombe, Joseph Patrice)
Lacretelle, Jacques de 1888-1985 .... DLB-65
Lacy, Ed 1911-1968 .... DLB-226

Lacy, Sam 1903-2003 .... DLB-171
Ladd, Joseph Brown 1764-1786 .... DLB-37
La Farge, Oliver 1901-1963 .... DLB-9
Lafayette, Marie-Madeleine, comtesse de
   1634-1693 .... DLB-268
Laferrière, Dany 1953- DLB-334
Laffan, Mrs. R. S. de Courcy
   (see Adams, Bertha Leith)
Lafferty, R. A. 1914-2002 .... DLB-8
La Flesche, Francis 1857-1932 .... DLB-175
La Fontaine, Jean de 1621-1695 .... DLB-268
Laforet, Carmen 1921-2004 .... DLB-322
Laforge, Jules 1860-1887 .... DLB-217
Lagerkvist, Pär 1891-1974 .... DLB-259, 331
Lagerlöf, Selma 1858-1940 .... DLB-259, 331
Lagorio, Gina 1922- DLB-196
La Guma, Alex
   1925-1985 .... DLB-117, 225; CDWLB-3
Lahaise, Guillaume (see Delahaye, Guy)
La Harpe, Jean-François de 1739-1803 .... DLB-313
Lahiri, Jhumpa 1967- DLB-323
Lahontan, Louis-Armand de Lom d'Arce,
   Baron de 1666-1715? DLB-99
Lai He 1894-1943 .... DLB-328
Laing, Kojo 1946- DLB-157
Laird, Carobeth 1895-1983 .... Y-82
Laird and Lee DLB-49
Lake, Paul 1951- DLB-282
Lalić, Ivan V. 1931-1996 .... DLB-181
Lalić, Mihailo 1914-1992 .... DLB-181
Lalonde, Michèle 1937- DLB-60
Lamantia, Philip 1927-2005 .... DLB-16
Lamartine, Alphonse de
   1790-1869 .... DLB-217
Lamb, Lady Caroline 1785-1828 ..... DLB-116
Lamb, Charles
   1775-1834 ...... DLB-93, 107, 163; CDBLB-3
Lamb, Mary 1764-1874 .... DLB-163
Lambert, Angela 1940- DLB-271
Lambert, Anne-Thérèse de (Anne-Thérèse de
   Marguenat de Courcelles, marquise de Lambert)
   1647-1733 .... DLB-313
Lambert, Betty 1933-1983 .... DLB-60
La Mettrie, Julien Offroy de
   1709-1751 .... DLB-313
Lamm, Donald
   Goodbye, Gutenberg? A Lecture at
   the New York Public Library,
   18 April 1995 .... Y-95
Lamming, George 1927- ...DLB-125; CDWLB-3
La Mothe Le Vayer, François de
   1588-1672 .... DLB-268
L'Amour, Louis 1908-1988 .... DLB-206; Y-80
Lampman, Archibald 1861-1899 ...... DLB-92
Lamson, Wolffe and Company DLB-49
Lancer Books DLB-46
Lanchester, John 1962- DLB-267

Lander, Peter (see Cunningham, Peter)

Landesman, Jay 1919- and
Landesman, Fran 1927-..............DLB-16

Landolfi, Tommaso 1908-1979..........DLB-177

Landon, Letitia Elizabeth 1802-1838......DLB-96

Landor, Walter Savage 1775-1864 .... DLB-93, 107

Landry, Napoléon-P. 1884-1956 ....DLB-92

Landvik, Lorna 1954- DLB-292

Lane, Charles 1800-1870 ....DLB-1, 223; DS-5

Lane, F. C. 1885-1984 ....DLB-241

Lane, Laurence W. 1890-1967...........DLB-91

Lane, M. Travis 1934- DLB-60

Lane, Patrick 1939- DLB-53

Lane, Pinkie Gordon 1923- DLB-41

John Lane Company DLB-49

Laney, Al 1896-1988 ....DLB-4, 171

Lang, Andrew 1844-1912 ......DLB-98, 141, 184

Langer, Susanne K. 1895-1985 ....DLB-270

Langevin, André 1927- DLB-60

Langford, David 1953- DLB-261

Langgässer, Elisabeth 1899-1950.........DLB-69

Langhorne, John 1735-1779 ....DLB-109

Langland, William
circa 1330-circa 1400..............DLB-146

Langton, Anna 1804-1893 ....DLB-99

Lanham, Edwin 1904-1979 ....DLB-4

Lanier, Sidney 1842-1881 ....DLB-64; DS-13

Lanyer, Aemilia 1569-1645 ....DLB-121

Lao She 1899-1966 ....DLB-328

Lapine, James 1949- DLB-341

Lapointe, Gatien 1931-1983............DLB-88

Lapointe, Paul-Marie 1929- DLB-88

La Ramée, Pierre de (Petrus Ramus, Peter Ramus)
1515-1572 ....DLB-327

Larcom, Lucy 1824-1893..........DLB-221, 243

Lardner, John 1912-1960 ....DLB-171

Lardner, Ring 1885-1933
...... DLB-11, 25, 86, 171; DS-16; CDALB-4

Lardner 100: Ring Lardner
Centennial Symposium............Y-85

Lardner, Ring, Jr. 1915-2000 .... DLB-26, Y-00

Larivey, Pierre de 1541-1619...........DLB-327

Larkin, Philip 1922-1985 ......DLB-27; CDBLB-8

The Philip Larkin Society Y-99

La Roche, Sophie von 1730-1807........DLB-94

La Rochefoucauld, François duc de
1613-1680......................DLB-268

La Rocque, Gilbert 1943-1984..........DLB-60

Laroque de Roquebrune, Robert
(see Roquebrune, Robert de)

Laroui, Abdallah 1933- DLB-346

Larrick, Nancy 1910-2004.............DLB-61

Lars, Claudia 1899-1974 ....DLB-283

Larsen, Nella 1893-1964 ....DLB-51

Larsen, Thøger 1875-1928 ....DLB-300

Larson, Clinton F. 1919-1994 ....DLB-256

La Sale, Antoine de
circa 1386-1460/1467 ....DLB-208

Las Casas, Fray Bartolomé de
1474-1566 ....DLB-318

Lasch, Christopher 1932-1994..........DLB-246

Lasdun, James 1958- DLB-319

Lasker-Schüler, Else 1869-1945 ......DLB-66, 124

Lasnier, Rina 1915-1997 ....DLB-88

Lassalle, Ferdinand 1825-1864..........DLB-129

Last Orders, 1996 Booker Prize winner,
Graham Swift DLB-326

La Taille, Jean de 1534?-1611? DLB-327

Late-Medieval Castilian Theater DLB-286

Latham, Robert 1912-1995 ....DLB-201

Lathan, Emma (Mary Jane Latsis [1927-1997] and
Martha Henissart [1929-   ]) DLB-306

Lathrop, Dorothy P. 1891-1980.........DLB-22

Lathrop, George Parsons 1851-1898 ......DLB-71

Lathrop, John, Jr. 1772-1820 ....DLB-37

Latimer, Hugh 1492?-1555 ....DLB-136

Latimore, Jewel Christine McLawler
(see Amini, Johari M.)

Latin Histories and Chronicles of
Medieval Spain DLB-337

Latin Literature, The Uniqueness of DLB-211

La Tour du Pin, Patrice de 1911-1975 ....DLB-258

Latymer, William 1498-1583...........DLB-132

Laube, Heinrich 1806-1884............DLB-133

Laud, William 1573-1645..............DLB-213

Laughlin, James 1914-1997 ..... DLB-48; Y-96, 97

A Tribute [to Henry Miller]............Y-80

Tribute to Albert Erskine Y-93

Tribute to Kenneth Rexroth Y-82

Tribute to Malcolm Cowley Y-89

Laumer, Keith 1925-1993 ....DLB-8

Lauremberg, Johann 1590-1658 ....DLB-164

Laurence, Margaret 1926-1987 ....DLB-53

Laurentius von Schnüffis 1633-1702 .....DLB-168

Laurents, Arthur 1917- DLB-26, 341

Laurie, Annie (see Black, Winifred)

Laut, Agnes Christiana 1871-1936........DLB-92

Lauterbach, Ann 1942- DLB-193

Lautréamont, Isidore Lucien Ducasse,
Comte de 1846-1870..............DLB-217

Lavater, Johann Kaspar 1741-1801 ....DLB-97

Lavin, Mary 1912-1996...........DLB-15, 319

Law, John (see Harkness, Margaret)

Lawes, Henry 1596-1662..............DLB-126

Lawler, Ray 1922- DLB-289

Lawless, Anthony (see MacDonald, Philip)

Lawless, Emily (The Hon. Emily Lawless)
1845-1913 ....DLB-240

Lawless, Gary 1951- DLB-342

Lawrence, D. H. 1885-1930
..... DLB-10, 19, 36, 98, 162, 195; CDBLB-6

The D. H. Lawrence Society of
North America Y-00

Lawrence, David 1888-1973 ....DLB-29

Lawrence, Jerome 1915-2004...........DLB-228

Lawrence, Seymour 1926-1994 ....Y-94

Tribute to Richard Yates Y-92

Lawrence, T. E. 1888-1935 ....DLB-195

The T. E. Lawrence Society Y-98

Lawson, George 1598-1678.............DLB-213

Lawson, Henry 1867-1922..............DLB-230

Lawson, John ?-1711 ....DLB-24

Lawson, John Howard 1894-1977 ....DLB-228

Lawson, Louisa Albury 1848-1920 ......DLB-230

Lawson, Robert 1892-1957 ....DLB-22

Lawson, Victor F. 1850-1925............DLB-25

Layard, Austen Henry 1817-1894 ....DLB-166

Layton, Irving 1912-2006 ....DLB-88

LaZamon fl. circa 1200 ....DLB-146

Lazarević, Laza K. 1851-1890 ....DLB-147

Lazarus, George 1904-1997............DLB-201

Lazhechnikov, Ivan Ivanovich
1792-1869 ....DLB-198

Lea, Henry Charles 1825-1909 ....DLB-47

Lea, Sydney 1942- DLB-120, 282

Lea, Tom 1907-2001....................DLB-6

Leacock, John 1729-1802...............DLB-31

Leacock, Stephen 1869-1944 ....DLB-92

Lead, Jane Ward 1623-1704............DLB-131

Leadenhall Press DLB-106

"The Greatness of Southern Literature":
League of the South Institute for the
Study of Southern Culture and History
...............................Y-02

Leakey, Caroline Woolmer 1827-1881 .... DLB-230

Leapor, Mary 1722-1746 ....DLB-109

Lear, Edward 1812-1888 ....DLB-32, 163, 166

Leary, Timothy 1920-1996 ....DLB-16

W. A. Leary and Company DLB-49

Léautaud, Paul 1872-1956 ....DLB-65

Leavis, F. R. 1895-1978 ....DLB-242

Leavitt, David 1961- DLB-130

Leavitt and Allen DLB-49

Le Blond, Mrs. Aubrey 1861-1934 ......DLB-174

le Carré, John (David John Moore Cornwell)
1931- DLB-87; CDBLB-8

Tribute to Graham Greene Y-91

Tribute to George Greenfield Y-00

Lécavelé, Roland (see Dorgeles, Roland)

Lechlitner, Ruth 1901-1989 .... DLB-48

Leclerc, Félix 1914-1988 .... DLB-60

Le Clézio, J. M. G. 1940- DLB-83

Leder, Rudolf (see Hermlin, Stephan)

Lederer, Charles 1910-1976 .... DLB-26

Ledwidge, Francis 1887-1917 .... DLB-20

Lee, Chang-rae 1965- DLB-312

Lee, Cherylene 1953- DLB-312

Lee, Dennis 1939- DLB-53

Lee, Don L. (see Madhubuti, Haki R.)

Lee, George W. 1894-1976 .... DLB-51

Lee, Gus 1946- DLB-312

Lee, Harper 1926- DLB-6; CDALB-1

Lee, Harriet 1757-1851 and
   Lee, Sophia 1750-1824 .... DLB-39

Lee, Laurie 1914-1997 .... DLB-27

Lee, Leslie 1935- DLB-266

Lee, Li-Young 1957- DLB-165, 312

Lee, Manfred B. 1905-1971 .... DLB-137

Lee, Nathaniel circa 1645-1692 .... DLB-80

Lee, Robert E. 1918-1994 .... DLB-228

Lee, Sir Sidney 1859-1926 .... DLB-149, 184

   "Principles of Biography," in
   Elizabethan and Other Essays DLB-149

Lee, Tanith 1947- DLB-261

Lee, Vernon
   1856-1935 ...... DLB-57, 153, 156, 174, 178

Lee and Shepard DLB-49

Le Fanu, Joseph Sheridan
   1814-1873 .... DLB-21, 70, 159, 178

Lefèvre d'Etaples, Jacques
   1460?-1536 .... DLB-327

Leffland, Ella 1931- Y-84

le Fort, Gertrud von 1876-1971 .... DLB-66

Le Gallienne, Richard 1866-1947 .... DLB-4

Legaré, Hugh Swinton
   1797-1843 .... DLB-3, 59, 73, 248

Legaré, James Mathewes 1823-1859 ... DLB-3, 248

Léger, Antoine-J. 1880-1950 .... DLB-88

Leggett, William 1801-1839 .... DLB-250

Le Guin, Ursula K.
   1929- DLB-8, 52, 256, 275; CDALB-6

Lehman, Ernest 1915-2005 .... DLB-44

Lehmann, John 1907-1989 .... DLB-27, 100

John Lehmann Limited DLB-112

Lehmann, Rosamond 1901-1990 .... DLB-15

Lehmann, Wilhelm 1882-1968 .... DLB-56

Leiber, Fritz 1910-1992 .... DLB-8

Leibniz, Gottfried Wilhelm 1646-1716 ... DLB-168

Leicester University Press DLB-112

Leigh, Carolyn 1926-1983 .... DLB-265

Leigh, W. R. 1866-1955 .... DLB-188

Leinster, Murray 1896-1975 .... DLB-8

Leiser, Bill 1898-1965 .... DLB-241

Leisewitz, Johann Anton 1752-1806 ...... DLB-94

Leitch, Maurice 1933- DLB-14

Leithauser, Brad 1943- DLB-120, 282

Leivick, H[alper] (H. Leyvik)
   1888-1962 .... DLB-333

Leland, Charles G. 1824-1903 .... DLB-11

Leland, John 1503?-1552 .... DLB-136

Leland, Thomas 1722-1785 .... DLB-336

Lemaire de Belges, Jean 1473-? DLB-327

Lemay, Pamphile 1837-1918 .... DLB-99

Lemelin, Roger 1919-1992 .... DLB-88

Lemercier, Louis-Jean-Népomucène
   1771-1840 .... DLB-192

Le Moine, James MacPherson 1825-1912 . DLB-99

Lemon, Mark 1809-1870 .... DLB-163

Le Moyne, Jean 1913-1996 .... DLB-88

Lemperly, Paul 1858-1939 .... DLB-187

Leñero, Vicente 1933- DLB-305

L'Engle, Madeleine 1918-2007 .... DLB-52

Lennart, Isobel 1915-1971 .... DLB-44

Lennox, Charlotte 1729 or 1730-1804 ... DLB-39

Lenox, James 1800-1880 .... DLB-140

Lenski, Lois 1893-1974 .... DLB-22

Lentricchia, Frank 1940- DLB-246

Lenz, Hermann 1913-1998 .... DLB-69

Lenz, J. M. R. 1751-1792 .... DLB-94

Lenz, Siegfried 1926- DLB-75

León, Fray Luis de 1527-1591 .... DLB-318

Leonard, Elmore 1925- DLB-173, 226

Leonard, Hugh 1926- DLB-13

Leonard, William Ellery 1876-1944 ..... DLB-54

Leong, Russell C. 1950- DLB-312

Leonov, Leonid Maksimovich
   1899-1994 .... DLB-272

Leonowens, Anna 1834-1914 .... DLB-99, 166

Leont'ev, Konstantin Nikolaevich
   1831-1891 .... DLB-277

Leopold, Aldo 1887-1948 .... DLB-275

LePan, Douglas 1914-1998 .... DLB-88

Lepik, Kalju 1920-1999 .... DLB-232

Leprohon, Rosanna Eleanor 1829-1879 ... DLB-99

Le Queux, William 1864-1927 .... DLB-70

Lermontov, Mikhail Iur'evich
   1814-1841 .... DLB-205

Lerner, Alan Jay 1918-1986 .... DLB-265

Lerner, Max 1902-1992 .... DLB-29

Lernet-Holenia, Alexander 1897-1976 .... DLB-85

Le Rossignol, James 1866-1969 .... DLB-92

Lesage, Alain-René 1668-1747 .... DLB-313

Lescarbot, Marc circa 1570-1642 .... DLB-99

LeSeur, William Dawson 1840-1917 ..... DLB-92

LeSieg, Theo. (see Geisel, Theodor Seuss)

Leskov, Nikolai Semenovich
   1831-1895 .... DLB-238

Leslie, Doris before 1902-1982 .... DLB-191

Leslie, Eliza 1787-1858 .... DLB-202

Leslie, Frank (Henry Carter)
   1821-1880 .... DLB-43, 79

Frank Leslie [publishing house] DLB-49

Leśmian, Bolesław 1878-1937 .... DLB-215

Lesperance, John 1835?-1891 .... DLB-99

Lespinasse, Julie de 1732-1776 .... DLB-313

Lessing, Bruno 1870-1940 .... DLB-28

Lessing, Doris
   1919- DLB-15, 139; Y-85; CDBLB-8

Lessing, Gotthold Ephraim
   1729-1781 .... DLB-97; CDWLB-2

The Lessing Society Y-00

L'Estoile, Pierre de 1546-1611 .... DLB-327

Le Sueur, Meridel 1900-1996 .... DLB-303

Lettau, Reinhard 1929-1996 .... DLB-75

Letters from a Peruvian Woman, Françoise d'Issembourg
   de Graffigny DLB-314

The Hemingway Letters Project Finds
   an Editor Y-02

Lever, Charles 1806-1872 .... DLB-21

Lever, Ralph ca. 1527-1585 .... DLB-236

Leverson, Ada 1862-1933 .... DLB-153

Levertov, Denise
   1923-1997 ...... DLB-5, 165, 342; CDALB-7

Levi, Peter 1931-2000 .... DLB-40

Levi, Primo 1919-1987 .... DLB-177, 299

Levien, Sonya 1888-1960 .... DLB-44

Levin, Meyer 1905-1981 .... DLB-9, 28; Y-81

Levin, Phillis 1954- DLB-282

Lévinas, Emmanuel 1906-1995 .... DLB-296

Levine, Norman 1923- DLB-88

Levine, Philip 1928- DLB-5

Levis, Larry 1946- DLB-120

Lévi-Strauss, Claude 1908- DLB-242

Levitov, Aleksandr Ivanovich
   1835?-1877 .... DLB-277

Levy, Amy 1861-1889 .... DLB-156, 240

Levy, Benn Wolfe 1900-1973 .... DLB-13; Y-81

Levy, Deborah 1959- DLB-310

Lewald, Fanny 1811-1889 .... DLB-129

Lewes, George Henry 1817-1878 .... DLB-55, 144

   "Criticism in Relation to Novels"
   (1863) DLB-21

   The Principles of Success in Literature
   (1865) [excerpt] DLB-57

Lewis, Agnes Smith 1843-1926 .... DLB-174

Lewis, Alfred H. 1857-1914 .... DLB-25, 186

Lewis, Alun 1915-1944 .... DLB-20, 162

Lewis, C. Day (see Day Lewis, C.)

Lewis, C. I. 1883-1964 . . . . DLB-270

Lewis, C. S. 1898-1963
. . . . DLB-15, 100, 160, 255; CDBLB-7

    The New York C. S. Lewis Society Y-99

Lewis, Charles B. 1842-1924 . . . . DLB-11

Lewis, David 1941-2001 . . . . DLB-279

Lewis, Henry Clay 1825-1850 . . . . DLB-3, 248

Lewis, Janet 1899-1999 . . . . Y-87

    Tribute to Katherine Anne Porter Y-80

Lewis, Matthew Gregory
1775-1818 . . . . DLB-39, 158, 178

Lewis, Meriwether 1774-1809 . . . . . . DLB-183, 186

Lewis, Norman 1908-2003 . . . . DLB-204

Lewis, R. W. B. 1917-2002 . . . . DLB-111

Lewis, Richard circa 1700-1734 . . . . DLB-24

Lewis, Saunders 1893-1985 . . . . DLB-310

Lewis, Sinclair 1885-1951
. . . . DLB-9, 102, 331; DS-1; CDALB-4

    Sinclair Lewis Centennial Conference Y-85

    The Sinclair Lewis Society Y-99

Lewis, Wilmarth Sheldon 1895-1979 . . . . . DLB-140

Lewis, Wyndham 1882-1957 . . . . DLB-15

    Time and Western Man
    [excerpt] (1927) DLB-36

Lewisohn, Ludwig 1882-1955 . . . DLB-4, 9, 28, 102

Leyendecker, J. C. 1874-1951 . . . . DLB-188

Leyner, Mark 1956- DLB-292

Lezama Lima, José 1910-1976 . . . . . . DLB-113, 283

Lézardière, Marie-Charlotte-Pauline Robert de
1754-1835 . . . . DLB-313

L'Heureux, John 1934- DLB-244

Libbey, Laura Jean 1862-1924 . . . . DLB-221

Libedinsky, Iurii Nikolaevich
1898-1959 . . . . DLB-272

The Liberator DLB-303

Library History Group Y-01

    E-Books' Second Act in Libraries Y-02

The Library of America DLB-46

The Library of America: An Assessment
After Two Decades Y-02

Libro de Alexandre
(early thirteenth century) DLB-337

Libro de Apolonio (late thirteenth century) . . DLB-337

Libro del Caballero Zifar
(circa 1300-1325) DLB-337

Libro de miserio d'omne (circa 1300-1340) . . . DLB-337

Licensing Act of 1737 . . . . DLB-84

Leonard Lichfield I [publishing house] . . . DLB-170

Lichtenberg, Georg Christoph
1742-1799 . . . . DLB-94

The Liddle Collection Y-97

Lidman, Sara 1923-2004 . . . . DLB-257

Lieb, Fred 1888-1980 . . . . DLB-171

Liebling, A. J. 1904-1963 . . . . DLB-4, 171

Lieutenant Murray (see Ballou, Maturin Murray)

Life and Times of Michael K, 1983 Booker Prize winner,
J. M. Coetzee DLB-326

Life of Pi, 2002 Booker Prize winner,
Yann Martel DLB-326

Lighthall, William Douw 1857-1954 . . . . . . DLB-92

Lihn, Enrique 1929-1988 . . . . DLB-283

Lilar, Françoise (see Mallet-Joris, Françoise)

Lili'uokalani, Queen 1838-1917 . . . . DLB-221

Lillo, George 1691-1739 . . . . DLB-84

Lilly, J. K., Jr. 1893-1966 . . . . DLB-140

Lilly, Wait and Company DLB-49

Lily, William circa 1468-1522 . . . . DLB-132

Lim, Shirley Geok-lin 1944- DLB-312

Lima, Jorge de 1893-1953 . . . . DLB-307

Lima Barreto, Afonso Henriques de
1881-1922 . . . . DLB-307

Limited Editions Club DLB-46

Limón, Graciela 1938- DLB-209

Limonov, Eduard 1943- DLB-317

Lincoln and Edmands DLB-49

Lind, Jakov 1927-2007 . . . . DLB-299

Linda Vilhjálmsdóttir 1958- DLB-293

Lindesay, Ethel Forence
(see Richardson, Henry Handel)

Lindgren, Astrid 1907-2002 . . . . DLB-257

Lindgren, Torgny 1938- DLB-257

Lindsay, Alexander William, Twenty-fifth
Earl of Crawford 1812-1880 . . . . DLB-184

Lindsay, Sir David circa 1485-1555 . . . . . . DLB-132

Lindsay, David 1878-1945 . . . . DLB-255

Lindsay, Jack 1900-1990 . . . . Y-84

Lindsay, Lady (Caroline Blanche
Elizabeth Fitzroy Lindsay)
1844-1912 . . . . DLB-199

Lindsay, Norman 1879-1969 . . . . DLB-260

Lindsay, Vachel
1879-1931 . . . . DLB-54; CDALB-3

The Line of Beauty, 2004 Booker Prize winner,
Alan Hollinghurst DLB-326

Linebarger, Paul Myron Anthony
(see Smith, Cordwainer)

Ling Shuhua 1900-1990 . . . . DLB-328

Link, Arthur S. 1920-1998 . . . . DLB-17

Linn, Ed 1922-2000 . . . . DLB-241

Linn, John Blair 1777-1804 . . . . DLB-37

Lins, Osman 1924-1978 . . . . DLB-145, 307

Linton, Eliza Lynn 1822-1898 . . . . DLB-18

Linton, William James 1812-1897 . . . . DLB-32

Barnaby Bernard Lintot
[publishing house] DLB-170

Lion Books DLB-46

Lionni, Leo 1910-1999 . . . . DLB-61

Lippard, George 1822-1854 . . . . DLB-202

Lippincott, Sara Jane Clarke
1823-1904 . . . . DLB-43

J. B. Lippincott Company DLB-49

Lippmann, Walter 1889-1974 . . . . DLB-29

Lipton, Lawrence 1898-1975 . . . . DLB-16

Lisboa, Irene 1892-1958 . . . . DLB-287

Liscow, Christian Ludwig
1701-1760 . . . . DLB-97

Lish, Gordon 1934- DLB-130

    Tribute to Donald Barthelme Y-89

    Tribute to James Dickey Y-97

Lisle, Charles-Marie-René Leconte de
1818-1894 . . . . DLB-217

Lispector, Clarice
1925?-1977 . . . . DLB-113, 307; CDWLB-3

LitCheck Website Y-01

Literary Awards and Honors Y-81–02

    Booker Prize Y-86, 96–98

    The Drue Heinz Literature Prize Y-82

    The Elmer Holmes Bobst Awards
in Arts and Letters Y-87

    The Griffin Poetry Prize Y-00

    Literary Prizes [British] DLB-15, 207

    National Book Critics Circle
Awards Y-00–01

    The National Jewish
Book Awards Y-85

    Nobel Prize Y-80–02

    Winning an Edgar Y-98

The Literary Chronicle and Weekly Review
1819-1828 . . . . DLB-110

Literary Periodicals:

    Callaloo Y-87

    Expatriates in Paris DS-15

    New Literary Periodicals:
A Report for 1987 . . . . Y-87

    A Report for 1988 . . . . Y-88

    A Report for 1989 . . . . Y-89

    A Report for 1990 . . . . Y-90

    A Report for 1991 . . . . Y-91

    A Report for 1992 . . . . Y-92

    A Report for 1993 . . . . Y-93

Literary Research Archives
The Anthony Burgess Archive at
the Harry Ransom Humanities
Research Center Y-98

    Archives of Charles Scribner's Sons DS-17

    Berg Collection of English and
American Literature of the
New York Public Library Y-83

    The Bobbs-Merrill Archive at the
Lilly Library, Indiana University Y-90

    Die Fürstliche Bibliothek Corvey Y-96

    Guide to the Archives of Publishers,
Journals, and Literary Agents in
North American Libraries Y-93

    The Henry E. Huntington Library Y-92

    The Humanities Research Center,
University of Texas Y-82

    The John Carter Brown Library Y-85

Cumulative Index

Kent State Special Collections Y-86
The Lilly Library Y-84
The Modern Literary Manuscripts
    Collection in the Special
    Collections of the Washington
    University Libraries Y-87
A Publisher's Archives: G. P. Putnam Y-92
Special Collections at Boston
    University Y-99
The University of Virginia Libraries Y-91
The William Charvat American Fiction
    Collection at the Ohio State
    University Libraries Y-92
Literary Societies Y-98–02
The Margery Allingham Society Y-98
The American Studies Association
    of Norway Y-00
The Arnold Bennett Society Y-98
The Association for the Study of
    Literature and Environment
    (ASLE) Y-99
Belgian Luxembourg American Studies
    Association Y-01
The E. F. Benson Society Y-98
The Elizabeth Bishop Society Y-01
The [Edgar Rice] Burroughs
    Bibliophiles Y-98
The Byron Society of America Y-00
The Lewis Carroll Society
    of North America Y-00
The Willa Cather Pioneer Memorial
    and Education Foundation Y-00
New Chaucer Society Y-00
The Wilkie Collins Society Y-98
The James Fenimore Cooper Society Y-01
The Stephen Crane Society Y-98, 01
The E. E. Cummings Society Y-01
The James Dickey Society Y-99
John Dos Passos Newsletter Y-00
The Priory Scholars [Sir Arthur Conan
    Doyle] of New York Y-99
The International Theodore Dreiser
    Society Y-01
The Friends of the Dymock Poets Y-00
The George Eliot Fellowship Y-99
The T. S. Eliot Society: Celebration and
    Scholarship, 1980-1999 . . . . Y-99
The Ralph Waldo Emerson Society Y-99
The William Faulkner Society Y-99
The C. S. Forester Society Y-00
The Hamlin Garland Society Y-01
The [Elizabeth] Gaskell Society Y-98
The Charlotte Perkins Gilman Society Y-99
The Ellen Glasgow Society Y-01
Zane Grey's West Society Y-00
The Ivor Gurney Society Y-98
The Joel Chandler Harris Association Y-99
The Nathaniel Hawthorne Society Y-00
The [George Alfred] Henty Society Y-98

George Moses Horton Society Y-99
The William Dean Howells Society Y-01
WW2 HMSO Paperbacks Society Y-98
American Humor Studies Association Y-99
International Society for Humor Studies . . . Y-99
The W. W. Jacobs Appreciation Society . . . Y-98
The Richard Jefferies Society Y-98
The Jerome K. Jerome Society Y-98
The D. H. Lawrence Society of
    North America Y-00
The T. E. Lawrence Society Y-98
The [Gotthold] Lessing Society Y-00
The New York C. S. Lewis Society Y-99
The Sinclair Lewis Society Y-99
The Jack London Research Center Y-00
The Jack London Society Y-99
The Cormac McCarthy Society Y-99
The Melville Society Y-01
The Arthur Miller Society Y-01
The Milton Society of America Y-00
International Marianne Moore Society . . . Y-98
International Nabokov Society Y-99
The Vladimir Nabokov Society Y-01
The Flannery O'Connor Society Y-99
The Wilfred Owen Association Y-98
Penguin Collectors' Society Y-98
The [E. A.] Poe Studies Association Y-99
The Katherine Anne Porter Society Y-01
The Beatrix Potter Society Y-98
The Ezra Pound Society Y-01
The Powys Society Y-98
Proust Society of America Y-00
The Dorothy L. Sayers Society Y-98
The Bernard Shaw Society Y-99
The Society for the Study of
    Southern Literature Y-00
The Wallace Stevens Society Y-99
The Harriet Beecher Stowe Center Y-00
The R. S. Surtees Society Y-98
The Thoreau Society Y-99
The Tilling [E. F. Benson] Society Y-98
The Trollope Societies Y-00
H. G. Wells Society Y-98
The Western Literature Association Y-99
The William Carlos Williams Society Y-99
The Henry Williamson Society Y-98
The [Nero] Wolfe Pack Y-99
The Thomas Wolfe Society Y-99
Worldwide Wodehouse Societies Y-98
The W. B. Yeats Society of N.Y. Y-99
The Charlotte M. Yonge Fellowship Y-98
Literary Theory
    The Year in Literary Theory Y-92–Y-93
Literature at Nurse, or Circulating Morals (1885),
    by George Moore DLB-18

Litt, Toby 1968- DLB-267, 319
Littell, Eliakim 1797-1870 . . . . DLB-79
Littell, Robert S. 1831-1896 . . . . DLB-79
Little, Brown and Company DLB-49
Little Magazines and Newspapers DS-15
    Selected English-Language Little
        Magazines and Newspapers
        [France, 1920-1939] DLB-4
The Little Magazines of the
    New Formalism DLB-282
The Little Review 1914-1929 . . . . DS-15
Littlewood, Joan 1914-2002 . . . . DLB-13
Liu, Aimee E. 1953- DLB-312
Liu E 1857-1909 . . . . DLB-328
Lively, Penelope 1933- . . . DLB-14, 161, 207, 326
Liverpool University Press DLB-112
The Lives of the Poets (1753) DLB-142
Livesay, Dorothy 1909-1996 . . . . DLB-68
Livesay, Florence Randal 1874-1953 . . . . . . DLB-92
Livings, Henry 1929-1998 . . . . DLB-13
Livingston, Anne Home 1763-1841 . . . DLB-37, 200
Livingston, Jay 1915-2001 . . . . DLB-265
Livingston, Myra Cohn 1926-1996 . . . . . . DLB-61
Livingston, William 1723-1790 . . . . DLB-31
Livingstone, David 1813-1873 . . . . DLB-166
Livingstone, Douglas 1932-1996 . . . . DLB-225
Livshits, Benedikt Konstantinovich
    1886-1938 or 1939 . . . . DLB-295
Livy 59 B.C.-A.D. 17 . . . . DLB-211; CDWLB-1
Liyong, Taban lo (see Taban lo Liyong)
Lizárraga, Sylvia S. 1925- DLB-82
Llamazares, Julio 1955- DLB-322
Llewellyn, Kate 1936- DLB-325
Llewellyn, Richard 1906-1983 . . . . DLB-15
Lloréns Torres, Luis 1876-1944 . . . . DLB-290
Edward Lloyd [publishing house] DLB-106
Llull, Ramon (1232?-1316?) DLB-337
Lobato, José Bento Monteiro
    1882-1948 . . . . DLB-307
Lobel, Arnold 1933- DLB-61
Lochhead, Liz 1947- DLB-310
Lochridge, Betsy Hopkins (see Fancher, Betsy)
Locke, Alain 1886-1954 . . . . DLB-51
Locke, David Ross 1833-1888 . . . . DLB-11, 23
Locke, John 1632-1704 . . . . DLB-31, 101, 213, 252
Locke, Richard Adams 1800-1871 . . . . DLB-43
Locker-Lampson, Frederick
    1821-1895 . . . . DLB-35, 184
Lockhart, John Gibson
    1794-1854 . . . . DLB-110, 116 144
Locklin, Gerald 1941- DLB-335
Lockridge, Francis 1896-1963 . . . . DLB-306
Lockridge, Richard 1898-1982 . . . . DLB-306

Lockridge, Ross, Jr. 1914-1948 .... DLB-143; Y-80
Locrine and Selimus DLB-62
Lodge, David 1935- DLB-14, 194
Lodge, George Cabot 1873-1909.......... DLB-54
Lodge, Henry Cabot 1850-1924 .... DLB-47
Lodge, Thomas 1558-1625 .... DLB-172
    Defence of Poetry (1579) [excerpt] DLB-172
Loeb, Harold 1891-1974 .... DLB-4; DS-15
Loeb, William 1905-1981 .... DLB-127
Loesser, Frank 1910-1969 .... DLB-265
Lofting, Hugh 1886-1947.............. DLB-160
Logan, Deborah Norris 1761-1839 ...... DLB-200
Logan, James 1674-1751............ DLB-24, 140
Logan, John 1923-1987 .... DLB-5
Logan, Martha Daniell 1704?-1779 ...... DLB-200
Logan, William 1950- DLB-120
Logau, Friedrich von 1605-1655 .... DLB-164
Logue, Christopher 1926- DLB-27
Lohenstein, Daniel Casper von
    1635-1683 .... DLB-168
Lohrey, Amanda 1947- DLB-325
Lo-Johansson, Ivar 1901-1990 .... DLB-259
Lokert, George (or Lockhart)
    circa 1485-1547 .... DLB-281
Lomonosov, Mikhail Vasil'evich
    1711-1765...................... DLB-150
London, Jack
    1876-1916 ..... DLB-8, 12, 78, 212; CDALB-3
    The Jack London Research Center....... Y-00
    The Jack London Society Y-99
The London Magazine 1820-1829 .... DLB-110
Long, David 1948- DLB-244
Long, H., and Brother DLB-49
Long, Haniel 1888-1956 .... DLB-45
Long, Ray 1878-1935.................. DLB-137
Longfellow, Henry Wadsworth
    1807-1882 .... DLB-1, 59, 235; CDALB-2
Longfellow, Samuel 1819-1892 .... DLB-1
Longford, Elizabeth 1906-2002 .... DLB-155
    Tribute to Alfred A. Knopf Y-84
Longinus circa first century DLB-176
Longley, Michael 1939- DLB-40
T. Longman [publishing house] DLB-154
Longmans, Green and Company......... DLB-49
Longmore, George 1793?-1867 .... DLB-99
Longstreet, Augustus Baldwin
    1790-1870............... DLB-3, 11, 74, 248
D. Longworth [publishing house] DLB-49
Lønn, Øystein 1936- DLB-297
Lonsdale, Frederick 1881-1954 .... DLB-10
Loos, Anita 1893-1981..... DLB-11, 26, 228; Y-81
Lopate, Phillip 1943- Y-80

Lope de Rueda 1510?-1565? DLB-318
Lopes, Fernão 1380/1390?-1460?........ DLB-287
Lopez, Barry 1945- DLB-256, 275, 335
López, Diana (see Isabella, Ríos)
López, Josefina 1969- DLB-209
López de Ayala, Pero (1332-1407) DLB-337
López de Córdoba, Leonor (1362 or
    1363-1412?/1430? DLB-337
López de Mendoza, Íñigo
    (see Santillana, Marqués de)
López Velarde, Ramón 1888-1921....... DLB-290
Loranger, Jean-Aubert 1896-1942 .... DLB-92
Lorca, Federico García 1898-1936....... DLB-108
Lord, John Keast 1818-1872............. DLB-99
Lorde, Audre 1934-1992 .... DLB-41
Lorimer, George Horace 1867-1937....... DLB-91
A. K. Loring [publishing house].......... DLB-49
Loring and Mussey DLB-46
Lorris, Guillaume de (see *Roman de la Rose*)
Lossing, Benson J. 1813-1891 .... DLB-30
Lothar, Ernst 1890-1974................ DLB-81
D. Lothrop and Company.............. DLB-49
Lothrop, Harriet M. 1844-1924.......... DLB-42
Loti, Pierre 1850-1923 .... DLB-123
Lotichius Secundus, Petrus 1528-1560.... DLB-179
Lott, Emmeline fl. nineteenth century DLB-166
Louisiana State University Press Y-97
Lounsbury, Thomas R. 1838-1915 .... DLB-71
Louÿs, Pierre 1870-1925 .... DLB-123
Løveid, Cecile 1951- DLB-297
Lovejoy, Arthur O. 1873-1962.......... DLB-270
Lovelace, Earl 1935- DLB-125; CDWLB-3
Lovelace, Richard 1618-1657 .... DLB-131
John W. Lovell Company DLB-49
Lovell, Coryell and Company.......... DLB-49
Lover, Samuel 1797-1868 .... DLB-159, 190
Lovesey, Peter 1936- DLB-87
    Tribute to Georges Simenon Y-89
Lovinescu, Eugen
    1881-1943 .... DLB-220; CDWLB-4
Lovingood, Sut
    (see Harris, George Washington)
Low, Samuel 1765-? DLB-37
Lowell, Amy 1874-1925 .... DLB-54, 140
Lowell, James Russell 1819-1891
    ...... DLB-1, 11, 64, 79, 189, 235; CDALB-2
Lowell, Robert
    1917-1977............ DLB-5, 169; CDALB-7
Lowenfels, Walter 1897-1976 .... DLB-4
Lowndes, Marie Belloc 1868-1947........ DLB-70
Lowndes, William Thomas
    1798-1843 .... DLB-184

Humphrey Lownes [publishing house] ... DLB-170
Lowry, Lois 1937- DLB-52
Lowry, Malcolm 1909-1957.... DLB-15; CDBLB-7
Lowry, Robert 1919-1994 .... DLB-335
Lowther, Pat 1935-1975................ DLB-53
Loy, Mina 1882-1966................ DLB-4, 54
Loynaz, Dulce María 1902-1997 .... DLB-283
Lozeau, Albert 1878-1924 .... DLB-92
Lu Ling 1923-1994 .... DLB-328
Lu Xun 1881-1936 .... DLB-328
Lu Yin 1898?-1934 .... DLB-328
Lubbock, Percy 1879-1965............. DLB-149
Lubrano, Giacomo
    1619-1692 or 1693 .... DLB-339
Lucan A.D. 39-A.D. 65 .... DLB-211
Lucas, E. V. 1868-1938 .... DLB-98, 149, 153
Fielding Lucas Jr. [publishing house] DLB-49
Luce, Clare Booth 1903-1987 .... DLB-228
Luce, Henry R. 1898-1967 .... DLB-91
John W. Luce and Company DLB-46
Lucena, Juan de ca. 1430-1501 .... DLB-286
Lucian circa 120-180 .... DLB-176
Lucie-Smith, Edward 1933- DLB-40
Lucilius circa 180 B.C.-102/101 B.C....... DLB-211
Lucini, Gian Pietro 1867-1914 .... DLB-114
Luco Cruchaga, Germán 1894-1936 ..... DLB-305
Lucretius circa 94 B.C.-circa 49 B.C.
    .... DLB-211; CDWLB-1
Luder, Peter circa 1415-1472 .... DLB-179
Ludlam, Charles 1943-1987............ DLB-266
Ludlum, Robert 1927-2001 .... Y-82
Ludus de Antichristo circa 1160 .... DLB-148
Ludvigson, Susan 1942- DLB-120
Ludwig, Jack 1922- DLB-60
Ludwig, Otto 1813-1865 .... DLB-129
Ludwigslied 881 or 882 .... DLB-148
Luera, Yolanda 1953- DLB-122
Luft, Lya 1938- DLB-145
Lugansky, Kazak Vladimir
    (see Dal', Vladimir Ivanovich)
Lugn, Kristina 1948- DLB-257
Lugones, Leopoldo 1874-1938.......... DLB-283
Luhan, Mabel Dodge 1879-1962 .... DLB-303
Lukács, Georg (see Lukács, György)
Lukács, György
    1885-1971 .... DLB-215, 242; CDWLB-4
Luke, Peter 1919-1995................. DLB-13
Lummis, Charles F. 1859-1928 .... DLB-186
Lundkvist, Artur 1906-1991 .... DLB-259
Lunts, Lev Natanovich
    1901-1924..................... DLB-272
F. M. Lupton Company................ DLB-49

Cumulative Index

Lupus of Ferrières
circa 805-circa 862 .... DLB-148
Lurie, Alison 1926- DLB-2
Lussu, Emilio 1890-1975............... DLB-264
Lustig, Arnošt 1926- DLB-232, 299
Luther, Martin
1483-1546 .... DLB-179; CDWLB-2
Luzi, Mario 1914-2005............... DLB-128
L'vov, Nikolai Aleksandrovich
1751-1803 .... DLB-150
Lyall, Gavin 1932-2003 .... DLB-87
Lydgate, John circa 1370-1450 .... DLB-146
Lyly, John circa 1554-1606........ DLB-62, 167
Lynch, Martin 1950- DLB-310
Lynch, Patricia 1898-1972 .... DLB-160
Lynch, Richard fl. 1596-1601.......... DLB-172
Lynd, Robert 1879-1949............... DLB-98
Lynds, Dennis (Michael Collins)
1924-2005 .... DLB-306
   Tribute to John D. MacDonald Y-86
   Tribute to Kenneth Millar Y-83
   Why I Write Mysteries: Night and Day... Y-85
Lynes, Jeanette 1956- DLB-334
Lyon, Matthew 1749-1822 .... DLB-43
Lyotard, Jean-François 1924-1998 ..... DLB-242
Lyricists
   Additional Lyricists: 1920-1960..... DLB-265
Lysias circa 459 B.C.-circa 380 B.C....... DLB-176
Lytle, Andrew 1902-1995.......... DLB-6; Y-95
   Tribute to Caroline Gordon........... Y-81
   Tribute to Katherine Anne Porter Y-80
Lytton, Edward
(see Bulwer-Lytton, Edward)
Lytton, Edward Robert Bulwer
1831-1891 .... DLB-32

M

Maalouf, Amin 1949- DLB-346
Maass, Joachim 1901-1972 .... DLB-69
Mabie, Hamilton Wright 1845-1916...... DLB-71
Mac A'Ghobhainn, Iain (see Smith, Iain Crichton)
MacArthur, Charles 1895-1956 .... DLB-7, 25, 44
Macaulay, Catherine 1731-1791 .... DLB-104, 336
Macaulay, David 1945- DLB-61
Macaulay, Rose 1881-1958............. DLB-36
Macaulay, Thomas Babington
1800-1859........... DLB-32, 55; CDBLB-4
Macaulay Company DLB-46
MacBeth, George 1932-1992 .... DLB-40
Macbeth, Madge 1880-1965 .... DLB-92
MacCaig, Norman 1910-1996 .... DLB-27
MacDiarmid, Hugh
1892-1978............. DLB-20; CDBLB-7
MacDonald, Ann-Marie 1958- DLB-334

MacDonald, Cynthia 1928- DLB-105
MacDonald, George 1824-1905.... DLB-18, 163, 178
MacDonald, John D.
1916-1986 ....DLB-8, 306; Y-86
MacDonald, Philip 1899?-1980 .... DLB-77
Macdonald, Ross (see Millar, Kenneth)
Macdonald, Sharman 1951- DLB-245
MacDonald, Wilson 1880-1967 .... DLB-92
Macdonald and Company (Publishers) .. DLB-112
MacEwen, Gwendolyn 1941-1987 ... DLB-53, 251
Macfadden, Bernarr 1868-1955 ...... DLB-25, 91
MacGregor, John 1825-1892.......... DLB-166
MacGregor, Mary Esther (see Keith, Marian)
Macherey, Pierre 1938- DLB-296
Machado, Antonio 1875-1939.......... DLB-108
Machado, Manuel 1874-1947 .... DLB-108
Machado de Assis, Joaquim Maria
1839-1908 .... DLB-307
Machar, Agnes Maule 1837-1927 .... DLB-92
Machaut, Guillaume de
circa 1300-1377................. DLB-208
Machen, Arthur Llewelyn Jones
1863-1947................DLB-36, 156, 178
MacIlmaine, Roland fl. 1574........... DLB-281
MacInnes, Colin 1914-1976 .... DLB-14
MacInnes, Helen 1907-1985 .... DLB-87
Mac Intyre, Tom 1931- DLB-245
Mačiulis, Jonas (see Maironis, Jonas)
MacIvor, Daniel 1962- DLB-334
Mack, Maynard 1909-2001 .... DLB-111
Mackall, Leonard L. 1879-1937 .... DLB-140
MacKay, Isabel Ecclestone 1875-1928..... DLB-92
Mackay, Shena 1944- DLB-231, 319
MacKaye, Percy 1875-1956........... DLB-54
Macken, Walter 1915-1967............ DLB-13
MacKenna, John 1952- DLB-319
Mackenzie, Alexander 1763-1820........ DLB-99
Mackenzie, Alexander Slidell
1803-1848 .... DLB-183
Mackenzie, Compton 1883-1972 .... DLB-34, 100
Mackenzie, Henry 1745-1831.......... DLB-39
   The Lounger, no. 20 (1785)........... DLB-39
Mackenzie, Kenneth (Seaforth Mackenzie)
1913-1955 .... DLB-260
Mackenzie, William 1758-1828......... DLB-187
Mackey, Nathaniel 1947- DLB-169
Mackey, William Wellington 1937- DLB-38
Mackintosh, Elizabeth (see Tey, Josephine)
Mackintosh, Sir James 1765-1832....... DLB-158
Macklin, Charles 1699-1797 .... DLB-89
Maclaren, Ian (see Watson, John)
Maclaren-Ross, Julian 1912-1964 .... DLB-319

MacLaverty, Bernard 1942- DLB-267
MacLean, Alistair 1922-1987 ....DLB-276
MacLean, Katherine Anne 1925- DLB-8
Maclean, Norman 1902-1990.......... DLB-206
MacLeish, Archibald 1892-1982
.... DLB-4, 7, 45; Y-82; DS-15; CDALB-7
MacLennan, Hugh 1907-1990 .... DLB-68
MacLeod, Alistair 1936- DLB-60
Macleod, Fiona (see Sharp, William)
Macleod, Norman 1906-1985........... DLB-4
Mac Low, Jackson 1922-2004.......... DLB-193
MacMahon, Bryan 1909-1998 .... DLB-319
Macmillan and Company............. DLB-106
The Macmillan Company DLB-49
Macmillan's English Men of Letters,
First Series (1878-1892) DLB-144
MacNamara, Brinsley 1890-1963........ DLB-10
MacNeice, Louis 1907-1963 .... DLB-10, 20
Macphail, Andrew 1864-1938 .... DLB-92
Macpherson, James 1736-1796 ..... DLB-109, 336
Macpherson, Jay 1931- DLB-53
Macpherson, Jeanie 1884-1946......... DLB-44
Macrae Smith Company............... DLB-46
MacRaye, Lucy Betty (see Webling, Lucy)
John Macrone [publishing house]....... DLB-106
MacShane, Frank 1927-1999.......... DLB-111
Macy-Masius DLB-46
Madden, David 1933- DLB-6
Madden, Sir Frederic 1801-1873........ DLB-184
Maddow, Ben 1909-1992 .... DLB-44
Maddux, Rachel 1912-1983 .....DLB-234; Y-93
Madgett, Naomi Long 1923- DLB-76
Madhubuti, Haki R. 1942- DLB-5, 41; DS-8
Madison, James 1751-1836............ DLB-37
Madsen, Svend Åge 1939- DLB-214
Madrigal, Alfonso Fernández de (El Tostado)
ca. 1405-1455.................. DLB-286
Maeterlinck, Maurice 1862-1949 ... DLB-192, 331
The Little Magazines of the
New Formalism DLB-282
Magee, David 1905-1977 ....DLB-187
Maginn, William 1794-1842........DLB-110, 159
Maggi, Carlo Maria 1630-1699 .... DLB-339
Magoffin, Susan Shelby 1827-1855...... DLB-239
Mahan, Alfred Thayer 1840-1914 .... DLB-47
Mahapatra, Jayanta 1928- DLB-323
Maheux-Forcier, Louise 1929- DLB-60
Mahfouz, Naguib (Najīb Mahfūz)
1911-2006 ....DLB-331, 346; Y-88
   Nobel Lecture 1988 .... Y-88
Mahin, John Lee 1902-1984........... DLB-44
Mahon, Derek 1941- DLB-40

Maiakovsky, Vladimir Vladimirovich
    1893-1930....................DLB-295

Maikov, Apollon Nikolaevich
    1821-1897......................DLB-277

Maikov, Vasilii Ivanovich 1728-1778.....DLB-150

Mailer, Norman 1923-2007
    ....DLB-2, 16, 28, 185, 278; Y-80, 83, 97;
    DS-3; CDALB-6

    Tribute to Isaac Bashevis Singer.........Y-91

    Tribute to Meyer Levin................Y-81

Maillart, Ella 1903-1997..............DLB-195

Maillet, Adrienne 1885-1963..........DLB-68

Maillet, Antonine 1929-..............DLB-60

Maillu, David G. 1939-..............DLB-157

Maimonides, Moses 1138-1204.........DLB-115

Main Selections of the Book-of-the-Month
    Club, 1926-1945....................DLB-9

Mainwaring, Daniel 1902-1977.........DLB-44

Mair, Charles 1838-1927..............DLB-99

Mair, John circa 1467-1550............DLB-281

Maironis, Jonas 1862-1932...DLB-220; CDWLB-4

Mais, Roger 1905-1955.....DLB-125; CDWLB-3

Maitland, Sara 1950-..............DLB-271

Major, Andre 1942-..............DLB-60

Major, Charles 1856-1913............DLB-202

Major, Clarence 1936-..............DLB-33

Major, Kevin 1949-..............DLB-60

Major Books......................DLB-46

Makanin, Vladimir Semenovich
    1937-......................DLB-285

Makarenko, Anton Semenovich
    1888-1939......................DLB-272

Makemie, Francis circa 1658-1708........DLB-24

The Making of Americans Contract............Y-98

Makovsky, Sergei 1877-1962...........DLB-317

Maksimov, Vladimir Emel'ianovich
    1930-1995......................DLB-302

Maksimović, Desanka
    1898-1993............DLB-147; CDWLB-4

Malamud, Bernard 1914-1986
    ....DLB-2, 28, 152; Y-80, 86; CDALB-1

    Bernard Malamud Archive at the
    Harry Ransom Humanities
    Research Center.................Y-00

Mălăncioiu, Ileana 1940-............DLB-232

Malaparte, Curzio
    (Kurt Erich Suckert) 1898-1957.....DLB-264

Malerba, Luigi 1927-..............DLB-196

Malet, Lucas 1852-1931..............DLB-153

Malherbe, François de 1555-1628.......DLB-327

Mallarmé, Stéphane 1842-1898........DLB-217

Malleson, Lucy Beatrice (see Gilbert, Anthony)

Mallet-Joris, Françoise (Françoise Lilar)
    1930-......................DLB-83

Mallock, W. H. 1849-1923..........DLB-18, 57

"Every Man His Own Poet; or,
    The Inspired Singer's Recipe
    Book" (1877)..................DLB-35

"Le Style c'est l'homme" (1892)......DLB-57

Memoirs of Life and Literature (1920),
    [excerpt]..................DLB-57

Malone, Dumas 1892-1986............DLB-17

Malone, Edmond 1741-1812...........DLB-142

Malory, Sir Thomas
    circa 1400-1410 - 1471....DLB-146; CDBLB-1

Malouf, David 1934-..............DLB-289

Malpede, Karen 1945-..............DLB-249

Malraux, André 1901-1976............DLB-72

The Maltese Falcon (Documentary).......DLB-280

Malthus, Thomas Robert
    1766-1834..................DLB-107, 158

Maltz, Albert 1908-1985............DLB-102

Malzberg, Barry N. 1939-..............DLB-8

Mamet, David 1947-..............DLB-7

Mamin, Dmitrii Narkisovich
    1852-1912......................DLB-238

Manaka, Matsemela 1956-............DLB-157

Mañas, José Ángel 1971-............DLB-322

Manchester University Press..........DLB-112

Mandel, Eli 1922-1992..............DLB-53

Mandel'shtam, Nadezhda Iakovlevna
    1899-1980......................DLB-302

Mandel'shtam, Osip Emil'evich
    1891-1938......................DLB-295

Mandeville, Bernard 1670-1733........DLB-101

Mandeville, Sir John
    mid fourteenth century...........DLB-146

Mandiargues, André Pieyre de
    1909-1991......................DLB-83

Manea, Norman 1936-..............DLB-232

Manfred, Frederick 1912-1994....DLB-6, 212, 227

Manfredi, Gianfranco 1948-..........DLB-196

Mangan, Sherry 1904-1961............DLB-4

Manganelli, Giorgio 1922-1990........DLB-196

Manger, Itzik (Itsik Manger)
    1901-1969......................DLB-333

Mani Leib (Mani Leyb Brahinsky)
    1883-1953......................DLB-333

Manilius fl. first century A.D............DLB-211

Mankiewicz, Herman 1897-1953........DLB-26

Mankiewicz, Joseph L. 1909-1993........DLB-44

Mankowitz, Wolf 1924-1998............DLB-15

Manley, Delarivière 1672?-1724.......DLB-39, 80

    Preface to *The Secret History, of Queen
    Zarah, and the Zarazians* (1705).....DLB-39

Mann, Abby 1927-..............DLB-44

Mann, Charles 1929-1998..............Y-98

Mann, Emily 1952-..............DLB-266

Mann, Heinrich 1871-1950.........DLB-66, 118

Mann, Horace 1796-1859............DLB-1, 235

Mann, Klaus 1906-1949..............DLB-56

Mann, Mary Peabody 1806-1887.......DLB-239

Mann, Thomas
    1875-1955.........DLB-66, 331; CDWLB-2

Mann, William D'Alton 1839-1920......DLB-137

Mannin, Ethel 1900-1984.........DLB-191, 195

Manning, Emily (see Australie)

Manning, Frederic 1882-1935..........DLB-260

Manning, Laurence 1899-1972.........DLB-251

Manning, Marie 1873?-1945.............DLB-29

Manning and Loring....................DLB-49

Mannyng, Robert fl.
    1303-1338......................DLB-146

Mano, D. Keith 1942-..............DLB-6

Manor Books......................DLB-46

Manrique, Gómez 1412?-1490.........DLB-286

Manrique, Jorge ca. 1440-1479..........DLB-286

Mansfield, Katherine 1888-1923........DLB-162

Mantel, Hilary 1952-..............DLB-271

Manuel, Niklaus circa 1484-1530.......DLB-179

Manzini, Gianna 1896-1974............DLB-177

Mao Dun 1896-1981..............DLB-328

Mapanje, Jack 1944-..............DLB-157

Maraini, Dacia 1936-..............DLB-196

Maraise, Marie-Catherine-Renée Darcel de
    1737-1822......................DLB-314

Maramzin, Vladimir Rafailovich
    1934-......................DLB-302

March, William (William Edward Campbell)
    1893-1954..................DLB-9, 86, 316

Marchand, Leslie A. 1900-1999.........DLB-103

Marchant, Bessie 1862-1941............DLB-160

Marchant, Tony 1959-..............DLB-245

Marchenko, Anastasiia Iakovlevna
    1830-1880......................DLB-238

Marchessault, Jovette 1938-............DLB-60

Marcinkevičius, Justinas 1930-........DLB-232

Marcos, Plínio (Plínio Marcos de Barros)
    1935-1999......................DLB-307

Marcus, Frank 1928-..............DLB-13

Marcuse, Herbert 1898-1979...........DLB-242

Marden, Orison Swett 1850-1924......DLB-137

Marechera, Dambudzo 1952-1987......DLB-157

Marcy, Mary E. 1877-1922............DLB-345

Marek, Richard, Books..............DLB-46

Mares, E. A. 1938-..............DLB-122

Margolin, Anna (Rosa Lebensbaum [Roza
    Lebensboym]) 1887-1952)).........DLB-333

Margoshes, Dave 1941-..............DLB-334

Marguerite de Navarre 1492-1549......DLB-327

Margulies, Donald 1954-............DLB-228

Mariana, Juan de 1535 or 1536-1624....DLB-318

Mariani, Paul 1940-..............DLB-111

Marías, Javier 1951- DLB-322

Marie de France fl. 1160-1178 .... DLB-208

Marie-Victorin, Frère (Conrad Kirouac)
   1885-1944 .... DLB-92

Marin, Biagio 1891-1985 .... DLB-128

Marinella, Lucrezia 1571?-1653 .... DLB-339

Marinetti, Filippo Tommaso
   1876-1944 .... DLB-114, 264

Marinina, Aleksandra (Marina Anatol'evna
   Alekseeva) 1957- DLB-285

Marinković, Ranko
   1913-2001 .... DLB-147; CDWLB-4

Marino, Giambattista 1569-1625 .... DLB-339

Marion, Frances 1886-1973 .... DLB-44

Marius, Richard C. 1933-1999 .... Y-85

Marivaux, Pierre Carlet de Chamblain de
   1688-1763 .... DLB-314

Markandaya, Kamala 1924-2004 .... DLB-323

Markevich, Boleslav Mikhailovich
   1822-1884 .... DLB-238

Markfield, Wallace 1926-2002 .... DLB-2, 28

Markham, E. A. 1939- DLB-319

Markham, Edwin 1852-1940 .... DLB-54, 186

Markish, David 1938- DLB-317

Markish, Peretz (Perets Markish)
   1895-1952 .... DLB-333

Markle, Fletcher 1921-1991 .... DLB-68; Y-91

Marlatt, Daphne 1942- DLB-60

Marlitt, E. 1825-1887 .... DLB-129

Marlowe, Christopher
   1564-1593 .... DLB-62; CDBLB-1

Marlyn, John 1912-1985 .... DLB-88

Marmion, Shakerley 1603-1639 .... DLB-58

Marmontel, Jean-François 1723-1799 .... DLB-314

Der Marner before 1230-circa 1287 ..... DLB-138

Marnham, Patrick 1943- DLB-204

Marot, Clément 1496-1544 .... DLB-327

The *Marprelate Tracts* 1588-1589 ...... DLB-132

Marquand, John P. 1893-1960 .... DLB-9, 102

Marques, Helena 1935- DLB-287

Marqués, René 1919-1979 ...... DLB-113, 305

Marquis, Don 1878-1937 .... DLB-11, 25

Marriott, Anne 1913-1997 .... DLB-68

Marryat, Frederick 1792-1848 .... DLB-21, 163

Marsé, Juan 1933- DLB-322

Marsh, Capen, Lyon and Webb DLB-49

Marsh, George Perkins
   1801-1882 .... DLB-1, 64, 243

Marsh, James 1794-1842 .... DLB-1, 59

Marsh, Narcissus 1638-1713 .... DLB-213

Marsh, Ngaio 1899-1982 .... DLB-77

Marshall, Alan 1902-1984 .... DLB-260

Marshall, Edison 1894-1967 .... DLB-102

Marshall, Edward 1932- DLB-16

Marshall, Emma 1828-1899 .... DLB-163

Marshall, James 1942-1992 .... DLB-61

Marshall, Joyce 1913- DLB-88

Marshall, Paule 1929- DLB-33, 157, 227

Marshall, Tom 1938-1993 .... DLB-60

Marsilius of Padua
   circa 1275-circa 1342 .... DLB-115

Mars-Jones, Adam 1954- DLB-207, 319

Marson, Una 1905-1965 .... DLB-157

Marston, John 1576-1634 .... DLB-58, 172

Marston, Philip Bourke 1850-1887 .... DLB-35

Marston, Westland 1819-1890 .... DLB-344

Martel, Yann 1963- DLB-326, 334

Martens, Kurt 1870-1945 .... DLB-66

Martí, José 1853-1895 .... DLB-290

Martial circa A.D. 40-circa A.D. 103
   .... DLB-211; CDWLB-1

William S. Martien [publishing house] DLB-49

Martin, Abe (see Hubbard, Kin)

Martin, Catherine ca. 1847-1937 .... DLB-230

Martin, Charles 1942- DLB-120, 282

Martin, Claire 1914- DLB-60

Martin, David 1915-1997 .... DLB-260

Martin, Jay 1935- DLB-111

Martin, Johann (see Laurentius von Schnüffis)

Martin, Thomas 1696-1771 .... DLB-213

Martin, Violet Florence (see Ross, Martin)

Martin du Gard, Roger 1881-1958 ... DLB-65, 331

Martineau, Harriet
   1802-1876 ..... DLB-21, 55, 159, 163, 166, 190

Martínez, Demetria 1960- DLB-209

Martínez de Toledo, Alfonso
   1398?-1468 .... DLB-286

Martínez, Eliud 1935- DLB-122

Martínez, Max 1943- DLB-82

Martínez, Rubén 1962- DLB-209

Martín Gaite, Carmen 1925-2000 .... DLB-322

Martín-Santos, Luis 1924-1964 .... DLB-322

Martinson, Harry 1904-1978 ...... DLB-259, 331

Martinson, Moa 1890-1964 .... DLB-259

Martone, Michael 1955- DLB-218

Martyn, Edward 1859-1923 .... DLB-10

Marvell, Andrew
   1621-1678 .... DLB-131; CDBLB-2

Marvin X 1944- DLB-38

Marx, Karl 1818-1883 .... DLB-129

Marzials, Theo 1850-1920 .... DLB-35

Masefield, John 1878-1967
   .... DLB-10, 19, 153, 160; CDBLB-5

Masham, Damaris Cudworth, Lady
   1659-1708 .... DLB-252

Masino, Paola 1908-1989 .... DLB-264

Mason, A. E. W. 1865-1948 .... DLB-70

Mason, Bobbie Ann
   1940- DLB-173; Y-87; CDALB-7

Mason, F. van Wyck (Geoffrey Coffin, Frank W.
   Mason, Ward Weaver) 1901-1978 .... DLB-306

Mason, William 1725-1797 .... DLB-142

Mason Brothers DLB-49

The Massachusetts Quarterly Review
   1847-1850 .... DLB-1

The Masses DLB-303

Massey, Gerald 1828-1907 .... DLB-32

Massey, Linton R. 1900-1974 .... DLB-187

Massie, Allan 1938- DLB-271

Massinger, Philip 1583-1640 .... DLB-58

Masson, David 1822-1907 .... DLB-144

Masters, Edgar Lee
   1868-1950 .... DLB-54; CDALB-3

Masters, Hilary 1928- DLB-244

Masters, Olga 1919-1986 .... DLB-325

Mastronardi, Lucio 1930-1979 .... DLB-177

Mat' Maria (Elizaveta Kuz'mina-Karavdeva
   Skobtsova, née Pilenko) 1891-1945..... DLB-317

Matevski, Mateja 1929- ... DLB-181; CDWLB-4

Mather, Cotton
   1663-1728 .... DLB-24, 30, 140; CDALB-2

Mather, Increase 1639-1723 .... DLB-24

Mather, Richard 1596-1669 .... DLB-24

Matheson, Annie 1853-1924 .... DLB-240

Matheson, Richard 1926- DLB-8, 44

Matheus, John F. 1887-1986 .... DLB-51

Mathews, Aidan 1956- DLB-319

Mathews, Cornelius 1817?-1889 .. DLB-3, 64, 250

Elkin Mathews [publishing house] DLB-112

Mathews, John Joseph 1894-1979 .... DLB-175

Mathias, Roland 1915-2007 .... DLB-27

Mathis, June 1892-1927 .... DLB-44

Mathis, Sharon Bell 1937- DLB-33

Matković, Marijan 1915-1985 .... DLB-181

Matoš, Antun Gustav 1873-1914 .... DLB-147

Matos Paoli, Francisco 1915-2000 ...... DLB-290

Matsumoto Seichō 1909-1992 .... DLB-182

The Matter of England 1240-1400 ...... DLB-146

The Matter of Rome early twelfth to late
   fifteenth century DLB-146

Matthew of Vendôme
   circa 1130-circa 1200 .... DLB-208

Matthews, Brander
   1852-1929 .... DLB-71, 78; DS-13

Matthews, Brian 1936- DLB-325

Matthews, Jack 1925- DLB-6

Matthews, Victoria Earle 1861-1907 ..... DLB-221

Matthews, William 1942-1997 .... DLB-5

Matthías Jochumsson 1835-1920 .... DLB-293

Matthías Johannessen 1930- DLB-293

Matthiessen, F. O. 1902-1950 ....DLB-63

Matthiessen, Peter 1927- DLB-6, 173, 275

Maturin, Charles Robert 1780-1824 .....DLB-178

Matute, Ana María 1926- DLB-322

Maugham, W. Somerset 1874-1965
....DLB-10, 36, 77, 100, 162, 195; CDBLB-6

Maupassant, Guy de 1850-1893 ....DLB-123

Maupertuis, Pierre-Louis Moreau de
1698-1759 ....DLB-314

Maupin, Armistead 1944- DLB-278

Mauriac, Claude 1914-1996..........DLB-83

Mauriac, François 1885-1970.......DLB-65, 331

Maurice, Frederick Denison 1805-1872....DLB-55

Maurois, André 1885-1967 ....DLB-65

Maury, James 1718-1769 ....DLB-31

Mavor, Elizabeth 1927- DLB-14

Mavor, Osborne Henry (see Bridie, James)

Maxwell, Gavin 1914-1969 ....DLB-204

Maxwell, William
1908-2000 ....DLB-218, 278; Y-80

Tribute to Nancy Hale Y-88

H. Maxwell [publishing house] DLB-49

John Maxwell [publishing house]........DLB-106

May, Elaine 1932- DLB-44

May, Karl 1842-1912.................DLB-129

May, Thomas 1595/1596-1650 ....DLB-58

Mayer, Bernadette 1945- DLB-165

Mayer, Mercer 1943- DLB-61

Mayer, O. B. 1818-1891............DLB-3, 248

Mayes, Herbert R. 1900-1987 ....DLB-137

Mayes, Wendell 1919-1992 ....DLB-26

Mayfield, Julian 1928-1984 ....DLB-33; Y-84

Mayhew, Henry 1812-1887 ......DLB-18, 55, 190

Mayhew, Jonathan 1720-1766............DLB-31

Mayne, Ethel Colburn 1865-1941.......DLB-197

Mayne, Jasper 1604-1672.............DLB-126

Mayne, Seymour 1944- DLB-60

Mayor, Flora Macdonald 1872-1932.....DLB-36

Mayröcker, Friederike 1924- DLB-85

Mayr, Suzette 1967- DLB-334

Mazrui, Ali A. 1933- DLB-125

Mažuranić, Ivan 1814-1890 ....DLB-147

Mazursky, Paul 1930- DLB-44

McAlmon, Robert 1896-1956 ...DLB-4, 45; DS-15

"A Night at Bricktop's" Y-01

McArthur, Peter 1866-1924 ....DLB-92

McAuley, James 1917-1976 ....DLB-260

Robert M. McBride and Company DLB-46

McCabe, Patrick 1955- DLB-194

McCafferty, Owen 1961- DLB-310

McCaffrey, Anne 1926- DLB-8

McCaffrey, Steve 1947- DLB-334

McCann, Colum 1965- DLB-267

McCarthy, Cormac 1933- DLB-6, 143, 256

The Cormac McCarthy Society Y-99

McCarthy, Mary 1912-1989 ....DLB-2; Y-81

McCarthy, Shaun Lloyd (see Cory, Desmond)

McCay, Winsor 1871-1934 ....DLB-22

McClane, Albert Jules 1922-1991 ....DLB-171

McClatchy, C. K. 1858-1936...........DLB-25

McClellan, George Marion 1860-1934 ....DLB-50

"The Negro as a Writer"............DLB-50

McCloskey, Robert 1914-2003 ....DLB-22

McCloy, Helen 1904-1992............DLB-306

McClung, Nellie Letitia 1873-1951 ....DLB-92

McClure, James 1939-2006 ....DLB-276

McClure, Joanna 1930- DLB-16

McClure, Michael 1932- DLB-16

McClure, Phillips and Company DLB-46

McClure, S. S. 1857-1949.............DLB-91

A. C. McClurg and Company...........DLB-49

McCluskey, John A., Jr. 1944- DLB-33

McCollum, Michael A. 1946- Y-87

McConnell, William C. 1917- DLB-88

McCord, David 1897-1997.............DLB-61

McCord, Louisa S. 1810-1879 ....DLB-248

McCorkle, Jill 1958- DLB-234; Y-87

McCorkle, Samuel Eusebius 1746-1811....DLB-37

McCormick, Anne O'Hare 1880-1954 ....DLB-29

McCormick, Kenneth Dale 1906-1997 ....Y-97

McCormick, Robert R. 1880-1955 ....DLB-29

McCourt, Edward 1907-1972...........DLB-88

McCoy, Horace 1897-1955............DLB-9

McCrae, Hugh 1876-1958 ....DLB-260

McCrae, John 1872-1918..............DLB-92

McCrumb, Sharyn 1948- DLB-306

McCullagh, Joseph B. 1842-1896.......DLB-23

McCullers, Carson
1917-1967 .....DLB-2, 7, 173, 228; CDALB-1

McCulloch, Thomas 1776-1843..........DLB-99

McCunn, Ruthanne Lum 1946- DLB-312

McDermott, Alice 1953- DLB-292

McDonald, Forrest 1927- DLB-17

McDonald, Walter 1934- DLB-105, DS-9

"Getting Started: Accepting the
Regions You Own–or Which
Own You"..................DLB-105

Tribute to James Dickey Y-97

McDougall, Colin 1917-1984...........DLB-68

McDowell, Katharine Sherwood Bonner
1849-1883 ....DLB-202, 239

Obolensky McDowell
[publishing house].................DLB-46

McEwan, Ian 1948- DLB-14, 194, 319, 326

McFadden, David 1940- DLB-60

McFall, Frances Elizabeth Clarke
(see Grand, Sarah)

McFarland, Ron 1942- DLB-256

McFarlane, Leslie 1902-1977 ....DLB-88

McFee, William 1881-1966 ....DLB-153

McGahan, Andrew 1966- DLB-325

McGahern, John 1934- DLB-14, 231, 319

McGee, Thomas D'Arcy 1825-1868 ......DLB-99

McGeehan, W. O. 1879-1933 ....DLB-25, 171

McGill, Ralph 1898-1969 ....DLB-29

McGinley, Phyllis 1905-1978 ....DLB-11, 48

McGinniss, Joe 1942- DLB-185

McGirt, James E. 1874-1930 ....DLB-50

McGlashan and Gill..................DLB-106

McGough, Roger 1937- DLB-40

McGrath, John 1935- DLB-233

McGrath, Patrick 1950- DLB-231

McGraw, Erin 1957- DLB-335

McGraw-Hill DLB-46

McGuane, Thomas 1939- DLB-2, 212; Y-80

Tribute to Seymour Lawrence..........Y-94

McGuckian, Medbh 1950- DLB-40

McGuffey, William Holmes 1800-1873 ....DLB-42

McGuinness, Frank 1953- DLB-245

McHenry, James 1785-1845 ....DLB-202

McIlvanney, William 1936- DLB-14, 207

McIlwraith, Jean Newton 1859-1938......DLB-92

McInerney, Jay 1955- DLB-292

McInerny, Ralph 1929- DLB-306

McIntosh, Maria Jane 1803-1878....DLB-239, 248

McIntyre, James 1827-1906 ....DLB-99

McIntyre, O. O. 1884-1938 ....DLB-25

McKay, Claude 1889-1948 ....DLB-4, 45, 51, 117

The David McKay Company DLB-49

McKay, Don 1942- DLB-334

McKean, William V. 1820-1903.........DLB-23

McKenna, Stephen 1888-1967..........DLB-197

The McKenzie Trust Y-96

McKerrow, R. B. 1872-1940............DLB-201

McKinley, Robin 1952- DLB-52

McKnight, Reginald 1956- DLB-234

McLachlan, Alexander 1818-1896........DLB-99

McLaren, Floris Clark 1904-1978 ....DLB-68

McLaverty, Michael 1907-1992 ....DLB-15

McLean, Duncan 1964- DLB-267

McLean, John R. 1848-1916 ....DLB-23

McLean, William L. 1852-1931.........DLB-25

McLennan, William 1856-1904 .... DLB-92

McLoughlin Brothers DLB-49

McLuhan, Marshall 1911-1980 .... DLB-88

McMaster, John Bach 1852-1932 .... DLB-47

McMillan, Terry 1951- DLB-292

McMurtry, Larry 1936-
.... DLB-2, 143, 256; Y-80, 87; CDALB-6

McNally, Terrence 1939- DLB-7, 249

McNeil, Florence 1937- DLB-60

McNeile, Herman Cyril 1888-1937 ...... DLB-77

McNickle, D'Arcy 1904-1977 .... DLB-175, 212

McPhee, John 1931- DLB-185, 275

McPherson, James Alan 1943- DLB-38, 244

McPherson, Sandra 1943- Y-86

McTaggart, J. M. E. 1866-1925 .... DLB-262

McWhirter, George 1939- DLB-60

McWilliam, Candia 1955- DLB-267

McWilliams, Carey 1905-1980........ DLB-137

"*The Nation's* Future," Carey
McWilliams's Editorial Policy
in *Nation* DLB-137

Mda, Zakes 1948- DLB-225

Mead, George Herbert 1863-1931 ......DLB-270

Mead, L. T. 1844-1914................ DLB-141

Mead, Matthew 1924- DLB-40

Mead, Taylor circa 1931- DLB-16

Meany, Tom 1903-1964 ....DLB-171

Mears, Gillian 1964- DLB-325

Mechthild von Magdeburg
circa 1207-circa 1282 .... DLB-138

Medieval Galician-Portuguese Poetry DLB-287

Medieval Spanish Debate Literature DLB-337

Medieval Spanish Epics DLB-337

Medieval Spanish Exempla Literature ... DLB-337

Medieval Spanish Spiritual Literature.... DLB-337

Medill, Joseph 1823-1899.............. DLB-43

Medoff, Mark 1940- DLB-7

Meek, Alexander Beaufort
1814-1865................. DLB-3, 248

Meeke, Mary ?-1816................ DLB-116

Mehta, Ved 1934- DLB-323

Mei, Lev Aleksandrovich 1822-1862 .....DLB-277

Meinke, Peter 1932- DLB-5

Meireles, Cecília 1901-1964 .... DLB-307

Mejía, Pedro 1497-1551 .... DLB-318

Mejia Vallejo, Manuel 1923- DLB-113

Melanchthon, Philipp 1497-1560 ....DLB-179

Melançon, Robert 1947- DLB-60

Melfi, Leonard 1935-2001 .... DLB-341

Mell, Max 1882-1971 .... DLB-81, 124

Mellow, James R. 1926-1997........ DLB-111

Mel'nikov, Pavel Ivanovich
1818-1883 .... DLB-238

Meltzer, David 1937- DLB-16

Meltzer, Milton 1915- DLB-61

Melville, Elizabeth, Lady Culross
circa 1585-1640 ....DLB-172

Melville, Herman
1819-1891 ...... DLB-3, 74, 250; CDALB-2

The Melville Society Y-01

Melville, James
(Roy Peter Martin) 1931- DLB-276

"Memorandum on Local Government," Anne-
Robert-Jacques Turgot, bacon de
l'Aulne DLB-314

Mena, Juan de 1411-1456............ DLB-286

Mena, María Cristina 1893-1965 ... DLB-209, 221

Menaker, Daniel 1941- DLB-335

Menander 342-341 B.C.-circa 292-291 B.C.
.... DLB-176; CDWLB-1

Menantes (see Hunold, Christian Friedrich)

Mencke, Johann Burckhard 1674-1732... DLB-168

Mencken, H. L. 1880-1956
.... DLB-11, 29, 63, 137, 222; CDALB-4

"Berlin, February, 1917"............. Y-00

From the Initial Issue of *American Mercury*
(January 1924) DLB-137

Mencken and Nietzsche: An
Unpublished Excerpt from H. L.
Mencken's *My Life as Author and
Editor* Y-93

Mendele Moyhker Sforim (Solomon Jacob
Abramowitz [Sholem Yankev Abramovitsch])
1836-1917.................... DLB-333

Mendelssohn, Moses 1729-1786 .... DLB-97

Mendes, Catulle 1841-1909 .... DLB-217

Méndez M., Miguel 1930- DLB-82

Mendoza, Diego Hurtado de
1504-1575................... DLB-318

Mendoza, Eduardo 1943- DLB-322

Menzini, Benedetto 1646-1704 .... DLB-339

The Mercantile Library of New York....... Y-96

Mercer, Cecil William (see Yates, Dornford)

Mercer, David 1928-1980.......... DLB-13, 310

Mercer, John 1704-1768 .... DLB-31

Mercer, Johnny 1909-1976 .... DLB-265

Mercier, Louis-Sébastien 1740-1814 ..... DLB-314

Le Tableau de Paris DLB-314

Meredith, George
1828-1909 ....DLB-18, 35, 57, 159; CDBLB-4

Meredith, Louisa Anne 1812-1895 .. DLB-166, 230

Meredith, Owen
(see Lytton, Edward Robert Bulwer)

Meredith, William 1919- DLB-5

Meres, Francis
Palladis Tamia, Wits Treasurie (1598)
[excerpt].................DLB-172

Merezhkovsky, Dmitrii Sergeevich
1865-1941 .... DLB-295

Mergerle, Johann Ulrich
(see Abraham ä Sancta Clara)

Mérimée, Prosper 1803-1870 .... DLB-119, 192

Merino, José María 1941- DLB-322

Merivale, John Herman 1779-1844....... DLB-96

Meriwether, Louise 1923- DLB-33

Merleau-Ponty, Maurice 1908-1961 ..... DLB-296

Merlin Press DLB-112

Mernissi, Fatima 1940- DLB-346

Merriam, Eve 1916-1992 .... DLB-61

The Merriam Company DLB-49

Merril, Judith 1923-1997 .... DLB-251

Tribute to Theodore Sturgeon Y-85

Merrill, Christopher 1957- DLB-342

Merrill, James 1926-1995 .... DLB-5, 165; Y-85

Merrill and Baker................ DLB-49

The Mershon Company............... DLB-49

Merton, Thomas 1915-1968........DLB-48; Y-81

Merwin, W. S. 1927- DLB-5, 169, 342

Julian Messner [publishing house] DLB-46

Mészöly, Miklós 1921-2001 .... DLB-232

J. Metcalf [publishing house]........... DLB-49

Metcalf, John 1938- DLB-60

The Methodist Book Concern DLB-49

Methuen and Company DLB-112

Meun, Jean de (see *Roman de la Rose*)

Mew, Charlotte 1869-1928......... DLB-19, 135

Mewshaw, Michael 1943- Y-80

Tribute to Albert Erskine............ Y-93

Meyer, Conrad Ferdinand 1825-1898.... DLB-129

Meyer, E. Y. 1946- DLB-75

Meyer, Eugene 1875-1959.............. DLB-29

Meyer, Michael 1921-2000............. DLB-155

Meyers, Jeffrey 1939- DLB-111

Meynell, Alice 1847-1922 .... DLB-19, 98

Meynell, Viola 1885-1956 .... DLB-153

Meyrink, Gustav 1868-1932............ DLB-81

Mézières, Philipe de circa 1327-1405..... DLB-208

Michael, Ib 1945- DLB-214

Michael, Livi 1960- DLB-267

Michaëlis, Karen 1872-1950 .... DLB-214

Michaels, Anne 1958- DLB-299

Michaels, Leonard 1933-2003 .... DLB-130

Michaux, Henri 1899-1984 .... DLB-258

Micheaux, Oscar 1884-1951............ DLB-50

Michel of Northgate, Dan
circa 1265-circa 1340 .... DLB-146

Micheline, Jack 1929-1998 .... DLB-16

Michener, James A. 1907?-1997 .... DLB-6

Micklejohn, George circa 1717-1818 ...... DLB-31

Middle Hill Press DLB-106

Middleton, Christopher 1926- DLB-40

Middleton, Conyers 1683-1750 ....DLB-336

Middleton, Richard 1882-1911 ....DLB-156

Middleton, Stanley 1919- DLB-14, 326

Middleton, Thomas 1580-1627 ....DLB-58

Midnight's Children, 1981 Booker Prize winner, Salman Rushdie.........DLB-326

Miegel, Agnes 1879-1964 ....DLB-56

Miežalaitis, Eduardas 1919-1997 ....DLB-220

Miguéis, José Rodrigues 1901-1980 ....DLB-287

Mihailović, Dragoslav 1930- DLB-181

Mihalić, Slavko 1928- DLB-181

Mikhailov, A. (see Sheller, Aleksandr Konstantinovich)

Mikhailov, Mikhail Larionovich 1829-1865 ....DLB-238

Mikhailovsky, Nikolai Konstantinovich 1842-1904 ....DLB-277

Miles, Josephine 1911-1985 ....DLB-48

Miles, Susan (Ursula Wyllie Roberts) 1888-1975 ....DLB-240

Miliković, Branko 1934-1961 ....DLB-181

Milius, John 1944- DLB-44

Mill, James 1773-1836 ....DLB-107, 158, 262

Mill, John Stuart 1806-1873 ....DLB-55, 190, 262; CDBLB-4

Thoughts on Poetry and Its Varieties (1833) DLB-32

Andrew Millar [publishing house] DLB-154

Millar, John 1735-1801 ....DLB-336

Millar, Kenneth 1915-1983 ....DLB-2, 226; Y-83; DS-6

Millás, Juan José 1946- DLB-322

Millay, Edna St. Vincent 1892-1950 ....DLB-45, 249; CDALB-4

Millen, Sarah Gertrude 1888-1968 ....DLB-225

Miller, Andrew 1960- DLB-267

Miller, Arthur 1915-2005 ....DLB-7, 266; CDALB-1

The Arthur Miller Society Y-01

Miller, Caroline 1903-1992 ....DLB-9

Miller, Eugene Ethelbert 1950- DLB-41

Tribute to Julian Mayfield Y-84

Miller, Heather Ross 1939- DLB-120

Miller, Henry 1891-1980 ....DLB-4, 9; Y-80; CDALB-5

Miller, Hugh 1802-1856 ....DLB-190

Miller, J. Hillis 1928- DLB-67

Miller, Jane 1949- DLB-342

Miller, Jason 1939- DLB-7

Miller, Joaquin 1839-1913 ....DLB-186

Miller, May 1899-1995 ....DLB-41

Miller, Paul 1906-1991 ....DLB-127

Miller, Perry 1905-1963 ....DLB-17, 63

Miller, Sue 1943- DLB-143

Miller, Vassar 1924-1998 ....DLB-105

Miller, Walter M., Jr. 1923-1996 ....DLB-8

Miller, Webb 1892-1940 ....DLB-29

James Miller [publishing house] DLB-49

Millett, Kate 1934- DLB-246

Millhauser, Steven 1943- DLB-2

Millican, Arthenia J. Bates 1920- DLB-38

Milligan, Alice 1866-1953 ....DLB-240

Mills, Magnus 1954- DLB-267

Mills and Boon DLB-112

Milman, Henry Hart 1796-1868 ....DLB-96

Milne, A. A. 1882-1956 ....DLB-10, 77, 100, 160

Milner, Ron 1938- DLB-38

William Milner [publishing house] DLB-106

Milnes, Richard Monckton (Lord Houghton) 1809-1885 ....DLB-32, 184

Milton, John 1608-1674 ....DLB-131, 151, 281; CDBLB-2

The Milton Society of America Y-00

Miłosz, Czesław 1911-2004 ....DLB-215, 331; CDWLB-4

Minakami Tsutomu 1919-2004 ....DLB-182

Minamoto no Sanetomo 1192-1219 ....DLB-203

Minco, Marga 1920- DLB-299

The Minerva Press DLB-154

Mina, Hanna 1924- DLB-346

Minnesang circa 1150-1280 ....DLB-138

The Music of *Minnesang* DLB-138

Minns, Susan 1839-1938 ....DLB-140

Minsky, Nikolai 1855-1937 ....DLB-317

Minton, Balch and Company DLB-46

Minyana, Philippe 1946- DLB-321

Mirbeau, Octave 1848-1917 ....DLB-123, 192

Mirikitani, Janice 1941- DLB-312

Mirk, John died after 1414? DLB-146

Miró, Gabriel 1879-1930 ....DLB-322

Miró, Ricardo 1883-1940 ....DLB-290

Miron, Gaston 1928-1996 ....DLB-60

A Mirror for Magistrates DLB-167

Mirsky, D. S. 1890-1939 ....DLB-317

Mishima Yukio 1925-1970 ....DLB-182

Mistral, Frédéric 1830-1914 ....DLB-331

Mistral, Gabriela 1889-1957 ....DLB-283, 331

Mistry, Rohinton 1952- DLB-334

Mitchel, Jonathan 1624-1668 ....DLB-24

Mitchell, Adrian 1932- DLB-40

Mitchell, Donald Grant 1822-1908 ....DLB-1, 243; DS-13

Mitchell, Gladys 1901-1983 ....DLB-77

Mitchell, H. L. 1906-1989 ....DLB-345

Mitchell, James Leslie 1901-1935 ....DLB-15

Mitchell, John (see Slater, Patrick)

Mitchell, John Ames 1845-1918 ....DLB-79

Mitchell, Joseph 1908-1996 ....DLB-185; Y-96

Mitchell, Julian 1935- DLB-14

Mitchell, Ken 1940- DLB-60

Mitchell, Langdon 1862-1935 ....DLB-7

Mitchell, Loften 1919-2001 ....DLB-38

Mitchell, Margaret 1900-1949 ....DLB-9; CDALB-7

Mitchell, S. Weir 1829-1914 ....DLB-202

Mitchell, W. J. T. 1942- DLB-246

Mitchell, W. O. 1914-1998 ....DLB-88

Mitchison, Naomi Margaret (Haldane) 1897-1999 ....DLB-160, 191, 255, 319

Mitford, Mary Russell 1787-1855 ....DLB-110, 116

Mitford, Nancy 1904-1973 ....DLB-191

Mitford, William 1744-1827 ....DLB-336

Mittelholzer, Edgar 1909-1965 ....DLB-117; CDWLB-3

Mitterer, Erika 1906-2001 ....DLB-85

Mitterer, Felix 1948- DLB-124

Mitternacht, Johann Sebastian 1613-1679 ....DLB-168

Miyamoto Yuriko 1899-1951 ....DLB-180

Mizener, Arthur 1907-1988 ....DLB-103

Mo, Timothy 1950- DLB-194

Moberg, Vilhelm 1898-1973 ....DLB-259

Las Mocedades de Rodrigo (circa 1300) DLB-337

Modern Age Books DLB-46

Modern Language Association of America
The Modern Language Association of America Celebrates Its Centennial Y-84

The Modern Library DLB-46

Modern School Movement, The DLB-345

Modiano, Patrick 1945- DLB-83, 299

Modjeska, Drusilla 1946- DLB-325

Moffat, Yard and Company DLB-46

Moffet, Thomas 1553-1604 ....DLB-136

Mofolo, Thomas 1876-1948 ....DLB-225

Mohr, Nicholasa 1938- DLB-145

Moix, Ana María 1947- DLB-134

Molesworth, Louisa 1839-1921 ....DLB-135

Molière (Jean-Baptiste Poquelin) 1622-1673 ....DLB-268

Møller, Poul Martin 1794-1838 ....DLB-300

Möllhausen, Balduin 1825-1905 ....DLB-129

Molnár, Ferenc 1878-1952 ....DLB-215; CDWLB-4

Molnár, Miklós (see Mészöly, Miklós)

Molodowsky, Kadya (Kadye Molodovski) 1894-1975 ....DLB-333

Momaday, N. Scott 1934- DLB-143, 175, 256; CDALB-7

Mommsen, Theodor 1817-1903 ....DLB-331

Moncrieff, W. T. (William Thomas Thomas) 1794-1857 . . . . DLB-344

Monkhouse, Allan 1858-1936 . . . . DLB-10

Monro, Harold 1879-1932 . . . . DLB-19

Monroe, Harriet 1860-1936 . . . . DLB-54, 91

Monsarrat, Nicholas 1910-1979 . . . . DLB-15

Montagu, Lady Mary Wortley 1689-1762 . . . . DLB-95, 101

Montague, C. E. 1867-1928 . . . . DLB-197

Montague, John 1929- DLB-40

Montaigne, Michel de 1533-1592 . . . . . . DLB-327

Montale, Eugenio 1896-1981 . . . . . . DLB-114, 331

Montalvo, Garci Rodríguez de ca. 1450?-before 1505 . . . . DLB-286

Montalvo, José 1946-1994 . . . . DLB-209

Montemayor, Jorge de 1521?-1561? DLB-318

Montero, Rosa 1951- DLB-322

Monterroso, Augusto 1921-2003 . . . . DLB-145

Montesquieu, Charles-Louis de Secondat, baron de 1689-1755 . . . . DLB-314

The Spirit of Laws DLB-314

Montesquiou, Robert de 1855-1921 . . . . . DLB-217

Montgomerie, Alexander circa 1550?-1598 . . . . DLB-167

Montgomery, James 1771-1854 . . . . . . DLB-93, 158

Montgomery, John 1919- DLB-16

Montgomery, Lucy Maud 1874-1942 . . . . DLB-92; DS-14

Montgomery, Marion 1925- DLB-6

Montgomery, Robert Bruce (see Crispin, Edmund)

Montherlant, Henry de 1896-1972 . . . DLB-72, 321

The Monthly Review 1749-1844 . . . . DLB-110

Monti, Ricardo 1944- DLB-305

Montigny, Louvigny de 1876-1955 . . . . . . DLB-92

Montoya, José 1932- DLB-122

Moodie, John Wedderburn Dunbar 1797-1869 . . . . DLB-99

Moodie, Susanna 1803-1885 . . . . DLB-99

Moody, Joshua circa 1633-1697 . . . . DLB-24

Moody, William Vaughn 1869-1910 . . . . DLB-7, 54

Moon Tiger, 1987 Booker Prize winner, Penelope Lively DLB-326

Moorcock, Michael 1939- DLB-14, 231, 261, 319

Moore, Alan 1953- DLB-261

Moore, Brian 1921-1999 . . . . DLB-251

Moore, Catherine L. 1911-1987 . . . . DLB-8

Moore, Clement Clarke 1779-1863 . . . . . . DLB-42

Moore, Dora Mavor 1888-1979 . . . . DLB-92

Moore, G. E. 1873-1958 . . . . DLB-262

Moore, George 1852-1933 . . . . DLB-10, 18, 57, 135

Literature at Nurse, or Circulating Morals (1885) DLB-18

Moore, J. Howard 1862-1916 . . . . DLB-345

Moore, Lorrie 1957- DLB-234

Moore, Marianne 1887-1972 . . . . DLB-45; DS-7; CDALB-5

International Marianne Moore Society . . . Y-98

Moore, Mavor 1919- DLB-88

Moore, Richard 1927- DLB-105

"The No Self, the Little Self, and the Poets" DLB-105

Moore, T. Sturge 1870-1944 . . . . DLB-19

Moore, Thomas 1779-1852 . . . . DLB-96, 144

Moore, Ward 1903-1978 . . . . DLB-8

Moore, Wilstach, Keys and Company DLB-49

Moorehead, Alan 1901-1983 . . . . DLB-204

Moorhouse, Frank 1938- DLB-289

Moorhouse, Geoffrey 1931- DLB-204

Moorish Novel of the Sixteenth Century, The DLB-318

The Moorland-Spingarn Research Center DLB-76

Moorman, Mary C. 1905-1994 . . . . DLB-155

Mora, Pat 1942- DLB-209

Moraes, Dom 1938-2004 . . . . DLB-323

Moraes, Vinicius de 1913-1980 . . . . DLB-307

Moraga, Cherríe 1952- DLB-82, 249

Morales, Alejandro 1944- DLB-82

Morales, Mario Roberto 1947- DLB-145

Morales, Rafael 1919- DLB-108

Morality Plays: *Mankind* circa 1450-1500 and *Everyman* circa 1500 . . . . DLB-146

Morand, Paul 1888-1976 . . . . DLB-65

Morante, Elsa 1912-1985 . . . . DLB-177

Morata, Olympia Fulvia 1526-1555 . . . . . DLB-179

Moravia, Alberto 1907-1990 . . . . DLB-177

Mordaunt, Elinor 1872-1942 . . . . DLB-174

Mordovtsev, Daniil Lukich 1830-1905 . . . DLB-238

More, Hannah 1745-1833 . . . . DLB-107, 109, 116, 158

More, Henry 1614-1687 . . . . DLB-126, 252

More, Sir Thomas 1477/1478-1535 . . . . DLB-136, 281

Morejón, Nancy 1944- DLB-283

Morellet, André 1727-1819 . . . . DLB-314

Morency, Pierre 1942- DLB-60

Moreno, Dorinda 1939- DLB-122

Moretti, Marino 1885-1979 . . . . DLB-114, 264

Morgan, Berry 1919-2002 . . . . DLB-6

Morgan, Charles 1894-1958 . . . . DLB-34, 100

Morgan, Edmund S. 1916- DLB-17

Morgan, Edwin 1920- DLB-27

Morgan, John Pierpont 1837-1913 . . . . . . DLB-140

Morgan, John Pierpont, Jr. 1867-1943 . . . . DLB-140

Morgan, Robert 1944- DLB-120, 292

Morgan, Sally 1951- DLB-325

Morgan, Sydney Owenson, Lady 1776?-1859 . . . . DLB-116, 158

Morgner, Irmtraud 1933-1990 . . . . DLB-75

Morhof, Daniel Georg 1639-1691 . . . . . . DLB-164

Mori, Kyoko 1957- DLB-312

Mori Ōgai 1862-1922 . . . . DLB-180

Mori, Toshio 1910-1980 . . . . DLB-312

Móricz, Zsigmond 1879-1942 . . . . DLB-215

Morier, James Justinian 1782 or 1783?-1849 . . . . DLB-116

Mörike, Eduard 1804-1875 . . . . DLB-133

Morin, Paul 1889-1963 . . . . DLB-92

Morison, Richard 1514?-1556 . . . . DLB-136

Morison, Samuel Eliot 1887-1976 . . . . DLB-17

Morison, Stanley 1889-1967 . . . . DLB-201

Moritz, Karl Philipp 1756-1793 . . . . DLB-94

Moriz von Craûn circa 1220-1230 . . . . DLB-138

Morley, Christopher 1890-1957 . . . . DLB-9

Morley, John 1838-1923 . . . . DLB-57, 144, 190

Moro, César 1903-1956 . . . . DLB-290

Morris, George Pope 1802-1864 . . . . DLB-73

Morris, James Humphrey (see Morris, Jan)

Morris, Jan 1926- DLB-204

Morris, Lewis 1833-1907 . . . . DLB-35

Morris, Margaret 1737-1816 . . . . DLB-200

Morris, Mary McGarry 1943- DLB-292

Morris, Richard B. 1904-1989 . . . . DLB-17

Morris, William 1834-1896 . . . . . DLB-18, 35, 57, 156, 178, 184; CDBLB-4

Morris, Willie 1934-1999 . . . . Y-80

Tribute to Irwin Shaw Y-84

Tribute to James Dickey Y-97

Morris, Wright 1910-1998 . . . . DLB-2, 206, 218; Y-81

Morrison, Arthur 1863-1945 . . . . DLB-70, 135, 197

Morrison, Charles Clayton 1874-1966 . . . . DLB-91

Morrison, John 1904-1998 . . . . DLB-260

Morrison, Toni 1931- DLB-6, 33, 143, 331; Y-81, 93; CDALB-6

Nobel Lecture 1993 . . . . Y-93

Morrissy, Mary 1957- DLB-267

William Morrow and Company DLB-46

Morse, James Herbert 1841-1923 . . . . DLB-71

Morse, Jedidiah 1761-1826 . . . . DLB-37

Morse, John T., Jr. 1840-1937 . . . . DLB-47

Morselli, Guido 1912-1973 . . . . DLB-177

Morte Arthure, the *Alliterative* and the *Stanzaic* circa 1350-1400 . . . . DLB-146

Mortimer, Favell Lee 1802-1878 . . . . DLB-163

Mortimer, John 1923- DLB-13, 245, 271; CDBLB-8

Morton, Carlos 1942- DLB-122

Morton, H. V. 1892-1979 . . . . DLB-195

Morton, John Maddison 1811-1891......DLB-344

John P. Morton and Company..........DLB-49

Morton, Nathaniel 1613-1685............DLB-24

Morton, Sarah Wentworth 1759-1846.....DLB-37

Morton, Thomas circa 1579-circa 1647....DLB-24

Moscherosch, Johann Michael 1601-1669..................DLB-164

Humphrey Moseley [publishing house]................DLB-170

Möser, Justus 1720-1794................DLB-97

Moses, Daniel David 1952-............DLB-334

Mosley, Nicholas 1923-...........DLB-14, 207

Mosley, Walter 1952-................DLB-306

Moss, Arthur 1889-1969.................DLB-4

Moss, Howard 1922-1987.................DLB-5

Moss, Thylias 1954-..................DLB-120

Mother Earth 1906-1918..............DLB-345

Motion, Andrew 1952-..................DLB-40

Motley, John Lothrop 1814-1877............DLB-1, 30, 59, 235

Motley, Willard 1909-1965........DLB-76, 143

Mott, Lucretia 1793-1880.............DLB-239

Benjamin Motte Jr. [publishing house]................DLB-154

Motteux, Peter Anthony 1663-1718......DLB-80

Mottram, R. H. 1883-1971..............DLB-36

Mount, Ferdinand 1939-...............DLB-231

Mouré, Erin 1955-.....................DLB-60

Mourning Dove (Humishuma) between 1882 and 1888?-1936.........DLB-175, 221

Movies
 Fiction into Film, 1928-1975: A List of Movies Based on the Works of Authors in British Novelists, 1930-1959..................DLB-15

 Movies from Books, 1920-1974........DLB-9

Mowat, Farley 1921-..................DLB-68

A. R. Mowbray and Company, Limited........................DLB-106

Mowrer, Edgar Ansel 1892-1977........DLB-29

Mowrer, Paul Scott 1887-1971.........DLB-29

Edward Moxon [publishing house]......DLB-106

Joseph Moxon [publishing house].......DLB-170

Moyes, Patricia 1923-2000............DLB-276

Mphahlele, Es'kia (Ezekiel) 1919-2008........DLB-125, 225; CDWLB-3

Mrożek, Sławomir 1930-...DLB-232; CDWLB-4

Mtshali, Oswald Mbuyiseni 1940-.................DLB-125, 225

Mu Shiying 1912-1940.................DLB-328

al-Mubarrad 826-898 or 899..........DLB-311

Mucedorus..............................DLB-62

Mudford, William 1782-1848...........DLB-159

Mudrooroo (see Johnson, Colin)

Mueller, Lisel 1924-.................DLB-105

Muhajir, El (see Marvin X)

Muhajir, Nazzam Al Fitnah (see Marvin X)

Muhammad the Prophet circa 570-632...DLB-311

Mühlbach, Luise 1814-1873............DLB-133

Muir, Edwin 1887-1959........DLB-20, 100, 191

Muir, Helen 1937-.....................DLB-14

Muir, John 1838-1914............DLB-186, 275

Muir, Percy 1894-1979................DLB-201

Mujū Ichien 1226-1312................DLB-203

Mukherjee, Bharati 1940-....DLB-60, 218, 323

Mulcaster, Richard 1531 or 1532-1611...DLB-167

Muldoon, Paul 1951-...................DLB-40

Mulisch, Harry 1927-.................DLB-299

Mulkerns, Val 1925-..................DLB-319

Müller, Friedrich (see Müller, Maler)

Müller, Heiner 1929-1995.............DLB-124

Müller, Maler 1749-1825...............DLB-94

Muller, Marcia 1944-.................DLB-226

Müller, Wilhelm 1794-1827.............DLB-90

Mumford, Lewis 1895-1990..............DLB-63

Munby, A. N. L. 1913-1974............DLB-201

Munby, Arthur Joseph 1828-1910.......DLB-35

Munday, Anthony 1560-1633.......DLB-62, 172

Mundt, Clara (see Mühlbach, Luise)

Mundt, Theodore 1808-1861............DLB-133

Munford, Robert circa 1737-1783.......DLB-31

Mungoshi, Charles 1947-..............DLB-157

Munif, Abdelrahman 1933-2004........DLB-346

Munk, Kaj 1898-1944..................DLB-214

Munonye, John 1929-..................DLB-117

Muñoz Molina, Antonio 1956-.........DLB-322

Munro, Alice 1931-....................DLB-53

George Munro [publishing house].......DLB-49

Munro, H. H. 1870-1916..........DLB-34, 162; CDBLB-5

Munro, Neil 1864-1930................DLB-156

Norman L. Munro [publishing house]....DLB-49

Munroe, Kirk 1850-1930...............DLB-42

Munroe and Francis....................DLB-49

James Munroe and Company.............DLB-49

Joel Munsell [publishing house].......DLB-49

Munsey, Frank A. 1854-1925........DLB-25, 91

Frank A. Munsey and Company.........DLB-49

Mura, David 1952-....................DLB-312

Murakami Haruki 1949-................DLB-182

Muratov, Pavel 1881-1950.............DLB-317

Murayama, Milton 1923-...............DLB-312

Murav'ev, Mikhail Nikitich 1757-1807....DLB-150

Murdoch, Iris 1919-1999 ....DLB-14, 194, 233, 326; CDBLB-8

Murdock, James
 From *Sketches of Modern Philosophy*........DS-5

Murdoch, Rupert 1931-...............DLB-127

Murfree, Mary N. 1850-1922........DLB-12, 74

Murger, Henry 1822-1861..............DLB-119

Murger, Louis-Henri (see Murger, Henry)

Murnane, Gerald 1939-................DLB-289

Murner, Thomas 1475-1537.............DLB-179

Muro, Amado 1915-1971.................DLB-82

Murphy, Arthur 1727-1805.........DLB-89, 142

Murphy, Beatrice M. 1908-1992.........DLB-76

Murphy, Dervla 1931-.................DLB-204

Murphy, Emily 1868-1933...............DLB-99

Murphy, Jack 1923-1980...............DLB-241

John Murphy and Company..............DLB-49

Murphy, John H., III 1916-...........DLB-127

Murphy, Richard 1927-1993............DLB-40

Murphy, Tom 1935-....................DLB-310

Murray, Albert L. 1916-...............DLB-38

Murray, Gilbert 1866-1957.............DLB-10

Murray, Jim 1919-1998................DLB-241

John Murray [publishing house].......DLB-154

Murray, Judith Sargent 1751-1820..............DLB-37, 200

Murray, Les 1938-....................DLB-289

Murray, Pauli 1910-1985...............DLB-41

Murry, John Middleton 1889-1957......DLB-149

 "The Break-Up of the Novel" (1922).....................DLB-36

Murry, John Middleton, Jr. (see Cowper, Richard)

Musäus, Johann Karl August 1735-1787......................DLB-97

al-Musawi, Muhsin 1945-..............DLB-346

Muschg, Adolf 1934-...................DLB-75

Musil, Robert 1880-1942.........DLB-81, 124; CDWLB-2

Muspilli circa 790-circa 850..........DLB-148

Musset, Alfred de 1810-1857......DLB-192, 217

Benjamin B. Mussey and Company...................DLB-49

Muste, A. J. 1885-1967...............DLB-303

Mutafchieva, Vera 1929-..............DLB-181

Mutis, Alvaro 1923-..................DLB-283

Mwangi, Meja 1948-...................DLB-125

Myers, Frederic W. H. 1843-1901......................DLB-190

Myers, Gustavus 1872-1942.............DLB-47

Myers, L. H. 1881-1944................DLB-15

Myers, Walter Dean 1937-..............DLB-33

Myerson, Julie 1960-.................DLB-267

Mykle, Agnar 1915-1994...............DLB-297

Mykolaitis-Putinas, Vincas 1893-1967................DLB-220

Myles, Eileen 1949- DLB-193

Myrdal, Jan 1927- DLB-257

Mystery
   1985: The Year of the Mystery:
     A Symposium Y-85
   Comments from Other Writers Y-85
   The Second Annual New York Festival
     of Mystery Y-00
   Why I Read Mysteries Y-85
   Why I Write Mysteries: Night and Day,
     by Michael Collins Y-85

N

Na Prous Boneta circa 1296-1328 .... DLB-208

Nabl, Franz 1883-1974 .... DLB-81

Nabakov, Véra 1902-1991 .... Y-91

Nabokov, Vladimir 1899-1977 .... DLB-2, 244,
     278, 317; Y-80, 91; DS-3; CDALB-1
   International Nabokov Society Y-99
   An Interview [On Nabokov], by
     Fredson Bowers Y-80
   Nabokov Festival at Cornell Y-83
   The Vladimir Nabokov Archive in the
     Berg Collection of the New York
     Public Library: An Overview Y-91
   The Vladimir Nabokov Society Y-01

Nádaši, Ladislav (see Jégé)

Naden, Constance 1858-1889 .... DLB-199

Nader, Ralph 1934- DLB-345

Nadezhdin, Nikolai Ivanovich
   1804-1856 .... DLB-198

Nadir, Moshe (Moyshe Nadir; Isaac Reis [Yitskhok
   Reyz]) 1885-1943 .... DLB-333

Nadson, Semen Iakovlevich 1862-1887 ... DLB-277

Naevius circa 265 B.C.-201 B.C. DLB-211

Nafis and Cornish DLB-49

Nagai Kafū 1879-1959 .... DLB-180

Nagel, Ernest 1901-1985 .... DLB-279

Nagibin, Iurii Markovich 1920-1994 .... DLB-302

Nagrodskaia, Evdokiia Apollonovna
   1866-1930 .... DLB-295

Nahman of Bratslav (Nakhmen Bratslaver)
   1772-1810 .... DLB-333

Naidus, Leib (Leyb Naydus)
   1890-1918 .... DLB-333

Naipaul, Shiva 1945-1985 .... DLB-157; Y-85

Naipaul, V. S. 1932-
   .... DLB-125, 204, 207, 326, 331;
     Y-85, 01; CDBLB-8; CDWLB-3
   Nobel Lecture 2001: "Two Worlds" Y-01

Nakagami Kenji 1946-1992 .... DLB-182

Nakano-in Masatada no Musume (see Nijō, Lady)

Nałkowska, Zofia 1884-1954 .... DLB-215

Namora, Fernando 1919-1989 .... DLB-287

Joseph Nancrede [publishing house] DLB-49

Naranjo, Carmen 1930- DLB-145

Narayan, R. K. 1906-2001 .... DLB-323

Narbikova, Valeriia Spartakovna
   1958- DLB-285

Narezhny, Vasilii Trofimovich
   1780-1825 .... DLB-198

Narrache, Jean (Emile Coderre)
   1893-1970 .... DLB-92

Nasby, Petroleum Vesuvius (see Locke, David Ross)

Eveleigh Nash [publishing house] DLB-112

Nash, Ogden 1902-1971 .... DLB-11

Nashe, Thomas 1567-1601? DLB-167

Nason, Jerry 1910-1986 .... DLB-241

Nasr, Seyyed Hossein 1933- DLB-279

Nasrallah, Emily 1931- DLB-346

Nast, Condé 1873-1942 .... DLB-91

Nast, Thomas 1840-1902 .... DLB-188

Nastasijević, Momčilo 1894-1938 .... DLB-147

Nathan, George Jean 1882-1958 .... DLB-137

Nathan, Leonard 1924- DLB-342

Nathan, Robert 1894-1985 .... DLB-9

Nation, Carry A. 1846-1911 .... DLB-303

National Book Critics Circle Awards Y-00–01

The National Jewish Book Awards Y-85

Natsume Sōseki 1867-1916 .... DLB-180

Naughton, Bill 1910-1992 .... DLB-13

Nava, Michael 1954- DLB-306

Navarro, Joe 1953- DLB-209

Naylor, Gloria 1950- DLB-173

Nazor, Vladimir 1876-1949 .... DLB-147

Ndebele, Njabulo 1948- DLB-157, 225

Neagoe, Peter 1881-1960 .... DLB-4

Neal, John 1793-1876 .... DLB-1, 59, 243

Neal, Joseph C. 1807-1847 .... DLB-11

Neal, Larry 1937-1981 .... DLB-38

The Neale Publishing Company DLB-49

Nearing, Scott 1883-1983 .... DLB-303

Nebel, Frederick 1903-1967 .... DLB-226

Nebrija, Antonio de 1442 or 1444-1522 .. DLB-286

Nedreaas, Torborg 1906-1987 .... DLB-297

F. Tennyson Neely [publishing house] DLB-49

Negoițescu, Ion 1921-1993 .... DLB-220

Negri, Ada 1870-1945 .... DLB-114

Nehru, Pandit Jawaharlal 1889-1964 .... DLB-323

Neihardt, John G. 1881-1973 ..... DLB-9, 54, 256

Neidhart von Reuental
   circa 1185-circa 1240 .... DLB-138

Neilson, John Shaw 1872-1942 .... DLB-230

Nekrasov, Nikolai Alekseevich
   1821-1877 .... DLB-277

Nekrasov, Viktor Platonovich
   1911-1987 .... DLB-302

Neledinsky-Meletsky, Iurii Aleksandrovich
   1752-1828 .... DLB-150

Nelligan, Emile 1879-1941 .... DLB-92

Nelson, Alice Moore Dunbar 1875-1935 .. DLB-50

Nelson, Antonya 1961- DLB-244

Nelson, Kent 1943- DLB-234

Nelson, Richard 1950- DLB-341

Nelson, Richard K. 1941- DLB-275

Nelson, Thomas, and Sons [U.K.] DLB-106

Nelson, Thomas, and Sons [U.S.] DLB-49

Nelson, William 1908-1978 .... DLB-103

Nelson, William Rockhill 1841-1915 ..... DLB-23

Nemerov, Howard 1920-1991 ..... DLB-5, 6; Y-83

Németh, László 1901-1975 .... DLB-215

Nepos circa 100 B.C.-post 27 B.C. DLB-211

Nėris, Salomėja 1904-1945 .. DLB-220; CDWLB-4

Neruda, Pablo 1904-1973 .... DLB-283, 331

Nerval, Gérard de 1808-1855 .... DLB-217

Nervo, Amado 1870-1919 .... DLB-290

Nesbit, E. 1858-1924 .... DLB-141, 153, 178

Ness, Evaline 1911-1986 .... DLB-61

Nestroy, Johann 1801-1862 .... DLB-133

Nettleship, R. L. 1846-1892 .... DLB-262

Neugeboren, Jay 1938- DLB-28, 335

Neukirch, Benjamin 1655-1729 .... DLB-168

Neumann, Alfred 1895-1952 .... DLB-56

Neumann, Ferenc (see Molnár, Ferenc)

Neumark, Georg 1621-1681 .... DLB-164

Neumeister, Erdmann 1671-1756 ...... DLB-168

Nevins, Allan 1890-1971 .... DLB-17; DS-17

Nevinson, Henry Woodd 1856-1941 .... DLB-135

The New American Library DLB-46

New Directions Publishing Corporation ... DLB-46

The New Monthly Magazine 1814-1884 .... DLB-110

New York Times Book Review Y-82

John Newbery [publishing house] DLB-154

Newbolt, Henry 1862-1938 .... DLB-19

Newbound, Bernard Slade (see Slade, Bernard)

Newby, Eric 1919-2006 .... DLB-204

Newby, P. H. 1918-1997 .... DLB-15, 326

Thomas Cautley Newby
   [publishing house] DLB-106

Newcomb, Charles King 1820-1894 ... DLB-1, 223

Newell, Peter 1862-1924 .... DLB-42

Newell, Robert Henry 1836-1901 .... DLB-11

Newhouse, Edward 1911-2002 .... DLB-335

Newhouse, Samuel I. 1895-1979 .... DLB-127

Newman, Cecil Earl 1903-1976 .... DLB-127

Newman, David 1937- DLB-44

Newman, Frances 1883-1928 .... Y-80

Newman, Francis William 1805-1897 .... DLB-190

Newman, G. F. 1946- DLB-310

Newman, John Henry
   1801-1890 .... DLB-18, 32, 55

Mark Newman [publishing house]........DLB-49
Newmarch, Rosa Harriet 1857-1940.....DLB-240
George Newnes Limited DLB-112
Newsome, Effie Lee 1885-1979 ....DLB-76
Newton, A. Edward 1864-1940........DLB-140
Newton, Sir Isaac 1642-1727 ....DLB-252
Nexø, Martin Andersen 1869-1954......DLB-214
Nezval, Vítěslav
   1900-1958............DLB-215; CDWLB-4
Ngugi wa Thiong'o
   1938- DLB-125; CDWLB-3
Niatum, Duane 1938- DLB-175
The *Nibelungenlied* and the *Klage*
   circa 1200 ....DLB-138
Nichol, B. P. 1944-1988................DLB-53
Nicholas of Cusa 1401-1464 ....DLB-115
Nichols, Ann 1891?-1966...........DLB-249
Nichols, Beverly 1898-1983...........DLB-191
Nichols, Dudley 1895-1960............DLB-26
Nichols, Grace 1950- DLB-157
Nichols, John 1940- Y-82
Nichols, Mary Sargeant (Neal) Gove
   1810-1884 ....DLB-1, 243
Nichols, Peter 1927- DLB-13, 245
Nichols, Roy F. 1896-1973.............DLB-17
Nichols, Ruth 1948- DLB-60
Nicholson, Edward Williams Byron
   1849-1912 ....DLB-184
Nicholson, Geoff 1953- DLB-271
Nicholson, Norman 1914-1987 ....DLB-27
Nicholson, William 1872-1949.........DLB-141
Ní Chuilleanáin, Eiléan 1942- DLB-40
Nicol, Eric 1919- DLB-68
Nicolai, Friedrich 1733-1811 ....DLB-97
Nicolas de Clamanges circa 1363-1437 ...DLB-208
Nicolay, John G. 1832-1901 and
   Hay, John 1838-1905...............DLB-47
Nicole, Pierre 1625-1695 ....DLB-268
Nicolson, Adela Florence Cory (see Hope, Laurence)
Nicolson, Harold 1886-1968 ....DLB-100, 149
   "The Practice of Biography," in
   *The English Sense of Humour and
   Other Essays* DLB-149
Nicolson, Nigel 1917-2004 ....DLB-155
Ní Dhuibhne, Éilís 1954- DLB-319
Niebuhr, Reinhold 1892-1971 ..... DLB-17; DS-17
Niedecker, Lorine 1903-1970 ....DLB-48
Nieman, Lucius W. 1857-1935..........DLB-25
Nietzsche, Friedrich
   1844-1900 ....DLB-129; CDWLB-2
   Mencken and Nietzsche: An Unpublished
   Excerpt from H. L. Mencken's *My Life
   as Author and Editor* Y-93
Nievo, Stanislao 1928- DLB-196

Niggli, Josefina 1910-1983 ....Y-80
Nightingale, Florence 1820-1910 ....DLB-166
Nijō, Lady (Nakano-in Masatada no Musume)
   1258-after 1306 ....DLB-203
Nijō Yoshimoto 1320-1388............DLB-203
Nikitin, Ivan Savvich 1824-1861 ....DLB-277
Nikitin, Nikolai Nikolaevich 1895-1963 ..DLB-272
Nikolev, Nikolai Petrovich 1758-1815 ....DLB-150
Niles, Hezekiah 1777-1839..............DLB-43
Nims, John Frederick 1913-1999 ....DLB-5
   Tribute to Nancy Hale Y-88
Nin, Anaïs 1903-1977............DLB-2, 4, 152
Nína Björk Árnadóttir 1941-2000 ....DLB-293
Niño, Raúl 1961- DLB-209
Nissenson, Hugh 1933- DLB-28, 335
Der Nister (Pinchas Kahanovitch [Pinkhes
   Kahanovitsh]) 1884-1950 ....DLB-333
Niven, Frederick John 1878-1944........DLB-92
Niven, Larry 1938- DLB-8
Nixon, Howard M. 1909-1983 ....DLB-201
Nizan, Paul 1905-1940................DLB-72
Njegoš, Petar II Petrović
   1813-1851 ....DLB-147; CDWLB-4
Nkosi, Lewis 1936- DLB-157, 225
Noah, Mordecai M. 1785-1851 ....DLB-250
Noailles, Anna de 1876-1933 ....DLB-258
Nobel Peace Prize
   The Nobel Prize and Literary Politics.....Y-88
   Elie Wiesel Y-86
Nobel Prize in Literature
   Shmuel Yosef Agnon...............DLB-329
   Vicente Aleixandre DLB-108, 329
   Ivo Andrić........ DLB-147, 329; CDWLB-4
   Miguel Ángel Asturias....... DLB-113, 290,
      329; CDWLB-3
   Samuel Beckett DLB-13, 15, 233, 319,
      321, 329; Y-90; CDBLB-7
   Saul Bellow DLB-2, 28, 299, 329;
      Y-82; DS-3; CDALB-1
   Jacinto Benavente DLB-329
   Henri Bergson...................DLB-329
   Bjørnstjerne Bjørnson DLB-329
   Heinrich Böll ...DLB-69, 329; Y-85; CDWLB-2
   Joseph Brodsky DLB-285, 329; Y-87
   Pearl S. Buck.....DLB-9, 102, 329; CDALB-7
   Ivan Bunin................. DLB-317, 329
   Albert Camus DLB-72, 321, 329
   Elias Canetti ... DLB-85, 124, 329; CDWLB-2
   Giosuè Carducci DLB-329
   Camilo José Cela....... DLB-322, 329; Y-89
   Sir Winston Churchill........ DLB-100, 329;
      DS-16; CDBLB-5
   J. M. Coetzee............DLB-225, 326, 329
   Grazia Deledda DLB-264, 329
   Jose Echegaray DLB-329

T. S. Eliot DLB-7, 10, 45, 63, 245, 329;
      Y-88, 99; CDALB-5
Odysseus Elytis.................DLB-329
Rudolf Eucken DLB-329
William Faulkner DLB-9, 11, 44, 102, 316,
      330; DS-2; Y-86; CDALB-5
Dario Fo DLB-330; Y-97
Anatole France DLB-123, 330
John Galsworthy........DLB-10, 34, 98, 162,
      330; DS-16; CDBLB-5
Gao Xingjian................ DLB-330; Y-00
Gabriel García Márquez DLB-13,
      330; Y-82; CDWLB-3
André Gide DLB-65, 321, 330
Karl Gjellerup DLB-300, 330
William Golding DLB-15, 100, 255,
      326, 330; Y-83; CDBLB-7
Nadine Gordimer DLB-225, 326, 330;
      Y-91
Günter Grass........ DLB-75, 124, 330; Y-99
Halldór Laxness DLB-293, 331
Knut Hamsun DLB-297, 330
Gerhart Hauptmann DLB-66, 118,
      330; CDWLB-2
Seamus Heaney.........DLB-40, 330; Y-95;
      CDBLB-8
Verner von Heidenstam DLB-330
Ernest Hemingway DLB-4, 9, 102,
     210, 316, 330; Y-81, 87, 99; DS-1, 15, 16;
      CDALB-4
Hermann Hesse DLB-66, 330; CDWLB-2
Paul Heyse DLB-129, 330
Elfriede Jelinek DLB-85, 330
Johannes V. Jensen DLB-214, 330
Juan Ramón Jiménez...........DLB-134, 330
Eyvind Johnson................DLB-259, 330
Erik Axel Karlfeldt DLB-330
Yasunari Kawabata DLB-180, 330
Imre Kertész DLB-299, 330; Y-02
Rudyard Kipling........DLB-19, 34, 141, 156,
      330; CDBLB-5
Pär Lagerkvist.................DLB-259, 331
Selma Lagerlöf DLB-259, 331
Sinclair Lewis
     ....DLB-9, 102, 331; DS-1; CDALB-4
Maurice Maeterlinck..........DLB-192, 331
Najīb Mahfūz Y-88, 331; Y-88
Thomas Mann DLB-66, 331; CDWLB-2
Roger Martin du Gard DLB-65, 331
Harry Martinson.............DLB-259, 331
François Mauriac...............DLB-65, 331
Czesław Miłosz....DLB-215, 331; CDWLB-4
Frédéric Mistral........... DLB-215, 331; D
Gabriela Mistral DLB-283, 331
Theodor Mommsen DLB-331
Eugenio Montale................DLB-114, 331
Toni Morrison
  .. DLB-6, 33, 143, 331; Y-81, 93; CDALB-6

Cumulative Index

V. S. Naipaul
....DLB-125, 204, 207, 326, 331; Y-85, 01; CDBLB-8; CDWLB-3
Pablo Neruda.............. DLB-283, 331
Kenzaburō Ōe DLB-182, 331; Y-94
Eugene O'Neill....... DLB-7, 331; CDALB-5
Boris Pasternak DLB-302, 331
Octavio Paz DLB-290, 331; Y-90, 98
Saint-John Perse DLB-258, 331
Harold Pinter ... DLB-13, 310, 331; CDBLB-8
Luigi Pirandello DLB-264, 331
Henrik Pontoppidan.......... DLB-300, 331
Salvatore Quasimodo......... DLB-114, 332
Władysław Stanisław Reymont..... DLB-332
Romain Rolland............. DLB-65, 332
Bertrand Russell........ DLB-100, 262, 332
Nelly Sachs.................... DLB-332
José Saramago DLB-287, 332; Y-98
Jean-Paul Sartre DLB-72, 296, 321, 332
George Seferis DLB-332
Jaroslav Seifert
........DLB-215, 332; Y-84; CDBLB-4
George Bernard Shaw
........DLB-10, 57, 190, 332; CDBLB-6
Mikhail Aleksandrovich Sholokov
.....................DLB-272, 332
Henryk Sienkiewicz DLB-332
Frans Eemil Sillanpää............ DLB-332
Claude Simon..........DLB-83, 332; Y-85
Isaac Bashevis Singer
...DLB-6, 28, 52, 278, 332; Y-91; CDALB-1
Aleksandr Solzhenitsyn DLB-302, 332
Wole Soyinka
.....DLB-125, 332; Y-86, 87; CDWLB-3
Carl Spitteler DLB-129, 332
John Steinbeck
.....DLB-7, 9, 212, 275, 309, 332; DS-2; CDALB-5
Sully Prudhomme DLB-332
Wisława Szymborska.... DLB-232, 332; Y-96; CDWLB-4
Rabindranath Tagore......... DLB-323, 332
Sigrid Undset..............DLB-297, 332
Derek Walcott
.... DLB-117, 332; Y-81, 92; CDWLB-3
Patrick White.............. DLB-260, 332
William Butler Yeats
.... DLB-10, 19, 98, 156, 332; CDBLB-5
Nobre, António 1867-1900 .... DLB-287
Nodier, Charles 1780-1844 .... DLB-119
Noël, Marie (Marie Mélanie Rouget) 1883-1967................... DLB-258
Noel, Roden 1834-1894 .... DLB-35
Nogami Yaeko 1885-1985............ DLB-180
Nogo, Rajko Petrov 1945- DLB-181
Nolan, William F. 1928- DLB-8
   Tribute to Raymond Chandler.......... Y-88
Noland, C. F. M. 1810?-1858......... DLB-11

Noma Hiroshi 1915-1991............. DLB-182
Nonesuch Press..................... DLB-112
Creative Nonfiction Y-02
Nonni (Jón Stefán Sveinsson or Svensson) 1857-1944.................. DLB-293
Noon, Jeff 1957- DLB-267
Noonan, Robert Phillipe (see Tressell, Robert)
Noonday Press DLB-46
Noone, John 1936- DLB-14
Nora, Eugenio de 1923- DLB-134
Nordan, Lewis 1939- DLB-234
Nordbrandt, Henrik 1945- DLB-214
Nordhoff, Charles 1887-1947 .... DLB-9
Norén, Lars 1944- DLB-257
Norfolk, Lawrence 1963- DLB-267
Norman, Charles 1904-1996 .... DLB-111
Norman, Marsha 1947- DLB-266; Y-84
Norris, Charles G. 1881-1945 .... DLB-9
Norris, Frank 1870-1902....... DLB-12, 71, 186; CDALB-3
Norris, Helen 1916- DLB-292
Norris, John 1657-1712 .... DLB-252
Norris, Leslie 1921-2006...........DLB-27, 256
Norse, Harold 1916- DLB-16
Norte, Marisela 1955- DLB-209
North, Marianne 1830-1890 ....DLB-174
North, Roger 1651-1734............. DLB-336
North Point Press DLB-46
NorthSun, Nila 1951- DLB-342
Nortje, Arthur 1942-1970 .... DLB-125, 225
Norton, Alice Mary (see Norton, Andre)
Norton, Andre 1912-2005 .... DLB-8, 52
Norton, Andrews 1786-1853.... DLB-1, 235; DS-5
Norton, Caroline 1808-1877........ DLB-21, 159, 199
Norton, Charles Eliot 1827-1908................ DLB-1, 64, 235
Norton, John 1606-1663.............. DLB-24
Norton, Mary 1903-1992 .... DLB-160
Norton, Thomas 1532-1584........... DLB-62
W. W. Norton and Company......... DLB-46
Norwood, Robert 1874-1932 .... DLB-92
Nosaka Akiyuki 1930- DLB-182
Nossack, Hans Erich 1901-1977......... DLB-69
Notker Balbulus circa 840-912 .... DLB-148
Notker III of Saint Gall circa 950-1022 .... DLB-148
Notker von Zweifalten ?-1095......... DLB-148
Nourse, Alan E. 1928-1992 .... DLB-8
Novak, Slobodan 1924- DLB-181
Novak, Vjenceslav 1859-1905 .... DLB-147
Novakovich, Josip 1956- DLB-244

Novalis 1772-1801.......... DLB-90; CDWLB-2
Novaro, Mario 1868-1944 .... DLB-114
Novás Calvo, Lino 1903-1983 .... DLB-145
Novelists
   Library Journal Statements and
      Questionnaires from First Novelists.... Y-87
Novels
   The Columbia History of the American Novel
      A Symposium on.................. Y-92
   The Great Modern Library Scam Y-98
   Novels for Grown-Ups................ Y-97
   The Proletarian Novel DLB-9
   Novel, The "Second-Generation" Holocaust
   .... DLB-299
   The Year in the Novel Y-87–88, Y-90–93
Novels, British
   "The Break-Up of the Novel" (1922),
      by John Middleton Murry....... DLB-36
   The Consolidation of Opinion: Critical
      Responses to the Modernists..... DLB-36
   "Criticism in Relation to Novels"
      (1863), by G. H. Lewes......... DLB-21
   "Experiment in the Novel" (1929)
      [excerpt], by John D. Beresford ... DLB-36
   "The Future of the Novel" (1899), by
      Henry James DLB-18
   The Gay Science (1866), by E. S. Dallas
      [excerpt]..................... DLB-21
   A Haughty and Proud Generation
      (1922), by Ford Madox Hueffer .. DLB-36
   Literary Effects of World War II DLB-15
   "Modern Novelists –Great and Small"
      (1855), by Margaret Oliphant DLB-21
   The Modernists (1932),
      by Joseph Warren Beach........ DLB-36
   A Note on Technique (1926), by
      Elizabeth A. Drew [excerpts]..... DLB-36
   Novel-Reading: The Works of Charles
      Dickens; The Works of W. Makepeace
      Thackeray (1879),
      by Anthony Trollope........... DLB-21
   Novels with a Purpose (1864), by
      Justin M'Carthy............... DLB-21
   "On Art in Fiction" (1838),
      by Edward Bulwer............ DLB-21
   The Present State of the English Novel
      (1892), by George Saintsbury DLB-18
   Representative Men and Women:
      A Historical Perspective on
      the British Novel, 1930-1960..... DLB-15
   "The Revolt" (1937), by Mary Colum
      [excerpts] DLB-36
   "Sensation Novels" (1863), by
      H. L. Manse DLB-21
   Sex, Class, Politics, and Religion [in
      the British Novel, 1930-1959] ... DLB-15
   Time and Western Man (1927),
      by Wyndham Lewis [excerpts] ... DLB-36
Noventa, Giacomo 1898-1960 .... DLB-114
Novikov, Nikolai Ivanovich 1744-1818................... DLB-150
Novomeský, Laco 1904-1976 .... DLB-215

Nowlan, Alden 1933-1983 . . . . DLB-53

Nowra, Louis 1950- DLB-325

Noyes, Alfred 1880-1958 . . . . DLB-20

Noyes, Crosby S. 1825-1908 . . . . DLB-23

Noyes, Nicholas 1647-1717 . . . . DLB-24

Noyes, Theodore W. 1858-1946 . . . . DLB-29

Nozick, Robert 1938-2002 . . . . DLB-279

N-Town Plays circa 1468 to early
  sixteenth century DLB-146

Nugent, Frank 1908-1965 . . . . DLB-44

Nunez, Sigrid 1951- DLB-312

Nušić, Branislav
  1864-1938 . . . . DLB-147; CDWLB-4

David Nutt [publishing house] DLB-106

Nwapa, Flora
  1931-1993 . . . . DLB-125; CDWLB-3

Nye, Edgar Wilson (Bill)
  1850-1896 . . . . DLB-11, 23, 186

Nye, Naomi Shihab 1952- DLB-120

Nye, Robert 1939- DLB-14, 271

Nyka-Niliūnas, Alfonsas 1919- DLB-220

O

Oakes, Urian circa 1631-1681 . . . . DLB-24

Oakes Smith, Elizabeth
  1806-1893 . . . . DLB-1, 239, 243

Oakley, Violet 1874-1961 . . . . DLB-188

Oates, Joyce Carol 1938-
  . . . . DLB-2, 5, 130; Y-81; CDALB-6

  Tribute to Michael M. Rea Y-97

Ōba Minako 1930- DLB-182

Ober, Frederick Albion 1849-1913 . . . . . . DLB-189

Ober, William 1920-1993 . . . . Y-93

Oberholtzer, Ellis Paxson 1868-1936 . . . . . . DLB-47

The Obituary as Literary Form Y-02

Obradović, Dositej 1740?-1811 . . . . DLB-147

O'Brien, Charlotte Grace 1845-1909 . . . . . DLB-240

O'Brien, Edna
  1932- DLB-14, 231, 319; CDBLB-8

O'Brien, Fitz-James 1828-1862 . . . . DLB-74

O'Brien, Flann (see O'Nolan, Brian)

O'Brien, Kate 1897-1974 . . . . DLB-15

O'Brien, Tim
  1946- DLB-152; Y-80; DS-9; CDALB-7

Ó Cadhain, Máirtín 1905-1970 . . . . DLB-319

O'Casey, Sean 1880-1964 . . . . . DLB-10; CDBLB-6

Occom, Samson 1723-1792 . . . . DLB-175

Occomy, Marita Bonner 1899-1971 . . . . . . DLB-51

Ochs, Adolph S. 1858-1935 . . . . DLB-25

Ochs-Oakes, George Washington
  1861-1931 . . . . DLB-137

Ockley, Simon 1678-1720 . . . . DLB-336

O'Connor, Flannery 1925-1964
  . . . . DLB-2, 152; Y-80; DS-12; CDALB-1

The Flannery O'Connor Society Y-99

O'Connor, Frank 1903-1966 . . . . DLB-162

O'Connor, Joseph 1963- DLB-267

O'Conor, Charles, of Belanagare
  1709/1710-1791 . . . . DLB-336

Octopus Publishing Group DLB-112

Oda Sakunosuke 1913-1947 . . . . DLB-182

Odell, Jonathan 1737-1818 . . . . DLB-31, 99

O'Dell, Scott 1903-1989 . . . . DLB-52

Odets, Clifford 1906-1963 . . . . DLB-7, 26

Odhams Press Limited DLB-112

Odio, Eunice 1922-1974 . . . . DLB-283

Odoevsky, Aleksandr Ivanovich
  1802-1839 . . . . DLB-205

Odoevsky, Vladimir Fedorovich
  1804 or 1803-1869 . . . . DLB-198

Odoevtseva, Irina 1895-1990 . . . . DLB-317

O'Donnell, Peter 1920- DLB-87

O'Donovan, Michael (see O'Connor, Frank)

O'Dowd, Bernard 1866-1953 . . . . DLB-230

Ōe, Kenzaburō 1935- DLB-182, 331; Y-94

  Nobel Lecture 1994: Japan, the
    Ambiguous, and Myself Y-94

Oehlenschläger, Adam 1779-1850 . . . . DLB-300

O'Faolain, Julia 1932- DLB-14, 231, 319

O'Faolain, Sean 1900-1991 . . . . DLB-15, 162

Off-Loop Theatres DLB-7

Offord, Carl Ruthven 1910-1990 . . . . DLB-76

Offshore, 1979 Booker Prize winner,
  Penelope Fitzgerald DLB-326

Offutt, Chris 1958- DLB-335

O'Flaherty, Liam 1896-1984 . . . DLB-36, 162; Y-84

Ogarev, Nikolai Platonovich 1813-1877 . . . DLB-277

J. S. Ogilvie and Company DLB-49

Ogilvy, Eliza 1822-1912 . . . . DLB-199

Ogot, Grace 1930- DLB-125

O'Grady, Desmond 1935- DLB-40

Ogunyemi, Wale 1939- DLB-157

O'Hagan, Howard 1902-1982 . . . . DLB-68

O'Halloran, Sylvester 1728-1807 . . . . DLB-336

O'Hara, Frank 1926-1966 . . . . DLB-5, 16, 193

O'Hara, John
  1905-1970 . . . DLB-9, 86, 324; DS-2; CDALB-5

  John O'Hara's Pottsville Journalism Y-88

O'Hare, Kate Richards 1876-1948 . . . . DLB-303

O'Hegarty, P. S. 1879-1955 . . . . DLB-201

Ohio State University
  The William Charvat American Fiction
    Collection at the Ohio State
    University Libraries Y-92

Okada, John 1923-1971 . . . . DLB-312

Okara, Gabriel 1921- DLB-125; CDWLB-3

O'Keeffe, John 1747-1833 . . . . DLB-89

Nicholas Okes [publishing house] DLB-170

Okigbo, Christopher
  1930-1967 . . . . DLB-125; CDWLB-3

Okot p'Bitek 1931-1982 . . . . . DLB-125; CDWLB-3

Okpewho, Isidore 1941- DLB-157

Okri, Ben 1959- DLB-157, 231, 319, 326

Ólafur Jóhann Sigurðsson 1918-1988 . . . . DLB-293

The Old Devils, 1986 Booker Prize winner,
  Kingsley Amis DLB-326

Old Dogs / New Tricks? New Technologies,
  the Canon, and the Structure of
  the Profession Y-02

Old Franklin Publishing House DLB-49

Old German Genesis and *Old German Exodus*
  circa 1050-circa 1130 . . . . DLB-148

The *Old High German Isidor*
  circa 790-800 . . . . DLB-148

Older, Fremont 1856-1935 . . . . DLB-25

Oldham, John 1653-1683 . . . . DLB-131

Oldman, C. B. 1894-1969 . . . . DLB-201

Oldmixon, John 1673?-1742 . . . . DLB-336

Olds, Sharon 1942- DLB-120

Olearius, Adam 1599-1671 . . . . DLB-164

O'Leary, Ellen 1831-1889 . . . . DLB-240

O'Leary, Juan E. 1879-1969 . . . . DLB-290

Olesha, Iurii Karlovich 1899-1960 . . . . DLB-272

Oliphant, Laurence 1829?-1888 . . . . . . DLB-18, 166

Oliphant, Margaret 1828-1897 . . . DLB-18, 159, 190

  "Modern Novelists–Great and Small"
    (1855) DLB-21

Oliveira, Carlos de 1921-1981 . . . . DLB-287

Oliver, Chad 1928-1993 . . . . DLB-8

Oliver, Mary 1935- DLB-5, 193, 342

Ollier, Claude 1922- DLB-83

Olsen, Tillie 1912/1913-2007
  . . . . DLB-28, 206; Y-80; CDALB-7

Olson, Charles 1910-1970 . . . . DLB-5, 16, 193

Olson, Elder 1909-1992 . . . . DLB-48, 63

Olson, Sigurd F. 1899-1982 . . . . DLB-275

The Omega Workshops DS-10

Omotoso, Kole 1943- DLB-125

Omulevsky, Innokentii Vasil'evich
  1836 [or 1837]-1883 . . . . DLB-238

Ondaatje, Michael 1943- DLB-60, 323, 326

O'Neill, Eugene
  1888-1953 . . . . DLB-7, 331; CDALB-5

  Eugene O'Neill Memorial Theater
    Center DLB-7

  Eugene O'Neill's Letters: A Review Y-88

Onetti, Juan Carlos
  1909-1994 . . . . DLB-113; CDWLB-3

Onions, George Oliver 1872-1961 . . . . DLB-153

Onofri, Arturo 1885-1928 . . . . DLB-114

O'Nolan, Brian 1911-1966 . . . . DLB-231

Oodgeroo of the Tribe Noonuccal
  (Kath Walker) 1920-1993 . . . . DLB-289

Opie, Amelia 1769-1853 . . . . DLB-116, 159

Opitz, Martin 1597-1639. . . . . DLB-164

Oppen, George 1908-1984 . . . . DLB-5, 165

Oppenheim, E. Phillips 1866-1946 . . . . DLB-70

Oppenheim, James 1882-1932 . . . . DLB-28

Oppenheimer, Joel 1930-1988. . . . . . . DLB-5, 193

Optic, Oliver (see Adams, William Taylor)

Orczy, Emma, Baroness 1865-1947 . . . . . . DLB-70

Oregon Shakespeare Festival Y-00

Origo, Iris 1902-1988. . . . . DLB-155

O'Riordan, Kate 1960- DLB-267

Orlovitz, Gil 1918-1973. . . . . DLB-2, 5

Orlovsky, Peter 1933- DLB-16

Ormond, John 1923-1990 . . . . DLB-27

Ornitz, Samuel 1890-1957 . . . . DLB-28, 44

O'Rourke, P. J. 1947- DLB-185

Orozco, Olga 1920-1999. . . . . DLB-283

Orten, Jiří 1919-1941 . . . . DLB-215

Ortese, Anna Maria 1914-1998 . . . . .DLB-177

Ortiz, Lourdes 1943- DLB-322

Ortiz, Simon J. 1941- . . .DLB-120, 175, 256, 342

Ortnit and *Wolfdietrich* circa 1225-1250 . . . . DLB-138

Orton, Joe 1933-1967 . . . . DLB-13, 310; CDBLB-8

Orwell, George (Eric Arthur Blair)
 1903-1950 . . DLB-15, 98, 195, 255; CDBLB-7

 The Orwell Year. Y-84

 (Re-)Publishing Orwell. Y-86

Ory, Carlos Edmundo de 1923- DLB-134

Osbey, Brenda Marie 1957- DLB-120

Osbon, B. S. 1827-1912. . . . . DLB-43

Osborn, Sarah 1714-1796 . . . . DLB-200

Osborne, John 1929-1994. . . . DLB-13; CDBLB-7

Oscar and Lucinda, 1988 Booker Prize winner,
 Peter Carey DLB-326

Osgood, Frances Sargent 1811-1850. . . . . DLB-250

Osgood, Herbert L. 1855-1918. . . . . DLB-47

James R. Osgood and Company DLB-49

Osgood, McIlvaine and Company DLB-112

O'Shaughnessy, Arthur 1844-1881 . . . . . . DLB-35

Patrick O'Shea [publishing house] DLB-49

Osipov, Nikolai Petrovich
 1751-1799 . . . . DLB-150

Oskison, John Milton 1879-1947 . . . . . . .DLB-175

Osler, Sir William 1849-1919 . . . . DLB-184

Osofisan, Femi 1946- DLB-125; CDWLB-3

Ostenso, Martha 1900-1963 . . . . DLB-92

Ostrauskas, Kostas 1926- DLB-232

Ostriker, Alicia 1937- DLB-120

Ostrovsky, Aleksandr Nikolaevich
 1823-1886 . . . . .DLB-277

Ostrovsky, Nikolai Alekseevich
 1904-1936 . . . . DLB-272

Osundare, Niyi 1947- DLB-157; CDWLB-3

Oswald, Eleazer 1755-1795 . . . . DLB-43

Oswald von Wolkenstein
 1376 or 1377-1445 . . . . .DLB-179

Otero, Blas de 1916-1979 . . . . DLB-134

Otero, Miguel Antonio 1859-1944 . . . . DLB-82

Otero, Nina 1881-1965. . . . . DLB-209

Otero Silva, Miguel 1908-1985. . . . . DLB-145

Otfried von Weißenburg
 circa 800-circa 875? DLB-148

Otis, Broaders and Company DLB-49

Otis, James (see Kaler, James Otis)

Otis, James, Jr. 1725-1783 . . . . DLB-31

Otsup, Nikolai 1894-1958. . . . . DLB-317

Ottaway, James 1911-2000 . . . . DLB-127

Ottendorfer, Oswald 1826-1900 . . . . DLB-23

Ottieri, Ottiero 1924-2002 . . . . .DLB-177

Otto-Peters, Louise 1819-1895 . . . . DLB-129

Otway, Thomas 1652-1685 . . . . DLB-80

Ouellette, Fernand 1930- DLB-60

Ouida 1839-1908 . . . . DLB-18, 156

Outing Publishing Company DLB-46

Overbury, Sir Thomas
 circa 1581-1613 . . . . DLB-151

The Overlook Press DLB-46

Ovid 43 B.C.-A.D. 17 . . . . . DLB-211; CDWLB-1

Oviedo, Gonzalo Fernández de
 1478-1557 . . . . DLB-318

Owen, Guy 1925-1981 . . . . DLB-5

Owen, John 1564-1622 . . . . DLB-121

John Owen [publishing house] DLB-49

Peter Owen Limited DLB-112

Owen, Robert 1771-1858 . . . . .DLB-107, 158

Owen, Wilfred
 1893-1918 . . . . DLB-20; DS-18; CDBLB-6

 A Centenary Celebration. Y-93

 The Wilfred Owen Association Y-98

The Owl and the Nightingale
 circa 1189-1199 . . . . DLB-146

Owsley, Frank L. 1890-1956. . . . . DLB-17

Oxenford, John 1812-1877 . . . . DLB-344

Oxford, Seventeenth Earl of, Edward
 de Vere 1550-1604 . . . . .DLB-172

OyamO (Charles F. Gordon)
 1943- DLB-266

Ozerov, Vladislav Aleksandrovich
 1769-1816. DLB-150

Ozick, Cynthia
 1928- DLB-28, 152, 299; Y-82

 First Strauss "Livings" Awarded
  to Cynthia Ozick and
  Raymond Carver
  An Interview with Cynthia Ozick Y-83

 Tribute to Michael M. Rea. Y-97

P

Pace, Richard 1482?-1536 . . . . DLB-167

Pacey, Desmond 1917-1975. . . . . DLB-88

Pacheco, José Emilio 1939- DLB-290

Pack, Robert 1929- DLB-5

Paddy Clarke Ha Ha Ha, 1993 Booker Prize winner,
 Roddy Doyle DLB-326

Padell Publishing Company DLB-46

Padgett, Ron 1942- DLB-5

Padilla, Ernesto Chávez 1944- DLB-122

L. C. Page and Company. DLB-49

Page, Louise 1955- DLB-233

Page, P. K. 1916- DLB-68

Page, Thomas Nelson
 1853-1922 . . . . .DLB-12, 78; DS-13

Page, Walter Hines 1855-1918 . . . . . . .DLB-71, 91

Paget, Francis Edward 1806-1882 . . . . . . DLB-163

Paget, Violet (see Lee, Vernon)

Pagliarani, Elio 1927- DLB-128

Pagnol, Marcel 1895-1974. . . . . DLB-321

Pain, Barry 1864-1928 . . . . .DLB-135, 197

Pain, Philip ?-circa 1666 . . . . DLB-24

Paine, Robert Treat, Jr. 1773-1811 . . . . . . DLB-37

Paine, Thomas
 1737-1809 . . . . DLB-31, 43, 73, 158; CDALB-2

Painter, George D. 1914-2005 . . . . DLB-155

Painter, William 1540?-1594. . . . . DLB-136

Palazzeschi, Aldo 1885-1974 . . . . DLB-114, 264

Palei, Marina Anatol'evna 1955- DLB-285

Palencia, Alfonso de 1424-1492 . . . . DLB-286

Palés Matos, Luis 1898-1959 . . . . DLB-290

Paley, Grace 1922-2007 . . . . DLB-28, 218

Paley, William 1743-1805 . . . . DLB-252

Palfrey, John Gorham
 1796-1881. . . . . DLB-1, 30, 235

Palgrave, Francis Turner 1824-1897 . . . . . . DLB-35

Palissy, Bernard 1510?-1590? DLB-327

Palmer, Joe H. 1904-1952. . . . . .DLB-171

Palmer, Michael 1943- DLB-169

Palmer, Nettie 1885-1964 . . . . DLB-260

Palmer, Vance 1885-1959 . . . . DLB-260

Paltock, Robert 1697-1767 . . . . DLB-39

Paludan, Jacob 1896-1975. . . . . DLB-214

Paludin-Müller, Frederik 1809-1876 . . . . . . DLB-300

Pan Books Limited. DLB-112

Panaev, Ivan Ivanovich 1812-1862 . . . . . . DLB-198

Panaeva, Avdot'ia Iakovlevna
 1820-1893 . . . . DLB-238

Panama, Norman 1914-2003 and
 Frank, Melvin 1913-1988. . . . . DLB-26

Pancake, Breece D'J 1952-1979. . . . . DLB-130

Panduro, Leif 1923-1977 . . . . .DLB-214	Parley, Peter (see Goodrich, Samuel Griswold)	Pattillo, Henry 1726-1801 . . . . .DLB-37
Panero, Leopoldo 1909-1962. . . . . .DLB-108	Parmenides late sixth-fifth century B.C. . . .DLB-176	Paul, Elliot 1891-1958 . . . . .DLB-4; DS-15
Pangborn, Edgar 1909-1976. . . . . .DLB-8	Parnell, Thomas 1679-1718 . . . . .DLB-95	Paul, Jean (see Richter, Johann Paul Friedrich)
Panizzi, Sir Anthony 1797-1879 . . . . .DLB-184	Parnicki, Teodor 1908-1988. . . . . .DLB-215	Paul, Kegan, Trench, Trubner and Company Limited. DLB-106
Panneton, Philippe (see Ringuet)	Parnok, Sofiia Iakovlevna (Parnokh) 1885-1933 . . . . .DLB-295	Peter Paul Book Company. DLB-49
Panova, Vera Fedorovna 1905-1973. . . . . .DLB-302	Parr, Catherine 1513?-1548 . . . . .DLB-136	Stanley Paul and Company Limited DLB-112
Panshin, Alexei 1940- DLB-8	Parra, Nicanor 1914- DLB-283	Paulding, James Kirke 1778-1860 . . . . DLB-3, 59, 74, 250
Pansy (see Alden, Isabella)	Parrington, Vernon L. 1871-1929. . . . . .DLB-17, 63	Paulin, Tom 1949- DLB-40
Pantheon Books. .DLB-46	Parrish, Maxfield 1870-1966 . . . . .DLB-188	Pauper, Peter, Press DLB-46
Papadat-Bengescu, Hortensia 1876-1955 . . . . .DLB-220	Parronchi, Alessandro 1914- DLB-128	Paustovsky, Konstantin Georgievich 1892-1968. . . . . .DLB-272
Papantonio, Michael 1907-1976 . . . . .DLB-187	Parshchikov, Aleksei Maksimovich (Raiderman) 1954- DLB-285	Pavese, Cesare 1908-1950 . . . . .DLB-128, 177
Paperback Library DLB-46	Parsons, Albert R. 1848-1887 . . . . .DLB-345	Pavić, Milorad 1929- DLB-181; CDWLB-4
Paperback Science Fiction DLB-8	Parsons, Lucy E. 1853?-1942. . . . . .DLB-345	Pavlov, Konstantin 1933- DLB-181
Papini, Giovanni 1881-1956. . . . . .DLB-264	*Partisan Review*. DLB-303	Pavlov, Nikolai Filippovich 1803-1864 . . . . .DLB-198
Paquet, Alfons 1881-1944 . . . . .DLB-66	Parton, James 1822-1891 . . . . .DLB-30	Pavlova, Karolina Karlovna 1807-1893. . . . .DLB-205
Paracelsus 1493-1541. . . . . .DLB-179	Parton, Sara Payson Willis 1811-1872 . . . . .DLB-43, 74, 239	Pavlović, Miodrag 1928- DLB-181; CDWLB-4
Paradis, Suzanne 1936- DLB-53	S. W. Partridge and Company. DLB-106	Pavlovsky, Eduardo 1933- DLB-305
Páral, Vladimír, 1932- DLB-232	Parun, Vesna 1922- DLB-181; CDWLB-4	Paxton, John 1911-1985. . . . . .DLB-44
Pardoe, Julia 1804-1862. . . . . .DLB-166	Pascal, Blaise 1623-1662. . . . . .DLB-268	Payn, James 1830-1898 . . . . .DLB-18
Paré, Ambroise 1510 or 1517?-1590 . . . . .DLB-327	Pasinetti, Pier Maria 1913-2006. . . . . .DLB-177	Payne, John 1842-1916 . . . . .DLB-35
Paredes, Américo 1915-1999 . . . . .DLB-209	Tribute to Albert Erskine Y-93	Payne, John Howard 1791-1852. . . . . .DLB-37
Pareja Diezcanseco, Alfredo 1908-1993 . . .DLB-145	Pasolini, Pier Paolo 1922-1975. . . . . .DLB-128, 177	Payson and Clarke. DLB-46
Parents' Magazine Press. DLB-46	Pastan, Linda 1932- DLB-5	Paz, Octavio 1914-1998 . . . DLB-290, 331; Y-90, 98
Paretsky, Sara 1947- DLB-306	Pasternak, Boris 1890-1960 . . . . .DLB-302, 331	Nobel Lecture 1990. . . . . .Y-90
Parfit, Derek 1942- DLB-262	Paston, George (Emily Morse Symonds) 1860-1936 . . . . .DLB-149, 197	Pazzi, Roberto 1946- DLB-196
Parise, Goffredo 1929-1986 . . . . .DLB-177	*The Paston Letters* 1422-1509 . . . . .DLB-146	Pea, Enrico 1881-1958. . . . . .DLB-264
Parish, Mitchell 1900-1993 . . . . .DLB-265	Pastoral Novel of the Sixteenth Century, The. DLB-318	Peabody, Elizabeth Palmer 1804-1894 . . . . .DLB-1, 223
Parizeau, Alice 1930-1990 . . . . .DLB-60	Pastorius, Francis Daniel 1651-circa 1720 . . . . .DLB-24	Preface to *Record of a School: Exemplifying the General Principles of Spiritual Culture*. DS-5
Park, Ruth 1923?- DLB-260	Patchen, Kenneth 1911-1972 . . . . .DLB-16, 48	
Parke, John 1754-1789 . . . . .DLB-31	Pater, Walter 1839-1894. . . DLB-57, 156; CDBLB-4	Elizabeth Palmer Peabody [publishing house] DLB-49
Parker, Dan 1893-1967 . . . . .DLB-241	Aesthetic Poetry (1873) DLB-35	Peabody, Josephine Preston 1874-1922 . . .DLB-249
Parker, Dorothy 1893-1967 . . . . . . .DLB-11, 45, 86	"Style" (1888) [excerpt] DLB-57	Peabody, Oliver William Bourn 1799-1848 . . . . .DLB-59
Parker, Gilbert 1860-1932 . . . . .DLB-99	Paterson, A. B. "Banjo" 1864-1941 . . . . . .DLB-230	Peace, Roger 1899-1968. . . . . .DLB-127
Parker, James 1714-1770. . . . . .DLB-43	Paterson, Katherine 1932- DLB-52	Peacham, Henry 1578-1644? DLB-151
Parker, John [publishing house] DLB-106	Patmore, Coventry 1823-1896. . . . . . . .DLB-35, 98	Peacham, Henry, the Elder 1547-1634 . . . . .DLB-172, 236
Parker, Matthew 1504-1575 . . . . .DLB-213	Paton, Alan 1903-1988 . . . . .DLB-225; DS-17	
Parker, Robert B. 1932- DLB-306	Paton, Joseph Noel 1821-1901. . . . . .DLB-35	Peachtree Publishers, Limited DLB-46
Parker, Stewart 1941-1988 . . . . .DLB-245	Paton Walsh, Jill 1937- DLB-161	Peacock, Molly 1947- DLB-120
Parker, Theodore 1810-1860 . . . .DLB-1, 235; DS-5	Patrick, Edwin Hill ("Ted") 1901-1964 . . .DLB-137	Peacock, Thomas Love 1785-1866. . . .DLB-96, 116
Parker, William Riley 1906-1968. . . . . . . .DLB-103	Patrick, John 1906-1995. . . . . .DLB-7	Pead, Deuel ?-1727. . . . . .DLB-24
J. H. Parker [publishing house] DLB-106	Patrick, Robert 1937- DLB-341	Peake, Mervyn 1911-1968. . . . . .DLB-15, 160, 255
Parkes, Bessie Rayner (Madame Belloc) 1829-1925 . . . . .DLB-240	Pattee, Fred Lewis 1863-1950 . . . . .DLB-71	Peake, Richard Brinsley 1792-1847 . . . . . .DLB-344
Parkman, Francis 1823-1893 . . . . DLB-1, 30, 183, 186, 235	Patterson, Alicia 1906-1963 . . . . .DLB-127	Peale, Rembrandt 1778-1860 . . . . .DLB-183
Parks, Gordon 1912-2006 . . . . .DLB-33	Patterson, Eleanor Medill 1881-1948. . . . . .DLB-29	Pear Tree Press. .DLB-112
Parks, Suzan-Lori 1964- DLB-341	Patterson, Eugene 1923- DLB-127	Pearce, Philippa 1920-2006 . . . . .DLB-161
Parks, Tim 1954- DLB-231	Patterson, Joseph Medill 1879-1946 . . . . . .DLB-29	H. B. Pearson [publishing house]. DLB-49
Parks, William 1698-1750 . . . . .DLB-43		
William Parks [publishing house]. DLB-49		

Pearson, Hesketh 1887-1964 . . . . DLB-149

Peattie, Donald Culross 1898-1964 . . . . . . .DLB-275

Pechersky, Andrei (see Mel'nikov, Pavel Ivanovich)

Peck, George W. 1840-1916 . . . . DLB-23, 42

H. C. Peck and Theo. Bliss
    [publishing house] DLB-49

Peck, Harry Thurston 1856-1914 . . . . . DLB-71, 91

Peden, William 1913-1999 . . . . DLB-234

    Tribute to William Goyen Y-83

Peele, George 1556-1596 . . . . DLB-62, 167

Pegler, Westbrook 1894-1969 . . . . .DLB-171

Péguy, Charles 1873-1914 . . . . DLB-258

Peirce, Charles Sanders 1839-1914 . . . . . . .DLB-270

Pekić, Borislav 1930-1992 . . . DLB-181; CDWLB-4

Pelecanos, George P. 1957- DLB-306

Peletier du Mans, Jacques 1517-1582 . . . . DLB-327

Pelevin, Viktor Olegovich 1962- DLB-285

Pellegrini and Cudahy DLB-46

Pelletier, Aimé (see Vac, Bertrand)

Pelletier, Francine 1959- DLB-251

Pellicer, Carlos 1897?-1977 . . . . DLB-290

Pemberton, Sir Max 1863-1950 . . . . DLB-70

de la Peña, Terri 1947- DLB-209

Penfield, Edward 1866-1925 . . . . DLB-188

Penguin Books [U.K.] DLB-112

    Fifty Penguin Years Y-85

    Penguin Collectors' Society Y-98

Penguin Books [U.S.] DLB-46

Penn, William 1644-1718 . . . . DLB-24

Penn Publishing Company DLB-49

Penna, Sandro 1906-1977 . . . . DLB-114

Pennell, Joseph 1857-1926 . . . . DLB-188

Penner, Jonathan 1940- Y-83

Pennington, Lee 1939- Y-82

Penton, Brian 1904-1951 . . . . DLB-260

Pepper, Stephen C. 1891-1972 . . . . .DLB-270

Pepys, Samuel
    1633-1703 . . . . DLB-101, 213; CDBLB-2

Percy, Thomas 1729-1811 . . . . DLB-104

Percy, Walker 1916-1990 . . . . .DLB-2; Y-80, 90

    Tribute to Caroline Gordon Y-81

Percy, William 1575-1648 . . . . .DLB-172

Perec, Georges 1936-1982 . . . . DLB-83, 299

Perelman, Bob 1947- DLB-193

Perelman, S. J. 1904-1979 . . . . DLB-11, 44

Peretz, Isaac Leib (Yitskhok Leybush Perets)
    1852-1915 . . . . DLB-333

Perez, Raymundo "Tigre" 1946- DLB-122

Pérez de Ayala, Ramón 1880-1962 . . . . . . DLB-322

Pérez de Guzmán, Fernán
    ca. 1377-ca. 1460 . . . . DLB-286

Pérez-Reverte, Arturo 1951- DLB-322

Peri Rossi, Cristina 1941- DLB-145, 290

Perkins, Eugene 1932- DLB-41

Perkins, Maxwell
    The Claims of Business and Literature:
    An Undergraduate Essay Y-01

Perkins, William 1558-1602 . . . . DLB-281

Perkoff, Stuart Z. 1930-1974 . . . . DLB-16

Perley, Moses Henry 1804-1862 . . . . DLB-99

Permabooks DLB-46

Perovsky, Aleksei Alekseevich
    (Antonii Pogorel'sky) 1787-1836 . . . . . DLB-198

Perrault, Charles 1628-1703 . . . . .DLB-268

Perri, Henry 1561-1617 . . . . DLB-236

Perrin, Alice 1867-1934 . . . . DLB-156

Perruchi, Andrea 1651-1704 . . . . DLB-339

Perry, Anne 1938- DLB-276

Perry, Bliss 1860-1954 . . . . DLB-71

Perry, Eleanor 1915-1981 . . . . DLB-44

Perry, Henry (see Perri, Henry)

Perry, Matthew 1794-1858 . . . . DLB-183

Perry, Sampson 1747-1823 . . . . DLB-158

Pers, Ciro di 1599-1663 . . . . DLB-339

Perse, Saint-John 1887-1975 . . . . DLB-258, 331

Persius A.D. 34-A.D. 62 . . . . DLB-211

Perutz, Leo 1882-1957 . . . . DLB-81

Pesetsky, Bette 1932- DLB-130

Pessanha, Camilo 1867-1926 . . . . DLB-287

Pessoa, Fernando 1888-1935 . . . . DLB-287

Pestalozzi, Johann Heinrich 1746-1827 . . . . DLB-94

Peter, Laurence J. 1919-1990 . . . . DLB-53

Peter of Spain circa 1205-1277 . . . . DLB-115

Peterkin, Julia 1880-1961 . . . . DLB-9

Peters, Ellis (Edith Pargeter)
    1913-1995 .DLB-276

Peters, Lenrie 1932- DLB-117

Peters, Robert 1924- DLB-105

    "Foreword to *Ludwig of Bavaria*" DLB-105

Petersham, Maud 1889-1971 and
    Petersham, Miska 1888-1960 . . . . DLB-22

Peterson, Charles Jacobs 1819-1887 . . . . . DLB-79

Peterson, Len 1917-2008 . . . . DLB-88

Peterson, Levi S. 1933- DLB-206

Peterson, Louis 1922-1998 . . . . DLB-76

Peterson, T. B., and Brothers DLB-49

Petitclair, Pierre 1813-1860 . . . . DLB-99

Petrescu, Camil 1894-1957 . . . . DLB-220

Petronius circa A.D. 20-A.D. 66
    . . . . DLB-211; CDWLB-1

Petrov, Aleksandar 1938- DLB-181

Petrov, Evgenii (Evgenii Petrovich Kataev)
    1903-1942 .DLB-272

Petrov, Gavriil 1730-1801 . . . . DLB-150

Petrov, Valeri 1920- DLB-181

Petrov, Vasilii Petrovich 1736-1799 . . . . . . DLB-150

Petrović, Rastko
    1898-1949 . . . . .DLB-147; CDWLB-4

Petrus Alfonsi (Pedro Alfonso, Pierre Alphonse)
    fl. 1106-circa 1125 . . . . DLB-337

Petrushevskaia, Liudmila Stefanovna
    1938- DLB-285

Petruslied circa 854? DLB-148

Petry, Ann 1908-1997 . . . . DLB-76

Pettie, George circa 1548-1589 . . . . DLB-136

Pétur Gunnarsson 1947- DLB-293

Peyton, K. M. 1929- DLB-161

Pfaffe Konrad fl. circa 1172 . . . . DLB-148

Pfaffe Lamprecht fl. circa 1150 . . . . DLB-148

Pfeiffer, Emily 1827-1890 . . . . DLB-199

Pforzheimer, Carl H. 1879-1957 . . . . DLB-140

Phaedrus circa 18 B.C.-circa A.D. 50 . . . . . DLB-211

Phaer, Thomas 1510?-1560 . . . . DLB-167

Phaidon Press Limited DLB-112

Pharr, Robert Deane 1916-1992 . . . . DLB-33

Phelps, Elizabeth Stuart 1815-1852 . . . . . . DLB-202

Phelps, Elizabeth Stuart 1844-1911 . . .DLB-74, 221

Philander von der Linde
    (see Mencke, Johann Burckhard)

Philby, H. St. John B. 1885-1960 . . . . DLB-195

Philip, Marlene Nourbese 1947- . . .DLB-157, 334

Philippe, Charles-Louis 1874-1909 . . . . DLB-65

Philips, John 1676-1708 . . . . DLB-95

Philips, Katherine 1632-1664 . . . . DLB-131

Phillipps, Sir Thomas 1792-1872 . . . . DLB-184

Phillips, Caryl 1958- DLB-157

Phillips, David Graham
    1867-1911 . . . . DLB-9, 12, 303

Phillips, Jayne Anne 1952- DLB-292; Y-80

    Tribute to Seymour Lawrence Y-94

Phillips, Robert 1938- DLB-105

    "Finding, Losing, Reclaiming: A Note
    on My Poems" DLB-105

    Tribute to William Goyen Y-83

Phillips, Stephen 1864-1915 . . . . DLB-10

Phillips, Ulrich B. 1877-1934 . . . . .DLB-17

Phillips, Wendell 1811-1884 . . . . DLB-235

Phillips, Willard 1784-1873 . . . . DLB-59

Phillips, William 1907-2002 . . . . .DLB-137

Phillips, Sampson and Company DLB-49

Phillpotts, Adelaide Eden (Adelaide Ross)
    1896-1993 . . . . DLB-191

Phillpotts, Eden 1862-1960 . . .DLB-10, 70, 135, 153

Philo circa 20-15 B.C.-circa A.D. 50 . . . . . . .DLB-176

Philosophical Dictionary, Voltaire DLB-314

Philosophical Library DLB-46

Philosophy
    Eighteenth-Century Philosophical
    Background DLB-31

Philosophic Thought in Boston......DLB-235

Translators of the Twelfth Century:
Literary Issues Raised and
Impact Created..............DLB-115

Elihu Phinney [publishing house].......DLB-49

Phoenix, John (see Derby, George Horatio)

PHYLON (Fourth Quarter, 1950),
The Negro in Literature:
The Current Scene...............DLB-76

Physiologus circa 1070-circa 1150........DLB-148

II.O. (Pi O, Peter Oustabasides)
1951-...................DLB-325

Piccolo, Lucio 1903-1969..............DLB-114

Pichette, Henri 1924-2000............DLB-321

Pickard, Tom 1946-...............DLB-40

William Pickering [publishing house].....DLB-106

Pickthall, Marjorie 1883-1922..........DLB-92

Picoult, Jodi 1966-...............DLB-292

Pictorial Printing Company............DLB-49

Piel, Gerard 1915-2004..............DLB-137

"An Announcement to Our Readers,"
Gerard Piel's Statement in *Scientific
American* (April 1948)..........DLB-137

Pielmeier, John 1949-..............DLB-266

Piercy, Marge 1936-.........DLB-120, 227

Pierre, DBC 1961-...............DLB-326

Pierro, Albino 1916-1995.............DLB-128

Pignotti, Lamberto 1926-...........DLB-128

Pike, Albert 1809-1891..............DLB-74

Pike, Zebulon Montgomery 1779-1813...DLB-183

Pillat, Ion 1891-1945................DLB-220

Pil'niak, Boris Andreevich (Boris Andreevich
Vogau) 1894-1938................DLB-272

Pilon, Jean-Guy 1930-..............DLB-60

Pinar, Florencia fl. ca. late
fifteenth century..............DLB-286

Pinckney, Eliza Lucas 1722-1793........DLB-200

Pinckney, Josephine 1895-1957..........DLB-6

Pindar circa 518 B.C.-circa 438 B.C.
..............DLB-176; CDWLB-1

Pindar, Peter (see Wolcot, John)

Pineda, Cecile 1942-...............DLB-209

Pinero, Arthur Wing 1855-1934.....DLB-10, 344

Piñero, Miguel 1946-1988............DLB-266

Pinget, Robert 1919-1997..............DLB-83

Pinkerton, John 1758-1825.............DLB-336

Pinkney, Edward Coote
1802-1828....................DLB-248

Pinnacle Books....................DLB-46

Piñon, Nélida 1935-...........DLB-145, 307

Pinski, David (Dovid Pinski)
1872-1959....................DLB-333

Pinsky, Robert 1940-...............Y-82

Reappointed Poet Laureate............Y-98

Pinter, Harold 1930-
............DLB-13, 310, 331; CDBLB-8

Writing for the Theatre............DLB-13

Pinto, Fernão Mendes 1509/1511?-1583..DLB-287

Piontek, Heinz 1925-...............DLB-75

Piozzi, Hester Lynch [Thrale]
1741-1821...................DLB-104, 142

Piper, H. Beam 1904-1964..............DLB-8

Piper, Watty....................DLB-22

Pirandello, Luigi 1867-1936........DLB-264, 331

Pirckheimer, Caritas 1467-1532.........DLB-179

Pirckheimer, Willibald 1470-1530.......DLB-179

Pires, José Cardoso 1925-1998..........DLB-287

Pisar, Samuel 1929-...................Y-83

Pisarev, Dmitrii Ivanovich 1840-1868....DLB-277

Pisemsky, Aleksei Feofilaktovich
1821-1881...................DLB-238

Pitkin, Timothy 1766-1847..............DLB-30

Pitt, George Dibdin 1795-1855.........DLB-344

Pitter, Ruth 1897-1992................DLB-20

Pix, Mary 1666-1709..................DLB-80

Pixerécourt, René Charles Guilbert de
1773-1844....................DLB-192

Pizarnik, Alejandra 1936-1972.......DLB-283

Plá, Josefina 1909-1999..............DLB-290

Plaatje, Sol T. 1876-1932.........DLB-125, 225

Planchon, Roger 1931-..............DLB-321

Plante, David 1940-..................Y-83

Plantinga, Alvin 1932-..............DLB-279

Platen, August von 1796-1835...........DLB-90

Plath, Sylvia
1932-1963........DLB-5, 6, 152; CDALB-1

Plato circa 428 B.C.-348-347 B.C.
.................DLB-176; CDWLB-1

Plato, Ann 1824-?.................DLB-239

Platon 1737-1812..................DLB-150

Platonov, Andrei Platonovich (Andrei
Platonovich Klimentev)
1899-1951....................DLB-272

Platt, Charles 1945-...............DLB-261

Platt and Munk Company.............DLB-46

Plautus circa 254 B.C.-184 B.C.
.................DLB-211; CDWLB-1

Playboy Press......................DLB-46

John Playford [publishing house]........DLB-170

Der Pleier fl. circa 1250..............DLB-138

Pleijel, Agneta 1940-..............DLB-257

Plenzdorf, Ulrich 1934-..............DLB-75

Pleshcheev, Aleksei Nikolaevich
1825?-1893...................DLB-277

Plessen, Elizabeth 1944-.............DLB-75

Pletnev, Petr Aleksandrovich
1792-1865....................DLB-205

Pliekšāne, Elza Rozenberga (see Aspazija)

Pliekšāns, Jānis (see Rainis, Jānis)

Plievier, Theodor 1892-1955............DLB-69

Plimpton, George 1927-2003..DLB-185, 241; Y-99

Pliny the Elder A.D. 23/24-A.D. 79.......DLB-211

Pliny the Younger
circa A.D. 61-A.D. 112.............DLB-211

Plomer, William
1903-1973..........DLB-20, 162, 191, 225

Plotinus 204-270..........DLB-176; CDWLB-1

Plowright, Teresa 1952-.............DLB-251

Plume, Thomas 1630-1704.............DLB-213

Plumly, Stanley 1939-............DLB-5, 193

Plumpp, Sterling D. 1940-.............DLB-41

Plunkett, James 1920-2003.............DLB-14

Plutarch
circa 46-circa 120........DLB-176; CDWLB-1

Plymell, Charles 1935-..............DLB-16

Pocket Books.......................DLB-46

Pocock, Isaac 1782-1835..............DLB-344

Podestá, José J. 1858-1937.............DLB-305

Poe, Edgar Allan 1809-1849
..........DLB-3, 59, 73, 74, 248; CDALB-2

The Poe Studies Association............Y-99

Poe, James 1921-1980.................DLB-44

Poema de Alfonso XI (1348)...............DLB-337

Poema de Fernán González
(between 1251 and 1258)..........DLB-337

The Poet Laureate of the United States........Y-86

Statements from Former Consultants
in Poetry........................Y-86

Poetry
Aesthetic Poetry (1873).............DLB-35

A Century of Poetry, a Lifetime of
Collecting: J. M. Edelstein's
Collection of Twentieth-
Century American Poetry...........Y-02

"Certain Gifts," by Betty Adcock....DLB-105

Concrete Poetry...................DLB-307

Contempo Caravan: Kites in a
Windstorm......................Y-85

"Contemporary Verse Story-telling,"
by Jonathan Holden..........DLB-105

"A Detail in a Poem," by Fred
Chappell....................DLB-105

"The English Renaissance of Art"
(1908), by Oscar Wilde.........DLB-35

"Every Man His Own Poet; or,
The Inspired Singer's Recipe
Book" (1877), by
H. W. Mallock................DLB-35

"Eyes Across Centuries: Contemporary
Poetry and 'That Vision Thing,'"
by Philip Dacey...............DLB-105

A Field Guide to Recent Schools
of American Poetry................Y-86

"Finding, Losing, Reclaiming:
A Note on My Poems,
by Robert Phillips"............DLB-105

"The Fleshly School of Poetry and Other
Phenomena of the Day" (1872)....DLB-35

"The Fleshly School of Poetry:
   Mr. D. G. Rossetti" (1871)....... DLB-35

The G. Ross Roy Scottish Poetry Collection
   at the University of South Carolina... Y-89

"Getting Started: Accepting the Regions
   You Own–or Which Own You,"
   by Walter McDonald......... DLB-105

"The Good, The Not So Good," by
   Stephen Dunn............. DLB-105

The Griffin Poetry Prize............. Y-00

The Hero as Poet. Dante; Shakspeare
   (1841), by Thomas Carlyle...... DLB-32

"Images and 'Images,'" by Charles
   Simic................... DLB-105

"Into the Mirror," by Peter Cooley.. DLB-105

"Knots into Webs: Some Autobiographical
   Sources," by Dabney Stuart..... DLB-105

"L'Envoi" (1882), by Oscar Wilde.... DLB-35

"Living in Ruin," by Gerald Stern... DLB-105

Looking for the Golden Mountain:
   Poetry Reviewing.............. Y-89

Lyric Poetry (French)............. DLB-268

Medieval Galician-Portuguese
   Poetry................... DLB-287

"The No Self, the Little Self, and the
   Poets," by Richard Moore...... DLB-105

On Some of the Characteristics of Modern
   Poetry and On the Lyrical Poems of
   Alfred Tennyson (1831)......... DLB-32

The Pitt Poetry Series: Poetry Publishing
   Today...................... Y-85

"The Poetry File," by Edward
   Field................... DLB-105

Poetry in Nineteenth-Century France:
   Cultural Background and Critical
   Commentary............... DLB-217

The Poetry of Jorge Luis Borges........ Y-86

"The Poet's Kaleidoscope: The Element
   of Surprise in the Making of the
   Poem" by Madeline DeFrees.... DLB-105

The Pre-Raphaelite Controversy..... DLB-35

Protest Poetry in Castile........... DLB-286

"Reflections: After a Tornado,"
   by Judson Jerome............ DLB-105

Statements from Former Consultants
   in Poetry..................... Y-86

Statements on the Art of Poetry...... DLB-54

The Study of Poetry (1880), by
   Matthew Arnold............. DLB-35

A Survey of Poetry Anthologies,
   1879-1960................. DLB-54

Thoughts on Poetry and Its Varieties
   (1833), by John Stuart Mill...... DLB-32

Under the Microscope (1872), by
   A. C. Swinburne............. DLB-35

The Unterberg Poetry Center of the
   92nd Street Y.................. Y-98

Victorian Poetry: Five CriticalViews... DLBV-35

Year in Poetry............. Y-83–92, 94–01

Year's Work in American Poetry....... Y-82

Poets
   The Lives of the Poets (1753).......... DLB-142

Minor Poets of the Earlier
   Seventeenth Century.......... DLB-121

Other British Poets Who Fell
   in the Great War............ DLB-216

Other Poets [French]............. DLB-217

Second-Generation Minor Poets of
   the Seventeenth Century....... DLB-126

Third-Generation Minor Poets of
   the Seventeenth Century....... DLB-131

Pogodin, Mikhail Petrovich 1800-1875... DLB-198

Pogorel'sky, Antonii
   (see Perovsky, Aleksei Alekseevich)

Pohl, Frederik 1919-............. DLB-8

   Tribute to Isaac Asimov............. Y-92

   Tribute to Theodore Sturgeon......... Y-85

Poirier, Louis (see Gracq, Julien)

Poláček, Karel 1892-1945... DLB-215; CDWLB-4

Polanyi, Michael 1891-1976......... DLB-100

Pole, Reginald 1500-1558............ DLB-132

Polevoi, Nikolai Alekseevich 1796-1846.. DLB-198

Polezhaev, Aleksandr Ivanovich
   1804-1838................ DLB-205

Poliakoff, Stephen 1952-............ DLB-13

Polidori, John William 1795-1821....... DLB-116

Polite, Carlene Hatcher 1932-......... DLB-33

Pollard, Alfred W. 1859-1944......... DLB-201

Pollard, Edward A. 1832-1872........ DLB-30

Pollard, Graham 1903-1976......... DLB-201

Pollard, Percival 1869-1911.......... DLB-71

Pollard and Moss................. DLB-49

Pollock, Sharon 1936-............. DLB-60

Polonsky, Abraham 1910-1999......... DLB-26

Polonsky, Iakov Petrovich 1819-1898.....DLB-277

Polotsky, Simeon 1629-1680......... DLB-150

Polybius circa 200 B.C.-118 B.C..........DLB-176

Pomialovsky, Nikolai Gerasimovich
   1835-1863................ DLB-238

Pomilio, Mario 1921-1990..........DLB-177

Pompéia, Raul (Raul d'Avila Pompéia)
   1863-1895................ DLB-307

Ponce, Mary Helen 1938-......... DLB-122

Ponce-Montoya, Juanita 1949-...... DLB-122

Ponet, John 1516?-1556........... DLB-132

Ponge, Francis 1899-1988........DLB-258; Y-02

Poniatowska, Elena
   1933-..............DLB-113; CDWLB-3

Ponsard, François 1814-1867......... DLB-192

William Ponsonby [publishing house].....DLB-170

Pontiggia, Giuseppe 1934-......... DLB-196

Pontoppidan, Henrik 1857-1943.... DLB-300, 331

Pony Stories, Omnibus Essay on...... DLB-160

Poole, Ernest 1880-1950............. DLB-9

Poole, Sophia 1804-1891........... DLB-166

Poore, Benjamin Perley 1820-1887....... DLB-23

Popa, Vasko 1922-1991.....DLB-181; CDWLB-4

Pope, Abbie Hanscom 1858-1894....... DLB-140

Pope, Alexander
   1688-1744...... DLB-95, 101, 213; CDBLB-2

Poplavsky, Boris 1903-1935............DLB-317

Popov, Aleksandr Serafimovich
   (see Serafimovich, Aleksandr Serafimovich)

Popov, Evgenii Anatol'evich 1946-.... DLB-285

Popov, Mikhail Ivanovich
   1742-circa 1790................ DLB-150

Popović, Aleksandar 1929-1996........ DLB-181

Popper, Karl 1902-1994.............. DLB-262

Popular Culture Association/
   American Culture Association........ Y-99

Popular Library..................... DLB-46

Poquelin, Jean-Baptiste (see Molière)

Porete, Marguerite ?-1310............. DLB-208

Porlock, Martin (see MacDonald, Philip)

Porpoise Press..................... DLB-112

Porta, Antonio 1935-1989............. DLB-128

Porter, Anna Maria 1780-1832......DLB-116, 159

Porter, Cole 1891-1964................ DLB-265

Porter, David 1780-1843.............. DLB-183

Porter, Dorothy 1954-................ DLB-325

Porter, Eleanor H. 1868-1920............ DLB-9

Porter, Gene Stratton (see Stratton-Porter, Gene)

Porter, Hal 1911-1984................ DLB-260

Porter, Henry circa sixteenth century..... DLB-62

Porter, Jane 1776-1850.............DLB-116, 159

Porter, Katherine Anne 1890-1980
   ....DLB-4, 9, 102; Y-80; DS-12; CDALB-7

   The Katherine Anne Porter Society...... Y-01

Porter, Peter 1929-............. DLB-40, 289

Porter, William Sydney (O. Henry)
   1862-1910........DLB-12, 78, 79; CDALB-3

Porter, William T. 1809-1858..... DLB-3, 43, 250

Porter and Coates.................... DLB-49

Portillo Trambley, Estela 1927-1998..... DLB-209

Portis, Charles 1933-................. DLB-6

Medieval Galician-Portuguese Poetry.... DLB-287

Posey, Alexander 1873-1908............DLB-175

Possession, 1990 Booker Prize winner,
   A. S. Byatt.................. DLB-326

Postans, Marianne circa 1810-1865..... DLB-166

Postgate, Raymond 1896-1971.........DLB-276

Postl, Carl (see Sealsfield, Carl)

Postmodern Holocaust Fiction......... DLB-299

Poston, Ted 1906-1974................ DLB-51

Potekhin, Aleksei Antipovich
   1829-1908.................. DLB-238

Potok, Chaim 1929-2002.......... DLB-28, 152

   A Conversation with Chaim Potok...... Y-84

   Tribute to Bernard Malamud.......... Y-86

Potter, Beatrix 1866-1943 . . . . .DLB-141
    The Beatrix Potter Society. Y-98
Potter, David M. 1910-1971 . . . . .DLB-17
Potter, Dennis 1935-1994. . . . . .DLB-233
John E. Potter and Company. DLB-49
Pottle, Frederick A. 1897-1987 . . . . . DLB-103; Y-87
Poulin, Jacques 1937- DLB-60
Pound, Ezra 1885-1972
    . . . . .DLB-4, 45, 63; DS-15; CDALB-4
    The Cost of the *Cantos*: William Bird
        to Ezra Pound. Y-01
    The Ezra Pound Society Y-01
Poverman, C. E. 1944- DLB-234
Povey, Meic 1950- DLB-310
Povich, Shirley 1905-1998 . . . . .DLB-171
Powderly, Terence V. 1849-1924 . . . . . . .DLB-345
Powell, Anthony 1905-2000. . . DLB-15; CDBLB-7
    The Anthony Powell Society: Powell and
        the First Biennial Conference Y-01
Powell, Dawn 1897-1965
    Dawn Powell, Where Have You Been
        All Our Lives?. Y-97
Powell, Adam Clayton, Jr. 1908-1973. . . . .DLB-345
Powell, John Wesley 1834-1902. . . . . .DLB-186
Powell, Padgett 1952- DLB-234
Powers, J. F. 1917-1999. . . . . .DLB-130
Powers, Jimmy 1903-1995 . . . . .DLB-241
Pownall, David 1938- DLB-14
Powys, John Cowper 1872-1963 . . . . .DLB-15, 255
Powys, Llewelyn 1884-1939. . . . . .DLB-98
Powys, T. F. 1875-1953 . . . . .DLB-36, 162
    The Powys Society Y-98
Poynter, Nelson 1903-1978. . . . . .DLB-127
Prada, Juan Manuel de 1970- DLB-322
Prado, Adélia 1935- DLB-307
Prado, Pedro 1886-1952. . . . . .DLB-283
Prados, Emilio 1899-1962 . . . . .DLB-134
Praed, Mrs. Caroline (see Praed, Rosa)
Praed, Rosa (Mrs. Caroline Praed)
    1851-1935 . . . . .DLB-230
Praed, Winthrop Mackworth 1802-1839. . .DLB-96
Praeger Publishers DLB-46
Praetorius, Johannes 1630-1680. . . . . .DLB-168
Pratolini, Vasco 1913-1991. . . . . .DLB-177
Pratt, E. J. 1882-1964. . . . . .DLB-92
Pratt, Samuel Jackson 1749-1814 . . . . .DLB-39
Preciado Martin, Patricia 1939- DLB-209
Préfontaine, Yves 1937- DLB-53
Prelutsky, Jack 1940- DLB-61
Prentice, George D. 1802-1870 . . . . .DLB-43
Prentice-Hall DLB-46
Prescott, Orville 1906-1996 . . . . .Y-96

Prescott, William Hickling
    1796-1859 . . . . .DLB-1, 30, 59, 235
Prešeren, Francè
    1800-1849 . . . . DLB-147; CDWLB-4
Presses (*See also* Publishing)
    Small Presses in Great Britain and
        Ireland, 1960-1985 . . . . .DLB-40
    Small Presses I: Jargon Society Y-84
    Small Presses II: The Spirit That Moves
        Us Press Y-85
    Small Presses III: Pushcart Press. Y-87
Preston, Margaret Junkin
    1820-1897 . . . . .DLB-239, 248
Preston, May Wilson 1873-1949 . . . . . . .DLB-188
Preston, Thomas 1537-1598. . . . . .DLB-62
Preti, Girolamo 1582-1626. . . . . .DLB-339
Prévert, Jacques 1900-1977 . . . . .DLB-258
Prévost d'Exiles, Antoine François
    1697-1763. . . . . .DLB-314
Price, Anthony 1928- DLB-276
Price, Reynolds 1933- DLB-2, 218, 278
Price, Richard 1723-1791 . . . . .DLB-158
Price, Richard 1949- Y-81
Prichard, Katharine Susannah
    1883-1969 . . . . .DLB-260
Prideaux, John 1578-1650 . . . . .DLB-236
Priest, Christopher 1943- DLB-14, 207, 261
Priestley, J. B. 1894-1984
    . . . .DLB-10, 34, 77, 100, 139; Y-84; CDBLB-6
Priestley, Joseph 1733-1804 . . . . .DLB-252, 336
Prigov, Dmitrii Aleksandrovich 1940- . .DLB-285
Prime, Benjamin Young 1733-1791. . . . . . .DLB-31
Primrose, Diana floruit circa 1630 . . . . . .DLB-126
Prince, F. T. 1912-2003 . . . . .DLB-20
Prince, Nancy Gardner
    1799-circa 1856 . . . . .DLB-239
Prince, Thomas 1687-1758. . . . . .DLB-24, 140
Pringle, Thomas 1789-1834 . . . . .DLB-225
Printz, Wolfgang Casper 1641-1717 . . . . . .DLB-168
Prior, Matthew 1664-1721 . . . . .DLB-95
Prisco, Michele 1920-2003. . . . . DLB-177
Prishvin, Mikhail Mikhailovich
    1873-1954 . . . . .DLB-272
Pritchard, William H. 1932- DLB-111
Pritchett, V. S. 1900-1997. . . . . .DLB-15, 139
Probyn, May 1856 or 1857-1909 . . . . . . .DLB-199
Procter, Adelaide Anne 1825-1864. . . .DLB-32, 199
Procter, Bryan Waller 1787-1874 . . . . .DLB-96, 144
Proctor, Robert 1868-1903. . . . . .DLB-184
Prokopovich, Feofan 1681?-1736. . . . . . .DLB-150
Prokosch, Frederic 1906-1989 . . . . .DLB-48
Pronzini, Bill 1943- DLB-226
Propertius circa 50 B.C.-post 16 B.C.
    .DLB-211; CDWLB-1
Propper, Dan 1937- DLB-16

Prose, Francine 1947- DLB-234
Protagoras circa 490 B.C.-420 B.C.. . . . . . . .DLB-176
Protest Poetry in Castile
    ca. 1445-ca. 1506. . . . . .DLB-286
Proud, Robert 1728-1813. . . . . .DLB-30
Proulx, Annie 1935- DLB-335
Proust, Marcel 1871-1922 . . . . .DLB-65
    Marcel Proust at 129 and the Proust
        Society of America Y-00
    Marcel Proust's *Remembrance of Things Past*:
        The Rediscovered Galley Proofs Y-00
Prutkov, Koz'ma Petrovich
    1803-1863 . . . . .DLB-277
Prynne, J. H. 1936- DLB-40
Przybyszewski, Stanislaw 1868-1927 . . . . .DLB-66
Pseudo-Dionysius the Areopagite floruit
    circa 500 . . . . .DLB-115
Public Lending Right in America
    PLR and the Meaning of Literary
        Property Y-83
    Statement by Sen. Charles
        McC. Mathias, Jr. PLR. Y-83
    Statements on PLR by American Writers. . . .Y-83
Public Lending Right in the United Kingdom
    The First Year in the United Kingdom Y-83
Publishers [listed by individual names]
Publishers, Conversations with:
    An Interview with Charles Scribner III . . Y-94
    An Interview with Donald Lamm. Y-95
    An Interview with James Laughlin Y-96
    An Interview with Patrick O'Connor Y-84
Publishing
    The Art and Mystery of Publishing:
        Interviews. Y-97
    Book Publishing Accounting: Some Basic
        Concepts. Y-98
    1873 Publishers' Catalogues DLB-49
    The Literary Scene 2002: Publishing, Book
        Reviewing, and Literary Journalism. . .Y-02
    Main Trends in Twentieth-Century
        Book Clubs. DLB-46
    Overview of U.S. Book Publishing,
        1910-1945. .DLB-9
    The Pitt Poetry Series: Poetry Publishing
        Today Y-85
    Publishing Fiction at LSU Press Y-87
    The Publishing Industry in 1998:
        Sturm-und-drang.com Y-98
    The Publishing Industry in 1999 . . . . .Y-99
    Publishers and Agents: The Columbia
        Connection. .Y-87
    Responses to Ken Auletta Y-97
    Southern Writers Between the Wars DLB-9
    The State of Publishing Y-97
    Trends in Twentieth-Century
        Mass Market Publishing. DLB-46
    The Year in Book Publishing. Y-86
Pückler-Muskau, Hermann von
    1785-1871 . . . . DLB-133
Puértolas, Soledad 1947- DLB-322

Pufendorf, Samuel von 1632-1694 ...... DLB-168

Pugh, Edwin William 1874-1930 .... DLB-135

Pugin, A. Welby 1812-1852 .... DLB-55

Puig, Manuel 1932-1990. ... DLB-113; CDWLB-3

Puisieux, Madeleine d'Arsant de
1720-1798 .... DLB-314

Pulgar, Hernando del (Fernando del Pulgar)
ca. 1436-ca. 1492 .... DLB-286

Pulitzer, Joseph 1847-1911. .... DLB-23

Pulitzer, Joseph, Jr. 1885-1955. .... DLB-29

Pulitzer Prizes for the Novel, 1917-1945 .... DLB-9

Pulliam, Eugene 1889-1975. .... DLB-127

Purcell, Deirdre 1945- DLB-267

Purchas, Samuel 1577?-1626. .... DLB-151

Purdy, Al 1918-2000. .... DLB-88

Purdy, James 1923- DLB-2, 218

Purdy, Ken W. 1913-1972. .... DLB-137

Pusey, Edward Bouverie 1800-1882 ...... DLB-55

Pushkin, Aleksandr Sergeevich
1799-1837 .... DLB-205

Pushkin, Vasilii L'vovich
1766-1830 .... DLB-205

Putnam, George Palmer
1814-1872 .... DLB-3, 79, 250, 254

G. P. Putnam [publishing house]. DLB-254

G. P. Putnam's Sons [U.K.] DLB-106

G. P. Putnam's Sons [U.S.] DLB-49

A Publisher's Archives: G. P. Putnam Y-92

Putnam, Hilary 1926- DLB-279

Putnam, Samuel 1892-1950 .... DLB-4; DS-15

Puttenham, George 1529?-1590 .... DLB-281

Puzo, Mario 1920-1999 .... DLB-6

Pyle, Ernie 1900-1945. .... DLB-29

Pyle, Howard
1853-1911. .... DLB-42, 188; DS-13

Pyle, Robert Michael 1947- DLB-275

Pym, Barbara 1913-1980 .... DLB-14, 207; Y-87

Pynchon, Thomas 1937- DLB-2, 173

Pyramid Books DLB-46

Pyrnelle, Louise-Clarke 1850-1907. .... DLB-42

Pythagoras circa 570 B.C.-? DLB-176

Q

Qasim, 'Abd al-Hakim 1935-1990 ...... DLB-346

Qays ibn al-Mulawwah circa 680-710 .... DLB-311

Qian Zhongshu 1910-1998. .... DLB-328

Quad, M. (see Lewis, Charles B.)

Quaritch, Bernard 1819-1899. .... DLB-184

Quarles, Francis 1592-1644 .... DLB-126

The Quarterly Review 1809-1967 .... DLB-110

Quasimodo, Salvatore 1901-1968. ... DLB-114, 332

Queen, Ellery (see Dannay, Frederic, and Manfred B. Lee)

Queen, Frank 1822-1882 .... DLB-241

The Queen City Publishing House DLB-49

Queirós, Eça de 1845-1900. .... DLB-287

Queneau, Raymond 1903-1976 ..... DLB-72, 258

Quennell, Peter 1905-1993 .... DLB-155, 195

Quental, Antero de
1842-1891 .... DLB-287

Quesada, José Luis 1948- DLB-290

Quesnel, Joseph 1746-1809. .... DLB-99

Quiller-Couch, Sir Arthur Thomas
1863-1944 .... DLB-135, 153, 190

Quin, Ann 1936-1973 .... DLB-14, 231

Quinault, Philippe 1635-1688 .... DLB-268

Quincy, Samuel, of Georgia
fl. eighteenth century DLB-31

Quincy, Samuel, of Massachusetts
1734-1789 .... DLB-31

Quindlen, Anna 1952- DLB-292

Quine, W. V. 1908-2000 .... DLB-279

Quinn, Anthony 1915-2001 .... DLB-122

Quinn, John 1870-1924. .... DLB-187

Quiñónez, Naomi 1951- DLB-209

Quintana, Leroy V. 1944- DLB-82

Quintana, Miguel de 1671-1748
A Forerunner of Chicano
Literature. DLB-122

Quintilian circa A.D. 40-circa A.D. 96 .... DLB-211

Quintus Curtius Rufus
fl. A.D. 35 .... DLB-211

Harlin Quist Books. DLB-46

Quoirez, Françoise (see Sagan, Françoise)

Qutb, Sayyid 1906-1966. .... DLB-346

R

Raabe, Wilhelm 1831-1910 .... DLB-129

Raban, Jonathan 1942- DLB-204

Rabe, David 1940- DLB-7, 228; Y-91

Rabelais, François 1494?-1593 .... DLB-327

Rabi'ah al-'Adawiyyah circa 720-801 .... DLB-311

Raboni, Giovanni 1932- DLB-128

Rachilde 1860-1953 .... DLB-123, 192

Racin, Kočo 1908-1943. .... DLB-147

Racine, Jean 1639-1699 .... DLB-268

Rackham, Arthur 1867-1939. .... DLB-141

Raczymow, Henri 1948- DLB-299

Radauskas, Henrikas
1910-1970. .... DLB-220; CDWLB-4

Radcliffe, Ann 1764-1823 .... DLB-39, 178

Raddall, Thomas 1903-1994 .... DLB-68

Radford, Dollie 1858-1920 .... DLB-240

Radichkov, Yordan 1929-2004 .... DLB-181

Radiguet, Raymond 1903-1923 .... DLB-65

Radishchev, Aleksandr Nikolaevich
1749-1802. .... DLB-150

Radnóti, Miklós 1909-1944 . . DLB-215; CDWLB-4

Radrigán, Juan 1937- DLB-305

Radványi, Netty Reiling (see Seghers, Anna)

Rafat, Taufiq 1927-1998 .... DLB-323

Rahv, Philip 1908-1973. .... DLB-137

Raich, Semen Egorovich 1792-1855 ..... DLB-205

Raičković, Stevan 1928- DLB-181

Raiderman (see Parshchikov, Aleksei Maksimovich)

Raimund, Ferdinand Jakob 1790-1836 .... DLB-90

Raine, Craig 1944- DLB-40

Raine, Kathleen 1908-2003. .... DLB-20

Rainis, Jānis 1865-1929 .... DLB-220; CDWLB-4

Rainolde, Richard
circa 1530-1606 .... DLB-136, 236

Rainolds, John 1549-1607. .... DLB-281

Rakić, Milan 1876-1938 ..... DLB-147; CDWLB-4

Rakosi, Carl 1903-2004 .... DLB-193

Ralegh, Sir Walter
1554?-1618. .... DLB-172; CDBLB-1

Raleigh, Walter
Style (1897) [excerpt] DLB-57

Ralin, Radoy 1923-2004 .... DLB-181

Ralph, Julian 1853-1903 .... DLB-23

Ramanujan, A. K. 1929-1993 .... DLB-323

Ramat, Silvio 1939- DLB-128

Ramée, Marie Louise de la (see Ouida)

Ramírez, Sergío 1942- DLB-145

Ramke, Bin 1947- DLB-120

Ramler, Karl Wilhelm 1725-1798 .... DLB-97

Ramon Ribeyro, Julio 1929-1994 ...... DLB-145

Ramos, Graciliano 1892-1953 .... DLB-307

Ramos, Manuel 1948- DLB-209

Ramos Sucre, José Antonio 1890-1930. . . DLB-290

Ramous, Mario 1924- DLB-128

Rampersad, Arnold 1941- DLB-111

Ramsay, Allan 1684 or 1685-1758 .... DLB-95

Ramsay, David 1749-1815 .... DLB-30

Ramsay, Martha Laurens 1759-1811 .... DLB-200

Ramsey, Frank P. 1903-1930 .... DLB-262

Ranch, Hieronimus Justesen
1539-1607 .... DLB-300

Ranck, Katherine Quintana 1942- DLB-122

Rand, Avery and Company DLB-49

Rand, Ayn 1905-1982 . . . DLB-227, 279; CDALB-7

Rand McNally and Company DLB-49

Randall, David Anton 1905-1975 .... DLB-140

Randall, Dudley 1914-2000 .... DLB-41

Randall, Henry S. 1811-1876 .... DLB-30

Randall, James G. 1881-1953 .... DLB-17

The Randall Jarrell Symposium: A Small
  Collection of Randall Jarrells Y-86

Excerpts From Papers Delivered at the
  Randall Jarrel Symposium Y-86

Randall, John Herman, Jr. 1899-1980 . . . . DLB-279

Randolph, A. Philip 1889-1979 . . . . DLB-91

Anson D. F. Randolph
  [publishing house] DLB-49

Randolph, Thomas 1605-1635 . . . . . . DLB-58, 126

Random House DLB-46

Rankin, Ian (Jack Harvey) 1960- DLB-267

Henry Ranlet [publishing house] DLB-49

Ransom, Harry 1908-1976 . . . . DLB-187

Ransom, John Crowe
  1888-1974 . . . . DLB-45, 63; CDALB-7

Ransome, Arthur 1884-1967 . . . . DLB-160

Rao, Raja 1908-2006 . . . . DLB-323

Raphael, Frederic 1931- DLB-14, 319

Raphaelson, Samson 1896-1983 . . . . DLB-44

Rare Book Dealers
  Bertram Rota and His Bookshop Y-91

  An Interview with Glenn Horowitz Y-90

  An Interview with Otto Penzler Y-96

  An Interview with Ralph Sipper Y-94

  New York City Bookshops in the
    1930s and 1940s: The Recollections
    of Walter Goldwater Y-93

Rare Books
  Research in the American Antiquarian
    Book Trade Y-97

  Two Hundred Years of Rare Books and
    Literary Collections at the
    University of South Carolina Y-00

Rascón Banda, Víctor Hugo 1948- DLB-305

Rashi circa 1040-1105 . . . . DLB-208

Raskin, Ellen 1928-1984 . . . . DLB-52

Rasputin, Valentin Grigor'evich
  1937- DLB-302

Rastell, John 1475?-1536 . . . . DLB-136, 170

Rattigan, Terence
  1911-1977 . . . . DLB-13; CDBLB-7

Raven, Simon 1927-2001 . . . . DLB-271

Ravenhill, Mark 1966- DLB-310

Ravnkilde, Adda 1862-1883 . . . . DLB-300

Rawicz, Piotr 1919-1982 . . . . DLB-299

Rawlings, Marjorie Kinnan 1896-1953
  . . . . DLB-9, 22, 102; DS-17; CDALB-7

Rawlins, C. L. 1949- DLB-342

Rawlinson, Richard 1690-1755 . . . . DLB-213

Rawlinson, Thomas 1681-1725 . . . . DLB-213

Rawls, John 1921-2002 . . . . DLB-279

Raworth, Tom 1938- DLB-40

Ray, David 1932- DLB-5

Ray, Gordon Norton 1915-1986 . . . . DLB-103, 140

Ray, Henrietta Cordelia 1849-1916 . . . . . DLB-50

Raymond, Ernest 1888-1974 . . . . DLB-191

Raymond, Henry J. 1820-1869 . . . . . . DLB-43, 79

Raymond, René (see Chase, James Hadley)

Razaf, Andy 1895-1973 . . . . DLB-265

al-Razi 865?-925? DLB-311

Razón de amor con los denuestos del agua y el vino
  (1230-1250) DLB-337

Rea, Michael 1927-1996 . . . . Y-97

  Michael M. Rea and the Rea Award for
    the Short Story Y-97

Reach, Angus 1821-1856 . . . . DLB-70

Read, Herbert 1893-1968 . . . . DLB-20, 149

Read, Martha Meredith
  fl. nineteenth century DLB-200

Read, Opie 1852-1939 . . . . DLB-23

Read, Piers Paul 1941- DLB-14

Reade, Charles 1814-1884 . . . . DLB-21

Reader's Digest Condensed Books DLB-46

Readers Ulysses Symposium Y-97

Reading, Peter 1946- DLB-40

Reading Series in New York City Y-96

Reaney, James 1926- DLB-68

Rebhun, Paul 1500?-1546 . . . . DLB-179

Rèbora, Clemente 1885-1957 . . . . DLB-114

Rebreanu, Liviu 1885-1944 . . . . DLB-220

Rechy, John 1934- DLB-122, 278; Y-82

Redding, J. Saunders 1906-1988 . . . . . DLB-63, 76

Rede, William Leman 1802-1847 . . . . . . DLB-344

J. S. Redfield [publishing house] DLB-49

Redgrove, Peter 1932-2003 . . . . DLB-40

Redmon, Anne 1943- Y-86

Redmond, Eugene B. 1937- DLB-41

Redol, Alves 1911-1969 . . . . DLB-287

James Redpath [publishing house] DLB-49

Reed, Henry 1808-1854 . . . . DLB-59

Reed, Henry 1914-1986 . . . . DLB-27

Reed, Ishmael
  1938- DLB-2, 5, 33, 169, 227; DS-8

Reed, Rex 1938- DLB-185

Reed, Sampson 1800-1880 . . . . DLB-1, 235

Reed, Talbot Baines 1852-1893 . . . . DLB-141

Reedy, William Marion 1862-1920 . . . . . . DLB-91

Reese, Lizette Woodworth 1856-1935 . . . . DLB-54

Reese, Thomas 1742-1796 . . . . DLB-37

Reeve, Clara 1729-1807 . . . . DLB-39

  Preface to *The Old English Baron*
    (1778) DLB-39

  The Progress of Romance (1785)
    [excerpt] DLB-39

Reeves, James 1909-1978 . . . . DLB-161

Reeves, John 1926- DLB-88

Reeves-Stevens, Garfield 1953- DLB-251

Régio, José (José Maria dos Reis Pereira)
  1901-1969 . . . . DLB-287

Henry Regnery Company DLB-46

Rêgo, José Lins do 1901-1957 . . . . DLB-307

Rehberg, Hans 1901-1963 . . . . DLB-124

Rehfisch, Hans José 1891-1960 . . . . DLB-124

Reich, Ebbe Kløvedal 1940- DLB-214

Reid, Alastair 1926- DLB-27

Reid, B. L. 1918-1990 . . . . DLB-111

Reid, Christopher 1949- DLB-40

Reid, Forrest 1875-1947 . . . . DLB-153

Reid, Helen Rogers 1882-1970 . . . . DLB-29

Reid, James fl. eighteenth century DLB-31

Reid, Mayne 1818-1883 . . . . DLB-21, 163

Reid, Thomas 1710-1796 . . . . DLB-31, 252

Reid, V. S. (Vic) 1913-1987 . . . . DLB-125

Reid, Whitelaw 1837-1912 . . . . DLB-23

Reilly and Lee Publishing Company DLB-46

Reimann, Brigitte 1933-1973 . . . . DLB-75

Reinmar der Alte circa 1165-circa 1205 . . . DLB-138

Reinmar von Zweter
  circa 1200-circa 1250 . . . . DLB-138

Reisch, Walter 1903-1983 . . . . DLB-44

Reizei Family DLB-203

Religion
  A Crisis of Culture: The Changing
    Role of Religion in the
    New Republic DLB-37

The Remains of the Day, 1989 Booker Prize winner,
  Kazuo Ishiguro DLB-326

Remarque, Erich Maria
  1898-1970 . . . . DLB-56; CDWLB-2

Remington, Frederic
  1861-1909 . . . . DLB-12, 186, 188

Remizov, Aleksei Mikhailovich
  1877-1957 . . . . DLB-295

Renaud, Jacques 1943- DLB-60

Renault, Mary 1905-1983 . . . . Y-83

Rendell, Ruth (Barbara Vine)
  1930- DLB-87, 276

Rensselaer, Maria van Cortlandt van
  1645-1689 . . . . DLB-200

Repplier, Agnes 1855-1950 . . . . DLB-221

Reshetnikov, Fedor Mikhailovich
  1841-1871 . . . . DLB-238

Restif (Rétif) de La Bretonne, Nicolas-Edme
  1734-1806 . . . . DLB-314

Rettenbacher, Simon 1634-1706 . . . . DLB-168

Retz, Jean-François-Paul de Gondi,
  cardinal de 1613-1679 . . . . DLB-268

Reuchlin, Johannes 1455-1522 . . . . DLB-179

Reuter, Christian 1665-after 1712 . . . . . . DLB-168

Fleming H. Revell Company DLB-49

Reverdy, Pierre 1889-1960 . . . . DLB-258

Cumulative Index

Reuter, Fritz 1810-1874 .... DLB-129

Reuter, Gabriele 1859-1941 .... DLB-66

Reventlow, Franziska Gräfin zu
    1871-1918 .... DLB-66

Review of Reviews Office DLB-112

Rexroth, Kenneth 1905-1982
    .... DLB-16, 48, 165, 212; Y-82; CDALB-1

    The Commercialization of the Image
       of Revolt DLB-16

Rey, H. A. 1898-1977 .... DLB-22

Reyes, Carlos José 1941- DLB-305

Reymont, Władysław Stanisław
    1867-1925 .... DLB-332

Reynal and Hitchcock DLB-46

Reynolds, G. W. M. 1814-1879 .... DLB-21

Reynolds, John Hamilton
    1794-1852 .... DLB-96

Reynolds, Sir Joshua 1723-1792 .... DLB-104

Reynolds, Mack 1917-1983 .... DLB-8

Reza, Yazmina 1959- DLB-321

Reznikoff, Charles 1894-1976 .... DLB-28, 45

Rhetoric
    Continental European Rhetoricians,
      1400-1600, and Their Influence
      in Reaissance England DLB-236

    A Finding Guide to Key Works on
      Microfilm DLB-236

    Glossary of Terms and Definitions of
      Rhetoic and Logic DLB-236

Rhett, Robert Barnwell 1800-1876 .... DLB-43

Rhode, John 1884-1964 .... DLB-77

Rhodes, Eugene Manlove 1869-1934 .... DLB-256

Rhodes, James Ford 1848-1927 .... DLB-47

Rhodes, Richard 1937- DLB-185

Rhys, Jean 1890-1979
    ..... DLB-36, 117, 162; CDBLB-7; CDWLB-3

Ribeiro, Bernadim
    fl. ca. 1475/1482-1526/1544 .... DLB-287

Ricardo, David 1772-1823 .... DLB-107, 158

Ricardou, Jean 1932- DLB-83

Riccoboni, Marie-Jeanne (Marie-Jeanne de
    Heurles Laboras de Mézières Riccoboni)
    1713-1792 .... DLB-314

Rice, Anne (A. N. Roquelare, Anne Rampling)
    1941- DLB-292

Rice, Christopher 1978- DLB-292

Rice, Elmer 1892-1967 .... DLB-4, 7

Rice, Grantland 1880-1954 .... DLB-29, 171

Rich, Adrienne 1929- DLB-5, 67; CDALB-7

Richard, Mark 1955- DLB-234

Richard de Fournival
    1201-1259 or 1260 .... DLB-208

Richards, David Adams 1950- DLB-53

Richards, George circa 1760-1814 ...... DLB-37

Richards, I. A. 1893-1979 .... DLB-27

Richards, Laura E. 1850-1943 .... DLB-42

Richards, William Carey 1818-1892 ..... DLB-73

Grant Richards [publishing house] DLB-112

Richardson, Charles F. 1851-1913 ...... DLB-71

Richardson, Dorothy M. 1873-1957 ...... DLB-36

    The Novels of Dorothy Richardson
      (1918), by May Sinclair DLB-36

Richardson, Henry Handel
    (Ethel Florence Lindesay Robertson)
    1870-1946 .... DLB-197, 230

Richardson, Jack 1935- DLB-7

Richardson, John 1796-1852 .... DLB-99

Richardson, Samuel
    1689-1761 .... DLB-39, 154; CDBLB-2

    Introductory Letters from the Second
      Edition of *Pamela* (1741) DLB-39

    Postscript to [the Third Edition of]
      Clarissa (1751) DLB-39

    Preface to the First Edition of
      Pamela (1740) DLB-39

    Preface to the Third Edition of
      Clarissa (1751) [excerpt] DLB-39

    Preface to Volume 1 of *Clarissa*
      (1747) DLB-39

    Preface to Volume 3 of *Clarissa*
      (1748) DLB-39

Richardson, Willis 1889-1977 .... DLB-51

Riche, Barnabe 1542-1617 .... DLB-136

Richepin, Jean 1849-1926 .... DLB-192

Richler, Mordecai 1931-2001 .... DLB-53

Richter, Conrad 1890-1968 .... DLB-9, 212

Richter, Hans Werner 1908-1993 .... DLB-69

Richter, Johann Paul Friedrich
    1763-1825 .... DLB-94; CDWLB-2

Joseph Rickerby [publishing house] DLB-106

Rickword, Edgell 1898-1982 .... DLB-20

Riddell, Charlotte 1832-1906 .... DLB-156

Riddell, John (see Ford, Corey)

Ridge, John Rollin 1827-1867 .... DLB-175

Ridge, Lola 1873-1941 .... DLB-54

Ridge, William Pett 1859-1930 .... DLB-135

Riding, Laura (see Jackson, Laura Riding)

Ridler, Anne 1912-2001 .... DLB-27

Ridruego, Dionisio 1912-1975 .... DLB-108

Riel, Louis 1844-1885 .... DLB-99

Riemer, Johannes 1648-1714 .... DLB-168

Riera, Carme 1948- DLB-322

Rifbjerg, Klaus 1931- DLB-214

Riffaterre, Michael 1924-2006 .... DLB-67

Rifkin, Jeremy 1945- DLB-345

A Conversation between William Riggan
    and Janette Turner Hospital Y-02

Riggs, Lynn 1899-1954 .... DLB-175

Riis, Jacob 1849-1914 .... DLB-23

John C. Riker [publishing house] DLB-49

Riley, James 1777-1840 .... DLB-183

Riley, John 1938-1978 .... DLB-40

Rilke, Rainer Maria
    1875-1926 .... DLB-81; CDWLB-2

Rimanelli, Giose 1926- DLB-177

Rimbaud, Jean-Nicolas-Arthur
    1854-1891 .... DLB-217

Rinehart and Company DLB-46

Ringuet 1895-1960 .... DLB-68

Ringwood, Gwen Pharis 1910-1984 ...... DLB-88

Rinser, Luise 1911-2002 .... DLB-69

Rinuccini, Ottavio 1562-1621 .... DLB-339

Ríos, Alberto 1952- DLB-122

Ríos, Isabella 1948- DLB-82

Ripley, Arthur 1895-1961 .... DLB-44

Ripley, George 1802-1880 ..... DLB-1, 64, 73, 235

The Rising Glory of America:
    Three Poems DLB-37

The Rising Glory of America: Written in 1771
    (1786), by Hugh Henry Brackenridge
    and Philip Freneau DLB-37

Riskin, Robert 1897-1955 .... DLB-26

Risse, Heinz 1898-1989 .... DLB-69

Rist, Johann 1607-1667 .... DLB-164

Ristikivi, Karl 1912-1977 .... DLB-220

Ritchie, Anna Mowatt 1819-1870 ..... DLB-3, 250

Ritchie, Anne Thackeray 1837-1919 ..... DLB-18

Ritchie, Thomas 1778-1854 .... DLB-43

Rites of Passage, 1980 Booker Prize winner,
    William Golding DLB-326

The Ritz Paris Hemingway Award Y-85

    Mario Varga Llosa's Acceptance Speech .. Y-85

Rivard, Adjutor 1868-1945 .... DLB-92

Rive, Richard 1931-1989 .... DLB-125, 225

Rivera, José 1955- DLB-249

Rivera, Marina 1942- DLB-122

Rivera, Tomás 1935-1984 .... DLB-82

Rivers, Conrad Kent 1933-1968 .... DLB-41

Riverside Press DLB-49

Rivington, James circa 1724-1802 ...... DLB-43

Charles Rivington [publishing house] ... DLB-154

Rivkin, Allen 1903-1990 .... DLB-26

Rno, Sung J. 1967- DLB-341

Roa Bastos, Augusto 1917-2005 .... DLB-113

Robbe-Grillet, Alain 1922-2008 .... DLB-83

Robbins, Tom 1936- Y-80

Roberts, Charles G. D. 1860-1943 ...... DLB-92

Roberts, Dorothy 1906-1993 .... DLB-88

Roberts, Elizabeth Madox
    1881-1941 .... DLB-9, 54, 102

Roberts, John (see Swynnerton, Thomas)

Roberts, Kate 1891-1985 .... DLB-319

Roberts, Keith 1935-2000 .... DLB-261

Roberts, Kenneth 1885-1957 .... DLB-9

Roberts, Michèle 1949- DLB-231

Roberts, Theodore Goodridge
1877-1953 ....DLB-92

Roberts, Ursula Wyllie (see Miles, Susan)

Roberts, William 1767-1849............DLB-142

James Roberts [publishing house] DLB-154

Roberts Brothers DLB-49

A. M. Robertson and Company DLB-49

Robertson, Ethel Florence Lindesay
(see Richardson, Henry Handel)

Robertson, T. W. 1829-1871 ....DLB-344

Robertson, William 1721-1793......DLB-104, 336

Robin, Leo 1895-1984................DLB-265

Robins, Elizabeth 1862-1952...........DLB-197

Robinson, A. Mary F. (Madame James
Darmesteter, Madame Mary
Duclaux) 1857-1944...............DLB-240

Robinson, Casey 1903-1979............DLB-44

Robinson, Derek 1932- Y-02

Robinson, Edwin Arlington
1869-1935 ....DLB-54; CDALB-3

Review by Derek Robinson of George
Greenfield's *Rich Dust* Y-02

Robinson, Henry Crabb 1775-1867 ......DLB-107

Robinson, James Harvey 1863-1936 ......DLB-47

Robinson, Lennox 1886-1958 ....DLB-10

Robinson, Mabel Louise 1874-1962......DLB-22

Robinson, Marilynne 1943- DLB-206

Robinson, Mary 1758-1800 ....DLB-158

Robinson, Richard circa 1545-1607......DLB-167

Robinson, Therese 1797-1870.......DLB-59, 133

Robison, Mary 1949- DLB-130

Roblès, Emmanuel 1914-1995..........DLB-83

Roccatagliata Ceccardi, Ceccardo
1871-1919 ....DLB-114

Rocha, Adolfo Correira da (see Torga, Miguel)

Roche, Billy 1949- DLB-233

Rochester, John Wilmot, Earl of
1647-1680 ....DLB-131

Rochon, Esther 1948- DLB-251

Rock, Howard 1911-1976 ....DLB-127

Rockwell, Norman Perceval 1894-1978 ...DLB-188

Rodgers, Carolyn M. 1945- DLB-41

Rodgers, W. R. 1909-1969.............DLB-20

Rodney, Lester 1911- DLB-241

Rodoreda, Mercé 1908-1983 ....DLB-322

Rodrigues, Nelson 1912-1980 ....DLB-307

Rodríguez, Claudio 1934-1999 ....DLB-134

Rodríguez, Joe D. 1943- DLB-209

Rodriguez, Judith 1936- DLB-325

Rodríguez, Luis J. 1954- DLB-209

Rodriguez, Richard 1944- DLB-82, 256

Rodríguez Julia, Edgardo 1946- DLB-145

Roe, E. P. 1838-1888.................DLB-202

Roethke, Theodore
1908-1963 ....DLB-5, 206; CDALB-1

Rogers, Jane 1952- DLB-194

Rogers, Pattiann 1940- DLB-105

Rogers, Samuel 1763-1855.............DLB-93

Rogers, Will 1879-1935................DLB-11

Rohmer, Sax 1883-1959................DLB-70

Roig, Montserrat 1946-1991 ....DLB-322

Roiphe, Anne 1935- Y-80

Rojas, Arnold R. 1896-1988 ....DLB-82

Rojas, Fernando de ca. 1475-1541 ......DLB-286

Roland de la Platière, Marie-Jeanne
(Madame Roland) 1754-1793 ....DLB-314

Rolfe, Edwin (Solomon Fishman)
1909-1954 ....DLB-303

Rolfe, Frederick William
1860-1913 ....DLB-34, 156

Rolland, Romain 1866-1944 ....DLB-65, 332

Rolle, Richard circa 1290-1300 - 1349....DLB-146

Rölvaag, O. E. 1876-1931 ....DLB-9, 212

Romains, Jules 1885-1972 ....DLB-65, 321

A. Roman and Company...............DLB-49

Roman de la Rose: Guillaume de Lorris
1200/1205-circa 1230, Jean de
Meun 1235-1240-circa 1305 ....DLB-208

Romano, Lalla 1906-2001 ....DLB-177

Romano, Octavio 1923-2005...........DLB-122

Rome, Harold 1908-1993 ....DLB-265

Romero, Leo 1950- DLB-122

Romero, Lin 1947- DLB-122

Romero, Orlando 1945- DLB-82

Ronsard, Pierre de 1524-1585 ....DLB-327

Rook, Clarence 1863-1915 ....DLB-135

Roosevelt, Theodore
1858-1919 ....DLB-47, 186, 275

Root, Waverley 1903-1982 ....DLB-4

Root, William Pitt 1941- DLB-120

Roquebrune, Robert de 1889-1978 ......DLB-68

Rorty, Richard 1931-2007 ....DLB-246, 279

Rosa, João Guimarães 1908-1967...DLB-113, 307

Rosales, Luis 1910-1992 ....DLB-134

Roscoe, William 1753-1831 ....DLB-163

Rose, Dilys 1954- DLB-319

Rose, Ernestine 1810-1892.............DLB-345

Rose, Reginald 1920-2002 ....DLB-26

Rose, Wendy 1948- DLB-175

Rosegger, Peter 1843-1918............DLB-129

Rosei, Peter 1946- DLB-85

Rosen, Norma 1925- DLB-28

Rosenbach, A. S. W. 1876-1952........DLB-140

Rosenbaum, Ron 1946- DLB-185

Rosenbaum, Thane 1960- DLB-299

Rosenberg, Isaac 1890-1918 ....DLB-20, 216

Rosenfarb, Chava (Khave Roznfarb)
1923- DLB-333

Rosenfeld, Isaac 1918-1956 ....DLB-28

Rosenfeld, Morris (Moris Roznfeld)
1862-1923 ....DLB-333

Rosenthal, Harold 1914-1999 ....DLB-241

Jimmy, Red, and Others: Harold
Rosenthal Remembers the Stars of
the Press Box Y-01

Rosenthal, M. L. 1917-1996.............DLB-5

Rosenwald, Lessing J. 1891-1979........DLB-187

Rospigliosi, Giulio (Pope Clement IX)
1600-1669 ....DLB-339

Ross, Alexander 1591-1654............DLB-151

Ross, Harold 1892-1951 ....DLB-137

Ross, Jerry 1926-1955 ....DLB-265

Ross, Leonard Q. (see Rosten, Leo)

Ross, Lillian 1927- DLB-185

Ross, Martin 1862-1915..............DLB-135

Ross, Sinclair 1908-1996 ....DLB-88

Ross, W. W. E. 1894-1966.............DLB-88

Rosselli, Amelia 1930-1996 ....DLB-128

Rossen, Robert 1908-1966............DLB-26

Rosset, Barney 1922- Y-02

Rossetti, Christina 1830-1894 ...DLB-35, 163, 240

Rossetti, Dante Gabriel
1828-1882 ....DLB-35; CDBLB-4

The Stealthy School of
Criticism (1871) DLB-35

Rossner, Judith 1935- DLB-6

Rostand, Edmond 1868-1918 ....DLB-192

Rosten, Leo 1908-1997 ....DLB-11

Rostenberg, Leona 1908-2005..........DLB-140

Rostopchina, Evdokiia Petrovna
1811-1858 ....DLB-205

Rostovsky, Dimitrii 1651-1709 ....DLB-150

Rota, Bertram 1903-1966 ....DLB-201

Bertram Rota and His Bookshop Y-91

Roth, Gerhard 1942- DLB-85, 124

Roth, Henry 1906?-1995...............DLB-28

Roth, Joseph 1894-1939...............DLB-85

Roth, Philip
1933- DLB-2, 28, 173; Y-82; CDALB-6

Rothenberg, Jerome 1931- DLB-5, 193

Rothschild Family DLB-184

Rotimi, Ola 1938-2000 ....DLB-125

Rotrou, Jean 1609-1650 ....DLB-268

Rousseau, Jean-Jacques 1712-1778 ....DLB-314

The Social Contract................DLB-314

Routhier, Adolphe-Basile 1839-1920 ......DLB-99

Routier, Simone 1901-1987 ....DLB-88

George Routledge and Sons DLB-106

Roversi, Roberto 1923- DLB-128

Rowe, Elizabeth Singer 1674-1737 .... DLB-39, 95
Rowe, Nicholas 1674-1718 .... DLB-84
Rowlands, Ian 1964- DLB-310
Rowlands, Samuel circa 1570-1630...... DLB-121
Rowlandson, Mary
　circa 1637-circa 1711........... DLB-24, 200
Rowley, William circa 1585-1626 .... DLB-58
Rowling, J. K.
　The Harry Potter Phenomenon Y-99
Rowse, A. L. 1903-1997 .... DLB-155
Rowson, Susanna Haswell
　circa 1762-1824................DLB-37, 200
Roy, Arundhati 1961- DLB-323, 326
Roy, Camille 1870-1943 .... DLB-92
The G. Ross Roy Scottish Poetry Collection
　at the University of South Carolina Y-89
Roy, Gabrielle 1909-1983 .... DLB-68
Roy, Jules 1907-2000.................. DLB-83
The Royal Court Theatre and the English
　Stage Company DLB-13
The Royal Court Theatre and the New
　Drama DLB-10
The Royal Shakespeare Company
　at the Swan........................ Y-88
Royall, Anne Newport 1769-1854.... DLB-43, 248
Royce, Josiah 1855-1916................DLB-270
The Roycroft Printing Shop DLB-49
Royde-Smith, Naomi 1875-1964 .... DLB-191
Royster, Vermont 1914-1996 .... DLB-127
Richard Royston [publishing house]......DLB-170
Rozanov, Vasilii Vasil'evich
　1856-1919..................... DLB-295
Różewicz, Tadeusz 1921- DLB-232
Ruark, Gibbons 1941- DLB-120
Ruban, Vasilii Grigorevich 1742-1795.... DLB-150
Rubens, Bernice 1928-2004 ..... DLB-14, 207, 326
Rubião, Murilo 1916-1991 .... DLB-307
Rubina, Dina Il'inichna 1953- DLB-285
Rubinshtein, Lev Semenovich 1947- ... DLB-285
Rudd and Carleton................. DLB-49
Rudd, Steele (Arthur Hoey Davis) DLB-230
Rudkin, David 1936- DLB-13
Rudnick, Paul 1957- DLB-266
Rudnicki, Adolf 1909-1990............ DLB-299
Rudolf von Ems circa 1200-circa 1254 ... DLB-138
Ruffhead, Owen 1723-1769............ DLB-336
Ruffin, Josephine St. Pierre 1842-1924 .... DLB-79
Rufo, Juan Gutiérrez 1547?-1620? DLB-318
Ruganda, John 1941- DLB-157
Ruggles, Henry Joseph 1813-1906 .... DLB-64
Ruiz, Juan, Arcipreste de Hita
　1330-1343 .... DLB-337
Ruiz de Burton, María Amparo
　1832-1895 .... DLB-209, 221

Rukeyser, Muriel 1913-1980............ DLB-48
Rule, Jane 1931-2007 .... DLB-60
Rulfo, Juan 1918-1986 .....DLB-113; CDWLB-3
Rumaker, Michael 1932- DLB-16, 335
Rumens, Carol 1944- DLB-40
Rummo, Paul-Eerik 1942- DLB-232
Runyon, Damon 1880-1946......DLB-11, 86, 171
Ruodlieb circa 1050-1075 .... DLB-148
Rush, Benjamin 1746-1813............. DLB-37
Rush, Rebecca 1779-?................ DLB-200
Rushdie, Salman 1947- DLB-194, 323, 326
Rusk, Ralph L. 1888-1962 .... DLB-103
Ruskin, John
　1819-1900...... DLB-55, 163, 190; CDBLB-4
Russ, Joanna 1937- DLB-8
Russell, Benjamin 1761-1845 .... DLB-43
Russell, Bertrand 1872-1970 ....DLB-100, 262, 332
Russell, Charles Edward 1860-1941....... DLB-25
Russell, Charles M. 1864-1926......... DLB-188
Russell, Eric Frank 1905-1978 .... DLB-255
Russell, Fred 1906-2003 .... DLB-241
Russell, George William (see AE)
Russell, Countess Mary Annette Beauchamp
　(see Arnim, Elizabeth von)
Russell, Willy 1947- DLB-233
B. B. Russell and Company DLB-49
R. H. Russell and Son DLB-49
Rutebeuf fl.1249-1277................ DLB-208
Rutherford, Mark 1831-1913 .... DLB-18
Ruxton, George Frederick
　1821-1848 .... DLB-186
R-va, Zeneida
　(see Gan, Elena Andreevna)
Ryan, Gig 1956- DLB-325
Ryan, James 1952- DLB-267
Ryan, Michael 1946- Y-82
Ryan, Oscar 1904-1988 .... DLB-68
Rybakov, Anatolii Naumovich
　1911-1994 .... DLB-302
Ryder, Jack 1871-1936 .... DLB-241
Ryga, George 1932-1987 .... DLB-60
Rylands, Enriqueta Augustina Tennant
　1843-1908 .... DLB-184
Rylands, John 1801-1888 .... DLB-184
Ryle, Gilbert 1900-1976 .... DLB-262
Ryleev, Kondratii Fedorovich 1795-1826 . DLB-205
Rymer, Thomas 1643?-1713........ DLB-101, 336
Ryskind, Morrie 1895-1985 .... DLB-26
Rzhevsky, Aleksei Andreevich
　1737-1804..................... DLB-150

S

El Saadawi, Nawal 1931- DLB-346

The Saalfield Publishing Company DLB-46
Saba, Umberto 1883-1957 .... DLB-114
Sábato, Ernesto 1911- DLB-145; CDWLB-3
Saberhagen, Fred 1930-2007............ DLB-8
Sabin, Joseph 1821-1881.............DLB-187
Sabino, Fernando (Fernando Tavares Sabino)
　1923-2004 .... DLB-307
Sacer, Gottfried Wilhelm 1635-1699..... DLB-168
Sachs, Hans 1494-1576......DLB-179; CDWLB-2
Sachs, Nelly 1891-1970............... DLB-332
Sá-Carneiro, Mário de 1890-1916 ...... DLB-287
Sack, John 1930-2004................ DLB-185
Sackler, Howard 1929-1982 .... DLB-7
Sackville, Lady Margaret 1881-1963 .... DLB-240
Sackville, Thomas 1536-1608 and
　Norton, Thomas 1532-1584 .... DLB-62
Sackville, Thomas 1536-1608.......... DLB-132
Sackville-West, Edward 1901-1965...... DLB-191
Sackville-West, Vita 1892-1962...... DLB-34, 195
Sacred Hunger, 1992 Booker Prize winner,
　Barry Unsworth................. DLB-326
Sá de Miranda, Francisco de
　1481-1588?.................... DLB-287
Sade, Marquis de (Donatien-Alphonse-François,
　comte de Sade) 1740-1814 .... DLB-314
　"Dialogue entre un prêtre et un
　　moribond".................. DLB-314
Sadlier, Mary Anne 1820-1903.......... DLB-99
D. and J. Sadlier and Company DLB-49
Sadoff, Ira 1945- DLB-120
Sadoveanu, Mihail 1880-1961 .... DLB-220
al-Sadr, Muhammad Baqir 1935-1980 ... DLB-346
Sadur, Nina Nikolaevna 1950- DLB-285
Sáenz, Benjamin Alire 1954- DLB-209
Saenz, Jaime 1921-1986 .... DLB-145, 283
Saffin, John circa 1626-1710 .... DLB-24
Sagan, Françoise 1935-2004 .... DLB-83
Sage, Robert 1899-1962 .... DLB-4
Sagel, Jim 1947- DLB-82
Sagendorph, Robb Hansell 1900-1970 ....DLB-137
Sahagún, Carlos 1938- DLB-108
Sahgal, Nayantara 1927- DLB-323
Sahkomaapii, Piitai (see Highwater, Jamake)
Sahl, Hans 1902-1993................ DLB-69
Said, Edward W. 1935-2003.........DLB-67, 346
Saigyō 1118-1190 .... DLB-203
Saijo, Albert 1926- DLB-312
Saiko, George 1892-1962 .... DLB-85
Sainte-Beuve, Charles-Augustin
　1804-1869 ....DLB-217
Saint-Exupéry, Antoine de 1900-1944 .... DLB-72
Saint-Gelais, Mellin de 1490?-1558 ..... DLB-327
St. John, J. Allen 1872-1957 .... DLB-188

St John, Madeleine 1942- DLB-267

St. Johns, Adela Rogers 1894-1988 .... DLB-29

St. Omer, Garth 1931- DLB-117

Saint Pierre, Michel de 1916-1987 .... DLB-83

Saintsbury, George 1845-1933 .... DLB-57, 149

   "Modern English Prose" (1876) DLB-57

   The Present State of the English
      Novel (1892), ... DLB-18

Saint-Simon, Louis de Rouvroy, duc de
   1675-1755 .... DLB-314

St. Dominic's Press.................... DLB-112

The St. John's College Robert Graves Trust ... Y-96

St. Martin's Press DLB-46

St. Nicholas 1873-1881 .... DS-13

Saiokuken Sōchō 1448-1532 .... DLB-203

Saki (see Munro, H. H.)

Salaam, Kalamu ya 1947- DLB-38

Salacrou, Armand 1899-1989.......... DLB-321

Šalamun, Tomaž 1941- DLB-181; CDWLB-4

Salas, Floyd 1931- DLB-82

Sálaz-Marquez, Rubén 1935- DLB-122

Salcedo, Hugo 1964- DLB-305

Salemson, Harold J. 1910-1988 .... DLB-4

Salesbury, William 1520?-1584? DLB-281

Salih, Tayeb 1929- DLB-346

Salinas, Luis Omar 1937- DLB-82

Salinas, Pedro 1891-1951 .... DLB-134

Salinger, J. D.
   1919- DLB-2, 102, 173; CDALB-1

Salkey, Andrew 1928-1995 .... DLB-125

Sallust circa 86 B.C.-35 B.C.
   .... DLB-211; CDWLB-1

Salt, Waldo 1914-1987 .... DLB-44

Salter, James 1925- DLB-130

Salter, Mary Jo 1954- DLB-120

Saltus, Edgar 1855-1921 .... DLB-202

Saltykov, Mikhail Evgrafovich
   1826-1889 .... DLB-238

Salustri, Carlo Alberto (see Trilussa)

Salverson, Laura Goodman 1890-1970 .... DLB-92

Samain, Albert 1858-1900 .... DLB-217

Sampson, Richard Henry (see Hull, Richard)

Samuels, Ernest 1903-1996 .... DLB-111

Sanborn, Franklin Benjamin
   1831-1917 .... DLB-1, 223

Sánchez, Florencio 1875-1910.......... DLB-305

Sánchez, Luis Rafael 1936- DLB-145, 305

Sánchez, Philomeno "Phil" 1917- DLB-122

Sánchez, Ricardo 1941-1995 .... DLB-82

Sánchez, Saúl 1943- DLB-209

Sanchez, Sonia 1934- DLB-41; DS-8

Sánchez de Arévalo, Rodrigo
   1404-1470 .... DLB-286

Sánchez de Badajoz, Diego ?-1552? DLB-318

Sánchez Ferlosio, Rafael 1927- DLB-322

Sand, George 1804-1876 .... DLB-119, 192

Sandburg, Carl
   1878-1967 .... DLB-17, 54; CDALB-3

Sandel, Cora (Sara Fabricius)
   1880-1974 .... DLB-297

Sandemose, Aksel 1899-1965.......... DLB-297

Sanders, Edward 1939- DLB-16, 244

Sanderson, Robert 1587-1663 .... DLB-281

Sandoz, Mari 1896-1966 .... DLB-9, 212

Sandwell, B. K. 1876-1954 .... DLB-92

Sandy, Stephen 1934- DLB-165

Sandys, George 1578-1644 .... DLB-24, 121

Sanger, Margaret 1878-1933 .... DLB-345

Sangster, Charles 1822-1893 .... DLB-99

Sanguineti, Edoardo 1930- DLB-128

Sanjōnishi Sanetaka 1455-1537 .... DLB-203

San Pedro, Diego de fl. ca. 1492 .... DLB-286

Sansay, Leonora ?-after 1823 .... DLB-200

Sansom, William 1912-1976 .... DLB-139

Santa Maria Egipçiaca thirteenth-fourteenth
   centuries DLB-337

Sant'Anna, Affonso Romano de
   1937- DLB-307

Santayana, George
   1863-1952 ..... DLB-54, 71, 246, 270; DS-13

Santiago, Danny 1911-1988........... DLB-122

Santillana, Marqués de (Íñigo López de Mendoza)
   1398-1458 .... DLB-286

Santmyer, Helen Hooven 1895-1986 .... Y-84

Santos, Bienvenido 1911-1996 .... DLB-312

Sanvitale, Francesca 1928- DLB-196

Sapidus, Joannes 1490-1561........... DLB-179

Sapir, Edward 1884-1939.............. DLB-92

Sapper (see McNeile, Herman Cyril)

Sappho circa 620 B.C.-circa 550 B.C.
   .... DLB-176; CDWLB-1

Saramago, José 1922- DLB-287, 332; Y-98

   Nobel Lecture 1998: How Characters
      Became the Masters and the Author
      Their Apprentice Y-98

Sarban (John W. Wall) 1910-1989....... DLB-255

Sardou, Victorien 1831-1908 .... DLB-192

Sarduy, Severo 1937-1993 .... DLB-113

Sargent, Pamela 1948- DLB-8

Saro-Wiwa, Ken 1941- DLB-157

Saroyan, Aram
   Rites of Passage [on William Saroyan] Y-83

Saroyan, William
   1908-1981 ..... DLB-7, 9, 86; Y-81; CDALB-7

Sarraute, Nathalie 1900-1999 .... DLB-83, 321

Sarrazin, Albertine 1937-1967 .... DLB-83

Sarris, Greg 1952- DLB-175

Sarrocchi, Margherita 1560-1617........ DLB-339

Sarton, May 1912-1995 .... DLB-48; Y-81

Sartre, Jean-Paul
   1905-1980.......... DLB-72, 296, 321, 332

Sassoon, Siegfried
   1886-1967 .... DLB-20, 191; DS-18

   A Centenary Essay Y-86

   Tributes from Vivien F. Clarke and
      Michael Thorpe Y-86

Sata Ineko 1904-1998 .... DLB-180

Saturday Review Press................. DLB-46

Saunders, George W. 1958- DLB-335

Saunders, James 1925-2004 .... DLB-13

Saunders, John Monk 1897-1940......... DLB-26

Saunders, Margaret Marshall
   1861-1947 .... DLB-92

Saunders and Otley DLB-106

Saussure, Ferdinand de 1857-1913 .... DLB-242

Savage, James 1784-1873 .... DLB-30

Savage, Marmion W. 1803?-1872 .... DLB-21

Savage, Richard 1697?-1743 .... DLB-95

Savard, Félix-Antoine 1896-1982......... DLB-68

Savery, Henry 1791-1842 .... DLB-230

Saville, (Leonard) Malcolm 1901-1982 ... DLB-160

Saville, 1976 Booker Prize winner,
   David Storey DLB-326

Savinio, Alberto 1891-1952 .... DLB-264

Sawyer, Robert J. 1960- DLB-251

Sawyer, Ruth 1880-1970 .... DLB-22

Sayer, Mandy 1963- DLB-325

Sayers, Dorothy L.
   1893-1957 .... DLB-10, 36, 77, 100; CDBLB-6

   The Dorothy L. Sayers Society Y-98

Sayle, Charles Edward 1864-1924....... DLB-184

Sayles, John Thomas 1950- DLB-44

Sbarbaro, Camillo 1888-1967 .... DLB-114

Scala, Flaminio (Flavio) 1552-1624 ...... DLB-339

Scalapino, Leslie 1947- DLB-193

Scannell, Vernon 1922-2007............. DLB-27

Scarry, Richard 1919-1994............. DLB-61

Scève, Maurice circa 1502-circa 1564 .... DLB-327

Schack, Hans Egede 1820-1859......... DLB-300

Schaefer, Jack 1907-1991 .... DLB-212

Schaeffer, Albrecht 1885-1950 .... DLB-66

Schaeffer, Susan Fromberg 1941- ... DLB-28, 299

Schaff, Philip 1819-1893 .... DS-13

Schaper, Edzard 1908-1984 .... DLB-69

Scharf, J. Thomas 1843-1898............ DLB-47

Schede, Paul Melissus 1539-1602 .... DLB-179

Scheffel, Joseph Viktor von 1826-1886 ... DLB-129

Scheffler, Johann 1624-1677............ DLB-164

Schéhadé, Georges 1905-1999 .... DLB-321

Cumulative Index

Schelling, Andrew 1953- DLB-342
Schelling, Friedrich Wilhelm Joseph von
  1775-1854 .... DLB-90
Scherer, Wilhelm 1841-1886 .... DLB-129
Schenkkan, Robert 1953- DLB-341
Scherfig, Hans 1905-1979 .... DLB-214
Schickele, René 1883-1940 .... DLB-66
Schiff, Dorothy 1903-1989 .... DLB-127
Schiller, Friedrich
  1759-1805 .... DLB-94; CDWLB-2
Schindler's Ark, 1982 Booker Prize winner,
  Thomas Keneally DLB-326
Schirmer, David 1623-1687 .... DLB-164
Schlaf, Johannes 1862-1941 .... DLB-118
Schlegel, August Wilhelm 1767-1845 ..... DLB-94
Schlegel, Dorothea 1763-1839 .... DLB-90
Schlegel, Friedrich 1772-1829 .... DLB-90
Schleiermacher, Friedrich 1768-1834 ..... DLB-90
Schlesinger, Arthur M., Jr. 1917-2007 .... DLB-17
Schlumberger, Jean 1877-1968 .... DLB-65
Schmid, Eduard Hermann Wilhelm
  (see Edschmid, Kasimir)
Schmidt, Arno 1914-1979 .... DLB-69
Schmidt, Johann Kaspar (see Stirner, Max)
Schmidt, Michael 1947- DLB-40
Schmidtbonn, Wilhelm August
  1876-1952 .... DLB-118
Schmitz, Aron Hector (see Svevo, Italo)
Schmitz, James H. 1911-1981 .... DLB-8
Schnabel, Johann Gottfried 1692-1760 ... DLB-168
Schnackenberg, Gjertrud 1953- DLB-120
Schnitzler, Arthur
  1862-1931 .... DLB-81, 118; CDWLB-2
Schnurre, Wolfdietrich 1920-1989 .... DLB-69
Schocken Books DLB-46
Scholartis Press DLB-112
Scholderer, Victor 1880-1971 .... DLB-201
The Schomburg Center for Research
  in Black Culture DLB-76
Schönbeck, Virgilio (see Giotti, Virgilio)
Schönherr, Karl 1867-1943 .... DLB-118
Schoolcraft, Jane Johnston 1800-1841 .... DLB-175
School Stories, 1914-1960 .... DLB-160
Schopenhauer, Arthur 1788-1860 .... DLB-90
Schopenhauer, Johanna 1766-1838 ...... DLB-90
Schorer, Mark 1908-1977 .... DLB-103
Schottelius, Justus Georg 1612-1676 .... DLB-164
Schouler, James 1839-1920 .... DLB-47
Schoultz, Solveig von 1907-1996 .... DLB-259
Schrader, Paul 1946- DLB-44
Schreiner, Olive
  1855-1920 .... DLB-18, 156, 190, 225
Schroeder, Andreas 1946- DLB-53

Schubart, Christian Friedrich Daniel
  1739-1791 .... DLB-97
Schubert, Gotthilf Heinrich 1780-1860 ... DLB-90
Schücking, Levin 1814-1883 .... DLB-133
Schulberg, Budd 1914- DLB-6, 26, 28; Y-81
  Excerpts from USC Presentation
    [on F. Scott Fitzgerald] Y-96
F. J. Schulte and Company DLB-49
Schulz, Bruno 1892-1942 ... DLB-215; CDWLB-4
Schulze, Hans (see Praetorius, Johannes)
Schupp, Johann Balthasar 1610-1661 .... DLB-164
Schurz, Carl 1829-1906 .... DLB-23
Schuyler, George S. 1895-1977 ...... DLB-29, 51
Schuyler, James 1923-1991 .... DLB-5, 169
Schwartz, Delmore 1913-1966 .... DLB-28, 48
Schwartz, Jonathan 1938- Y-82
Schwartz, Lynne Sharon 1939- DLB-218
Schwarz, Sibylle 1621-1638 .... DLB-164
Schwarz-Bart, Andre 1928-2006 .... DLB-299
Schwerner, Armand 1927-1999 .... DLB-165
Schwob, Marcel 1867-1905 .... DLB-123
Sciascia, Leonardo 1921-1989 .... DLB-177
Science Fiction and Fantasy
  Documents in British Fantasy and
    Science Fiction DLB-178
  Hugo Awards and Nebula Awards DLB-8
  The Iconography of Science-Fiction
    Art DLB-8
  The New Wave DLB-8
  Paperback Science Fiction DLB-8
  Science Fantasy DLB-8
  Science-Fiction Fandom and
    Conventions DLB-8
  Science-Fiction Fanzines: The Time
    Binders DLB-8
  Science-Fiction Films DLB-8
  Science Fiction Writers of America
    and the Nebula Award DLB-8
  Selected Science-Fiction Magazines and
    Anthologies DLB-8
  A World Chronology of Important Science
    Fiction Works (1818-1979) DLB-8
  The Year in Science Fiction
    and Fantasy Y-00, 01
Scot, Reginald circa 1538-1599 .... DLB-136
Scotellaro, Rocco 1923-1953 .... DLB-128
Scott, Alicia Anne (Lady John Scott)
  1810-1900 .... DLB-240
Scott, Catharine Amy Dawson
  1865-1934 .... DLB-240
Scott, Dennis 1939-1991 .... DLB-125
Scott, Dixon 1881-1915 .... DLB-98
Scott, Duncan Campbell 1862-1947 ..... DLB-92
Scott, Evelyn 1893-1963 .... DLB-9, 48
Scott, F. R. 1899-1985 .... DLB-88
Scott, Frederick George 1861-1944 ..... DLB-92

Scott, Geoffrey 1884-1929 .... DLB-149
Scott, Harvey W. 1838-1910 .... DLB-23
Scott, John 1948- DLB-325
Scott, Lady Jane (see Scott, Alicia Anne)
Scott, Paul 1920-1978 .... DLB-14, 207, 326
Scott, Sarah 1723-1795 .... DLB-39
Scott, Tom 1918-1995 .... DLB-27
Scott, Sir Walter 1771-1832
  .... DLB-93, 107, 116, 144, 159; CDBLB-3
Scott, William Bell 1811-1890 .... DLB-32
Walter Scott Publishing Company
  Limited DLB-112
William R. Scott [publishing house] DLB-46
Scott-Heron, Gil 1949- DLB-41
Scribe, Eugène 1791-1861 .... DLB-192
Scribner, Arthur Hawley 1859-1932 ..... DS-13, 16
Scribner, Charles 1854-1930 .... DS-13, 16
Scribner, Charles, Jr. 1921-1995 .... Y-95
  Reminiscences DS-17
Charles Scribner's Sons DLB-49; DS-13, 16, 17
  Archives of Charles Scribner's Sons DS-17
Scribner's Magazine DS-13
Scribner's Monthly DS-13
Scripps, E. W. 1854-1926 .... DLB-25
Scudder, Horace Elisha 1838-1902 ..... DLB-42, 71
Scudder, Vida Dutton 1861-1954 .... DLB-71
Scudéry, Madeleine de 1607-1701 .... DLB-268
Scupham, Peter 1933- DLB-40
The Sea, 2005 Booker Prize winner,
  John Banville DLB-326
The Sea, The Sea, 1978 Booker Prize winner,
  Iris Murdoch DLB-326
Seabrook, William 1886-1945 .... DLB-4
Seabury, Samuel 1729-1796 .... DLB-31
Seacole, Mary Jane Grant 1805-1881 .... DLB-166
The Seafarer circa 970 .... DLB-146
Sealsfield, Charles (Carl Postl)
  1793-1864 .... DLB-133, 186
Searle, John R. 1932- DLB-279
Sears, Edward I. 1819?-1876 .... DLB-79
Sears Publishing Company DLB-46
Seaton, George 1911-1979 .... DLB-44
Seaton, William Winston 1785-1866 ..... DLB-43
Sebillet, Thomas 1512-1589 .... DLB-327
Martin Secker [publishing house] DLB-112
Martin Secker, and Warburg Limited ... DLB-112
The "Second Generation" Holocaust
  Novel DLB-299
Sedgwick, Arthur George 1844-1915 .... DLB-64
Sedgwick, Catharine Maria
  1789-1867 .... DLB-1, 74, 183, 239, 243
Sedgwick, Ellery 1872-1960 .... DLB-91
Sedgwick, Eve Kosofsky 1950- DLB-246

Sedley, Sir Charles 1639-1701 ....DLB-131

Seeberg, Peter 1925-1999...............DLB-214

Seeger, Alan 1888-1916 ....DLB-45

Seers, Eugene (see Dantin, Louis)

Seferis, George 1900-1971 ....DLB-332

Segal, Erich 1937- Y-86

Segal, Lore 1928- DLB-299

Šegedin, Petar 1909-1998...............DLB-181

Seghers, Anna 1900-1983.....DLB-69; CDWLB-2

Seid, Ruth (see Sinclair, Jo)

Seidel, Frederick Lewis 1936- Y-84

Seidel, Ina 1885-1974 ....DLB-56

Seifert, Jaroslav
   1901-1986 ... DLB-215, 332; Y-84; CDWLB-4

   Jaroslav Seifert Through the Eyes of
     the English-Speaking Reader Y-84

   Three Poems by Jaroslav Seifert Y-84

Seifullina, Lidiia Nikolaevna 1889-1954 ..DLB-272

Seigenthaler, John 1927- DLB-127

Seizin Press.........................DLB-112

Séjour, Victor 1817-1874................DLB-50

Séjour Marcou et Ferrand, Juan Victor
   (see Séjour, Victor)

Sekowski, Józef-Julian, Baron Brambeus
   (see Senkovsky, Osip Ivanovich)

Selby, Bettina 1934- DLB-204

Selby, Hubert Jr. 1928-2004.........DLB-2, 227

Selden, George 1929-1989 ....DLB-52

Selden, John 1584-1654 ....DLB-213

Selenić, Slobodan 1933-1995 ....DLB-181

Self, Edwin F. 1920- DLB-137

Self, Will 1961- DLB-207

Seligman, Edwin R. A. 1861-1939........DLB-47

Selimović, Meša
   1910-1982 ....DLB-181; CDWLB-4

Sellars, Wilfrid 1912-1989 ....DLB-279

Sellings, Arthur (Arthur Gordon Ley)
   1911-1968 ....DLB-261

Selous, Frederick Courteney 1851-1917...DLB-174

Seltzer, Chester E. (see Muro, Amado)

Thomas Seltzer [publishing house] DLB-46

Selvadurai, Shyam 1965- DLB-323

Selvon, Sam 1923-1994 .....DLB-125; CDWLB-3

Semel, Nava 1954- DLB-299

Semmes, Raphael 1809-1877 ....DLB-189

Senancour, Etienne de 1770-1846........DLB-119

Sena, Jorge de 1919-1978...............DLB-287

Sendak, Maurice 1928- DLB-61

Sender, Ramón J. 1901-1982 ....DLB-322

Seneca the Elder
   circa 54 B.C.-circa A.D. 40 ....DLB-211

Seneca the Younger
   circa 1 B.C.-A.D. 65 .....DLB-211; CDWLB-1

Senécal, Eva 1905-1988 ....DLB-92

Sengstacke, John 1912-1997............DLB-127

Senior, Olive 1941- DLB-157

Senkovsky, Osip Ivanovich
   (Józef-Julian Sekowski, Baron Brambeus)
   1800-1858 ....DLB-198

Šenoa, August 1838-1881 ...DLB-147; CDWLB-4

Sentimental Fiction of the Sixteenth
   Century.........................DLB-318

Sepamla, Sipho 1932-2007 ....DLB-157, 225

Serafimovich, Aleksandr Serafimovich
   (Aleksandr Serafimovich Popov)
   1863-1949 ....DLB-272

Serao, Matilde 1856-1927 ....DLB-264

Seredy, Kate 1899-1975 ....DLB-22

Sereni, Vittorio 1913-1983 ....DLB-128

William Seres [publishing house]........DLB-170

Sergeev-Tsensky, Sergei Nikolaevich (Sergei
   Nikolaevich Sergeev) 1875-1958 ....DLB-272

Serling, Rod 1924-1975 ....DLB-26

Sernine, Daniel 1955- DLB-251

Serote, Mongane Wally 1944- DLB-125, 225

Serraillier, Ian 1912-1994...............DLB-161

Serrano, Nina 1934- DLB-122

Service, Robert 1874-1958 ....DLB-92

Sessler, Charles 1854-1935...............DLB-187

Seth, Vikram 1952- DLB-120, 271, 323

Seton, Elizabeth Ann 1774-1821.........DLB-200

Seton, Ernest Thompson
   1860-1942 ....DLB-92; DS-13

Seton, John circa 1509-1567.............DLB-281

Setouchi Harumi 1922- DLB-182

Settle, Mary Lee 1918-2005...............DLB-6

Seume, Johann Gottfried 1763-1810.......DLB-94

Seuse, Heinrich 1295?-1366............DLB-179

Seuss, Dr. (see Geisel, Theodor Seuss)

Severianin, Igor' 1887-1941 ....DLB-295

Severin, Timothy 1940- DLB-204

Sévigné, Marie de Rabutin Chantal,
   Madame de 1626-1696 ....DLB-268

Sewall, Joseph 1688-1769................DLB-24

Sewall, Richard B. 1908-2003 ....DLB-111

Sewall, Samuel 1652-1730 ....DLB-24

Sewell, Anna 1820-1878................DLB-163

Sewell, Stephen 1953- DLB-325

Sexton, Anne 1928-1974 ...DLB-5, 169; CDALB-1

Seymour-Smith, Martin 1928-1998 ......DLB-155

Sgorlon, Carlo 1930- DLB-196

Shaara, Michael 1929-1988 ....Y-83

Shabel'skaia, Aleksandra Stanislavovna
   1845-1921 ....DLB-238

Shadwell, Thomas 1641?-1692 ....DLB-80

Shaffer, Anthony 1926-2001 ....DLB-13

Shaffer, Peter 1926- DLB-13, 233; CDBLB-8

Muhammad ibn Idris al-Shafi'i 767-820...DLB-311

Shaftesbury, Anthony Ashley Cooper,
   Third Earl of 1671-1713 ....DLB-101, 336

Shaginian, Marietta Sergeevna
   1888-1982 ....DLB-272

Shairp, Mordaunt 1887-1939 ....DLB-10

Shakespeare, Nicholas 1957- DLB-231

Shakespeare, William
   1564-1616 ......DLB-62, 172, 263; CDBLB-1

   The New Variorum Shakespeare Y-85

   Shakespeare and Montaigne: A Symposium
     by Jules Furthman.................Y-02

   $6,166,000 for a *Book!* Observations on
     *The Shakespeare First Folio: The History
     of the Book* Y-01

   Taylor-Made Shakespeare? Or Is
     "Shall I Die?" the Long-Lost Text
     of Bottom's Dream? Y-85

   The Shakespeare Globe Trust Y-93

Shakespeare Head Press................DLB-112

Shakhova, Elisaveta Nikitichna
   1822-1899 ....DLB-277

Shakhovskoi, Aleksandr Aleksandrovich
   1777-1846........................DLB-150

Shalamov, Varlam Tikhonovich
   1907-1982 ....DLB-302

Shammas, Anton 1950- DLB-346

al-Shanfara fl. sixth century DLB-311

Shange, Ntozake 1948- DLB-38, 249

Shanley, John Patrick 1950- DLB-341

Shapcott, Thomas W. 1935- DLB-289

Shapir, Ol'ga Andreevna 1850-1916 .....DLB-295

Shapiro, Gerald 1950- DLB-335

Shapiro, Karl 1913-2000 ....DLB-48

Sharon Publications DLB-46

Sharov, Vladimir Aleksandrovich
   1952- DLB-285

Sharp, Margery 1905-1991 ....DLB-161

Sharp, William 1855-1905..............DLB-156

Sharpe, Tom 1928- DLB-14, 231

Shaw, Albert 1857-1947 ....DLB-91

Shaw, George Bernard
   1856-1950 ... DLB-10, 57, 190, 332; CDBLB-6

   The Bernard Shaw Society Y-99

   "Stage Censorship: The Rejected
     Statement" (1911) [excerpts] DLB-10

Shaw, Henry Wheeler 1818-1885 ....DLB-11

Shaw, Irwin
   1913-1984 ......DLB-6, 102; Y-84; CDALB-1

Shaw, Joseph T. 1874-1952 ....DLB-137

   "As I Was Saying," Joseph T. Shaw's
     Editorial Rationale in *Black Mask*
     (January 1927)................DLB-137

Shaw, Mary 1854-1929 ....DLB-228

Shaw, Robert 1927-1978.............DLB-13, 14

Shaw, Robert B. 1947- DLB-120

Cumulative Index

Shawn, Wallace 1943- DLB-266

Shawn, William 1907-1992 .... DLB-137

Frank Shay [publishing house] DLB-46

al-Shaykh, Hanan 1945- DLB-346

Shchedrin, N. (see Saltykov, Mikhail Evgrafovich)

Shcherbakova, Galina Nikolaevna 1932- DLB-285

Shcherbina, Nikolai Fedorovich 1821-1869 .... DLB-277

Shea, John Gilmary 1824-1892......... DLB-30

Sheaffer, Louis 1912-1993............. DLB-103

Sheahan, Henry Beston (see Beston, Henry)

Shearing, Joseph 1886-1952 .... DLB-70

Shebbeare, John 1709-1788 .... DLB-39

Sheckley, Robert 1928-2005 .... DLB-8

Shedd, William G. T. 1820-1894 .... DLB-64

Sheed, Wilfrid 1930- DLB-6

Sheed and Ward [U.S.] DLB-46

Sheed and Ward Limited [U.K.] DLB-112

Sheldon, Alice B. (see Tiptree, James, Jr.)

Sheldon, Edward 1886-1946............ DLB-7

Sheldon and Company................ DLB-49

Sheller, Aleksandr Konstantinovich 1838-1900................. DLB-238

Shelley, Mary Wollstonecraft 1797-1851 .... DLB-110, 116, 159, 178; CDBLB-3

    Preface to *Frankenstein; or, The Modern Prometheus* (1818) DLB-178

Shelley, Percy Bysshe 1792-1822...... DLB-96, 110, 158; CDBLB-3

Shelnutt, Eve 1941- DLB-130

Shelton, Richard 1933- DLB-342

Shem Tov de Carrión (Isaac Ibn Ardutiel) fl. circa 1350-1360 .... DLB-337

Shen Congwen 1902-1988 .... DLB-328

Shenshin (see Fet, Afanasii Afanas'evich)

Shenstone, William 1714-1763 .... DLB-95

Shepard, Clark and Brown............. DLB-49

Shepard, Ernest Howard 1879-1976 ..... DLB-160

Shepard, Sam 1943- DLB-7, 212, 341

Shepard, Thomas, I, 1604 or 1605-1649 .. DLB-24

Shepard, Thomas, II, 1635-1677......... DLB-24

Shepherd, Luke fl. 1547-1554 .... DLB-136

Sherburne, Edward 1616-1702 .... DLB-131

Sheridan, Frances 1724-1766 .... DLB-39, 84

Sheridan, Richard Brinsley 1751-1816.............DLB-89; CDBLB-2

Sherman, Francis 1871-1926 .... DLB-92

Sherman, Martin 1938- DLB-228

Sherriff, R. C. 1896-1975 ...... DLB-10, 191, 233

Sherrod, Blackie 1919- DLB-241

Sherry, Norman 1935- DLB-155

    Tribute to Graham Greene............ Y-91

Sherry, Richard 1506-1551 or 1555 ..... DLB-236

Sherwood, Mary Martha 1775-1851..... DLB-163

Sherwood, Robert E. 1896-1955....DLB-7, 26, 249

Shevyrev, Stepan Petrovich 1806-1864 .... DLB-205

Shi Tuo (Lu Fen) 1910-1988.......... DLB-328

Shiel, M. P. 1865-1947 .... DLB-153

Shields, Carol 1935-2003 .... DLB-334

Shiels, George 1886-1949 .... DLB-10

Shiga Naoya 1883-1971 .... DLB-180

Shiina Rinzō 1911-1973 .... DLB-182

Shikishi Naishinnō 1153?-1201....... DLB-203

Shillaber, Benjamin Penhallow 1814-1890 .... DLB-1, 11, 235

Shimao Toshio 1917-1986............ DLB-182

Shimazaki Tōson 1872-1943 .... DLB-180

Shimose, Pedro 1940- DLB-283

Shine, Ted 1931- DLB-38

Shinkei 1406-1475................. DLB-203

Ship, Reuben 1915-1975 .... DLB-88

Shirer, William L. 1904-1993 .... DLB-4

Shirinsky-Shikhmatov, Sergii Aleksandrovich 1783-1837..................... DLB-150

Shirley, James 1596-1666 .... DLB-58

Shishkov, Aleksandr Semenovich 1753-1841..................... DLB-150

Shmelev, I. S. 1873-1950............ DLB-317

Shockley, Ann Allen 1927- DLB-33

Sholem Aleichem (Sholem Aleykhem; Sholem Yakov Rabinowitz [Sholem Yankev Rabinovitsch]) 1859-1916 .... DLB-333

Sholokhov, Mikhail Aleksandrovich 1905-1984 ....DLB-272, 332

Shōno Junzō 1921- DLB-182

Shore, Arabella 1820?-1901 .... DLB-199

Shore, Louisa 1824-1895 .... DLB-199

Short, Luke (see Glidden, Frederick Dilley)

Peter Short [publishing house] DLB-170

Shorter, Dora Sigerson 1866-1918 ...... DLB-240

Shorthouse, Joseph Henry 1834-1903 .... DLB-18

Short Stories

    Michael M. Rea and the Rea Award for the Short Story................ Y-97

    The Year in Short Stories Y-87

    The Year in the Short Story Y-88, 90–93

Shōtetsu 1381-1459 .... DLB-203

Showalter, Elaine 1941- DLB-67

Shreve, Anita 1946- DLB-292

Shteiger, Anatolii 1907-1944 .... DLB-317

Shukshin, Vasilii Makarovich 1929-1974 .... DLB-302

Shulevitz, Uri 1935- DLB-61

Shulman, Max 1919-1988.............. DLB-11

Shute, Henry A. 1856-1943 .... DLB-9

Shute, Nevil (Nevil Shute Norway) 1899-1960 .... DLB-255

Shuttle, Penelope 1947- DLB-14, 40

Shvarts, Evgenii L'vovich 1896-1958 .....DLB-272

Sibawayhi circa 750-circa 795 .... DLB-311

Sibbes, Richard 1577-1635 .... DLB-151

Sibiriak, D. (see Mamin, Dmitrii Narkisovich)

Siddal, Elizabeth Eleanor 1829-1862 .... DLB-199

Sidgwick, Ethel 1877-1970............DLB-197

Sidgwick, Henry 1838-1900........... DLB-262

Sidgwick and Jackson Limited DLB-112

Sidhwa, Bapsi 1939- DLB-323

Sidney, Margaret (see Lothrop, Harriet M.)

Sidney, Mary 1561-1621.............. DLB-167

Sidney, Sir Philip 1554-1586 .... DLB-167; CDBLB-1

    An Apologie for Poetrie (the Olney edition, 1595, of *Defence of Poesie*)........ DLB-167

Sidney's Press DLB-49

The Siege of Krishnapur, 1973 Booker Prize winner, J. G. Farrell..................... DLB-326

Sienkiewicz, Henryk 1846-1916 .... DLB-332

Sierra, Rubén 1946- DLB-122

Sierra Club Books DLB-49

Siger of Brabant circa 1240-circa 1284 ... DLB-115

Sigourney, Lydia Huntley 1791-1865.......DLB-1, 42, 73, 183, 239, 243

Silkin, Jon 1930-1997 .... DLB-27

Silko, Leslie Marmon 1948- DLB-143, 175, 256, 275

Sillanpää, Frans Eemil 1888-1964....... DLB-332

Silliman, Benjamin 1779-1864.......... DLB-183

Silliman, Ron 1946- DLB-169

Silliphant, Stirling 1918-1996 .... DLB-26

Sillitoe, Alan 1928- DLB-14, 139; CDBLB-8

    Tribute to J. B. Priestly................ Y-84

Silman, Roberta 1934- DLB-28

Silone, Ignazio (Secondino Tranquilli) 1900-1978..................... DLB-264

Silva, Beverly 1930- DLB-122

Silva, Clara 1905-1976 .... DLB-290

Silva, José Asunció 1865-1896 .... DLB-283

Silverberg, Robert 1935- DLB-8

Silverman, Kaja 1947- DLB-246

Silverman, Kenneth 1936- DLB-111

Simak, Clifford D. 1904-1988........... DLB-8

Simcoe, Elizabeth 1762-1850 .... DLB-99

Simcox, Edith Jemima 1844-1901....... DLB-190

Simcox, George Augustus 1841-1905..... DLB-35

Sime, Jessie Georgina 1868-1958 .... DLB-92

Simenon, Georges 1903-1989.......DLB-72; Y-89

Simic, Charles 1938- DLB-105

    "Images and 'Images'" DLB-105

Simionescu, Mircea Horia 1928- DLB-232

Simmel, Georg 1858-1918 ....DLB-296

Simmel, Johannes Mario 1924- DLB-69

Valentine Simmes [publishing house].....DLB-170

Simmons, Ernest J. 1903-1972 ....DLB-103

Simmons, Herbert Alfred 1930- DLB-33

Simmons, James 1933- DLB-40

Simms, William Gilmore
1806-1870 ....DLB-3, 30, 59, 73, 248

Simms and M'Intyre DLB-106

Simon, Claude 1913-2005 .....DLB-83, 332; Y-85

   Nobel Lecture Y-85

Simon, Neil 1927- DLB-7, 266

Simon and Schuster DLB-46

Simonov, Konstantin Mikhailovich
1915-1979 ....DLB-302

Simons, Katherine Drayton Mayrant
1890-1969 ....Y-83

Simović, Ljubomir 1935- DLB-181

Simpkin and Marshall
[publishing house] DLB-154

Simpson, Helen 1897-1940...........DLB-77

Simpson, John Palgrave 1807-1887.......DLB-344

Simpson, Louis 1923- DLB-5

Simpson, N. F. 1919- DLB-13

Sims, George 1923-1999 ....DLB-87; Y-99

Sims, George Robert 1847-1922...DLB-35, 70, 135

Sinán, Rogelio 1902-1994 ....DLB-145, 290

Sinclair, Andrew 1935- DLB-14

Sinclair, Bertrand William 1881-1972.....DLB-92

Sinclair, Catherine 1800-1864 ....DLB-163

Sinclair, Clive 1948- DLB-319

Sinclair, Jo 1913-1995................DLB-28

Sinclair, Lister 1921-2006..............DLB-88

Sinclair, May 1863-1946...........DLB-36, 135

   The Novels of Dorothy Richardson
(1918) DLB-36

Sinclair, Upton 1878-1968 ......DLB-9; CDALB-5

Upton Sinclair [publishing house] DLB-46

Singer, Isaac Bashevis 1904-1991
...DLB-6, 28, 52, 278, 332, 333; Y-91; CDALB-1

Singer, Israel Joshua (Yisroel-Yehoyshue Zinger)
1893-1944 ....DLB-333

Singer, Mark 1950- DLB-185

Singh, Khushwant 1915- DLB-323

Singmaster, Elsie 1879-1958 ....DLB-9

Siniavsky, Andrei (Abram Tertz)
1925-1997 ....DLB-302

Sinisgalli, Leonardo 1908-1981 ....DLB-114

Siodmak, Curt 1902-2000 ....DLB-44

Sîrbu, Ion D. 1919-1989..............DLB-232

Siringo, Charles A. 1855-1928 ....DLB-186

Sissman, L. E. 1928-1976 ....DLB-5

Sisson, C. H. 1914-2003 ....DLB-27

Sitwell, Edith 1887-1964...... DLB-20; CDBLB-7

Sitwell, Osbert 1892-1969 ....DLB-100, 195

Sivanandan, Ambalavaner 1923- DLB-323

Sixteenth-Century Spanish Epic, The DLB-318

Skácel, Jan 1922-1989 ....DLB-232

Skalbe, Kārlis 1879-1945 ....DLB-220

Skármeta, Antonio
1940- DLB-145; CDWLB-3

Skavronsky, A. (see Danilevsky, Grigorii Petrovich)

Skeat, Walter W. 1835-1912 ....DLB-184

William Skeffington [publishing house]...DLB-106

Skelton, John 1463-1529 ....DLB-136

Skelton, Robin 1925-1997 .... DLB-27, 53

Škėma, Antanas 1910-1961 ....DLB-220

Skinner, Constance Lindsay
1877-1939 ....DLB-92

Skinner, John Stuart 1788-1851 ....DLB-73

Skipsey, Joseph 1832-1903 ....DLB-35

Skou-Hansen, Tage 1925- DLB-214

Skrzynecki, Peter 1945- DLB-289

Škvorecký, Josef 1924- ...DLB-232; CDWLB-4

Slade, Bernard 1930- DLB-53

Slamnig, Ivan 1930- DLB-181

Slančeková, Božena (see Timrava)

Slataper, Scipio 1888-1915 ....DLB-264

Slater, Patrick 1880-1951 ....DLB-68

Slaveykov, Pencho 1866-1912 ....DLB-147

Slaviček, Milivoj 1929- DLB-181

Slavitt, David 1935- DLB-5, 6

Sleigh, Burrows Willcocks Arthur
1821-1869 ....DLB-99

Sleptsov, Vasilii Alekseevich 1836-1878 ...DLB-277

Slesinger, Tess 1905-1945.............DLB-102

Slessor, Kenneth 1901-1971 ....DLB-260

Slick, Sam (see Haliburton, Thomas Chandler)

Sloan, John 1871-1951 ....DLB-188

Sloane, William, Associates DLB-46

Slonimsky, Mikhail Leonidovich
1897-1972......................DLB-272

Sluchevsky, Konstantin Konstantinovich
1837-1904 ....DLB-277

Small, Maynard and Company DLB-49

Smart, Christopher 1722-1771 ....DLB-109

Smart, David A. 1892-1957 ....DLB-137

Smart, Elizabeth 1913-1986............DLB-88

Smart, J. J. C. 1920- DLB-262

Smedley, Menella Bute 1820?-1877 ......DLB-199

William Smellie [publishing house] DLB-154

Smiles, Samuel 1812-1904 ....DLB-55

Smiley, Jane 1949- DLB-227, 234

Smith, A. J. M. 1902-1980 ....DLB-88

Smith, Adam 1723-1790.......DLB-104, 252, 336

Smith, Adam (George Jerome Waldo
Goodman) 1930- DLB-185

Smith, Alexander 1829-1867 ....DLB-32, 55

   "On the Writing of Essays" (1862) DLB-57

Smith, Amanda 1837-1915............DLB-221

Smith, Anna Deavere 1950- DLB-341

Smith, Betty 1896-1972 ....Y-82

Smith, Carol Sturm 1938- Y-81

Smith, Charles Henry 1826-1903 ....DLB-11

Smith, Charlotte 1749-1806 ....DLB-39, 109

Smith, Chet 1899-1973 ....DLB-171

Smith, Cordwainer 1913-1966...........DLB-8

Smith, Dave 1942- DLB-5

   Tribute to James Dickey Y-97

   Tribute to John Gardner Y-82

Smith, Dodie 1896-1990 ....DLB-10

Smith, Doris Buchanan 1934-2002 ....DLB-52

Smith, E. E. 1890-1965 ....DLB-8

Smith, Elihu Hubbard 1771-1798........DLB-37

Smith, Elizabeth Oakes (Prince)
(see Oakes Smith, Elizabeth)

Smith, Eunice 1757-1823 ....DLB-200

Smith, F. Hopkinson 1838-1915 .... DS-13

Smith, George D. 1870-1920 ....DLB-140

Smith, George O. 1911-1981.............DLB-8

Smith, Goldwin 1823-1910 ....DLB-99

Smith, H. Allen 1907-1976 ....DLB-11, 29

Smith, Harry B. 1860-1936 ....DLB-187

Smith, Hazel Brannon 1914-1994 ....DLB-127

Smith, Henry circa 1560-circa 1591......DLB-136

Smith, Horatio (Horace)
1779-1849 ....DLB-96, 116

Smith, Iain Crichton (Iain Mac A'Ghobhainn)
1928-1998 .... DLB-40, 139, 319

Smith, J. Allen 1860-1924 ....DLB-47

Smith, James 1775-1839 ....DLB-96

Smith, Jessie Willcox 1863-1935 ....DLB-188

Smith, John 1580-1631 ....DLB-24, 30

Smith, John 1618-1652................DLB-252

Smith, Josiah 1704-1781 ....DLB-24

Smith, Ken 1938- DLB-40

Smith, Lee 1944- DLB-143; Y-83

Smith, Logan Pearsall 1865-1946.........DLB-98

Smith, Margaret Bayard 1778-1844 ......DLB-248

Smith, Mark 1935- Y-82

Smith, Michael 1698-circa 1771 ....DLB-31

Smith, Pauline 1882-1959 ....DLB-225

Smith, Red 1905-1982 .... DLB-29, 171

Smith, Roswell 1829-1892 ....DLB-79

Smith, Samuel Harrison 1772-1845 ....DLB-43

Smith, Samuel Stanhope 1751-1819 ....DLB-37

Cumulative Index

Smith, Sarah (see Stretton, Hesba)

Smith, Sarah Pogson 1774-1870........ DLB-200

Smith, Seba 1792-1868 .... DLB-1, 11, 243

Smith, Stevie 1902-1971 .... DLB-20

Smith, Sydney 1771-1845 .... DLB-107

Smith, Sydney Goodsir 1915-1975 .... DLB-27

Smith, Sir Thomas 1513-1577.......... DLB-132

Smith, Vivian 1933- DLB-325

Smith, W. Gordon 1928-1996.......... DLB-310

Smith, Wendell 1914-1972 ....DLB-171

Smith, William fl. 1595-1597 .... DLB-136

Smith, William 1727-1803............. DLB-31

    A General Idea of the College of Mirania
    (1753) [excerpts]............... DLB-31

Smith, William 1728-1793............. DLB-30

Smith, William Gardner 1927-1974....... DLB-76

Smith, William Henry 1808-1872....... DLB-159

Smith, William Jay 1918- DLB-5

Smith, Winchell 1871-1933............ DLB-341

Smith, Elder and Company DLB-154

Harrison Smith and Robert Haas
    [publishing house] DLB-46

J. Stilman Smith and Company......... DLB-49

W. B. Smith and Company............. DLB-49

W. H. Smith and Son DLB-106

Leonard Smithers [publishing house] DLB-112

Smollett, Tobias
    1721-1771 .... DLB-39, 104; CDBLB-2

    Dedication to *Ferdinand Count Fathom*
    (1753)..................... DLB-39

    Preface to *Ferdinand Count Fathom*
    (1753)..................... DLB-39

    Preface to *Roderick Random* (1748) DLB-39

Smythe, Francis Sydney 1900-1949 ..... DLB-195

Snelling, William Joseph 1804-1848 ..... DLB-202

Snellings, Rolland (see Touré, Askia Muhammad)

Snodgrass, W. D. 1926- DLB-5

Snorri Hjartarson 1906-1986 .... DLB-293

Snow, C. P.
    1905-1980 .... DLB-15, 77; DS-17; CDBLB-7

Snyder, Gary
    1930- ... DLB-5, 16, 165, 212, 237, 275, 342

Sobiloff, Hy 1912-1970 .... DLB-48

The Social Contract, Jean-Jacques
    Rousseau DLB-314

The Society for Textual Scholarship and
    TEXT...................... Y-87

The Society for the History of Authorship,
    Reading and Publishing.............. Y-92

Söderberg, Hjalmar 1869-1941......... DLB-259

Södergran, Edith 1892-1923........... DLB-259

Soffici, Ardengo 1879-1964........ DLB-114, 264

Sofola, 'Zulu 1938- DLB-157

Sokhanskaia, Nadezhda Stepanovna
    (Kokhanovskaia) 1823?-1884........DLB-277

Sokolov, Sasha (Aleksandr Vsevolodovich
    Sokolov) 1943- DLB-285

Solano, Solita 1888-1975................ DLB-4

Soldati, Mario 1906-1999.............DLB-177

Soledad (see Zamudio, Adela)

Šoljan, Antun 1932-1993 .... DLB-181

Sollers, Philippe (Philippe Joyaux)
    1936- DLB-83

Sollogub, Vladimir Aleksandrovich
    1813-1882 .... DLB-198

Sollors, Werner 1943- DBL-246

Solmi, Sergio 1899-1981 .... DLB-114

Sologub, Fedor 1863-1927 .... DLB-295

Solomon, Carl 1928- DLB-16

Solórzano, Carlos 1922- DLB-305

Soloukhin, Vladimir Alekseevich
    1924-1997................... DLB-302

Solov'ev, Sergei Mikhailovich
    1885-1942 .... DLB-295

Solov'ev, Vladimir Sergeevich
    1853-1900 .... DLB-295

Solstad, Dag 1941- DLB-297

Solway, David 1941- DLB-53

Solzhenitsyn, Aleksandr
    1918-2008 .... DLB-302, 332
    Solzhenitsyn and America Y-85

Some Basic Notes on Three Modern Genres:
    Interview, Blurb, and Obituary Y-02

Somerville, Edith Œnone 1858-1949 .... DLB-135

Something to Answer For, 1969 Booker Prize winner,
    P. H. Newby.................... DLB-326

Somov, Orest Mikhailovich 1793-1833 ... DLB-198

Sønderby, Knud 1909-1966 .... DLB-214

Sone, Monica 1919- DLB-312

Song, Cathy 1955- DLB-169, 312

Sonnevi, Göran 1939- DLB-257

Sono Ayako 1931- DLB-182

Sontag, Susan 1933-2004 .... DLB-2, 67

Sophocles 497/496 B.C.-406/405 B.C.
    ....DLB-176; CDWLB-1

Šopov, Aco 1923-1982 .... DLB-181

Sorel, Charles ca.1600-1674............DLB-268

Sørensen, Villy 1929-2001 .... DLB-214

Sorensen, Virginia 1912-1991.......... DLB-206

Sorge, Reinhard Johannes 1892-1916.... DLB-118

Sorokin, Vladimir Georgievich
    1955- DLB-285

Sorrentino, Gilbert 1929-2006 ... DLB-5, 173; Y-80

Sosa, Roberto 1930- DLB-290

Sotheby, James 1682-1742............ DLB-213

Sotheby, John 1740-1807............. DLB-213

Sotheby, Samuel 1771-1842........... DLB-213

Sotheby, Samuel Leigh 1805-1861 ...... DLB-213

Sotheby, William 1757-1833 .... DLB-93, 213

Soto, Gary 1952- DLB-82

Soueif, Ahdaf 1950- DLB-267

Souster, Raymond 1921- DLB-88

The *South English Legendary* circa
    thirteenth-fifteenth centuries DLB-146

Southerland, Ellease 1943- DLB-33

Southern, Terry 1924-1995.............. DLB-2

Southern Illinois University Press.......... Y-95

Southern Literature
    Fellowship of Southern Writers Y-98

    The Fugitives and the Agrarians:
    The First Exhibition Y-85

    "The Greatness of Southern Literature":
    League of the South Institute for the
    Study of Southern Culture and
    History Y-02

    The Society for the Study of
    Southern Literature Y-00

    Southern Writers Between the Wars ... DLB-9

Southerne, Thomas 1659-1746.......... DLB-80

Southey, Caroline Anne Bowles
    1786-1854...................... DLB-116

Southey, Robert 1774-1843...... DLB-93, 107, 142

Southwell, Robert 1561?-1595 .... DLB-167

Southworth, E. D. E. N. 1819-1899 ..... DLB-239

Sowande, Bode 1948- DLB-157

Tace Sowle [publishing house] DLB-170

Soyfer, Jura 1912-1939 .... DLB-124

Soyinka, Wole 1934-
    .... DLB-125, 332; Y-86, 87; CDWLB-3

    Nobel Lecture 1986: This Past Must
    Address Its Present Y-86

Spacks, Barry 1931- DLB-105

Spalding, Frances 1950- DLB-155

Spanish Byzantine Novel, The DLB-318

Spanish Travel Writers of the
    Late Middle Ages.............. DLB-286

Spark, Muriel
    1918-2006 .... DLB-15, 139; CDBLB-7

Michael Sparke [publishing house].......DLB-170

Sparks, Jared 1789-1866 .... DLB-1, 30, 235

Sparshott, Francis 1926- DLB-60

Späth, Gerold 1939- DLB-75

Spatola, Adriano 1941-1988........... DLB-128

Spaziani, Maria Luisa 1924- DLB-128

Specimens of Foreign Standard Literature
    1838-1842 .... DLB-1

The Spectator 1828- DLB-110

Spedding, James 1808-1881 .... DLB-144

Spee von Langenfeld, Friedrich
    1591-1635 .... DLB-164

Speght, Rachel 1597-after 1630......... DLB-126

Speke, John Hanning 1827-1864........ DLB-166

Spellman, A. B. 1935- DLB-41

Spence, Catherine Helen 1825-1910..... DLB-230

Spence, Thomas 1750-1814 . . . . .DLB-158

Spencer, Anne 1882-1975. . . . . .DLB-51, 54

Spencer, Charles, third Earl of Sunderland
  1674-1722 . . . . .DLB-213

Spencer, Elizabeth 1921- DLB-6, 218

Spencer, George John, Second Earl Spencer
  1758-1834 . . . . .DLB-184

Spencer, Herbert 1820-1903. . . . . DLB-57, 262

  "The Philosophy of Style" (1852) DLB-57

Spencer, Scott 1945- Y-86

Spender, J. A. 1862-1942 . . . . .DLB-98

Spender, Stephen 1909-1995 . . DLB-20; CDBLB-7

Spener, Philipp Jakob 1635-1705 . . . . .DLB-164

Spenser, Edmund
  circa 1552-1599 . . . . .DLB-167; CDBLB-1

  Envoy from *The Shepheardes Calender* DLB-167

  "The Generall Argument of the
    Whole Booke," from
    The Shepheardes Calender DLB-167

  "A Letter of the Authors Expounding
    His Whole Intention in the Course
    of this Worke: Which for that It
    Giueth Great Light to the Reader,
    for the Better Vnderstanding
    Is Hereunto Annexed,"
    from *The Faerie Qveene* (1590) DLB-167

  "To His Booke," from
    The Shepheardes Calender (1579) DLB-167

  "To the Most Excellent and Learned
    Both Orator and Poete, Mayster
    Gabriell Haruey, His Verie Special
    and Singular Good Frend E. K.
    Commendeth the Good Lyking of
    This His Labour, and the Patronage
    of the New Poete," from
    The Shepheardes Calender DLB-167

Sperr, Martin 1944- DLB-124

Spewack, Bella Cowen 1899-1990 . . . . . . .DLB-266

Spewack, Samuel 1899-1971 . . . . .DLB-266

Spicer, Jack 1925-1965 . . . . .DLB-5, 16, 193

Spiegelman, Art 1948- DLB-299

Spielberg, Peter 1929- Y-81

Spielhagen, Friedrich 1829-1911 . . . . .DLB-129

"*Spielmannsepen*" (circa 1152-circa 1500) . . .DLB-148

Spier, Peter 1927- DLB-61

Spillane, Mickey 1918-2006 . . . . .DLB-226

Spink, J. G. Taylor 1888-1962 . . . . .DLB-241

Spinrad, Norman 1940- DLB-8

  Tribute to Isaac Asimov Y-92

Spires, Elizabeth 1952- DLB-120

The Spirit of Laws, Claude-Adrien
  Helvétius DLB-314

The Spirit of Laws, Charles-Louis de Secondat, baron
  de Montesquieu DLB-314

Spitteler, Carl 1845-1924 . . . . .DLB-129, 332

Spivak, Lawrence E. 1900-1994 . . . . .DLB-137

Spofford, Harriet Prescott
  1835-1921 . . . . .DLB-74, 221

Sponde, Jean de 1557-1595 . . . . .DLB-327

Sports
  Jimmy, Red, and Others: Harold
    Rosenthal Remembers the Stars
    of the Press Box Y-01

  The Literature of Boxing in England
    through Arthur Conan Doyle Y-01

  Notable Twentieth-Century Books
    about Sports DLB-241

Sprigge, Timothy L. S. 1932- DLB-262

Spring, Howard 1889-1965 . . . . .DLB-191

Springs, Elliott White 1896-1959 . . . . .DLB-316

Sproxton, Birk 1943-2007 . . . . .DLB-334

Squibob (see Derby, George Horatio)

Squier, E. G. 1821-1888 . . . . .DLB-189

Staal-Delaunay, Marguerite-Jeanne Cordier de
  1684-1750 . . . . .DLB-314

Stableford, Brian 1948- DLB-261

Stacpoole, H. de Vere 1863-1951 . . . . .DLB-153

Staël, Germaine de 1766-1817 . . . . . .DLB-119, 192

Staël-Holstein, Anne-Louise Germaine de
  (see Staël, Germaine de)

Staffeldt, Schack 1769-1826 . . . . .DLB-300

Stafford, Jean 1915-1979 . . . . DLB-2, 173

Stafford, William 1914-1993 . . . . .DLB-5, 206

Stallings, Laurence 1894-1968 . . . . . DLB-7, 44, 316

Stallworthy, Jon 1935- DLB-40

Stampp, Kenneth M. 1912- DLB-17

Stănescu, Nichita 1933-1983 . . . . .DLB-232

Stanev, Emiliyan 1907-1979 . . . . .DLB-181

Stanford, Ann 1916-1987 . . . . .DLB-5

Stangerup, Henrik 1937-1998 . . . . .DLB-214

Stanihurst, Richard 1547-1618 . . . . .DLB-281

Stanitsky, N. (see Panaeva, Avdot'ia Iakovlevna)

Stankevich, Nikolai Vladimirovich
  1813-1840 . . . . .DLB-198

Stanković, Borisav ("Bora")
  1876-1927 . . . . DLB-147; CDWLB-4

Stanley, Henry M. 1841-1904 . . . . DLB-189; DS-13

Stanley, Thomas 1625-1678 . . . . .DLB-131

Stannard, Martin 1947- DLB-155

William Stansby [publishing house] DLB-170

Stanton, Elizabeth Cady 1815-1902 . . . . . . .DLB-79

Stanton, Frank L. 1857-1927 . . . . .DLB-25

Stanton, Maura 1946- DLB-120

Stapledon, Olaf 1886-1950 . . . . .DLB-15, 255

Star Spangled Banner Office DLB-49

Stark, Freya 1893-1993 . . . . .DLB-195

Starkey, Thomas circa 1499-1538 . . . . .DLB-132

Starkie, Walter 1894-1976 . . . . .DLB-195

Starkweather, David 1935- DLB-7

Starrett, Vincent 1886-1974 . . . . .DLB-187

Stationers' Company of London, The DLB-170

Statius circa A.D. 45-A.D. 96 . . . . .DLB-211

Stavis, Barrie 1906-2007 . . . . .DLB-341

Staying On, 1977 Booker Prize winner,
  Paul Scott DLB-326

Stead, Christina 1902-1983 . . . . .DLB-260

Stead, Robert J. C. 1880-1959 . . . . .DLB-92

Steadman, Mark 1930- DLB-6

Stearns, Harold E. 1891-1943 . . . . . . DLB-4; DS-15

Stebnitsky, M. (see Leskov, Nikolai Semenovich)

Stedman, Edmund Clarence 1833-1908 . . .DLB-64

Steegmuller, Francis 1906-1994 . . . . .DLB-111

Steel, Flora Annie 1847-1929 . . . . . . .DLB-153, 156

Steele, Max 1922-2005 . . . . .Y-80

Steele, Richard
  1672-1729 . . . . .DLB-84, 101; CDBLB-2

Steele, Timothy 1948- DLB-120

Steele, Wilbur Daniel 1886-1970 . . . . .DLB-86

Wallace Markfield's "Steeplechase" Y-02

Steere, Richard circa 1643-1721 . . . . .DLB-24

Stefán frá Hvítadal (Stefán Sigurðsson)
  1887-1933 . . . . .DLB-293

Stefán Guðmundsson (see Stephan G. Stephansson)

Stefán Hörður Grímsson
  1919 or 1920-2002 . . . . .DLB-293

Steffens, Lincoln 1866-1936 . . . . .DLB-303

Stefanovski, Goran 1952- DLB-181

Stegner, Wallace
  1909-1993 . . . . DLB-9, 206, 275; Y-93

Stehr, Hermann 1864-1940 . . . . .DLB-66

Steig, William 1907-2003 . . . . .DLB-61

Stein, Gertrude 1874-1946
  . . . . . . .DLB-4, 54, 86, 228; DS-15; CDALB-4

Stein, Leo 1872-1947 . . . . .DLB-4

Stein and Day Publishers DLB-46

Steinbarg, Eliezer (Eliezer Shtaynbarg)
  1880-1932 . . . . .DLB-333

Steinbeck, John 1902-1968 . . . .
  DLB-7, 9, 212, 275, 309, 332; DS-2; CDALB-5

  John Steinbeck Research Center,
    San Jose State University Y-85

  The Steinbeck Centennial Y-02

Steinem, Gloria 1934- DLB-246

Steiner, George 1929- DLB-67, 299

Steinhoewel, Heinrich 1411/1412-1479 . . .DLB-179

Steinn Steinarr (Aðalsteinn Kristmundsson)
  1908-1958 . . . . .DLB-293

Steinunn Sigurðardóttir 1950- DLB-293

Steloff, Ida Frances 1887-1989 . . . . .DLB-187

Stendhal 1783-1842 . . . . .DLB-119

Stephan G. Stephansson (Stefán Guðmundsson)
  1853-1927 . . . . .DLB-293

Stephen, Leslie 1832-1904 . . . . . . DLB-57, 144, 190

Stephen Family (Bloomsbury Group) DS-10

Stephens, A. G. 1865-1933 . . . . .DLB-230

Stephens, Alexander H. 1812-1883 . . . . . . .DLB-47

Stephens, Alice Barber 1858-1932 . . . . . . .DLB-188

Cumulative Index

Stephens, Ann 1810-1886 . . . . DLB-3, 73, 250

Stephens, Charles Asbury 1844?-1931 . . . . DLB-42

Stephens, James 1882?-1950 . . . . DLB-19, 153, 162

Stephens, John Lloyd 1805-1852 . . . DLB-183, 250

Stephens, Michael 1946- DLB-234

Stephensen, P. R. 1901-1965 . . . . DLB-260

Sterling, George 1869-1926 . . . . DLB-54

Sterling, James 1701-1763 . . . . DLB-24

Sterling, John 1806-1844 . . . . DLB-116

Stern, Gerald 1925- DLB-105

  "Living in Ruin" DLB-105

Stern, Gladys B. 1890-1973 . . . . DLB-197

Stern, Madeleine B. 1912-2007 . . . . . DLB-111, 140

Stern, Richard 1928- DLB-218; Y-87

Stern, Stewart 1922- DLB-26

Sterne, Laurence 1713-1768 . . . DLB-39; CDBLB-2

Sternheim, Carl 1878-1942 . . . . DLB-56, 118

Sternhold, Thomas ?-1549 . . . . DLB-132

Steuart, David 1747-1824 . . . . DLB-213

Stevens, Henry 1819-1886 . . . . DLB-140

Stevens, Wallace 1879-1955
 . . . . DLB-54, 342; CDALB-5

  The Wallace Stevens Society Y-99

Stevenson, Anne 1933- DLB-40

Stevenson, D. E. 1892-1973 . . . . DLB-191

Stevenson, Lionel 1902-1973 . . . . DLB-155

Stevenson, Robert Louis
 1850-1894 . . . . DLB-18, 57, 141, 156, 174;
  DS-13; CDBLB-5

  "On Style in Literature:
   Its Technical Elements" (1885) . . . DLB-57

Stewart, Donald Ogden
 1894-1980 . . . . DLB-4, 11, 26; DS-15

Stewart, Douglas 1913-1985 . . . . DLB-260

Stewart, Dugald 1753-1828 . . . . DLB-31

Stewart, George, Jr. 1848-1906 . . . . DLB-99

Stewart, George R. 1895-1980 . . . . DLB-8

Stewart, Harold 1916-1995 . . . . DLB-260

Stewart, J. I. M. (see Innes, Michael)

Stewart, Maria W. 1803?-1879 . . . . DLB-239

Stewart, Randall 1896-1964 . . . . DLB-103

Stewart, Sean 1965- DLB-251

Stewart and Kidd Company DLB-46

Sthen, Hans Christensen 1544-1610 . . . . . DLB-300

Stickney, Trumbull 1874-1904 . . . . DLB-54

Stieler, Caspar 1632-1707 . . . . DLB-164

Stifter, Adalbert 1805-1868 . . DLB-133; CDWLB-2

Stiles, Ezra 1727-1795 . . . . DLB-31

Still, James 1906-2001 . . . . DLB-9; Y-01

Stirling, S. M. 1953- DLB-251

Stirner, Max 1806-1856 . . . . DLB-129

Stith, William 1707-1755 . . . . DLB-31

Stivens, Dal 1911-1997 . . . . DLB-260

Elliot Stock [publishing house] DLB-106

Stockton, Annis Boudinot 1736-1801 . . . . DLB-200

Stockton, Frank R. 1834-1902 . .DLB-42, 74; DS-13

Stockton, J. Roy 1892-1972 . . . . DLB-241

Ashbel Stoddard [publishing house] DLB-49

Stoddard, Charles Warren 1843-1909 . . . DLB-186

Stoddard, Elizabeth 1823-1902 . . . . DLB-202

Stoddard, Richard Henry
 1825-1903 . . . . DLB-3, 64, 250; DS-13

Stoddard, Solomon 1643-1729 . . . . DLB-24

Stoker, Bram
 1847-1912 . . . . DLB-36, 70, 178; CDBLB-5

  On Writing *Dracula,* from the
   Introduction to *Dracula* (1897) DLB-178

  Dracula (Documentary) DLB-304

Frederick A. Stokes Company DLB-49

Stokes, Rose Pastor 1879-1933 . . . . DLB-345

Stokes, Thomas L. 1898-1958 . . . . DLB-29

Stokesbury, Leon 1945- DLB-120

Stolberg, Christian Graf zu 1748-1821 . . . . DLB-94

Stolberg, Friedrich Leopold Graf zu
 1750-1819 . . . . DLB-94

Stone, Lucy 1818-1893 . . . . DLB-79, 239

Stone, Melville 1848-1929 . . . . DLB-25

Stone, Robert 1937- DLB-152

Stone, Ruth 1915- DLB-105

Stone, Samuel 1602-1663 . . . . DLB-24

Stone, William Leete 1792-1844 . . . . DLB-202

Herbert S. Stone and Company DLB-49

Stone and Kimball DLB-49

Stoppard, Tom
 1937- DLB-13, 233; Y-85; CDBLB-8

  Playwrights and Professors DLB-13

Storey, Anthony 1928- DLB-14

Storey, David 1933- . . DLB-13, 14, 207, 245, 326

Storm, Theodor
 1817-1888 . . . . DLB-129; CDWLB-2

Storni, Alfonsina 1892-1938 . . . . DLB-283

Story, Thomas circa 1670-1742 . . . . DLB-31

Story, William Wetmore 1819-1895 . . . DLB-1, 235

Storytelling: A Contemporary Renaissance . . . Y-84

Stoughton, William 1631-1701 . . . . DLB-24

Stout, Rex 1886-1975 . . . . DLB-306

Stow, John 1525-1605 . . . . DLB-132

Stow, Randolph 1935- DLB-260

Stowe, Harriet Beecher 1811-1896 . . . . . DLB-1,12,
  42, 74, 189, 239, 243; CDALB-3

  The Harriet Beecher Stowe Center Y-00

Stowe, Leland 1899-1994 . . . . DLB-29

Stoyanov, Dimitr Ivanov (see Elin Pelin)

Strabo 64/63 B.C.-circa A.D. 25 . . . . DLB-176

Strachey, Lytton 1880-1932 . . . . . DLB-149; DS-10

Preface to *Eminent Victorians* DLB-149

William Strahan [publishing house] DLB-154

Strahan and Company DLB-106

Strand, Mark 1934- DLB-5

The Strasbourg Oaths 842 . . . . DLB-148

Stratemeyer, Edward 1862-1930 . . . . DLB-42

Strati, Saverio 1924- DLB-177

Stratton and Barnard DLB-49

Stratton-Porter, Gene 1863-1924 . . DLB-221; DS-14

Straub, Peter 1943- Y-84

Strauß, Botho 1944- DLB-124

Strauß, David Friedrich 1808-1874 . . . . . DLB-133

Strauss, Jennifer 1933- DLB-325

The Strawberry Hill Press DLB-154

Strawson, P. F. 1919-2006 . . . . DLB-262

Streatfeild, Noel 1895-1986 . . . . DLB-160

Street, Cecil John Charles (see Rhode, John)

Street, G. S. 1867-1936 . . . . DLB-135

Street and Smith DLB-49

Streeter, Edward 1891-1976 . . . . DLB-11

Streeter, Thomas Winthrop 1883-1965 . . DLB-140

Stretton, Hesba 1832-1911 . . . . DLB-163, 190

Stribling, T. S. 1881-1965 . . . . DLB-9

Der Stricker circa 1190-circa 1250 . . . . . . DLB-138

Strickland, Samuel 1804-1867 . . . . DLB-99

Strindberg, August 1849-1912 . . . . DLB-259

Stringer, Arthur 1874-1950 . . . . DLB-92

Stringer and Townsend DLB-49

Strittmatter, Erwin 1912-1994 . . . . DLB-69

Strniša, Gregor 1930-1987 . . . . DLB-181

Strode, William 1630-1645 . . . . DLB-126

Strong, L. A. G. 1896-1958 . . . . DLB-191

Strother, David Hunter (Porte Crayon)
 1816-1888 . . . . DLB-3, 248

Strouse, Jean 1945- DLB-111

Strugatsky, Arkadii Natanovich
 1925- DLB-302

Strugatsky, Boris Natanovich 1933- . . . DLB-302

Strype, John 1643-1737 . . . . DLB-336

Stuart, Dabney 1937- DLB-105

  "Knots into Webs: Some
   Autobiographical Sources" DLB-105

Stuart, Gilbert 1743-1786 . . . . DLB-336

Stuart, Jesse 1906-1984 . . . . . . DLB-9, 48, 102; Y-84

Lyle Stuart [publishing house] DLB-46

Stuart, Ruth McEnery 1849?-1917 . . . . . DLB-202

Stub, Ambrosius 1705-1758 . . . . DLB-300

Stubbs, Harry Clement (see Clement, Hal)

Stubenberg, Johann Wilhelm von
 1619-1663 . . . . DLB-164

Stuckenberg, Viggo 1763-1905 . . . . DLB-300

Studebaker, William V. 1947- DLB-256

Studies in American Jewish Literature Y-02	Sutherland, Efua Theodora 1924-1996 . . . DLB-117	Szabó, Magda 1917-2007 . . . . DLB-215
Studio DLB-112	Sutherland, John 1919-1956 . . . . DLB-68	Sze, Arthur 1950- DLB-342
Stukeley, William 1687-1765 . . . . DLB-336	Sutro, Alfred 1863-1933 . . . . DLB-10	Szymborska, Wisława
Stump, Al 1916-1995 . . . . DLB-241	Sutzkever, Abraham (Avrom Sutzkever)	1923- DLB-232, 332; Y-96; CDWLB-4
Sturgeon, Theodore 1918-1985 . . . . DLB-8; Y-85	1913- DLB-333	Nobel Lecture 1996:
Sturges, Preston 1898-1959 . . . . DLB-26	Svava Jakobsdóttir 1930- DLB-293	The Poet and the World Y-96
Styron, William 1925-2006	Svendsen, Hanne Marie 1933- DLB-214	**T**
. . . . DLB-2, 143, 299; Y-80; CDALB-6	Svevo, Italo (Ettore Schmitz)	
Tribute to James Dickey Y-97	1861-1928 . . . . DLB-264	Taban lo Liyong 1939?- DLB-125
Suard, Jean-Baptiste-Antoine	Swados, Harvey 1920-1972 . . . . DLB-2, 335	al-Tabari 839-923 . . . . DLB-311
1732-1817 . . . . DLB-314	Swain, Charles 1801-1874 . . . . DLB-32	Tablada, José Juan 1871-1945 . . . . DLB-290
Suárez, Clementina 1902-1991 . . . . DLB-290	Swallow Press DLB-46	*Le Tableau de Paris*, Louis-Sébastien
Suárez, Mario 1925- DLB-82	Swan Sonnenschein Limited DLB-106	Mercier DLB-314
Suassuna, Ariano 1927- DLB-307	Swanberg, W. A. 1907-1992 . . . . DLB-103	Tabori, George 1914-2007 . . . . DLB-245
Such, Peter 1939- DLB-60	Swedish Literature	Tabucchi, Antonio 1943- DLB-196
Suckling, Sir John 1609-1641? DLB-58, 126	The Literature of the Modern	Taché, Joseph-Charles 1820-1894 . . . . DLB-99
Suckow, Ruth 1892-1960 . . . . DLB-9, 102	Breakthrough DLB-259	Tachihara Masaaki 1926-1980 . . . . DLB-182
Sudermann, Hermann 1857-1928 . . . . . . DLB-118	Swenson, May 1919-1989 . . . . DLB-5	Tacitus circa A.D. 55-circa A.D. 117
Sue, Eugène 1804-1857 . . . . DLB-119	Swerling, Jo 1897-1964 . . . . DLB-44	. . . . DLB-211; CDWLB-1
Sue, Marie-Joseph (see Sue, Eugène)	Swift, Graham 1949- DLB-194, 326	Tadijanović, Dragutin 1905-2007 . . . . DLB-181
Suetonius circa A.D. 69-post A.D. 122 . . . . . DLB-211	Swift, Jonathan	Tafdrup, Pia 1952- DLB-214
Suggs, Simon (see Hooper, Johnson Jones)	1667-1745 . . . . DLB-39, 95, 101; CDBLB-2	Tafolla, Carmen 1951- DLB-82
Sui Sin Far (see Eaton, Edith Maude)	Swinburne, A. C.	Taggard, Genevieve 1894-1948 . . . . DLB-45
Suits, Gustav 1883-1956 . . . . DLB-220; CDWLB-4	1837-1909 . . . . DLB-35, 57; CDBLB-4	Taggart, John 1942- DLB-193
Sukenick, Ronald 1932-2004 . . . . . . DLB-173; Y-81	Under the Microscope (1872) DLB-35	Tagger, Theodor (see Bruckner, Ferdinand)
An Author's Response Y-82	Swineshead, Richard floruit circa 1350 . . . DLB-115	Tagore, Rabindranath 1861-1941 . . . DLB-323, 332
Sukhovo-Kobylin, Aleksandr Vasil'evich	Swinnerton, Frank 1884-1982 . . . . DLB-34	Taher, Bahaa' 1935- DLB-346
1817-1903 . . . . DLB-277	Swisshelm, Jane Grey 1815-1884 . . . . DLB-43	Taiheiki late fourteenth century DLB-203
Suknaski, Andrew 1942- DLB-53	Swope, Herbert Bayard 1882-1958 . . . . DLB-25	Tait, J. Selwin, and Sons DLB-49
Sullam, Sara Copio circa 1592-1641 . . . DLB-339	Swords, James ?-1844 . . . . DLB-73	*Tait's Edinburgh Magazine* 1832-1861 . . . . . . DLB-110
Sullivan, Alan 1868-1947 . . . . DLB-92	Swords, Thomas 1763-1843 . . . . DLB-73	The Takarazaka Revue Company Y-91
Sullivan, C. Gardner 1886-1965 . . . . DLB-26	T. and J. Swords and Company DLB-49	al-Takarli, Fuad 1927-2008 . . . . DLB-346
Sullivan, Frank 1892-1976 . . . . DLB-11	Swynnerton, Thomas (John Roberts)	Talander (see Bohse, August)
Sully Prudhomme (René François-Armand	circa 1500-1554 . . . . DLB-281	Talese, Gay 1932- DLB-185
Prudhomme) 1839-1907 . . . . DLB-332	Sykes, Ella C. ?-1939 . . . . DLB-174	Tribute to Irwin Shaw Y-84
Sulte, Benjamin 1841-1923 . . . . DLB-99	Sylvester, Josuah 1562 or 1563-1618 . . . . . DLB-121	Talev, Dimitr 1898-1966 . . . . DLB-181
Sulzberger, Arthur Hays 1891-1968 . . . . . . DLB-127	Symonds, Emily Morse (see Paston, George)	Taliaferro, H. E. 1811-1875 . . . . DLB-202
Sulzberger, Arthur Ochs 1926- DLB-127	Symonds, John Addington	Tallent, Elizabeth 1954- DLB-130
Sulzer, Johann Georg 1720-1779 . . . . DLB-97	1840-1893 . . . . DLB-57, 144	TallMountain, Mary 1918-1994 . . . . DLB-193
Sumarokov, Aleksandr Petrovich	"Personal Style" (1890) DLB-57	Talvj 1797-1870 . . . . DLB-59, 133
1717-1777 . . . . DLB-150	Symons, A. J. A. 1900-1941 . . . . DLB-149	Tamási, Áron 1897-1966 . . . . DLB-215
Summers, Hollis 1916-1987 . . . . DLB-6	Symons, Arthur 1865-1945 . . . . . . DLB-19, 57, 149	Tamer, Zakaria 1931- DLB-346
Sumner, Charles 1811-1874 . . . . DLB-235	Symons, Julian 1912-1994 . . . . . . DLB-87, 155; Y-92	Tammsaare, A. H.
Sumner, William Graham 1840-1910 . . . . . DLB-270	Julian Symons at Eighty Y-92	1878-1940 . . . . DLB-220; CDWLB-4
Henry A. Sumner	Symons, Scott 1933- DLB-53	Tan, Amy 1952- DLB-173, 312; CDALB-7
[publishing house] DLB-49	Synge, John Millington	Tandori, Dezső 1938- DLB-232
Sundman, Per Olof 1922-1992 . . . . DLB-257	1871-1909 . . . . DLB-10, 19; CDBLB-5	Tanner, Thomas 1673/1674-1735 . . . . DLB-213
Supervielle, Jules 1884-1960 . . . . DLB-258	Synge Summer School: J. M. Synge	Tanizaki Jun'ichirō 1886-1965 . . . . DLB-180
Surtees, Robert Smith 1803-1864 . . . . DLB-21	and the Irish Theater, Rathdrum,	Tapahonso, Luci 1953- DLB-175
The R. S. Surtees Society Y-98	County Wiclow, Ireland Y-93	The Mark Taper Forum DLB-7
Sutcliffe, Matthew 1550?-1629 . . . . DLB-281	Syrett, Netta 1865-1943 . . . . DLB-135, 197	Taradash, Daniel 1913-2003 . . . . DLB-44
Sutcliffe, William 1971- DLB-271	*The System of Nature,* Paul Henri Thiry,	Tarasov-Rodionov, Aleksandr Ignat'evich
	baron d'Holbach (as Jean-Baptiste	1885-1938 . . . . DLB-272
	de Mirabaud) DLB-314	
	Szabó, Lőrinc 1900-1957 . . . . DLB-215	

Tarbell, Ida M. 1857-1944 . . . . DLB-47	Tendriakov, Vladimir Fedorovich 1923-1984 . . . . DLB-302	Off Broadway and Off-Off Broadway . . DLB-7
Tardieu, Jean 1903-1995 . . . . DLB-321	Tenn, William 1919- DLB-8	Oregon Shakespeare Festival Y-00
Tardivel, Jules-Paul 1851-1905 . . . . DLB-99	Tennant, Emma 1937- DLB-14	Plays, Playwrights, and Playgoers DLB-84
Targan, Barry 1932- DLB-130	Tenney, Tabitha Gilman 1762-1837 . . . DLB-37, 200	Playwrights on the Theater DLB-80
Tribute to John Gardner Y-82	Tennyson, Alfred 1809-1892. . . DLB-32; CDBLB-4	Playwrights and Professors DLB-13
Tarkington, Booth 1869-1946 . . . . DLB-9, 102	On Some of the Characteristics of Modern Poetry and On the Lyrical Poems of Alfred Tennyson (1831) DLB-32	Producing *Dear Bunny, Dear Volodya: The Friendship and the Feud* Y-97
Tashlin, Frank 1913-1972 . . . . DLB-44		Viewpoint: Politics and Performance, by David Edgar DLB-13
Tasma (Jessie Couvreur) 1848-1897 . . . . DLB-230		
Tassoni, Alessandro 1565-1635 . . . . DLB-339		Writing for the Theatre, by Harold Pinter DLB-13
Tate, Allen 1899-1979 . . . . DLB-4, 45, 63; DS-17	Tennyson, Frederick 1807-1898 . . . . DLB-32	
Tate, James 1943- DLB-5, 169	Tenorio, Arthur 1924- DLB-209	The Year in Drama Y-82–85, 87–98
Tate, Nahum circa 1652-1715 . . . . DLB-80	"The Tenth Stage," Marie-Jean-Antoine-Nicolas Caritat, marquis de Condorcet. DLB-314	The Year in U.S. Drama Y-00
Tatian circa 830 . . . . DLB-148		Theater, English and Irish Anti-Theatrical Tracts DLB-263
Taufer, Veno 1933- DLB-181	Tepl, Johannes von circa 1350-1414/1415 . . . . DLB-179	
Tauler, Johannes circa 1300-1361 . . . . . . .DLB-179		The Chester Plays circa 1505-1532; revisions until 1575 . . . . DLB-146
Tavares, Salette 1922-1994 . . . . DLB-287	Tepliakov, Viktor Grigor'evich 1804-1842 . . . . DLB-205	
Tavčar, Ivan 1851-1923 . . . . DLB-147		Dangerous Years: London Theater, 1939-1945 . . . . DLB-10
Taverner, Richard ca. 1505-1575 . . . . DLB-236	Terence circa 184 B.C.-159 B.C. or after DLB-211; CDWLB-1	
Taylor, Ann 1782-1866 . . . . DLB-163		A Defense of Actors DLB-263
Taylor, Bayard 1825-1878 . . . . DLB-3, 189, 250	St. Teresa of Ávila 1515-1582 . . . . DLB-318	The Development of Lighting in the Staging of Drama, 1900-1945 . . . . DLB-10
Taylor, Bert Leston 1866-1921 . . . . DLB-25	Terhune, Albert Payson 1872-1942 . . . . DLB-9	
Taylor, Charles H. 1846-1921 . . . . DLB-25	Terhune, Mary Virginia 1830-1922 . . . . . . .DS-13	Education DLB-263
Taylor, Edward circa 1642-1729 . . . . DLB-24	Terpigorev, Sergei Nikolaevich (S. Atava) 1841-1895 .DLB-277	The End of English Stage Censorship, 1945-1968 . . . . DLB-13
Taylor, Elizabeth 1912-1975 . . . . DLB-139		
Taylor, Sir Henry 1800-1886 . . . . DLB-32	Terry, Megan 1932- DLB-7, 249	Epigrams and Satires DLB-263
Taylor, Henry 1942- DLB-5	Terson, Peter 1932- DLB-13	Eyewitnesses and Historians DLB-263
Who Owns American Literature Y-94	Tesich, Steve 1943-1996 . . . . Y-83	Fringe and Alternative Theater in Great Britain DLB-13
Taylor, Jane 1783-1824 . . . . DLB-163	Tessa, Delio 1886-1939 . . . . DLB-114	
Taylor, Jeremy circa 1613-1667 . . . . DLB-151	Testi, Fulvio 1593-1646 . . . . DLB-339	The Great War and the Theater, 1914-1918 [Great Britain] DLB-10
Taylor, John 1577 or 1578 - 1653 . . . . DLB-121	Testori, Giovanni 1923-1993 . . . . .DLB-128, 177	
Taylor, Mildred D. 1943- DLB-52		Licensing Act of 1737 . . . . DLB-84
Taylor, Peter 1917-1994 . . . . DLB-218, 278; Y-81, 94	Texas The Year in Texas Literature Y-98	Morality Plays: *Mankind* circa 1450-1500 and *Everyman* circa 1500 . . . . DLB-146
Taylor, Susie King 1848-1912 . . . . DLB-221		
Taylor, Tom 1817-1880 . . . . DLB-344	Tey, Josephine 1896?-1952 . . . . DLB-77	The New Variorum Shakespeare Y-85
Taylor, William Howland 1901-1966 . . . . DLB-241	Thacher, James 1754-1844 . . . . DLB-37	N-Town Plays circa 1468 to early sixteenth century DLB-146
William Taylor and Company DLB-49	Thacher, John Boyd 1847-1909 . . . . DLB-187	
Teale, Edwin Way 1899-1980 . . . . .DLB-275	Thackeray, William Makepeace 1811-1863 . . DLB-21, 55, 159, 163; CDBLB-4	Politics and the Theater DLB-263
Teasdale, Sara 1884-1933 . . . . DLB-45		Practical Matters DLB-263
Teffi, Nadezhda 1872-1952 . . . . DLB-317	Thames and Hudson Limited DLB-112	Prologues, Epilogues, Epistles to Readers, and Excerpts from Plays DLB-263
Teillier, Jorge 1935-1996 . . . . DLB-283	Thanet, Octave (see French, Alice)	
Telles, Lygia Fagundes 1924- DLB-113, 307	Thaxter, Celia Laighton 1835-1894 . . . . DLB-239	The Publication of English Renaissance Plays DLB-62
The Temper of the West: William Jovanovich Y-02		
Temple, Sir William 1555?-1627 . . . . DLB-281	Thayer, Caroline Matilda Warren 1785-1844 . . . . DLB-200	Regulations for the Theater DLB-263
Temple, Sir William 1628-1699 . . . . DLB-101		Sources for the Study of Tudor and Stuart Drama DLB-62
Temple, William F. 1914-1989 . . . . DLB-255	Thayer, Douglas H. 1929- DLB-256	
Temrizov, A. (see Marchenko, Anastasia Iakovlevna)	Theater Black Theatre: A Forum [excerpts] . . . DLB-38	Stage Censorship: "The Rejected Statement" (1911), by Bernard Shaw [excerpts] DLB-10
Tench, Watkin ca. 1758-1833 . . . . DLB-230		
Tencin, Alexandrine-Claude Guérin de 1682-1749 . . . . DLB-314	Community and Commentators: Black Theatre and Its Critics DLB-38	Synge Summer School: J. M. Synge and the Irish Theater, Rathdrum, County Wiclow, Ireland Y-93
	German Drama from Naturalism to Fascism: 1889-1933 . . . . DLB-118	
Tender Is the Night (Documentary) DLB-273		The Theater in Shakespeare's Time . . DLB-62
	A Look at the Contemporary Black Theatre Movement DLB-38	The Theatre Guild DLB-7
		The Townely Plays fifteenth and sixteenth centuries DLB-146
	The Lord Chamberlain's Office and Stage Censorship in England DLB-10	
		The Year in British Drama Y-99–01
	New Forces at Work in the American Theatre: 1915-1925 . . . . DLB-7	The Year in Drama: London Y-90
		The Year in London Theatre Y-92
		A Yorkshire Tragedy DLB-58

Theaters
 The Abbey Theatre and Irish Drama,
  1900-1945..................DLB-10
 Actors Theatre of Louisville.........DLB-7
 American Conservatory Theatre.......DLB-7
 Arena Stage......................DLB-7
 Black Theaters and Theater
  Organizations in America,
  1961-1982: A Research List......DLB-38
 The Dallas Theater Center..........DLB-7
 Eugene O'Neill Memorial Theater
  Center....................DLB-7
 The Goodman Theatre..............DLB-7
 The Guthrie Theater DLB-7
 The Mark Taper Forum DLB-7
 The National Theatre and the Royal
  Shakespeare Company: The
  National Companies...........DLB-13
 Off-Loop Theatres.................DLB-7
 The Royal Court Theatre and the
  English Stage Company DLB-13
 The Royal Court Theatre and the
  New Drama DLB-10
 The Takarazaka Revue Company........Y-91

Thegan and the Astronomer
 fl. circa 850 ....DLB-148

Thelwall, John 1764-1834 ....DLB-93, 158

Theocritus circa 300 B.C.-260 B.C........DLB-176

Theodorescu, Ion N. (see Arghezi, Tudor)

Theodulf circa 760-circa 821 ....DLB-148

Theophrastus circa 371 B.C.-287 B.C......DLB-176

Thériault, Yves 1915-1983...............DLB-88

Thério, Adrien 1925- DLB-53

Theroux, Paul 1941- DLB-2, 218; CDALB-7

Thesiger, Wilfred 1910-2003..........DLB-204

They All Came to Paris.................DS-15

Thibaudeau, Colleen 1925- DLB-88

Thiele, Colin 1920-2006 ....DLB-289

Thielen, Benedict 1903-1965...........DLB-102

Thiong'o Ngugi wa (see Ngugi wa Thiong'o)

Thiroux d'Arconville, Marie-Geneviève
 1720-1805 ....DLB-314

This Quarter 1925-1927, 1929-1932 ....DS-15

Thoma, Ludwig 1867-1921 ....DLB-66

Thoma, Richard 1902-1974..............DLB-4

Thomas, Audrey 1935- DLB-60

Thomas, Brandon 1848-1914 ....DLB-344

Thomas, D. M.
 1935- ... DLB-40, 207, 299; Y-82; CDBLB-8
 The Plagiarism Controversy............Y-82

Thomas, Dylan
 1914-1953.......DLB-13, 20, 139; CDBLB-7
 The Dylan Thomas Celebration........Y-99

Thomas, Ed 1961- DLB-310

Thomas, Edward
 1878-1917..........DLB-19, 98, 156, 216
 The Friends of the Dymock Poets......Y-00

Thomas, Frederick William 1806-1866...DLB-202

Thomas, Gwyn 1913-1981 ....DLB-15, 245

Thomas, Isaiah 1750-1831....... DLB-43, 73, 187

Thomas, Johann 1624-1679............DLB-168

Thomas, John 1900-1932................DLB-4

Thomas, Joyce Carol 1938- DLB-33

Thomas, Lewis 1913-1993.............DLB-275

Thomas, Lorenzo 1944- DLB-41

Thomas, Norman 1884-1968............DLB-303

Thomas, R. S. 1915-2000 .....DLB-27; CDBLB-8

Isaiah Thomas [publishing house]........DLB-49

Thomasîn von Zerclære
 circa 1186-circa 1259..............DLB-138

Thomason, George 1602?-1666.........DLB-213

Thomasius, Christian 1655-1728.........DLB-168

Thompson, Daniel Pierce 1795-1868.....DLB-202

Thompson, David 1770-1857............DLB-99

Thompson, Dorothy 1893-1961 ....DLB-29

Thompson, E. P. 1924-1993 ....DLB-242

Thompson, Flora 1876-1947 ....DLB-240

Thompson, Francis
 1859-1907..............DLB-19; CDBLB-5

Thompson, George Selden (see Selden, George)

Thompson, Henry Yates 1838-1928 .....DLB-184

Thompson, Hunter S. 1939-2005 ....DLB-185

Thompson, Jim 1906-1977............DLB-226

Thompson, John 1938-1976.............DLB-60

Thompson, John R. 1823-1873 ....DLB-3, 73, 248

Thompson, Judith 1954- DLB-334

Thompson, Lawrance 1906-1973........DLB-103

Thompson, Maurice 1844-1901 ...... DLB-71, 74

Thompson, Ruth Plumly 1891-1976 ....DLB-22

Thompson, Thomas Phillips 1843-1933 ...DLB-99

Thompson, William 1775-1833 ....DLB-158

Thompson, William Tappan
 1812-1882 ....DLB-3, 11, 248

Thomson, Cockburn
 "Modern Style" (1857) [excerpt]......DLB-57

Thomson, Edward William 1849-1924....DLB-92

Thomson, James 1700-1748.............DLB-95

Thomson, James 1834-1882 ....DLB-35

Thomson, Joseph 1858-1895...........DLB-174

Thomson, Mortimer 1831-1875.........DLB-11

Thomson, Rupert 1955- DLB-267

Thon, Melanie Rae 1957- DLB-244

Thor Vilhjálmsson 1925-..............DLB-293

Þórarinn Eldjárn 1949- DLB-293

Þórbergur Þórðarson 1888-1974 ....DLB-293

Thoreau, Henry David 1817-1862 ... DLB-1, 183,
     223, 270, 298; DS-5; CDALB-2

The Thoreau Society Y-99

The Thoreauvian Pilgrimage: The
 Structure of an American Cult...DLB-223

Thorne, William 1568?-1630...........DLB-281

Thornton, John F.
 [Response to Ken Auletta]............Y-97

Thorpe, Adam 1956- DLB-231

Thorpe, Thomas Bangs
 1815-1878 ....DLB-3, 11, 248

Thorup, Kirsten 1942- DLB-214

Thotl, Birgitte 1610-1662..............DLB-300

Thrale, Hester Lynch
 (see Piozzi, Hester Lynch [Thrale])

The Three Marias: A Landmark Case in
 Portuguese Literary History
 (Maria Isabel Barreno, 1939-   ;
 Maria Teresa Horta, 1937-   ;
 Maria Velho da Costa, 1938-   ).....DLB-287

Thubron, Colin 1939- DLB-204, 231

Thucydides
 circa 455 B.C.-circa 395 B.C.........DLB-176

Thulstrup, Thure de 1848-1930 ....DLB-188

Thümmel, Moritz August von
 1738-1817 ....DLB-97

Thurber, James
 1894-1961.....DLB-4, 11, 22, 102; CDALB-5

Thurman, Wallace 1902-1934 ....DLB-51
 "Negro Poets and Their Poetry"..... DLB-50

Thwaite, Anthony 1930- DLB-40
 The Booker Prize, Address Y-86

Thwaites, Reuben Gold 1853-1913........DLB-47

Tibullus circa 54 B.C.-circa 19 B.C........DLB-211

Ticknor, George 1791-1871.....DLB-1, 59, 140, 235

Ticknor and Fields....................DLB-49

Ticknor and Fields (revived) DLB-46

Tieck, Ludwig 1773-1853.....DLB-90; CDWLB-2

Tietjens, Eunice 1884-1944 ....DLB-54

Tikkanen, Märta 1935- DLB-257

Tilghman, Christopher circa 1948.......DLB-244

Tilney, Edmund circa 1536-1610........DLB-136

Charles Tilt [publishing house] DLB-106

J. E. Tilton and Company DLB-49

Time-Life Books DLB-46

Times Books DLB-46

Timothy, Peter circa 1725-1782 ....DLB-43

Timrava 1867-1951 ....DLB-215

Timrod, Henry 1828-1867............DLB-3, 248

Tindal, Henrietta 1818?-1879 ....DLB-199

Tindal, Nicholas 1688-1774 ....DLB-336

Tinker, Chauncey Brewster 1876-1963 ....DLB-140

Tinsley Brothers DLB-106

Tiptree, James, Jr. 1915-1987 ....DLB-8

Tišma, Aleksandar 1924-2003 ....DLB-181

Titus, Edward William
 1870-1952 ....DLB-4; DS-15

Tiutchev, Fedor Ivanovich 1803-1873 ....DLB-205

381

Tlali, Miriam 1933- DLB-157, 225

Todd, Barbara Euphan 1890-1976 ...... DLB-160

Todorov, Tzvetan 1939- DLB-242

Tofte, Robert
  1561 or 1562-1619 or 1620 .... DLB-172

Tóibín, Colm 1955- DLB-271

Toklas, Alice B. 1877-1967 .... DLB-4; DS-15

Tokuda Shūsei 1872-1943............. DLB-180

Toland, John 1670-1722 .... DLB-252, 336

Tolkien, J. R. R.
  1892-1973...... DLB-15, 160, 255; CDBLB-6

Toller, Ernst 1893-1939................. DLB-124

Tollet, Elizabeth 1694-1754............. DLB-95

Tolson, Melvin B. 1898-1966 .... DLB-48, 76

Tolstaya, Tatyana 1951- DLB-285

Tolstoy, Aleksei Konstantinovich
  1817-1875 .... DLB-238

Tolstoy, Aleksei Nikolaevich 1883-1945 .. DLB-272

Tolstoy, Leo 1828-1910................. DLB-238

Tomalin, Claire 1933- DLB-155

Tómas Guðmundsson 1901-1983 ..... DLB-293

Tomasi di Lampedusa, Giuseppe
  1896-1957......................DLB-177

Tomlinson, Charles 1927- DLB-40

Tomlinson, H. M. 1873-1958 ....DLB-36, 100, 195

Abel Tompkins [publishing house] DLB-49

Tompson, Benjamin 1642-1714.......... DLB-24

Tomson, Graham R.
  (see Watson, Rosamund Marriott)

Ton'a 1289-1372 .... DLB-203

Tondelli, Pier Vittorio 1955-1991 .... DLB-196

Tonks, Rosemary 1932- DLB-14, 207

Tonna, Charlotte Elizabeth 1790-1846 ... DLB-163

Jacob Tonson the Elder
  [publishing house] DLB-170

Toole, John Kennedy 1937-1969............ Y-81

Toomer, Jean 1894-1967 ... DLB-45, 51; CDALB-4

Topsoe, Vilhelm 1840-1881 .... DLB-300

Tor Books.......................... DLB-46

Torberg, Friedrich 1908-1979 .... DLB-85

Torga, Miguel (Adolfo Correira da Rocha)
  1907-1995.....................DLB-287

Torre, Francisco de la ?-? DLB-318

Torrence, Ridgely 1874-1950 .... DLB-54, 249

Torrente Ballester, Gonzalo
  1910-1999.....................DLB-322

Torres-Metzger, Joseph V. 1933- DLB-122

Torres Naharro, Bartolomé de
  1485?-1523?.....................DLB-318

El Tostado (see Madrigal, Alfonso Fernández de)

Toth, Susan Allen 1940- Y-86

Richard Tottell [publishing house] DLB-170

  "The Printer to the Reader,"
    (1557) DLB-167

Tough-Guy Literature................. DLB-9

Touré, Askia Muhammad 1938- DLB-41

Tourgée, Albion W. 1838-1905.......... DLB-79

Tournemir, Elizaveta Sailhas de (see Tur, Evgeniia)

Tourneur, Cyril circa 1580-1626......... DLB-58

Tournier, Michel 1924- DLB-83

Frank Tousey [publishing house] DLB-49

Tower Publications DLB-46

Towers, Joseph 1737-1799 .... DLB-336

Towne, Benjamin circa 1740-1793........ DLB-43

Towne, Robert 1936- DLB-44

The Townely Plays fifteenth and sixteenth
  centuries....................... DLB-146

Townsend, Sue 1946- DLB-271

Townshend, Aurelian
  by 1583-circa 1651.............. DLB-121

Toy, Barbara 1908-2001 .... DLB-204

Tozzi, Federigo 1883-1920 .... DLB-264

Tracy, Honor 1913-1989................. DLB-15

Traherne, Thomas 1637?-1674......... DLB-131

Traill, Catharine Parr 1802-1899 .... DLB-99

Train, Arthur 1875-1945.......... DLB-86; DS-16

Tranquilli, Secondino (see Silone, Ignazio)

The Transatlantic Publishing Company ... DLB-49

The Transatlantic Review 1924-1925..........DS-15

The Transcendental Club
  1836-1840 ....DLB-1; DLB-223

Transcendentalism DLB-1; DLB-223; DS-5

  "A Response from America," by
    John A. Heraud..................DS-5

  Publications and Social Movements.... DLB-1

  The Rise of Transcendentalism,
    1815-1860 .... DS-5

  Transcendentalists, American...........DS-5

  "What Is Transcendentalism? By a
    Thinking Man," by James
    Kinnard Jr.....................DS-5

transition 1927-1938 ....DS-15

Translations (Vernacular) in the Crowns of
  Castile and Aragon 1352-1515...... DLB-286

Tranströmer, Tomas 1931- DLB-257

Tranter, John 1943- DLB-289

Traubel, Horace 1858-1919 .... DLB-345

Travel Writing
  American Travel Writing, 1776-1864
    (checklist)................. DLB-183

  British Travel Writing, 1940-1997
    (checklist)................. DLB-204

  Travel Writers of the Late
    Middle Ages DLB-286

  (1876-1909) DLB-174

  (1837-1875).................... DLB-166

  (1910-1939) DLB-195

Traven, B. 1882?/1890?-1969? DLB-9, 56

Travers, Ben 1886-1980 .... DLB-10, 233

Travers, P. L. (Pamela Lyndon)
  1899-1996 .... DLB-160

Trediakovsky, Vasilii Kirillovich
  1703-1769.................... DLB-150

Treece, Henry 1911-1966............ DLB-160

Treitel, Jonathan 1959- DLB-267

Trejo, Ernesto 1950-1991 .... DLB-122

Trelawny, Edward John
  1792-1881.............DLB-110, 116, 144

Tremain, Rose 1943- DLB-14, 271

Tremblay, Michel 1942- DLB-60

Trenchard, John 1662-1723............. DLB-336

Trent, William P. 1862-1939.........DLB-47, 71

Trescot, William Henry 1822-1898 ...... DLB-30

Tressell, Robert (Robert Phillipe Noonan)
  1870-1911....................DLB-197

Trevelyan, Sir George Otto
  1838-1928 .... DLB-144

Trevisa, John circa 1342-circa 1402 ..... DLB-146

Trevisan, Dalton 1925- DLB-307

Trevor, William 1928- DLB-14, 139

Triana, José 1931- DLB-305

Trierer Floyris circa 1170-1180........... DLB-138

Trifonov, Iurii Valentinovich
  1925-1981 .... DLB-302

Trillin, Calvin 1935- DLB-185

Trilling, Lionel 1905-1975........... DLB-28, 63

Trilussa 1871-1950 .... DLB-114

Trimmer, Sarah 1741-1810 .... DLB-158

Triolet, Elsa 1896-1970 .... DLB-72

Tripp, John 1927- DLB-40

Trocchi, Alexander 1925-1984 .... DLB-15

Troisi, Dante 1920-1989.............. DLB-196

Trollope, Anthony
  1815-1882 ....DLB-21, 57, 159; CDBLB-4

  Novel-Reading: *The Works of Charles
    Dickens; The Works of W. Makepeace
    Thackeray* (1879) DLB-21

  The Trollope Societies Y-00

Trollope, Frances 1779-1863......... DLB-21, 166

Trollope, Joanna 1943- DLB-207

Troop, Elizabeth 1931- DLB-14

Tropicália DLB-307

Trotter, Catharine 1679-1749 .... DLB-84, 252

Trotti, Lamar 1898-1952 .... DLB-44

Trottier, Pierre 1925- DLB-60

Trotzig, Birgitta 1929- DLB-257

Troupe, Quincy Thomas, Jr. 1943- DLB-41

John F. Trow and Company........... DLB-49

Trowbridge, John Townsend 1827-1916 .. DLB-202

Trudel, Jean-Louis 1967- DLB-251

True History of the Kelly Gang, 2001 Booker Prize winner,
  Peter Carey DLB-326

Truillier-Lacombe, Joseph-Patrice 1807-1863 ....DLB-99	Turner, Frederick Jackson 1861-1932 .... DLB-17, 186	Underhill, Evelyn 1875-1941 ....DLB-240
Trumbo, Dalton 1905-1976 ....DLB-26	A Conversation between William Riggan and Janette Turner Hospital Y-02	Undset, Sigrid 1882-1949 .... DLB-297, 332
Trumbull, Benjamin 1735-1820 ....DLB-30	Turner, Joseph Addison 1826-1868 ....DLB-79	Ungaretti, Giuseppe 1888-1970 ....DLB-114
Trumbull, John 1750-1831 ....DLB-31	Turpin, Waters Edward 1910-1968 ....DLB-51	Unger, Friederike Helene 1741-1813 ....DLB-94
Trumbull, John 1756-1843 ....DLB-183	Turrini, Peter 1944- DLB-124	United States Book Company DLB-49
Trunk, Yehiel Teshaia (Yekhiel Yeshayda Trunk) 1888-1961 ....DLB-333	Tusquets, Esther 1936- DLB-322	Universal Publishing and Distributing Corporation DLB-46
Truth, Sojourner 1797?-1883 ....DLB-239	Tutuola, Amos 1920-1997 ...DLB-125; CDWLB-3	University of Colorado Special Collections at the University of Colorado at Boulder................Y-98
Tscherning, Andreas 1611-1659.........DLB-164	Twain, Mark (see Clemens, Samuel Langhorne)	
Tsubouchi Shōyō 1859-1935 ....DLB-180	Tweedie, Ethel Brilliana circa 1860-1940 .... DLB-174	Indiana University Press Y-02
Tsvetaeva, Marina Ivanovna 1892-1941 ....DLB-295	A Century of Poetry, a Lifetime of Collecting: J. M. Edelstein's Collection of Twentieth- Century American Poetry............ YB-02	The University of Iowa Writers' Workshop Golden Jubilee Y-86
Tuchman, Barbara W. Tribute to Alfred A. Knopf Y-84		University of Missouri Press Y-01
Tucholsky, Kurt 1890-1935 ....DLB-56	Twombly, Wells 1935-1977 ....DLB-241	University of South Carolina The G. Ross Roy Scottish Poetry Collection....................Y-89
Tucker, Charlotte Maria 1821-1893 ....DLB-163, 190	Twysden, Sir Roger 1597-1672..........DLB-213	
Tucker, George 1775-1861 ....DLB-3, 30, 248	Tyard, Pontus de 1521?-1605 ....DLB-327	Two Hundred Years of Rare Books and Literary Collections at the University of South Carolina Y-00
Tucker, James 1808?-1866? DLB-230	Ty-Casper, Linda 1931- DLB-312	
Tucker, Nathaniel Beverley 1784-1851 ....DLB-3, 248	Tyler, Anne 1941- DLB-6, 143; Y-82; CDALB-7	The University of South Carolina Press Y-94
	Tyler, Mary Palmer 1775-1866..........DLB-200	University of Virginia The Book Arts Press at the University of Virginia Y-96
Tucker, St. George 1752-1827 ....DLB-37	Tyler, Moses Coit 1835-1900......... DLB-47, 64	
Tuckerman, Frederick Goddard 1821-1873 ....DLB-243	Tyler, Royall 1757-1826 ....DLB-37	The Electronic Text Center and the Electronic Archive of Early American Fiction at the University of Virginia Library........................Y-98
	Tylor, Edward Burnett 1832-1917 ....DLB-57	
Tuckerman, Henry Theodore 1813-1871 ....DLB-64	Tynan, Katharine 1861-1931........DLB-153, 240	
Tumas, Juozas (see Vaizgantas)	Tyndale, William circa 1494-1536.......DLB-132	University of Virginia Libraries Y-91
Tunis, John R. 1889-1975........... DLB-22, 171	Tynes, Maxine 1949- DLB-334	University of Wales Press DLB-112
Tunstall, Cuthbert 1474-1559 ....DLB-132	Tyree, Omar 1969- DLB-292	University Press of Florida Y-00
Tunström, Göran 1937-2000 ....DLB-257	**U**	University Press of Kansas Y-98
Tuohy, Frank 1925-1999 ....DLB-14, 139		University Press of Mississippi Y-99
Tupper, Martin F. 1810-1889 ....DLB-32	Uchida, Yoshiko 1921-1992...DLB-312; CDALB-7	Unnur Benediktsdóttir Bjarklind (see Hulda)
Tur, Evgeniia 1815-1892 ....DLB-238	Udall, Nicholas 1504-1556 ....DLB-62	Uno Chiyo 1897-1996 ....DLB-180
al-Turabi, Hasan 1932- DLB-346	Ugrešić, Dubravka 1949- DLB-181	Unruh, Fritz von 1885-1970.........DLB-56, 118
Turbyfill, Mark 1896-1991................DLB-45	Uhland, Ludwig 1787-1862 ....DLB-90	Unsworth, Barry 1930- DLB-194, 326
Turco, Lewis 1934- Y-84	Uhse, Bodo 1904-1963 ....DLB-69	Unt, Mati 1944- DLB-232
Tribute to John Ciardi................Y-86	Ujević, Augustin "Tin" 1891-1955 ....DLB-147	The Unterberg Poetry Center of the 92nd Street Y Y-98
Turgenev, Aleksandr Ivanovich 1784-1845 ....DLB-198		
	Ulenhart, Niclas fl. circa 1600 ....DLB-164	Untermeyer, Louis 1885-1977 ....DLB-303
Turgenev, Ivan Sergeevich 1818-1883 ....DLB-238	Ulfeldt, Leonora Christina 1621-1698....DLB-300	T. Fisher Unwin [publishing house]......DLB-106
Turgot, baron de l'Aulne, Anne-Robert-Jacques 1727-1781 ....DLB-314	Ulibarrí, Sabine R. 1919-2003 ....DLB-82	Upchurch, Boyd B. (see Boyd, John)
	Ulica, Jorge 1870-1926................DLB-82	Updike, John 1932- DLB-2, 5, 143, 218, 227; Y-80, 82; DS-3; CDALB-6
"Memorandum on Local Government" DLB-314	Ulitskaya, Liudmila Evgen'evna 1943- DLB-285	John Updike on the Internet Y-97
Turini Bufalini, Francesca 1553-1641.....DLB-339	Ulivi, Ferruccio 1912- DLB-196	Tribute to Alfred A. Knopf Y-84
Turnbull, Alexander H. 1868-1918 ......DLB-184	Ulizio, B. George 1889-1969 ....DLB-140	Tribute to John Ciardi.................Y-86
Turnbull, Andrew 1921-1970...........DLB-103	Ulrich von Liechtenstein circa 1200-circa 1275 ....DLB-138	Upīts, Andrejs 1877-1970 ....DLB-220
Turnbull, Gael 1928-2004 ....DLB-40		Uppdal, Kristofer 1878-1961 ....DLB-297
Turnèbe, Odet de 1552-1581 ....DLB-327	Ulrich von Zatzikhoven before 1194-after 1214..............DLB-138	Upton, Bertha 1849-1912 ....DLB-141
Turner, Arlin 1909-1980 ....DLB-103		Upton, Charles 1948- DLB-16
Turner, Charles (Tennyson) 1808-1879 ....DLB-32	'Umar ibn Abi Rabi'ah 644-712 or 721 ...DLB-311	Upton, Florence K. 1873-1922..........DLB-141
	Unaipon, David 1872-1967 ....DLB-230	Upward, Allen 1863-1926 ....DLB-36
Turner, Ethel 1872-1958................DLB-230	Unamuno, Miguel de 1864-1936....DLB-108, 322	Urban, Milo 1904-1982................DLB-215
Turner, Frederick 1943- DLB-40	Under, Marie 1883-1980 ....DLB-220; CDWLB-4	Ureña de Henríquez, Salomé 1850-1897 ..DLB-283

Urfé, Honoré d' 1567-1625 . . . . DLB-268
Urista, Alberto Baltazar (see Alurista)
Urquhart, Fred 1912-1995 . . . . DLB-139
Urquhart, Jane 1949- DLB-334
Urrea, Luis Alberto 1955- DLB-209
Urzidil, Johannes 1896-1970 . . . . DLB-85
U.S.A. (Documentary) DLB-274
Usigli, Rodolfo 1905-1979 . . . . DLB-305
Usk, Thomas died 1388 . . . . DLB-146
Uslar Pietri, Arturo 1906-2001 . . . . DLB-113
Uspensky, Gleb Ivanovich
  1843-1902 . . . . DLB-277
Ussher, James 1581-1656 . . . . DLB-213
Ustinov, Peter 1921-2004 . . . . DLB-13
Uttley, Alison 1884-1976 . . . . DLB-160
Uz, Johann Peter 1720-1796 . . . . DLB-97

V

Vadianus, Joachim 1484-1551 . . . . DLB-179
Vac, Bertrand (Aimé Pelletier) 1914- DLB-88
Vācietis, Ojārs 1933-1983 . . . . DLB-232
Vaculík, Ludvík 1926- DLB-232
Vaičiulaitis, Antanas 1906-1992 . . . . DLB-220
Vaičiūnaite, Judita 1937- DLB-232
Vail, Laurence 1891-1968 . . . . DLB-4
Vail, Petr L'vovich 1949- DLB-285
Vailland, Roger 1907-1965 . . . . DLB-83
Vaižgantas 1869-1933 . . . . DLB-220
Vajda, Ernest 1887-1954 . . . . DLB-44
Valdés, Alfonso de circa 1490?-1532 . . . . DLB-318
Valdés, Gina 1943- DLB-122
Valdes, Juan de 1508-1541 . . . . DLB-318
Valdez, Luis Miguel 1940- DLB-122
Valduga, Patrizia 1953- DLB-128
Vale Press DLB-112
Valente, José Angel 1929-2000 . . . . DLB-108
Valenzuela, Luisa 1938- . . DLB-113; CDWLB-3
Valera, Diego de 1412-1488 . . . . DLB-286
Valeri, Diego 1887-1976 . . . . DLB-128
Valerius Flaccus fl. circa A.D. 92 . . . . DLB-211
Valerius Maximus fl. circa A.D. 31 . . . . . . DLB-211
Valéry, Paul 1871-1945 . . . . DLB-258
Valesio, Paolo 1939- DLB-196
Valgardson, W. D. 1939- DLB-60
Valle, Luz 1899-1971 . . . . DLB-290
Valle, Víctor Manuel 1950- DLB-122
Valle-Inclán, Ramón del
  1866-1936 . . . . DLB-134, 322
Vallejo, Armando 1949- DLB-122
Vallejo, César Abraham 1892-1938 . . . . . DLB-290
Vallès, Jules 1832-1885 . . . . DLB-123

Vallette, Marguerite Eymery (see Rachilde)
Valverde, José María 1926-1996 . . . . DLB-108
Vampilov, Aleksandr Valentinovich (A. Sanin)
  1937-1972 . . . . DLB-302
Van Allsburg, Chris 1949- DLB-61
Van Anda, Carr 1864-1945 . . . . DLB-25
Vanbrugh, Sir John 1664-1726 . . . . DLB-80
Vance, Jack 1916?- DLB-8
Vančura, Vladislav
  1891-1942 . . . . DLB-215; CDWLB-4
Vanderhaege, Guy 1951- DLB-334
van der Post, Laurens 1906-1996 . . . . . . DLB-204
Van Dine, S. S. (see Wright, Willard Huntington)
Van Doren, Mark 1894-1972 . . . . . DLB-45, 335
van Druten, John 1901-1957 . . . . DLB-10
Van Duyn, Mona 1921-2004 . . . . DLB-5
  Tribute to James Dickey Y-97
Van Dyke, Henry 1852-1933 . . . . . DLB-71; DS-13
Van Dyke, Henry 1928- DLB-33
Van Dyke, John C. 1856-1932 . . . . DLB-186
Vane, Sutton 1888-1963 . . . . DLB-10
Van Gieson, Judith 1941- DLB-306
Vanguard Press DLB-46
van Gulik, Robert Hans 1910-1967 . . . . . . DS-17
van Herk, Aritha 1954- DLB-334
van Itallie, Jean-Claude 1936- DLB-7
Van Loan, Charles E. 1876-1919 . . . . DLB-171
Vann, Robert L. 1879-1940 . . . . DLB-29
Van Rensselaer, Mariana Griswold
  1851-1934 . . . . DLB-47
Van Rensselaer, Mrs. Schuyler
  (see Van Rensselaer, Mariana Griswold)
Van Vechten, Carl 1880-1964 . . . . . . DLB-4, 9, 51
van Vogt, A. E. 1912-2000 . . . . DLB-8, 251
Varela, Blanca 1926- DLB-290
Vargas Llosa, Mario
  1936- DLB-145; CDWLB-3
  Acceptance Speech for the Ritz Paris
    Hemingway Award Y-85
Varley, John 1947- Y-81
Varnhagen von Ense, Karl August
  1785-1858 . . . . DLB-90
Varnhagen von Ense, Rahel
  1771-1833 . . . . DLB-90
Varro 116 B.C.-27 B.C. DLB-211
Vasilenko, Svetlana Vladimirovna
  1956- DLB-285
Vasiliu, George (see Bacovia, George)
Vásquez, Richard 1928- DLB-209
Vassa, Gustavus (see Equiano, Olaudah)
Vassalli, Sebastiano 1941- DLB-128, 196
Vassanji, M. G. 1950- DLB-334
Vaugelas, Claude Favre de 1585-1650 . . . DLB-268

Vaughan, Henry 1621-1695 . . . . DLB-131
Vaughan, Thomas 1621-1666 . . . . DLB-131
Vaughn, Robert 1592?-1667 . . . . DLB-213
Vaux, Thomas, Lord 1509-1556 . . . . DLB-132
Vazov, Ivan 1850-1921 . . . . . . DLB-147; CDWLB-4
Vázquez Montalbán, Manuel
  1939- DLB-134, 322
Véa, Alfredo, Jr. 1950- DLB-209
Veblen, Thorstein 1857-1929 . . . . DLB-246
Vedel, Anders Sørensen 1542-1616 . . . . . DLB-300
Vega, Janine Pommy 1942- DLB-16
Veiller, Anthony 1903-1965 . . . . DLB-44
Velásquez-Trevino, Gloria 1949- DLB-122
Veley, Margaret 1843-1887 . . . . DLB-199
Velleius Paterculus
  circa 20 B.C.-circa A.D. 30 . . . . DLB-211
Veloz Maggiolo, Marcio 1936- DLB-145
Vel'tman, Aleksandr Fomich
  1800-1870 . . . . DLB-198
Venegas, Daniel ?-? DLB-82
Venevitinov, Dmitrii Vladimirovich
  1805-1827 . . . . DLB-205
Verbitskaia, Anastasiia Alekseevna
  1861-1928 . . . . DLB-295
Verde, Cesário 1855-1886 . . . . DLB-287
Vergil, Polydore circa 1470-1555 . . . . DLB-132
Veríssimo, Erico 1905-1975 . . . . DLB-145, 307
Verlaine, Paul 1844-1896 . . . . DLB-217
Vernacular Translations in the Crowns of
  Castile and Aragon 1352-1515 . . . . . DLB-286
Verne, Jules 1828-1905 . . . . DLB-123
Vernon God Little, 2003 Booker Prize winner,
  DBC Pierre DLB-326
Verplanck, Gulian C. 1786-1870 . . . . DLB-59
Vertinsky, Aleksandr 1889-1957 . . . . DLB-317
Very, Jones 1813-1880 . . . . DLB-1, 243; DS-5
Vesaas, Halldis Moren 1907-1995 . . . . . . DLB-297
Vesaas, Tarjei 1897-1970 . . . . DLB-297
Vian, Boris 1920-1959 . . . . DLB-72, 321
Viazemsky, Petr Andreevich
  1792-1878 . . . . DLB-205
Vicars, Thomas 1591-1638 . . . . DLB-236
Vicente, Gil 1465-1536/1540? DLB-287, 318
Vickers, Roy 1888?-1965 . . . . DLB-77
Vickery, Sukey 1779-1821 . . . . DLB-200
Victoria 1819-1901 . . . . DLB-55
Victoria Press DLB-106
La vida de Lazarillo de Tormes DLB-318
Vidal, Gore 1925- DLB-6, 152; CDALB-7
Vidal, Mary Theresa 1815-1873 . . . . DLB-230
Vidmer, Richards 1898-1978 . . . . DLB-241
Viebig, Clara 1860-1952 . . . . DLB-66

Vieira, António, S. J. (Antonio Vieyra) 1608-1697 .... DLB-307

Viereck, George Sylvester 1884-1962 ..... DLB-54

Viereck, Peter 1916-2006 .... DLB-5

Vietnam War (ended 1975)
Resources for the Study of Vietnam War Literature DLB-9

Viets, Roger 1738-1811 .... DLB-99

Vigil-Piñon, Evangelina 1949- DLB-122

Vigneault, Gilles 1928- DLB-60

Vigny, Alfred de 1797-1863 .... DLB-119, 192, 217

Vigolo, Giorgio 1894-1983 .... DLB-114

Vik, Bjorg 1935- DLB-297

The Viking Press DLB-46

Vila-Matas, Enrique 1948- DLB-322

Vilde, Eduard 1865-1933 .... DLB-220

Vilinskaia, Mariia Aleksandrovna (see Vovchok, Marko)

Villa, José García 1908-1997 .... DLB-312

Villanueva, Alma Luz 1944- DLB-122

Villanueva, Tino 1941- DLB-82

Villard, Henry 1835-1900 .... DLB-23

Villard, Oswald Garrison 1872-1949 ... DLB-25, 91

Villarreal, Edit 1944- DLB-209

Villarreal, José Antonio 1924- DLB-82

Villaseñor, Victor 1940- DLB-209

Villedieu, Madame de (Marie-Catherine Desjardins) 1640?-1683 .... DLB-268

Villegas, Antonio de ?-? DLB-318

Villegas de Magnón, Leonor 1876-1955 .... DLB-122

Villehardouin, Geoffroi de circa 1150-1215 .... DLB-208

Villemaire, Yolande 1949- DLB-60

Villena, Enrique de ca. 1382/84-1432 .... DLB-286

Villena, Luis Antonio de 1951- DLB-134

Villiers, George, Second Duke of Buckingham 1628-1687 .... DLB-80

Villiers de l'Isle-Adam, Jean-Marie Mathias Philippe-Auguste, Comte de 1838-1889 .... DLB-123, 192

Villon, François 1431-circa 1463? DLB-208

Vinaver, Michel (Michel Grinberg) 1927- DLB-321

Vine Press DLB-112

Viorst, Judith 1931- DLB-52

Vipont, Elfrida (Elfrida Vipont Foulds, Charles Vipont) 1902-1992 .... DLB-160

Viramontes, Helena María 1954- DLB-122

Virgil 70 B.C.-19 B.C. DLB-211; CDWLB-1

Vischer, Friedrich Theodor 1807-1887 .... DLB-133

Vitier, Cintio 1921- DLB-283

Vitrac, Roger 1899-1952 .... DLB-321

Vitruvius circa 85 B.C.-circa 15 B.C. DLB-211

Vitry, Philippe de 1291-1361 .... DLB-208

Vittorini, Elio 1908-1966 .... DLB-264

Vivanco, Luis Felipe 1907-1975 .... DLB-108

Vives, Juan Luis 1493-1540 .... DLB-318

Vivian, E. Charles (Charles Henry Cannell, Charles Henry Vivian, Jack Mann, Barry Lynd) 1882-1947 .... DLB-255

Viviani, Cesare 1947- DLB-128

Vivien, Renée 1877-1909 .... DLB-217

Vizenor, Gerald 1934- DLB-175, 227

Vizetelly and Company DLB-106

Vladimov, Georgii 1931-2003 .... DLB-302

Voaden, Herman 1903-1991 .... DLB-88

Voß, Johann Heinrich 1751-1826 .... DLB-90

Vogau, Boris Andreevich (see Pil'niak, Boris Andreevich)

Vogel, Paula 1951- DLB-341

Voigt, Ellen Bryant 1943- DLB-120

Voinovich, Vladimir Nikolaevich 1932- DLB-302

Vojnović, Ivo 1857-1929 ..... DLB-147; CDWLB-4

Vold, Jan Erik 1939- DLB-297

Volkoff, Vladimir 1932-2005 .... DLB-83

P. F. Volland Company DLB-46

Vollbehr, Otto H. F. 1872?-1945 or 1946 .... DLB-187

Vologdin (see Zasodimsky, Pavel Vladimirovich)

Voloshin, Maksimilian Aleksandrovich 1877-1932 .... DLB-295

Volponi, Paolo 1924-1994 .... DLB-177

Voltaire (François-Marie Arouet) 1694-1778 .... DLB-314

"An account of the death of the chevalier de La Barre" DLB-314

Candide DLB-314

Philosophical Dictionary DLB-314

Vonarburg, Élisabeth 1947- DLB-251

von der Grün, Max 1926- DLB-75

Vonnegut, Kurt 1922-2007 .... DLB-2, 8, 152; Y-80; DS-3; CDALB-6

Tribute to Isaac Asimov Y-92

Tribute to Richard Brautigan Y-84

Voranc, Prežihov 1893-1950 .... DLB-147

Voronsky, Aleksandr Konstantinovich 1884-1937 .... DLB-272

Vorse, Mary Heaton 1874-1966 .... DLB-303

Vovchok, Marko 1833-1907 .... DLB-238

Voynich, E. L. 1864-1960 .... DLB-197

Vroman, Mary Elizabeth circa 1924-1967 .... DLB-33

W

Wace, Robert ("Maistre") circa 1100-circa 1175 .... DLB-146

Wackenroder, Wilhelm Heinrich 1773-1798 .... DLB-90

Wackernagel, Wilhelm 1806-1869 .... DLB-133

Waddell, Helen 1889-1965 .... DLB-240

Waddington, Miriam 1917-2004 .... DLB-68

Wade, Henry 1887-1969 .... DLB-77

Wagenknecht, Edward 1900-2004 .... DLB-103

Wägner, Elin 1882-1949 .... DLB-259

Wagner, Heinrich Leopold 1747-1779 ..... DLB-94

Wagner, Henry R. 1862-1957 .... DLB-140

Wagner, Richard 1813-1883 .... DLB-129

Wagoner, David 1926- DLB-5, 256

Wah, Fred 1939- DLB-60

Waiblinger, Wilhelm 1804-1830 .... DLB-90

Wain, John 1925-1994
.... DLB-15, 27, 139, 155; CDBLB-8
Tribute to J. B. Priestly Y-84

Wainwright, Jeffrey 1944- DLB-40

Waite, Peirce and Company DLB-49

Wakeman, Stephen H. 1859-1924 .... DLB-187

Wakoski, Diane 1937- DLB-5

Walahfrid Strabo circa 808-849 .... DLB-148

Henry Z. Walck [publishing house] DLB-46

Walcott, Derek 1930- DLB-117, 332; Y-81, 92; CDWLB-3
Nobel Lecture 1992: The Antilles: Fragments of Epic Memory Y-92

Robert Waldegrave [publishing house] ... DLB-170

Waldis, Burkhard circa 1490-1556? DLB-178

Waldman, Anne 1945- DLB-16

Waldrop, Rosmarie 1935- DLB-169

Walker, Alice 1900-1982 .... DLB-201

Walker, Alice 1944- DLB-6, 33, 143; CDALB-6

Walker, Annie Louisa (Mrs. Harry Coghill) circa 1836-1907 .... DLB-240

Walker, George F. 1947- DLB-60

Walker, John Brisben 1847-1931 .... DLB-79

Walker, Joseph A. 1935-2003 .... DLB-38

Walker, Kath (see Oodgeroo of the Tribe Noonuccal)

Walker, Margaret 1915-1998 .... DLB-76, 152

Walker, Obadiah 1616-1699 .... DLB-281

Walker, Ted 1934-2004 .... DLB-40

Walker, Evans and Cogswell Company DLB-49

Wall, John F. (see Sarban)

Wallace, Alfred Russel 1823-1913 ...... DLB-190

Wallace, Dewitt 1889-1981 .... DLB-137

Wallace, Edgar 1875-1932 .... DLB-70

Wallace, Lew 1827-1905 .... DLB-202

Wallace, Lila Acheson 1889-1984 .... DLB-137

"A Word of Thanks," From the Initial Issue of Reader's Digest (February 1922) DLB-137

Wallace, Naomi 1960- DLB-249

Cumulative Index

Wallace Markfield's "Steeplechase" Y-02
Wallace-Crabbe, Chris 1934- DLB-289
Wallant, Edward Lewis
   1926-1962 .... DLB-2, 28, 143, 299
Waller, Edmund 1606-1687 .... DLB-126
Walling, William English 1877-1936 ..... DLB-345
Walpole, Horace 1717-1797 ..... DLB-39, 104, 213
   Preface to the First Edition of
     The Castle of Otranto (1764) DLB-39, 178
   Preface to the Second Edition of
     The Castle of Otranto (1765) DLB-39, 178
Walpole, Hugh 1884-1941 .... DLB-34
Walrond, Eric 1898-1966 .... DLB-51
Walser, Martin 1927- DLB-75, 124
Walser, Robert 1878-1956 .... DLB-66
Walsh, Ernest 1895-1926 .... DLB-4, 45
Walsh, Robert 1784-1859 .... DLB-59
Walters, Henry 1848-1931 .... DLB-140
Waltharius circa 825 .... DLB-148
Walther von der Vogelweide
   circa 1170-circa 1230 .... DLB-138
Walton, Izaak
   1593-1683 .... DLB-151, 213; CDBLB-1
Walwicz, Ania 1951- DLB-325
Wambaugh, Joseph 1937- DLB-6; Y-83
Wand, Alfred Rudolph 1828-1891 ...... DLB-188
Wandor, Michelene 1940- DLB-310
Waniek, Marilyn Nelson 1946- DLB-120
Wanley, Humphrey 1672-1726 .... DLB-213
War of the Words (and Pictures):
   The Creation of a Graphic Novel Y-02
Warburton, William 1698-1779 .... DLB-104
Ward, Aileen 1919- DLB-111
Ward, Artemus (see Browne, Charles Farrar)
Ward, Arthur Henry Sarsfield (see Rohmer, Sax)
Ward, Douglas Turner 1930- DLB-7, 38
Ward, Mrs. Humphry 1851-1920........ DLB-18
Ward, James 1843-1925 .... DLB-262
Ward, Lynd 1905-1985................. DLB-22
Ward, Lock and Company............. DLB-106
Ward, Nathaniel circa 1578-1652 .... DLB-24
Ward, Theodore 1902-1983 .... DLB-76, 341
Wardle, Ralph 1909-1988 .... DLB-103
Ware, Henry, Jr. 1794-1843 .... DLB-235
Ware, William 1797-1852 .... DLB-1, 235
Warfield, Catherine Ann 1816-1877 ..... DLB-248
Waring, Anna Letitia 1823-1910 .... DLB-240
Frederick Warne and Company [U.K.].... DLB-106
Frederick Warne and Company [U.S.]..... DLB-49
Warner, Anne 1869-1913 .... DLB-202
Warner, Charles Dudley 1829-1900 ...... DLB-64
Warner, Marina 1946- DLB-194

Warner, Rex 1905-1986 .... DLB-15
Warner, Susan 1819-1885.... DLB-3, 42, 239, 250
Warner, Sylvia Townsend
   1893-1978................... DLB-34, 139
Warner, William 1558-1609 ....DLB-172
Warner Books...................... DLB-46
Warr, Bertram 1917-1943 .... DLB-88
Warren, John Byrne Leicester
   (see De Tabley, Lord)
Warren, Josiah 1798-1874 .... DLB-345
Warren, Lella 1899-1982 .... Y-83
Warren, Mercy Otis 1728-1814 ..... DLB-31, 200
Warren, Robert Penn 1905-1989
   ....DLB-2, 48, 152, 320; Y-80, 89; CDALB-6
   Tribute to Katherine Anne Porter Y-80
Warren, Samuel 1807-1877 .... DLB-190
Warszawski, Oser (Oyzer Varshavski)
   1898-1944 .... DLB-333
Die Wartburgkrieg circa 1230-circa 1280 ... DLB-138
Warton, Joseph 1722-1800 ....DLB-104, 109
Warton the Younger, Thomas
   1728-1790..............DLB-104, 109, 336
Warung, Price (William Astley)
   1855-1911 .... DLB-230
Washington, Booker T. 1856?-1915 ..... DLB-345
Washington, George 1732-1799 .... DLB-31
Washington, Ned 1901-1976........... DLB-265
Wassermann, Jakob 1873-1934......... DLB-66
Wasserstein, Wendy 1950-2006 .... DLB-228
Wassmo, Herbjørg 1942- DLB-297
Wasson, David Atwood 1823-1887 ... DLB-1, 223
Watanna, Onoto (see Eaton, Winnifred)
Waten, Judah 1911?-1985............. DLB-289
Waterhouse, Keith 1929- DLB-13, 15
Waterman, Andrew 1940- DLB-40
Waters, Frank 1902-1995 ....DLB-212; Y-86
Waters, Michael 1949- DLB-120
Watkins, Tobias 1780-1855............ DLB-73
Watkins, Vernon 1906-1967 .... DLB-20
Watmough, David 1926- DLB-53
Watson, Colin 1920-1983.............DLB-276
Watson, Ian 1943- DLB-261
Watson, James Wreford (see Wreford, James)
Watson, John 1850-1907.............. DLB-156
Watson, Rosamund Marriott
   (Graham R. Tomson) 1860-1911 .... DLB-240
Watson, Sheila 1909-1998 .... DLB-60
Watson, Thomas 1545?-1592.......... DLB-132
Watson, Wilfred 1911-1998 .... DLB-60
W. J. Watt and Company............. DLB-46
Watten, Barrett 1948- DLB-193
Watterson, Henry 1840-1921 .... DLB-25
Watts, Alan 1915-1973 .... DLB-16

Watts, Isaac 1674-1748 .... DLB-95
Franklin Watts [publishing house] DLB-46
Waugh, Alec 1898-1981 .... DLB-191
Waugh, Auberon 1939-2000 ... DLB-14, 194; Y-00
Waugh, Evelyn 1903-1966
   ....DLB-15, 162, 195; CDBLB-6
Way and Williams DLB-49
Wayman, Tom 1945- DLB-53
Wearne, Alan 1948- DLB-325
Weatherly, Tom 1942- DLB-41
Weaver, Gordon 1937- DLB-130
Weaver, Robert 1921-2008 .... DLB-88
Webb, Beatrice 1858-1943 .... DLB-190
Webb, Francis 1925-1973 .... DLB-260
Webb, Frank J. fl. 1857 .... DLB-50
Webb, James Watson 1802-1884 .... DLB-43
Webb, Mary 1881-1927 .... DLB-34
Webb, Phyllis 1927- DLB-53
Webb, Sidney 1859-1947 .... DLB-190
Webb, Walter Prescott 1888-1963 ....DLB-17
Webbe, William ?-1591 .... DLB-132
Webber, Charles Wilkins
   1819-1856?.................... DLB-202
Weber, Max 1864-1920 .... DLB-296
Webling, Lucy (Lucy Betty MacRaye)
   1877-1952..................... DLB-240
Webling, Peggy (Arthur Weston)
   1871-1949..................... DLB-240
Webster, Augusta 1837-1894........ DLB-35, 240
Webster, John
   1579 or 1580-1634? DLB-58; CDBLB-1
   The Melbourne Manuscript........... Y-86
Webster, Noah
   1758-1843......... DLB-1, 37, 42, 43, 73, 243
Webster, Paul Francis 1907-1984........ DLB-265
Charles L. Webster and Company DLB-49
Weckherlin, Georg Rodolf 1584-1653 ... DLB-164
Wedekind, Frank
   1864-1918 ....DLB-118; CDWLB-2
Weeks, Edward Augustus, Jr.
   1898-1989 ....DLB-137
Weeks, Stephen B. 1865-1918...........DLB-187
Weems, Mason Locke 1759-1825 ...DLB-30, 37, 42
Weerth, Georg 1822-1856 .... DLB-129
Weidenfeld and Nicolson DLB-112
Weidman, Jerome 1913-1998 .... DLB-28
Weigl, Bruce 1949- DLB-120
Weil, Jiří 1900-1959 .... DLB-299
Weinbaum, Stanley Grauman
   1902-1935 .... DLB-8
Weiner, Andrew 1949- DLB-251
Weintraub, Stanley 1929- DLB-111; Y82
Weise, Christian 1642-1708 .... DLB-168
Weisenborn, Gunther 1902-1969 .... DLB-69, 124

Weiss, John 1818-1879 . . . . DLB-1, 243

Weiss, Paul 1901-2002 . . . . DLB-279

Weiss, Peter 1916-1982 . . . . DLB-69, 124

Weiss, Theodore 1916-2003 . . . . DLB-5

Weissenberg, Isaac Meir (Yitskhok-Meyer Vaysenberg)
1878-1938 . . . . DLB-333

Weiß, Ernst 1882-1940 . . . . DLB-81

Weiße, Christian Felix 1726-1804 . . . . DLB-97

Weitling, Wilhelm 1808-1871 . . . . DLB-129

Welch, Denton 1915-1948 . . . . DLB-319

Welch, James 1940- DLB-175, 256

Welch, Lew 1926-1971? DLB-16

Weldon, Fay 1931-
. . . . DLB-14, 194, 319; CDBLB-8

Wellek, René 1903-1995 . . . . DLB-63

Weller, Archie 1957- DLB-325

Wells, Carolyn 1862-1942 . . . . DLB-11

Wells, Charles Jeremiah
circa 1800-1879 . . . . DLB-32

Wells, Gabriel 1862-1946 . . . . DLB-140

Wells, H. G. 1866-1946
. . . . DLB-34, 70, 156, 178; CDBLB-6
H. G. Wells Society Y-98
Preface to *The Scientific Romances of
H. G. Wells* (1933) DLB-178

Wells, Helena 1758?-1824 . . . . DLB-200

Wells, Rebecca 1952- DLB-292

Wells, Robert 1947- DLB-40

Wells-Barnett, Ida B. 1862-1931 . . . . DLB-23, 221

Welsh, Irvine 1958- DLB-271

Welty, Eudora 1909-2001 . . . . . . DLB-2, 102, 143;
Y-87, 01; DS-12; CDALB-1

Eudora Welty: Eye of the Storyteller Y-87

Eudora Welty Newsletter Y-99

Eudora Welty's Funeral Y-01

Eudora Welty's Ninetieth Birthday Y-99

Eudora Welty Remembered in
Two Exhibits Y-02

Wendell, Barrett 1855-1921 . . . . DLB-71

Wentworth, Patricia 1878-1961 . . . . DLB-77

Wentworth, William Charles
1790-1872 . . . . DLB-230

Wenzel, Jean-Paul 1947- DLB-321

Werder, Diederich von dem 1584-1657 . . . DLB-164

Werfel, Franz 1890-1945 . . . . DLB-81, 124

Werner, Zacharias 1768-1823 . . . . DLB-94

The Werner Company DLB-49

Wersba, Barbara 1932- DLB-52

Wescott, Glenway
1901-1987 . . . . DLB-4, 9, 102; DS-15

Wesker, Arnold
1932- DLB-13, 310, 319; CDBLB-8

Wesley, Charles 1707-1788 . . . . DLB-95

Wesley, John 1703-1791 . . . . DLB-104

Wesley, Mary 1912-2002 . . . . DLB-231

Wesley, Richard 1945- DLB-38

Wessel, Johan Herman 1742-1785 . . . . DLB-300

A. Wessels and Company DLB-46

Wessobrunner Gebet circa 787-815 . . . . DLB-148

West, Anthony 1914-1988 . . . . DLB-15

Tribute to Liam O'Flaherty Y-84

West, Cheryl L. 1957- DLB-266

West, Cornel 1953- DLB-246

West, Dorothy 1907-1998 . . . . DLB-76

West, Jessamyn 1902-1984 . . . . DLB-6; Y-84

West, Mae 1892-1980 . . . . DLB-44, 341

West, Michael Lee 1953- DLB-292

West, Michelle Sagara 1963- DLB-251

West, Morris 1916-1999 . . . . DLB-289

West, Nathanael
1903-1940 . . . . DLB-4, 9, 28; CDALB-5

West, Paul 1930- DLB-14

West, Rebecca 1892-1983 . . . . DLB-36; Y-83

West, Richard 1941- DLB-185

West and Johnson DLB-49

Westcott, Edward Noyes 1846-1898 . . . . . DLB-202

The Western Literature Association Y-99

The Western Messenger
1835-1841 . . . . DLB-1; DLB-223

Western Publishing Company DLB-46

Western Writers of America Y-99

The Westminster Review 1824-1914 . . . . DLB-110

Weston, Arthur (see Webling, Peggy)

Weston, Elizabeth Jane circa 1582-1612 . . . DLB-172

Wetherald, Agnes Ethelwyn 1857-1940 . . . . DLB-99

Wetherell, Elizabeth (see Warner, Susan)

Wetherell, W. D. 1948- DLB-234

Wetzel, Friedrich Gottlob 1779-1819 . . . . . DLB-90

Weyman, Stanley J. 1855-1928 . . . . . DLB-141, 156

Wezel, Johann Karl 1747-1819 . . . . DLB-94

Whalen, Philip 1923-2002 . . . . DLB-16

Whalley, George 1915-1983 . . . . DLB-88

Wharton, Edith 1862-1937 . . . . DLB-4, 9, 12,
78, 189; DS-13; CDALB-3

Wharton, William 1925- Y-80

Whately, Mary Louisa 1824-1889 . . . . DLB-166

Whately, Richard 1787-1863 . . . . DLB-190

Elements of Rhetoric (1828;
revised, 1846) [excerpt] DLB-57

Wheatley, Dennis 1897-1977 . . . . DLB-77, 255

Wheatley, Phillis
circa 1754-1784 . . . . DLB-31, 50; CDALB-2

Wheeler, Anna Doyle 1785-1848? DLB-158

Wheeler, Charles Stearns 1816-1843 . . . DLB-1, 223

Wheeler, Monroe 1900-1988 . . . . DLB-4

Wheelock, John Hall 1886-1978 . . . . DLB-45

From John Hall Wheelock's
Oral Memoir Y-01

Wheelwright, J. B. 1897-1940 . . . . DLB-45

Wheelwright, John circa 1592-1679 . . . . . . DLB-24

Whetstone, George 1550-1587 . . . . DLB-136

Whetstone, Colonel Pete (see Noland, C. F. M.)

Whewell, William 1794-1866 . . . . DLB-262

Whichcote, Benjamin 1609?-1683 . . . . DLB-252

Whicher, Stephen E. 1915-1961 . . . . DLB-111

Whipple, Edwin Percy 1819-1886 . . . . . . DLB-1, 64

Whitaker, Alexander 1585-1617 . . . . DLB-24

Whitaker, Daniel K. 1801-1881 . . . . DLB-73

Whitcher, Frances Miriam
1812-1852 . . . . DLB-11, 202

White, Andrew 1579-1656 . . . . DLB-24

White, Andrew Dickson 1832-1918 . . . . . . DLB-47

White, E. B. 1899-1985 . . . . . DLB-11, 22; CDALB-7

White, Edgar B. 1947- DLB-38

White, Edmund 1940- DLB-227

White, Ethel Lina 1887-1944 . . . . DLB-77

White, Hayden V. 1928- DLB-246

White, Henry Kirke 1785-1806 . . . . DLB-96

White, Horace 1834-1916 . . . . DLB-23

White, James 1928-1999 . . . . DLB-261

White, Patrick 1912-1990 . . . . DLB-260, 332

White, Phyllis Dorothy James (see James, P. D.)

White, Richard Grant 1821-1885 . . . . DLB-64

White, T. H. 1906-1964 . . . . DLB-160, 255

White, Walter 1893-1955 . . . . DLB-51

Wilcox, James 1949- DLB-292

William White and Company DLB-49

White, William Allen 1868-1944 . . . . DLB-9, 25

White, William Anthony Parker
(see Boucher, Anthony)

White, William Hale (see Rutherford, Mark)

Whitchurch, Victor L. 1868-1933 . . . . DLB-70

Whitehead, Alfred North
1861-1947 . . . . DLB-100, 262

Whitehead, E. A. (Ted Whitehead)
1933- DLB-310

Whitehead, James 1936-2003 . . . . Y-81

Whitehead, William 1715-1785 . . . . . . DLB-84, 109

Whitfield, James Monroe 1822-1871 . . . . . DLB-50

Whitfield, Raoul 1898-1945 . . . . DLB-226

Whitgift, John circa 1533-1604 . . . . DLB-132

Whiting, John 1917-1963 . . . . DLB-13

Whiting, Samuel 1597-1679 . . . . DLB-24

Whitlock, Brand 1869-1934 . . . . DLB-12

Whitman, Albery Allson 1851-1901 . . . . . . DLB-50

Whitman, Alden 1913-1990 . . . . Y-91

Whitman, Sarah Helen (Power)
1803-1878 . . . . DLB-1, 243

Cumulative Index

Whitman, Walt
    1819-1892.... DLB-3, 64, 224, 250; CDALB-2

Albert Whitman and Company DLB-46

Whitman Publishing Company DLB-46

Whitney, Geoffrey
    1548 or 1552?-1601 .... DLB-136

Whitney, Isabella fl. 1566-1573......... DLB-136

Whitney, John Hay 1904-1982 .... DLB-127

Whittemore, Reed 1919-1995........... DLB-5

Whittier, John Greenleaf
    1807-1892 .... DLB-1, 243; CDALB-2

Whittlesey House.................... DLB-46

Whyte, John 1941-1992 .... DLB-334

Wickham, Anna (Edith Alice Mary Harper)
    1884-1947..................... DLB-240

Wickram, Georg circa 1505-circa 1561....DLB-179

Wicomb, Zoë 1948- DLB-225

Wideman, John Edgar 1941- DLB-33, 143

Widener, Harry Elkins 1885-1912 ...... DLB-140

Wiebe, Rudy 1934- DLB-60

Wiechert, Ernst 1887-1950 .... DLB-56

Wied, Gustav 1858-1914 .... DLB-300

Wied, Martina 1882-1957.............. DLB-85

Wiehe, Evelyn May Clowes (see Mordaunt, Elinor)

Wieland, Christoph Martin 1733-1813.... DLB-97

Wienbarg, Ludolf 1802-1872 .... DLB-133

Wieners, John 1934-2002................ DLB-16

Wier, Ester 1910-2000 .... DLB-52

Wiesel, Elie
    1928- DLB-83, 299; Y-86, 87; CDALB-7

    Nobel Lecture 1986: Hope, Despair and
        Memory....................... Y-86

Wiggin, Kate Douglas 1856-1923........ DLB-42

Wiggins, Marianne 1947- DLB-335

Wigglesworth, Michael 1631-1705 .... DLB-24

Wilberforce, William 1759-1833......... DLB-158

Wilbrandt, Adolf 1837-1911 .... DLB-129

Wilbur, Richard 1921- .. DLB-5, 169; CDALB-7

    Tribute to Robert Penn Warren Y-89

Wilcox, James 1949- DLB-292

Wild, Peter 1940- DLB-5

Wilde, Lady Jane Francesca Elgee
    1821?-1896.................... DLB-199

Wilde, Oscar 1854-1900
    ....DLB-10, 19, 34, 57, 141, 156, 190, 344;
                             CDBLB-5
    "The Critic as Artist" (1891) DLB-57
    "The Decay of Lying" (1889)........ DLB-18
    "The English Renaissance of
        Art" (1908) DLB-35
    "L'Envoi" (1882) DLB-35
    Oscar Wilde Conference at Hofstra
        University..................... Y-00

Wilde, Richard Henry 1789-1847...... DLB-3, 59

W. A. Wilde Company................. DLB-49

Wilder, Billy 1906-2002 .... DLB-26

Wilder, Laura Ingalls 1867-1957...... DLB-22, 256

Wilder, Thornton
    1897-1975 ....DLB-4, 7, 9, 228; CDALB-7

    Thornton Wilder Centenary at Yale Y-97

Wildgans, Anton 1881-1932........... DLB-118

Wilding, Michael 1942- DLB-325

Wiley, Bell Irvin 1906-1980 .... DLB-17

John Wiley and Sons DLB-49

Wilhelm, Kate 1928- DLB-8

Wilkes, Charles 1798-1877 .... DLB-183

Wilkes, George 1817-1885 .... DLB-79

Wilkins, John 1614-1672............... DLB-236

Wilkinson, Anne 1910-1961 .... DLB-88

Wilkinson, Christopher 1941- DLB-310

Wilkinson, Eliza Yonge 1757-circa 1813 .. DLB-200

Wilkinson, Sylvia 1940- Y-86

Wilkinson, William Cleaver 1833-1920 ... DLB-71

Willard, Barbara 1909-1994 .... DLB-161

Willard, Emma 1787-1870.............. DLB-239

Willard, Frances E. 1839-1898 .... DLB-221

Willard, Nancy 1936- DLB-5, 52

Willard, Samuel 1640-1707 .... DLB-24

L. Willard [publishing house] DLB-49

Willeford, Charles 1919-1988.......... DLB-226

William of Auvergne 1190-1249........ DLB-115

William of Conches
    circa 1090-circa 1154 .... DLB-115

William of Ockham circa 1285-1347 .... DLB-115

William of Sherwood
    1200/1205-1266/1271.............. DLB-115

The William Charvat American Fiction
    Collection at the Ohio State
    University Libraries................. Y-92

Williams, Ben Ames 1889-1953 .... DLB-102

Williams, C. K. 1936- DLB-5

Williams, Chancellor 1905-1992 .... DLB-76

Williams, Charles 1886-1945 ...DLB-100, 153, 255

Williams, Denis 1923-1998............. DLB-117

Williams, Emlyn 1905-1987 ....DLB-10, 77

Williams, Garth 1912-1996............. DLB-22

Williams, George Washington 1849-1891 . DLB-47

Williams, Heathcote 1941- DLB-13

Williams, Helen Maria 1761-1827 ...... DLB-158

Williams, Hugo 1942- DLB-40

Williams, Isaac 1802-1865 .... DLB-32

Williams, Joan 1928-2004............... DLB-6

Williams, Joe 1889-1972 .... DLB-241

Williams, John A. 1925- DLB-2, 33

Williams, John E. 1922-1994 .... DLB-6

Williams, Jonathan 1929- DLB-5

Williams, Joy 1944- DLB-335

Williams, Miller 1930- DLB-105

Williams, Nigel 1948- DLB-231

Williams, Raymond 1921-1988 . DLB-14, 231, 242

Williams, Roger circa 1603-1683 .... DLB-24

Williams, Rowland 1817-1870.......... DLB-184

Williams, Samm-Art 1946- DLB-38

Williams, Sherley Anne 1944-1999 ...... DLB-41

Williams, T. Harry 1909-1979 ....DLB-17

Williams, Tennessee 1911-1983
    .... DLB-7, 341; Y-83; DS-4; CDALB-1

Williams, Terry Tempest 1955- DLB-206, 275

Williams, Ursula Moray 1911-2006..... DLB-160

Williams, Valentine 1883-1946......... DLB-77

Williams, William Appleman 1921-1990 ..DLB-17

Williams, William Carlos
    1883-1963 ..... DLB-4, 16, 54, 86; CDALB-4

    The William Carlos Williams Society Y-99

Williams, Wirt 1921-1986 .... DLB-6

A. Williams and Company............. DLB-49

Williams Brothers..................... DLB-49

Williamson, David 1942- DLB-289

Williamson, Henry 1895-1977 .... DLB-191

    The Henry Williamson Society Y-98

Williamson, Jack 1908-2006............ DLB-8

Willingham, Calder Baynard, Jr.
    1922-1995 .... DLB-2, 44

Williram of Ebersberg circa 1020-1085 .. DLB-148

Willis, Browne 1682-1760.............. DLB-336

Willis, John circa 1572-1625 .... DLB-281

Willis, Nathaniel Parker 1806-1867
    ....DLB-3, 59, 73, 74, 183, 250; DS-13

Willis, Ted 1918-1992................. DLB-310

Willkomm, Ernst 1810-1886 .... DLB-133

Wills, Garry 1934- DLB-246

    Tribute to Kenneth Dale McCormick Y-97

Wills, W. G. 1828-1891 .... DLB-344

Willson, Meredith 1902-1984.......... DLB-265

Willumsen, Dorrit 1940- DLB-214

Wilmer, Clive 1945- DLB-40

Wilson, A. N. 1950- DLB-14, 155, 194

Wilson, Angus 1913-1991 ......DLB-15, 139, 155

Wilson, Arthur 1595-1652 .... DLB-58

Wilson, August 1945-2005 .... DLB-228

Wilson, Augusta Jane Evans 1835-1909... DLB-42

Wilson, Colin 1931- DLB-14, 194

    Tribute to J. B. Priestly................ Y-84

Wilson, Edmund 1895-1972............ DLB-63

Wilson, Ethel 1888-1980 .... DLB-68

Wilson, F. P. 1889-1963 .... DLB-201

Wilson, Harriet E.
    1827/1828?-1863? DLB-50, 239, 243

Wilson, Harry Leon 1867-1939 .... DLB-9

Wilson, John 1588-1667............... DLB-24

Wilson, John 1785-1854 .... DLB-110

Wilson, John Anthony Burgess
    (see Burgess, Anthony)

Wilson, John Dover 1881-1969 .... DLB-201

Wilson, Lanford 1937- DLB-7, 341

Wilson, Margaret 1882-1973 ....DLB-9

Wilson, Michael 1914-1978 ....DLB-44

Wilson, Mona 1872-1954................DLB-149

Wilson, Robert Charles 1953- DLB-251

Wilson, Robert McLiam 1964- DLB-267

Wilson, Robley 1930- DLB-218

Wilson, Romer 1891-1930...............DLB-191

Wilson, Thomas 1524-1581........DLB-132, 236

Wilson, Woodrow 1856-1924 ....DLB-47

Effingham Wilson [publishing house] DLB-154

Wimpfeling, Jakob 1450-1528 ....DLB-179

Wimsatt, William K., Jr. 1907-1975 ....DLB-63

Winchell, Walter 1897-1972 ....DLB-29

J. Winchester [publishing house] DLB-49

Winckelmann, Johann Joachim
1717-1768....................DLB-97

Winckler, Paul 1630-1686 ....DLB-164

Wind, Herbert Warren 1916-2005.......DLB-171

John Windet [publishing house]............DLB-170

Windham, Donald 1920- DLB-6

Windsor, Gerard 1944- DLB-325

Wing, Donald Goddard 1904-1972 ......DLB-187

Wing, John M. 1844-1917...............DLB-187

Allan Wingate [publishing house] DLB-112

Winnemucca, Sarah 1844-1921 ....DLB-175

Winnifrith, Tom 1938- DLB-155

Winsloe, Christa 1888-1944 ....DLB-124

Winslow, Anna Green 1759-1780........DLB-200

Winsor, Justin 1831-1897................DLB-47

John C. Winston Company DLB-49

Winters, Yvor 1900-1968...............DLB-48

Winterson, Jeanette 1959- DLB-207, 261

Winther, Christian 1796-1876 ....DLB-300

Winthrop, John 1588-1649 ....DLB-24, 30

Winthrop, John, Jr. 1606-1676 ....DLB-24

Winthrop, Margaret Tyndal
1591-1647 ....DLB-200

Winthrop, Theodore 1828-1861........DLB-202

Winton, Tim 1960- DLB-325

Wirt, William 1772-1834 ....DLB-37

Wise, Francis 1695-1767................DLB-336

Wise, John 1652-1725 ....DLB-24

Wise, Thomas James 1859-1937 ....DLB-184

Wiseman, Adele 1928-1992.............DLB-88

Wishart and Company DLB-112

Wisner, George 1812-1849 ....DLB-43

Wister, Owen 1860-1938......DLB-9, 78, 186

Wister, Sarah 1761-1804 ....DLB-200

Wither, George 1588-1667.............DLB-121

Witherspoon, John 1723-1794 ....DLB-31

The Works of the Rev. John Witherspoon
(1800-1801) [excerpts]...........DLB-31

Withrow, William Henry 1839-1908......DLB-99

Witkacy (see Witkiewicz, Stanisław Ignacy)

Witkiewicz, Stanisław Ignacy
1885-1939...........DLB-215; CDWLB-4

Wittenwiler, Heinrich before 1387-
circa 1414?...................DLB-179

Wittgenstein, Ludwig 1889-1951........DLB-262

Wittig, Monique 1935- DLB-83

Witting, Amy (Joan Austral Levick, née Fraser)
1918-2001 ....DLB-325

Wodehouse, P. G.
1881-1975 ....DLB-34, 162; CDBLB-6

Worldwide Wodehouse Societies.........Y-98

Wodrow, Robert 1679-1734 ....DLB-336

Wohmann, Gabriele 1932- DLB-75

Woiwode, Larry 1941- DLB-6

Tribute to John Gardner Y-82

Wolcot, John 1738-1819................DLB-109

Wolcott, Roger 1679-1767 ....DLB-24

Wolf, Christa 1929- DLB-75; CDWLB-2

Wolf, Friedrich 1888-1953 ....DLB-124

Wolfe, Gene 1931- DLB-8

Wolfe, Thomas 1900-1938....................
DLB-9, 102, 229; Y-85; DS-2, DS-16; CDALB-5

"All the Faults of Youth and Inexperience":
A Reader's Report on
Thomas Wolfe's *O Lost*...........Y-01

Emendations for *Look Homeward, Angel* Y-00

Eugene Gant's Projected Works Y-01

Fire at the Old Kentucky Home
[Thomas Wolfe Memorial] Y-98

Thomas Wolfe Centennial
Celebration in Asheville...........Y-00

The Thomas Wolfe Collection at
the University of North Carolina
at Chapel Hill..................Y-97

The Thomas Wolfe Society.......... Y-97, 99

Wolfe, Tom 1931- DLB-152, 185

John Wolfe [publishing house] DLB-170

Reyner (Reginald) Wolfe
[publishing house] DLB-170

Wolfenstein, Martha 1869-1906.........DLB-221

Wolff, David (see Maddow, Ben)

Wolff, Egon 1926- DLB-305

Wolff, Helen 1906-1994..................Y-94

Wolff, Tobias 1945- DLB-130

Tribute to Michael M. Rea Y-97

Tribute to Raymond Carver Y-88

Wolfram von Eschenbach
circa 1170-after 1220 ....DLB-138; CDWLB-2

Wolfram von Eschenbach's *Parzival*:
Prologue and Book 3 ....DLB-138

Wolker, Jiří 1900-1924................DLB-215

Wollstonecraft, Mary 1759-1797
.........DLB-39, 104, 158, 252; CDBLB-3

Women

Women's Work, Women's Sphere:
Selected Comments from Women
Writers DLB-200

Women Writers in Sixteenth-Century
Spain........................DLB-318

Wondratschek, Wolf 1943- DLB-75

Wong, Elizabeth 1958- DLB-266

Wong, Nellie 1934- DLB-312

Wong, Shawn 1949- DLB-312

Wongar, B. (Sreten Bozic) 1932- DLB-325

Wood, Anthony à 1632-1695..........DLB-213

Wood, Benjamin 1820-1900.............DLB-23

Wood, Charles 1932-1980...............DLB-13

The Charles Wood Affair:
A Playwright Revived..............Y-83

Wood, Mrs. Henry 1814-1887..........DLB-18

Wood, Joanna E. 1867-1927............DLB-92

Wood, Sally Sayward Barrell Keating
1759-1855 ....DLB-200

Wood, William fl. seventeenth century DLB-24

Samuel Wood [publishing house].........DLB-49

Woodberry, George Edward
1855-1930 .... DLB-71, 103

Woodbridge, Benjamin 1622-1684 ....DLB-24

Woodbridge, Frederick J. E. 1867-1940 ...DLB-270

Woodcock, George 1912-1995............DLB-88

Woodhull, Victoria C. 1838-1927 ....DLB-79

Woodmason, Charles circa 1720-?........DLB-31

Woodress, James Leslie, Jr. 1916- DLB-111

Woods, Margaret L. 1855-1945........DLB-240

Woodson, Carter G. 1875-1950.........DLB-17

Woodward, C. Vann 1908-1999 ....DLB-17

Woodward, Stanley 1895-1965 ....DLB-171

Woodworth, Samuel 1785-1842........DLB-250

Wooler, Thomas 1785 or 1786-1853 .....DLB-158

Woolf, David (see Maddow, Ben)

Woolf, Douglas 1922-1992 ....DLB-244

Woolf, Leonard 1880-1969 ...... DLB-100; DS-10

Woolf, Virginia 1882-1941
........DLB-36, 100, 162; DS-10; CDBLB-6

"The New Biography," *New York Herald
Tribune*, 30 October 1927 ....DLB-149

Woollcott, Alexander 1887-1943 ....DLB-29

Woolman, John 1720-1772..............DLB-31

Cumulative Index

Woolner, Thomas 1825-1892 . . . . DLB-35

Woolrich, Cornell 1903-1968 . . . . DLB-226

Woolsey, Sarah Chauncy 1835-1905 . . . . . DLB-42

Woolson, Constance Fenimore
   1840-1894 . . . . DLB-12, 74, 189, 221

Worcester, Joseph Emerson
   1784-1865 . . . . DLB-1, 235

Wynkyn de Worde [publishing house] DLB-170

Wordsworth, Christopher 1807-1885 . . . . DLB-166

Wordsworth, Dorothy 1771-1855 . . . . DLB-107

Wordsworth, Elizabeth 1840-1932 . . . . . . DLB-98

Wordsworth, William
   1770-1850 . . . . DLB-93, 107; CDBLB-3

Workman, Fanny Bullock
   1859-1925 . . . . DLB-189

World Literatue Today: A Journal for the
   New Millennium Y-01

World Publishing Company DLB-46

World War I (1914-1918) DS-18

   The Great War Exhibit and Symposium
      at the University of South Carolina . . . Y-97

   The Liddle Collection and First World
      War Research Y-97

   Other British Poets Who Fell
      in the Great War DLB-216

   The Seventy-Fifth Anniversary of
      the Armistice: The Wilfred Owen
      Centenary and the Great War Exhibit
      at the University of Virginia Y-93

World War II (1939–1945)

   Literary Effects of World War II DLB-15

   World War II Writers Symposium
      at the University of South Carolina,
      12–14 April 1995 . . . . Y-95

   WW2 HMSO Paperbacks Society Y-98

R. Worthington and Company DLB-49

Wotton, Sir Henry 1568-1639 . . . . DLB-121

Wouk, Herman 1915- Y-82; CDALB-7

   Tribute to James Dickey Y-97

Wreford, James 1915-1990 . . . . DLB-88

Wren, Sir Christopher 1632-1723 . . . . . . DLB-213

Wren, Percival Christopher 1885-1941 . . . DLB-153

Wrenn, John Henry 1841-1911 . . . . DLB-140

Wright, C. D. 1949- DLB-120

Wright, Charles 1935- DLB-165; Y-82

Wright, Charles Stevenson 1932- DLB-33

Wright, Chauncey 1830-1875 . . . . DLB-270

Wright, Frances 1795-1852 . . . . DLB-73

Wright, Harold Bell 1872-1944 . . . . DLB-9

Wright, James 1927-1980
   . . . . DLB-5, 169, 342; CDALB-7

Wright, Jay 1935- DLB-41

Wright, Judith 1915-2000 . . . . DLB-260

Wright, Louis B. 1899-1984 . . . . DLB-17

Wright, Richard 1908-1960
   . . . . DLB-76, 102; DS-2; CDALB-5

Wright, Richard B. 1937- DLB-53

Wright, S. Fowler 1874-1965 . . . . DLB-255

Wright, Sarah Elizabeth 1928- DLB-33

Wright, T. H. "Style" (1877) [excerpt] DLB-57

Wright, Willard Huntington (S. S. Van Dine)
   1887-1939 . . . . DLB-306; DS-16

Wrightson, Patricia 1921- DLB-289

Wrigley, Robert 1951- DLB-256

Writers' Forum Y-85

Writing

   A Writing Life Y-02

   On Learning to Write Y-88

   The Profession of Authorship:
      Scribblers for Bread Y-89

   A Writer Talking: A Collage Y-00

Wroth, Lawrence C. 1884-1970 . . . . DLB-187

Wroth, Lady Mary 1587-1653 . . . . DLB-121

Wu Jianren (Wo Foshanren)
   1866-1910 . . . . DLB-328

Wu Zuxiang 1908-1994 . . . . DLB-328

Wumingshi (Bu Baonan) 1917-2002 . . . . . DLB-328

Wurlitzer, Rudolph 1937- DLB-173

Wyatt, Sir Thomas circa 1503-1542 . . . . . DLB-132

Wycherley, William
   1641-1715 . . . . DLB-80; CDBLB-2

Wyclif, John circa 1335-1384 . . . . DLB-146

Wyeth, N. C. 1882-1945 . . . . DLB-188; DS-16

Wyle, Niklas von circa 1415-1479 . . . . . . DLB-179

Wylie, Elinor 1885-1928 . . . . DLB-9, 45

Wylie, Philip 1902-1971 . . . . DLB-9

Wyllie, John Cook 1908-1968 . . . . DLB-140

Wyman, Lillie Buffum Chace
   1847-1929 . . . . DLB-202

Wymark, Olwen 1934- DLB-233

Wynd, Oswald Morris (see Black, Gavin)

Wyndham, John (John Wyndham Parkes
   Lucas Beynon Harris) 1903-1969 . . . DLB-255

Wynne-Tyson, Esmé 1898-1972 . . . . DLB-191

X

Xenophon circa 430 B.C.-circa 356 B.C. DLB-176

Xiang Kairan (Pingjiang Buxiaoshengj
   Buxiaosheng) 1890-1957 . . . . DLB-328

Xiao Hong 1911-1942 . . . . DLB-328

Xu Dishan (Luo Huasheng)
   1893-1941 . . . . DLB-328

Xu Zhenya 1889-1937 . . . . DLB-328

Y

Yahp, Beth 1964- DLB-325

Yamamoto, Hisaye 1921- DLB-312

Yamanaka, Lois-Ann 1961- DLB-312

Yamashita, Karen Tei 1951- DLB-312

Yamauchi, Wakako 1924- DLB-312

Yang Kui 1905-1985 . . . . DLB-328

Yasuoka Shōtarō 1920- DLB-182

Yates, Dornford 1885-1960 . . . . DLB-77, 153

Yates, J. Michael 1938- DLB-60

Yates, Richard 1926-1992 . . . . DLB-2, 234; Y-81, 92

Yau, John 1950- DLB-234, 312

Yavorov, Peyo 1878-1914 . . . . DLB-147

Ye Shaojun (Ye Shengtao) 1894-1988 . . . . DLB-328

Yearsley, Ann 1753-1806 . . . . DLB-109

Yeats, William Butler 1865-1939
   . . . . DLB-10, 19, 98, 156, 332; CDBLB-5

Yehoash (Yehoyesh; Solomon Bloomgarden
   [Shloyme Blumgarten]) 1872-1927 . . . DLB-333

   The W. B. Yeats Society of N.Y. Y-99

Yellen, Jack 1892-1991 . . . . DLB-265

Yep, Laurence 1948- DLB-52, 312

Yerby, Frank 1916-1991 . . . . DLB-76

Yezierska, Anzia 1880-1970 . . . . DLB-28, 221

Yolen, Jane 1939- DLB-52

Yonge, Charlotte Mary 1823-1901 . . . DLB-18, 163

   The Charlotte M. Yonge Fellowship Y-98

The York Cycle circa 1376-circa 1569 . . . . DLB-146

A Yorkshire Tragedy DLB-58

Thomas Yoseloff [publishing house] DLB-46

Youd, Sam (see Christopher, John)

Young, A. S. "Doc" 1919-1996 . . . . DLB-241

Young, Al 1939- DLB-33

Young, Arthur 1741-1820 . . . . DLB-158

Young, Dick 1917 or 1918-1987 . . . . DLB-171

Young, Edward 1683-1765 . . . . DLB-95

Young, Frank A. "Fay" 1884-1957 . . . . . . DLB-241

Young, Francis Brett 1884-1954 . . . . DLB-191

Young, Gavin 1928-2001 . . . . DLB-204

Young, Stark 1881-1963 . . . . . . DLB-9, 102; DS-16
Young, Waldeman 1880-1938 . . . . DLB-26
William Young [publishing house] DLB-49
Young Bear, Ray A. 1950- DLB-175
Yourcenar, Marguerite 1903-1987 . . . DLB-72; Y-88
Yovkov, Yordan 1880-1937 . . . . DLB-147; CDWLB-4
Yu Dafu 1896-1945 . . . . DLB-328
Yushkevich, Semen 1868-1927 . . . . DLB-317
Yver, Jacques 1520?-1570? DLB-327

Z

Zachariä, Friedrich Wilhelm 1726-1777 . . . . DLB-97
Zagajewski, Adam 1945- DLB-232
Zagoskin, Mikhail Nikolaevich
   1789-1852 . . . . DLB-198
Zaitsev, Boris 1881-1972 . . . . DLB-317
Zajc, Dane 1929-2005 . . . . DLB-181
Zālīte, Māra 1952- DLB-232
Zalygin, Sergei Pavlovich 1913-2000 . . . . DLB-302
Zamiatin, Evgenii Ivanovich 1884-1937 . . . DLB-272
Zamora, Bernice 1938- DLB-82
Zamudio, Adela (Soledad) 1854-1928 . . . . DLB-283
Zand, Herbert 1923-1970 . . . . DLB-85
Zangwill, Israel 1864-1926 . . . . . . DLB-10, 135, 197
Zanzotto, Andrea 1921- DLB-128
Zapata Olivella, Manuel 1920- DLB-113
Zapoev, Timur Iur'evich
   (see Kibirov, Timur Iur'evich)
Zasodimsky, Pavel Vladimirovich
   1843-1912 . . . . DLB-238
al-Zayyat, Latifa 1923-1996 . . . . DLB-346
Zebra Books DLB-46
Zebrowski, George 1945- DLB-8

Zech, Paul 1881-1946 . . . . DLB-56
Zeidner, Lisa 1955- DLB-120
Zeidonis, Imants 1933- DLB-232
Zeimi (Kanze Motokiyo) 1363-1443 . . . . DLB-203
Zelazny, Roger 1937-1995 . . . . DLB-8
Zeng Pu 1872-1935 . . . . DLB-328
Zenger, John Peter 1697-1746 . . . . DLB-24, 43
Zepheria DLB-172
Zernova, Ruf' 1919-2004 . . . . DLB-317
Zesen, Philipp von 1619-1689 . . . . DLB-164
Zhadovskaia, Iuliia Valerianovna
   1824-1883 . . . . DLB-277
Zhang Ailing (Eileen Chang)
   1920-1995 . . . . DLB-328
Zhang Henshui 1895-1967 . . . . DLB-328
Zhang Tianyi 1906-1985 . . . . DLB-328
Zhao Shuli 1906-1970 . . . . DLB-328
Zhukova, Mar'ia Semenovna
   1805-1855 . . . . DLB-277
Zhukovsky, Vasilii Andreevich
   1783-1852 . . . . DLB-205
Zhvanetsky, Mikhail Mikhailovich
   1934- DLB-285
G. B. Zieber and Company DLB-49
Ziedonis, Imants 1933- CDWLB-4
Zieroth, Dale 1946- DLB-60
Zigler und Kliphausen, Heinrich
   Anshelm von 1663-1697 . . . . DLB-168
Zil'ber, Veniamin Aleksandrovich
   (see Kaverin, Veniamin Aleksandrovich)
Zimmer, Paul 1934- DLB-5
Zinberg, Len (see Lacy, Ed)
Zincgref, Julius Wilhelm 1591-1635 . . . . . DLB-164
Zindel, Paul 1936- DLB-7, 52; CDALB-7

Zinnes, Harriet 1919- DLB-193
Zinov'ev, Aleksandr Aleksandrovich
   1922- DLB-302
Zinov'eva-Annibal, Lidiia Dmitrievna
   1865 or 1866-1907 . . . . DLB-295
Zinzendorf, Nikolaus Ludwig von
   1700-1760 . . . . DLB-168
Zitkala-Ša 1876-1938 . . . . DLB-175
Zīverts, Mārtiņš 1903-1990 . . . . DLB-220
Zlatovratsky, Nikolai Nikolaevich
   1845-1911 . . . . DLB-238
Zola, Emile 1840-1902 . . . . DLB-123
Zolla, Elémire 1926- DLB-196
Zolotow, Charlotte 1915- DLB-52
Zoshchenko, Mikhail Mikhailovich
   1895-1958 . . . . DLB-272
Zschokke, Heinrich 1771-1848 . . . . DLB-94
Zubly, John Joachim 1724-1781 . . . . DLB-31
Zu-Bolton, Ahmos, II 1935-2005 . . . . DLB-41
Zuckmayer, Carl 1896-1977 . . . . DLB-56, 124
Zukofsky, Louis 1904-1978 . . . . DLB-5, 165
Zupan, Vitomil 1914-1987 . . . . DLB-181
Župančič, Oton 1878-1949 . . . DLB-147; CDWLB-4
zur Mühlen, Hermynia 1883-1951 . . . . DLB-56
Zurayk, Constantine K. 1909-2000 . . . . . . DLB-346
Zweig, Arnold 1887-1968 . . . . DLB-66
Zweig, Stefan 1881-1942 . . . . DLB-81, 118
Zwicky, Fay 1933- DLB-325
Zwicky, Jan 1955- DLB-334
Zwinger, Ann 1925- DLB-275
Zwingli, Huldrych 1484-1531 . . . . DLB-179

Ø

Øverland, Arnulf 1889-1968 . . . . DLB-297

ISBN-13: 978-0-7876-8164-7
ISBN-10: 0-7876-8164-4

PJ
7521
.T84

2009